Survey of Accounting, Eighth Edition, is designed for a one-term introductory accounting course. Written for students who have no prior knowledge of accounting, this text emphasizes how managers, investors, and other business stakeholders use accounting reports. It provides an overview of the basic topics in financial and managerial accounting.

Hallmark Features

The Eighth Edition of this text continues to emphasize elements designed to help instructors and enhance the learning experience of students. These features include the following:

- **Integrated Financial Statement Framework** shows how transactions impact each of the three primary financial statements and stresses the integrated nature of accounting.
- **Infographic art** examples help students visualize important accounting concepts within the chapter.

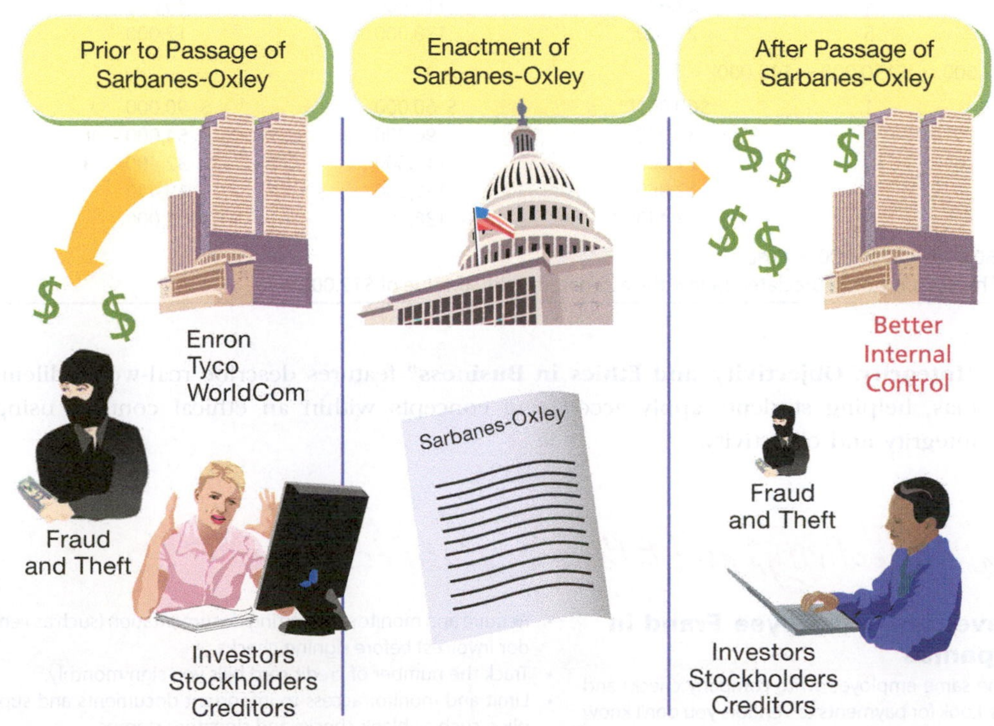

- **Illustrative Problems** help students apply what they learn by walking them through problems that cover the most important concepts addressed within the chapter.

Illustrative Problem

McCollum Company, a furniture wholesaler, acquired new equipment at a cost of $150,000 at the beginning of the fiscal year. The equipment has an estimated life of five years and an estimated residual value of $12,000. Ellen McCollum, the president, has requested information regarding alternative depreciation methods.

Instructions

Determine the annual depreciation for each of the five years of estimated useful life of the equipment, the accumulated depreciation at the end of each year, and the book value of the equipment at the end of each year by (a) the straight-line method and (b) the double-declining-balance method.

Solution

	Year	Depreciation Expense	Accumulated Depreciation, End of Year	Book Value, End of Year
a.	1	$27,600*	$ 27,600	$122,400
	2	27,600	55,200	94,800
	3	27,600	82,800	67,200
	4	27,600	110,400	39,600
	5	27,600	138,000	12,000
*$27,600 = ($150,000 − $12,000) ÷ 5				
b.	1	$60,000**	$ 60,000	$ 90,000
	2	36,000	96,000	54,000
	3	21,600	117,600	32,400
	4	12,960	130,560	19,440
	5	7,440***	138,000	12,000

**$60,000 = $150,000 × 40%.
***The asset is not depreciated below the estimated residual value of $12,000.

- **"Integrity, Objectivity, and Ethics in Business"** features describe real-world dilemmas, helping students apply accounting concepts within an ethical context, using integrity and objectivity.

Integrity, Objectivity, and Ethics in Business

Tips on Preventing Employee Fraud in Small Companies

- Do not have the same employee write company checks and keep the books. Look for payments to vendors you don't know or payments to vendors whose names appear to be misspelled.
- If your business has a computer system, restrict access to accounting files as much as possible. Also, keep a backup copy of your accounting files and store it at an off-site location.
- Be wary of anybody working in finance that declines to take vacations. They may be afraid that a replacement will uncover fraud.
- Require and monitor supporting documentation (such as vendor invoices) before signing checks.
- Track the number of credit card bills you sign monthly.
- Limit and monitor access to important documents and supplies, such as blank checks and signature stamps.
- Check W-2 forms against your payroll annually to make sure you're not carrying any fictitious employees.
- Rely on yourself, not on your accountant, to spot fraud.

Source: Steve Kaufman, "Embezzlement Common at Small Companies," Knight-Ridder Newspapers, reported in *Athens Daily News/Athens Banner-Herald*, March 10, 1996, p. 4D.

Survey of Accounting 8e

Carl S. Warren*
Professor Emeritus of Accounting
University of Georgia, Athens

* A special thanks to Amanda Farmer, Andrea Meyer, and Mark Sears for their contributions to this edition.

Australia • Brazil • Japan • Korea • Mexico • Singapore • Spain • United Kingdom • United States

Survey of Accounting, Eighth Edition

Carl S. Warren

Vice President, General Manager, Science, Math & Quantitative Business: Erin Joyner

Executive Product Director: Mike Schenk

Product Director: Jason Fremder

Product Manager: Matt Filimonov

Content Developer: Andrea Meyer

Product Assistant: Audrey Jacobs

Marketing Manager: Robin LeFevre

Marketing Coordinator: Eileen Corcoran

Production Management and Composition: Cenveo Publisher Services

Intellectual Property

Analyst: Brittani Morgan

Project Manager: Reba Frederics

Manufacturing Planner: Doug Wilke

Senior Art Director: Michelle Kunkler

Cover Designer: Ke Design

Internal Designer: Ke Design

Cover Image(s): Glowimages/Getty Images

For product information and technology assistance, contact us at **Cengage Learning Customer & Sales Support, 1-800-354-9706**

For permission to use material from this text or product, submit all requests online at **www.cengage.com/permissions**
Further permissions questions can be emailed to **permissionrequest@cengage.com**

Library of Congress Control Number: 2016947594

ISBN: 978-1-305-96188-3

Cengage Learning
20 Channel Center Street
Boston, MA 02210
USA

Cengage Learning is a leading provider of customized learning solutions with employees residing in nearly 40 different countries and sales in more than 125 countries around the world. Find your local representative at **www.cengage.com.**

Cengage Learning products are represented in Canada by Nelson Education, Ltd.

To learn more about Cengage Learning Solutions, visit **www.cengage.com**

Purchase any of our products at your local college store or at our preferred online store **www.cengagebrain.com**

Printed at CLDPC, USA, 08-18

- **"Business Insight Make Money"** vignettes emphasize practical ways in which businesses apply accounting concepts when generating profit strategies.

Got the Flu? Why Not Chew Some Gum?

Facing a slumping market for sugared chewing gum—such as Juicy Fruit™ and Doublemint™—**Wm. Wrigley Jr. Company**, a subsidiary of **Mars Incorporated**, is reinventing itself by expanding its product lines and introducing new chewing gum applications. Wrigley's new products include sugarless breath mints and more powerful flavored mint chewing gum, like Extra Polar Ice™. In addition, Wrigley is experimenting with health-care applications of chewing gum. For example, the company founded the Wrigley Science Institute™ with the objective of promoting scientific research on the benefits of chewing gum. Specifically, the Institute sponsors research in such areas as weight reduction, management and stress relief, and cognitive focus. The Institute provides grants to leading researchers who investigate the role of chewing gum in health and wellness.

Source: Wrigley.com and *USA Today*, "Wrigley Wants Science to Prove Gum-Chewing Benefits," by Dave Carpenter, The Associated Press, March 28, 2006.

- The **"International Connections"** feature, in select chapters, highlights key differences between international accounting standards and U.S. GAAP.

International Connection

Adoption or Convergence?

The largest public accounting firms, known as the Big Four, have pushed for the "adoption" of IFRS in the United States within a relatively short period of time. Such a strategy of adoption would generate millions of dollars of consulting and accounting work within the U.S. for the Big Four: Deloitte Touche Tohmatsu, PwC (PriceWaterhouseCoopers), Ernst & Young, and KPMG.

In contrast, others have argued for a strategy of gradual "convergence" to IFRS over time. Currently, it appears that regulators within the United States and the FASB are favoring convergence rather than adoption. For example, since November 2010, the FASB and IASB have completed several projects to converge U.S. and IFRS standards.[1]

1. FASB.org, "Progress Report on IASB-FASB Convergence Work," April 21, 2011.

- **An attractive design** engages students and clearly presents the material. The Integrated Financial Statement Framework benefits from this pedagogically sound use of color, as each statement within the framework is shaded to reinforce the integrated nature of accounting.

Integrated Financial Statement (IFS) Approach

This framework clearly demonstrates the impact of transactions on the balance sheet, income statement, and the statement of cash flows and the corresponding relationship among these financial statements. The IFS framework moves the student from the simple to the complex and explains the how and why of financial statements.

Chapter 1 introduces students to this integration in the form of actual company financials from **The Hershey Company**, a well-known manufacturer of chocolates.

Exhibit 10 Integrated Financial Statements

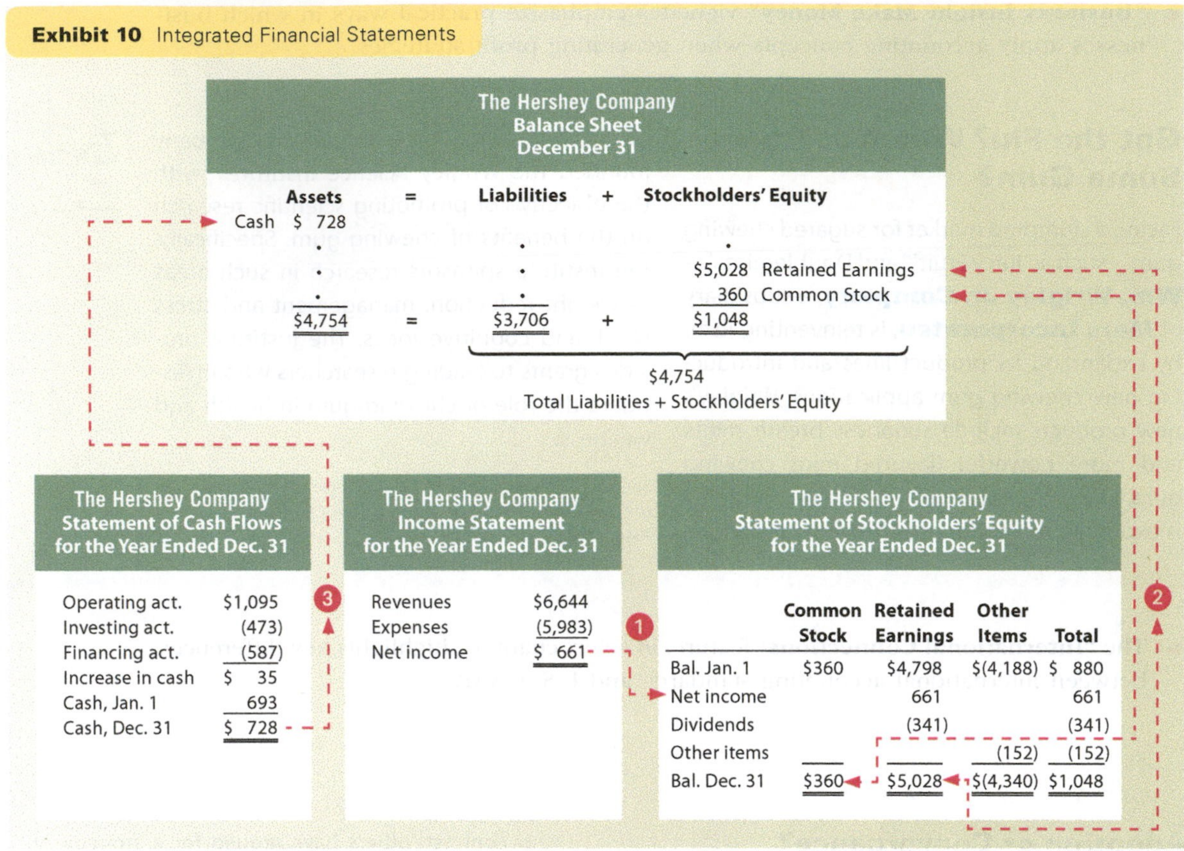

Chapter 2 begins with an example format of the integrated framework used throughout the financial chapters. Early in the course, students will gain a greater understanding of how important trends or events can impact a company's financial statements, which add valuable insight into the financial condition and performance of a business.

Exhibit 1 Integrated Financial Statement Framework

Integrated Financial Statement Framework

BALANCE SHEET

	Assets	=	Liabilities	+	Stockholders' Equity	
	Assets	**=**	**Liabilities**	**+**	**Capital Stock +**	**Retained Earnings**
Transaction	XXX		XXX		XXX	XXX
	XXX					
	XXX		XXX		XXX	XXX

STATEMENT OF CASH FLOWS

+/– Operating activities	XXX
+/– Investing activities	XXX
+/– Financing activities	XXX
Increase or decrease in cash	XXX
Beginning cash	XXX
Ending cash	XXX

INCOME STATEMENT

Revenues	XXX
Expenses	XXX
Net income or loss	XXX

The primary focus in Chapter 2 is on cash transactions, which helps eliminate confusion for students who may have difficulty determining whether an event or transaction should be recorded.

Transaction (d)

During the first month of operations, Family Health Care earned patient fees of $5,500, receiving the fees in cash.

The effects of this transaction on Family Health Care's financial statements are recorded as follows:

1. Under the Statement of Cash Flows column, Cash from Operating activities is increased by $5,500.
2. Under the Balance Sheet column, Cash under Assets is increased by $5,500. To balance the accounting equation, Retained Earnings under Stockholders' Equity is also increased by $5,500.
3. Under the Income Statement column, Fees earned is increased by $5,500.

This transaction illustrates an inflow of cash from operating activities by earning revenues (fees earned) of $5,500. Retained Earnings is increased under Stockholders' Equity by $5,500 because fees earned contribute to net income and net income increases stockholders' equity. Since fees earned are a type of revenue, Fees earned of $5,500 is also entered under the Income Statement column.

The effects of this transaction on Family Health Care's financial statements are shown below.

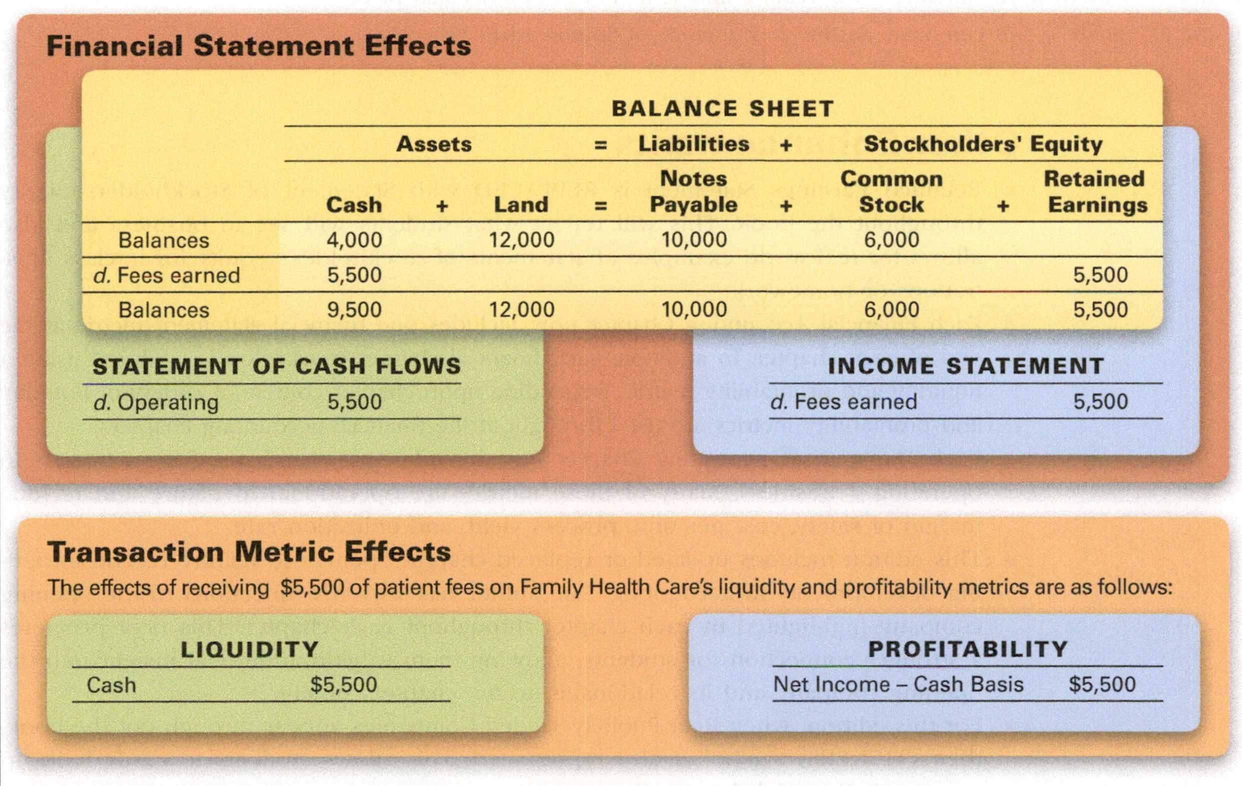

Financial Statement Effects

	BALANCE SHEET								
	Assets			=	Liabilities	+	Stockholders' Equity		
	Cash	+	Land	=	Notes Payable	+	Common Stock	+	Retained Earnings
Balances	4,000		12,000		10,000		6,000		
d. Fees earned	5,500								5,500
Balances	9,500		12,000		10,000		6,000		5,500

STATEMENT OF CASH FLOWS	
d. Operating	5,500

INCOME STATEMENT	
d. Fees earned	5,500

Transaction Metric Effects

The effects of receiving $5,500 of patient fees on Family Health Care's liquidity and profitability metrics are as follows:

LIQUIDITY	
Cash	$5,500

PROFITABILITY	
Net Income – Cash Basis	$5,500

Eighth Edition: Changes and Enhancements

NEW! Warren's Metric Analyses

As illustrated above, the Eighth Edition of Survey of Accounting introduces and incorporates Warren's Metric Analyses throughout. It uses common business metrics to assess a company's financial condition and performance. Metrics are assessed at three levels: the Transaction Level, Financial Statement level, and Managerial Decision-Making Level.

To accompany the addition of Warren's Metric Analyses, end-of-chapter problems have been added to test the students knowledge and understanding of the concepts.

Metric Analyses are clearly identified wtih a separate screen of color. This allows for quick identification of the analyses through the chapters and text. This separate screen of color also identifies the end-of-chapter section for assigning homework.

MBA 2-4 Common-Sized Statements **Obj. 6**

Southwest Airlines Co. (LUV) provides passenger services throughout the United States, Mexico, Jamaica, The Bahamas, Aruba, and the Dominican Republic. The following operating data (in millions) were adapted from recent financial statements of Southwest.

	Year 1	Year 2
Revenue	$ 17,699	$ 18,605
Operating expenses:		
Fuel	$(5,763)	$(5,293)
Aircraft-related	(3,411)	(3,322)
Selling and general	(5,035)	(5,434)
Other expenses	(2,212)	(2,331)
Total operating expenses	$(16,421)	$(16,380)
Operating income	$ 1,278	$ 2,225

1. Prepare common-sized statements for Years 2 and 1. Round to one decimal place.
2. Using (1), analyze and comment on the performance of Southwest in Year 2.

Other Enhancements

- Retained Earnings Statement is REPLACED with Statement of Stockholders Equity throughout the book. This will reflect what students will see in business and also allows for real-world examples of statements of stockholder's equity for in-class illustrations or homework.
- Each Financial Accounting Chapter now includes one financial statement metric at the end of each chapter. In addition, each financial chapter transaction is analyzed using a liquidity and profitability metric. Depending upon chapter content, a variety of liquidity and profitability metrics are used throughout the financial accounting chapters.
- Each Managerial Accounting Chapter now includes one metric used by managers in operating a business. Many of these metrics are operational in nature and include margin of safety, cost per unit, process yield, and utilization rate.
- This edition includes updated or replaced chapter openers to feature recent, intriguing developments in accounting. The author has woven connections to the opening company highlighted in each chapter throughout each chapter. This now promotes a stronger connection for students, allowing them to gain additional insight into the opening company and its relationship to the chapter content.
- For this edition, when Real Publicly Traded Companies appear through out the book, their (TICKERS) symbol is also represented. This allows students to easily look up company's financial data on the internet.

Technology

What is CengageNOWv2?

CengageNOWv2 is a powerful course management and online homework tool that provides robust intructor control and customization to optimize the student learning experience and meet desired outcomes.

CengageNOWv2 includes

- Integrated eBook
- End-of-Chapter homework with static and algorithmic version
- Adaptive Study Plan with quizzing and multimedia study tools
- Test Bank
- Course management tools and flexible assignment options
- Reporting and grade book options
- Mastery Problems
- Tell Me More eLectures
- Show Me How Demonstration Videos
- Animated Activities

CengageNOWv2 for Warren's *Survey of Accounting, 8e* is designed to help students learn more effectively by providing engaging resources at unique points in the learning process:

When to use it?	What to use?	How will it help?
Preparing for Class	Lecture Activities Animated Activities	Recall Understand
Completing Homework	Solutions Videos Enhanced Feedback	Apply
Going Further	Mastery Assignments Conceptual Conversions	Analyze Evaluate

Preparing for Class

CengageNOWv2 helps you motivate students and prepare them for class with a host of resources. These resources were developed with visual learners and those that don't like to read textbooks in mind. Available in the Study Tools tab in CengageNOWv2, students may access these resources on demand. Each resource is fully assignable and gradable!

Tell Me More Lecture Activities are available and correlate to each Learning Objective (LO). These Lecture Assignments review the material covered in each LO, giving students a way to review what is covered in each objective in a digestible video activity format so they come to class more prepared and ready to participate.

Animated Activities are available on a chapter-by-chapter basis. Animated Activities are assignable/gradable illustrations that visually explain and guide students through selected core topics. Each activity uses a realistic company example to illustrate how the concepts relate to the everyday activities of a business. After finishing the video, a student is expected to answer questions based on what they've seen. These activities offer excellent resources for students prior to coming to lecture and will especially appeal to visual learners.

By using these resources, you have a powerful suite of content to help you ensure students can familiarize themselves with content prior to coming to class, which is an excellent way to help you flip the classroom!

Financial Analysis and Interpretation: Fixed Asset Turnover Ratio

- A measure of a company's efficiency in using its fixed assets to generate revenue is the fixed asset turnover ratio. The **fixed asset turnover ratio** measures the number of dollars of sales earned per dollar of fixed assets.
- The fixed asset turnover ratio is computed as follows:

$$\text{Fixed Asset Turnover Ratio} = \frac{\text{Sales}}{\text{Average Book Value of Fixed Assets}}$$

- The higher the fixed asset turnover, the more efficiently a company is using its fixed assets in generating sales. the better a company is at using its fixed assets

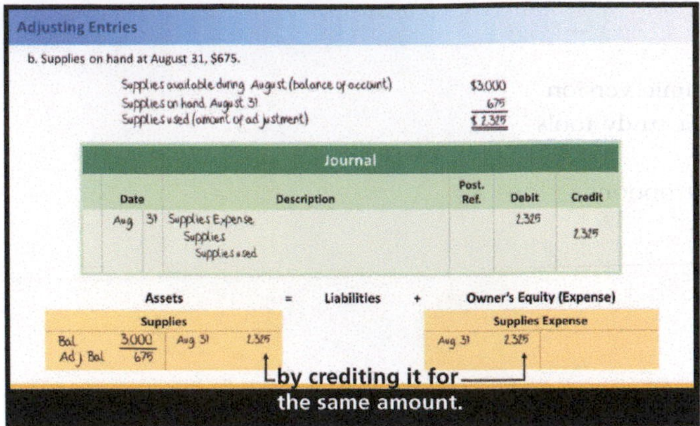

Completing Homework

Students sometimes struggle with accounting homework. By using CengageNOWv2's powerful instructor tools you can fine-tune the amount of help that your students receive as they work on their homework. Help your students succeed by making the right amount of assistance available at the right time!

Show Me How Videos are available for the most commonly assigned end-of-chapter assignments. *Linked only to algorithms*, these Videos provide students with both a detailed walk-through of a similar problem and problem-solving strategies.

Made without giving away the answer.

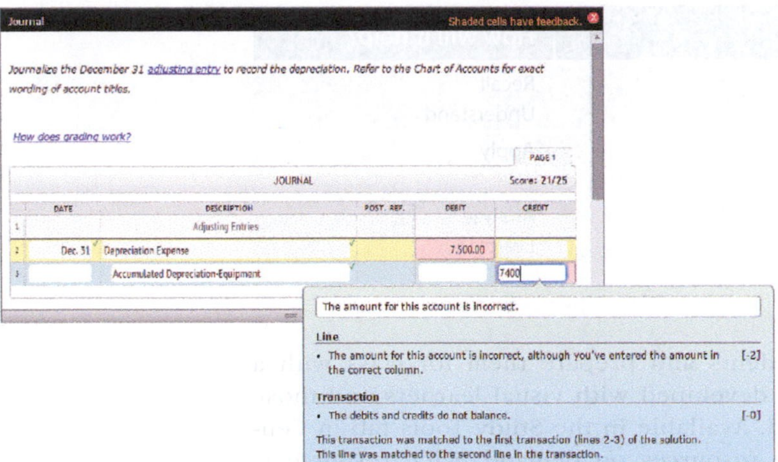

CengageNOWv2 provides multiple layers of guidance to keep students on track and progressing.

- Check My Work Feedback provides general guidance and hints as students work through homework assignments.
- Check My Work Feedback in CengageNOWv2 only reports on what students have attempted, which prevents them from "guessing" their way through assignments.
- Explanations are available after the assignment has been submitted and provide a detailed description of how the student should have arrived at the solution.

Going Further

Mastering accounting includes making connections between concepts and asking students to apply what they've learned to different scenarios. CengageNOWv2 has the tools that help you assess your students' abilities in these key skill areas!

In CengageNOWv2, all of the special activities in Warren, *Survey of Accounting, 8th Edition* are available for you to assign to your students. These **Mastery Assignments** do more than test your students' ability to recall, understand and apply. These assignments challenge your students to go further by demonstrating their ability to analyze and evaluate accounting information.

Conceptual Conversions are open-ended requirements from the end-of-chapter homework that have been converted into automatically gradable formats in CengageNOWv2. Now you can assess your students' understanding of more conceptual, open-ended questions previously not available to assign in an online environment.

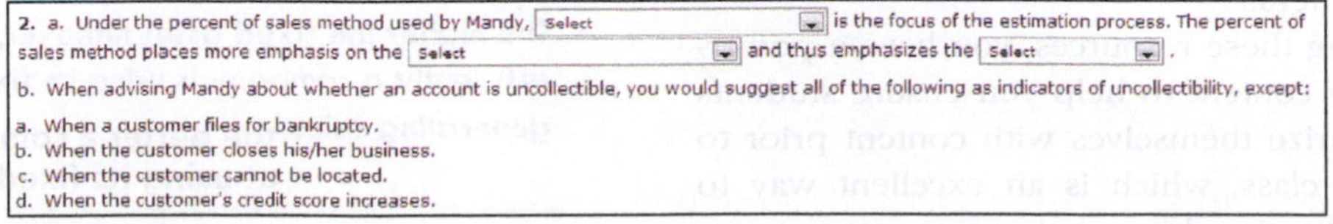

2. a. Under the percent of sales method used by Mandy, [Select] is the focus of the estimation process. The percent of sales method places more emphasis on the [Select] and thus emphasizes the [Select].

b. When advising Mandy about whether an account is uncollectible, you would suggest all of the following as indicators of uncollectibility, except:

a. When a customer files for bankruptcy.
b. When the customer closes his/her business.
c. When the customer cannot be located.
d. When the customer's credit score increases.

To view a demo of CengageNOWv2, please visit: **http://services.cengage.com/dcs/cengagenowv2/learn/**

Supplements for the Instructor

- **Product Companion Site** includes convenient downloads of the instructor supplements, including PowerPoint presentations, Instructor's Manual, Solutions Manual, and Excel® template solutions. Log in at www.cengage.com/login.
- **Test Bank Available with Cengage Learning Testing Powered by Cognero** is a flexible, online system that allows you to:
  - author, edit, and manage test bank content from multiple Cengage Learning solutions
  - create multiple test versions in an instant
  - deliver tests from your LMS, your classroom, or wherever you want.
- **PowerPoint® Presentation Slides** Included on the product companion site. Each presentation enhances lectures and simplifies class preparation.
- **Instructor Excel® Templates** This resource provides the solutions for the problems and exercises that have enhanced Excel® templates for students.
- **Instructor's Manual** Each chapter contains a number of resources designed to aid instructors as they prepare lectures, assign homework, and teach in the classroom.
- **Solutions Manual** The Solutions Manual contains answers to all exercises, problems, and cases that appear in the text. As always, the solutions are author-written and verified multiple times for numerical accuracy and consistency with the core text.

Acknowledgments

Many people deserve thanks for their contributions to this text. For the Eighth edition Amanda Farmer and Mark Sears provided a thorough technical review and verification of the end-of-chapter materials. Robin Browning and Tomeika Williams did a thorough review of the CNOWv2 content. Andrea Meyer, the Content Developer from Cengage who helped to manage the timeline and development process for this edition. The comments from the following reviewers also influenced recent edition of the text as well as the current edition:

Sharon Agee, *Rollins College*
Tim Alzheimer, *Montana State University, Bozeman*
Scott R. Berube, *University of New Hampshire, Whittemore School of Business & Economics*
Jekabs Bikis, *Dallas Baptist University*
Jerold Braun, *Daytona State College*
Suzanne Lyn Cercone, *Keystone College*
H. Edward Gallatin, *Indiana State University*
Robert E. Holtfreter, *Central Washington University*
José Luis Hortensi, *Miami Dade College*
Daniel Kerch, *Pennsylvania Highlands Community College*
William J. Lavelle, *Ave Maria University*
Ann E. Martel, *Marquette University*
Edna C. Mitchell, *Polk State College*
Tami Park, *University of Great Falls*
Craig Pence, *Highland Community College*
Patricia G. Roshto, *University of Louisiana at Monroe*
Geeta Shankar, *University of Dayton*
Alice Sineath, *Forsyth Technical Community College*
Hans Sprohge, *Wright State University*
Gary Volk, *Wayne State College*

Your comments and suggestions as you use this text are sincerely appreciated.

Carl S. Warren

About the Author

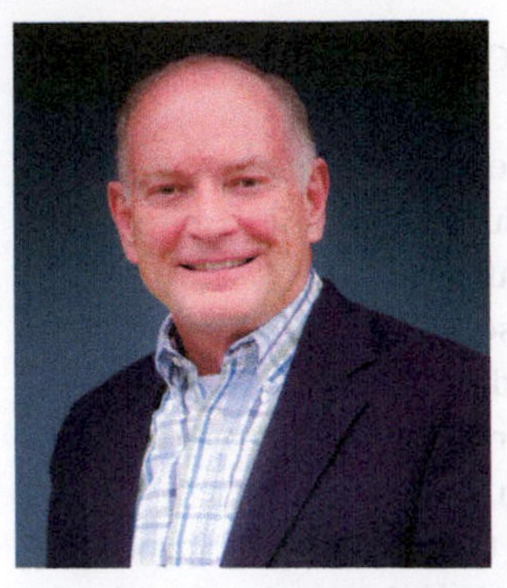

Carl S. Warren

Dr. Carl S. Warren is Professor Emeritus of Accounting at the University of Georgia, Athens. For over twenty-five years, Professor Warren has taught all levels of accounting classes. In recent years, Professor Warren has focused his teaching efforts on principles of accounting and auditing courses. Professor Warren has taught classes at the University of Iowa, Michigan State University, and University of Chicago. Professor Warren received his doctorate degree (PhD) from Michigan State University and his undergraduate (BBA) and master's (MA) degrees from the University of Iowa. During his career, Professor Warren published numerous articles in professional journals, including *The Accounting Review, Journal of Accounting Research, Journal of Accountancy, The CPA Journal,* and *Auditing: A Journal of Practice & Theory*. Professor Warren's outside interests include handball, skiing, hiking, fly-fishing, and golf. Professor Warren also spends time backpacking U.S. national parks (Yellowstone and the Grand Canyon), playing with his grandchildren, and riding ATVs and motorcycles.

Brief Contents

Contents

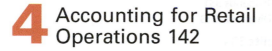

13 Budgeting and Standard Costs 546

14 Decentralized Operations 609

15 Capital Investment Analysis 651

Chapter 1

The Role of Accounting in Business

What's Covered:

Topics: The Role of Accounting in Business

Nature of Business
- Types of Business (Obj. 1)
- Forms of Business (Obj. 1)
- Business Strategies (Obj. 1)
- Business Stakeholders (Obj. 1)
- Business Activities (Obj. 2)

Role of Accounting
- Financial and Managerial Accounting (Obj. 3)
- Income Statement (Obj. 4)
- Statement of Changes in Stockholders' Equity (Obj. 4)
- Balance Sheet (Obj. 4)
- Statement of Cash Flows (Obj. 4)
- Accounting Concepts (Obj. 5)

Metric-Based Analysis
- Types of Analyses (Obj. 6)
- Return on Assets (Obj. 6)

Learning Objectives

Obj.1 Describe the types and forms of businesses, how businesses make money, and business stakeholders.

Obj.2 Describe the three business activities of financing, investing, and operating.

Obj.3 Define accounting and describe its role in business.

Obj.4 Describe and illustrate the basic financial statements and how they interrelate.

Obj.5 Describe eight accounting concepts underlying financial reporting.

Obj.6 Describe types of metrics and analyze a company's performance using return on assets.

Chapter Metrics

Use the following metrics to analyze transactions and financial statements

TRANSACTIONS*

Liquidity: N/A

Profitability: N/A

FINANCIAL STATEMENTS

Return on Assets

* There are no transactions in this chapter.

LinkedIn

LinkedIn

Evan Lorne/Shutterstock.com

How much are you willing to pay for stock of a company that has never been traded on a public market? Investors must come up with an answer to this question for companies that offer stock to the public for the first time, which is called an *initial public offering*.

In the United States, before such companies can offer stock for sale, they must file a prospectus (Form S-1) with the Securities and Exchange Commission. The prospectus includes background information on the company, including its business strategy and the range of prices that the stock is expected to sell for in the market. Also included in the prospectus are the company's financial statements for the past three years.

LinkedIn Corporation (LNKD) offered its stock for sale to the public in May 2011. At that time, LinkedIn was the world's largest professional network on the Internet with more than 100 million members in over 200 countries. Members join the network free of cost and are able to create and manage their professional identity online. LinkedIn generates its revenues by offering premium services to its members and by selling services such as hiring and marketing solutions to businesses and professional organizations.

In its prospectus filed with the Securities and Exchange Commission in 2011, LinkedIn indicated that it anticipated a price for its stock of between $42.00 and $45.00 per share. On the first day the stock was publicly traded, LinkedIn's stock rose to a high of $122.70, more than two and a half times its highest anticipated price of $45.00. LinkedIn recently traded on the New York Exhange for over $135.

Is LinkedIn's stock really worth over $100 per share? To answer this question, investors analyze LinkedIn's financial condition and performance using public information, including its financial statements.*

In this chapter, the nature, types, and activities of businesses, such as LinkedIn, are described and illustrated. In addition, the role of accounting in business, including financial statements, basic accounting concepts, and how to use metrics to evaluate a business's performance, are also described and illustrated.

* In June 2016 Microsoft and LinkedIn entered into an agreement in which Microsoft (MSFT) would acquire LinkedIn for $196 per share.

Objective 1
Describe the types and forms of businesses, how businesses make money, and business stakeholders.

Nature of Business and Accounting

A **business**[1] is an organization in which basic resources (inputs), such as materials and labor, are assembled and processed to provide goods or services (outputs) to customers. Businesses come in all sizes, from a local coffee house to **Starbucks**, which sells over $19 billion of coffee and related products each year.

The objective of most businesses is to earn a profit. **Profit** is the difference between the amounts received from customers for goods or services and the amounts paid for the inputs used to provide the goods or services. In this text, we focus on businesses operating to earn a profit. However, many of the same concepts and principles also apply to not-for-profit organizations such as hospitals, churches, and government agencies.

Types of Businesses

Three types of businesses operated for profit include service, merchandising, and manufacturing businesses. Each type of business and some examples are described below.

Service businesses provide services rather than products to customers.

Delta Air Lines (transportation services)
The Walt Disney Company (entertainment services)

Merchandising businesses sell products they purchase from other businesses to customers.

Wal-Mart (general merchandise)
Amazon.com (books, music, videos)

1. A complete glossary of terms appears at the end of the text.

Manufacturing businesses change basic inputs into products that are sold to customers.

General Motors Corporation (cars, trucks, vans)
Dell Inc. (personal computers)

LinkedIn is a service business that provides value to its members by connecting them to people, knowledge, and opportunities to advance their careers.

LinkedIn Connection

Forms of Business

A business is normally organized in one of the following four forms:

- proprietorship
- partnership
- corporation
- limited liability company

A **proprietorship** is owned by one individual. More than 70% of the businesses in the United States are organized as proprietorships. The frequency of this form is due to the ease and low cost of organizing. The primary disadvantage of proprietorships is that the financial resources are limited to the individual owner's resources. In addition, the owner has unlimited liability to creditors for the debts of the company.

A **partnership** is owned by two or more individuals. About 10% of the businesses in the United States are organized as partnerships. Like a proprietorship, a partnership may outgrow the financial resources of its owners. Also, the partners have unlimited liability to creditors for the debts of the company.

A **corporation** is organized under state or federal statutes as a separate legal entity. The ownership of a corporation is divided into shares of stock. A corporation issues the stock to individuals or other companies, who then become owners or stockholders of the corporation. A primary advantage of the corporate form is the ability to obtain large amounts of resources by issuing shares of stock. In addition, the stockholders' liability to creditors for the debts of the company is limited to their investment in the corporation.

LinkedIn is organized as a corporation in Delaware even though its offices are in Mountain View, California. Many companies incorporate in Delaware because of its favorable legal and business environment.

LinkedIn Connection

A **limited liability company (LLC)** combines attributes of a partnership and a corporation. The primary advantage of the limited liability company form is that it operates similar to a partnership, but its owners' (or members') liability for the debts of the company is limited to their investment. Many professional practices such as, lawyers, doctors, and accountants are organized as limited liability companies.

In addition to the ease of formation, ability to raise capital, and liability for the debts of the business, other factors such as taxes and legal life of the business should be considered when forming a business. For example, corporations are taxed as separate legal entities, while the income of sole proprietorships, partnerships, and limited liability companies is passed through to the owners and taxed on the owners' tax returns. As separate legal entities, corporations also continue on, regardless of the lives of the individual owners. In contrast, sole proprietorships, partnerships, and limited liability companies may terminate their existence with the death of an individual owner.

The characteristics of sole proprietorships, partnerships, corporations, and limited liability companies are summarized below.

Organizational Form	Ease of Formation	Legal Liability	Taxation	Limitation on Life of Entity	Access to Capital
Proprietorship	Simple	No limitation	Nontaxable (pass-through) entity	Yes	Limited
Partnership	Simple	No limitation	Nontaxable (pass-through) entity	Yes	Average
Corporation	Complex	Limited liability	Taxable entity	No	Extensive
Limited Liability Company	Moderate	Limited liability	Nontaxable (pass-through) entity by election	Yes	Average

The three types of businesses we discussed earlier—manufacturing, merchandising, and service—may be proprietorships, partnerships, corporations, or limited liability companies. However, businesses that require a large amount of resources, such as many manufacturing businesses, are corporations. Likewise, most large retailers such as **Wal-Mart**, **Target**, and **Macy's** are corporations.

Because most large businesses are corporations, they tend to dominate the economic activity in the United States. For this reason, this text focuses on the corporate form of organization. However, many of the concepts and principles discussed also apply to proprietorships, partnerships, and limited liability companies.

How Do Businesses Make Money?

The objective of a business is to earn a profit by providing goods or services to customers. How does a company decide which products or services to offer its customers? Many factors influence this decision. Ultimately, however, the decision is based on how the company plans to gain an advantage over its competitors and, in doing so, maximize its profits.

Companies try to maximize their profits by generating high revenues while maintaining low costs, which results in high profits. However, a company's competitors are also trying to do the same, and thus, a company can only maximize its profits by gaining an advantage over its competitors.

Generally, companies gain an advantage over their competitors by using one of the following strategies:

- A **low-cost strategy**, where a company designs and produces products or services at a lower cost than its competitors. Such companies often sell no-frills, standardized products and services.
- A **premium-price strategy**, where a company tries to design and produce products or services that serve unique market needs, allowing it to charge premium prices. Such companies often design and market their products so that customers perceive their products or services as having a unique quality, reliability, or image.

Wal-Mart and **Southwest Airlines** are examples of companies using a low-cost strategy. **John Deere**, **Tommy Hilfiger**, and **BMW** are examples of companies using a premium-price strategy.

Since business is highly competitive, it is difficult for a company to sustain a competitive advantage over time. For example, a competitor of a company using a low-cost strategy may copy the company's low-cost methods or develop new methods that achieve even lower costs. Likewise, a competitor of a company using a premium-price strategy may develop products that are perceived as more desirable by customers.

Examples of companies utilizing low-cost and premium-price strategies include:

- Local pharmacies who develop personalized relationships with their customers. By doing so, they are able to charge premium (higher) prices. In contrast, Wal-Mart's pharmacies use the low-cost emphasis and compete on cost.
- Grocery stores such as **Kroger** and **Safeway** develop relationships with their customers by issuing preferred customer cards. These cards allow the stores to track consumer preferences and buying habits for use in purchasing and advertising campaigns.

- **Honda** promotes the reliability and quality ratings of its automobiles and thus charges premium prices. Similarly, **Volvo** promotes the safety characteristics of its automobiles. In contrast, **Kia** uses a low-cost strategy.
- **Harley-Davidson** emphasizes that its motorcycles are "Made in America" and promotes its "rebel" image as a means of charging higher prices than its competitors **Honda**, **Yamaha**, or **Suzuki**.

Companies sometimes struggle to find a competitive advantage. For example, **JCPenney** and **Macy's** have difficulty competing on low costs against **Wal-Mart**, **Kohl's**, **T.J. Maxx**, and **Target**. At the same time, JCPenney and Sears have difficulty charging premium prices against competitors such as **The Gap**, **Eddie Bauer**, and **Talbot's**. Likewise, **Delta Air Lines** and **United Airlines** have difficulty competing against low-cost airlines such as **Southwest**. At the same time, Delta and United don't offer any unique services for which their passengers are willing to pay a premium price.

Exhibit 1 summarizes low-cost and premium-price strategies with common examples of companies that employ each strategy.

Exhibit 1 Business Strategies and Industries

	Industry					
Business Strategy	Airline	Freight	Automotive	Retail	Financial Services	Hotel
Low cost	Southwest	Union Pacific	Hyundai	Sam's Club	Ameritrade	Super 8
Premium price	Virgin Atlantic	FedEx	BMW	Talbot's	Morgan Stanley	Ritz-Carlton

LinkedIn's strategy is to be the premier online professional network that allows its members to be more productive and successful. It provides a free platform for members to manage their professional identify and engage in professional networks. To make money (monetize itself), it provides recruiting and marketing services to organizations and enterprises for a fee.

LinkedIn Connection

Business Stakeholders

A **business stakeholder** is a person or entity with an interest in the economic performance and well-being of a company. For example, owners, suppliers, customers, and employees are all stakeholders in a company.

Business stakeholders can be classified into one of the four categories illustrated in Exhibit 2.

Exhibit 2 Business Stakeholders

Business Stakeholder	Interest in the Business	Examples
Capital market stakeholders	Providers of major financing for the business	Banks, owners, stockholders
Product or service market stakeholders	Buyers of products or services and vendors to the business	Customers and suppliers
Government stakeholders	Collect taxes and fees from the business and its employees	Federal, state, and city governments
Internal stakeholders	Individuals employed by the business	Employees and managers

Capital market stakeholders provide the financing for a company to begin and continue its operations. Banks and other long-term creditors have an economic interest in receiving the amount loaned plus interest. Owners want to maximize the economic value of their investments.

Product or service market stakeholders purchase the company's products or services or sell their products or services to the company. Customers have an economic interest in the continued success of the company. For example, customers who purchase advance tickets on **Delta Air Lines** are depending on Delta continuing in business. Likewise, suppliers depend on continued success of their customers. For example, if a customer fails or cuts back on purchases, the supplier's business will also decline.

Government stakeholders, such as federal, state, county, and city governments, collect taxes from companies. The better a company does, the more taxes the government collects. In addition, workers who are laid off by a company can file claims for unemployment compensation, which results in a financial burden for the state and federal governments.

Internal stakeholders, such as managers and employees, depend upon the continued success of the company for keeping their jobs. Managers of companies that perform poorly are often fired by the owners. Likewise, during economic downturns companies often lay off workers. Stakeholders are illustrated in Exhibit 3.

LinkedIn Connection LinkedIn's stakeholders include common stockholders, bondholders, network members, employees, and U.S. and state governments who receives taxes.

Exhibit 3 Business Stakeholders

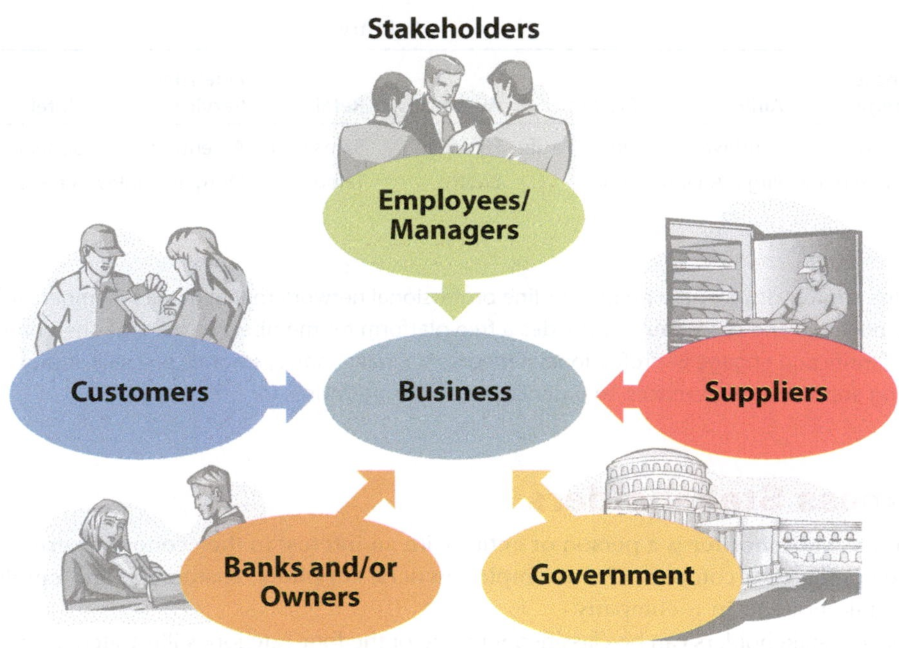

Integrity, Objectivity, and Ethics in Business

The Hershey Trust Company

Milton Snavely Hershey founded **The Hershey Company** after serving as a candy apprentice in Philadelphia, running a failing candy shop, and finally succeeding at caramel making. Milton started The Hershey Company in the early 1900s after selling his caramel company.

Milton and his wife, Catherine, couldn't have children, and in 1909, they created the Milton Hershey School. After Catherine's death, Milton willed virtually his entire fortune, including his interest in The Hershey Company, to the School. Today, the School provides free education, meals, clothing, health care, and a home to almost 2,000 children in financial and social need. The School is run by The Hershey Trust Company, which is the largest shareholder of The Hershey Company.

Finnbarr Webster/Alamy Stock Photo

A public uproar was created in 2002 when the trustees of The Hershey Trust Company tried to sell their controlling stock interest in The Hershey Company. As a result of the public outcry, the majority of the trustees were forced to resign.

Source: Adapted from www.thehersheycompany.com.

Business Activities

Objective 2
Describe the three business activities of financing, investing, and operating.

All companies engage in the following three business activities:

- **Financing activities** to obtain the necessary funds (monies) to organize and operate the company
- **Investing activities** to obtain assets such as buildings and equipment to begin and operate the company
- **Operating activities** to earn revenues and profits

The preceding business activities are illustrated in Exhibit 4.

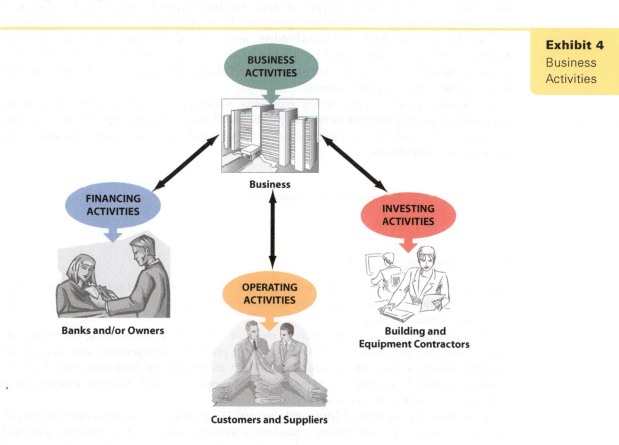

Exhibit 4 Business Activities

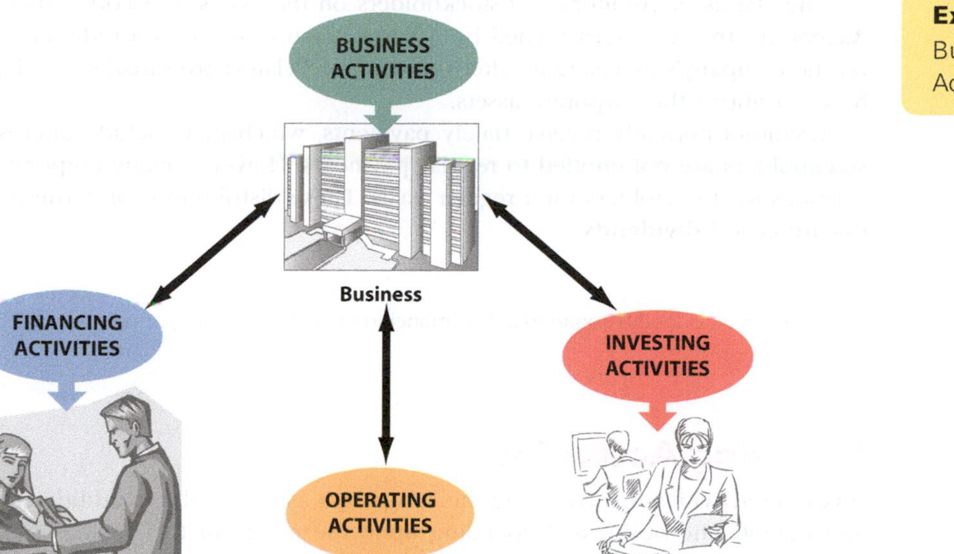

Financing Activities

Financing activities involve obtaining funds to begin and operate a business. Companies obtain financing through the use of capital markets by:

- borrowing
- issuing shares of ownership

When a company borrows money, it incurs a liability. A **liability** is a legal obligation to repay the amount borrowed according to the terms of the borrowing agreement. When a company borrows from a vendor or supplier, the liability is called an **account payable**. In such cases, the company promises to pay according to the terms set by the vendor or supplier. Most vendors and suppliers require payment within a relatively short time, such as 30 days.

On a recent balance sheet, LinkedIn reported $100.3 million of accounts payable.

LinkedIn Connection

A company may also borrow money by issuing bonds. *Bonds* are sold to investors and require repayment normally with interest. The amount of the bonds, called the *face value*, usually requires repayment several years in the future. Thus, bonds are a form of long-term financing. The interest on the bonds, however, is normally paid semiannually. Bond obligations are reported as **bonds payable**, and any interest that is due is reported as **interest payable**.

Many companies borrow by issuing notes payable. A **note payable** requires payment of the amount borrowed plus interest. Notes payable are similar to bonds except that they may be issued on either a short-term or a long-term basis.

A company may finance its operations by issuing shares of ownership. For a corporation, shares of ownership are issued in the form of shares of stock. Although corporations may issue a variety of different types of stock, the basic type of stock issued to owners is called **common stock**.[2] Investors who purchase the stock are referred to as **stockholders**.

The claims of creditors and stockholders on the assets of a corporation are different. **Assets** are the resources owned by a corporation (company). Creditors have first claim on the company's assets. Only after the creditors' claims are satisfied do the stockholders have a right to the corporate assets.

Creditors normally receive timely payments, which may include interest. In contrast, stockholders are not entitled to regular payments. However, many corporations distribute earnings to stockholders on a regular basis. These distributions of earnings to stockholders are called **dividends**.

LinkedIn Connection

In a recent year, LinkedIn engaged in the financing activities of issuing bonds and stock.

Investing Activities

Investing activities involve using the company's assets to obtain additional assets to start and operate the business. Depending upon the nature of the business, a variety of different assets must be acquired.

Most businesses need assets such as machinery, buildings, computers, office furnishings, trucks, and automobiles. These assets have physical characteristics and as such are **tangible assets**. Long-term tangible assets such as machinery, buildings, and land are reported separately as property, plant, and equipment. Short-term tangible assets such as cash and inventories are reported separately.

A business may also need **intangible assets**. For example, a business may obtain patent rights to use in manufacturing a product. Long-term assets such as patents, goodwill, and copyrights are reported separately as intangible assets.

A company may also prepay for items such as insurance or rent. Such items, which are assets until they are consumed, are reported as **prepaid expenses**. In addition, rights to payments from customers who purchase merchandise or services on credit are reported as **accounts receivable**.

LinkedIn Connection

For a recent year, LinkedIn engaged in the investing activities of purchasing property and equipment as well as acquiring other companies, including Bizo, Inc. and Bright Media Corporation.

Operating Activities

Operating activities involve using assets to earn revenues and profits. The management of a company does this by implementing one of the business strategies discussed earlier.

2. Other types of stock are discussed in Chapter 8, "Liabilities and Stockholders' Equity."

Revenue is the increase in assets from selling products or services. Revenues are normally identified according to their source. For example, revenues received from selling products are called **sales**. Revenues received from providing services are called **fees earned**.

In a recent year, LinkedIn reported $2.2 billiion of revenue.

LinkedIn Connection

To earn revenue, a business incurs costs, such as wages of employees, salaries of managers, rent, insurance, advertising, freight, and utilities. Costs used to earn revenue are called **expenses** and are identified and reported in a variety of ways. For example, the cost of products sold is referred to as the **cost of goods sold, cost of merchandise sold, or cost of sales**. Other expenses are normally classified as either selling expenses or administrative expenses. **Selling expenses** include those costs directly related to the selling of a product or service. For example, selling expenses include such costs as sales salaries, sales commissions, freight, and advertising costs. **Administrative expenses** include other costs not directly related to the selling such as officer salaries and other costs of the corporate office.

By comparing the revenues for a period to the related expenses, it can be determined whether the company has earned net income or incurred a net loss. **Net income** results when revenues exceed expenses. A **net loss** results when expenses exceed revenues.

In a recent year, LinkedIn reported income from operations of $36.1 million and a net loss of $15.3 million after taxes.

LinkedIn Connection

As discussed next, the major role of accounting is to provide stakeholders with information on the financing, investing, and operating activities of businesses. Financial statements are one source of such information.

What Is Accounting and Its Role in Business?

Objective 3
Define accounting and describe its role in business.

The *role of accounting* is to provide information about the financing, investing, and operating activities of a company to its stakeholders. For example, accounting provides information for managers to use in operating the business. In addition, accounting provides information to other stakeholders, such as creditors, for assessing the economic performance and condition of the company.

Accounting is often called the "language of business." In a general sense, **accounting** is defined as an information system that provides reports to stakeholders about the economic activities and condition of a business. This text focuses on accounting and its role in business. However, many of the concepts discussed also apply to individuals, governments, and not-for-profit organizations. For example, individuals must account for their hours worked, checks written, and bills paid. Stakeholders for individuals include creditors, dependents, and the government.

A primary purpose of accounting is to summarize the financial performance of a business for external stakeholders, such as banks and governmental agencies. The branch of accounting that is associated with preparing reports for users external to the business is called **financial accounting**. Accounting also can be used to guide management in making financing, investing, and operations decisions for the company. This branch of accounting is called **managerial accounting**. Financial and managerial accounting may overlap. For example, financial reports for external stakeholders are often used by managers in assessing the potential impact of their decisions on the company. The head of the accounting department in a company is called **comptroller** or **chief financial officer** (CFO).

LinkedIn Connection The chief financial officer (CFO) of LinkedIn is Steven J. Sordello (age 46), who earns a salary of $1 million.

The two major objectives of financial accounting are:

- To report the financial condition of a business at a point in time
- To report changes in the financial condition of a business over a period of time

The relationship between these two financial accounting objectives is shown in Exhibit 5.

Exhibit 5 Objectives of Financial Accounting

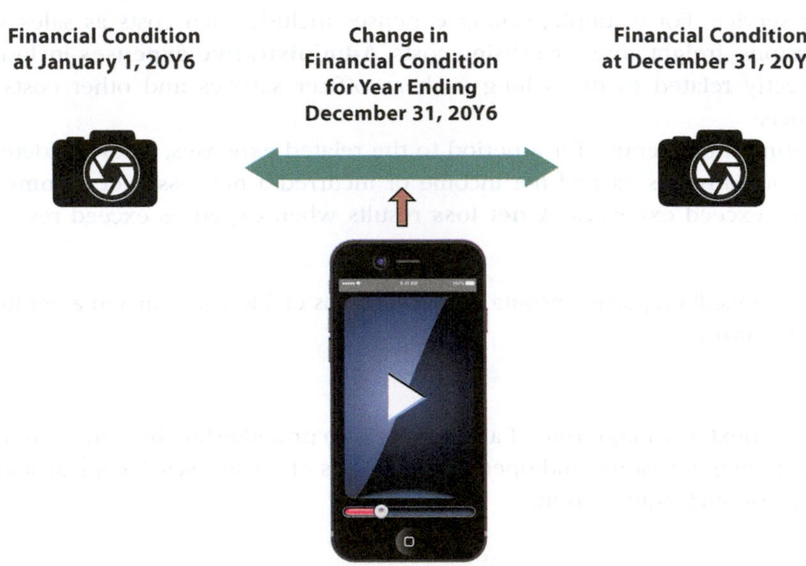

The first objective can be thought of as a still photograph (snapshot) of the company's financial (economic) condition as of a point in time. The second objective can be thought of as a moving picture (video) of the company's financial (economic) performance over time.

The objectives of accounting are achieved by (1) recording the economic events affecting a business and then (2) summarizing the impact of these events on the business in financial reports, called **financial statements**.

Objective 4 Describe and illustrate the basic financial statements and how they are integrated.

Financial Statements

Financial statements report the financial condition of a business at a point in time and changes in the financial condition over a period of time. The four basic financial statements and their relationship to the objectives of financial accounting are listed below.

Financial Statement	Financial Accounting Objective
Income Statement	Reports change in financial condition
Statement of Stockholders' Equity	Reports change in financial condition
Balance Sheet	Reports financial condition
Statement of Cash Flows	Reports change in financial condition

The order in which each financial statement is prepared and the nature of each statement is described below.

Order Prepared	Financial Statement	Description of Statement
1	Income Statement	A summary of the revenue and expenses for a specific period of time, such as a month or a year.
2	Statement of Stockholders' Equity	A summary of the changes in the stockholders' equity in the corporation for a specific period of time, such as a month or a year.
3	Balance Sheet	A list of the assets, liabilities, and stockholders' equity as of a specific date, usually at the close of the last day of a month or a year.
4	Statement of Cash Flows	A summary of the cash receipts and cash payments for a specific period of time, such as a month or a year.

The preceding four financial statements are described and illustrated in Exhibits 6 through 9 using **The Hershey Company (HSY)**. These illustrations will introduce you to the financial statements that you will be studying throughout this text. The data for the statements are adapted from a recent annual report of The Hershey Company.[3]

Income Statement

The **income statement** reports the change in financial condition due to the operations of the company. The time period covered by the income statement may vary depending upon the needs of stakeholders. Public corporations are required to file quarterly and annual income statements with the Securities and Exchange Commission (SEC). The income statement for a year ending December 31 for The Hershey Company is shown in Exhibit 6.

Since the objective of business operations is to generate revenues, the income statement begins by listing the revenues for the period. During the year, Hershey generated sales of $6,644 million. These sales are listed under "Revenues." The numbers shown in Exhibit 6 are expressed in millions of dollars. It is common for large companies to express their financial statements in thousands or millions of dollars.

Exhibit 6 Income Statement: The Hershey Company

The Hershey Company Income Statement For the Year Ended December 31 (in millions)		
Revenues:		
Sales		$6,644
Expenses:		
Cost of sales	$3,784	
Selling and administrative expenses	1,704	
Interest expense	96	
Income taxes expense	354	
Other expenses	45	(5,983)
Net income		$ 661

3. The financial statements for Hershey shown in Exhibits 6–9 are for the year ended December 31, 2015. The most up to date statements may be found at http://www.sec.gov/edgar/searchedgar/companysearch.html, enter Hershey's stock market symbol HSY in the Fast Search box, enter 10-K in the Filing Type box, and click on the latest 10-K.

Following the revenues, the expenses used in generating the revenues are listed. For Hershey, these expenses include cost of sales, selling and administrative, interest, income taxes, and other expenses. By reporting the expenses and the related revenues for a period, the expenses are said to be matched against the revenues. This is known in accounting as the *matching concept*, which is discussed later in this chapter.

When revenues exceed expenses for a period, the company has *net income*. If expenses exceed revenues, the company has a *net loss*. Net income means that the business increased its net assets through its operations. That is, the assets created by the revenues exceeded the assets used in generating those revenues.

The objective of most companies is to maximize net income or profit. A net loss means that the business decreased its net assets through its operations. While a business might survive in the short run by reporting net losses, in the long run a business must earn net income to survive.

Exhibit 6 shows that Hershey earned net income of $661 million. Is this good or bad? Certainly, net income is better than a net loss. However, the stakeholders must assess net income according to their objectives. For example, a creditor might be satisfied that the net income is sufficient to ensure that it will be repaid. In contrast, a stockholder might assess the corporation's profitability as less than its competitors' profits and thus be disappointed. Throughout this text, various methods of assessing corporate performance will be described and illustrated.

Statement of Stockholders' Equity

The **statement of stockholders' equity** reports the changes in financial condition due to changes in stockholders' equity for a period. Changes to stockholders' equity normally involve common stock and retained earnings. **Retained earnings** are the portion of a corporation's net income retained in the business. A corporation may retain all of its net income for expanding operations, or it may pay a portion or all of its net income as dividends. For example, high-growth companies often do not distribute dividends but instead retain profits for future expansion. In contrast, more mature corporations normally pay a regular dividend.

LinkedIn Connection

LinkedIn has never paid a dividend and doesn't intend to in the foreseeable future. Instead, it retains all its income to use in the development of its operations.

Since retained earnings depend upon net income, the period covered by the statement of stockholders' equity is the same period as the income statement. The statement of stockholders' equity for Hershey for the year ended December 31 is shown in Exhibit 7.

Exhibit 7 Statement of Stockholders' Equity

The Hershey Company
Statement of Stockholders' Equity
For the Year Ended December 31 (in millions)

	Common Stock	Retained Earnings	Other Items	Total
Balances, January 1	$360	$4,708	$(4,188)	$ 880
Net income		661		661
Dividends		(341)		(341)
Other items			(152)	(152)
Balances, December 31	$360	$5,028	$(4,340)	$1,048

There was no change in common stock during the year. During the year, Hershey earned net income of $661 million and distributed (declared) dividends of $341 million. Thus, Hershey's retained earnings increased from $4,188 million to $4,340 million during the year. Dividends are reported in the statement of stockholders' equity rather than the income statement. This is because dividends are not an expense but a distribution of net income to stockholders.

Exhibit 7 includes a column for other equity items. Items in this category include paid-in capital (amounts contributed in excess of the par value of stock) and Treasury stock (repurchased common stock) that will be discussed in a later chapter.

Balance Sheet

The balance sheet reports the financial condition *as of a point in time*. This is in contrast to the income statement, statement of stockholders' equity, and statement of cash flows, which report changes in financial condition *for a period of time*. The financial condition of a business as of a point in time is measured by its total assets and claims or rights to those assets.

The claims on a company's assets consist of rights of creditors and stockholders. The rights of creditors are *liabilities*. The rights of stockholders are referred to as **stockholders' equity** or **owners' equity**. Thus, the financial condition of a business can be expressed in equation form as:

Assets = Liabilities + Stockholders' Equity

This equation is called the **accounting equation**. This equation is the foundation of accounting information systems, which are discussed in later chapters.

The **balance sheet**, sometimes called the **statement of financial condition**, is prepared using the accounting equation. The balance sheet is prepared by listing the accounting equation in vertical rather than horizontal form as follows:

Step 1. Each *asset* is listed and added to arrive at *total assets*.
Step 2. Each *liability* is listed and added to arrive at *total liabilities*.
Step 3. Each *stockholders' equity* item is listed and added to arrive at *total stockholders' equity*.
Step 4. Total liabilities and total stockholders' equity is added to arrive at *total liabilities and stockholders' equity*.
Step 5. Total assets must equal total liabilities and stockholders' equity.

The accounting equation must balance in Step 5; hence, the name balance sheet. The balance sheet for The Hershey Company as of December 31 is shown in Exhibit 8.

Exhibit 8 reports total assets of $4,754 million equal its total liabilities of $3,706 million plus its total stockholders' equity of $1,048 million.

Statement of Cash Flows

The **statement of cash flows** reports the change in financial condition due to the changes in cash during a period. The statement of cash flows is organized around the three business activities of financing, investing, and operating. Any changes in cash must be related to one or more of these activities.

The *net cash flows from operating activities* is reported first. This is because cash flows from operating activities is a primary focus of the company's stakeholders. In the short term, creditors use cash flows from operating activities to assess whether the company's operating activities are generating enough cash to repay them. In the long term, a company cannot survive unless it generates positive cash flows from operating activities. Thus, cash flows from operating activities is also a focus of employees, managers, suppliers, customers, and other stakeholders who are interested in the long-term success of the company.

The *net cash flows from investing activities* is reported second. This is because investing activities directly impact the operations of the company. Cash receipts from

Exhibit 8 Balance Sheet: The Hershey Company

The Hershey Company Balance Sheet December 31 (in millions)	
Assets	
Cash	$ 728
Accounts receivable	461
Inventories	633
Prepaid expenses	168
Property, plant, and equipment	1,674
Intangibles	803
Other assets	287
Total assets	$4,754
Liabilities	
Accounts payable	$ 442
Accrued liabilities	651
Notes and other debt	2,611
Income taxes payable	2
Total liabilities	$3,706
Stockholders' Equity	
Capital stock	$ 579
Retained earnings	5,028
Repurchased capital stock and other equity items	(4,559)
Total stockholders' equity	$1,048
Total liabilities and stockholders' equity	$4,754

selling property, plant, and equipment are reported in this section. Likewise, any purchases of property, plant, and equipment are reported as cash payments. Companies that are expanding rapidly, such as start-up companies, normally report negative net cash flows from investing activities. In contrast, companies that are downsizing or selling segments of the business may report positive net cash flows from investing activities.

The *net cash flows from financing activities* is reported third. Any cash receipts from issuing debt or stock are reported in this section as cash receipts. Likewise, cash payments of debt and dividends are reported in this section.

The statement of cash flows is completed by adding the net cash flows from operating, investing, and financing activities to determine the *net increase or decrease in cash* for the period. This net increase or decrease in cash is then added to the *cash at the beginning of the period* to arrive at the *cash at the end of the period.*

The statement of cash flows for The Hershey Company for the year ended December 31 is shown in Exhibit 9.

During the year, Hershey's *operating activities* generated a positive net cash flow of $1,095 million. Hershey's *investing activities* used $473 million of cash primarily to purchase property, plant, equipment, and other long-term assets. Hershey's *financing activities* used $587 million of cash. This cash was used to pay dividends of $341 million, pay debt of $115 million, and purchase $511 million of its own stock. A company may purchase its own common stock if the corporate management believes its stock is undervalued or for providing stock to employees or managers as part of an incentive (stock option) plan.[4] Hershey received cash of $380 million primarily by borrowing from creditors.

4. The accounting for a company's purchase of its own stock, termed treasury stock, is discussed in a later chapter.

Exhibit 9 Statement of Cash Flows: The Hershey Company

The Hershey Company Statement of Cash Flows For the Year Ended December 31 (in millions)		
Net cash flows from operating activities		$1,095
Cash flows used in investing activities:		
Investments in property, plant, equipment, and other long-term assets	$ (473)	
Net cash flows used in investing activities		(473)
Cash flows from financing activities:		
Cash receipts from financing activities, including debt	$ 380	
Dividends paid to stockholders	(341)	
Repurchase of stock	(511)	
Other, including repayment of debt	(115)	
Net cash flows used in financing activities		(587)
Net increase in cash during year		$ 35
Cash as of January 1		693
Cash as of December 31		$ 728

During the year Hershey increased its cash by $35 million. This increase is added to the cash at the beginning of the period of $693 million to arrive at net cash at the end of the period of $728 million.

Overall, Hershey's statement of cash flows indicates that Hershey generated over $1,095 million in cash flows from its operations. It used this cash to expand its operations and pay dividends to stockholders. Thus, Hershey appears to be in a strong operating position.

Integrated Financial Statements

The financial statements are prepared in the following order:

1. income statement
2. statement of stockholders' equity
3. balance sheet
4. statement of cash flows

Preparing the financial statements in the preceding order is important because the financial statements are integrated as follows:[5]

1. The income statement and statement of stockholders' equity are integrated. The net income or net loss reported on the income statement also appears on the statement of stockholders' equity as either an addition (net income) to or deduction (net loss) from the beginning retained earnings.
2. The statement of stockholders' equity and the balance sheet are integrated. The common stock and retained earnings at the end of the period on the statement of stockholders' equity also appear on the balance sheet.
3. The balance sheet and statement of cash flows are integrated. The cash on the balance sheet also appears as the end-of-period cash on the statement of cash flows.

5. Depending upon the method of preparing cash flows from operating activities, net income may also appear on the statement of cash flows. This method of preparing the statement of cash flows is called the indirect method. This method is illustrated in a later chapter. In addition, Chapter 2 illustrates how cash flows from operating activities may equal net income.

To illustrate, The Hershey Company's financial statements in Exhibits 6 through 9 are integrated as follows:

1. *Net income* of $661 million is also reported on the statement of stockholders' equity as an addition to the beginning retained earnings.
2. *Retained earnings* of $5,028 million and common stock of $360 as of December 31 are also reported on the balance sheet.
3. *Cash* of $728 million on the December 31 balance sheet is also reported as the end-of-period cash on the statement of cash flows.

The preceding integrations are shown in Exhibit 10. These integrations are important in analyzing (1) financial statements and (2) the impact of transactions on the financial statements. In addition, these integrations serve as a check on whether the financial statements have been prepared correctly. For example, if the ending cash on the statement of cash flows doesn't agree with the balance sheet cash, then an error has occurred.

Exhibit 10 Integrated Financial Statements

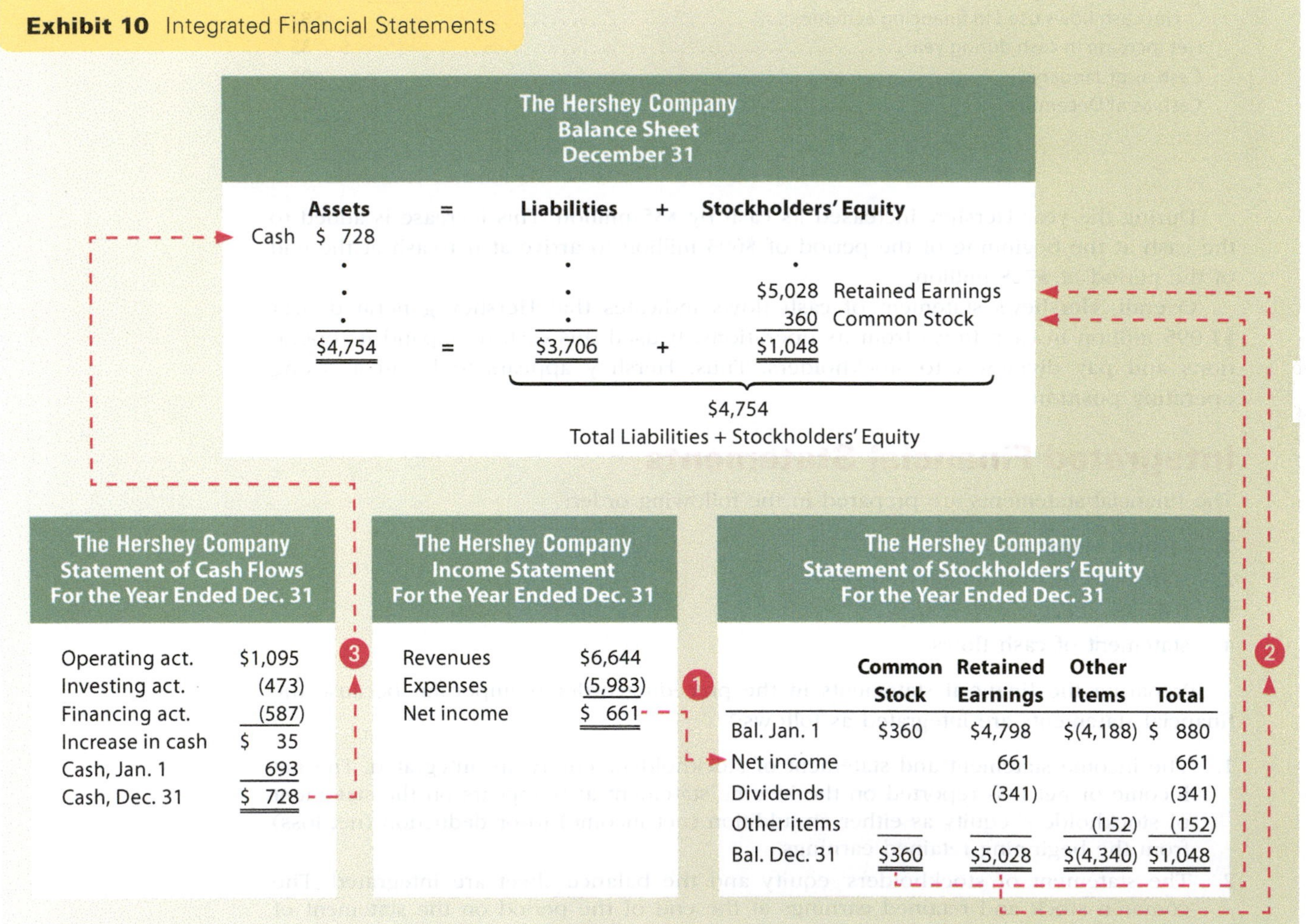

The Hershey Company
Balance Sheet
December 31

	Assets	=	Liabilities	+	Stockholders' Equity	
Cash	$ 728					
	•		•		•	
	•		•		$5,028	Retained Earnings
	•		•		360	Common Stock
	$4,754	=	$3,706	+	$1,048	

$4,754
Total Liabilities + Stockholders' Equity

The Hershey Company
Statement of Cash Flows
For the Year Ended Dec. 31

Operating act.	$1,095
Investing act.	(473)
Financing act.	(587)
Increase in cash	$ 35
Cash, Jan. 1	693
Cash, Dec. 31	$ 728

The Hershey Company
Income Statement
For the Year Ended Dec. 31

Revenues	$6,644
Expenses	(5,983)
Net income	$ 661

The Hershey Company
Statement of Stockholders' Equity
For the Year Ended Dec. 31

	Common Stock	Retained Earnings	Other Items	Total
Bal. Jan. 1	$360	$4,798	$(4,188)	$ 880
Net income		661		661
Dividends		(341)		(341)
Other items			(152)	(152)
Bal. Dec. 31	$360	$5,028	$(4,340)	$1,048

Accounting Concepts

Objective 5
Describe eight accounting concepts underlying financial reporting.

The four corporate financial statements described and illustrated in the preceding section were prepared using accounting "rules," called **generally accepted accounting principles (GAAP)**. Generally accepted accounting principles (GAAP) are necessary so that stakeholders can compare companies across time. If the management of a company could prepare financial statements as they saw fit, the comparability between companies and across time would be impossible.

Accounting principles and concepts develop from research, accepted accounting practices, and pronouncements of regulators. Within the United States, the **Financial Accounting Standards Board (FASB)** has the primary responsibility for developing accounting principles. The FASB publishes *Statements of Financial Accounting Standards* as well as interpretations of these *Standards*.

The **Securities and Exchange Commission (SEC)**, an agency of the U.S. government, also has authority over the accounting and financial disclosures for corporations whose stock is traded and sold to the public. The SEC normally accepts the accounting principles set forth by the FASB. However, the SEC may issue *Staff Accounting Bulletins* on accounting matters that may not have been addressed by the FASB.

Many countries outside the United States use generally accepted accounting principles adopted by the **International Accounting Standards Board (IASB)**. The IASB issues *International Financial Reporting Standards (IFRS)*. Significant differences currently exist between FASB and IASB accounting principles. However, the FASB and IASB are working together to reduce and eliminate these differences towards the goal of developing a single set of accounting principles. Such a set of worldwide accounting principles would help facilitate investment and business in an increasingly global economy.

Generally accepted accounting principles (GAAP) rely upon eight supporting accounting concepts, as shown in Exhibit 11. Throughout this text, emphasis is on accounting principles and concepts. In this way, you will gain an understanding of "why" as well as "how" accounting is applied in business. Such an understanding is essential for analyzing and interpreting financial statements.

Business Entity Concept

The **business entity concept** limits the economic data recorded in an accounting system to data related to the activities of that company. In other words, the company is viewed as an entity separate from its owners, creditors, or other companies. For example, a company with one owner records the activities of only that company and does not record the personal activities, property, or debts of the owner. A business entity may take the form of a proprietorship, partnership, corporation, or limited liability company (LLC).

To illustrate, the accounting for The Hershey Company, a corporation, is separate from the accounting of its stakeholders. In other words, the accounting for transactions and events of individual stockholders, creditors, or other Hershey stakeholders is not included in The Hershey Company's financial statements. Only the transactions and events of the corporation are included.

International Connection

Adoption or Convergence?

The largest public accounting firms, known as the Big Four, have pushed for the "adoption" of IFRS in the United States within a relatively short period of time. Such a strategy of adoption would generate millions of dollars of consulting and accounting work within the U.S. for the Big Four: Deloitte Touche Tohmatsu, PwC (PriceWaterhouseCoopers), Ernst & Young, and KPMG.

In contrast, others have argued for a strategy of gradual "convergence" to IFRS over time. Currently, it appears that regulators within the United States and the FASB are favoring convergence rather than adoption. For example, the FASB and IASB have completed several projects to converge U.S. and IFRS standards.[1]

1. FASB.org, "Progress Report on IASB-FASB Convergence Work," April 21, 2011.

Exhibit 11
Accounting Principles and Concepts

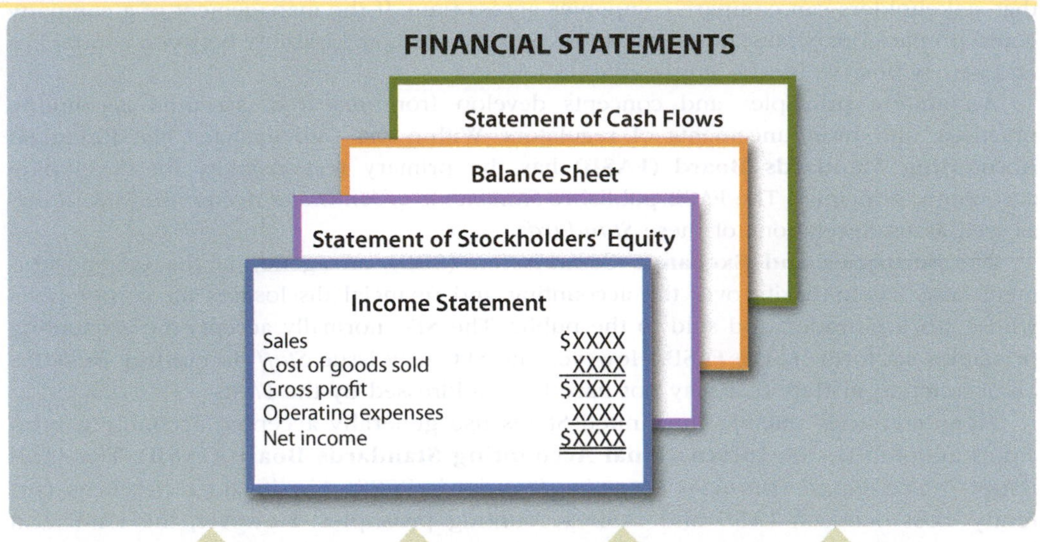

Generally Accepted Accounting Principles (GAAP)

ACCOUNTING CONCEPTS

- **Business Entity Concept**
- **Cost Concept**
- **Going Concern Concept**
- **Matching Concept**
- **Objectivity Concept**
- **Unit of Measure Concept**
- **Adequate Disclosure Concept**
- **Accounting Period Concept**

Cost Concept

The **cost concept** initially records assets in the accounting records at their cost or purchase price. To illustrate, assume that Aaron Publishers purchased the following land on August 3, 20Y4, for $150,000:

Price listed by seller on March 1, 20Y4	$160,000
Aaron Publishers' initial offer to buy on January 31, 20Y4	140,000
Estimated selling price on December 31, 20Y8	220,000
Assessed value for property taxes, December 31, 20Y8	190,000

Under the cost concept, Aaron Publishers records the purchase of the land on August 3, 20Y4, at the purchase price of $150,000. The other amounts listed above have no effect on the accounting records.

The fact that the land has an estimated selling price of $220,000 on December 31, 20Y8, indicates that the land has increased in value. However, to use the $220,000 in the accounting records would be to record an illusory or unrealized profit. If Aaron Publishers sells the land on January 9, 20Y9, for $240,000, a profit of $90,000 ($240,000 − $150,000) is then realized and recorded. The new owner would record $240,000 as its cost of the land.

Going Concern Concept

The **going concern concept** assumes that a company will continue in business indefinitely. This assumption is made because the amount of time that a company will continue in business is not known.

The going concern concept justifies the use of the cost concept for recording purchases, such as land. For example, in the preceding illustration Aaron Publishers plans to build a plant on the land. Since Aaron Publishers does not plan to sell the land, reporting changes in the market value of the land is irrelevant. That is, the amount Aaron Publishers could sell the land for if it went out of business is not important. This is because Aaron Publishers plans to continue its operations.

If, however, there is strong evidence that a company is planning on discontinuing its operations, then the accounting records are revised. To illustrate, the assets and liabilities of businesses in receivership or bankruptcy are valued from a quitting concern or liquidation point of view, rather than from the going concern point of view.

Matching Concept

The **matching concept** reports the revenues earned by a company for a period with the expenses incurred in generating the revenues. That is, expenses are *matched* against the revenues they generated.

Revenues are normally recorded at the time a product is sold or a service is rendered, which is referred to as the **revenue recognition principle**. At the point of sale, the sale price has been agreed upon, the buyer acquires ownership of the product or acquires the service, and the seller has a legal claim against the buyer for payment.

The expenses incurred in generating revenue should be reported in the same period as the related revenue. This is called the **expense recognition principle**. By matching revenues and expenses, net income or loss for the period can properly be determined and reported.

LinkedIn Connection

LinkedIn recognizes (records) revenue when (1) evidence of a contract exists, (2) delivery of a product or services has been provided to the customer, (3) the fee is fixed or determinable, and (4) the fee is reasonably collectible.

Objectivity Concept

The **objectivity concept** requires that entries in the accounting records and the data reported on financial statements be based on verifiable or objective evidence. For example, invoices, bank statements, and a physical count of supplies on hand are all objective and verifiable. Thus, they can be used for entering amounts in the accounting system. In some cases, judgments, estimates, and other subjective factors may have to be used in preparing financial statements. In such situations, the most objective evidence available is used.

Unit of Measure Concept

In the United States, the **unit of measure concept** requires that all economic data be recorded in dollars. Other relevant, nonfinancial information may also be recorded, such as terms of contracts. However, it is only through using dollar amounts that the various transactions and activities of a business can be measured, summarized, reported, and compared. Money is common to all business transactions and thus is the unit of measurement for financial reporting.

Adequate Disclosure Concept

The **adequate disclosure concept** requires that the financial statements, including related notes, contain all relevant data a stakeholder needs to understand the financial condition and performance of the company. Nonessential data are excluded to avoid clutter.

Accounting Period Concept

The **accounting period concept** requires that accounting data be recorded and summarized in financial statements for periods of time. For example, transactions are recorded for a period of time such as a month or a year. The accounting records are then summarized and updated before preparing the financial statements.

The financial history of a company may be shown by a series of balance sheets and income statements. If the life of a company is expressed by a line moving from left to right, the financial history of the company may be graphed as shown in Exhibit 12.

Exhibit 12 Financial History of a Company

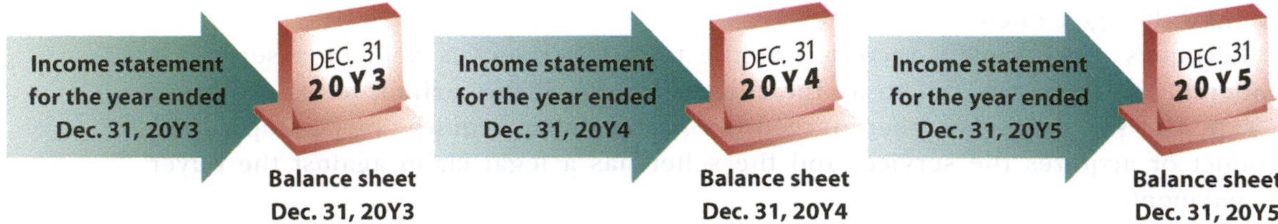

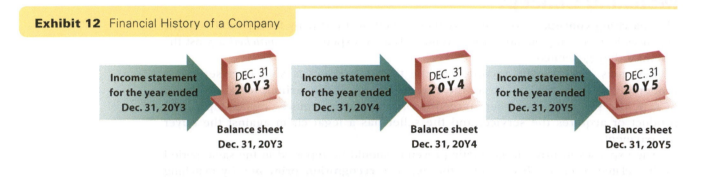

Responsible Reporting

The reliability of the financial reporting system is important to the economy and for the ability of businesses to raise money from investors. That is, stockholders and creditors require accurate financial reporting before they will invest their money. Scandals and financial reporting frauds threaten the confidence of investors. Exhibit 13 is a list of some financial reporting frauds and abuses.

The companies listed in Exhibit 13 were caught in the midst of ethical lapses that led to fines, firings, and criminal or civil prosecution. The second column of Exhibit 13 identifies the accounting concept that was violated in committing these unethical business practices. For example, the **WorldCom** fraud involved reporting various expense items as though they were assets. This is a violation of the matching concept and resulted in overstating income and assets. The third column of the exhibit identifies some of the results of these events. In most cases, senior and mid-level executives lost their jobs and were sued by upset stakeholders. In some cases, the executives also were criminally prosecuted and are serving prison terms.

Integrity, Objectivity, and Ethics in Business

Doing the Right Thing

Time magazine named three women as "Persons of the Year 2002." Each of these not-so-ordinary women had the courage, determination, and integrity to do the right thing. Each risked their personal careers to expose shortcomings in their organizations. Sherron Watkins, an **Enron** vice president, wrote a letter to Enron's chairman, Kenneth Lay, warning him of improper accounting that eventually led to Enron's collapse. Cynthia Cooper, an internal accountant, informed **WorldCom**'s Board of Directors of phony accounting that allowed WorldCom to cover up over $3 billion in losses and forced WorldCom into bankruptcy. Coleen Rowley, an FBI staff attorney, wrote a memo to FBI Director Robert Mueller, exposing how the Bureau brushed off her pleas to investigate Zacarias Moussaoui, who was indicted as a co-conspirator in the September 11 terrorist attacks.

Exhibit 13 Accounting Frauds

Company	Concept Violated	Result
Adelphia	*Business Entity Concept:* Rigas family treated the company assets as their own.	Bankruptcy. Rigas family members convicted of fraud and lost their investment in the company.
AIG	*Business Entity Concept:* Compensation transactions with an off-shore company that should have been disclosed on AIG's books.	CEO (Chief Executive Officer) resigned. AIG paid out $126 million in fines.
AOL and PurchasePro	*Matching Concept:* Back-dated contracts to inflate revenues.	Civil charges filed against senior executives of both companies. Fined $500 million.
Computer Associates	*Matching Concept:* Fraudulently inflating revenues.	CEO and senior executives indicted. Five executives pled guilty. Fined $225 million.
Enron	*Business Entity Concept:* Treated transactions as revenue, when they should have been treated as debt.	Bankruptcy. Criminal charges against senior executives. Over $60 billion in stock market losses.
Fannie Mae	*Accounting Period Concept:* Managing earnings by shifting expenses between periods.	CEO and CFO fired. $9 billion in restated earnings.
HealthSouth	*Matching Concept:* $4 billion in false entries to overstate revenues.	Senior executives faced regulatory and civil charges.
Quest	*Matching Concept:* Improper recognition of $3 billion in revenue.	CEO and six other executives charged with "massive financial fraud." Fined $250 million by SEC.
Tyco	*Adequate Disclosure Concept:* Failure to disclose secret loans to executives that were subsequently forgiven.	CEO forced to resign and was convicted in criminal proceedings.
WorldCom	*Matching Concept:* Improperly treated expenses as assets.	Bankruptcy. Criminal conviction of CEO and CFO. Over $100 billion in stock market losses. Directors fined $18 million.
Xerox	*Matching Concept:* Recognized $3 billion in revenue in periods earlier than should have been recognized.	Fined $10 million by SEC. Six executives fined $22 million.

What went wrong for the managers and companies listed in Exhibit 13? The answer normally involved one or both of the following factors:

- *Failure of Individual Character.* Ethical managers and accountants are honest and fair. However, managers and accountants often face pressures from supervisors to meet company and investor expectations. In many of the cases in Exhibit 13, managers and accountants justified small ethical violations to avoid such pressures. However, these small violations became big violations as the company's financial problems became worse.
- *Culture of Greed and Ethical Indifference.* By their behavior and attitude, senior managers set the company culture. In most of the companies listed in Exhibit 13, the senior managers created a culture of greed and indifference to the truth.

Ponzi Schemes

Business Insight

A Ponzi scheme is a scam or fraudulent operation where to attract investors an individual or entity promises high returns with little or no risk. To meet their claims, the perpetrators (fraudsters) pay early investors with monies obtained from attracting new investors. To succeed, a Ponzi scheme requires a constant stream of money from new investors. Eventually, Ponzi schemes become so large that they collapse. One of the most recent Ponzi schemes was perpetrated by Bernard Madoff, who admitted to defrauding clients of up to $50 billion over a number of years. He is serving a sentence of 150 years in prison.

As a result of accounting and business frauds, the United States Congress passed laws to monitor the behavior of accounting and business. For example, the Sarbanes-Oxley Act of 2002 (SOX) was enacted. SOX established a new oversight body for the accounting profession called the Public Company Accounting Oversight Board (PCAOB). In addition, SOX established standards for independence, corporate responsibility, and disclosure.

How does one behave ethically when faced with financial or other types of pressure? Guidelines for behaving ethically are shown in Exhibit 14.

Exhibit 14
Guidelines for Ethical Conduct

1. Identify an ethical decision by using your personal ethical standards of honesty and fairness.
2. Identify the consequences of the decision and its effect on others.
3. Consider your obligations and responsibilities to those that will be affected by your decision.
4. Make a decision that is ethical and fair to those affected by it.

Many companies have ethical standards of conduct for managers and employees. In addition, the Institute of Management Accountants and the American Institute of Certified Public Accountants have professional codes of conduct.

Objective 6
Describe types of metrics and analyze a company's performance using return on assets.

Metric-Based Analysis: Return on Assets

In analyzing and assessing a company's financial condition and performance, a variety of quantitative measures may be used. Quantitative measures are referred to as **metrics.** Throughout this text, we use a variety of metrics to assess a company's financial condition and performance. In addition, the effects of management's decisions on metrics are also described and illustrated. We call this use of metrics to assess financial condition, performance, and decisions **metric-based analysis.**

Types of Metrics

The two basic types of metrics used in this text are ratios and amounts. For example, the return on assets ratio is described and illustrated in this chapter. An example of a metric amount is passenger miles flown by an airline or grade point average of a student.

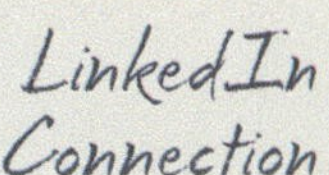

Some ratio metrics that LinkedIn uses to assess its performance include its price to earnings ratio (common stock price divided by earnings per share) and net revenue growth rate. Some of its amount metrics include number of registered members and number of member page views.

Level of Application

We apply metric analysis at the following three levels:

1. Financial statement level
2. Transaction level
3. Managerial decision level

Financial statement level. Metric-based analysis is commonly applied at the financial statement level. At this level, various financial ratios are computed and analyzed. In the next section, we apply metric-based analysis at the financial statement level using the ratio return on assets (net income divided by average total assets).

Transaction level. We also apply metric-based analysis at the transaction level. When a company enters into a transaction, it changes the company's assets, liabilities, and stockholders' equity. Since we assume companies operate to maximize their profits, we assess the effects of a transaction on one or more of a company's profitability metrics.

Companies also attempt to maintain a minimum degree of liquidity so they can pay their liabilities and respond quickly to new opportunities to expand or enhance their operations. **Liquidity** refers to the degree to which a company has cash or assets that can be readily converted to cash. For example, investments in marketable securities can readily be converted to cash. In contrast, property, plant, and equipment are less liquid and could take months or years to convert to cash.

Liquidity differs from solvency. **Solvency** refers to the ability of a company to pay its long-term debts. Companies that cannot pay their debts are said to be insolvent, which usually involves filing for bankruptcy. Liquidity affects a company's ability to pay its debts. However, a company may have a large portion of assets that cannot be readily converted to cash but still be profitable and solvent.

In addition to assessing the effects of a transaction on one or more of a company's profitability metrics, we also assess the effects on one or more of a company's liquidity metrics. In Chapter 2, we begin our metric-based analysis of transactions by assessing the effects of each transaction on cash and net income. In later chapters, we expand this analysis to include a variety of profitability and liquidity metrics.

Managerial decision level. In the managerial chapters of this text, metric-basis analysis assesses the effects of decisions on a variety of operating metrics. For example, a managerial decision to increase selling prices (assuming no decrease in units sold) would decrease its break-even point, which is the level at which operations may neither profit nor experience a loss. In this case, the metric being assessed is the break-even point.

Return on Assets

In the remainder of this chapter, we describe and illustrate metric-based analysis at the financial statement level using return on assets. The return on assets is a profitability metric often used to compare a company's performance over time and with competitors.

Return on assets is normally expressed as a percent such as 12%. However, it may also be expressed as an amount per dollar invested. For example, a 12% return on assets could also be expressed as $0.12 return per $1 invested. In other words, the company is earning 12 cents per dollar invested.

The **return on assets** percentage is computed as follows:

$$\textbf{Return on Assets} = \frac{\textbf{Net Income}}{\textbf{Average Total Assets}}$$

To illustrate, return on assets is computed for **Apple Inc. (AAPL)** and **HP Inc. (HPQ)** (formerly **Hewlett-Packard)**. The computations use data (in millions) from recent financial statements.

	Apple Inc.	HP Inc.
Net income	$ 53,394	$ 5,013
Total assets at beginning of year	$231,839	$105,676
Total assets at end of year	$290,479	$103,206
Average total assets:		
Apple Inc. [($231,839 + $290,479) ÷ 2]	$261,159	
HP Inc. [($105,676 + $103,206) ÷ 2]		$104,441
Return on assets:*		
Apple Inc. ($53,394 ÷ $261,159)	20.4%	
HP Inc. ($5,013 ÷ $104,441)		4.8%

* Rounded to one decimal place.

As shown above, Apple is over 4 (20.4% ÷ 4.8%) times more profitable, as measured by return on assets, than is HP Inc. Apple's profitability is largely due to its innovative technology, including its iPad, iPhone, iPod, and Mac computers.

Comparing rates of return among companies that use different tax strategies or different methods of financing their operations may be misleading. In the case of companies using different tax strategies, tax expense may be added to net income to reduce the impact of taxes. Likewise, some companies finance their operations primarily by debt, while other companies finance their operations primarily by equity. In this case, interest expense may be added to net income to reduce the impact of differences in financing.

Key Points

1. Describe the types and forms of businesses, how businesses make money, and business stakeholders.

The three types of businesses operated for profit include manufacturing, merchandising, and service businesses. Such businesses may be organized as proprietorships, partnerships, corporations, and limited liability companies. A business may make money (profits) by gaining an advantage over its competitors using a low-cost or a premium-price emphasis. Under a *low-cost emphasis*, a business designs and produces products or services at a lower cost than its competitors. Under a *premium-price emphasis*, a business tries to design products or services that possess unique attributes or characteristics for which customers are willing to pay more. A business' economic performance is of interest to its stakeholders. Business stakeholders include four categories: capital market stakeholders, product or service market stakeholders, government stakeholders, and internal stakeholders.

2. Describe the three business activities of financing, investing, and operating.

All businesses engage in financing, investing, and operating activities. Financing activities involve obtaining funds to begin and operate a business. Investing activities involve obtaining the necessary resources to start and operate the business. Operating activities involve using the business's resources according to its business emphasis.

3. Define accounting and describe its role in business.

Accounting is an information system that provides reports to stakeholders about the economic activities and condition of a business. Accounting is the "language of business."

4. Describe and illustrate the basic financial statements and how they interrelate.

The principal financial statements of a corporation are the income statement, the statement of stockholders' equity, the balance sheet, and the statement of cash flows. The income statement reports a period's net income or net loss, which also appears on the statement of stockholders' equity. The ending reported on the statement of stockholders' equity is also reported on the balance sheet. The ending cash balance is reported on the balance sheet and the statement of cash flows.

5. Describe eight accounting concepts underlying financial reporting.

The eight accounting concepts discussed in this chapter include the business entity, cost, going concern, matching, objectivity, unit of measure, adequate disclosure, and accounting period concepts.

6. Describe types of metrics and analyze a company's performance using return on assets.

A metric is any quantitative measure. Metric analysis may be performed at the financial statement, transaction, or managerial decision level. At the financial statement level, return on assets is computed by dividing net income by average total assets. Return on assets is useful in assessing the percentage (rate) that a company is earnings on its invested assets. Return on assets can also be expressed as dollars earned for each dollar invested.

Key Terms

Accounting (9)
Accounting equation (13)
Accounting period concept (20)
Accounts payable (7)
Accounts receivable (8)
Adequate disclosure concept (19)
Administrative expenses (9)
Assets (8)
Balance sheet (13)
Bonds payable (8)
Business (2)
Business entity concept (17)
Business stakeholder (5)
Chief financial officer (10)
Common stock (8)
Comptroller (10)
Corporation (3)
Cost concept (18)
Cost of goods sold (9)
Cost of merchandise sold (9)
Cost of sales (9)
Dividends (8)
Expenses (9)
Expense recognition principle (19)
Fees earned (9)
Financial accounting (9)
Financial Accounting Standards Board (FASB) (17)
Financial statements (10)
Financing activities (7)
Generally accepted accounting principles (GAAP) (16)
Going concern concept (18)
Income statement (11)
Intangible assets (8)
Interest payable (8)
International Accounting Standards Board (IASB) (17)
Investing activities (7)
Liabilities (7)
Limited liability company (LLC) (3)
Liquidity (23)
Low-cost strategy (4)
Managerial accounting (9)
Manufacturing business (3)
Matching concept (19)
Merchandising business (2)
Metric (22)
Metric-based analysis (22)
Net income (9)
Net loss (9)
Note payable (8)
Objectivity concept (19)
Operating activities (7)
Owner's equity (13)
Partnership (3)
Premium-price strategy (4)
Prepaid expenses (8)
Profit (2)
Proprietorship (3)
Retained earnings (12)
Return on assets (23)
Revenue (9)
Revenue recognition principle (19)
Sales (9)
Securities and Exchange Commission (SEC) (17)
Selling expenses (9)
Service business (2)
Solvency (23)
Statement of cash flows (13)
Statement of financial condition (13)
Statement of stockholders' equity (12)
Stockholders (8)
Stockholders' equity (13)
Tangible assets (8)
Unit of measure concept (19)

Illustrative Problem

The financial statements at the end of Spratlin Consulting's first month of operations follow.

SPRATLIN CONSULTING
Income Statement
For the Month Ended June 30, 20Y8

Fees earned		$ 36,000
Operating expenses:		
Wages expense	$12,000	
Rent expense	7,640	
Utilities expense	(a)	
Miscellaneous expense	1,320	
Total operating expenses		(23,120)
Net income		$ (b)

SPRATLIN CONSULTING
Statement of Stockholders' Equity
For the Month Ended June 30, 20Y8

	Common Stock	Retained Earnings
Balances, June 1, 20Y8	$ 0	$ 0
Issued common stock	48,000	
Net income		(c)
Dividends		(d)
Balances, June 30, 20Y8	$48,000	$(e)

SPRATLIN CONSULTING
Balance Sheet
June 30, 20Y8

Assets	
Cash	$ 5,600
Land	50,000
Total assets	$ (f)
Liabilities	
Accounts payable	$ 1,920
Stockholders' Equity	
Common stock	$ (g)
Retained earnings	(h)
Total stockholders' equity	$ (i)
Total liabilities and stockholders' equity	$ (j)

SPRATLIN CONSULTING
Statement of Cash Flows
For the Month Ended June 30, 20Y8

Cash flows from operating activities:		
Cash received from customers	$36,000	
Cash paid for operating expenses	(k)	
Net cash flows from operating activities		$14,800
Cash flows from investing activities:		
Cash paid for acquisition of land		(l)
Cash flows from financing activities:		
Cash received from issuing common stock	$48,000	
Dividends paid to stockholders	(7,200)	
Net cash flows from financing activities		(m)
Net increase in cash during month		$ (n)
Cash as of June 1		0
Cash as of June 30		$ (n)

Instructions

By analyzing how the four financial statements are integrated, determine the proper amounts for (a) through (n).

Solution

a. Utilities expense, $2,160 ($23,120 − $12,000 − $7,640 − $1,320)
b. Net income, $12,880 ($36,000 − $23,120)
c. Net income, $12,880 [same as (b)]
d. Dividends, $(7,200) (from statement of cash flows)
e. Retained earnings, $5,680 ($12,880 − $7,200)
f. Total assets, $55,600 ($5,600 + $50,000)
g. Common stock, $48,000 (from the statement of stockholders' equity or statement of cash flows)
h. Retained earnings, $5,680 [same as (e)]
i. Total stockholders' equity, $53,680 ($48,000 + $5,680)
j. Total liabilities and stockholders' equity, $55,600 ($1,920 + $53,680) [same as (f)]

k. Cash payments for operating expenses, $21,200 ($36,000 − $14,800)
l. Cash payments for acquisition of land, $50,000 (from balance sheet)
m. Net cash flows from financing activities, $40,800 ($48,000 − $7,200)
n. Net increase in cash and June 30, 20Y8, cash balance, $5,600 ($14,800 − $50,000 + $40,800)

Self-Examination Questions

(Answers appear at the end of chapter.)

1. A profit-making business operating as a separate legal entity and in which ownership is divided into shares of stock is known as a:
   A. proprietorship.
   B. service business.
   C. partnership.
   D. corporation.
2. The resources owned by a business are called:
   A. assets.
   B. liabilities.
   C. the accounting equation.
   D. stockholders' equity.
3. A listing of a business entity's assets, liabilities, and stockholders' equity as of a specific date is:
   A. a balance sheet.
   B. an income statement.
   C. a statement of changes in stockholders' equity.
   D. a statement of cash flows.
4. If total assets are $20,000 and total liabilities are $12,000, the amount of stockholders' equity is:
   A. $32,000.
   B. $(32,000).
   C. $(8,000).
   D. $8,000.
5. If revenue was $45,000, expenses were $37,500, and dividends were $10,000, the amount of net income or net loss would be:
   A. $45,000 net income.
   B. $7,500 net income.
   C. $37,500 net loss.
   D. $2,500 net loss.

Class Discussion Questions

1. What is the objective of most businesses?
2. What is the difference between a manufacturing business and a merchandising business? Give an example of each type of business.
3. What is the difference between a manufacturing business and a service business? Is a restaurant a manufacturing business, a service business, or both?
4. Why are most large companies like Apple, Pepsi, General Electric, and Intel organized as corporations?
5. Both KIA and BMW produce and sell automobiles. Describe and contrast the business emphasis of KIA and BMW.
6. Assume that a friend of yours operates a family-owned pharmacy. A super Wal-Mart, scheduled to open in the next several months, will also offer pharmacy services. What business emphasis would your friend use to compete with the Super Walmart pharmacy?
7. What services does eBay offer its customers?
8. A business's stakeholders can be classified into capital market, product or service market, government, and internal stakeholders. Will the interests of all the stakeholders within a classification be the same? Use bankers and stockholders of the capital market as an example in answering this question.

9. The three business activities are financing, investing, and operating. Using Southwest Airlines, give an example of each type of activity.
10. What is the role of accounting in business?
11. Briefly describe the nature of the information provided by each of the following financial statements: the income statement, the statement of stockholders' equity, the balance sheet, and the statement of cash flows. In your descriptions, indicate whether each of the financial statements covers a period of time or is for a specific date.
12. For a recent year ending January 31, Target Corporation had revenues of $72,618 million and total expenses of $74,254 million. Did Target Corporation report a net loss or a net income?
13. What particular item of financial or operating data appears on both the income statement and the statement of stockholders' equity? What items appear on both the balance sheet and the statement of stockholders' equity? What item appears on both the balance sheet and statement of cash flows?
14. Billy Jessop is the owner of Valley Delivery Service. Recently, Billy paid interest of $6,000 on a personal loan of $75,000 that he used to begin the business. Should Valley Delivery Service record the interest payment? Explain.
15. On October 1, Wok Repair Service extended an offer of $100,000 for land that had been priced for sale at $150,000. On December 19, Wok Repair Service accepted the seller's counteroffer of $110,000. Describe how Wok Repair Service should record the land.
16. Land with an assessed value of $500,000 for property tax purposes is acquired by a business for $600,000. Four years later, the plot of land has an assessed value of $750,000 and the business receives an offer of $975,000 for it. Should the monetary amount assigned to the land in the business records now be increased?

Exercises

Obj. 1

E1-1 Types of businesses

Indicate whether each of the following companies is primarily a service, merchandise, or manufacturing business. If you are unfamiliar with the company, you may use the Internet to locate the company's home page or use the finance Web site of Yahoo.com.

1. AFLAC
2. Best Buy
3. Boeing
4. Caterpillar
5. Citigroup
6. CVS Caremark
7. Dow Chemical
8. Exxon Mobil
9. Facebook
10. Ford Motor
11. General Electric
12. Hilton Hotels
13. H&R Block Inc.
14. Oracle
15. Target

Obj. 1

E1-2 Business emphasis

Identify the primary business emphasis of each of the following companies as (a) a low-cost emphasis or (b) a premium-price emphasis. If you are unfamiliar with the company, you may use the Internet to locate the company's home page or use the finance Web site of Yahoo.com.

1. Allegiant Travel Services
2. Best Buy
3. BMW
4. Dollar Tree
5. E*TRADE
6. Goldman Sachs Group
7. Lowe's
8. Nike
9. Pepsi
10. Staples
11. Sub-Zero
12. Mercedes-Benz

E1-3 Accounting equation

Obj. 4

✔ Best Buy, $4,995

The total assets and total liabilities for a recent year of Best Buy (BBY) and Gamestop (GME) are shown below.

	Best Buy (in millions)	Gamestop (in millions)
Assets	$15,256	$4,246
Liabilities	10,261	2,179

Determine the stockholders' equity of each company.

E1-4 Accounting equation

Obj. 4

✔ Apple, $119,355

The total assets and total liabilities for a recent year of Apple (AAPL) and HP (HPQ) formerly Hewlett-Packard are shown here.

	Apple (in millions)	HP (in millions)
Assets	$290,479	$103,206
Liabilities	171,124	76,475

Determine the stockholders' equity of each company.

E1-5 Accounting equation

Obj. 4

✔ a. $475,000

Determine the missing amount for each of the following:

	Assets	=	Liabilities	+	Stockholders' Equity
a.	X	=	$ 175,000	+	$300,000
b.	$ 880,000	=	X	+	$525,000
c.	$2,100,000	=	$600,000	+	X

E1-6 Accounting equation

Obj. 4

✔ a. $10,617

Determine the missing amounts (in millions) for the condensed balance sheets shown below.

	Costco (COST)	Target (TGT)	Wal-Mart (WMT)
Assets	$33,440	$41,404	$ (c)
Liabilities	22,823	(b)	122,312
Stockholders' equity	(a)	13,997	81,394

E1-7 Net income and dividends

Obj. 4

The income statement of a corporation for the month of November indicates a net income of $90,000. During the same period, $100,000 in cash dividends were paid. Would it be correct to say that the business incurred a net loss of $10,000 during the month? Discuss.

Obj. 4

✔ Company Chang: Net income, $225,000

E1-8 Net income and stockholders' equity for four businesses

Four different companies—Chang, Henry, Nagel, and Wilcox—show the same balance sheet data at the beginning and end of a year. These data, exclusive of the amount of stockholders' equity, are summarized as follows:

	Total Assets	Total Liabilities
Beginning of the year	$775,000	$400,000
End of the year	900,000	300,000

On the basis of the preceding data and the following additional information for the year, determine the net income (or loss) of each company for the year. (*Hint:* First determine the amount of increase or decrease in stockholders' equity during the year.)

Company Chang: No additional capital stock was issued, and no dividends were paid.

Company Henry: No additional capital stock was issued, but dividends of $90,000 were paid.

Company Nagel: Capital stock of $125,000 was issued, but no dividends were paid.

Company Wilcox: Capital stock of $125,000 was issued, and dividends of $90,000 were paid.

Obj. 4

✔ a. (1) $5,008,669

E1-9 Accounting equation and income statement

Staples, Inc., (SPLS) is a leading office products distributor, with retail stores in the United States, Canada, Asia, Europe, and South America. The following financial statement data were adapted from recent financial statements of Staples:

	Year 2 (in thousands)	Year 1 (in thousands)
Total assets	$10,313,728	$11,174,876
Total liabilities	(1)	5,042,613
Total stockholders' equity	5,305,059	(2)
Sales	22,492,360	
Cost of goods sold	16,691,324	
Operating expenses	5,518,665	
Other expense (net)	14,236	
Income tax expense	133,609	

a. Determine the missing data indicated for (1) and (2).

b. Using the income statement data for Year 2, determine the amount of net income or loss.

Obj. 4

E1-10 Balance sheet items

From the following list of selected items taken from the records of Flip Flop Sandals Inc. as of a specific date, identify those that would appear on the balance sheet.

1. Accounts Receivable
2. Common Stock
3. Cash
4. Fees Earned
5. Rent Expense
6. Salaries Expense
7. Salaries Payable
8. Supplies
9. Supplies Expense
10. Utilities Expense

Obj. 4

E1-11 Income statement items

Based on the data presented in Exercise 1-10, identify those items that would appear on the income statement.

E1-12 Financial statement items

Obj. 4

Identify each of the following items as (a) an asset, (b) a liability, (c) revenue, (d) an expense, or (e) a dividend:

1. Amounts due from customers
2. Amounts owed suppliers
3. Cash on hand
4. Cash paid to stockholders
5. Cash sales
6. Equipment
7. Note payable owed to the bank
8. Rent paid for the month
9. Sales commissions paid to salespersons
10. Wages paid to employees

E1-13 Statement of stockholders' equity

Obj. 4

✔ Retained earnings, June 30, 20Y7, $435,000

Financial information related to Webber Company for the month ended June 30, 20Y7, is as follows:

Common Stock, June 1, 20Y7	$ 60,000
Stock issued in June	40,000
Net income for June	175,000
Dividends during June	30,000
Retained earnings, June 1, 20Y7	290,000

Prepare a statement of stockholders' equity for the month ended June 30, 20Y7.

E1-14 Income statement

Obj. 4

✔ Net income: $845,000

Maynard Services was organized on August 1, 20Y5. A summary of the revenue and expense transactions for August follows:

Fees earned	$3,400,000
Wages expense	2,150,000
Miscellaneous expense	55,000
Rent expense	320,000
Supplies expense	30,000

Prepare an income statement for the month ended August 31.

E1-15 Missing amounts from balance sheet and income statement data

Obj. 4

✔ (a) $90,000

One item is omitted in each of the following summaries of balance sheet and income statement data for four different corporations, AL, CO, KS, and MT.

	AL	CO	KS	MT
Beginning of the year:				
Assets	$400,000	$300,000	$550,000	$ (d)
Liabilities	200,000	130,000	325,000	350,000
End of the year:				
Assets	800,000	460,000	660,000	1,200,000
Liabilities	450,000	110,000	360,000	700,000
During the year:				
Additional issue of capital stock	(a)	50,000	100,000	100,000
Dividends	50,000	20,000	(c)	90,000
Revenue	175,000	(b)	115,000	420,000
Expenses	65,000	70,000	130,000	480,000

Determine the missing amounts, identifying them by letter. [*Hint:* First determine the amount of increase or decrease in stockholders' equity during the year.]

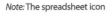

Note: The spreadsheet icon  indicates an Excel template is available on the student companion site at www.cengagebrain.com.

Obj. 4

E1-16 Balance sheets, net income

✔ b. $53,000

Financial information related to Montana Interiors for October and November 20Y8 is as follows:

	October 31, 20Y8	November 30, 20Y8
Accounts payable	$ 40,000	$ 65,000
Accounts receivable	75,000	118,000
Capital stock	60,000	60,000
Retained earnings	?	?
Cash	110,000	140,000
Supplies	15,000	20,000

a. Prepare balance sheets for Montana Interiors as of October 31 and as of November 30, 20Y8.

b. Determine the amount of net income for November, assuming that no additional capital stock was issued and no dividends were paid during the month.

c. Determine the amount of net income for November, assuming that no additional capital stock was issued but dividends of $20,000 were paid during the month.

Obj. 4

E1-17 Financial statements

Each of the following items is shown in the financial statements of ExxonMobil Corporation. Identify the financial statement (balance sheet or income statement) in which each item would appear.

a. Accounts payable
b. Cash equivalents
c. Crude oil inventory
d. Equipment
e. Exploration expenses
f. Income taxes payable
g. Investments
h. Long-term debt
i. Marketable securities
j. Notes and loans payable
k. Operating expenses
l. Prepaid taxes
m. Retained earnings
n. Sales
o. Selling expenses

Obj. 4

E1-18 Statement of cash flows

Indicate whether each of the following cash activities would be reported on the statement of cash flows as (a) an operating activity, (b) an investing activity, or (c) a financing activity.

1. Issued common stock
2. Paid rent
3. Paid for office equipment
4. Sold services
5. Issued a note payable
6. Sold excess office equipment
7. Paid officers' salaries
8. Paid for advertising
9. Paid insurance
10. Paid dividends

Obj. 4

E1-19 Statement of cash flows

Indicate whether each of the following activities would be reported on the statement of cash flows as (a) an operating activity, (b) an investing activity, or (c) a financing activity.

1. Cash received from investment by stockholders
2. Cash received from fees earned
3. Cash paid for expenses
4. Cash paid for land

E1-20 Statement of cash flows

Obj. 4

Looney Inc. was organized on July 1, Year 1. A summary of cash flows for July follows.

Cash receipts:	
Cash received from customers	$600,000
Cash received from issuance of common stock	200,000
Cash received from note payable	75,000
Cash payments:	
Cash paid out for expenses	$380,000
Cash paid out for purchase of equipment	95,000
Cash paid as dividends	25,000

✔ Net cash flows from operating activities, $220,000

Prepare a statement of cash flows for the month ended July 31, Year 1.

E1-21 Using financial statements

Obj. 4

A company's stakeholders often differ in their financial statement focus. For example, some stakeholders focus primarily on the income statement, while others focus primarily on the statement of cash flows or the balance sheet. For each of the following situations, indicate which financial statement would be the likely focus for the stakeholder. Choose either the income statement, balance sheet, or statement of cash flows, and justify your choice.

Situation 1: Assume that you are considering purchasing a personal computer from Dell.

Situation 2: Assume that you are considering investing in LinkedIn (capital market stakeholder).

Situation 3: Assume that you are employed by Campbell Soup Co. (product market stakeholder) and are considering whether to extend credit for a 60-day period to a new grocery store chain that has recently opened throughout the Midwest.

Situation 4: Assume that you are considering taking a job (internal stakeholder) with either Sears or JCPenney.

Situation 5: Assume that you are a banker for US Bank (capital market stakeholder), and you are considering whether to grant a major credit line (loan) to Target. The credit line will allow Target to borrow up to $400 million for a five-year period at the market rate of interest.

E1-22 Financial statement items

Obj. 4

Amazon.com, Inc., (AMZN) operates as an online retailer in North America and internationally. Both Amazon and third parties, via the Amazon.com Web site, sell products across various product categories.

The following items were adapted from a recent annual report of Amazon.com for the year ending December 31:

	In millions
1. Accounts payable	$16,459
2. Accounts receivable	5,612
3. Cash	14,557
4. Cost of sales	62,752
5. Income tax expense	167
6. Interest expense	210
7. Inventories	8,299
8. Net cash provided by operating activities	6,842
9. Net cash flows used for investing activities	(5,065)
10. Net sales	88,988
11. Other expense	118
12. Other income	76
13. Property, plant, and other long-term assets	16,967
14. Selling, general, and administrative expenses	26,058
15. Retained earnings (Dec. 31)	2,190

Using the following notations, indicate on which financial statement you would find each of the preceding items. (*Note:* An item may appear on more than one statement.)

IS	Income statement
SE	Statement of stockholders' equity
BS	Balance sheet
SCF	Statement of cash flows

Obj. 4

✔ Net loss, $241

E1-23 Income statement

Based on the Amazon.com, Inc.,financial statement data shown in Exercise 1-22, prepare an income statement for the year ending December 31.

Obj. 4

E1-24 Financial statement items

Though the McDonald's (MCD) menu of hamburgers, cheeseburgers, the Big Mac®, Quarter Pounder®, Filet-O-Fish®, and Chicken McNuggets® is easily recognized, McDonald's financial statements may not be as familiar. The following items were adapted from a recent annual report of McDonald's Corporation:

1. Accounts payable
2. Accrued interest payable
3. Cash
4. Cash provided by operations
5. Common Stock
6. Food and packaging costs used in operations
7. Income tax expense
8. Interest expense
9. Inventories
10. Long-term debt payable
11. Net income
12. Net increase in cash
13. Notes payable
14. Notes receivable
15. Occupancy and rent expense
16. Payroll expense
17. Prepaid expenses not yet used in operations
18. Property and equipment
19. Retained earnings
20. Sales

Identify the financial statement on which each of the preceding items would appear. An item may appear on more than one statement. Use the following notations:

IS	Income statement
SE	Statement of stockholders' equity
BS	Balance sheet
SCF	Statement of cash flows

Obj. 4

✔ Correct amount of total assets is $200,000

E1-25 Financial statements

Outlaw Realty, organized August 1, 20Y7, is owned and operated by Julie Baxter. How many errors can you find in the following financial statements for Outlaw Realty, prepared after its first month of operations? Assume that the cash balance on August 31, 20Y7, is $51,600 and that cash flows from operating activities is reported correctly.

OUTLAW REALTY
Income Statement
August 31, 20Y7

Sales commissions		$ 408,400
Operating expenses:		
Office salaries expense	$272,600	
Rent expense	31,200	
Miscellaneous expense	2,200	
Automobile expense	7,900	
Total operating expenses		(313,900)
Net income		$ 134,500

JULIE BAXTER
Statement of Stockholders' Equity
August 31, Year 1

	Common Stock	Retained Earnings	Total
Balances, August 1, 20Y7	$ 0	$ 7,800	$ 7,800
Issuance of common stock			100,000
Net income		134,500	134,500
Dividends		12,000	12,000
Balances, August 30, 20Y7	$100,000	$154,300	$254,300

Balance Sheet
For the Month Ended August 31, 20Y7

Assets		
Cash		$ 51,600
Accounts payable		17,500
Land		60,000
Total assets		$129,100
Liabilities		
Accounts receivable		$ 81,200
Prepaid expenses		7,200
Stockholders' Equity		
Common stock	$100,000	
Retained earnings	140,300	240,300
Total liabilities and stockholders' equity		$328,700

Statement of Cash Flows
August 31, 20Y7

Cash flows from operating activities:		
Cash received from customers	$327,200	
Cash paid for operating expenses	303,600	
Net cash flows from operating activities		$ 23,600
Cash flows from financing activities:		
Cash received from issuance of common stock	$100,000	
Dividends paid to stockholders	(12,000)	
Net cash flows from financing activities		88,000
Net cash flow and cash balance as of August 31, 20Y7		$111,600

E1-26 Accounting concepts

Obj. 5

Match each of the following statements with the appropriate accounting concept. Some concepts may be used more than once, while others may not be used at all. Use the notations shown to indicate the appropriate accounting concept.

Accounting Concept	Notation
Accounting period concept	P
Adequate disclosure concept	D
Business entity concept	B
Cost concept	C
Going concern concept	G
Matching concept	M
Objectivity concept	O
Unit of measure concept	U

Statements

1. Assume that a business will continue forever.
2. Material litigation involving the corporation is described in a note.
3. Monthly utilities costs are reported as expenses along with the monthly revenues.
4. Personal transactions of owners are kept separate from the business.
5. This concept supports relying on an independent actuary (statistician), rather than the chief operating officer of the corporation, to estimate a pension liability.
6. Changes in the use of accounting methods from one period to the next are described in the notes to the financial statements.
7. Land worth $800,000 is reported at its original purchase price of $220,000.
8. This concept justifies recording only transactions that are expressed in dollars.
9. If this concept was ignored, the confidence of users in the financial statements could not be maintained.
10. The changes in financial condition are reported at the end of the month.

Obj. 5

E1-27 Business entity concept

Crazy Mountain Sports sells hunting and fishing equipment and provides guided hunting and fishing trips. Crazy Mountain is owned and operated by Karl Young, a well-known sports enthusiast and hunter. Karl's wife, Mila, owns and operates Mila's Boutique, a women's clothing store. Karl and Mila have established a trust fund to finance their children's college education. The trust fund is maintained by First Bank in the names of their children, Steve and Isabelle.

For each of the following transactions, identify which of the entities listed should record the transaction in its records.

Entities	
C	Crazy Mountain Sports
B	First Bank Trust Fund
M	Mila's Boutique
X	None of the above

1. Karl paid a local doctor for a physical, which was required by the workmen's compensation insurance policy carried by Crazy Mountain Sports.
2. Karl received a cash advance from customers for a guided hunting trip.
3. Mila paid her dues to the YWCA.
4. Karl paid a breeder's fee for an English Springer spaniel to be used as a hunting guide dog.
5. Mila deposited a $10,000 personal check in the trust fund at First Bank.
6. Karl paid for an advertisement in a hunters' magazine.
7. Mila authorized the trust fund to purchase mutual fund shares.
8. Mila donated several dresses from the store's inventory to a local charity auction for the benefit of a women's abuse shelter.
9. Karl paid for dinner and a movie to celebrate the couple's fifteenth wedding anniversary.
10. Mila purchased two dozen spring dresses from a Boise designer for a special spring sale.

Problems

P1-1 Income statement, retained earnings statement, and balance sheet

Obj. 4

✔ 1. Net income: $115,000

The amounts of the assets and liabilities of Glacier Travel Service as of September 30, 20Y6, the end of the current year, and its revenue and expenses for the year are listed below. The retained earnings were $150,000 and the common stock was $50,000 as of October 1, 20Y5, the beginning of the current year. Dividends of $10,000 were paid during the year.

Accounts payable	$ 175,000
Accounts receivable	321,000
Cash	166,000
Common stock	70,000
Fees earned	900,000
Miscellaneous expense	37,000
Rent expense	180,000
Supplies	13,000
Supplies expense	38,000
Taxes expense	30,000
Utilities expense	75,000
Wages expense	425,000

Instructions

1. Prepare an income statement for the current year ended September 30, 20Y6.
2. Prepare a statement of stockholders' equity for the current year ended September 30, 20Y6.
3. Prepare a balance sheet as of September 30, 20Y6.

P1-2 Missing amounts from financial statements

Obj. 4

✔ j. $314,000

The financial statements at the end of Paradise Realty's first month of operations are shown below.

PARADISE REALTY
Income Statement
For the Month Ended November 30, 20Y3

Fees earned		$149,300
Operating expenses:		
Wages expense	$ (a)	
Rent expense	14,400	
Supplies expense	12,000	
Utilities expense	8,100	
Miscellaneous expense	4,950	
Total operating expenses		(69,300)
Net income		$ (b)

PARADISE REALTY
Statement of Stockholders' Equity
For the Month Ended November 30, 20Y3

	Common Stock	Retained Earnings	Total
Balances, Nov. 1, 20Y3	$ 0	$ 0	$ 0
Issuance of common stock	270,000		270,000
Net income		(c)	(c)
Dividends		(d)	(d)
Balances, Nov. 30, 20Y3	$270,000	$(e)	$314,000

PARADISE REALTY
Balance Sheet
November 30, 20Y3

Assets		
Cash		$ 99,200
Supplies		6,000
Land		(f)
Total assets		$ (g)
Liabilities		
Note payable		$ 7,200
Stockholders' Equity		
Common stock	$ (h)	
Retained earnings	(i)	
Total stockholders' equity		(j)
Total liabilities and stockholders' equity		$ (k)

PARADISE REALTY
Statement of Cash Flows
For the Month Ended November 30, 20Y3

Cash flows from operating activities:		
Cash received from customers	$ (l)	
Cash paid for expenses and to creditors	(68,100)	
Net cash flows from operating activities		$ (m)
Cash flows used for investing activities:		
Cash paid for acquisition of land		(216,000)
Cash flows from financing activities:		
Cash received from issuing common stock	$270,000	
Deduct dividends	(36,000)	
Net cash flows from financing activities		(n)
Net increase in cash during month		$ (o)
Cash as of November 1		0
Cash as of November 30		$ (o)

Instructions

1. Would you classify a realty business such as Hamel Realty as a manufacturing, merchandising, or service business?
2. By analyzing the interrelationships among the financial statements, determine the proper amounts for (a) through (o).

Obj. 4

✔ 1. Net loss (1,636)

P1-3 Income statement, retained earnings statement, and balance sheet

The following financial data were adapted from a recent annual report of Target Corporation (TGT) for the year ending January 31.

	In millions
Accounts payable	$ 7,759
Cash	2,210
Common stock	53
Cost of goods sold	51,278
Debt and other borrowings	12,705
Income tax expense	1,204
Interest expense	882
Inventories	8,790
Other assets	4,446
Other expenses	6,214
Other liabilities	6,943
Property, plant, and equipment	25,958
Sales	72,618
Selling, general, and administrative expenses	14,676

Instructions

1. Prepare Target's income statement for the year ending January 31.
2. Prepare Target's statement of stockholders' equity for the year ending January 31.

   Use the following additional information for the year:

No common stock was issue during the year	
Retained earnings Feb. 1 of prior year	$12,599
Dividends	1,319
Other stockholder equity items on Feb. 1 of prior year	3,579
Increase in other stockholder equity items	721

3. Prepare a balance sheet as of January 31.

P1-4 Statement of cash flows

Obj. 4

✔ Net decrease in cash, $(1,798)

The following cash data for the year ended December 31 were adapted from a recent annual report of Alphabet (GOOG), formerly known as Google. The cash balance as of January 1 was $18,347 (in millions).

	In millions
Payments on debt	$ 4,111
Purchases of property, plant, and equipment	9,915
Purchases of investments (marketable securities)	13,796
Cash flows from operating activities	26,024

Instructions

Prepare Alphabet's statement of cash flows for the year ended December 31.

P1-5 Financial statements, including statement of cash flows

Obj. 4

✔ 1. Net income, $335,000

Pendray Systems Corporation began operations on January 1, 20Y5 as an online retailer of computer software and hardware. The following financial statement data were taken from Pendray's records at the end of its first year of operations, December 31, 20Y5.

Accounts payable	$ 40,000
Accounts receivable	88,000
Cash	?
Cash payments for operating activities	896,000
Cash receipts from operating activities	1,087,000
Common stock	120,000
Cost of sales	650,000
Dividends	90,000
Income tax expense	87,000
Income taxes payable	15,000
Interest expense	3,000
Inventories	111,000
Note payable (due in ten years)	80,000
Property, plant, and equipment	265,000
Retained earnings	?
Sales	1,175,000
Selling and administrative expenses	100,000

Instructions

1. Prepare an income statement for the year ended December 31, 20Y5.
2. Prepare a statement of stockholders' equity for the year ended December 31, 20Y5.
3. Prepare a balance sheet as of December 31, 20Y5.
4. Prepare a statement of cash flows for the year ended December 31, 20Y5.

Metric-Based Analysis

Obj. 6

MBA 1-1 Quantitative metrics

Interpublic Group of Companies Inc. (IPG) is an advertising and marketing service company that operates throughout the world. In addition, the company provides event planning, public relations, and brand management services. Twitter Inc. (TWTR) operates as a worldwide platform for individuals to communicate with each other by sending Tweets using their mobile devices.

For each company, go to the Securities and Exchange Commission (SEC) Internet site *http://www.sec.gov/edgar/searchedgar/companysearch.html.* In the search box "Fast Search," enter the Central Index Key (stock market ticker symbol) shown next to the company name. Once the EDGAR Search screen appears, type in 10-K for Filing Type. Open the most recent 10-K file and search the file for "metric" using the "Edit and Find" functions.

1. List the quantitative metrics that appear in each company's 10-K.
2. Comment on the differences in the metrics for each company listed in (1).

Obj. 6

MBA 1-2 Quantitative metrics

JetBlue Airways Corporation (JBLU) is a passenger airline with flights to destinations throughout the United States, the Caribbean, and Latin America. Costco (COST) operates membership retail warehouses offering a variety of products including foods, electronics, appliances, and clothing.

For each company, go to the Securities and Exchange Commission (SEC) Internet site *http://www.sec.gov/edgar/searchedgar/companysearch.html.* In the search box "Fast Search," enter the Central Index Key (stock market ticker symbol) shown next to the company name. Once the EDGAR Search screen appears, type in 10-K for Filing Type. Open the most recent 10-K file and search the file for "metric" using the "Edit and Find" functions.

1. List the quantitative metrics that appear in each company's 10-K.
2. Comment on the differences in the metrics for each company listed in (1).

Obj. 6

MBA 1-3 Return on assets

The financial statements of The Hershey Company (HSY) are shown in Exhibits 6 through 9 of this chapter. Based upon these statements, answer the following questions.

1. What are Hershey's sales (in millions)?
2. What is Hershey's cost of sales (in millions)?
3. What is Hershey's net income (in millions)?
4. What is Hershey's percent of cost of sales to sales? Round to one decimal place.
5. The percent that a company adds to its cost of sales to determine the selling price is called a markup. What is Hershey's markup percent? Round to one decimal place.
6. What is the percentage of net income to sales for Hershey? Round to one decimal place.
7. Hershey had total assets of $4,412 (million) at the beginning of the year. Compute the return on assets for Hershey for the year shown in Exhibits 6–9.

MBA 1-4 Return on assets

Obj. 6

The following data (in millions) were adapted from recent financial statements of Tootsie Roll Industries Inc. (TR):

Sales	$543
Cost of goods sold	342
Net income	63
Average total assets	899

1. What is Tootsie Roll's percent of the cost of sales to sales? Round to one decimal place.
2. The percent a company adds to its cost of sales to determine selling price is called a markup. What is Tootsie Roll's markup percent? Round to one decimal place.
3. What is the percentage of net income to sales for Tootsie Roll? Round to one decimal place.
4. Compute the return on assets for Tootsie Roll.
5. Using your answers to MBA 1-3, compare the markup percentages and return on assets for Hershey and Tootsie Roll.

MBA 1-5 Return on assets

Obj. 6

Pfizer Inc. (PFE) discovers, produces, and distributes medicines, including Celebrex and Lipitor. Ford (F) Motor Co. develops, markets, and produces automobiles and trucks. Microsoft Corporation (MSFT) develops, produces, and distributes a variety of computer software and hardware products including Windows, Office, Excel, and the Xbox.

1. Without computing the return on assets, rank from highest to lowest Pfizer, Ford, and Microsoft in terms of their return on assets.
2. The following data (in millions) were taken from recent financial statements of each company:

	Pfizer	Ford	Microsoft
Net income	$ 9,135	$ 3,187	$ 12,193
Total assets at the beginning of the year	172,101	202,179	172,384
Total assets at the end of the year	169,274	208,527	176,223

Compute the return on assets for each company using the preceding data, and rank the companies' return on assets from highest to lowest. Round the return on assets to one decimal place.

3. Analyze and explain the rankings in (2).

MBA 1-6 Return on assets

Obj. 6

ExxonMobil Corporation (XOM) explores, produces, and distributes oil and natural gas. The Coca-Cola Company (KO) produces and distributes soft drink beverages, including Coke. Wal-Mart Stores, Inc., (WMT) operates retail stores and supermarkets.

1. Without computing the return on assets, rank from highest to lowest Exxon-Mobil, Coca-Cola, and Wal-Mart in terms of their return on assets.
2. The following data (in millions) were taken from recent financial statements of each company:

	ExxonMobil	Coca-Cola	Wal-Mart
Net income	$ 32,520	$ 7,098	$ 16,363
Total assets at the beginning of the year	346,808	90,055	204,751
Total assets at the end of the year	349,493	92,023	203,706

Compute the return on assets for each company using the preceding data, and rank the companies' return on assets from highest to lowest. Round the return on assets to one decimal place.

3. Analyze and explain the rankings in (2).

Obj. 6

MBA 1-7 Return on assets

Tiffany & Co. (TIF) designs and sells jewelry including rings, watches, and necklaces throughout the world. The following data (in millions) were taken from recent financial statements of Tiffany:

Net income	$ 891
Total assets at the beginning of the year	4,752
Total assets at the end of the year	5,181

1. Compute the return on assets for Tiffany using the preceding data. Round to one decimal place.
2. Using your answers to MBA 1-6, compare the return on assets for Wal-Mart to that of Tiffany.

Cases

Case 1-1 Integrity, objectivity, and ethics at The Hershey Company

The management of The Hershey Company (HSY) has asked union workers in two of its highest-cost Pennsylvania plants to accept higher health insurance premiums and take a wage cut. The workers' portion of the insurance cost would double from 6% of the premium to 12%. In addition, workers hired after January 2000 would have their hourly wages cut by $4, which would be partially offset by a 2% annual raise. Management says that the plants need to be more cost competitive. Management has indicated that if the workers accept the proposal, the company would invest $30 million to modernize the plants and move future projects to the plants. Management has refused, however, to guarantee more work at the plants even if the workers approve the proposal. If the workers reject the proposal, management implies that it would move future projects to other plants and that layoffs might be forthcoming. Do you consider management's actions ethical?

Source: Susan Govzdas, "Hershey to Cut Jobs or Wages," *Central Penn Business Journal*, September 24, 2004.

GROUP PROJECT

Case 1-2 Ethics and professional conduct in business

Loretta Smith, president and owner of Custom Enterprises, applied for a $250,000 loan from City National Bank. The bank requested financial statements from Custom Enterprises as a basis for granting the loan. Loretta has told her accountant to provide the bank with a balance sheet. Loretta has decided to omit the other financial statements because there was a net loss during the past year.

In groups of three or four, discuss the following questions:

1. Is Loretta behaving in a professional manner by omitting some of the financial statements?
2. a. What types of information about their businesses would owners be willing to provide bankers? What types of information would owners not be willing to provide?
   b. What types of information about a business would bankers want before extending a loan?
   c. What common interests are shared by bankers and business owners?

GROUP PROJECT

Case 1-3 How businesses make money

Assume that you are the chief executive officer for a national poultry producer. The company's operations include hatching chickens through the use of breeder stock and feeding, raising, and processing the mature chicks into finished products. The finished products include breaded chicken nuggets and patties and deboned, skinless, and marinated chicken. The company sells its products to schools, military services, fast-food chains, and grocery stores.

In groups of four or five, discuss the following business emphasis and risk issues:

1. In a commodity business like poultry production, what do you think is the dominant business emphasis? What are the implications in this dominant emphasis for how you would run the company?
2. Identify at least two major business risks for operating the company.
3. How could the company try to differentiate its products?

Case 1-4 Net income versus cash flow

On January 9, 20--, Dr. Susan Tempkin established DocMed, a medical practice organized as a professional corporation. The below conversation took place the following September between Dr. Tempkin and a former medical school classmate, Dr. Phil Anzar, at an American Medical Association convention in London.

Dr. Anzar: Susan, good to see you again. Why didn't you call when you were in Chicago? We could have had dinner together.

Dr. Tempkin: Actually, I never made it to Chicago this year. My husband and kids went to our Wisconsin Dells condo twice, but I got stuck in New York. I opened a new consulting practice this January and haven't had any time for myself since.

Dr. Anzar: I heard about it . . . Doc . . . something . . . right?

Dr. Tempkin: Yes, DocMed. My husband chose the name.

Dr. Anzar: I've thought about doing something like that. Are you making any money? I mean, is it worth your time?

Dr. Tempkin: You wouldn't believe it. I started by opening a bank account with $40,000, and my August bank statement shows a balance of $215,000. Not bad for eight months—all pure profit.

Dr. Anzar: Maybe I'll try it in Chicago. Let's have breakfast together tomorrow and you can fill me in on the details.

Comment on Dr. Tempkin's statement that the difference between the opening bank balance ($40,000) and the August statement balance ($215,000) is pure profit.

Case 1-5 The accounting equation

Review financial statements for three well-known companies, such as Ford Motor Co. (F), General Motors (GM), International Business Machines (IBM), Microsoft (MSFT), or Amazon (AMZ). The financial statements may be found at http://www.sec.gov/edgar/searchedgar/companysearch.html. Enter the company's stock market symbol in the Fast Search box, enter 10-K in the Filing Type box, and click on the latest 10-K. If you wish, you can save the whole 10-K report to your computer.

Examine the balance sheet for each company and determine the total assets, liabilities, and stockholders' equity. Verify that total assets equal the total of the liabilities plus stockholders' equity.

Case 1-6 Financial analysis of Enron Corporation

Enron Corporation, headquartered in Houston, Texas, provided products and services for natural gas, electricity, and communications to wholesale and retail customers. Enron's operations were conducted through a variety of subsidiaries and affiliates that involved transporting gas through pipelines, transmitting electricity, and managing energy commodities. The following data were taken from Enron's December 31, 2000, financial statements:

	In millions
Total revenues	$100,789
Total costs and expenses	98,836
Operating income	1,953
Net income	979
Total assets	65,503
Total liabilities	54,033
Total stockholders' equity	11,470
Net cash flows from operating activities	4,779
Net cash flows from investing activities	(4,264)
Net cash flows from financing activities	571
Net increase in cash	1,086

At the end of 2000, the market price of Enron's stock was approximately $83 per share. Eventually, however, Enron's stock was selling for $0.22 per share.

Review the preceding financial statement data and search the Internet for articles on Enron Corporation. Briefly explain why Enron's stock dropped so dramatically in such a short time.

Answers to Self-Examination Questions

1. **D** A corporation, organized in accordance with state or federal statutes, is a separate legal entity in which ownership is divided into shares of stock (answer D). A proprietorship (answer A) is an unincorporated business owned by one individual. A service business (answer B) provides services to its customers. It can be organized as a proprietorship, partnership, or corporation. A partnership (answer C) is an unincorporated business owned by two or more individuals.

2. **A** The resources owned by a business are called assets (answer A). The debts of the business are called liabilities (answer B), and the equity of the owners is called stockholders' equity (answer D). The relationship among assets, liabilities, and stockholders' equity is expressed as the accounting equation (answer C).

3. **A** The balance sheet is a listing of the assets, liabilities, and stockholders' equity of a business at a specific date (answer A). The income statement (answer B) is a summary of the revenue and expenses of a business for a specific period of time. The retained earnings statement (answer C) summarizes the changes in retained earnings during a specific period of time. The statement of cash flows (answer D) summarizes the cash receipts and cash payments for a specific period of time.

4. **D** The accounting equation is:

   Assets = Liabilities + Stockholders' Equity

   Therefore, if assets are $20,000 and liabilities are $12,000, stockholders' equity is $8,000 (answer D), as indicated in the following computation:

Assets	= Liabilities + Stockholders' Equity
+$20,000	= $12,000 + Stockholders' Equity
+$20,000 − $12,000	= Stockholders' Equity
+$8,000	= Stockholders' Equity

5. **B** Net income is the excess of revenue over expenses, or $7,500 (answer B). If expenses exceed revenue, the difference is a net loss. Dividends are the opposite of the stockholders investing in the business and do not affect the amount of net income or net loss.

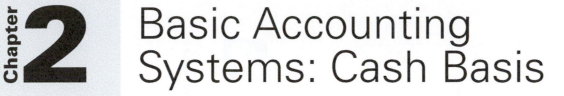

Chapter 2 Basic Accounting Systems: Cash Basis

What's Covered:

Topics: Basic Accounting Systems: Cash Basis

Systems Elements
- Rules (Obj. 1)
- Framework (Obj. 1)
- Controls (Obj. 1)

Recording Transactions
- First-Period Transactions (Obj. 2)
- First-Period Financial Statements (Obj. 3)
- Second-Period Transactions (Obj. 4)
- Second-Period Financial Statements (Obj. 5)

Metric-Based Analysis
- Transactions
  - Liquidity: Cash (Obj. 2,4)
  - Profitability: Net Income (Obj. 2,4)
- Financial Statements
  - Common-Sized Statements (Obj. 6)

Learning Objectives

Obj.1 Describe the basic elements of a financial accounting system.

Obj.2 Analyze, record, and summarize transactions for a corporation's first period of operations.

Obj.3 Prepare financial statements for a corporation's first period of operations.

Obj.4 Analyze, record, and summarize transactions for a corporation's second period of operations.

Obj.5 Prepare financial statements for a corporation's second period of operations.

Obj.6 Describe and illustrate the use of common-sized income statements in assessing a company's performance.

Chapter Metrics

Use the following metrics to analyze transactions and financial statements.

TRANSACTIONS

- Liquidity: Cash
- Profitability: Net Income—Cash Basis

FINANCIAL STATEMENTS

- Common-Sized Statements

x9626/Shutterstock.com

Twitter Connection

Every day it seems like you get an incredible amount of incoming e-mail messages; you get them from your friends, relatives, subscribed e-mail lists, and even spammers! But how do you organize all of these messages? You might create folders to sort messages by sender, topic, or project. Perhaps you use keyword search utilities. You might even use filters or rules to automatically delete spam or send messages from your best friend to a special folder. In any case, you are organizing information so that it is simple to retrieve and allows you to more easily understand, respond to, or refer to the messages.

In the same way that you organize your e-mail, companies develop an organized method for processing, recording, and summarizing financial transactions. For example, **Twitter** is an information network used by millions to share messages of up to 140 characters. Such messages, called Tweets, are available free to the public. Twitter earns revenue by selling advertisements on the Internet as "Promoted Tweets, "Promoted Trends," or "Promoted Accounts." In order to analyze revenue by these three sources, Twitter records and summarizes its revenues by each advertising category. In addition, Twitter records and summarizes various metrics for its customers such as Retweets, clicks, replies, mentions, and follows. In doing so, Twitter has an integrated information system that includes an accounting component.

This chapter describes the basic elements of financial accounting systems. Such systems process, record, and summarize financial transactions, allowing for the preparation of financial statements, as discussed in Chapter 1.

The simplest form of an accounting system records and summarizes only transactions involving the receipt and payment of cash. For this reason, this chapter describes and illustrates a cash basis accounting system. This serves as a foundation for later discussions of more complex accounting systems and financial reporting issues.

Objective 1

Describe the basic elements of a financial accounting system.

Elements of an Accounting System

A financial accounting system is designed to produce financial statements. The financial statements include the income statement, statement of stockholders' equity, balance sheet, and statement of cash flows.

The basic elements of a **financial accounting system** include:

- *Rules* for determining what, when, and the amount that should be recorded
- A *framework* for preparing financial statements
- *Controls* to determine whether errors may have arisen in the recording process

Rules

The rules for determining what, when, and the amount recorded are derived from the eight concepts discussed in Chapter 1. These concepts are the basis of generally accepted accounting principles (GAAP), which require the recording of transactions affecting elements of the financial statements.

A **transaction** is an economic event that under GAAP affects the financial statements. A transaction may affect one, two, or more items within the financial statements. For example, equipment purchased for cash affects only assets. That is, one asset (equipment) increases while another asset (cash) decreases. If, on the other hand, the equipment is purchased on credit, assets (equipment) and liabilities (accounts or notes payable) increase.

Twitter Connection

Twitter records transactions using generally accepted accounting principles (GAAP).

Framework

Transactions must be analyzed, recorded, and summarized using a framework. The accounting equation is the basis for all such frameworks. The accounting equation is expressed as follows:

Assets = Liabilities + Stockholders' Equity

Twitter Connection

Using the accounting equation as a framework, **Twitter** reported in recent financial statements (in millions) assets of \$5,583, liabilities of \$1,957, and stockholders equity of \$3,626, which can be expressed in the form of the accounting equation as: \$5,583 = \$1,957 + \$3,626.

By expanding the accounting equation, as shown in Exhibit 1, an integrated financial statement approach can be designed for analyzing, recording, and summarizing transactions. This is done by including columns for the statement of cash flows, balance sheet, and income statement.

The *left-hand* column in Exhibit 1 shows the effects of transactions on the statement of cash flows. Each cash transaction is recorded and classified as an operating, investing, or financing activity. This serves as a basis for preparing the statement of cash flows.

The cash at the beginning of the period plus or minus the cash flows from operating, investing, and financing activities equals the end-of-period cash. This end-of-period cash amount is reported as an asset on the balance sheet. Thus, the statement of cash flows is integrated with the balance sheet in Exhibit 1.

Twitter Connection

Twitter reported cash of \$1,511 million on its balance sheet and statement of cash flows.

Exhibit 1 Integrated Financial Statement Framework

Integrated Financial Statement Framework

BALANCE SHEET

	Assets	=	Liabilities	+	Stockholders' Equity	
	Assets	**=**	**Liabilities**	**+**	**Capital Stock +**	**Retained Earnings**
Transaction	XXX		XXX		XXX	XXX
	XXX					
	XXX		XXX		XXX	XXX

STATEMENT OF CASH FLOWS

+/– Operating activities	XXX
+/– Investing activities	XXX
+/– Financing activities	XXX
Increase or decrease in cash	XXX
Beginning cash	XXX
Ending cash	XXX

INCOME STATEMENT

Revenues	XXX
Expenses	XXX
Net income or loss	XXX

The *right-hand* column in Exhibit 1 shows the effects of transactions on the income statement. Each revenue and expense transaction is recorded and classified as a revenue or expense. This serves as a basis for preparing the income statement.

Net income for the period (revenues less expenses) is added to beginning retained earnings.[1] Thus, revenue and expense transactions are also recorded under the Retained Earnings column of the balance sheet. By doing so, the balance sheet is integrated with the income statement in Exhibit 1.

Exhibit 1 also illustrates the importance of the balance sheet as the connecting link between the statement of cash flows and the income statement.[2] This integrated financial statement approach for analyzing, recording, and summarizing transactions is illustrated later in this chapter.

The integrated financial statement approach shown in Exhibit 1 is an invaluable tool for analyzing transactions and their effects on the financial statements. It is also an aid for analyzing and interpreting a company's financial statements. This is because, without understanding how a company's financial statements are integrated, important trends or events may be missed or misinterpreted.

To illustrate, assume a company reports net income (profits) on its income statement. As a result, it might be mistakenly concluded that the company's operations are doing well and no major changes are necessary. In fact, the company might be experiencing a continuing negative net cash flow from operations and thus be headed towards bankruptcy. This is why it is essential to analyze all the financial statements and their integration.

Controls

The integrated financial statement approach shown in Exhibit 1 has built-in controls to ensure that all transactions are correctly analyzed, recorded, and summarized. These controls include the following:[3]

1. The accounting equation must balance.
2. The ending cash on the statement of cash flows must equal the cash on the balance sheet.
3. The net income on the income statement must equal the net effects of revenues and expenses on retained earnings.

First, the accounting equation requires that total assets equal total liabilities plus total stockholders' equity. If at the end of the period this equality does not hold, an error has occurred.

To illustrate, assume that a cash purchase of equipment for $10,000 is incorrectly recorded as a $10,000 increase in equipment and a $10,000 increase (instead of decrease) in cash. In this case, the total assets exceed the total liabilities plus stockholders' equity by $20,000. Likewise, assume that the equipment was increased by $10,000, but the $10,000 decrease in cash was omitted. In this case, the total assets exceed total liabilities plus stockholders' equity by $10,000. In both cases, the inequality of the equation indicates that an error has occurred.

The equality of the equation doesn't necessarily mean that no errors have occurred. To illustrate, assume that a business purchased $10,000 of equipment on credit and recorded the transaction as an increase in equipment of $10,000. However, instead of increasing the liabilities by $10,000, the transaction was recorded as a $10,000 decrease in cash. In this case, the accounting equation still balances, even though cash and liabilities are understated by $10,000.

Second, the ending Cash shown in the Statement of Cash Flows column must equal the ending cash under Assets in the Balance Sheet column. If these two amounts do not agree, an error has occurred.

To illustrate, assume that a $5,000 cash receipt was recorded as an increase in Cash in the Balance Sheet column under Assets but was omitted from the Statement of Cash Flows column. In this case, the ending cash shown in the Statement of Cash Flows column would be $5,000 less than the balance of Cash under Assets in the Balance Sheet column.

1. A net loss for the period, which occurs when expenses exceed revenues, is subtracted from beginning retained earnings.
2. In Chapter 3, the use of the balance sheet to reconcile net cash flows from operating activities with net income is described and illustrated.
3. Additional accounting controls are discussed in Chapter 5.

Third, the net income or loss from the Income Statement column must equal the net effects of revenues and expenses on retained earnings. If these two amounts do not agree, an error has occurred.

To illustrate, assume that a $7,500 payment for rent expense was recorded under Retained Earnings in the Balance Sheet column but was omitted from the Income Statement column. In this case, the Net income in the Income Statement column would be $7,500 more than the net effects of revenues and expenses on retained earnings.

In **Twitter's** annual report, it includes a report on its controls and procedures for preparing accurate financial statements.

Twitter Connection

Recording a Corporation's First Period of Operations

Objective 2
Analyze, record, and summarize transactions for a corporation's first period of operations.

The integrated financial statement framework shown in Exhibit 1 is illustrated using the transactions for a corporation's first period of operations. Assume that on September 1, 20Y5, Lee Landry, M.D., organizes a professional corporation to practice general medicine. The business is to be known as Family Health Care, P.C., where P.C. refers to a *professional corporation.*

Each of Family Health Care's transactions during September is described and recorded in this section. The transactions begin with Dr. Landry's investment to establish the business.

Transaction (a)

Dr. Landry deposits $6,000 in a bank account in the name of Family Health Care, P.C., in return for shares of common stock in the corporation.

In recording this transaction, increases are recorded as positive numbers, while decreases are recorded as negative numbers. Negative amounts are shown in parentheses.

The effects of this transaction on Family Health Care's financial statements are recorded as follows:

1. Under the Statement of Cash Flows column, Cash from Financing activities is increased by $6,000.
2. Under the Balance Sheet column, Cash under Assets is increased by $6,000. To balance the accounting equation, **Common Stock** under Stockholders' Equity is also increased by $6,000.

Got the Flu? Why Not Chew Some Gum?

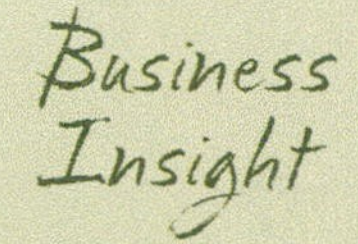

Facing a slumping market for sugared chewing gum—such as Juicy Fruit™ and Doublemint™—**Wm. Wrigley Jr. Company**, a subsidiary of **Mars Incorporated**, is reinventing itself by expanding its product lines and introducing new chewing gum applications. Wrigley's new products include sugarless breath mints and more powerful flavored mint chewing gum, like Extra Polar Ice™. In addition, Wrigley is experimenting with health-care applications of chewing gum. For example, the company founded the Wrigley Science Institute™ with the objective of promoting scientific research on the benefits of chewing gum. Specifically, the Institute sponsors research in such areas as weight reduction, management and stress relief, and cognitive focus. The Institute provides grants to leading researchers who investigate the role of chewing gum in health and wellness.

Source: Wrigley.com and *USA Today*, "Wrigley Wants Science to Prove Gum-Chewing Benefits," by Dave Carpenter, The Associated Press, March 28, 2006.

Since no revenues or expenses are affected, there are no entries under the Income Statement column. The recording of transaction (a) relates only to the business, Family Health Care, P.C. Dr. Landry's personal assets (such as a home or a personal bank account) and personal liabilities are excluded. This is because under the business entity concept, Family Health Care is treated as a separate entity, with cash of $6,000 and stockholders' equity of $6,000.

The effects of this transaction on Family Health Care's financial statements are as follows:

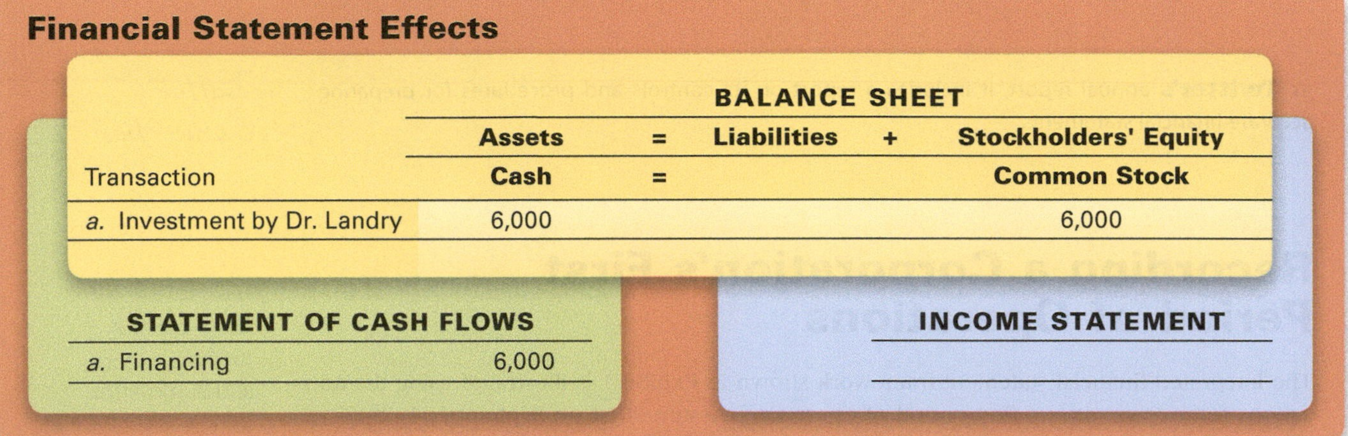

Financial Statement Effects

BALANCE SHEET

Transaction	Assets	=	Liabilities	+	Stockholders' Equity
	Cash	=			**Common Stock**
a. Investment by Dr. Landry	6,000				6,000

STATEMENT OF CASH FLOWS	
a. Financing	6,000

INCOME STATEMENT

Transaction Metric Effects

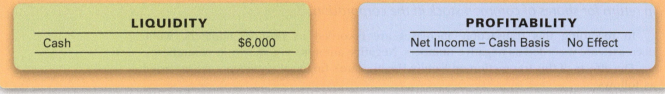

The effects of each transaction on liquidity and profitability metrics for Family Health Care are also illustrated. Cash is used as the liquidity metric and net income (revenues less expenses) as the profitability metric. Since this chapter illustrates only cash transactions, the profitability metric is termed Net Income – Cash Basis.

The effects of issuing $6,000 of common stock on Family Health Care's liquidity and profitability metrics are as follows:

LIQUIDITY	
Cash	$6,000

PROFITABILITY	
Net Income – Cash Basis	No Effect

Transaction (b)

Family Health Care borrows $10,000 from First National Bank to finance its operations.

To borrow the $10,000, Dr. Landry signs a note payable with First National Bank in the name of Family Health Care. The note payable is a liability that Family Health Care must pay in the future. The note payable also requires the payment of interest of $100 per month until the note of $10,000 is paid on September 30, 20Y9. The interest is to be paid at the end of each month.

The effects of this transaction on Family Health Care's financial statements are recorded as follows:

1. Under the Statement of Cash Flows column, Cash from Financing activities is increased by $10,000.
2. Under the Balance Sheet column, Cash under Assets is increased by $10,000. To balance the accounting equation, Notes Payable under Liabilities is also increased by $10,000.

This transaction changes assets and liabilities on the balance sheet but does not change Family Health Care's stockholders' equity of $6,000. Since no revenues or expenses are affected, no entries are made under the Income Statement column.

The effects of this transaction on Family Health Care's financial statements are shown below.

Financial Statement Effects

BALANCE SHEET

	Assets	=	Liabilities	+	Stockholders' Equity
	Cash	=	**Notes Payable**	+	**Common Stock**
Balances	6,000				6,000
b. Issued note pay.	10,000		10,000		
Balances	16,000		10,000		6,000

STATEMENT OF CASH FLOWS	
b. Financing	10,000

INCOME STATEMENT

Transaction Metric Effects

The effects of borrowing $10,000 on Family Health Care's liquidity and profitability metrics are as follows:

LIQUIDITY	
Cash	$10,000

PROFITABILITY	
Net Income – Cash Basis	No Effect

Transaction (c)

Family Health Care buys land for $12,000 cash.

The land is located near a new suburban hospital that is under construction. Dr. Landry plans to rent office space and equipment for several months. When the hospital is completed, Family Health Care will build on the land.

The effects of this transaction on Family Health Care's financial statements are recorded as follows:

1. Under the Statement of Cash Flows column, Cash from Investing activities is decreased by $12,000.
2. Under the Balance Sheet column, Cash under Assets is decreased by $12,000. To balance the accounting equation, Land under Assets is increased by $12,000.

This transaction illustrates the use of cash for an investing activity. As a result, $12,000 was entered under the Statement of Cash Flows column. In addition, the mix of assets changes on the balance sheet. Since no revenues or expenses are affected, no entries are made under the Income Statement column.

The effects of this transaction on Family Health Care's financial statements are shown below.

Financial Statement Effects

BALANCE SHEET

	Assets			=	Liabilities	+	Stockholders' Equity
	Cash	+	**Land**	=	**Notes Payable**	+	**Common Stock**
Balances	16,000				10,000		6,000
c. Purchase of land	(12,000)		12,000				
Balances	4,000		12,000		10,000		6,000

STATEMENT OF CASH FLOWS	
c. Investing	(12,000)

INCOME STATEMENT

Transaction Metric Effects

The effects of the $12,000 purchase of the land on Family Health Care's liquidity and profitability metrics are as follows:

LIQUIDITY	
Cash	$(12,000)

PROFITABILITY	
Net Income – Cash Basis	No Effect

Transaction (d)

During the first month of operations, Family Health Care earned patient fees of $5,500, receiving the fees in cash.

The effects of this transaction on Family Health Care's financial statements are recorded as follows:

1. Under the Statement of Cash Flows column, Cash from Operating activities is increased by $5,500.
2. Under the Balance Sheet column, Cash under Assets is increased by $5,500. To balance the accounting equation, Retained Earnings under Stockholders' Equity is also increased by $5,500.
3. Under the Income Statement column, Fees earned is increased by $5,500.

This transaction illustrates an inflow of cash from operating activities by earning revenues (fees earned) of $5,500. Retained Earnings is increased under Stockholders' Equity by $5,500 because fees earned contribute to net income and net income increases stockholders' equity. Since fees earned are a type of revenue, Fees earned of $5,500 is also entered under the Income Statement column.

The effects of this transaction on Family Health Care's financial statements are shown below.

Financial Statement Effects

BALANCE SHEET

	Assets			=	Liabilities	+	Stockholders' Equity		
	Cash	**+**	**Land**	**=**	**Notes Payable**	**+**	**Common Stock**	**+**	**Retained Earnings**
Balances	4,000		12,000		10,000		6,000		
d. Fees earned	5,500								5,500
Balances	9,500		12,000		10,000		6,000		5,500

STATEMENT OF CASH FLOWS	
d. Operating	5,500

INCOME STATEMENT	
d. Fees earned	5,500

Transaction Metric Effects

The effects of receiving $5,500 of patient fees on Family Health Care's liquidity and profitability metrics are as follows:

LIQUIDITY	
Cash	$5,500

PROFITABILITY	
Net Income – Cash Basis	$5,500

Transaction (e)

Family Health Care paid expenses during September as follows: wages, $1,125; rent, $950; utilities, $450; interest, $100; and miscellaneous, $275.

Miscellaneous expenses include small amounts paid for such items as postage, newspapers, and magazines. The effects of this transaction on Family Health Care's financial statements are recorded as follows:

1. Under the Statement of Cash Flows column, Cash from Operating activities is decreased by $2,900, which is the sum of the expenses ($1,125 + $950 + $450 + $100 + $275).
2. Under the Balance Sheet column, Cash under Assets is decreased by $2,900. To balance the accounting equation, Retained Earnings under Stockholders' Equity is also decreased by $2,900.
3. Under the Income Statement column, each expense is listed as a negative amount.

This transaction illustrates an outflow of cash of $2,900 for operating activities (paying expenses). Thus, $2,900 is entered in the Statement of Cash Flows column as an Operating activity. Expenses have the opposite effect from revenues on net income and retained earnings. As a result, $2,900 is entered for Retained Earnings under Stockholders' Equity. In addition, each expense is listed under the Income Statement column as a negative amount.

The effects of this transaction on Family Health Care's financial statements are shown below.

Financial Statement Effects

BALANCE SHEET

	Assets			=	Liabilities	+	Stockholders' Equity		
	Cash	+	Land	=	Notes Payable	+	Common Stock	+	Retained Earnings
Balances	9,500		12,000		10,000		6,000		5,500
e. Paid expenses	(2,900)								(2,900)
Balances	6,600		12,000		10,000		6,000		2,600

STATEMENT OF CASH FLOWS

e. Operating	(2,900)

INCOME STATEMENT

e. Wages expense	(1,125)
Rent expense	(950)
Utilities expense	(450)
Interest expense	(100)
Misc. expense	(275)

Transaction Metric Effects

The effects of paying $2,900 in expenses on Family Health Care's liquidity and profitability metrics are as follows:

LIQUIDITY

Cash	$(2,900)

PROFITABILITY

Net Income – Cash Basis	$(2,900)

Transaction (f)

Family Health Care paid $1,500 to stockholders (Dr. Lee Landry) as dividends.

Dividends are distributions of a company's earnings to stockholders. Dividends should not be confused with expenses. Dividends do not represent assets consumed or services used in earning revenues. Instead, dividends are a distribution of earnings to the stockholders.

The effects of this transaction on Family Health Care's financial statements are recorded as follows:

1. Under the Statement of Cash Flows column, Cash from Financing activities is decreased by $1,500.
2. Under the Balance Sheet column, Cash under Assets is decreased by $1,500. To balance the accounting equation, Retained Earnings under Stockholders' Equity is also decreased by $1,500.

This transaction illustrates an outflow of cash of $1,500 for financing activities (paying dividends). Thus, $1,500 is entered in the Statement of Cash Flows column as a Financing activity. Dividends decrease retained earnings; thus, $1,500 is entered for Retained Earnings under Stockholders' Equity. Since dividends are not an expense, no entry is made under the Income Statement column.

The effects of this transaction on Family Health Care's financial statements are shown below.

Financial Statement Effects

BALANCE SHEET

	Assets			=	Liabilities	+	Stockholders' Equity		
	Cash	+	**Land**	=	**Notes Payable**	+	**Common Stock**	+	**Retained Earnings**
Balances	6,600		12,000		10,000		6,000		2,600
f. Paid dividends	(1,500)								(1,500)
Balances	5,100		12,000		10,000		6,000		1,100

STATEMENT OF CASH FLOWS

f. Financing	(1,500)

INCOME STATEMENT

Transaction Metric Effects

The effects of paying dividends of $1,500 on Family Health Care's liquidity and profitability metrics are as follows:

LIQUIDITY

Cash	$(1,500)

PROFITABILITY

Net Income – Cash Basis	No Effect

Family Heath Care's September transactions are summarized in Exhibit 2 using the integrated financial statement format. Each transaction is identified by letter.

Exhibit 2 illustrates the three controls that are built into the integrated financial statement approach. These controls are as follows:

1. The accounting equation under the Balance Sheet column balances. That is, total assets of $17,100 ($5,100 + $12,000) equals total liabilities plus stockholders' equity of $17,100 ($10,000 + $6,000 + $1,100).
2. The ending cash under the Statement of Cash Flows column of $5,100 equals the cash balance under the Balance Sheet column of $5,100.
3. The net income under the Income Statement column of $2,600 equals the net effects of revenues of $5,500 and expenses of $2,900 on retained earnings ($5,500 − $2,900).

Exhibit 2 Family Health Care Summary of Transactions for September

Financial Statement Effects for September

BALANCE SHEET

	Assets			=	Liabilities	+	Stockholders' Equity		
	Cash	+	Land	=	Notes Payable	+	Common Stock	+	Retained Earnings
a. Investment by Dr. Landry	6,000						6,000		
b. Issued note pay.	10,000				10,000				
c. Purchase of land	(12,000)		12,000						
d. Fees earned	5,500								5,500
e. Paid expenses	(2,900)								(2,900)
f. Paid dividends	(1,500)								(1,500)
Balances, Sept. 30	5,100		12,000		10,000		6,000		1,100

STATEMENT OF CASH FLOWS

a. Financing	6,000
b. Financing	10,000
c. Investing	(12,000)
d. Operating	5,500
e. Operating	(2,900)
f. Financing	(1,500)
Increase in cash and Sept. 30 cash	5,100

INCOME STATEMENT

d. Fees earned	5,500
e. Wages expense	(1,125)
Rent expense	(950)
Utilities expense	(450)
Interest expense	(100)
Misc. expense	(275)
Net income	2,600

Integrity, Objectivity, and Ethics in Business

A History of Ethical Conduct

The **Wm. Wrigley Jr. Company**, which is now a subsidiary of **Mars Incorporated**, has a long history of integrity, objectivity, and ethical conduct. When pressured to become part of a cartel, known as the Chewing Gum Trust, the company founder, William Wrigley Jr., said, "We prefer to do business by fair and square methods or we prefer not to do business at all." In 1932, Phillip K. Wrigley, called "PK" by his friends, became president of the Wrigley Company after his father, William Wrigley Jr., died. PK also was president of the Chicago Cubs, which played in Wrigley Field. He was financially generous to his players and frequently gave them advice on and off the field. However, as a man of integrity and high ethical standards, PK docked (reduced) his salary as president of the Wrigley Company for the time he spent working on Cubs-related activities and business.

Richard B. Levine/Newscom

Source: St. Louis Post-Dispatch, "Sports—Backpages," January 26, 2003.

In reviewing Exhibit 2, you should note that the following apply to all companies:

- The Balance Sheet column reflects the accounting equation (Assets = Liabilities + Stockholders' Equity).
- The two sides of the accounting equation are always equal.
- Every transaction affects (increases or decreases) one or more of the balance sheet elements—assets, liabilities, or stockholders' equity.
- A transaction may or may not affect (increase or decrease) an element of the statement of cash flows or the income statement. Some transactions affect elements of both statements, some transactions affect only one statement and not the other, and some transactions affect neither statement.
- Every cash transaction increases or decreases the asset (cash) on the balance sheet. Every cash transaction also increases or decreases an operating, investing, or financing activity on the statement of cash flows.
- The ending balance of Cash under the Statement of Cash Flows column ($5,100 in Exhibit 2) agrees with the ending cash balance shown on the balance sheet. Since September was Family Health Care's first period of operations, this ending cash balance equals the net increase in cash for the period. In future periods, the net increase (decrease) in cash is added to (or subtracted from) the beginning cash balance to equal the ending cash balance. This ending cash balance is reported in the statement of cash flows and balance sheet.
- The stockholders' equity is increased by amounts invested by stockholders (common stock).
- Revenues increase stockholders' equity (retained earnings) and expenses decrease stockholders' equity (retained earnings). The effects of revenue and expense transactions are also shown in the Income Statement column.
- Stockholders' equity (retained earnings) is decreased by dividends paid to stockholders.
- The change in retained earnings for the period is the net income minus dividends. For a net loss, the change in retained earnings is the net loss plus dividends.
- The statement of cash flows is linked to the balance sheet through cash.
- The income statement is linked to the balance sheet through revenues and expenses (net income or loss), which affects retained earnings.

Exhibit 3 summarizes the effects of the various transactions affecting stockholders' equity.

Exhibit 3 Effects of Transactions on Stockholders' Equity

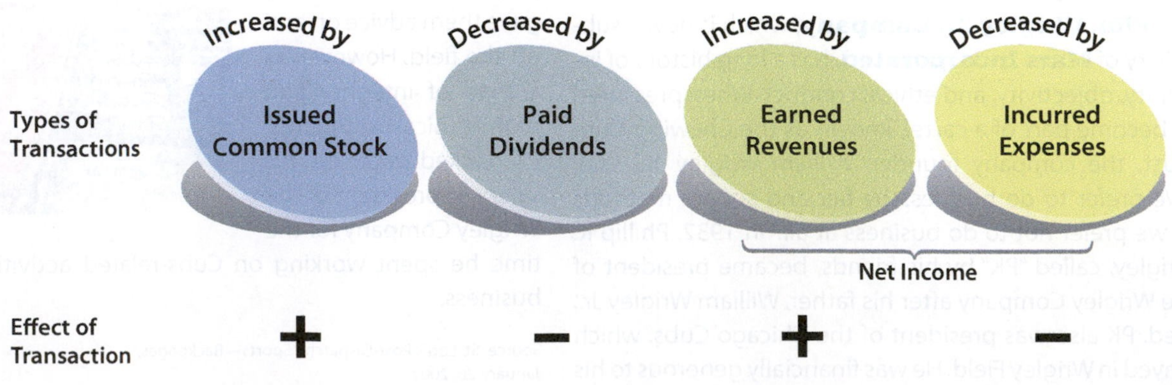

Transaction Metric Effects

The effects of September's transactions on Family Health Care's liquidity and profitability metrics are shown as follows:

LIQUIDITY	
Transaction	**Cash**
a. Issued stock	$6,000
b. Issued note pay.	10,000
c. Purchased land	(12,000)
d. Earned fees	5,500
e. Paid expenses	(2,900)
f. Paid dividends	(1,500)
Total	$5,100

PROFITABILITY	
Net Income – Cash Basis	
a. Issued stock	—
b. Issued note pay.	—
c. Purchased land	—
d. Earned fees	$5,500
e. Paid expenses	(2,900)
f. Paid dividends	—
Total	$2,600

September's transactions had the effect of increasing Family Health Care's liquidity metric (Cash) by $5,100. Since this is Family Health Care's first period of operations, this is also the ending balance of cash. September's transactions increased Family Health Care's profitability metric, Net Income – Cash Basis, by $2,600, which is also the amount that will be reported as net income on the income statement for September.

Financial Statements for a Corporation's First Period of Operations

Objective 3

Prepare financial statements for a corporation's first period of operations.

Exhibit 2 lists Family Health Care's September transactions in the order they occurred. Exhibit 2, however, does not group and summarize like transactions together. The accounting reports that provide this summarized information are financial statements.

Family Health Care's September financial statements can be prepared from Exhibit 2. These financial statements are shown in Exhibit 4.

The financial statements shown in Exhibit 4 are prepared from Exhibit 2 as follows:

1. The income statement is prepared using the Income Statement column.
2. The statement of stockholders' equity is prepared next because the ending balance of common stock and retained earnings is needed to prepare the balance sheet. The retained earnings column is prepared using net income from the income statement and the amount recorded for dividends.
3. The balance sheet is prepared next using the balances shown under the Balance Sheet column.
4. The statement of cash flows is prepared last using the Statement of Cash Flows column.

Each financial statement is identified by the name of the business, the title of the statement, and the date or period of time covered by the statement.

Income Statement

The income statement for Family Health Care shown in Exhibit 4 reports fees earned of $5,500, total operating expenses of $2,900, and net income of $2,600. The $5,500 of fees earned is taken from the Income Statement column of Exhibit 2. Likewise, the expenses are summarized from the Income Statement column of Exhibit 2. These expenses are reported under the heading "Operating expenses." Operating expenses are normally listed in order of size, beginning with the largest expense. Miscellaneous expense is usually shown as the last item, regardless of amount.

Statement of Stockholders' Equity

The statement of stockholders' equity shown in Exhibit 4 reports two columns for common stock and retained earnings. Since this is the first month of Family Health Care's operations, the beginning balances of common stock and retained earnings are zero. Common stock of $6,000 is taken from Exhibit 2. Ending retained earnings of $1,100 is created by net income of $2,600 less dividends of $1,500.

Exhibit 4 Family Health Care Financial Statements for September

Family Health Care, P.C.
Income Statement
For the Month Ended September 30, 20Y5

Fees earned		$5,500
Operating expenses:		
Wages expense	$1,125	
Rent expense	950	
Utilities expense	450	
Interest expense	100	
Miscellaneous expense	275	
Total operating expenses		(2,900)
Net income		$2,600

Family Health Care, P.C.
Statement of Stockholders' Equity
For the Month Ended September 30, 20Y5

	Common Stock	Retained Earnings	Total
Balances, Sept. 1, 20Y5	$ 0	$ 0	$ 0
Issuance of common stock	6,000		6,000
Net income		2,600	2,600
Dividends		(1,500)	(1,500)
Balances, Sept. 30, 20Y5	$ 6,000	$ 1,100	$7,100

Family Health Care, P.C.
Balance Sheet
September 30, 20Y5

Assets		
Cash		$ 5,100
Land		12,000
Total assets		$17,100
Liabilities		
Notes payable		$10,000
Stockholders' Equity		
Common stock	$6,000	
Retained earnings	1,100	
Total stockholders' equity		7,100
Total liabilities and stockholders' equity		$17,100

(Continued)

Exhibit 4 Family Health Care Financial Statements for September (Concluded)

Family Health Care, P.C.
Statement of Cash Flows
For the Month Ended September 30, 20Y5

Cash flows from operating activities:		
Cash received from customers	$ 5,500	
Cash paid for expenses	(2,900)	
Net cash flow from operating activities		$ 2,600
Cash flows used in investing activities:		
Cash paid for acquisition of land		(12,000)
Cash flows from financing activities:		
Cash received from issuing common stock	$ 6,000	
Cash received from notes payable	10,000	
Cash dividends paid to stockholder	(1,500)	
Net cash flow from financing activities		14,500
Net increase in cash		$ 5,100
September 1, 20Y5, cash balance		0
September 30, 20Y5, cash balance		$ 5,100

Balance Sheet

Family Health Care's assets, liabilities, and stockholders' equity as of September 30, 20Y5, are taken from the last line of the Balance Sheet column of Exhibit 2. The September 30, 20Y5, balance sheet is shown in Exhibit 4.

In the Assets section of the balance sheet, assets are normally listed in order of liquidity, starting with cash. **Liquidity** refers to the ability to convert an asset to cash. Land is less liquid than cash and thus would be listed second in Family Health Care's balance sheet.

In the Liabilities section of Family Health Care's balance sheet, notes payable is the only liability. When there are two or more categories of liabilities, each should be listed and the total amount reported. Liabilities should be presented in the order that they will be paid in cash. Thus, the notes payable due in 20Y9 would be listed after the liabilities that are due earlier.

The stockholders' equity for Family Health Care as of September 30, 20Y5, consists of $6,000 of common stock and retained earnings of $1,100. The retained earnings is the ending retained earnings reported on the statement of stockholders' equity.

Statement of Cash Flows

Family Health Care's statement of cash flows for September is prepared from the Statement of Cash Flows column of Exhibit 2. Cash increased from a zero balance at the beginning of the month to $5,100 at the end of the month.

The $5,100 increase in cash during September was created by:

1. Operating activities that generated $2,600 of cash
2. Investing activities that used $12,000 of cash
3. Financing activities that generated $14,500 of cash

The details of how the operating, investing, and financing activities generated or used cash is reported in the statement of cash flows. For example, financing activities generated $6,000 from the sale of common stock and $10,000 from borrowing by issuing a note payable. Financing activities used $1,500 for paying dividends.

Integration of Financial Statements

Exhibit 5 shows how Family Health Care's financial statements for September are integrated. As shown in Exhibit 5, these statements are integrated as follows:

1. The ending cash balance of $5,100 on the balance sheet equals the ending cash balance reported on the statement of cash flows.

2. The net income of $2,600 is reported on the income statement and the statement of stockholders' equity.
3. The ending common stock of $6,000 and retained earnings of $1,100 are reported in the statement of stockholders' equity and balance sheet.
4. The cash flows from operating activities of $2,600 reported on the statement of cash flows equals the net income on the income statement. The relationship between cash flows from operating activities and net income is further described and illustrated in Chapter 3.

Exhibit 5 Family Health Care Integrated Financial Statements for September

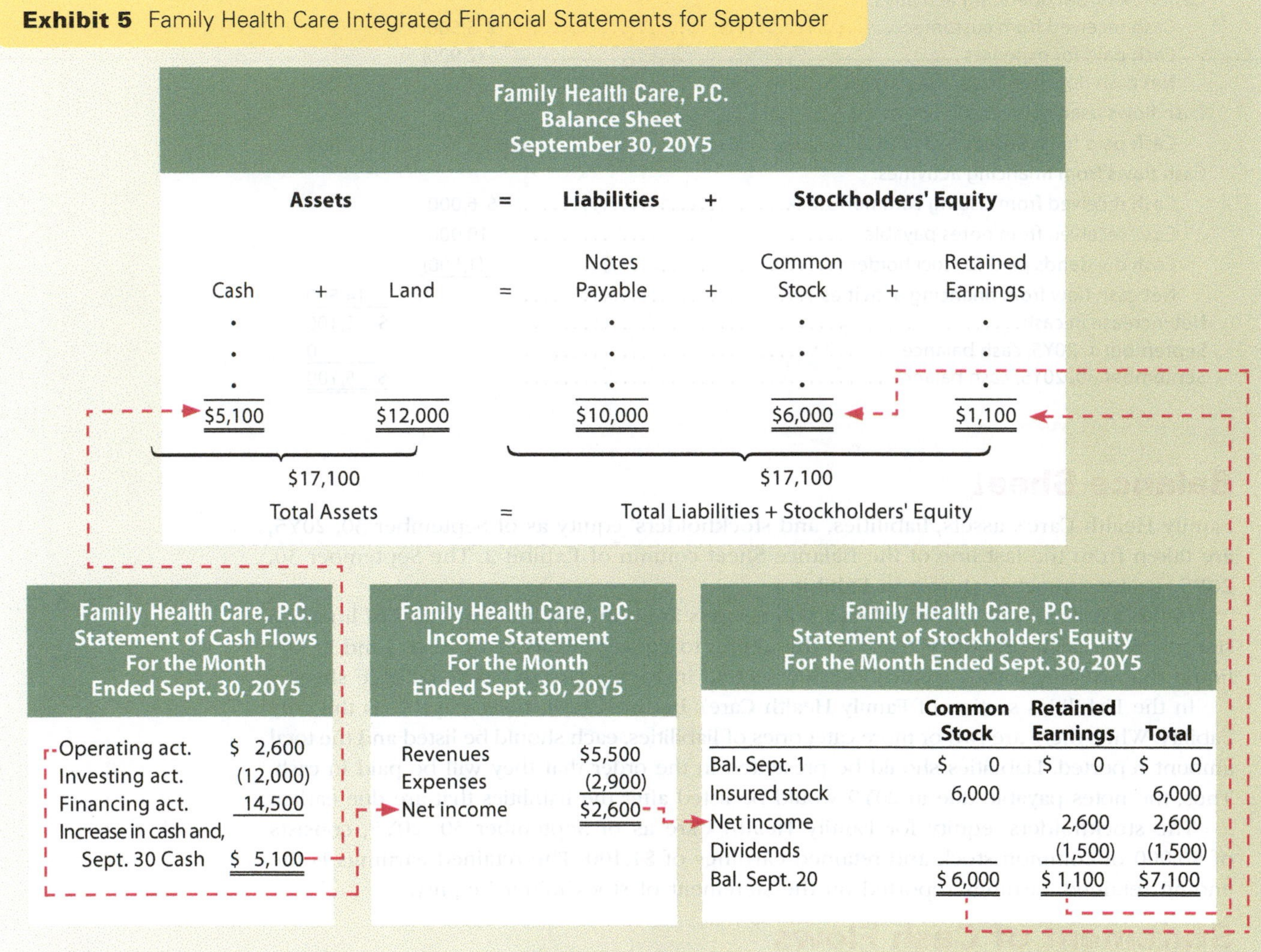

Family Health Care, P.C.
Balance Sheet
September 30, 20Y5

Assets			=	Liabilities	+	Stockholders' Equity		
Cash	+	Land	=	Notes Payable	+	Common Stock	+	Retained Earnings
$5,100		$12,000		$10,000		$6,000		$1,100
$17,100 Total Assets			=	$17,100 Total Liabilities + Stockholders' Equity				

Family Health Care, P.C.
Statement of Cash Flows
For the Month Ended Sept. 30, 20Y5

Operating act.	$ 2,600
Investing act.	(12,000)
Financing act.	14,500
Increase in cash and, Sept. 30 Cash	$ 5,100

Family Health Care, P.C.
Income Statement
For the Month Ended Sept. 30, 20Y5

Revenues	$5,500
Expenses	(2,900)
Net income	$2,600

Family Health Care, P.C.
Statement of Stockholders' Equity
For the Month Ended Sept. 30, 20Y5

	Common Stock	Retained Earnings	Total
Bal. Sept. 1	$ 0	$ 0	$ 0
Insured stock	6,000		6,000
Net income		2,600	2,600
Dividends		(1,500)	(1,500)
Bal. Sept. 20	$ 6,000	$ 1,100	$7,100

Recording a Corporation's Second Period of Operations

Objective 4

Analyze, record, and summarize transactions for a corporation's second period of operations.

During October, Family Health Care entered into the following transactions:

a. Received cash fees of $6,400
b. Paid expenses as follows: wages, $1,370; rent, $950; utilities, $540; interest, $100; and miscellaneous, $220
c. Paid cash dividends of $1,000

Family Heath Care's October transactions are summarized in Exhibit 6 using the integrated financial statement format. Each transaction is identified by letter.

The Balance Sheet column of Exhibit 6 begins with the ending balances as of September 30, 20Y5, taken from Exhibit 2. This is because the balance sheet is the cumulative total of the entity's assets, liabilities, and stockholders' equity since the company's inception.

As of October 1, 20Y5, Family Health Care has cash of $5,100, land of $12,000, notes payable of $10,000, common stock of $6,000, and retained earnings of $1,100. In contrast, the statement of cash flows and the income statement report only transactions for a period and are not cumulative.

Exhibit 6 Family Health Care Summary of Transactions for October

Financial Statement Effects for October

BALANCE SHEET

	Assets			=	Liabilities	+	Stockholders' Equity		
	Cash	+	Land	=	Notes Payable	+	Common Stock	+	Retained Earnings
Balances, Oct. 1	5,100		12,000		10,000		6,000		1,100
a. Fees earned	6,400								6,400
b. Paid expenses	(3,180)								(3,180)
c. Paid dividends	(1,000)								(1,000)
Balances, Oct. 31	7,320		12,000		10,000		6,000		3,320

STATEMENT OF CASH FLOWS

a. Operating	6,400
b. Operating	(3,180)
c. Financing	(1,000)
Increase in cash	2,220

INCOME STATEMENT

a. Fees earned	6,400
b. Wages expense	(1,370)
Rent expense	(950)
Utilities expense	(540)
Interest expense	(100)
Misc. expense	(220)
Net income	3,220

Transaction Metric Effects

The effects of October's transactions on Family Health Care's liquidity and profitability metrics are as follows:

October Effects

LIQUIDITY

Transaction	Cash
a. Fees earned	$6,400
b. Paid expenses	(3,180)
c. Paid dividends	(1,000)
Total	$2,220

PROFITABILITY

Net Income – Cash Basis	
a. Fees earned	$6,400
b. Paid expenses	(3,180)
c. Paid dividends	—
Total	$3,220

October's transactions had the effect of increasing Family Health Care's liquidity metric (Cash) by $2,220. Since the beginning cash balance on October 1 was $5,100, the increase of $2,220 yields an ending cash balance of $7,320, which will be reported on the balance sheet. October's transactions increased Family Health Care's profitability metric, Net Income – Cash Basis, by $3,220, which is also the amount that will be reported as net income on the income statement.

Financial Statements for a Corporation's Second Period of Operations

Objective 5
Prepare financial statements for a corporation's second period of operations.

Family Health Care's financial statements for October are shown in Exhibit 7. These statements were prepared from Exhibit 6.

Income Statement

The income statement for October reports net income of $3,220. This is an increase of $620, or 23.8% ($620÷$2,600), from September's net income of $2,600. The increase in net income was due to fees increasing from $5,500 to $6,400, a $900, or 16.4% ($900÷$5,500), increase from September. At the same time, total operating expenses increased only $280 ($3,180 – $2,900), or 9.7% ($280÷$2,900). This suggests that Family Health Care's operations are profitable and expanding.

Statement of Stockholders' Equity

The statement of stockholders' equity shown in Exhibit 7 starts with the balances of common stock and retained earnings as of October 1, 20Y5. These are the same balances as of September 30, 20Y5 shown in Exhibit 4. Since no common stock was issued during October, the common stock balance on October 31, 20Y5 is $6,000. October's net income of $3,220 is added and dividends of $1,000 are deducted from the beginning retained earnings of $1,100 to yield retained earnings of $3,320 as of October 31, 20Y5.

Exhibit 7 Family Health Care Financial Statements for October

Family Health Care, P.C.
Income Statement
For the Month Ended October 31, 20Y5

Fees earned		$6,400
Operating expenses:		
Wages expense	$1,370	
Rent expense	950	
Utilities expense	540	
Interest expense	100	
Miscellaneous expense	220	
Total operating expenses		(3,180)
Net income		$3,220

Family Health Care, P.C.
Statement of Stockholders' Equity
For the Month Ended October 31, 20Y5

	Common Stock	Retained Earnings	Total
Balances, Oct. 1, 20Y5	$6,000	$1,100	$7,100
Net income		3,220	3,220
Dividends		(1,000)	(1,000)
Balances, Oct. 31, 20Y5	$6,000	$3,320	$9,320

(Continued)

Exhibit 7 Family Health Care Financial Statements for October (Concluded)

Family Health Care, P.C.
Balance Sheet
October 31, 20Y5

Assets		
Cash		$ 7,320
Land		12,000
Total assets		$19,320
Liabilities		
Notes payable		$10,000
Stockholders' Equity		
Common stock	$6,000	
Retained earnings	3,320	
Total stockholders' equity		9,320
Total liabilities and stockholders' equity		$19,320

Family Health Care, P.C.
Statement of Cash Flows
For the Month Ended October 31, 20Y5

Cash flows from operating activities:		
Cash received from customers	$6,400	
Cash paid for expenses	(3,180)	
Net cash flow from operating activities		$ 3,220
Cash flows from investing activities		0
Cash flows used for financing activities:		
Cash dividends paid to stockholder		(1,000)
Net increase in cash		$ 2,220
October 1, 20Y5, cash balance		5,100
October 31, 20Y5, cash balance		$ 7,320

Balance Sheet

The total assets increased from $17,100 on September 30, 20Y5 (Exhibit 4), to $19,320 on October 31 (Exhibit 7). This increase of $2,220 ($19,320 − $17,100) was due to an increase in cash from $5,100 to $7,320. Total liabilities of $10,000 remained the same.

Since total assets increased by $2,220 and total liabilities remained the same, total stockholders' equity must also have increased by $2,220. This is because the accounting equation must always balance. Exhibit 7 shows that total stockholders' equity did increase by $2,220, which is the increase in retained earnings.

Statement of Cash Flows

Family Health Care's statement of cash flows for October indicates that cash increased by $2,220. This increase is cash generated from operating activities of $3,220 less cash used by financing activities to pay dividends of $1,000.

The net increase in cash of $2,220 is added to the beginning cash balance of $5,100 to yield the ending cash balance of $7,320. This ending cash balance of $7,320 also appears on the October 31, 20Y5, balance sheet.

Integration of Financial Statements

Exhibit 8 illustrates that Family Health Care's financial statements for October are integrated as follows:

1. The ending cash balance of $7,320 on the balance sheet equals the ending cash balance reported on the statement of cash flows.
2. The net income of $3,220 is reported on the income statement and the statement of stockholders' equity.
3. The ending common stock of $6,000 and retained earnings of $3,320 are reported in the statement of stockholders' equity and the balance sheet.
4. The cash flows from operating activities of $3,220 reported on the statement of cash flows equals the net income on the income statement. The relationship between cash flows from operating activities and net income is further described and illustrated in Chapter 3.

Exhibit 8 Family Health Care Integrated Financial Statements for October

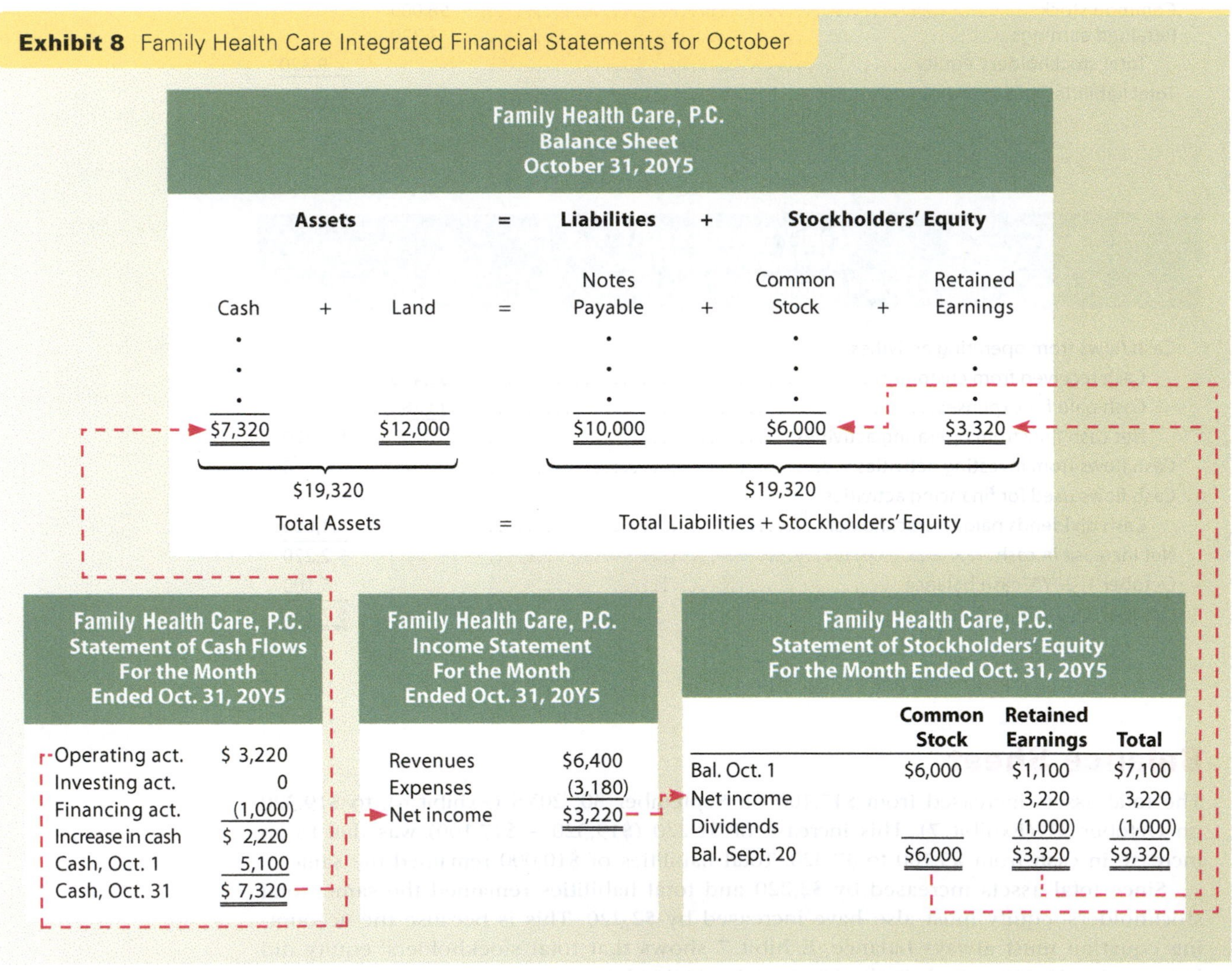

Family Health Care, P.C.
Balance Sheet
October 31, 20Y5

Assets			=	**Liabilities**	+	**Stockholders' Equity**		
Cash	+	Land	=	Notes Payable	+	Common Stock	+	Retained Earnings
$7,320		$12,000		$10,000		$6,000		$3,320

$19,320 Total Assets = $19,320 Total Liabilities + Stockholders' Equity

Family Health Care, P.C.
Statement of Cash Flows
For the Month Ended Oct. 31, 20Y5

Operating act.	$ 3,220
Investing act.	0
Financing act.	(1,000)
Increase in cash	$ 2,220
Cash, Oct. 1	5,100
Cash, Oct. 31	$ 7,320

Family Health Care, P.C.
Income Statement
For the Month Ended Oct. 31, 20Y5

Revenues	$6,400
Expenses	(3,180)
Net income	$3,220

Family Health Care, P.C.
Statement of Stockholders' Equity
For the Month Ended Oct. 31, 20Y5

	Common Stock	Retained Earnings	Total
Bal. Oct. 1	$6,000	$1,100	$7,100
Net income		3,220	3,220
Dividends		(1,000)	(1,000)
Bal. Sept. 20	$6,000	$3,320	$9,320

Metric-Based Analysis: Common-Sized Statements

Objective 6

Describe and illustrate the use of common-sized income statements in assessing a company's performance.

Common-sized financial statements are useful in assessing a company's financial condition and performance over time. Common-sized financial statements are also useful in comparing companies with one another.

Common-sized financial statements are prepared by expressing financial statement amounts as a percent of a base amount. A **common-sized income statement** is prepared by expressing income statement amounts as a percent of sales. A **common-sized balance sheet** is prepared by expressing each asset as a percent of total assets. Each liability and stockholders' equity item is expressed as a percent of total liabilities plus stockholders' equity.[4]

To illustrate common-sized income statements, we use data (in millions) adapted from recent financial statements of The Kroger Co. (KR). Kroger operates over 2,600 supermarkets, over 1,300 fueling centers, and over 700 convenience stores. The following operating data were adapted from recent income statements of Kroger.

	Year 1	Year 2
Sales	$ 98,375	$108,465
Cost of sales	(78,138)	(85,512)
Gross profit	$ 20,237	$ 22,953
Operating expenses:		
Selling and administrative	$(15,196)	$ (17,161)
Other expenses	(2,316)	(2,655)
Total operating expenses	$(17,512)	$ (19,816)
Operating income	$ 2,725	$ 3,137

Kroger's common-sized income statements (rounded to one decimal place) for Year 1 and Year 2 are shown below. Each item is expressed as a percent of sales. For example, the cost of sales for Year 2 of 78.8% is computed as $85,512 ÷ $108,465.

	Year 1	Year 2	Increase (Decrease)
Sales	100.0%	100.0%	n/a
Cost of sales	(79.4)	(78.8)	(0.6)%
Gross profit	20.6%	21.2%	0.6%
Operating expenses:			
Selling and administrative	(15.4)%	(15.8)%	0.4%
Other expenses	(2.4)	(2.5)	0.1
Total operating expenses	(17.8)%	(18.3)%	0.5%
Operating income	2.8%	2.9%	(0.1)%

The common-sized income statements for Kroger indicate that the cost of sales decreased by 0.6% between Year 1 and Year 2. This decrease in cost of goods sold in Year 2 was partially offset by an increase in operating expenses of 0.5%. As a result, Kroger's operating income increased by only 0.1% between Year 1 and Year 2. These results imply that Kroger's operations did not change significantly between years.

When comparing operating performance across companies within the same industry, common-sized income statements are often prepared only through operating income rather than through net income. This is because other income and expenses are influenced by a variety of factors that are independent of operations and that can vary significantly across companies. For example, differences in the financing and tax strategies used by companies affect the comparability.

4. Since total assets equals total liabilities plus total stockholders' equity, common-sized balance sheets can be prepared simply by expressing each balance sheet item as a percent of total assets.

Key Points

1. Describe the basic elements of a financial accounting system.

The basic elements of a financial accounting system include (1) a set of rules for determining what, when, and the amount that should be recorded; (2) a framework for preparing financial statements; and (3) one or more controls to determine whether errors may have arisen in the recording process.

2. Analyze, record, and summarize transactions for a corporation's first period of operations.

Using the integrated financial statement framework, September transactions for Family Health Care are recorded and summarized in Exhibit 2.

3. Prepare financial statements for a corporation's first period of operations.

The financial statements for Family Health Care for September, its first period of operations, are shown in Exhibit 4.

4. Analyze, record, and summarize transactions for a corporation's second period of operations.

Using the accounting equation as a basic framework, October transactions for Family Health Care are recorded and summarized in Exhibit 6.

5. Prepare financial statements for a corporation's second period of operations.

The financial statements for Family Health Care for October, its second period of operations, are shown in Exhibit 7.

6. Describe and illustrate the use of common-sized income statements in assessing a company's performance.

A common-sized income statement is prepared by expressing each income statement amount as a percent of sales.

Key Terms

Common stock (49)
Common-sized balance sheet (65)
Common-sized financial statements (65)
Common-sized income statement (65)
Financial accounting system (46)
Liquidity (59)
Transaction (46)

Illustrative Problem

Beth Sumner established an insurance agency on April 1, 20Y4, and completed the following transactions during April:

a. Opened a business bank account in the name of Sumner Insurance Inc., with a deposit of $15,000 in exchange for common stock.
b. Borrowed $8,000 by issuing a note payable.
c. Received cash from fees earned, $11,500.
d. Paid rent on office and equipment for the month, $3,500.
e. Paid automobile expenses for the month, $650, and miscellaneous expenses, $300.
f. Paid office salaries, $1,400.
g. Paid interest on the note payable, $60.
h. Purchased land as a future building site, $20,000.
i. Paid dividends, $1,000.

Instructions

1. Indicate the effect of each transaction and the balances after each transaction, using the integrated financial statement framework.
2. Indicate the effects of each transaction on liquidity metric Cash and profitability metric Net Income – Cash Basis.
3. Prepare an income statement and statement of stockholders' equity for April.
4. Prepare a balance sheet as of April 30, 20Y4.
5. Prepare a statement of cash flows for April.

Solution

1.

Financial Statement Effects

BALANCE SHEET

	Assets		= Liabilities +	Stockholders' Equity	
	Cash +	Land =	Notes Payable +	Common Stock +	Retained Earnings
a. Investment	15,000			15,000	
b. Issued note payable	8,000		8,000		
Balances	23,000		8,000	15,000	
c. Fees earned	11,500				11,500
Balances	34,500		8,000	15,000	11,500
d. Rent expense	(3,500)				(3,500)
Balances	31,000		8,000	15,000	8,000
e. Paid expenses	(950)				(950)
Balances	30,050		8,000	15,000	7,050
f. Paid salary expense	(1,400)				(1,400)
Balances	28,650		8,000	15,000	5,650
g. Paid interest expense	(60)				(60)
Balances	28,590		8,000	15,000	5,590
h. Purchased land	(20,000)	20,000			
Balances	8,590	20,000	8,000	15,000	5,590
i. Paid dividends	(1,000)				(1,000)
Balances, April 30	7,590	20,000	8,000	15,000	4,590

STATEMENT OF CASH FLOWS

a. Financing	15,000
b. Financing	8,000
c. Operating	11,500
d. Operating	(3,500)
e. Operating	(950)
f. Operating	(1,400)
g. Operating	(60)
h. Investing	(20,000)
i. Financing	(1,000)
Increase in cash and April 30 cash	7,590

INCOME STATEMENT

c. Fees earned	11,500
d. Rent expense	(3,500)
e. Auto expense	(650)
e. Misc. expense	(300)
f. Salary expense	(1,400)
g. Interest expense	(60)
Net income	5,590

2.

Transaction Metric Effects

LIQUIDITY	
Transaction	**Cash**
a. Issued stock	$15,000
b. Issued note pay.	8,000
c. Earned fees	11,500
d. Paid rent exp.	(3,500)
e. Paid expenses	(950)
f. Paid salaries	(1,400)
g. Paid interest	(60)
h. Purchased land	(20,000)
i. Paid dividends	(1,000)
Total	$ 7,590

PROFITABILITY	
Net Income – Cash Basis	
a. Issued stock	—
b. Issued note pay.	—
c. Earned fees	$11,500
d. Paid rent exp.	(3,500)
e. Paid expenses	(950)
f. Paid salaries	(1,400)
g. Paid interest	(60)
h. Purchased land	—
i. Paid dividends	—
Total	$ 5,590

3.

SUMNER INSURANCE, INC.
Income Statement
For the Month Ended April 30, 20Y4

Revenues:		
Fees earned		$11,500
Expenses:		
Rent expense	$3,500	
Salaries expense	1,400	
Automotive expense	650	
Interest expense	60	
Miscellaneous expense	300	
Total expenses		(5,910)
Net income		$ 5,590

SUMNER INSURANCE, INC.
Statement of Stockholders' Equity
For the Month Ended April 30, 20Y4

	Common Stock	Retained Earnings	Total
Balances, Apr. 1, 20Y4	$ 0	$ 0	$ 0
Issued common stock	15,000		15,000
Net income		5,590	5,590
Dividends		(1,000)	(1,000)
Balances, Apr. 30, 20Y4	$15,000	$ 4,590	$19,590

4.

SUMNER INSURANCE, INC.
Balance Sheet
April 30, 20Y4

Assets		
Cash		$ 7,590
Land		20,000
Total assets		$27,590
Liabilities		
Note payable		$ 8,000
Stockholders' Equity		
Common stock	$15,000	
Retained earnings	4,590	
Total stockholders' equity		19,590
Total liabilities and stockholders' equity		$27,590

5.

SUMNER INSURANCE, INC.
Statement of Cash Flows
For the Month Ended April 30, 20Y4

Cash flows from operating activities:		
Cash receipts from operating activities	$11,500	
Cash payments for operating activities	(5,910)	
Net cash flows from operating activities		$ 5,590
Cash flows used for investing activities:		
Cash payments for land		(20,000)
Cash flows from financing activities:		
Cash receipts from issuing common stock	$15,000	
Cash receipts from issuing note payable	8,000	
Cash payments for dividends	(1,000)	
Net cash flows from financing activities		22,000
Net increase in cash during April		$ 7,590
Cash as of April 1, 20Y4		0
Cash as of April 30, 20Y4		$ 7,590

Self-Examination Questions

(Answers appear at the end of chapter)

1. The purchase of land for $50,000 cash was incorrectly recorded as an increase in land and an increase in notes payable. Which of the following statements is correct?
   A. The accounting equation will not balance because cash is overstated by $50,000.
   B. The accounting equation will not balance because notes payable are overstated by $50,000.
   C. The accounting equation will not balance because assets will exceed liabilities by $50,000.
   D. Even though a recording error has been made, the accounting equation will balance.

2. The receipt of $8,000 cash for fees earned was recorded by Langley Consulting as an increase in cash of $8,000 and a decrease in retained earnings (revenues) of $8,000. What is the effect of this error on the accounting equation?
   A. Total assets will exceed total liabilities and stockholders' equity by $8,000.
   B. Total assets will be less than total liabilities and stockholders' equity by $8,000.
   C. Total assets will exceed total liabilities and stockholders' equity by $16,000.
   D. The error will not affect the accounting equation.

3. If total assets increased $20,000 during a period and total liabilities increased $12,000 during the same period, the amount and direction (increase or decrease) of the change in stockholders' equity for that period is:
   A. a $32,000 increase.
   B. a $32,000 decrease.
   C. an $8,000 increase.
   D. an $8,000 decrease.

4. If revenue was $90,000, expenses were $75,000, and dividends were $20,000, the amount of net income or net loss would be:
   A. $90,000 net income.
   B. $15,000 net income.
   C. $75,000 net loss.
   D. $5,000 net loss.

5. Which of the following transactions changes only the mix of assets and does not affect liabilities or stockholders' equity?
   A. Borrowed $40,000 from First National Bank
   B. Purchased land for $50,000 cash
   C. Received $3,800 for fees earned
   D. Paid $4,000 for office salaries

Class Discussion Questions

1. What are the basic elements of a financial accounting system? Do these elements apply to all businesses, from a local restaurant to Alphabet (Google) Inc.? Explain.

2. Provide an example of a transaction that affects (a) only one element of the accounting equation, (b) two elements of the accounting equation, (c) three elements of the accounting equation.

3. Indicate whether the following error would cause the accounting equation to be out of balance and, if so, indicate how it would be out of balance. The payment of utilities of $1,200 was recorded as a decrease in cash of $1,200 and a decrease in retained earnings (utilities expense) of $2,100.

4. For each of the following errors, indicate whether the error would cause the accounting equation to be out of balance and, if so, indicate how it would be out of balance. (a) The purchase of land for $85,000 cash was recorded as an increase in land of $85,000 and a decrease in cash of $58,000. (b) The receipt of $7,000 for fees earned was recorded as an increase in cash of $7,000 and an increase in liabilities of $7,000.

5. What is a primary control for determining the accuracy of a business's record keeping?

6. Capstone Consulting Services acquired land 5 years ago for $200,000. Capstone recently signed an agreement to sell the land for $375,000. In accordance with the sales agreement, the buyer transferred $375,000 to Capstone's bank account on February 20. How would elements of the accounting equation be affected by the sale?

7. (a) How does the payment of dividends of $15,000 affect the three elements of the accounting equation? (b) Is net income affected by the payment of dividends? Explain.

8. Assume that Esquire Consulting erroneously recorded the payment of $30,000 of dividends as salary expense. (a) How would this error affect the equality of the accounting equation? (b) How would this error affect the income statement, statement of stockholders' equity, balance sheet, and statement of cash flows?

9. Assume that Larsh Realty Inc. borrowed $75,000 from Country Bank and Trust. In recording the transaction, Larsh erroneously recorded the receipt as an increase in cash, $75,000, and an increase in fees earned, $75,000. (a) How would this error affect the equality of the accounting equation? (b) How would this error affect the income statement, statement of stockholders' equity, balance sheet, and statement of cash flows?

10. Assume that as of January 1, 20Y8, Sylvester Consulting has total assets of $500,000 and total liabilities of $150,000. As of December 31, 20Y8, Sylvester has total liabilities of $200,000 and total stockholders' equity of $400,000. (a) What was Sylvester's stockholders' equity as of January 1, 20Y8? (b) Assume that Sylvester did not pay any dividends during 20Y8. What was the amount of net income for 20Y8?

11. Using the January 1 and December 31, 20Y8, data given in Question 10, answer the following question: If Sylvester Consulting paid $18,000 of dividends during 20Y8, what was the amount of net income for 20Y8?

Exercises

Obj. 1

✔ a. $1,900,000

E2-1 Accounting equation

Determine the missing amount for each of the following:

	Assets	=	Liabilities	+	Stockholders' Equity
a.	X	=	$715,000	+	$1,185,000
b.	$600,000	=	X	+	$ 510,000
c.	$112,400	=	$23,750	+	X

E2-2 Accounting equation

Obj. 1

✔ **a. $44,958**

The Walt Disney Company (DIS) had the following assets and liabilities (in millions) at the end of Year 1.

Assets	$84,141
Liabilities	39,183

a. Determine the stockholders' equity of Walt Disney at the end of Year 1.

b. If assets increased by $4,041 million and stockholders' equity decreased by $433 million, what was the increase or decrease in liabilities for the Year 2?

c. What were the total assets, liabilities, and stockholders' equity at the end of Year 2?

d. Based upon your answer to (c), does the accounting equation balance?

E2-3 Accounting equation

Obj. 1

✔ **a. $1,615**

Campbell Soup Co. (CPB) had the following assets and liabilities (in millions) at the end of Year 1.

Assets	$8,113
Liabilities	6,498

a. Determine the stockholders' equity of Campbell Soup at the end of Year 1.

b. If assets decreased by $24 million and liabilities increased by $211 million, what was the increase or decrease in stockholders' equity for the Year 2?

c. What were the total assets, liabilities, and stockholders' equity at the end of Year 2?

d. Based upon your answer to (c), does the accounting equation balance?

E2-4 Accounting equation

Obj. 1

✔ **(a) $120,292**

The following are recent year summaries of balance sheet and income statement data (in millions) for Apple Inc. (AAPL) and Verizon Communications (VZ).

	Apple	Verizon
Year 1:		
Assets	$231,839	(e)
Liabilities	(a)	(f)
Stockholders' equity	(b)	$ 38,836
Increase (Decrease) in assets, liabilities, and stockholders' equity during Year 2:		
Assets	$ 58,640	(g)
Liabilities	50,832	$(14,852)
Stockholders' equity	7,808	(h)
Year 2:		
Assets	(c)	$232,708
Liabilities	$171,124	(i)
Stockholders' equity	(d)	12,298

Determine the amounts of the missing items (a) through (i).

E2-5 Accounting equation

Obj. 1

✔ **b. $895,000**

Alex Hayden is the sole stockholder and operator of Elevate and Succeed, a motivational consulting business. At the end of its accounting period, December 31, 20Y7, Elevate and Succeed has assets of $1,200,000 and liabilities of $375,000. Using the accounting equation and considering each case independently, determine the following amounts:

a. Stockholders' equity, as of December 31, 20Y7.
b. Stockholders' equity, as of December 31, 20Y8, assuming that assets increased by $150,000 and liabilities increased by $80,000 during 20Y8.
c. Stockholders' equity, as of December 31, 20Y8, assuming that assets decreased by $200,000 and liabilities increased by $100,000 during 20Y8.
d. Stockholders' equity, as of December 31, 20Y8, assuming that assets increased by $400,000 and liabilities decreased by $75,000 during 20Y8.
e. Net income (or net loss) during 20Y8, assuming that as of December 31, 20Y8, assets were $1,275,000, liabilities were $290,000, and there were no dividends and no additional common stock was issued.

Obj. 2, 4

E2-6 Effects of transactions on stockholders' equity

For Target Corporation (TGT), indicate whether the following transactions would (1) increase, (2) decrease, or (3) have no effect on stockholders' equity.

a. Borrowed money from the bank.
b. Paid creditors.
c. Made cash sales to customers.
d. Purchased store equipment.
e. Paid dividends.
f. Paid store rent.
g. Paid interest expense.
h. Sold store equipment at a gain.
i. Received interest revenue.
j. Paid taxes.

Obj. 1, 2, 4

E2-7 Effects of transactions on accounting equation

Describe how the following business transactions affect the three elements of the accounting equation.

a. Received cash for services performed.
b. Paid for utilities used in the business.
c. Borrowed cash at local bank.
d. Issued common stock for cash.
e. Purchased land for cash.

Obj. 1, 2, 4

✔ (1) Assets decreased by $140,000

E2-8 Effects of transactions on accounting equation

A vacant lot acquired for $500,000, on which there is a balance owed of $300,000, is sold for $660,000 in cash. The seller pays the $300,000 owed. What is the effect of these transactions on the total amount of the seller's (1) assets, (2) liabilities, and (3) stockholders' equity?

Obj. 2, 4

E2-9 Effects of transactions on stockholders' equity

Indicate whether each of the following types of transactions will (a) increase stockholders' equity or (b) decrease stockholders' equity.

a. Issued common stock for cash.
b. Received cash for fees earned.
c. Paid cash for utilities expense.
d. Paid cash for rent expense.
e. Paid cash dividends.

E2-10 Effects of transactions on accounting equation

Obj. 1, 2, 4

On Time Delivery Service had the following selected transactions during November:

1. Received cash from issuance of common stock, $75,000.
2. Paid rent for November, $5,000.
3. Paid advertising expense, $3,000.
4. Received cash for providing delivery services, $34,500.
5. Borrowed $10,000 from Second National Bank to finance its operations.
6. Purchased a delivery van for cash, $25,000.
7. Paid interest on note from Second National Bank, $75.
8. Paid salaries and wages for November, $10,000.
9. Paid dividends, $2,000.

Indicate the effect of each transaction on the accounting equation by listing the numbers identifying the transactions, (1) through (9), in a vertical column, and inserting at the right of each number the appropriate letter from the following list:

a. Increase in an asset, decrease in another asset.
b. Increase in an asset, increase in a liability.
c. Increase in an asset, increase in stockholders' equity.
d. Decrease in an asset, decrease in a liability.
e. Decrease in an asset, decrease in stockholders' equity.

E2-11 Nature of transactions

Obj. 1, 2, 4

✔ b. $11,000 decrease

Cheryl Alder operates her own catering service. Summary financial data for March are presented in the following equation form. Each line, designated by a number, indicates the effect of a transaction on the balance sheet. Each increase and decrease in retained earnings, except transaction (4), affects net income.

	Cash	+	Land	=	Liabilities	+	Common Stock	+	Retained Earnings
Bal.	40,000		100,000		16,000		24,000		100,000
1.	28,000								28,000
2.	(20,000)		20,000						
3.	(18,000)								(18,000)
4.	(1,000)								(1,000)
Bal.	29,000		120,000		16,000		24,000		109,000

a. Describe each transaction.
b. What is the net decrease in cash during the month?
c. What is the net increase in retained earnings during the month?
d. What is the net income for the month?
e. How much of the net income for the month was retained in the business?
f. What are the net cash flows from operating activities?
g. What are the net cash flows from investing activities?
h. What are the net cash flows from financing activities?

E2-12 Net income and dividends

Obj. 3, 5

The income statement of a corporation for the month of February indicates a net income of $32,000. During the same period, $40,000 in cash dividends were paid.

Would it be correct to say that the business incurred a net loss of $8,000 during the month? Discuss.

Obj. 1, 3, 5

✔ Company Yankee: Net income, $86,000

E2-13 Net income and stockholders' equity for four businesses

Four different companies, Sierra, Tango, Yankee, and Zulu, show the same balance sheet data at the beginning and end of a year. These data, exclusive of the amount of stockholders' equity, are summarized as follows:

	Total Assets	Total Liabilities
Beginning of the year	$490,000	$175,000
End of the year	770,000	294,000

On the basis of the preceding data and the following additional information for the year, determine the net income (or loss) of each company for the year. (*Suggestion:* First determine the amount of increase or decrease in stockholders' equity during the year.)

Sierra:	No additional common stock was issued, and no dividends were paid.
Tango:	No additional common stock was issued, but dividends of $55,000 were paid.
Yankee:	Common stock of $75,000 was issued, but no dividends were paid.
Zulu:	Common stock of $75,000 was issued, and dividends of $55,000 were paid.

Obj. 1, 3, 5

✔ (a) 76,500

E2-14 Missing amounts from balance sheet and income statement data

One item is omitted from each of the following summaries of balance sheet and income statement data for four different corporations.

	Carbon	Krypton	Fluorine	Radium
Beginning of the year:				
Assets	$333,000	$250,000	$100,000	(d)
Liabilities	118,000	130,000	76,000	$120,000
End of the year:				
Assets	495,000	350,000	90,000	248,000
Liabilities	160,000	110,000	80,000	136,000
During the year:				
Additional issuance of common stock	(a)	50,000	10,000	40,000
Dividends	7,500	16,000	(c)	60,000
Revenue	90,000	(b)	115,000	112,000
Expenses	39,000	64,000	122,500	128,000

Determine the amounts of the missing items, identifying them by letter. (*Suggestion:* First determine the amount of increase or decrease in stockholders' equity during the year.)

Obj. 3, 5

✔ a. $538

E2-15 Net income, retained earnings, and dividends

Use the following data (in millions) for Oracle Corporation (ORCL), for a recent year to answer the questions below:

Retained earnings, beginning of year	$25,503
Retained earnings, end of year	26,503
Net cash flows from operating activities	14,336
Net increase in cash	3,947
Net cash flows from financing activities	8,658

a. Determine the amount of earnings retained in Oracle for the year, assuming no dividends were paid during the year.

b. Determine the net cash flows used for investing activities for the year.

E2-16 Balance sheet, net income, and cash flows

Obj. 3, 5

✔ b. $147,000

Financial information related to Abby's Interiors for October and November of 20Y6 is as follows:

	October 31, 20Y6	November 30, 20Y6
Notes payable	$200,000	$250,000
Land	500,000	575,000
Common stock	75,000	90,000
Retained earnings	?	?
Cash	50,000	175,000

a. Prepare balance sheets for Abby's Interiors as of October 31 and November 30, 20Y6.

b. Determine the amount of net income for November, assuming that dividends of $12,000 were paid.

c. Determine the net cash flows from operating activities for November.

d. Determine the net cash flows from investing activities for November.

e. Determine the net cash flows from financing activities for November.

f. Determine the net increase or decrease in cash for November.

E2-17 Income statement

Obj. 1, 3

✔ Net income, $20,000

After its first month of operations, the following amounts were taken from the accounting records of Big Mountain Realty Inc. as of June 30, 20Y9.

Cash	$ 43,000	Notes payable	$ 50,000
Common stock	75,000	Rent expense	8,000
Dividends	2,000	Retained earnings	0
Interest expense	300	Salaries expense	50,000
Land	100,000	Sales commissions	90,000
Miscellaneous expense	1,700	Utilities expense	10,000

Prepare an income statement for the month ending June 30, 20Y9.

E2-18 Statement of stockholders' equity

Obj. 3, 5

Using the financial data shown in Exercise 2-17 for Big Mountain Realty Inc., prepare a statement of stockholders' equity for the month ending June 30, 20Y9.

E2-19 Balance sheet

Obj. 3, 5

Using the financial data shown in Exercise 2-17 for Big Mountain Realty Inc., prepare a balance sheet as of June 30, 20Y9.

E2-20 Statement of cash flows

Obj. 3, 5

✔ Net cash flows from financing activities, $123,000

Using the financial data shown in Exercise 2-17 for Big Mountain Realty Inc., prepare a statement of cash flows for the month ending June 30, 20Y9.

Note: The spreadsheet icon indicates an Excel template is available on the student companion site at www.cengagebrain.com.

Obj. 1, 2, 4

E2-21 Effects of transactions on accounting equation

Describe how the following transactions of McDonald's Corp. (MCD), would affect the three elements of the accounting equation.

a. Paid research and development expenses for the current year.
b. Purchased machinery and equipment for cash.
c. Received cash from issuing stock.
d. Received cash from the issuance of long-term debt.
e. Made cash sales.
f. Paid selling expenses.
g. Paid employee pension expenses for the current year.
h. Received cash from selling manufacturing equipment for a gain on the sale.
i. Paid officer salaries.
j. Paid taxes.
k. Paid off long-term debt.
l. Paid dividends.

Obj. 3, 5

E2-22 Statement of cash flows

Based upon the financial transactions for McDonald's Corp. (MCD), shown in Exercise 2-21, indicate whether the transaction would be reported in the cash flows from operating, investing, or financing sections of the statement of cash flows.

Problems

Obj. 1, 2, 3

✔ 3. Net income, $14,500

P2-1 Transactions and financial statements

Les Stanley established an insurance agency on July 1, 20Y5, and completed the following transactions during July:

a. Opened a business bank account in the name of Stanley Insurance Inc., with a deposit of $60,000 in exchange for common stock.
b. Borrowed $100,000 by issuing a note payable.
c. Received cash from fees earned, $30,000.
d. Paid rent on office and equipment for the month, $5,000.
e. Paid automobile expense for the month, $2,500, and miscellaneous expense, $1,000.
f. Paid office salaries, $6,500.
g. Paid interest on the note payable, $500.
h. Purchased land as a future building site, paying cash of $120,000.
i. Paid dividends, $3,000.

Instructions

1. Indicate the effect of each transaction and the balances after each transaction, using the integrated financial statement framework.
2. Briefly explain why the stockholders' investments and revenues increased stockholders' equity, while dividends and expenses decreased stockholders' equity.
3. Prepare an income statement and statement of stockholders' equity for July.
4. Prepare a balance sheet as of July 31, 20Y5.
5. Prepare a statement of cash flows for July.

P2-2 Transactions and financial statements

Obj. 1, 2, 3

James Nesbitt established Up-Date Computer Services on August 1, 20Y4. The effect of each transaction and the balances after each transaction for August are shown below in the integrated financial statement framework.

✔ 4. Net cash flows from financing activities, $32,000

Instructions

1. Prepare an income statement for the month ended August 31, 20Y4.
2. Prepare a statement of stockholders' equity for the month ended August 31, 20Y4.
3. Prepare a balance sheet as of August 31, 20Y4.
4. Prepare a statement of cash flows for the month ended August 31, 20Y4.

Financial Statement Effects

BALANCE SHEET

	Assets		=	Liabilities	+	Stockholders' Equity		
	Cash	+ Land	=	Notes Payable	+	Common Stock	+	Retained Earnings
a. Issued common stock	25,000					25,000		
b. Fees earned	27,000							27,000
Balances	52,000					25,000		27,000
c. Rent expense	(2,500)							(2,500)
Balances	49,500					25,000		24,500
d. Issued notes payable	10,000			10,000				
Balances	59,500			10,000		25,000		24,500
e. Purchased land	(40,000)	40,000						
Balances	19,500	40,000		10,000		25,000		24,500
f. Paid expenses	(1,900)							(1,900)
Balances	17,600	40,000		10,000		25,000		22,600
g. Paid salary expense	(4,600)							(4,600)
Balances	13,000	40,000		10,000		25,000		18,000
i. Paid dividends	(3,000)							(3,000)
Balances, Aug. 31	10,000	40,000		10,000		25,000		15,000

STATEMENT OF CASH FLOWS

a. Financing	25,000
b. Operating	27,000
c. Operating	(2,500)
d. Financing	10,000
e. Investing	(40,000)
f. Operating	(1,900)
g. Operating	(4,600)
h. Financing	(3,000)
Increase in cash	10,000

INCOME STATEMENT

b. Fees earned	27,000
c. Rent expense	(2,500)
f. Auto expense	(1,200)
f. Misc. expense	(700)
g. Salary expense	(4,600)
Net income	18,000

Obj. 3

✔ 1. Net income, $135,000

P2-3 Financial statements

The following amounts were taken from the accounting records of Padget Home Services, Inc., as of December 31, 20Y7. Padget Home Services began its operations on January 1, 20Y7.

Cash	$ 60,000
Common stock	75,000
Dividends	15,000
Fees earned	620,000
Interest expense	4,800
Land	215,000
Miscellaneous expense	10,200
Notes payable	80,000
Rent expense	70,000
Salaries expense	272,000
Taxes expense	43,000
Utilities expense	85,000

Instructions

1. Prepare an income statement for the year ending December 31, 20Y7.
2. Prepare a statement of stockholders' equity for the year ending December 31, 20Y7.
3. Prepare a balance sheet as of December 31, 20Y7.
4. Prepare a statement of cash flows for the year ending December 31, 20Y7.

Obj. 5

✔ 1. Net income, $200,000

P2-4 Financial statements

Padget Home Services began its operations on January 1, 20Y7 (see Problem 2-3). After its second year of operations, the following amounts were taken from the accounting records of Padget Home Services, Inc., as of December 31, 20Y8.

Cash	?
Common stock	$110,000
Dividends	50,000
Fees earned	886,000
Interest expense	7,200
Land	340,000
Miscellaneous expense	13,800
Notes payable	120,000
Rent expense	100,000
Salaries expense	380,000
Taxes expense	65,000
Utilities expense	120,000

Instructions

1. Prepare an income statement for the year ending December 31, 20Y8.
2. Prepare a statement of stockholders' equity for the year ending December 31, 20Y8. (*Note:* The retained earnings at January 1, 20Y8, was $120,000.)
3. Prepare a balance sheet as of December 31, 20Y8.
4. Prepare a statement of cash flows for the year ending December 31, 20Y8. (*Hint:* You should compare the asset and liability amounts of December 31, 20Y8, with those of December 31, 20Y7, to determine cash used in investing and financing activities. See Problem 2-3 for the December 31, 20Y7, balance sheet amounts.)

P2-5 Missing amounts from financial statements

Obj. 3, 5

✔ a. $125,000

The financial statements at the end of Network Realty, Inc.'s first month of operations are shown below. By analyzing the interrelationships among the financial statements, fill in the proper amounts for (a) through (s).

NETWORK REALTY, INC.
Income Statement
For the Month Ended December 31, 20Y4

Fees earned		$ (a)
Operating expenses:		
Wages expense	$33,120	
Rent expense	18,000	
Utilities expense	(b)	
Interest expense	1,800	
Miscellaneous expense	3,960	
Total operating expenses		67,500
Net income		$ (c)

NETWORK REALTY, INC.
Statement of Stockholders' Equity
For the Month Ended December 31, 20Y4

	Common Stock	Retained Earnings	Total
Balances, Dec. 1, 20Y4	$ 0	$ (d)	$ 0
Issued common stock	75,000		75,000
Net income		57,500	57,500
Dividends		(e)	(e)
Balances, Dec. 31, 20Y4	$75,000	$ (f)	$ (g)

NETWORK REALTY, INC.
Balance Sheet
December 31, 20Y4

Assets		
Cash		$ (h)
Land		175,000
Total assets		$225,500
Liabilities		
Notes payable		$105,000
Stockholders' Equity		
Common stock	$(i)	
Retained earnings	(j)	
Total stockholders' equity		(k)
Total liabilities and stockholders' equity		$ (l)

NETWORK REALTY, INC.
Statement of Cash Flows
For the Month Ended December 31, 20Y4

Cash flows from operating activities:		
Cash received from customers	$125,000	
Cash paid for expenses	(67,500)	
Net cash flows from operating activities		$ (m)
Cash flows used in investing activities:		
Cash paid for purchase of land		(175,000)
Cash flows from financing activities:		
Cash received from issuing common stock	$ 75,000	
Cash received from issuing notes payable	(n)	
Cash dividends paid to stockholders	(12,000)	
Net cash flows from financing activities		(o)
Net increase in cash		$ (p)
December 1, 20Y4, cash balance		(q)
December 31, 20Y4, cash balance		$ (r)

Obj. 3, 5

P2-6 Financial statements

Alpine Realty, Inc., organized July 1, 20Y8, is operated by Angela Griffin. How many errors can you find in the following financial statements for Alpine Realty, Inc., prepared after its first month of operations?

ALPINE REALTY, INC.
Income Statement
July 31, 20Y8

Sales commissions		$60,000
Operating expenses:		
Office salaries expense	$20,000	
Rent expense	6,000	
Automobile expense	3,500	
Dividends	2,000	
Miscellaneous expense	1,500	
Total operating expenses		(33,000)
Net income		$27,000

ANGELA GRIFFIN
Statement of Stockholders' Equity
July 31, 20Y7

Net income for the month	$27,000
Retained earnings, July 31, 20Y7	$27,000

Balance Sheet
For the Month Ended July 31, 20Y7

Assets		
Cash		$32,000
Notes payable		20,000
Total assets		$52,000
Liabilities		
Land		$30,000
Stockholders' Equity		
Common stock	$15,000	
Retained earnings	27,000	
Total stockholders' equity		42,000
Total liabilities and stockholders' equity		$72,000

ALPINE REALTY, INC.
Statement of Cash Flows
July 31, 20Y8

Cash flows from operating activities:	
Cash receipts from sales commissions	$ 60,000
Cash flows used for investing activities:	
Cash payments for land	(30,000)
Cash flows from financing activities:	
Cash receipts from retained earnings	27,000
Net increase in cash during July	$ 57,000
Cash as of July 1, 20Y8	0
Cash as of July 31, 20Y8	$ 57,000

Metric-Based Analysis

MBA 2-1 Metric analysis of transactions

Obj. 2, 4

Using transactions listed in P2-1 for Stanley Insurance Inc. indicate the effects of each transaction on the liquidity metric Cash and profitability metric Net Income – Cash Basis.

MBA 2-2 Metric analysis of transactions

Obj. 2, 4

Using transactions listed in P2-2 for Up-Date Computer Services indicate the effects of each transaction on the liquidity metric Cash and profitability metric Net Income – Cash Basis.

MBA 2-3 Common-sized income statements

Obj. 6

Delta Air Lines, Inc. (DAL) provides cargo and passenger services throughout the world. The following operating data (in millions) were adapted from recent financial statements of Delta.

	Year 1	Year 2
Revenue	$ 37,773	$ 40,362
Operating expenses:		
Fuel	$ (9,397)	$(11,668)
Aircraft related	(13,225)	(13,070)
Selling and general	(9,829)	(10,905)
Other expenses	(1,922)	(2,513)
Total operating expenses	$(34,373)	$(38,156)
Operating income	$ 3,400	$ 2,206

1. Prepare common-sized income statements for Years 1 and 2. Round to one decimal place.
2. Using your answer to (1), analyze and comment on the performance of Delta in Year 2.

MBA 2-4 Common-sized income statements

Obj. 6

Southwest Airlines Co. (LUV) provides passenger services throughout the United States, Mexico, Jamaica, The Bahamas, Aruba, and the Dominican Republic. The following operating data (in millions) were adapted from recent financial statements of Southwest.

	Year 1	Year 2
Revenue	$ 17,699	$ 18,605
Operating expenses:		
Fuel	$(5,763)	$(5,293)
Aircraft related	(3,411)	(3,322)
Selling and general	(5,035)	(5,434)
Other expenses	(2,212)	(2,331)
Total operating expenses	$(16,421)	$(16,380)
Operating income	$ 1,278	$ 2,225

1. Prepare common-sized income statements for Years 1 and 2. Round to one decimal place.
2. Using your answer to (1), analyze and comment on the performance of Southwest in Year 2.

MBA 2-5 Common-sized income statements

Obj. 6

Using your answers to MBA 2-3 and MBA 2-4, compare and comment on the operating results of Delta and Southwest.

Obj. 6

MBA 2-6 Common-sized income statements

Kellogg Company (K) produces, markets, and distributes cereal and food products including Cheez-It, Coco Pops, Rice Krispies, and Pringles. The following partial income statements (in millions) were adapted from recent financial statements.

	Year 1	Year 2
Sales	$14,792	$14,580
Cost of goods sold	(8,689)	(9,517)
Gross profit	$ 6,103	$ 5,063
Selling and administrative expenses	(3,266)	(4,039)
Operating income	$ 2,837	$ 1,024

1. Prepare common-sized income statements for Years 1 and 2. Round to one decimal place.
2. Using your answer to (1), analyze the performance of Kellogg in Year 2.

Obj. 6

MBA 2-7 Common-sized income statements

General Mills Inc. (GIS) produces, markets, and distributes cereal and food products including Cheerios, Wheaties, Cocoa Puffs, Yoplait, and Pillsbury branded products. The following partial income statements (in millions) were adapted from recent financial statements.

	Year 1	Year 2
Sales	$ 17,910	$ 17,630
Cost of goods sold	(11,540)	(11,681)
Gross profit	$ 6,370	$ 5,949
Selling and administrative expenses	(3,474)	(3,328)
Operating income	$ 2,896	$ 2,621

1. Prepare common-sized income statements for Years 1 and 2. Round to one decimal place.
2. Using your answer to (1), analyze the performance of General Mills in Year 2.

Obj. 6

MBA 2-8 Common-sized income statements

Using your answers to MBA 2-6 and MBA 2-7, compare and analyze Year 2 common-sized income statements of Kellogg (K) to those of General Mills (GIS).

Obj. 6

MBA 2-9 Common-sized balance sheets

The following end-of-the-year balance sheets (in millions) were adapted from recent financial statements of Apple (AAPL).

	Year 1	Year 2
Current assets:		
Cash	$ 13,844	$ 21,120
Marketable securities	11,233	20,481
Accounts receivable	27,219	30,343
Inventory	2,111	2,349
Other	14,124	15,085
Total current assets	$ 68,531	$ 89,378
Long-term assets:		
Long-term marketable securities	$130,162	$164,065
Property, plant, and equipment	20,624	22,471
Other long-term assets	12,522	14,565
Total long-term assets	$163,308	$201,101
Total assets	$231,839	$290,479

Current liabilities:		
Accounts payable and similar liabilities	$ 48,649	$ 60,671
Current portion of long-term debt	0	2,500
Other	14,799	17,439
Total current liabilities	$ 63,448	$ 80,610
Long-term liabilities	56,844	90,514
Total liabilities	$120,292	$171,124
Stockholders' equity		
Common stock	$ 23,313	$ 27,416
Retained earnings	87,152	92,284
Other items	1,082	(345)
Total stockholders' equity	$111,547	$119,355
Total liabilities and stockholders' equity	$231,839	$290,479

1. Prepare common-sized balance sheets for Apple for Years 1 and 2. Round to one decimal place.
2. Comment on your answer in (1).

Cases

Case 2-1 Business emphasis

Assume that you are considering developing a nationwide chain of women's clothing stores. You have contacted a Seattle-based firm that specializes in financing new business ventures and enterprises. Such firms, called venture capital firms, finance new businesses in exchange for a percentage of the ownership.

1. In groups of four or five, discuss the different business emphases that you might use in your venture.
2. For each emphasis you listed in (1), provide an example of a real-world business using the same emphasis.
3. What percentage of the ownership would you be willing to give the venture capital firm in exchange for its financing?

Case 2-2 Cash accounting

On August 1, 20Y7, Dr. Ruth Turner established SickCo, a medical practice organized as a professional corporation. The following conversation occurred the following February between Dr. Turner and a former medical school classmate, Dr. Shonna Rees, at an American Medical Association convention in New York City.

Dr. Rees: Ruth, good to see you again. Why didn't you call when you were in Denver? We could have had dinner together.

Dr. Turner: Actually, I never made it to Denver this year. My husband and kids went up to our Vail condo twice, but I got stuck in Fort Lauderdale. I opened a new consulting practice this August and haven't had any time for myself since.

Dr. Rees: I heard about it ... Sick... something ... right?

Dr. Turner: Yes, SickCo. My husband chose the name.

Dr. Rees: I've thought about doing something like that. Are you making any money? I mean, is it worth your time?

Dr. Turner: You wouldn't believe it. I started by opening a bank account with $45,000, and my January bank statement shows a balance of $100,000. Not bad for six months—all pure profit.

Dr. Rees: Maybe I'll try it in Denver! Let's have breakfast together tomorrow and you can fill me in on the details.

Comment on Dr. Turner's statement that the difference between the opening bank balance ($45,000) and the January statement balance ($100,000) is pure profit.

Case 2-3 Business emphasis

Amazon.com (AMZN), an Internet retailer, was incorporated in the early 1990s and opened its virtual doors on the Web shortly thereafter. On its statement of cash flows, would you expect Amazon.com's net cash flows from operating, investing, and financing activities to be positive or negative for its first three years of operations? Use the following format for your answers, and briefly explain your logic.

	Year 1	Year 2	Year 3
Net cash flows from operating activities	negative		
Net cash flows from investing activities			
Net cash flows from financing activities			

Case 2-4 Financial information

Yahoo.com's (YHOO) finance Internet site provides summary financial information about public companies, such as stock quotes, recent financial filings with the Securities and Exchange Commission, and recent news stories. Go to Yahoo.com's financial Web site (**http://finance.yahoo.com/**) and enter Apple, Inc.'s (AAPL). Answer the following questions concerning Apple, Inc. by clicking on the various items under the tab "More On AAPL."

1. At what price did Apple's stock last trade?
2. What is the 52-week range of Apple's stock?
3. When was the last time Apple's stock hit a 52-week high?
4. Over the last six months, has there been any insider selling or buying of Apple's stock?
5. Who is the chief executive officer of Apple Inc., and how old is the president?
6. What was the salary of the president of Apple Inc.?
7. What is the annual dividend of Apple's stock?
8. How many current broker recommendations are strong buy, buy, hold, sell, or strong sell? What is the average of the broker recommendations?
9. What is the net cash flow from operations for this year?
10. What is the operating margin for this year?

Answers to Self-Examination Questions

1. **D** Even though a recording error has been made, the accounting equation will balance (answer D). However, assets (cash) will be overstated by $50,000, and liabilities (notes payable) will be overstated by $50,000. Answer A is incorrect because although cash is overstated by $50,000, the accounting equation will balance. Answer B is incorrect because although notes payable are overstated by $50,000, the accounting equation will balance. Answer C is incorrect because the accounting equation will balance and assets will not exceed liabilities.

2. **C** Total assets will exceed total liabilities and stockholders' equity by $16,000. This is because stockholders' equity (retained earnings) was decreased instead of increased by $8,000. Thus, stockholders' equity will be understated by a total of $16,000.

3. **C** The accounting equation is:

   Assets = Liabilities + Stockholders' Equity

   Therefore, if assets increased by $20,000 and liabilities increased by $12,000, stockholders' equity must have increased by $8,000 (answer C), as indicated in the following computation:

Assets	**= Liabilities + Stockholders' Equity**
+$20,000	= $12,000 + Stockholders' Equity
+$20,000 − $12,000	= Stockholders' Equity
+$8,000	= Stockholders' Equity

4. **B** Net income is the excess of revenue over expenses, or $15,000 (answer B). If expenses exceed revenue, the difference is a net loss. Dividends are the opposite of the stockholders investing in the business and do not affect the amount of net income or net loss.

5. **B** The purchase of land for cash (answer B) changes the mix of assets and does not affect liabilities or stockholders' equity. Borrowing cash from a bank (answer A) increases assets and liabilities. Receiving cash for fees earned (answer C) increases cash and stockholders' equity (retained earnings). Paying office salaries (answer D) decreases cash and stockholders' equity (retained earnings).

Chapter 3

Basic Accounting Systems: Accrual Basis

What's Covered:

Topics: Basic Accounting Systems: Accrual Basis

Accrual Concepts
- Matching Concept (Obj. 1)
- Revenue Recognition (Obj. 1)
- Expense Recognition (Obj. 1)

Accrual Accounting
- Transactions (Obj. 2)
- Adjustment Process (Obj. 3)
- Financial Statements (Obj. 4)

Why Accrual Basis is Used
- Cash vs. Accrual Basis (Obj. 5)
- Advantage of Accrual Basis (Ob. 5)
- Accounting Cycle (Obj. 5)

Metric-Based Analysis
- Transactions
  - Liquidity: Quick Assets (Obj. 2,3)
  - Profitability: Net Income (Obj. 2,3)
- Financial Statements
  - Quick Ratio (Obj. 6)

Learning Objectives

Obj.1 Describe accrual accounting concepts, including the matching concept, revenue recognition, and expense recognition principles.

Obj.2 Use the accrual basis of accounting to analyze, record, and summarize transactions.

Obj.3 Describe and illustrate the end-of-period adjustment process.

Obj.4 Prepare financial statements using the accrual basis of accounting, including a classified balance sheet.

Obj.5 Describe why generally accepted accounting principles (GAAP) requires the accrual basis of accounting.

Obj.6 Describe and illustrate the use of the quick ratio in assessing a company's liquidity.

Chapter Metrics

Use the following metrics to analyze transactions and financial statements.

TRANSACTIONS

Liquidity: Quick Assets

Profitability: Net Income – Accrual Basis

FINANCIAL STATEMENTS

Quick Ratio

Apple Inc.

Have you ever purchased an iTunes gift card that can be redeemed online at the iTunes Store? If so, when do you think **Apple Inc. (AAPL)** should record the revenue from the sale of the gift card?

As we discussed and illustrated in Chapter 2, sometimes revenues are earned at the point cash is received. However, in some cases, a company renders a service or delivers a product before cash is received. In other cases, cash is received before a company renders a service or delivers a product. In these cases, companies normally record revenue when the service is rendered or the product is delivered to the customer.

One company that receives cash before the service is rendered or the product delivered is Apple Inc. In the case of iTunes gift cards, Apple receives cash before the customer downloads music, movies, or other content from its online iTunes Store. When cash is received for the gift card, Apple defers recording the revenue until the customer redeems the card. Likewise, revenue from AppleCare, which provides computer support and repair services, is recorded over the service period covered by the AppleCare contract. For example, Apple offers AppleCare on its iPads for up to a two-year period.

In this chapter, we continue our discussion of financial statements and financial reporting systems. In doing so, we focus on accrual concepts of accounting such as how Apple would record revenue. In addition, our discussions will include how to record transactions under accrual accounting concepts, update accounting records, and prepare accrual financial statements. Because all large companies, and many small ones, use accrual concepts of accounting, a thorough understanding of this topic is important for your business studies and future career.

Accrual Accounting Concepts

Objective 1

Describe accrual accounting concepts, including the matching concept, revenue recognition, and expense recognition principles.

Family Health Care's transactions and financial statements for September and October were illustrated in Chapter 2. These illustrations used many of the eight accounting concepts described in Chapter 1. For example, the business entity concept was used to account for Family Health Care as a separate entity, independent of the owner-manager, Dr. Lee Landry. The cost, unit of measure, going concern, accounting period, full disclosure, and objectivity concepts were also used.

The one accounting concept not used in Chapter 2 was the matching concept. This is because all the transactions in Chapter 2 were structured so that cash was either received or paid. This was done to simplify the recording of transactions and preparing of the financial statements. For example, all revenues were received in cash at the time the services were rendered and all expenses were paid in cash at the time they were incurred. In doing so, this allowed us to illustrate the cash basis of accounting in its simplest form.

In the real world, cash may be received or paid at a different time from when revenues are earned or expenses are incurred. In fact, companies often earn revenue before or after cash is received and incur expenses before or after cash is paid.

To illustrate, a real estate company might spend months or years developing land for a business complex or subdivision. During this period, the company earns no revenues but makes payments for materials, wages, insurance, and other construction items. Thus, if revenues were recorded only when cash is received and expenses recorded only when cash is paid, the company would report a series of losses on its income statement while the land is being developed. In such cases, the income statements would not provide a realistic picture of the company's operations. In fact, the development might become highly successful and the early losses misleading.

Accrual basis accounting is designed to avoid misleading information arising from the timing of cash receipts and payments. Under accrual accounting, transactions are recorded as they occur and thus affect the accounting equation (assets, liabilities, and stockholders' equity). Specifically, the **accrual basis of accounting** records revenue as it is earned and matches expenses against the revenue they generate. Since the receipt or payment of cash affects assets (cash), all cash receipts and payments are recorded in the accounts under accrual accounting. Additionally, under accrual accounting, transactions are recorded even though cash is not received or paid until a later point.

To illustrate, Family Health Care may provide services to patients who are covered by health insurance. Periodically, Family Health Care files claims with the insurance companies requesting payment. In this case, revenue is recorded, referred to as *recognized*, when the services are provided even though the cash is to be received later. When services are provided with the cash to be received at a later time, the services are said to be provided *on account*. In such cases, an *account receivable* for the amount of the services is recorded as an asset.

Likewise, a company may purchase supplies from a supplier (vendor), with terms that allow the company to pay for the purchase at a later time. In this case, the supplies are said to be purchased *on account* and an *account payable* for the amount to be paid is recorded as a liability.

In accounting, the term *recognized* is used to refer to when a transaction is recorded. Under the **revenue recognition principle**, revenue is recorded when services have been provided or when a product has been delivered to a customer. For Family Health Care, revenue is recorded when services have been provided to the patient. At this point, the revenue-earning process is complete and the patient is legally obligated to pay for the services.

Under the **expense recognition principle**, expenses are recorded in the same period that they generate. This is required by the **matching concept** so net income or net loss for the period is properly determined.

Accrual accounting also recognizes liabilities at the time the business incurs the obligation to pay for the services or goods purchased. For example, the purchase of supplies on account is recorded when the supplies are received and the business has incurred the obligation to pay for the supplies.

Apple uses the accrual basis of accounting in recording transactions and reporting its financial statements.

Family Health Care's November Transactions

Objective 2

Use accrual concepts of accounting to analyze, record, and summarize transactions.

To illustrate accrual accounting, the following November 20Y5 Family Health Care transactions are used:

a. On November 1, received $1,800 from ILS Company as rent for the use of Family Health Care's land as a temporary parking lot from November 20Y5 through March 20Y6.

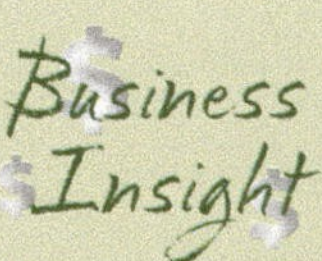

Not Cutting Corners

Have you ever ordered a hamburger from **Wendy's** and noticed that the meat patty is square? The square meat patty reflects a business emphasis instilled in Wendy's by its founder, Dave Thomas. Mr. Thomas emphasized offering high-quality products at a fair price in a friendly atmosphere, without "cutting corners"; hence, the square meat patty. In the highly competitive fast-food industry, Dave Thomas's approach has enabled Wendy's to become one of the largest fast-food restaurant chains in the world.

Source: Douglas Martin, "Dave Thomas, 69, Wendy's Founder, Dies," *New York Times*, January 9, 2002.

b. On November 1, paid a premium of $2,400 for a two-year general business insurance policy that covers risks from fire and theft.

c. On November 1, paid $6,000 for an insurance premium on a six-month medical malpractice policy.

d. Dr. Landry invested an additional $5,000 in the business in exchange for common stock.

e. Purchased supplies for $240 on account.

f. Purchased $8,500 of office equipment. Paid $1,700 cash as a down payment, with the remaining $6,800 ($8,500 – $1,700) due in five monthly installments of $1,360 ($6,800 ÷ 5) beginning January 1, 20Y6.

g. Provided services of $6,100 to patients on account.

h. Received $5,500 for services provided to patients who paid cash.

i. Received $4,200 from insurance companies on patients' accounts for services that were provided in transaction g.

j. Paid $100 on account for supplies that were purchased in transaction e.

k. Expenses paid during November were as follows: wages, $2,790; rent, $800; utilities, $580; interest, $100; and miscellaneous, $420.

l. Paid dividends of $1,200 to stockholder (Dr. Landry).

In analyzing and recording the November transactions for Family Health Care, the integrated financial statement framework is used. Transactions that increase or decrease a financial statement element are recorded. These financial statement elements are referred to as **accounts**.

In addition, the effects of each transaction on liquidity and profitability metrics for Family Health Care are illustrated. In this chapter, we use quick assets as our liquidity metric. **Quick assets** include cash and other assets that can be readily converted to cash such as receivables and marketable securities. Inventory is normally not included as a quick asset since inventory must be sold and any related receivable collected before it is converted to cash. Since Family Health Care is a service business with no marketable securities, quick assets consist of cash and account receivable.

In this chapter, we use net income (revenue – expenses) as our profitability metric. Since this chapter illustrates accrual transactions, the profitability metric is termed **Net Income – Accrual Basis.**

Transaction (a)

On November 1, received $1,800 from ILS Company as rent for the use of Family Health Care's land as a temporary parking lot from November 20Y5 through March 20Y6.

In this transaction, Family Health Care entered into a rental agreement for the use of its land for five months. The agreement requires a payment of a rental fee of $1,800 in advance. The rental agreement also gives ILS Company the option of renewing the agreement for an additional four months.

By entering into this rental agreement and accepting the $1,800, Family Health Care has incurred a liability to make the land available for ILS's use. If Family Health Care canceled the agreement on November 1, after accepting the $1,800, it would have to repay the $1,800.

Family Health Care records this transaction as an increase in Cash and an increase in a liability for $1,800. Because the liability relates to rent that has not yet been earned, it is recorded as Unearned Revenue.

The effects of this transaction on Family Health Care's financial statements are recorded as follows.

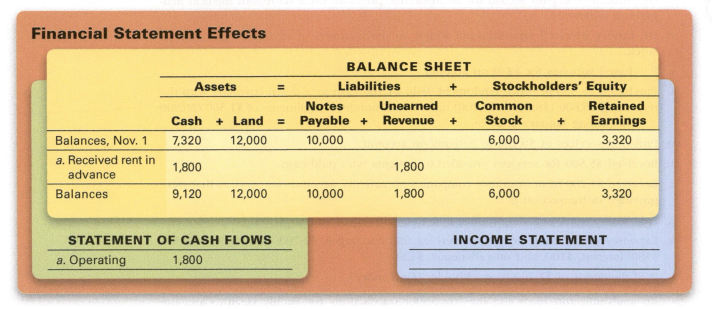

Financial Statement Effects

BALANCE SHEET

	Assets		=	Liabilities		+	Stockholders' Equity	
	Cash	**+ Land**	**=**	**Notes Payable**	**+ Unearned Revenue**	**+**	**Common Stock**	**+ Retained Earnings**
Balances, Nov. 1	7,320	12,000		10,000			6,000	3,320
a. Received rent in advance	1,800				1,800			
Balances	9,120	12,000		10,000	1,800		6,000	3,320

STATEMENT OF CASH FLOWS	
a. Operating	1,800

INCOME STATEMENT

The November 1 balances shown in the preceding integrated financial statement spreadsheet are the ending balances from October 31. That is, the cash balance of $7,320 is the ending cash balance as of October 31, 20Y5. Likewise, the other balances are carried forward from the preceding month. In this sense, the Balance Sheet column is a cumulative financial history of Family Health Care.

The receipt of the $1,800 of cash from ILS Company increases cash flows from Operating activities under the Statement of Cash Flows column. Since no rental revenue has yet been earned, there are no entries under the Income Statement column.

As time passes, Family Health Care will earn the rental revenue. For example, at the end of November, $360 ($1,800 ÷ 5 months) will be earned. Recording the $360 of earned rent revenue at the end of November is described and illustrated later in this chapter.

Transaction Metric Effects

The effects of each transaction on liquidity and profitability metrics for Family Health Care are illustrated throughout the chapter. Quick assets is used as the liquidity metric. Quick assets include cash and other assets that can be readily converted to cash such as receivables and marketable securities. Inventory is normally not included in quick assets. Since Family Health Care is a service business with no marketable securities, quick assets consist of cash and accounts receivable.

Net income (revenue – expenses) is used as the profitability metric. Since this chapter illustrates accrual transactions, the profitability metric is **Net Income – Accrual Basis.**

The effects of the receipt of the rent of $1,800 on the liquidity and profitability metrics are as follows:

LIQUIDITY	
Quick Assets	$1,800

PROFITABILITY	
Net Income – Accrual Basis	No Effect

Transaction (b)

On November 1, paid a premium of $2,400 for a two-year general business insurance policy that covers risks from fire and theft.

By paying the premium, Family Health Care has purchased an asset, insurance coverage, in exchange for cash. The effects of this transaction on Family Health Care's financial statements are recorded as follows.

Financial Statement Effects

BALANCE SHEET

	Assets			=	Liabilities		+ Stockholders' Equity	
	Cash	+ Prepaid Insurance	+ Land	=	Notes Payable	+ Unearned Revenue	+ Common Stock	+ Retained Earnings
Balances	9,120		12,000		10,000	1,800	6,000	3,320
b. Paid insurance for two years	(2,400)	2,400						
Balances	6,720	2,400	12,000		10,000	1,800	6,000	3,320

STATEMENT OF CASH FLOWS	
b. Operating	(2,400)

INCOME STATEMENT

Under the Balance Sheet column the mix of assets has changed, with Cash decreasing by $2,400 and Prepaid Insurance increasing by $2,400. The payment of cash also decreases cash flows from Operating activities under the Statement of Cash Flows column. Since no revenue or expenses are affected, there are no entries under the Income Statement column.

Prepaid insurance is unique in that it expires with the passage of time. For example, $100 ($2,400 ÷ 24 months) of Family Health Care's insurance will expire each month. Such assets are called **prepaid expenses** or **deferred expenses**.

Transaction Metric Effects

The effects of paying the insurance premium of $2,400 on the liquidity and profitability metrics are as follows:

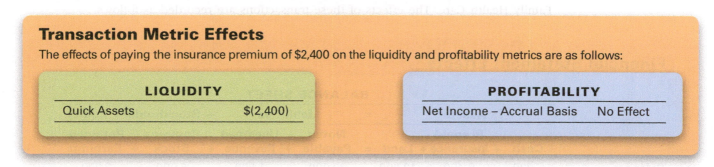

LIQUIDITY	
Quick Assets	$(2,400)

PROFITABILITY	
Net Income – Accrual Basis	No Effect

Transaction (c)

On November 1, paid $6,000 for an insurance premium on a six-month medical malpractice policy.

This transaction is similar to transaction (b), except that Family Health Care has purchased medical malpractice insurance that is renewable every 6 months. The effects of this transaction on Family Health Care's financial statements are recorded as follows.

Financial Statement Effects

BALANCE SHEET

	Assets			=	Liabilities		+ Stockholders' Equity	
	Cash	+ Prepaid Insurance	+ Land	=	Notes Payable	+ Unearned Revenue	+ Common Stock	+ Retained Earnings
Balances	6,720	2,400	12,000		10,000	1,800	6,000	3,320
c. Paid insurance for two years	(6,000)	6,000						
Balances	720	8,400	12,000		10,000	1,800	6,000	3,320

STATEMENT OF CASH FLOWS	
c. Operating	(6,000)

INCOME STATEMENT

Transaction Metric Effects

The effects of paying the insurance premium of $6,000 on the liquidity and profitability metrics are as follows:

LIQUIDITY	
Quick Assets	$(6,000)

PROFITABILITY	
Net Income – Accrual Basis	No Effect

Apple Connection

Apple maintains insurance coverage for cyber risks.

Transaction (d)

Dr. Landry invested an additional $5,000 in the business in exchange for common stock.

This transaction is similar to the initial transaction in which Dr. Landry established Family Health Care. The effects of these transactions are recorded as follows:

Financial Statement Effects

BALANCE SHEET

	Assets			=	Liabilities		+ Stockholders' Equity	
	Cash	+ Prepaid Insurance	+ Land	=	Notes Payable	+ Unearned Revenue	+ Common Stock	+ Retained Earnings
Balances	720	8,400	12,000		10,000	1,800	6,000	3,320
d. Issued common stock	5,000						5,000	
Balances	5,720	8,400	12,000		10,000	1,800	11,000	3,320

STATEMENT OF CASH FLOWS	
d. Financing	5,000

INCOME STATEMENT

Transaction Metric Effects

The effects of issuing $5,000 of common stock on the liquidity and profitability metrics are as follows:

LIQUIDITY	
Quick Assets	$5,000

PROFITABILITY	
Net Income – Accrual Basis	No Effect

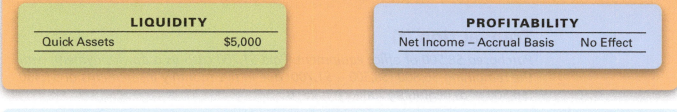

On a recent balance sheet, **Apple** reported 5,575,331,000 shares of common stock outstanding.

Apple Connection

Transaction (e)

Purchased supplies for $240 on account.

This transaction is similar to transactions (b) and (c), in that purchased supplies are assets until they are used in the generation of revenue. Family Health Care has purchased and received the supplies, with a promise to pay in the near future. Such liabilities that are incurred in the normal operations are called **accounts payable**. The effects of this transaction on Family Health Care's financial statements are recorded as follows.

Financial Statement Effects

BALANCE SHEET

	Assets				=	Liabilities		+	Stockholders' Equity	
	Cash +	Prepaid Insurance +	Supplies +	Land	=	Notes Payable +	Accounts Payable	+ Unearned Revenue +	Common Stock +	Retained Earnings
Balances	5,720	8,400		12,000		10,000		1,800	11,000	3,320
e. Purchased supplies			240				240			
Balances	5,720	8,400	240	12,000		10,000	240	1,800	11,000	3,320

STATEMENT OF CASH FLOWS

INCOME STATEMENT

Under the Balance Sheet column, the asset Supplies increases by $240 and the liability Accounts Payable increases by $240. Since no cash is paid or received, there are no entries under the Statement of Cash Flows column. Likewise, since no revenue or expenses are affected, there are no entries under the Income Statement column.

Transaction Metric Effects

The effects of purchasing $240 of supplies on credit on the liquidity and profitability metrics are as follows:

LIQUIDITY	
Quick Assets	No Effect

PROFITABILITY	
Net Income – Accrual Basis	No Effect

On a recent balance sheet, Apple reported $35,490 million of accounts payable.

Transaction (f)

Purchased $8,500 of office equipment. Paid $1,700 cash as a down payment, with the remaining $6,800 ($8,500 – $1,700) due in five monthly installments of $1,360 ($6,800 ÷ 5) beginning January 1, 20Y6.

In this transaction, the asset Office Equipment increases by $8,500, Cash decreases by $1,700, and Notes Payable increases by $6,800. Since cash was paid, cash flows from Investing activities is decreased by $1,700 under the Statement of Cash Flows column. No revenues or expenses are affected, so no entries under the Income Statement column are necessary.

The effects of transaction (f) on Family Health Care's financial statements are recorded as shown below.

Financial Statement Effects

BALANCE SHEET

	Assets					=	Liabilities			+ Stockholders' Equity	
	Cash +	Prepaid Insur. +	Supp. +	Office Equip. +	Land	=	Notes Pay. +	Accts. Pay. +	Unearned Revenue +	Common Stock +	Retained Earnings
Balances	5,720	8,400	240		12,000		10,000	240	1,800	11,000	3,320
f. Purchased office equipment	(1,700)			8,500			6,800				
Balances	4,020	8,400	240	8,500	12,000		16,800	240	1,800	11,000	3,320

STATEMENT OF CASH FLOWS

f. Investing	(1,700)

INCOME STATEMENT

Transaction Metric Effects

The effects of purchasing $8,500 of office equipment by paying cash of $1,700 and issuing $6,800 in notes payable on the liquidity and profitability metrics are as follows:

LIQUIDITY

Quick Assets	$(1,700)

PROFITABILITY

Net Income – Accrual Basis	No Effect

Transaction (g)

Provided services of $6,100 to patients on account.

This transaction is similar to the revenue transactions recorded for Family Health Care in September and October. This transaction is different in that instead of receiving cash, the services were provided *on account.*

Family Health Care will collect cash from the patients' insurance companies in the future. Such amounts that are to be collected in the future and that arise from the normal operations are called **accounts receivable**. Since a valid claim exists for future collection, accounts receivable are assets. Thus, the asset Accounts Receivable is increased by $6,100 under the Balance Sheet column. In addition, Retained Earnings are increased under the Balance Sheet column and Fees earned is increased under the Income Statement column.

The effects of transaction (g) on Family Health Care's financial statements are recorded as follows.

Financial Statement Effects

BALANCE SHEET

	Assets						=	Liabilities			+ Stockholders' Equity	
	Cash +	Accts. Rec. +	Prepaid Insur. +	Supp. +	Office Equip. +	Land	=	Notes Pay. +	Accts. Pay. +	Unearned Revenue +	Common Stock +	Retained Earnings
Balances	4,020		8,400	240	8,500	12,000		16,800	240	1,800	11,000	3,320
g. Fees earned on acct.		6,100										6,100
Balances	4,020	6,100	8,400	240	8,500	12,000		16,800	240	1,800	11,000	9,420

STATEMENT OF CASH FLOWS

INCOME STATEMENT

g. Fees earned	6,100

Transaction Metric Effects

The effects of earning $6,100 of patient fees on account on the liquidity and profitability metrics are as follows:

LIQUIDITY

Quick Assets	$6,100

PROFITABILITY

Net Income – Accrual Basis	$6,100

On a recent balance sheet, Apple reported $16,931 million of accounts receivable.

Apple Connection

Transaction (h)

Received $5,500 for services provided to patients who paid cash.

This transaction is similar to the revenue transactions that Family Health Care recorded in September and October. The effects of this transaction on Family Health Care's financial statements are recorded as shown:

Financial Statement Effects

BALANCE SHEET

	Assets						=	Liabilities			+ Stockholders' Equity	
	Cash +	Accts. Rec. +	Prepaid Insur. +	Supp. +	Office Equip. +	Land	=	Notes Pay. +	Accts. Pay. +	Unearned Revenue +	Common Stock +	Retained Earnings
Balances	4,020	6,100	8,400	240	8,500	12,000		16,800	240	1,800	11,000	9,420
h. Fees earned for cash	5,500											5,500
Balances	9,520	6,100	8,400	240	8,500	12,000		16,800	240	1,800	11,000	14,920

STATEMENT OF CASH FLOWS	
h. Operating	5,500

INCOME STATEMENT	
h. Fees earned	5,500

Transaction Metric Effects

The effects of earning cash patient fees of $5,500 on the liquidity and profitability metrics are as follows:

LIQUIDITY	
Quick Assets	$5,500

PROFITABILITY	
Net Income – Accrual Basis	$5,500

Transaction (i)

Received $4,200 from insurance companies on patients' accounts for services that were provided in transaction g.

This transaction is similar to transaction (b) in that only the mix of assets changes. Cash is increased and Accounts Receivable is decreased by $4,200 under the Balance Sheet column. The effects of this transaction on Family Health Care's financial statements are recorded as follows.

Financial Statement Effects

BALANCE SHEET

	Assets						=	Liabilities			+ Stockholders' Equity	
	Cash +	Accts. Rec. +	Prepaid Insur. +	Supp. +	Office Equip. +	Land	=	Notes Pay. +	Accts. Pay. +	Unearned Revenue +	Common Stock +	Retained Earnings
Balances	9,520	6,100	8,400	240	8,500	12,000		16,800	240	1,800	11,000	14,920
i. Collected receivables	4,200	(4,200)										
Balances	13,720	1,900	8,400	240	8,500	12,000		16,800	240	1,800	11,000	14,920

STATEMENT OF CASH FLOWS	
i. Operating	4,200

INCOME STATEMENT

Transaction Metric Effects

The effects of receiving $4,200 from insurance companies for payments on account on the liquidity and profitability metrics are as follows:

LIQUIDITY	
Quick Assets	No Effect

PROFITABILITY	
Net Income – Accrual Basis	No Effect

Since cash and accounts receivable are quick assets, the increase in cash and decrease in accounts receivable offset each other, with the result that there is no effect on quick assets.

Transaction (j)

Paid $100 on account for supplies that were purchased in transaction e.

The cash was paid for supplies purchased on account. Thus, this transaction decreases Cash and Accounts Payable by $100 under the Balance Sheet column. Since the supplies are used in the normal operations of Family Health Care, cash flows from Operating activities is also decreased under the Statement of Cash Flows column.

The effects of transaction (j) on Family Health Care's financial statements are recorded as follows.

Financial Statement Effects

BALANCE SHEET

	Assets						= Liabilities			+ Stockholders' Equity	
	Cash +	Accts. Rec. +	Prepaid Insur. +	Supp. +	Office Equip. +	Land =	Notes Pay. +	Accts. Pay. +	Unearned Revenue +	Common Stock +	Retained Earnings
Balances	13,720	1,900	8,400	240	8,500	12,000	16,800	240	1,800	11,000	14,920
j. Paid on acct.	(100)							(100)			
Balances	13,620	1,900	8,400	240	8,500	12,000	16,800	140	1,800	11,000	14,920

STATEMENT OF CASH FLOWS	
j. Operating	(100)

INCOME STATEMENT

Transaction Metric Effects

The effects of paying $100 on accounts payable on the liquidity and profitability metrics are as follows:

LIQUIDITY	
Quick Assets	$(100)

PROFITABILITY	
Net Income – Accrual Basis	No Effect

Transaction (k)

Expenses paid during November were as follows: wages, $2,790; rent, $800; utilities, $580; interest, $100; and miscellaneous, $420.

This transaction is similar to the September and October expense transactions for Family Health Care. The effects of this transaction on Family Health Care's financial statements are recorded as follows.

Financial Statement Effects

BALANCE SHEET

	Assets						=	Liabilities			+ Stockholders' Equity	
	Cash +	Accts. Rec. +	Prepaid Insur.	+ Supp. +	Office Equip. +	Land	=	Notes Pay. +	Accts. Pay.	+ Unearned Revenue +	Common Stock +	Retained Earnings
Balances	13,620	1,900	8,400	240	8,500	12,000		16,800	140	1,800	11,000	14,920
k. Paid expenses	(4,690)											(4,690)
Balances	8,930	1,900	8,400	240	8,500	12,000		16,800	140	1,800	11,000	10,230

STATEMENT OF CASH FLOWS

k. Operating	(4,690)

INCOME STATEMENT

k. Wages expense	(2,790)
Rent expense	(800)
Utilities expense	(580)
Interest expense	(100)
Misc. expense	(420)

Transaction Metric Effects

The effects of paying expenses of $4,690 on the liquidity and profitability metrics are as follows:

LIQUIDITY

Quick Assets	$(4,690)

PROFITABILITY

Net Income – Accrual Basis	$(4,690)

Transaction (l)

Paid dividends of $1,200 to stockholder (Dr. Landry).

This transaction is similar to Family Health Care's dividend transactions in September and October. The effects of this transaction on Family Health Care's financial statements are recorded as follows.

Financial Statement Effects

BALANCE SHEET

	Assets						=	Liabilities			+ Stockholders' Equity	
	Cash +	Accts. Rec. +	Prepaid Insur.	+ Supp. +	Office Equip. +	Land	=	Notes Pay. +	Accts. Pay.	+ Unearned Revenue +	Common Stock +	Retained Earnings
Balances	8,930	1,900	8,400	240	8,500	12,000		16,800	140	1,800	11,000	10,230
l. Paid dividends	(1,200)											(1,200)
Balances	7,730	1,900	8,400	240	8,500	12,000		16,800	140	1,800	11,000	9,030

STATEMENT OF CASH FLOWS

l. Financing	(1,200)

INCOME STATEMENT

Transaction Metric Effects

The effects of paying $1,200 in dividends on liquidity and profitability metrics are as follows:

LIQUIDITY	
Quick Assets	$(1,200)

PROFITABILITY	
Net Income – Accrual Basis	No Effect

For a recent year, Apple paid dividends of $11,561 million.

Apple Connection

The Adjustment Process

Objective 3

Describe and illustrate the end-of-period adjustment process.

Accrual accounting requires the updating of the accounting records prior to preparing financial statements. This updating is called the **adjustment process**. The adjustment process is needed to match revenues and expenses, which is an application of the matching concept and the revenue and expense recognition principles.

Adjustments are necessary because, at any point in time, some accounts (elements) of the accounting equation are not up to date. For example, as time passes, prepaid insurance expires and supplies are used. However, it is not efficient to record the daily expiration of prepaid insurance or the daily use of supplies. Instead, the accounting records are normally updated just prior to preparing financial statements.

Family Health Care's September and October financial statements were prepared in Chapter 2 without recording any adjustments. This is because Family Health Care only entered into cash transactions in September and October. When all of a company's transactions are cash transactions, no adjustments are necessary.

During November, however, Family Health Care entered into several accrual transactions. As a result, Family Health must adjust its accounts before preparing financial statements.

Deferrals and Accruals

Two types of accounts require adjustments as follows:

- **Deferrals**, which are created by recording a transaction in a way that delays or defers the recognition of an expense or revenue.
- **Accruals**, which are created when a revenue or expense has been earned or incurred but has not been recorded.

Common deferrals include prepaid expenses and unearned revenues.

Prepaid expenses or **deferred expenses** are initially recorded as assets but become expenses over time or through normal operations of the business. For Family Health Care, prepaid insurance is an example of a deferral that requires adjustment. Other examples include supplies, prepaid advertising, and prepaid interest.

Unearned revenues or **deferred revenues** are initially recorded as liabilities but become revenues over time or through normal operations of the business. For Family Health Care, unearned rent is an example of a deferral that requires adjustment. Other examples include tuition received in advance, an attorney's annual retainer fee, insurance premiums received in advance, and magazine subscriptions received in advance.

On a recent balance sheet, Apple reported unearned revenue of over $12 billion as a liability, which includes cash received for Apple gift cards.

Apple Connection

Integrity, Objectivity, and Ethics in Business

Dave's Legacy

When Dave Thomas, founder of **Wendy's**, died in 2002, he left behind a corporate culture of integrity and high ethical conduct. When asked to comment on Dave's death, Jack Schuessler, chairman and chief executive officer of Wendy's, stated:

"People (could) relate to Dave, that he was honest and has integrity and he really cares about people. . . . There is no replacing Dave Thomas. . . . So you are left with . . . the values that he gave us . . . and you take care of the customer every day like Dave would want us to and good things will happen. He's [Dave Thomas] taught us so much that when we get stuck, we can always look back and ask ourselves, how would Dave handle it?"

In a recent discussion of corporate earnings with analysts, Kerrii Anderson, then chief financial officer of Wendy's, stated: "We're confident about the future because of our unwavering commitment to our core values, such as quality food, superior restaurant operations, continuous improvement, and *integrity to doing the right thing* [emphasis added]."

Sources: Neil Cavuto, "Wendy's CEO—Interview," *Fox News: Your World*, February 11, 2002; "Q1 2003 Wendy's International Earnings Conference Call—Final," *Financial Disclosure Wire*, April 24, 2003.

Common accruals include accrued expenses and accrued revenues. **Accrued expenses** or **accrued liabilities** are expenses that have been incurred but are not recorded in the accounts. For Family Health Care, unpaid wages at the end of November are an example of an accrued expense. Other examples include accrued interest, utility expenses, and taxes.

Accrued revenues or **accrued assets** are revenues that have been earned but are not recorded in the accounts. For Family Health Care, revenue for patient services that have been earned but not billed at the end of November is an example of accrued revenue. Other examples include accrued interest on notes receivable and accrued rent on property rented to others.

Deferrals are normally the result of cash being received or paid *before* the revenue is earned or the expense is incurred. In contrast, accruals are normally the result of cash being received or paid *after* revenue has been earned or an expense has been incurred. Exhibit 1 summarizes the nature of deferrals and accruals.

Exhibit 1
Deferrals and Accruals

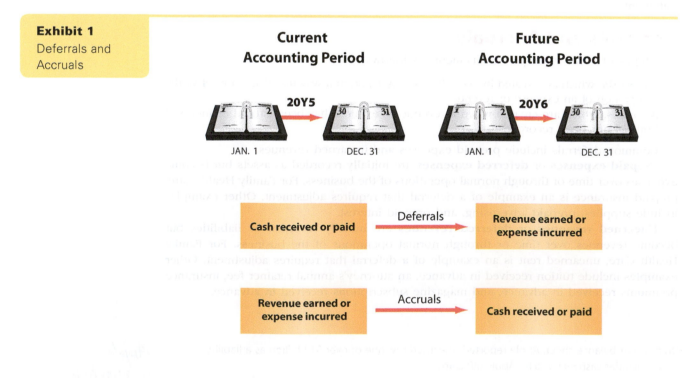

Current Accounting Period | **Future Accounting Period**

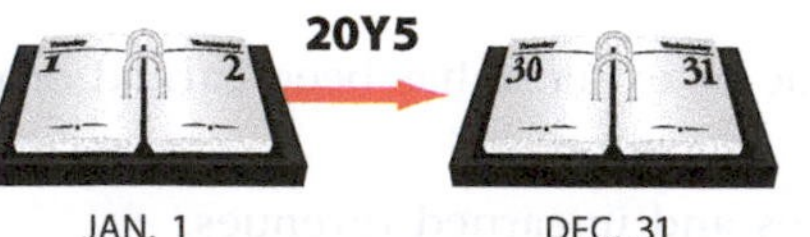

Cash received or paid → Deferrals → Revenue earned or expense incurred

Revenue earned or expense incurred → Accruals → Cash received or paid

Adjustments for Family Health Care

On November 30, 20Y5, the following adjustment data have been gathered for Family Health Care.

DEFERRALS

Deferred expenses:

a1. Prepaid insurance expired, $1,100.

a2. Supplies used, $150.

a3. Depreciation on office equipment, $160.

Deferred revenue:

a4. Unearned revenue earned, $360.

ACCRUALS

Accrued expense:

a5. Wages owed but not paid to employees, $220.

Accrued revenue:

a6. Services provided to patients but not billed to insurance companies, $750.

Adjustment a1

Prepaid insurance expired, $1,100.

During November, a portion of the prepaid insurance purchased on November 1 has expired. On November 1, Family Health Care paid for the following two policies:

1. General business policy for $2,400 (transaction b)
2. Malpractice policy for $6,000 (transaction c)

The general business policy is a two-year policy expiring at a rate of $100 ($2,400 ÷ 24) per month. The malpractice policy is a six-month policy that expires at a rate of $1,000 ($6,000 ÷ 6) per month. Thus, a total of $1,100 ($100 + $1,000) of prepaid insurance has expired by the end of November.

Adjustment a1 is recorded by decreasing the asset Prepaid Insurance and decreasing Retained Earnings under the Balance Sheet column. In addition, Insurance expense under the Income Statement column is recorded as $(1,100). Since no cash was received or paid, no entries are necessary in the Statement of Cash Flows column.

The effects of Adjustment 1 on Family Health Care's financial statements are recorded as shown below.

Financial Statement Effects

BALANCE SHEET

	Assets						=	Liabilities			+ Stockholders' Equity	
	Cash +	Accts. Rec. +	Prepaid Insur.	+ Supp.	+ Office Equip.	+ Land	= Notes Pay.	+ Accts. Pay.	+ Unearned Revenue	+ Common Stock	+ Retained Earnings
Balances	7,730	1,900	8,400	240	8,500	12,000	16,800	140	1,800	11,000	9,030
a1. Insurance expense			(1,100)								(1,100)
Balances	7,730	1,900	7,300	240	8,500	12,000	16,800	140	1,800	11,000	7,930

STATEMENT OF CASH FLOWS

INCOME STATEMENT

a1. Insurance exp.	(1,100)

All adjustments affect the balance sheet and income statement, and thus, adjusting entries are recorded in the Balance Sheet and Income Statement columns. In contrast, *no adjustment* affects cash or the statement of cash flows, and thus, no adjusting entries are recorded in the Statement of Cash Flows column.

Adjustment Metric Effects

The effects of Adjustment a1 for $1,100 of expiring prepaid insurance on the liquidity and profitability metrics are as follows:

LIQUIDITY	
Quick Assets	No Effect

PROFITABILITY	
Net Income – Accrual Basis	$(1,100)

Prepaid insurance is not classified as a quick asset (cash or receivable). Thus, Adjustment a1 has no effect on quick assets. All adjustments will affect net income, and since insurance expense is increased by $1,100, net income decreases by $(1,100).

Adjustment a2

Supplies used, $150.

For November, supplies of $150 were used. This leaves $90 ($240 − $150) of supplies on hand as of November 30.

Adjustment a2 is recorded by decreasing the asset Supplies and decreasing Retained Earnings under the Balance Sheet column. In addition, Supplies expense under the Income Statement column is recorded as $(150).

The effects of Adjustment a2 on Family Health Care's financial statements are recorded as shown below.

Financial Statement Effects

BALANCE SHEET

	Assets						=	Liabilities		+ Stockholders' Equity	
	Cash +	Accts. Rec. +	Prepaid Insur. +	Supp. +	Office Equip. +	Land =	Notes Pay. +	Accts. Pay. +	Unearned Revenue +	Common Stock +	Retained Earnings
Balances	7,730	1,900	7,300	240	8,500	12,000	16,800	140	1,800	11,000	7,930
a2. Supplies expense				(150)							(150)
Balances	7,730	1,900	7,300	90	8,500	12,000	16,800	140	1,800	11,000	7,780

STATEMENT OF CASH FLOWS

INCOME STATEMENT	
a2. Supplies exp.	(150)

Adjustment Metric Effects

The effects of Adjustment a2 for $150 of supplies used on the liquidity and profitability metrics are as follows:

LIQUIDITY	
Quick Assets	No Effect

PROFITABILITY	
Net Income – Accrual Basis	$(150)

Supplies are not a quick asset and thus, there is no effect on the liquidity metric.

Adjustment a3

Depreciation on office equipment, $160.

Fixed assets such as office equipment lose their ability to provide service over time. This reduction in the ability of a fixed asset to provide service is called **depreciation**. However, it is difficult to objectively determine the physical decline in a fixed asset's ability to provide service. For this reason, depreciation is estimated based on the asset's useful life. Methods of estimating depreciation are covered in Chapter 7. In this chapter, the November depreciation for the office equipment is assumed to be $160.

A record of the initial cost of a fixed asset must be maintained for tax and other purposes. For this reason, the fixed asset account is not reduced directly for depreciation. Instead, an offsetting or *contra asset account*, called **accumulated depreciation**, is added to the Balance Sheet column. On the balance sheet, the accumulated depreciation is subtracted from the cost of the fixed asset.

Adjustment 3a is recorded in the Accumulated Depreciation (Acc. Dep.) column under Assets in the Balance Sheet column as $(160). Retained Earnings is also decreased under the Balance Sheet column by $(160). In addition, Depreciation expense under the Income Statement column is recorded as $(160).

The effects of Adjustment 3a on Family Health Care's financial statements are recorded as shown below.

Financial Statement Effects

BALANCE SHEET

	Assets							=	Liabilities			+ Stockholders' Equity	
	Cash +	Accts. Rec. +	Prepaid Insur. +	Supp. +	Office Equip. −	Acc. Depr. +	Land	=	Notes Pay. +	Accts. Pay. +	Unearned Revenue +	Common Stock +	Retained Earnings
Balances	7,730	1,900	7,300	90	8,500		12,000		16,800	140	1,800	11,000	7,780
a3. Depr. exp.						(160)							(160)
Balances	7,730	1,900	7,300	90	8,500	(160)	12,000		16,800	140	1,800	11,000	7,620

STATEMENT OF CASH FLOWS

INCOME STATEMENT

a3. Depreciation exp.	(160)

In recent financial statements, Apple reported depreciation expense of $11,257 million.

Apple Connection

Three other points related to depreciation are:

1. Land is not depreciated, because it usually does not lose its ability to provide service.
2. The cost of the equipment is a type of deferred expense that is recognized as an expense over the fixed asset's useful life.
3. The cost of the fixed asset less the balance of its accumulated depreciation is called the asset's **book value**, or *carrying value*. For example, the book value of Family Health Care's office equipment, after the preceding adjustment, is $8,340 ($8,500 − $160).

In recent financial statements, **Apple** reported property, plant, and equipment of $49,257 million and accumulated depreciation of $26,786 million for a book value of $22,471 million.

Adjustment Metric Effects

The effects of Adjustment a3 for depreciation of $160 on the liquidity and profitability metrics are as follows:

LIQUIDITY	
Quick Assets	No Effect

PROFITABILITY	
Net Income – Accrual Basis	$(160)

Adjustment a4

Unearned revenue earned, $360.

This adjustment recognizes that a portion of the unearned revenue is earned by the end of November. That is, of the $1,800 received for rental of the land for five months (November through March), one-fifth, or $360, would have been earned as of November 30.

Adjustment a4 is recorded by decreasing the liability Unearned Revenue by $360 under the Balance Sheet column. In addition, Rent revenue is increased by $360 under the Income Statement column.

The effects of Adjustment a4 on Family Health Care's financial statements are recorded as shown below.

Financial Statement Effects

BALANCE SHEET

	Assets							=	Liabilities			+ Stockholders' Equity	
	Cash +	Accts. Rec. +	Prepaid Insur.	+ Supp. +	Office Equip. –	Acc. Depr. +	Land =		Notes Pay. +	Accts. Pay. +	Unearned Revenue +	Common Stock +	Retained Earnings
Balances	7,730	1,900	7,300	90	8,500	(160)	12,000		16,800	140	1,800	11,000	7,620
a4. Rent rev.											(360)		360
Balances	7,730	1,900	7,300	90	8,500	(160)	12,000		16,800	140	1,440	11,000	7,980

STATEMENT OF CASH FLOWS

INCOME STATEMENT

a4. Rent revenue	360

Adjustment Metric Effects

The effects of Adjustment a4 for rent earned of $360 on the liquidity and profitability metrics are as follows:

LIQUIDITY	
Quick Assets	No Effect

PROFITABILITY	
Net Income – Accrual Basis	$360

Adjustment a5

Wages owed but not paid to employees, $220.

It is rare that employees are paid the same day that the accounting period ends. Thus, at the end of an accounting period, it is normal for businesses to owe wages to their employees.

Adjustment a5 recognizes that as of November 30, employees of Family Health Care have not been paid $220 for work they have performed. This adjustment is recorded by increasing the liability Wages Payable by $220 and decreasing Retained Earnings by $220 under the Balance Sheet column. In addition, Wages expense under the Income Statement column is recorded as $(220).

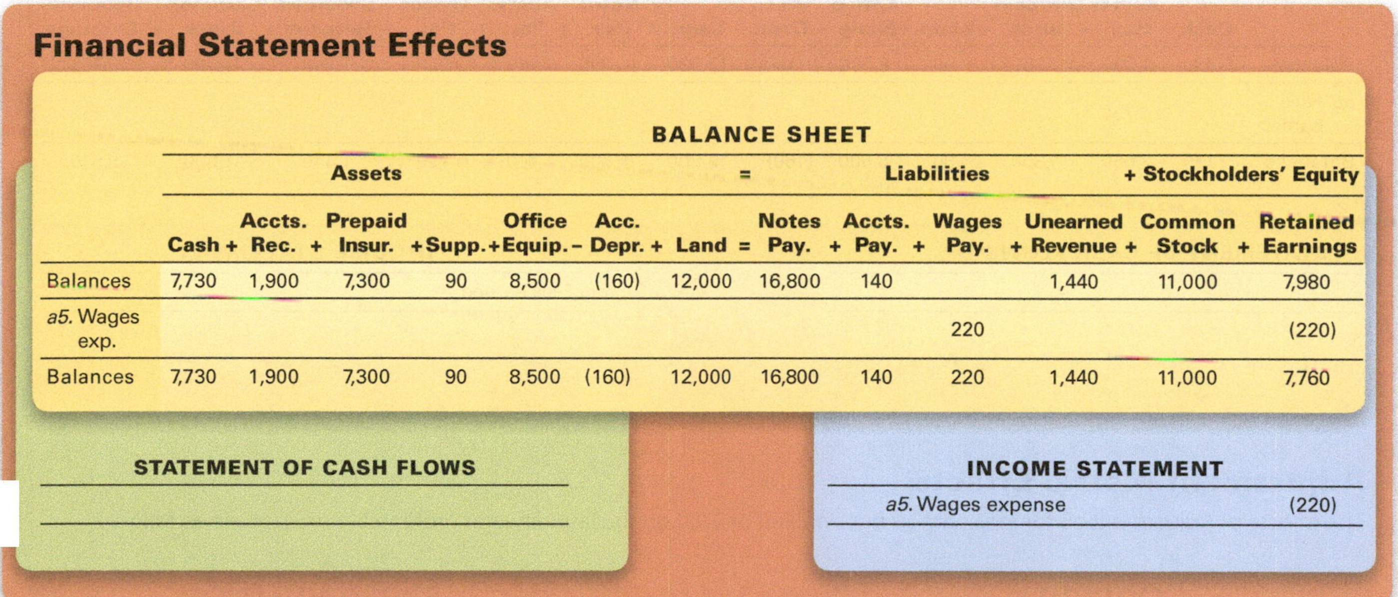

Financial Statement Effects

BALANCE SHEET

	Assets							= Liabilities				+ Stockholders' Equity	
	Cash +	Accts. Rec. +	Prepaid Insur. +	Supp. +	Office Equip. −	Acc. Depr. +	Land =	Notes Pay. +	Accts. Pay. +	Wages Pay. +	Unearned Revenue +	Common Stock +	Retained Earnings
Balances	7,730	1,900	7,300	90	8,500	(160)	12,000	16,800	140		1,440	11,000	7,980
a5. Wages exp.										220			(220)
Balances	7,730	1,900	7,300	90	8,500	(160)	12,000	16,800	140	220	1,440	11,000	7,760

STATEMENT OF CASH FLOWS

INCOME STATEMENT

a5. Wages expense	(220)

Adjustment Metric Effects

The effects of Adjustment a5 for accrued wages of $220 on the liquidity and profitability metrics are as follows:

LIQUIDITY

Quick Assets	No Effect

PROFITABILITY

Net Income – Accrual Basis	$(220)

Apple has over 100,000 full-time equivalent employees.

Apple Connection

Adjustment a6

Services provided but not billed to insurance companies, $750.

This adjustment recognizes that Family Health Care has provided services of $750 to patients who have not yet been billed. Such services are usually provided near the end of the month.

This adjustment is recorded by increasing the asset Accounts Receivable (Accts. Rec.) and increasing Retained Earnings by $750 under the Balance Sheet column. In addition, Fees earned under the Income Statement column is recorded as $750.

The effects of Adjustment a6 on Family Health Care's financial statements are as shown below.

Financial Statement Effects

BALANCE SHEET

	Assets							=	Liabilities			+ Stockholders' Equity		
	Cash +	Accts. Rec. +	Prepaid Insur. +	Supp. +	Office Equip. –	Acc. Depr. +	Land	=	Notes Pay. +	Accts. Pay. +	Wages Pay. +	Unearned Revenue +	Common Stock +	Retained Earnings
Balances	7,730	1,900	7,300	90	8,500	(160)	12,000		16,800	140	220	1,440	11,000	7,760
a6. Fees earned		750												750
Balances	7,730	2,650	7,300	90	8,500	(160)	12,000		16,800	140	220	1,440	11,000	8,510

STATEMENT OF CASH FLOWS

INCOME STATEMENT

a6. Fees earned	750

Adjustment Metric Effects

The effects of Adjustment a6 for fees earned but unbilled of $750 on the liquidity and profitability metrics are as follows:

LIQUIDITY

Quick Assets	$750

PROFITABILITY

Net Income – Accrual Basis	$750

Since Adjustment 6a increases accounts receivable by $750, the liquidity metric quick assets increases by $750. The profitability metric Net Income – Accrual Basis also increases for the fees earned of $750.

The November transactions and adjustments for Family Health Care are summarized in Exhibit 2. The net effects of November's transactions and adjustments on the Family Health Care's liquidity and profitability metrics are also shown in Exhibit 3.

Objective 4

Prepare financial statements using accrual concepts of accounting, including a classified balance sheet.

Financial Statements

Based on the summary of transactions and adjustments shown in Exhibit 2, Family Health Care's financial statements for November are described and illustrated in this section. These financial statements are shown in Exhibits 4, 5, 6, and 7.

Exhibit 2 Family Health Care Summary of Transactions and Adjustments for November

Financial Statement Effects

BALANCE SHEET

	Assets							=	Liabilities				+ Stockholders' Equity	
	Cash	+ Accts. Rec.	+ Prepaid Insur.	+ Supp.	+ Office Equip.	− Acc. Depr.	+ Land	=	Notes Pay.	+ Accts. Pay.	+ Wages Pay.	+ Unearned Revenue	+ Common Stock	+ Retained Earnings
Balances, Nov 1	7,320						12,000		10,000				6,000	3,320
a. Received rent	1,800											1,800		
b. Paid insurancec	(2,400)		2,400											
c. Paid insurance	(6,000)		6,000											
d. Issued stock	5,000												5,000	
e. Pur. supplies				240						240				
f. Pur. off. equip.	(1,700)				8,500				6,800					
g. Fees earned		6,100												6,100
h. Fees earned	5,500													5,500
i. Collected rec.	4,200	(4,200)								(100)				
j. Paid on acct.	(100)													
k. Paid expenses	(4,690)													(4,690)
l. Dividends	(1,200)													(1,200)
a1. Insurance exp.			(1,100)											(1,100)
a2. Supplies exp.				(150)										(150)
a3. Depr. exp.						(160)								(160)
a4. Rent revenue												(360)		360
a5. Wages exp.											220			(220)
a6. Fees earned		750												750
Balances Nov.30	7,730	2,650	7,300	90	8,500	(160)	12,000		16,800	140	220	1,440	11,000	8,510

STATEMENT OF CASH FLOWS

a. Operating	1,800
b. Operating	(2,400)
c. Operating	(6,000)
d. Financing	5,000
f. Investing	(1,700)
h. Operating	5,500
i. Operating	4,200
j. Operating	(100)
k. Operating	(4,690)
l. Financing	(1,200)
Increase in cash	410
Nov. 1 cash bal.	7,320
Nov. 30 cash bal.	7,730

INCOME STATEMENT

g. Fees earned	6,100
h. Fees earned	5,500
k. Wages exp	(2,790)
Rent exp.	(800)
Utilities exp.	(580)
Interest exp.	(100)
Misc exp.	(420)
a1. Insur. exp.	(1,100)
a2. Supplies exp.	(150)
a3. Depr. exp.	(160)
a4. Rent revenue	360
a5. Wages exp.	(220)
a6. Fees earned	750
Net income	6,390

Exhibit 3 Family Health Care Summary of Metric Effects for November

LIQUIDITY		PROFITABILITY
Transaction and Adjustments	**Quick Assets**	**Net Income – Accrual Basis**
a. Received rent	$1,800	–
b. Paid insurance	(2,400)	–
c. Paid insurance	(6,000)	–
d. Issued stock	5,000	–
e. Pur. supplies	–	–
f. Pur. office equip.	(1,700)	–
g. Fees earned	6,100	$6,100
h. Fees earned	5,500	5,500
i. Collected receivable	–	–
j. Paid on account	(100)	–
k. Paid expenses	(4,690)	(4,690)
l. Paid dividends	(1,200)	–
Adjustments		
Adj. a1. Insurance exp.	–	(1,100)
Adj. a2. Supplies exp.	–	(150)
Adj. a3. Depr. exp.	–	(160)
Adj. a4. Rent revenue	–	360
Adj. a5. Wages exp.	–	(220)
Adj. a6. Fees earned	750	750
Total	$3,060	$6,390

Quick Assets increased by $3,060 and Net Income – Accrual Basis was $6,390 for November. The net income of $6,390 will be reported on Family Health Care's November income statement.

Income Statement

The income statement is shown in Exhibit 4. It is prepared by summarizing the revenue and expense transactions listed under the Income Statement column of Exhibit 2.

Revenues are a result of providing services or selling products to customers. Examples of revenues include fees earned, fares earned, commissions revenue, interest revenue, and rent revenue.

Revenues from the primary operations of the business are reported separately from other revenue. For example, Family Health Care has two types of revenues for November fees earned and rent revenue. Since the primary operation of the business is providing services to patients, rent revenue is reported under the heading of "Other revenue."

Expenses are assets used up or services consumed in the process of generating revenues. Expenses are matched against their related revenues to determine the net income or net loss for a period. Examples of typical expenses include wages expense, rent expense,

Exhibit 4 Family Health Care Income Statement for November

Family Health Care, P.C. Income Statement For the Month Ended November 30, 20Y5		
Fees earned		$12,350
Operating expenses:		
Wages expense	$3,010	
Insurance expense	1,100	
Rent expense	800	
Utilities expense	580	
Depreciation expense	160	
Supplies expense	150	
Interest expense	100	
Miscellaneous expense	420	
Total operating expenses		(6,320)
Operating income		$ 6,030
Other revenue:		
Rent revenue		360
Net income		$ 6,390

utilities expense, supplies expense, and miscellaneous expense. Expenses are normally listed on the income statement from largest to smallest except for miscellaneous expense, which is always listed last. Expenses not related to the primary operations of the business are reported as "Other expenses."

Operating income is determined by deducting the operating expenses from the fees earned. Family Health Care has operating income of $6,030 in November. Other income consisting of $360 in rental revenue is then added to determine the net income for November of $6,390.

In a recent income statement, Apple reported operating income of $71,230 million and net income of $53,394 million.

Apple Connection

Statement of Stockholders' Equity

The statement of stockholders' equity shown in Exhibit 5 is prepared by adding the common stock issued in Transaction d of $5,000 to the November 1 balance of common stock of $6,000. This yields the November 30 balance of common stock of $11,000. The November net income of $6,390 (from the income statement), less dividends of $1,200, to the November 1 balance of retained earnings of $3,320. The result is the November 30 retained earnings of $8,510. The November 30 balances of common stock and retained earnings are also reported on Family Health Care's November 30, 20Y5, balance sheet.

In a recent statement of stockholders' equity, Apple reported common stock of $27,416 million, retained earnings of $92,284 million, other equity items of $(345) million, and total stockholders' equity of $119,355 million.

Apple Connection

Exhibit 5 Family Health Care Statement of Stockholders' Equity for November

Family Health Care, P.C.
Statement of Stockholders' Equity
For the Month Ended November 30, 20Y5

	Common Stock	Retained Earnings	Total
Balances, Nov. 1, 20Y5	$ 6,000	$3,320	$ 9,320
Common stock issued	5,000		5,000
Net income		6,390	6,390
Dividends		(1,200)	(1,200)
Balances, Nov. 30, 20Y5	$11,000	$8,510	$19,510

Balance Sheet

The balance sheet shown in Exhibit 6 is prepared from the ending balances shown in the Balance Sheet columns of Exhibit 2. The balance sheet shown in Exhibit 6 is a **classified balance sheet**. As the term implies, a classified balance sheet is prepared with various sections, subsections, and captions.

Exhibit 6 Family Health Care Balance Sheet for November

Family Health Care, P.C.
Balance Sheet
November 30, 20Y5

Assets			
Current assets:			
Cash		$ 7,730	
Accounts receivable		2,650	
Prepaid insurance		7,300	
Supplies		90	
Total current assets			$17,770
Fixed assets:			
Office equipment	$8,500		
Less accumulated depreciation	(160)	$ 8,340	
Land		12,000	
Total fixed assets			20,340
Total assets			$38,110
Liabilities			
Current liabilities:			
Accounts payable		$ 140	
Wages payable		220	
Notes payable		6,800	
Unearned revenue		1,440	
Total current liabilities			$ 8,600
Long-term liabilities:			
Notes payable			10,000
Total liabilities			$18,600
Stockholders' Equity			
Common stock		$11,000	
Retained earnings		8,510	
Total stockholders' equity			19,510
Total liabilities and stockholders' equity			$38,110

A classified balance sheet normally reports assets as the following:

- Current assets
- Fixed assets
- Intangible assets

Current assets are cash and other assets that are expected to be converted to cash or sold or used up within one year or less, through normal operations. In addition to cash, the current assets normally include accounts receivable, notes receivable, supplies, and prepaid expenses.

Accounts receivable and notes receivable are current assets because they are normally converted to cash within one year or less. **Notes receivable** are written claims against debtors who promise to pay the amount of the note plus interest. From the creditor's point of view, a note receivable is a note payable.

Exhibit 6 indicates that Family Health Care has current assets of cash, accounts receivable, prepaid insurance, and supplies as of November 30, 20Y5. These current assets total $17,770.

Fixed assets are physical assets of a long-term nature. The fixed assets may also be reported on the balance sheet as *property, plant, and equipment* or *plant assets.* Fixed assets include equipment, machinery, buildings, and land. Except for land, fixed assets depreciate over a period of time. The cost less accumulated depreciation for each major type of fixed asset is normally reported on the classified balance sheet.

Exhibit 6 indicates that Family Health Care has fixed assets of office equipment and land. The book value, cost less accumulated depreciation, of the office equipment is $8,340. The land is reported at its cost of $12,000, which when added to the book value of the office equipment yields total fixed assets of $20,340.

Intangible assets represent rights of a long-term nature, such as patent rights, copyrights, and goodwill. Goodwill arises from such factors as name recognition, location, product quality, reputation, and managerial skill. Goodwill is recorded and reported on the balance sheet when a company purchases another company at a price above the normal market value of the purchased company's assets. As shown in Exhibit 6, Family Health Care has no intangible assets.

In a recent balance sheet, Apple reported current assets of $89,378 million: property, plant and equipment of $22,471 million, and intangible assets of $27,587 million. *Apple Connection*

A classified balance sheet normally reports liabilities as:

1. Current liabilities
2. Long-term liabilities

Current liabilities are due within a short time (usually one year or less) and are to be paid out of current assets. Common current liabilities include accounts payable and notes payable. Other current liabilities include wages payable, interest payable, taxes payable, and unearned revenue.

Exhibit 6 indicates that Family Health Care has total current liabilities of $8,600 that include accounts payable, wages payable, and notes payable. Unearned revenue (rent) is also reported as a current liability, since the revenue has not yet been earned.

Long-term liabilities are not due for a long time (usually more than one year). Long-term liabilities are reported following the current liabilities.

As long-term liabilities come due and are to be paid within one year, they are reported as current liabilities. If they are to be renewed rather than paid, they would continue to be classified as long term. When an asset is pledged as security for a long-term liability, the obligation may be called a *mortgage note payable* or a *mortgage payable.*

In a recent balance sheet, Apple reported current liabilities of $80,610 million and long-term debt of $53,463 million. *Apple Connection*

Exhibit 6 indicates that Family Health Care has total long-term liabilities of $10,000, which consists of notes payable. These notes payable are not due until 20Y9. However, $6,800 of notes payable are due within the next year and thus are reported as a current liability.

A classified balance sheet normally reports stockholders' equity as:

1. Common stock, which has been invested in the company by the stockholders
2. Retained earnings, which is net income that has been retained in the corporation

Exhibit 6 reports common stock of $11,000 and the retained earnings of $8,510. These amounts are the November 30 balances for common stock and retained earnings reported on the statement of stockholders' equity in Exhibit 6.

Statement of Cash Flows

The statement of cash flows shown in Exhibit 7 is prepared by summarizing the November cash transactions. These cash transactions are shown in the Statement of Cash Flows column of Exhibit 2.

The *Cash flows from operating activities* section is prepared from the Statement of Cash Flows column of Exhibit 2 by summarizing the *Operating* activity transactions. The cash receipts from revenue transactions are added, and the cash payments for operating transactions are subtracted to determine the cash flows from operating activities.

Exhibit 7 indicates that the cash received from revenue transactions consists of $9,700 ($5,500 + $4,200) received from patients and $1,800 received from rental of the land. The cash payments for operating transactions of $13,190 ($2,400 + $6,000 + $100 + $4,690) is determined by adding the negative cash payments for operating activities shown in Exhibit 2.

The *Cash flows from investing activities* is prepared from the Statement of Cash Flows column of Exhibit 2 by summarizing the *Investing* activity transactions. During November, Family Health Care has only one investing transaction of $1,700 for the purchase of office equipment.

The *Cash flows from financing activities* section is prepared from the Statement of Cash Flows column of Exhibit 2 by summarizing the *Financing* activity transactions. During November, Family Health Care received an additional investment from Dr. Landry of $5,000 and paid dividends of $1,200.

Exhibit 7 Family Health Care Statement of Cash Flows for November

Family Health Care, P.C.
Statement of Cash Flows
For the Month Ended November 30, 20Y5

Cash flows used for operating activities:		
Cash received from patients	$ 9,700	
Cash received from rental of land	1,800	
Cash paid for expenses	(13,190)	
Net cash flows used in operating activities		$ (1,690)
Cash flows used for investing activities:		
Cash paid for office equipment		(1,700)
Cash flows from financing activities:		
Cash received from issuing common stock	$ 5,000	
Dividends paid	(1,200)	
Net cash flows from financing activities		3,800
Net increase in cash		$ 410
November 1, 20Y5, cash balance		7,320
November 30, 20Y5, cash balance		$ 7,730

In a recent statement of cash flows, Apple reported net cash flows from operating activities of $81,266 million, net cash flows used in investing activities of $(56,274) million, and net cash flows used in financing activities of $(17,716) million for a net increase in cash of $7,276 million.

Integration of Financial Statements

Exhibit 8 shows the integration of Family Health Care's financial statements for November. The reconciliation of net income and net cash flows from operations is shown in the appendix at the end of this chapter.

Exhibit 8 Integrated Financial Statements—Family Health Care

Family Health Care, P.C.
Balance Sheet
November 30, 20Y5

Assets			=	Liabilities	+	Stockholders' Equity		
Cash	+	Noncash Assets	=			Common Stock	+	Retained Earnings
$7,730		$30,380		$18,600		$11,000		$8,510
$38,110 Total Assets			=	$38,110 Total Liabilities + Stockholders' Equity				

Family Health Care, P.C.
Statement of Cash Flows
For the Month Ended Nov. 30, 20Y5

Operating act.	$(1,690)
Investing act.	(1,700)
Financing act.	3,800
Increase in cash	$ 410
Cash, Oct. 1	7,320
Cash, Oct. 31	$ 7,730

Family Health Care, P.C.
Income Statement
For the Month Ended Nov. 30, 20Y5

Revenues	$12,350
Expenses	6,320
Net income	$ 6,030
Other revenue	360
Net income	$ 6,390

Family Health Care, P.C.
Statement of Stockholders' Equity
For the Month Ended Nov. 30, 20Y5

	Common Stock	Retained Earnings	Total
Bal. Nov. 1	$ 6,000	$3,320	$ 9,320
Issued common stock	5,000		5,000
Net income		6,390	6,390
Dividends		(1,200)	(1,200)
Bal. Nov. 30	$11,000	$8,510	$19,510

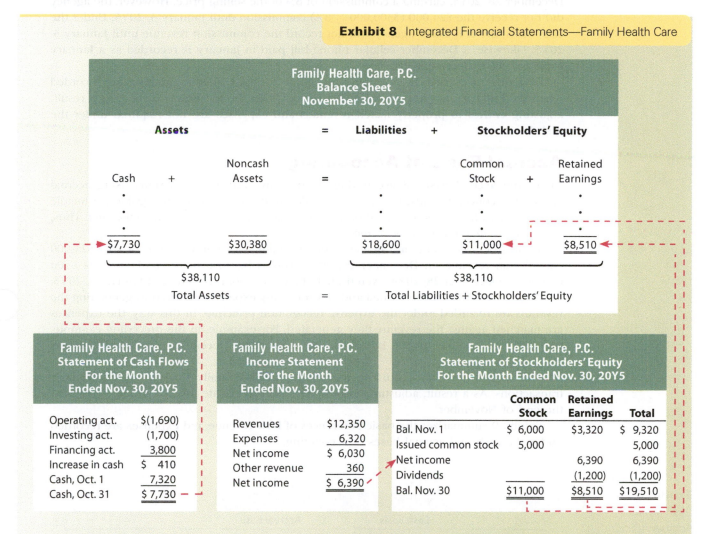

Accrual and Cash Bases of Accounting

Objective 5
Describe why generally accepted accounting principles (GAAP) requires the accrual basis of accounting is required by.

The financial statements of Family Health Care for November were prepared under accrual accounting concepts. Companies that use accrual accounting concepts for recording transactions and preparing financial statements are said to use the **accrual basis of accounting**. The accrual basis of accounting is required by generally accepted accounting principles (GAAP) and is used by large companies, such as corporations whose stock is publicly traded. Companies that record transactions only when cash is received or paid are said to use the **cash basis of accounting**.[1] Individuals and small businesses often use the cash basis of accounting.

Cash Basis of Accounting

Under the cash basis of accounting, a company records only transactions involving increases or decreases of cash. Thus, revenue is recorded only when cash is received, and expenses are recorded only when cash is paid.

To illustrate, assume that a real estate agency sells a $300,000 piece of property on December 28, 20Y4, earning a commission of 8% of the selling price. However, the agency did not receive the $24,000 ($300,000 × 8%) commission until January 3, 20Y5. Under the cash basis, the real estate agency will not record the commission revenue until January 3, 20Y5. Likewise, a December cellular phone bill paid in January is recorded as a January expense, not a December expense.

Under the cash basis, the matching concept is not used. That is, expenses are recorded when paid in cash, not necessarily in the period when the revenue is earned. As a result, adjusting entries to properly match revenues and expenses are not required under the cash basis.

Accrual Basis of Accounting

Under the accrual basis of accounting, a company records transactions using accrual accounting concepts. Thus, revenue is recorded under the revenue recognition principle when services have been rendered or a product has been delivered to the customer. Thus, cash may or may not have been received.

To illustrate, the real estate agency in the preceding example would record the $24,000 commission revenue on December 28, 20Y4. This is because the commission has been earned on December 28, 20Y4, even though the cash is not received until January 3, 20Y5.

Once revenue has been earned and recorded, any expenses incurred in generating the revenue are recorded under the expense recognition principle. In this way, the expenses are matched against the revenue they generated. For example, in the preceding example, the December cellular phone bill would be recorded in December even though it was not paid until January.

The accrual basis of accounting was used to record Family Health Care's November transactions. As a result, adjusting entries were used to update the accounting records at the end of November.

Exhibit 9 summarizes the basic differences of how revenue and expenses are recorded under the cash and accrual bases of accounting.

Exhibit 9 Cash versus Accrual Accounting

	Cash Basis	Accrual Basis
Revenue is recorded	When cash is received	When revenue is earned
Expense is recorded	When cash is paid	When expense is incurred in generating revenue
Adjusting entries	Not required	Required in order to prepare financial statements

Family Health Care Transactions

All the September and October transactions for Family Health Care in Chapter 2 involved the receipt or payment of cash. As a result, the financial statements shown in Exhibit 4

1. Some small, privately owned companies use a modified-cash basis of accounting, which includes some accrual accounting concepts. These hybrid bases of accounting are covered in advanced accounting texts.

and Exhibit 7 in Chapter 2 are the same as those that would be reported under the cash basis of accounting.

In November, Family Health Care entered into transactions that used accrual accounting concepts. As a result, the November financial statements shown in Exhibits 4 through 7 of this chapter use the accrual basis of accounting.

One of the major differences between accrual and cash basis financial statements is the reporting of net income and net cash flows from operations. Specifically, the following differences exist:

- Under the cash basis of accounting, net income and net cash flows from operating activities are equal.
- Under the accrual basis of accounting, net income and net cash flows from operating activities may be significantly different.

The net income and net cash flows from operating activities for Family Health Care are shown below.

	Net Cash Flows from Operating Activities	Net Income
September (Cash basis)	$ 2,600	$2,600
October (Cash basis)	3,220	3,220
November (Accrual basis)	(1,690)	6,390

The difference between the November net cash flows from operating activities and net income is due to the effects of accruals and deferrals.[2]

Why the Accrual Basis is Required by GAAP

Understanding why the accrual basis of accounting is required is essential to assessing and interpreting the financial condition and performance of a company. To illustrate, we use Family Health Care's November financial statements.

If the *cash basis* of accounting is used, Family Health Care's November financial statements would report negative net cash flows from operating activities and net income (loss) of $(1,690). This is because under the cash basis, net cash flows from operating activities are equal to net income. When compared to September's net income of $2,600 and October's net income of $3,220, November's operations would suggest an unfavorable trend.

If the *accrual basis* of accounting is used, Family Health Care's November financial statements report negative net cash flows from operating activities of $(1,690) but a positive net income of $6,390. When compared to September's net income of $2,600 and October's net income of $3,220, November's operations indicate a favorable trend. For example, since September, revenues have more than doubled, increasing from $5,500 to $12,350. As a result, net income has also more than doubled. Thus, Family Health Care is a profitable, rapidly expanding business.

The preceding Family Health Care illustration shows why generally accepted accounting principles (GAAP) require accrual accounting. That is, accrual accounting is generally a better predictor of the profitability of a company than is net cash flows from operating activities and the cash basis of accounting.

Net cash flow from operating activities, however, is useful. For example, in the long run, a business cannot survive if it continually reports negative cash flows from operating activities. This is true even though the company may report net income. In other words, a business *must* generate positive cash flows from operating activities in the long term in order to survive. For this reason, generally accepted accounting principles (GAAP) require reporting net cash flows from operating activities as well as net income.

Family Health Care's negative cash flows from operations of $(1,690) for November was largely due to prepaying insurance premiums of $8,400. This suggests that Family Health Care's negative cash flows from operations is temporary and not a major concern.

Family Health Care also illustrates why the financial statements must be analyzed and interpreted together rather than individually. This is the primary reason the integrated finan-

2. A reconciliation of net cash flows from operations and the net income is shown in the appendix at the end of this chapter.

cial statements approach is used throughout this text. For example, long-run profitability is best analyzed using accrual accounting and net income. The ability of the company to pay debts as they become due is best analyzed using net cash flows from operating activities.

The Accounting Cycle

The **accounting cycle** is the process that begins with analyzing transactions and ends with preparing financial statements. Using the Integrated Financial Statement Framework, the accounting cycle for the cash basis of accounting consists of the following two steps:

1. Identify, analyze, and record the effects each *cash transaction* on the balances sheet, statement of cash flows, and income statement elements (accounts).
2. Prepare financial statements.

The preceding steps for Family Health Care's September and October transactions were illustrated in Chapter 2.

Using the Integrated Financial Statement Framework, the accounting cycle for the accrual basis of accounting consists of the following three steps:

1. Using the matching concept, including the revenue and expense recognition principles, identify, analyze, and record the effects each transaction on the balances sheet, statement of cash flows, and income statement elements (accounts).
2. Assemble adjustment data and record end-of-the period adjustments.
3. Prepare financial statements.

The preceding steps for Family Health Care's November transactions were illustrated in this chapter. The Illustrative Problem at the end of this chapter illustrates these steps for Family Health Care's December transactions.

When using the Integrated Financial Statement Framework for recording transactions, the balances of the Balance Sheet columns carry forward from period to period. In contrast, the Statement of Cash Flows and Income Statement columns begin each period with no amounts or balances. This is because the statement of cash flows and income statement report the company's performance for each period independent of other periods. The balance sheet, however, reports the cumulative results of the company's performance on its financial condition.

Advanced accounting systems use a double-entry accounting system where transactions are recorded separate accounts using rules of debit and credit. The accounting cycle for a double-entry accounting system is more complex and involves more steps than the Integrated Financial Statement Framework.[3]

The double-entry accounting system is taught in accounting courses where the focus is on the mechanics of recording transactions and preparing financial statements. This focus is especially relevant for accounting majors. In contrast, we use the Integrated Financial Statement Framework to focus more on the effects of transactions on financial statements and metrics used to assess a company's performance and condition.

Objective 6

Describe and illustrate the use of the quick ratio in assessing a company's liquidity.

Metric-Based Analysis: Quick Ratio

An important aspect of a company's financial condition is its ability to pay its short-term liabilities as they become due. The liquidity metric quick assets measures the "amount" of cash and other assets that a company has on hand to pay its current liabilities. The quick ratio is a related metric used to assess a company's ability to pay its current liabilities.

The **quick ratio** is computed as quick assets divided by current liabilities. The quick ratio is a better metric than quick assets for comparing companies because, as a ratio, it eliminates the effect of size differences among companies.

3. A double-entry accounting system is described and illustrated in Appendix A at the end of this text.

To illustrate, the following data for Fly Creek Company and Huron Inc. are used.

	Fly Creek Company	Huron Inc.
Current assets:		
Cash	$ 60,000	$ 120,000
Accounts receivable	120,000	600,000
Inventories	202,000	300,000
Prepaid assets	18,000	60,000
Total current assets	$400,000	$1,080,000
Current liabilities	$150,000	$ 800,000

Fly Creek Company has $180,000 ($60,000 + $120,00) of quick assets compared to Huron Inc.'s quick assets of $720,000 ($120,000 + $600,000). Since Huron has four times ($720,000 ÷ $180,000) the amount of quick assets as Fly Creek, it would appear that Huron is in a stronger liquidity position.

However, the quick ratios for each company differ significantly, as shown below.

Fly Creek Company

$$\text{Quick Ratio} = \frac{\text{Quick Assets}}{\text{Current Liabilities}} = \frac{(\$60{,}000 + \$120{,}000)}{\$150{,}000} = \frac{\$180{,}000}{\$150{,}000} = 1.2$$

Huron Inc.

$$\text{Quick Ratio} = \frac{\text{Quick Assets}}{\text{Current Liabilities}} = \frac{(\$120{,}000 + \$600{,}000)}{\$800{,}000} = \frac{\$720{,}000}{\$800{,}000} = 0.9$$

The quick ratios indicate that Fly Creek is in a stronger liquidity position than Huron Inc. Huron's quick ratio of less than 1.0 raises concerns as to whether it will be able to pay its current liabilities on time.

Although quick ratios vary by industry, a quick ratio of at least 1.0 is normal. A quick ratio of less than 1.0, such as Huron Inc.'s ratio of 0.9, raises liquidity concerns for creditors.

Appendix

Reconciliation: Net Cash Flows from Operations and Net Income[4]

Chapter 2 illustrates the financial statements for Family Health Care for September and October 20Y5. Because all the September and October transactions were cash transactions, the net cash flows from operating activities shown on the statement of cash flows equals the net income shown in the income statements as follows:

	Net Cash Flows from Operating Activities	Net Income
September (cash basis)	$2,600	$2,600
October (cash basis)	3,220	3,220

When all of a company's transactions are cash transactions or when a company uses the cash basis of accounting, net cash flows from operating activities always equals net income. This is not true, however, under the accrual basis of accounting.

During November and December, Family Health Care used the accrual basis of accounting. The November financial statements are illustrated in Exhibits 4 through 7 of this chapter.

4. This reconciliation is referred to as the indirect method of reporting cash flows from operations.

The December financial statements for Family Health Care are illustrated in the Illustrative Problem at the end of this chapter. The net cash flows from operating activities and net income for November and December are as follows.

	Net Cash Flows from Operating Activities	Net Income
November (Accrual basis)	$(1,690)	$ 6,390
December (Accrual basis)	8,760	10,825

As shown above, net cash flows from operating activities will normally not be the same as net income under accrual accounting. Any difference can be reconciled by considering the effects of deferrals and accruals on the income statement.

Exhibit 10 illustrates the November reconciliation of Family Health Care's net income with operating cash flows from operations.

Exhibit 10 November's Reconciliation of Net Income and Cash Flows from Operations

Net income		$ 6,390
Depreciation expense	$ 160	
Changes in noncash current operating assets and liabilities:		
Increase in accounts receivable	(2,650)	
Increase in prepaid insurance	(7,300)	
Increase in supplies	(90)	
Increase in accounts payable	140	
Increase in wages payable	220	
Increase in unearned revenue	1,440	(8,080)
Net cash flows used for operating activities		$(1,690)

Exhibit 10 begins with net income and then adds or deducts the effects of accruals or deferrals that affect net income but do not result in the receipt or payment of cash. By doing so, Exhibit 10 ends with net cash flows from operating activities.

The effect of an accrual or deferral on net income is a net increase or decrease during the period. For example, during November, depreciation expense of $160 was recorded (a deferred expense) and thus deducted in arriving at net income. Yet no cash was paid. Thus, to arrive at cash flows from operations, depreciation expense is added back to net income.

Accounts receivable increased by $2,650 during November and thus was recorded as part of revenue in arriving at net income. However, no cash was received. Thus, this increase in accounts receivable is deducted in arriving at net cash flows from operations.

Prepaid insurance increased by $7,300 during November. This represents an $8,400 payment of cash for insurance premiums less $1,100 of premiums deducted in arriving at net income. Thus, the remaining $7,300 (the increase in prepaid insurance) is deducted in arriving at net cash flows from operations. Similarly, the increase in supplies of $90 is deducted.

Accounts payable also increased during November by $140, and a related expense was recorded. But, no cash was paid. Similarly, wages payable increased during November by $220, and the related wages expense was deducted in arriving at net income. However, the $220 was not paid until the next month. Thus, for November, the increases of $140 in accounts payable and $220 in wages payable are added back to net income.

Unearned revenue increased by $1,440 during November, which represents land rented to ILS Company. ILS Company initially paid Family Health Care $1,800 in advance. Of the $1,800, one-fifth ($360) was recorded as revenue for November. However, under the cash basis, the entire $1,800 would have been recorded as revenue. Thus, $1,440 (the increase in the unearned revenue) is added back to net income to arrive at net cash flows from operating activities.

During November, all the current assets are related to Family Health Care's operations. In addition, current liabilities for accounts payable and wages payable are also related to Family Health Care's operations. However, the increase in the current liability for notes payable, which increased by $6,800, is not included in the reconciliation shown in Exhibit 10. This is because the notes payable is related to the purchase of office equipment, which is an investing activity rather than an operating activity.

During November, Family Health Care did not have any decreases in current assets or current liabilities. Thus, the effects of these items are not shown in Exhibit 10. Normally, however, both increases and decreases in current assets and liabilities are included in reconciling net income and net cash flows from operating activities. For example, Family Health Care's December reconciliation, shown in the Illustrative Problem includes increases and decreases in current assets and current liabilities.

The reconciliation of net income to net cash flows from operations is normally prepared as shown in Exhibit 11.

Exhibit 11 Reconciling Items

Net income		$XXX
Depreciation expense	$XXX	
Changes in noncash current operating assets and liabilities:		
Decreases in current assets	XXX	
Increases in current liabilities	XXX	
Increases in current assets	(XXX)	
Decreases in current liabilities	(XXX)	XXX
Net cash flows from (used for) operating activities		$XXX

Key Points

1. Describe basic accrual accounting concepts, including the matching concept.

Under accrual concepts of accounting, revenue is recognized when it is earned. When revenues are earned and recorded, all expenses incurred in generating the revenues are recorded so that revenues and expenses are properly matched in determining the net income or loss for the period. Liabilities are recorded at the time a business incurs the obligation to pay for the services or goods purchased.

2. Use accrual concepts of accounting to analyze, record, and summarize transactions.

Using the integrated financial statement framework, November transactions for Family Health Care were recorded. Family Health Care's November transactions involved accrual accounting transactions.

3. Describe and illustrate the end-of-period adjustment process.

The accrual concepts of accounting require the accounting records to be updated prior to preparing financial statements. This updating process, called the adjustment process, is necessary to match revenues and expenses. The adjustment process involves two types of adjustments—deferrals and accruals. Adjustments for deferrals may involve deferred expenses or deferred revenues. Adjustments for accruals may involve accrued expenses or accrued revenues.

4. Prepare financial statements using accrual concepts of accounting, including a classified balance sheet.

A classified balance sheet includes sections for current assets; property, plant, and equipment (fixed assets); and intangible assets. Liabilities are classified as current liabilities or long-term liabilities. The income statement normally reports sections for revenues, operating expenses, other income and expense, and net income.

5. Describe how the accrual basis of accounting enhances the interpretation of financial statements.

The net cash flows from operating activities and net income will differ under the accrual basis of accounting. Under the accrual basis, net income is a better indicator of the long-term profitability of a business. For this reason, the accrual basis of accounting is required by generally accepted accounting principles (GAAP), except for very small businesses. The accrual basis reports the effects of operations on cash flows through the reporting of net cash flows from operating activities on the statement of cash flows.

The accounting cycle is the process that begins with analyzing transactions and ends with preparing the accounting records for the next accounting period. The basic steps in the accounting cycle are (1) identifying, analyzing, and recording the effects of transactions on the accounting equation; (2) identifying, analyzing, and recording adjustment data; and (3) preparing financial statements.

6. Metric-Based Analysis: Describe and illustrate the use of the quick ratio in assessing a company's liquidity.

A company's liquidity is its ability to convert assets to cash. The quick ratio is quick assets divided by current liabilities. Quick assets are normally cash, receivables, and short-term investments. The higher the quick ratio the more liquid the company and the better its ability to pay current liabilities as they become due.

Key Terms

Account (89)
Accounting cycle (116)
Accounts payable (93)
Accounts receivable (94)
Accrual basis of accounting (87)
Accruals (99)
Accrued assets (100)
Accrued expenses (100)
Accrued liabilities (100)
Accrued revenues (100)
Accumulated depreciation (103)
Adjustment process (99)
Book value (103)
Cash basis of accounting (114)
Classified balance sheet (110)
Current assets (111)
Current liabilities (111)
Deferrals (99)
Deferred expenses (91)
Deferred revenues (99)
Depreciation (103)
Expense recognition principle (88)
Fixed assets (111)
Intangible assets (111)
Long-term liabilities (111)
Matching concept (88)
Net Income – Accrual Basis (89)
Notes receivable (111)
Prepaid expenses (91)
Quick assets (89)
Quick ratio (116)
Revenue recognition principle (88)
Unearned revenues (99)

Illustrative Problem

Assume that the December transactions for Family Health Care are as follows:

a. Received cash of $1,900 from patients for services provided on account during November.
b. Provided services of $10,800 on account.
c. Received $6,500 for services provided for patients who paid cash.
d. Purchased supplies on account, $400.
e. Received $6,900 from insurance companies that paid on patients' accounts for services that had been previously billed.
f. Paid $310 on account for supplies that had been purchased.
g. Expenses paid during December were as follows: wages, $4,200, including $220 accrued at the end of November; rent, $800; utilities, $610; interest, $100; and miscellaneous, $520.
h. Paid dividends of $1,200 to stockholder (Dr. Landry).

Instructions

1. Record the December transactions, using the integrated financial statement framework as shown below. The beginning balances of December 1 have already been entered. After each transaction, you should enter a balance for each item. The transactions are recorded similarly to those for November. You should note that in transaction (g), the $4,200 of wages paid includes wages of $220 that were accrued at the end of November. Thus, only $3,980 ($4,200 – $220) should be recorded as wages expense for December. The remaining $220 reduces the wages payable.

Financial Statement Effects

BALANCE SHEET

	Assets							=	Liabilities				+ Stockholders' Equity	
	Cash +	Accts. Rec. +	Prepaid Insur	+ Supp.	+ Office Equip. –	Acc. Depr. +	Land =		Notes Pay. +	Accts. Pay. +	Wages Pay. +	Unearned Revenue +	Common Stock +	Retained Earnings
Balances, Dec. 1	7,730	2,650	7,300	90	8,500	(160)	12,000		16,800	140	220	1,440	11,000	8,510

STATEMENT OF CASH FLOWS

INCOME STATEMENT

2. The adjustment data for December are as follows:

Deferred expenses:

a1 Prepaid insurance expired, $1,100.

a2 Supplies used, $275.

a3 Depreciation on office equipment, $160.

Deferred revenues:

a4 Unearned revenue earned, $360.

Accrued expense:

a5 Wages owed employees but not paid, $340.

Accrued revenue:

a6 Services provided but not billed to insurance companies, $1,050.

Enter the adjustments in the integrated financial statement framework. Identify each adjustment by "a" and the number of the related adjustment item. For example, the adjustment for prepaid insurance should be identified as (a1).

3. Prepare the December financial statements, including the income statement, statement of stockholders' equity, balance sheet, and statement of cash flows. Note that the current portion of notes payable is $6,800.
4. Indicate the effects of each transaction on liquidity metric Quick Assets and profitability metric Net Income—Accrual Basis.
5. (Appendix) Reconcile the December net income with the net cash flows from operations. (*Note:* In computing increases and decreases in amounts, use adjusted balances.)

Solution

1. and 2. Family Health Care summary of transactions and adjustments for December:

Financial Statement Effects

BALANCE SHEET

	Assets							= Liabilities				+ Stockholders' Equity	
	Cash +	Accts. Rec. +	Prepaid Insur.	+ Supp.	+ Office Equip. –	Acc. Depr. +	Land =	Notes Pay. +	Accts. Pay. +	Wages Pay.	+ Unearned Revenue +	Common Stock +	Retained Earnings
Balances,Dec. 1	7,730	2,650	7,300	90	8,500	(160)	12,000	16,800	140	220	1,440	11,000	8,510
a. Collected rece.	1,900	(1,900)											
Balances	9,630	750	7,300	90	8,500	(160)	12,000	16,800	140	220	1,440	11,000	8,510
b. Earned fees		10,800											10,800
Balances	9,630	11,550	7,300	90	8,500	(160)	12,000	16,800	140	220	1,440	11,000	19,310
c. Earned fees	6,500												6,500
Balances	16,130	11,550	7,300	90	8,500	(160)	12,000	16,800	140	220	1,440	11,000	25,810
d. Pur. supplies				400					400				
Balances	16,130	11,550	7,300	490	8,500	(160)	12,000	16,800	540	220	1,440	11,000	25,810
e. Collected cash	6,900	(6,900)											
Balances	23,030	4,650	7,300	490	8,500	(160)	12,000	16,800	540	220	1,440	11,000	25,810
f. Paid accts. pay.	(310)								(310)				
Balances	22,720	4,650	7,300	490	8,500	(160)	12,000	16,800	230	220	1,440	11,000	25,810
g. Paid expenses	(6,230)									(220)			(6,010)
Balances	16,490	4,650	7,300	490	8,500	(160)	12,000	16,800	230	0	1,440	11,000	19,800
h. Paid dividends	(1,200)												(1,200)
Balances	15,290	4,650	7,300	490	8,500	(160)	12,000	16,800	230	0	1,440	11,000	18,600
a1. Insurance exp.			(1,100)										(1,100)
Balances	15,290	4,650	6,200	490	8,500	(160)	12,000	16,800	230	0	1,440	11,000	17,500
a2. Supplies exp.				(275)									(275)
Balances	15,290	4,650	6,200	215	8,500	(160)	12,000	16,800	230	0	1,440	11,000	17,225
a3. Depr. exp.						(160)							(160)
Balances	15,290	4,650	6,200	215	8,500	(320)	12,000	16,800	230	0	1,440	11,000	17,065
a4. Rent revenue											(360)		360
Balances	15,290	4,650	6,200	215	8,500	(320)	12,000	16,800	230	0	1,080	11,000	17,425
a5. Wages exp.										340			(340)
Balances	15,290	4,650	6,200	215	8,500	(320)	12,000	16,800	230	340	1,080	11,000	17,085
a6. Fees earned		1,050											1,050
Balances Dec. 31	15,290	5,700	6,200	215	8,500	(320)	12,000	16,800	230	340	1,080	11,000	18,135

STATEMENT OF CASH FLOWS

a. Operating	1,900
b. Operating	6,500
c. Operating	6,900
d. Operating	(310)
f. Operating	(6,230)
h. Financing	(1,200)
Net increase in cash	7,560
Beginning cash bal.	7,730
Ending cash bal.	15,290

INCOME STATEMENT

g. Fees earned	10,800
h. Fees earned	6,500
k. Wages exp.	(3,980)
Rent exp.	(800)
Utilities exp.	(610)
Interest exp.	(100)
Misc exp.	(520)
a1. Insur. exp.	(1,100)
a2. Supplies exp.	(275)
a3. Depr. exp.	(160)
a4. Rent revenue	360
a5. Wages exp.	(340)
a6. Fees earned	1,050
Net income	10,825

3.

FAMILY HEALTH CARE, P.C.
Income Statement
For the Month Ended December 31, 20Y5

Fees earned		$18,350
Operating expenses:		
Wages expense	$4,320	
Insurance expense	1,100	
Rent expense	800	
Utilities expense	610	
Supplies expense	275	
Depreciation expense	160	
Interest expense	100	
Miscellaneous expense	520	
Total operating expenses		(7,885)
Operating income		$10,465
Other revenue		
Rent revenue		360
Net income		$10,825

FAMILY HEALTH CARE, P.C.
Statement of Stockholders' Equity
For the Month Ended December 31, 20Y5

	Common Stock	Retained Earnings	Total
Bal. Dec. 1	$11,000	$ 8,510	$19,510
Net income		10,825	10,825
Dividends		(1,200)	(1,200)
Bal. Dec. 31	$11,000	$18,135	$29,135

FAMILY HEALTH CARE, P.C.
Balance Sheet
December 31, 20Y5

Assets			
Current assets:			
Cash		$15,290	
Accounts receivable		5,700	
Prepaid insurance		6,200	
Supplies		215	
Total current assets			$27,405
Fixed assets:			
Office equipment	$8,500		
Less accumulated depreciation	(320)	$ 8,180	
Land		12,000	
Total fixed assets			20,180
Total assets			$47,585
Liabilities			
Current liabilities:			
Accounts payable		$ 230	
Wages payable		340	
Notes payable		6,800	
Unearned revenue		1,080	
Total current liabilities			$ 8,450
Long-term liabilities:			
Notes payable			10,000
Total liabilities			$18,450
Stockholders' Equity			
Capital stock		$11,000	
Retained earnings		18,135	
Total stockholders' equity			29,135
Total liabilities and stockholders' equity			$47,585

FAMILY HEALTH CARE, P.C.
Statement of Cash Flows
For the Month Ended December 31, 20Y5

Cash flows from operating activities:		
Cash received from patients	$15,300	
Cash paid for expenses	(6,540)	
Net cash flows from operating activities		$ 8,760
Cash flows from financing activities:		
Cash dividends paid		(1,200)
Net increase in cash		$ 7,560
December 1, 20Y5, cash balance		7,730
December 31, 20Y5, cash balance		$15,290

4.

Metric Effects

LIQUIDITY

Transaction and Adjustments	Quick Assets
a. Collected receivables	–
b. Earned fees	$10,800
c. Earned fees	6,500
d. Pur. supplies	–
e. Collected receivables	–
f. Paid accts. pay.	(310)
g. Paid expenses	(6,230)
h. Paid dividends	(1,200)
Adjustments	
a1 Insurance exp.	–
a2 Supplies exp.	–
a3 Depr. exp.	–
a4 Rent revenue	–
a5 Wages exp.	–
a6 Earned fees	1,050
Total	$10,610

PROFITABILITY

	Net Income – Accrual Basis
a. Collected receivables	
b. Earned fees	$10,800
c. Earned fees	6,500
d. Pur. Supplies	–
e. Collected receivables	–
f. Paid accts. pay.	–
g. Paid expenses	(6,010)
h. Paid dividends	–
Adjustments	
a1 Insurance exp.	(1,100)
a2 Supplies exp.	(275)
a3 Depr. exp.	(160)
a4 Rent revenue	360
a5 Wages exp.	(340)
a6 Earned fees	1,050
Total	$10,825

Note: The December 31 balance sheet indicates quick assets of $20,990 ($15,290 + $5,700), which equals the December 1 quick assets of $10,380 plus the December increase in quick assets of $10,610.

Appendix

5. December's reconciliation of net income with net cash flows from operations:

Net income		$10,825
Depreciation expense	$ 160	
Changes in noncash current operating assets and liabilities:		
Increase in accounts receivable	(3,050)	
Decrease in prepaid insurance	1,100	
Increase in supplies	(125)	
Increase in accounts payable	90	
Increase in wages payable	120	
Decrease in unearned revenue	(360)	(2,065)
Net cash flows from operating activities		$ 8,760

Self-Examination Questions

(Answers appear at the end of chapter)

1. Assume that a lawyer bills her clients $15,000 on June 30, for services rendered during June. The lawyer collects $8,500 of the billings during July and the remainder in August. Under the accrual basis of accounting, when would the lawyer record the revenue for the fees?
   A. June, $15,000; July, $0; and August, $0
   B. June, $0; July, $6,500; and August, $8,500
   C. June, $8,500; July, $6,500; and August, $0
   D. June, $0; July, $8,500; and August, $6,500
2. On January 24, 20Y8, Niche Consulting collected $5,700 it had billed its clients for services rendered on December 31, 20Y7. How would you record the January 24 transaction, using the accrual basis?
   A. Increase Cash, $5,700; decrease Fees Earned, $5,700
   B. Increase Accounts Receivable, $5,700; increase Fees Earned, $5,700
   C. Increase Cash, $5,700; decrease Accounts Receivable, $5,700
   D. Increase Cash, $5,700; increase Fees Earned, $5,700
3. Which of the following items represents a deferral?
   A. Prepaid insurance
   B. Wages payable
   C. Fees earned
   D. Accumulated depreciation
4. If the supplies account indicated a balance of $2,250 before adjustment on May 31 and supplies on hand at May 31 totaled $950, the adjustment would be:
   A. Increase Supplies, $950; decrease Supplies Expense, $950.
   B. Increase Supplies, $1,300; decrease Supplies Expense, $1,300.
   C. Increase Supplies Expense, $950; decrease Supplies, $950.
   D. Increase Supplies Expense, $1,300; decrease Supplies, $1,300.
5. The balance in the unearned rent account for Jones Co. as of December 31 is $1,200. If Jones Co. failed to record the adjusting entry for $600 of rent earned during December, the effect on the balance sheet and income statement for December would be:
   A. Assets understated by $600; net income overstated by $600.
   B. Liabilities understated by $600; net income understated by $600.
   C. Liabilities overstated by $600; net income understated by $600.
   D. Liabilities overstated by $600; net income overstated by $600.

Class Discussion Questions

1. Would AT&T and Microsoft use the cash basis or the accrual basis of accounting? Explain.
2. How are revenues and expenses reported on the income statement under (a) the cash basis of accounting and (b) the accrual basis of accounting?
3. Fees for services provided are billed to a customer during 20Y6. The customer remits the amount owed in 20Y7. During which year would the revenues be reported on the income statement under (a) the cash basis? (b) the accrual basis?
4. Employees performed services in 20Y8, but the wages were not paid until 20Y9. During which year would the wages expense be reported on the income statement under (a) the cash basis? (b) the accrual basis?
5. Which of the following accounts would appear only in an accrual basis accounting system, and which could appear in either a cash basis or an accrual basis accounting system? (a) Common Stock, (b) Fees Earned, (c) Accounts Receivable, (d) Land, (e) Utilities Expense, and (f) Wages Payable.
6. Is the Land balance before the accounts have been adjusted the amount that should normally be reported on the balance sheet? Explain.
7. Is the Supplies balance before the accounts have been adjusted the amount that should normally be reported on the balance sheet? Explain.
8. Why are adjustments needed at the end of an accounting period?

9. Identify the four different categories of adjustments frequently required at the end of an accounting period.
10. If the effect of an adjustment is to increase the balance of a liability account, which of the following statements describes the effect of the adjustment on the other account?
    a. Increases the balance of a revenue account
    b. Increases the balance of an expense account
    c. Increases the balance of an asset account
11. If the effect of an adjustment is to increase the balance of an asset account, which of the following statements describes the effect of the adjustment on the other account?
    a. Increases the balance of a revenue account
    b. Increases the balance of a liability account
    c. Increases the balance of an expense account
12. Does every adjustment have an effect on determining the amount of net income for a period? Explain.
13. (a) Explain the purpose of the accounts Depreciation Expense and Accumulated Depreciation. (b) Is it customary for the balances of the two accounts to be equal? (c) In what financial statements, if any, will each account appear?
14. Describe the nature of the assets that compose the following sections of a balance sheet: (a) current assets, (b) property, plant, and equipment.

Exercises

Obj. 2

E3-1 Transactions using accrual accounting

Terry Mason organized The Fifth Season at the beginning of February 20Y4. During February, The Fifth Season entered into the following transactions:

a. Terry Mason invested $15,000 in The Fifth Season in exchange for common stock.
b. Paid $2,700 on February 1 for an insurance premium on a 1-year policy.
c. Purchased supplies on account, $900.
d. Received fees of $28,500 during February.
e. Paid expenses as follows: wages, $10,800; rent, $3,200; utilities, $1,400; and miscellaneous, $1,600.
f. Paid dividends of $4,000.

Record the preceding transactions using the integrated financial statement framework. After each transaction, you should enter a balance for each item.

Obj. 3

E3-2 Adjustment process

Using the data from Exercise 3-1, record the adjusting entries at the end of February to record the insurance expense and supplies expense. There was $150 of supplies on hand as of February 28. Identify the adjusting entry for insurance as (a1) and supplies as (a2).

Obj. 4

✔ Net income, $10,525

app

E3-3 Financial statements

Using the data from Exercises 3-1 and 3-2, prepare financial statements for February, including income statement, statement of stockholders' equity, balance sheet, and statement of cash flows.

E3-4 Reconcile net income and net cash flows from operations.

Using the income statement and statement of cash flows you prepared in Exercise 3-3, reconcile net income with the net cash flows from operations.

Note: The spreadsheet icon  indicates an Excel template is available on the student companion site at www.cengagebrain.com.

E3-5 Accrual basis of accounting **Obj. 2**

Margie Van Epps established Health Services, P.C., a professional corporation, in March of the current year. Health Services offers healthy living advice to its clients. The effect of each transaction on the balance sheet and the balances after each transaction for March are as follows. Each increase or decrease in stockholders' equity, except transaction (h), affects net income.

Financial Statement Effects

BALANCE SHEET

	Assets			= Liabilities +	Stockholders' Equity	
	Cash	+ Accounts Receivable	+ Supplies =	Accounts Payable +	Common Stock +	Retained Earnings
a.	35,000				35,000	
b.			1,800	1,800		
Bal.	35,000		1,800	1,800	35,000	
c.	(800)			(800)		
Bal.	34,200		1,800	1,000	35,000	
d.	31,300					31,300
Bal.	65,500		1,800	1,000	35,000	31,300
e.	(25,000)					(25,000)
Bal.	40,500		1,800	1,000	35,000	6,300
f.			(1,250)			(1,250)
Bal.	40,500		550	1,000	35,000	5,050
g.		8,900				8,900
Bal.	40,500	8,900	550	1,000	35,000	13,950
h.	(6,000)					(6,000)
Bal.	34,500	8,900	550	1,000	35,000	7,950

STATEMENT OF CASH FLOWS

a. Financing	35,000
c. Operating	(800)
d. Operating	31,300
e. Operating	(25,000)
h. Financing	(6,000)
	34,500

INCOME STATEMENT

d. Fees earned	31,300
e. Expenses	(25,000)
f. Expenses	(1,250)
g. Fees earned	8,900
	13,950

a. Describe each transaction.

b. What is the amount of the net income for March?

Obj. 3

E3-6 Classify accruals and deferrals

Classify the following items as (a) deferred expense (prepaid expense), (b) deferred revenue (unearned revenue), (c) accrued expense (accrued liability), or (d) accrued revenue (accrued asset).

1. Subscriptions received in advance by a magazine publisher.
2. A three-year premium paid on a fire insurance policy.
3. Fees received but not yet earned.
4. Fees earned but not yet received.
5. Utilities owed but not yet paid.
6. Supplies on hand.
7. Salary owed but not yet paid.
8. Taxes owed but payable in the following period.

Obj. 3

E3-7 Classify adjustments

The following accounts were taken from the unadjusted trial balance of Inter Circle Co., a congressional lobbying firm. Indicate whether or not each account would normally require an adjusting entry. If the account normally requires an adjusting entry, use the following notations to indicate the type of adjustment:

AE—Accrued Expense
AR—Accrued Revenue
DR—Deferred Revenue
DE—Deferred Expense

To illustrate, the answer for the first account is as follows.

Account	Answer
Accounts Receivable	Normally requires adjustment (AR)
Accumulated Depreciation	
Common Stock	
Dividends	
Interest Payable	
Interest Receivable	
Land	
Office Equipment	
Prepaid Rent	
Supplies	
Unearned Fees	
Wages Expense	

Obj. 3
✔ a. $2,400

E3-8 Adjustment for supplies

Answer each of the following independent questions concerning supplies and the adjustment for supplies.

a. The balance in the supplies account, before adjustment at the end of the year, is $3,500. What is the amount of the adjustment if the amount of supplies on hand at the end of the year is $1,100?

b. The supplies account has a balance of $650, and the supplies expense account has a balance of $1,950 at the end of the first year of operations. What was the amount of supplies purchased during the year?

E3-9 Adjustment for prepaid insurance

Obj. 3

The prepaid insurance account had a balance of $9,600 at the beginning of the year. The account was increased for $28,800 for premiums on policies purchased during the year. What is the adjustment required at the end of the year for each of the following independent situations? Indicate each account affected, whether the account is increased or decreased, and the amount of the increase or decrease.

a. The amount of unexpired insurance applicable to future periods is $12,000.

b. The amount of insurance expired during the year is $31,200.

E3-10 Adjustment for unearned fees

Obj. 3

The balance in the unearned fees account, before adjustment at the end of the year, is $1,375,000. What is the adjustment if the amount of unearned fees at the end of the year is $1,100,000? Indicate each account affected, whether the account is increased or decreased, and the amount of the increase or decrease.

E3-11 Adjustment for unearned revenue

Obj. 3

For a recent year, Microsoft Corporation (MSFT) reported short-term unearned revenue of $23,223 million. For the same year, Microsoft also reported total revenues of $93,580 million.

a. Assume that Microsoft recognized $2,000 million of unearned revenue as revenue during the year, what entry for unearned revenue did Microsoft make during the year? Indicate each account affected, whether the account is increased or decreased, and the amount of the increase or decrease.

b. What percentage of total revenues is the short-term unearned revenue? Round to one decimal place.

E3-12 Effect of omitting adjustment

Obj. 3

At the end of August, the first month of the business year, the usual adjustment transferring rent earned of $36,750 to a revenue account from the unearned rent account was omitted. Indicate which items will be incorrectly stated because of the error on (a) the income statement for August and (b) the balance sheet as of August 31. Also indicate whether the items in error will be overstated or understated.

E3-13 Adjustment for accrued salaries

Obj. 3

Laguna Realty Co. pays weekly salaries of $8,000 on Friday for a five-day week ending on that day. What is the adjustment at the end of the accounting period, assuming that the period ends (a) on Monday or (b) on Wednesday? Indicate each account affected, whether the account is increased or decreased, and the amount of the increase or decrease.

E3-14 Determine wages paid

Obj. 3

The balances of the two accounts related to wages at October 31, after adjustments at the end of the first year of operations, are Wages Payable, $11,900, and Wages Expense, $825,000. Determine the amount of wages paid during the year.

E3-15 Effect of omitting adjustment

Obj. 3

Accrued salaries of $6,750 owed to employees for December 30 and 31 were not considered when preparing the financial statements for the year ended December 31, 20Y6. Indicate which items will be erroneously stated because of the error on (a) the income statement for December 20Y6 and (b) the balance sheet as of December 31, 20Y6. Also indicate whether the items in error will be overstated or understated.

Obj. 3

E3-16 Effect of omitting adjustment

Assume that the error in Exercise 3-15 was not corrected and that the $6,750 of accrued salaries was included in the first salary payment in January 20Y7. Indicate which items will be erroneously stated because of failure to correct the initial error on (a) the income statement for January 20Y7 and (b) the balance sheet as of January 31, 20Y7.

Obj. 3

E3-17 Effects of errors on financial statements

For a recent year, the balance sheet for The Campbell Soup Company (CPB) includes accrued expenses of $553 million. The income before taxes for the year was $1,073 million.

a. Assume the accruals apply to the current year and were not recorded at the end of the year. By how much would income before taxes have been misstated?

b. What is the percentage of the misstatement in (a) to the reported income of $1,073 million? Round to one decimal place.

Obj. 3

✔ 1. (a) Revenue understated, $175,000

E3-18 Effects of errors on financial statements

The accountant for Healthy Medical Co., a medical services consulting firm, mistakenly omitted adjusting entries for (a) unearned revenue earned during the year ($175,000) and (b) accrued wages ($12,300). Indicate the effect of each error, considered individually, on the income statement for the current year ended August 31. Also indicate the effect of each error on the August 31 balance sheet. Set up a table similar to the following, and record your answers by inserting the dollar amount in the appropriate spaces. Insert a zero if the error does not affect the item.

	Error (a)		Error (b)	
	Over-stated	Under-stated	Over-stated	Under-stated
1. Revenue for the year would be	$ ____	$ ____	$ ____	$ ____
2. Expenses for the year would be	$ ____	$ ____	$ ____	$ ____
3. Net income for the year would be	$ ____	$ ____	$ ____	$ ____
4. Assets at August 31 would be	$ ____	$ ____	$ ____	$ ____
5. Liabilities at August 31 would be	$ ____	$ ____	$ ____	$ ____
6. Stockholders' equity at August 31 would be	$ ____	$ ____	$ ____	$ ____

Obj. 3

E3-19 Effects of errors on financial statements

If the net income for the current year had been $2,224,600 in Exercise 3-18, what would have been the correct net income if the proper adjustments had been made?

Obj. 3

E3-20 Adjustment for accrued fees

At the end of the current year, $47,700 of fees have been earned but not billed to clients.

a. What is the adjustment to record the accrued fees? Indicate each account affected, whether the account is increased or decreased, and the amount of the increase or decrease.

b. If the cash basis rather than the accrual basis had been used, would an adjustment have been necessary? Explain.

Obj. 3

E3-21 Adjustments for unearned and accrued fees

The balance in the unearned fees account, before adjustment at the end of the year, is $900,000. Of these fees, $775,000 have been earned. In addition, $289,500 of fees have been earned but not billed to clients. What are the adjustments (a) to adjust the unearned fees account and (b) to record the accrued fees? Indicate each account affected, whether the account is increased or decreased, and the amount of the increase or decrease.

E3-22 Effect on financial statements of omitting adjustment

Obj. 3

The adjustment for accrued fees of $13,400 was omitted at July 31, the end of the current year. Indicate which items will be in error because of the omission on (a) the income statement for the current year and (b) the balance sheet as of July 31. Also indicate whether the items in error will be overstated or understated.

E3-23 Adjustment for depreciation

Obj. 3

The estimated amount of depreciation on equipment for the current year is $133,000.

a. How is the adjustment recorded? Indicate each account affected, whether the account is increased or decreased, and the amount of the increase or decrease.

b. If the adjustment in (a) was omitted, which items would be erroneously stated on (1) the income statement for the year and (2) the balance sheet as of December 31?

E3-24 Adjustments

Obj. 3

Clean Air Company is a consulting firm specializing in pollution control. The following adjustments were made for Clean Air Company:

Account	Adjustments Increase (Decrease)
Accounts Receivable	$11,250
Supplies	(1,350)
Prepaid Insurance	(1,800)
Accumulated Depreciation—Equipment	7,500
Wages Payable	4,500
Unearned Rent	(9,000)
Fees Earned	11,250
Wages Expense	4,500
Supplies Expense	1,350
Rent Revenue	9,000
Insurance Expense	1,800
Depreciation Expense	7,500

Identify each of the six pairs of adjustments. For each adjustment, indicate the account, whether the account is increased or decreased, and the amount of the adjustment. No account is affected by more than one adjustment. Use the following format. The first adjustment is shown as an example.

Adjustment	Account	Increase or Decrease	Amount
1.	Accounts Receivable	Increase	$11,250
	Fees Earned	Increase	11,250

E3-25 Book value of fixed assets

Obj. 4

For a recent year, Barnes & Noble Inc. (BKS) reported (in thousands) *Property and Equipment* of $3,076,299 and *Accumulated Depreciation* of $2,627,007.

a. What was the book value of the fixed assets?

b. Would the book values of Barnes & Noble's fixed assets normally approximate their fair market values?

E3-26 Classify assets

Obj. 4

Identify each of the following as (a) a current asset or (b) property, plant, and equipment:

1. Accounts Receivable
2. Building
3. Cash
4. Office Equipment
5. Prepaid Insurance
6. Supplies

Obj. 4

E3-27 Balance sheet classification

At the balance sheet date, a business owes a five-year mortgage note payable of $480,000, the terms of which provide for monthly payments of $8,000. Explain how the liability should be classified on the balance sheet.

Obj. 4

✔ Total assets, $1,185,000

E3-28 Classified balance sheet

Pounds-Away Services Co. offers personal weight reduction consulting services to individuals. On November 30, 20Y9, the balances of selected accounts of Pounds-Away Services Co. are as follows:

Accounts Payable	$135,600	Prepaid Insurance	$ 28,800
Accounts Receivable	129,000	Prepaid Rent	21,600
Accum. Depreciation—Equipment	120,000	Retained Earnings	855,000
Cash	?	Salaries Payable	26,400
Common Stock	150,000	Supplies	48,000
Equipment	990,000	Unearned Fees	18,000

Prepare a classified balance sheet that includes the correct balance for Cash.

Obj. 4

✔ Total assets, $774,604

E3-29 Classified balance sheet

La-Z-Boy Inc. (LZB) is one of the world's largest manufacturer of furniture and is best known for its reclining chairs. The following data (in thousands) were adapted from recent financial statements:

Accounts payable	$ 46,168
Accounts receivable	158,548
Accrued expenses	108,326
Accumulated depreciation	325,993
Common stock	50,747
Cash	107,938
Intangible assets	20,622
Inventories	156,789
Debt due within one year	397
Long-term debt	433
Other current assets	53,176
Other long-term assets	103,495
Other long-term liabilities	86,180
Other stockholders' equity items	246,847
Property, plant, and equipment	500,029
Retained earnings	235,506

Prepare a classified balance sheet as of April 25.

Obj. 4

E3-30 Balance sheet

List any errors you can find in the following balance sheet. Prepare a corrected balance sheet.

ATLAS SERVICES CO.
Balance Sheet
For the Year Ended May 31, 20Y5

Assets

Current assets:		
Cash	$ 12,000	
Accounts payable	47,900	
Supplies	4,800	
Prepaid insurance	17,400	
Land	400,000	
Total current assets		$482,100
Property, plant, and equipment:		
Building	$225,000	
Equipment	90,000	
Total property, plant, and equipment		315,000
Total assets		$797,100

Liabilities		
Current liabilities:		
Accounts receivable	$ 40,800	
Accumulated depreciation—building	54,600	
Accumulated depreciation—equipment	32,400	
Net loss	44,200	
Total liabilities		$172,000
Stockholders' Equity		
Wages payable	$ 8,100	
Common stock	200,000	
Retained earnings	447,000	
Total stockholders' equity		655,100
Total liabilities and stockholders' equity		$797,100

Problems

P3-1 Accrual basis accounting

Obj. 2

San Mateo Health Care Inc. is owned and operated by Rachel Fields, the sole stockholder. During January 20Y6, San Mateo Health Care entered into the following transactions:

- Jan. 1 Received $27,000 from Hillard Company as rent for the use of a vacant office in San Mateo Health Care's building. Hillard paid the rent nine months in advance.
- 1 Paid $6,000 for a one-year general insurance business policy.
- 6 Purchased supplies of $1,800 on account.
- 9 Collected $32,000 for services provided to customers on account.
- 11 Paid creditors $5,000 on account.
- 18 Invested an additional $10,000 in the business in exchange for common stock.
- 20 Billed patients $52,000 for services provided on account.
- 25 Received $15,000 for services provided to customers who paid cash.
- 30 Paid expenses as follows: wages, $31,000; utilities, $8,500; rent on medical equipment, $5,300; interest, $200; and miscellaneous, $3,000.
- 30 Paid dividends of $8,000 to stockholder (Dr. Fields).

Instructions

Analyze and record the January transactions for San Mateo Health Care Inc., using the integrated financial statement framework. Record each transaction by date, and show the balance for each item after each transaction. The January 1, 20Y6, balances for the balance sheet are shown below.

	Assets						**=**	**Liabilities**				**+**	**Stockholders' Equity**	
	Cash +	Accts. Rec. +	Pre. Ins. +	Supp. +	Building −	Acc. Depr. +	Land =	Accts. Pay. +	Un. Rev. +	Wages Pay. +	Notes Pay. +		Common Stock +	Retained Earnings
Bal., Jan.1	20,000	44,500	700	1,200	150,000	(11,200)	120,000	7,700	0	0	30,000		50,000	237,500

Obj. 3

P3-2 Adjustment process

Adjustment data for San Mateo Health Care Inc. for January are as follows:

1. Insurance expired, $900.
2. Supplies on hand on January 31, $1,200.
3. Depreciation on building, $2,300.
4. Unearned rent revenue earned, $3,000.
5. Wages owed employees but not paid, $2,900.
6. Services provided but not billed to patients, $5,000.

Instructions

Based on the transactions recorded in January for Problem 3-1, record the adjustments for January using the integrated financial statement framework.

Obj. 4

✔ 1. Net income, $19,100

P3-3 Financial statements

Data for San Mateo Health Care for January are provided in Problems 3-1 and 3-2.

Instructions

Prepare an income statement, statement of stockholders' equity, and a classified balance sheet for January. The note payable is due in ten years.

Obj. 4

✔ Net cash flows from operating activities, $15,000

P3-4 Statement of cash flows

Data for San Mateo Health Care for January are provided in Problems 3-1, 3-2, and 3-3.

Instructions

1. Prepare a statement of cash flows for January.
2. Reconcile the net cash flows from operating activities with the net income for January. (*Hint:* See the appendix to this chapter and use adjusted balances in computing increases and decreases in accounts.)

Obj. 3

✔ Corrected net income, $127,075

P3-5 Adjustments and errors

At the end of May, the first month of operations, the following selected data were taken from the financial statements of Julie Mortenson, Attorney at Law, P.C.:

Net income for May	$127,500
Total assets at May 31	480,000
Total liabilities at May 31	150,000
Total stockholders' equity at May 31	330,000

In preparing the financial statements, adjustments for the following data were overlooked:

a. Unbilled fees earned at May 31, $9,700
b. Depreciation of equipment for May, $8,000
c. Accrued wages at May 31, $1,150
d. Supplies used during May, $975

Instructions

Determine the correct amount of net income for May and the total assets, liabilities, and stockholders' equity at May 31. In addition to indicating the corrected amounts, indicate the effect of each omitted adjustment by setting up and completing a columnar table similar to the one shown below. Adjustment (a) is presented as an example.

	Net Income	Total Assets	=	Total Liabilities	+	Total Stockholders' Equity
Reported amounts	$127,500	$480,000		$150,000		$330,000
Corrections:						
Adjustment (a)	+9,700	+9,700		0		+9,700
Adjustment (b)	______	______		______		______
Adjustment (c)	______	______		______		______
Adjustment (d)	______	______		______		______
Corrected amounts	______	______		______		______

P3-6 Adjustment process and financial statements

Obj. 3, 4

✔ 2. Net income, $82,750

Adjustment data for Ms. Ellen's Laundry Inc. for the year ended December 31, 20Y8, are as follows:

a. Wages accrued but not paid at December 31, $2,150

b. Depreciation of equipment during the year, $12,500

c. Laundry supplies on hand at December 31, $1,500

d. Insurance premiums expired, $4,600

Instructions

1. Using the following integrated financial statement framework, record each adjustment to the appropriate accounts, identifying each adjustment by its letter. After all adjustments are recorded, determine the balances.

Financial Statement Effects

BALANCE SHEET

	Assets					= Liabilities		+ Stockholders' Equity	
	Cash	+ Laundry Supplies	+ Prepaid Insurance	+ Laundry Equip.	− Acc. Depr.	= Accts. Payable	+ Wages Payable	+ Common Stock	+ Retained Earnings
Unadjusted Balances Dec. 31, 20Y8	53,000	9,000	6,000	250,000	(65,000)	7,000	0	50,000	196,000

STATEMENT OF CASH FLOWS

Operating (Revenues)	275,000
Financing (Common Stock)	25,000
Operating (Expenses)	(200,000)
Investing (Equipment)	(50,000)
Financing (Dividends)	(15,000)
Net increase in cash	35,000
Beginning cash bal., Jan. 1, 20Y8	18,000
Ending cash bal., Dec. 31, 2018	53,000

INCOME STATEMENT

Laundry revenue	275,000
Wages expense	(110,000)
Rent expense	(30,000)
Utilities expense	(18,000)
Misc. expense	(7,500)

2. Prepare an income statement and statement of stockholders' equity for the year ended December 31, 20Y8. The common stock balance as of January 1, 20Y8, was $25,000. The retained earnings balance as of January 1, 20Y8, was $101,500.
3. Prepare a classified balance sheet as of December 31, 20Y8.
4. Prepare a statement of cash flows for the year ended December 31, 20Y8.

Metric-Based Analysis

Obj. 2

MBA 3-1 Metric analysis of transactions

Using the transactions listed in E3-5 for Health Services, P.C., indicate the effects of each transaction on the liquidity metric Quick Assets and profitability metric Net Income – Accrual Basis.

Obj. 2

MBA 3-2 Metric analysis of transactions

Using the transactions listed in P3-1 for San Mateo Health Care, indicate the effects of each transaction on the liquidity metric Quick Assets and profitability metric Net Income – Accrual Basis.

Obj. 3

MBA 3-3 Metric analysis of transactions

Using the adjustment data listed in P3-2 for San Mateo Health Care, indicate the effects of each adjustment on the liquidity metric Quick Assets and profitability metric Net Income – Accrual Basis.

Obj. 3

MBA 3-4 Metric analysis of transactions

Using the adjustment data listed in P3-6 for Ms. Ellen's Laundry, indicate the effects of each adjustment on the liquidity metric Quick Assets and profitability metric Net Income – Accrual Basis.

Obj. 6

MBA 3-5 Quick ratio

GameStop Corporation (GME) has over 6,500 retail stores worldwide and sells new and used video games. The following asset and liability data (in millions) were adapted from recent financial statements.

	Year 2	Year 1
Current assets:		
Cash	$ 610	$ 536
Accounts receivable	114	85
Inventory	1,145	1,199
Prepaid and other current assets	194	130
Total current assets	$2,063	$1,950
Total current liabilities	$1,640	$1,726

1. Compute quick assets for Years 2 and 1.
2. Compute the quick ratio for Years 2 and 1. Round to two decimal places.
3. Analyze and assess any changes in liquidity for Years 2 and 1.
4. Comment on any competitive pressures that you think GameStop may be experiencing.

MBA 3-6 Quick ratio

Obj. 6

The Gap Inc. (GPS) operates specialty retail stores under such brand names as GAP, Old Navy, and Banana Republic. The following asset and liability data (in millions) were adapted from recent financial statements.

	Year 2	Year 1
Current assets:		
Cash	$1,515	$1,510
Accounts receivable	275	462
Inventory	1,889	1,928
Prepaid and other current assets	638	530
Total current assets	$4,317	$4,430
Total current liabilities	$2,234	$2,342

1. Compute quick assets for Years 2 and 1.
2. Compute the quick ratio for Years 2 and 1. Round to two decimal places.
3. Analyze and assess any changes in liquidity for Years 2 and 1.

MBA 3-7 Quick ratio

Obj. 6

American Eagle Outfitters Inc. (AEO) operates specialty retail stores, selling clothing such as denim, sweaters, t-shirts, and fleece outerwear that targets 15 to 25 year old men and women. that targets 15 to 25 year old men and women. The following asset and liability data (in millions) were adapted from recent financial statements.

	Year 2	Year 1
Current assets:		
Cash	$ 411	$ 429
Accounts receivable	68	74
Inventory	279	291
Prepaid and other current assets	133	134
Total current assets	$ 891	$ 928
Total current liabilities	$ 459	$ 415

1. Compute quick assets for Years 2 and 1.
2. Compute the quick ratio for Years 2 and 1. Round to two decimal places.
3. Analyze and assess any changes in liquidity for Years 2 and 1.

MBA 3-8 Quick ratios

Obj. 6

Compare The Gap Inc. (MBA 3-6) and American Eagle Outfitters Inc. (MBA 3-7) liquidity positions for Year 2. Comment on the differences.

MBA 3-9 Quick ratios

Obj. 6

Wal-Mart Stores Inc. (WMT) operates over retail stores throughout the world. In contrast, Alphabet Inc. (GOOG) is a technology company, formerly known as Google, that provides a variety of online services.

1. Do you think Wal-Mart or Alphabet has a higher quick ratio?
2. Using the following data (in millions) adapted from financial statements of a recent year, compute the quick ratios for Wal-mart and Alphabet. Round to two decimal places.

	Alphabet (Google)	Wal-Mart
Current assets	$72,886	$63,278
Quick assets	67,699	15,913
Total current liabilities	15,908	65,272

3. Explain the results in (2).

Cases

Case 3-1 Accrued revenue

The following is an excerpt from a conversation between Monte Trask and Jamie Palk just before they boarded a flight to Berlin on American Airlines. They are going to Berlin to attend their company's annual sales conference.

Monte: Jamie, aren't you taking an introductory accounting course at college?

Jamie: Yes, I decided it's about time I learned something about accounting. You know, our annual bonuses are based on the sales figures that come from the accounting department.

Monte: I guess I never really thought about it.

Jamie: You should think about it! Last year, I placed a $900,000 order on December 27. But when I got my bonus, the $900,000 sale wasn't included. They said it didn't ship until January 5, so it would have to count in next year's bonus.

Monte: A real bummer!

Jamie: Right! I was counting on that bonus including the $900,000 sale.

Monte: Did you complain?

Jamie: Yes, but it didn't do any good. Sophia, the head accountant, said something about matching revenues and expenses. Also, something about not recording revenues until the sale is final. I figured I'd take the accounting course and find out whether she's just jerking me around.

Monte: I never really thought about it. When do you think American Airlines will record its revenues from this flight?

Jamie: Hmmm, I guess it could record the revenue when it sells the ticket … or when the boarding passes are taken at the door … or when we get off the plane … or when our company pays for the tickets … or I don't know. I'll ask my accounting instructor.

Discuss when American Airlines should recognize the revenue from ticket sales to properly match revenues and expenses.

Case 3-2 Adjustments for financial statements

Several years ago, your brother opened Ready Appliance Repairs. He made a small initial investment and added money from his personal bank account as needed. He withdrew money for living expenses at irregular intervals. As the business grew, he hired an assistant. He is now considering adding more employees, purchasing additional service trucks, and purchasing the building he now rents. To secure funds for the expansion, your brother submitted a loan application to the bank and included the most recent financial statements (shown below) prepared from accounts maintained by a part-time bookkeeper.

READY APPLIANCE REPAIRS
Income Statement
For the Year Ended March 31, 20Y6

Service revenue		$182,500
Less: Rent paid	$41,200	
Wages paid	34,750	
Supplies paid	7,000	
Utilities paid	6,500	
Insurance paid	3,600	
Miscellaneous payments	9,100	102,150
Net income		$ 80,350

READY APPLIANCE REPAIRS
Balance Sheet
March 31, 20Y6

Assets	
Cash	$ 25,900
Amounts due from customers	18,750
Truck	55,350
Total assets	$100,000
Equities	
Owner's equity	$100,000

After reviewing the financial statements, the loan officer at the bank asked your brother if he used the accrual basis of accounting for revenues and expenses. Your brother responded that he did and that is why he included an account for "Amounts Due from Customers." The loan officer then asked whether or not the accounts were adjusted prior to the preparation of the statements. Your brother answered that they had not been adjusted.

a. Why do you think the loan officer suspected that the accounts had not been adjusted prior to the preparation of the statements?

b. Indicate possible accounts that might need to be adjusted before an accurate set of financial statements could be prepared.

Case 3-3 Business emphasis

GROUP PROJECT

Assume that you and two friends are debating whether to open an automotive and service retail chain that will be called Auto-Mart. Initially, Auto-Mart will open three stores locally, but the business plan anticipates going nationwide within five years.

Currently, you and your future business partners are debating whether to focus Auto-Mart on a "do-it-yourself" or "do-it-for-me" business. A do-it-yourself business emphasizes the sale of retail auto parts that customers will use themselves to repair and service their cars. A do-it-for-me business emphasizes the offering of maintenance and service for customers.

1. In groups of three or four, discuss whether to implement a do-it-yourself or do-it-for-me business emphasis. List the advantages of each emphasis, and arrive at a conclusion as to which emphasis to implement.
2. Provide examples of real-world businesses that use do-it-yourself or do-it-for-me business emphases.

Case 3-4 Accrual versus cash net income.

Cigna Corp. (CI) provides insurance services, and Deere & Company (DE) manufactures and sells farm and construction equipment. The following data (in millions) were adapted from recent financial statements of each company.

	Cigna	Deere
Net income (accrual basis)	$2,102	$1,940
Cash flows from operating activities	1,994	3,740
Depreciation	588	1,382

1. Compute the difference between cash flows from operating activities and net income.
2. Express the difference in (1) as a percent of accrual net income. Round to one decimal place.
3. Which company's accrual based net income is closer to what would be reported if the company used the cash basis? Why?

Case 3-5 Analysis of income and cash flows

The following data (in millions) were taken from http://finance.yahoo.com.

	Year 3	Year 2	Year 1
Company A			
Revenues	$ 12,466	$ 7,872	$ 5,089
Operating income	4,994	2,804	538
Net income	2,925	1,491	32
Net cash flows from operating activities	5,457	4,222	1,612
Net cash flows from investing activities	(5,913)	(2,624)	(7,024)
Net cash flows from financing activities	1,571	(667)	6,283
Total assets	40,184	17,895	15,103
Company B			
Revenues	$ 92,793	$ 98,367	$102,874
Operating income (loss)	18,532	20,312	22,156
Net income (loss)	12,022	16,483	16,604
Net cash flows from operating activities	16,868	17,485	19,586
Net cash flows from investing activities	(3,001)	(7,326)	(9,004)
Net cash flows from financing activities	(15,452)	(9,883)	(11,976)
Total assets	117,532	126,223	119,213
Company C			
Revenues	$233,715	$182,795	$170,910
Operating income	71,230	52,503	48,999
Net income	53,394	39,510	37,037
Net cash flows from operating activities	81,266	59,713	53,666
Net cash flows from investing activities	(56,274)	(22,579)	(33,774)
Net cash flows from financing activities	(17,716)	(37,549)	(16,379)
Total assets	290,479	231,839	207,000
Company D			
Revenues	$108,465	$ 98,375	$ 96,619
Operating income (loss)	3,137	2,725	2,764
Net income (loss)	1,728	1,519	1,497
Net cash flows from operating activities	4,163	3,573	2,954
Net cash flows from investing activities	(3,060)	(4,771)	(2,183)
Net cash flows from financing activities	(1,236)	1,361	(721)
Total assets	30,556	29,281	24,634

1. Match each of the following companies with the data for Company A, B, C, or D:
   Apple Inc. (AAPL)
   Facebook, Inc. (FB)
   International Business Machines Corporation (IBM)
   Kroger (KR)
2. Explain the logic underlying your matches.

Answers to Self-Examination Questions

1. **A** Under the accrual basis of accounting, revenues are recorded when the services are rendered. Since the services were rendered during June, all the fees should be recorded in June (answer A). This is an example of accrued revenue. Under the cash basis of accounting, revenues are recorded when the cash is collected, not necessarily when the fees are earned. Thus, no revenue would be recorded in June, $8,500 of revenue would be recorded in July, and $6,500 of revenue would be recorded in August (answer D). Answers B and C are incorrect and are not used under either the accrual or cash basis.

2. **C** The collection of a $5,700 accounts receivable is recorded as an increase in Cash, $5,700, and a decrease in Accounts Receivable, $5,700 (answer C). The initial recording of the fees earned on account is recorded as an increase in Accounts Receivable and an increase in Fees Earned (answer B). Services rendered for cash are recorded as an increase in Cash and an increase in Fees Earned (answer D). Answer A is incorrect and would result in the accounting equation being out of balance because total assets would exceed total liabilities and stockholders' equity by $11,400.

3. **A** A deferral is the delay in recording an expense already paid, such as prepaid insurance (answer A). Wages payable (answer B) is considered an accrued expense or accrued liability. Fees earned (answer C) is a revenue item. Accumulated depreciation (answer D) is a contra account to a fixed asset.

4. **D** The balance in the supplies account, before adjustment, represents the amount of supplies available during the period. From this amount, $2,250, is subtracted the amount of supplies on hand, $950, to determine the supplies used, $1,300. The used supplies is recorded as an increase in Supplies Expense, $1,300, and a decrease in Supplies, $1,300 (answer D).

5. **C** The failure to record the adjusting entry increasing Rent Revenue, $600, and decreasing Unearned Rent, $600, would have the effect of overstating liabilities by $600 and understating net income by $600 (answer C).

Chapter 4

Accounting for Retail Operations

What's Covered:

Topics: Accounting for Retail Operations

Nature
- Operating cycle (Obj. 1)
- Financial statement components (Obj. 1)

Transactions
- Purchases (Obj. 2)
- Sales (Obj. 3)
- Freight (Obj. 4)
- Sales taxes (Obj. 4)
- Buyer and seller (Obj. 5)

Financial Statements
- Adjustments (Obj. 6)
- Income statement (Obj. 7)
- Statement of stockholders' equity (Obj. 7)
- Balance sheet (Obj. 7)
- Statement of cash flows (Obj. 7)

Metric-Based Analysis
- Transactions:
  Liquidity: Working capital (Obj. 2, 3, 6)
  Profitability: Gross profit percent (Obj. 2, 3, 6)
- Financial Statements:
  Markup percent (Obj. 8)

Learning Objectives

Obj.1 Distinguish the operations and financial statements of a service business from those of a retail business.

Obj.2 Describe the accounting for the purchase of merchandise.

Obj.3 Describe the accounting for the sale of merchandise.

Obj.4 Describe the accounting for freight and sales taxes.

Obj.5 Illustrate the dual nature of merchandising transactions.

Obj.6 Describe and illustrate adjustments for retail operations.

Obj.7 Describe and illustrate the financial statements of a retail company.

Obj.8 Describe and illustrate the markup percent.

Chapter Metrics

Use the following metrics to analyze transactions and financial statements.

TRANSACTIONS

- **Liquidity: Working Capital**
- **Profitabililty: Gross Profit Percent**

FINANCIAL STATEMENTS

- **Markup Percent**

Amazon.com

Jeff Bezos, the founder of Amazon.com, started Amazon's operations from the garage of his two-bedroom home in Seattle where he set up 3 workstations and designed a computer code that would work across various computer platforms. **Amazon.com (AMZN)** began its operations in July, 1995, by selling books over the Internet. By September, Amazon was growing rapidly and was selling $20,000 books per week. To expand, Jeff solicited monies from friends and family with a 70% chance that investors would lose everything.

When Amazon started its retail operations, its primary competitors were Borders and Barnes and Noble. Neither company, however, had developed Internet operations. To continue its growth, Amazon.com offered its common stock for sale to the public on May 15, 1997, at $16 per share. Assuming you purchased one share at $16, you would now have 12 shares worth over $7,000.

Amazon is guided by four principles: customer obsession rather than competitor focus, passion for invention, commitment to operational excellence, and long-term thinking. Amazon, which was named after the South American river that has numerous branches, has expanded its products beyond books to various products, including electronics, movies, clothing, Kindle e-readers, and Fire tablets. In addition, Amazon allows sellers to offer their products on its website as well as offering digital services, such as cloud storage.

This chapter focuses on accounting issues unique to retailers. This discussion includes the recording of purchase and sales transactions as well as how retail financial statements differ from those of a service business.

Nature of Retail Operations

Objective 1
Distinguish the operations and financial statements of a service business from those of a retail business.

The operating activities of a retail and service businesses differ. These differences are reflected in the operating cycle of each business as well as in their financial statements.

Operating Cycle

The **operating cycle** of a business is the process it takes for the business to spend cash to generate revenue, earn revenues, and receive cash from customers. The operating cycle for a retail business differs from a service business in that it must purchase merchandise for sale to customers. The operating cycle for a retail business is shown in Exhibit 1.

Exhibit 1
Retail Operating Cycle

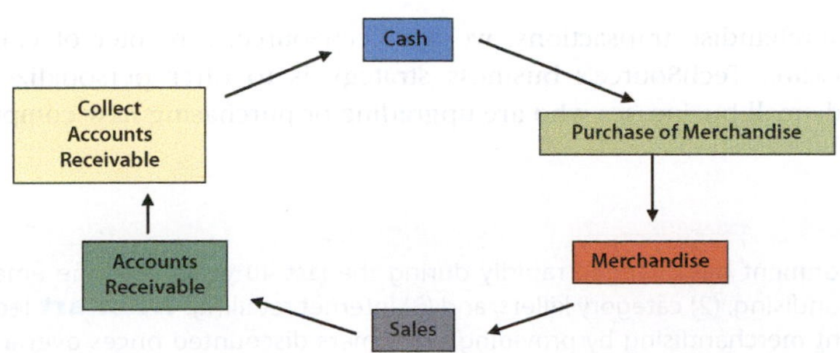

The length of time to complete an operating cycle differs among retail businesses. Grocery stores normally have short operating cycles because much of their merchandise is perishable with fixed selling dates. For example, milk has an expiration date of a week or two by which it must be sold. In contrast, jewelry stores carry expensive items often displayed months before being sold to customers.

Amazon.com Connection Because Amazon.com sells its inventory quickly, it has a short operating cycle.

Financial Statements

The differences between retail and service businesses are also reflected in their financial statements. These differences are illustrated in the following income statements:

Retail Business		Service Business	
Sales	$XXX	Fees earned	$XXX
Cost of goods sold	(XXX)	Operating expenses	(XXX)
Gross profit	$XXX	Operating income	$XXX
Operating expenses	(XXX)		
Operating income	$XXX		

The revenue activities of a retail business involve the buying and selling of merchandise. A retail business first purchases merchandise to sell to its customers. When this merchandise is sold, the revenue is reported as **sales**. The cost of the merchandise sold is reported as **cost of goods sold** or *cost of merchandise sold.* The cost of goods sold is subtracted from sales to arrive at **gross profit** or *gross margin.* This amount is called gross profit because it is the profit *before* deducting operating expenses. The operating expenses are subtracted from gross profit to arrive at **operating income**.

Amazon.com Connection In a recent income statement, Amazon.com reported sales of $70,080 million and cost of goods sold of $62,752 million, resulting in a gross profit of $7,328 million.

In contrast, the revenue activities of a service business involve providing services to customers. These revenues from services are reported on the income statement as *fees earned.* The operating expenses incurred in providing the services are subtracted from the fees earned to arrive at *operating income.*

The balance sheet of a retail business differs from a service business in that there is normally merchandise on hand (not sold) at the end of a period. This merchandise is reported as **inventory** or *merchandise inventory* in the current asset section of the balance sheet.

Objective 2 Describe the accounting for the purchase of merchandise.

Purchase Transactions

To illustrate merchandise transactions, we use TechSource, a retailer of computer hardware and software. TechSource's business strategy is to offer personalized service to individuals and small businesses who are upgrading or purchasing new computer systems.

Business Insight The retail environment has changed rapidly during the last 40 years with the emergence of (1) discount merchandising, (2) category killers, and (3) Internet retailing. **Walmart** led the development of discount merchandising by providing consumers discounted prices over a wide array of grocery, household, and electronic products. Category killers include **Toys "R" Us** (toys), Best Buy (electronics), **Home Depot** (home improvement), and **Office Depot** (office supplies). Each of these companies provides a wide selection of competitively priced goods within their market segment. Internet retailers, such as **Amazon.com**, allow consumers to shop quickly for a wide variety of products using online platforms. Retailing will continue to evolve as consumer tastes, lifestyles, and technology change.

TechSource's personal service includes a no-obligation, on-site assessment of the customer's computer needs. By providing personalized service and follow-up, TechSource hopes to compete effectively against retailers, such as **Best Buy**.

The effects of each merchandise transaction on TechSource's financial statements are illustrated using the Integrated Financial Statement Framework. In addition, the effects of each transaction on liquidity and profitability metrics are illustrated. In this chapter, we use **Working Capital** as our liquidity metric. Working capital is defined as current assets minus current liabilities. We use **Gross Profit Percent** as our profitability metric. The gross profit percent is computed as follows:

$$\text{Gross profit percent} = \frac{\text{Sales} - \text{Cost of Goods Sold}}{\text{Sales}} = \frac{\text{Gross Profit}}{\text{Sales}}$$

To illustrate, assume Crane Company has sales of $4,500,000 and cost of goods sold of $3,375,000. Crane's gross profit percent is 25%, computed as follows:

$$\text{Gross profit percent} = \frac{\text{Sales} - \text{Cost of Goods Sold}}{\text{Sales}} = \frac{\$4{,}500{,}000 - \$3{,}375{,}000}{\$4{,}500{,}000} = \frac{\$1{,}125{,}000}{\$4{,}500{,}000} = 25\%$$

In analyzing the effects of transactions, we assume that TechSource desires a minimum gross profit percent of 20%.

Perpetual and Periodic Inventory Systems

Two systems for recording and accounting for merchandise transactions exist: perpetual and periodic. In a **perpetual inventory system**, each purchase and sale of merchandise is recorded. In this way, the amount of merchandise available for sale (on hand), and the amount sold are continuously (perpetually) updated in the inventory records. Perpetual inventory records consist of the Inventory account, called the **controlling account**, and a subsidiary record of each item of inventory, called a **subsidiary ledger**. The sum of the balances of the inventory items in the subsidiary ledger equals the balance of the Inventory (controlling) account. The Inventory account and related items in the subsidiary ledger are updated for each purchase and sale.

In a **periodic inventory system**, the inventory does not show the amount of merchandise available for sale (on hand) and the amount sold. Instead, a listing of inventory on hand, called a **physical inventory**, is prepared at the end of the accounting period. This physical inventory is used to determine the cost of inventory on hand at the end of the period, which is the amount reported as Inventory on the balance sheet.

The cost of goods sold for the period is determined as follows:

Beginning inventory	$XXX
Purchases	XXX
Merchandise available for sale	$XXX
Ending inventory (from physical count)	(XXX)
Cost of goods sold	$XXX

To illustrate, assume that on January 1, 20Y5, Jones Inc. had $250,000 of inventory on hand and purchased $3,140,000 of merchandise during 20Y5. On December 31, 20Y5, Jones Inc. conducted its physical inventory and determined that $315,000 of inventory was on hand. Jones Inc.'s cost of goods sold for 20Y5 is $3,075,000, computed as follows:

Inventory, Jan. 1, 20Y5	$ 250,000
Purchases	3,140,000
Merchandise available for sale	$3,390,000
Inventory (from physical count) Dec. 31, 20Y5	(315,000)
Cost of goods sold	$3,075,000

Because many retailers use computerized systems, the perpetual inventory system is widely used. Such systems typically use bar codes, such as the one on the back of this textbook, or radio frequency identification codes embedded in each product. An optical scanner reads the bar or radio code to record merchandise when it is received (purchased). Likewise, optical scanners at cash registers record when the merchandise is sold. Because of its wide use, the perpetual inventory system is used in the remainder of this chapter.

Purchase of Merchandise for Cash

Assume that TechSource purchases $5,000 of merchandise for cash on September 3. The effects of the purchase on the TechSource's financial statements are recorded as follows:

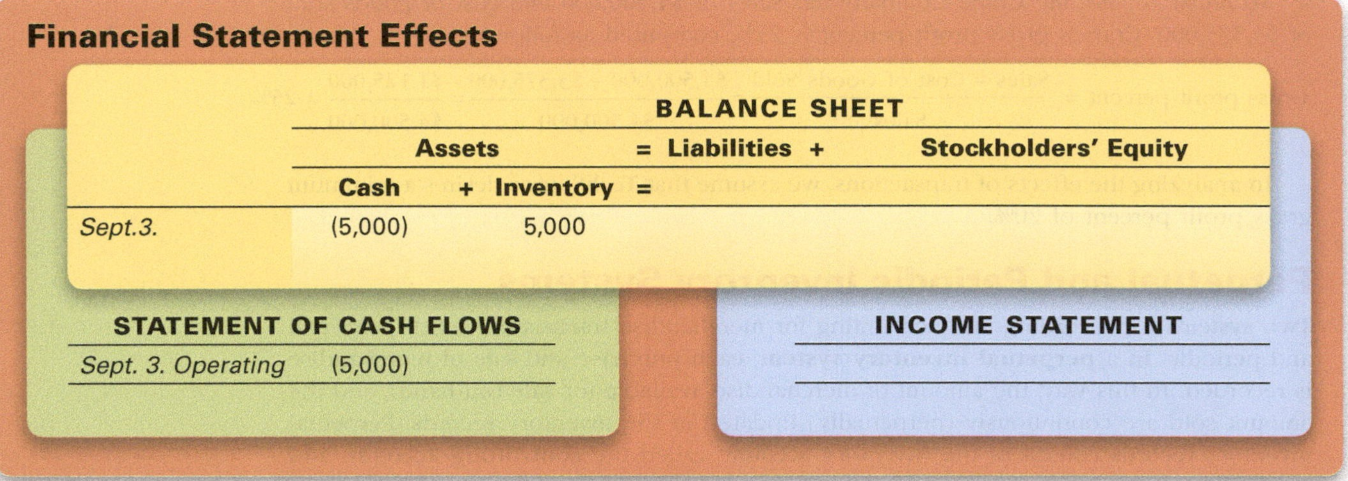

Financial Statement Effects
BALANCE SHEET
Assets = Liabilities + Stockholders' Equity
Cash + Inventory =
Sept.3. (5,000) 5,000
STATEMENT OF CASH FLOWS
Sept. 3. Operating (5,000)
INCOME STATEMENT

Transaction Metric Effects

The effects of purchasing $5,000 of merchandise for cash on the liquidity and profitability metrics are as follows:

LIQUIDITY	
Working Capital	No Effect

PROFITABILITY	
Gross Profit Percent	No Effect

Since cash and inventory are both current assets, there was no effect on working capital. Likewise, since no sale of merchandise occurred, there was no effect on the gross profit percent.

Purchase of Merchandise on Account

When merchandise is purchased on account, the terms of the purchase are normally indicated on the **invoice** or bill that the seller sends the buyer. An example of an invoice from ABC Printers for a purchase by TechSource of printers on May 29, 20Y7 is shown in Exhibit 2.

The terms for when payments for merchandise are to be made, agreed on by the buyer and the seller, are called the **credit terms**. If payment is required on delivery, the terms are *cash* or *net cash*. Otherwise, the buyer is allowed an amount of time in which to pay, known as the **credit period**.

Exhibit 2 Invoice

ABC Printers
1000 Matrix PWY
San Jose, CA 95116-1000

Invoice
106-891

SOLD TO		**CUSTOMER'S ORDER NO.**	**DATE**
TechSource 5101 Washington Ave. Cincinnati, OH 45227-5101		10537	May 29, 20Y7
DATE SHIPPED	**HOW SHIPPED AND ROUTE**	**TERMS**	**INVOICE DATE**
June 3, 20Y7	US Express Trucking Co.	2/10, n/30	June 3, 20Y7
FROM	**F.O.B.**		
Cincinnati	Cincinnati		
QUANTITY	**DESCRIPTION**	**UNIT PRICE**	**AMOUNT**
10	Printer/Fax/Scanner/Copier	150.00	1,500.00

The credit period usually begins with the date of the sale as shown on the invoice. If payment is due within a stated number of days after the date of the invoice, such as 30 days, the terms will be *net 30 days*. These terms may be written as *n/30*. If payment is due by the end of the month in which the sale was made, the terms are written as *n/eom*.

As a means of encouraging the buyer to pay before the end of the credit period, the seller may offer a discount. For example, a seller may offer a 2% discount if the buyer pays within 10 days of the invoice date. If the buyer does not take the discount, the total amount is due within 30 days. These terms are expressed as *2/10, n/30* and are read as *2% discount if paid within 10 days, net amount due within 30 days*. Using the information from the invoice in Exhibit 2, the credit terms of 2/10, n/30 are summarized in Exhibit 3.

Discounts taken by the buyer for early payment of an invoice are called **purchases discounts**. Even if the buyer has to borrow to pay within a discount period, it is normally to the buyer's advantage to take the discount.

To illustrate, the invoice shown in Exhibit 2 is used. The last day of the discount period is June 13 (invoice date of June 3 plus 10 days). Assume, that to pay the invoice on June 13, TechSource borrows $1,470, which is $1,500 less the discount of $30 ($1,500 × 2%). If an annual interest rate of 6% and a 360-day year is also assumed, the interest on the loan of $1,470 for the remaining 20 days of the credit period is $4.90 ($1,470 × 6% × 20 ÷ 360).[1]

The net savings to NetSolutions of taking the discount is $25.10, computed as follows:

Discount of 2% on $1,500	$30.00
Interest for 20 days at a rate of 6% on $1,470	(4.90)
Savings from taking the discount	$25.10

The advantage of taking the discount can also be illustrated by comparing the interest rate on the money *saved* by taking the discount and the interest rate on the money *borrowed* to take the discount. The interest rate earned by taking the discount the prior example is approximately 36%, estimated by converting 2% for 20 days to a yearly rate as follows:

$$2\% \times \frac{360 \text{ days}}{20 \text{ days}} = 2\% \times 18 = 36\%$$

1 To simplify computations and rounding, we use a 360-day year rather than a 365-year.

Exhibit 3 Credit Terms

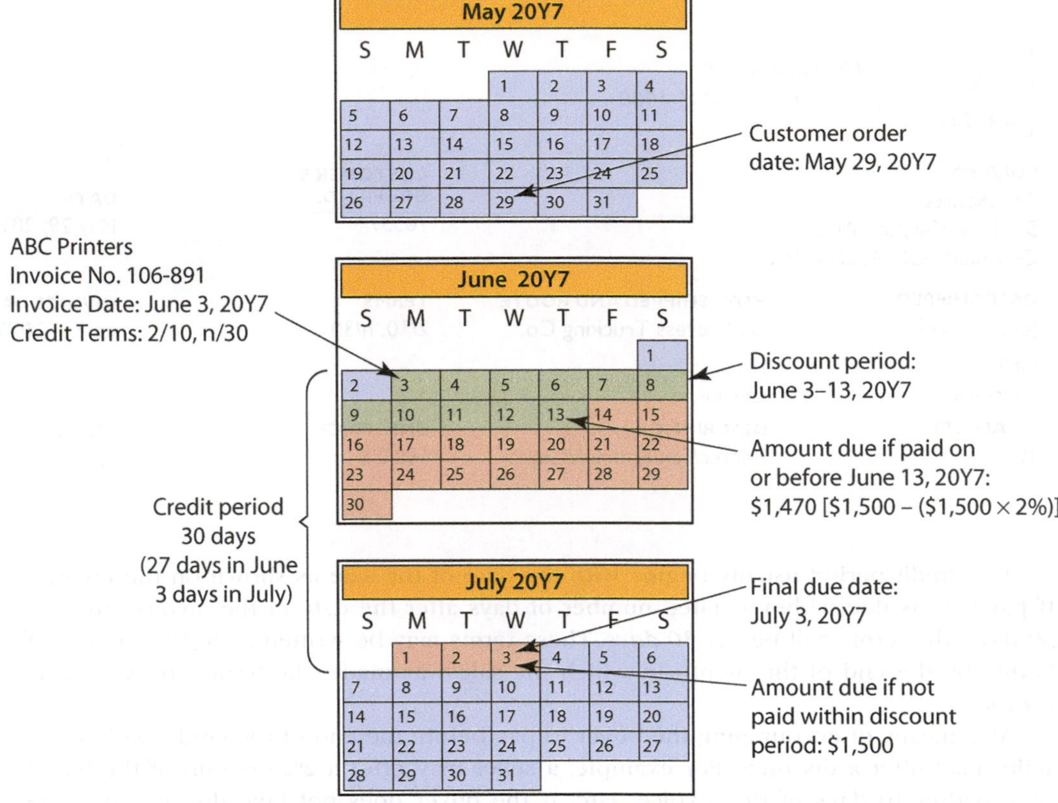

If TechSource borrows to take the discount it pays 6%, but earns 36% by paying within the discount period. Thus, buyers normally take all available purchase discounts and design their accounting systems to do so. For this reason, we assume all purchase discounts are taken throughout the remainder of this chapter.

Purchases discounts reduce the cost of the merchandise purchased. As a result, under the perpetual inventory system, purchases of merchandise are recorded by increasing Inventory for the net purchase price (invoice amount less the purchase discount).

To illustrate, the effects of the purchase shown in Exhibit 2 on the accounts and financial statements of TechSource are as follows:

Financial Statement Effects

BALANCE SHEET

	Assets	=	Liabilities	+	Stockholders' Equity
	Inventory	=	**Accounts Payable**		
June 3.	1,470		1,470		

STATEMENT OF CASH FLOWS

INCOME STATEMENT

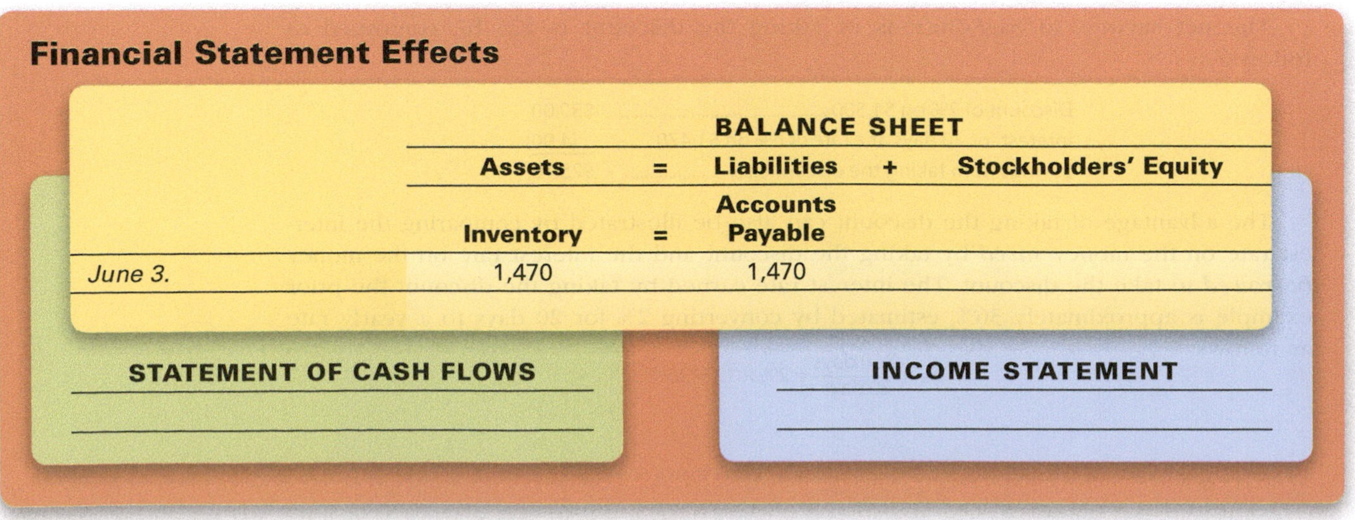

Transaction Metric Effects

The effects of purchasing merchandise on account with credit terms 2/10, n/30 on the liquidity and profitability metrics are as follows:

LIQUIDITY	
Working Capital	No Effect

PROFITABILITY	
Gross Profit Percent	No Effect

Working capital is not changed since Inventory and Accounts Payable are increased by the same amount of $1,470. Since no sale occurred, the gross profit percent is also unaffected.

The effects of paying the invoice shown in Exhibit 2 on the accounts and financial statements of TechSource are as follows:

Financial Statement Effects

	BALANCE SHEET				
	Assets	=	Liabilities	+	Stockholders' Equity
	Cash	=	Accounts Payable		
June 13.	(1,470)		(1,470)		

STATEMENT OF CASH FLOWS	
June 13. Operating	(1,470)

INCOME STATEMENT

Transaction Metric Effects

The effects of paying the invoice within the discount period on the liquidity and profitability metrics are as follows:

LIQUIDITY	
Working Capital	No Effect

PROFITABILITY	
Gross Profit Percent	No Effect

Working capital is not changed since Cash and Accounts Payable are decreased by the same amount of $1,470. Since no sale occurred, the gross profit percent is also unaffected.

Purchase Returns and Allowances

Purchases returns and allowances result when merchandise received by a buyer is defective, damaged in shipment, or not what was ordered. In these cases, the buyer may request a price adjustment or return the merchandise for full credit. The buyer normally notifies the seller of his or her intent by issuing a **debit memorandum**. The debit memorandum, sometimes called a debit memo, informs the seller of the amount the buyer proposes to decrease the account payable due the seller and why.

To illustrate, assume that TechSource issued the debit memo shown in Exhibit 4.

Exhibit 4 Debit Memorandum

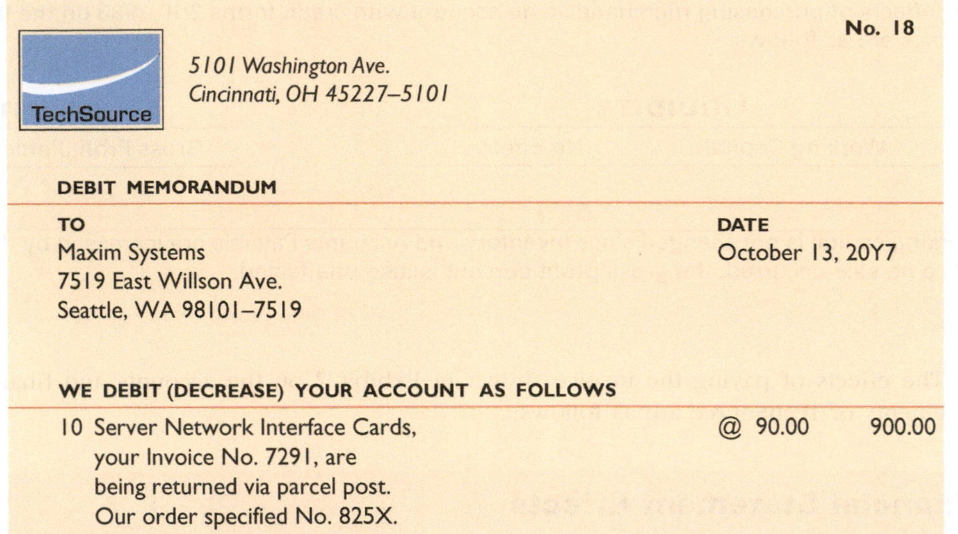
No. 18

TechSource
5101 Washington Ave.
Cincinnati, OH 45227–5101

DEBIT MEMORANDUM

TO
Maxim Systems
7519 East Willson Ave.
Seattle, WA 98101–7519

DATE
October 13, 20Y7

WE DEBIT (DECREASE) YOUR ACCOUNT AS FOLLOWS

10 Server Network Interface Cards, your Invoice No. 7291, are being returned via parcel post. Our order specified No. 825X.	@ 90.00	900.00

The effects of the purchase shown in Exhibit 3 on the accounts and financial statements of TechSource are as follows:

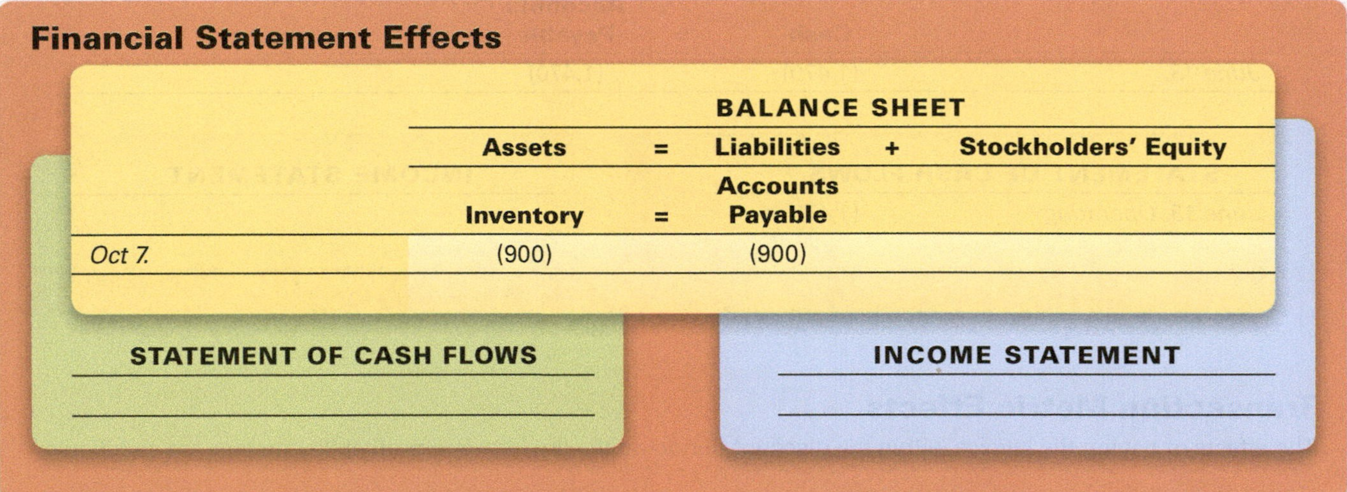

Financial Statement Effects

BALANCE SHEET

	Assets	=	Liabilities	+	Stockholders' Equity
	Inventory	=	Accounts Payable		
Oct 7.	(900)		(900)		

STATEMENT OF CASH FLOWS

INCOME STATEMENT

Transaction Metric Effects

The effects of the return of merchandise on the liquidity and profitability metrics are as follows:

LIQUIDITY	
Working Capital	No Effect

PROFITABILITY	
Gross Profit Percent	No Effect

Working capital is not changed since Inventory and Accounts Payable are decreased by the same amount of $900. Since no sale occurred, the gross profit percent is also unaffected.

If Maxim Systems' Invoice #7291 had credit terms of 2/10, n/30, TechSource would have recorded the receipt of the merchandise as $882 [$900 – ($900 x 2%)]. In addition, if instead of returning the merchandise, TechSource kept the merchandise and requested an allowance of $100, both Inventory and Accounts Payable would decrease by $100.

Integrity, Objectivity, and Ethics in Business

The Case of the Fraudulent Price Tags
One of the challenges for a retailer is policing its sales return policy. There are many ways in which customers can unethically or illegally abuse such policies. In one case, a couple was accused of attaching Marshall's store price tags to cheaper merchandise bought or obtained elsewhere. The couple then returned the cheaper goods and received the substantially higher refund amount. Company security officials discovered the fraud and had the couple arrested after they had allegedly bilked the company for over $1 million.

Sales Transactions

Objective 3
Describe the accounting for the sale of merchandise.

A retail business may sell merchandise for cash. Cash sales are normally rung up (entered) on a cash register and recorded in the accounts by increasing cash and sales. Under the perpetual inventory system, the increase in cost of goods sold and the decrease in inventory should also be recorded at the time of sale.

To illustrate, assume that on January 3, TechSource sells merchandise for $1,800 that cost $1,200 with credit terms n/30. The effect on the accounts and financial statements of these cash sales are as follows:

Financial Statement Effects

BALANCE SHEET

	Assets			= Liabilities	+	Stockholders' Equity
	Cash	+ Inventory	=			Retained Earnings
Jan 3.	1,800	(1,200)				600

STATEMENT OF CASH FLOWS

Jan. 3. Operating	1,800

INCOME STATEMENT

Jan. 3. Sales	1,800
Cost of goods sold	(1,200)

Transaction Metric Effects

The effects of the cash sale on the liquidity and profitability metrics are as follows:

LIQUIDITY

Working Capital	$600

PROFITABILITY

Gross Profit Percent (33%)	Increases ability to achieve minimum of 20%

Since Cash increased by $1,800 and Inventory decreased by $1,200, working capital increased by $600 ($1,800 – $1,200). Assume TechSource desires a minimum overall gross profit percent of 20%. Since the gross profit percent for this sale is 33% [($1,800 – $1,200) ÷ $1,800], as shown in parentheses, this sale increases TechSource's ability to achieve its overall minimum gross profit percent of 20%.

Sales made to customers using credit cards, such as MasterCard, VISA, or American Express, are treated as *cash sales*. Any processing fees charged to the retailer for use of credit cards are recorded as an expense. This expense is normally reported on the income statement as an administrative expense.

A retailer may sell merchandise on credit (on account). The effects of sales on account are similar to those for cash sales except that Accounts Receivable is increased instead of Cash. When the customer pays the amount, Accounts Receivable is decreased and Cash is increased.

Customer Discounts

A retailer may grant customers various discounts as incentives to encourage customer actions benefiting the seller. For example, a seller may offer discounts to encourage customers to purchase in volume or to order early.

Amazon.com Connection Amazon offers various customer and promotional discounts, including percentage discounts off future purchases based upon current purchases.

A common discount, called a **sales discount**, encourages customers to pay their invoices early. For example, a seller may offer credit terms of 2/10, n/30, which provides a 2% sales discount if the invoice is paid within 10 days. If not paid within 10 days, the total invoice amount is due within 30 days. As we discussed earlier in this chapter, a buyer refers to a sales discount as a purchases discount.

Generally accepted accounting principles (GAAP) require that revenue be recorded in the amount expected to be received from selling a product or rendering services.[2] As illustrated earlier in this chapter, it is advantageous for buyers to take sales discounts such as 2/10, n/30. In addition, most computerized accounting systems are designed so that all sales discounts are taken. For these reasons, a seller offering a sales discount, such as 2/10, n/30, should record the sale "net" of the discount.

To illustrate, assume that TechSource sells $15,000 of merchandise on account to Medical Health Services Inc. on August 7 with terms 2/10, n/30. The cost of the merchandise sold was $12,495. The sale is recorded for $14,700 [$15,000 – ($15,000 × 2%)], which is net of the sales discount. The effects of this sale on the accounts and financial statements of TechSource are as follows:

Financial Statement Effects

BALANCE SHEET

	Assets			= Liabilities +	Stockholders' Equity
	Accounts Recivable	+ Inventory	=		Retained Earnings
Aug 7.	14,700	(12,495)			2,205

STATEMENT OF CASH FLOWS

INCOME STATEMENT

Aug 7. Sales	14,700
Cost of goods sold	(12,495)

2 This is consistent with *Revenue from Contracts with Customers, Topic 606, FASB Accounting Standards Update*, Financial Accounting Standards Board, Norwalk, CT, May 2014.

Transaction Metric Effects

The effects of the sale on account on liquidity and profitability metrics are as follows:

LIQUIDITY	
Working Capital	$2,205

PROFITABILITY	
Gross Profit Percent (15%)	Decreases ability to achieve minimum of 20%

Since Accounts Receivable increased by $14,700 and Inventory decreased by $12,495, working capital increases by $2,205 ($14,700 – $12,495). Assume TechSource desires a minimum overall gross profit percent of 20%. Since the gross profit percent for this sale is 15% [($14,700 – $12,495) ÷ $14,700], as shown in parentheses, the sale has the effect of decreasing TechSource's ability to achieve an overall gross profit percent of at least 20%.

Customer Refunds and Allowances

Customers may receive merchandise that is defective, damaged during shipment, or does not meet their expectations. In these cases, the seller may pay customers a refund or grant an allowance that reduces the accounts receivable owed by the customers.

In a recent annual report, Amazon reported an allowance for customer returns of $147 million.

Amazon.com Connection

As discussed earlier, generally accepted accounting principles (GAAP) require that revenue be recorded in the amount expected to be received. As a result, at the end of each accounting period, a seller must estimate the amount of refunds and allowances expected to be granted in the future. This estimate is used in the adjusting process to record a liability, called **Customer Refunds Payable**. This adjustment is described and illustrated later in this chapter.

When a seller pays a customer a refund, the seller decreases Cash and Customer Refunds Payable. To illustrate, assume, that on August 13, TechSource pays Krier Company a refund of $225 for merchandise damaged in shipment. Krier Company has agreed to keep the merchandise.

The effects of paying the refund on the accounts and financial statements are as follows:

Financial Statement Effects

	BALANCE SHEET				
	Assets	**=**	**Liabilities**	**+**	**Stockholders' Equity**
	Cash	**=**	**Customer Refunds Payable**		**Retained Earnings**
Aug. 13.	(225)		(225)		

STATEMENT OF CASH FLOWS		
Aug. 13.	Operating	(225)

INCOME STATEMENT

Transaction Metric Effects

The effects of paying the $225 cash refund on the liquidity and profitability metrics are as follows:

LIQUIDITY	
Working Capital	No Effect

PROFITABILITY	
Gross Profit Percent	No Effect

Working capital is not changed since Cash and Customer Refunds Payable are decreased by the same amount of $225. Since no sale occurred, the gross profit percent is also unaffected.

A customer who is due a refund may have an account receivable balance due to the seller. In this case, instead of paying a cash refund to the customer, the seller may decrease the customer's account receivable. When this is done, the seller sends the customer a **credit memorandum**, or credit memo, indicating its intent to decrease the customer's account receivable.

To illustrate, assume that instead of paying a cash refund to Krier Company, TechSource issues the credit memo shown in Exhibit 5.

Exhibit 5
Credit Memorandum

No. 32

TechSource

5101 Washington Ave.
Cincinnati, OH 45227-5101

CREDIT MEMORANDUM

TO	**DATE**
Krier Company 7608 Melton Avenue Los Angeles, CA 90025–3942	August 13, 20Y7

WE CREDIT YOUR ACCOUNT AS FOLLOWS

Allowance for merchandise damaged in shipment	225.00

The effects of issuing the credit memo shown in Exhibit 5 on the accounts and financial statements are as follows:

Financial Statement Effects

	BALANCE SHEET				
	Assets	=	Liabilities	+	Stockholders' Equity
	Accounts Receivable	=	Customer Refunds Payable		Retained Earnings
Aug. 13.	(225)		(225)		

STATEMENT OF CASH FLOWS

INCOME STATEMENT

Transaction Metric Effects

The effects of issuing the $225 credit memo on the liquidity and profitability metrics are as follows:

LIQUIDITY	
Working Capital	No Effect

PROFITABILITY	
Gross Profit Percent	No Effect

Working capital is not changed since Accounts Receivable and Customer Refunds Payable are decreased by the same amount of $225. Since no sale occurred, the gross profit percent is also unaffected.

Merchandise Returns

A customer may return merchandise for a cash refund or allowance. In this case, the receipt of the returned inventory must also be recorded. To illustrate, assume that, on September 2, Wallis Co. returned merchandise with a selling price of $4,000, terms n/30, that had a cost of goods sold of $3,000. TechSource accepted the return and issued Wallis Co. a credit memo for $4,000.

TechSource would record the credit memo of $4,000 in the same manner as the prior illustration. In addition, Inventory is increased by the cost of the goods returned of $3,000, and **Estimated Returns Inventory** is decreased by the same amount. Estimated Returns Inventory represents inventory expected to be returned in the future, which is estimated at the end of the period as part of the adjusting process. This adjustment is illustrated later in this chapter.

The effects of the $4,000 return and credit memo on the accounts and financial statements are as follows:

Financial Statement Effects

BALANCE SHEET

	Assets			=	Liabilities	+	Stockholders' Equity
	Accounts Receivable	+ Inventory	+ Estimated Returns Inventory	=	Customer Refunds Payable	+	Retained Earnings
Sept. 2	(4,000)	3,000	(3,000)		(4,000)		

STATEMENT OF CASH FLOWS

INCOME STATEMENT

Transaction Metric Effects

The effects of the return and credit memo on the liquidity and profitability metrics are as follows:

LIQUIDITY	
Working Capital	No Effect

PROFITABILITY	
Gross Profit Percent (25%)	Decreases ability to achieve minimum of 20%

No change occurs to working capital since the increases and decreases in current assets and current liabilities offset. Assume that TechSource desires a minimum overall gross profit percent of 20%. Since the gross profit percent for the sale that was returned was 25% [($4,000 – $3,000) ÷ $4,000], as shown in parentheses, the effect of the return decreases TechSource's ability to achieve an overall gross profit percent of at least 20%.

Objective 4

Describe the accounting for freight and sales taxes.

Freight and Sales Taxes

Retail businesses incur **freight** in selling and purchasing merchandise. In addition, a retailer must collect sales taxes in most states. In this section, the accounting for freight costs and sales taxes are discussed.

Freight

The terms of a sale should indicate when the ownership (title) of the merchandise passes to the buyer. This point determines which party, the buyer or the seller, must pay the transportation costs.[3]

The ownership of the merchandise may pass to the buyer when the seller delivers the merchandise to the freight carrier or transportation company. In this case, the terms are said to be **FOB (free on board) shipping point**. This term means that the buyer pays the freight costs from the shipping point (factory) to the final destination. Such costs are part of the buyer's total cost of purchasing inventory and should be added to the cost of the inventory by increasing Inventory.

To illustrate, assume that on December 10, TechSource buys merchandise from Magna Data on account, $900, terms FOB shipping point, and pays the freight cost of $50. The effect on the accounts and financial statements of these transactions is as follows:

Financial Statement Effects

	BALANCE SHEET					
	Assets		=	Liabilities	+	Stockholders' Equity
	Cash	+ Inventory	=	Accounts Payable		
Dec. 10.	(50)	950		900		

STATEMENT OF CASH FLOWS	
Dec. 10. Operating	(50)

INCOME STATEMENT

3 The passage of title also determines whether the buyer or seller must pay other costs, such as the cost of insurance, while the merchandise is in transit.

Transaction Metric Effects

The effects on the liquidity and profitability metrics are as follows:

LIQUIDITY	
Working Capital	No Effect

PROFITABILITY	
Gross Profit Percent	No Effect

Working capital is not changed since the net increase of $900 ($950 – $50) in current assets equals the increase in Accounts Payable. Since no sale occurred, the gross profit percent is also unaffected.

The ownership of the merchandise may pass to the buyer when the buyer receives the merchandise. In this case, the terms are said to be **FOB (free on board) destination**. This term means that the seller delivers the merchandise to the buyer's final destination, free of freight charges to the buyer. The seller thus pays the freight costs to the final destination. The seller increases Delivery Expense, or Freight Out, which is reported on the seller's income statement as an expense.

Shipping terms, the passage of title, and whether the buyer or seller is to pay the transportation costs are summarized in Exhibit 6.

Exhibit 6
Freight Terms

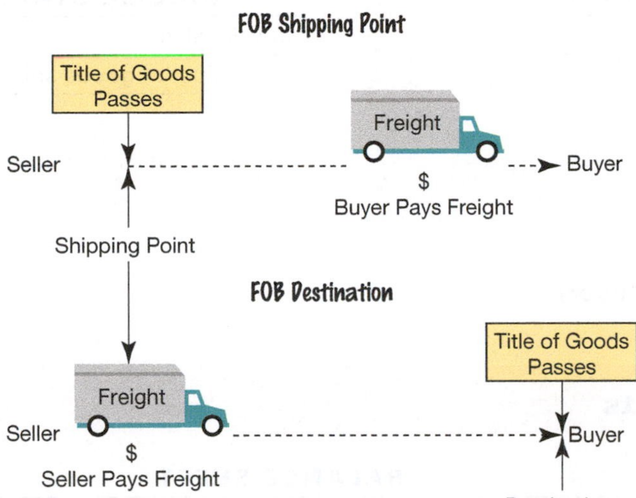

Sales Taxes

Almost all states and many other taxing units levy a tax on sales of merchandise.[4] The liability for the sales tax is incurred when the sale is made. At the time of a cash sale, the seller collects the sales tax. When a sale is made on account, the seller charges the buyer by increasing Accounts Receivable. The seller increases the sales account for the amount of the sale and increases Sales Tax Payable for the amount of the tax. Normally on a regular basis, the seller pays to the taxing unit the amount of the sales tax collected. The seller records such a payment by decreasing Sales Tax Payable and Cash.

In a recent financial report, Amazon reported it collects sales taxes on approximately half of its revenue.

Amazon.com Connection

4 Businesses that purchase merchandise for resale to others are normally exempt from paying sales taxes on their purchases. Only final buyers of merchandise normally pay sales taxes.

Objective 5
Illustrate the dual nature of merchandising transactions.

Dual Nature of Merchandise Transactions

Each merchandising transaction affects a buyer and a seller. The following illustration shows how the same transactions would be recorded by both the seller and the buyer. In this example, the seller is Scully Company and the buyer is Burton Co.[5]

On July 1, Scully Company sold merchandise on account to Burton Co., $7,500, terms FOB destination; 2/10, n/30. The cost of the merchandise sold was $4,500.

Scully Company (Seller)

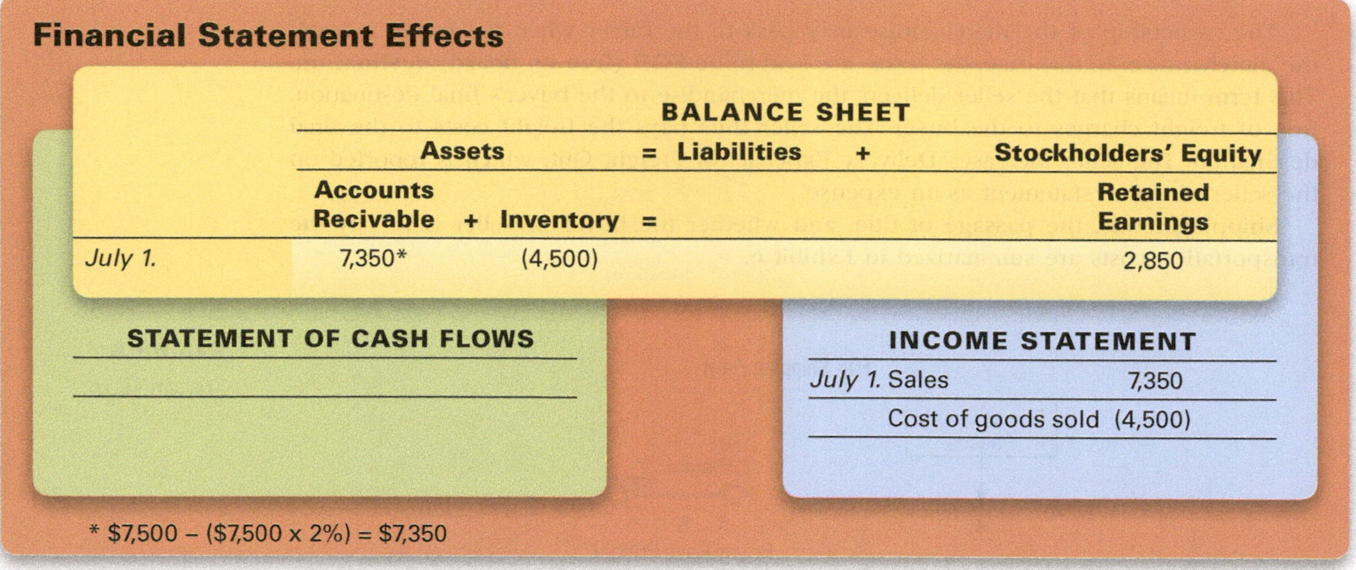

Financial Statement Effects

BALANCE SHEET

	Assets			=	Liabilities	+	Stockholders' Equity
	Accounts Recivable	**+**	**Inventory**	**=**			**Retained Earnings**
July 1.	7,350*		(4,500)				2,850

STATEMENT OF CASH FLOWS

INCOME STATEMENT

July 1.	Sales	7,350
	Cost of goods sold	(4,500)

* $7,500 – ($7,500 x 2%) = $7,350

Burton Co. (Buyer)

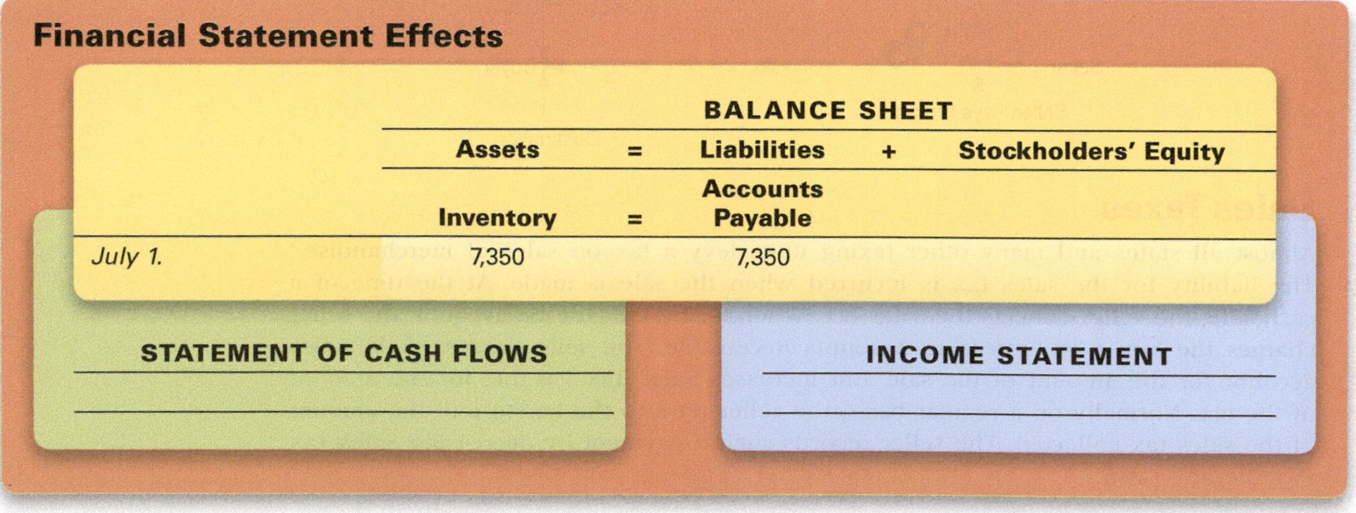

Financial Statement Effects

BALANCE SHEET

	Assets	=	Liabilities	+	Stockholders' Equity
	Inventory	**=**	**Accounts Payable**		
July 1.	7,350		7,350		

STATEMENT OF CASH FLOWS

INCOME STATEMENT

On July 5, Scully Company pays transportation charges of $300 for delivery of the merchandise sold on July 1 to Burton Co.

5 The metric effects of the transactions are not shown.

Scully Company (Seller)

Financial Statement Effects

	BALANCE SHEET				
	Assets	**=**	**Liabilities**	**+**	**Stockholders' Equity**
	Cash	**=**			**Retained Earnings**
July 5.	(300)				(300)

STATEMENT OF CASH FLOWS	
July 5. Operating	(300)

INCOME STATEMENT	
July 5. Delivery exp.	(300)

Burton Co. (Buyer) No effect on the accounts and financial statements.

On July 6, Scully Company issues a credit memorandum for $400 for damaged merchandise. The merchandise was not returned.

Scully Company (Seller)

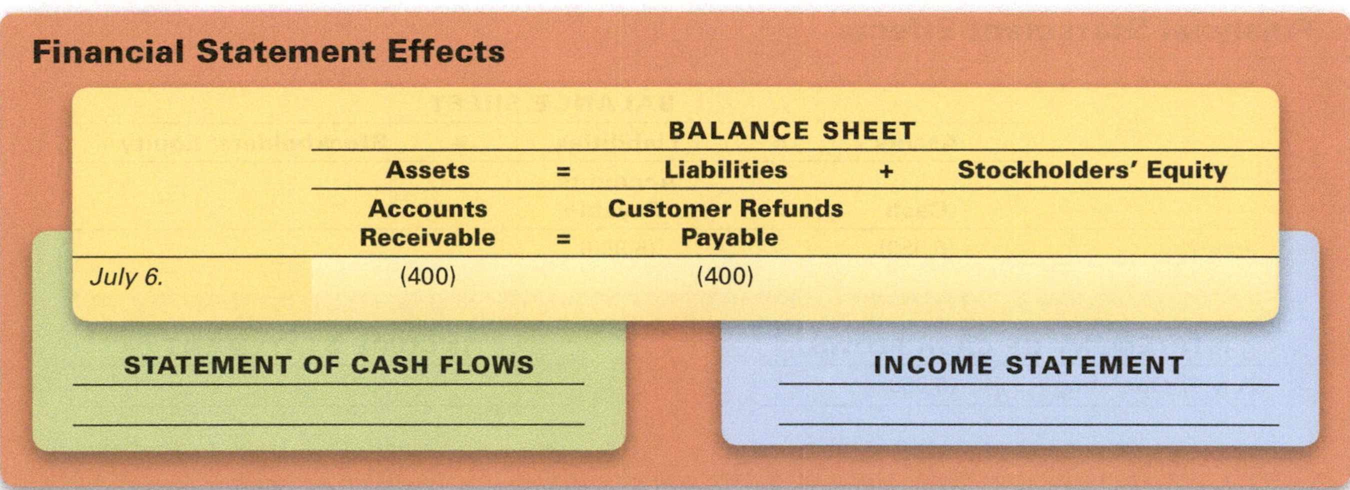

Financial Statement Effects

	BALANCE SHEET				
	Assets	**=**	**Liabilities**	**+**	**Stockholders' Equity**
	Accounts Receivable	**=**	**Customer Refunds Payable**		
July 6.	(400)		(400)		

STATEMENT OF CASH FLOWS

INCOME STATEMENT

Burton Co. (Buyer)

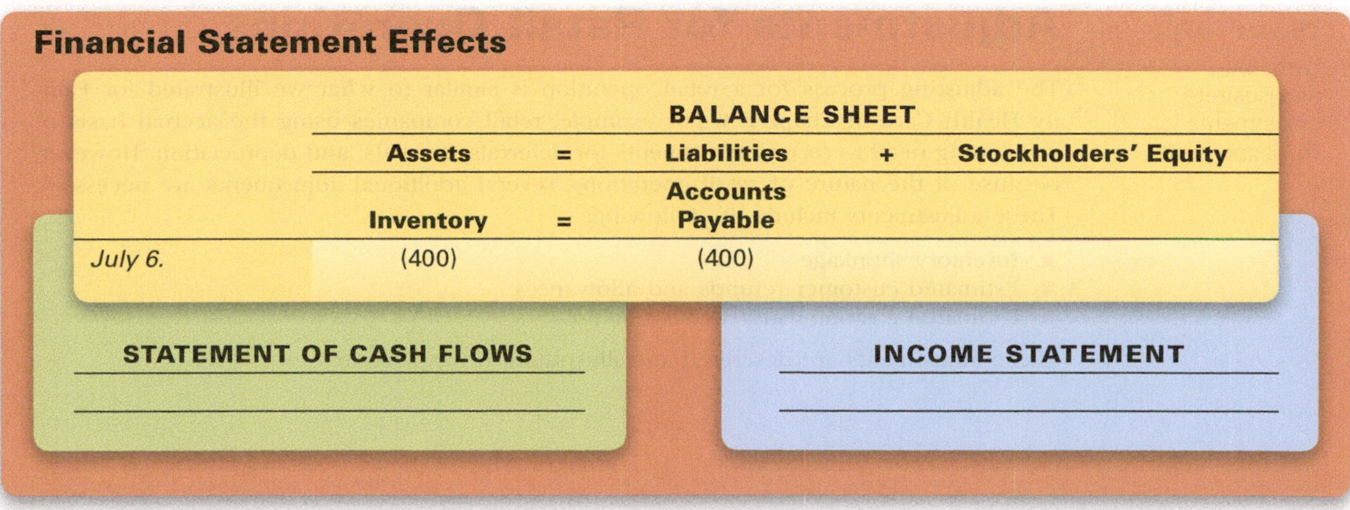

Financial Statement Effects

	BALANCE SHEET				
	Assets	**=**	**Liabilities**	**+**	**Stockholders' Equity**
	Inventory	**=**	**Accounts Payable**		
July 6.	(400)		(400)		

STATEMENT OF CASH FLOWS

INCOME STATEMENT

On July 11, Scully Company received payment from Burton Co.

Scully Company (Seller)

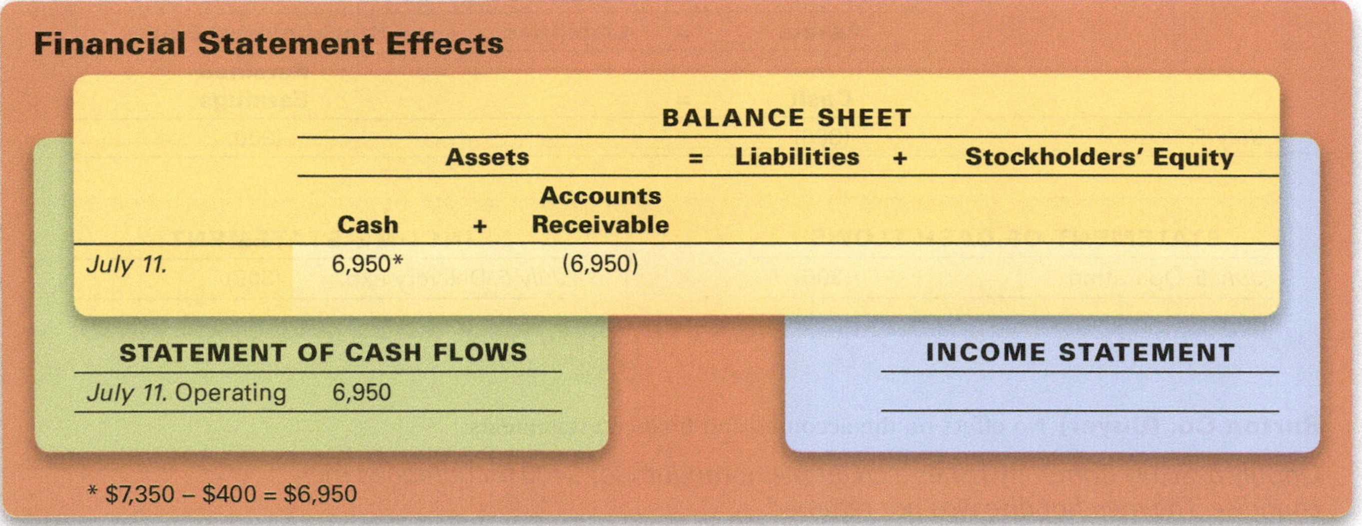

Financial Statement Effects

BALANCE SHEET

	Assets			=	Liabilities	+	Stockholders' Equity
	Cash	+	Accounts Receivable				
July 11.	6,950*		(6,950)				

STATEMENT OF CASH FLOWS	
July 11. Operating	6,950

INCOME STATEMENT

* $7,350 – $400 = $6,950

Burton Co. (Buyer)

Financial Statement Effects

BALANCE SHEET

	Assets	=	Liabilities	+	Stockholders' Equity
	Cash	=	Accounts Payable		
July 11.	(6,950)		(6,950)		

STATEMENT OF CASH FLOWS	
July 11. Operating	(6,950)

INCOME STATEMENT

Objective 6
Describe and illustrate adjustments for retail operations.

Adjustments for Retail Operations

The adjusting process for a retail operation is similar to what we illustrated for Family Health Care in Chapter 3. For example, retail companies using the accrual basis of accounting need to record adjustments for deferrals, accruals, and depreciation. However, because of the nature of retail operations, several additional adjustments are necessary. These adjustments include the following:

- Inventory shrinkage
- Estimated customer refunds and allowances
- Estimated customer merchandise returns

These adjustments are described and illustrated in this section.

Inventory Shrinkage

Under the perpetual inventory system, the inventory account is continually updated for purchase and sales transactions. As a result, the balance of the inventory account is the amount of merchandise available for sale at that point in time. However, retailers normally experience some loss of inventory due to shoplifting, employee theft, or errors. Thus, the physical inventory on hand at the end of the accounting period is usually less than the balance of Inventory. This difference is called **inventory shrinkage** or **inventory shortage**.

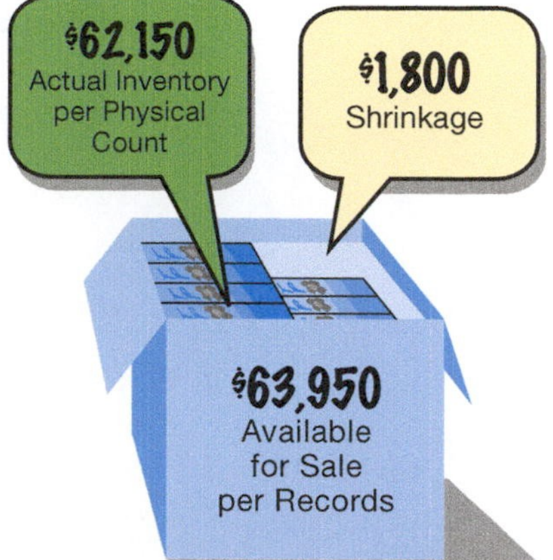

To illustrate, TechSource's inventory records indicate the following on December 31, 20Y7:

	Dec. 31, 20Y7
Account balance of Inventory	$ 63,950
Physical merchandise inventory on hand	(62,150)
Inventory shrinkage	$ 1,800

The effect of the shrinkage on the accounts and financial statements is as follows.

Financial Statement Effects

BALANCE SHEET

	Assets	=	Liabilities	+	Stockholders' Equity
	Inventory	=			**Retained Earnings**
Dec. 31. Adjustments	(1,800)				(1,800)

STATEMENT OF CASH FLOWS

INCOME STATEMENT

Dec. 31. Cost of goods sold	1,800

After the shrinkage is recorded, the balance of Inventory agrees with the physical inventory on hand at the end of the period. Since inventory shrinkage cannot be totally eliminated, it is considered a normal cost of operations and is included in the cost of goods sold.

Transaction Metric Effects

The effects of the shrinkage adjustment on the liquidity and profitability metrics are as follows:

LIQUIDITY

Working Capital	$(1,800)

PROFITABILITY

Gross Profit Percent	Decrease ability to achieve minimum of 20%

Since Inventory decreased by $1,800, working capital will decrease by $1,800. Since cost of goods sold increased by $1,800, gross profit will decrease by $1,800, which will have the effect of decreasing TechSource's ability to achieve an overall gross profit percent of at least 20%.

Customer Refunds, Allowances, and Returns

Retailers can normally estimate, based upon past operations, the percent of sales resulting in customer refunds and allowances. Using this percent, the Customer Refund Payable account is adjusted to reflect future refunds and allowances. An adjustment is also made to reflect estimated customer merchandise returns occurring in the future.

To illustrate, assume the following data for TechSource for the year ending December 31, 20Y7.

Unadjusted Balances
December 31, 20Y7

Account	**Balances***
Estimated Returns Inventory	$ 300
Customer Refunds Payable	800
Sales	523,505
Cost of Goods Sold	
Adjustment Data	
Estimated percent of sales that is expected to be refunded or issued an allowance in 20Y8	1%
Estimated cost of inventory that is expected to be return in 20Y8	$ 5,000

* Assume all normal balances (positive amounts)

Based upon the preceding data, TechSource expects that customers of 20Y7 sales will be issued refunds or allowances of $7,154 ($715,409 × 1%) in 20Y8. As a result, an adjustment increasing Customer Refunds Payable by $7,154 and decreasing Sales by $7,154 is necessary. In addition, inventory costing $5,000 is expected to be returned in 20Y8. As a result, an adjustment increasing Estimated Returns Inventory by $5,000 and decreasing Cost of Goods Sold by $5,000 is necessary.[6]

The effects of these adjustments on the accounts and financial statements are as follows:

Financial Statement Effects

BALANCE SHEET

	Assets	=	**Liabilities**	+	**Stockholders' Equity**
	Estimated Returns Inventory	=	**Customer Refunds Payable**	+	**Retained Earnings**
Dec. 31.	5,000		7,154		(2,154)

STATEMENT OF CASH FLOWS

INCOME STATEMENT

Dec. 31. Sales	(7,154)
Cost of goods sold	5,000

6 Because the specific items of inventory that will be returned in 20Y8 is unknown, Estimated Returns Inventory is increased rather than Inventory. In this way, the controlling account Inventory will still equal the sum of the Inventory subsidiary ledger accounts.

After the preceding adjustments, Estimated Returns Inventory will have a balance of \$5,300 (\$300 + \$5,000) and Customer Refunds Payable will have a balance of \$7,954 (\$800 + \$7,154). Estimated Returns Inventory is reported on the balance sheet as a current asset following Inventory. Customer Refunds Payable is reported on the balance sheet as a current liability following Accounts Payable.

Transaction Metric Effects

The effects of the preceding adjustments on liquidity and profitability metrics are as follows:

LIQUIDITY	
Working Capital	\$(2,154)

PROFITABILITY	
Gross Profit Percent (30.1%)	Decrease ability to achieve minimum of 20%

Current assets (Estimated Returns Inventory) increased by \$5,000 and current liabilities (Customer Refunds Payable) increased by \$7,154. As a result, working capital decreased by \$2,154. TechSource desires a minimum gross profit percent of 20%. The gross profit percent on Sales of \$7,154 and Cost of Goods Sold of \$5,000 is 30.1% [(\$7,154 – \$5,000) ÷ \$7,154), as shown in parentheses. As a result, the adjustments decrease TechSource's ability to achieve a gross profit percent of at least 20%.

Financial Statements for a Retail Business

Objective 7
Describe and illustrate the financial statements of a retail company.

The financial statements for a retail company are illustrated in this section. As a basis for illustration, we use the financial statements of TechSource. We begin by illustrating multiple-step and single-step income statements.

Multiple-Step Income Statement

The 20Y7 income statement for TechSource is shown in Exhibit 7. This form of income statement, called a **multiple-step income statement**, contains several sections, subsections, and subtotals.

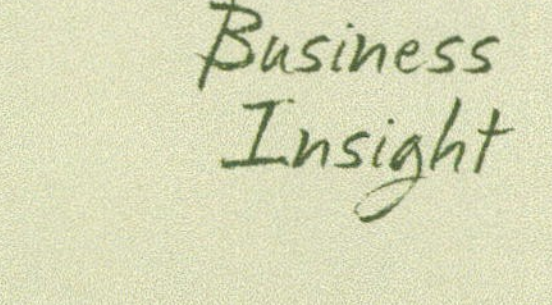

Under One Roof at JCPenney

Matthew Staver/Bloomberg/Getty Images

Most businesses cannot be all things to all people. Businesses must seek a position in the marketplace to serve a unique customer need. Companies that are unable to do this can be squeezed out of the marketplace. The mall-based department store has been under pressure from both ends of the retail spectrum. At the discount store end of the market, **Wal-Mart** has been a formidable competitor. At the high end, specialty retailers have established strong presence in identifiable niches, such as electronics and apparel. Over a decade ago, **JCPenney** abandoned its "hard goods," such as electronics and sporting goods, in favor of providing "soft goods" because of the emerging strength of specialty retailers in the hard goods segments. JCPenney is positioning itself against these forces by *"exceeding the fashion, quality, selection, and service components of the discounter, equaling the merchandise intensity of the specialty store, and providing the selection and 'under one roof' shopping convenience of the department store."* JCPenney's merchandise emphasis is focused toward customers it terms the "modern spender" and "starting outs." It views these segments as most likely to value its higher-end merchandise offered under the convenience of "one roof."

Exhibit 7 Multiple-Step Income Statement for Retail Company

TechSource Income Statement For the Year Ended December 31, 20Y7			
Sales			$ 708,255
Cost of goods sold			(520,305)
Gross profit			$ 187,950
Operating expenses:			
Selling expenses:			
Sales salaries expense	$53,430		
Advertising expense	10,860		
Depreciation expense—store equipment	3,100		
Delivery expense	2,800		
Miscellaneous selling expense	630		
Total selling expenses		$70,820	
Administrative expenses:			
Office salaries expense	$21,020		
Rent expense	8,100		
Depreciation expense—office equipment	2,490		
Insurance expense	1,910		
Office supplies expense	610		
Miscellaneous administrative expense	760		
Total administrative expenses		34,890	
Total operating expenses			(105,710)
Operating income			$ 82,240
Other revenue and expense:			
Rent revenue		$ 600	
Interest expense		(2,440)	(1,840)
Net income			$ 80,400

Sales is the total amount charged customers for merchandise sold, including cash sales and sales on account. During 20Y7, TechSource sold merchandise of $708,255.

Cost of Goods Sold

The cost of goods sold, sometimes called *cost of merchandise sold*, is the cost of the goods sold to customers. TechSource reported cost of goods sold of $520,305 during 20Y7.

Gross Profit

Gross profit is computed by subtracting the cost of goods sold from sales.

Sales	$708,255
Cost of goods sold	(520,305)
Gross profit	$187,950

Operating Income

Operating income, sometimes called *income from operations*, is determined by subtracting operating expenses from gross profit. Operating expenses are normally classified as either selling expenses or administrative expenses.

Selling expenses are incurred directly in the selling of merchandise. Examples of selling expenses include sales salaries, store supplies used, depreciation of store equipment, delivery expense, and advertising.

Administrative expenses, sometimes called **general expenses**, are incurred in the administration or general operations of the business. Examples of administrative expenses include office salaries, depreciation of office equipment, and office supplies used.

Each selling and administrative expense may be reported separately, as shown in Exhibit 7. However, many companies report selling, administrative, and operating expenses as single line items, as follows for TechSource.

Gross profit		$ 187,950
Operating expenses:		
Selling expenses	$70,820	
Administrative expenses	34,890	
Total operating expenses		(105,710)
Operating income		$ 82,240

Other Revenue and Expense

Other revenue and expense items are not related to the primary operations of the business. **Other revenue** is revenue from sources other than the primary operating activity of a business. Examples of other revenue include income from interest, rent, and gains resulting from the sale of fixed assets. **Other expense** is an expense that cannot be traced directly to the normal operations of the business. Examples of other expenses include interest expense and losses from disposing of fixed assets.

Other revenue and other expense are offset against each other on the income statement. If the total of other revenue exceeds the total of other expense, the difference is added to operating income to determine net income. If the reverse is true, the difference is subtracted from operating income. The other revenue and expense items of TechSource are reported as follows.

Operating income		$82,240
Other revenue and expense:		
Rent revenue	$ 600	
Interest expense	(2,440)	(1,840)
Net income		$80,400

Amazon's income staement uses the multiple-step form.

Amazon.com Connection

Single-Step Income Statement

An alternate form of income statement is the **single-step income statement**. As shown in Exhibit 8, the income statement for TechSource deducts the total of all expenses *in one step* from the total of all revenues.

The single-step form emphasizes total revenues and total expenses in determining net income. A criticism of the single-step form is that gross profit and operating income are not reported.

Exhibit 8 Single-Step Income Statement for Retail Company

TechSource
Income Statement
For the Year Ended December 31, 20Y7

Revenues:		
Sales		$708,255
Rent revenue		600
Total revenues		$708,855
Expenses:		
Cost of goods sold	$520,305	
Selling expenses	70,820	
Administrative expenses	34,890	
Interest expense	2,440	
Total expenses		(628,455)
Net income		$ 80,400

Statement of Stockholders' Equity

The statement of stockholders' equity for TechSource is shown in Exhibit 9. This statement is prepared in the same manner as for a service business.

Exhibit 9 Statement of Stockholders' Equity for Retail Company

	Common Stock	Retained Earnings	Total
Balances, Jan. 1, 20Y7	$25,000	$128,800	$153,800
Net income		80,400	80,400
Dividends		(18,000)	(18,000)
Balances, Dec. 31, 20Y7	$25,000	$191,200	$216,200

Amazon.com Connection Amazon reported total stockholders' equity of $10,741 million on a recent statement of stockholders' equity.

Balance Sheet

As discussed and illustrated in Chapters 1–3, the balance sheet is presented in a downward sequence in three sections. The balance sheet for TechSource is shown in Exhibit 10. Inventory and estimated returns inventory are reported as current assets. Customer refunds payable and the current portion of the note payable of $5,000 are reported as a current liabilities.

Amazon.com Connection In a recent balance sheet, Amazon reported Inventories of $8,299 million and total current assets of $31,327 million.

Exhibit 10 Balance Sheet for Retail Company

TechSource Balance Sheet December 31, 20Y7			
Assets			
Current assets:			
Cash			$ 52,650
Accounts receivable			91,080
Inventory			62,150
Estimated returns inventory			5,300
Office supplies			480
Prepaid insurance			2,650
Total current assets			$214,310
Property, plant, and equipment:			
Land		$ 20,000	
Store equipment	$27,100		
Less accumulated depreciation	(5,700)	21,400	
Office equipment	$15,570		
Less accumulated depreciation	(4,720)	10,850	
Total property, plant, and equipment			52,250
Total assets			$266,560
Liabilities			
Current liabilities:			
Accounts payable			$ 14,466
Customer refunds payable			7,954
Note payable (current portion)			5,000
Salaries payable			1,140
Unearned rent			1,800
Total current liabilities			$ 30,360
Long-term liabilities:			
Note payable (final payment due in ten years)			20,000
Total liabilities			$ 50,360
Stockholders' Equity			
Common stock		$ 25,000	
Retained earnings		191,200	
Total stockholders' equity			216,200
Total liabilities and stockholders' equity			$266,560

Statement of Cash Flows

The statement of cash flows for TechSource is shown in Exhibit 11. It indicates that cash increased during 20Y7 by $16,450. This increase is generated from a positive cash flow from operating activities of $52,120 which is partially offset by negative cash flows from investing and financing activities of $(12,670) and $(23,000).

Amazon.com Connection

In a recent statement of cash flows, Amazon reported cash from operating activities of $6,842 million, cash used for investing activities of $(5,065) million, cash from financing activities of $4,122 million, and a net increase in cash of $5,899 million.

The net cash flows from operating activities is shown in Exhibit 11 using a method known as the **indirect method**. This method, which reconciles net income with net cash flows from operating activities, is widely used among publicly held corporations.[8] Note that the December 31, 20Y7, cash balance reported on the statement of cash flows agrees with the amount reported for cash on the December 31, 20Y7, balance sheet shown in Exhibit 10.

Exhibit 11 Statement of Cash Flows for Retail Company

TechSource
Statement of Cash Flows
For the Year Ended December 31, 20Y7

Cash flows from operating activities:		
Net income		$80,400
Depreciation expense—store equipment	$ 3,100	
Depreciation expense—office equipment	2,490	
Changes in noncash current operating assets and liabilities:		
Increase in accounts receivable	(38,080)	
Increase in inventory	(2,450)	
Increase in estimated returns inventory	(1,000)	
Decrease in office supplies	120	
Decrease in prepaid insurance	350	
Increase in accounts payable	7,650	
Increase in customer refunds payable	500	
Decrease in salaries payable	(360)	
Decrease in unearned rent	(600)	(28,280)
Net cash flows from operating activities		$52,120
Cash flows used for investing activities:		
Purchase of store equipment	$ (7,100)	
Purchase of office equipment	(5,570)	
Net cash flows from investing activities		(12,670)
Cash flows used for financing activities:		
Payment of note payable	$ (5,000)	
Payment of dividends	(18,000)	
Net cash flows from financing activities		(23,000)
Net increase in cash		$ 16,450
January 1, 20Y7, cash balance		36,200
December 31, 20Y7, cash balance		$ 52,650

Amazon.com Connection Amazon uses the indirect method for preparing its statement of cash flows.

The integration of TechUSA's financial statements is shown in Exhibit 12.

8 The preparation of the statement of cash flows shown in Exhibit 11 is further discussed and illustrated in the appendix to this chapter.

Exhibit 12 Integrated Financial Statements for Retail Company

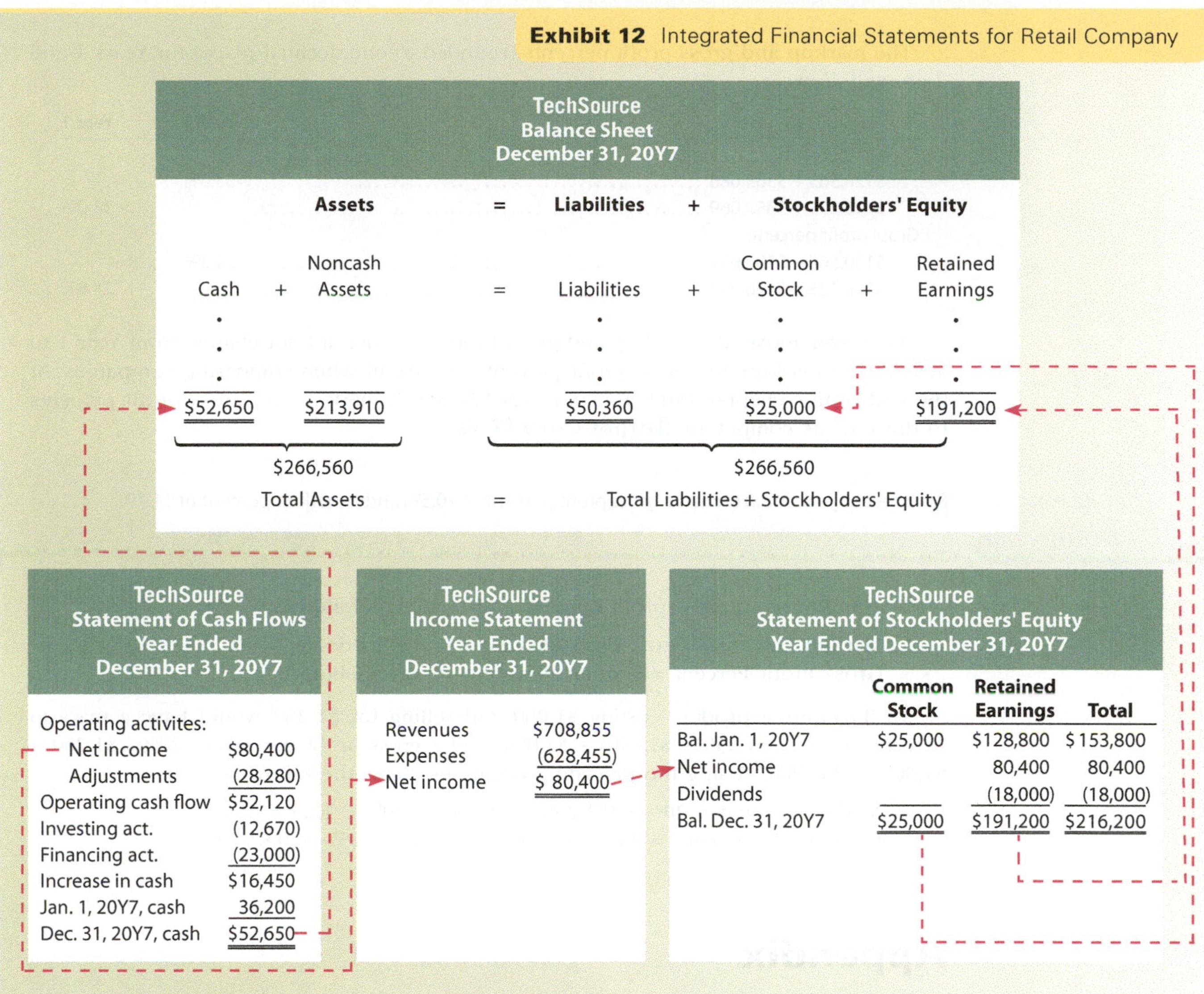

TechSource
Balance Sheet
December 31, 20Y7

Assets		=	Liabilities	+	Stockholders' Equity		
Cash	+ Noncash Assets	=	Liabilities	+	Common Stock	+	Retained Earnings
$52,650	$213,910		$50,360		$25,000		$191,200
$266,560 Total Assets		=	$266,560 Total Liabilities + Stockholders' Equity				

TechSource
Statement of Cash Flows
Year Ended December 31, 20Y7

Operating activites:	
Net income	$80,400
Adjustments	(28,280)
Operating cash flow	$52,120
Investing act.	(12,670)
Financing act.	(23,000)
Increase in cash	$16,450
Jan. 1, 20Y7, cash	36,200
Dec. 31, 20Y7, cash	$52,650

TechSource
Income Statement
Year Ended December 31, 20Y7

Revenues	$708,855
Expenses	(628,455)
Net income	$ 80,400

TechSource
Statement of Stockholders' Equity
Year Ended December 31, 20Y7

	Common Stock	Retained Earnings	Total
Bal. Jan. 1, 20Y7	$25,000	$128,800	$153,800
Net income		80,400	80,400
Dividends		(18,000)	(18,000)
Bal. Dec. 31, 20Y7	$25,000	$191,200	$216,200

Metric-Based Analysis: Markup Percent

Objective 8
Describe and illustrate the markup percent.

A related metric to the gross profit percent is the markup percent. The **markup percent** is multiplied by a product's cost to determine the product's selling price. For example, assuming a product costs $1,000 and the desired markup percent is 25%, the selling price would be $1,250 [$1,000 + ($1,000 × 25%)].

The markup percent is computed as follows:

$$\text{Markup Percent} = \frac{\text{Gross Profit}}{\text{Cost of Goods Sold}}$$

To illustrate, data (in millions) for **Wal-Mart Stores Inc. (WMT)** are used. The following data were taken from two recent years financial statements of Wal-Mart.

	Year 2	Year 1
Sales	$485,651	$476,294
Cost of goods sold	(365,086)	(358,069)
Gross profit	$120,565	$118,225

The markup and gross profit percents (rounded to one decimal place) for Years 1 and 2 are as follows:

	Year 2	Year 1
Markup percent:		
$120,565 ÷ $365,086	33.0%	
$118,225 ÷ $358,069		33.0%
Gross profit percent:		
$120,565 ÷ $485,651	24.8%	
$118,225 ÷ $476,294		24.8%

As shown above, the markup and gross profit percents did not change from Year 1 to Year 2. The markup and gross profit percents are useful when comparing companies. At the end of this chapter, MBA 4-6 compares Wal-Mart's markup and gross profit percents to those of its competitor, **Target Corp (TGT)**.

Amazon.com Connection For a recent year, Amazon had a gross profit percent of 10.5% and a markup percent of 11.7%.

The markup and gross profit percents are related as follows:

Markup Percent = Gross Profit Percent × (Selling Price ÷ Cost)
Gross Profit Percent = Markup Percent × (Cost ÷ Selling Price)

To illustrate, a product costing $1,000 and selling for $1,250 would have a markup percent of 25% [($1,250 − $1,000) ÷ $1,000] and a gross profit percent of 20% [($1,250 − $1,000) ÷ $1,250]. Using the preceding equations yields the following:

Markup Percent = 20% × ($1,250 ÷ $1,000) = 20% × 1.25 = 25%
Gross Profit Percent = 25% × ($1,000 ÷ $1,250) = 25% × 0.8 = 20%

Appendix

Statement of Cash Flows: The Indirect Method

TechUSA's statement of cash flows for the year ended December 31, 20Y7, is shown in Exhibit 11. The operating activities section of this statement was prepared using a method known as the indirect method. This method is used by over 90% of publicly held companies.

The use of the indirect method only affects net cash flows from operating activities. The other method of preparing the net cash flows from operating activities section is called the *direct method*. The direct method analyzes each transaction and its effect on cash flows. The direct method was used in preparing the statement of cash flows in Chapters 2 and 3. In contrast, the indirect method analyzes only the changes in accounts.

A major reason that the indirect method is so popular is that it is normally less costly to use. However, regardless of whether the indirect or direct method is used, the reporting of net cash flows from investing and financing activities is not affected. In this appendix, the use of the indirect method of preparing the statement of cash flows is illustrated.

The indirect method reconciles net income with net cash flows from operating activities. Net income is adjusted for the effects of accruals and deferrals that affected the net income but did not result in the receipt or payment of cash. The resulting amount is the net cash flows from operating activities.

The indirect method converts net income determined under the accrual basis of accounting to what it would have been under the cash basis of accounting. In other words, net cash flows from operating activities is equivalent to net income using the cash basis of accounting.

The typical adjustments to convert net income to net cash flows from operating activities, using the indirect method, are shown in Exhibit 13.

Exhibit 13 Indirect Method

		Increase (Decrease)
Net income (loss)		$XXX
Depreciation of fixed assets	$XXX	
Changes in noncash current operating assets and liabilities:		
Increases in noncash current operating assets	(XXX)	
Decreases in noncash current operating assets	XXX	
Increases in current operating liabilities	XXX	
Decreases in current operating liabilities	(XXX)	XXX
Net cash flow from operating activities		$XXX

Subtract	Add
Increases in accounts receivable	Decreases in accounts receivable
Increases in inventory	Decreases in inventory
Increases in estimated returns inventory	Decreases in estimated returns inventory
Increases in prepaid expenses	Decreases in prepaid expenses
Decreases in accounts payable	Increases in accounts payable
Decreases in customer refunds payable	Increases in customer refunds payable
Decreases in accrued expenses payable	Increases in accrued expenses payable

You should note that, except for depreciation, the adjustments in Exhibit 13 are for changes in the current assets and the current liabilities. This is because changes in the noncash current assets and the current liabilities are related to operations and thus net income. For example, changes in inventories are related to sales, while changes in accounts payable are related to expenses.

Depreciation expense is deducted in arriving at net income but does not involve any cash payments. Thus, depreciation expense is added to net income under the indirect method. Likewise, assume that accounts receivable increases during the period by $10,000. This increase is included in the period's revenue and thus increases net income. However, cash was not collected. Thus, an increase in accounts receivable must be deducted from net income under the indirect method.

Cash Flows from Operating Activities

To prepare the operating activities section for TechSource's statement of cash flows, depreciation and the changes in the current assets and the current liabilities during the year must be determined using comparative balance sheets.

Comparative balance sheets for TechSource as of December 31, 20Y7 and 20Y6 and related changes are shown in Exhibit 14. Based on Exhibit 14, the net cash flows from operating activities is shown below.

Net income		$80,400
Depreciation expense—store equipment	$ 3,100	
Depreciation expense—office equipment	2,490	
Changes in current operating assets and liabilities:		
Increase in accounts receivable	(38,080)	
Increase in inventory	(2,450)	
Increase in estimated returns inventory	(1,000)	
Decrease in office supplies	120	
Decrease in prepaid insurance	350	
Increase in accounts payable	7,650	
Increase in customer refunds payable	500	
Decrease in salaries payable	(360)	
Decrease in unearned rent	(600)	(28,280)
Net cash flows from operating activities		$ 52,120

Exhibit 14 TechSource Comparative Balance Sheets

TechSource
Balance Sheet

	December 31, 20Y7	December 31, 20Y6	Changes Increase (Decrease)
Assets			
Current assets:			
Cash	$ 52,650	$ 36,200	$16,450
Accounts receivable	91,080	53,000	38,080
Inventory	62,150	59,700	2,450
Estimated returns inventory	5,300	4,300	1,000
Office supplies	480	600	(120)
Prepaid insurance	2,650	3,000	(350)
Total current assets	$214,310	$156,800	$57,510
Property, plant, and equipment:			
Land	$ 20,000	$ 20,000	$ 0
Store equipment	27,100	20,000	7,100
Accumulated depreciation—store equipment	(5,700)	(2,600)	(3,100)
Office equipment	15,570	10,000	5,570
Accumulated depreciation—office equipment	(4,720)	(2,230)	(2,490)
Total property, plant, and equipment	$ 52,250	$ 45,170	$ 7,080
Total assets	$266,560	$201,970	$64,590
Liabilities			
Current liabilities:			
Accounts payable	$ 14,466	$ 6,816	$ 7,650
Customer refunds payable	7,954	7,454	500
Notes payable (current portion)	5,000	5,000	0
Salaries payable	1,140	1,500	(360)
Unearned rent	1,800	2,400	(600)
Total current liabilities	$ 30,360	$ 23,170	$ 7,190
Long-term liabilities:			
Notes payable (final payment due in ten years)	20,000	25,000	(5,000)
Total liabilities	$ 50,360	$ 48,170	$ 2,190
Stockholders' Equity			
Capital stock	$ 25,000	$ 25,000	$ 0
Retained earnings	191,200	128,800	62,400
Total stockholders' equity	$216,200	$153,800	$62,400
Total liabilities and stockholders' equity	$266,560	$201,970	$64,590

The depreciation expense of $3,100 for store equipment is determined from the increase in the accumulated depreciation for store equipment. Likewise, the depreciation expense of $2,490 for office equipment is determined from the increase in the accumulated depreciation for office equipment. The changes in the current assets and the current liabilities are also taken from Exhibit 14.

Cash Flows Used for Investing Activities

The cash flows for investing activities section can also be prepared by analyzing the changes in the accounts shown in Exhibit 14. For TechSource, the cash flows used for investing activities is composed of two items. First, additional store equipment of $7,100 was purchased, as shown by the increase in the store equipment. Likewise, additional office equipment of $5,570 was purchased. Thus, cash of $12,670 was used for investing activities, as shown in Exhibit 11.

Cash Flows Used for Financing Activities

The cash flows for financing activities can also be determined from Exhibit 13. For TechSource, the cash flows used for financing activities is composed of two items. First, dividends of $18,000 are reported on the statement of stockholders' equity shown in Exhibit 9. Since no dividends payable appears on the balance sheets, cash dividends of $18,000 must have been paid during the year. In addition, notes payable decreased by $5,000 during the year, so cash must have been used in paying off $5,000 of the notes. Thus, cash of $23,000 was used for financing activities, as shown in Exhibit 11.

Key Points

1. Distinguish the operations and financial statements of a service business from those of a retail business.

The operating cycle of a business is the process it takes for the business to spend cash to generate revenue, earn revenues, and receive cash from customers. The operating cycle for a retail business differs from a service business in that it must purchase merchandise for sale to customers. The differences between retail and service businesses are also reflected in their financial statements. A retail business reports sales, cost of goods sold, and gross profit on its income statement and inventory on its balance sheet.

2. Describe the accounting for the purchase of merchandise.

Purchases of merchandise for cash or on account are recorded in a perpetual inventory system by increasing Inventory. For purchases of merchandise on account, the credit terms can allow cash discounts for early payment. Such purchases discounts are recorded net of the discount. When merchandise is returned or a price adjustment is granted, the buyer decreases Inventory.

3. Describe the accounting for the sale of merchandise.

Sales of merchandise for cash or on account are recorded in a perpetual inventory system by increasing Sales. The cost of goods sold and the reduction in inventory are also recorded for the sale. For sales of on account, the credit terms can allow sales discounts for early payment. Such discounts are recorded by the seller net of the discount. Cash refunds and allowances are recorded by decreasing customer refunds payable and cash or accounts receivable. When merchandise is returned by a customer, Inventory is increased and Estimated Returns Inventory is decreased.

4. Describe the accounting for freight and sales taxes.

When merchandise is shipped FOB shipping point, the buyer pays the freight and increases Inventory. When merchandise is shipped FOB destination, the seller pays the freight and increases Delivery Expense or Freight Out.

The liability for sales tax is incurred when the sale is made and is recorded by the seller as an increase in the sales tax payable account. When the amount of the sales tax is paid to the taxing unit, Sales Tax Payable and Cash are decreased.

5. Illustrate the dual nature of merchandising transactions.

Each merchandising transaction affects a buyer and a seller. The illustration in this chapter shows how the same transactions would be recorded by both.

6. Describe and illustrate adjustments for retail operations.

Because of the nature of retail operations adjustments are necessary for inventory shrinkage, estimated customer refunds and allowances, and estimated customer merchandise returns.

The physical inventory taken at the end of the accounting period could differ from the amount of inventory shown in the inventory records. The difference, called *inventory shrinkage*, requires an adjusting entry increasing Cost of Goods Sold and decreasing Inventory. After this entry has been recorded, the adjusted Inventory (book inventory) in the accounting records agrees with the actual physical inventory at the end of the period.

The adjustment for estimated customer refunds or allowances decreases Sales and increases Customer Refunds Payable. The adjustment for estimated customer returns increases Estimated Returns Inventory and decreases Cost of Goods Sold.

7. Describe and illustrate the financial statements of a retail company.

The multiple-step income statement of a retail company reports sales, cost of goods sold, and gross profit. Operating income is determined by subtracting operating expenses from gross profit. Operating expenses are normally classified as selling or administrative expenses. Net income is determined by subtracting income taxes and other expense and adding other revenue. The income statement may also be reported in a single-step form. The statement of stockholders' equity and the statement of cash flows are similar to those for a service business. The balance sheet reports inventory and estimated returns inventory at the end of the period as current assets. In addition, customer returns payable is reported as a current liability.

8. Describe and illustrate the markup percent.

The markup percent is computed by dividing gross profit by cost of goods sold. It is useful for analyzing a company's performance and is related to the gross profit percent.

Key Terms

Administrative expenses (165)
Controlling account (145)
Cost of goods sold (144)
Credit memorandum (154)
Credit period (146)
Credit terms (146)
Customer Refunds Payable (153)
Debit memorandum (149)
Estimated Returns Inventory (155)
FOB (free on board) destination (157)
FOB (free on board) shipping point (156)
Freight (156)
General expenses (165)
Gross profit (144)
Gross profit percent (145)
Indirect method (168)
Inventory (144)
Inventory shortage (161)
Inventory shrinkage (161)
Invoice (146)
Markup percent (169)
Multiple-step income statement (163)
Operating cycle (143)
Operating income (144)
Other expense (165)
Other revenue (165)
Periodic inventory system (145)
Perpetual inventory system (145)
Physical inventory (145)
Purchases discounts (147)
Purchases returns and allowances (149)
Sales (144)
Sales discount (152)
Selling expenses (165)
Single-step income statement (165)
Subsidiary ledger (145)
Working capital (145)

Illustrative Problem

The following selected accounts and their current balances appear in the ledger of Sciatic Co. for the fiscal year ended July 31, 20Y5:

Cash	$123,000	Retained earnings	301,600
Accounts receivable	96,800	Dividends	28,000
Inventory	125,000	Sales	$992,000
Estimated returns inventory	15,000	Cost of goods sold	620,000
Office supplies	4,480	Sales salaries expense	138,560
Prepaid insurance	2,720	Advertising expense	35,040
Office equipment	68,000	Depreciation expense—store equipment	5,120
Accumulated depreciation—office equipment	10,240	Miscellaneous selling expense	1,280
Store equipment	122,400	Office salaries expense	67,320
Accumulated depreciation—store equipment	27,360	Rent expense	25,080
Accounts payable	32,480	Depreciation expense—office equipment	10,160
Customer refunds payable	12,000	Insurance expense	3,120
Salaries payable	1,920	Office supplies expense	1,040
Note payable (final payment due in seven years)	44,800	Miscellaneous administrative expense	1,280
Common stock	75,000	Interest expense	4,000

Instructions

1. Prepare a single-step income statement.
2. Prepare a multiple-step income statement.
3. Prepare a statement of stockholders' equity. Common stock of $15,000 was issued during the year. The retained earnings balance on August 1, 20Y4 was $301,600.
4. Prepare a balance sheet, assuming that the current portion of the note payable is $6,400

Solution

1.

SCIATIC CO.
Income Statement
For the Year Ended July 31, 20Y5

Sales		$ 992,000
Expenses:		
Cost of goods sold	$620,000	
Selling expenses	180,000	
Administrative expenses	108,000	
Interest expense	4,000	
Total expenses		(912,000)
Net income		$ 80,000

2.

SCIATIC CO.
Income Statement
For the Year Ended July 31, 20Y5

Sales			$ 992,000
Cost of goods sold			(620,000)
Gross profit			$ 372,000
Operating expenses:			
Selling expenses:			
Sales salaries expense	$138,560		
Advertising expense	35,040		
Depreciation expense—store equipment	5,120		
Miscellaneous selling expense	1,280		
Total selling expenses		$180,000	
Administrative expenses:			
Office salaries expense	$ 67,320		
Rent expense	25,080		
Depreciation expense—office equipment	10,160		
Insurance expense	3,120		
Office supplies expense	1,040		
Miscellaneous administrative expense	1,280		
Total administrative expenses		108,000	
Total operating expenses			(288,000)
Operating income			$ 84,000
Other expense:			
Interest expense			4,000
Net income			$ 80,000

3.

SCIATIC CO.
Statement of Stockholders' Equity
For the Year Ended July 31, 20Y5

	Common Stock	Retained Earnings	Total
Balances, Aug. 1, 20Y4	$60,000	$301,600	$361,600
Issued common stock	15,000		15,000
Net income		80,000	80,000
Dividends		(28,000)	(28,000)
Balances, July 31, 20Y5	$75,000	$353,600	$428,600

4.

SCIATIC CO.
Balance Sheet
July 31, 20Y5

Assets

Current assets:			
Cash		$123,000	
Accounts receivable		96,800	
Inventory		125,000	
Estimated returns inventory		15,000	
Office supplies		4,480	
Prepaid insurance		2,720	
Total current assets			$367,000
Property, plant, and equipment:			
Office equipment	$ 68,000		
Less accumulated depreciation	(10,240)	$ 57,760	
Store equipment	$122,400		
Less accumulated depreciation	(27,360)	95,040	
Total property, plant, and equipment			152,800
Total assets			$519,800

Liabilities		
Current liabilities:		
Accounts payable	$ 32,480	
Customer refunds payable	12,000	
Note payable (current portion)	6,400	
Salaries payable	1,920	
Total current liabilities		$ 52,800
Long-term liabilities:		
Note payable (final payment due in seven years)		38,400
Total liabilities		$ 91,200
Stockholders' Equity		
Common stock	$ 75,000	
Retained earnings	353,600	
Total stockholders' equity		428,600
Total liabilities and stockholders' equity		$519,800

Self-Examination Questions

(Answers appear at the end of chapter)

1. If merchandise purchased on account is returned, the buyer can inform the seller of the details by issuing:
   A. A debit memorandum
   B. A credit memorandum
   C. An invoice
   D. A bill

2. If merchandise is sold on account to a customer for $1,000, terms FOB shipping point, 1/10, n/30, and the seller prepays $50 in freight, the amount of the discount for early payment would be:
   A. $0
   B. $5.00
   C. $10.00
   D. $10.50

3. The income statement in which the total of all expenses is deducted from the total of all revenues is termed:
   A. Multiple-step form
   B. Single-step form
   C. Account form
   D. Report form

4. On a multiple-step income statement, the excess of sales over the cost of goods sold is called:
   A. Operating income
   B. Income from operations
   C. Gross profit
   D. Net income

5. As of December 31, 20Y4, Ames Corporation's physical inventory was $275,000, and its book inventory was $290,000. The effect of the inventory shrinkage on the accounts is:
   A. To increase Cost of Goods Sold and Inventory by $15,000
   B. To increase Cost of Goods Sold and decrease Inventory by $15,000
   C. To decrease Cost of Goods Sold and increase Inventory by $15,000
   D. To decrease Cost of Goods Sold and Inventory by $15,000

Class Discussion Questions

1. What distinguishes a retail business from a service business?
2. Describe how the periodic method differs from the perpetual method of accounting for merchandise inventory.
3. What is the meaning of (a) 2/10, n/30; (b) n/90; (c) n/eom?
4. What is the nature of (a) a credit memorandum issued by the seller of merchandise and (b) a debit memorandum issued by the buyer of merchandise?
5. Who bears the freight when the terms of sale are (a) FOB shipping point or (b) FOB destination?
6. When you purchase a new car, the "sticker price" includes a "destination" charge. Are you purchasing the car FOB shipping point or FOB destination? Explain.
7. How are sales to customers using MasterCard and VISA recorded?
8. Differentiate between the multiple and single-step forms of the income statement.
9. What are the major advantages and disadvantages of the single-step form of the income statement compared to the multiple-step form?
10. Can a business earn a gross profit but incur a net loss? Explain.
11. What type of revenue is reported in the "Other revenue" section of the multiple-step income statement?
12. Office Outfitters Inc., which uses a perpetual inventory system, experienced a inventory shrinkage of $3,750. What accounts would be increased and decreased to record the adjustment for the inventory shrinkage at the end of the accounting period?

Exercises

Obj. 1

E4-1 Determining gross profit

During the current year, merchandise is sold for $6,400,000. The cost of the goods sold is $5,376,000.

a. What is the amount of the gross profit?

b. Compute the gross profit percent.

c. Will the income statement necessarily report a net income? Explain.

Obj. 1

E4-2 Determining cost of goods sold

For a recent year, Target Corporation (TGT) reported revenue of $72,618 million. Its gross profit was $21,340 million. What was the amount of Target's cost of goods sold?

Obj. 2

E4-3 Purchase-related transaction

Burr Company purchased merchandise on account from a supplier for $18,000, terms 2/10, n/30. Burr Company returned $3,000 of the merchandise before payment was made and received full credit.

a. If Burr Company pays the invoice within the discount period, what is the amount of cash required for the payment?

b. What account is decreased by Burr Company to record the return?

E4-4 Purchase-related transactions

Obj. 2

A retailer is considering the purchase of 100 units of a specific item from either of two suppliers. Their offers are as follows:

A: $390 a unit, total of $39,000, 1/10, n/30, plus freight of $750.

B: $400 a unit, total of $40,000, 2/10, n/30, no charge for freight.

Which of the two offers, A or B, yields the lower price?

E4-5 Purchase-related transactions

Obj. 2

✔ c. Cash, decreased $101,920

Milan Co., a women's clothing store, purchased $120,000 of merchandise from a supplier on account, terms FOB destination, 2/10, n/30. Milan Co. returned $16,000 of the merchandise, receiving a credit memorandum, and then paid the amount due within the discount period. Illustrate the effects on the accounts and financial statements of Milan Co. to record (a) the purchase, (b) the merchandise return, and (c) the payment.

E4-6 Purchase-related transactions

Obj. 2

✔ e. Cash, increased $24,750

Illustrate the effects on the accounts and financial statements of the following related transactions of Bowen Inc.

a. Purchased $400,000 of merchandise from Swanson Co. on account, terms 1/10, n/30.

b. Paid the amount owed on the invoice within the discount period.

c. Discovered that $60,000 of the merchandise was defective and returned items, receiving credit.

d. Purchased $35,000 of merchandise from Swanson Co. on account, terms 1/10, n/30.

e. Received a check from Swanson Co. for the balance owed from the return in (c), after deducting for the purchase in (d).

E4-7 Determining amounts to be paid on invoices

Obj. 2, 4

✔ a. $11,682

Determine the amount to be paid in full settlement of each of the following invoices, assuming that credit for returns and allowances was received prior to payment and that all invoices were paid within the discount period.

	Merchandise	Freight Paid by Seller		Returns and Allowances
a.	$ 12,800	—	FOB shipping point, 1/10, n/30	$ 1,000
b.	6,000	$175	FOB shipping point, 2/10, n/30	500
c.	30,000	2,500	FOB destination, n/30	5,000
d.	28,500	1,100	FOB shipping point, 2/10, n/30	2,500
e.	7,700	250	FOB destination, 2/10, n/30	—

E4-8 Sales-related transactions, including the use of credit cards

Obj. 3

Illustrate the effects on the accounts and financial statements of recording the following transactions:

a. Sold merchandise for cash, $62,500. The cost of the goods sold was $30,000.

b. Sold merchandise on account, $27,800. The cost of the goods sold was $16,000.

c. Sold merchandise to customers who used MasterCard and VISA, $287,500. The cost of the merchandise sold was $170,000.

Obj. 3

E4-9 Sales-related transactions

After the amount due on a sale of $16,000, terms 2/10, n/eom, is received from a customer within the discount period, the seller consents to the return of the entire shipment. The cost of the merchandise returned was $10,000. (a) What is the amount of the refund owed to the customer? (b) Illustrate the effects on the accounts and financial statements of the return and the refund.

Obj. 3, 4

✔ d. $8,220

E4-10 Sales-related transactions

Merchandise is sold on account to a customer for $8,000, terms FOB shipping point, 1/10, n/30. The seller paid the freight of $300. Determine the following: (a) amount of the sale, (b) amount debited to Accounts Receivable, (c) amount of the discount for early payment, and (d) amount due within the discount period.

Obj. 4

✔ c. $5,400

E4-11 Sales tax

A sale of merchandise on account for $5,000 is subject to an 8% sales tax. (a) Should the sales tax be recorded at the time of sale or when payment is received? (b) What is the amount of the sale? (c) What is the amount of the increase to Accounts Receivable? (d) What is the title of the account in which the $400 ($5,000 × 8%) is recorded?

Obj. 4

E4-12 Sales tax transactions

Illustrate the effects on the accounts and financial statements of recording the following selected transactions:

a. Sold $11,250 of merchandise on account, subject to a sales tax of 6%. The cost of the merchandise sold was $6,750.

b. Paid $63,120 to the state sales tax department for taxes collected.

Obj. 3, 5

E4-13 Sales-related transactions

Steritech Co., a furniture wholesaler, sells merchandise to Butler Co. on account, $86,000, terms 2/10, n/30. The cost of the merchandise sold is $51,600. Steritech Co. issues a credit memorandum for $5,000 ($4,900 net of the 2% discount) for merchandise that was damaged in shipment. Butler Co. agreed to keep the damaged merchandiise. Illustrate the effects on the accounts and financial statements of Steritech Co. for (a) the sale, including the cost of the merchandise sold, (b) the credit memorandum and (c) the receipt of the check for the amount due from Butler Co.

Obj. 2, 5

E4-14 Purchase-related transactions

Based on the data presented in Exercise 4-13, illustrate the effects on the accounts and financial statements of Butler Co. for (a) the purchase, (b) the credit for damaged merchandise, and (c) the payment of the invoice within the discount period.

Obj. 6

E4-15 Adjustment for merchandise inventory shrinkage

Intrax Inc.'s perpetual inventory records indicate that $815,400 of merchandise should be on hand on December 31, 20Y4. The physical inventory indicates that $798,300 of merchandise is actually on hand. Illustrate the effects on the accounts and financial statements of the inventory shrinkage for Intrax Inc. for the year ended December 31, 20Y4.

E 4-16 Adjustment for Customer Refunds and Returns

Obj. 6

Assume the following data for Alpine Technologies for the year ending July 31, 20Y2.

Sales	$900,000
Estimated percent of sales expected to be refunded or issued an allowance in 20Y3	1.5%
Estimated cost of inventory expected to be returned in 20Y3	$6,000

Illustrate the effects of the adjustments for customer refunds and returns on the accounts and financial statements of Alpine Technologies for the year ended July 31, 20Y2.

E4-17 Income statement for merchandiser

Obj. 7

The following expenses were incurred by a retail business during the year. In which expense section of the income statement should each be reported: (a) selling, (b) administrative, or (c) other?

1. Advertising expense
2. Depreciation expense on store equipment
3. Insurance expense on office equipment
4. Interest expense on notes payable
5. Rent expense on office building
6. Salaries of office personnel
7. Salary of sales manager
8. Sales supplies used

E4-18 Multiple-step income statement

Obj. 7

✔ a. Net income: $4,855,000

On March 31, 20Y5, the balances of the accounts appearing in the ledger of Lange Daughters Inc. are as follows:

Administrative Expenses	$ 950,000	Inventory	$ 800,000
Accumulated Dep. - Building	4,000,000	Notes Payable	900,000
Building	19,000,000	Office Supplies	50,000
Common Stock	1,000,000	Retained Earnings	12,365,000
Cash	2,970,000	Sales	17,850,000
Cost of Goods Sold	10,350,000	Selling Expenses	1,650,000
Dividends	200,000	Store Supplies	150,000
Interest Expense	45,000		

a. Prepare a multiple-step income statement for the year ended March 31, 20Y5.

b. Compare the major advantages and disadvantages of the multiple-step and single-step forms of income statements.

E4-19 Single-step income statement

Obj. 7

✔ Net income: $4,100,000

Summary operating data for Loma Company during the current year ended April 30, 20Y6, are as follows: cost of goods sold, $7,500,000; administrative expenses, $750,000; interest expense, $100,000; rent revenue, $120,000; sales, $13,580,000 and selling expenses, $1,250,000. Prepare a single-step income statement.

Obj. 7

E4-20 Multiple-step income statement

Identify the errors in the following income statement and prepare a corrected income statement:

CARLSBAD COMPANY
Income Statement
For the Year Ended February 28, 20Y8

Sales		$4,220,000
Cost of goods sold		(2,650,000)
Operating income		$1,930,000
Expenses:		
Selling expenses	$ 800,000	
Administrative expenses	600,000	
Delivery expense	50,000	
Total expenses		(1,450,000)
Other expense:		$ 480,000
Interest revenue		40,000
Gross profit		$ 440,000

Problems

Obj. 2, 4

P4-1 Purchase-related transactions

The following selected transactions were completed by Epic Co. during August of the current year:

Aug. 3. Purchased merchandise on account for $33,400, terms FOB destination, 2/10, n/30.
9. Issued debit memorandum for $2,500 ($2,450 net of 2% discount) for merchandise from the August 3 purchase that was damaged in shipment.
10. Purchased merchandise on account, $25,000, terms FOB shipping point, n/eom. Paid $600 cash to the freight company for delivery of the merchandise.
13. Paid for invoice of August 3, less debit memorandum of August 9.
31. Paid for invoice of August 10.

Instructions

Illustrate the effects of each of the preceding transactions on the accounts and financial statements of Epic Co. Identify each transaction by date.

Obj. 3, 4

P4-2 Sales-related transactions

The following selected transactions were completed by Affordable Supplies Co., which sells supplies primarily to wholesalers and occasionally to retail customers.

Jan. 6. Sold merchandise on account, $14,000, terms FOB shipping point, n/eom. The cost of merchandise sold was $8,400.
8. Sold merchandise on account, $20,000, terms FOB destination, 1/10, n/30. The cost of merchandise sold was $14,000.
16. Sold merchandise on account, $19,500, terms FOB shipping point, n/30. The cost of merchandise sold was $11,700.
18. Received check for amount due for sale on January 8.
19. Issued credit memorandum for $4,500 for merchandise returned from sale on January 16. The cost of the merchandise returned was $2,700.
26. Received check for amount due for sale on January 16 less credit memorandum of January 19.
31. Paid Cashell Delivery Service $3,000 for merchandise delivered during January to customers under shipping terms of FOB destination.
31. Received check for amount due for sale of January 6.

Instructions

Illustrate the effects of each of the preceding transactions on the accounts and financial statements of Affordable Supplies Co. Identify each transaction by date.

P4-3 Sales and purchase-related transactions for seller and buyer

Obj. 4, 5

The following selected transactions were completed during June between Snipes Company and Beejoy Company:

June 8. Snipes Company sold merchandise on account to Beejoy Company, $18,250, terms FOB destination, 2/15, n/eom. The cost of the merchandise sold was $10,000.
8. Snipes Company paid transportation costs of $400 for delivery of merchandise sold to Beejoy Company on June 8.
12. Beejoy Company returned merchandise with a selling price of $5,000 ($4,900 net of discount) purchased on June 8 from Snipes Company. The cost of the merchandise returned was $3,000.
23. Beejoy Company paid Snipes Company for purchase of June 8, less refund on return of June 12.
24. Snipes Company sold merchandise on account to Beejoy Company, $15,000, terms FOB shipping point, n/eom. The cost of the merchandise sold was $9,000.
26. Beejoy Company paid transportation charges of $375 on June 24 purchase from Snipes Company.
30. Beejoy Company paid Snipes Company on account for purchase of June 24.

Instructions

Illustrate the effects of each of the preceding transactions on the accounts and financial statements of (1) Snipes Company and (2) Beejoy Company. Identify each transaction by date.

P4-4 Multiple-step income statement and report form of balance sheet

Obj. 7

✔ **1. Net income, $1,550,000**

The following selected accounts and their current balances appear in the ledger of Prescott Inc. for the fiscal year ended September 30, 20Y8:

Cash	$ 167,000	Retained Earnings	$ 507,600
Accounts Receivable	300,000	Dividends	250,000
Inventory	735,000	Sales	7,134,000
Estimated Returns Inventory	25,000	Cost of Goods Sold	4,350,000
Office Supplies	30,000	Sales Salaries Expense	777,600
Prepaid Insurance	24,000	Advertising Expense	91,800
Office Equipment	230,400	Depreciation Expense— Store Equipment	16,600
Accumulated Depreciation— Office Equipment	99,000	Miscellaneous Selling Expense	4,000
Store Equipment	1,023,000	Office Salaries Expense	154,800
Accumulated Depreciation— Store Equipment	373,400	Rent Expense	79,800
		Insurance Expense	45,900
Accounts Payable	67,000	Depreciation Expense— Office Equipment	32,400
Customer Refunds Payable	30,200		
Salaries Payable	19,200	Office Supplies Expense	3,300
Note Payable (final payment due in five years)	108,000	Miscellaneous Administrative Expense	3,800
Common Stock	30,000	Interest Expense	24,000

Instructions

1. Prepare a multiple-step income statement.
2. Prepare a statement of stockholders' equity. No common stock was issued during the year.
3. Prepare a balance sheet, assuming that the current portion of the note payable is $16,000.
4. Briefly explain how multiple-step and single-step income statements differ.

Note: The spreadsheet icon  indicates an Excel template is available on the student companion site at www.cengagebrain.com.

Obj. 7

P4-5 Single-step income statement

Selected accounts and related amounts for Prescott Inc. for the fiscal year ended September 30, 20Y8, are presented in Problem 4-4.

Instructions

1. Prepare a single-step income statement in the format shown in Exhibit 8.
2. Prepare a statement of stockholders' equity. No common stock was issued during the year.

P4-6 Appendix Statement of cash flows using indirect method

✔ 1. Net cash flows from operating activities: $98,605

app

For the year ending March 31, 20Y5, Omega Systems Inc. reported net income of $105,450 and paid dividends of $7,500. Comparative balance sheets as of March 31, 20Y5 and 20Y4, are as follows:

OMEGA SYSTEMS INC.
Balance Sheets

	March 31, 20Y5	March 31, 20Y4	Changes Increase (Decrease)
Assets			
Current assets:			
Cash	$ 39,500	$ 29,250	$ 10,250
Accounts receivable	114,120	78,000	36,120
Inventory	126,550	117,550	9,000
Estimated Returns Inventory	6,600	5,000	1,600
Office supplies	4,255	4,435	(180)
Prepaid insurance	3,975	4,500	(525)
Total current assets	$ 295,000	$238,735	$ 56,265
Property, plant, and equipment:			
Land	$ 30,000	$ 30,000	$ 0
Store equipment	350,000	285,000	65,000
Accumulated depreciation—store equipment	(118,550)	(93,900)	(24,650)
Office equipment	23,355	15,000	8,355
Accumulated depreciation—office equipment	(7,080)	(3,345)	(3,735)
Total property, plant, and equipment	$ 277,725	$232,755	$ 44,970
Total assets	$ 572,725	$471,490	$101,235
Liabilities			
Current liabilities:			
Accounts payable	$ 24,630	$ 13,905	$ 10,725
Customer refunds payable	9,000	7,500	1,500
Notes payable (current portion)	7,500	7,500	0
Salaries payable	1,710	2,250	(540)
Unearned rent	2,700	3,600	(900)
Total current liabilities	$ 45,540	$ 34,755	$ 10,785
Long-term liabilities:			
Notes payable (final payment due in eight years)	30,000	37,500	(7,500)
Total liabilities	$ 75,540	$ 72,255	$ 3,285
Stockholders' Equity			
Common stock	$ 37,500	$ 37,500	$ 0
Retained earnings	459,685	361,735	97,950
Total stockholders' equity	$ 497,185	$399,235	$ 97,950
Total liabilities and stockholders' equity	$ 572,725	$471,490	$101,235

Instructions

1. Prepare a statement of cash flows, using the indirect method.
2. Why is depreciation added to net income in determining net cash flows from operating activities? Explain.

Metric-Based Analysis

MBA 4-1 Purchase transactions

Obj. 2, 8

Using transactions listed in P4-1, indicate the effects of each transaction on the liquidity metric working capital and profitability metric gross profit percent.

MBA 4-2 Sales transactions

Obj. 3, 8

Using transactions listed in P4-2, indicate the effects of each transaction on the liquidity metric working capital and profitability metric gross profit percent. Indicate the gross profit percent for each sale (rounding to one decimal place) in parentheses next to the effect of the sale on the company's ability to attain an overall gross profit percent of 30%.

MBA 4-3 Inventory shrinkage

Obj. 6, 8

Using adjustment data listed in E4-15, indicate the effects the inventory shrinkage adjustment on the liquidity metric working capital and profitability metric gross profit percent.

MBA 4-4 Customer refunds and returns

Obj. 6, 8

Using adjustment data listed in E4-16, indicate the effects the adjustment for estimated customer refunds and returns on the liquidity metric working capital and profitability metric gross profit percent. Indicate in parentheses the effect of the adjustment for sales and cost of goods sold on the company's ability to attain an overall gross profit percent of 30%.

MBA 4-5 Gross margin percent and markup percent

Obj. 8

Target Corp. (TGT) operates retail stores throughout the United States and is a major competitor of Wal-Mart. The following data (in millions) were adapted from recent financial statements of Target.

	Year 2	Year 1
Sales	$72,618	$71,279
Cost of goods sold	(51,278)	(50,039)
Gross profit	$21,340	$21,240

1. Compute the gross profit percent for Years 1 and 2. Round to one decimal place.
2. Compute the average markup percent for Years 1 and 2. Round to one decimal place.
3. Compare the results in parts (1) and (2) for Years 1 and 2. Comment on your comparison.

MBA 4-6 Gross profit percent and markup percent

Obj. 8

Compare the Target results in MBA 4-5 with those of Wal-Mart (WMT) shown in the chapter illustration. Comment on the differences.

Obj. 8

MBA 4-7 Gross profit percent and markup percent

Deere & Company (DE) produces and sells tractors, loaders, combines, lawnmowers, and a variety of other equipment. The following data (in millions) were adapted from recent financial statements of Deere.

	Year 2	Year 1
Sales	$28,863	$36,067
Cost of goods sold	(20,143)	(24,776)
Gross profit	$ 8,720	$11,291

1. Compute the gross profit percent for Years 1 and 2. Round to one decimal place.
2. Compute the average markup percent for Years 1 and 2. Round to one decimal place.
3. Compare the results in parts (1) and (2) for Years 1 and 2. Comment on your comparison.

Obj. 8

MBA 4-8 Gross profit percent and markup percent

Caterpillar Inc. (CAT) produces and sells various types of equipment, including tractors, loaders, and mining equipment. The following data (in millions) were adapted from recent financial statements of Caterpillar.

	Year 2	Year 1
Sales	$55,184	$55,656
Cost of goods sold	(40,391)	(41,454)
Gross profit	$14,793	$14,202

1. Compute the gross profit percent for Years 1 and 2. Round to one decimal place.
2. Compute the average markup percent for Years 1 and 2. Round to one decimal place.
3. Compare the results in parts (1) and (2) for Years 1 and 2. Comment on your comparison.

Obj. 8

MBA 4-9 Gross profit percent, markup percent, and ratio of sales to assets

Compare the gross profit percent, average markup percent, and ratio of sales to assets for Deere & Company and Caterpillar Inc. using the results of MBA 4-7 and MBA 4-8. Comment on any differences.

Obj. 8

MBA 4-10 Gross profit percent and markup percent

Companies with low gross profit and markup percents often have higher volumes of sales than companies with high gross profit and markup percents.

1. Comment on the preceding statement.
2. The following data (in millions) were adapted from recent financial statements of The Kroger Co. (KR) and Tiffany & Co. (TIF) Kroger operates supermarkets, while Tiffany designs and sells jewelry, china, watches, and other expensive merchandise.

	Kroger	Tiffany
Sales	$108,465	$4,250
Cost of goods sold	(85,512)	(1,713)
Gross profit	$22,953	$2,537

   Compute the gross profit percent and average markup percent Kroger and Tiffany. Round to one decimal place.
3. Comment on the results in part (2).

Cases

Case 4-1 Ethics and professional conduct in business

On July 29, 20Y1, Ever Green Company, a garden retailer, purchased $12,000 of seed, terms 2/10, n/30, from Fleck Seed Co. Even though the discount period had expired, Mary Jasper subtracted the discount of $240 when she processed the documents for payment on August 13, 20Y1.

Discuss whether Mary Jasper behaved in a professional manner by subtracting the discount, even though the discount period had expired.

Case 4-2 Purchases discounts and accounts payable

The Laurel Co. is owned and operated by Paul Laurel. The following is an excerpt from a conversation between Paul Laurel and Maria Fuller, the chief accountant for Laurel Co.

Paul: Maria, I've got a question about this recent balance sheet.

Maria: Sure, what's your question?

Paul: Well, as you know, I'm applying for a bank loan to finance our new store in Clinton, and I noticed that the accounts payable are listed as $180,000.

Maria: That's right. Approximately $150,000 of that represents amounts due our suppliers, and the remainder is miscellaneous payables to creditors for utilities, office equipment, supplies, etc.

Paul: That's what I thought. But we normally receive a 2% discount from our suppliers for earlier payment, and we always try to take the discount.

Maria: That's right. I can't remember the last time we missed a discount.

Paul: Well, in that case, it seems to me the accounts payable should be listed minus the 2% discount. Let's list the accounts payable due suppliers as $147,000, rather than $150,000. Every little bit helps. You never know. It might make the difference between getting the loan and not.

How would you respond to Paul Laurel's request?

Case 4-3 Determining cost of purchase

The following is an excerpt from a conversation between Eric Jackson and Carlie Miller. Eric is debating whether to buy a stereo system from First Audio, a locally owned electronics store, or Dynamic Sound Systems, an online electronics company.

Eric: Carlie, I don't know what to do about buying my new stereo.

Carlie: What's the problem?

Eric: Well, I can buy it locally at First Audio for $890.00. But Dynamic Sound Systems has the same system listed for $899.99.

Carlie: So what's the big deal? Buy it from First Audio.

Eric: It's not quite that simple. Dynamic Sound Systems said something about not having to pay sales tax, since I was out of state.

Carlie: Yes, that's a good point. If you buy it at First Audio, they'll charge you 6% sales tax.

Eric: But Dynamic Sound Systems charges $13.99 for shipping and handling. If I have them send it next-day air, it'll cost $44.99 for shipping and handling.

Carlie: I guess it is a little confusing.

Eric: That's not all. First Audio will give an additional 1% discount if I pay cash. Otherwise, they will let me use my VISA, or I can pay it off in three monthly installments.

Carlie: Anything else???

Eric: Well ... Dynamic Sound Systems says I have to charge it on my VISA. They don't accept checks.

Carlie: I am not surprised. Many online stores don't accept checks.

Eric: I give up. What would you do?

1. Assuming that Dynamic Sound Systems doesn't charge sales tax on the sale to Eric, which company is offering the best buy?
2. What might be some considerations other than price that might influence Eric's decision on where to buy the stereo system?

Case 4-4 Sales discounts

Your sister operates Harbor Ready Parts Company, an online boat parts distributorship that is in its third year of operation. The income statement is shown below and was recently prepared for the year ended October 31, 20Y6.

HARBOR READY PARTS COMPANY
Income Statement
For the Year Ended October 31, 20Y6

Revenues:		
Sales		$1,200,000
Interest revenue		15,000
Total revenues		$1,215,000
Expenses:		
Cost of goods sold	$800,000	
Selling expenses	135,000	
Administrative expenses	75,000	
Interest expense	21,650	
Total expenses		(1,031,650)
Net income		$ 183,350

Your sister is considering a proposal to increase net income by offering sales discounts of 2/15, n/30 and by shipping all merchandise FOB shipping point. Currently, no sales discounts are allowed and merchandise is shipped FOB destination. It is estimated that these credit terms will increase sales by 15%. The ratio of the cost of goods sold to sales is expected to be 65%. All selling and administrative expenses are expected to remain unchanged, except for store supplies, miscellaneous selling, office supplies, and miscellaneous administrative expenses, which are expected to increase proportionately with increased sales. The amounts of these preceding items for the year ended October 31, 20Y6, were as follows:

Store supplies expense	$18,000	Office supplies expense	$4,000
Miscellaneous selling expense	5,000	Miscellaneous administrative expense	2,000

The other revenue and other expense items will remain unchanged. The shipment of all merchandise FOB shipping point will eliminate all delivery expenses, which for the year ended October 31, 20Y6, were $28,000.

1. Prepare a projected single-step income statement for the year ending October 31, 20Y7, based on the proposal. Assume all sales are collected within the discount period.
2. Based on the projected income statement in part (1), would you recommend implementation of the proposed changes?
3. Describe any possible concerns you may have related to the proposed changes described in part (1).

Case 4-5 Shopping for a television

Assume that you are planning to purchase a Samsung LED-LCD, 55-inch television. In groups of three or four, determine the lowest cost for the television, considering the available alternatives and the advantages and disadvantages of each alternative. For example, you could purchase locally, through mail order, or through an Internet shopping service. Consider such factors as delivery charges, interest-free financing, discounts, coupons, and availability of warranty services. Prepare a report for presentation to the class.

Answers to Self-Examination Questions

1. **A** A debit memorandum (answer A), issued by the buyer, indicates the amount the buyer proposes to decrease the accounts payable account. A credit memorandum (answer B), issued by the seller, indicates the amount the seller proposes to decrease the accounts receivable account. An invoice (answer C) or a bill (answer D), issued by the seller, indicates the amount and terms of the sale.
2. **C** The amount of discount for early payment is $10 (answer C), or 1% of $1,000. Although the $50 of transportation costs paid by the seller increases the customer's account, the customer is not entitled to a discount on that amount.
3. **B** The single-step form of income statement (answer B) is so named because the total of all expenses is deducted in one step from the total of all revenues. The multiple-step form (answer A) includes numerous sections and subsections with several subtotals. The account form (answer C) and the report form (answer D) are two common forms of the balance sheet.
4. **C** Gross profit (answer C) is the excess of sales over the cost of goods sold. Operating income (answer A) or income from operations (answer B) is the excess of gross profit over operating expenses. Net income (answer D) is the final figure on the income statement after all revenues and expenses have been reported.
5. **B** The inventory shrinkage, $15,000, is the difference between the book inventory, $290,000, and the physical inventory, $275,000. The effect of the inventory shrinkage on the accounts is to increase Cost of Goods Sold and decrease Inventory by $15,000.

Chapter **5**

Internal Control and Cash

What's Covered:

Topics: Internal Control and Cash

Internal Control
- Sarbanes-Oxley Act (Obj. 1)
- Control objectives (Obj. 2)
- Control elements (Obj. 2)
- Controls for cash receipts (Obj. 3)
- Controls for cash payments (Obj. 3)

Bank Accounts
- Bank statement (Obj. 4)
- Bank reconciliation (Obj. 5)
- Special-purpose funds (Obj. 6)

Financial Reporting
- Cash (Obj. 7)
- Cash equivalents (Obj.7)

Metric-Based Analysis
- Financial statements: Cash to monthly cash expenses (Obj. 8)

Learning Objectives

Obj.1 Describe the Sarbanes-Oxley Act and its impact on internal controls and financial reporting.

Obj.2 Describe and illustrate the objectives and elements of internal control.

Obj.3 Describe and illustrate the application of internal controls to cash.

Obj.4 Describe the nature of a bank account and its use in controlling cash.

Obj.5 Describe and illustrate the use of a bank reconciliation in controlling cash.

Obj.6 Describe the accounting for special-purpose cash funds.

Obj.7 Describe and illustrate the reporting of cash and cash equivalents in the financial statements.

Obj.8 Describe and illustrate the ratio of cash to net monthly operating cash flows in assessing the ability of a company to continue operating.

Chapter Metrics

Use the following metrics to analyze transactions and financial statements:

TRANSACTIONS*

Liquidity: N/A

Profitability: N/A

FINANCIAL STATEMENTS

Ratio of Cash to Monthly Cash Expenses

* Because of the few number of transactions in this chapter, liquidity and profitablity metrics are not illustrated.

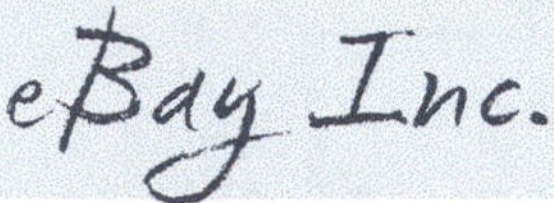

ebay

rvlsoft/Shutterstock.com

Controls are a part of your everyday life. At one extreme, laws are used to limit your behavior. For example, the speed limit is a control on your driving, designed for traffic safety. In addition, you are also affected by many nonlegal controls. For example, recording checks in your checkbook is a control that you can use at the end of the month to verify the accuracy of your bank statement. In addition, banks give you a personal identification number (PIN) as a control against unauthorized access to your cash if you lose your automated teller machine (ATM) card. As you can see, you use and encounter controls every day.

Just as there are many examples of controls throughout society, businesses must also implement controls to help guide the behavior of their managers, employees, and customers. For example, **eBay Inc. (EBAY)** maintains an Internet-based marketplace for the sale of goods and services. Using eBay's online platform, buyers and sellers can browse, buy, and sell a wide variety of items including antiques and used cars. However, in order to maintain the integrity and trust of its buyers and sellers, eBay must have controls to ensure that buyers pay for their items and sellers don't misrepresent their items or fail to deliver sales. One such control eBay uses is a feedback forum that estabilishes buyer and seller reputations. A prospective buyer or seller can view the member's reputation and feedback comments before completing a transaction. Dishonest or unfair trading can lead to a negative reputation and even suspension or cancellation.

This chapter discusses controls that can be included in accounting systems to provide reasonable assurance that the financial statements are reliable. Controls over cash that you can use to determine whether your bank has made any errors in your account are also discussed. This chapter begins by discussing the Sarbanes-Oxley Act and its impact on controls and financial reporting.

Sarbanes-Oxley Act

Objective 1
Describe the Sarbanes-Oxley Act and its impact on internal controls and financial reporting.

When companies commit financial fraud, stockholders, creditors, and other investors often lose billions of dollars.[1] To reduce the likelihood and mitigate the impact of financial fraud, the U.S. Congress passed the **Sarbanes-Oxley Act**. This act, often referred to as *Sarbanes-Oxley,* is one of the most important laws affecting U.S. companies. The purpose of Sarbanes-Oxley is to restore public confidence and trust in the financial reporting of companies.

Sarbanes-Oxley applies only to companies whose stock is traded on public exchanges, referred to as *publicly held companies.* However, Sarbanes-Oxley highlights the importance of assessing the financial controls and reporting of all companies. As a result, companies of all sizes have been influenced by Sarbanes-Oxley.

eBay Connection

eBay designs and maintains its internal controls in conformity with Sarbanes-Oxley.

Sarbanes-Oxley emphasizes the importance of effective internal control.[2] **Internal control** is defined as the procedures and processes used by a company to:

1. Safeguard its assets.
2. Process information accurately.
3. Ensure compliance with laws and regulations.

Sarbanes-Oxley requires companies to maintain effective internal controls over the recording of transactions and the preparing of financial statements. Such controls are important because they deter fraud and prevent misleading financial statements as shown in Exhibit 1.

1. Exhibit 13 in Chapter 1 briefly summarizes these scandals.
2. Sarbanes-Oxley also has important implications for corporate governance and the regulation of the public accounting profession. This chapter, however, focuses on the internal control implications of Sarbanes-Oxley.

Exhibit 1 Effect of Sarbanes-Oxley

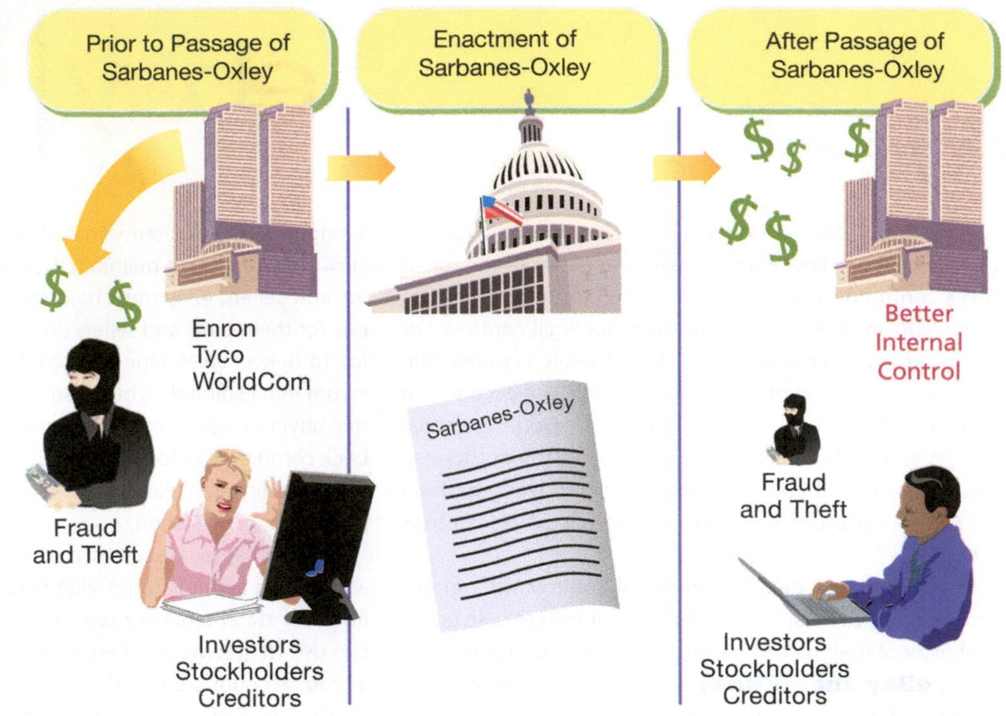

Sarbanes-Oxley also requires companies and their independent accountants to report on the effectiveness of the company's internal controls.[3] These reports are required to be filed with the company's annual 10-K report with the Securities and Exchange Commission. Companies are also encouraged to include these reports in their annual reports to stockholders. An example of such a report by the management of **eBay** is shown in Exhibit 2.

Exhibit 2 Sarbanes-Oxley Report of eBay

eBay Connection

Management's Report on Internal Control over Financial Reporting

Our management is responsible for establishing and maintaining adequate internal control over financial reporting. Our management, including our principal executive officer and principal financial officer, conducted an evaluation of the effectiveness of our internal control over financial reporting based on the framework in Internal Control - Integrated Framework (2013) issued by the Committee of Sponsoring Organizations of the Treadway Commission.

Based on its evaluation under the framework in Internal Control - Integrated Framework, our management concluded that our internal control over financial reporting was effective . . .

Source: eBay Inc., Form 10-K.

Exhibit 2 indicates that **eBay, Inc. (EBAY)** based its evaluation of internal controls on *Internal Control—Integrated Framework,* which was issued by the Committee of Sponsoring Organizations (COSO) of the Treadway Commission. This framework is the standard by which companies design, analyze, and evaluate internal controls.

3. These reporting requirements are required under Section 404 of the act. As a result, these requirements and reports are often referred to as 404 requirements and 404 reports.

Internal Control

Objective 2
Describe and illustrate the objectives and elements of internal control.

Internal Control—Integrated Framework is used as the basis for discussing internal controls.[4] In this section, the objectives of internal control are described, followed by a discussion of how these objectives can be achieved through the *Integrated Framework*'s five elements of internal control.

Objectives of Internal Control

The objectives of internal control are to provide reasonable assurance that:

1. Assets are safeguarded and used for business purposes.
2. Business information is accurate.
3. Employees and managers comply with laws and regulations.

These objectives are illustrated in Exhibit 3.

Exhibit 3
Objectives of Internal Control

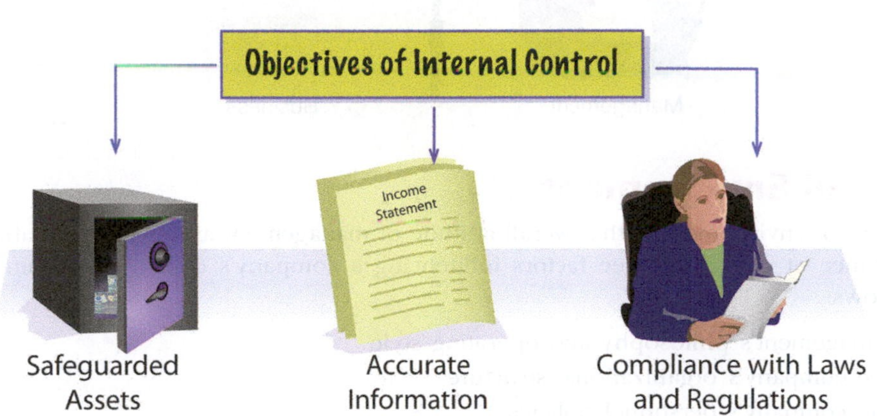

Internal control can safeguard assets by preventing theft, fraud, misuse, or misplacement. A serious concern of internal control is preventing employee fraud. **Employee fraud** is the intentional act of deceiving an employer for personal gain. Such fraud may range from minor overstating of a travel expense report to stealing millions of dollars. Employees stealing from a business often adjust the accounting records in order to hide their fraud. Thus, employee fraud usually affects the accuracy of business information.

Accurate information is necessary to successfully operate a business. Businesses must also comply with laws, regulations, and financial reporting standards. Examples of such standards include environmental regulations, safety regulations, and generally accepted accounting principles (GAAP).

Elements of Internal Control

The three internal control objectives can be achieved by applying the five **elements of internal control** set forth by the *Integrated Framework*.[5] These elements are as follows:

1. Control environment
2. Risk assessment
3. Control procedures
4. Monitoring
5. Information and communication

The elements of internal control are illustrated in Exhibit 4. In this exhibit, the elements of internal control form an umbrella over the business to protect it from control threats.

4. Internal Control—Integrated Framework by the Committee of Sponsoring Organizations of the Treadway Commission, 1992.
5. Ibid., pp. 12–14.

The control environment is the size of the umbrella. Risk assessment, control procedures, and monitoring are the fabric of the umbrella, which keep it from leaking. Information and communication connect the umbrella to management.

Exhibit 4
Elements of Internal Control

Control Environment

The control environment is the overall attitude of management and employees about the importance of controls. Three factors influencing a company's control environment are as follows:

1. Management's philosophy and operating style
2. The company's organizational structure
3. The company's personnel policies

Management's philosophy and operating style relates to whether management emphasizes the importance of internal controls. An emphasis on controls and adherence to control policies creates an effective control environment. In contrast, overemphasizing operating goals and tolerating deviations from control policies creates an ineffective control environment.

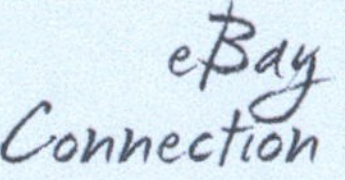

eBay has a *Code of Business Conduct and Ethics* that applies to all employees.

A business's *organizational structure* is the framework for planning and controlling operations. For example, a retail store chain might organize each of its stores as separate business units. Each store manager has full authority over pricing and other operating activities. In such a structure, each store manager has the responsibility for establishing an effective control environment.

A business's *personnel policies* involve the hiring, training, evaluation, compensation, and promotion of employees. In addition, job descriptions, employee codes of ethics, and conflict-of-interest policies are part of the personnel policies. Such policies can enhance the internal control environment if they provide reasonable assurance that only competent, honest employees are hired and retained.

Risk Assessment

All businesses face risks such as changes in customer requirements, competitive threats, regulatory changes, and changes in economic factors. Management should identify such risks, analyze their significance, assess their likelihood of occurring, and take any necessary actions to minimize them.

eBay faces competitive risks from *various* online companies including Amazon.com and Home Shopping Network.

eBay Connection

Control Procedures

Control procedures provide reasonable assurance that business goals will be achieved, including the prevention of fraud. Control procedures, which constitute one of the most important elements of internal control, include the following:

1. Competent personnel, rotating duties, and mandatory vacations
2. Separating responsibilities for related operations
3. Separating operations, custody of assets, and accounting
4. Proofs and security measures

Competent Personnel, Rotating Duties, and Mandatory Vacations A successful company needs competent employees who are able to perform the duties that they are assigned. Procedures should be established for properly training and supervising employees. It is also advisable to rotate duties of accounting personnel and mandate vacations for all employees. In this way, employees are encouraged to adhere to procedures. Cases of employee fraud are often discovered when a long-term employee, who never took vacations, missed work because of an illness or another unavoidable reason.

Separating Responsibilities for Related Operations The responsibility for related operations should be divided among two or more persons. This decreases the possibility of errors and fraud. For example, if the same person orders supplies, verifies the receipt of the supplies, and pays the supplier, the following abuses may occur:

1. Orders may be placed on the basis of friendship with a supplier, rather than on price, quality, and other objective factors.
2. The quantity and quality of supplies received may not be verified; thus, the company may pay for supplies not received or that are of poor quality.
3. Supplies may be stolen by the employee.
4. The validity and accuracy of invoices may not be verified; hence, the company may pay false or inaccurate invoices.

Separating Operations, Custody of Assets, and Accounting The responsibilities for operations, custody of assets, and accounting should be separated. In this way, the accounting records serve as an independent check on the operating managers and the employees who have custody of assets.

To illustrate, employees who handle cash receipts should not record cash receipts in the accounting records. To do so would allow employees to borrow or steal cash and hide the theft in the accounting records. Likewise, operating managers should not also record the results of operations. To do so would allow the managers to distort the accounting reports to show favorable results, which might allow them to receive larger bonuses.

Proofs and Security Measures Proofs and security measures are used to safeguard assets and ensure reliable accounting data. Proofs involve procedures such as authorization, approval, and reconciliation. For example, an employee planning to travel on company business may be required to complete a "travel request" form for a manager's authorization and approval.

Documents used for authorization and approval should be prenumbered, accounted for, and safeguarded. Prenumbering of documents helps prevent transactions from being recorded more than once or not at all. In addition, accounting for and safeguarding prenumbered documents helps prevent fraudulent transactions from being recorded. For example, blank checks are prenumbered and safeguarded. Once a payment has been properly authorized and approved, the checks are filled out and issued.

Reconciliations are also an important control. Later in this chapter, the use of bank reconciliations as an aid in controlling cash is described and illustrated.

Security measures involve measures to safeguard assets. For example, cash on hand should be kept in a cash register or safe. Inventory not on display should be stored in a locked storeroom or warehouse. Accounting records such as the accounts receivable subsidiary ledger should also be safeguarded to prevent their loss. For example, electronically maintained accounting records should be safeguarded with access codes and backed up so that any lost or damaged files could be recovered if necessary.

Monitoring

Monitoring the internal control system is used to locate weaknesses and improve controls. Monitoring often includes observing employees' behavior and the accounting system for indicators of control problems. Some such indicators are shown in Exhibit 5.[6]

Exhibit 5 Warning Signs of Internal Control Problems

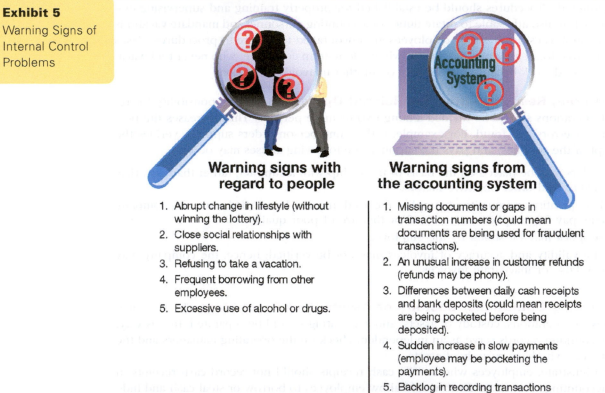

Warning signs with regard to people

1. Abrupt change in lifestyle (without winning the lottery).
2. Close social relationships with suppliers.
3. Refusing to take a vacation.
4. Frequent borrowing from other employees.
5. Excessive use of alcohol or drugs.

Warning signs from the accounting system

1. Missing documents or gaps in transaction numbers (could mean documents are being used for fraudulent transactions).
2. An unusual increase in customer refunds (refunds may be phony).
3. Differences between daily cash receipts and bank deposits (could mean receipts are being pocketed before being deposited).
4. Sudden increase in slow payments (employee may be pocketing the payments).
5. Backlog in recording transactions (possibly an attempt to delay detection of fraud).

Evaluations of controls are often performed when there are major changes in strategy, senior management, business structure, or operations. Internal auditors, who are independent of operations, usually perform such evaluations. Internal auditors are also responsible for day-to-day monitoring of controls. External auditors evaluate and report on internal control as part of their annual financial statement audit.

6. Edwin C. Bliss, "Employee Theft," Boardroom Reports, July 15, 1994, pp. 5–6.

Information and Communication

Information and communication is an essential element of internal control. Information about the control environment, risk assessment, control procedures, and monitoring is used by management for guiding operations and ensuring compliance with reporting, legal, and regulatory requirements. Management also uses external information to assess events and conditions that impact decision making and external reporting. For example, management uses pronouncements of the Financial Accounting Standards Board (FASB) to assess the impact of changes in reporting standards on the financial statements.

In its annual 10-K filing with the Securities and Exchange Commission, **eBay** reports on its business strategies, risk factors affecting its business, legal matters, and analysis of its current operating results and condition. Its financial statements are also Included in the filing.

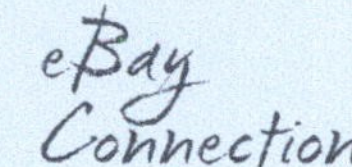

Limitations of Internal Control

Internal control systems can provide only reasonable assurance for safeguarding assets, processing accurate information, and complying with laws and regulations. In other words, internal controls are not a guarantee. This is due to the following factors:

1. The human element of controls
2. Cost-benefit considerations

The *human element* recognizes that controls are applied and used by humans. As a result, human errors can occur because of fatigue, carelessness, confusion, or misjudgment. For example, an employee may unintentionally shortchange a customer or miscount the amount of inventory received from a supplier. In addition, two or more employees may collude together to defeat or circumvent internal controls. This latter case often involves fraud and the theft of assets. For example, the cashier and the accounts receivable clerk might collude to steal customer payments on account.

Cost-benefit considerations recognize that the costs of internal controls should not exceed their benefits. For example, retail stores could eliminate shoplifting by searching all customers before they leave the store. However, such a control procedure would upset customers and result in lost sales. Instead, retailers use cameras or signs saying they prosecute all shoplifters.

Integrity, Objectivity, and Ethics in Business

Tips on Preventing Employee Fraud in Small Companies

- Do not have the same employee write company checks and keep the books. Look for payments to vendors you don't know or payments to vendors whose names appear to be misspelled.
- If your business has a computer system, restrict access to accounting files as much as possible. Also, keep a backup copy of your accounting files and store it at an off-site location.
- Be wary of any employee working in finance that declines to take vacations. They may be afraid that a replacement will uncover fraud.
- Require and monitor supporting documentation (such as vendor invoices) before signing checks.
- Track the number of credit card bills you sign monthly.
- Limit and monitor access to important documents and supplies, such as blank checks and signature stamps.
- Check W-2 forms against your payroll annually to make sure you're not carrying any fictitious employees.
- Rely on yourself, not on your accountant, to spot fraud.

Source: Steve Kaufman, "Embezzlement Common at Small Companies," Knight-Ridder Newspapers, reported in *Athens Daily News/Athens Banner-Herald,* March 10, 1996, p. 4D.

Cash Controls Over Receipts and Payments

Objective 3
Describe and illustrate the application of internal controls to cash.

Cash includes coins, currency (paper money), checks, and money orders. Money on deposit with a bank or other financial institution that is available for withdrawal is also considered cash. Normally, you can think of cash as anything that a bank would accept for deposit in your account. For example, a check made payable to you could normally be deposited in a bank and thus is considered cash.

Businesses usually have several bank accounts. For example, a business might have one bank account for general cash payments and another for payroll. For example, a general bank account at City Bank could be identified as *Cash in Bank—City Bank*. To simplify, we will assume that a company has only one bank account, which is identified as *Cash*.

Cash is the asset most likely to be stolen or used improperly in a business. For this reason, businesses must carefully control cash and cash transactions.

Control of Cash Receipts

To protect cash from theft and misuse, a business must control cash from the time it is received until it is deposited in a bank. Businesses normally receive cash from two main sources:

1. Customers purchasing products or services
2. Customers making payments on account

Cash Received from Cash Sales An important control to protect cash received in over-the-counter sales is a cash register. The use of a cash register to control cash is shown in Exhibit 6.

Exhibit 6
Receipts from Cash Registers

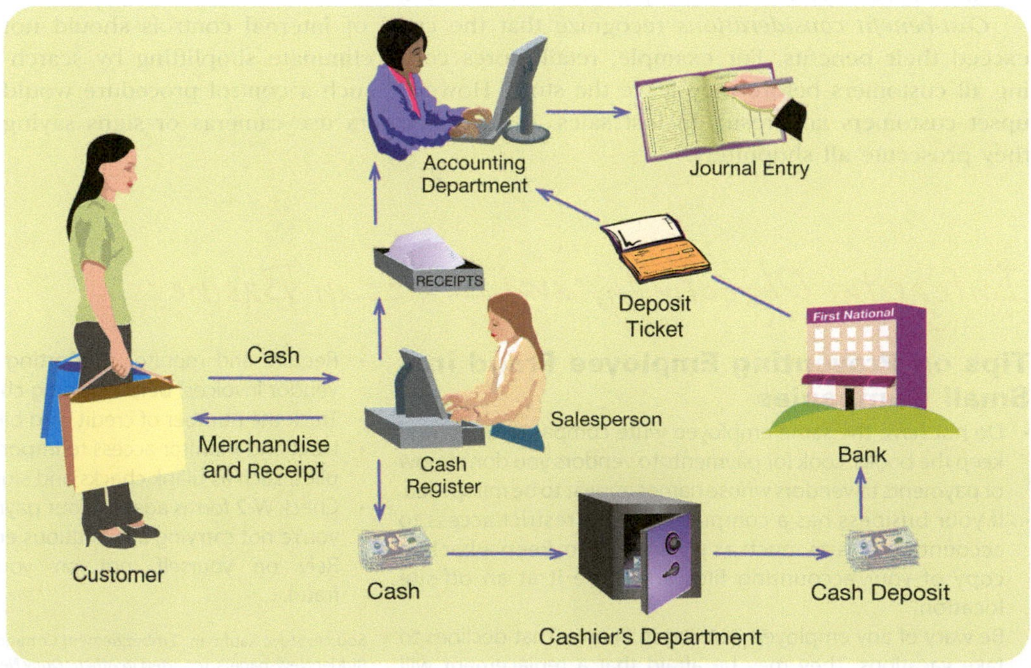

A cash register controls cash as follows:

1. Each cash register clerk is given a cash drawer containing a predetermined amount of cash. This amount is used for making change for customers and is sometimes called a *change fund*.

2. When the clerk enters the amount of a sale, the cash register displays the amount to the customer. This allows the customer to verify that the clerk has charged the correct amount. The customer also receives a cash receipt.
3. The clerk and a supervisor count the cash in the clerk's cash drawer each time a new clerk takes control of the cash register. The amount of cash in the clerk's drawer should equal the beginning amount of cash plus the cash sales.
4. The supervisor takes the cash to the Cashier's Department where it is placed in a safe.
5. The supervisor forwards the clerk's cash register receipts to the Accounting Department.
6. The cashier prepares a bank deposit ticket.
7. The cashier deposits the cash in the bank, or the cash is picked up by an armored car service, such as **Wells Fargo**.
8. The Accounting Department summarizes the cash receipts and records the day's cash sales.
9. When cash is deposited in the bank, the bank normally stamps a duplicate copy of the deposit ticket or sends an electronic receipt of the amount received. The bank receipt is returned to the Accounting Department, where it is compared to the total amount that should have been deposited. This control helps ensure that all the cash is deposited and that no cash is lost or stolen on the way to the bank. Any shortages are thus promptly detected.

Cash register clerks may make errors in making change for customers or in ringing up cash sales. As a result, the amount of cash on hand may differ from the amount of cash sales. Such differences are recorded in a **cash short and over**.

To illustrate, assume the following cash register data for May 3:

Cash register total for cash sales	$35,690
Cash receipts from cash sales	35,668

The cash sales are recorded in the normal manner. The cash shortage of $22 ($35,690 − $35,668) is recorded as a normal operating expense. This is done by recording a negative $22 under the account titled Cash Short and Over.

A cash overage is recorded as a positive amount in Cash Short and Over. At the end of the period, a negative balance in Cash Short and Over is reported as a Miscellaneous operating expense. A positive balance in Cash Short and Over is reported as Other revenue.

Cash Received in the Mail Cash is received in the mail when customers pay their bills. This cash is usually in the form of checks and money orders. Most companies design their invoices so that customers return a portion of the invoice, called a *remittance advice,* with their payment. Remittance advices may be used to control cash received in the mail as follows:

1. An employee opens the incoming mail and compares the amount of cash received with the amount shown on the remittance advice. If a customer does not return a remittance advice, the employee prepares one. The remittance advice serves as a record of the cash initially received. It also helps ensure that the posting to the customer's account is for the amount of cash received.
2. The employee opening the mail stamps checks and money orders "For Deposit Only" in the bank account of the business.
3. The remittance advices and their summary totals are delivered to the Accounting Department.
4. All cash and money orders are delivered to the Cashier's Department.
5. The cashier prepares a bank deposit ticket.
6. The cashier deposits the cash in the bank, or the cash is picked up by an armored car service, such as **Wells Fargo**.
7. An accounting clerk records the cash received and posts the amounts to the customer accounts.
8. When cash is deposited in the bank, the bank normally stamps a duplicate copy of the deposit ticket with the amount received. This bank receipt is returned to the Accounting Department, where it is compared to the total amount that should have been deposited. This control helps ensure that all cash is deposited and that no cash is lost or stolen on the way to the bank. Any shortages are thus promptly detected.

Separating the duties of the Cashier's Department, which handles cash, and the Accounting Department, which records cash, is a control. If Accounting Department employees both handle and record cash, an employee could steal cash and change the accounting records to hide the theft.

Cash Received by EFT Cash also may be received from customers through **electronic funds transfer (EFT)**. For example, customers may authorize automatic electronic transfers from their checking accounts to pay monthly bills for such items as cell phone, Internet services, and utilities. In such cases, the company sends the customer's bank a signed form from the customer authorizing the monthly electronic transfers. Each month, the company notifies the customer's bank of the amount of the transfer and the date the transfer should take place. On the due date, the company records the electronic transfer as a receipt of cash to its bank account and posts the amount paid to the customer's account.

Companies encourage customers to use EFT for the following reasons:

1. EFTs cost less than receiving cash payments through the mail.
2. EFTs enhance internal controls over cash since the cash is received directly by the bank without any employees handling cash.
3. EFTs reduce late payments from customers and speed up the processing of cash receipts.

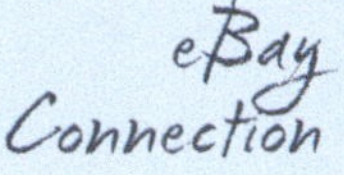

In a recent year, **eBay** generated over $5 billion of cash from its operations.

Control of Cash Payments

The control of cash payments should provide reasonable assurance that:

1. Payments are made for only authorized transactions.
2. Cash is used effectively and efficiently. For example, controls should ensure that all available purchase discounts are taken.

In a small business, an owner/manager may authorize payments based on personal knowledge. In a large business, however, purchasing goods, inspecting the goods received, and verifying the invoices are usually performed by different employees. These duties must be coordinated to ensure that proper payments are made to creditors. One system used for this purpose is the voucher system.

Voucher System A **voucher system** is a set of procedures for authorizing and recording liabilities and cash payments. A **voucher** is any document that serves as proof of authority to pay cash or issue an electronic funds transfer. An invoice that has been approved for payment could be considered a voucher. In many businesses, however, a voucher is a special form used to record data about a liability and the details of its payment.

In a manual system, a voucher is normally prepared after all necessary supporting documents have been received. For the purchase of goods, a voucher is supported by the supplier's invoice, a purchase order, and a receiving report. After a voucher is prepared, it is submitted for approval. Once approved, the voucher is recorded in the accounts and filed by due date. Upon payment, the voucher is recorded in the same manner as the payment of an account payable.

In a computerized system, data from the supporting documents (such as purchase orders, receiving reports, and suppliers' invoices) are entered directly into computer files. At the due date, the checks are automatically generated and mailed to creditors. At that time, the voucher is electronically transferred to a paid voucher file.

Cash Paid by EFT Cash can also be paid by electronic funds transfer systems. For example, many companies pay their employees by EFT. Under such a system, employees authorize the deposit of their payroll checks directly into their checking accounts. Each pay period, the company transfers the employees' net pay to their checking accounts through the use of EFT. Many companies also use EFT systems to pay their suppliers and other vendors.

PayPal provides **eBay** customers a convenient way for eBay users to receive and pay cash. In 2015, PayPal was spun off by eBay into a separate company.

Bank Accounts

Objective 4
Describe the nature of a bank account and its use in controlling cash.

A major reason that companies use bank accounts is for internal control. Some of the control advantages of using bank accounts are as follows:

1. Bank accounts reduce the amount of cash on hand.
2. Bank accounts provide an independent recording of cash transactions. Reconciling the balance of the cash account in the company's records with the cash balance according to the bank is an important control.
3. Use of bank accounts facilitates the transfer of funds using EFT systems.

Bank Statement

Banks usually maintain a record of all checking account transactions. A summary of all transactions, called a **bank statement**, is mailed, usually each month, to the company (depositor) or made available online. The bank statement shows the beginning balance, additions, deductions, and the ending balance. A typical bank statement is shown in Exhibit 7.

Exhibit 7
Bank Statement

MEMBER FDIC

PAGE 1

Mariner National Bank
5000 NE 75th Street
Bellevue, WA 98005

ACCOUNT NUMBER 1627042

FROM 6/30/20Y7 TO 7/31/20Y7

	BALANCE	4,218.60
22	DEPOSITS	13,749.75
52	WITHDRAWALS	14,698.57
3	OTHER DEBITS AND CREDITS	90.00CR
	NEW BALANCE	3,359.78

Colter Inc.
200 West Main Street
Bozeman, MT 59715

CHECKS AND OTHER DEBITS						DEPOSITS	DATE	BALANCE
No. 850	819.40	No. 852	122.54			585.75	07/01	3,862.41
No. 854	369.50	No. 853	20.15			421.53	07/02	3,894.29
No. 851	600.00	No. 856	190.70	No. 857	52.50	781.30	07/03	3,832.39
No. 855	25.93	No. 858	160.00			662.50	07/05	4,308.96
No. 860	921.20	NSF	300.00			503.18	07/07	3,590.94
No. 880	32.26	No. 877	535.09			ACH 932.00	07/29	4,136.66
No. 881	21.10	No. 879	732.26	No. 882	126.20	705.21	07/30	3,962.31
		SC	18.00			MS 408.00	07/30	4,352.31
No. 874	26.12	ACH	1,615.13			648.72	07/31	3,359.78

EC — ERROR CORRECTION
MS — MISCELLANEOUS
NSF — NOT SUFFICIENT FUNDS
ACH — AUTOMATED CLEARING HOUSE
SC — SERVICE CHARGE

*** *** ***

THE RECONCILEMENT OF THIS STATEMENT WITH YOUR RECORDS IS ESSENTIAL.
ANY ERROR OR EXCEPTION SHOULD BE REPORTED IMMEDIATELY.

Checks or copies of the checks listed in the order that they were paid by the bank may accompany the bank statement. If paid checks are returned, they are stamped "Paid," together with the date of payment. Many banks no longer return checks or check copies. Instead, the check payment information is available online.

The depositor's checking account balance in the bank records is a liability. A credit memo entry on the bank statement indicates an increase in the depositor's account. Likewise, a debit memo entry on the bank statement indicates a decrease in the depositor's account.

A bank issues credit memos for the following:

1. Deposits made by electronic funds transfer (EFT)
2. Collections of note receivable for the company
3. Proceeds for a loan made to the company by the bank
4. Interest earned on the company's account
5. Correction (if any) of bank errors

A bank issues debit memos for the following:

1. Payments made by electronic funds transfer (EFT)
2. Service charges
3. Customer checks returned for not sufficient funds
4. Correction (if any) of bank errors

Customers' checks returned for not sufficient funds, called *NSF checks,* are customer checks that were initially deposited but not paid by the customer's bank. Since the company's bank increased the company's account when the customer's check was deposited, the bank decreases the company's account (issues a debit memo) when the check is returned without payment.

The reason for a credit or debit memo entry is indicated on the bank statement. Exhibit 7 identifies the following types of credit and debit memo entries:

EC: Error correction to correct bank error
NSF: Not sufficient funds check
SC: Service charge
ACH: Automated clearing house entry for electronic funds transfer
MS: Miscellaneous item such as collection of a note receivable on behalf of the company or receipt of a loan by the company from the bank

The above list includes the notation "ACH" for electronic funds transfers. ACH is a network for clearing electronic funds transfers among individuals, companies, and banks.[7] Because electronic funds transfers may be either deposits or payments, ACH entries may indicate either a positive or negative entry to the company's account. Likewise, entries to correct bank errors and miscellaneous items may indicate a positive or negative entry to the company's account.

The relationship between the company's cash in bank asset account and the bank's liability account is shown in Exhibit 8.

Integrity, Objectivity, and Ethics in Business

Check Fraud

Check fraud involves counterfeiting, altering, or otherwise manipulating the information on checks in order to fraudulently cash a check. According to the **National Check Fraud Center**, check fraud and counterfeiting are among the growing problems affecting the financial system, generating over $10 billion in losses annually. Criminals perpetrate the fraud by taking blank checks from your checkbook, finding a canceled check in the garbage, or removing a check you have mailed to pay bills. Consumers can prevent check fraud by carefully storing blank checks, placing outgoing mail in postal mailboxes, and shredding canceled checks.

7. For further information on ACH, go to http://www.nacha.org/. Click on "ACH Network" and then click on "Intro to the ACH Network."

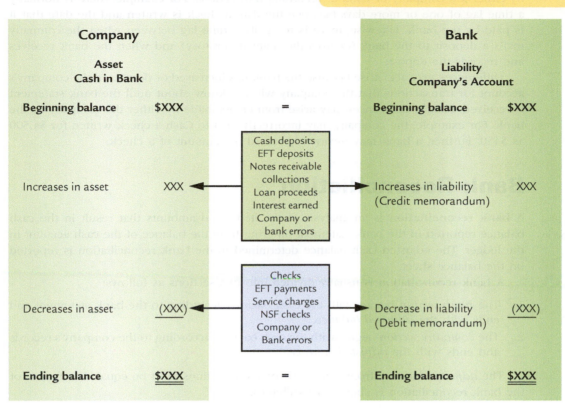

Exhibit 8 Relationship Between Bank and Company

Company			**Bank**	
Asset Cash in Bank			**Liability Company's Account**	
Beginning balance	**$XXX**	=	**Beginning balance**	**$XXX**
Increases in asset	XXX ←	Cash deposits EFT deposits Notes receivable collections Loan proceeds Interest earned Company or bank errors	→ Increases in liability (Credit memorandum)	XXX
Decreases in asset	(XXX) ←	Checks EFT payments Service charges NSF checks Company or Bank errors	→ Decrease in liability (Debit memorandum)	(XXX)
Ending balance	**$XXX**	=	**Ending balance**	**$XXX**

Using the Bank Statement as a Control Over Cash

The bank statement is a primary control that a company uses over cash. A company uses the bank's statement as a control by comparing the company's recording of cash transactions to those recorded by the bank.

The cash balance shown by a bank statement is usually different from the company's cash balance, as shown in Exhibit 9.

Exhibit 9 Colter Inc.'s Records and Bank Statement

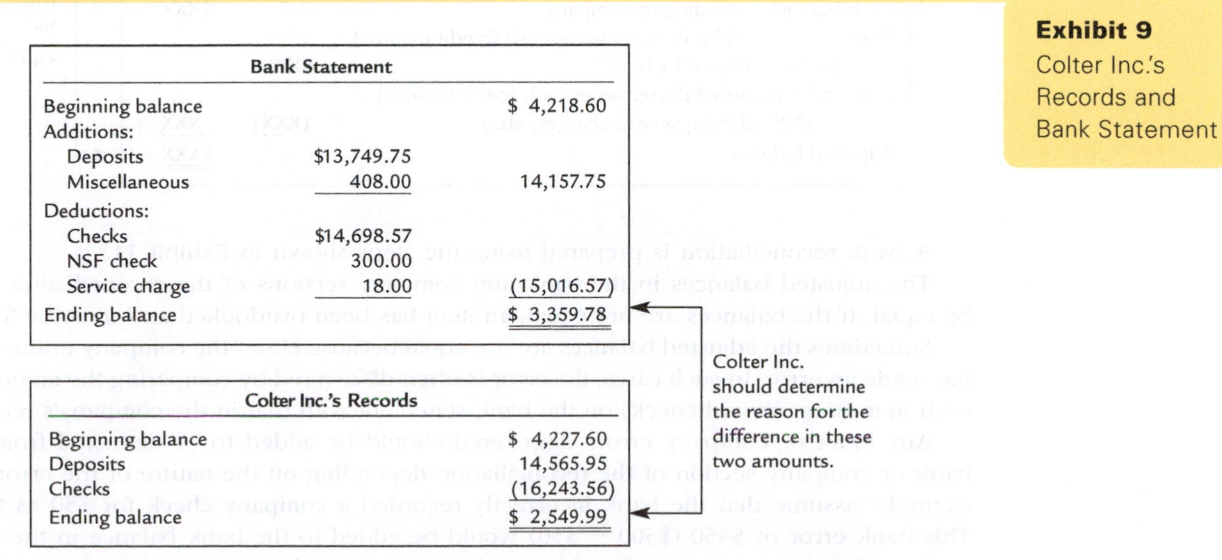

Bank Statement		
Beginning balance		$ 4,218.60
Additions:		
Deposits	$13,749.75	
Miscellaneous	408.00	14,157.75
Deductions:		
Checks	$14,698.57	
NSF check	300.00	
Service charge	18.00	(15,016.57)
Ending balance		$ 3,359.78

Colter Inc.'s Records	
Beginning balance	$ 4,227.60
Deposits	14,565.95
Checks	(16,243.56)
Ending balance	$ 2,549.99

Colter Inc. should determine the reason for the difference in these two amounts.

Differences between the company and bank balances may arise because of a delay by either the company or bank in recording transactions. For example, there is normally a time lag of one or more days between the date a check is written and the date that it is paid by the bank. Likewise, there is normally a time lag between when the company mails a deposit to the bank (or uses the night depository) and when the bank receives and records the deposit.

Differences may also arise because the bank has increased or decreased the company's account for transactions that the company will not know about until the bank statement is received. Finally, differences may arise from errors made by either the company or the bank. For example, the company may incorrectly post to Cash a check written for $4,500 as $450. Further, a bank may incorrectly record the amount of a check.

Objective 5

Describe and illustrate the use of a bank reconciliation in controlling cash.

Bank Reconciliation

A **bank reconciliation** is an analysis of the items and amounts that result in the cash balance reported in the bank statement differing from the balance of the cash account in the ledger. The adjusted cash balance determined in the bank reconciliation is reported on the balance sheet.

A bank reconciliation is usually divided into two sections as follows:

1. The *bank section* begins with the cash balance according to the bank statement and ends with the *adjusted balance.*
2. The *company section* begins with the cash balance according to the company's records and ends with the *adjusted balance.*

The *adjusted balance* from bank and company sections must be equal. The format of the bank reconciliation is shown in Exhibit 10.

Exhibit 10

Bank Reconciliation Format

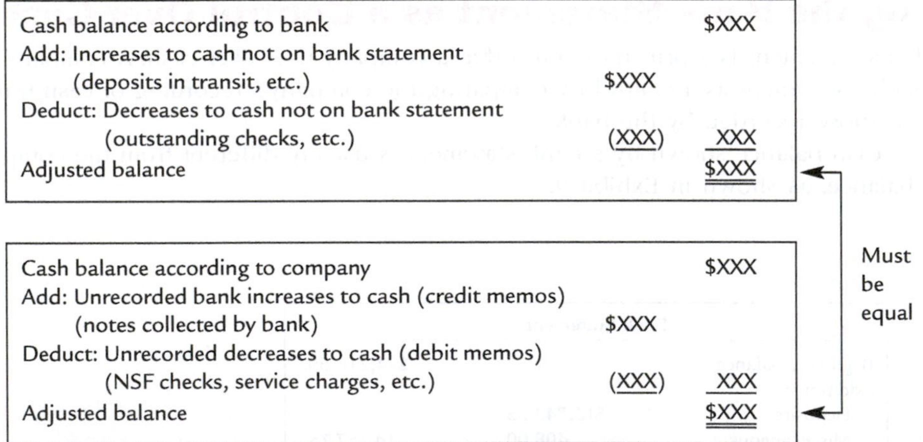

Cash balance according to bank		$XXX
Add: Increases to cash not on bank statement (deposits in transit, etc.)	$XXX	
Deduct: Decreases to cash not on bank statement (outstanding checks, etc.)	(XXX)	XXX
Adjusted balance		$XXX

Cash balance according to company		$XXX
Add: Unrecorded bank increases to cash (credit memos) (notes collected by bank)	$XXX	
Deduct: Unrecorded decreases to cash (debit memos) (NSF checks, service charges, etc.)	(XXX)	XXX
Adjusted balance		$XXX

A bank reconciliation is prepared using the steps shown in Exhibit 11.

The adjusted balances in the bank and company sections of the reconciliation must be equal. If the balances are not equal, an item has been overlooked and must be found.

Sometimes the adjusted balances are not equal because either the company or the bank has made an error. In such cases, the error is often discovered by comparing the amount of each item (deposit and check) on the bank statement with that in the company's records.

Any bank or company errors discovered should be added to or deducted from the bank or company section of the reconciliation depending on the nature of the error. For example, assume that the bank incorrectly recorded a company check for $50 as $500. This bank error of $450 ($500 − $50) would be added to the bank balance in the bank section of the reconciliation. In addition, the bank would be notified of the error so that it could be corrected. On the other hand, assume that the company recorded a deposit

Exhibit 11 Bank Reconciliation Steps

Bank Section of Reconciliation

Step 1. Enter the *Cash balance according to bank* from the ending cash balance according to the bank statement.

Step 2. *Add deposits not recorded by the bank.* Identify deposits not recorded by the bank by comparing each deposit listed on the bank statement with unrecorded deposits appearing in the preceding period's reconciliation and with the current period's deposits. Examples: Deposits in transit at the end of the period.

Step 3. *Deduct outstanding checks that have not been paid by the bank.* Identify outstanding checks by comparing paid checks with outstanding checks appearing on the preceding period's reconciliation and with recorded checks. Examples: Outstanding checks at the end of the period.

Step 4. Determine the *Adjusted balance* by adding Step 2 and deducting Step 3.

Company Section of Reconciliation

Step 5. Enter the *Cash balance according to company* from the ending cash balance in the ledger.

Step 6. *Add increases to cash (credit memos) that have not been recorded.* Identify the bank credit memos that have not been recorded by comparing the bank statement credit memos to entries in the journal. Examples: A note receivable and interest that the bank has collected for the company.

Step 7. *Deduct decreases to cash (debit memos) that have not been recorded.* Identify the bank debit memos that have not been recorded by comparing the bank statement debit memos to entries in the journal. Examples: Customers' not sufficient funds (NSF) checks and bank service charges.

Step 8. Determine the *Adjusted balance* by adding Step 6 and deducting Step 7.

Verify that Adjusted Balances Are Equal

Step 9. Verify that the Adjusted balances determined in Steps 4 and 8 are equal.

of $1,200 as $2,100. This company error of $900 ($2,100 − $1,200) would be deducted from the cash balance in the company section of the bank reconciliation. The company would later correct the error in its records.

To illustrate, we will use the bank statement for Colter Inc. in Exhibit 7. This bank statement shows a balance of $3,359.78 as of July 31. The cash balance in Colter Inc.'s ledger on the same date is $2,549.99. Using the preceding steps, the following reconciling items were identified:

Step 2. Deposit of July 31, not recorded on bank statement: $816.20

Step 3. Outstanding checks:

Check No. 812	$1,061.00
Check No. 878	435.39
Check No. 883	48.60
Total	$1,544.99

Step 6. Note receivable of $400 plus interest of $8 collected by bank but not recorded by the company as indicated by a credit memo of $408.

Step 7. Check from customer (Thomas Ivey) for $300 returned by bank because of not sufficient funds (NSF) as indicated by a debit memo of $300.00. Bank service charges of $18 not recorded by the company as indicated by a debit memo of $18.00.

In addition, an error of $9 was discovered. This error occurred when Check No. 879 for $732.26 to Taylor Co., on account, was recorded by the company as $723.26.

The bank reconciliation, based on the Exhibit 7 bank statement and the preceding reconciling items, is shown in Exhibit 12.

Exhibit 12 Bank Reconciliation for Colter Inc.

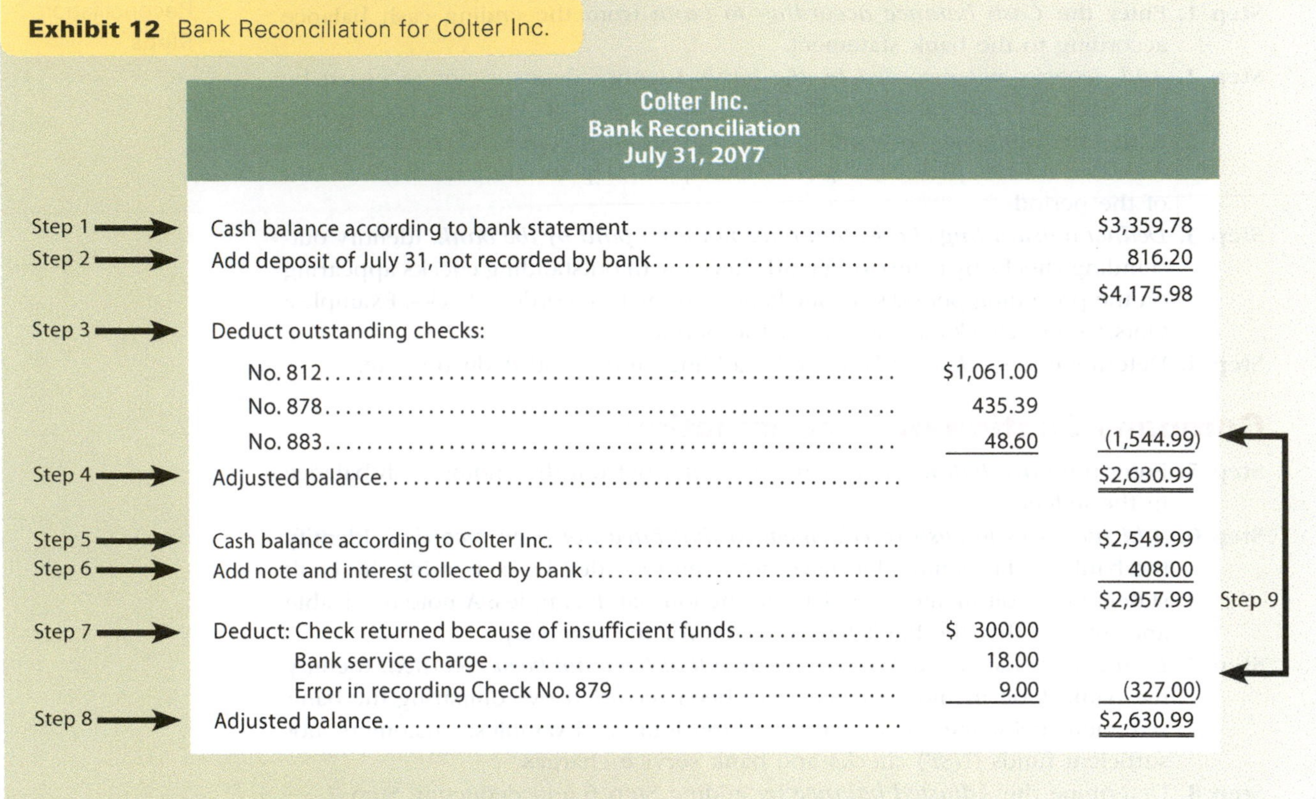

	Colter Inc. Bank Reconciliation July 31, 20Y7		
Step 1	Cash balance according to bank statement		$3,359.78
Step 2	Add deposit of July 31, not recorded by bank		816.20
			$4,175.98
Step 3	Deduct outstanding checks:		
	No. 812	$1,061.00	
	No. 878	435.39	
	No. 883	48.60	(1,544.99)
Step 4	Adjusted balance		$2,630.99
Step 5	Cash balance according to Colter Inc.		$2,549.99
Step 6	Add note and interest collected by bank		408.00
			$2,957.99
Step 7	Deduct: Check returned because of insufficient funds	$ 300.00	
	Bank service charge	18.00	
	Error in recording Check No. 879	9.00	(327.00)
Step 8	Adjusted balance		$2,630.99

The company's records do not need to be updated for any items in the *bank section* of the reconciliation. This section begins with the cash balance according to the bank statement. However, the bank should be notified of any errors that need to be corrected.

The company's records do need to be updated for any items in the *company section* of the bank reconciliation. For example, entries should be made for any unrecorded bank memos and any company errors.

The effects on the accounts and financial statements of Colter Inc. of the bank reconciliation in Exhibit 12 are as follows:

Increases to Cash

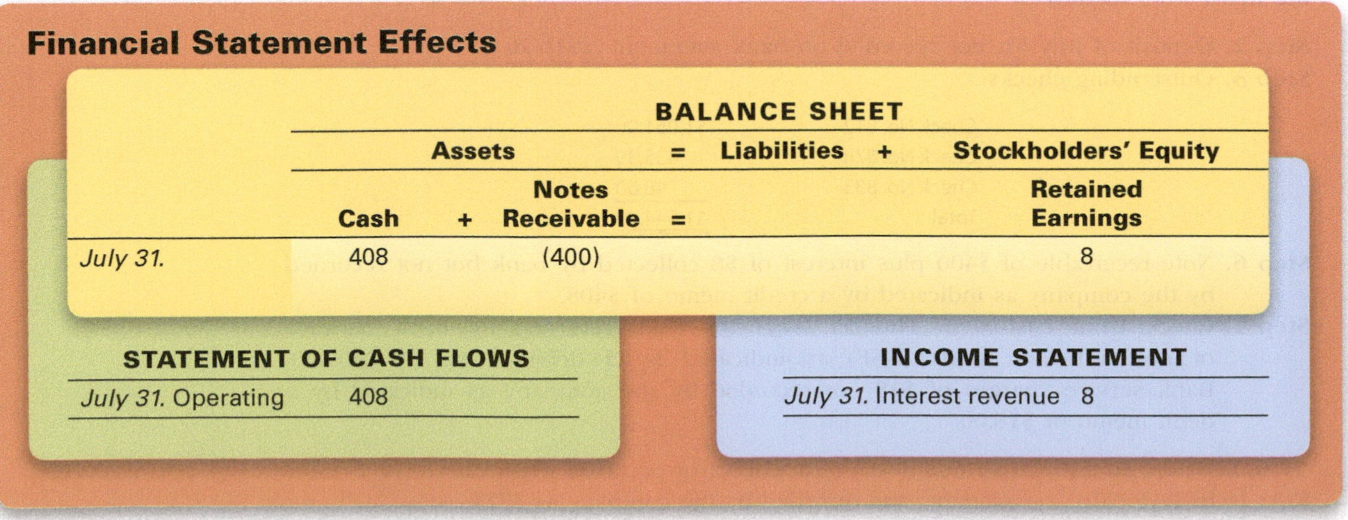

Financial Statement Effects

	BALANCE SHEET			
	Assets		= Liabilities +	Stockholders' Equity
	Cash	+ Notes Receivable	=	Retained Earnings
July 31.	408	(400)		8

STATEMENT OF CASH FLOWS	
July 31. Operating	408

INCOME STATEMENT	
July 31. Interest revenue	8

Decreases to Cash

Financial Statement Effects

	BALANCE SHEET				
	Assets		= Liabilities	+	Stockholders' Equity
	Cash	+ Accounts Receivable	= Accounts Payable	+	Retained Earnings
July 31.	(327)	300	(9)		(18)

STATEMENT OF CASH FLOWS	
July 31. Operating	(327)

INCOME STATEMENT	
July 31. Misc. expense	(18)

After the preceding entries are recorded, the cash account will have a balance of $2,630.99. This cash balance agrees with the adjusted balance shown on the bank reconciliation. This is the amount of cash on July 31 and is the amount that is reported on Colter Inc.'s July 31 balance sheet.

Businesses may reconcile their bank accounts in a slightly different format from that shown in Exhibit 12. Regardless, the objective is to control cash by reconciling the company's records with the bank statement. In doing so, any errors or misuse of cash may be detected.

To enhance internal control, the bank reconciliation should be prepared by an employee who does not take part in or record cash transactions. Otherwise, mistakes may occur, and it is more likely that cash will be stolen or misapplied. For example, an employee who handles cash and also reconciles the bank statement could steal a cash deposit, omit the deposit from the accounts, and omit it from the reconciliation.

Bank reconciliations are also important in computerized systems where deposits and checks are stored in electronic files and records. Some systems use computer software to determine the difference between the bank statement and company cash balances. The software then adjusts for deposits in transit and outstanding checks. Any remaining differences are reported for further analysis.

Special-Purpose Cash Funds

Objective 6
Describe the accounting for special-purpose cash funds.

A company often has to pay small amounts for such items as postage, office supplies, or minor repairs. Although small, such payments may occur often enough to total a significant amount. Thus, it is desirable to control such payments. However, writing a check for each small payment is not practical. Instead, a special cash fund, called a **petty cash fund**, is used.

Integrity, Objectivity, and Ethics in Business

stephenkirsh/Shutterstock.com

Bank Error in Your Favor

At some point, you might experience a bank error in your favor, such as a misposted deposit. Such errors are not a case of "found money," as in the Monopoly® game. Bank control systems quickly discover most errors and make automatic adjustments. Even so, you have a legal responsibility to report the error and return the money to the bank.

A petty cash fund is established by estimating the amount of payments needed from the fund during a period, such as a week or a month. A check is then written and cashed for this amount. The money obtained from cashing the check is then given to an employee, called the *petty cash custodian*. The petty cash custodian disburses monies from the fund as needed. For control purposes, the company may place restrictions on the maximum amount and the types of payments that can be made from the fund. Each time money is paid from petty cash, the custodian records the details on a petty cash receipts form.

The petty cash fund is normally replenished at periodic intervals, when it is depleted, or reaches a minimum amount. When a petty cash fund is replenished, the accounts are updated by summarizing the petty cash receipts. A check is then written for this amount, payable to Petty Cash.

To illustrate normal petty cash fund entries, assume that a petty cash fund of $500 is established on August 1. The effect on the accounts and financial statements of recording this transaction is as follows:

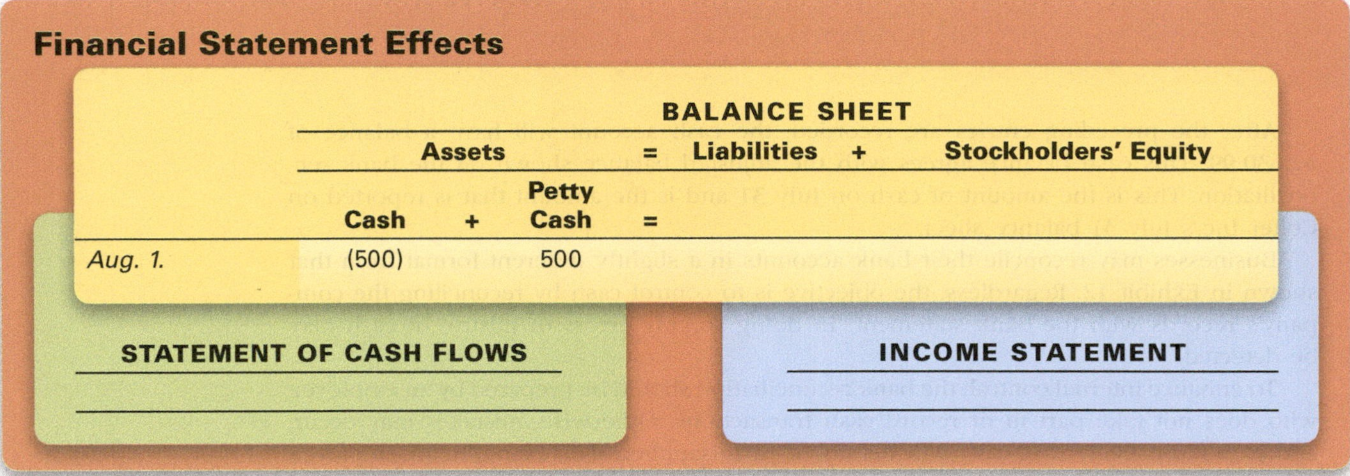

At the end of August, the petty cash receipts indicate expenditures for the following items:

Office supplies	$380
Postage (debit Office Supplies)	22
Store supplies	35
Miscellaneous administrative expense	30
Total	$467

The effect on the accounts and financial statements of replenishing the petty cash fund on August 31 is as follows:

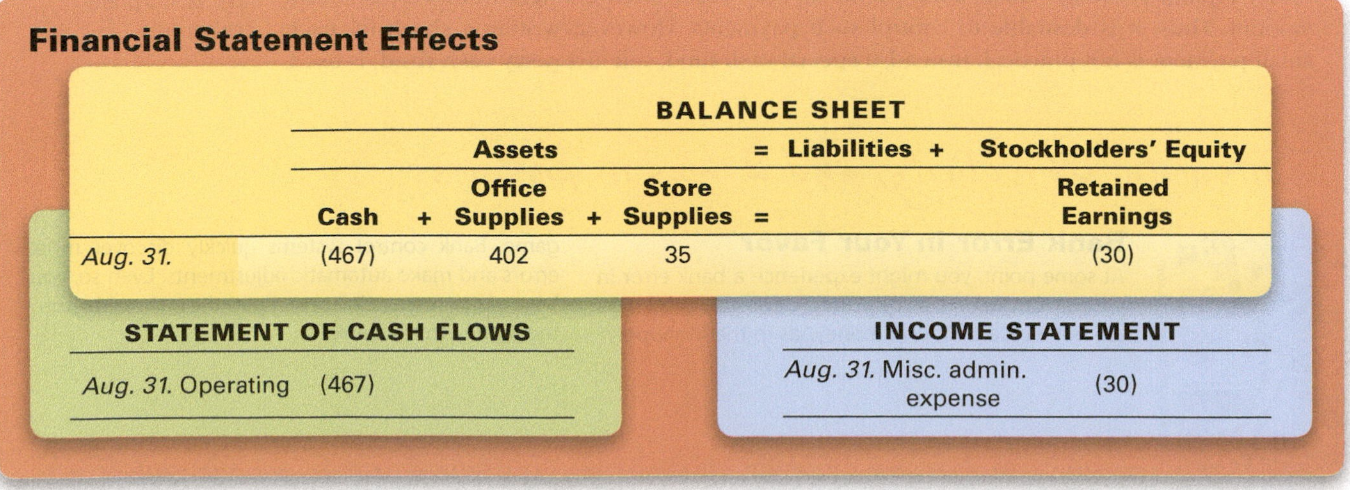

Replenishing the petty cash fund restores the fund to its original amount of $500. There is no adjustment to Petty Cash when the fund is replenished. Petty Cash is adjusted only if the amount of the fund is later increased or decreased.

Companies often use other cash funds for special needs, such as payroll or travel expenses. Such funds are called **special-purpose funds**. For example, each salesperson might be given $1,000 for travel-related expenses. Periodically, each salesperson submits an expense report, and the fund is replenished. Special-purpose funds are established and controlled in a manner similar to that of the petty cash fund.

Financial Statement Reporting of Cash

Objective 7
Describe and illustrate the reporting of cash and cash equivalents in the financial statements.

Cash is normally listed as the first asset in the Current Assets section of the balance sheet. Most companies present only a single cash amount on the balance sheet by combining all their bank and cash fund accounts.

A company may temporarily have excess cash. In such cases, the company normally invests in highly liquid investments in order to earn interest. These investments are called **cash equivalents**.[8] Examples of cash equivalents include U.S. Treasury bills, notes issued by major corporations (referred to as commercial paper), and money market funds. In such cases, companies usually report *Cash and cash equivalents* as one amount on the balance sheet.

In a recent balance sheet, **eBay** reported cash and cash equivalents of $6,328 million.

eBay Connection

Banks may require that companies maintain minimum cash balances in their bank accounts. Such a balance is called a **compensating balance**. This is often required by the bank as part of a loan agreement or line of credit. A *line of credit* is a preapproved amount the bank is willing to lend to a customer upon request. Compensating balance requirements are normally disclosed in notes to the financial statements.

8. To be classified as a cash equivalent, according to *FASB Accounting Standards Codification*, Section 305.10, the investment is expected to be converted to cash within three months.

Metric-Based Analysis: Ratio of Cash to Monthly Cash Expenses

Objective 8
Describe and illustrate the ratio of cash to monthly cash expenses in assessing the ability of a company to continue operating.

The statement of cash flows reports "Net cash flows from operating activities." It is generally expected that a company will generate positive cash flows from operations. While a company may occasionally experience economic downturns that generate negative cash flows from operations, a company must generate positive cash flows from operations over the long term to remain in business.

When a company reports *negative* net cash flows from operations, one measure that is useful in assessing the ability of the company to continue to operate is the ratio of cash to monthly cash expenses. The **ratio of cash to monthly cash expenses** is computed as follows:

$$\text{Ratio of Cash to Monthly Cash Expenses} = \frac{\text{Cash and Cash Equivalents}}{\text{Monthly Cash Expenses}}$$

In the preceding formula, the numerator includes short-term investments that are reported under current assets as cash equivalents. Cash and cash equivalents is the amount reported on the end-of-period balance sheet for which the net cash flows from operations is reported.

The **monthly cash expenses**, sometimes called **monthly cash burn**, are computed as follows:

$$\text{Monthly Cash Expenses} = \frac{\text{Net Cash Flows from Operations}}{12}$$

The ratio of cash to monthly cash expenses is especially useful when assessing the ability of new companies to continue operating. A primary cause of failure of new companies is that they are undercapitalized. That is, the companies don't have sufficient funding (cash) from debt or equity financing to operate long enough to generate positive cash flows from operations.

To illustrate, assume the following data for Ztech Inc., a new biotechnology startup company.

	Year 2	Year 1
Net cash flows from operating activities	$(3,420,000)	$(3,600,000)
Cash and cash equivalents at end of year	1,824,000	2,550,000

The monthly cash expenses and ratio of cash to monthly cash expenses for Year 2 and Year 1 are as follows:

	Year 2	Year 1
Monthly cash expenses:		
$3,420,000 ÷ 12	$(285,000)	
$3,600,000 ÷ 12		$(300,000)
Ratio of cash to monthly cash expenses:		
$1,824,000 ÷ $285,000	6.4 months	
$2,550,000 ÷ $300,000		8.5 months

At the end of Year 1, Ztech had enough cash to continue operating for 8.5 months. To continue beyond 8.5 months, Ztech needed to do one or more of the following:

- Generate positive net cash flows from operations
- Obtain additional financing from issuing stock or debt

Assume that during Year 2 Ztech continued to operate by issuing additional common stock and debt. As a result, at the end of Year 2, the company had cash and cash equivalents of $1,824,000. Based on this amount and its monthly cash expenses, the company can continue to operate 6.4 months into Year 3. Ultimately, Ztech's ability to survive depends upon its ability to generate positive cash flows from its operations.

Startup companies, like Ztech, often experience negative cash flows from operations as they establish a customer base, generate revenue, and earn profits. As a result, startup companies must raise enough funds or have commitments from investors for additional funding to survive until they can generate positive cash flows from their operations.

Key Points

1. Describe the Sarbanes-Oxley Act and its impact on internal controls and financial reporting.

Sarbanes-Oxley requires companies to maintain strong and effective internal controls over the recording of transactions and the preparing of financial statements. Sarbanes-Oxley also requires companies and their independent accountants to report on the effectiveness of a company's internal controls.

2. Describe and illustrate the objectives and elements of internal control.

The objectives of internal control are to provide reasonable assurance that (1) assets are safeguarded and used for business purposes, (2) business information is accurate, and (3) compliance with laws and regulations is met. The elements of internal control are the control environment, risk assessment, control procedures, monitoring, and information and communication.

3. Describe and illustrate the application of internal controls to cash.

One of the most important controls to protect cash received in over-the-counter sales is a cash register. A remittance advice is a control for cash received through the mail. Separating the duties of handling cash and recording cash is also a control. A voucher system is a control system for cash payments that uses a set of procedures for authorizing and recording liabilities and cash payments. Many companies use electronic funds transfers to enhance their control over cash receipts and cash payments.

4. Describe the nature of a bank account and its use in controlling cash.

Businesses use bank accounts as a means of controlling cash. Bank accounts reduce the amount of cash on hand and facilitate the transfer of cash between businesses and locations. In addition, banks send monthly statements to their customers, summarizing all of the transactions for the month. The bank statement allows a business to reconcile the cash transactions recorded in the accounting records to those recorded by the bank.

5. Describe and illustrate the use of a bank reconciliation in controlling cash.

The first section of the bank reconciliation begins with the cash balance according to the bank statement. This balance is adjusted for the company's changes in cash that do not appear on the bank statement and for any bank errors. The second section begins with the cash balance according to the company's records. This balance is adjusted for the bank's changes in cash that do not appear on the company's records and for any company errors. The adjusted balances for the two sections must be equal. No adjustments are necessary on the company's records as a result of the information included in the bank section of the bank reconciliation. However, the items in the company section require adjustments on the company's records.

6. Describe the accounting for special-purpose cash funds.

Businesses often use special-purpose cash funds, such as a petty cash fund or travel funds, to meet specific needs. Each fund is initially established by cashing a check for the amount of cash needed. The cash is then given to a custodian who is authorized to disburse monies from the fund. At periodic intervals or when it is depleted or reaches a minimum amount, the fund is replenished and the disbursements recorded.

7. Describe and illustrate the reporting of cash and cash equivalents in the financial statements.

Cash is listed as the first asset in the Current Assets section of the balance sheet. Companies that have invested excess cash in highly liquid investments usually report *Cash and cash equivalents* on the balance sheet.

8. Metric-Based Analysis: Describe and illustrate the ratio of cash to monthly cash expenses in assessing the ability of a company to continue operating.

The ratio of cash to monthly cash expenses can be used to assess how long a company with negative cash flows from operations can continue to operate. It is computed as cash and cash equivalents divided by monthly cash expenses. Monthly cash expenses are computed as net cash flows from operations divided by 12.

Key Terms

Bank reconciliation (204)
Bank statement (201)
Cash (198)
Cash equivalents (209)
Cash short and over (199)
Compensating balance (209)
Electronic funds transfer (EFT) (200)
Elements of internal control (193)
Employee fraud (193)
Internal control (191)
Monthly cash burn (210)
Monthly cash expenses (210)
Petty cash fund (207)
Ratio of cash to monthly cash expenses (209)
Sarbanes-Oxley Act (191)
Special-purpose funds (209)
Voucher (200)
Voucher system (200)

Illustrative Problem

The bank statement for Urethane Company for June 30, 20Y5, indicates a balance of $9,143.11. All cash receipts are deposited each evening in a night depository, after banking hours.

The accounting records indicate the following summary data for cash receipts and payments for June:

Cash balance as of June 1	$ 3,943.50
Total cash receipts for June	28,971.60
Total amount of checks issued in June	28,388.85

Comparing the bank statement and the accompanying canceled checks and memorandums with the records reveals the following reconciling items:

a. The bank had collected for Urethane Company $1,030 on a customer's note left for collection. The face of the note was $1,000.

b. A deposit of $1,852.21, representing receipts of June 30, had been made too late to appear on the bank statement.

c. Checks outstanding totaled $5,265.27.

d. A check drawn for $157 had been incorrectly charged by the bank as $175.

e. A check for $30 returned with the statement had been recorded in the company's records as $300. The check was for the payment of an obligation to Avery Equipment Company for the purchase of office supplies on account.

f. Bank service charges for June amounted to $78.20.

Instructions

1. Prepare a bank reconciliation for June.
2. Record the effects on the accounts and financial statements that should be made by Urethane Company based upon the bank reconciliation.

Solution

1.

URETHANE COMPANY
Bank Reconciliation
June 30, 20Y5

Cash balance according to bank statement		$ 9,143.11
Add: Deposit of June 30 not recorded by bank	$1,852.21	
Bank error in charging check as $175 instead of $157	18.00	1,870.21
		$11,013.32
Deduct: Outstanding checks		(5,265.27)
Adjusted balance		$ 5,748.05
Cash balance according to company's records		$ 4,526.25*
Add: Proceeds of note collected by bank, including $30 interest	$1,030.00	
Error in recording check	270.00	1,300.00
		$ 5,826.25
Deduct: Bank service charges		(78.20)
Adjusted balance		$ 5,748.05

*$3,943.50 + $28,971.60 − $28,388.85

2.

Increases to Cash

Financial Statement Effects

BALANCE SHEET

	Assets		=	Liabilities	+	Stockholders' Equity
	Cash	+ Notes Receivable	=	Accounts Payable	+	Retained Earnings
June 30.	1,300.00	(1,000.00)		270.00		30.00

STATEMENT OF CASH FLOWS

June 30.	Operating	1,300.00

INCOME STATEMENT

June 30.	Interest revenue	30.00

Decreases to Cash

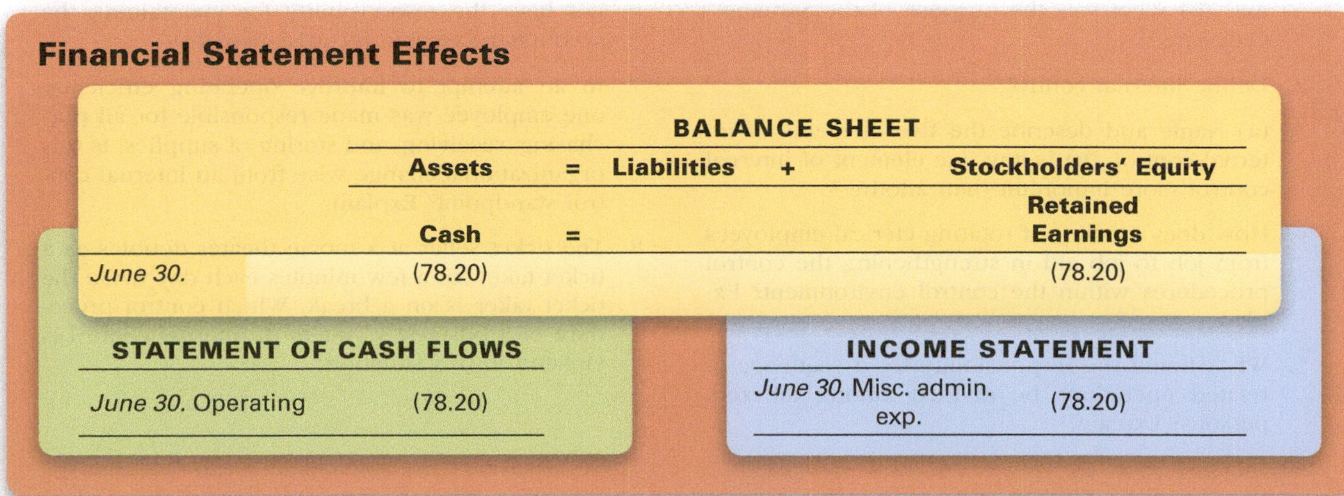

Self-Examination Questions

(Answers appear at the end of chapter)

1. Which of the following is not an element of internal control?
   A. Control environment
   B. Monitoring
   C. Compliance with laws and regulations
   D. Control procedures

2. The bank erroneously charged Tropical Services' account for $450.50 for a check that was correctly written and recorded by Tropical Services as $540.50. To reconcile the bank account of Tropical Services at the end of the month, you would:
   A. add $90 to the cash balance according to the bank statement.
   B. add $90 to the cash balance according to Tropical Services' records.
   C. deduct $90 from the cash balance according to the bank statement.
   D. deduct $90 from the cash balance according to Tropical Services' records.

3. In preparing a bank reconciliation, the amount of checks outstanding would be:
   A. added to the cash balance according to the bank statement.
   B. deducted from the cash balance according to the bank statement.
   C. added to the cash balance according to the company's records.
   D. deducted from the cash balance according to the company's records.

4. Adjustments to the company's records based on the bank reconciliation are required for:
   A. additions to the cash balance according to the company's records.
   B. deductions from the cash balance according to the company's records.
   C. both A and B.
   D. neither A nor B.

5. A petty cash fund is:
   A. used to pay relatively small amounts.
   B. established by estimating the amount of cash needed for disbursements of relatively small amounts during a specified period.
   C. reimbursed when the amount of money in the fund is reduced to a predetermined minimum amount.
   D. all of the above.

Class Discussion Questions

1. (a) Why did Congress pass the Sarbanes-Oxley Act? (b) What was the purpose of the Sarbanes-Oxley Act?
2. Define internal control.
3. (a) Name and describe the five elements of internal control. (b) Is any one element of internal control more important than another?
4. How does a policy of rotating clerical employees from job to job aid in strengthening the control procedures within the control environment? Explain.
5. Why should the responsibility for a sequence of related operations be divided among different persons? Explain.
6. Why should the employee who handles cash receipts not have the responsibility for maintaining the accounts receivable records? Explain.
7. In an attempt to improve operating efficiency, one employee was made responsible for all purchasing, receiving, and storing of supplies. Is this organizational change wise from an internal control standpoint? Explain.
8. The ticket seller at a movie theater doubles as a ticket taker for a few minutes each day while the ticket taker is on a break. Which control procedure of a business's system of internal control is violated in this situation?

9. Why should the responsibility for maintaining the accounting records be separated from the responsibility for operations?
10. Assume that Leslie Hunter, accounts payable clerk for Campland Inc., stole $185,000 by paying fictitious invoices for goods that were never received. The clerk set up accounts in the names of fictitious companies and cashed the checks at a local bank. Describe a control procedure that would have prevented or detected the fraud.
11. Before a voucher for the purchase of merchandise is approved for payment, supporting documents should be compared to verify the accuracy of the liability. Give an example of a supporting document for the purchase of merchandise.
12. The accounting clerk pays all obligations by prenumbered checks. What are the strengths and weaknesses in the internal control over cash payments in this situation?
13. The balance of Cash is likely to differ from the bank statement balance. What two factors are likely to be responsible for the difference?
14. What is the purpose of preparing a bank reconciliation?
15. Do items reported as a credit memorandum on the bank statement represent (a) additions made by the bank to the company's balance or (b) deductions made by the bank from the company's balance? Explain.
16. Seatow Inc. has a petty cash fund of $2,500. (a) Since the petty cash fund is only $2,500, should Seatow Inc. implement controls over petty cash? (b) What controls, if any, could be used for the petty cash fund?
17. (a) How are cash equivalents reported on the financial statements? (b) What are some examples of cash equivalents?

Exercises

E5-1 Sarbanes-Oxley internal control report

Obj. 1

Using Wikipedia (www.wikipedia.org.), look up the entry for the Sarbanes-Oxley Act. Look over the table of contents and find the section that describes Section 404. What does Section 404 require of management's internal control report?

E5-2 Internal controls

Obj. 2, 3

Lyle Steinberg has recently been hired as the manager of Laramie Coffee, a national chain of franchised coffee shops. During her first month as store manager, Lyle encountered the following internal control situations:

a. Laramie Coffee has one cash register. Prior to Lyle's joining the coffee shop, each employee working on a shift would take a customer order, accept payment, and then prepare the order. Lyle made one employee on each shift responsible for taking orders and accepting the customer's payment. Other employees prepare the orders.

b. Since only one employee uses the cash register, that employee is responsible for counting the cash at the end of the shift and verifying that the cash in the drawer matches the amount of cash sales recorded by the cash register. Lyle expects each cashier to balance the drawer to the penny *every* time—no exceptions.

c. Lyle caught an employee putting a case of single-serving tea bags in her car. Not wanting to create a scene, Lyle smiled and said, "I don't think you're putting those tea bags on the right shelf. Don't they belong inside the coffee shop?" The employee returned the tea bags to the stockroom.

State whether you agree or disagree with Lyle's method of handling each situation and explain your answer.

E5-3 Internal controls

Obj. 2, 3

Sherry's Fashions is a retail store specializing in women's clothing. The store has established a liberal return policy for the holiday season in order to encourage gift purchases.

Any item purchased during November and December may be returned through January 31, with a receipt, for cash or exchange. If the customer does not have a receipt, cash will still be refunded for any item under $100. If the item is more than $100, a check is mailed to the customer.

Whenever an item is returned, a store clerk completes a return slip, which the customer signs. The return slip is placed in a special box. The store manager visits the return counter approximately once every two hours to authorize the return slips. Clerks are instructed to place the returned merchandise on the proper rack on the selling floor as soon as possible.

This year, returns at Sherry's Fashions reached an all-time high. There are a large number of returns under $100 without receipts.

a. How can sales clerks employed at Sherry's Fashions use the store's return policy to steal money from the cash register?

b. What internal control weaknesses do you see in the return policy that make cash thefts easier?

c. Would issuing a store credit in place of a cash refund for all merchandise returned without a receipt reduce the possibility of theft? List some advantages and disadvantages of issuing a store credit in place of a cash refund.

d. Assume that Sherry's Fashions is committed to the current policy of issuing cash refunds without a receipt. What changes could be made in the store's procedures regarding customer refunds in order to improve internal control?

Obj. 2, 3

E5-4 Internal controls

Republic City Bank provides loans to businesses in the community through its Commercial Lending Department. Small loans (less than $250,000) may be approved by an individual loan officer, while larger loans (greater than $250,000) must be approved by a board of loan officers. Once a loan is approved, the funds are made available to the loan applicant under agreed-upon terms. The president of Republic City Bank has instituted a policy whereby he has the individual authority to approve loans up to $4,000,000. The president believes that this policy will allow flexibility to approve loans to valued clients much quicker than under the previous policy.

As an internal auditor of Republic City Bank, how would you respond to this change in policy?

Obj. 2, 3

E5-5 Internal controls

One of the largest losses in history from unauthorized securities trading involved a securities trader for a French bank. The trader was able to circumvent internal controls and create over a billion in trading losses. The trader apparently escaped detection by using knowledge of the bank's internal control systems learned from a previous back-office monitoring job. Much of this monitoring involved the use of software to monitor trades. The traders were usually kept to tight spending limits. However, these controls failed in this case.

What general weaknesses in internal controls contributed to the occurrence and size of the losses?

Obj. 2, 3

E5-6 Internal controls

An employee of a trucking company was responsible for resolving roadway accident claims under $25,000. The employee created fake accident claims and wrote settlement checks of between $5,000 and $25,000 to friends or acquaintances acting as phony "victims." One friend recruited subordinates at his place of work to cash some of the checks. Beyond this, the employee also recruited lawyers, who he paid to represent both the trucking company and the fake victims in the bogus accident settlements. When the lawyers cashed the checks, they allegedly split the money with the corrupt employee. This fraud went undetected for two years.

Why would it take so long to discover such a fraud?

E5-7 Internal controls

Obj. 2, 3

Awesome Sound Inc. discovered a fraud wherein one of its front office administrative employees used company funds to purchase goods, such as computers, digital cameras, DVD players, and other electronic items, for her own use. The fraud was discovered when employees noticed an increase in delivery frequency from vendors and the use of unusual vendors. After some investigation, it was discovered that the employee would alter the description or change the quantity on an invoice in order to explain the cost on the bill.

Comment on control strengths and weaknesses related to this fraud.

E5-8 Financial statement fraud

Obj. 2, 3

A former chairman, chief financial officer, and controller of an apparel company pleaded guilty to financial statement fraud. These managers used false journal entries to record fictitious sales, hid inventory in public warehouses so that it could be recorded as "sold," and required sales orders to be backdated so that the sale could be moved back to an earlier period. The combined effect of these actions caused millions in phony quarterly sales.

a. Why might control procedures listed in this chapter be insufficient in stopping this type of fraud?

b. How could this type of fraud be stopped?

E5-9 Internal control of cash receipts

Obj. 2, 3

At the close of each day's business, the sales clerks count the cash in their respective cash drawers and compare the total cash to the cash register tapes. They then prepare a cash memo noting any discrepancies between the actual cash and the cash tapes. An employee from the cashier's office then recounts the cash, compares the total with the memo, and takes the cash to the cashier's office.

a. Indicate the weak link in internal control.

b. How can the weakness be corrected?

E5-10 Internal control of cash receipts

Obj. 2, 3

Jodi Rostad works at the drive-through window of Mamma's Burgers. Occasionally, when a drive-through customer orders, Jodi fills the order and pockets the customer's money. She does not ring up the order on the cash register.

Identify the internal control weaknesses that exist at Mamma's Burgers, and discuss what can be done to prevent this theft.

E5-11 Internal control of cash receipts

Obj. 2, 3

The mailroom employees send all remittances and remittance advices to the cashier. The cashier deposits the cash in the bank and forwards the remittance advices and duplicate deposit slips to the Accounting Department.

a. Indicate the weak link in internal control in the handling of cash receipts.

b. How can the weakness be corrected?

E5-12 Entry for cash sales; cash short

Obj. 2, 3

The actual cash received from the day's cash sales was $18,125 and the amount indicated by the cash register total was $18,200.

a. What is the amount deposited in the bank for the day's sales?

b. What is the amount recorded for the day's sales?

c. How should the difference be recorded?

d. If a cashier is consistently over or short, what action should be taken?

Obj. 2, 3

E5-13 Recording cash sales; cash over

The actual cash received from the day's cash sales was $9,380 and the amount indicated by the cash register total was $9,300.

a. What is the amount deposited in the bank for the day's sales?

b. What is amount recorded for the day's sales?

c. How should the difference be recorded?

d. If a cashier is consistently over or short, what action should be taken?

Obj. 2, 3

E5-14 Internal control of cash payments

Greenleaf Co. is a small merchandising company with a manual accounting system. An investigation revealed that in spite of a sufficient bank balance, a significant amount of available cash discounts had been lost because of failure to make timely payments. In addition, it was discovered that the invoices for several purchases had been paid twice.

Outline procedures for the payment of vendors' invoices, so that the possibilities of losing available cash discounts and of paying an invoice a second time will be minimized.

Obj. 2, 3

E5-15 Internal control of cash payments

Torpedo Digital Company, a communications equipment manufacturer, recently fell victim to a fraud scheme developed by one of its employees. To understand the scheme, it is necessary to review Torpedo's procedures for the purchase of services.

The purchasing agent is responsible for ordering services (such as repairs to a photocopy machine or office cleaning) after receiving a service requisition from an authorized manager. However, since no tangible goods are delivered, a receiving report is not prepared. When the Accounting Department receives an invoice billing Torpedo for a service call, the accounts payable clerk calls the manager who requested the service in order to verify that it was performed.

The fraud scheme involves Ross Dunbar, the manager of plant and facilities. Ross arranged for his uncle's company, Capo Industrial Supplies and Service, to be placed on Torpedo's approved vendor list. Ross did not disclose the family relationship.

On several occasions, Ross would submit a requisition for services to be provided by Capo Industrial Supplies and Service. However, the service requested was really not needed, and it was never performed. Capo Industrial Supplies and Service would bill Torpedo for the service and then split the cash payment with Ross.

Explain what changes should be made to Torpedo's procedures for ordering and paying for services in order to prevent such occurrences in the future.

Obj. 5

E5-16 Bank reconciliation

Identify each of the following reconciling items as: (a) an addition to the cash balance according to the bank statement, (b) a deduction from the cash balance according to the bank statement, (c) an addition to the cash balance according to the company's records, or (d) a deduction from the cash balance according to the company's records. (None of the transactions reported by bank debit and credit memos have been recorded by the company.)

1. Bank service charges, $36.
2. Check drawn by company for $375 but incorrectly recorded by company as $735.
3. Check for $50 incorrectly charged by bank as $500.
4. Check of a customer returned by bank to company because of insufficient funds, $1,200.
5. Deposit in transit, $12,375.
6. Outstanding checks, $14,770.
7. Note collected by bank, $10,600.

E5-17 Entries based on bank reconciliation

Obj. 5

Which of the reconciling items listed in Exercise 5-16 are required to be recorded in the company's accounts?

E5-18 Bank reconciliation

Obj. 5

✔ **Adjusted balance: $14,770**

The following data were accumulated for use in reconciling the bank account of Kaycee Sisters Inc. for August 20Y9:

a. Cash balance according to the company's records at August 31, $14,190.

b. Cash balance according to the bank statement at August 31, $18,330.

c. Checks outstanding, $5,710.

d. Deposit in transit, not recorded by bank, $2,150.

e. A check for $180 in payment of an account was erroneously recorded by Kaycee Sisters Inc. as $810.

f. Bank debit memo for service charges, $50.

Prepare a bank reconciliation, using the format shown in Exhibit 8.

E5-19 Entries for bank reconciliation

Obj. 5

Using the data presented in Exercise 5-18, record the effects on the accounts and financial statements of the company based upon the bank reconciliation.

E5-20 Entries for note collected by bank

Obj. 5

Accompanying a bank statement for Nite Lighting Company is a credit memo for $26,500, representing the principal ($25,000) and interest ($1,500) on a note that had been collected by the bank. The company had been notified by the bank at the time of the collection but had made no recording. Record the adjustment that should be made by the company to bring the accounting records up to date.

E5-21 Bank reconciliation

Obj. 5

✔ **Adjusted balance: $15,310**

An accounting clerk for Westwind Co. prepared the following bank reconciliation:

WESTWIND CO.
Bank Reconciliation
August 31, 20Y6

Cash balance according to company's records		$ 6,800
Add: Outstanding checks	$4,190	
Error by Westwind Co. in recording Check No. 01-115 as $830 instead of $380	450	
Note for $7,500 collected by bank, including interest	8,100	12,740
		$19,540
Deduct: Deposit in transit on August 31	$2,175	
Bank service charges	40	(2,215)
Cash balance according to bank statement		$17,325

a. From the bank reconciliation data, prepare a new bank reconciliation for Westwind Co., using the format shown in Exhibit 10.

b. If a balance sheet were prepared for Westwind Co. on August 31, 20Y6, what amount should be reported for cash?

Obj. 5

✔ Corrected adjusted balance: $24,110

E5-22 Bank reconciliation

Identify the errors in the following bank reconciliation:

DAKOTA CO.
Bank Reconciliation
For the Month Ended June 30, 20Y3

Cash balance according to bank statement			$22,900
Add outstanding checks:			
No. 7715		$1,450	
7760		915	
7764		1,850	
7765		775	4,990
			$27,890
Deduct deposit of June 30, not recorded by bank			(6,200)
Adjusted balance			$21,690
Cash balance according to company's records			$15,625
Add: Proceeds of note collected by bank:			
Principal	$6,000		
Interest	360	$6,360	
Service charges		30	6,390
			$22,015
Deduct: Check returned because of insufficient funds		$ 545	
Error in recording June 20 deposit of $5,200 as $2,500		2,700	(3,245)
Adjusted balance			$18,770

Obj. 2, 3, 5

E5-23 Using bank reconciliation to determine cash receipts stolen

Pala Co. records all cash receipts on the basis of its cash register tapes. Pala Co. discovered during April 20Y1 that one of its sales clerks had stolen an undetermined amount of cash receipts when she took the daily deposits to the bank. The following data have been gathered for April:

Cash in bank according to the company records	$19,565
Cash according to the April 30, 20Y1, bank statement	28,175
Outstanding checks as of April 30, 20Y1	12,100
Bank service charges for April	75
Note receivable, including interest collected by bank in April	3,710

No deposits were in transit on April 30.

a. Determine the amount of cash receipts stolen by the sales clerk.

b. What accounting controls would have prevented or detected this theft?

Obj. 6

E5-24 Recording petty cash fund transactions

Illustrate the effect on the accounts and financial statements of the following transactions:

a. Established a petty cash fund of $750.

b. The amount of cash in the petty cash fund is now $140. Replenished the fund, based on the following summary of petty cash receipts: office supplies, $325; miscellaneous selling expense, $200; miscellaneous administrative expense, $85.

Obj. 6

E5-25 Recording petty cash fund transactions

Illustrate the effect on the accounts and financial statements of the following transactions:

a. Established a petty cash fund of $500.

b. The amount of cash in the petty cash fund is now $45. Replenished the fund, based on the following summary of petty cash receipts: office supplies purchased, $175; miscellaneous selling expense, $190; miscellaneous administrative expense, $90.

Problems

P5-1 Evaluate internal control of cash

Obj. 2, 3

The following procedures were recently implemented by Wind Rivers Clothing Co.:

a. Each cashier is assigned a separate cash register drawer to which no other cashier has access.

b. All sales are rung up on the cash register, and a receipt is given to the customer. All sales are recorded on a record locked inside the cash register.

c. At the end of a shift, each cashier counts the cash in his or her cash register, unlocks the cash register record, and compares the amount of cash with the amount on the record to determine cash shortages and overages.

d. Checks received through the mail are given daily to the accounts receivable clerk for recording collections on account and for depositing in the bank.

e. Vouchers and all supporting documents are stamped PAID after being paid by the treasurer.

f. Disbursements are made from the petty cash fund only after a petty cash receipt has been completed and signed by the payee.

g. The bank reconciliation is prepared by the accountant.

Instructions

Indicate whether each of the procedures of internal control over cash represents (1) a strength or (2) a weakness. For each weakness, indicate why it exists.

P5-2 Bank reconciliation and entries

Obj. 5

✔ 1. Adjusted balance: $25,000

The cash account for Deaver Consulting at October 31, 20Y6, indicated a balance of $15,750. The bank statement indicated a balance of $31,095 on October 31, 20Y6. Comparing the bank statement and the accompanying canceled checks and memos with the records revealed the following reconciling items:

a. Checks outstanding totaled $10,125.

b. A deposit of $4,120, representing receipts from October 31, had been made too late to appear on the bank statement.

c. The bank had collected $10,400 on a note left for collection. The face of the note was $10,000.

d. A check for $1,200 returned with the statement had been incorrectly recorded by Deaver Consulting as $120. The check was for the payment of an obligation to Oxford Office Supplies Co. for the purchase of office supplies on account.

e. A check drawn for $320 had been incorrectly charged by the bank as $230.

f. Bank service charges for October amounted to $70.

Instructions

1. Prepare a bank reconciliation.
2. Illustrate the effects on the accounts and financial statements of the bank reconciliation.

Note: The spreadsheet icon indicates an Excel template is available on the student companion site at www.cengagebrain.com.

Obj. 5

✔ 1. Adjusted balance: $34,885

P5-3 Bank reconciliation and entries

The cash account for All American Sports Co. on April 1, 20Y5, indicated a balance of $23,600. During April, the total cash deposited was $80,150, and checks written totaled $72,800. The bank statement indicated a balance of $40,360 on April 30, 20Y5. Comparing the bank statement, the canceled checks, and the accompanying memos with the records revealed the following reconciling items:

a. Checks outstanding totaled $14,300.

b. A deposit of $9,275, representing receipts of April 30, had been made too late to appear on the bank statement.

c. A check for $720 had been incorrectly charged by the bank as $270.

d. A check for $110 returned with the statement had been recorded by All American Sports Co. as $1,100. The check was for the payment of an obligation to Garber Co. on account.

e. The bank had collected for All American Sports Co. $4,320 on a note left for collection. The face of the note was $4,000.

f. Bank service charges for April amounted to $75.

g. A check for $1,300 from Bishop Co. was returned by the bank because of insufficient funds.

Instructions

1. Prepare a bank reconciliation as of April 30.
2. Illustrate the effects on the accounts and financial statements of the bank reconciliation.

Obj. 5

✔ 1. Adjusted balance: $10,798.88

P5-4 Bank reconciliation and entries

Rancho Foods deposits all cash receipts each Wednesday and Friday in a night depository, after banking hours. The data required to reconcile the bank statement as of May 31 have been taken from various documents and records and are reproduced as follows. The sources of the data are printed in capital letters.

CASH ACCOUNT:

Balance as of May 1 $9,578.00

CASH RECEIPTS FOR MONTH OF MAY $5,255.89

DUPLICATE DEPOSIT TICKETS:

Date and amount of each deposit in May:

Date	Amount	Date	Amount	Date	Amount
May 2	$569.50	May 12	$580.70	May 23	$ 731.45
5	701.80	16	600.10	26	601.50
9	189.24	19	701.26	31	580.34

CHECKS WRITTEN:

Number and amount of each check issued in May:

Check No.	Amount	Check No.	Amount	Check No.	Amount
614	$243.50	621	$309.50	628	$ 837.70
615	350.10	622	Void	629	329.90
616	279.90	623	Void	630	882.80
617	395.50	624	707.01	631	1,081.56
618	435.40	625	185.63	632	62.40
619	320.10	626	550.03	633	310.08
620	238.87	627	318.73	634	503.30

Total amount of checks issued in May $8,342.01

MEMBER FDIC

AMERICAN NATIONAL BANK
OF DETROIT

DETROIT, MI 48201-2500 (313)933-8547

Rancho Foods

	PAGE 1
ACCOUNT NUMBER	
FROM 5/01/20Y8	TO 5/31/20Y8
BALANCE	9,422.80
9 DEPOSITS	6,086.35
20 WITHDRAWALS	7,462.11
4 OTHER DEBITS AND CREDITS	3,650.00CR
NEW BALANCE	11,697.04

CHECKS AND OTHER DEBITS					DEPOSITS	DATE	BALANCE
No.580	310.10	No.612	92.50		780.80	05/01	9,801.00
No.602	85.50	No.614	243.50		569.50	05/03	10,041.50
No.615	350.10	No.616	279.90		701.80	05/06	10,113.30
No.617	395.50	No.618	435.40		819.24	05/11	10,101.64
No.619	320.10	No.620	238.87		580.70	05/13	10,123.37
No.621	309.50	No.624	707.01		MS 4,000.00	05/14	13,106.86
No.625	158.63	No.626	550.03		MS 160.00	05/14	12,558.20
No.627	318.73	No.629	329.90		600.10	05/17	12,509.67
No.630	882.80	No.631	1,081.56	NSF 450.00		05/20	10,095.31
No.632	62.40	No.633	310.08		701.26	05/21	10,424.09
					731.45	05/24	11,155.54
					601.50	05/28	11,757.04
		SC	60.00			05/31	11,697.04

EC — ERROR CORRECTION OD — OVERDRAFT
MS — MISCELLANEOUS PS — PAYMENT STOPPED
NSF — NOT SUFFICIENT FUNDS SC — SERVICE CHARGE

* * * * * * * * *

THE RECONCILEMENT OF THIS STATEMENT WITH YOUR RECORDS IS ESSENTIAL.
ANY ERROR OR EXCEPTION SHOULD BE REPORTED IMMEDIATELY.

BANK RECONCILIATION FOR PRECEDING MONTH (DATED APRIL 30):

Cash balance according to bank statement		$ 9,422.80
Add deposit of April 30, not recorded by bank		780.80
		$10,203.60
Deduct outstanding checks:		
No. 580	$310.10	
No. 602	85.50	
No. 612	92.50	
No. 613	137.50	625.60
Adjusted balance		$ 9,578.00
Cash balance according to company's records		$ 9,605.70
Deduct service charges		27.70
Adjusted balance		$ 9,578.00

Instructions

1. Prepare a bank reconciliation as of May 31. If errors in recording deposits or checks are discovered, assume that the errors were made by the company. Assume that all deposits are from cash sales except for the note receivable of $4,000 and interest of $160 collected on May 14. All checks were written to satisfy accounts payable.
2. Illustrate the effects on the accounts and financial statements of the bank reconciliation.
3. What is the amount of Cash that should appear on the balance sheet as of May 31?
4. Assume that a canceled check for $50 has been incorrectly recorded by the bank as $500. Briefly explain how the error would be included in a bank reconciliation and how it should be corrected.

Metric-Based Analysis

MBA 5-1 Ratio of cash to monthly cash expenses

AcelRx Pharmaceuticals, Inc. (ACRX), develops therapies for pain relief for a variety of patients, including cancer and trauma patients. The following data (in thousands) were adapted from financial statements of a recent year.

Net cash flows from operating activities	$(34,456)
End of the year cash and cash equivalents	60,038
Short-term investments*	15,312

*Includes U.S. short-term government securities that are readily convertible to cash.

1. Compute the monthly cash expenses. Round to nearest thousand.
2. Compute the ratio of cash to monthly cash expenses, excluding short-term investments. Round to one decimal place.
3. Including short-term investments as part of cash and cash equivalents, compute the ratio of cash to monthly cash expenses. Round to one decimal place.
4. Comment on the results from parts (2) and (3).
5. AcelRx had negative cash flows from operations for the past seven years, yet cash, cash equivalents, and short-term investments are $75,350 ($60,038 + $15,312). How could this have happened?

MBA 5-2 Ratio of cash to monthly cash expenses

Pacira Pharmaceuticals Inc. (PCRX) develops, produces, and sells products used in hospitals and surgery centers.

The following data (in thousands) were adapted from recent financial statements.

	Year 3	Year 2	Year 1
Operations:			
Net income (loss)	$(13,716)	$(63,909)	$(52,281)
Net cash flows from operating activities	25,469	(43,216)	(70,130)
Balance sheet:			
End of the year cash and cash equivalents	39,029	14,148	11,649
Short-term investments*	119,138	59,637	30,924
Financing activities:			
Issued common stock	118,875	—	62,855
Issued long-term debt	—	120,000	—

*Includes various short-term securities that are readily convertible to cash.

1. Compute the monthly cash expenses for Years 1 and 2. Round to nearest thousand.
2. Compute the ratio of cash to monthly cash expenses for Years 1 and 2. Round to one decimal place.
3. Including short-term investments as part of cash and cash equivalents, compute the ratio of cash to monthly cash expenses for Years 1 and 2. Round to one decimal place.
4. Comment on the results from parts (2) and (3).
5. Comment on Year 3 results.

MBA 5-3 Ratio of cash to monthly cash expenses

Kips Bay Medical Inc. is a medical device company that develops, produces, and sells products used in coronary surgery. The following data (in thousands) were adapted from recent financial statements.

	Year 4	Year 3	Year 2	Year 1
Operations:				
Net income (loss)	$(5,607)	$(6,060)	$(5,507)	$(4,250)
Net cash flows from operating activities	(5,026)	(5,537)	(4,203)	(8,105)
Balance sheet:				
End of the year cash and cash equivalents	3,138	2,316	9,403	6,211
Short-term investments*	457	2,684	947	2,957
Financing activities:				
Issued common stock	3,643	—	5,441	13,632

*Includes various short-term securities that are readily convertible to cash.

1. Compute the monthly cash expenses for Years 1–4. Round to nearest thousand.
2. Compute the ratio of cash to monthly cash expenses for Years 1–4. Round to one decimal place.
3. Including short-term investments as part of cash and cash equivalents, compute the ratio of cash to monthly cash expenses for Years 1–4. Round to one decimal place.
4. Comment on the results from parts (2) and (3).
5. Kips Bay Medical issued common stock in Year 4. Based upon (2) and (3), would you invest in Kips common stock in Year 4?

MBA 5-4 Ratio of cash to monthly cash expenses

Boston Scientific Corporation (BSX) is a competitor of Kips Bay Medical (MBA 5-3). It was organized in 1979 and also develops, produces, and sells medical devices. The following data (in thousands) were adapted from Boston Scientific's recent financial statements.

	Year 2	Year 1
Net cash flows from operating activities	$1,269	$1,110
End of the year cash and cash equivalents	587	217

1. Compare the preceding data for Boston Scientific with Kips Bay Medical's data shown in MBA 5-3.
2. Would the computation of the ratio of cash to monthly cash expenses be meaningful for Boston Scientific?

Cases

Case 5-1 Ethics and professional conduct in business

During the preparation of the bank reconciliation for Apache Grading Co., Sarah Ferrari, the assistant controller, discovered that Rocky Spring Bank incorrectly recorded a $610 check written by Apache Grading Co. as $160. Sarah has decided not to notify the bank but wait for the bank to detect the error. Sarah plans to record the $450 error as Other Income if the bank fails to detect the error within the next three months.

Discuss whether Sarah is behaving in a professional manner.

Case 5-2 Internal controls

The following is an excerpt from a conversation between two sales clerks, Tracy Rawlin and Jeff Weimer. Both Tracy and Jeff are employed by Magnum Electronics, a locally owned and operated electronics retail store.

Tracy: Did you hear the news?

Jeff: What news?

Tracy: Bridget and Ken were both arrested this morning.

Jeff: What? Arrested? You're putting me on!

Tracy: No, really! The police arrested them first thing this morning. Put them in handcuffs, read them their rights—the whole works. It was unreal!

Jeff: What did they do?

Tracy: Well, apparently they were filling out merchandise refund forms for fictitious customers and then taking the cash.

Jeff: I guess I never thought of that. How did they catch them?

Tracy: The store manager noticed that returns were twice that of last year and seemed to be increasing. When he confronted Bridget, she became flustered and admitted to taking the cash, apparently over $15,000 in just three months. They're going over the last six months' transactions to try to determine how much Ken stole. He apparently started stealing first.

Suggest appropriate control procedures that would have prevented or detected the theft of cash.

Case 5-3 Internal controls

The following is an excerpt from a conversation between the store manager of La Food Grocery Stores, Amy Locke, and Steve Meyer, president of La Food Grocery Stores.

Steve: Amy, I'm concerned about this new scanning system.

Amy: What's the problem?

Steve: Well, how do we know the clerks are ringing up all the merchandise?

Amy: That's one of the strong points about the system. The scanner automatically rings up each item, based on its bar code. We update the prices daily, so we're sure that the sale is rung up for the right price.

Steve: That's not my concern. What keeps a clerk from pretending to scan items and then simply not charging his friends? If his friends were buying 10–15 items, it would be easy for the clerk to pass through several items with his finger over the bar code or just pass the merchandise through the scanner with the wrong side showing. It would look normal for anyone observing. In the old days, we at least could hear the cash register ringing up each sale.

Amy: I see your point.

Suggest ways that La Food Grocery Stores could prevent or detect the theft of merchandise as described.

Case 5-4 Ethics and professional conduct in business

Javier Meza and Sue Quan are both cash register clerks for Healthy Markets. Ingrid Perez is the store manager for Healthy Markets. The following is an excerpt of a conversation between Javier and Sue:

Javier: Sue, how long have you been working for Healthy Markets?

Sue: Almost five years this June. You just started two weeks ago, right?

Javier: Yes. Do you mind if I ask you a question?

Sue: No, go ahead.

Javier: What I want to know is, have they always had this rule that if your cash register is short at the end of the day, you have to make up the shortage out of your own pocket?

Sue: Yes, as long as I've been working here.

Javier: Well, it's the pits. Last week I had to pay in almost $30.

Sue: It's not that big a deal. I just make sure that I'm not short at the end of the day.

Javier: How do you do that?

Sue: I just shortchange a few customers early in the day. There are a few jerks that deserve it anyway. Most of the time, their attention is elsewhere and they don't think to check their change.

Javier: What happens if you're over at the end of the day?

Sue: Ingrid lets me keep it as long as it doesn't get to be too large. I've not been short in over a year. I usually clear about $10 to $40 extra per day.

Discuss this case from the viewpoint of proper controls and professional behavior.

Case 5-5 Bank reconciliation and internal control

The records of Clairemont Company indicate an August 31, 20Y1 cash balance of $6,675, which includes undeposited receipts for August 30 and 31. The cash balance on the bank statement as of August 31 is $5,350. This balance includes a note of $3,000 plus $210 interest collected by the bank but not recorded in the journal. Checks outstanding on August 31 were as follows: No. 370, $580; No. 379, $615; No. 390, $900; No. 1148, $225; No. 1149, $300; and No. 1151, $750.

On August 9, the cashier resigned, effective at the end of the month. Before leaving on August 31, the cashier prepared the following bank reconciliation:

Cash balance per books, August 31, 20Y1		$ 6,675
Add outstanding checks:		
No. 1148	$225	
1149	300	
1151	750	1,175
		$ 7,850
Less undeposited receipts		(2,500)
Cash balance per bank, August 31, 20Y1		$ 5,350
Deduct unrecorded note with interest		(3,210)
True cash, August 31, 20Y1		$ 2,140

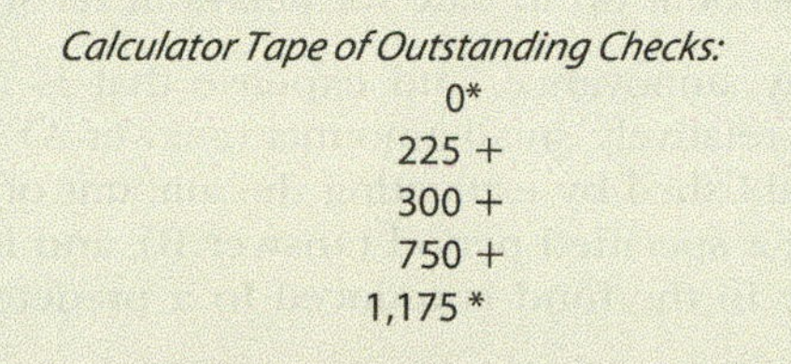
Calculator Tape of Outstanding Checks:
0*
225 +
300 +
750 +
1,175 *

Subsequently, the owner of Clairemont Company discovered that the cashier had stolen an unknown amount of undeposited receipts, leaving only $2,500 to be deposited on August 31. The owner, a close family friend, has asked for your help in determining the amount that the former cashier has stolen.

1. Determine the amount the cashier stole from Clairemont Company. Show your computations in good form.
2. How did the cashier attempt to conceal the theft?
3. a. Identify two major weaknesses in internal controls that allowed the cashier to steal the undeposited cash receipts.

   b. Recommend improvements in internal controls, so that similar types of thefts of undeposited cash receipts can be prevented.

Case 5-6 Observe internal controls over cash

Select a business in your community and observe its internal controls over cash receipts and cash payments. The business could be a bank or a bookstore, restaurant, department store, or other retailer. In groups of three or four, identify and discuss the similarities and differences in each business's cash internal controls.

Answers to Self-Examination Questions

1. **C** Compliance with laws and regulations (answer C) is an objective, not an element, of internal control. The control environment (answer A), monitoring (answer B), control procedures (answer D), risk assessment, and information and communication are the five elements of internal control.
2. **C** The error was made by the bank, so the cash balance according to the bank statement needs to be adjusted. Since the bank deducted $90 ($540.50 − $450.50) too little, the error of $90 should be deducted from the cash balance according to the bank statement (answer C).
3. **B** On any specific date, the cash account in a company's records may not agree with the account in the bank's records because of delays and/or errors by either party in recording transactions. The purpose of a bank reconciliation, therefore, is to determine the reasons for any differences between the two account balances. All errors should then be corrected by the company or the bank, as appropriate. In arriving at the adjusted cash balance according to the bank statement, outstanding checks must be deducted (answer B) to adjust for checks that have been written by the company but that have not yet been presented to the bank for payment.
4. **C** All reconciling items that are added to and deducted from the cash balance according to the company's records on the bank reconciliation (answer C) require that adjustments be recorded by the company to correct errors made in recording transactions or to bring the cash account up to date for delays in recording transactions.
5. **D** To avoid the delay, annoyance, and expense that is associated with paying all obligations by check, relatively small amounts (answer A) are paid from a petty cash fund. The fund is established by estimating the amount of cash needed to pay these small amounts during a specified period (answer B), and it is then reimbursed when the amount of money in the fund is reduced to a predetermined minimum amount (answer C).

Chapter 6

Receivables and Inventories

What's Covered:

Topics: Receivables and Inventories

Receivables

- Classifications (Obj. 1)
- Uncollectible Receivables (Obj. 2)
- Direct write-off method (Obj. 3)
- Allowance method (Obj. 4)

Inventories

- Classifications (Obj. 5)
- Cost flow assumptions (Obj. 6)
- Cost flow comparisons (Obj. 7)

Financial Reporting

- Receivables (Obj. 8)
- Inventories (Obj. 8)

Metric-Based Analysis

- Transactions:
  - Liquidity: Days' sales in receivables (Obj. 3, 4)
    Days' sales in inventory (Obj. 7, 8)
  - Profitability: Return on sales (Obj. 3, 4, 7, 8)
- Financial Statements:
  - Receivable turnover (Obj. 9)
  - Inventory turnover (Obj. 9)

Learning Objectives

Obj.1 Describe the common classifications of receivables.

Obj.2 Describe the nature of and the accounting for uncollectible receivables.

Obj.3 Describe the direct write-off method of accounting for uncollectible receivables.

Obj.4 Describe the allowance method of accounting for uncollectible receivables.

Obj.5 Describe the common classifications of inventories.

Obj.6 Describe three inventory cost flow assumptions.

Obj.7 Compare and contrast the use of the three inventory costing methods.

Obj.8 Describe how receivables and inventory are reported on the financial statements.

Obj.9 Metric-Based Analysis: Describe and illustrate the accounts receivable turnover and inventory turnover in assessing a company's liquidity and operations.

Chapter Metrics

Use the following metrics to analyze transactions and financial statements.

TRANSACTIONS

Liquidity: Days' Sales in Receivables
Days' Sales in Inventory

Profitability: Return on Sales

FINANCIAL STATEMENTS

Accounts Receivable Turnover
Inventory Turnover

Susan Montgomery/ Shutterstock.com

CVS Health Care Corporation (CVS) operates over 7,500 retail pharmacies and 900 walk-in medical clinics. In addition, CVS provides a mail-order pharmacy where customers can fill prescriptions using the mail, telephone, fax, or the Internet. Finally, CVS serves as a pharmacy benefits plan manager for employers, insurance companies, and health plans offered by private insurance exchanges. In this role, CVS serves more than 65 million customers.

CVS faces many operational challenges and risks. For example, in its pharmacy operations, CVS must comply with laws regulating the purchase, distribution, tracking, and dispensing of prescription drugs and other controlled substances. It must comply with privacy laws on the collection, disclosure, and transmission of customers' personal information. It must monitor patent expirations of brand drugs and the availability of generic substitutes. Finally, CVS must protect against the possibility of product tampering and incorrectly dispensing drugs to customers. In its retail operations, CVS faces various competitive pressures from companies like Walgreens and Wal-Mart as well as changing customer lifestyles and preferences.

As a provider of medical services and medications, CVS generates accounts receivables from insurance companies, health plans, and governmental agencies, including the U.S. government's Centers for Medicare and Medicaid Services (CMS). As a retail business, CVS maintains inventories of prescription drugs as well as general merchandise including cosmetics, snack foods, greeting cards, and soft drinks.

In this chapter, accounting and reporting issues related to receivables and inventories are described and illustrated. In doing so, the effects on the financial statements of estimating uncollectible receivables and inventory cost flow assumptions are emphasized.

Objective 1
Describe the common classifications of receivables.

Classification of Receivables

The receivables that result from sales on account are normally accounts receivable or notes receivable. The term **receivables** includes all money claims against other entities, including people, companies, and other organizations. Receivables are usually a significant portion of the total current assets.

Accounts Receivable

The most common transaction creating a receivable is selling merchandise or services on account (on credit). The receivable is recorded as an increase to Accounts Receivable. Such **accounts receivable** are normally collected within a short period, such as 30 or 60 days. They are classified on the balance sheet as a current asset.

In a recent balance sheet, **CVS** reported $9,943 million of accounts receivable.

Notes Receivable

Notes receivable are amounts that customers owe for which a formal, written instrument of credit has been issued. If notes receivable are expected to be collected within a year, they are classified on the balance sheet as a current asset.

Notes are often used for credit periods of more than 60 days. For example, an automobile dealer may require a down payment at the time of sale and accept a note or a series of notes for the remainder. Such notes usually provide for monthly payments.

A note has some advantages over an account receivable. By signing a note, the debtor recognizes the debt and agrees to pay it according to its terms. Thus, a note is a stronger legal claim.

Integrity, Objectivity, and Ethics in Business

Receivables Fraud

Financial reporting frauds are often tied to accounts receivable, because receivables allow companies to record revenue before cash is received. Take, for example, the case of entrepreneur Michael Weinstein, who acquired **Coated Sales, Inc.**, with the dream of growing the small specialty company into a major corporation. To acquire funding that would facilitate this growth, Weinstein had to artificially boost the company's sales. He accomplished this by adding millions in false accounts receivable to existing customer accounts.

The company's auditors began to sense a problem when they called one of the company's customers to confirm a large order. When the customer denied placing the order, the auditors began to investigate the company's receivables more closely. Their analysis revealed a fraud which overstated profits by $55 million and forced the company into bankruptcy, costing investors and creditors over $160 million.

Source: Joseph T. Wells, "Follow Fraud to the Likely Perpetrator," *The Journal of Accountancy*, March 2001.

A promissory note receivable is a written promise to pay the face amount, usually with interest, on demand or at a date in the future.[1] Characteristics of a promissory note are as follows:

1. The *maker* is the party making the promise to pay.
2. The *payee* is the party to whom the note is payable.
3. The *face amount* is the amount the note is written for on its face.
4. The *issuance date* is the date a note is issued.
5. The *due date* or *maturity date* is the date the note is to be paid.
6. The *term* of a note is the amount of time between the issuance and due dates.
7. The *interest rate* is that rate of interest that must be paid on the face amount for the term of the note.

Exhibit 1 illustrates a promissory note.

Exhibit 1 Promissory Note

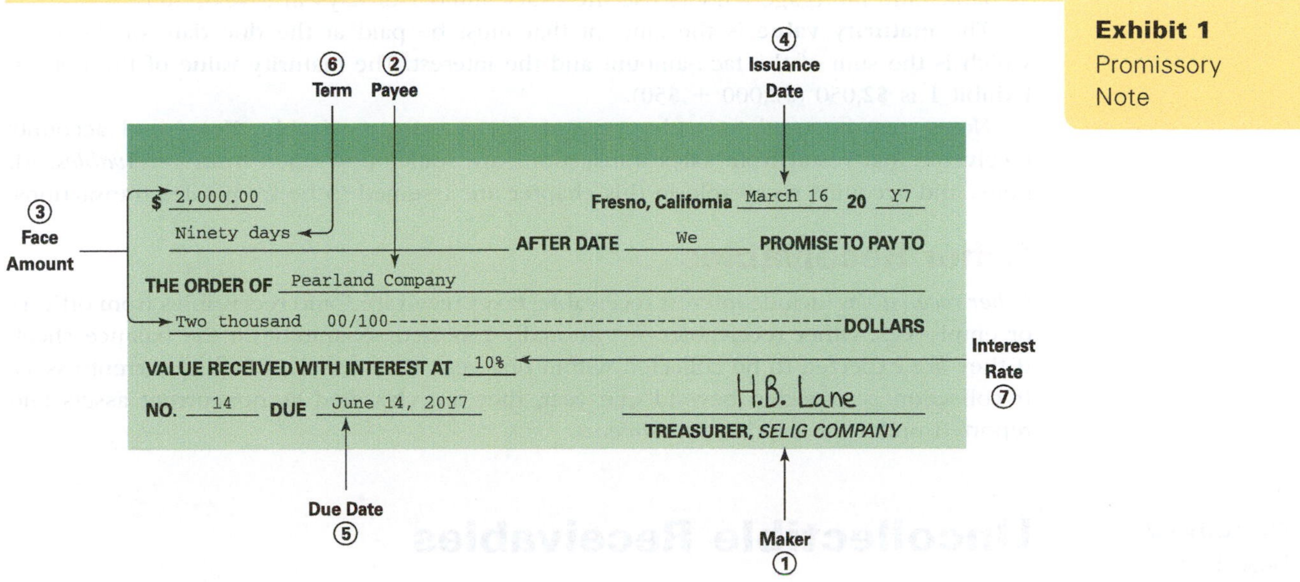

1. You may see references to non-interest-bearing notes. Such notes are not widely used and carry an assumed or implicit interest rate.

The maker of the note is Selig Company, and the payee is Pearland Company. The face value of the note is $2,000, and the issuance date is March 16, 20Y7. The term of the note is 90 days, which results in a due date of June 14, 20Y7, as follows.

Days in March	31 days
Minus issuance date of note	(16)
Days remaining in March	15 days
Add days in April	30
Add days in May	31
Add days in June (due date of June 14)	14
Term of note	90 days

Due Date of 90-Day Note

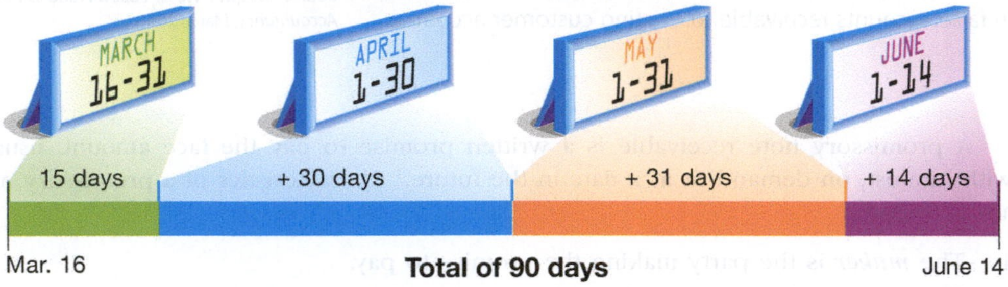

MARCH 16-31 | APRIL 1-30 | MAY 1-31 | JUNE 1-14

15 days | + 30 days | + 31 days | + 14 days

Mar. 16 — **Total of 90 days** — June 14

In Exhibit 1, the term of the note is 90 days and it has an interest rate of 10%. The interest on a note is computed as follows:

Interest = Face Amount × Interest Rate × (Term/360 days)

The interest rate is stated on an annual (yearly) basis, while the term is expressed in days. Thus, the interest on the note in Exhibit 1 is computed as follows:

Interest = $2,000 × 10% × (90/360) = $50

To simplify, 360 days per year are used in this chapter. In practice, companies such as banks and mortgage lenders use the exact number of days in a year, 365.

The **maturity value** is the amount that must be paid at the due date of the note, which is the sum of the face amount and the interest. The maturity value of the note in Exhibit 1 is $2,050 ($2,000 + $50).

Notes may be used to settle a customer's account receivable. Notes and accounts receivable that result from sales transactions are sometimes called *trade receivables*. All notes and accounts receivable in this chapter are assumed to be from sales transactions.

Other Receivables

Other receivables include interest receivable, taxes receivable, and receivables from officers or employees. Other receivables are normally reported separately on the balance sheet. If they are expected to be collected within one year, they are classified as current assets. If collection is expected beyond one year, they are classified as noncurrent assets and reported under the caption *Investments*.

Objective 2
Describe the nature of and the accounting for uncollectible receivables.

Uncollectible Receivables

In prior chapters, the accounting for sales of merchandise or services on account (on credit) was described and illustrated. A major issue that has not yet been discussed is that some customers will not pay their accounts. That is, some accounts receivable will be uncollectible.

Companies may shift the risk of uncollectible receivables to other companies. For example, some retailers do not accept sales on account but will only accept cash or credit cards. Such policies shift the risk to the credit card companies.

Companies may also sell their receivables. This is often the case when a company issues its own credit card. For example, **Macy's** and **JCPenney** issue their own credit cards. Selling receivables is called *factoring* the receivables. The buyer of the receivables is called a *factor.* An advantage of factoring is that the company selling its receivables immediately receives cash for operating and other needs. Also, depending on the factoring agreement, some of the risk of uncollectible accounts is shifted to the factor.

Regardless of how careful a company is in granting credit, some credit sales will be uncollectible. The operating expense recorded from uncollectible receivables is called **bad debt expense**, *uncollectible accounts expense,* or *doubtful accounts expense.*

There is no general rule for when an account becomes uncollectible. Some indications that an account may be uncollectible include the following:

- The receivable is past due.
- The customer does not respond to the company's attempts to collect.
- The customer files for bankruptcy.
- The customer closes its business.
- The company cannot locate the customer.

If a customer doesn't pay, a company may turn the account over to a collection agency. After the collection agency attempts to collect payment, any remaining balance in the account is considered worthless.

The two methods of accounting for uncollectible receivables are as follows:

1. The **direct write-off method** records bad debt expense only when an account is determined to be worthless.
2. The **allowance method** records bad debt expense by estimating uncollectible accounts at the end of the accounting period.

The direct write-off method is often used by small companies and companies with few receivables.[2] Generally accepted accounting principles (GAAP), however, require companies with a large amount of receivables to use the allowance method. As a result, most well-known companies such as **General Electric**, **Pepsi**, **Intel**, and **FedEx** use the allowance method.

CVS uses the allowance method of accounting for uncollectible receivables.

CVS Connection

Direct Write-Off Method for Uncollectible Accounts

Objective 3

Describe the direct write-off method of accounting for uncollectible receivables.

Under the direct write-off method, bad debt expense is not recorded until the customer's account is determined to be worthless. At that time, the customer's account receivable is written off.

To illustrate, assume that on May 10 a $4,200 account receivable from Markieff Carson has been determined to be uncollectible. The effect on the accounts and financial statements of writing off the account is as follows:

2. The direct write-off method is also required for federal income tax purposes.

Financial Statement Effects

BALANCE SHEET

	Assets	=	Liabilities	+	Stockholders' Equity
	Accounts Receivable	=			**Retained Earnings**
May 10.	(4,200)				(4,200)

STATEMENT OF CASH FLOWS

INCOME STATEMENT

May 10. Bad debt expense (4,200)

The liquidity metric related to accounts receivable transactions used throughout the chapter is days' sales in receivables. **Days' sales in receivables** estimates the average number of days it takes to collect accounts receivable. For example, a company with credit terms of n/30 would expect to collect receivables every 30 days and have 30 days of accounts receivable outstanding.

Days' sales in accounts receivable is computed as follows:[3]

$$\textbf{Days' Sales in Receivables} = \frac{\textbf{Average Accounts Receivables}}{\textbf{Average Daily Sales}}$$

Average daily sales is computed by dividing annual sales by 365 days. To illustrate, assume the following data for Downing Inc. for the year ending December 31, 20Y4.

Sales for year ending Dec. 31, 20Y4	$9,125,000
Accounts Receivable, Jan. 1, 20Y4	400,000
Accounts Receivable, Dec. 31, 20Y4	600,000

The days' sales in receivables of 20 days is computed as follows:

$$\textbf{Days' Sales in Receivables} = \frac{\textbf{Average Accounts Receivables}}{\textbf{Average Daily Sales}} = \frac{\textbf{(\$400,000 + \$600,000)} \div \textbf{2}}{\textbf{\$9,125,000} \div \textbf{365 days}}$$

$$= \frac{\textbf{\$500,000}}{\textbf{\$25,000}} = \textbf{20 days}$$

The profitability metric related to accounts receivable transactions used throughout the chapter is **return on sales**. Return on sales is computed as follows:

$$\textbf{Return on Sales} = \frac{\textbf{Operating Income}}{\textbf{Sales}}$$

To illustrate, assume that Downing Inc. reported operating income of $1,460,000 for the year ending December 31, 20Y4. The return on sales of 16% is computed as follows:

$$\textbf{Return on Sales} = \frac{\textbf{Operating Income}}{\textbf{Sales}} = \frac{\textbf{\$1,460,000}}{\textbf{\$9,125,000}} = \textbf{16\%}$$

3. Although accounts receivable are just related to "credit" sales, total sales is normally used to compute accounts receivable turnover. This is because credit sales are normally not reported to external users.

Transaction Metric Effects

The effects of writing off an uncollectible account of $4,200 using the direct write-off method on the liquidity and profitability metrics are as follows:

LIQUIDITY	
Days' Sales in Receivables	Decrease

PROFITABILITY	
Return on Sales	Decrease

Writing off accounts receivable under the direct method increases bad debt expense and decreases accounts receivables. Sales are not affected. However, because of the increase in bad debt expense, operating income decreases. As a result, the days' sales in receivables will decrease and the return on sales will decrease.

An account receivable that has been written off may be later collected. In such cases, the account is reinstated by reversing the write-off. The cash received in payment is then recorded as a receipt on account.

To illustrate, assume that the Markieff Carson account of $4,200 written off on May 10 is later collected on November 21. The effect on the accounts and financial statements of the reinstatement and the receipt of cash is as follows:

Reinstate Account

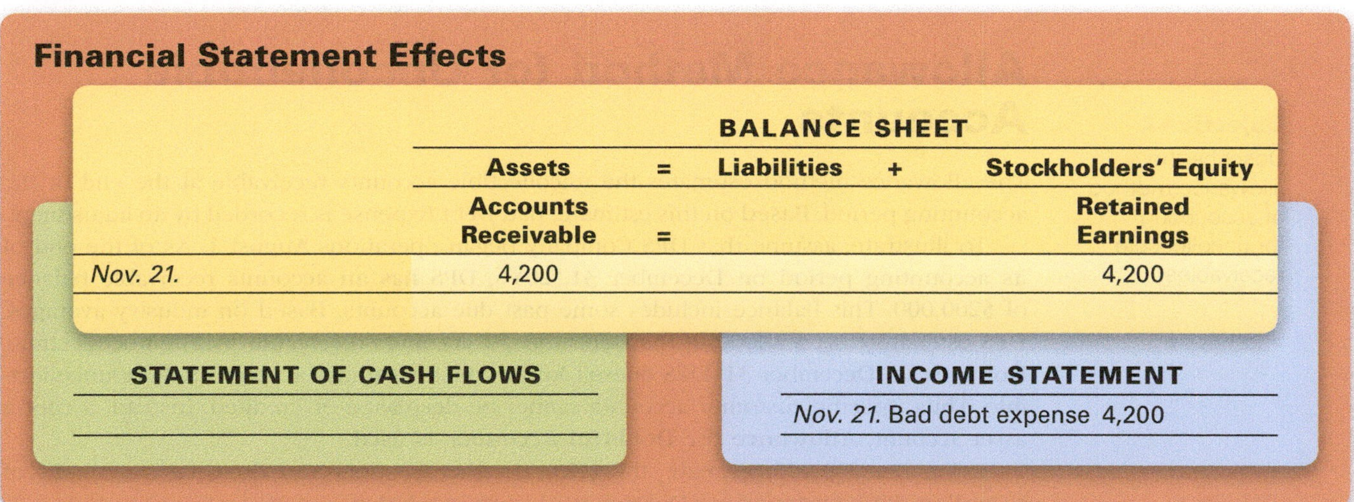

Financial Statement Effects

	BALANCE SHEET				
	Assets	=	Liabilities	+	Stockholders' Equity
	Accounts Receivable	=			Retained Earnings
Nov. 21.	4,200				4,200

STATEMENT OF CASH FLOWS

INCOME STATEMENT	
Nov. 21. Bad debt expense	4,200

Collected Cash

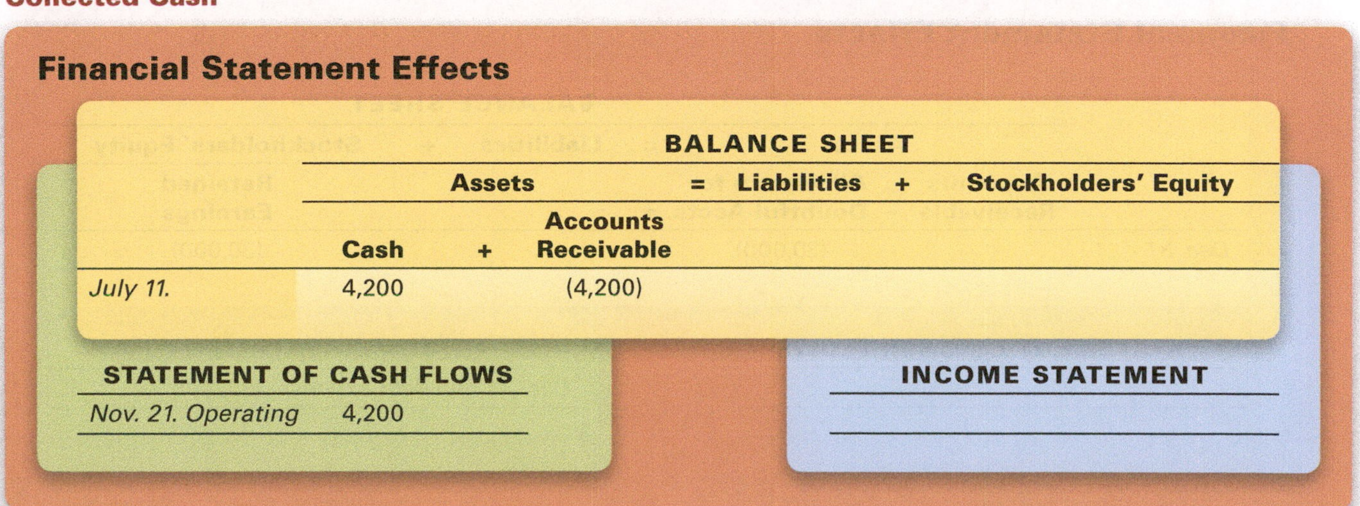

Financial Statement Effects

	BALANCE SHEET					
	Assets			=	Liabilities +	Stockholders' Equity
	Cash	+	Accounts Receivable			
July 11.	4,200		(4,200)			

STATEMENT OF CASH FLOWS	
Nov. 21. Operating	4,200

INCOME STATEMENT

Transaction Metric Effects

The effects of the reinstatement and collection of the $4,200 account on the liquidity and profitability metrics are as follows:

Date	Description	Liquidity Days' Sales in Receivables	Profitability Return on Sales
Nov. 21	Reinstate account	Increase	Increase
21	Collected cash	Decrease	No effect

Days' sales in receivables is increased by the reinstatement of the account and decreased by its collection. Since bad debt expense is reduced by the reinstatement of the account, operating income and return on sales increase. Operating income and return on sales are not affected by collection of the account.

The direct write-off method is used by businesses that sell most of their goods or services for cash and accept only credit cards such as MasterCard or Visa, which are recorded as cash sales. In such cases, receivables are a small part of the current assets and any bad debt expense would be small. Examples of such businesses are a local restaurant or convenience store.

Allowance Method for Uncollectible Accounts

Objective 4

Describe the allowance method of accounting for uncollectible receivables.

The allowance method estimates the uncollectible accounts receivable at the end of the accounting period. Based on this estimate, Bad Debt Expense is recorded by an adjustment.

To illustrate, assume that DPS Company began operations August 1. As of the end of its accounting period on December 31, 20Y6, DPS has an accounts receivable balance of $200,000. This balance includes some past due accounts. Based on industry averages, DPS estimates that $30,000 of the December 31 accounts receivable will be uncollectible. However, on December 31, DPS doesn't know which customer accounts will be uncollectible. Thus, specific customer accounts cannot be decreased or credited. Instead, a contra asset account, **Allowance for Doubtful Accounts**, is used.

Using the $30,000 estimate, the effect on the accounts and financial statements of recording the adjustment on December 31 is shown below.

Financial Statement Effects

BALANCE SHEET

	Assets			=	Liabilities	+	Stockholders' Equity
	Accounts Receivable	–	Allowance for Doubtful Accts.	=			Retained Earnings
Dec. 31.			(30,000)				(30,000)

STATEMENT OF CASH FLOWS

INCOME STATEMENT

Dec. 31. Bad debt expense (30,000)

The preceding adjustment affects the income statement and balance sheet. On the income statement, the $30,000 of Bad Debt Expense will be matched against the related revenues of the period. On the balance sheet, the value of the receivables is reduced to the amount that is expected to be collected or realized. This amount, $170,000 ($200,000 − $30,000), is called the **net realizable value** of the receivables.

After the preceding adjustment is recorded, Accounts Receivable still has a balance of $200,000. This balance is the total amount owed by customers on account at December 31 and is supported by the individual customer accounts.[4] The accounts receivable contra account, Allowance for Doubtful Accounts, has a negative balance of $(30,000).

Adjustment Metric Effects

The effects of the adjustment of $30,000 on the liquidity and profitability metrics are as follows:

LIQUIDITY	
Days' Sales in Receivables	Decrease

PROFITABILITY	
Return on Sales	Decrease

Days' sales in receivables is normally computed using net realizable value of receivables (accounts receivable less the allowance for doubtful accounts). Since allowance for doubtful accounts increases, the net realizable value of receivables decreases and the days' sales in receivables decreases. Since Bad Debt Expense increases, operating income decreases, which results in a decrease in the return on sales.

Write-Offs to the Allowance Account

When a customer's account is identified as uncollectible, it is written off against the allowance account. This requires the company to remove the specific accounts receivable and an equal amount from the allowance account. For example, the effect on the accounts and financial statements on January 21, 20Y7, of writing off Chandler Somers's account of $6,000 with DPS Company is as follows:

Financial Statement Effects

	BALANCE SHEET				
	Assets		=	Liabilities +	Stockholders' Equity
	Accounts Receivable	− Allowance for Doubtful Accts.	=		
Jan. 21.	(6,000)	6,000			

STATEMENT OF CASH FLOWS

INCOME STATEMENT

4. The individual customer accounts are often maintained in a separate file or record called a subsidiary ledger. The sum of the individual customer accounts equals the balance of the accounts receivable, called the control account, reported on the balance sheet.

Transaction Metric Effects

The write-off of the $6,000 account receivable on the liquidity and profitability metrics are as follows:

LIQUIDITY	
Days' Sales in Receivables	No Effect

PROFITABILITY	
Return on Sales	No Effect

Since the net realizable value of receivables does not change, the write-off has no effect on the days' sales in receivables. Since the write-off does not affect operating income, there is no effect on the profitability metric return on sales.

At the end of a period, the Allowance for Doubtful Accounts will normally have a balance. This is because the Allowance for Doubtful Accounts is based upon an estimate. As a result, the total write-offs to the allowance account during the period will rarely equal the balance of the account at the beginning of the period. The allowance account will have a negative balance at the end of the period if the write-offs during the period are less than the beginning balance. It will have a positive balance if the write-offs exceed the beginning balance. However, after the end-of-period adjustment is recorded, Allowance for Doubtful Accounts should always have a negative balance.

In a recent year, **CVS** wrote of $185 million of receivables to its allowance account.

An account receivable that has been written off against the allowance account may be collected later. Like the direct write-off method, the account is reinstated by reversing the write-off. The cash received in payment is then recorded as a receipt on account.

To illustrate, assume that Nancy Smith's account of $5,000, which was written off on April 2, is later collected on June 10. DPS Company records the reinstatement and the collection as follows:

Reinstate Account

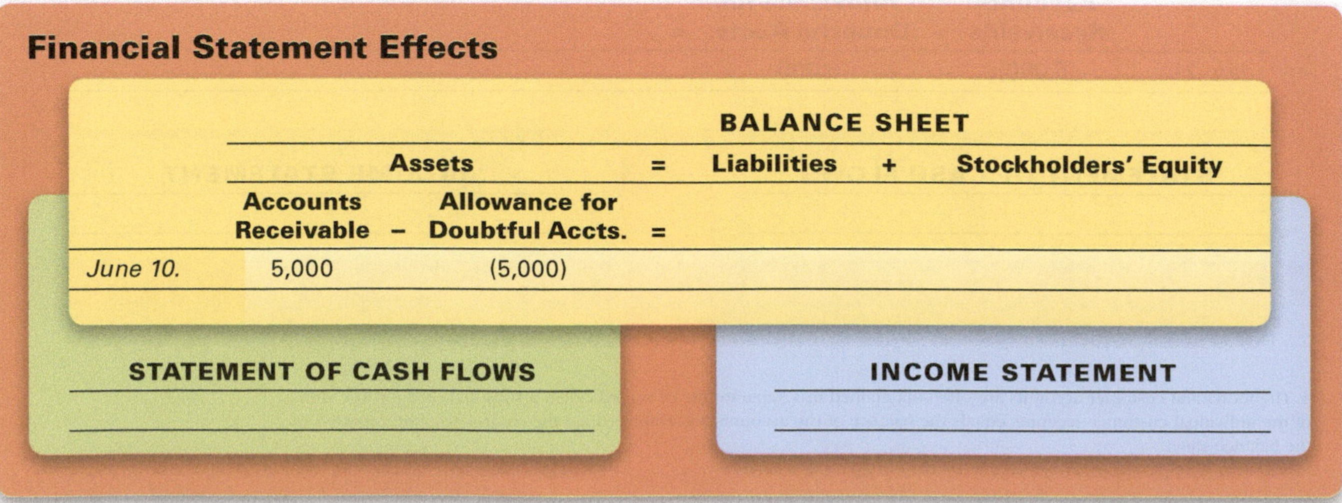

Financial Statement Effects

	BALANCE SHEET					
	Assets		=	Liabilities	+	Stockholders' Equity
	Accounts Receivable	– Allowance for Doubtful Accts.	=			
June 10.	5,000	(5,000)				

STATEMENT OF CASH FLOWS

INCOME STATEMENT

Collected Cash

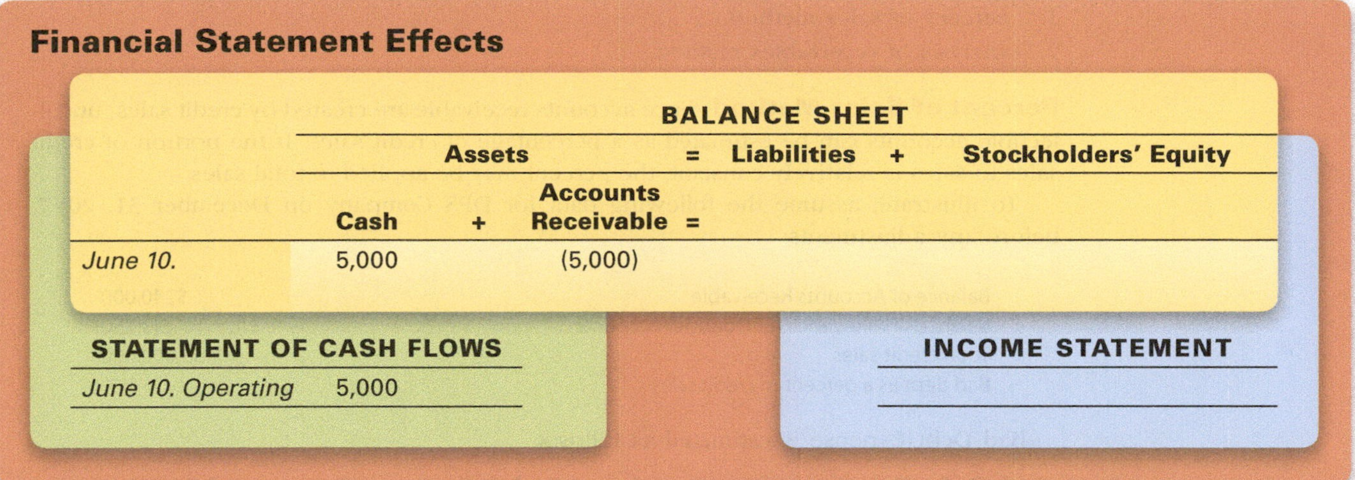

Financial Statement Effects

BALANCE SHEET

	Assets			= Liabilities +	Stockholders' Equity
	Cash	+	Accounts Receivable	=	
June 10.	5,000		(5,000)		

STATEMENT OF CASH FLOWS

June 10. Operating	5,000

INCOME STATEMENT

Transaction Metric Effects

The effects of the reinstatement and collection of the $5,000 account on the liquidity and profitability metrics are as follows:

Date	Description	Liquidity Days' Sales in Receivables	Profitability Return on Sales
June 10	Reinstate account	No Effect	No Effect
10	Collected cash	Decrease	No Effect

The reinstatement of the account increases accounts receivable and the allowance for doubtful accounts. Since days' sales in receivables is normally computed using net accounts receivable, there is no effect on the liquidity metric as a result of the reinstatement. However, the collection of cash for the accounts receivable reduces accounts receivable and thus, decrease days' sales in receivables. Since revenues and expenses are not affected, there is no effect on return on sales.

Estimating Uncollectibles

The allowance method requires an estimate of uncollectible accounts at the end of the period. This estimate is normally based on past experience, industry averages, and forecasts of the future.

Integrity, Objectivity, and Ethics in Business

Seller Beware

A company in financial distress will still try to purchase goods and services on account. In these cases, rather than "buyer beware," it is more like "seller beware." Sellers must be careful in advancing credit to such companies, because trade creditors have low priority for cash payments in the event of bankruptcy. To help suppliers, third-party services specialize in evaluating financially distressed customers. These services analyze credit risk for these firms by evaluating recent management payment decisions (who is getting paid and when), court actions (if in bankruptcy), and other supplier credit tightening or suspension actions. Such information helps monitor and adjust trade credit amounts and terms with the financially distressed customer.

The two methods used to estimate uncollectible accounts are as follows:

1. percent of sales method
2. analysis of receivables method

Percent of Sales Method Since accounts receivable are created by credit sales, uncollectible accounts can be estimated as a percentage of credit sales. If the portion of credit sales to sales is relatively constant, the percent may be applied to total sales.

To illustrate, assume the following data for DPS Company on December 31, 20Y7, before any adjustments:

Balance of Accounts Receivable	$240,000
Balance of Allowance for Doubtful Accounts	$(3,250)
Total credit sales	$3,000,000
Bad debt as a percent of credit sales	¾%

Bad Debt Expense is estimated as follows:

Bad Debt Expense = Credit Sales × Bad Debts as a Percent of Credit Sales

Bad Debt Expense = $3,000,000 × ¾% = $22,500

Under the percent of sales method, the amount of the adjustment is always the amount estimated for Bad Debt Expense, which in this case is $22,500.

The effect of the adjustment on the accounts and financial statements on December 31 is as follows:

Financial Statement Effects

BALANCE SHEET

	Assets			=	Liabilities	+	Stockholders' Equity
	Accounts Receivable	–	Allowance for Doubtful Accts.	=			Retained Earnings
Dec. 31.			(22,500)				(22,500)

STATEMENT OF CASH FLOWS

INCOME STATEMENT

Dec. 31. Bad debt expense (22,500)

After the adjustment, Bad Debt Expense will have an adjusted balance of $22,500. Allowance for Doubtful Accounts will have a negative adjusted balance of $(25,750) ($3,250 + $22,500).

Adjustment Metric Effects

The effects of the adjustment for uncollectible accounts using the allowance method on the liquidity and profitability metrics are as follows:

LIQUIDITY	
Days' Sales in Receivables	Decrease

PROFITABILITY	
Return on Sales	Decrease

The increase in the allowance for doubtful accounts decreases the net realizable value of the receivables and thus, the liquidity metric decreases. Since the increase in Bad Debt Expense decreases operating income, return on sales also decreases.

> In a recent year, **CVS** reported Bad Debt Expense of $185 million.
>
> *CVS Connection*

Analysis of Receivables Method The analysis of receivables method is based on the assumption that the longer an account receivable is outstanding, the less likely that it will be collected. The analysis of receivables method is applied as follows:

Step 1. The due date of each account receivable is determined.

Step 2. The number of days each account is past due is determined. This is the number of days between the due date of the account and the date of the analysis.

Step 3. Each account is placed in an aged class according to its days past due. Typical aged classes include the following:

Not past due
1–30 days past due
31–60 days past due
61–90 days past due
91–180 days past due
181–365 days past due
Over 365 days past due

Step 4. The totals for each aged class are determined.

Step 5. The total for each aged class is multiplied by an estimated percentage of uncollectible accounts for that class.

Step 6. The estimated total of uncollectible accounts is determined as the sum of the uncollectible accounts for each aged class.

The preceding steps are summarized in an aging schedule, and this overall process is called **aging the receivables**.

To illustrate, assume that DPS Company uses the analysis of receivables method instead of the percent of sales method. DPS prepared an aging schedule for its accounts receivable of $240,000 as of December 31, 20Y7, as shown in Exhibit 2.

Exhibit 2 Aging of Receivables Schedule, December 31, 20Y7

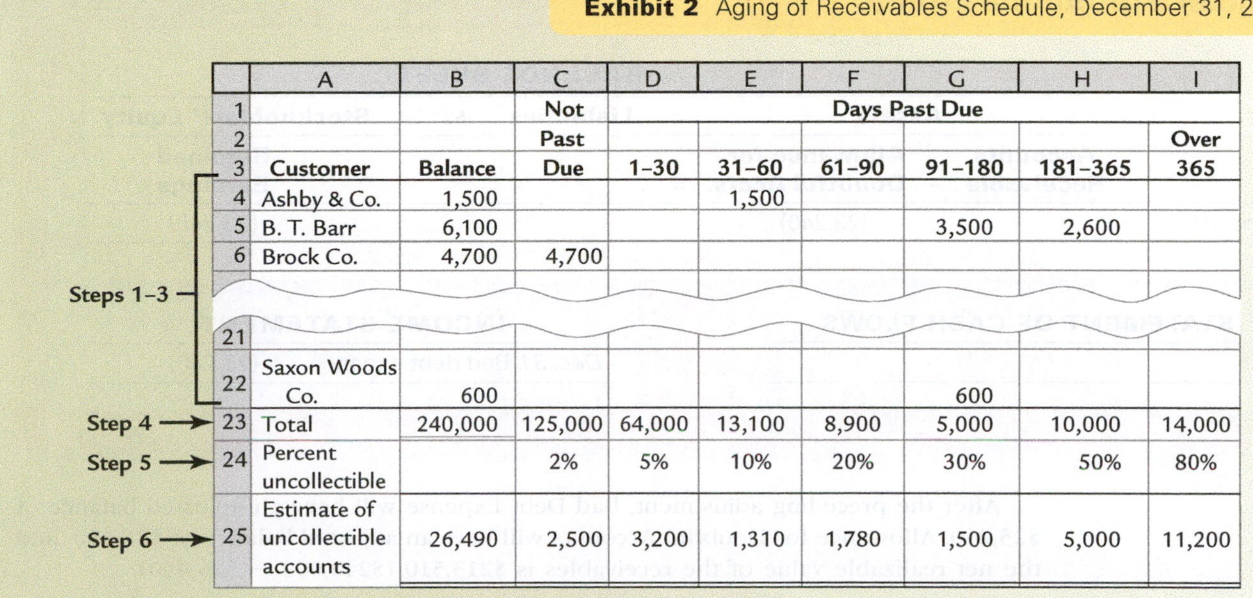

		A	B	C	D	E	F	G	H	I
	1			Not		Days Past Due				
	2			Past						Over
Steps 1–3	3	Customer	Balance	Due	1–30	31–60	61–90	91–180	181–365	365
	4	Ashby & Co.	1,500			1,500				
	5	B. T. Barr	6,100					3,500	2,600	
	6	Brock Co.	4,700	4,700						
	21									
	22	Saxon Woods Co.	600					600		
Step 4 →	23	Total	240,000	125,000	64,000	13,100	8,900	5,000	10,000	14,000
Step 5 →	24	Percent uncollectible		2%	5%	10%	20%	30%	50%	80%
Step 6 →	25	Estimate of uncollectible accounts	26,490	2,500	3,200	1,310	1,780	1,500	5,000	11,200

Assume that DPS Company sold merchandise to Saxon Woods Co. on August 29, 20Y7, with terms 2/10, n/30. Thus, the due date (Step 1) of Saxon Woods' account is September 28, as shown below.

Credit terms, net	30 days
Less two days in August (31 – 29)	(2) days
Days in September	28 days

As of December 31, Saxon Woods' account is 94 days past due (Step 2), as shown below.

Number of days past due in September	2 days	(30 – 28)
Number of days past due in October	31 days	
Number of days past due in November	30 days	
Number of days past due in December	31 days	
Total number of days past due	94 days	

Exhibit 2 shows that the $600 account receivable for Saxon Woods Co. was placed in the 91–180 days past due class (Step 3).

The total for each of the aged classes is determined (Step 4). Exhibit 2 shows that $125,000 of the accounts receivable are not past due, while $64,000 are 1–30 days past due. DPS Company applies a different estimated percentage of uncollectible accounts to the totals of each of the aged classes (Step 5). As shown in Exhibit 2, the percent is 2% for accounts not past due, while the percent is 80% for accounts over 365 days past due.

The sum of the estimated uncollectible accounts for each aged class (Step 6) is the estimated uncollectible accounts on December 31, 20Y7. This is the desired adjusted balance for Allowance for Doubtful Accounts. For DPS Company, this amount is $26,490, as shown in Exhibit 2.

The amount of the adjustment for Bad Debt Expense is the amount that will yield an adjusted balance for Allowance for Doubtful Accounts equal to that estimated by the aging schedule. For DPS, the unadjusted balance of the allowance account is a negative balance of $(3,250). The amount to be added to this balance is therefore $(23,240) ($26,490 – $3,250).

The effect of the adjustment of $23,240 on the accounts and financial statements of DPS Company is shown below.

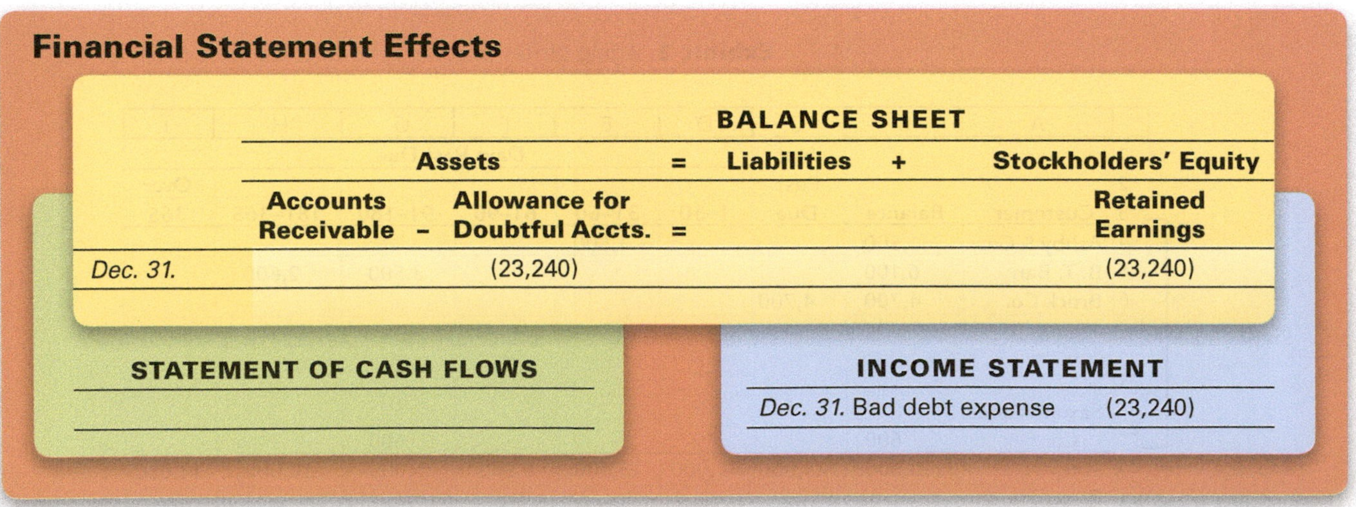

Financial Statement Effects
BALANCE SHEET
Assets = Liabilities + Stockholders' Equity
Accounts Receivable – Allowance for Doubtful Accts. = Retained Earnings
Dec. 31. (23,240) (23,240)
STATEMENT OF CASH FLOWS
INCOME STATEMENT
Dec. 31. Bad debt expense (23,240)

After the preceding adjustment, Bad Debt Expense will have an adjusted balance of $23,240. Allowance for Doubtful Accounts will have an adjusted balance of $26,490, and the net realizable value of the receivables is $213,510 ($240,000 – $26,490).

Adjustment Metric Effects

The effects of the adjustment of $23,240 for uncollectible accounts on the liquidity and profitability metrics are as follows:

LIQUIDITY	
Days' Sales in Receivables	Decrease

PROFITABILITY	
Return on Sales	Decrease

The increase in the allowance for doubtful accounts decreases the net realizable value of the receivables, and thus, the liquidity metric decreases. Since the increase in Bad Debt Expense decreases operating income, return on sales also decreases.

CVS Connection

For a recent year, **CVS** reported accounts receivable of $9,943 million, allowance for doubtful accounts of $256 million, and net accounts receivable of $9,687 million.

Comparing Estimation Methods Both the percent of sales and analysis of receivables methods estimate uncollectible accounts. However, each method has a slightly different focus and financial statement emphasis.

Under the percent of sales method, Bad Debt Expense is the focus of the estimation process. The percent of sales method places more emphasis on matching revenues and expenses and thus emphasizes the income statement. That is, the amount of the adjusting entry is based on the estimate of Bad Debt Expense for the period. Allowance for Doubtful Accounts is then adjusted by this amount.

Under the analysis of receivables method, Allowance for Doubtful Accounts is the focus of the estimation process. The analysis of receivables method places more emphasis on the net realizable value of the receivables and thus emphasizes the balance sheet. That is, the amount of the adjusting entry is the amount that will yield an adjusted balance for Allowance for Doubtful Accounts equal to that estimated by the aging schedule. Bad Debt Expense is then adjusted by this amount.

Exhibit 3 summarizes these differences between the percent of sales and the analysis of receivables methods. Exhibit 3 also shows the results of the DPS Company illustration for the percent of sales and analysis of receivables methods. The amounts shown in

Exhibit 3 Differences Between Estimation Methods

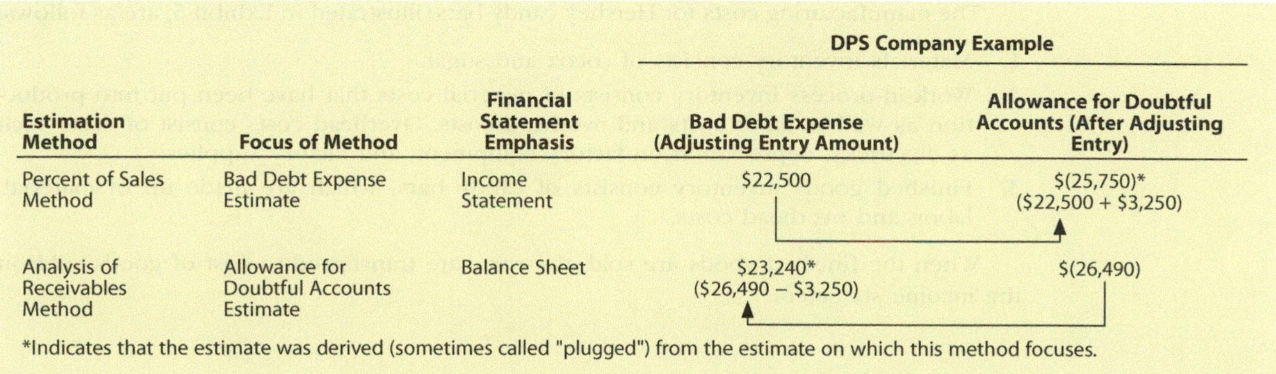

			DPS Company Example	
Estimation Method	**Focus of Method**	**Financial Statement Emphasis**	**Bad Debt Expense (Adjusting Entry Amount)**	**Allowance for Doubtful Accounts (After Adjusting Entry)**
Percent of Sales Method	Bad Debt Expense Estimate	Income Statement	$22,500	$(25,750)* ($22,500 + $3,250)
Analysis of Receivables Method	Allowance for Doubtful Accounts Estimate	Balance Sheet	$23,240* ($26,490 – $3,250)	$(26,490)

*Indicates that the estimate was derived (sometimes called "plugged") from the estimate on which this method focuses.

Exhibit 3 assume an unadjusted negative balance of $(3,250) for Allowance for Doubtful Accounts. While the methods normally yield different amounts for any one period, over several periods the amounts should be similar.

Inventory Classification for Retailers and Manufacturers

Objective 5
Describe the common classifications of inventories.

In Chapter 4, a retail business was defined as a company that purchases products for resale, such as apparel, consumer electronics, hardware, or food items. Merchandise on hand (not sold) at the end of the period is a current asset called **inventory** or merchandise inventory. Inventory sold becomes *cost of goods sold*. Inventory is a large asset for most retail companies, as illustrated for some well-known retailers in Exhibit 4.

Exhibit 4
Size of Inventory for Retail Businesses

	Inventory as a Percentage of Current Assets	Inventory as a Percentage of Total Assets
Wal-Mart	71%	22%
Best Buy	44	34
Home Depot	72	28
Kroger	64	19

CVS Connection

CVS reported $11,930 million in inventories on a recent balance sheet, which was 46% of its current assets.

As illustrated in earlier chapters, the cost of inventory is its purchase price less any purchase discounts. Inventory also includes other costs, such as freight, import duties, property taxes, and insurance costs.

Manufacturing companies convert raw materials into final products, which are often sold to retail businesses. A manufacturing company has three types of inventory:

1. **Materials inventory** consists of the cost of raw materials used in manufacturing a product.
2. **Work-in-process (WIP) inventory** consists of the costs for partially completed product.
3. **Finished goods inventory** consists of all the costs for completed product.

The manufacturing costs for Hershey candy bars, illustrated in Exhibit 5, are as follows:

1. Materials inventory consists of cocoa and sugar.
2. Work-in-process inventory consists of material costs that have been put into production as well as labor costs and overhead costs. Overhead costs consist of costs such as electricity, depreciation on factory equipment, and factory supplies.
3. Finished goods inventory consists of candy bars, which are made up of material, labor, and overhead costs.

When the finished goods are sold, the costs are transferred to cost of goods sold on the income statement.

Exhibit 5 Manufacturing Inventories

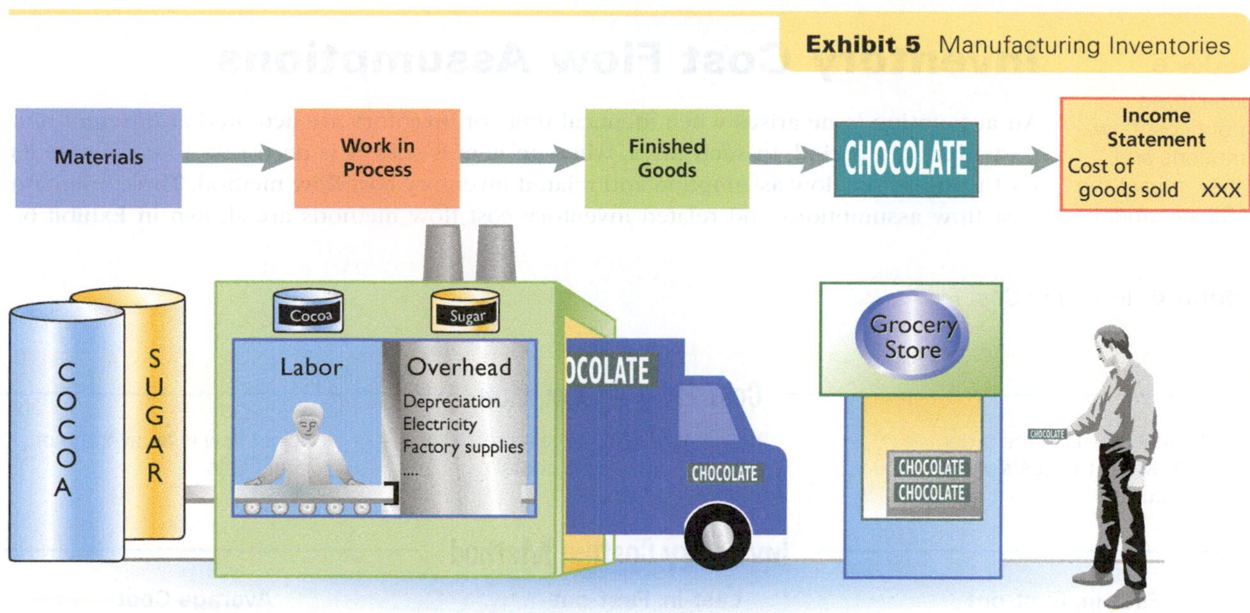

Manufacturing inventories are normally disclosed in the notes to the financial statements. For example, **The Hershey Company** recently reported inventories of $973,144 (in thousands) as follows:

Materials	$377,620
Work in process	63,916
Finished goods	531,608
Total inventories	$973,144

In this chapter, inventory accounting and analysis issues for a retail company are described and illustrated. However, much of this discussion also applies to manufacturing companies.

Business Insight

THE CONSUMER ELECTRONIC WARS: BEST BUY VERSUS AMAZON.COM

Adam Hunger/Reuters

How does **Best Buy** compete against online retailers such as **Amazon.com** in the intensely competitive consumer electronic market? Best Buy believes that by offering high-quality customer service in its retail stores that it can compete effectively with online retailers like Amazon.com. An important part of this strategy is hiring, training, and retaining high-quality store employees and managers. In addition, Best Buy recently announced a "Perfect Match Promise" that provides customers (1) 30 days of free telephone support for any products purchased, (2) 30-day return policy with no restocking fees, and (3) 30 days of competitor price matching. Finally, Best Buy plans to enhance its customer loyalty program with free shipping, access to new products and technologies, free access to the Geek Squad, and extended return and price-matching options.

Source: Adapted from Best Buy Co., Inc.'s 10-K report.

Objective 6
Describe three inventory cost flow assumptions and how they impact the financial statements.

Inventory Cost Flow Assumptions

An accounting issue arises when identical units of inventory are acquired at different unit costs during a period. In such cases, when an item is sold, it is necessary to determine its cost using a cost flow assumption and related inventory cost flow method. Three common cost flow assumptions and related inventory cost flow methods are shown in Exhibit 6.

Exhibit 6 Inventory Cost Flows

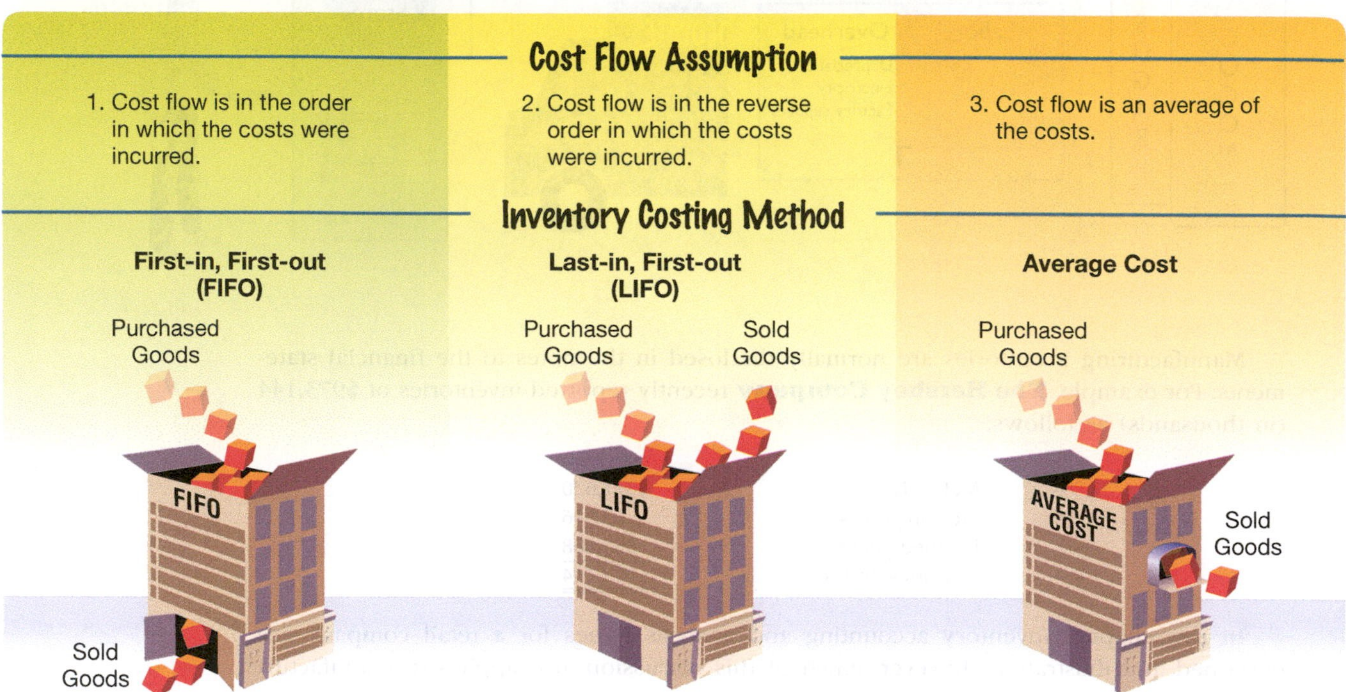

Cost Flow Assumption
1. Cost flow is in the order in which the costs were incurred.
2. Cost flow is in the reverse order in which the costs were incurred.
3. Cost flow is an average of the costs.
Inventory Costing Method
First-in, First-out (FIFO)
Last-in, First-out (LIFO)
Average Cost
Purchased Goods
Sold Goods
FIFO
LIFO
AVERAGE COST

To illustrate, assume that three identical units of merchandise are purchased during May, as follows:

			Units	Cost
May	10	Purchase	1	$ 9
	18	Purchase	1	13
	24	Purchase	1	14
Total			3	$36

Average cost per unit: $12 ($36 ÷ 3 units)

Assume that one unit is sold on May 30 for $20. Depending upon which unit was sold, the gross profit varies from $11 to $6, as shown below.

	May 10 Unit Sold	May 18 Unit Sold	May 24 Unit Sold
Sales	$20	$20	$20
Cost of goods sold	(9)	(13)	(14)
Gross profit	$11	$ 7	$ 6
Ending inventory*	$27	$23	$22
	*($13 + $14)	*($9 + $14)	*($9 + $13)

Under the **specific identification inventory cost flow method**, the unit sold is identified with a specific purchase. The ending inventory is made up of the remaining units on hand. Thus, the gross profit, cost of goods sold, and ending inventory can vary as shown above. For example, if the May 18 unit was sold, the cost of goods sold is $13, the gross profit is $7, and the ending inventory is $23.

The specific identification method is not practical unless each inventory unit can be separately identified. For example, an automobile dealer may use the specific identification method since each automobile has a unique serial number. However, most businesses cannot identify each inventory unit separately. In such cases, one of the following three inventory cost flow methods is used.

Under the **first-in, first-out (FIFO) inventory cost flow method**, the first units purchased are assumed to be sold and the ending inventory is made up of the most recent purchases. In the preceding example, the May 10 unit would be assumed to have been sold. Thus, the gross profit would be $11, and the ending inventory would be $27 ($13 + $14).

Under the **last-in, first-out (LIFO) inventory cost flow method**, the last units purchased are assumed to be sold and the ending inventory is made up of the first purchases. In the preceding example, the May 24 unit would be assumed to have been sold. Thus, the gross profit would be $6, and the ending inventory would be $22 ($9 + $13).

Under the **weighted average cost inventory cost flow method**, the cost of the units sold and in ending inventory is an average of the purchase costs. In the preceding example, the cost of the unit sold would be $12 ($36 ÷ 3 units), the gross profit would be $8 ($20 − $12), and the ending inventory would be $24 ($12 × 2 units).

The three inventory cost flow methods—FIFO, LIFO, and average cost—are shown in Exhibit 7.

Exhibit 7 Inventory Costing Methods

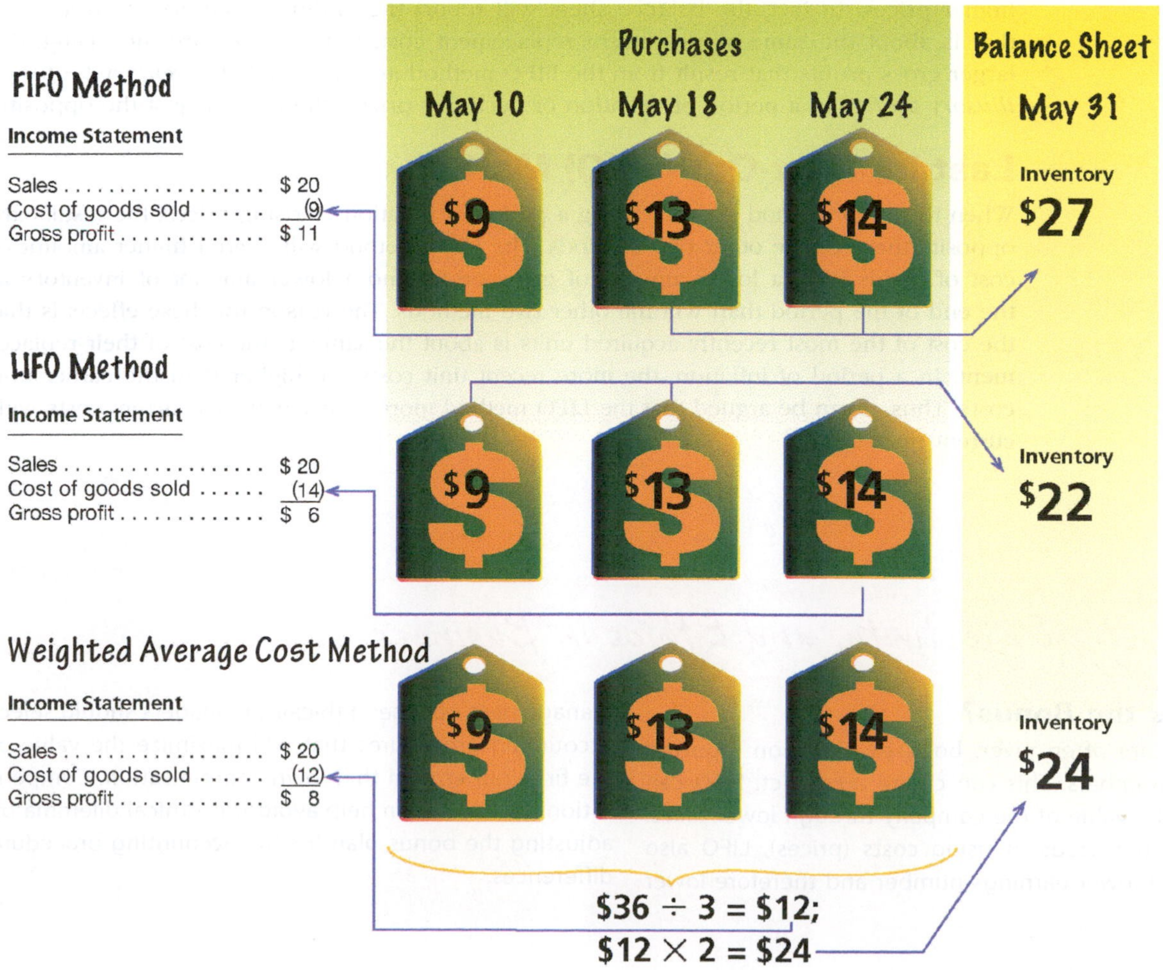

International Connection

IFRS Prohibits LIFO

While the FIFO, LIFO, and average cost methods are permitted within the United States, International Financial Reporting Standards (IFRS) prohibit the LIFO method. If IFRS were adopted within the United States, this could have a significant impact on a company's income. For example, **Deere & Company** reports its inventories using LIFO. If Deere & Company were to switch to FIFO, its income before taxes would decrease by approximately $1,398 million, which is over a 40% decrease.

Objective 7

Compare and contrast the use of the three inventory costing methods.

Comparing Inventory Costing Methods

As illustrated in Exhibit 7, when prices change, the different inventory costing methods affect the income statement and balance sheet differently. That is, the methods yield different amounts for (1) the cost of the goods sold for the period, (2) the gross profit (and net income) for the period, and (3) the ending inventory.

First-In, First-Out (FIFO) Method

When the FIFO method is used during a period of inflation or rising prices, the earlier unit costs are lower than the more recent unit costs. Much of the benefit of the larger amount of gross profit is lost, however, because the inventory must be replaced at ever higher prices. In fact, the balance sheet will report the ending inventory at an amount that is about the same as its current replacement cost. When prices are increasing, the larger gross profits that result from the FIFO method are often called *inventory profits* or *illusory profits*. In a period of deflation or declining prices, the effect is just the opposite.

Last-In, First-Out (LIFO) Method

When the LIFO method is used during a period of inflation or rising prices, the results are opposite those of the other two methods. The LIFO method will yield a higher amount of cost of goods sold, a lower amount of gross profit, and a lower amount of inventory at the end of the period than will the other two methods. The reason for these effects is that the cost of the most recently acquired units is about the same as the cost of their replacement. In a period of inflation, the more recent unit costs are higher than the earlier unit costs. Thus, it can be argued that the LIFO method more nearly matches current costs with current revenues.

Integrity, Objectivity, and Ethics in Business

Where's the Bonus?

Managers are often given bonuses based on reported earnings numbers. This can create a conflict. LIFO can improve the value of the company through lower taxes. However, in periods of rising costs (prices), LIFO also produces a lower earnings number and therefore lower management bonuses. Ethically, managers should select accounting procedures that will maximize the value of the firm, rather than their own compensation. Compensation specialists can help avoid this ethical dilemma by adjusting the bonus plan for the accounting procedure differences.

LIFO and Taxes

The rules used for external financial reporting need not be the same as those used for income tax reporting. One exception to this general rule is the use of LIFO. If a company elects to use LIFO inventory valuation for tax purposes, then the company must also use LIFO for external financial reporting. This is called the **LIFO conformity rule**. Thus, in periods of rising prices, LIFO offers an income tax savings because it reports the lowest amount of net income of the three methods. Many managers elect to use LIFO because of the tax savings, even though the reported earnings will be lower.

Under LIFO, the ending inventory on the balance sheet may be quite different from its current replacement cost (or FIFO estimate).[5] In such cases, the financial statements will include a note that states the estimated difference between the LIFO inventory and the inventory if FIFO had been used. This difference is called the **LIFO reserve**. An example of such a note for **Deere & Company** is shown below.

> ***Most inventories owned by Deere & Company and its U.S. equipment subsidiaries are valued at cost, on the "last-in, first-out" (LIFO) basis. .... If all inventories had been valued on a FIFO basis, estimated inventories by major classification at October 31 in millions of dollars would have been as follows:***

INVENTORIES

	Year 2	Year 1
Raw materials and supplies	$ 1,559	$ 1,724
Work in process	450	654
Finished goods and parts	3,234	3,360
Total FIFO value	$ 5,243	$ 5,738
Less adjustment to LIFO value	(1,426)	(1,528)
Inventories	$ 3,817	$ 4,210

As shown above, the LIFO reserve may be quite large. For Deere & Company, the LIFO reserve is 27.2% ($1,426 ÷ $5,243) of the total FIFO inventory for Year 2 and 26.6% ($1,528 ÷ $5,738) in Year 1.

The wide differences in the percent of LIFO reserve to FIFO are a result of two major factors: (1) price inflation of the inventory and (2) the age of the inventory. Generally, old LIFO inventory combined with rapid price inflation will result in large LIFO reserves.

If a business sells some of its old LIFO inventory, the LIFO reserve is said to be liquidated. Since old LIFO inventory is normally at low prices, selling old LIFO inventory will result in a lower cost of goods sold and a higher gross profit and net income.

Whenever LIFO inventory is liquidated, investors and analysts should be careful in interpreting the income statement. In such cases, most investors and analysts will adjust earnings to what they would have been under FIFO.

Weighted Average Cost Method

As you might have already reasoned, the weighted average cost method is, in a sense, a compromise between FIFO and LIFO. The effect of price trends is averaged in determining the cost of goods sold and the ending inventory. For a series of purchases, the average cost will be the same, regardless of the direction of price trends. For example, reversing the sequence of unit costs presented in Exhibit 7 would not affect the reported cost of goods sold, gross profit, or ending inventory.

5. The FIFO estimate is often very close to replacement cost.

Financial Statement Effects

The preceding paragraphs describe the effects on the financial statements of the FIFO, LIFO, and weighted average cost flow methods. The effects on the accounts and financial statements of using FIFO rather than LIFO with *rising prices* are as follows:

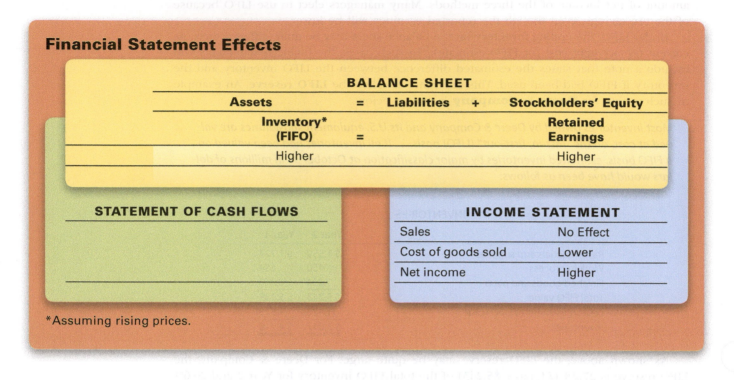

Financial Statement Effects

BALANCE SHEET

Assets	=	Liabilities	+	Stockholders' Equity
Inventory* (FIFO)	=			Retained Earnings
Higher				Higher

STATEMENT OF CASH FLOWS

INCOME STATEMENT

Sales	No Effect
Cost of goods sold	Lower
Net income	Higher

*Assuming rising prices.

The effects of using the weighted average method on the financial statements would be in between the FIFO and LIFO methods

The selection of an inventory cost flow method also affects a company's liquidity and profitability metrics. For inventory, the liquidity metric **days' sales in inventory** is used. Days' sales in inventory estimates the average number of days it takes to sell inventory. For example, if a company's days' sales in inventory is 30, the company would expect to sell its inventory every 30 days. In other words, it expects to turnover its entire inventory 12 times a year.

Days' sales in inventory is computed as follows:

$$\textbf{Days' Sales in Inventory} = \frac{\textbf{Average Inventory}}{\textbf{Average Daily Cost of Goods Sold}}$$

Average daily cost of goods sold is computed as yearly cost of goods sold divided by 365 days. To illustrate, assume the following data for Downing Inc. for the year ending December 31, 20Y4.

Cost of goods sold for 20Y4	$4,745,000
Inventory, Jan. 1, 20Y4	285,000
Inventory, Dec. 31, 20Y4	339,000

Days' sales in inventory of 24 days is computed as follows:

$$\textbf{Days' Sales in Inventory} = \frac{\textbf{Average Inventory}}{\textbf{Average Cost of Goods Sold}} = \frac{(\$285{,}000 + \$339{,}000) \div 2}{\$4{,}745{,}000 \div 365 \text{ days}}$$

$$= \frac{\$312{,}000}{\$13{,}000} = 24 \text{ days}$$

The profitability metric is return on sales. The computation of return on sales was illustrated in an earlier section of this chapter.

Transaction Metric Effects

Assuming rising prices, the effects of selecting FIFO rather than LIFO on the liquidity and profitability metrics are as follows:

LIQUIDITY	
Days' Sales in Inventory	Increase

PROFITABILITY	
Return on Sales	Increase

Since ending inventory using FIFO will be higher than ending inventory using LIFO during periods of rising prices, days' sales in inventory will increase. Since cost of goods sold will be lower using FIFO rather than LIFO, operating income will be higher under FIFO and therefore, return on sales will increase.

Days' sales in inventory is higher using FIFO rather than LIFO. This implies that since the dollar amount of inventory is higher, the company's overall liquidity, which is the ability to convert assets to cash, will be higher. The inventory items being valued, however, are the same regardless of whether FIFO or LIFO is used. Since the inventory items are the same, the ability to sell the items and convert them to cash is the same regardless of whether FIFO or LIFO is used. For this reason, managers must distinguish between the "metric" used to assess liquidity and the "actual" liquidity, which is the ability to convert assets to cash.

CVS uses the weighted average cost method for its prescription drugs. It uses the FIFO method for retail inventories.

CVS Connection

Reporting Receivables and Inventory

Objective 8

Describe how receivables and inventory are reported on the financial statements.

Receivables and inventory are reported as current assets on the balance sheet, as shown in Exhibit 8. In addition, generally accepted accounting principles require that supplementary information for these accounts be reported in the notes accompanying the financial statements. This section focuses on the financial statement and note reporting requirements for receivables and inventory.

Exhibit 8 Receivables and Inventory on the Balance Sheet

Crabtree co.
Balance Sheet
December 31, 20Y3

Assets		
Current assets:		
Cash and cash equivalents		$119,500
Notes receivable		250,000
Accounts receivable	$445,000	
Less allowance for doubtful accounts	(15,000)	430,000
Interest receivable		14,500
Inventory—at lower of cost (first-in, first-out method) or market		216,300

Receivables

All receivables expected to be realized in cash within a year are presented in the Current Assets section of the balance sheet. These assets are normally listed in the order of their liquidity, that is, the order in which they are expected to be converted to cash during normal operations. The receivables reported on a recent Johnson & Johnson balance sheet are shown below.[6]

Assets (in millions)	Year 2	Year 1
Current assets:		
Cash and cash equivalents	$14,523	$20,927
Marketable securities	18,566	8,279
Accounts receivable, net of allowances of $275 in Year 2 and $333 in Year 1	10,985	11,713
Inventories	8,184	7,878
Prepaid expenses and other current assets	7,053	7,610
Total current assets	$59,311	$56,407

Johnson & Johnson reports net accounts receivable of $10,985 and $11,713. The allowances for doubtful accounts of $275 and $333 are subtracted from the total accounts receivable to arrive at the net receivables. Alternatively, the allowances for each year could be shown in a note to the financial statements.

Other disclosures related to receivables are presented either on the face of the financial statements or in the accompanying notes. Such disclosures include the market (fair) value of the receivables if significantly different from the reported value. In addition, if unusual credit risks exist within the receivables, the nature of the risks should be disclosed. For example, if the majority of the receivables are due from one customer or are due from customers located in one area of the country or one industry, these facts should be disclosed.

To illustrate, **Johnson & Johnson** reported the following related to credit risks in its recent financial statements:

> ***Concentration of Credit Risk***
>
> ***Global concentration of credit risk with respect to trade accounts receivables continues to be limited due to the large number of customers globally ....***

6. Adapted from Johnson & Johnson Form 10-K.

Inventory

Cost is the primary basis for valuing and reporting inventories in the financial statements. However, inventory may be valued at other than cost in the following cases:

- The cost of replacing items in inventory is below the recorded cost.
- The inventory cannot be sold at normal prices due to imperfections, style changes, spoilage, damage, obsolescence, or other causes.

Valuing at Lower of Cost or Market. If the market is lower than the purchase cost, the **lower-of-cost-or-market (LCM) method** is used to value the inventory. *Market*, as used in *lower of cost or market*, is the **net realizable value** of the inventory.[7] Net realizable value is determined as follows:

Net Realizable Value = Estimated Selling Price − Direct Costs of Disposal

Direct costs of disposal include selling expenses such as special advertising or sales commissions on the sale. To illustrate, assume the following data about an item of damaged merchandise:

Original cost	$1,000
Estimated selling price	800
Selling expenses	150

The merchandise should be valued at its net realizable value of $650 as follows.

Net Realizable Value = $800 − $150 = $650

The lower-of-cost-or-market method can be applied in one of three ways by determining the cost, market price, and any declines for one of the following:

- each item in the inventory
- each major class or category of inventory
- total inventory as a whole

The amount of any price decline is included in the cost of goods sold. This in turn reduces gross profit and net income in the period in which the price declines occur. This matching of price declines to the period in which they occur is the primary advantage of using the lower-of-cost-or-market method.

To illustrate, assume the following data for 400 identical units of Item A in inventory on December 31, 20Y4:

Unit purchased cost	$10.25
Replacement cost on December 31, 20Y4	9.50

Since Item A could be replaced at $9.50 a unit, $9.50 is used under the lower-of-cost-or-market method.

Exhibit 9 illustrates applying the lower-of-cost-or-market method to each inventory item (A, B, C, and D). As applied on an item-by-item basis, the total lower of cost or market is $15,070, which is a market decline of $450 ($15,520 – $15,070). This market decline of $450 is included in the cost of goods sold.

In Exhibit 9, Items A, B, C, and D could be viewed as a class of inventory items. If the lower-of-cost-or-market method is applied to the class, the inventory would be valued at $15,472, which is a market decline of $48 ($15,520 – $15,472). Likewise, if Items A, B, C, and D make up the total inventory, the lower-of-cost-or-market method as applied to the total inventory would be the same amount, $15,472.

7. Accounting Standards Update, *Inventory (Topic 330): Simplifying the Measurement of Inventory*, July 2015, FASB.

Exhibit 9
Determining Inventory at Lower of Cost or Market

	A	B	C	D	E	F	G
1			Cost	Market Value	Total		
2		Inventory	per	per Unit			
3	Item	Quantity	Unit	(Net Realizable Value)	Cost	Market	LCM
4	A	400	$10.25	$ 9.50	$ 4,100	$ 3,800	$ 3,800
5	B	120	22.50	24.10	2,700	2,892	2,700
6	C	600	8.00	7.75	4,800	4,650	4,650
7	D	280	14.00	14.75	3,920	4,130	3,920
8	Total				$15,520	$15,472	$15,070
9							

The effects of lower of cost or market on the financial statements are as follows:

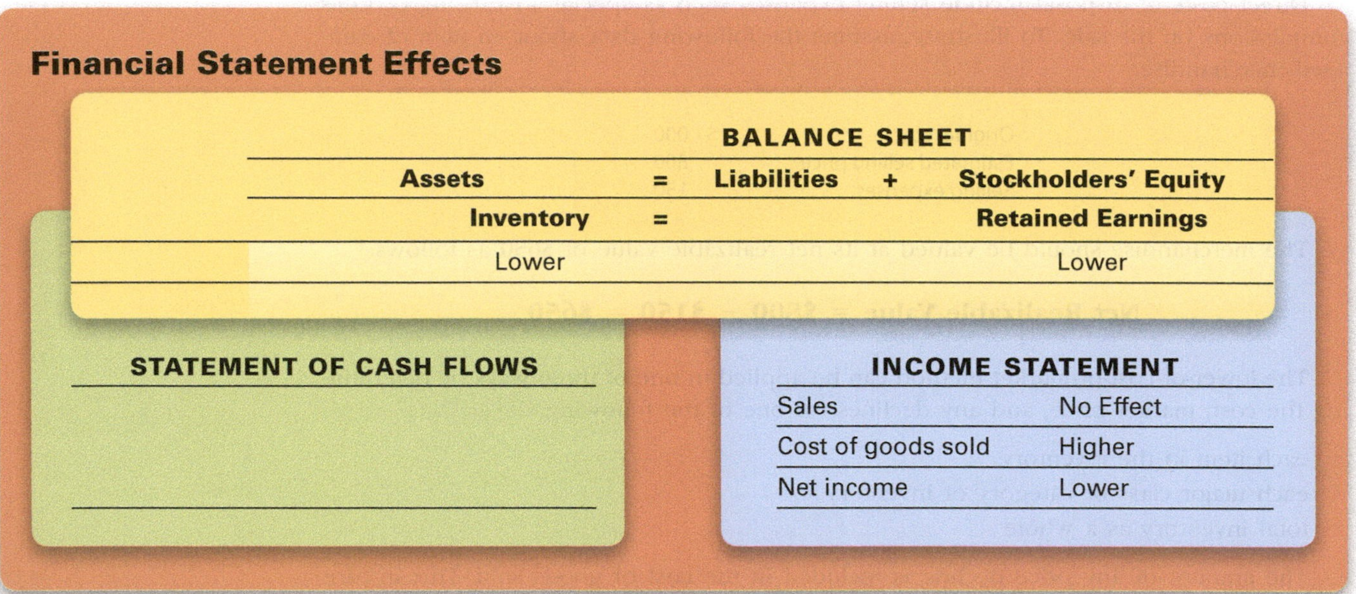

Financial Statement Effects
BALANCE SHEET
Assets = Liabilities + Stockholders' Equity
Inventory = Retained Earnings
Lower
Lower
STATEMENT OF CASH FLOWS
INCOME STATEMENT
Sales No Effect
Cost of goods sold Higher
Net income Lower

Transaction Metric Effects

The effects of lower of cost or market on liquidity and profitability metrics are as follows:

LIQUIDITY	
Days' Sales in Inventory	Decrease

PROFITABILITY	
Return on Sales	Decrease

Since lower of cost or market reduces the dollar amount of inventory, lower of cost or market decrease the days' sales in inventory. Since cost of goods sold is increased, return on sales is decreased.

CVS Connection

CVS values all its inventories using lower of cost or market.

Metric-Based Analysis: Accounts Receivable Turnover and Inventory Turnover

Objective 9

Describe and illustrate the accounts receivable turnover and inventory turnover in assessing a company's liquidity and operations.

Accounts receivable and inventory are large current assets for many companies. One of the primary objectives in managing receivables and inventory is to convert them to cash by collecting receivables and selling inventory. Accounts receivable and inventory turnover are two useful measures of liquidity and how efficiently a company is managing its operations.

Accounts Receivable Turnover

The **accounts receivable turnover** is computed as follows:

$$\textbf{Accounts Receivable Turnover} = \frac{\textbf{Sales}}{\textbf{Average Accounts Receivable}}$$

Although accounts receivable are just related to "credit" sales, total sales is normally used to compute accounts receivable turnover. This is because credit sales are normally not reported to external users. The average accounts receivable is computed as the beginning accounts receivable plus the ending accounts receivable for the period divided by two.

To illustrate, assume the following data for Downing Inc. for the year ending December 31, 20Y4.

Sales for 20Y4	$9,125,000
Accounts Receivable, Jan. 1, 20Y4	400,000
Accounts Receivable, Dec. 31, 20Y4	600,000

The accounts receivable turnover of 18.3 for Downing Inc. is computed as follows:

$$\textbf{Accounts Receivable Turnover} = \frac{\$9{,}125{,}000}{(\$400{,}000 + \$600{,}000) \div 2} = \frac{\$9{,}125{,}000}{\$500{,}000} = 18.3^{*}$$

* **Rounded to one decimal place.**

An accounts receivable turnover ratio of 18.3 means that Downing Inc. is converting its accounts receivable to cash 18.3 times per year. Assuming that Downing Inc.'s credit terms are net 30 days, a turnover of 18.3 is favorable. In other words, customers are paying within the credit period. When customers are paying faster and within the credit period, a company's liquidity is increased (improved).

For a recent year, **CVS** had an average accounts receivable turnover of 14.4.

Accounts receivable turnover is related to the liquidity metric days' sales in accounts receivable described earlier in this chapter. Specifically, these two metrics are related as follows.

$$\textbf{Days' Sales in Receivables} = \frac{\textbf{365 Days}}{\textbf{Accounts Receivable Turnover}}$$

To illustrate, the days' sales in accounts receivable of 20 days for Downing Inc. can be computed as follows.

$$\textbf{Days' Sales in Receivables} = \frac{\textbf{365 Days}}{\textbf{Accounts Receivable Turnover}} = \frac{\textbf{365 Days}}{\textbf{18.3}} = \textbf{20 days}^{*}$$

* **Rounded to nearest day.**

CVS Connection For a recent year, **CVS** had an average days' sales in accounts receivable of 26 days.

Inventory Turnover

The **inventory turnover** is computed as follows:

$$\textbf{Inventory Turnover} = \frac{\textbf{Cost of Goods Sold}}{\textbf{Average Inventory}}$$

The average inventory is computed as the beginning inventory plus the ending inventory for the period divided by two.

To illustrate, assume the following data for Downing Inc. for the year ending December 31, 20Y4.

Cost of goods sold for 20Y4	$4,745,000
Inventory, Jan. 1, 20Y4	285,000
Inventory, Dec. 31, 20Y4	339,000

The inventory turnover of 15.2 times for Downing Inc. is computed as follows:

$$\textbf{Inventory Turnover} = \frac{\$4{,}745{,}000}{(\$285{,}000 + \$339{,}000) \div 2} = \frac{\$4{,}745{,}000}{\$312{,}000} = 15.2^*$$

*Rounded to one decimal place.

An inventory turnover ratio of 15.2 means that Downing Inc. is converting (or turning over) its inventory 15.2 times a year. A comparison of the current period's inventory turnover with the prior period or industry averages provides feedback on how efficiently the company is managing its inventory. For example, if Downing Inc.'s inventory turnover was 14.0 in the prior period, then the company has improved its management of inventory. In other words, it is selling its inventory faster. When a company is selling inventory faster, its liquidity is also increased (improved).

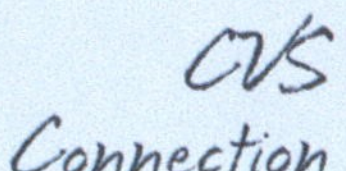

For a recent year, **CVS** had an average inventory turnover of 9.6.

Inventory turnover is related to the liquidity metric days' sales in inventory described earlier in this chapter. Specifically, these two metrics are related as follows.

$$\textbf{Days' Sales in Inventory} = \frac{\textbf{365 Days}}{\textbf{Inventory Turnover}}$$

To illustrate, the days' sales in inventory of 24 days for Downing Inc. can be computed as follows.

$$\textbf{Sales in Receivables} = \frac{\textbf{365 Days}}{\textbf{Inventory Turnover}} = \frac{\textbf{365 Days}}{\textbf{15.2}} = \textbf{24 days}^*$$

*Rounded to nearest day.

CVS Connection For a recent year, **CVS** had an average days' sales in inventory of 38 days.

Key Points

1. Describe the common classifications of receivables.

The term *receivables* includes all money claims against other entities, including people, business firms, and other organizations. Receivables are normally classified as accounts receivable, notes receivable, or other receivables.

2. Describe the nature of and the accounting for uncollectible receivables.

The two methods of accounting for uncollectible receivables are the direct write-off method and the allowance method. The direct write-off method recognizes the expense only when the account is judged to be uncollectible. The allowance method provides in advance for uncollectible receivables.

3. Describe the direct write-off method of accounting for uncollectible receivables.

Under the direct write-off method, writing off an account increases Bad Debt Expense and decreases Accounts Receivable. Neither an allowance account nor an adjustment is needed at the end of the period.

4. Describe the allowance method of accounting for uncollectible receivables.

A year-end adjustment provides for (1) the reduction of the value of the receivables to the amount of cash expected to be realized from them in the future and (2) the allocation to the current period of the expected expense resulting from such reduction. The adjustment affects Bad Debt Expense and the Allowance for Doubtful Accounts. When an account is believed to be uncollectible, it is written off against the allowance account.

When the estimate of uncollectibles is based on the amount of sales for the period, the adjustment is made without regard to the balance of the allowance account. When the estimate of uncollectibles is based on the amount and the age of the receivable accounts at the end of the period, the adjustment is recorded so that the balance of the allowance account will equal the estimated uncollectibles at the end of the period.

The allowance account, which will have a negative balance after the adjustment has been posted, is a contra asset account. The bad debt expense is generally reported on the income statement as an operating expense.

5. Describe the common classifications of inventories.

The goods held for sale by a retailer are called inventory. The cost of merchandise inventory sold is reported on the income statement. Manufacturers typically have three types of inventory: materials, work in process, and finished goods. When finished goods are sold, the cost is reported on the income statement as cost of goods sold.

6. Describe three inventory cost flow assumptions and how they impact the financial statements.

The three common cost flow assumptions used in business are the (1) first-in, first-out method, (2) last-in, first-out method, and (3) average cost method. Each method normally yields different amounts for the cost of goods sold and the ending inventory. Thus, the choice of a cost flow assumption directly affects the financial statements.

7. Compare and contrast the use of the three inventory costing methods.

The three inventory costing methods will normally yield different amounts for (1) the ending inventory, (2) the cost of goods sold for the period, and (3) the gross profit (and net income) for the period. During periods of inflation, the FIFO method yields the lowest amount for the cost of goods sold, the highest amount for gross profit (and net income), and the highest amount for the ending inventory. The LIFO method yields the opposite results. During periods of deflation, the preceding effects are reversed. The average cost method yields results that are between those of FIFO and LIFO.

8. Describe how receivables and inventory are reported on the financial statements.

All receivables that are expected to be realized in cash within a year are presented in the Current Assets section of the balance sheet. It is normal to list the assets in the order of their liquidity, which is the order in which they can be converted to cash in normal operations. In addition to the allowance for doubtful accounts, additional receivable disclosures include the market value and unusual credit risks.

Inventory is normally presented in the Current Assets section of the balance sheet following receivables. If the market price of an item of inventory is lower than its cost, the lower market price is used to compute the value of the item. Market price is the net realizable value of the inventory. The lower of cost or market can be applied to each item in the inventory, to major classes or categories, or to the inventory as a whole.

9. Metric-Based Analysis: Describe and illustrate the accounts receivable turnover and inventory turnover in assessing a company's liquidity and operations.

The accounts receivable and inventory turnovers are useful in assessing a company's liquidity and operations. The accounts receivable turnover is computed as sales divided by average accounts receivable. The inventory turnover is computed as cost of goods sold divided by average inventory. Higher receivable and inventory turnovers imply that a company is efficient in managing its operations.

Key Terms

Accounts receivable (230)
Accounts receivable turnover (255)
Aging the receivables (241)
Allowance for Doubtful Accounts (236)
Allowance method (233)
Bad debt expense (233)
Days' sales in inventory (250)
Days' sales in receivables (234)
Direct write-off method (233)
Finished goods inventory (244)
First-in, first-out (FIFO) inventory cost flow method (247)
Inventory (244)
Inventory turnover (256)
Last-in, first-out (LIFO) inventory cost flow method (247)
LIFO conformity rule (249)
LIFO reserve (249)
Lower-of-cost-or-market (LCM) method (253)
Materials inventory (244)
Maturity value (232)
Net realizable value of accounts receivable (237)
Net realizable value of inventory (253)
Notes receivable (230)
Receivables (230)
Return on sales (234)
Specific identification inventory cost flow method (246)
Weighted average cost inventory cost flow method (247)
Work-in-process (WIP) inventory (244)

Illustrative Problem

Stewart Co. is a construction supply company that uses the allowance method of accounting for uncollectible accounts receivable. It is estimated that 3% of the credit sales of $1,375,000 for the year ended December 31 will be uncollectible. In addition, Stewart Co.'s beginning inventory and purchases during the year ended December 31, 20Y5, were as follows:

		Units	Unit Cost	Total Cost
January 1	Inventory	1,000	$50.00	$ 50,000
March 10	Purchase	1,200	52.50	63,000
August 30	Purchase	800	55.00	44,000
November 26	Purchase	2,000	56.00	112,000
Total		5,000		$269,000

Instructions

1. Determine the amount of the adjustment for uncollectible accounts as of December 31, 20Y5.
2. Illustrate the effects of the adjustment for uncollectible accounts on the accounts and financial statements of Stewart Co.
3. If the balance of Allowance for Doubtful Accounts was a negative $7,500, would the amount of adjustment determined in (1) change?

4. Assuming that 3,300 units were sold during the year, determine the cost of inventory on December 31, 20Y5, using each of the following inventory costing methods:
   a. First-in, first-out
   b. Last-in, first-out
   c. Weighted average cost

Solution

1. $41,250 ($1,375,000 × 3%)
2.

Financial Statement Effects

	BALANCE SHEET				
	Assets	=	Liabilities	+	Stockholders' Equity
	Allowance for – Doubtful Accts.	=			Retained Earnings
Dec. 31.	(41,250)				(41,250)

STATEMENT OF CASH FLOWS

INCOME STATEMENT	
Dec. 31. Bad debt expense	(41,250)

3. No. Under the percent of sales method, the amount of the adjustment is determined without considering the balance of Allowance for Doubtful Accounts. Under the analysis of receivables method, however, the balance of Allowance for Doubtful Accounts does affect the amount of the adjustment.
4. a. First-in, first-out method: 1,700 units at $56 = $95,200
   b. Last-in, first-out method:

1,000	units at $50.00	$50,000
700	units at $52.50	36,750
1,700		$86,750

   c. Weighted average cost method:

   Weighted average cost per unit: $269,000 ÷ 5,000 units = $53.80

   Inventory, December 31, 20Y5: 1,700 units at $53.80 = $91,460

Self-Examination Questions

(Answers appear at the end of chapter)

1. At the end of the fiscal year, before the accounts are adjusted, Accounts Receivable has a balance of $200,000 and Allowance for Doubtful Accounts has a negative balance of $(2,500). If the estimate of uncollectible accounts determined by aging the receivables is $8,500, the amount of bad debt expense is:
   A. $2,500
   B. $6,000
   C. $8,500
   D. $11,000

2. At the end of the fiscal year, Accounts Receivable has a balance of $100,000 and Allowance for Doubtful Accounts has a negative balance of $(7,000). The expected net realizable value of the accounts receivable is:
   A. $7,000
   B. $93,000
   C. $100,000
   D. $107,000

3. The direct labor cost should be recognized first in which inventory account?
   A. Materials Inventory
   B. Merchandise Inventory
   C. Finished Goods Inventory
   D. Work-in-Process Inventory

4. The following units of a particular item were available for sale during the period:

Beginning inventory	40 units at $20
First purchase	50 units at $21
Second purchase	50 units at $22
Third purchase	50 units at $23

   What is the unit cost of the 35 units on hand at the end of the period as determined under the FIFO costing method?
   A. $20
   B. $21
   C. $22
   D. $23

5. If inventory is being valued at cost and the price level is steadily rising, the method of costing that will yield the highest net income is:
   A. LIFO
   B. FIFO
   C. Weighted average
   D. Periodic

Class Discussion Questions

1. What are the three classifications of receivables?
2. What types of transactions give rise to accounts receivable?
3. In what section of the balance sheet should a note receivable be listed if its term is (a) 90 days, (b) 12 years?
4. Give two examples of other receivables.
5. Carter's Hardware is a small hardware store in the rural township of Oglethorpe that rarely extends credit to its customers in the form of an account receivable. The few customers that are allowed to carry accounts receivable are long-time residents of Oglethorpe and have a history of doing business at Carter's. What method of accounting for uncollectible receivables should Carter's Hardware use? Why?
6. Which of the two methods of accounting for uncollectible accounts provides for the recognition of the expense at the earlier date?
7. What kind of an account (asset, liability, etc.) is Allowance for Doubtful Accounts?
8. After the accounts are adjusted at the end of the fiscal year, Accounts Receivable has a balance of $475,000 and Allowance for Doubtful Accounts has a negative balance of $(46,800). Describe how Accounts Receivable and Allowance for Doubtful Accounts are reported on the balance sheet.
9. A firm has consistently adjusted its allowance account at the end of the fiscal year by adding a fixed percent of the period's sales on account. After 10 years, the balance in Allowance for Doubtful Accounts has become very large in relationship to the balance in Accounts Receivable. Give two possible explanations.
10. How are manufacturing inventories different from those of a retailer?
11. Do the terms *FIFO* and *LIFO* refer to techniques used in determining quantities of the various classes of merchandise on hand? Explain.
12. Does the term *last-in* in the LIFO method mean that the items in the inventory are assumed to be the most recent (last) acquisitions? Explain.
13. If inventory is being valued at cost and the price level is steadily rising, which of the three methods of costing—FIFO, LIFO, or average cost—will yield (a) the highest inventory cost, (b) the lowest inventory cost, (c) the highest gross profit, (d) the lowest gross profit?

14. Which of the three methods of inventory costing—FIFO, LIFO, or average cost—will in general yield an inventory cost most nearly approximating current replacement cost?

15. If inventory is being valued at cost and the price level is steadily rising, which of the three methods of costing—FIFO, LIFO, or average cost—will yield the lowest annual income tax expense? Explain.

16. What is the LIFO reserve, and why would an analyst be careful in interpreting the earnings of a company that has liquidated some of its LIFO reserve?

17. Under what section should accounts receivable be reported on the balance sheet?

18. How is the method of determining the cost of inventory and the method of valuing it disclosed in the financial statements?

Exercises

E6-1 Classifications of receivables

Obj. 1

Boeing (BA) is one of the world's major aerospace firms, with operations involving commercial aircraft, military aircraft, missiles, satellite systems, and information and battle management systems. Recently, Boeing reported $4,281 million of receivables involving U.S. government contracts and $1,749 million of receivables involving commercial aircraft customers, such as Delta Air Lines (DAL) and United Airlines (UAL).

Should Boeing report these receivables separately in the financial statements, or combine them into one overall accounts receivable amount? Explain.

E6-2 Determine due date and interest on notes

Obj. 1

✔ a. Feb. 14, $250

Determine the due date and the amount of interest due at maturity on the following notes:

	Date of Note	Face Amount	Interest Rate	Term of Note
a.	January 15	$50,000	6%	30 days
b.	April 1	27,000	4	90 days
c.	June 22	30,000	6	45 days
d.	August 30	90,000	8	120 days
e.	October 16	72,000	5	50 days

To simplify, use 360 days per year to compute interest.

E6-3 Nature of uncollectible accounts

Obj. 2

✔ a. 15.9%

MGM Resorts International (MGM) owns and operates casinos including the MGM Grand and the Bellagio in Las Vegas, Nevada. For a recent year, the MGM Resorts International reported accounts and notes receivable of $562,947,000 and allowance for doubtful accounts of $89,602,000.

International Business Machines (IBM) provides information technology services, including software, worldwide. For a recent year, IBM reported notes and accounts receivable of $9,426,000,000 and allowance for doubtful accounts of $336,000,000.

a. Compute the percentage of the allowance for doubtful accounts to the accounts and notes receivable for MGM.

b. Compute the percentage of the allowance for doubtful accounts to the accounts receivable for IBM.

c. Discuss possible reasons for the difference in the two ratios computed in (a) and (b).

Note: The spreadsheet icon  indicates an Excel template is available on the student companion site.

Obj. 3

E6-4 Uncollectible accounts, using direct write-off method

Illustrate the effects on the accounts and financial statements of the following transactions in the accounts of Valley Care & Supplies Co., a local hospital supply company that uses the direct write-off method of accounting for uncollectible receivables:

March 18 Received $5,000 on an account and wrote off the remainder owed of $10,000 as uncollectible.

Aug. 29 Reinstated the account that had been written off on March 18 and received $10,000 cash in full payment.

Obj. 4

E6-5 Uncollectible receivables, using allowance method

Illustrate the effects on the accounts and financial statements of the following transactions in the accounts of Kitchen Depot Company, a restaurant supply company that uses the allowance method of accounting for uncollectible receivables:

July 3 Received $2,500 on an account and wrote off the remainder owed of $11,000 as uncollectible.

Oct. 8 Reinstated the account that had been written off on July 3 and received $11,000 cash in full payment.

Obj. 3, 4

E6-6 Writing off accounts receivable

Quantum Technologies, a computer consulting firm, has decided to write off the $13,000 balance of an account owed by a customer. Illustrate the effects on the accounts and financial statements to record the write-off (a) assuming that the direct write-off method is used, and (b) assuming that the allowance method is used.

Obj. 4

E6-7 Estimating doubtful accounts

Easy Rider International is a wholesaler of motorcycle supplies. An aging of the company's accounts receivable on December 31, 20Y3, and a historical analysis of the percentage of uncollectible accounts in each age category are as follows:

Age Interval	Balance	Percent Uncollectible
Not past due	$1,850,000	1%
1–30 days past due	750,000	2
31–60 days past due	100,000	6
61–90 days past due	60,000	14
91–180 days past due	45,000	60
Over 180 days past due	25,000	90
	$2,830,000	

Estimate what the balance of Allowance for Doubtful Accounts should be as of December 31, 20Y3.

Obj. 4

E6-8 Entry for uncollectible accounts

Using the data in Exercise 6-7, assume that the allowance for doubtful accounts for Easy Rider International had a negative balance of $(13,300) as of December 31, 20Y3.

Illustrate the effects of the adjustment for uncollectible accounts as of December 31, 20Y3, on the accounts and financial statements.

Obj. 4

✔ a. $172,500

✔ b. $181,500

E6-9 Providing for doubtful accounts

At the end of the current year, the accounts receivable account has a balance of $2,875,000 and sales for the year total $34,500,000. Determine the amount of the adjusting entry to provide for doubtful accounts under each of the following independent assumptions:

a. The allowance account before adjustment has a negative balance of $(18,500). Bad debt expense is estimated at ½ of 1% of sales.

b. The allowance account before adjustment has a negative balance of $(18,500). An aging of the accounts in the customer ledger indicates estimated doubtful accounts of $200,000.

c. The allowance account before adjustment has a positive balance of $9,000. Bad debt expense is estimated at ¾ of 1% of sales.

d. The allowance account before adjustment has a positive balance of $9,000. An aging of the accounts in the customer ledger indicates estimated doubtful accounts of $255,000.

E6-10 Effect of doubtful accounts on net income

Obj. 3, 4

During its first year of operations, Fisher Plumbing Supply Co. had sales of $2,780,000, wrote off $16,000 of accounts as uncollectible using the direct write-off method, and reported net income of $120,000. Determine what the net income would have been if the allowance method had been used, and the company estimated that 1% of sales would be uncollectible.

E6-11 Effect of doubtful accounts on net income

Obj. 3, 4

✔ b. $21,800

Using the data in Exercise 6-10, assume that during the second year of operations Fisher Plumbing Supply Co. had sales of $3,000,000, wrote off $20,000 of accounts as uncollectible using the direct write-off method, and reported net income of $140,000.

a. Determine what net income would have been in the second year if the allowance method (using 1% of sales) had been used in both the first and second years.

b. Determine what the balance of Allowance for Doubtful Accounts would have been at the end of the second year if the allowance method had been used in both the first and second years.

E6-12 Manufacturing inventories

Obj. 5

Qualcomm Incorporated (QCOM) is a leading developer and manufacturer of digital wireless telecommunications products and services. Qualcomm reported the following inventories (in millions) in the notes to recent financial statements:

Raw materials	$ 1
Work in process	550
Finished goods	941
	$1,492

a. Why does Qualcomm report three different inventories?

b. What costs are included in each of the three inventory accounts?

E6-13 Film costs of DreamWorks

Obj. 5

DreamWorks Animation SKG Inc. (DWA) shows "film costs" as an asset on its balance sheet. In the notes to its financial statements, the following disclosure was made:

	December 31,	
Film Costs (in thousands)	Year 2	Year 1
In release:		
Animated feature films	$392,186	$285,238
Television specials	67,803	58,631
In production:		
Animated feature films	206,240	474,609
Television specials	62,426	15,332

(Continued on next page)

In development:		
Feature films	$88,200	$75,498
Television series and specials	1,118	1,500
Product inventory	9,917	32,678
Total film costs	$827,890	$943,486

a. Interpret the film cost asset categories.

b. How are these classifications similar or dissimilar to the inventory classifications used in a manufacturing firm?

Obj. 6

✔ **b. $19,080**

E6-14 Inventory by three methods

The units of an item available for sale during the year were as follows:

Jan. 1	Inventory	27 units at $400
Feb. 19	Purchase	54 units at $460
June 8	Purchase	63 units at $520
Oct. 7	Purchase	56 units at $550

There are 45 units of the item in the physical inventory at December 31. Determine the cost of ending inventory using (a) the first-in, first-out method, (b) the last-in, first-out method, and (c) the weighted average cost method.

Obj. 6

✔ **a. Inventory, $37,620**

E6-15 Inventory by three methods; cost of goods sold

The units of an item available for sale during the year were as follows:

Jan. 1	Inventory	21 units at $1,800
May 15	Purchase	29 units at $1,950
Aug. 7	Purchase	10 units at $2,040
Nov. 20	Purchase	15 units at $2,100

There are 18 units of the item in the physical inventory at December 31. Determine the cost of ending inventory and the cost of goods sold by three methods, presenting your answers in the following form:

Inventory Method	Ending Inventory	Cost of Goods Sold
a. First-in, first-out	$	$
b. Last-in, first-out		
c. Weighted average		

Obj. 7

E6-16 Comparing inventory methods

Assume that a firm separately determined inventory under FIFO and LIFO and then compared the results.

1. In each space below, place the correct sign [less than (<), greater than (>), or equal (=)] for each comparison, assuming periods of rising prices.
   a. FIFO ending inventory ______ LIFO ending inventory
   b. FIFO cost of goods sold ______ LIFO cost of goods sold
   c. FIFO net income ______ LIFO net income
   d. FIFO income tax ______ LIFO income tax
2. Why would management prefer to use LIFO over FIFO in periods of rising prices?

E6-17 Receivables in the balance sheet

Obj. 8

List any errors you can find in the following partial balance sheet:

ZABEL COMPANY
Balance Sheet
December 31, 20Y4

Assets		
Current assets:		
Cash		$ 75,000
Notes receivable	$115,000	
Less interest receivable	9,000	106,000
Account receivable	$475,000	
Plus allowance for doubtful accounts	11,150	486,150

E6-18 Lower-of-cost-or-market inventory

Obj. 8

✔ LCM: $250,370

On the basis of the following data, determine the value of the inventory at the lower of cost or market. Assemble the data in the form illustrated in Exhibit 9.

Product	Inventory Quantity	Cost per Unit	Market Value per Unit (Net Realizable Value)
Adams	100	$140	$125
Coolidge	375	90	112
McKinley	220	60	59
Garfield	900	120	115
Lincoln	626	140	145

E6-19 Inventory on the balance sheet

Obj. 8

Based on the data in Exercise 6-18 and assuming that cost was determined by the FIFO method, show how the inventory would appear on the balance sheet.

Problems

P6-1 Allowance method for doubtful accounts

Obj. 4

✔ 1. Estimate of uncollectible accounts, $59,350

Averys All-Natural Company supplies wigs and hair care products to beauty salons throughout Texas and the Southwest. The accounts receivable clerk for Averys All-Natural prepared the following aging-of-receivables schedule as of the end of business on December 31, 20Y7:

	A	B	C	D	E	F	G	H
1			Not		Days Past Due			
2			Past					
3	Customer	Balance	Due	1–30	31–60	61–90	91–120	Over 120
4	AAA Beauty	27,500	27,500					
5	Amelia's Wigs	3,750			3,750			
30	Zim's Beauty	1,650		1,650				
31	Totals	1,100,000	750,000	180,000	75,000	45,000	22,000	28,000

Averys All-Natural Company has a past history of uncollectible accounts by age category, as follows:

Age Class	Percent Uncollectible
Not past due	1%
1–30 days past due	3
31–60 days past due	7
61–90 days past due	16
91–120 days past due	40
Over 120 days past due	90

Instructions

1. Estimate the allowance for doubtful accounts, based on the aging-of-receivables schedule.
2. Assume that the allowance for doubtful accounts for Averys All-Natural Company has a negative balance of $(2,250) before adjustment on December 31, 20Y7. Illustrate the effect on the accounts and financial statements of the adjustment for uncollectible accounts.
3. Averys All-Natural Company reported credit sales of $2,400,000 during 20Y7. Assume that instead of using the analysis of receivables method of estimating uncollectible accounts, Natural Hair Company uses the percent of sales method and estimates that 2.5% of sales will be uncollectible. Illustrate the effect on the accounts and financial statements of the adjustment for uncollectible accounts using the percent of sales method.
4. Assume that on March 4, 20Y8, Averys All-Natural wrote off the $2,950 account of Superior Images as uncollectible. Illustrate the effect on the accounts and financial statements of the write-off of the Superior Images account.
5. Assume that on August 17, 20Y8, Superior Images paid $2,950 on its account. Illustrate the effect on the accounts and financial statements of reinstating and collecting the Superior Images account.
6. Assume that instead of using the allowance method, Averys All-Natural uses the direct write-off method. Illustrate the effect on the accounts and financial statements of the following:
   a. The write-off of the Superior Images account on March 4, 20Y8.
   b. The reinstatement and collection of the Superior Images account on August 17, 20Y8.

Obj. 4

P6-2 Estimate uncollectible accounts

✔ 1. a. 20Y2, $31,250

For several years, EquiPrime Co.'s sales have been on a "cash only" basis. On January 1, 20Y2, however, EquiPrime Co. began offering credit on terms of n/30. The amount of the adjusting entry to record the estimated uncollectible receivables at the end of each year has been ¼ of 1% of credit sales, which is the rate reported as the average for the industry. Credit sales and the year-end credit balances in Allowance for Doubtful Accounts for the past four years are as follows:

Year	Credit Sales	Allowance for Doubtful Accounts
20Y2	$12,500,000	$12,800
20Y3	12,600,000	23,000
20Y4	12,800,000	34,000
20Y5	13,000,000	49,000

Mandy Pulaski, president of EquiPrime Co., is concerned that the method used to account for and write off uncollectible receivables is unsatisfactory. She has asked for your advice in the analysis of past operations in this area and for recommendations for change.

1. Determine the amount of (a) the addition to Allowance for Doubtful Accounts and (b) the accounts written off for each of the four years.

2. a. Advise Mandy Pulaski as to whether the estimate of ¼ of 1% of credit sales appears reasonable.
   b. Assume that after discussing (a) with Mandy Pulaski, she asked you what action might be taken to determine what the balance of Allowance for Doubtful Accounts should be at December 31, 20Y5, and what possible changes, if any, you might recommend in accounting for uncollectible receivables. How would you respond?

P6-3 Compare two methods of accounting for uncollectible receivables

Obj. 3, 4

✔ 1. Year 4: Balance of allowance account, end of year, $53,750

Cyber Space Company, which operates a chain of 65 electronics supply stores, has just completed its fourth year of operations. The direct write-off method of recording bad debt expense has been used during the entire period. Because of substantial increases in sales volume and the amount of uncollectible accounts, the firm is considering changing to the allowance method. Information is requested as to the effect that an annual provision of ½% of sales would have had on the amount of bad debt expense reported for each of the past four years. It is also considered desirable to know what the balance of Allowance for Doubtful Accounts would have been at the end of each year. The following data have been obtained from the accounts:

			Year of Origin of Accounts Receivable Written Off as Uncollectible			
Year	**Sales**	**Uncollectible Accounts Written Off**	**1**	**2**	**3**	**4**
1	$2,300,000	$ 5,000	$5,000			
2	4,750,000	9,000	4,000	$ 5,000		
3	9,000,000	23,000	2,000	12,000	$ 9,000	
4	9,600,000	37,500		5,500	14,500	$17,500

Instructions

1. Assemble the desired data, using the following column headings:

	Bad Debt Expense			
Year	**Expense Actually Reported**	**Expense Based on Estimate**	**Increase (Decrease) in Amount of Expense**	**Balance of Allowance Account, End of Year**

2. Experience during the first four years of operations indicated that the receivables were either collected within two years or had to be written off as uncollectible. Does the estimate of ½% of sales appear to be reasonably close to the actual experience with uncollectible accounts originating during the first two years? Explain.

P6-4 Inventory by three cost flow methods

Obj. 6, 7

✔ 1. $10,700

Details regarding the inventory of appliances on January 1, 20Y7, purchases invoices during the year, and the inventory count on December 31, 20Y7, of Amsterdam Appliances are summarized as follows:

		Purchases Invoices			
Model	**Inventory, January 1**	**1st**	**2nd**	**3rd**	**Inventory Count, December 31**
A10	—	4 at $ 64	4 at $ 70	4 at $ 76	6
B15	8 at $176	4 at 158	3 at 170	6 at 184	8
E60	3 at 75	3 at 65	15 at 68	9 at 70	5
G83	7 at 242	6 at 250	5 at 260	10 at 259	9
J34	12 at 240	10 at 246	16 at 267	16 at 270	15
M90	2 at 108	2 at 110	3 at 128	3 at 130	5
Q70	5 at 160	4 at 170	4 at 175	7 at 180	8

Instructions

1. Determine the cost of the inventory on December 31, 20Y7, by the first-in, first-out method. Present data in columnar form, using the following headings:

Model	Quantity	Unit Cost	Total Cost

If the inventory of a particular model comprises one entire purchase plus a portion of another purchase acquired at a different unit cost, use a separate line for each purchase.

2. Determine the cost of the inventory on December 31, 20Y7, by the last-in, first-out method, following the procedures indicated in (1).
3. Determine the cost of the inventory on December 31, 20Y7, by the average cost method, using the columnar headings indicated in (1).
4. Discuss which method (FIFO or LIFO) would be preferred for income tax purposes in periods of (a) rising prices and (b) declining prices.

Obj. 8

✔ Total LCM, $41,855

P6-5 Lower-of-cost-or-market inventory

Data on the physical inventory of Moyer Company as of December 31, 20Y9, are presented below.

Description	Inventory Quantity	Unit Market Price
112Aa	38	$ 83
B300t	33	115
C39f	41	64
Echo9	125	26
F900w	18	550
H687	60	15
J023	5	390
L33y	375	6
R66b	90	18
S77x	6	235
T882m	130	18
Z55p	12	746

Quantity and cost data from the last purchases invoice of the year and the next-to-the-last purchases invoice are summarized as follows:

	Last Purchases Invoice		Next-to-the-Last Purchases Invoice	
Description	Quantity Purchased	Unit Cost	Quantity Purchased	Unit Cost
112Aa	25	$ 80	30	$ 78
B300t	35	118	20	117
C39f	20	66	25	70
Echo9	150	25	100	24
F900w	10	565	10	560
H687	100	15	100	14
J023	10	385	5	384
L33y	500	6	500	6
R66b	80	22	50	21
S77x	5	250	4	260
T882m	100	20	75	19
Z55p	9	750	9	749

Instructions

Determine the inventory at cost and also at the lower of cost or market, using the first-in, first-out method. Record the appropriate unit costs on an inventory sheet and complete the pricing of the inventory. When there are two different unit costs applicable to an item, proceed as follows:

1. Draw a line through the quantity, and insert the quantity and unit cost of the last purchase.
2. On the following line, insert the quantity and unit cost of the next-to-the-last purchase.
3. Total the cost and market columns and insert the lower of the two totals in the LCM column. The first item on the inventory sheet has been completed below as an example.

Inventory Sheet
December 31, 20Y9

				Total		
Description	Inventory Quantity	Unit Cost Price	Unit Market Price	Cost	Market	LCM
112Aa	~~38~~ 25	$80	$83	$2,000	$2,075	
	13	78		1,014	1,079	
				$3,014	$3,154	$3,014

Metric-Based Analysis

MBA 6-1 Direct write-off method — Obj. 3

Using transactions listed in E6-4, indicate the effects of each transaction on the liquidity metric days' sales in receivables and profitability metric return on sales.

MBA 6-2 Allowance method — Obj. 4

Using transactions listed in E6-5, indicate the effects of each transaction on the liquidity metric days' sales in receivables and profitability metric return on sales.

MBA 6-3 Allowance method: adjustment — Obj. 4

Using transactions listed in E6-8, indicate the effects of the adjustment on the liquidity metric days' sales in receivables and profitability metric return on sales.

MBA 6-4 FIFO and LIFO — Obj. 6

Using data in E6-16, indicate the effects of selecting FIFO and LIFO on the liquidity metric days' sales in inventory and profitability metric return on sales.

Obj. 6

MBA 6-5 Lower of cost or market

Using data in E6-18, indicate the effects of valuing inventory using lower of cost or market on the liquidity metric days' sales in inventory and profitability metric return on sales.

Obj. 9

MBA 6-6 Accounts receivable and inventory turnover

The following data (in millions) were adapted from recent financial statements of Apple Inc (AAPL).

	Year 2	Year 1
Sales	$233,715	$182,795
Cost of goods sold	140,089	112,258
Operating income	71,230	52,503
Average accounts receivable	33,713	27,816
Average inventory	2,230	1,938

1. Compute the accounts receivable turnover for Years 1 and 2. Round to one decimal place.
2. Compute days' sales in receivables for Years 1 and 2. Round to the nearest day.
3. Compute the inventory turnover for Years 1 and 2. Round to one decimal place.
4. Compute days' sales in inventory for Years 1 and 2. Round to nearest day.
5. Compute the return on sales for Years 1 and 2. Round to one decimal place.
6. Comment on Apple's operations based upon the results in parts (1), (2), (3), (4), and (5).

Obj. 9

MBA 6-7 Accounts receivable and inventory turnover

The following data (in millions) were adapted from recent financial statements of HP Inc. (HPQ) formerly Hewlett-Packard Company.

	Year 2	Year 1
Sales	$103,355	$111,454
Cost of goods sold	78,596	84,839
Operating income	5,471	7,185
Average accounts receivable	16,530	17,899
Average inventory	6,450	6,231

1. Compute the accounts receivable turnover for Years 1 and 2. Round to one decimal place.
2. Compute days' sales in receivables for Years 1 and 2. Round to nearest day.
3. Compute the inventory turnover for Years 1 and 2. Round to nearest day.
4. Compute days' sales in inventory for Years 1 and 2. Round to nearest day.
5. Compute the return on sales for Years 1 and 2. Round to one decimal place.
6. Comment on HP's operations based upon the results in parts (1), (2), (3), (4) and (5).

Obj. 9

MBA 6-8 Accounts receivable and inventory turnover

Compare and comment on Apple and HP using the results of MBA 6-6 and MBA 6-7.

MBA 6-9 Accounts receivable and inventory turnover

Obj. 9

The following data (in millions) were adapted from recent financial statements of CVS Health Corporation (CVS).

	Year 2	Year 1
Sales	$139,367	$126,761
Cost of goods sold	114,000	102,978
Operating income	8,799	8,037
Average accounts receivable	10,152	8,402
Average inventory	11,488	11,039

1. Compute the accounts receivable turnover for Years 1 and 2. Round to one decimal place.
2. Compute the days' sales in receivables for Years 1 and 2. Round to the nearest day.
3. Compute the inventory turnover for Years 1 and 2. Round to one decimal place.
4. Compute the days' sales in inventory for Years 1 and 2. Round to one decimal place.
5. Compute the return on sales for Years 1 and 2. Round to one decimal place.
6. Comment on CVS' operations based upon the results in parts (1), (2), (3), (4) and (5).

MBA 6-10 Accounts receivable and inventory turnover

Obj. 9

The following data (in millions) were adapted from recent financial statements of International Paper Company (IP) and Wal-Mart Stores Inc. (WMT)

	International Paper	Wal-Mart
Sales	$23,617	$484,651
Cost of goods sold	16,254	365,086
Operating income	1,517	27,147
Accounts receivable:		
Beginning of year	4,058	6,677
End of year	3,414	6,778
Inventory:		
Beginning of year	2,825	44,858
End of year	2,424	45,141

1. Compute the accounts receivable turnover for International Paper and Wal-Mart. Round to one decimal place.
2. Compute the days' sales in receivables for International Paper and Wal-Mart. Round to nearest day.
3. Compute the inventory turnover for International Paper and Wal-Mart. Round to one decimal place.
4. Compute the days' sales in inventory for International Paper and Wal-Mart. Round to nearest day.
5. Compute the return on sales for International Paper and Wal-Mart. Round to one decimal place.
6. Comment on and explain any differences in International Paper's and Wal-Mart's management of inventories and receivables based upon the results in parts (1), (2), (3), (4), and (5).

Cases

Case 6-1 Ethics and professional conduct in business

Sybil Crumpton, vice president of operations for Bob Marshall Wilderness Bank, has instructed the bank's computer programmer to use a 365-day year to compute interest on depository accounts (payables). Sybil also instructed the programmer to use a 360-day year to compute interest on loans (receivables).

Discuss whether Sybil is behaving in a professional manner.

Case 6-2 Collecting accounts receivable

The following is an excerpt from a conversation between the office manager, Terry Holland, and the president of Northern Construction Supplies Co., Janet Austel. Northern Construction Supplies sells building supplies to local contractors.

Terry: Janet, we're going to have to do something about these overdue accounts receivable. One-third of our accounts are over 60 days past due, and I've had accounts that have stayed open for almost a year!

Janet: I didn't realize it was that bad. Any ideas?

Terry: Well, we could stop giving credit. Make everyone pay with cash or a credit card. We accept MasterCard and Visa already, but only the walk-in customers use them. Almost all of the contractors put purchases on their bills.

Janet: Yes, but we've been allowing credit for years. As far as I know, all of our competitors allow contractors credit. If we stopped giving credit, we'd lose many of our contractors. They'd just go elsewhere. You know, some of these guys run up bills as high as $50,000 or $75,000. There's no way they could put that kind of money on a credit card.

Terry: That's a good point. But we've got to do something.

Janet: How many of the contractor accounts do you actually end up writing off as uncollectible?

Terry: Not many. Almost all eventually pay. It's just that they take so long!

Suggest one or more solutions to Northern Construction Supplies Co.'s problem concerning the collection of accounts receivable.

Case 6-3 Ethics and professional conduct in business

Mitchell Co. is experiencing a decrease in sales and operating income for the fiscal year ending December 31, 20Y1. Gene Lumpkin, controller of Mitchell Co., has suggested that all orders received before the end of the fiscal year be shipped by midnight, December 31, 20Y1, even if the shipping department must work overtime. Since Mitchell Co. ships all merchandise FOB shipping point, it would record all such shipments as sales for the year ending December 31, 20Y1, thereby offsetting some of the decreases in sales and operating income.

Discuss whether Gene Lumpkin is behaving in a professional manner.

Case 6-4 LIFO and inventory flow

The following is an excerpt from a conversation between Evan Eberhard, the warehouse manager for Greenbriar Wholesale Co., and its accountant, Marty Hayes. Greenbriar operates a large regional warehouse that supplies produce and other grocery products to grocery stores in smaller communities.

Evan: Marty, can you explain what's going on here with these monthly statements?

Marty: Sure, Evan. How can I help you?

Evan: I don't understand this last-in, first-out inventory procedure. It just doesn't make sense.

Marty: Well, what it means is that we assume that the last goods we receive are the first ones sold. So the inventory is made up of the items we purchased first.

Evan: Yes, but that's my problem. It doesn't work that way! We always distribute the oldest produce first. Some of that produce is perishable! We can't keep any of it very long or it'll spoil.

Marty: Evan, you don't understand. We only assume that the products we distribute are the last ones received. We don't actually have to distribute the goods in this way.

Evan: I always thought that accounting was supposed to show what really happened. It all sounds like "make believe" to me! Why not report what really happens?

Respond to Evan's concerns.

Answers to Self-Examination Questions

1. **B** The estimate of uncollectible accounts, $8,500 (answer C), is the amount of the desired balance of Allowance for Doubtful Accounts after adjustment. The amount of the current provision to be made for bad debt expense is thus $6,000 (answer B), which is the amount that must be added to the Allowance for Doubtful Accounts negative balance of $2,500 (answer A), so that the account will have the desired balance of $8,500.

2. **B** The amount expected to be realized from accounts receivable is the balance of Accounts Receivable, $100,000, less the balance of Allowance for Doubtful Accounts, $7,000, or $93,000 (answer B).

3. **D** The direct labor costs are introduced into production initially as work in process. Once the units are completed, these costs are transferred to finished goods inventory (answer C). Materials inventory (answer A) includes only material costs, not direct labor cost. Merchandise inventory (answer B) is not used in a manufacturing setting and thus does not include direct labor cost.

4. **D** The FIFO method of costing is based on the assumption that costs should be charged against revenue in the order in which they were incurred (first-in, first-out). Thus, the most recent costs are assigned to inventory. The 35 units would be assigned a unit cost of $23 (answer D).

5. **B** When the price level is steadily rising, the earlier unit costs are lower than recent unit costs. Under the FIFO method (answer B), these earlier costs are matched against revenue to yield the highest possible net income.

Chapter 7

Fixed Assets, Natural Resources, and Intangible Assets

What's Covered:

Topics: Fixed Assets, Natural Resources, and Intangible Assets

Fixed Assets
- Nature (Obj. 1)
- Depreciation (Obj. 2)
- Repairs and improvements (Obj. 2)
- Disposal (Obj. 3)

Natural Resources
- Cost (Obj. 4)
- Depletion (Obj. 4)

Intangible Assets
- Patents, copyrights, trade-marks , goodwill (Obj. 5)
- Amortization and impairment (Obj.5)

Financial Reporting
- Income statement (Obj. 6)
- Balance sheet (Obj. 6)

Metric-Based Analysis
- Transactions:
  - Liquidity: Free cash flow (Obj. 1, 2, 3, 4, 5)
  - Profitability: Asset turn-over (Obj. 1, 2, 3, 4, 5)
- Financial Statements:
  - Asset turnover (Obj. 7)

Learning Objectives

Obj.1 Define, classify, and account for the cost of fixed assets.

Obj.2 Compute depreciation using the straight-line and double-declining-balance methods.

Obj.3 Describe the accounting for the disposal of fixed assets.

Obj.4 Describe the accounting for natural resources.

Obj.5 Describe the accounting for intangible assets.

Obj.6 Describe the reporting of fixed assets, natural resources, and intangible assets on the income statement and balance sheet.

Obj.7 Describe and illustrate asset turnover in assessing a company's operating results.

Chapter Metrics

Use the following metrics to analyze transactions and financial statements:

TRANSACTIONS

- **Liquidity: Free Cash Flow**
- **Profitability: Asset Turnover**

FINANCIAL STATEMENTS

- **Asset Turnover**

Chipotle Mexican Grill Inc.

Jonathan Weiss/ Shutterstock.com

Steve Ells is a graduate of Boulder High School, University of Colorado (majoring in Art History), and the Culinary Institute of America. After spending several years working as a cook in San Francisco, he returned to Colorado with a dream of opening a high-end Denver restaurant. In 1993, he opened a small restaurant serving burritos near the University of Denver with hopes of earning enough to finance his dream of a "high-end, fine-dining" restaurant. He never fulfilled his dream. Instead, this first restaurant was the start of what is now Chipotle Mexican Grill (CMG).

Currently, Chipotle (pronounced chi-POAT-lay) has over 1,700 restaurants worldwide and has expanded its operations to include ShopHouse Southeast Asian Kitchen and Pizzeria Locale restaurants. Chipotle's overriding business philosophy is "Food With Integrity" using carefully selected, quality ingredients while avoiding genetically modified ingredients. Consistent with its philosophy of "a few things, thousands of ways", it serves a simple menu including burritos, burrito bowls (without a tortilla), tacos, and salads. In addition, Chipotle implemented a restaurateur training program for its "crew members" that emphasizes a high-energy, conscientious, and motivated employee environment.

Within the United States, a new Chipotle restaurant costs approximately $800,000 to start. To finance its early expansion, Ells solicited funding from McDonald's Corp., which at the time was attempting to diversify its operations. In 2006 Chipotle offered its stock to the public and McDonald's sold its shares. In the coming years, Chipotle plans to open hundreds of new restaurants.

This chapter discusses the accounting for the costs of fixed assets, such as Chipotle's restaurants. In addition, methods of depreciating fixed asset costs are discussed. Finally, the accounting for the disposal of fixed assets as well as the accounting for natural resources and intangible assets, such as the trademark "Chipotle," is discussed.

Sources: Chipotle Mexican Grill 10-K; "Steve Ells, Chipotle Founder, Reflects on McDonald's, GMOs And The First 20 Year of His Chain," Joe Satran, Huffingtonpost.com, July 12, 2013; https://chipotle.com/company.

Nature of Fixed Assets

Objective 1
Define, classify, and account for the cost of fixed assets.

Fixed assets are long-term or relatively permanent assets such as equipment, machinery, buildings, and land. Other descriptive titles for fixed assets are *plant assets* or *property, plant, and equipment*. Fixed assets have the following characteristics:

- They exist physically and thus are *tangible* assets.
- They are owned and used by the company in its normal operations.
- They are not offered for sale as part of normal operations.

Exhibit 1 shows the percent of fixed assets to total assets for some select companies. As shown in Exhibit 1, fixed assets are often a significant portion of the total assets of a company.

Exhibit 1
Fixed Assets as a Percent of Total Assets—Selected Companies

	Fixed Assets as a Percent of Total Assets
Alcoa Inc.	44%
Exxon Mobil Corporation	72
Hyatt Hotels Corporation	51
Kroger	59
Starbucks Corporation	33
The Walt Disney Company	29
United Parcel Service, Inc.	47
Verizon Communications	39
Wal-Mart Stores, Inc.	57

Chipotle Connection On a recent balance sheet, property, plant, and equipment made up 43% of Chipotle's total assets.

Classifying Costs

A cost that has been incurred may be classified as a fixed asset, an investment, or an expense. Exhibit 2 shows how to determine the proper classification of a cost and thus how it should be recorded.

Exhibit 2 Classifying Costs

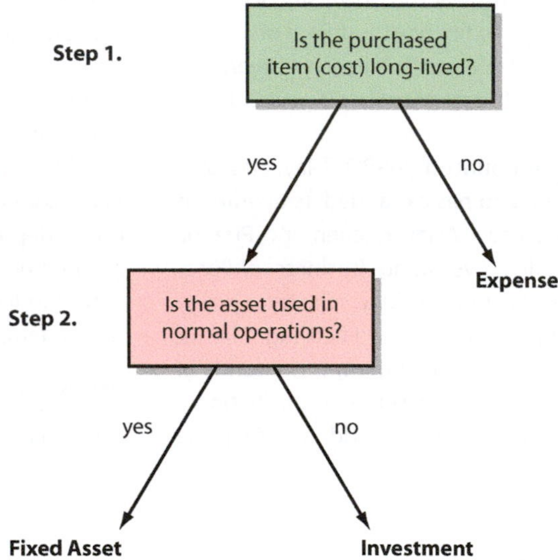

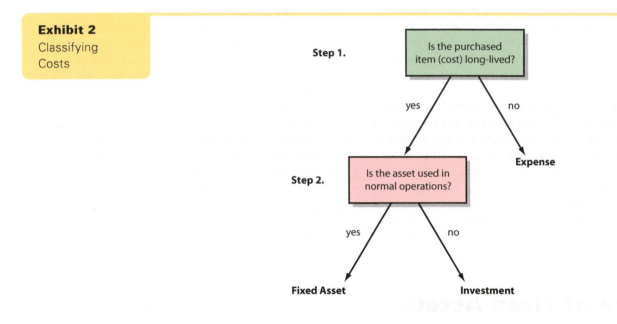

As shown in Exhibit 2, classifying a cost involves the following steps:

Step 1. Is the purchased item (cost) long-lived?

If *yes,* the item is capitalized as an asset on the balance sheet as either a fixed asset or an investment. Proceed to Step 2.

If *no,* the item is classified and recorded as an *expense.*

Step 2. Is the asset used in normal operations?

If *yes,* the asset is classified and recorded as a *fixed asset.*

If *no,* the asset is classified and recorded as an *investment.*

Costs that are classified and recorded as fixed assets include the purchase of land, buildings, or equipment. Such assets normally last more than a year and are used in normal operations. However, standby equipment for use during peak periods or when other equipment breaks down is still classified as a fixed asset even though it is not used very often. In contrast, fixed assets that have been abandoned or are no longer used in operations are not fixed assets.

Although fixed assets may be sold, they should not be offered for sale as part of normal operations. For example, cars and trucks offered for sale by an automotive dealership are not fixed assets of the dealership. On the other hand, a tow truck used in the normal operations of the dealership is a fixed asset of the dealership.

Investments are long-lived assets that are not used in the normal operations and are held for future resale. Such assets are reported on the balance sheet in a section entitled *Investments.* For example, undeveloped land acquired for future resale would be classified and reported as an investment, not land.

The Cost of Fixed Assets

The costs of acquiring fixed assets include all amounts spent to get the asset in place and ready for use. For example, freight costs and the costs of installing equipment are part of the asset's total cost.

Exhibit 3 summarizes some of the common costs of acquiring fixed assets. These costs are recorded by increasing the related fixed asset account, such as Building, Machinery and Equipment, Land,[1] and Land Improvements.

Exhibit 3 Costs of Acquiring Fixed Assets

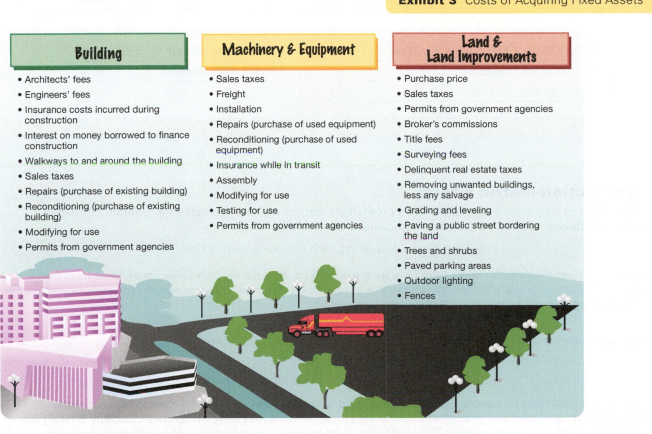

Building
- Architects' fees
- Engineers' fees
- Insurance costs incurred during construction
- Interest on money borrowed to finance construction
- Walkways to and around the building
- Sales taxes
- Repairs (purchase of existing building)
- Reconditioning (purchase of existing building)
- Modifying for use
- Permits from government agencies

Machinery & Equipment
- Sales taxes
- Freight
- Installation
- Repairs (purchase of used equipment)
- Reconditioning (purchase of used equipment)
- Insurance while in transit
- Assembly
- Modifying for use
- Testing for use
- Permits from government agencies

Land & Land Improvements
- Purchase price
- Sales taxes
- Permits from government agencies
- Broker's commissions
- Title fees
- Surveying fees
- Delinquent real estate taxes
- Removing unwanted buildings, less any salvage
- Grading and leveling
- Paving a public street bordering the land
- Trees and shrubs
- Paved parking areas
- Outdoor lighting
- Fences

Only costs necessary for preparing the fixed asset for use are included as a cost of the asset. Unnecessary costs that do not increase the asset's usefulness are recorded as an expense. For example, the following costs are recorded as an expense:

- Vandalism
- Mistakes in installation
- Uninsured theft
- Damage during unpacking and installing
- Fines for not obtaining proper permits from governmental agencies

To illustrate, assume that Southwest Needle Inc. purchased the following equipment on June 5 and that all costs were paid in cash.

Purchase price	$30,000
Freight costs (FOB shipping point)	1,100
Installation costs	2,750 *

* Includes cost of $900 incurred to repair equipment damaged during installation.

The equipment would be recorded at a cost of $32,950 ($30,000 + $1,100 + $2,750 – $900). The cost of the $900 damage incurred during installation is recorded as an expense.

1. As discussed here, land is assumed to be used only as a location or site and not for its mineral deposits or other natural resources.

The effects of purchasing the equipment on the financial statements are as follows:

Financial Statement Effects

BALANCE SHEET

	Assets		=	**Liabilities** + **Stockholders' Equity**
	Cash +	**Equipment**	=	**Retained Earnings**
June 5.	(33,850)	32,950		(900)

STATEMENT OF CASH FLOWS

June 5. Investing	(32,950)
June 5. Operating	(900)

INCOME STATEMENT

June 5. Misc. expense	(900)

Transaction Metric Effects

The effects of transactions on liquidity and profitability metrics are also illustrated throughout the chapter. **Free cash flow** is used as the liquidity metric and is computed as follows:

$$\text{Free Cash Flow} = \text{Operating Cash Flows} - \text{Investing Cash Flows}$$

Operating cash flows (cash flows from operating activities) and investing cash flows (cash flows used for investing activities) are reported on the statement of cash flows. Free cash flow represents the cash available after maintaining and expanding current operating capacity.

Asset turnover is used as the profitability metric and is computed as follows:

$$\text{Asset Turnover} = \frac{\text{Sales}}{\text{Average Long-Term Operating Assets}}$$

Long-term operating assets consist of property, plant, and equipment (net of accumulated depreciation) plus natural resources and intangible assets. Asset turnover measures how efficiently a company is using its operating assets to generate sales. The higher the asset turnover the more efficient assets are being used.

The effects of purchasing the above equipment on the liquidity and profitability metrics are as follows:

LIQUIDITY

Free Cash Flow	$(33,850)

PROFITABILITY

Asset Turnover	Decrease

Since the equipment purchase decreases operating and investing cash flows, free cash flow decreases. Since equipment increases with no increase in sales, asset turnover decreases.

A company may incur costs associated with constructing a fixed asset such as a new building. The direct costs incurred in the construction, such as labor and materials, should be capitalized by increasing an account entitled Construction in Progress. When the construction is complete, the costs are reclassified by decreasing Construction in Progress and increasing the proper fixed asset account such as Building. For some companies, construction in progress can be significant.

Fixed Asset Leases

A **lease** is a contract for the use of an asset for a period of time. Leases are often used in business. For example, automobiles, computers, medical equipment, buildings, and airplanes are often leased.

The two parties to a lease contract are as follows:

- The *lessor* is the party who owns the asset.
- The *lessee* is the party to whom the rights to use the asset are granted by the lessor.

Under a lease contract, the lessee pays rent on a periodic basis for the lease term. An advantage of leasing an asset is that the lessee has use of the asset without having to buy the asset. In addition, the lessor may be responsible for expenses, such as maintenance and repair costs. Finally, the risk that the asset may become obsolete is mitigated.

Chipotle leases its main office in Denver as well as almost all the properties on which its restaurants are located. The leases terms are five to ten years with two or more five-year renewal extensions.

Chipotle Connection

The accounting for leases was the focus of a joint project by the Financial Accounting Standards (FASB) and the International Accounting Standards Board (IASB) to merge U.S. and international standards.[2] Under the Standard, lessors and lessees would be required to record assets and liabilities related to certain long-term lease contracts.

To simplify, we assume that leases are short-term and the rental contracts do not extend beyond one year. In such cases lease payments are recorded as Rent Expense, which is consistent with earlier chapters. The lease terms, such as a renewal option, are normally disclosed in notes to the financial statements.

Accounting for Depreciation

Objective 2
Compute depreciation using the straight-line and double-declining-balance methods.

Fixed assets, with the exception of land, lose their ability, over time, to provide services. Thus, the cost of fixed assets such as equipment and buildings should be recorded as an expense over their useful lives. This periodic recording of the cost of fixed assets as an expense is called **depreciation**. Because land has an unlimited life, it is not depreciated.[3]

The adjustment to record depreciation was illustrated in earlier chapters. This adjustment increases *Depreciation Expense* and a *contra asset* account entitled *Accumulated Depreciation* or *Allowance for Depreciation*. The use of a contra asset account allows the original cost to remain unchanged in the fixed asset account.

Depreciation can be caused by physical or functional factors.

- *Physical depreciation* factors include wear and tear during use or from exposure to weather.
- *Functional depreciation* factors include obsolescence and changes in customer needs that cause the asset to no longer provide services for which it was intended. For example, equipment may become obsolete due to changing technology.

Two common misunderstandings that exist about *depreciation* as used in accounting include:

- Depreciation does not measure a decline in the market value of a fixed asset. Instead, depreciation is an allocation of a fixed asset's cost to expense over the asset's useful life. Thus, the **book value of a fixed asset** (cost less accumulated depreciation) usually

2. Accounting Standards Update, *Leases (Topic 842)*, Financial Accounting Standards Board, 2016.
3. Land on which natural resources are extracted is discussed later in this chapter.

does not agree with the asset's market value. This is justified in accounting because a fixed asset is for use in a company's operations rather than for resale.

- Depreciation does not provide cash to replace fixed assets as they wear out. This misunderstanding may occur because depreciation, unlike most expenses, does not require an outlay of cash when it is recorded.

Factors in Computing Depreciation Expense

Three factors determine the depreciation expense for a fixed asset. These three factors are as follows:

- The asset's initial cost
- The asset's expected useful life
- The asset's estimated residual value

The **initial cost of a fixed asset** is the purchase price of the asset plus all costs to obtain and ready it for use. This initial cost is determined using the concepts discussed and illustrated earlier in this chapter.

The **expected useful life** of a fixed asset is estimated at the time the asset is placed into service. Estimates of expected useful lives are available from industry trade associations. The Internal Revenue Service also publishes guidelines for useful lives, which may be helpful for financial reporting purposes. However, it is not uncommon for different companies to use a different useful life for similar assets.

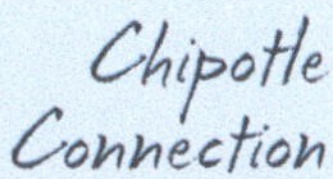

Chipotle uses estimated useful lives of 4-7 years for furniture and fixtures and 3-10 years for equipment.

The **residual value** of a fixed asset is the estimated value of the asset at the end of its useful life. It is estimated at the time the asset is placed into service. Residual value is sometimes referred to as *scrap value*, *salvage value*, or *trade-in value*.

The difference between a fixed asset's initial cost and its residual value is called the asset's **depreciable cost**. The depreciable cost is the amount of the asset's cost that is allocated over its useful life as depreciation expense. If a fixed asset has no residual value, then its entire cost should be allocated to depreciation.

To illustrate, assume the following used delivery van was purchased on January 1.

Initial cost	$24,000
Expected useful life	5 years
Estimated residual value	$2,000

Exhibit 4 shows the relationship among the van's initial cost, residual value, depreciable cost, expected useful life, and depreciation expense.

The two depreciation methods often used are:

1. Straight-line depreciation
2. Double-declining-balance depreciation

It is not necessary that a company use one method of computing depreciation for all of its fixed assets. For example, a company may use one method for depreciating equipment and another method for depreciating buildings. A company may also use different methods for determining income and property taxes.

Exhibit 4 Depreciation

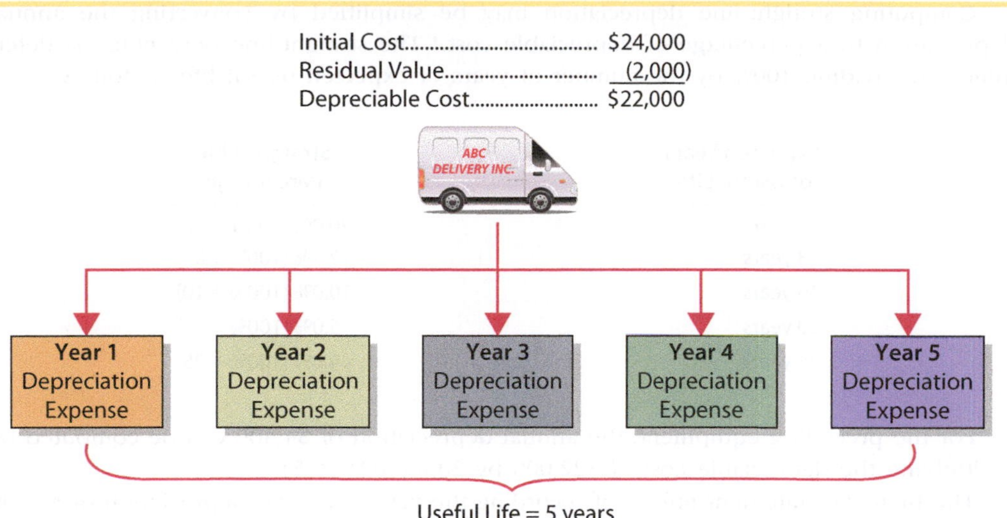

Straight-Line Method

The **straight-line method** provides for the same amount of depreciation expense for each year of the asset's useful life. The straight-line method is the most widely used depreciation method.

To illustrate, assume that the van was purchased on January 1 as follows:

Initial cost	$24,000
Expected useful life	5 years
Estimated residual value	$2,000

The annual straight-line depreciation of $4,400 is computed below.

$$\textbf{Annual Depreciation} = \frac{\textbf{Cost} - \textbf{Residual Value}}{\textbf{Useful Life}} = \frac{\$24{,}000 - \$2{,}000}{5\ \textbf{Years}} = \$4{,}400$$

The straight-line method reports the same amount of depreciation expense each year, as illustrated in Exhibit 5.

Exhibit 5 Straight-Line Method

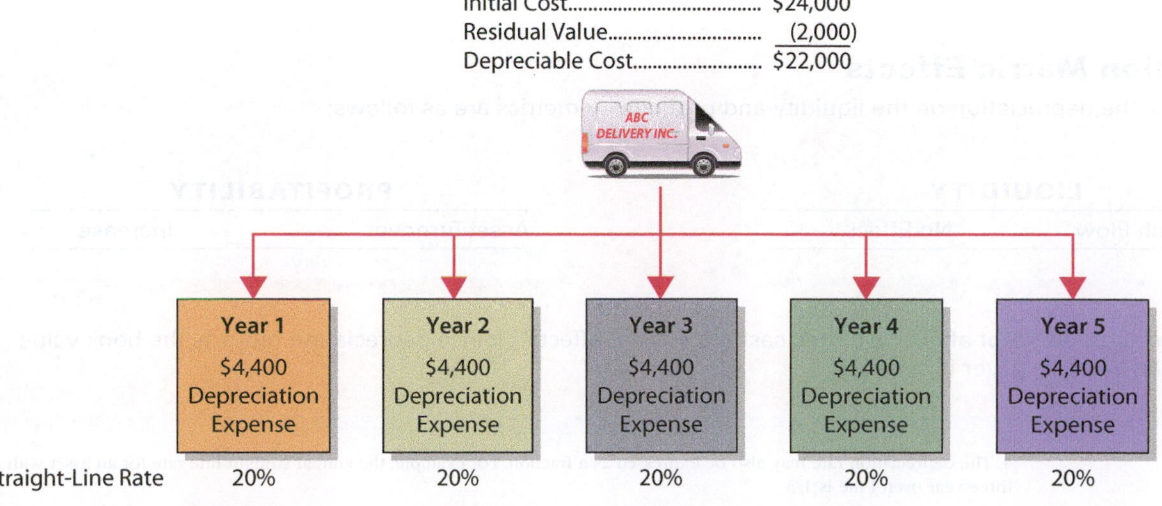

Computing straight-line depreciation may be simplified by converting the annual depreciation to a percentage of depreciable cost.[4] The straight-line percentage is determined by dividing 100% by the number of years of expected useful life, as follows:

Expected Years of Useful Life	Straight-Line Percentage
5 years	20.0% (100% ÷ 5)
8 years	12.5% (100% ÷ 8)
10 years	10.0% (100% ÷ 10)
20 years	5.0% (100% ÷ 20)
25 years	4.0% (100% ÷ 25)

For the preceding equipment, the annual depreciation of $4,400 can be computed by multiplying the depreciable cost of $22,000 by 20% (100% ÷ 5).

The financial statement effects of recording the van's first year depreciation of $4,400 on December 31 are as follows:

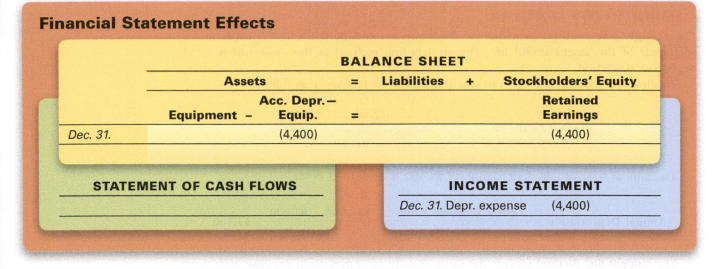

Financial Statement Effects

BALANCE SHEET

	Assets			=	Liabilities	+	Stockholders' Equity
	Equipment	–	Acc. Depr.—Equip.	=			Retained Earnings
Dec. 31.			(4,400)				(4,400)

STATEMENT OF CASH FLOWS

INCOME STATEMENT

Dec. 31. Depr. expense	(4,400)

The book value of the van at the end of the first year is $19,600 as follows:

Equipment	$24,000
Accumulated depreciation	(4,400)
Book value	$19,600

Transaction Metric Effects

The effects of the depreciation on the liquidity and profitability metrics are as follows:

LIQUIDITY	
Free Cash Flow	No Effect

PROFITABILITY	
Asset Turnover	Increase

Since depreciation does not affect cash, free cash flow is not affected. Since depreciation reduces the book value of the van, the asset turnover increases.

4. The depreciation rate may also be expressed as a fraction. For example, the annual straight-line rate for an asset with a three-year useful life is 1/3.

As illustrated, the straight-line method is simple to use. When an asset's revenues are about the same from period to period, straight-line depreciation provides a good matching of depreciation expense with the revenues generated by the asset.

Chipotle uses the straight-line method of depreciation.

Chipotle Connection

Double-Declining-Balance Method

The **double-declining-balance method** provides for a declining periodic expense over the expected useful life of the asset. The double-declining-balance method is applied in three steps.

Step 1. Determine the straight-line percentage using the expected useful life.

Step 2. Determine the double-declining-balance rate by multiplying the straight-line rate from Step 1 by two.

Step 3. Compute the depreciation expense by multiplying the double-declining-balance rate from Step 2 by the book value of the asset.

To illustrate, the van purchased in the preceding example is used to compute double-declining-balance depreciation. For the first year, the depreciation is $9,600, as shown below.

Step 1. Straight-line percentage = 20% (100% ÷ 5)

Step 2. Double-declining-balance rate = 40% (20% × 2)

Step 3. Depreciation expense = $9,600 ($24,000 × 40%)

For the first year, the book value of the equipment is its initial cost of $24,000. After the first year, the book value (cost minus accumulated depreciation) declines and thus the depreciation also declines. The double-declining-balance depreciation for the full five-year life of the equipment is shown below.

Year	Cost	Acc. Depr. at Beginning of Year	Book Value at Beginning of Year		Double-Declining-Balance Rate	Depreciation for Year	Book Value at End of Year
1	$24,000		$24,000.00	×	40%	$9,600.00	$14,400.00
2	24,000	$ 9,600.00	14,400.00	×	40%	5,760.00	8,640.00
3	24,000	15,360.00	8,640.00	×	40%	3,456.00	5,184.00
4	24,000	18,816.00	5,184.00	×	40%	2,073.60	3,110.40
5	24,000	20,889.60	3,110.40	×	—	1,110.40	2,000.00

When the double-declining-balance method is used, the estimated residual value is *not* considered. However, the asset should not be depreciated below its estimated residual value. In the above example, the estimated residual value was $2,000. Therefore, the depreciation for the fifth year is $1,110.40 ($3,110.40 − $2,000.00) instead of $1,244.16 (40% × $3,110.40).

Exhibit 6 illustrates the depreciation expense and book value of the van over its five-year life using the double-declining-balance method.

As shown in Exhibit 6, the double-declining-balance method has higher depreciation in the first year of the asset's life, followed by declining depreciation amounts. For this reason, the double-declining-balance method is called an **accelerated depreciation method**.

Exhibit 6 Double-Declining-Balance Method

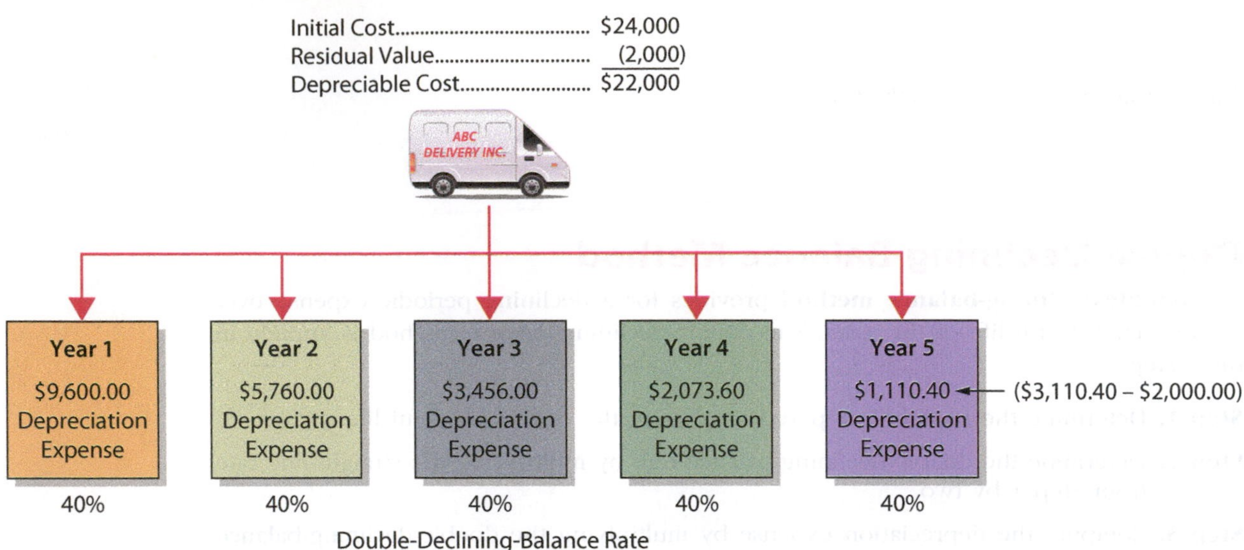

Except for the amount of depreciation, the effects of recording double-declining-balance depreciation on the financial statements are the same as those illustrated for the straight-line method. The liquidity and profitability metric effects are also the same.

An asset's revenues are often greater in the early years of its use than in later years. In such cases, the double-declining-balance method provides a good matching of depreciation expense with the asset's revenues.

Comparing Depreciation Methods

The depreciation methods are summarized in Exhibit 7. Both methods allocate a portion of the total cost of an asset to an accounting period, while never depreciating an asset below its residual value. The straight-line method provides for the same periodic amounts of depreciation expense over the life of the asset. The double-declining-balance method provides for a higher depreciation amount in the first year of the asset's use, followed by declining amounts.

Exhibit 7 Summary of Depreciation Methods

Method	Useful Life	Depreciable Cost	Depreciation Rate	Depreciation Expense
Straight-line	Years	Cost less residual value	Straight-line rate*	Constant
Double-declining-balance	Years	Declining book value, but not below residual value	Straight-line rate* × 2	Declining

*Straight-line rate = (1/Useful life)

Exhibit 8 illustrates depreciation expense for each depreciation method over the five-year life of the van.

Exhibit 8 Comparing Depreciation Methods

	Depreciation Expense	
Year	**Straight-Line Method**	**Double-Declining-Balance Method**
1	$ 4,400.00*	$ 9,600.00 ($24,000 × 40%)
2	4,400.00	5,760.00 ($14,400 × 40%)
3	4,400.00	3,456.00 ($8,640 × 40%)
4	4,400.00	2,073.60 ($5,184 × 40%)
5	4,400.00	1,110.40**
Total	$22,000.00	$22,000.00

*$4,400 = ($24,000 − $2,000) ÷ 5 years
**$3,110.40 − $2,000.00 because the equipment cannot be depreciated below its residual value.

Partial Year Depreciation

A fixed asset may be purchased and placed in service other than the first month of an accounting period. In such cases, depreciation is prorated based on the month the asset is placed in service. For example, assume an asset is placed in service on March 1. For an accounting period ending December 31, depreciation would be computed (prorated) for 10 months (March 1 to December 31).

Assets may also be placed in service other than the first day of a month. In such cases, assets placed in service during the first half of a month are normally treated as having been purchased on the first day of *that* month. Likewise, asset purchases during the second half of a month are treated as having been purchased on the first day of the next month.

Straight-Line Method Under the straight-line method, depreciation is prorated based on the number of months the asset is in service. To illustrate, assume the van in the preceding illustration was purchased on October 1 instead of January 1. The first-year depreciation would be based upon three months (October, November, December). Thus, the first-year depreciation would be $1,100, computed as follows:

Annual Depreciation = ($22,000 – $2,000) ÷ 5 years = $4,400
First-Year Depreciation = $4,400 × (3 ÷ 12) = $1,100

The second year's depreciation would be for a full year and would be $4,400.

Double-Declining-Balance Method Like the straight-line method, if an asset is used for only part of a year, the annual double-declining-balance depreciation is prorated based on the number of months the asset is in service. To illustrate, assume the van was purchased on October 1 instead of January 1. The first-year depreciation would be based upon three months (October, November, December). First-year depreciation would be $2,400, computed as follows:

Double-Declining Balance Rate = (100 ÷ 5) × 2 = 40%
First-Year Annual Depreciation = $24,000 × 40% = $9,600
First-Year Partial Depreciation = $9,600 × (3 ÷ 12) = $2,400

The second-year depreciation would be computed by multiplying the book value on January 1 of the second year by the double-declining-balance rate. To illustrate, assume partial depreciation on the van of $2,400 was recorded on December 31. Thus, the book value of the van on January 1 of the second year is $21,600 ($24,000 – $2,400). The second-year depreciation of $8,640 is computed as follows:

Second-Year Annual Depreciation = $21,600 × 40% = $8,640

Maintenance, Repair, and Improvement Costs

After a fixed asset has been purchased and placed into service, additional costs are often incurred. These costs include the following:

- Routine maintenance and repairs
- Extraordinary repairs
- Improvements

Routine maintenance and repair costs are often referred to as **revenue expenditures**. This is because these costs primarily benefit the current period. Extraordinary repairs and improvement costs are often referred to as **capital expenditures**. The benefits of these costs normally extend to multiple periods.

Routine Maintenance and Repairs Costs related to the routine maintenance and repairs are recorded as a revenue expenditure by increasing the repairs and maintenance expense account.

Extraordinary Repairs Costs incurred to extend the asset's useful life are recorded as a capital expenditure by decreasing the asset's accumulated depreciation account.

Improvements Costs incurred to improve the asset are recorded as a capital expenditure by increasing the fixed asset account.

To illustrate, assume that on January 8 of Year 2, the van used in the preceding examples incurred the following costs:

Tune-up engine and oil change	$ 300
Repaired transmission	900
Installed new hydraulic lift	1,500

The tune-up and oil change costs of $300 are recorded as an increase to Repairs and Maintenance Expense. The cost of repairing the transmission is recorded as a decrease in Accumulated Depreciation. The cost of installing the new hydraulic lift of $1,500 is recorded as an increase to the fixed asset account Delivery Van.[5]

The effects on the financial statements of incurring the preceding costs are as follows:

Financial Statement Effects

BALANCE SHEET

	Assets					=	Liabilities	+	Stockholders' Equity
	Cash	+	Delivery Van	–	Acc. Depr.—Delivery Van	=			Retained Earnings
Jan. 8.	(2,700)		1,500		900				(300)

STATEMENT OF CASH FLOWS

Jan. 8. Investing	(2,400)
Jan. 8. Operating	(300)

INCOME STATEMENT

Jan. 8. Repairs & maint. exp.	(300)

5. The costs of installing the lift (increase in Delivery Van) and repairing the transmission (decrease in Acc. Depr.) will change (revise) the depreciation expense in future years.

Transaction Metric Effects

The effects of the costs on liquidity and profitability metrics are as follows:

LIQUIDITY	
Free Cash Flow	$(2,700)

PROFITABILITY	
Asset Turnover	Decrease

Since the operating cash flows are $(300) and the investing cash flows are $(2,400), the free cash flow decreases by $2,700. Since the costs of the lift and transmission increase the book value of the van, asset turnover will decrease.

Chipotle Connection

In its financial statements, Chipotle reports that "...Expenditures for major improvements are capitalized *(treated as capital expenditures)* while expenditures for minor replacements, maintenance, and repairs are expensed as incurred.

The accounting for revenue and capital expenditures is summarized in Exhibit 9.

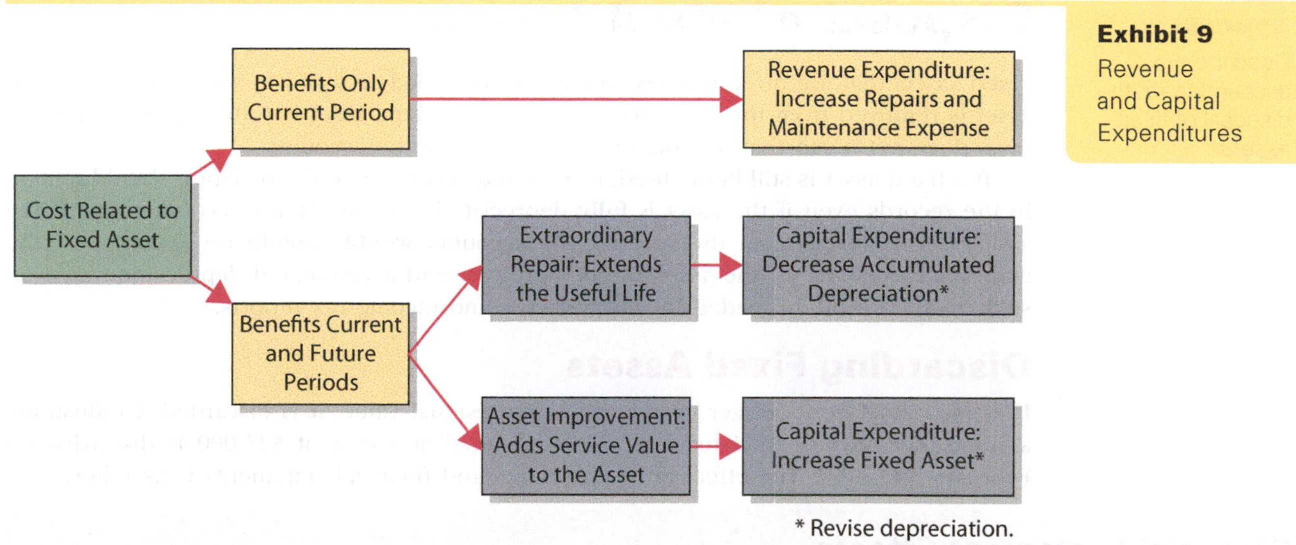

Exhibit 9 Revenue and Capital Expenditures

Integrity, Objectivity, and Ethics in Business

Capital Crime

One of the largest alleged accounting frauds in history involved the improper accounting for capital expenditures. **WorldCom**, the second largest telecommunications company in the United States at the time, improperly treated maintenance expenditures on its telecommunications network as capital expenditures. As a result, the company had to restate its prior years' earnings downward by nearly $4 billion to correct this error. The company declared bankruptcy within months of disclosing the error, and the CEO was sentenced to 25 years in prison.

Depreciation for Federal Income Tax

The Internal Revenue Code uses the *Modified Accelerated Cost Recovery System (MACRS)* to compute depreciation for tax purposes. MACRS has eight classes of useful lives and depreciation rates for each class. Two of the most common classes are the five-year class and the seven-year class.[6] The five-year class includes automobiles and light-duty trucks. The seven-year class includes most machinery and equipment. Depreciation for these two classes is similar to that computed using the double-declining-balance method.

In using the MACRS rates, residual value is ignored. Also, all fixed assets are assumed to be put in and taken out of service in the middle of the year. For the five-year-class of assets, depreciation is spread over six years, as shown below.

Year	MACRS 5-Year-Class Depreciation Rates
1	20.0%
2	32.0
3	19.2
4	11.5
5	11.5
6	5.8
	100.0%

To simplify, a company will sometimes use MACRS for both financial statement and tax purposes. This is acceptable if MACRS does not result in significantly different amounts than would have been reported using one of the depreciation methods discussed in this chapter.

Objective 3
Describe the accounting for the disposal of fixed assets.

Disposal of Fixed Assets

Fixed assets that are no longer useful may be discarded or sold.[7] In such cases, the fixed asset is removed from the accounts. Just because a fixed asset is fully depreciated, however, does not mean that it should be removed from the accounts.

If a fixed asset is still being used, its cost and accumulated depreciation should remain in the records even if the asset is fully depreciated. This maintains accountability. If the asset was removed from the records, the accounts would contain no evidence of the continued existence of the asset. In addition, cost and accumulated depreciation data on such assets are often needed for property tax and income tax reports.

Discarding Fixed Assets

If a fixed asset is no longer used and has no residual value, it is discarded. To illustrate, assume that fully depreciated equipment acquired at a cost of $25,000 is discarded on February 14, 20Y7. The effect on the accounts and financial statements is as follows:

Financial Statement Effects

	BALANCE SHEET				
	Assets		=	Liabilities +	Stockholders' Equity
	Equipment –	Acc. Depr.—Equip.			
Feb. 14.	(25,000)	25,000			

STATEMENT OF CASH FLOWS

INCOME STATEMENT

6. Real estate is in either a 27½-year or a 31½-year class and is depreciated by the straight-line method.

7. The accounting for the exchange of fixed assets is described and illustrated in advanced accounting courses.

Transaction Metric Effects

The effects of discarding the asset on liquidity and profitability metrics are as follows:

LIQUIDITY	
Free Cash Flow	No Effect

PROFITABILITY	
Asset Turnover	No Effect

Since there are no cash flows related to the transaction, there is no effect on free cash flow. Since the equipment was fully depreciated, discarding the asset has no effect on asset turnover.

If an asset has not been fully depreciated, depreciation should be recorded before removing the asset from the accounting records. To illustrate, assume that equipment costing $6,000 with no estimated residual value is depreciated at a straight-line rate of 10%. On December 31, 20Y6, the accumulated depreciation balance, after adjusting entries, is $4,750. On March 24, 20Y7, the asset is removed from service and discarded. The effect of recording the depreciation for the three months of 20Y7 before the asset is discarded is as follows:

Financial Statement Effects

BALANCE SHEET

	Assets			=	Liabilities	+	Stockholders' Equity
	Equipment	–	Acc. Depr.—Equip.	=			Retained Earnings
Mar. 24.			(150)*				(150)

STATEMENT OF CASH FLOWS

INCOME STATEMENT

Mar. 24. Depr. expense	(150)

*($6,000 x 10%) x (3 ÷ 12) = $150

The effect on the accounts and financial statements of discarding the equipment is as follows:

Financial Statement Effects

BALANCE SHEET

	Assets			=	Liabilities	+	Stockholders' Equity
	Equipment	–	Acc. Depr.—Equip.	=			Retained Earnings
Mar. 24.	(6,000)		4,900*				(1,100)

STATEMENT OF CASH FLOWS

INCOME STATEMENT

Mar. 24. Loss on disposal of equip.	(1,100)

*$4,750 + $150 = $4,900

The loss of $1,100 is recorded because the balance of the accumulated depreciation account ($4,900) is less than the balance in the equipment account ($6,000). Losses on the discarding of fixed assets are nonoperating items and are normally reported in the Other expense (loss) section of the income statement.

Transaction Metric Effects

The effects of updating depreciation and discarding the asset on liquidity and profitability metrics are as follows:

LIQUIDITY	
Free Cash Flow	No Effect

PROFITABILITY	
Asset Turnover	Increase

Since there are no cash flows, there is no effect on free cash flow. After updating depreciation, the equipment has a book value of $1,100 ($6,000 – $4,900). Discarding the equipment reduces the operating assets and increases asset turnover.

Selling Fixed Assets

The entry to record the sale of a fixed asset is similar to the entries for discarding an asset. The only difference is that the receipt of cash is also recorded. If the selling price is more than the book value of the asset, a gain is recorded. If the selling price is less than the book value, a loss is recorded.

To illustrate, assume that equipment is purchased at a cost of $10,000 with no estimated residual value and is depreciated at a straight-line rate of 10%. The equipment is sold for cash on October 12 of the eighth year of its use. The balance of the accumulated depreciation account as of the preceding December 31 is $7,000. The effect on the accounts and financial statements of updating depreciation for the nine months of the current year is as follows:

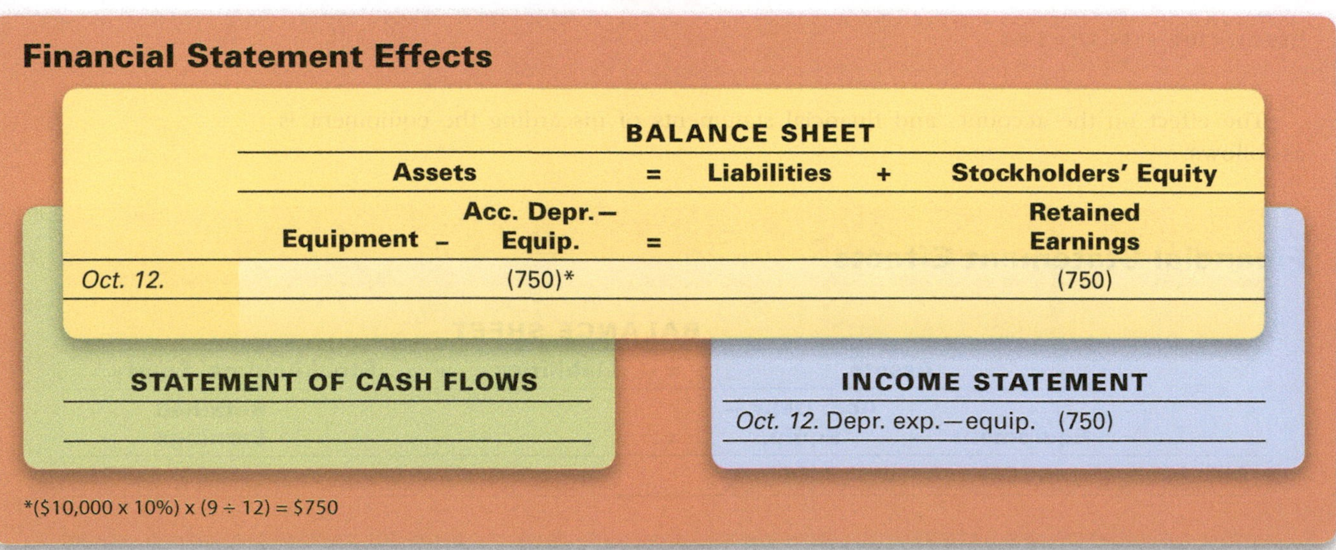

Financial Statement Effects

	BALANCE SHEET					
	Assets		=	Liabilities	+	Stockholders' Equity
	Equipment –	Acc. Depr.—Equip.	=			Retained Earnings
Oct. 12.		(750)*				(750)

STATEMENT OF CASH FLOWS

INCOME STATEMENT
Oct. 12. Depr. exp.—equip. (750)

*($10,000 x 10%) x (9 ÷ 12) = $750

After the current depreciation is recorded, the book value of the asset is $2,250 ($10,000 – $7,750). The effect of the sale, assuming three different selling prices, is as follows:

Sold at book value, for $2,250. No gain or loss.

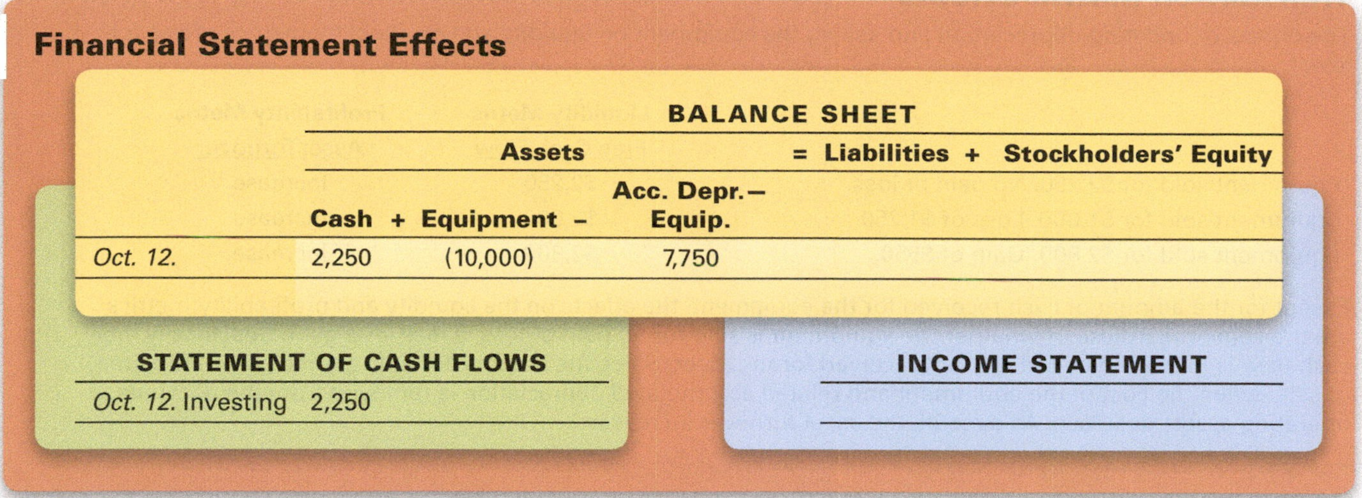

Financial Statement Effects

BALANCE SHEET

	Assets			= Liabilities + Stockholders' Equity
	Cash +	**Equipment –**	**Acc. Depr.—Equip.**	
Oct. 12.	2,250	(10,000)	7,750	

STATEMENT OF CASH FLOWS

Oct. 12. Investing 2,250

INCOME STATEMENT

Sold below book value, for $1,000. Loss of $1,250.

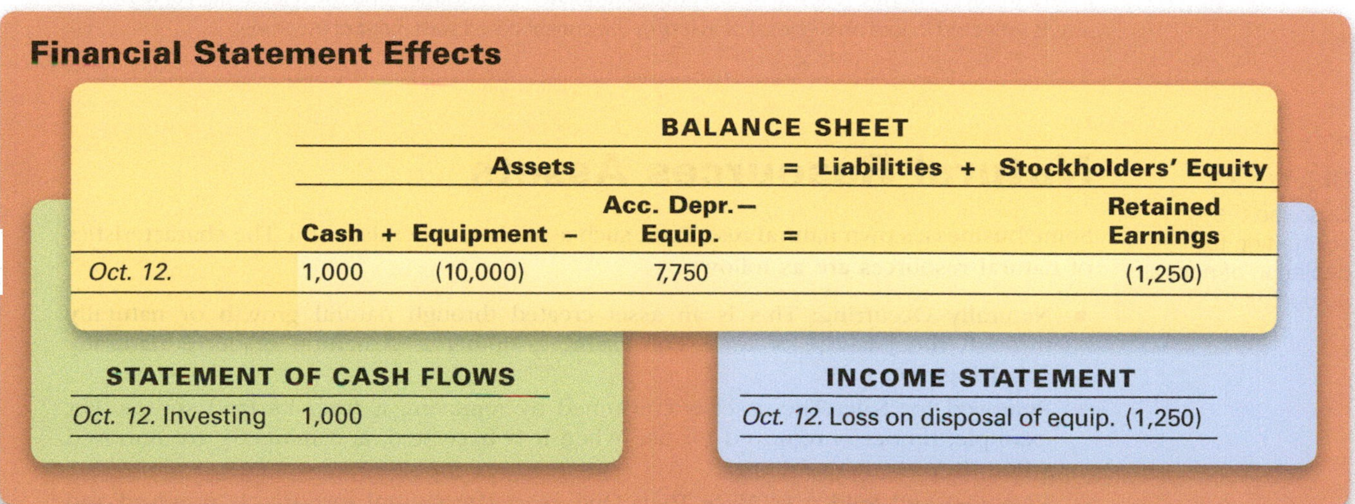

Financial Statement Effects

BALANCE SHEET

	Assets			= Liabilities + Stockholders' Equity
	Cash +	**Equipment –**	**Acc. Depr.—Equip. =**	**Retained Earnings**
Oct. 12.	1,000	(10,000)	7,750	(1,250)

STATEMENT OF CASH FLOWS

Oct. 12. Investing 1,000

INCOME STATEMENT

Oct. 12. Loss on disposal of equip. (1,250)

Sold above book value, for $2,800. Gain of $550.

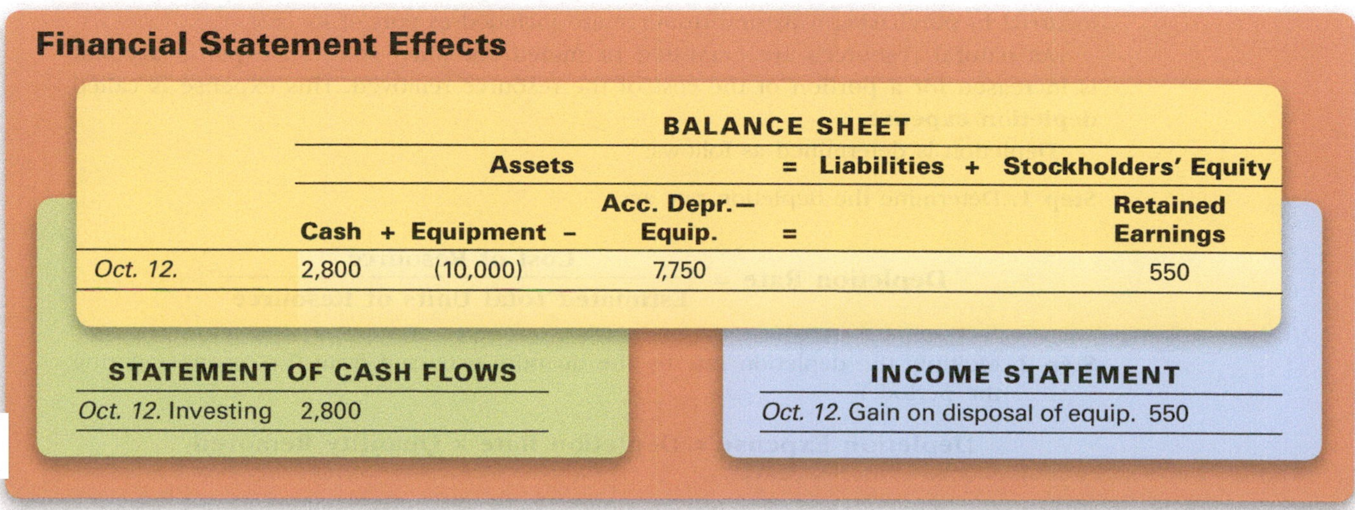

Financial Statement Effects

BALANCE SHEET

	Assets			= Liabilities + Stockholders' Equity
	Cash +	**Equipment –**	**Acc. Depr.—Equip. =**	**Retained Earnings**
Oct. 12.	2,800	(10,000)	7,750	550

STATEMENT OF CASH FLOWS

Oct. 12. Investing 2,800

INCOME STATEMENT

Oct. 12. Gain on disposal of equip. 550

Transaction Metric Effects

The effects of updating depreciation and selling the equipment on liquidity and profitability metrics are as follows:

	Liquidity Metric	Profitability Metric
	Free Cash Flow	Asset Turnover
Equipment sold for $2,250. No gain or loss.	$2,250	Increase
Equipment sold for $1,000. Loss of $1,250.	$1,000	Increase
Equipment sold for $2,800. Gain of $550.	$2,800	Increase

Except for the amount of cash received for the equipment, the effects on the liquidity and profitability metrics are the same regardless of whether the equipment is sold for no gain or loss, a loss, or a gain. Specifically, free cash flow is increased by the amount received for the asset. Since the asset is not fully depreciated at the time of sale, when the cost of the equipment and related accumulated depreciation is removed from the accounts, operating assets decrease. As a result, the asset turnover increases.

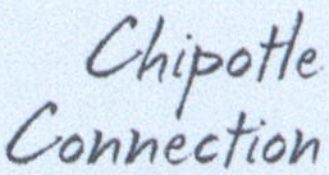

In notes to its financial statements, Chipotle stated the following: "Upon retirement or disposal of assets, the accounts are relieved of cost and accumulated depreciation and the related gain or loss, if any, is reflected in loss on disposal of assets in the consolidated statement of income..."

Objective 4

Describe the accounting for depletion of natural resources.

Natural Resources Assets

Some businesses own natural resources, such as timber, minerals, or oil. The characteristics of natural resources are as follows:

- Naturally Occurring: This is an asset created through natural growth or naturally through the passage of time. For example, timber is a natural resource naturally occurring over time.
- Removed for Sale: The asset is consumed by removing it from its land source. For example, timber is removed for use when it is harvested, and minerals are removed when they are mined.
- Removed and Sold over More Than One Year: The natural resource is removed and sold over a period of more than one year.

Natural resources are classified as a type of long-term asset. The cost of a natural resource includes the cost of obtaining and preparing it for use. For example, legal fees incurred in purchasing a natural resource are included as part of its cost.

As natural resources are harvested or mined and then sold, an expense account is increased for a portion of the cost of the resource removed. This expense is called **depletion expense**.

Depletion is determined as follows:[8]

Step 1. Determine the depletion rate as:

$$\textbf{Depletion Rate} = \frac{\textbf{Cost of Resource}}{\textbf{Estimated Total Units of Resource}}$$

Step 2. Multiply the depletion rate by the quantity extracted from the resource during the period.

$$\textbf{Depletion Expense} = \textbf{Depletion Rate} \times \textbf{Quantity Removed}$$

8. It is assumed that there is no significant residual value left after all the natural resource is extracted.

To illustrate, assume that Karst Company purchased mining rights as follows:

Cost of mineral deposit	$400,000
Estimated total units of resource	1,000,000 tons
Tons mined during year	90,000 tons

The depletion expense of $36,000 for the year is computed as shown below.

Step 1.

$$\textbf{Depletion Rate} = \frac{\textbf{Cost of Resource}}{\textbf{Estimated Total Units of Resource}}$$

$$= \frac{\$400{,}000}{1{,}000{,}000 \text{ Tons}} = \$0.40 \text{ per Ton}$$

Step 2.

$$\textbf{Depletion Expense} = \$0.40 \text{ per Ton} \times 90{,}000 \text{ Tons} = \$36{,}000$$

The effect of the depletion on the accounts and financial statements is shown below.

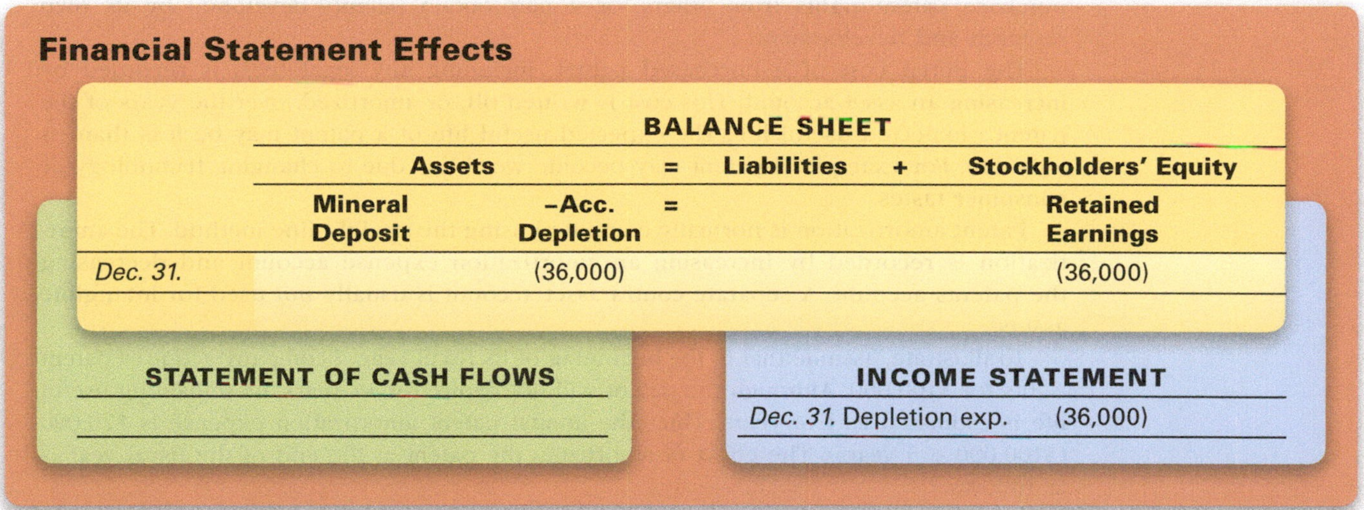

Like the accumulated depreciation account, Accumulated Depletion is a *contra asset* account. It is reported on the balance sheet as a deduction from the cost of the mineral deposit.

Transaction Metric Effects

The effects of depletion on the liquidity and profitability metrics are as follows:

LIQUIDITY	
Free Cash Flow	No Effect

PROFITABILITY	
Asset Turnover	Increase

Depletion has no effect on free cash flow. Depletion decreases operating assets, which increases asset turnover.

Objective 5
Describe the accounting for intangible assets.

Intangible Assets

Long-term assets that are used in the operations of the business but do not exist physically are called intangible assets. **Intangible assets** may be acquired through innovative, creative activities or from purchasing the rights from another company. Examples of intangible assets include patents, copyrights, trademarks, and goodwill.

The accounting for intangible assets is similar to that for fixed assets. The major issues are:

- Determining the initial cost
- Determining the **amortization**, which is the amount of cost to transfer to expense

Amortization results from the passage of time or a decline in the usefulness of the intangible asset.

Patents

Manufacturers may acquire exclusive rights to produce and sell goods with one or more unique features. Such rights are granted by **patents**, which the federal government issues to inventors. These rights continue in effect for 20 years. A business may purchase patent rights from others, or it may obtain patents developed by its own research and development.

The initial cost of a purchased patent, including any legal fees, is recorded by increasing an asset account. This cost is written off, or amortized, over the years of the patent's expected useful life. The expected useful life of a patent may be less than its legal life. For example, a patent may become worthless due to changing technology or consumer tastes.

Patent amortization is normally computed using the straight-line method. The amortization is recorded by increasing an amortization expense account and decreasing the patents account. A separate contra asset account is usually *not* used for intangible assets.

To illustrate, assume that at the beginning of its fiscal year, a company acquires patent rights for $100,000. Although the patent will not expire for 14 years, its remaining useful life is estimated as five years. Thus, the annual patent amortization expense is $20,000 ($100,000 ÷ 5 years). The effect of amortizing the patent at the end of the fiscal year is as follows:

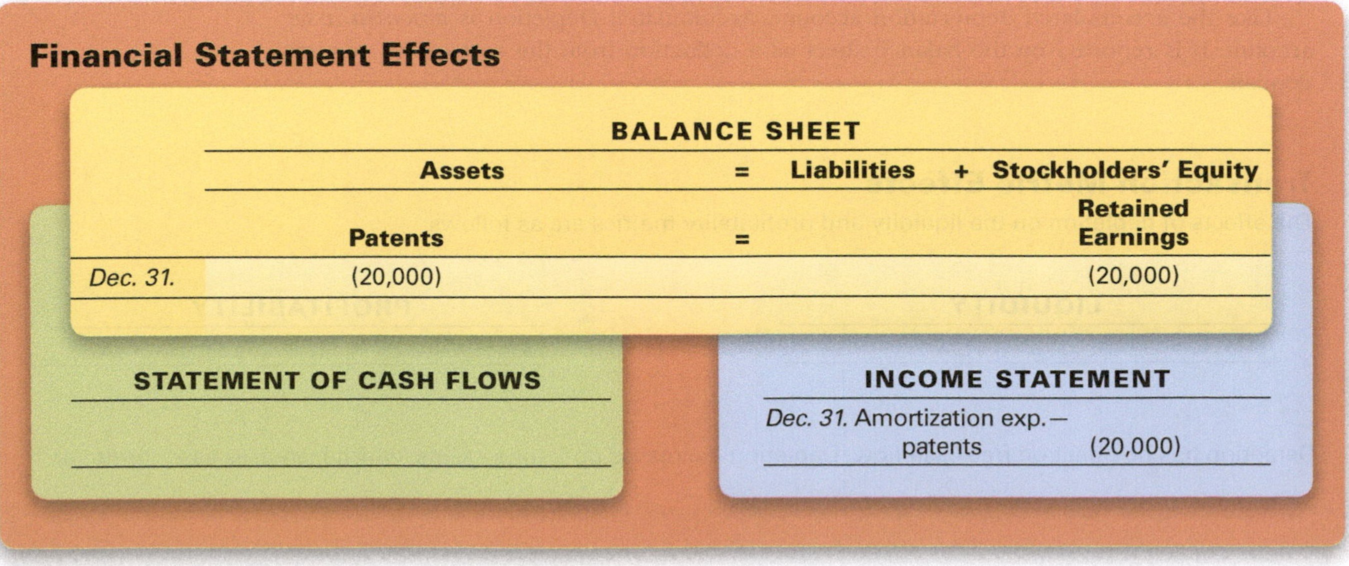

Financial Statement Effects

BALANCE SHEET

	Assets	=	Liabilities	+ Stockholders' Equity
	Patents	=		Retained Earnings
Dec. 31.	(20,000)			(20,000)

STATEMENT OF CASH FLOWS

INCOME STATEMENT

Dec. 31. Amortization exp.—patents	(20,000)

Transaction Metric Effects

The effects of amortizing the patent on the liquidity and profitability metrics are as follows:

LIQUIDITY	
Free Cash Flow	No Effect

PROFITABILITY	
Asset Turnover	Increase

Amortizing the patent has no effect on free cash flow. Amortizing the patent decreases operating assets, which increases asset turnover.

Some companies develop their own patents through research and development. In such cases, any *research and development costs* are usually recorded as current operating expenses in the period in which they are incurred. This accounting for research and development costs is justified on the basis that any future benefits from research and development are highly uncertain.

Copyrights and Trademarks

The exclusive right to publish and sell a literary, artistic, or musical composition is granted by a **copyright**. Copyrights are issued by the federal government and extend for 70 years beyond the author's death. The costs of a copyright include all costs of creating the work plus any other costs of obtaining the copyright. A copyright that is purchased is recorded at the price paid for it. Copyrights are amortized over their estimated useful lives.

A **trademark** is a name, term, or symbol used to identify a business and its products. Most businesses identify their trademarks with the symbol ® in their advertisements and on their products.

Under federal law, businesses can protect their trademarks by registering them for 10 years and renewing the registration for 10-year periods. Like a copyright, the legal costs of registering a trademark are recorded as an asset.

If a trademark is purchased from another business, its cost is recorded as an asset. In such cases, the cost of the trademark is considered to have an indefinite useful life. Thus, trademarks are not amortized. Instead, trademarks are reviewed periodically for impaired value. When a trademark is impaired, the trademark should be written down and a loss recognized.

Chipotle Connection

A number of names, designs, and logos are trademarks of Chipotle including the following: Chipotle, Chipotle Mexican Grill, Unburritable, Food With Intregity, and ShopHouse.

International Connection

Development Costs Under IFRS

In the United States, research and development costs must be expensed in the period in which they are incurred. IFRS, however, allow certain development costs to be recorded as an asset if specific criteria are met. Included in the criteria are the technical feasibility of completing the development of the intangible asset and whether the company intends to use or sell the asset. Whether development costs are recorded as an asset or expensed can have a significant impact on the financial statements. For example, **Nokia Corporation** reported €40 million of development costs as an asset on a recent balance sheet. [€ stands for the euro, the common currency of the European Economic Union.]

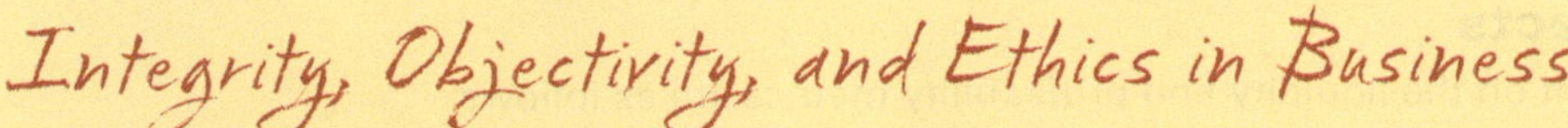

21st Century Pirates

Pirated software is a major concern of software companies. For example, during a recent global sweep, **Microsoft Corporation** seized nearly 5 million units of counterfeit Microsoft software with an estimated retail value of $1.7 billion. U.S. copyright laws and practices are sometimes ignored or disputed in other parts of the world.

Businesses must honor the copyrights held by software companies by eliminating pirated software from corporate computers. **The Business Software Alliance** (BSA) represents the largest software companies in campaigns to investigate illegal use of unlicensed software by businesses. The BSA estimates software industry losses of nearly $12 billion annually from software piracy. Employees using pirated software on business assets risk bringing legal penalties to themselves and their employers.

Goodwill

Goodwill refers to an intangible asset of a business that is created from such favorable factors as location, product quality, reputation, and managerial skill. Goodwill allows a business to earn a greater rate of return than normal.

Generally accepted accounting principles (GAAP) allow goodwill to be recorded only if it is objectively determined by a transaction. An example of such a transaction is the purchase of a business at a price in excess of the fair value of its net assets (assets – liabilities). The excess is recorded as goodwill and reported as an intangible asset.

Chipotle Connection

In a recent balance sheet, Chipotle reported goodwill of $21,939,000.

Unlike patents and copyrights, goodwill is not amortized. However, a loss should be recorded if the future prospects of the purchased firm become impaired. This loss would normally be disclosed in the Other expense section of the income statement.

To illustrate, assume that on December 31 FaceCard Company has determined that $250,000 of the goodwill created from the purchase of Electronic Systems is impaired. The effect on the accounts and financial statements is as follows:

Financial Statement Effects

BALANCE SHEET

	Assets	=	Liabilities	+	Stockholders' Equity
	Goodwill	=			Retained Earnings
Dec. 31.	(250,000)				(250,000)

STATEMENT OF CASH FLOWS

INCOME STATEMENT

Dec. 31. Loss from impaired goodwill	(250,000)

Transaction Metric Effects

The effects the impaired goodwill has on liquidity and profitability metrics are as follows:

LIQUIDITY	
Free Cash Flow	No Effect

PROFITABILITY	
Asset Turnover	Increase

The impairment of the goodwill has no effect on free cash flow. Recording the impairment decreases operating assets, which increases asset turnover.

Chipotle Connection

In recent financial statements, Chipotle reported that the goodwill reported on its balance sheet is not impaired.

Exhibit 9 shows intangible asset disclosures for 500 large firms. Goodwill is the most often reported intangible asset. This is because goodwill arises from companies acquiring one another.

Exhibit 10
Intangibles

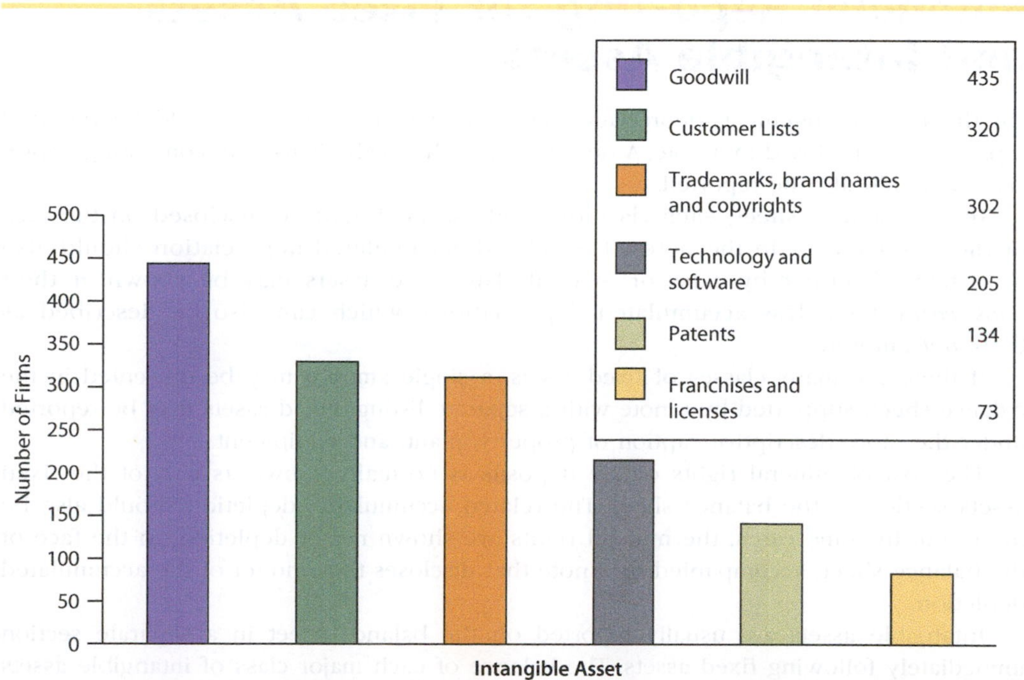

Source: *Accounting Trends & Techniques*, 66th ed., American Institute of Certified Public Accountants, New York, 2012.

Integrity, Objectivity, and Ethics in Business

When Does Goodwill Become Worthless?

The timing and amount of goodwill write-offs can be very subjective. Managers and their accountants should fairly estimate the value of goodwill and record goodwill impairment when it occurs. It would be unethical to delay a write-down of goodwill when it is determined that the asset is impaired.

Exhibit 11 summarizes the characteristics of intangible assets.

Exhibit 11
Comparison of Intangible Assets

Intangible Asset	Description	Amortization Period	Periodic Expense
Patent	Exclusive right to benefit from an innovation	Estimated useful life not to exceed legal life	Amortization expense
Copyright	Exclusive right to benefit from a literary, artistic, or musical composition	Estimated useful life not to exceed legal life	Amortization expense
Trademark	Exclusive use of a name, term, or symbol	None	Impairment loss if fair value less than carrying value (impaired)
Goodwill	Excess of purchase price of a business over the fair value of its net assets (assets – liabilities)	None	Impairment loss if fair value less than carrying value (impaired)

Objective 6
Describe the reporting of fixed assets, natural resources, and intangible assets on the income statement and balance sheet.

Financial Reporting for Fixed Assets and Intangible Assets

On the income statement, depreciation and amortization expense should be reported separately or disclosed in a note. A description of the methods used in computing depreciation should also be reported.

In the balance sheet, each class of fixed assets should be disclosed on the face of the statement or in the notes. The related accumulated depreciation should also be disclosed, either by class or in total. The fixed assets may be shown at their *book value* (cost less accumulated depreciation), which can also be described as their *net* amount.

If there are many classes of fixed assets, a single amount may be presented in the balance sheet, supported by a note with a separate listing. Fixed assets may be reported under the more descriptive caption of property, plant, and equipment.

The cost of mineral rights or ore deposits is normally shown as part of the fixed assets section of the balance sheet. The related accumulated depletion should also be disclosed. In some cases, the mineral rights are shown net of depletion on the face of the balance sheet, accompanied by a note that discloses the amount of the accumulated depletion.

Intangible assets are usually reported on the balance sheet in a separate section immediately following fixed assets. The balance of each major class of intangible assets should be disclosed at an amount net of amortization taken to date. Exhibit 12 is a partial balance sheet that shows the reporting of fixed assets and intangible assets.

Exhibit 12
Fixed Assets and Intangible Assets on the Balance Sheet

Assets					
Total current assets					$ 462,500
Property, plant, and equipment:	Cost	Acc. Depr.	Book Value		
Land	$ 30,000	—	$ 30,000		
Buildings	110,000	$ 26,000	84,000		
Factory equipment	650,000	192,000	458,000		
Office equipment	120,000	13,000	107,000		
	$ 910,000	$ 231,000		$ 679,000	
Mineral deposits:	Cost	Acc. Depl.	Book Value		
Alaska deposit	$1,200,000	$ 800,000	$ 400,000		
Wyoming deposit	750,000	200,000	550,000		
	$1,950,000	$ 1,000,000		950,000	
Total property, plant, and equipment					1,629,000
Intangible assets:					
Patents				$ 75,000	
Goodwill				50,000	
Total intangible assets					125,000

Hub-and-Spoke or Point-to-Point?

Business Insight

AP Images/Matt Slocum

Southwest Airlines Co. uses a simple fare structure, featuring low, unrestricted, unlimited, everyday coach fares. These fares are made possible by Southwest's use of a point-to-point, rather than a hub-and-spoke, business approach. **United Airlines, Inc.**, **Delta Air Lines**, and **American Airlines** employ a hub-and-spoke approach in which an airline establishes major hubs that serve as connecting links to other cities. For example, Delta has established major connecting hubs in Atlanta and Salt Lake City. In contrast, Southwest focuses on point-to-point service between select cities with over 450 one-way, nonstop city pairs with an average length of just over 640 miles and average flying time of 1.8 hours. As a result, Southwest minimizes connections, delays, and total trip time. Southwest also focuses on serving conveniently located satellite or downtown airports, such as Dallas Love Field, Houston Hobby, and Chicago Midway. Because these airports are normally less congested than hub airports, Southwest is better able to maintain high employee productivity and reliable on-time performance. This operating approach permits the company to achieve high utilization of its fixed assets, such as its 737 aircraft. For example, aircraft are scheduled to minimize time spent at the gate, thereby reducing the number of aircraft and gate facilities that would otherwise be required.

Objective 7
Describe and illustrate asset turnover in assessing a company's operating results.

Metric-Based Analysis: Asset Turnover

Long-term fixed, operating assets, such as property, plant, and equipment are a large percent of total assets for many companies. For example, over 40% of Delta Air Lines' total assets are composed of property, plant, and equipment. For such companies, maximizing the use of these assets to generate sales is an important operating objective.

Chipotle Connection

In a recent balance sheet, Chipotle reported that over 43% of its total assets were composed of property, plant, and equipment.

One metric that measures how efficiently a company is using its operating assets to generate sales is **asset turnover**. Asset turnover computes the sales per dollar generated by each dollar of invested long-term operating assets. Normally, a high or increasing fixed asset turnover is considered favorable. It is computed as follows:

$$\textbf{Asset Turnover} = \frac{\textbf{Sales}}{\textbf{Average of Long-term Operating Assets}}$$

Long-term operating assets consist of property, plant, and equipment (net of accumulated depreciation) plus natural resources and intangible assets.

To illustrate, assume the following data (in millions) adapted from recent financial statements for Delta Air Lines.

	Year 2	Year 1
Sales	$40,362	$37,773
Operating assets (average for year):		
Property, plant, equipment	21,892	21,284
Intangible	14,425	14,463

The asset turnover (rounded to two decimal places) for Delta Air Lines is computed as follows:

	Year 2	Year 1
Asset turnover:		
$40,362 ÷ ($21,892 + $14,425)	1.11	
$37,773 ÷ ($21,284 + $14,463)		1.06

Delta Air Lines increased its asset turnover between Year 1 and Year 2. In Year 1, Delta earned $1.06 in sales revenue for each dollar of long-term operating assets invested. In Year 2, Delta earned $1.11 in sales revenue for each dollar of long-term operating assets invested. Thus, Delta improved its management of long-term operating assets in generating sales between years.

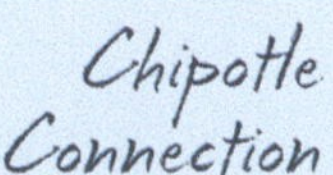

For the recent two years, Chipotle generated an average of $3.50 per dollar of invested long-term operating assets.

Key Points

1. Define, classify, and account for the cost of fixed assets.

Fixed assets are long-term tangible assets that are owned by the business and are used in the normal operations of the business. Examples of fixed assets are equipment, buildings, and land. The initial cost of a fixed asset includes all amounts spent to get the asset in place and ready for use. For example, sales tax, freight, insurance in transit, and installation costs are all included in the cost of a fixed asset. Rather than purchase an asset, a company (lessee) may lease the asset from a lessor.

2. Compute depreciation using the straight-line and double-declining-balance methods.

In computing depreciation, three factors need to be considered: (1) the fixed asset's initial cost, (2) the useful life of the asset, and (3) the residual value of the asset.

The straight-line method spreads the initial cost less the residual value equally over the asset's useful life. The double-declining-balance method is applied by multiplying the declining book value of the asset by twice the straight-line rate.

When an asset is purchased during the year, annual depreciation must be prorated based upon the month the asset is placed in service. After an asset is placed in service, maintenance, repair, and improvement costs may be incurred. Routine maintenance and repair costs, called revenue expenditures, are recorded as expenses when incurred. Extraordinary repairs and improvement costs, called capital expenditures, are recorded as decreases in accumulated depreciation (extraordinary repairs) or as increases to the asset (improvements).

3. Describe the accounting for the disposal of fixed assets.

The recording of disposals of fixed assets will vary. In all cases, however, any depreciation for the current period should be recorded, and the book value of the asset removed from the accounts. For assets retired from service, a loss may be recorded for any remaining book value of the asset. When a fixed asset is sold, the book value is removed and the cash or other asset received is also recorded. If the selling price is more than the book value of the asset, the transaction results in a gain. If the selling price is less than the book value, there is a loss.

4. Describe the accounting for depletion of natural resources.

The amount of periodic depletion is computed by multiplying the quantity of minerals extracted during the period by a depletion rate. The depletion rate is computed by dividing the cost of the mineral deposit by its estimated size. Recording depletion increases a depletion expense account and an accumulated depletion account.

5. Describe the accounting for intangible assets.

Long-term assets that are without physical attributes but are used in the business are classified as intangible assets. Examples of intangible assets are patents, copyrights, trademarks, and goodwill. The initial cost of an intangible asset should be recorded by increasing an asset account. For patents and copyrights, this cost should be written off, or amortized, over the years of the asset's expected usefulness by increasing an expense account and decreasing the intangible asset account. Trademarks and goodwill are not amortized but are written down only on impairment.

6. Describe the reporting of fixed assets, natural resources, and intangible assets on the income statement and balance sheet.

The amount of depreciation expense and the method or methods used in computing depreciation should be disclosed in the financial statements. In addition, each major class of fixed assets should be disclosed, along with the related accumulated depreciation. Intangible assets are usually presented in the balance sheet in a separate section immediately following fixed assets. Each major class of intangible assets should be disclosed at an amount net of the amortization recorded to date.

7. Describe and illustrate asset turnover in assessing a company's operating results.

The asset turnover is a measure of a company's use of its long-term operating assets to generate sales. It is computed by dividing sales by the average long-term operating assets for the period.

Key Terms

Accelerated depreciation method (283)
Amortization (294)
Asset turnover (278)
Book value of a fixed asset (279)
Capital expenditures (286)
Copyright (295)
Depletion expense (292)
Depreciable cost (280)
Depreciation (279)
Double-declining-balance method (283)
Expected useful life (280)
Fixed assets (275)
Free cash flow (278)
Goodwill (296)
Initial cost of a fixed asset (280)
Intangible assets (294)
Lease (279)
Patents (294)
Residual value (280)
Revenue expenditures (286)
Straight-line method (281)
Trademark (295)

Illustrative Problem

McCollum Company, a furniture wholesaler, acquired new equipment at a cost of $150,000 at the beginning of the fiscal year. The equipment has an estimated life of five years and an estimated residual value of $12,000. Ellen McCollum, the president, has requested information regarding alternative depreciation methods.

Instructions

Determine the annual depreciation for each of the five years of estimated useful life of the equipment, the accumulated depreciation at the end of each year, and the book value of the equipment at the end of each year by (a) the straight-line method and (b) the double-declining-balance method.

Solution

	Year	Depreciation Expense	Accumulated Depreciation, End of Year	Book Value, End of Year
a.	1	$27,600*	$ 27,600	$122,400
	2	27,600	55,200	94,800
	3	27,600	82,800	67,200
	4	27,600	110,400	39,600
	5	27,600	138,000	12,000

*$27,600 = ($150,000 − $12,000) ÷ 5

	Year	Depreciation Expense	Accumulated Depreciation, End of Year	Book Value, End of Year
b.	1	$60,000**	$ 60,000	$ 90,000
	2	36,000	96,000	54,000
	3	21,600	117,600	32,400
	4	12,960	130,560	19,440
	5	7,440***	138,000	12,000

**$60,000 = $150,000 × 40%

***The asset is not depreciated below the estimated residual value of $12,000.

Self-Examination Questions

(Answers appear at the end of chapter)

1. Which of the following expenditures incurred in connection with acquiring machinery is a proper addition to the asset account?
   A. Freight
   B. Installation costs
   C. Both A and B
   D. Neither A nor B
2. What is the amount of depreciation, using the double-declining-balance method (twice the straight-line rate), for the second year of use for equipment costing $9,000, with an estimated residual value of $600 and an estimated life of three years?
   A. $6,000
   B. $3,000
   C. $2,000
   D. $400
3. An example of an accelerated depreciation method is:
   A. Straight-line
   B. Double-declining-balance
   C. Units-of-activity
   D. Depletion balance
4. Hyde Inc. purchased mineral rights estimated at 2,500,000 tons near Great Falls, Montana, for $3,600,000 on August 7, 20Y4. During the remainder of the year, Hyde mined 175,000 tons of ore. What is the depletion expense for 20Y4?
   A. $121,528
   B. $252,000
   C. $1,500,000
   D. $3,600,000
5. Which of the following is an example of an intangible asset?
   A. Patents
   B. Goodwill
   C. Copyrights
   D. All of the above

Class Discussion Questions

1. Which of the following qualities are characteristic of fixed assets? (a) tangible, (b) capable of repeated use in the normal operations of the business, (c) not held for sale in the normal course of business, (d) not used in the operations of the business, (e) useful life must be greater than 10 years.
2. Enterprise Supplies Co. has a fleet of automobiles and trucks for use by salespersons and for delivery of office supplies and equipment. Bizarro Auto Sales Co. has automobiles and trucks for sale. Under what caption would the automobiles and trucks be reported on the balance sheet of (a) Enterprise Supplies Co. and (b) Bizarro Auto Sales Co.?
3. The Stone Store Co. acquired an adjacent vacant lot with the hope of selling it in the future at a gain. The lot is not intended to be used in The Stone Store's business operations. Where should such real estate be listed in the balance sheet?
4. Lanier Company solicited bids from several contractors to construct an addition to its office building. The lowest bid received was for $600,000. Lanier Company decided to construct the addition itself at a cost of $475,000. What amount should be recorded in the building account?
5. Are the amounts at which fixed assets are reported on the balance sheet their approximate market values as of the balance sheet date? Discuss.
6. a. Does the recognition of depreciation in the accounts provide a special cash fund for the replacement of fixed assets? Explain.
   b. Describe the nature of depreciation as the term is used in accounting.

7. Backyard Company purchased a machine that has a manufacturer's suggested life of 30 years. The company plans to use the machine on a special project that will last 18 years. At the completion of the project, the machine will be sold. Over how many years should the machine be depreciated?

8. Is it necessary for a business to use the same method of computing depreciation (a) for all classes of its depreciable assets and (b) in the financial statements and in determining income taxes?

9. Distinguish between the accounting for capital expenditures and revenue expenditures.

10. Immediately after a used truck is acquired, a new motor is installed and the tires are replaced at a total cost of $4,300. Is this a capital expenditure or a revenue expenditure?

11. Classify each of the following expenditures as either a revenue or capital expenditure: (a) installation of a video messaging system on a semitrailer, (b) changing oil in a delivery truck, (c) purchase of a color copier.

12. a. Under what conditions is the use of an accelerated depreciation method most appropriate?
    b. Why is an accelerated depreciation method often used for income tax purposes?
    c. What is the Modified Accelerated Cost Recovery System (MACRS), and under what conditions is it used?

13. For some of the fixed assets of a business, the balance in Accumulated Depreciation is exactly equal to the cost of the asset. (a) Is it permissible to record additional depreciation on the assets if they are still useful to the company? Explain. (b) When should the cost and the accumulated depreciation be removed from the accounts?

14. How is depletion determined?

15. a. Over what period of time should the cost of a patent acquired by purchase be amortized?
    b. In general, what is the required accounting treatment for research and development costs?
    c. How should goodwill be amortized?

Exercises

Obj. 1

E7-1 Costs of acquiring fixed assets

Summer Wilks owns and operates Wilks Services. During July, Wilks Services incurred the following costs in acquiring two printing presses. One printing press was new, and the other was used by a business that recently filed for bankruptcy.

Costs related to new printing press:

1. Fee paid to factory representative for installation
2. Freight
3. Insurance while in transit
4. New parts to replace those damaged in unloading
5. Sales tax on purchase price
6. Special foundation

Costs related to used printing press:

7. Amount paid to attorney to review purchase agreement
8. Freight
9. Installation
10. Repair of vandalism during installation
11. Replacement of worn-out parts
12. Repair of damage incurred in reconditioning the press

a. Indicate which costs incurred in acquiring the new printing press should be recorded as an increase to the asset account.

b. Indicate which costs incurred in acquiring the used printing press should be recorded as an increase to the asset account.

E7-2 Determine cost of land

Obj. 1

Snowy Ridges Ski Co. has developed a tract of land into a ski resort. The company has cut the trees, cleared and graded the land and hills, and constructed ski lifts. (a) Should the tree cutting, land clearing, and grading costs of constructing the ski slopes be recorded as an increase in the land account? (b) If such costs are recorded as an increase in Land, should they be depreciated?

E7-3 Determine cost of land

Obj. 1

✔ $598,000

Four Corners Delivery Company acquired an adjacent lot to construct a new warehouse, paying $200,000 and giving a short-term note for $375,000. Legal fees paid were $6,000, delinquent taxes assumed were $4,100, and fees paid to remove an old building from the land were $15,500. Materials salvaged from the demolition of the building were sold for $2,600. A contractor was paid $900,000 to construct a new warehouse. Determine the cost of the land to be reported on the balance sheet.

E7-4 Nature of depreciation

Obj. 2

Custer Construction Co. reported $8,300,000 for equipment and $4,950,000 for accumulated depreciation—equipment on its balance sheet.

Does this mean (a) that the replacement cost of the equipment is $8,300,000 and (b) that $4,950,000 is set aside in a special fund for the replacement of the equipment? Explain.

E7-5 Straight-line depreciation rates

Obj. 2

✔ c. 10%

Convert each of the following estimates of useful life to a straight-line depreciation rate, stated as a percentage, assuming that the residual value of the fixed asset is to be ignored: (a) 2 years, (b) 4 years, (c) 10 years, (d) 20 years, (e) 25 years, (f) 40 years, (g) 50 years.

E7-6 Straight-line depreciation

Obj. 2

A refrigerator used by a meat processor has a cost of $90,000, an estimated residual value of $15,000, and an estimated useful life of 20 years. What is the amount of the annual depreciation computed by the straight-line method?

E7-7 Depreciation by two methods

Obj. 2

✔ a. First Year, $7,200

A Caterpillar tractor acquired on January 12 at a cost of $180,000 has an estimated useful life of 25 years. Assuming that it will have no residual value, determine the depreciation for each of the first two years by (a) the straight-line method and (b) the double-declining-balance method.

E7-8 Depreciation by two methods

Obj. 2

✔ a. $31,500

Equipment acquired at the beginning of the fiscal year at a cost of $360,000 has an estimated residual value of $45,000 and an estimated useful life of 10 years. Determine the following: (a) the amount of annual depreciation by the straight-line method and (b) the amount of depreciation for the first and second years computed by the double-declining-balance method.

Obj. 2

✔ a. 20Y5, $900

E7-9 Partial-year depreciation

Sandblasting equipment acquired at a cost of $42,000 has an estimated residual value of $6,000 and an estimated useful life of 10 years. It was placed in service on October 1 of the current fiscal year, which ends on December 31, 20Y5. Determine the depreciation for 20Y5 and for 20Y6 by (a) the straight-line method and (b) the double-declining-balance method.

Obj. 2

E7-10 Capital and revenue expenditures

About Time Delivery Co. incurred the following costs related to trucks and vans used in operating its delivery service:

1. Changed the oil and greased the joints of all the trucks and vans.
2. Changed the radiator fluid on a truck that had been in service for the past four years.
3. Installed a hydraulic lift to a van.
4. Installed security systems on four of the newer trucks.
5. Overhauled the engine on one of the trucks purchased three years ago.
6. Rebuilt the transmission on one of the vans that had been driven 40,000 miles. The van was no longer under warranty.
7. Removed a two-way radio from one of the trucks and installed a new radio with a greater range of communication.
8. Repaired a flat tire on one of the vans.
9. Replaced a truck's suspension system with a new suspension system that allows for the delivery of heavier loads.
10. Tinted the back and side windows of one of the vans to discourage theft of contents.

Classify each of the costs as a capital expenditure or a revenue expenditure.

Obj. 2

E7-11 Capital and revenue expenditures

Debra Bundy owns and operates DB Transport Co. During the past year, Debra incurred the following costs related to an 18-wheel truck:

1. Changed engine oil.
2. Installed a television in the sleeping compartment of the truck.
3. Installed a wind deflector on top of the cab to increase fuel mileage.
4. Modified the factory-installed turbo charger with a special-order kit designed to add 50 more horsepower to the engine performance.
5. Removed the old GPS navigation system and replaced it with a newer model.
6. Replaced fog and cab light bulbs.
7. Replaced a headlight that had burned out.
8. Replaced a shock absorber that had worn out.
9. Replaced the hydraulic brake system that had begun to fail during her latest trip through the Rocky Mountains.
10. Replaced the old radar detector with a newer model that detects additional frequencies now used by many of the state patrol radar guns. The detector is wired directly into the cab, so that it is partially hidden. In addition, Debra fastened the detector to the truck with a locking device that prevents its removal.

Classify each of the costs as a capital expenditure or a revenue expenditure.

E7-12 Book value of fixed assets

Obj. 2

The following data (in millions) were adapted from recent annual reports of United Parcel Service, Inc. (UPS). UPS provides delivery and freight services throughout the world.

	Year 2	Year 1
Vehicles	$ 7,542	$ 6,762
Aircraft	15,801	15,772
Land	1,145	1,163
Buildings	6,542	6,376
Equipment	9,291	8,834
Construction in progress	299	244
Less accumulated depreciation	(22,339)	(21,190)

a. Compute the net property, plant, and equipment (book value) for Years 1 and 2

b. Compare Years 1 and 2; comment on changes between years.

E7-13 Sale of asset

Obj. 3

✔ a. $430,000

Equipment acquired on January 9, 20Y3, at a cost of $560,000, has an estimated useful life of 20 years, an estimated residual value of $40,000, and is depreciated by the straight-line method.

a. What was the book value of the equipment at the end of the fifth year, December 31, 20Y7?

b. Assuming that the equipment was sold on July 1, 20Y8, for $400,000, illustrate the effects on the accounts and financial statements of (1) depreciation for the six months until the sale date and (2) the sale of the equipment.

E7-14 Disposal of fixed asset

Obj. 3

✔ a. $31,250

Equipment acquired on January 8, 20Y1, at a cost of $280,000, has an estimated useful life of 8 years and an estimated residual value of $30,000.

a. What was the annual amount of depreciation for the years 20Y1, 20Y2, and 20Y3, using the straight-line method of depreciation?

b. What was the book value of the equipment on January 1, 20Y4?

c. Assuming that the equipment was sold on January 7, 20Y4, for $185,000, illustrate the effects on the accounts and financial statements of the sale.

d. Assuming that the equipment was sold on January 7, 20Y4, for $192,400 instead of $185,000, illustrate the effects on the accounts and financial statements of the sale.

E7-15 Recording depletion

Obj. 4

✔ a. $26,400,000

MacLean Mining Co. acquired mineral rights for $72,000,000. The mineral deposit is estimated at 120,000,000 tons. During the current year, 44,000,000 tons were mined and sold.

a. Determine the amount of depletion expense for the current year.

b. Illustrate the effects on the accounts and financial statements of the depletion expense.

E7-16 Recording amortization

Obj. 4

✔ a. $223,500

Dovetail Technologies Company acquired patent rights on January 6, 20Y5, for $1,500,000. The patent has a useful life of 8 years. On January 7, 20Y6, Dovetail Technologies successfully defended the patent in a lawsuit at a cost of $252,000.

a. Determine the patent amortization expense for the current year ended December 31, 20Y6.

b. Illustrate the effects on the accounts and financial statements to recognize the amortization.

Obj. 5

E7-17 Goodwill impairment

On January 1, 20Y3, The Simmons Group, Inc., purchased the assets of NWS Insurance Co. for $36,000,000, a price reflecting an $8,000,000 goodwill premium. On December 31, 20Y9, The Simmons Group determined that the goodwill from the NWS acquisition was impaired and had a value of only $2,300,000.

a. Determine the book value of the goodwill on December 31, 20Y9, prior to making the impairment adjustment.

b. Illustrate the effects on the accounts and financial statements of the December 31, 20Y9, adjustment for the goodwill impairment.

Obj. 6

E7-18 Book value of fixed assets

Apple, Inc., designs, manufactures, and markets personal computers (iPad™) and related software. Apple also manufactures and distributes music players (iPod™) along with related accessories and services, including the online distribution of third-party music. The following information was adapted from a recent annual report of Apple:

Property, Plant, and Equipment (in millions):

	Year 2	Year 1
Land and buildings	$ 2,439	$ 2,059
Machinery, equipment, and internal-use software	15,743	6,926
Office furniture and equipment	241	184
Other fixed assets related to leases	3,464	2,599
Accumulated depreciation and amortization	(6,435)	(3,991)

a. Compute the book value of the fixed assets for Years 1 and 2 and explain the differences, if any.

b. Would you normally expect the book value of fixed assets to increase or decrease during the year?

Obj. 6

E7-19 Balance sheet presentation

List the errors you find in the following partial balance sheet:

CHICO COMPANY
Balance Sheet
December 31, 20Y7

Assets

	Replacement Cost	Accumulated Depreciation	Book Value	
Total current assets				$350,000
Property, plant, and equipment:				
Land	$ 250,000	$ 20,000	$230,000	
Buildings	400,000	150,000	250,000	
Factory equipment	330,000	175,200	154,800	
Office equipment	72,000	48,000	24,000	
Patents	48,000	—	48,000	
Goodwill	90,000	3,000	87,000	
Total property, plant, and equipment	$1,190,000	$ 396,200		793,800

Problems

P7-1 Allocate payments and receipts to fixed asset accounts

Obj. 1

✔ Land, $473,500

The following payments and receipts are related to land, land improvements, and buildings acquired for use in a wholesale apparel business. The receipts are identified by an asterisk.

a. Architect's and engineer's fees for plans and supervision	$ 80,000
b. Cost of filling and grading land	30,000
c. Cost of removing building purchased with land in (e)	10,000
d. Cost of paving parking lot to be used by customers	25,000
e. Cost of real estate acquired as a plant site: Land ($375,000) and Building ($25,000)	400,000
f. Cost of repairing windstorm damage during construction	5,000
g. Cost of repairing vandalism damage during construction	1,800
h. Cost of trees and shrubbery planted	12,000
i. Delinquent real estate taxes on property, assumed by purchaser	20,000
j. Fee paid to attorney for title search	3,000
k. Finder's fee paid to real estate agency	4,000
l. Interest incurred on building loan during construction	40,000
m. Money borrowed to pay building contractor	775,000*
n. Payment to building contractor for new building	750,000
o. Proceeds from insurance company for windstorm and vandalism damage	3,600*
p. Premium on one-year insurance policy during construction	7,500
q. Proceeds from sale of salvage materials from old building	4,000*
r. Refund of premium on insurance policy (p) canceled after 10 months	1,250*
s. Special assessment paid to city for extension of water main to the property	10,500

Instructions

1. Assign each payment and receipt to Land (unlimited life), Land Improvements (limited life), Building, or Other Accounts. Indicate receipts by an asterisk. Identify each item by letter and list the amounts in columnar form, as follows:

Item	Land	Land Improvements	Building	Other Accounts

2. Determine the increases to Land, Land Improvements, and Building.
3. The costs assigned to the land, which is used as a plant site, will not be depreciated, while the costs assigned to land improvements will be depreciated. Explain this seemingly contradictory application of the concept of depreciation.

P7-2 Compare three depreciation methods

Obj. 2

✔ a. 20Y4: straight-line depreciation, $45,250

Bayside Coatings Company purchased waterproofing equipment on January 2, 20Y4, for $190,000. The equipment was expected to have a useful life of four years and a residual value of $9,000.

Instructions

Determine the amount of depreciation expense for the years ended December 31, 20Y4, 20Y5, 20Y6, and 20Y7, by (a) the straight-line method and (b) the double-declining-balance method. Also determine the total depreciation expense for the four years by each method. The following columnar headings are suggested for recording the depreciation expense amounts:

	Depreciation Expense	
Year	Straight-Line Method	Double-Declining-Balance Method

Note: The spreadsheet icon  indicates an Excel template is available on the student companion site.

Obj. 2

✔ a. 20Y5, $2,550

P7-3 Depreciation by two methods; partial years

Knife Edge Company purchased tool sharpening equipment on July 1, 20Y5, for $16,200. The equipment was expected to have a useful life of three years and a residual value of $900.

Instructions

Determine the amount of depreciation expense for the years ended December 31, 20Y5, 20Y6, 20Y7, and 20Y8, by (a) the straight-line method and (b) the double-declining-balance method.

Obj. 2, 3

✔ 1. b. Year 1, $70,000 depreciation expense

P7-4 Depreciation by two methods; sale of fixed asset

New tire retreading equipment, acquired at a cost of $140,000 at the beginning of a fiscal year, has an estimated useful life of four years and an estimated residual value of $10,000. The manager requested information regarding the effect of alternative methods on the amount of depreciation expense each year. On the basis of the data presented to the manager, the double-declining-balance method was selected.

In the first week of the fourth year, the equipment was sold for $23,300.

Instructions

1. Determine the annual depreciation expense for each of the estimated four years of use, the accumulated depreciation at the end of each year, and the book value of the equipment at the end of each year by (a) the straight-line method and (b) the double-declining-balance method. The following columnar headings are suggested for each schedule:

Year	Depreciation Expense	Accumulated Depreciation, End of Year	Book Value, End of Year

2. Illustrate the effects on the accounts and financial statements of the sale.
3. Illustrate the effects on the accounts and financial statements of the sale, assuming a sales price of $15,250 instead of $23,300.

Obj. 4, 5

✔ 1. b. $57,500

P7-5 Amortization and depletion entries

Data related to the acquisition of timber rights and intangible assets of Gemini Company during the current year ended December 31 are as follows:

a. On December 31, Gemini Company determined that $3,000,000 of goodwill was impaired.

b. Governmental and legal costs of $920,000 were incurred by Gemini Company on June 30 in obtaining a patent with an estimated economic life of eight years. Amortization is to be for one-half year.

c. Timber rights on a tract of land were purchased for $1,350,000 on March 6. The stand of timber is estimated at 15,000,000 board feet. During the current year, 3,300,000 board feet of timber were cut and sold.

Instructions

1. Determine the amount of the amortization, depletion, or impairment for the current year for each of the foregoing items.
2. Illustrate the effects on the accounts and financial statements of the adjustments for each item.

Metric-Based Analysis

MBA 7-1 Purchase of land — Obj. 1

Using the data from E7-3, indicate the effects of purchasing the land on the liquidity metric free cash flow and profitability metric asset turnover. Assume all costs were paid in cash and cash was received for the salvaged materials.

MBA 7-2 Comparing depreciation methods — Obj. 2

Use the data from E7-9 to answer each of the following:

1. Using the integrated financial statement framework, indicate the effects (higher or lower) of using double-declining-balance depreciation rather than straight-line depreciation on accumulated depreciation, retained earnings, and depreciation expense at the beginning of the asset's useful life.
2. Indicate the effects (higher, lower, or no effect) of using double-declining-balance depreciation rather than straight-line depreciation on the liquidity metric free cash flow and profitability metric asset turnover at the beginning of the asset's useful life.

MBA 7-3 Disposal of fixed assets — Obj. 3

Using the data from P7-4, indicate the effects on the liquidity metric free cash flow and profitability metric asset turnover for each of the following:

1. The equipment was sold in the first week of the fourth year for $23,300.
2. The equipment was sold in the first week of the fourth year for $15,250 instead of $23,300.
3. The equipment was sold at the end of four years for its estimated residual value of $10,000.
4. The equipment was discarded at the end of its useful life with no residual value. The balance of the equipment and its related accumulated depreciation is $140,000.

MBA 7-4 Depletion, patent amortization, goodwill impairment — Obj. 4, 5

Using the data from P7-5, indicate the effects on the liquidity metric free cash flow and profitability metric asset turnover for each of the following:

- Impaired goodwill
- Patent amortization
- Natural resource depletion

MBA 7-5 Asset turnover — Obj. 7

United Continental Holdings, Inc., (UAL), operates passenger service throughout the world. The following data (in millions) were adapted from a recent financial statement of United.

Sales (revenue)	$38,901
Average property, plant, and equipment	17,219
Average intangible assets	8,883

1. Compute the asset turnover. Round to two decimal places.
2. Compare the results from part (1) with **Delta**'s asset turnover of 1.11.

MBA 7-6 Asset turnover

Southwest Airlines (LUV) operates passenger services throughout the United States. The following data (in millions) were adapted from a recent financial statement of Southwest.

Sales (revenue)	$18,605
Average property, plant, and equipment	13,841
Average intangible assets	970

1. Compute the asset turnover. Round to two decimal places.
2. Compare the results from part (1) with the asset turnover calculated for United in MBA 7-5 and Delta's asset turnover of 1.11.

MBA 7-7 Asset turnover

JetBlue Airways Corporation (JBLU) operates passenger services throughout the United States. The following data (in millions) were adapted from recent financial statements of JetBlue.

	Year 2	Year 1
Sales	$5,817	$5,441
Operating assets (average for year):		
Property, plant, and equipment	5,431	5,043

1. Compute the asset turnover for Years 1 and 2. Round to two decimal places.
2. Comment on the asset turnover results from part (1).

MBA 7-8 Asset turnover

1. Compare the asset turnover ratios for Delta Air Lines (see the chapter illustration), United (MBA 7-5), Southwest (MBA 7-6), and JetBlue (MBA 7-7). Use Year 2 of Delta and JetBlue for your comparison.
2. Comment on the results from part (1).

MBA 7-9 Asset turnover

Marriott International Inc. (MAR) and Hilton Wordwide Holdings Inc. (HLT) operate hotels worldwide. The following data (in millions) were adapted from recent financial statements of Marriott and Hilton.

	Marriott	Hilton
Sales (revenue)	$13,796	$10,502
Average property, plant, and equipment	1,501	9,042
Average intangible assets	2,125	6,900

1. Compute the asset turnover for Marriott and Hilton. Round to two decimal places.
2. Comment on the asset turnover results from part (1).

Cases

Case 7-1 Ethics and professional conduct in business

Rowel Baylon, CPA, is an assistant to the controller of Arches Consulting Co. In his spare time, Rowel also prepares tax returns and performs general accounting services for clients. Frequently, Rowel performs these services after his normal working hours, using Arches Consulting Co.'s computers and laser printers. Occasionally, Rowel's clients will call him at the office during regular working hours.

Discuss whether Rowel is performing in a professional manner.

Case 7-2 Financial vs. tax depreciation

The following is an excerpt from a conversation between two employees of Linquest Technologies, Don Corbet and Rita Shevlin. Don is the accounts payable clerk, and Rita is the cashier.

Don: Rita, could I get your opinion on something?

Rita: Sure, Don.

Don: Do you know Margaret, the fixed assets clerk?

Rita: I know who she is, but I don't know her real well. Why?

Don: Well, I was talking to her at lunch last Tuesday about how she liked her job, etc. You know, the usual ... and she mentioned something about having to keep two sets of books ... one for taxes and one for the financial statements. That can't be good accounting, can it? What do you think?

Rita: Two sets of books? It doesn't sound right.

Don: It doesn't seem right to me either. I was always taught that you had to use generally accepted accounting principles. How can there be two sets of books? What could be the difference between the two?

How would you respond to Rita and Don if you were Margaret?

Case 7-3 Effect of depreciation on net income

Einstein Construction Co. specializes in building replicas of historic houses. Bree Andrus, president of Einstein Construction, is considering the purchase of various items of equipment on July 1, 20Y2, for $300,000. The equipment would have a useful life of five years and no residual value. In the past, all equipment has been leased. For tax purposes, Bree is considering depreciating the equipment by the straight-line method. She discussed the matter with her CPA and learned that although the straight-line method could be elected, it was to her advantage to use the Modified Accelerated Cost Recovery System (MACRS) for tax purposes. She asked for your advice as to which method to use for tax purposes.

1. Compute depreciation for each of the years (20Y2, 20Y3, 20Y4, 20Y5, 20Y6, and 20Y7) of useful life by (a) the straight-line method and (b) MACRS. In using the straight-line method, one-half year's depreciation should be computed for 20Y2 and 20Y7. Use the MACRS rates presented in the chapter.
2. Assuming that income before depreciation and income tax is estimated to be $800,000 uniformly per year and that the income tax rate is 40%, compute the net income for each of the years 20Y2, 20Y3, 20Y4, 20Y5, 20Y6, and 20Y7 if (a) the straight-line method is used and (b) MACRS is used.
3. What factors would you present for Bree's consideration in the selection of a depreciation method?

Case 7-4 Lease or buy

INTERNET PROJECT

You are planning to acquire an asset for use in your business. In groups of three or four, use the Internet to research some factors that should be considered in deciding whether to purchase or lease an asset. Summarize the considerations you have identified on purchasing or leasing an asset.

Case 7-5 Applying for patents, copyrights, and trademarks

INTERNET PROJECT

Go to the Internet and review the procedures for applying for a patent, a copyright, and a trademark. One Internet site that is useful for this purpose is **www.idresearch.com**. Prepare a written summary of these procedures.

Case 7-6 Ethics and professional conduct in business

The following is an excerpt from a conversation between the chief executive officer, Kim Jenkins, and the chief financial officer, Steve Mueller, of Quatro Group Inc.:

Kim: Steve, as you know, the auditors are coming in to audit our year-end financial statements pretty soon. Do you see any problems on the horizon?

Steve: Well, you know about our "famous" Scher Company acquisition from a couple of years ago. We booked $9,000,000 of goodwill from that acquisition, and the accounting rules require us to recognize any impairment of goodwill.

Kim: Uh-oh.

Steve: Yeah, right. We had to shut the old Scher Company operations down this year because those products were no longer selling. Thus, our auditor is going to insist that we write off the $9,000,000 of goodwill to reflect the impaired value.

Kim: We can't have that—at least not this year! Do everything you can to push back on this one. We just can't take that kind of a hit this year. The most we could stand is $5,000,000. Steve, keep the write-off to $5,000,000 and promise anything in the future. Then we'll deal with that down the road.

How should Steve respond to Kim?

Answers to Self-Examination Questions

1. **C** All amounts spent to get a fixed asset (such as machinery) in place and ready for use are proper additions to the asset account. In the case of machinery acquired, the freight (answer A) and the installation costs (answer B) are both (answer C) proper charges to the machinery account.

2. **C** The periodic charge for depreciation under the double-declining-balance method for the second year is determined by first computing the depreciation charge for the first year. The depreciation for the first year of $6,000 (answer A) is computed by multiplying the cost of the equipment, $9,000, by 2/3 (the straight-line rate of 1/3 multiplied by 2). The depreciation for the second year of $2,000 (answer C) is then determined by multiplying the book value at the end of the first year, $3,000 (the cost of $9,000 minus the first-year depreciation of $6,000), by 2/3. The third year's depreciation is $400 (answer D). It is determined by multiplying the book value at the end of the second year, $1,000, by 2/3, thus yielding $667. However, the equipment cannot be depreciated below its residual value of $600; thus, the third-year depreciation is $400 ($1,000 − $600).

3. **B** A depreciation method that provides for a higher depreciation amount in the first year of the use of an asset and a gradually declining periodic amount thereafter is called an accelerated depreciation method. The double-declining-balance method (answer B) is an example of such a method.

4. **B** $252,000. The depletion expense is determined by first computing a depletion rate. For Hyde Inc., the depletion rate is $1.44 per ton ($3,600,000/2,500,000 tons). The depletion rate of $1.44 per ton is then multiplied by the number of tons mined during the year, or 175,000 tons, to determine the depletion expense of $252,000 (175,000 tons × $1.44).

5. **D** Long-lived assets that are useful in operations, not held for sale, and without physical qualities are called intangible assets. Patents, goodwill, and copyrights are examples of intangible assets (answer D).

Chapter **8**

Liabilities and Stockholders' Equity

What's Covered:

Topics: Liabilities and Stockholders' Equity

Financing Corporations
- Short-term debt (Obj. 1)
- Long-term debt (Obj. 1)
- Equity (Obj. 1)
- Earnings per share (Obj. 1)

Liabilities
- Current liabilities (Obj. 2)
- Notes payable (Obj. 2)
- Payroll (Obj. 2)
- Bonds (Obj. 3)
- Contingent (Obj. 4)

Stockholders' Equity
- Common stock (Obj. 5)
- Preferred stock (Obj. 5)
- Treasury stock (Obj. 5)
- Dividends (Obj. 6)
- Stock splits (Obj. 7)

Financial Reporting
- Liabilities (Obj. 8)
- Stockholders' equity (Obj. 8)

Metric-Based Analysis
- Transactions:
  - Solvency: Net assets
  - Profitability: Earnings per share (Obj. 1, 2, 3, 4, 5, 6)
- Financial Statements:
  - Debt and Price-earnings ratios (Obj. 9)

Learning Objectives

Obj. 1 Describe how corporations finance their operations and its impact on earnings per share.

Obj. 2 Describe and illustrate the accounting for current liabilities, notes payable, and payroll.

Obj. 3 Describe the accounting for bonds payable.

Obj. 4 Describe types of contingent liabilities and how the related accounting.

Obj. 5 Describe and illustrate transactions involving stock.

Obj. 6 Describe and illustrate the accounting for dividends.

Obj. 7 Describe and illustrate stock splits.

Obj. 8 Describe and illustrate the reporting of liabilities and stockholders' equity.

Obj. 9 Describe and illustrate the debt and price-earnings ratios.

Chapter Metrics

Use the following metrics to analyze transactions and financial statements.

TRANSACTIONS

Solvency*: Net Assets

Profitability: Earnings per Share

FINANCIAL STATEMENTS

Debt and Price-Earnings Ratios

*As will be discussed, a solvency rather than a liquidity metric is used in this chapter.

Panera Bread

Juli Hansen/ Shutterstock.com

Banks and other financial institutions provide loans or credit to buyers for purchases of various items. Using credit to purchase items is probably as old as commerce itself. In fact, the Babylonians were lending money to support trade as early as 1300 B.C. The use of credit provides individuals convenience and buying power. Credit cards provide individuals convenience over using cash and make purchasing over the Internet easier. Credit cards also provide individuals control over cash by providing documentation of their purchases through receipt of monthly credit card statements and by allowing them to avoid carrying large amounts of cash.

Short-term credit is also used by *businesses* to provide convenience in purchasing items for manufacture or resale. More importantly, short-term credit gives a business control over the payment for goods and services. For example, **Panera Bread Company (PNRA)**, a chain of bakery-cafés located throughout the United States, uses short-term trade credit, or accounts payable, to purchase ingredients for making bread products in its bakeries. In addition to accounts payable, a business like Panera Bread has current liabilities related to payroll, payroll taxes, short-term notes, and contingencies. Each of these types of current liabilities is described and illustrated in this chapter.

Panera Bread also uses long-term debt and stock to finance its operations and to raise funds for future expansion of its business. In this chapter, the use of bond and stock financing is described and illustrated.

Objective 1

Describe how corporations finance their operations and its impact on earnings per share.

Financing Corporations

Corporations finance their operations using the following sources:

- Short-term debt
- Long-term debt
- Equity

Short-term debt includes the purchasing of goods and services on account as well as issuing short-term notes payable. Long-term debt includes issuing long-term notes payable or bonds payable. A **bond** is a form of an interest-bearing note requiring periodic interest payments with the face amount due at the maturity date.

Equity includes issuing common stock and preferred stock. Preferred stock has preference to (is paid) dividends before common stock.

Panera Bread Connection

Panera Bread is financed with long-term debt of $100 million. In addition, Panera Bread has common stock outstanding and is authorized to issue preferred stock.

A factor influencing whether a company's operations should be financed with debt or equity is the impact of the financing decision on the company's earnings per share (EPS). **Earnings per share (EPS)** measures the income earned for each share of common stock outstanding. It is computed as follows:

$$\textbf{Earnings per Share} = \frac{\textbf{Net Income} - \textbf{Preferred Dividends}}{\textbf{Number of Common Shares Outstanding}}$$

Panera Bread Connection

Panera Bread reported earnings per share of $6.67 on a recent income statement. Panera Bread is authorized to issue preferred stock, but no preferred stock is outstanding. Thus, no preferred dividends are deducted in computing its earnings per share.

To illustrate the effects of financing with debt or equity, assume that Reedy Corporation needs to raise $4,000,000 to begin its operations. Reedy Corporation is considering the three financing alternatives shown in Exhibit 1.

Exhibit 1
Reedy Corporation Financing Alternatives

	Alternative One		Alternative Two		Alternative Three	
	Amount	Percent	Amount	Percent	Amount	Percent
Issue 12% bonds	—	0%	—	0%	$2,000,000	50%
Issue preferred 9% stock, $50 par value	—	0	$2,000,000	50	1,000,000	25
Issue common stock, $10 par value	$4,000,000	100	2,000,000	50	1,000,000	25
Total amount of financing	$4,000,000	100%	$4,000,000	100%	$4,000,000	100%

Each alternative in Exhibit 1 finances a percent of the corporation's operations with common stock. However, this percent varies from 100% (Alternative One) to 25% (Alternative Three). The par value of a stock in Exhibit 1 is the dollar amount assigned to each share of stock. For example, in Alternative One Reedy issues 40,000 shares of common stock with a par value of $10 per share for a total of $4,000,000 (40,000 shares x $10 per share).[1]

Assume that during its first year of operations, Reedy Corporation earned income of $800,000 before interest and income taxes. Also, assume that the bonds were issued at their face amount and an income tax rate of 40%. The effect on earnings per share of financing Reedy's operations with each of the Exhibit 1 alternatives is shown in Exhibit 2.

Exhibit 2
Earnings per Share $800,000*

	Alternative One	Alternative Two	Alternative Three
12% bonds	—	—	$2,000,000
Preferred 9% stock, $50 par	—	$2,000,000	1,000,000
Common stock, $10 par	$4,000,000	2,000,000	1,000,000
Total	$4,000,000	$4,000,000	$4,000,000
Earnings before interest and income tax	$ 800,000	$ 800,000	$ 800,000
Deduct interest on bonds	—	—	(240,000)[a]
Income before income tax	$ 800,000	$ 800,000	$ 560,000
Deduct income tax	(320,000)[b]	(320,000)[b]	(224,000)[b]
Net income	$ 480,000	$ 480,000	$ 336,000
Dividends on preferred stock	—	(180,000)[c]	(90,000)[c]
Available for dividends on common stock	$ 480,000	$ 300,000	$ 246,000
Shares of common stock outstanding	÷ 400,000[d]	÷ 200,000[d]	÷ 100,000[d]
Earnings per share on common stock	$ 1.20	$ 1.50	$ 2.46

[a]$2,000,000 bonds × 12%
[b]Income before income tax × 40%
[c]Preferred stock × 9%
[d]Common stock ÷ $10 par value per share

*Earnings before interest and taxes

Exhibit 1 indicates that when earnings are $800,000, Alternative Three has the highest earnings per share. Thus, Alternative Three is most attractive for common shareholders. This is because $800,000 of income is enough to pay the bondholders their interest and the preferred shareholder their dividends.

For income more than $800,000, the earnings per share for each of the alternatives is even greater with Alternative Three still the highest. However, lowering the income will

1. Later in this chapter, we discuss the issuing stock for amounts other than par value.

have the opposite effect. For example, if income is lowered to $440,000 Alternatives One and Two become more attractive to common stockholders. This is shown in Exhibit 3.

Exhibit 3
Earnings per Share $440,000*

	Alternative One	Alternative Two	Alternative Three
12% bonds	—	—	$2,000,000
Preferred 9% stock, $50 par	—	$2,000,000	1,000,000
Common stock, $10 par	$4,000,000	2,000,000	1,000,000
Total	$4,000,000	$4,000,000	$4,000,000
Earnings before interest and income tax	$ 440,000	$ 440,000	$ 440,000
Deduct interest on bonds	—	—	(240,000)
Income before income tax	$ 440,000	$ 440,000	$ 200,000
Deduct income tax	(176,000)	(176,000)	(80,000)
Net income	$ 264,000	$ 264,000	$ 120,000
Dividends on preferred stock	—	(180,000)	(90,000)
Available for dividends on common stock	$ 264,000	$ 84,000	$ 30,000
Shares of common stock outstanding	÷ 400,000	÷ 200,000	÷ 100,000
Earnings per share on common stock	$ 0.66	$ 0.42	$ 0.30

*Earnings before interest and taxes

In Exhibit 3, earnings per share is lowest for Alternative Three because the income must first be used to pay bond interest and preferred stock dividends. What's left then becomes available to common stockholders.

In addition to earnings per share, a corporation should consider other factors in deciding among the financing plans. For example, if bonds are issued, periodic interest and the face value of the bonds at maturity must be paid. If these payments are not made, the bondholders could seek court action and force the company into bankruptcy. In contrast, a corporation is not legally obligated to pay dividends on preferred or common stock.

Objective 2
Describe and illustrate the accounting for current liabilities, notes payable, and payroll.

Current Liabilities

Liabilities are debts owed to others called **creditors**. Liabilities that are to be paid out of current assets and are due within a short time are reported as **current liabilities** on the balance sheet. Liabilities due beyond one year are classified as **long-term liabilities.** When a long-term liability becomes due within one year, it is reclassified as a current liability.

Accounts Payable and Accruals

Accounts payable transactions have been described and illustrated in earlier chapters. These transactions involve a variety of purchases on account, including the purchase of merchandise and supplies. Accruals have also been described and illustrated in earlier chapters. Accrued liabilities are an obligation to pay current assets in the future. Accrued liabilities are normally recorded at the end of an accounting period as part of the adjustment process. For example, wages due employees at the end of the period are recorded as an expense (Wages Expense) and an accrued liability (Wages Payable). For many companies, accounts payable and accrued liabilities make up most of their current liabilities.

Panera Bread Connection

In a recent balance sheet, accounts payable of $19,511,000 and accrued expenses (liabilities) of $333,201,000 make up all of **Panera Bread**'s current liabilities.

Notes Payable

Notes payable are often issued to:

1. Satisfy an account payable
2. Purchase merchandise or other assets

The issuer of the note is called the borrower, while the party receiving the note is called the lender. The lender accounts for the note as a note receivable, which was described and illustrated in Chapter 6.[2]

To illustrate the effects on the accounts and financial statements of issuing a note to satisfy an accounts payable, assume the following:

Face value of note:	$1,000
Interest rate:	6%
Date of note:	August 1, 20Y5
Term of note:	90 days
Due date of note:	October 30

The effects on the accounts and financial statements of issuing and paying the note are as follows:

Issuing a 90-day, 6%, $1,000 note on account on August 1.

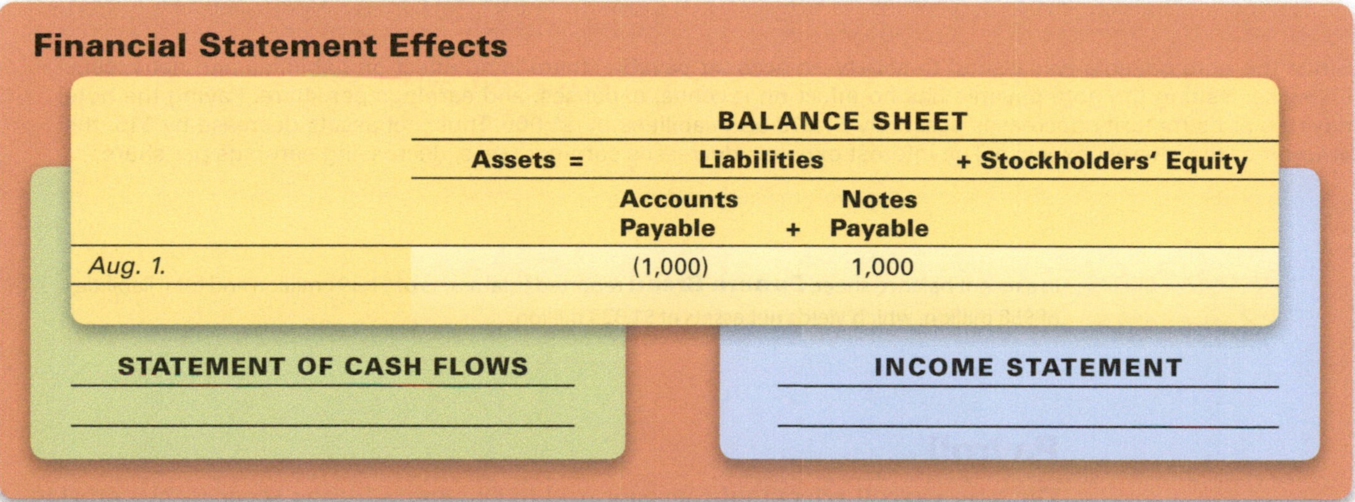

Paying of note on October 30 including interest of $15 [$1,000 x 6% x (90 ÷360)].

Financial Statement Effects

BALANCE SHEET

	Assets	=	Liabilities	+	Stockholders' Equity
	Cash	=	Notes Payable	+	Retained Earnings
Oct. 30.	(1,015)		(1,000)		(15)

STATEMENT OF CASH FLOWS	
Oct. 30. Operating	(1,015)

INCOME STATEMENT	
Oct. 30. Interest expense	(15)

2. The effect on the accounts and financial statements by a lender who accepts a note is exactly opposite that for the issuer of the note.

The interest expense is reported in the Other expense section of the income statement for the year ended December 31, 20Y5. If the accounting period ends before the maturity date of the note, interest expense to the end of the period is recorded by an adjustment.

The transaction metric effects of issuing and paying the note payable are also illustrated. Earnings per share (EPS) is used as the profitability metric. Since this chapter focuses on total liabilities, current as well as long-term, the solvency metric rather than a liquidity metric is used. Net assets (Total assets – Total liabilities) is used as the solvency metric. A company is said to be **insolvent** if it cannot pay its liabilities as they become due or if its total liabilities exceed its total assets.

Transaction Metric Effects

The effects of issuing and paying the $1,000 note payable, including interest, on solvency and profitability metrics are as follows:

SOLVENCY	
Net Assets	
Issuing note payable	No Effect
Paying note payable	$(15)

PROFITABILITY	
Earnings per Share	
Issuing note payable	No Effect
Paying note payable	Decreases

Since the note payable was issued to satisfy an account payable, there is no effect on liabilities and net assets. Likewise, issuing the note payable has no effect on revenue, expenses, and earnings per share. Paying the note payable at its maturity decreases assets by $1,015 and liabilities by $1,000. Thus, net assets decrease by $15, the amount of the interest expense. The interest expense decreases earnings, thus, decreasing earnings per share.

Panera Bread Connection

In a recent balance sheet, **Panera Bread** reported total assets of $1,391 million and total liabilities of $58 million, which yields net assets of $1,333 million.

Payroll

The term **payroll** refers to the amount paid to employees for the services they provide during a period. Payroll can include salaries or wages. The rate of salary is normally expressed in terms of a month or a year. *Wages* refers to payment for manual labor, both skilled and unskilled. The rate of wages is normally stated on an hourly or a weekly basis.

The total earnings of an employee for a payroll period, including bonuses and overtime pay, is called **gross pay**. From this amount is subtracted one or more deductions to arrive at the net pay. **Net pay** is the amount the employer must pay the employee. The deductions for federal income taxes are usually the largest deduction. Deductions may also be required for state or local income taxes. Still other deductions may be made for FICA tax, medical insurance, contributions to pensions, and items authorized by individual employees.

The FICA tax withheld from employees contributes to two federal programs. The first program, called *Social Security,* is for old age, survivors, and disability insurance (OASDI). The second program, called *Medicare,* is health insurance for senior citizens. The FICA tax rate and the amounts subject to the tax are established annually by law.[3]

To illustrate recording payroll, assume that McDermott Co. had a gross payroll of $13,800 for the week ending April 11. Assume that the FICA tax was 7.5% of the gross payroll and

3. The social security tax portion of the FICA tax is limited to a specific amount of the annual compensation for each individual. The Medicare portion is not subject to a limitation. To simplify, it is assumed that all compensation is within the social security limitation. By doing so, we express social security and Medicare as a single assumed rate of 7.5%.

that federal and state withholding were $1,655 and $280, respectively. The effect on the accounts and financial statements of McDermott Co. of recording the payroll follows:

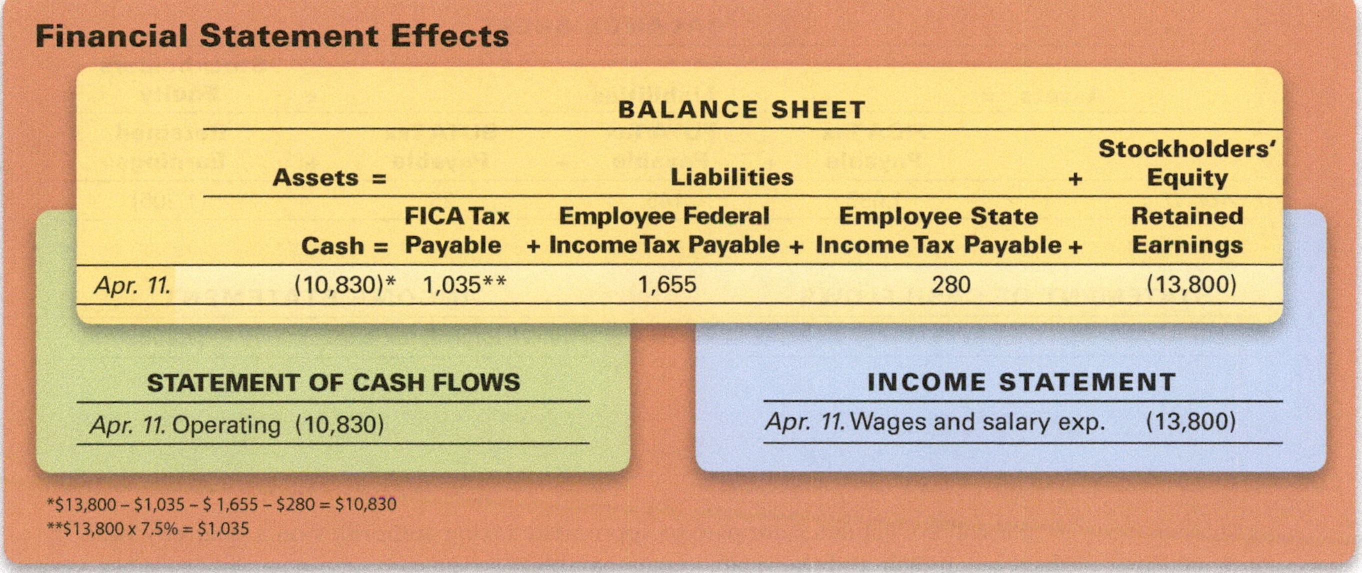

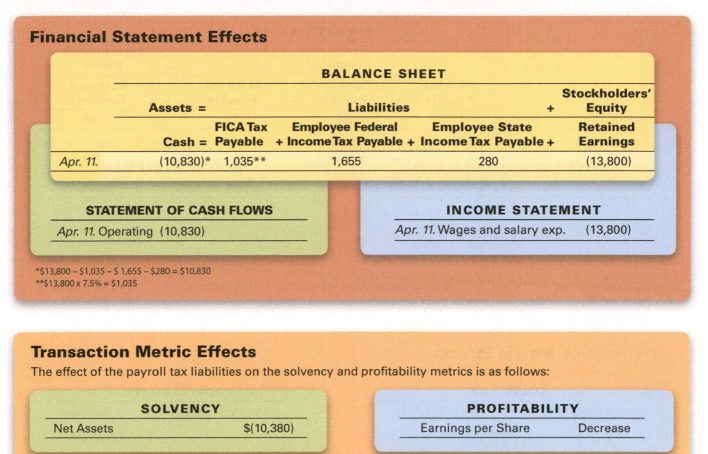

Financial Statement Effects

BALANCE SHEET

	Assets =	Liabilities			+ Stockholders' Equity
	Cash =	FICA Tax Payable	+ Employee Federal Income Tax Payable	+ Employee State Income Tax Payable +	Retained Earnings
Apr. 11.	(10,830)*	1,035**	1,655	280	(13,800)

STATEMENT OF CASH FLOWS	
Apr. 11. Operating	(10,830)

INCOME STATEMENT	
Apr. 11. Wages and salary exp.	(13,800)

*$13,800 – $1,035 – $ 1,655 – $280 = $10,830
**$13,800 x 7.5% = $1,035

Transaction Metric Effects

The effect of the payroll tax liabilities on the solvency and profitability metrics is as follows:

SOLVENCY	
Net Assets	$(10,380)

PROFITABILITY	
Earnings per Share	Decrease

Net assets decrease by $10,830 ($13,800 – $1,035 – $1,655 – $280). The increase in payroll tax expense decreases net income, thus, decreasing earnings per share (EPS).

The FICA, federal, and state taxes withheld from the employees' earnings are not expenses to the employer. Rather, these amounts are withheld on the behalf of employees. These amounts must be remitted periodically to the state and federal agencies.

Most employers are subject to federal and state payroll taxes. Such taxes are an operating expense of the business. For example, employers are required to match employees' contributions to Social Security and Medicare. In addition, most businesses must pay federal and state unemployment taxes.

The Federal Unemployment Tax Act (FUTA) provides for temporary payments to those who become unemployed as a result of layoffs or other causes beyond their control. The FUTA tax rate and maximum earnings of each employee subject to the tax are established annually by law.

State Unemployment Tax Acts (SUTA) provide for payments to unemployed workers. The amounts paid as benefits are obtained, for the most part, from a tax on employers only. The employment experience and the status of each employer's tax account are reviewed annually, and the tax rates are adjusted accordingly by each state.

The employer's payroll taxes become liabilities when the related payroll is *paid* to employees. The prior payroll information of McDermott Co. indicates that the amount of FICA tax withheld is $1,035 on April 11. Since the employer must match the employees' FICA contributions, the employer's social security payroll tax will also be $1,035. Furthermore, assume that the FUTA and SUTA taxes are $145 and $25, respectively. The effect on the accounts and financial statements of McDermott Co. of recording the payroll tax liabilities for the week follows:

Financial Statement Effects

BALANCE SHEET

	Assets	=	Liabilities					+	Stockholders' Equity
			FICA Tax Payable	+	FUTA Tax Payable	+	SUTA Tax Payable	+	Retained Earnings
Apr. 11.			1,035		145		25		(1,205)

STATEMENT OF CASH FLOWS

INCOME STATEMENT

Apr. 11. Payroll tax exp.	(1,205)

Payroll tax liabilities are paid to appropriate taxing authorities on a quarterly basis by decreasing Cash and the related taxes payable.

Transaction Metric Effects

SOLVENCY

Net Assets	$(1,205)

PROFITABILITY

Earnings per Share	Decrease

Net assets decrease by the total of the payroll tax liabilities of $1,205. The increase in payroll tax expense decreases earnings, thus decreasing earnings per share.

Many companies provide their employees a variety of benefits in addition to salary and wages earned. Such **fringe benefits** can take many forms, including vacations, pension plans, and health, life, and disability insurance coverage. When the employer pays part or all of the cost of the fringe benefits, these costs must be recognized as expenses. To properly match revenues and expenses, the estimated cost of these benefits should be recorded as an expense during the period in which the employee earns the benefit. In recording the expense, the related liability is also recorded.

Objective 3

Describe the accounting for bonds payable.

Bonds

Many large corporations finance their long-term operations through the issuance of bonds. A **bond** is simply a form of an interest-bearing note. Like a note, a bond requires periodic interest payments, with the face amount payable at the maturity date.

A corporation that issues bonds enters into a contract, called a **bond indenture** or trust indenture, with the bondholders. A bond issue is normally divided into a number of individual bonds. Usually, the face value of each bond, called the *principal,* is $1,000 or a multiple of $1,000. The interest on bonds may be payable annually, semiannually, or quarterly. Most bonds pay interest semiannually.

The prices of bonds are quoted on bond exchanges as a percentage of the bonds' face value. Thus, investors could purchase or sell bonds quoted at 109⅞ for $1,098.75. Likewise, bonds quoted at 110 could be purchased or sold for $1,100.

When a corporation issues bonds, the price that buyers are willing to pay for the bonds depends on these three factors:

1. The face amount of the bonds due at the maturity date
2. The periodic interest to be paid on the bonds
3. The market rate of interest

The periodic interest to be paid on the bonds is identified in the bond indenture and is expressed as a percentage of the face amount of the bond. This percentage or rate of interest is called the **contract rate** or *coupon rate.* The **market rate of interest**, sometimes called the *effective rate of interest,* is determined by transactions between buyers and sellers of similar bonds. If the contract rate of interest is the same as the market rate of interest, the bonds sell for their face amount.

To illustrate, assume that on January 1 a corporation issues for cash $100,000 of 6%, 5-year bonds, with interest of $3,000 payable semiannually. The market rate of interest at the time the bonds are issued is 6%. Since the contract rate and the market rate of interest are the same, the bonds will sell at their face amount. The effect on the accounts and financial statements of issuing the bonds, paying the semiannual interest, and paying off the bonds at the maturity date is shown as follows.

Issuance of $100,000 bonds payable at face amount on January 1.

Financial Statement Effects

	BALANCE SHEET				
	Assets	=	Liabilities	+	Stockholders' Equity
	Cash	=	Bonds Payable		
Jan. 1.	100,000		100,000		

STATEMENT OF CASH FLOWS	
Jan. 1. Financing	100,000

INCOME STATEMENT

Integrity, Objectivity, and Ethics in Business

A Résumé Padding

Misrepresenting your accomplishments on your résumé could come back to haunt you. In one case, the chief financial officer (CFO) of **Veritas Software** was forced to resign his position when it was discovered that he had lied about earning an MBA from Stanford University, when in actuality he had earned only an undergraduate degree from Idaho State University.

Source: Reuters News Service, October 4, 2002.

Payment of semiannual interest on June 30. (Interest: $100,000 × 0.06 × ½ = $3,000)

Financial Statement Effects

BALANCE SHEET

	Assets	=	Liabilities	+	Stockholders' Equity
	Cash	=			Retained Earnings
June 30.	(3,000)				(3,000)

STATEMENT OF CASH FLOWS

June 30. Operating	(3,000)

INCOME STATEMENT

June 30. Interest expense (3,000)

Payment of face value of $100,000 bond at maturity.

BALANCE SHEET

	Assets	=	Liabilities	+	Stockholders' Equity
	Cash	=	Bonds Payable		
Dec. 31.	(100,000)		(100,000)		

STATEMENT OF CASH FLOWS

Dec. 31. Financing	(100,000)

INCOME STATEMENT

Transaction Metric Effects

The effects of the bond payable transactions on the solvency and profitability metrics are as follows:

SOLVENCY

Net Assets	
Issuing bonds payable	No Effect
Payment of interest	$(3,000)
Paying note payable	No Effect

PROFITABILITY

Earnings per Share	
Issuing bonds payable	No Effect
Payment of interest	Decrease
Paying note payable	No Effect

Issuing bonds payable increases assets and liabilities by $100,000 and thus, has no effect on net assets. Since revenue and expenses are unaffected by issuing bonds payable, there is no effect on the earnings per share (EPS). Payment of interest decreases assets and increases expenses but does not change liabilities. Thus, paying interest decreases net assets by $3,000 and decreases earnings per share. Paying the bonds at their maturity has no effect on net assets or earnings per share.

The market and contract rates of interest determine whether the selling price of a bond will be equal to, less than, or more than the bond's face amount.

1. Market Rate = Contract Rate
   Selling Price = Face Amount of Bonds
2. Market Rate > Contract Rate
   Selling Price < Face Amount of Bonds
   The face amount of bonds less the selling price is called a **discount on bonds payable**.
3. Market Rate < Contract Rate
   Selling Price > Face Amount of Bonds
   The selling price less the face amount of the bonds is called a **premium on bonds payable**.

A bond sells at a discount because buyers are willing to pay less than the face amount for bonds whose contract rate is less than the market rate. A bond sells at a premium because buyers are willing to pay more than the face amount for bonds whose contract rate is higher than the market rate.

Generally accepted accounting principles require that bond discounts and premiums be amortized to Interest Expense over the life of the bond. The amortization of a discount increases Interest Expense, and the amortization of a premium decreases Interest Expense.

Contingent Liabilities

Objective 4
Describe types of contingent liabilities and the related accounting.

Some liabilities may arise from past transactions if certain events occur in the future. These *potential* liabilities are called **contingent liabilities.**

The accounting for contingent liabilities depends on the following two factors:

1. Likelihood of occurring
2. Measurement

The likelihood of the potential liability occurring is classified as *probable*, *reasonably possible*, or *remote*. The ability to measure the potential liability is classified as *estimable* or *not estimable*.

Probable and Estimable

If a contingent liability is *probable* and the amount of the liability can be *reasonably estimated,* it is recorded and disclosed. The liability is recorded by increasing an expense and a liability.

To illustrate, assume that during June a company sold a product for $60,000 that includes a 36-month warranty for repairs. The average cost of repairs over the warranty period is 5% of the sales price.

Warranty expense of $3,000 ($60,000 × 5%) is recorded by increasing Warranty Expense and increasing Product Warranty Payable. In doing so, the warranty expense is recorded in the same period in which the related product sale is recorded. In other words, the warranty expense is matched with the related revenue (sales). When a defective product is repaired, the repair costs are recorded by decreasing Product Warranty Payable and decreasing Cash, Supplies, or other appropriate accounts.

Probable and Not Estimable

A contingent liability may be probable but cannot be estimated. In this case, the contingent liability is disclosed in the notes to the financial statements. For example, a company may have accidentally polluted a local river by dumping waste products. At the end of the period, the cost of the cleanup and any fines may not be able to be estimated.

Reasonably Possible

A contingent liability may be only possible. For example, a company may have lost a lawsuit for infringing on another company's patent rights. However, the verdict is under appeal and the company's lawyers feel that the verdict will be reversed or significantly reduced. In this case, the contingent liability is disclosed in the notes to the financial statements.

Remote

A contingent liability may be remote. For example, a ski resort may be sued for injuries incurred by skiers. In most cases, the courts have found that a skier accepts the risk of injury when participating in the activity of skiing. Thus, unless the ski resort is grossly negligent, the resort will not incur a liability for ski injuries. In such cases, no disclosure needs to be made in the notes to the financial statements.

The accounting for contingencies is summarized in Exhibit 4.

Exhibit 4 Accounting for Contingent Liabilities

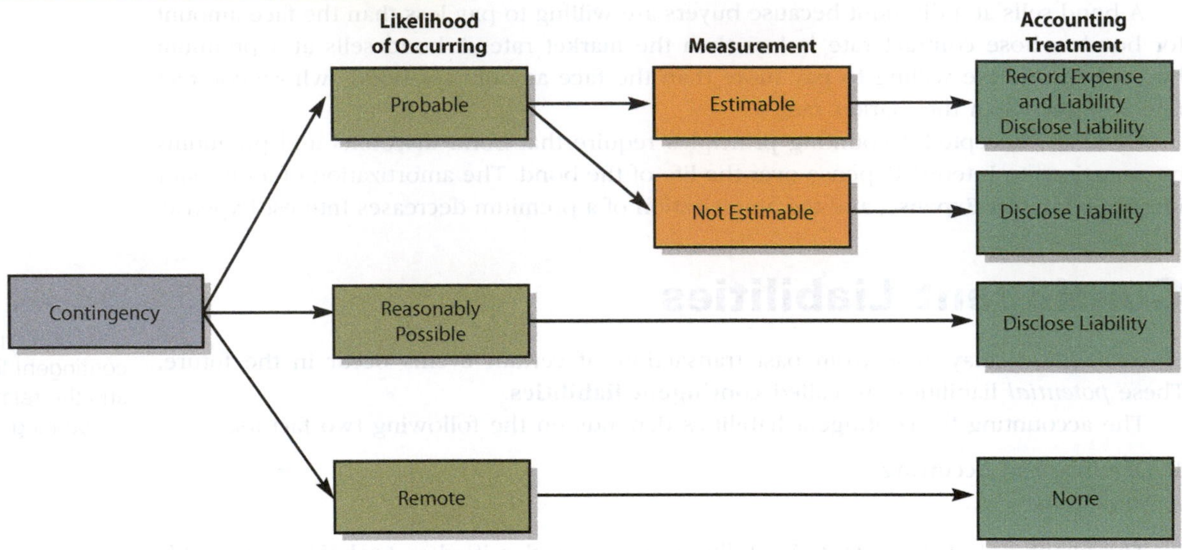

Disclosure of Contingent Liabilities

Common examples of contingent liabilities disclosed in notes to the financial statements are litigation, environmental matters, guarantees, and contingencies from the sale of receivables.

Professional judgment is necessary in distinguishing among classes of contingent liabilities. This is especially the case when distinguishing between probable and reasonably possible contingent liabilities.

Panera Bread Connection

In notes to recent financial statements, **Panera Bread** disclosed the following contingency:

... a purported class action lawsuit was filed (by) ... a former employee ... The complaint alleges ... failure to pay overtime, failure to provide meal and rest periods, and violations of California's Unfair Competition Law. The complaint seeks ... unspecified damages, costs and expenses, including attorneys' fees, and such other relief as the Court might find just and proper. The Company believes its subsidiary has meritorious defenses to each of the claims in the lawsuit and is prepared to vigorously defend the lawsuit. There can be no assurance, however, that the Company's subsidiary will be successful, and an adverse resolution of the lawsuit could have a material adverse effect on the Company's consolidated financial position and results of operations in the period in which the lawsuit is resolved. The Company is not presently able to reasonably estimate potential losses, if any, related to the lawsuit.

Integrity, Objectivity, and Ethics in Business

Today's Mistakes Can Be Tomorrow's Liability

Environmental and public health claims are quickly growing into some of the largest contingent liabilities facing companies. As a result, managers must be careful that today's decisions do not become tomorrow's liabilities. For example, tobacco, asbestos, and environmental cleanup claims have reached billions of dollars and have led to a number of corporate bankruptcies.

Durabla Manufacturing Co., which produced sealing products, had over 100,000 asbestos lawsuits filed against it. As a result, Durabla filed for bankruptcy.

Stock

Objective 5
Describe and illustrate transactions involving stock.

A major means of equity financing for a corporation is issuing stock. The equity that results from issuing stock is called *paid-in capital* or *contributed capital.* Another major means of equity financing for a corporation's operations is through retaining net income in the business, called *retained earnings.* The accounting for retained earnings has been described and illustrated in earlier chapters.

The number of shares of stock that a corporation is authorized to issue is stated in its charter filed in its state of incorporation. The term *issued* refers to the shares issued to the stockholders. A corporation may reacquire some of the stock that it has issued. The stock remaining in the hands of stockholders is then called **outstanding stock**. The relationship between authorized, issued, and outstanding stock is shown in Exhibit 5.

Exhibit 5
Authorized, Issued, and Outstanding Shares of Stock

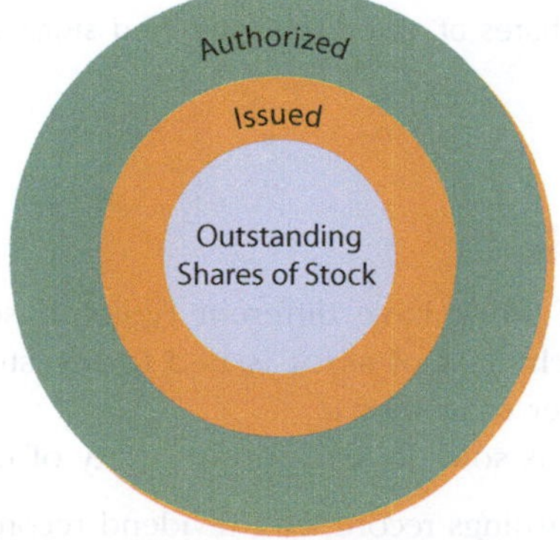

Shares of stock are often assigned a monetary amount, called **par**. Upon request, a corporation may issue stock certificates to stockholders to document their ownership. Printed on a stock certificate is the par value of the stock, the name of the stockholder, and the number of shares owned. Stock can also be issued without par, in which case it is called *no-par stock.* Some states require the board of directors to assign a **stated value** to no-par stock.

Because corporations have limited liability, creditors have no claim against the personal assets of stockholders. However, some state laws require that corporations maintain a minimum stockholder contribution to protect creditors. This minimum amount is called *legal capital.* The amount of required legal capital varies among the states, but it usually includes the amount of par or stated value of the shares of stock issued. For this reason, the par value of most common stocks of public companies is a low amount such as $0.01 or $0.001.

Panera Bread Connection

Each share of **Panera Bread**'s common stock has a par value of $.0001.

The major rights that accompany ownership of a share of stock are as follows:

- The right to vote in matters concerning the corporation
- The right to share in distributions of earnings
- The right to share in assets upon liquidation

Common and Preferred Stock

When only one class of stock is issued, it is called **common stock**. Each share of common stock has equal rights.

A corporation may also issue one or more classes of stock with various preference rights such as a preference to dividends. Such stock is called **preferred stock**. The dividend rights of preferred stock are stated either as dollars per share or as a percent of par. For example, a $50 par value preferred stock with a $4-per-share dividend may be described as either:

$4 preferred stock, $50 par

or

8% preferred stock, $50 par

The payment of dividends is authorized by the corporation's board of directors. When authorized, the directors are said to have *declared* a dividend. Because they have first rights (preference) to any dividends, preferred stockholders have a greater chance of receiving dividends than common stockholders. However, since dividends are normally based on earnings, a corporation cannot guarantee dividends even to preferred stockholders.

Panera Bread Connection

Panera Bread has 2,000,000 shares of authorized preferred stock but has no shares issued or outstanding.

Issuance of Stock

Because different classes of stock have different rights, a separate account is used for recording the amount of each class of stock issued to investors. Stock is often issued by a corporation at a price other than its par.

The price at which stock is sold depends on a variety of factors such as the following:

- The financial condition, earnings record, and dividend record of the corporation
- Investor expectations of the corporation's potential earning power
- General business and economic conditions and prospects

Normally, stock is issued for a price that is more than its par. In this case, it is sold at a **premium**.[4] Thus, if stock with a par of $50 is issued for a price of $60, the stock is sold at a premium of $10.

When stock is issued at a premium, Cash (or other asset) is increased for the amount received. Common Stock or Preferred Stock is then increased for the par amount. The excess of the amount received over par is a part of the capital contributed by the stockholders of the corporation. This amount is recorded in an account entitled Paid-In Capital in Excess of Par.

To illustrate, assume that Caldwell Company issues 2,000 shares of $1 par common stock for cash at $55 on November 1. The effects on the accounts and financial statements follow:

4. When stock is issued for a price that is less than its par, the stock is sold at a discount. Many states do not permit stock to be issued at a discount, and most companies issue stock with very low par values such as $0.001. For these reasons, we assume that stock is sold at par or at a premium in this text.

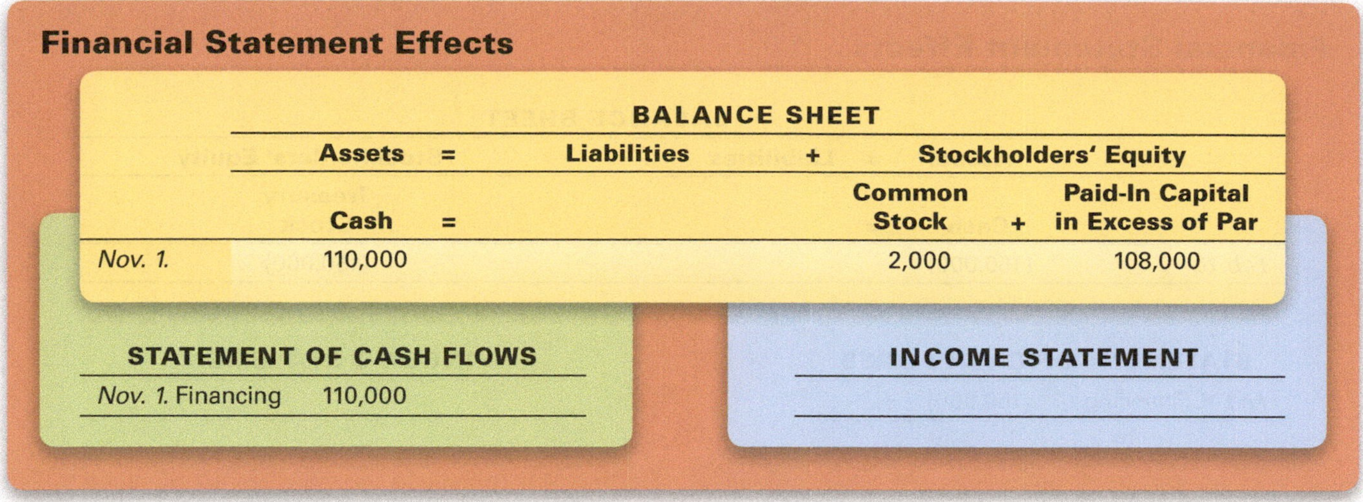

Financial Statement Effects

	BALANCE SHEET						
	Assets	**=**	**Liabilities**	**+**	**Stockholders' Equity**		
	Cash	**=**			**Common Stock**	**+**	**Paid-In Capital in Excess of Par**
Nov. 1.	110,000				2,000		108,000

STATEMENT OF CASH FLOWS	
Nov. 1. Financing	110,000

INCOME STATEMENT

Transaction Metric Effects

The effect issuing common stock on the solvency and profitability metrics is as follows:

SOLVENCY	
Net Assets	$110,000

PROFITABILITY	
Earnings per Share	Decrease

Issuing common stock increases assets and equity with no change in liabilities. Thus, net assets increase by $110,000. Revenues and expenses are not affected, but the number of common shares outstanding increases. As result, the earnings per share (EPS) decreases.

When stock is issued in exchange for assets other than cash, such as land, buildings, and equipment, the assets acquired are recorded at their fair market value. If this value cannot be objectively determined, the fair market price of the stock issued may be used.

In most states, both preferred and common stock may be issued without a par value. When no-par stock is issued, the entire proceeds are recorded in the stock account. In some states, no-par stock may be assigned a stated value per share. The stated value is recorded like a par value, and the excess of the amount received over the stated value is recorded in Paid-In Capital in Excess of Stated Value.

Treasury Stock

Treasury stock is stock that a corporation has issued and then reacquired. A corporation may reacquire (purchase) its own stock for a variety of reasons including the following:

- To provide shares for resale to employees
- To reissue as bonuses to employees
- To support the market price of the stock

The purchase of treasury stock increases Treasury Stock and decreases Cash by the cost of the repurchased shares. To illustrate, assume that, on February 6, Hoffman Inc. purchases 10,000 shares of its outstanding common stock for $150,000. The effects of the treasury stock purchase on the accounts and financial statements are as follows:

Financial Statement Effects

BALANCE SHEET

	Assets	=	Liabilities	+	Stockholders' Equity
	Cash	=			Treasury Stock
Feb. 6.	(150,000)				(150,000)

STATEMENT OF CASH FLOWS

Feb. 6. Financing	(150,000)

INCOME STATEMENT

Transaction Metric Effects

The effect purchasing on the solvency and profitability metrics is as follows:

SOLVENCY

Net Assets	$(150,000)

PROFITABILITY

Earnings per Share	Increase

Purchasing $150,000 of treasury stock decreases cash and stockholders' equity. Thus, net assets decreases by $150,000. Since the number of shares of common stock outstanding decreases while revenue and expense are unaffected, earnings per share increases. Public corporations often purchase treasury stock and, in doing so, increase their earnings per share.

At the end of the year, the balance of the Treasury stock account is reported as a reduction of stockholders' equity. When the Treasury stock is sold or reissued, cash is increased by the proceeds from the sale and Treasury stock is decreased by the cost of its repurchase. Any difference increases or decreases an account called Paid-In Capital from Treasury Stock.

Panera Bread Connection

On a recent balance sheet, **Panera Bread** reported Treasury stock of 5,260,744 shares at a cost of $706,073,000.

Objective 6

Describe and illustrate the accounting for cash and stock dividends.

Dividends

When a board of directors declares a cash dividend, it authorizes the distribution of cash to stockholders. When a board of directors declares a stock dividend, it authorizes the distribution of its stock. In both cases, declaring a dividend decreases the retained earnings of the corporation.[5]

5. In rare cases, when a corporation is reducing its operations or going out of business, a dividend may be a distribution of paid-in capital. Such a dividend is called a liquidating dividend.

Cash Dividends

A cash distribution of earnings by a corporation to its shareholders is a **cash dividend**. Although dividends may be paid in other assets, cash dividends are the most common.

Three conditions for a cash dividend are as follows:

1. Sufficient retained earnings
2. Sufficient cash
3. Formal action by the board of directors

There must be a sufficient (large enough) balance in Retained Earnings to declare a cash dividend. However, a large Retained Earnings balance does not mean that there is cash available to pay dividends. This is because the balances of Cash and Retained Earnings are often unrelated.

Even if there are sufficient retained earnings and cash, a corporation's board of directors is not required to pay dividends. Nevertheless, many corporations pay quarterly cash dividends to make their stock more attractive to investors. *Special* or *extra* dividends may also be paid when a corporation experiences higher than normal profits.

Three dates included in a dividend announcement are as follows:

1. Date of declaration
2. Date of record
3. Date of payment

The *date of declaration* is the date the board of directors formally authorizes the payment of the dividend. On this date, the corporation incurs the liability to pay the amount of the dividend.

The *date of record* is the date the corporation uses to determine which stockholders will receive the dividend. During the period of time between the date of declaration and the date of record, the stock price is quoted as selling *with-dividends*. This means that any investors purchasing the stock before the date of record will receive the dividend.

The *date of payment* is the date the corporation will pay the dividend to the stockholders who owned the stock on the date of record. During the period of time between the record date and the payment date, the stock price is quoted as selling *ex-dividends*. This means that since the date of record has passed, any new investors will not receive the dividend.

To illustrate, assume that on *December 1*, Hiber Corporation's board of directors declares the cash dividends of $42,500 as shown in Exhibit 6. The date of record is *January 10*, and the date of payment is *February 2*.

Exhibit 6
Cash Dividend Dates

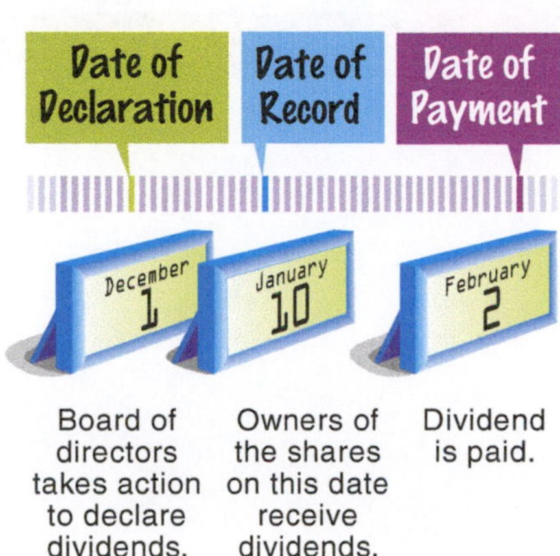

The effect of the declaration of the dividend on the accounts and financial statements is as follows:

Financial Statement Effects

	BALANCE SHEET				
	Assets	=	Liabilities	+	Stockholders' Equity
			Dividends Payable	+	Retained Earnings
Dec. 1.			42,500		(42,500)

STATEMENT OF CASH FLOWS

INCOME STATEMENT

Note that the date of record, January 10, does not affect the accounts or the financial statements, since this date merely determines which stockholders will receive the dividend. The payment of the dividend on February 2 decreases Cash and Dividends Payable.

The effect of payment of the cash dividend on the accounts and financial statements is as follows:

Financial Statement Effects

	BALANCE SHEET				
	Assets	=	Liabilities	+	Stockholders' Equity
	Cash	=	Dividends Payable		
Feb. 2.	(42,500)		(42,500)		

STATEMENT OF CASH FLOWS

Feb. 2. Financing	(42,500)

INCOME STATEMENT

Transaction Metric Effects

The effects of declaring and paying a cash dividend on the solvency and profitability metrics are as follows:

SOLVENCY Net Assets	
Declaring cash dividend	$(42,500)
Payment of cash dividend	No Effect

PROFITABILITY Earnings per Share	
Declaring cash dividend	No Effect
Payment of cash dividend	No Effect

Declaring the cash dividend increases a liability and, thus, decreases net assets by $42,500. Payment of the cash dividend decreases cash and decreases a liability by $42,500 and thus, has no effect on net assets. Since revenue and expenses are unaffected by dividends, there is no effect on earnings per share of declaring or paying a cash dividend.

If a corporation holding treasury stock declares a cash dividend, the dividends are not paid on the treasury shares. To do so would place the corporation in the position of earning income through dealing with itself. For example, assume a corporation with 100,000 shares of outstanding common stock holds 5,000 of its shares as treasury stock. Declaration of a $0.30 per share cash dividend results in paying dividends of $28,500 [(100,000 shares – 5,000 shares) × $0.30] rather than $30,000 (100,000 shares × $0.30).

Panera Bread Connection

In recent financial statements, **Panera Bread** stated that "... we have never paid cash dividends ... and we do not have current plans to do so."

Integrity, Objectivity, and Ethics in Business

The Professor Who Knew Too Much

A major Midwestern university released a quarterly "American Customer Satisfaction Index" based on its research of customers of popular U.S. products and services. Before the release of the index to the public, the professor in charge of the research bought and sold stocks of some of the companies in the report. The professor was quoted as saying that he thought it was important to test his theories of customer satisfaction with "real" [his own] money.

Is this proper or ethical? Apparently, the dean of the Business School didn't think so. In a statement to the press, the dean stated: "I have instructed anyone affiliated with the (index) not to make personal use of information gathered in the course of producing the quarterly index, prior to the index's release to the general public, and they [the researchers] have agreed."

Sources: Jon E. Hilsenrath and Dan Morse, "Researcher Uses Index to Buy, Short Stocks," *The Wall Street Journal*, February 18, 2003; and Jon E. Hilsenrath, "Satisfaction Theory: Mixed Results," *The Wall Street Journal*, February 19, 2003.

Stock Dividends

A **stock dividend** is a distribution of shares of stock to stockholders. Stock dividends are normally declared only on common stock and issued to common stockholders.

The effect of a stock dividend on the stockholders' equity of the issuing corporation is to transfer retained earnings to paid-in capital. For public corporations, the amount transferred from the retained earnings account to the paid-in capital account is normally the fair value (market price) of the shares issued in the stock dividend.[6]

A stock dividend does not change the assets, liabilities, or total stockholders' equity of a corporation. Likewise, a stock dividend does not change an individual stockholder's proportionate interest (equity) in the corporation.

6. The use of fair market value is justified as long as the number of shares issued for the stock dividend is small (less than 25% of the shares outstanding).

To illustrate, assume a stockholder owns 1,000 of a corporation's 10,000 shares outstanding. If the corporation declares a 6% stock dividend, the stockholder's proportionate interest will not change, as shown in Exhibit 7.

Exhibit 7
Effects of Stock Dividend

	Before Stock Dividend	After Stock Dividend
Total shares issued	10,000	10,600 [10,000 + (10,000 × 6%)]
Number of shares owned	1,000	1,060 [1,000 + (1,000 × 6%)]
Proportionate ownership	10% (1,000/10,000)	10% (1,060/10,600)

Transaction Metric Effects

Since stock dividends do not affect assets, liabilities, revenues, or expenses, but only stockholders' equity, the solvency and profitability metrics are not affected.

Objective 7
Describe and illustrate stock splits.

Stock Splits

A **stock split** is a process by which a corporation reduces the par or stated value of its common stock and issues a proportionate number of additional shares. A stock split applies to all common shares including the unissued, issued, and treasury shares.

A major objective of a stock split is to reduce the market price per share of the stock. This, in turn, attracts more investors to the stock and broadens the types and numbers of stockholders.

To illustrate, assume that Rojek Corporation has 10,000 shares of $100 par common stock outstanding with a current market price of $150 per share. The board of directors declares the following stock split:

1. Each common shareholder will receive 5 shares for each share held. This is called a 5-for-l stock split. As a result, 50,000 shares (10,000 shares × 5) will be outstanding.
2. The par of each share of common stock will be reduced to $20 ($100/5).

The par value of the common stock outstanding before and after the stock split is as follows:

	Before Split	After Split
Number of shares	10,000	50,000
Par value per share	× $100	× $20
Total	$1,000,000	$1,000,000

Exhibit 8 shows that each Rojek Corporation shareholder owns the same total par amount of stock before and after the stock split. For example, a stockholder who owned 4 shares of $100 par stock before the split (total par of $400) would own 20 shares of $20 par stock after the split (total par of $400). Only the number of shares and the par value per share have changed.

Since there are more shares outstanding after the stock split, the market price of the stock should decrease. For example, in the preceding example, there would be 5 times as many shares outstanding after the split. Thus, the market price of the stock would be expected to fall from $150 to about $30 ($150/5).

Stock splits do not affect any financial statement accounts, since only the par (or stated) value and number of shares outstanding have changed. However, the details of stock splits are normally disclosed in the notes to the financial statements.

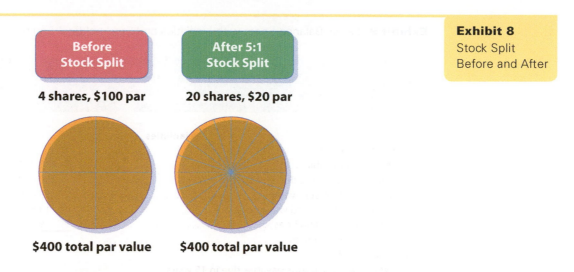

Exhibit 8
Stock Split Before and After

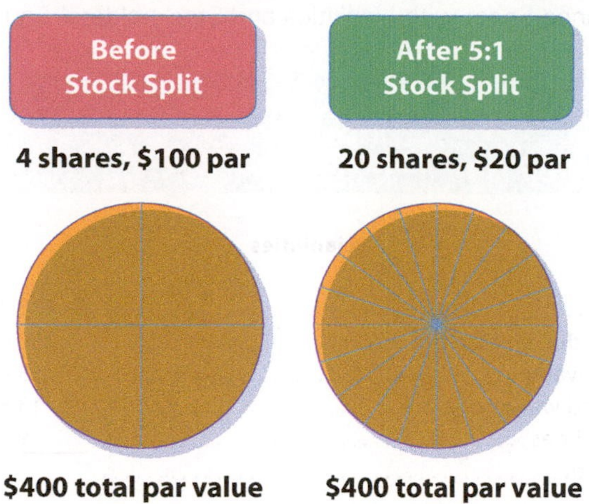

Transaction Metric Effects
Since stock splits do affect assets, liabilities, revenues, or expenses, but only stockholders' equity, the solvency and profitability metrics are not affected.

Reporting Liabilities and Stockholders' Equity

Objective 8
Describe and illustrate the reporting of liabilities and stockholders' equity.

Liabilities that are expected to be paid within one year are presented in the Current Liabilities section of the balance sheet. Thus, any notes or bonds payable maturing within one year are reported as current liabilities. However, if the notes or bonds are to be paid from noncurrent assets or if the notes or bonds are going to be refinanced, they are reported as long-term liabilities. The detailed descriptions, including terms, due dates, and interest rates for notes or bonds, are reported either on the balance sheet or in a note. Also, the fair market value of notes or bonds is disclosed. Exhibit 9 illustrates the reporting of liabilities on the balance sheet.

Contingent liabilities that are probable but cannot be reasonably estimated or are only possible are disclosed in the notes to the financial statements.

A separate statement of stockholders' equity should report changes in common stock, preferred stock, treasury stock, paid-in capital, and retained earnings. An example of a statement of stockholders' equity is shown in Exhibit 10.

International Connection

Reporting Liabilities and Stockholders' Equity Under IFRS

In the United States, liabilities are reported in the order that they will become due, with current liabilities reported first followed by long-term liabilities. On the balance sheet, stockholders' equity is reported after liabilities. Typically, companies reporting under IFRS report stockholders' equity before liabilities on the balance sheet. In addition, long-term liabilities are reported before current liabilities. That is, liabilities are reported in the reverse order in which they become due, with liabilities due within one year reported last.

Exhibit 9 Partial Balance Sheet with Liabilities and Stockholders' Equity

Bergstom Corporation
Balance Sheet
December 31, 20Y8

Liabilities		
Current liabilities:		
Accounts payable	$ 488,200	
Notes payable (9% due on March 1, 20Y9)	250,000	
Accrued interest payable	15,000	
Accrued salaries and wages payable	13,500	
Other accrued liabilities	9,850	
Total current liabilities		$ 776,550
Long-term liabilities:		
Debenture 8% bonds payable, due in 15 years (Market value, $950,000)		1,000,000
Total liabilities		$1,776,550
Stockholders' Equity		
Paid-in capital:		
Preferred 10% stock, $50 par (20,000 shares authorized and issued)	$1,000,000	
Common stock, $20 par (250,000 shares authorized, 100,000 shares issued)	2,000,000	
Additional paid-in capital in excess of par	520,000	
Total paid-in capital	$3,520,000	
Retained earnings	4,580,500	
Total	$8,100,500	
Deduct treasury stock (1,000 shares at cost)	(75,000)	
Total stockholders' equity		8,025,500
Total liabilities and stockholders' equity		$9,802,050

Exhibit 10 Statement of Stockholders' Equity

Heise Inc.
Statement of Stockholders' Equity
For the Year Ended December 31, 20Y8

	Preferred Stock	Common Stock	Paid-In Capital in Excess of Par—Common Stock	Retained Earnings	Treasury (Common) Stock	Total
Balance, January 1	$5,000,000	$10,000,000	$3,000,000	$2,000,000	$(500,000)	$19,500,000
Net income				850,000		850,000
Dividends on preferred stock				(250,000)		(250,000)
Dividends on common stock				(400,000)		(400,000)
Issuance of additional common stock		500,000	50,000			550,000
Purchase of treasury stock					(30,000)	(30,000)
Balance, December 31	$5,000,000	$10,500,000	$3,050,000	$ 2,200,000	$(530,000)	$20,220,000

Financial Statement Metric-Analysis: Debt and Price-Earnings Ratios

Objective 9
Describe and illustrate the debt and price-earnings ratios.

Two ratios useful in assessing solvency and future earnings potential of a company are the debt ratio and the price-earnings ratio.

Debt Ratio

The **debt ratio**, sometimes called the debt to assets ratio, is a useful solvency metric. It is normally expressed as a percent and is computed as follows:

$$\text{Debt Ratio} = \frac{\text{Total Liabilities}}{\text{Total Assets}}$$

The debt ratio measures the percent of the company's assets financed by debt. The debt ratio also may be used to measure how a company is using debt to generate income. However, the higher the debt ratio (financial leverage), the more risk a company is taking in managing its operations.

To illustrate, the following data (in millions) from recent financial statements of **Apple (AAPL)** and **Microsoft (MSFT)** are used.

	Assets	Total Liabilities	Stockholders' Equity
Apple	$290,479	$171,124	$119,355
Microsoft	176,223	96,140	80,083

The debt ratios (rounded to one decimal place) for Apple and Microsoft are as follows:

Apple:	58.9% ($171,124 ÷ $290,479)
Microsoft:	54.6% ($96,140 ÷ $176,223)

Apple and Microsoft finance over half of their operations using debt. Apple finances 58.9% of its assets using debt, while Microsoft finances 54.6% of its assets using debt. While Apple has slightly more solvency risk than Microsoft, both companies have strong operating results and generate significant cash flows from operations.

Exhibit 2 illustrate the effects of how issuing bonds can increase earnings per share. This use of debt to enhance the earnings of stockholders is called **financial leverage**. With over half of their operations financed by debt, Apple and Microsoft are using financial leverage to enhance earnings for their shareholders.

Price-Earnings Ratio

The market's assessment of the future earnings potential of a company is indicated by the **price-earnings ratio**. The price-earnings ratio, sometimes called the earnings multiple, is computed as follows:

$$\text{Price-Earnings Ratio} = \frac{\text{Market Price per Share of Common Stock}}{\text{Earnings per Share of Common Stock}}$$

The higher a company's price-earnings ratio, the more favorable the market's assessment of the future earnings potential and growth of the company. A price-earnings ratio of less than 10 is often interpreted as indicating a company that has declining earnings or is undervalued. A price-earnings ratio of over 25 usually indicates an expanding company with high earnings potential or a company that is overvalued.

Price-earnings ratios are often compared over time or with other companies within the same industry. To illustrate, recent earnings per share (EPS) of common stock and stock prices of **Apple Inc. (AAPL)** and **Microsoft Corporation (MSFT)** are as follows:

	Year 3	Year 2	Year 1
Apple Inc.			
Earnings per share	$ 9.28	$ 6.49	$ 5.72
Common stock price at end of year*	114.22	98.63	66.03
Microsoft			
Earnings per share	1.49	2.66	2.61
Common stock price at end of year*	43.57	40.09	32.25

* Adjusted for dividends and stock splits.

The price-earnings ratios (P/E) for each year (rounded to one decimal place) are as follows:

	Year 3	Year 2	Year 1
Apple Inc.			
$114.22 ÷ $9.28	12.3		
$98.63 ÷ $6.49		15.2	
$66.03 ÷ $5.72			11.5
Microsoft			
$43.57 ÷ $1.49	29.2		
$40.09 ÷ $2.66		15.1	
$32.25 ÷ $2.61			12.4

The P/Es for Apple suggest mixed signals from the market. The P/E of 12.3 in Year 3 decreased from the P/E of 15.2 in Year 2. The Year 3 P/E of 12.3 is slightly better than the Year 1 P/E of 11.5. In contrast, the P/E for Microsoft has improved in each of the three years from 12.4 in Year 1 to 15.1 in Year 2 and 29.2 in Year 3.

These results suggest that the market has a more favorable outlook for Microsoft than for Apple. This may be due to market concerns that Apple will be unable to continue its innovations without the leadership of Steve Jobs. On the other hand, Microsoft hired a new chief executive officer and was releasing its new operating software Windows 10 during this time.

Key Points

1. Describe how businesses finance their operations.

A business must finance its operations through either debt or equity. Debt financing includes all liabilities owed by a business, including both current and long-term liabilities. A corporation may also finance its operations by issuing equity (common stock and preferred stock). The method of financing impacts earnings per share for common stock.

2. Describe and illustrate the accounting for current liabilities, notes payable, and payroll.

Liabilities that are to be paid out of current assets and are due within a short time, usually within one year, are called *current liabilities*. Most current liabilities arise from either receiving goods or services prior to making payment or receiving payment prior to delivering goods or services. Current liabilities can also arise from accruals, notes payable, and payroll. Wages and salaries payable and employee and employer payroll taxes are examples of liabilities arising from payroll.

3. Describe and illustrate the accounting for bonds payable.

Many large corporations finance their operations through the issuance of bonds. A bond is simply a form of an interest-bearing note that requires periodic interest payments and the repayment of the face amount at the maturity date. When the contract rate of interest differs from the market rate of interest, bonds are issued at discounts or premiums. The amortization of discounts and premiums affects interest expense.

4. A contingent liability is a potential obligation that results from a past transaction but depends on a future event.

The accounting for contingent liabilities depends upon their likelihood of occurrence and the ability to measure the amount of the contingency. The accounting for contingent liabilities is summarized in Exhibit 4.

5. Describe and illustrate transactions involving stock.

A corporation may finance its operations by issuing either preferred or common stock. Preferred stock has preferential rights, including the right to receive dividends ahead of the common stockholders. When stock is issued at a premium, Cash or another asset account is increased for the amount received. Common Stock or Preferred Stock is increased for the par amount. The excess of the amount paid over par is a part of the paid-in capital and is normally recorded in an account entitled Paid-In Capital in Excess of Par.

Stock that a corporation has once issued and then reacquired is called *treasury stock*, which decreases stockholders' equity.

6. Describe and illustrate the accounting for dividends.

When a board of directors declares a cash dividend, it authorizes the distribution of a portion of the corporation's cash to stockholders. When a board of directors declares a stock dividend, it authorizes the distribution of a portion of the stock. In both cases, the declaration of a dividend reduces the retained earnings of the corporation.

7. Describe and illustrate stock splits.

Corporations sometimes reduce the par or stated value of their common stock and issue a proportionate number of additional shares in what is called a *stock split*. Since a stock split changes only the par or stated value and the number of shares outstanding, it is not recorded. However, the details of stock splits are normally disclosed in the notes to the financial statements.

8. Describe and illustrate reporting of liabilities and stockholders' equity.

Liabilities that are expected to be paid within one year are presented in the Current Liabilities section of the balance sheet. Notes or bonds payable not maturing within one year should be shown as long-term liabilities. The detailed descriptions including terms, due dates, and interest rates for notes or bonds should be reported either on the balance sheet or in an accompanying note. Also, the fair market value of notes or bonds should be disclosed. The notes should disclose any contingent liabilities that cannot be reasonably estimated or are only possible. Significant changes in stockholders' equity during the year should also be reported in the statement of stockholders' equity.

9. Describe and illustrate the debt and price-earnings ratios.

The debt ratio indicates the percent of a company's operations that are financed by debt. The higher the ratio, the higher the financial leverage and more risk to creditors. The price-earnings ratio measures the market's assessment of the future earnings potential of the company. It is computed as the market price per share of common stock divided by the earnings per share of common stock. The higher the price-earnings ratio, the greater the market's expectations of future earnings.

Key Terms

Bond (316)
Bond indenture (323)
Cash dividend (331)
Common stock (328)
Contingent liabilities (325)
Contract rate (323)
creditors (318)
Current liabilities (318)
Debt ratio (337)
Discount on bonds payable (325)
Earnings per share (EPS) (316)
Financial leverage (337)
Fringe benefits (322)
Gross pay (320)
Insolvent (320)
Long-term liabilities (318)
Market rate of interest (323)
Net pay (320)
Outstanding stock (327)
Par (327)
Payroll (320)
Preferred stock (328)
Premium on bonds payable (325)
Premium (328)
Price-earnings ratio (337)
Stated value (327)
Stock dividend (333)
Stock split (334)
Treasury stock (329)

Illustrative Problem

Three different plans for financing an $18,000,000 corporation are under consideration by its organizers. Under each of the following plans, the securities will be issued at their par or face amount, and the income rax rate is estimated at 40% of income

	Plan1	Plan 2	Plan 3
8% bonds	—	—	$ 9,000,000
Preferred 4% stock, $20 par	—	$9,000,000	4,500,000
Common stock, $10 par	$18,000,000	9,000,000	4,500,000
Total	$18,000,000	$18,000,000	$18,000,000

Instructions

1. Determine the earnings per share of common stock for each plan, assuming that the income before bond interest and income tax is $2,100,000.
2. Determine the earnings per share of common stock for each plan, assuming that the income before bond interest and income tax is $1,050,000.
3. Discuss the advantages and disadvantages of each plan.

Solution

1.	Plan1	Plan 2	Plan 3
Earnings before interest and income tax	$2,100,000	$2,100,000	$2,100,000
Deduct interest on bonds	0	0	(720,000)
Income before income tax	$2,100,000	$2,100,000	$1,380,000
Deduct income tax	(840,000)	(840,000)	(552,000)
Net income	$1,260,000	$1,260,000	$ 828,000
Dividends on preferred stock	0	(360,000)	(180,000)
Available for dividends on common stock	$1,260,000	$ 900,000	$ 648,000
Shares of common stock outstanding	÷1,800,000	÷ 900,000	÷ 450,000
Earnings per share on common stock	$ 0.70	$ 1.00	$ 1.44

2.	Plan1	Plan 2	Plan 3
Earnings before interest and income tax	$1,050,000	$1,050,000	$1,050,000
Deduct interest on bonds	0	0	(720,000)
Income before income tax	$1,050,000	$1,050,000	$ 330,000
Deduct income tax	(420,000)	(420,000)	(132,000)
Net income	$ 630,000	$ 630,000	$ 198,000
Dividends on preferred stock	0	(360,000)	(180,000)
Available for dividends on common stock	$ 630,000	$ 270,000	$ 18,000
Shares of common stock outstanding	÷1,800,000	÷ 900,000	÷ 450,000
Earnings per share on common stock	$ 0.35	$ 0.30	$ 0.04

3. The principal advantage of Plan 1 is that it involves only the issuance of common stock, which does not require a periodic interest payment or return of principal, and a payment of preferred dividends is not required. It is also more attractive to common shareholders than is Plan 2 or 3 if earnings before interest and income tax is $1,050,000. In this case, it has the largest EPS ($0.35). The principal disadvantage of Plan 1 is that, if earnings before interest and income tax is $2,100,000, it offers the lowest EPS ($0.70) on common stock.

The principal advantage of Plan 3 is that less investment would need to be made by common shareholders. Also, it offers the largest EPS ($1.44) if earnings before interest and income tax is $2,100,000. Its principal disadvantage is that the bonds carry a fixed annual interest charge and require the payment of principal. It also requires a dividend payment to preferred stockholders before a common dividend can be paid. Finally, Plan 3 provides the lowest EPS ($0.04) if earnings before interest and income tax is $1,050,000.

Plan 2 provides a middle ground in terms of the advantages and disadvantages described in the preceding paragraphs for Plans 1 and 3.

Self-Examination Questions

(Answers appear at the end of chapter)

1. A business issued a $5,000, 60-day, 12% note to the bank. The amount due at maturity is:
   - A. $4,900
   - B. $5,000
   - C. $5,100
   - D. $5,600
2. Which of the following taxes are employers usually not required to withhold from employees?
   - A. Federal income tax
   - B. Federal unemployment compensation tax
   - C. FICA tax
   - D. State and local income taxes
3. Employers do not incur an expense for which of the following payroll taxes?
   - A. FICA tax
   - B. Federal unemployment compensation tax
   - C. State unemployment compensation tax
   - D. Employees' federal income tax
4. If a corporation plans to issue $1,000,000 of 7% bonds when the market rate for similar bonds is 6%, the bonds can be expected to sell at:
   - A. Their face amount
   - B. A premium
   - C. A discount
   - D. A price below their face amount
5. A corporation has issued 25,000 shares of $100 par common stock and holds 3,000 of these shares as treasury stock. If the corporation declares a $2-per-share cash dividend, what amount will be recorded as cash dividends?
   - A. $22,000
   - B. $25,000
   - C. $44,000
   - D. $50,000

Class Discussion Questions

1. For most companies, what two types of transactions make up the largest percent of their current liabilities?
2. When are short-term notes payable issued?
3. For each of the following payroll-related taxes, indicate whether it generally applies to (1) employees only, (2) employers only, or (3) both employees and employers:
   a. Federal income tax
   b. Federal unemployment compensation tax
   c. Medicare tax
   d. Social security tax
   e. State unemployment compensation tax
4. To match revenues and expenses properly, should the expense for employee vacation pay be recorded in the period during which the vacation privilege is earned or during the period in which the vacation is taken?
5. Identify the two distinct obligations incurred by a corporation when issuing bonds.
6. A corporation issues $40,000,000 of 6% bonds to yield an effective interest rate of 8%.
   a. Was the amount of cash received from the sale of the bonds more or less than $40,000,000?
   b. Identify the following amounts related to the bond issue: (1) face amount, (2) market rate of interest, (3) contract rate of interest, and (4) maturity amount.
7. The following data relate to an $8,000,000, 7% bond issue for a selected semiannual interest period:

Bond carrying amount at beginning of period	$8,190,000
Interest paid at end of period	560,000
Interest expense allocable to the period	540,500

a. Were the bonds issued at a discount or at a premium?

b. What expense account is affected by the amortization of the discount or premium?

8. When should the liability associated with a product warranty be recorded? Discuss.

9. Deere & Company (DE), a company well known for manufacturing farm equipment, reported more than $800 million of product warranties in recent financial statements. How would costs of repairing a defective product be recorded?

10. Delta Air Lines (DAL)' SkyMiles program allows frequent flyers to earn credit toward free tickets and other amenities.
    a. Does Delta Air Lines have a contingent liability for award redemption by its SkyMiles members?
    b. When should a contingent liability be recorded?

11. Of two corporations organized at approximately the same time and engaged in competing businesses, one issued $75 par common stock, and the other issued $1 par common stock. Do the par designations provide any indication as to which stock is preferable as an investment? Explain.

12. When a corporation issues stock at a premium, is the premium income? Explain.

13. a. In what respect does treasury stock differ from unissued stock?
    b. How should treasury stock be presented on the balance sheet?

14. A corporation reacquires 18,000 shares of its own $50 par common stock for $2,250,000, recording it at cost.
    a. What effect does this transaction have on revenue or expense of the period?
    b. What effect does it have on stockholders' equity?

15. The treasury stock in Question 14 is resold for $2,400,000.
    a. What is the effect on the corporation's revenue of the period?
    b. What is the effect on stockholders' equity?

16. A corporation with preferred stock and common stock outstanding has a substantial balance in its retained earnings account at the beginning of the current fiscal year. Although net income for the current year is sufficient to pay the preferred dividend of $150,000 each quarter and a common dividend of $40,000 each quarter, the board of directors declares dividends only on the preferred stock. Suggest possible reasons that the board did not declare dividends on the common stock.

17. An owner of 300 shares of Colorado Spring Company common stock receives a stock dividend of 6 shares.
    a. What is the effect of the stock dividend on the stockholder's proportionate interest (equity) in the corporation?
    b. How does the total equity of 306 shares compare with the total equity of 300 shares before the stock dividend?

18. What is the primary purpose of a stock split?

Exercises

Obj. 1

✔ a. $0.60

E8-1 Effect of financing on earnings per share

BSF Co., which produces and sells skiing equipment, is financed as follows:

Bonds payable, 8% (issued at face amount)	$7,500,000
Preferred 2% stock, $10 par	7,500,000
Common stock, $50 par	7,500,000

Income tax is estimated at 40% of income.

Determine the earnings per share of common stock, assuming that the income before bond interest and income tax is (a) $1,000,000, (b) $3,000,000, and (c) $4,500,000.

E8-2 Evaluate alternative financing plans

Obj. 1

Based on the data in Exercise E8-1, discuss factors other than earnings per share that should be considered in evaluating such financing plans.

E8-3 Current liabilities

Obj 2, 8

✔ Total current liabilities, $256,400

Zahn Inc. sold 16,000 annual magazine subscriptions for $15 during December 20Y4. These new subscribers will receive monthly issues, beginning in January 20Y5. Zahn Inc. issued a $48,000, 180–day, 5% note payable on December 1, 20Y4. On March 31, 20Y5, Zahn Inc. had accounts payable of $21,500 and accrued wages payable of $6,100.

Prepare the Current Liabilities section of the balance sheet for Zahn Inc. on March 31, 20Y5.

E8-4 Notes payable

Obj. 2

A business issued a 90-day, 7% note for $30,000 to a creditor on account. Illustrate the effects on the accounts and financial statements of recording (a) the issuance of the note and (b) the payment of the note at maturity, including interest.

E8-5 Compute payroll

Obj. 2

✔ b. Net pay, $1,069.10

An employee earns $28 per hour and 1.5 times that rate for all hours in excess of 40 hours per week. Assume that the employee worked 46 hours during the week. Assume that the FICA tax rate is 7.5% and that federal income tax of $200 was withheld.

a. Determine the gross pay for the week.

b. Determine the net pay for the week.

E8-6 Summary payroll data

Obj. 2

✔ (3) Total earnings, $840,000

In the following summary of data for a payroll period, some amounts have been intentionally omitted:

Earnings:	
1. At regular rate	?
2. At overtime rate	$120,000
3. Total earnings	?
Deductions:	
4. FICA tax	63,000
5. Income tax withheld	200,000
6. Medical insurance	37,000
7. Union dues	?
8. Total deductions	315,000
9. Net amount paid	525,000
Accounts increased:	
10. Wages	400,000
11. Sales Salaries	?
12. Office Salaries	150,000

Compute the amounts omitted in lines (1), (3), (7), and (11).

E8-7 Recording payroll taxes

Obj. 2

According to a summary of the payroll of Kirby Co., $180,000 in earnings were subject to the 7.5% FICA tax. Also, $60,000 in earnings were subject to state and federal unemployment taxes.

a. Calculate the employer's payroll taxes, using the following rates: state unemployment, 4.3%; federal unemployment, 0.8%.

b. Illustrate the effects on the accounts and financial statements of recording the accrual of payroll taxes.

Obj. 2

E8-8 Accrued vacation pay

ProTech Inc. provides its employees with varying amounts of vacation per year, depending on the length of employment. The estimated amount of the current year's vacation pay is $432,000. Illustrate the effects on the accounts and financial statements of the adjustment required on January 31, the end of the first month of the current year, to record the accrued vacation pay.

Obj. 3

E8-9 Bond price

CVS Caremark Corp. (CVS) 5.3% bonds due in 2043, sold for 113.04. Were the bonds selling at a premium or at a discount? Explain.

Obj. 3

E8-10 Issuing bonds

Cyber Tech Inc. produces and distributes fiber optic cable for use by telecommunications companies. Cyber Tech Inc. issued $50,000,000 of 20-year, 6% bonds on March 1 at their face amount, with interest payable on March 1 and September 1. The fiscal year of the company is the calendar year. Illustrate the effects on the accounts and financial statements of recording the following selected transactions for the current year:

Mar. 1. Issued the bonds for cash at their face amount.

Sept. 1. Paid the interest on the bonds.

Dec. 31. Recorded accrued interest for four months.

Obj. 4

E8-11 Accrued product warranty

Back in Time Inc. warrants its products for one year. The estimated product warranty is 2% of sales. Assume that sales were $1,250,000 for March. In April, a customer received warranty repairs requiring $750 of parts.

a. Determine the warranty liability at March 31, the end of the first month of the current fiscal year.

b. What accounts are decreased for the warranty work provided in April?

Obj. 4

E8-12 Accrued product warranty

Ford Motor Company (F) disclosed the following estimated product warranty payable for two recent years.

	December 31,	
	Year 2	Year 1
	(in millions)	
Product warranty payable	$4,786	$3,927

Ford's sales in its automotive sector were $135,782 million in Year 2 and $139,369 million in Year 1. Assume that the total paid on warranty claims during Year 2 was $2,850 million.

a. Illustrate the effects on the accounts and financial statements for the Year 2 product warranty expense.

b. Explain the $859 ($4,786 – $3,927) million increase in the total warranty liability from Year 1 to Year 2.

E8-13 Contingent liabilities

Obj. 4

Several months ago, Cinnabar Chemical Company experienced a hazardous materials spill at one of its plants. As a result, the Environmental Protection Agency (EPA) fined the company $1,000,000. The company is contesting the fine. In addition, an employee is seeking $150,000 damages related to injuries sustained while cleaning up the spill. Lastly, a homeowner has sued the company for $100,000. The homeowner lives 6 miles from the plant but believes that the incident has reduced the home's resale value by $100,000.

Cinnabar's legal counsel believes that it is probable that the EPA fine will stand. In addition, counsel indicates that an out-of-court settlement of $75,000 has recently been reached with the employee. The final papers will be signed next week. Counsel believes that the homeowner's case is much weaker and will be decided in favor of Cinnabar. Other litigation related to the spill is possible, but the damage amounts are uncertain.

a. Illustrate the effects of the contingent liabilities associated with the hazardous materials spill on the accounts and financial statements.

b. Prepare a note disclosure relating to this incident.

E8-14 Contingent liabilities

Obj. 4

The following note accompanied the financial statements for Goodyear Tire and Rubber Company (GT):

> *We are a defendant in numerous lawsuits alleging various asbestos-related personal injuries purported to result from alleged exposure to certain asbestos products manufactured by us or present in certain of our facilities. Typically, these lawsuits have been brought against multiple defendants in state and federal courts. To date, we have disposed of approximately 109,500 claims by defending and obtaining the dismissal thereof or by entering into a settlement. The sum of our accrued asbestos-related liability, . . . including legal costs totaled approximately $458 million . . .*

a. Illustrate the effects on the accounts and financial statements of recording the contingent liability of $458,000,000.

b. Why was the contingent liability recorded?

E8-15 Issuing par stock

Obj. 5

On January 29, Quality Marble Inc., a marble contractor, issued 75,000 shares of $10 par common stock for cash at $23 per share, and on May 31, it issued 100,000 shares of $4 par preferred stock for cash at $6 per share.

a. Illustrate the effects on the accounts and financial statements of the January 29 and May 31 transactions.

b. What is the total amount invested (total paid-in capital) by all stockholders as of May 31?

E8-16 Issuing stock for assets other than cash

Obj. 5

On August 7, Easy Up Corporation, a wholesaler of hydraulic lifts, acquired land in exchange for 20,000 shares of $10 par common stock with a current market price of $14.

Illustrate the effect on the accounts and financial statements of the purchase of the land.

E8-17 Treasury stock transactions

Obj. 5

Blue Moon Water Supply Inc. bottles and distributes spring water. On July 17 of the current year, Blue Moon Water Supply reacquired 35,000 shares of its common stock at $60 per share.

a. What is the balance of Treasury Stock on December 31 of the current year?

b. Where will the balance of Treasury Stock be reported on the balance sheet?

c. For what reasons might Blue Moon Water Supply have purchased the treasury stock?

Obj. 5

E8-18 Treasury stock transactions

Sun Dance Gardens Inc. develops and produces spraying equipment for lawn maintenance and industrial uses. On June 3 of the current year, Sun Dance Gardens Inc. reacquired 28,000 shares of its common stock at $37 per share.

a. What is the balance of Treasury Stock on December 31 of the current year?

b. How will the balance in Treasury Stock be reported on the balance sheet?

c. Assume that Sun Dance Gardens sold 10,000 shares of its treasury stock at $40 on November 2. What accounts would be affected by the sale of the treasury stock?

Obj. 5

E8-19 Treasury stock transactions

Banff Water Inc. bottles and distributes spring water. On April 2 of the current year, Banff Water Inc. reacquired 30,000 shares of its common stock at $33 per share.

a. What is the balance of Treasury Stock on December 31 of the current year?

b. Where will the balance of Treasury Stock be reported on the balance sheet?

c. For what reasons might Banff Water Inc. have purchased the treasury stock?

d. Assume that on January 25 of the following year, Banff Water Inc. sold 20,000 shares of its treasury stock for $40 per share. Illustrate the effects on the accounts and financial statements of the sale of the treasury stock.

Obj. 6

E8-20 Cash dividends

The date of declaration, date of record, and date of payment in connection with a cash dividend of $1,200,000 on a corporation's common stock are June 1, July 15, and August 14, respectively. Illustrate the effects on the accounts and financial statements for each date.

Obj. 6, 7

E8-21 Effect of cash dividend, stock split, and stock dividend

Indicate whether the following actions would (+) increase, (–) decrease, or (0) not affect Ballistic Scientific Inc.'s total assets, liabilities, and stockholders' equity:

	Assets	Liabilities	Stockholders' Equity
(1) Declaring a cash dividend	______	______	______
(2) Paying the cash dividend declared in (1)	______	______	______
(3) Authorizing and issuing stock certificates in a stock split	______	______	______
(4) Declaring a stock dividend	______	______	______
(5) Issuing stock certificates for the stock dividend declared in (4)	______	______	______

Obj. 7

E8-22 Effect of stock split

Audrey's Restaurant Corporation wholesales ovens and ranges to restaurants throughout the Northwest. Audrey's Restaurant Corporation, which had 50,000 shares of common stock outstanding, declared a 6-for-1 stock split.

a. What will be the number of shares outstanding after the split?

b. If the common stock had a market price of $540 per share before the stock split, what would be an approximate market price per share after the split?

E8-23 Stockholders' Equity section of balance sheet

Obj. 7

✔ Total stockholders' equity, $15,055,000

The following accounts and their balances appear in the ledger of Young Properties Inc. on November 30 of the current year:

Common Stock, $40 par	$ 3,000,000
Paid-In Capital in Excess of Par	450,000
Paid-In Capital from Treasury Stock	125,000
Retained Earnings	12,000,000
Treasury Stock	520,000

Prepare the Stockholders' Equity section of the balance sheet as of November 30. One hundred thousand shares of common stock are authorized, and 10,000 shares have been reacquired.

E8-24 Stockholders' Equity section of balance sheet

Obj. 7

✔ Total stockholders' equity, $22,818,000

Premium Imports Inc. retails racing products for BMWs, Porsches, and Ferraris. The following accounts and their balances appear in the ledger of Premium Imports Inc. on November 30, the end of the current year:

Common Stock, $8 par	$ 3,200,000
Paid-In Capital in Excess of Par—Common Stock	700,000
Paid-In Capital in Excess of Par—Preferred Stock	182,000
Paid-In Capital from Treasury Stock—Common	150,000
Preferred 2% Stock, $80 par	2,080,000
Retained Earnings	17,250,000
Treasury Stock—Common	744,000

Forty thousand shares of preferred and 500,000 shares of common stock are authorized. There are 62,000 shares of common stock held as treasury stock.

Prepare the Stockholders' Equity section of the balance sheet as of November 30.

Problems

P8-1 Effect of financing on earnings per share

Obj. 1

✔ 1. Plan 3: $1.72

Three different plans for financing a $5,000,000 corporation are under consideration by its organizers. Under each of the following plans, the securities will be issued at their par or face amount, and the income tax rate is estimated at 40% of income.

	Plan 1	Plan 2	Plan 3
8% bonds	—	—	$2,500,000
Preferred 4% stock, $100 par	—	$2,500,000	1,250,000
Common stock, $5 par	$5,000,000	2,500,000	1,250,000
Total	$5,000,000	$5,000,000	$5,000,000

(Continued)

Note: The spreadsheet icon  indicates an Excel template is available on the student companion site at www.cengagebrain.com.

Instructions

1. Determine for each plan the earnings per share of common stock, assuming that the income before bond interest and income tax is $1,000,000.
2. Determine for each plan the earnings per share of common stock, assuming that the income before bond interest and income tax is $300,000.
3. Discuss the advantages and disadvantages of each plan.

Obj. 2

✔ 1. $6,750

P8-2 Recording payroll and payroll taxes

The following information about the payroll for the week ended October 4 was obtained from the records of Simkins Mining Co.:

Salaries:		Deductions:	
Sales salaries	$30,000	Income tax withheld	$17,000
Employee Wages	40,000	U.S. savings bonds	2,000
Office salaries	20,000	Group insurance	6,000
	$90,000		

Tax rates assumed:

FICA tax, 7.5% of employee annual earnings
State unemployment (employer only), 4.2%
Federal unemployment (employer only), 0.8%

Instructions

1. For the October 4 payroll, determine the employee FICA tax payable.
2. Illustrate the effect on the accounts and financial statements of recording the October 4 payroll.
3. Determine the following amounts for the employer payroll taxes related to the October 4 payroll: (a) FICA tax payable, (b) state unemployment tax payable, and (c) federal unemployment tax payable.
4. Illustrate the effect on the accounts and financial statements of recording the liability for the October 4 employer payroll taxes.

Obj. 3

P8-3 Bond premium; bonds payable transactions

Beaufort Vaults Corporation produces and sells burial vaults. On July 1, 20Y3, Beaufort Vaults Corporation issued $25,000,000 of 10-year, 8% bonds at par. Interest on the bonds is payable semiannually on December 31 and June 30. The fiscal year of the company is the calendar year.

Instructions

1. Illustrate the effects of the issuance of the bonds on July 1, 20Y3, on the accounts and financial statements.
2. Illustrate the effects of the first semiannual interest payment on December 31, 20Y3, on the accounts and financial statements.
3. Illustrate the effects of the payment of the face value of bonds at maturity on the accounts and financial statements.
4. If the market rate of interest had been 7% on July 1, 20Y3, would the bonds have sold at a discount or premium?

P8-4 Stock transactions for corporate expansion

Obj. 4

Vaga Optics produces medical lasers for use in hospitals. The following accounts and their balances appear in the ledger of Vaga Optics on December 31 of the current year:

Preferred 2% Stock, $120 par (50,000 shares authorized, 25,000 shares issued)	$ 3,000,000
Paid-In Capital in Excess of Par—Preferred Stock	400,000
Common Stock, $75 par (500,000 shares authorized, 300,000 shares issued)	22,500,000
Paid-In Capital in Excess of Par—Common Stock	540,000
Retained Earnings	55,000,000

At the annual stockholders' meeting on January 31, the board of directors presented a plan for modernizing and expanding plant operations at a cost of approximately $9,500,000. The plan provided (a) that the corporation borrow $4,500,000, (b) that 20,000 shares of the unissued preferred stock be issued through an underwriter, and (c) that a building, valued at $1,200,000, and the land on which it is located, valued at $900,000, be acquired in accordance with preliminary negotiations by the issuance of 27,400 shares of common stock. The plan was approved by the stockholders and accomplished by the following transactions:

Mar. 8. Borrowed $4,500,000 from Conrad National Bank, giving a 6% mortgage note.

13. Issued 20,000 shares of preferred stock, receiving $130 per share in cash.

26. Issued 27,400 shares of common stock in exchange for land and a building, according to the plan.

No other expansion-related transactions occurred during March.

Instructions

Illustrate the effects on the accounts and financial statements of each of the preceding transactions.

P8-5 Dividends on preferred and common stock

Obj. 4, 5

Yukon Bike Corp. manufactures mountain bikes and distributes them through retail outlets in Canada, Montana, Idaho, Oregon, and Washington. Yukon Bike Corp. declared the following annual dividends over a six-year period ending December 31 of each year: Year 1, $28,000; Year 2, $44,000; Year 3, $48,000; Year 4, $60,000; Year 5, $76,000; and Year 6, $140,000. During the entire period, the outstanding stock of the company was composed of 40,000 shares of 2% preferred stock, $65 par, and 50,000 shares of common stock, $1 par.

✔ 1. Preferred dividends in Year 2: $44,000

Instructions

1. Determine the total dividends and the per-share dividends declared on each class of stock for each of the six years. Assume that preferred dividends are paid before any common dividends. Summarize the data in tabular form, using the following column headings:

		Preferred Dividends		Common Dividends	
Year	**Total Dividends**	**Total**	**Per Share**	**Total**	**Per Share**
Year 1	$ 28,000				
Year 2	44,000				
Year 3	48,000				
Year 4	60,000				
Year 5	76,000				
Year 6	140,000				

2. Calculate the average annual dividend per share for each class of stock for the six-year period.
3. Assuming that the preferred stock was sold at $57.50 and common stock was sold at $5.00 at the beginning of the six-year period, calculate the average annual percentage return on initial shareholders' investment, based on the average annual dividend per share (a) for preferred stock and (b) for common stock.

Metric-Based Analysis

Obj. 2

MBA 8-1 Notes payable transactions

Using the data from E8-4, indicate the effects on net assets and earnings per share (EPS) of each of the following:

1. Issuing the notes payable.
2. Payment of the note at maturity, including interest.

Obj. 2

MBA 8-2 Recording payroll and payroll taxes

Using the data from P8-2, indicate the effects on net assets and EPS of each of the following:

1. Recording the payroll.
2. Recording the payroll taxes.
3. Paying the payroll and payroll taxes.

Obj. 3

MBA 8-3 Bonds payable transactions

Using the data from P8-3, indicate the effects on net assets and EPS of each of the following:

1. Issuing the bonds payable on July 1, 20Y3.
2. Interest payment on December 31, 20Y3.
3. Payment of the face value of the bonds at maturity.

Obj. 2, 5

MBA 8-4 Note payable and stock transactions

Using the data from P8-4, indicate the effects on net assets and EPS for the March 8, 13, and 26 transactions.

Obj. 5

MBA 8-5 Treasury stock purchase

Using the data from E8-19, indicate the effects on net assets and EPS for the following transactions:

1. Purchase of the Treasury stock on April 2.
2. Sale of the Treasury stock on January 25 of the following year.

Obj. 6

MBA 8-6 Dividends

Using the data from E8-20, indicate the effects on net assets and EPS for the following dates:

1. June 1 (date of declaration)
2. July 15 (date of record)
3. August 14 (date of payment)

Obj. 7

MBA 8-7 Stock split

Using the data from E8-22, indicate the effects on net assets and EPS of the stock split.

MBA 8-8 Debt and price-earnings ratios

Obj. 9

The Home Depot, Inc. (HD) operates over 2,200 home improvement retail stores and is a competitor of Lowe's (LOW). The following data (in millions) were adapted from recent financial statements of The Home Depot.

	Year 2	Year 1
Total assets	$39,946	$40,518
Total liabilities	30,624	27,996
Total stockholders' equity	9,322	12,522
Earnings per share	$4.74	$3.78

1. Compute the debt ratio for Years 1 and 2. Round to one decimal place.
2. Given your answer to part (1), what is the ratio of stockholders' equity to total assets? Round to one decimal place.
3. Compute the ratio of liabilities to stockholders' equity. Round to one decimal place.
4. Are Home Depot's operations financed primarily with liabilities or equity?
5. Comparing Years 1 and 2, should creditors feel more or less safe in Year 2?
6. With a market price of $104.43, compute the price-earnings ratio for Year 2.
7. With a market price of $75.09, compute the price-earnings ratio for Year 1.
8. Compare the results from parts (6) and (7). Comment on any differences.

MBA 8-9 Debt and price-earnings ratios

Obj. 9

Lowe's Companies Inc. (LOW) operates over 1,800 home improvement retail stores and is a competitor of The Home Depot (HD). The following data (in millions) were adapted from a recent financial statement of Lowe's:

Total assets	$31,827
Total liabilities	21,859
Total stockholders' equity	9,968
Earnings per share	$2.71

1. Compute the debt ratio. Round to one decimal place.
2. Given your answer to part (1), what is the ratio of stockholders' equity to total assets? Round to one decimal place.
3. Compute the ratio of liabilities to stockholders' equity. Round to one decimal place.
4. Are Lowe's operations financed primarily with liabilities or equity?
5. With a market price of $67.76, compute the price-earnings ratio.
6. Compare the ratios computed in (1)-(3) with those of Home Depot computed in MBA 8-8 for Year 2.
7. Compare the price-earnings ratios of Lowe's and The Home Depot (MBA 8-8). Comment on any differences.

Obj. 9

MBA 8-10 Debt and price-earnings ratios

Alphabet (formerly known as Google) (GOOG) is a technology company that offers users Internet search and e-mail services. Google also developed the Android operating system for use with cell phones and other mobile devices. The following data (in millions) were adapted from a recent financial statement of Alphabet.

	Year 2	Year 1
Total assets	$131,133	$110,920
Total liabilities	26,633	23,611
Total stockholders' equity	104,500	87,309
Earnings per share	21.02	19.07

1. Compute the debt ratio for Years 1 and 2. Round to one decimal place.
2. Given your answer to part (1), what is the ratio of stockholders' equity to total assets? Round to one decimal place.
3. Compute the ratio of liabilities to stockholders' equity. Round to one decimal place.
4. Are Google's operations financed primarily with liabilities or equity?
5. Comparing Years 1 and 2, should creditors feel more or less safe in Year 2?
6. With a market price of $526.40, compute the price-earnings ratio for Year 2.
7. With a market price of $560.36, compute the price-earnings ratio for Year 1.
8. Compare the results from parts (6) and (7). Comment on any differences.

Obj. 9

MBA 8-11 Debt and price-earnings ratios

For each of the following companies, indicate whether you think the ratio of liabilities to total assets is more than 50%. Also, indicate whether you think the price-earnings ratio is above 10.

	Debt Ratio More than 50% (Yes, No)	Price-Earnings Ratio Above 10 (Yes, No)
Alcoa (AA)		
Amazon.com (AMZN)		
Boeing (BA)		
Dell		
HP (formerly Hewlett-Packard) (HPQ)		
McDonald's (MCD)		
Nike (NKE)		
Wal-Mart (WMT)		

Cases

Case 8-1 Ethics and professional conduct in business

Jas Carillo was discussing summer employment with Maria Perez, president of Valparaiso Construction Service:

Maria: I'm glad that you're thinking about joining us for the summer. We could certainly use the help.

Jas: Sounds good. I enjoy outdoor work, and I could use the money to help with next year's school expenses.

Maria: I've got a plan that can help you out on that. As you know, I'll pay you $8 per hour; but in addition, I'd like to pay you with cash. Since you're only working for the summer, it really doesn't make sense for me to go to the trouble of formally putting you on our payroll system. In fact, I do some jobs for my clients on a strictly cash basis, so it would be easy to just pay you that way.

Jas: Well, that's a bit unusual, but I guess money is money.

Maria: Yeah, not only that, it's tax-free!

Jas: What do you mean?

Maria: Didn't you know? Any money that you receive in cash is not reported to the IRS on a W-2 form; therefore, the IRS doesn't know about the income—hence, it's the same as tax-free earnings.

1. Why does Maria Perez want to conduct business transactions using cash (not check or credit card)?
2. How should Jas respond to Maria's suggestion?

Case 8-2 Contingent liabilities

INTERNET PROJECT

Altria Group, Inc., has a note dedicated to describing contingent liabilities in its recent financial statements. This note includes extensive descriptions of multiple contingent liabilities. Go to the Web site **http://www.sec.gov/edgar/searchedgar/companysearch.html**, enter MO as the ticker symbol, click on 10-K Documents, and click on Form 10-K. Using the Table of Contents and excerpts from the annual report, answer the following questions.

1. What are the major business units of Altria Group?
2. Based on your understanding of this company, why would Altria Group require a note on contingent liabilities?

Case 8-3 Issuing stock

Sahara Unlimited Inc. began operations on January 2, 20Y4, with the issuance of 250,000 shares of $8 par common stock. The sole stockholders of Sahara Unlimited Inc. are Karina Takemoto and Dr. Noah Grove, who organized Sahara Unlimited Inc. with the objective of developing a new flu vaccine. Dr. Grove claims that the flu vaccine, which is nearing the final development stage, will protect individuals against 80% of the flu types that have been medically identified. To complete the project, Sahara Unlimited Inc. needs $25,000,000 of additional funds. The banks have been unwilling to loan the funds because of the lack of sufficient collateral and the riskiness of the business. The following is a conversation between Karina Takemoto, the chief executive officer of Sahara Unlimited Inc., and Dr. Noah Grove, the leading researcher:

Karina: What are we going to do? The banks won't loan us any more money, and we've got to have $25 million to complete the project. We are so close! It would be a disaster to quit now. The only thing I can think of is to issue additional stock. Do you have any suggestions?

Noah: I guess you're right. But if the banks won't loan us any more money, how do you think we can find any investors to buy stock?

Karina: I've been thinking about that. What if we promise the investors that we will pay them 2% of sales until they have received an amount equal to what they paid for the stock?

Noah: What happens when we pay back the $25 million? Do the investors get to keep the stock? If they do, it'll dilute our ownership.

Karina: How about, if after we pay back the $25 million, we make them turn in their stock for what they paid for it? Plus, we could pay them an additional $50 per share. That's a $50 profit per share for the investors.

Noah: It could work. We get our money, but don't have to pay any interest or dividends until we start generating sales. At the same time, the investors could get their money back plus $50 per share.

Karina: We'll need current financial statements for the new investors. I'll get our accountant working on them and contact our attorney to draw up a legally binding contract for the new investors. Yes, this could work.

In late 20Y4, the attorney and the various regulatory authorities approved the new stock offering, and shares of common stock were privately sold to new investors for $25,000,000.

In preparing financial statements for 20Y4, Karina Takemoto and Glenn Bergum, the controller for Sahara Unlimited Inc., have the following conversation:

Glenn: Karina, I've got a problem.

Karina: What's that, Glenn?

Glenn: Issuing common stock to raise that additional $25 million was a great idea. But ...

Karina: But what?

Glenn: I've got to prepare the 20Y4 annual financial statements, and I am not sure how to classify the common stock.

Karina: What do you mean? It's common stock.

Glenn: I'm not so sure. I called the auditor and explained how we are contractually obligated to pay the new stockholders 2% of sales until they receive what they paid for the stock. Then, we may be obligated to pay them $50 per share.

Karina: So ...

Glenn: So the auditor thinks that we should classify the additional issuance of $25 million as debt, not stock! And, if we put the $25 million on the balance sheet as debt, we will violate our other loan agreements with the banks. And, if these agreements are violated, the banks may call in all our debt immediately. If they do that, we are in deep trouble. We'll probably have to file for bankruptcy. We just don't have the cash to pay off the banks.

1. Discuss the arguments for and against classifying the issuance of the $25 million of stock as debt.
2. What do you think might be a practical solution to this classification problem?

Case 8-4 Preferred stock vs. bonds

Living Smart Inc. has decided to expand its operations to owning and operating long-term health care facilities. The following is an excerpt from a conversation between the chief executive officer, Mark Vierra, and the vice president of finance, Jolin Kilcup.

Mark: Jolin, have you given any thought to how we're going to finance the acquisition of St. George Health Care?

Jolin: Well, the two basic options, as I see it, are to issue either preferred stock or bonds. The equity market is a little depressed right now. The rumor is that the Federal Reserve Bank may increase the interest rates either this month or next.

Mark: Yes, I've heard the rumor. The problem is that we can't wait around to see what's going to happen. We'll have to move on this next week if we want any chance to complete the acquisition of St. George.

Jolin: Well, the bond market is strong right now. Maybe we should issue debt this time around.

Mark: That's what I would have guessed as well. St. George's financial statements look pretty good, except for the volatility of its income and cash flows. But that's characteristic of the industry.

Discuss the advantages and disadvantages of issuing preferred stock versus bonds.

Case 8-5 Financing business expansion

You hold a 30% common stock interest in the family-owned business, a vending machine company. Your sister, who is the manager, has proposed an expansion of plant facilities at an expected cost of $6,000,000. Two alternative plans have been suggested as methods of financing the expansion. Each plan is briefly described as follows:

Plan 1. Issue $6,000,000 of 15-year, 8% notes at face amount.

Plan 2. Issue an additional 100,000 shares of $20 par common stock at $25 per share, and $3,500,000 of 15-year, 8% notes at face amount.

The balance sheet as of the end of the previous fiscal year is as follows:

MOJAVE OASIS, INC.
Balance Sheet
December 31, 20Y6

Assets	
Current assets	$10,000,000
Property, plant, and equipment	15,000,000
Total assets	$25,000,000
Liabilities and Stockholders' Equity	
Liabilities	$ 7,000,000
Common stock, $20	8,000,000
Paid-in capital in excess of par	300,000
Retained earnings	9,700,000
Total liabilities and stockholders' equity	$25,000,000

Net income has remained relatively constant over the past several years. The expansion program is expected to increase yearly income before bond interest and income tax from $900,000 in the previous year to $1,200,000 for this year. Your sister has asked you, as the company treasurer, to prepare an analysis of each financing plan.

1. Prepare a table indicating the expected earnings per share on the common stock under each plan. Assume an income tax rate of 25%.
2. a. Discuss the factors that should be considered in evaluating the two plans.
   b. Which plan offers the greater benefit to the present stockholders? Give reasons for your opinion.

Answers to Self-Examination Questions

1. **C** The maturity value is $5,100, determined as follows:

Face amount of note	$5,000
Plus interest ($5,000 × 0.12 × 60/360)	100
Maturity value	$5,100

2. **B** Employers are usually required to withhold a portion of their employees' earnings for payment of federal income taxes (answer A), FICA tax (answer C), and state and local income taxes (answer D). Generally, federal unemployment compensation taxes (answer B) are levied against the employer only and thus are not withheld from employee earnings.

3. **D** The employer incurs an expense for FICA tax (answer A), federal unemployment compensation tax (answer B), and state unemployment compensation tax (answer C). The employees' federal income tax (answer D) is not an expense of the employer. It is withheld from the employees' earnings.

4. **B** Since the contract rate on the bonds is higher than the prevailing market rate, a rational investor would be willing to pay more than the face amount, or a premium (answer B), for the bonds. If the contract rate and the market rate were equal, the bonds could be expected to sell at their face amount (answer A). Likewise, if the market rate is higher than the contract rate, the bonds would sell at a price below their face amount (answer D) or at a discount (answer C).

5. **C** If a corporation that holds treasury stock declares a cash dividend, the dividends are not paid on the treasury shares. The corporation will record $44,000 (answer C) as cash dividends [(25,000 shares issued less 3,000 shares held as treasury stock) × $2 per share dividend].

Chapter 9 Metric-Analysis of Financial Statements

What's Covered:

Topics: Metric-Analysis of Financial Statements

Analysis of Financial Statements
- Usefulness of financial statements (Obj. 1)
- Methods of analysis (Obj. 1)

Global Analysis
- Horizontal analysis (Obj. 2)
- Vertical analysis (Obj. 2)
- Common-sized statements (Obj. 2)

Component Analysis: Liquidity
- Current position (Obj. 3)
- Accounts receivable (Obj. 3)
- Inventory (Obj. 3)

Component Analysis: Solvency
- Debt ratio (Obj. 4)
- Liabilities to stockholders' equity (Obj. 4)
- Fixed assets to long-term liabilities (Obj. 4)
- Times interest earned (Obj. 4)

Component Analysis: Profitability
- Asset turnover (Obj. 5)
- Return on total assets (Obj. 5)
- Return on stockholders' equity (Obj. 5)
- Return on common stockholders' Equity (Obj. 5)
- Earnings per share (Obj. 5)
- Price-earnings ratio (Obj. 5)
- Dividends per share (Obj. 5)
- Dividend yield (Obj. 5)

Corporate Annual Reports
- Management analysis (Obj. 6)
- Internal control report Obj. 6)
- Audit report (Obj. 6)

Learning Objectives

Obj.1 Describe the usefulness of financial statements and methods of analysis.

Obj.2 Describe and illustrate global analysis of financial statements.

Obj.3 Describe and illustrate metrics used to analyze liquidity.

Obj.4 Describe and illustrate metrics used to analyze solvency.

Obj.5 Describe and illustrate metrics used to analyze profitability.

Obj.6 Describe corporate annual reports.

Chapter Metrics

This chapter uses a variety of metrics to analyze financial statements to assess a company's liquidity, solvency, and profitability.

Nike Connection

Rose Carson/ Shutterstock.com

"Just do it." These three words identify one of the most recognizable brands in the world, Nike. While this phrase inspires athletes to "compete and achieve their potential," it also defines the company.

Nike (NKE) began in 1964 as a partnership between University of Oregon track coach Bill Bowerman and one of his former student-athletes, Phil Knight. The two began by selling shoes imported from Japan out of the back of Knight's car to athletes at track and field events. As sales grew, the company opened retail outlets and began to develop its own shoes. In 1971, the company, originally named Blue Ribbon Sports, commissioned a graphic design student at Portland State University to develop the Nike Swoosh logo for a fee of $35. In 1978, the company changed its name to Nike, and in 1980, it sold its first shares of stock to the public.

Nike would have been a great company in which to have invested. If you had invested in Nike's common stock back in 1990, you would have paid $5 per share. Recently, Nike's stock sold for $120 (adjusted for 2:1 stock split) per share. Unfortunately, you can't invest using hindsight.

How then should you select companies in which to invest? Like any significant purchase, you should do some research to guide your investment decision. If you were buying a car, for example, you might go to **Consumer Reports** or **Car and Driver magazine** to obtain reviews, ratings, prices, specifications, options, and fuel economy across a number of vehicles. In deciding whether to invest in a company, you can use financial analysis to gain insight into a company's past performance and future prospects. This chapter describes and illustrates metrics and analyses to assist you in making investment decisions such as whether or not to invest in Nike's stock.

Source: http://www.nikebiz.com/.

Objective 1
Describe the usefulness of financial statements and methods of analysis.

Analysis of Financial Statements

The objective of financial statements is to provide useful information to a company's stakeholders about the company's financial condition and performance. A company's stakeholders include a wide range of potential users including creditors, investors, managers, employees, suppliers, customers, and government agencies. Because of the wide range of potential users, the financial statements illustrated throughout this texts are often referred to as **general-purpose financial statements**.

Usefulness of Financial Statements

A company's financial condition and performance are normally analyzed and interpreted by focusing upon the following characteristics:

- Liquidity
- Solvency
- Profitability

Liquidity is the ability to convert assets to cash. Short-term creditors such as suppliers and banks often focus upon a company's liquidity as a means of evaluating the ability of the company to pay its accounts payable and short-term debt. The current assets and liabilities reported on the balance sheet provide useful information on a company's liquidity.

Solvency is the ability of a company to pay its debts as they become due over a long period of time. Long-term creditors, such as banks and bondholders, focus upon a company's solvency as a means of evaluating whether the company will continue to make its periodic interest payments and will be able to repay its loans at their maturity. The relationship among assets, liabilities, and equity reported on the balance sheet provides useful information on solvency. In addition, the income statement and statement of cash flows provide useful information on the ability of the company to generate cash to pay periodic interest and loans at maturity.

Profitability is the ability of a company to generate net income related to its invested assets. Stockholders, managers, and employees focus on profitability in evaluating whether a company's stock price will increase, whether the company will pay dividends, and whether the company will continue in business. The income statement and balance sheet provide useful information on the ability of a company to generate profits from its assets.

Methods of Analysis

Financial statements may be analyzed using a variety of methods and metrics. In this chapter, we focus upon the following two methods of analysis:

1. **Global analysis**, which computes changes in amounts, percentages of amounts, and percentage changes in amounts for each financial statement.
2. **Component analysis**, which computes metrics for liquidity, solvency, and profitability for components of financial statements.

Financial statement analysis is most effective when both methods of analyses are used and when results are compared over time and with competitors.

Global Analysis

Objective 2
Describe basic financial statement analytical methods.

Users analyze a company's financial statements using a variety of analytical methods. Three such methods are as follows:

1. Horizontal analysis
2. Vertical analysis
3. Common-sized statements

Horizontal Analysis

The percentage analysis of increases and decreases in related items in comparative financial statements is called **horizontal analysis**. Each item on the most recent statement is compared with the related item on one or more earlier statements in terms of the following:

1. *Amount* of increase or decrease
2. *Percent* of increase or decrease

When comparing statements, the earlier statement is normally used as the base for computing increases and decreases.

Exhibit 1 illustrates horizontal analysis for the December 31, 20Y6 and 20Y5 balance sheets of Mooney Company. In Exhibit 1, the December 31, 20Y5, balance sheet (the earliest year presented) is used as the base.

Exhibit 1 indicates that total assets decreased by $91,000 (7.4%), liabilities decreased by $133,000 (30.0%), and stockholders' equity increased by $42,000 (5.3%).

Exhibit 1 Comparative Balance Sheet—Horizontal Analysis

Mooney Company
Comparative Balance Sheet
December 31, 20Y6 and 20Y5

	Dec. 31, 20Y6	Dec. 31, 20Y5	Increase (Decrease) Amount	Increase (Decrease) Percent
Assets				
Current assets	$ 550,000	$ 533,000	$ 17,000	3.2%
Long-term investments	95,000	177,500	(82,500)	(46.5%)
Property, plant, and equipment (net)	444,500	470,000	(25,500)	(5.4%)
Intangible assets	50,000	50,000	—	—
Total assets	$1,139,500	$1,230,500	$ (91,000)	(7.4%)
Liabilities				
Current liabilities	$ 210,000	$ 243,000	$ (33,000)	(13.6%)
Long-term liabilities	100,000	200,000	(100,000)	(50.0%)
Total liabilities	$ 310,000	$ 443,000	$(133,000)	(30.0%)
Stockholders' Equity				
Preferred 6% stock, $100 par	$ 150,000	$ 150,000	—	—
Common stock, $10 par	500,000	500,000	—	—
Retained earnings	179,500	137,500	$ 42,000	30.5%
Total stockholders' equity	$ 829,500	$ 787,500	$ 42,000	5.3%
Total liabilities and stockholders' equity	$1,139,500	$1,230,500	$ (91,000)	(7.4%)

The balance sheets in Exhibit 1 may be expanded or supported by a separate schedule that includes the individual asset and liability accounts. For example, Exhibit 2 is a supporting schedule of Mooney's current asset accounts.

Exhibit 2 indicates that while cash and temporary investments increased, accounts receivable and inventories decreased. The decrease in accounts receivable could be caused by improved collection policies. The decrease in inventories could be caused by increased sales.

Exhibit 2 Comparative Schedule of Current Assets—Horizontal Analysis

Mooney Company
Comparative Schedule of Current Assets
December 31, 20Y6 and 20Y5

	Dec. 31, 20Y6	Dec. 31, 20Y5	Increase (Decrease) Amount	Increase (Decrease) Percent
Cash	$ 90,500	$ 64,700	$ 25,800	39.9%
Temporary investments	75,000	60,000	15,000	25.0%
Accounts receivable (net)	115,000	120,000	(5,000)	(4.2%)
Inventories	264,000	283,000	(19,000)	(6.7%)
Prepaid expenses	5,500	5,300	200	3.8%
Total current assets	$550,000	$533,000	$ 17,000	3.2%

In a recent balance sheet, Nike reported an increase in current assets of 14.3%.

Nike Connection

Exhibit 3 illustrates horizontal analysis for the 20Y6 and 20Y5 income statements of Mooney Company. Exhibit 3 indicates an increase in sales of $298,000, or 24.8%. However, the percentage increase in sales of 24.8% was accompanied by an even greater percentage increase in the cost of goods (merchandise) sold of 27.2%.[1] Thus, gross profit increased by only 19.7% rather than by the 24.8% increase in sales.

Exhibit 3 Comparative Income Statement—Horizontal Analysis

Mooney Company
Comparative Income Statement
For the Years Ended December 31, 20Y6 and 20Y5

			Increase (Decrease)	
	20Y6	**20Y5**	**Amount**	**Percent**
Sales	$ 1,498,000	$1,200,000	$ 298,000	24.8%
Cost of goods sold	(1,043,000)	(820,000)	223,000	27.2%
Gross profit	$ 455,000	$ 380,000	$ 75,000	19.7%
Selling expenses	$ (191,000)	$ (147,000)	$ 44,000	29.9%
Administrative expenses	(104,000)	(97,400)	6,600	6.8%
Total operating expenses	$ (295,000)	$ (244,400)	$ 50,600	20.7%
Income from operations	$ 160,000	$ 135,600	$ 24,400	18.0%
Other revenue and expense:				
Other revenue	8,500	11,000	(2,500)	(22.7%)
Other expense (interest)	(6,000)	(12,000)	(6,000)	(50.0%)
Income before income tax	$ 162,500	$ 134,600	$ 27,900	20.7%
Income tax expense	(71,500)	(58,100)	13,400	23.1%
Net income	$ 91,000	$ 76,500	$ 14,500	19.0%

Exhibit 3 also indicates that selling expenses increased by 29.9%. Thus, the 24.0% increase in sales could have been caused by an advertising campaign, which increased selling expenses. Administrative expenses increased by only 6.8%, total operating expenses increased by 20.7%, and income from operations increased by 18.0%. Interest expense decreased by 50.0%. This decrease was probably caused by the 50.0% decrease in long-term liabilities (Exhibit 1). Overall, net income increased by 19.0%, a favorable result.

In a recent income statement, Nike reported an increase in sales of 9.2%, an increase in gross profit of 11.5%, and an increase in net income of 17.7%.

Exhibit 4 illustrates horizontal analysis for the 20Y6 and 20Y5 statement of stockholders' equity of Mooney Company. Exhibit 4 shows that preferred stock and common stock did not change during the year. The 20Y6 ending balance of retained earnings increased by 30.5%. This increase was due to a 19.0% increase in net income, which was partially offset by a 33.3% increase in dividends to common stockholders.

1. The term *cost of goods sold* is often used in practice in place of *cost of merchandise sold*. Such usage is followed in this chapter.

Exhibit 4 Comparative Statement of Stockholders' Equity—Horizontal Analysis

Mooney Company
Comparative Statement of Stockholders' Equity
For the year ended December 31, 20Y6 and 20Y5

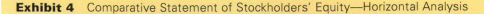

	Preferred Stock				Common Stock				Retained Earnings			
			Increase (Decrease)				Increase (Decrease)				Increase (Decrease)	
	20Y6	20Y5	Amount	Percent	20Y6	20Y5	Amount	Percent	20Y6	20Y5	Amount	Percent
Balances, Jan. 1	$150,000	$150,000	$0	0.0%	$500,000	$500,000	$0	0.0%	$137,500	$100,000	$37,500	37.5%
Net income									91,000	76,500	14,500	19.0%
Dividends:												
Preferred stock									(9,000)	(9,000)	0	0.0%
Common stock									(40,000)	(30,000)	(10,000)	33.3%
Balances, Dec. 31	$150,000	$150,000	$0	0.0%	$500,000	$500,000	$0	0.0%	$179,500	$137,500	$42,000	30.5%

Vertical Analysis

The percentage analysis of the relationship of each component in a financial statement to a total within the statement is called **vertical analysis**. Although vertical analysis is applied to a single statement, it may be applied to the same statement over time. This enhances the analysis by showing how the percentages of each item have changed.

In vertical analysis of the balance sheet, the percentages are computed as follows:

1. Each asset item is stated as a percent of the total assets.
2. Each liability and stockholders' equity item is stated as a percent of the total liabilities and stockholders' equity.

Exhibit 5 illustrates the vertical analysis of the December 31, 20Y6 and 20Y5 balance sheets of Mooney Company. Exhibit 5 indicates that current assets increased from 43.3% to 48.3% of total assets. Long-term investments decreased from 14.4% to 8.3% of total assets. Stockholders' equity increased from 64.0% to 72.8% with a comparable decrease in liabilities.

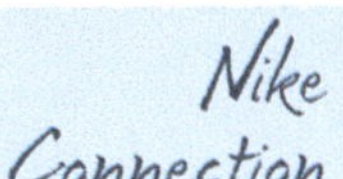

In a recent balance sheet, Nike reported that current assets were 74.0% of total assets.

In a vertical analysis of the income statement, each item is stated as a percent of sales. Exhibit 6 illustrates the vertical analysis of the 20Y6 and 20Y5 income statements of Mooney Company.

Exhibit 6 indicates a decrease of the gross profit rate from 31.7% in 20Y5 to 30.4% in 20Y6. Although this is only a 1.3 percentage points (31.7% − 30.4%) decrease, in dollars of potential gross profit, it represents a decrease of about $19,500 (1.3% × $1,498,000). Thus, a small percentage decrease can have a large dollar effect.

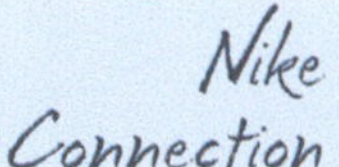

In an income statement, Nike reported that gross profit was 46.0% of sales, and sales and administrative expenses were 32.3% of sales.

Exhibit 5 Comparative Balance Sheet—Vertical Analysis

Mooney Company
Comparative Balance Sheet
December 31, 20Y6 and 20Y5

	Dec. 31, 20Y6		Dec. 31, 20Y5	
	Amount	**Percent**	**Amount**	**Percent**
Assets				
Current assets	$ 550,000	48.3%	$ 533,000	43.3%
Long-term investments	95,000	8.3	177,500	14.4
Property, plant, and equipment (net)	444,500	39.0	470,000	38.2
Intangible assets	50,000	4.4	50,000	4.1
Total assets	$1,139,500	100.0%	$1,230,500	100.0%
Liabilities				
Current liabilities	$ 210,000	18.4%	$ 243,000	19.7%
Long-term liabilities	100,000	8.8	200,000	16.3
Total liabilities	$ 310,000	27.2%	$ 443,000	36.0%
Stockholders' Equity				
Preferred 6% stock, $100 par	$ 150,000	13.2%	$ 150,000	12.2%
Common stock, $10 par	500,000	43.9	500,000	40.6
Retained earnings	179,500	15.7	137,500	11.2
Total stockholders' equity	$ 829,500	72.8%	$ 787,500	64.0%
Total liabilities and stockholders' equity	$1,139,500	100.0%	$1,230,500	100.0%

Exhibit 6 Comparative Income Statement—Vertical Analysis

Mooney Company
Comparative Income Statement
For the Years Ended December 31, 20Y6 and 20Y5

	20Y6		20Y5	
	Amount	**Percent**	**Amount**	**Percent**
Sales	$ 1,498,000	100.0%	$1,200,000	100.0%
Cost of goods sold	(1,043,000)	69.6	(820,000)	68.3
Gross profit	$ 455,000	30.4%	$ 380,000	31.7%
Selling expenses	$ (191,000)	12.8%	$ (147,000)	12.3%
Administrative expenses	(104,000)	6.9	(97,400)	8.1
Total operating expenses	$ (295,000)	19.7%	$ (244,400)	20.4%
Income from operations	$ 160,000	10.7%	$ 135,600	11.3%
Other revenue and expense:				
Other revenue	8,500	0.6	11,000	0.9
Other expense (interest)	(6,000)	0.4	(12,000)	1.0
Income before income tax	$ 162,500	10.9%	$ 134,600	11.2%
Income tax expense	(71,500)	4.8	(58,100)	4.8
Net income	$ 91,000	6.1%	$ 76,500	6.4%

Common-Sized Statements

In a **common-sized statement**, all items are expressed as percentages with no dollar amounts shown. Common-sized statements are often useful for comparing one company with another or for comparing a company with industry averages.

Exhibit 7 illustrates common-sized income statements for Mooney Company and Lowell Corporation.

Exhibit 7 Common-Sized Income Statement

	Mooney Company	Lowell Corporation
Sales	100.0%	100.0%
Cost of goods sold	(69.6)	(70.0)
Gross profit	30.4%	30.0%
Selling expenses	(12.8)%	(11.5)%
Administrative expenses	(6.9)	(4.1)
Total operating expenses	(19.7)%	(15.6)%
Income from operations	10.7%	14.4%
Other revenue and expense:		
Other revenue	0.6	0.6
Other expense (interest)	(0.4)	(0.5)
Income before income tax	10.9%	14.5%
Income tax expense	(4.8)	(5.5)
Net income	6.1%	9.0%

Exhibit 7 indicates that Mooney Company has a slightly higher rate of gross profit (30.4%) than Lowell Corporation (30.0%). However, Mooney has a higher percentage of selling expenses (12.8%) and administrative expenses (6.9%) than does Lowell (11.5% and 4.1%). As a result, the income from operations of Mooney (10.7%) is less than that of Lowell (14.4%).

The unfavorable difference of 3.7 (14.4% − 10.7%) percentage points in income from operations would concern the managers and other stakeholders of Mooney. The underlying causes of the difference should be investigated and possibly corrected. For example, Mooney Company may decide to outsource some of its administrative duties so that its administrative expenses are more comparative to those of Lowell Corporation.

Objective 3

Describe and illustrate metrics used to analyze liquidity.

Component Analysis: Liquidity Metrics

Liquidity is the ability of a company to convert assets into cash, which affects its ability to pay short-term debts such as accounts payable. The following three types of metrics are commonly used to assess liquidity:

1. Current position metrics
2. Accounts receivable metrics
3. Inventory metrics

Current Position Analysis

A company's ability to pay its current liabilities is called **current position analysis.** It is of special interest to short-term creditors and includes the computation and analysis of the following:

- Working capital
- Current ratio
- Quick ratio

Working Capital A company's **working capital** is computed as follows:

$$\textbf{Working Capital} = \textbf{Current Assets} - \textbf{Current Liabilities}$$

To illustrate, the working capital for Mooney Company for 20Y6 and 20Y5 is computed as follows:

	20Y6	20Y5
Current assets	$550,000	$533,000
Less current liabilities	(210,000)	(243,000)
Working capital	$340,000	$290,000

The working capital is used to evaluate a company's ability to pay current liabilities. A company's working capital is often monitored monthly, quarterly, and yearly by creditors and other debtors. However, it is difficult to use working capital to compare companies of different sizes. For example, working capital of $250,000 may be adequate for a local hardware store, but it would be inadequate for The Home Depot.

Current Ratio The **current ratio**, sometimes called the *working capital ratio* or *bankers' ratio,* is computed as follows:

$$\textbf{Current Ratio} = \frac{\textbf{Current Assets}}{\textbf{Current Liabilities}}$$

To illustrate, the current ratio for Mooney Company for 20Y6 and 20Y5 is computed as follows:

	20Y6	20Y5
Current assets	$550,000	$533,000
Current liabilities	$210,000	$243,000
Current ratio	2.6 ($550,000 ÷ $210,000)	2.2 ($533,000 ÷ $243,000)

The current ratio is a more reliable indicator of the ability to pay current liabilities than is working capital. To illustrate, assume that as of December 31, 20Y6, the working capital of a competitor is much greater than $340,000, but its current ratio is only 1.3. Considering these facts alone, Mooney Company, with its current ratio of 2.6, is in a more favorable position to obtain short-term credit than the competitor, which has the greater amount of working capital.

Quick Ratio One limitation of working capital and the current ratio is that they do not consider the makeup of the current assets. Because of this, two companies may have the same working capital and current ratios but differ significantly in their ability to pay their current liabilities.

To illustrate, the current assets and liabilities for Mooney Company and Wendt Corporation as of December 31, 20Y6, are as follows:

	Mooney Company	Wendt Corporation
Current assets:		
Cash	$ 90,500	$ 45,500
Temporary investments	75,000	25,000
Accounts receivable (net)	115,000	90,000
Inventories	264,000	380,000
Prepaid expenses	5,500	9,500
Total current assets	$550,000	$550,000
Total current assets	$550,000	$550,000
Less current liabilities	(210,000)	(210,000)
Working capital	$340,000	$340,000
Current ratio ($550,000/$210,000)	2.6	2.6

Mooney and Wendt both have a working capital of $340,000 and current ratios of 2.6. Wendt, however, has more of its current assets in inventories. These inventories must be sold and the receivables collected before all the current liabilities can be paid. This takes time. In addition, if the market for its product declines, Wendt may have difficulty selling its inventory. This, in turn, could impair its ability to pay its current liabilities.

In contrast, Mooney's current assets contain more cash, temporary investments, and accounts receivable, which can easily be converted to cash. Thus, Mooney is in a stronger current position than Wendt to pay its current liabilities.

A ratio that measures the "instant" debt-paying ability of a company is the **quick ratio**, sometimes called the *acid-test ratio*. The quick ratio is computed as follows:

$$\textbf{Quick Ratio} = \frac{\textbf{Quick Assets}}{\textbf{Current Liabilities}}$$

Quick assets are cash and other current assets that can be easily converted to cash. Quick assets normally include cash, temporary investments, and receivables.

To illustrate, the quick ratio for Mooney Company is computed as follows:

	20Y6	20Y5
Quick assets:		
Cash	$ 90,500	$ 64,700
Temporary investments	75,000	60,000
Accounts receivable (net)	115,000	120,000
Total quick assets	$280,500	$244,700
Current liabilities	$210,000	$243,000
Quick ratio	1.3*	1.0**

*1.3 = $280,500 ÷ $210,000
**1.0 = $244,700 ÷ $243,000

Nike Connection In a recent balance sheet, Nike reported working capital of $9,642 million, a current ratio of 2.5, and a quick ratio of 1.5.

Accounts Receivable Metrics

A company's accounts receivable metrics reflect the efficiency of collecting accounts receivable. These metrics include the following:

- Accounts receivable turnover
- Days' sales in receivables

Collecting accounts receivable as quickly as possible improves a company's liquidity. In addition, the cash collected from receivables may be used to improve or expand operations. Quick collection of receivables also reduces the risk of uncollectible accounts.

Accounts Receivable Turnover The **accounts receivable turnover** is computed as follows:

$$\textbf{Accounts Receivable Turnover} = \frac{\textbf{Sales}^2}{\textbf{Average Accounts Receivable}}$$

To illustrate, the accounts receivable turnover for Mooney Company for 20Y6 and 20Y5 is computed below.

	20Y6	20Y5
Sales	$ 1,498,000	$1,200,000
Accounts receivable (net):		
Beginning of year	$ 120,000	$ 140,000
End of year	115,000	120,000
Total	$ 235,000	$ 260,000
Average accounts receivable	$117,500 ($235,000 ÷ 2)	$130,000 ($260,000 ÷ 2)
Accounts receivable turnover	12.7 ($1,498,000 ÷ $117,500)	9.2 ($1,200,000 ÷ $130,000)

The increase in Mooney's accounts receivable turnover from 9.2 to 12.7 indicates that the collection of receivables has improved during 20Y6. This may be due to a change in how credit is granted, collection practices, or both.

For Mooney Company, the average accounts receivable was computed using the accounts receivable balance at the beginning and the end of the year. When sales are seasonal and thus vary throughout the year, monthly balances of receivables are often used. Also, if sales on account include notes receivable as well as accounts receivable, notes and accounts receivable are normally combined for analysis.

Days' Sales in Receivables The **days' sales in receivables** is computed as follows:[3]

$$\textbf{Days' Sales in Receivables} = \frac{\textbf{Average Accounts Receivable}}{\textbf{Average Daily Sales}}$$

where

$$\textbf{Average Daily Sales} = \frac{\textbf{Sales}}{\textbf{365 days}}$$

2. If known, credit sales should be used in the numerator. Because credit sales are not normally known by external users, sales is used in the numerator.

3. The days' sales in receivables can also be computed as: 365 Days ÷ Accounts Receivable Turnover

To illustrate, the days' sales in receivables for Mooney Company is computed below.

	20Y6	20Y5
Average accounts receivable	$117,500 ($235,000 ÷ 2)	$130,000 ($260,000 ÷ 2)
Average daily sales	$4,104 ($1,498,000 ÷ 365)	$3,288 ($1,200,000 ÷ 365)
Days' sales in receivables	28.6 ($117,500 ÷ $4,104)	39.5 ($130,000 ÷ $3,288)

The days' sales in receivables is an estimate of the time (in days) that the accounts receivable have been outstanding. The days' sales in receivables is often compared with a company's credit terms to evaluate the efficiency of the collection of receivables.

To illustrate, if Mooney's credit terms are 2/10, n/30, then Mooney was very *inefficient* in collecting receivables in 20Y5. In other words, receivables should have been collected in 30 days or less but were being collected in 39.5 days. Although collections improved during 20Y6 to 28.6 days, there is probably still room for improvement.

Days' sales in receivables and accounts receivable turnover are related. Specifically, days' sales in receivables can be computed by dividing 365 days by the accounts receivable turnover. To illustrate, Mooney Company's 20Y6 days' sales in receivable is computed as 28.7 days (365 days ÷ 12.7). The small difference of 28.7 days and the 28.6 days computed earlier is due to rounding.

In recent financial statements, Nike reported accounts receivable turnover of 9.0 and days' sales in receivables of 40.5 days.

Inventory Metrics

A company's inventory metrics reflect the efficiency of purchasing and selling inventory. These metrics include the following:

- Inventory turnover
- Days' sales in inventory

Excess inventory decreases liquidity by tying up funds (cash) in inventory. In addition, excess inventory increases insurance expense, property taxes, storage costs, and other related expenses. These expenses further reduce funds that could be used elsewhere to improve or expand operations.

Excess inventory also increases the risk of losses because of price declines or obsolescence of the inventory. On the other hand, a company should keep enough inventory in stock so that it doesn't lose sales because of lack of inventory.

Inventory Turnover The **inventory turnover** is computed as follows:

$$\textbf{Inventory Turnover} = \frac{\textbf{Cost of Goods Sold}}{\textbf{Average Inventory}}$$

To illustrate, the inventory turnover for Mooney Company for 20Y6 and 20Y5 is computed as follows:

	20Y6	20Y5
Cost of goods sold	$1,043,000	$820,000
Inventories:		
Beginning of year	$ 283,000	$311,000
End of year	264,000	283,000
Total	$ 547,000	$594,000
Average inventory	$273,500 ($547,000 ÷ 2)	$297,000 ($594,000 ÷ 2)
Inventory turnover	3.8 ($1,043,000 ÷ $273,500)	2.8 ($820,000 ÷ $297,000)

The increase in Mooney's inventory turnover from 2.8 to 3.8 indicates that the management of inventory has improved in 20Y6. The inventory turnover improved because of an increase in the cost of goods sold, which indicates more sales, and a decrease in the average inventories.

What is considered a good inventory turnover varies by type of inventory, companies, and industries. For example, grocery stores have a higher inventory turnover than jewelers or furniture stores. Likewise, within a grocery store, perishable foods have a higher turnover than the soaps and cleansers.

Days' Sales in Inventory The **days' sales in inventory** is computed as follows:[4]

$$\text{Days' Sales in Inventory} = \frac{\text{Average Inventory}}{\text{Average Daily Cost of Goods Sold}}$$

where

$$\text{Average Daily Cost of Goods Sold} = \frac{\text{Cost of Goods Sold}}{\text{365 days}}$$

To illustrate, the days' sales in inventory for Mooney Company is computed below.

	20Y6	20Y5
Average inventory	$273,500 ($547,000 ÷ 2)	$297,000 ($594,000 ÷ 2)
Average daily cost of goods sold	$2,858 ($1,043,000 ÷ 365)	$2,247 ($820,000 ÷ 365)
Days' sales in inventory	95.7 ($273,500 ÷ $2,858)	132.2 ($297,000 ÷ $2,247)

The days' sales in inventory is a rough measure of the length of time it takes to purchase, sell, and replace the inventory. Mooney's days' sales in inventory improved from 132.2 days to 95.7 days during 20Y6. This is a major improvement in managing inventory.

Days' sales in inventory and inventory turnover are related. Specifically, days' sales in inventory can be computed by dividing 365 days by the inventory turnover. To illustrate, Mooney Company's 20Y6 days' sales in inventory is computed as 96.1 days (365 days ÷ 3.8). The small difference of 96.1 days and the 95.7 days computed earlier is due to rounding.

In recent financial statements, Nike reported inventory turnover of 4.0 and days' sales in inventory of 91.4 days.

Nike Connection

4. The days' sales in inventory can also be computed as: 365 days ÷ Accounts Receivable Turnover

Objective 4

Describe and illustrate metrics used to analyze solvency.

Component Analysis: Solvency Metrics

Solvency is the ability of a company to pay its debts as they become due over a long period of time, which includes the company's ability to pay interest and loans as they mature. Metrics used to assess solvency include the following:

- Net assets
- Debt ratio
- Ratio of liabilities to stockholders' equity
- Ratio of fixed assets to long-term liabilities
- Times interest earned

Net Assets

A company's **net assets**, which equals the company's stockholders' equity, is computed as follows:

Net Assets = Total Assets − Total Liabilities

To illustrate, the net assets for Mooney Company for 20Y6 and 20Y5 are as follows:

	20Y6	20Y5
Total assets	$1,139,500	$1,230,000
Total liabilities	(310,000)	(443,000)
Net assets	$ 829,500	$ 787,000

Mooney's net assets increased $42,500 during 20Y6, which provides creditors an additional margin of safety.

Debt Ratio

The **debt ratio**, sometimes called the debt to assets ratio, is computed as follows:

$$\textbf{Debt Ratio} = \frac{\textbf{Total Liabilities}}{\textbf{Total Assets}}$$

To illustrate, the debt ratio for Mooney Company is computed as follows:

	20Y6	20Y5
Total liabilities	$310,000	$443,000
Total assets	$1,139,500	$1,230,000
Debt ratio	27.2% ($310,000 ÷ $1,139,500)	36.0% ($443,000 ÷$1,230,000)

Mooney's debt ratio decreased from 36.0% to 27.2% during 20Y6. This indicates Mooney decreased the percentage of its assets financed by debt. This provides creditors an additional margin of safety.

Ratio of Liabilities to Stockholders' Equity

Like the debt ratio, the **ratio of liabilities to stockholders' equity** measures how much of the company is financed by debt and equity. It is computed as follows:

$$\textbf{Ratio of Liabilities to Stockholders' Equity} = \frac{\textbf{Total Liabilities}}{\textbf{Total Stockholders' Equity}}$$

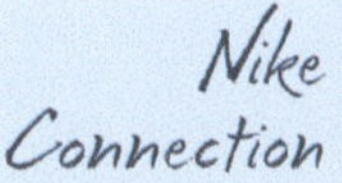

In recent financial statements, Nike reported a debt ratio of 41.2% and a ratio of liabilities to stockholders' equity of 0.7.

To illustrate, the ratio of liabilities to stockholders' equity for Mooney Company is computed as follows:

	20Y6	20Y5
Total liabilities	$310,000	$443,000
Total stockholders' equity	$829,500	$787,500
Ratio of liabilities to stockholders' equity	0.4 ($310,000 ÷ $829,500)	0.6 ($443,000 ÷ $787,500)

Mooney's ratio of liabilities to stockholders' equity decreased from 0.6 to 0.4 during 20Y6. This is an improvement and indicates that Mooney's creditors have an adequate margin of safety.

Ratio of Fixed Assets to Long-Term Liabilities

The **ratio of fixed assets to long-term liabilities** provides a measure of whether noteholders or bondholders will be paid. Since fixed assets are often pledged as security for long-term notes and bonds, it is computed as follows:

$$\textbf{Ratio of Fixed Assets to Long-Term Liabilities} = \frac{\textbf{Fixed Assets (net)}}{\textbf{Long-Term Liabilities}}$$

To illustrate, the ratio of fixed assets to long-term liabilities for Mooney Company is computed below.

	20Y6	20Y5
Fixed assets (net)	$444,500	$470,000
Long-term liabilities	$100,000	$200,000
Ratio of fixed assets to long-term liabilities	4.4 ($444,500 ÷ $100,000)	2.4 ($470,000 ÷ $200,000)

During 20Y6, Mooney's ratio of fixed assets to long-term liabilities increased from 2.4 to 4.4. This increase was due primarily to Mooney paying off one-half of its long-term liabilities in 20Y6.

Times Interest Earned

Times interest earned, sometimes called the *fixed charge coverage ratio,* measures the risk that interest payments will not be made if earnings decrease. It is computed as follows:

$$\textbf{Times Interest Earned} = \frac{\textbf{Income Before Income Tax + Interest Expense}}{\textbf{Interest Expense}}$$

Interest expense is paid before income taxes. In other words, interest expense is deducted in determining taxable income and, thus, income tax. For this reason, income *before taxes* is used in computing the times interest earned.

The *higher* the ratio, the more likely interest payments will be paid if earnings decrease. To illustrate, the times interest earned for Mooney Company is computed below.

	20Y6	20Y5
Income before income tax	$162,500	$134,600
Add interest expense	6,000	12,000
Amount available to pay interest	$168,500	$146,600
Times interest earned	28.1 ($168,500 ÷ $6,000)	12.2 ($146,600 ÷ $12,000)

The times interest earned ratio improved from 12.2 to 28.1 during 20Y6. This indicates that Mooney Company has sufficient earnings to pay interest expense.

The times interest earned ratio can be adapted for use with dividends on preferred stock. In this case, *times preferred dividends earned* is computed as follows:

$$\textbf{Times Preferred Dividends Earned} = \frac{\textbf{Net Income}}{\textbf{Preferred Dividends}}$$

Since dividends are paid after taxes, net income is used in computing the times preferred dividends earned. The *higher* the ratio, the more likely preferred dividend payments will be paid if earnings decrease.

Objective 5
Describe and illustrate metrics used to analyze profitability.

Component Analysis: Profitability Metrics

Profitability analysis focuses on the ability of a company to earn profits. This ability is reflected in the company's operating results, as reported on its income statement. The ability to earn profits also depends on the assets the company has available for use in its operations, as reported on its balance sheet. Thus, income statement and balance sheet relationships are often used in evaluating profitability.

Common profitability analyses include the following:

- Asset turnover
- Return on total assets
- Return on stockholders' equity
- Return on common stockholders' equity
- Earnings per share on common stock
- Price-earnings ratio
- Dividends per share
- Dividend yield

Asset Turnover

The **asset turnover** measures how effectively a company uses its long-term operating assets to generate sales. It is computed as follows:

$$\textbf{Asset Turnover} = \frac{\textbf{Sales}}{\textbf{Average Long-Term Operating Assets}}$$

A company's long-term operating assets consist of property, plant, and equipment (net of accumulated depreciation) plus natural resources and intangible assets.

To illustrate, the asset turnover for Mooney Company is computed below.

	20Y6	20Y5
Sales	$1,498,000	$1,200,000
Long-term operating assets:		
Beginning of year	$ 520,000[1]	$ 450,000
End of year	494,500[2]	520,000
Total	$1,014,500	$ 970,000
Average long-term operating assets	$507,250 ($1,014,500 ÷ 2)	$485,000 ($970,000 ÷ 2)
Asset turnover	3.0 ($1,498,000 ÷ $507,250)	2.5 ($1,200,000 ÷ $485,000)

1. $470,000 + $50,000
2. $444,500 + $50,000

The asset turnover indicates that Mooney's use of its operating assets has improved in 20Y6. This was primarily due to the increase in sales in 20Y6.

Return on Total Assets

The **return on total assets** measures the profitability of total assets, without considering how the assets are financed. In other words, this rate is not affected by the portion of assets financed by creditors or stockholders. It is computed as follows:

$$\textbf{Return on Total Assets} = \frac{\textbf{Net Income + Interest Expense}}{\textbf{Average Total Assets}}$$

The return on total assets is computed by adding interest expense to net income. By adding interest expense to net income, the effect of whether the assets are financed by creditors (debt) or stockholders (equity) is eliminated. Because net income includes any income earned from long-term investments, the average total assets includes long-term investments as well as the net operating assets.

To illustrate, the return on total assets by Mooney Company is computed below.

	20Y6	20Y5
Net income	$ 91,000	$ 76,500
Plus interest expense	6,000	12,000
Total	$ 97,000	$ 88,500
Total assets:		
Beginning of year	$1,230,500	$1,187,500
End of year	1,139,500	1,230,500
Total	$2,370,000	$2,418,000
Average total assets	$1,185,000 ($2,370,000 ÷ 2)	$1,209,000 ($2,418,000 ÷ 2)
Return on total assets	8.2% ($97,000 ÷ $1,185,000)	7.3% ($88,500 ÷ $1,209,000)

The return on total assets improved from 7.3% to 8.2% during 20Y6.

The *return on operating assets* is sometimes computed when there are large amounts of nonoperating income and expense. It is computed as follows:

$$\textbf{Return on Operating Assets} = \frac{\textbf{Income from Operations}}{\textbf{Average Operating Assets}}$$

Since Mooney Company does not have a significant amount of nonoperating income and expense, the return on operating assets is not illustrated.

Return on Stockholders' Equity

The **return on stockholders' equity** measures the rate of income earned on the amount invested by the stockholders. It is computed as follows:

$$\textbf{Return on Stockholders' Equity} = \frac{\textbf{Net Income}}{\textbf{Average Total Stockholders' Equity}}$$

To illustrate, the return on stockholders' equity for Mooney Company is computed below.

	20Y6	20Y5
Net income	$ 91,000	$ 76,500
Stockholders' equity:		
Beginning of year	$ 787,500	$ 750,000
End of year	829,500	787,500
Total	$1,617,000	$1,537,500
Average stockholders' equity	$808,500 ($1,617,000 ÷ 2)	$768,750 ($1,537,500 ÷ 2)
Return on stockholders' equity	11.3% ($91,000 ÷ $808,500)	10.0% ($76,500 ÷ $768,750)

The return on stockholders' equity improved from 10.0% to 11.3% during 20Y6.

Leverage involves using debt to increase the return on an investment. The return on stockholders' equity is normally higher than the return on total assets. This is because of the effect of leverage.

For Mooney Company, the effect of leverage for 20Y6 is 3.1%, computed as follows:

Return on stockholders' equity	11.3 %
Less return on total assets	(8.2)
Effect of leverage	3.1 %

Exhibit 8 shows the 20Y6 and 20Y5 effects of leverage for Mooney Company.

Exhibit 8
Effects of Leverage

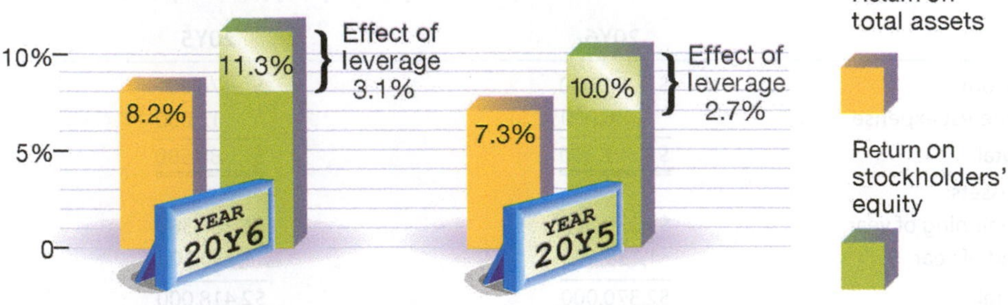

Return on Common Stockholders' Equity

The **return on common stockholders' equity** measures the rate of profits earned on the amount invested by the common stockholders. It is computed as follows:

$$\textbf{Return on Common Stockholders' Equity} = \frac{\textbf{Net Income} - \textbf{Preferred Dividends}}{\textbf{Average Common Stockholders' Equity}}$$

Because preferred stockholders rank ahead of the common stockholders in their claim on earnings, any preferred dividends are subtracted from net income in computing the return on common stockholders' equity.

Assuming $500,000 of common stock was outstanding in 20Y4, Mooney's common stockholders' equity determined from Exhibit 4 is as follows:

	December 31		
	20Y6	20Y5	20Y4
Common stock, $10 par	$500,000	$500,000	$500,000
Retained earnings	179,500	137,500	100,000
Common stockholders' equity	$679,500	$637,500	$600,000

The retained earnings on December 31, 20Y4, of $100,000 is the same as the retained earnings on January 1, 20Y5, as shown in Mooney's statement of stockholders' equity in Exhibit 4.

Mooney Company had $150,000 of 6% preferred stock outstanding on December 31, 20Y6 and 20Y5. Thus, preferred dividends of $9,000 ($150,000 × 6%) are deducted from net income.

The return on common stockholders' equity for Mooney Company is computed below.

	20Y6	20Y5
Net income	$ 91,000	$ 76,500
Less preferred dividends	(9,000)	(9,000)
Total	$ 82,000	$ 67,500
Common stockholders' equity:		
Beginning of year	$ 637,500	$ 600,000
End of year	679,500	637,500
Total	$1,317,000	$1,237,500
Average common stockholders' equity	$658,500 ($1,317,000 ÷ 2)	$618,750 ($1,237,500 ÷ 2)
Return on common stockholders' equity	12.5% ($82,000 ÷ $658,500)	10.9% ($67,500 ÷ $618,750)

Mooney Company's return on common stockholders' equity improved from 10.9% to 12.5% in 20Y6. This rate differs from the returns earned by Mooney Company on total assets and stockholders' equity as shown below.

	20Y6	20Y5
Return on total assets	8.2%	7.3%
Return on stockholders' equity	11.3%	10.0%
Return on common stockholders' equity	12.5%	10.9%

These returns differ because of leverage, as discussed in the preceding section.

In recent financial statements, Nike reported an asset turnover of 9.2, return on assets of 16.4%, and return on stockholders' equity of 27.8%. Nike has no preferred stock outstanding.

Earnings per Share on Common Stock

Earnings per share (EPS) on common stock measures the share of profits earned per share of common stock outstanding. Generally accepted accounting principles (GAAP) require the reporting of earnings per share on the income statement.[5] As a result, earnings per share (EPS) is often reported in the financial press. It is computed as follows:

$$\textbf{Earnings per Share (EPS) on Common Stock} = \frac{\textbf{Net Income} - \textbf{Preferred Dividends}}{\textbf{Shares of Common Stock Outstanding}}$$

When preferred and common stock are outstanding, preferred dividends are subtracted from net income to determine the income related to the common shares. Mooney Company had $150,000 of 6% preferred stock outstanding on December 31, 20Y6 and 20Y5. Thus, preferred dividends of $9,000 ($150,000 × 6%) are deducted from net income in computing earnings per share on common stock.

To illustrate, the earnings per share (EPS) of common stock for Mooney Company is computed below.

	20Y6	20Y5
Net income	$91,000	$76,500
Less preferred dividends	(9,000)	(9,000)
Total	$82,000	$67,500
Shares of common stock outstanding	50,000	50,000
Earnings per share on common stock	$1.64 ($82,000 ÷ 50,000)	$1.35 ($67,500 ÷ 50,000)

5. FASB, *Accounting Standards Codification*, Section 260.10.

As shown above, Mooney's earnings per share (EPS) on common stock improved from $1.35 to $1.64 during 20Y6. Mooney did not issue any additional shares of common stock in 20Y6. If Mooney had issued additional shares in 20Y6, a weighted average of common shares outstanding during the year would have been used.

Mooney Company has a simple capital structure with only common stock and preferred stock outstanding. Many corporations, however, have complex capital structures with various types of equity securities outstanding, such as convertible preferred stock, stock options, and stock warrants. In such cases, the possible effects of such securities on the shares of common stock outstanding are considered in reporting earnings per share. These possible effects are reported separately as *earnings per common share assuming dilution* or *diluted earnings per share*.[6] This topic is described and illustrated in advanced accounting courses and textbooks.

Price-Earnings Ratio

The **price-earnings (P/E) ratio** on common stock measures a company's future earnings prospects. It is often quoted in the financial press and is computed as follows:

$$\textbf{Price-Earnings (P/E) Ratio} = \frac{\textbf{Market Price per Share of Common Stock}}{\textbf{Earnings per Share on Common Stock}}$$

To illustrate, the price-earnings (P/E) ratio for Mooney Company is computed below.

	20Y6	20Y5
Market price per share of common stock	$41.00	$27.00
Earnings per share on common stock	$1.64	$1.35
Price-earnings ratio on common stock	25 ($41 ÷ $1.64)	20 ($27 ÷ $1.35)

The price-earnings ratio improved from 20 to 25 during 20Y6. In other words, a share of common stock of Mooney Company was selling for 20 times earnings per share at the end of 20Y5. At the end of 20Y6, the common stock was selling for 25 times earnings per share. This indicates that the market expects Mooney to experience favorable earnings in the future.

In recent financial statements, Nike reported earnings per share of $3.80, which with a recent stock price of $62.60 yields a price-earnings ratio of 16.5.

Dividends per Share

Dividends per share measures the extent to which earnings are being distributed to common shareholders. It is computed as follows:

$$\textbf{Dividends per Share} = \frac{\textbf{Common Stock Dividends}}{\textbf{Shares of Common Stock Outstanding}}$$

To illustrate, the dividends per share for Mooney Company are computed below.

	20Y6	20Y5
Common stock dividends	$40,000	$30,000
Shares of common stock outstanding	50,000	50,000
Dividends per share of common stock	$0.80 ($40,000 ÷ 50,000)	$0.60 ($30,000 ÷ 50,000)

The dividends per share of common stock increased from $0.60 to $0.80 during 20Y6.

6. Ibid., Section 260.10.

Dividends per share are often reported with earnings per share. Comparing the two per-share amounts indicates the extent to which earnings are being retained for use in operations. To illustrate, the dividends and earnings per share for Mooney Company are shown in Exhibit 9.

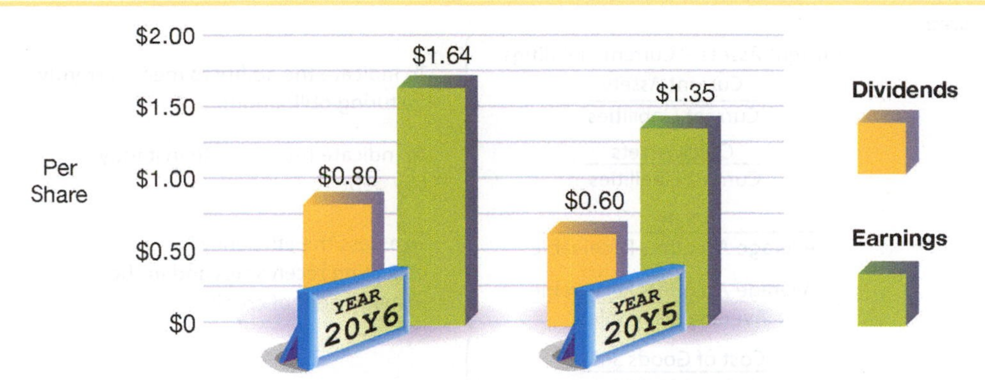

Exhibit 9 Dividends and Earnings per Share of Common Stock

Dividend Yield

The **dividend yield** on common stock measures the rate of return to common stockholders from cash dividends. It is of special interest to investors, whose objective is to earn revenue (dividends) from their investment. It is computed as follows:

$$\textbf{Dividend Yield} = \frac{\textbf{Dividends per Share of Common Stock}}{\textbf{Market Price per Share of Common Stock}}$$

To illustrate, the dividend yield for Mooney Company is computed below.

	20Y6	20Y5
Dividends per share of common stock	$ 0.80	$ 0.60
Market price per share of common stock	$41.00	$27.00
Dividend yield on common stock	2.0% ($0.80 ÷ $41)	2.2% ($0.60 ÷ $27)

The dividend yield declined slightly from 2.2% to 2.0% in 20Y6. This decline was primarily due to the increase in the market price of Mooney's common stock.

In recent years, Nike paid dividends of $0.64 per share with a dividend yield of 1.06%.

Nike Connection

Summary of Metrics

Exhibit 10 shows a summary of the liquidity, solvency, and profitability measures discussed in this chapter. The type of industry and the company's operations usually affect which measures are used. In many cases, additional measures are used for a specific industry. For example, airlines use *revenue per passenger mile* and *cost per available seat* as profitability measures. Likewise, hotels use *occupancy rates* as a profitability measure.

Exhibit 10 Summary of Metrics

	Method of Computation	
Liquidity and solvency measures:		
Working Capital	Current Assets − Current Liabilities	To indicate the ability to meet currently maturing obligations
Current Ratio	$\frac{\text{Current Assets}}{\text{Current Liabilities}}$	
Quick Ratio	$\frac{\text{Quick Assets}}{\text{Current Liabilities}}$	To indicate the ability to instantly pay debt
Accounts Receivable Turnover	$\frac{\text{Sales}}{\text{Average Accounts Receivable}}$	To assess the efficiency in collecting receivables and in the management of credit
Days' Sales in Receivables	$\frac{\text{Average Accounts Receivable}}{\text{Average Daily Sales}}$	
Inventory Turnover	$\frac{\text{Cost of Goods Sold}}{\text{Average Inventory}}$	To assess the efficiency in the management of inventory
Days' Sales in Inventory	$\frac{\text{Average Inventory}}{\text{Average Daily Cost of Goods Sold}}$	
Net Assets	Total Assets − Total Liabilities	To indicate the margin of safety of creditors
Debt Ratio	$\frac{\text{Total Liabilities}}{\text{Total Assets}}$	
Ratio of Liabilities to Stockholders' Equity	$\frac{\text{Total Liabilities}}{\text{Total Stockholders' Equity}}$	
Ratio of Fixed Assets to Long-Term Liabilities	$\frac{\text{Fixed Assets (net)}}{\text{Long-Term Liabilities}}$	To indicate the margin of safety of long-term creditors
Times Interest Earned	$\frac{\text{Income Before Income Tax + Interest Expense}}{\text{Interest Expense}}$	To assess the risk to creditors that interest will be paid if earnings decrease
Profitability measures:		
Asset Turnover	$\frac{\text{Sales}}{\text{Average Long-Term Operating Assets}}$	To assess the effectiveness in the use of operating assets
Return on Total Assets	$\frac{\text{Net Income + Interest Expense}}{\text{Average Total Assets}}$	To assess the profitability of the assets
Return on Stockholders' Equity	$\frac{\text{Net Income}}{\text{Average Total Stockholders' Equity}}$	To assess the profitability of the investment by stockholders
Return on Common Stockholders' Equity	$\frac{\text{Net Income − Preferred Dividends}}{\text{Average Common Stockholders' Equity}}$	To assess the profitability of the investment by common stockholders
Earnings per Share on Common Stock	$\frac{\text{Net Income − Preferred Dividends}}{\text{Shares of Common Stock Outstanding}}$	
Price-Earnings Ratio	$\frac{\text{Market Price per Share of Common Stock}}{\text{Earnings per Share on Common Stock}}$	To indicate future earnings prospects, based on the relationship between market value of common stock and earnings
Dividends per Share	$\frac{\text{Dividends}}{\text{Shares of Common Stock Outstanding}}$	To indicate the extent to which earnings are being distributed to common stockholders
Dividend Yield	$\frac{\text{Dividends per Share of Common Stock}}{\text{Market Price per Share of Common Stock}}$	To indicate the rate of return to common stockholders in terms of dividends

Integrity, Objectivity, and Ethics in Business

One Bad Apple

A recent survey by *CFO* magazine reported that 47% of chief financial officers have been pressured by the chief executive officer to use questionable accounting. In addition, only 38% of those surveyed feel less pressure to use aggressive accounting today than in years past, while 20% believe there is more pressure. Perhaps more troublesome is the chief financial officers' confidence in the quality of financial information, with only 27% being "very confident" in the quality of financial information presented by public companies.

Source: D. Durfee, "It's Better (and Worse) Than You Think," *CFO*, May 3, 2004.

The analytical measures shown in Exhibit 10 are a useful starting point for analyzing a company's liquidity, solvency, and profitability. However, they are not a substitute for sound judgment. For example, the general economic and business environment should always be considered in analyzing a company's future prospects. In addition, any trends and interrelationships among the measures should be carefully studied.

Corporate Annual Reports

Objective 6
Describe the corporate annual reports.

Public corporations issue annual reports summarizing their operating activities for the past year and plans for the future. Such annual reports include the financial statements and the accompanying notes. In addition, annual reports normally include the following sections:

- Management's Discussion and Analysis
- Report on Internal Control
- Report on Fairness of the Financial Statements

Management's Discussion and Analysis

Management's Discussion and Analysis (MD&A) is required in annual reports filed with the Securities and Exchange Commission. It includes management's analysis of current operations and its plans for the future. Typical items included in the MD&A are as follows:

- Management's analysis and explanations of any significant changes between the current and prior years' financial statements.
- Important accounting principles or policies that could affect interpretation of the financial statements, including the effect of changes in accounting principles or the adoption of new accounting principles.
- Management's assessment of the company's liquidity and the availability of capital to the company.
- Significant risk exposures that might affect the company.
- Any "off-balance-sheet" arrangements such as leases not included directly in the financial statements. Such arrangements are discussed in advanced accounting courses and textbooks.

Business Insight

Investing Strategies

How do people make investment decisions? Investment decisions, like any major purchase, must meet the needs of the buyer. For example, if you have a family of five and are thinking about buying a new car, you probably wouldn't buy a two-seat sports car. It just wouldn't meet your objectives or fit your lifestyle. Alternatively, if you are a young single person, a minivan might not meet your immediate needs. Investors buy stocks in the same way, buying stocks that match their investment style and their financial needs. Two common approaches are value and growth investing.

Value Investing

Value investors search for undervalued stocks. That is, the investor tries to find companies whose value is not reflected in their stock price. These are typically quiet, "boring" companies with excellent financial performance that are temporarily out of favor in the stock market. This investment approach assumes that the stock's price will eventually rise to match the company's value. The most successful investor of all time, Warren Buffett, uses this approach almost exclusively. Naturally, the key to successful value investing is to accurately determine a stock's value. This will often include analyzing a company's financial ratios, as discussed in this chapter, compared to target ratios and industry norms. For example, the stock of **Deckers Outdoor Corporation**, the maker of TEVA™ sport sandals, was selling for \$27.43 several years ago, a value relative to its earnings per share of \$2.58. Over the next two years, the company's stock price increased more than 500%, reaching \$166.50.

Kevork Djansezian/Getty Images News/Getty Images

Growth Investing

The growth investor tries to identify companies that have the potential to grow sales and earnings through new products, markets, or opportunities. Growth companies are often newer companies that are still unproven but that possess unique technologies or capabilities. The strategy is to purchase these companies before their potential becomes obvious, hoping to profit from relatively large increases in the company's stock price. This approach, however, carries the risk that the growth may not occur. Growth investors use many of the ratios discussed in this chapter to identify high-potential growth companies. For example, **Research in Motion Limited**, maker of the popular BlackBerry® handheld mobile device, reported earnings per share of \$0.37, when the company's stock price was trading near \$62 per share. In the following two years, the company's sales increased by 125%, earnings increased to \$1.14 per share, and the company's stock price rose above \$135 per share.

Report on Internal Control

The Sarbanes-Oxley Act requires management to prepare a report on internal control. The report states management's responsibility for establishing and maintaining internal control. In addition, management's assessment of the effectiveness of internal controls over financial reporting is included in the report.

Sarbanes-Oxley also requires a public accounting firm to verify management's conclusions on internal control. Thus, two reports on internal control, one by management and one by a public accounting firm, are included in the annual report. In some situations, these may be combined into a single report on internal control.

Audit Report

All publicly held corporations are required to have an independent audit (examination) of their financial statements. The Certified Public Accounting (CPA) firm that conducts the audit renders an opinion, called the *Report of Independent Registered Public Accounting Firm,* on the fairness of the statements.

An opinion stating that the financial statements present fairly the financial position, results of operations, and cash flows of the company is said to be an *unqualified opinion*, sometimes called a *clean opinion*. Any report other than an unqualified opinion raises a "red flag" for financial statement users and requires further investigation as to its cause.

In recent financial statements, Nike received a clean audit opinion from its auditors, Pricewater-houseCooopers.

Nike Connection

Appendix

Unusual Financial Statement Items

Generally accepted accounting principles require that unusual items be reported separately in the financial statements. This is because such items do not occur frequently and often are unrelated to current operations. Without separate reporting of these items, users of the financial statements might be misled about current and future operations.

Unusual items include the following:

- Discontinued operations
- Errors and changes generally accepted accounting principles

Discontinued Operations

A company may discontinue a segment of its operations by selling or abandoning the operations. For example, a retailer might decide to sell its product only online and thus discontinue selling its merchandise at its retail outlets (stores).

Any gain or loss on discontinued operations is reported on the income statement as a *Gain (or loss) from discontinued operations.* It is reported immediately following *Income from continuing operations.*[7]

To illustrate, assume that Jones Corporation produces and sells electrical products, hardware supplies, and lawn equipment. Because of lack of profits, Jones discontinues its electrical products operation and sells the remaining inventory and other assets at a loss of $100,000. Exhibit 11 illustrates the reporting of the loss on discontinued operations.[8]

A note accompanying the income statement should describe the operations sold, including such details as the date operations were discontinued, the assets sold, and the effect (if any) on current and future operations.

Exhibit 11 Unusual Items on the Income Statement

Jones Corporation Income Statement For the Year Ended December 31, 20Y6	
Sales	$12,350,000
Cost of goods sold	(5,800,000)
Gross profit	$ 6,550,000
Selling and administrative expenses	(5,240,000)
Income from continuing operations before income tax	$ 1,310,000
Income tax expense	(620,000)
Income from continuing operations	$ 690,000
Loss on discontinued operations	(100,000)
Net income	$ 590,000

7. FASB, *Accounting Standards Codification*, Section 260.20.

8. The gain or loss on discontinued operations is reported net of any tax effects. To simplify, the tax effects are not specifically identified in Exhibit 11.

Earnings per common share should also be reported separately for discontinued operations and extraordinary items. Assuming 200,000 shares of common stock are outstanding, a partial income statement for Jones Corporation is shown in Exhibit 12.

Exhibit 12 Income Statement with Earnings per Share

Jones Corporation Income Statement For the Year Ended December 31, 20Y6	
Earnings per common share:	
Income from continuing operations	$3.45
Loss on discontinued operations	(0.50)
Net income	$2.95

Exhibit 12 reports earnings per common share for income from continuing operations, discontinued operations, and net income. However, only earnings per share for income from continuing operations and net income are required by generally accepted accounting principles (GAAP). The other per-share amounts may be presented in the notes to the financial statements.[9]

Errors and Changes in Generally Accepted Accounting Principles

Unusual items may occur for each of the following:

- Errors in applying generally accepted accounting principles
- Changes from one generally accepted accounting principle to another

If an error is discovered, the current period and any prior-period financial statements must be corrected (restated). In addition, a company may change from one generally accepted accounting principle to another or a new accounting standard may be issued. Such changes affect the current period's financial statements and may require restatements of prior years' financial statements. Illustrations and reporting of these types of unusual items are discussed in advanced accounting textbooks.

Key Points

1. Describe the usefulness of financial statements and methods of analysis.

General-purpose financial statements are useful in analyzing and interpreting a company's financial condition and performance, including its liquidity, solvency, and profitability. Methods of analysis include global and component analysis.

2. Describe basic financial statement analytical methods.

Global analysis computes changes in amounts, percentage of amounts, and percentage changes in amounts. The analysis of percentage increases and decreases in related items in comparative financial statements is called horizontal analysis. The analysis of percentages of component parts to the total in a single statement is called vertical analysis. Financial statements in which all amounts are expressed in percentages for purposes of analysis are called common-sized statements.

3. Describe and illustrate metrics used to analyze liquidity.

Liquidity is the ability to convert assets to cash. Liquidity metrics include working capital, current ratio, quick ratio, accounts receivable turnover, days' sales in receivables, inventory turnover, and days' sales in inventory.

9. FASB, *Accounting Standards Codification*, Section 260.10.

4. Describe and illustrate metrics used to analyze solvency.

Solvency is the ability of a company to pay its debts as they become due over a long period of time. Solvency metrics include debt ratio, ratio of liabilities to stockholders' equity, ratio of fixed assets to long-term liabilities, and times interest earned.

5. Describe and illustrate metrics used to analyze profitability.

Profitability is the ability of a company to earn income (profits). Profitability metrics include asset turnover, return on total assets, return on stockholders' equity, earnings per share on common stock, price-earnings ratio, dividends per share, and dividend yield.

6. Describe the contents of corporate annual reports.

Corporate annual reports normally include financial statements and the accompanying notes, Management's Discussion and Analysis, the Report on Internal Control, and the Audit Report.

Key Terms

Accounts receivable turnover (367)
Asset turnover (372)
Common-sized statement (364)
Component analysis (359)
Current position analysis (365)
Current ratio (365)
Days' sales in inventory (369)
Days' sales in receivables (367)
Debt ratio (370)
Dividend yield (377)
Dividends per share (376)
Earnings per share (EPS) on common stock (375)
General-purpose financial statements (358)
Global analysis (359)
Horizontal analysis (359)
Inventory turnover (368)
Liquidity (358)
Management's Discussion and Analysis (MD&A) (379)
Net assets (370)
Price-earnings (P/E) ratio (376)
Profitability (359)
Quick assets (366)
Quick ratio (366)
Ratio of fixed assets to long-term liabilities (371)
Ratio of liabilities to stockholders' equity (370)
Return on common stockholders' equity (374)
Return on stockholders' equity (373)
Return on total assets (373)
Solvency (358)
Times interest earned (371)
Vertical analysis (362)
Working capital (365)

Illustrative Problem

Esmeralda Paint Co.'s comparative financial statements for the years ending December 31, 20Y4 and 20Y3, are as follows. The market price of Esmeralda Paint Co.'s common stock was $30 on December 31, 20Y3, and $25 on December 31, 20Y4.

ESMERALDA PAINT CO.
Comparative Income Statement
For the Years Ended December 31, 20Y4 and 20Y3

	20Y4	20Y3
Sales	$ 5,000,000	$3,200,000
Cost of goods sold	(3,400,000)	(2,080,000)
Gross profit	$ 1,600,000	$1,120,000
Selling expenses	$ (650,000)	$ (464,000)
Administrative expenses	(325,000)	(224,000)
Total operating expenses	$ (975,000)	$ (688,000)
Operating income	$ 625,000	$ 432,000
Other revenue and expense:		
Other revenue	25,000	19,200
Other expenses (interest)	(105,000)	(64,000)
Income before income tax	$ 545,000	$ 387,200
Income tax expenses	(300,000)	(176,000)
Net income	$ 245,000	$ 211,200

ESMERALDA PAINT CO.
Comparative Statement of Stockholders' Equity
For the Years Ended December 31, 20Y4 and 20Y3

	20Y4			20Y3		
	Preferred Stock	**Common Stock**	**Retained Earnings**	**Preferred Stock**	**Common Stock**	**Retained Earnings**
Balances, Jan. 1	$500,000	$500,000	$723,000	$500,000	$500,000	$581,800
Net income			245,000			211,200
Dividends:						
Preferred stock			(40,000)			(40,000)
Common stock			(45,000)			(30,000)
Balances, Dec. 31	$500,000	$500,000	$883,000	$500,000	$500,000	$723,000

ESMERALDA PAINT CO.
Comparative Balance Sheet
December 31, 20Y4 and 20Y3

	Dec. 31, 20Y4	Dec. 31, 20Y3
Assets		
Current assets:		
Cash	$ 175,000	$ 125,000
Temporary investments	150,000	50,000
Accounts receivable (net)	425,000	325,000
Inventories	720,000	480,000
Prepaid expenses	30,000	20,000
Total current assets	$1,500,000	$1,000,000
Long-term investments	250,000	225,000
Property, plant, and equipment (net)	2,093,000	1,948,000
Total assets	$3,843,000	$3,173,000
Liabilities		
Current liabilities	$ 750,000	$ 650,000
Long-term liabilities:		
Mortgage note payable, 10%, due in eight years	$ 410,000	—
Bonds payable, 8%, due in 15 years	800,000	$ 800,000
Total long-term liabilities	$1,210,000	$ 800,000
Total liabilities	$1,960,000	$1,450,000
Stockholders' Equity		
Preferred 8% stock, $100 par	$ 500,000	$ 500,000
Common stock, $10 par	500,000	500,000
Retained earnings	883,000	723,000
Total stockholders' equity	$1,883,000	$1,723,000
Total liabilities and stockholders' equity	$3,843,000	$3,173,000

Instructions

Compute the following metrics for 20Y4:

1. Working capital
2. Current ratio
3. Quick ratio
4. Accounts receivable turnover
5. Days' sales in receivables
6. Inventory turnover
7. Days' sales in inventory
8. Debt ratio
9. Ratio of liabilities to stockholders' equity
10. Ratio of fixed assets to long-term liabilities
11. Times interest earned
12. Times preferred dividends earned
13. Asset turnover
14. Return on total assets
15. Return on stockholders' equity
16. Return on common stockholders' equity
17. Earnings per share on common stock
18. Price-earnings ratio
19. Dividends per share
20. Dividend yield

Solution

(Metrics are rounded to the nearest single digit after the decimal point.)

1. Working capital: $750,000
   $1,500,000 − $750,000
2. Current ratio: 2.0
   $1,500,000 ÷ $750,000
3. Quick ratio: 1.0
   $750,000 ÷ $750,000
4. Accounts receivable turnover: 13.3
   $5,000,000 ÷ [($425,000 + $325,000) ÷ 2]
5. Days' sales in receivables: 27.4 days
   $5,000,000 ÷ 365 days = $13,699
   $375,000 ÷ $13,699
6. Inventory turnover: 5.7
   $3,400,000 ÷ [($720,000 + $480,000) ÷ 2]
7. Days' sales in inventory: 64.4 days
   $3,400,000 ÷ 365 days = $9,315
   $600,000 ÷ $9,315
8. Debt ratio: 51.0%
   $1,960,000 ÷ $3,843,000
9. Ratio of liabilities to stockholders' equity: 1.0
   $1,960,000 ÷ $1,883,000
10. Ratio of fixed assets to long-term liabilities: 1.7
    $2,093,000 ÷ $1,210,000
11. Times interest earned: 6.2
    ($545,000 + $105,000) ÷ $105,000
12. Times preferred dividends earned: 6.1
    $245,000 ÷ $40,000
13. Asset turnover: 2.5
    ($2,093,000 + $1,948,000) ÷ 2 = $2,020,500
    $5,000,000 ÷ $2,020,500
14. Return on total assets: 10.0%
    ($245,000 + $105,000) ÷ [($3,843,000 + $3,173,000) ÷ 2]
15. Return on stockholders' equity: 13.6%
    $245,000 ÷ [($1,883,000 + $1,723,000) ÷ 2]
16. Return on common stockholders' equity: 15.7%
    ($245,000 − $40,000) ÷ [($1,383,000 + $1,223,000) ÷ 2]
17. Earnings per share on common stock: $4.10
    ($245,000 − $40,000) ÷ 50,000 shares
18. Price-earnings ratio: 6.1
    $25 ÷ $4.10
19. Dividends per share: $0.90
    $45,000 ÷ 50,000 shares
20. Dividend yield: 3.6%
    $0.90 ÷ $25

Self-Examination Questions

(Answers appear at the end of chapter)

1. What type of analysis is indicated by the following?

	Amount	Percent
Current assets	$100,000	20%
Property, plant, and equipment	400,000	80
Total assets	$500,000	100%

A. Vertical analysis
B. Horizontal analysis
C. Profitability analysis
D. Contribution margin analysis

2. Which of the following measures indicates the ability of a firm to pay its current liabilities?

A. Working capital
B. Current ratio
C. Quick ratio
D. All of the above

3. The ratio determined by dividing total current assets by total current liabilities is:

A. The current ratio
B. The working capital ratio
C. The bankers' ratio
D. All of the above

4. The ratio of the quick assets to current liabilities, which indicates the "instant" debt-paying ability of a firm, is the:

A. Current ratio
B. Working capital ratio
C. Quick ratio
D. Bankers' ratio

5. A measure useful in evaluating efficiency in the management of inventories is the:

A. Working capital ratio
B. Quick ratio
C. Days' sales in inventory
D. Ratio of fixed assets to long-term liabilities

Class Discussion Questions

1. What is the difference between horizontal and vertical analysis of financial statements?
2. What is the advantage of using comparative statements for financial analysis rather than statements for a single date or period?
3. The current year's amount of net income (after income tax) is 9% larger than that of the preceding year. Does this indicate an improved operating performance? Discuss.
4. How would you respond to a horizontal analysis that showed an expense increasing by over 70%?
5. How would the current and quick ratios of a service business compare?
6. For Belzer Corporation, the working capital at the end of the current year is $24,000 more than the working capital at the end of the preceding year, reported as follows:

	Current Year	Preceding Year
Current assets:		
Cash, temporary investments, and receivables	$ 81,000	$ 72,000
Inventories	171,000	126,000
Total current assets	$252,000	$198,000
Current liabilities	(90,000)	(60,000)
Working capital	$162,000	$138,000

Has the current position improved? Explain.

7. Why would the accounts receivable turnover ratio be different between Wal-Mart (WMT) and Procter & Gamble (PG)?

8. A company that grants terms of n/30 on all sales has a yearly accounts receivable turnover, based on monthly averages, of 9. Is this a satisfactory turnover? Discuss.

9. a. Why is it advantageous to have a high inventory turnover?
   b. Is it possible for the inventory turnover to be too high? Discuss.
   c. Is it possible to have a high inventory turnover and a high days' sales in inventory? Discuss.

10. What do the following data taken from a comparative balance sheet indicate about the company's ability to borrow additional funds on a long-term basis in the current year as compared to the preceding year?

	Current Year	Preceding Year
Fixed assets (net)	$1,800,000	$1,260,000
Total long-term liabilities	450,000	350,000

11. a. How does the return on total assets differ from the return on stockholders' equity?
    b. Which return is normally higher? Explain.

12. a. Why is the return on stockholders' equity by a thriving business ordinarily higher than the return on total assets?
    b. Should the return on common stockholders' equity normally be higher or lower than the return on total stockholders' equity? Explain.

13. The net income (after income tax) of Fleming Inc. was $4.80 per common share in the latest year and $7.50 per common share for the preceding year. At the beginning of the latest year, the number of shares outstanding was doubled by a stock split. There were no other changes in the amount of stock outstanding. What were the earnings per share in the preceding year, adjusted for comparison with the latest year?

14. The price-earnings ratio for the common stock of In-Work Company was 15 at December 31, the end of the current fiscal year. What does the ratio indicate about the selling price of the common stock in relation to current earnings?

15. Why would the dividend yield differ significantly from the return on common stockholders' equity?

16. Favorable business conditions may bring about certain seemingly unfavorable ratios, and unfavorable business operations may result in apparently favorable ratios. For example, Shaddox Company increased its sales and net income substantially for the current year, yet the current ratio at the end of the year is lower than at the beginning of the year. Discuss some possible causes of the apparent weakening of the current position, while sales and net income have increased substantially.

17. Describe two reports provided by independent auditors in the annual report to shareholders.

Exercises

E9-1 Vertical analysis of income statement

Obj. 2

✔ a. 20Y8 net income: $85,500; 9.5% of sales

Revenue and expense data for Searle Technologies Co. are as follows:

	20Y8	20Y7
Sales	$900,000	$725,000
Cost of goods sold	558,000	435,000
Selling expenses	117,000	116,000
Administrative expenses	63,000	65,250
Income tax expense	76,500	58,000

a. Prepare an income statement in comparative form, stating each item for both 20Y8 and 20Y7 as a percent of sales. Round to one decimal place.

b. Comment on the significant changes disclosed by the comparative income statement.

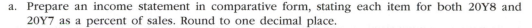

Note: The spreadsheet icon  indicates an Excel template is available on the student companion site.

Obj. 2

✔ a. Year 2 income from continuing operations before taxes, 8.5% of revenues

E9-2 Vertical analysis of income statement

The following comparative income statement (in thousands of dollars) for two recent years was adapted from the annual report of Speedway Motorsports, Inc. (TRK), owner and operator of several major motor speedways, such as the Atlanta, Bristol, Charlotte, Texas, and Las Vegas Motor Speedways.

	Year 2	Year 1
Revenues:		
Admissions	$ 100,798	$ 106,050
Event-related revenue	146,849	145,749
NASCAR broadcasting revenue	207,369	199,014
Other operating revenue	29,293	29,836
Total revenue	$ 484,309	$ 480,649
Expenses and other:		
Direct expense of events	$(102,196)	$ (99,500)
NASCAR purse and sanction fees	(128,254)	(125,003)
Other direct expenses	(18,513)	(18,640)
General and administrative	(194,120)	(286,069)
Total expenses	$(443,083)	$(529,212)
Income (loss) from continuing operations	$ 41,226	$ 48,563

a. Prepare a comparative income statement for Years 1 and 2 in vertical form, stating each item as a percent of revenues. Round to one decimal place.

b. Comment on the significant changes.

Obj. 2

E9-3 Common-sized income statement

Revenue and expense data for the current calendar year for Lyons Electronics Company and for the electronics industry are as follows. Lyons Electronics Company data are expressed in dollars. The electronics industry averages are expressed in percentages.

	Lyons Electronics Company	Electronics Industry Average
Sales	$ 7,500,000	100.0%
Cost of goods sold	(4,125,000)	(61.0)
Gross profit	$ 3,375,000	39.0%
Selling expenses	$(2,250,000)	(23.0)%
Administrative expenses	(525,000)	(10.0)
Total operating expenses	$(2,775,000)	(33.0)%
Operating income	$ 600,000	6.0%
Other revenue and expense:		
Other revenue	30,000	3.0
Other expense	$ (7,500)	(1.0)
Income before income tax	$ 622,500	8.0%
Income tax expense	(187,500)	(2.5)
Net income	$ 435,000	5.5%

a. Prepare a common-sized income statement comparing the results of operations for Lyons Electronics Company with the industry average.

b. Comment on significant relationships revealed by the comparisons.

E9-4 Vertical analysis of balance sheet

Obj. 2

✔ Retained earnings, Dec. 31, 20Y2, 59.4%

Balance sheet data for a company for the years ended December 31, 20Y2 and 20Y1, are shown below.

	20Y2	20Y1
Current assets	$ 1,500,000	$ 1,200,000
Property, plant, and equipment	12,500,000	10,800,000
Intangible assets	2,000,000	2,000,000
Current liabilities	1,000,000	850,000
Long-term liabilities	3,000,000	2,400,000
Common stock	2,500,000	2,500,000
Retained earnings	9,500,000	8,250,000

Prepare a comparative balance sheet for 20Y2 and 20Y1, stating each asset as a percent of total assets and each liability and stockholders' equity item as a percent of the total liabilities and stockholders' equity. Round to one decimal place.

E9-5 Horizontal analysis of the income statement

Obj. 2

✔ Net income increase, 36.4%

Income statement data for Yellowstone Images Inc. for the years ended December 31, 20Y5 and 20Y4, are as follows:

	20Y5	20Y4
Sales	$1,000,000	$ 800,000
Cost of goods sold	(640,000)	(500,000)
Gross profit	$ 360,000	$ 300,000
Selling expenses	$ (70,000)	$ (60,000)
Administrative expenses	(50,000)	(50,000)
Total operating expenses	$ (120,000)	$(110,000)
Income before income tax	$ 240,000	$ 190,000
Income tax expense	(90,000)	(80,000)
Net income	$ 150,000	$ 110,000

a. Prepare a comparative income statement with horizontal analysis, indicating the increase (decrease) for 20Y5 when compared with 20Y4. Round to one decimal place.

b. What conclusions can be drawn from the horizontal analysis?

E9-6 Current position analysis

Obj. 3

✔ 20Y9 working capital, $1,050,000

The following data were taken from the comparative balance sheet of Osborn Sisters Company for the years ended December 31, 20Y9 and December 31, 20Y8:

	Dec. 31, 20Y9	Dec. 31, 20Y8
Cash	$ 150,000	$ 100,000
Temporary investments	250,000	150,000
Accounts and notes receivable (net)	500,000	400,000
Inventories	850,000	610,000
Prepaid expenses	50,000	40,000
Total current assets	$1,800,000	$1,300,000
Accounts payable	$ 700,000	$ 460,000
Accrued liabilities	50,000	40,000
Total current liabilities	$ 750,000	$ 500,000

a. Determine for each year (1) the working capital, (2) the current ratio, and (3) the quick ratio.

b. What conclusions can be drawn from these data?

Obj. 3

✔ a. (1) Year 1 current ratio, 1.1

E9-7 Current position analysis

PepsiCo, Inc. (PEP), the parent company of Frito-Lay™ snack foods and Pepsi beverages, had the following current assets and current liabilities at the end of two recent years:

	Year 2 (in millions)	Year 1 (in millions)
Cash and cash equivalents	$ 9,096	$ 6,134
Short-term investments, at cost	2,913	2,592
Accounts and notes receivable, net	6,437	6,651
Inventories	2,720	3,143
Prepaid expenses and other current assets	1,865	2,143
Short-term obligations (liabilities)	4,071	5,076
Accounts payable and other current liabilities	13,507	13,016

a. Determine the (1) current ratio and (2) quick ratio for both years. Round to one decimal place.
b. What conclusions can you draw from these data?

Obj. 3

E9-8 Current position analysis

The bond indenture for the 10-year, 8% debenture bonds dated January 2, 20Y8, required working capital of $200,000, a current ratio of 2.0, and a quick ratio of 1.0 at the end of each calendar year until the bonds mature. At December 31, 20Y9, the three measures were computed as follows:

1. Current assets:			
Cash	$120,000		
Temporary investments	150,000		
Accounts receivable (net)	240,000		
Inventories	190,000		
Prepaid expenses	50,000		
Intangible assets	30,000		
Property, plant, and equipment	540,000		
Total current assets (net)			$1,320,000
Current liabilities:			
Accounts and short-term notes payable	$440,000		
Accrued liabilities	160,000		
Total current liabilities			(600,000)
Working capital			$ 720,000
2. Current ratio		2.2	$1,320,000 ÷ $600,000
3. Quick ratio		1.5	$660,000 ÷ $440,000

a. List the errors in the determination of the three measures of current position analysis.
b. Is the company satisfying the terms of the bond indenture?

Obj. 3

✔ a. Accounts receivable turnover, Year 3, 6.4

E9-9 Accounts receivable analysis

The following data are taken from the financial statements of Outdoor Patio Inc. Terms of all sales are 2/10, n/60.

	Year 3	Year 2	Year 1
Accounts receivable, end of year	$ 900,000	$ 750,000	$600,000
Sales	5,280,000	3,915,000	

a. For Years 2 and 3, determine (1) the accounts receivable turnover and (2) the days' sales in receivables. Round to nearest dollar and one decimal place.
b. What conclusions can be drawn from these data concerning accounts receivable and credit policies?

E9-10 Accounts receivable analysis

Obj. 3

Bassett Stores Company and Fox Stores Inc. are large retail department stores. Both companies offer credit to their customers through their own credit card operations. Information from the financial statements for both companies for two recent years is as follows (all numbers are in millions):

	Bassett	Fox
Merchandise sales	$726,000	$2,470,000
Credit card receivables—beginning	75,000	350,000
Credit card receviables—ending	90,000	410,000

a. Determine (1) the accounts receivable turnover and (2) the days' sales in receivables for both companies. Round to nearest dollar and one decimal place.

b. Compare the two companies with regard to their credit card policies.

E9-11 Inventory analysis

Obj. 3

✔ a. Inventory turnover, current year, 12.0

The following data were extracted from the income statement of Brecca Systems Inc.:

	Current Year	Preceding Year
Sales	$9,700,000	$7,175,000
Beginning inventories	420,000	400,000
Cost of goods sold	5,820,000	4,305,000
Ending inventories	550,000	420,000

a. Determine for each year (1) the inventory turnover and (2) the days' sales in inventory. Round to nearest dollar and one decimal place.

b. What conclusions can be drawn from these data concerning the inventories?

E9-12 Inventory analysis

Obj. 3

✔ a. Costco inventory turnover, 11.6

Costco Wholesale Corporation (COST) and Wal-Mart Stores Inc. (WMT) compete against each other in general merchandise retailing, gas stations, pharmacies, and optical centers. Below is selected financial information for both companies from a recent year's financial statements (in millions):

	Costco	Wal-Mart
Sales	$116,199	$485,651
Cost of goods sold	101,065	365,086
Inventory, beginning of period	8,456	44,858
Inventory, end of period	8,908	45,141

a. Determine for both companies (1) the inventory turnover and (2) the days' sales in inventory. Round to one decimal place.

b. Compare and interpret the inventory metrics computed in (a).

Obj. 4

✔ a. Ratio of liabilities to stockholders' equity, Dec. 31, 20Y6, 0.6

E9-13 Ratio of liabilities to stockholders' equity and times interest earned

The following data were taken from the financial statements of Starr Construction Inc. for December 31, 20Y6 and 20Y5:

	Dec. 31, 20Y6	Dec. 31, 20Y5
Accounts payable and other liabilities	$ 1,700,000	$2,325,000
Current maturities of bonds payable	500,000	500,000
Serial bonds payable, 8%, issued 2008, due in five years	5,000,000	5,500,000
Common stock, $5 par value	250,000	250,000
Paid-in capital in excess of par	1,500,000	1,500,000
Retained earnings	10,250,000	7,500,000

The income before income tax was $2,816,000 and $2,640,000 for the years 20Y6 and 20Y5, respectively.

a. Determine the ratio of liabilities to stockholders' equity at the end of each year.

b. Determine the times (bond) interest earned during the year for both years.

c. What conclusions can be drawn from these data as to the company's ability to meet its currently maturing debts?

Obj. 4

✔ a. Hasbro, 64.5%

E9-14 Debt ratio, ratio of liabilities to stockholders' equity, and times interest earned

Hasbro (HAS) and Mattel, Inc. (MAT), are the two largest toy companies in North America. Liability and stockholders' equity data from recent balance sheets are shown for each company below (in millions):

	Hasbro	Mattel
Current liabilities	$ 1,065	$ 1,646
Long-term debt	1,952	2,274
Total liabilities	$ 3,017	$ 3,920
Total stockholders' equity	1,704	2,633
Total liabilities and stockholders' equity	$ 4,721	$ 6,553

The income from operations and interest expense from the income statement for both companies were as follows (in millions):

	Hasbro	Mattel
Income from operations before tax	$604	$464
Interest expense	97	85

a. Determine the debt ratio for both companies. Round to one decimal place.

b. Determine the ratio of liabilities to stockholders' equity for both companies. Round to one decimal place.

c. Determine the times interest earned for both companies. Round to one decimal place.

d. Interpret the ratio differences between the two companies.

E9-15 Debt ratio, ratio of liabilities to stockholders' equity, and ratio of fixed assets to long-term liabilities

Obj. 4

✔ a. Hershey, 74.2%

Recent balance sheet information for two companies in the snack food industry, The Hershey Company (HSY) and Mondelez International, Inc. (MDLZ), is as follows (in millions of dollars):

	Hershey	Mondelez
Net property, plant, and equipment	$2,152	$ 8,362
Liabilities:		
Current liabilities	$1,936	$10,922
Long-term debt	1,549	14,557
Other long-term liabilities	690	9,352
Total liabilities	$4,175	$34,831
Stockholders' equity	1,455	28,012
Total liabilities and stockholders' equity	$5,630	$62,843

a. Determine the debt ratio for both companies. Round to one decimal place.

b. Determine the ratio of liabilities to stockholders' equity for both companies. Round to one decimal place.

c. Determine the ratio of fixed assets to long-term liabilities for both companies. Round to two decimal places.

d. Interpret the ratio differences between the two companies.

E9-16 Asset Turnover

Obj. 5

✔ a. YRC Worldwide, 4.76

Three major transportation segments and a major company within each segment are as follows:

Segment	Company
Motor carriers	YRC Worldwide Inc. (YRCW)
Railroads	Union Pacific Corporation (UNP)
Transportation Arrangement	C.H. Robinson Worldwide Inc. (CHRW)

	YRC Worldwide	Union Pacific	C.H. Robinson Worldwide
Sales	$4,832	$21,813	$13,470
Average long-term operating assets	1,016	47,569	1,092

a. Determine the asset turnover for all three companies. Round to two decimal places.

b. Interpret the differences in the asset turnover in terms of the operating characteristics of each of the respective segments.

E9-17 Profitability metrics

Obj. 5

✔ a. Return on total assets, 20Y5, 21.5%

The following selected data were taken from the financial statements of The O'Malley Group Inc. for December 31, 20Y5, 20Y4, and 20Y3:

	December 31		
	20Y5	20Y4	20Y3
Total assets	$2,900,000	$2,400,000	$2,000,000
Notes payable (5% interest)	800,000	800,000	800,000
Common stock	250,000	250,000	250,000
Preferred $4 stock, $50 par (no change during year)	400,000	400,000	400,000
Retained earnings	1,450,000	950,000	550,000
Net income	530,000	430,000	330,000

No dividends on common stock were declared between 20Y3 and 20Y5.

a. Determine the return on total assets, the return on stockholders' equity, and the return on common stockholders' equity for the years 20Y4 and 20Y5. Round to one decimal place.

b. What conclusions can be drawn from these data as to the company's profitability?

Obj. 5

✔ **a. Return on total assets, Year 3, 11.1%**

E9-18 Profitability metrics

Macy's, Inc. (M), sells merchandise through company-owned retail stores and Internet website. Recent financial information for Macy's is provided below (all numbers in millions).

	Year 3	Year 2
Net income	$1,526	$1,486
Interest expense	864	804

	Year 3	Year 2	Year 1
Total assets	$21,461	$21,620	$20,991
Total stockholders' equity	5,378	6,249	6,051

Assume the apparel industry's average return on total assets is 8.2%, and the average return on stockholders' equity is 10.0% for Year 3.

a. Determine the return on total assets for Macy's for Years 2 and 3. Round to one decimal place.

b. Determine the return on stockholders' equity for Macy's for Years 2 and 3. Round to one decimal place.

c. Evaluate the changes in the profitability ratios determined in (a) and (b).

Obj. 4, 5

✔ **d. Asset turnover 1.32**

E9-19 Seven metrics

The following data were taken from the financial statements of Woodwork Enterprises Inc. for the current fiscal year. Assuming that there are no intangible assets, determine the following: (a) debt ratio, (b) ratio of fixed assets to long-term liabilities, (c) ratio of liabilities to stockholders' equity, (d) asset turnover, (e) return on total assets, (f) return on stockholders' equity, and (g) return on common stockholders' equity. Round to two decimal places.

Property, plant, and equipment (net)			$ 5,000,000
Liabilities:			
Current liabilities		$ 400,000	
Mortgage note payable, 5%, ten-year note issued two years ago		3,600,000	
Total liabilities			$ 4,000,000
Stockholders' equity:			
Preferred $1 stock, $10 par (no change during year)			$ 1,000,000
Common stock, $5 par (no change during year)			2,000,000
Retained earnings:			
Balance, beginning of year	$8,000,000		
Net income	500,000	$8,500,000	
Preferred dividends	$ 100,000		
Common dividends	100,000	(200,000)	
Balance, end of year			8,300,000
Total stockholders' equity			$11,300,000
Sales			$ 6,250,000
Interest expense			$ 180,000
Beginning-of-the-year amounts:			
Property, plant, and equipment (net)			$ 4,500,000
Total assets			12,200,000
Retained earnings			8,000,000

E9-20 Six metrics

Obj. 4, 5

✔ d. Price-earnings ratio, 2.5

The balance sheet for Shryer Industries Inc. at the end of 20Y9 indicated the following:

Bonds payable, 5% (due in 30 years)	$ 8,000,000
Preferred $4 stock, $75 par	15,000,000
Common stock, $7 par	3,500,000

Income before income tax was $3,400,000, and income taxes were $1,000,000 for the current year. Cash dividends paid on common stock during the current year totaled $100,000. The common stock was selling for $8 per share at the end of the year. Determine each of the following: (a) times interest earned, (b) times preferred dividends earned, (c) earnings per share on common stock, (d) price-earnings ratio, (e) dividends per share of common stock, and (f) dividend yield. Round to one decimal place except earnings per share and dividends per share, which should be rounded to the nearest cent.

E9-21 Earnings per share, price-earnings ratio, dividend yield

Obj. 5

✔ b. Price-earnings ratio, 8.0

The following information was taken from the financial statements of Monarch Resources Inc. for December 31 of the current year:

Common stock, $125 par value (no change during the year)	$12,500,000
Preferred $6 stock, $90 par (no change during the year)	2,250,000

The net income was $1,300,000, and the declared dividends on the common stock were $460,000 for the current year. The market price of the common stock is $92 per share.

For the common stock, determine (a) the earnings per share, (b) the price-earnings ratio, (c) the dividends per share, and (d) the dividend yield.

E9-22 Price-earnings ratio, dividend yield

Obj. 5

The table below shows recent stock prices, earnings per share, and dividends per share for three companies.

	Price	Earnings per Share	Dividends per Share
McDonald's Corporation (MCD)	$51.79	$1.41	$1.44
eBay Inc. (EBAY)	24.32	1.42	0.00
The Coca-Cola Company (KO)	43.63	1.67	1.40

a. Determine the price-earnings ratio and dividend yield for the three companies. Round to one decimal place.

b. Discuss the differences in these ratios across the three companies.

E9-23 Unusual income statement items

app

Assume that the amount of each of the following items is material to the financial statements. Classify each item as either normally recurring (NR) or unusual (U) items. If unusual item, then specify if it is a discontinued operations item (DO).

a. Interest revenue on notes receivable.

b. Gain on sale of segment of the company's operations that manufactures bottling equipment.

c. Loss on sale of investments in stocks and bonds.

d. Uncollectible accounts expense.

e. Uninsured flood loss. (Flood insurance is unavailable because of periodic flooding in the area.)

app

E9-24 Income statement and earnings per share for extraordinary items and discontinued operations

Leadbetter Inc. reports the following for 20Y3:

Income from continuing operations before income tax	$766,250
Gain from discontinued operations	$180,000*
Applicable tax rate	40%

*Net of any tax effect.

a. Prepare a partial income statement for Leadbetter Inc. beginning with income from continuing operations before income tax.

b. Assuming 75,000 common shares and no preferred shares, calculate the earnings per share for Leadbetter Inc. including per-share amounts for unusual items.

Problems

Obj. 2

✔ 1. Sales 9.8% increase

P9-1 Horizontal analysis for income statement

For 20Y3, Greyhound Technology Company reported its most significant decline in net income in years. At the end of the year, Duane Vogel, the president, is presented with the following condensed comparative income statement:

GREYHOUND TECHNOLOGY COMPANY
Comparative Income Statement
For the Years Ended December 31, 20Y3 and 20Y2

	20Y3	20Y2
Sales	$ 862,000	$ 785,000
Cost of goods sold	(650,000)	(500,000)
Gross profit	$ 212,000	$ 285,000
Selling expenses	$ (44,000)	$ (40,000)
Administrative expenses	(27,000)	(25,000)
Total operating expenses	$ (71,000)	$ (65,000)
Income from operations	$ 141,000	$ 220,000
Other revenue	2,300	2,000
Income before income tax	$ 143,300	$ 222,000
Income tax expense	(13,000)	(20,000)
Net income	$ 130,300	$ 202,000

Instructions

1. Prepare a comparative income statement with horizontal analysis for the two-year period, using 20Y2 as the base year. Round to one decimal place.
2. Comment on the significant relationships revealed by the horizontal analysis prepared in (1).

P9-2 Vertical analysis for income statement

Obj. 2

✔ 1. Net income, 20Y6, 28.0%

For 20Y6, Fishing Experiences Inc. initiated a sales promotion campaign that included the expenditure of an additional $45,000 for advertising. At the end of the year, Colt Schultz, the president, is presented with the following condensed comparative income statement:

FISHING EXPERIENCES INC.
Comparative Income Statement
For the Years Ended December 31, 20Y6 and 20Y5

	20Y6	20Y5
Sales	$1,200,000	$1,000,000
Cost of goods sold	(624,000)	(558,000)
Gross profit	$ 576,000	$ 442,000)
Selling expenses	(120,000)	(75,000)
Administrative expenses	(50,000)	(50,000)
Total operating expenses	$ (170,000)	$ (125,000)
Operating income	$ 406,000	$ 317,000
Other revenue	30,000	30,000
Income before income tax	$ 436,000	$ 347,000
Income tax expense	(100,000)	(90,000)
Net income	$ 336,000	$ 257,000

Instructions

1. Prepare a comparative income statement for the two-year period, presenting a vertical analysis of each item in relationship to sales for each of the years.
2. Comment on the significant relationships revealed by the vertical analysis prepared in (1).

P9-3 Effect of transactions on current position analysis

Obj. 3

✔ 2. c. Current ratio, 2.3

Data pertaining to the current position of Newlan Company are as follows:

Cash	$ 80,000
Temporary investments	160,000
Accounts and notes receivable (net)	235,000
Inventories	190,000
Prepaid expenses	10,000
Accounts payable	158,000
Notes payable (short-term)	80,000
Accrued expenses	12,000

Instructions

1. Compute (a) the working capital, (b) the current ratio, and (c) the quick ratio.
2. List the following captions on a sheet of paper:

Transaction	Working Capital	Current Ratio	Quick Ratio

Compute the working capital, the current ratio, and the quick ratio after each of the following transactions, and record the results in the appropriate columns. Consider each transaction separately and assume that only that transaction affects the data given above. Round to one decimal place.

a. Sold temporary investments for cash at no gain or loss, $50,000.
b. Paid accounts payable, $40,000.
c. Purchased goods on account, $75,000.
d. Paid notes payable, $30,000.
e. Declared a cash dividend, $15,000.
f. Declared a stock dividend on common stock, $24,000.
g. Borrowed cash from bank on a long-term note, $150,000.

h. Received cash on account, $72,000.
i. Issued additional shares of stock for cash, $300,000.
j. Paid cash for prepaid expenses, $10,000.

Obj. 3, 4, 5

✔ 5. Days' sales in receivables, 22.8

P9-4 Twenty metrics of liquidity, solvency, and profitability

The comparative financial statements of Automotive Solutions Inc. are as follows. The market price of Automotive Solutions Inc. common stock was $119.70 on December 31, 20Y8.

AUTOMOTIVE SOLUTIONS INC.
Comparative Income Statement
For the Years Ended December 31, 20Y8 and 20Y7

	20Y8	20Y7
Sales	$10,000,000	$ 9,400,000
Cost of goods sold	(5,350,000)	(4,950,000)
Gross profit	$ 4,650,000	$ 4,450,000
Selling expenses	$ (2,000,000)	$(1,880,000)
Administrative expenses	(1,500,000)	(1,410,000)
Total operating expenses	$ (3,500,000)	$(3,290,000)
Operating income	$ 1,150,000	$ 1,160,000
Other revenue and expense:		
Other revenue	150,000	140,000
Other expense (interest)	(170,000)	(150,000)
Income before income tax	$ 1,130,000	$ 1,150,000
Income tax expense	(230,000)	(225,000)
Net income	$ 900,000	$ 925,000

AUTOMOTIVE SOLUTIONS INC.
Comparative Statement of Stockholders' Equity
For the Years Ended December 31, 20Y8 and 20Y7

	20Y8			20Y7		
	Preferred Stock	Common Stock	Retained Earnings	Preferred Stock	Common Stock	Retained Earnings
Balances, Jan. 1	$500,000	$500,000	$5,375,000	$500,000	$500,000	$4,545,000
Net income			900,000			925,000
Dividends:						
Preferred stock			(45,000)			(45,000)
Common stock			(50,000)			(50,000)
Balances, Dec. 31	$500,000	$500,000	$6,180,000	$500,000	$500,000	$5,375,000

AUTOMOTIVE SOLUTIONS INC.
Comparative Balance Sheet
December 31, 20Y8 and 20Y7

	Dec. 31, 20Y8	Dec. 31, 20Y7
Assets		
Current assets:		
Cash	$ 500,000	$ 400,000
Marketable securities	1,010,000	1,000,000
Accounts receivable (net)	740,000	510,000
Inventories	1,190,000	950,000
Prepaid expenses	250,000	229,000
Total current assets	$3,690,000	$3,089,000
Long-term investments	2,350,000	2,300,000
Property, plant, and equipment (net)	3,740,000	3,366,000
Total assets	$9,780,000	$8,755,000

Liabilities		
Current liabilities	$ 900,000	$ 880,000
Long-term liabilities:		
Mortgage note payable, 10%	$ 200,000	$ 0
Bonds payable, 10%	1,500,000	1,500,000
Total long-term liabilities	$1,700,000	$1,500,000
Total liabilities	$2,600,000	$2,380,000
Stockholders' Equity		
Preferred $0.90 stock, $10 par	$ 500,000	$ 500,000
Common stock, $5 par	500,000	500,000
Retained earnings	6,180,000	5,375,500
Total stockholders' equity	$7,180,000	$6,375,000
Total liabilities and stockholders' equity	$9,780,000	$8,755,000

Instructions

Determine the following measures for 20Y8. Round all ratios to one decimal place. Round earnings per share and dividends per share to the nearest cent.

1. Working capital
2. Current ratio
3. Quick ratio
4. Accounts receivable turnover
5. Days' sales in receivables
6. Inventory turnover
7. Days' sales in inventory
8. Debt ratio
9. Ratio of liabilities to stockholders' equity
10. Ratio of fixed assets to long-term liabilities
11. Times interest earned
12. Times preferred dividends earned
13. Asset turnover
14. Return on total assets
15. Return on stockholders' equity
16. Return on common stockholders' equity
17. Earnings per share on common stock
18. Price-earnings ratio
19. Dividends per share of common stock
20. Dividend yield

P9-5 Trend analysis Obj. 4, 5

Critelli Company has provided the following comparative information:

	Year 5	Year 4	Year 3	Year 2	Year 1
Net income	$1,785,000	$1,330,000	$ 990,000	$ 768,800	$ 664,000
Interest expense	400,000	350,000	300,000	240,000	200,000
Income tax expense	615,000	340,000	270,000	71,200	16,000
Average total assets	9,500,000	8,000,000	6,000,000	5,200,000	4,500,000
Average stockholders' equity	5,400,000	4,300,000	3,100,000	2,650,000	2,200,000

You have been asked to evaluate the historical performance of the company over the last five years.

Selected industry ratios have remained relatively steady at the following levels for the last five years:

	Industry Ratios
Return on total assets	15%
Return on stockholders' equity	18%
Times interest earned	3.5

Instructions

1. Prepare three line graphs, with the ratio on the vertical axis and the years on the horizontal axis for the following three ratios (rounded to one decimal place):
   a. Return on total assets
   b. Return on stockholders' equity
   c. Times interest earned

   Display both the company ratio and the industry benchmark on each graph. That is, each graph should have two lines.
2. Prepare an analysis of the graphs in (1).

Cases

Case 9-1 Analysis of financing corporate growth

Assume that the president of Elkhead Brewery made the following statement in the Annual Report to Shareholders:

> *"The founding family and majority shareholders of the company do not believe in using debt to finance future growth. The founding family learned from hard experience during Prohibition and the Great Depression that debt can cause loss of flexibility and eventual loss of corporate control. The company will not place itself at such risk. As such, all future growth will be financed either by stock sales to the public or by internally generated resources."*

As a public shareholder of this company, how would you respond to this policy?

Case 9-2 Receivables and inventory turnover

Thornby Inc. completed its fiscal year on December 31. The auditor, Kim Holmes, has approached the CFO, Brad Potter, regarding the year-end receivables and inventory levels of Thornby Inc. The following conversation takes place:

Kim: We are beginning our audit of Thornby Inc. and have prepared ratio analyses to determine if there have been significant changes in operations or financial position. This helps us guide the audit process. This analysis indicates that the inventory turnover has decreased from 5.1 to 3.8, while the accounts receivable turnover has decreased from 12.5 to 9. I was wondering if you could explain this change in operations.

Brad: There is little need for concern. The inventory represents computers that we were unable to sell during the holiday buying season. We are confident, however, that we will be able to sell these computers as we move into the next fiscal year.

Kim: What gives you this confidence?

Brad: We will increase our advertising and provide some very attractive price concessions to move these machines. We have no choice. Newer technology is already out there, and we have to unload this inventory.

Kim: ... and the receivables?

Brad: As you may be aware, the company is under tremendous pressure to expand sales and profits. As a result, we lowered our credit standards to our commercial customers so that we would be able to sell products to a broader customer base. As a result of this policy change, we have been able to expand sales by 28%.

Kim: Your responses have not been reassuring to me.

Brad: I'm a little confused. Assets are good, right? Why don't you look at our current ratio? It has improved, hasn't it? I would think that you would view that very favorably.

Why is Kim concerned about the inventory and accounts receivable turnover ratios and Brad's responses to them? What action may Kim need to take? How would you respond to Brad's last comment?

Case 9-3 Vertical analysis

The condensed income statements through operating income for Apple Inc. and Best Buy Co. Inc. (BBY) are reproduced below for recent fiscal years (numbers in millions of dollars).

	Apple	Best Buy
Sales	$ 233,715	$ 40,339
Cost of sales	(140,089)	(31,292)
Gross profit	$ 93,626	$ 9,047
Selling, general, and administrative expenses	(14,329)	(7,597)
Research and development expenses	(8,067)	—
Operating expenses	$ (22,396)	$ (7,597)
Operating income	$ 71,230	$ 1,450

Prepare comparative common-sized statements, rounding percents to one decimal place. Interpret the analyses.

Case 9-4 Profitability and stockholder ratios

Harley-Davidson, Inc. (HOG), is a leading motorcycle manufacturer in the United States. The company manufactures and sells a number of different types of motorcycles, a complete line of motorcycle parts, and brand-related accessories, clothing, and collectibles.

The following information is available for three recent years (in millions except per-share amounts):

	Year 3	Year 2	Year 1
Net income (loss)	$752	$845	$734
Preferred dividends	None	None	None
Interest expense	$12	$4	$45
Shares outstanding for computing earnings per share	203	216	222
Cash dividend per share	$1.24	$1.10	$0.84
Average total assets	$9,760	$9,467	$9,288
Average stockholders' equity	$2,374	$2,959	$2,784
Average stock price per share	$54.63	$64.58	$56.47

1. Calculate the following ratios for each year. Round to one decimal place except dollar amounts, which should be rounded to the nearest cent.
   a. Return on total assets
   b. Return on stockholders' equity
   c. Earnings per share
   d. Dividend yield
   e. Price-earnings ratio using the average price per share of stock.

2. What is the average debt ratio and the ratio of average liabilities to average stockholders' equity for Years 1, 2, and 3?
3. Comment on the results in (1) and (2).

Case 9-5 Comprehensive profitability and solvency analysis

Starwood Hotels & Resorts Worldwide Inc. (HOT) and Wyndham Worldwide Corporation (WYN) are two major owners and managers of lodging and resort properties in the United States. Financial data (in millions) for a recent year for the two companies are as follows:

	Starwood	Wyndham
Income statement data:		
Interest expense	$ 139	$ 125
Income before income tax	782	916
Net income	633	612
Balance sheet data:		
Total assets	$8,659	$9,716
Total liabilities	7,134	8,766
Total stockholders' equity	1,525	950

The average liabilities, stockholders' equity, and total assets were as follows:

	Starwood	Wyndham
Average total assets	$8,711	$9,698
Average total liabilities	6,268	8,595
Average total stockholders' equity	2,443	1,103

1. Determine the following ratios for both companies (round to one decimal place after the whole percent):
   a. Return on total assets
   b. Return on total stockholders' equity
   c. Times interest earned
   d. Debt ratio for the most recent year.
   e. Ratio of liabilities to stockholders' equity for the most recent year.
2. Analyze and compare the two companies, using the information in (1).

Answers to Self-Examination Questions

1. **A** Percentage analysis indicating the relationship of the component parts to the total in a financial statement, such as the relationship of current assets to total assets (20% to 100%) in the question, is called vertical analysis (answer A). Percentage analysis of increases and decreases in corresponding items in comparative financial statements is called horizontal analysis (answer B). An example of horizontal analysis would be the presentation of the amount of current assets in the preceding balance sheet, along with the amount of current assets at the end of the current year, with the increase or decrease in current assets between the periods expressed as a percentage. Profitability analysis (answer C) is the analysis of a firm's ability to earn income. Contribution margin analysis (answer D) is discussed in a later managerial accounting chapter.

2. **D** Various liquidity and solvency measures, categorized as current position analysis, indicate a firm's ability to meet currently maturing obligations. Each measure contributes to the analysis of a firm's current position and is most useful when viewed with other measures and compared with similar measures for other periods and for other firms. Working capital (answer A) is the excess of current assets over current liabilities; the current ratio (answer B) is the ratio of current assets to current liabilities; and the quick ratio (answer C) is the ratio of the sum of cash, receivables, and temporary investments to current liabilities.

3. **D** The ratio of current assets to current liabilities is usually called the current ratio (answer A). It is sometimes called the working capital ratio (answer B) or bankers' ratio (answer C).

4. **C** The ratio of the sum of cash, receivables, and temporary investments (sometimes called quick assets) to current liabilities is called the quick ratio (answer C) or acid-test ratio. The current ratio (answer A), working capital ratio (answer B), and bankers' ratio (answer D) are terms that describe the ratio of current assets to current liabilities.

5. **C** The days' sales in inventory (answer C), which is determined by dividing the average inventory by the average daily cost of goods sold, expresses the relationship between the cost of goods sold and inventory. It indicates the efficiency in the management of inventory. The working capital ratio (answer A) indicates the ability of the business to meet currently maturing obligations (debt). The quick ratio (answer B) indicates the "instant" debt-paying ability of the business. The ratio of fixed assets to long-term liabilities (answer D) indicates the margin of safety for long-term creditors.

Chapter 10

Accounting Systems for Manufacturing Operations

What's Covered:

Topics: Accounting Systems for Manufacturing Operations

Nature of Managerial Accounting
- Type of information (Obj. 1)
- When reported (Obj. 1)
- Focus of report (Obj. 1)
- Differences with financial accounting (Obj. 1)

Manufacturing Operations and Costs
- Nature of manufacturing (Obj. 2)
- Manufacturing costs (Obj. 2)
- Direct materials costs (Obj. 2)
- Direct labor costs (Obj. 2)
- Factory overhead cost (Obj. 2)
- Prime and conversion costs (Obj. 2)
- Product and period costs (Obj. 2)

Types of Cost Accounting Systems
- Job order cost systems (Obj. 3)
- Process cost systems (Obj. 3)

Job Order Cost Systems for Manufacturing Operations
- Direct materials (Obj. 4)
- Direct labor (Obj. 4)
- Factory overhead (Obj. 4)
- Work in process (Obj. 4)
- Finished goods (Obj. 4)
- Cost of goods sold (Obj. 4)
- Period costs (Obj. 4)

Job Order Cost System for Service Operations
- Job costs (Obj. 5)
- Flow of costs (Obj. 5)

Just-in-Time Processing
- Traditional (Obj. 6)
- Just-in-time (Obj. 6)

Activity-Based Costing
- Activity cost pools (Obj. 7)
- Allocating costs (Obj. 7)

Metric-Based Analysis
- Cost per unit (Obj. 8)

Learning Objectives

Obj.1 Describe the nature of managerial accounting.

Obj.2 Describe and illustrate manufacturing operations, including different types and classifications of costs.

Obj.3 Describe types of cost accounting systems.

Obj.4 Describe and illustrate a job order cost accounting system for manufacturing operations.

Obj.5 Describe a job order cost accounting system for service operations.

Obj.6 Describe just-in-time manufacturing processing.

Obj.7 Describe and illustrate activity based costing.

Obj.8 Describe and illustrate the use of cost per unit for managerial decision making and performance analysis.

Chapter Metrics

Transaction and financial statement metrics are not illustrated in the managerial accounting chapters. Instead, we focus on metrics useful for managerial decision-making and performance analysis. The metric for this chapter is cost per unit.

Gibson Guitar

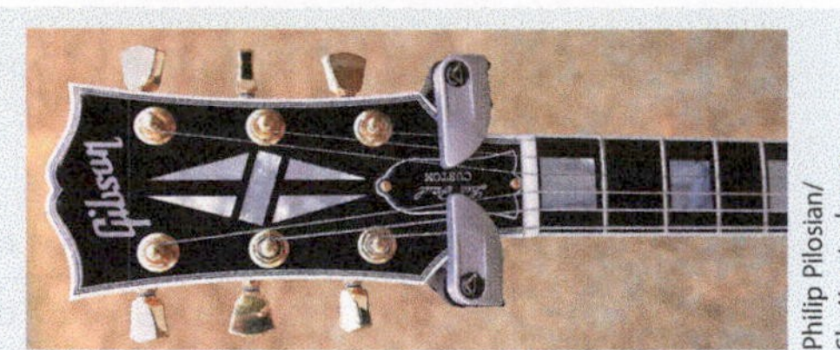

Philip Pilosian/ Shutterstock.com

Gibson guitars have been used by musical legends over the years, including B.B. King, Chet Atkins, Brian Wilson (Beach Boys), Jimmy Page (Led Zeppelin), Jackson Browne, John Fogerty, Jose Feliciano, Miranda Lambert, and Wynonna Judd. Known for its quality, Gibson Guitars celebrated its 120th anniversary in 2014.

Staying in business for 120 years requires a thorough understanding of how to manufacture high-quality guitars. In addition, it requires knowledge of how to account for the costs of making guitars. For example, Gibson needs cost information to answer the following questions:

- What should be the selling price of its guitars?
- How many guitars does it have to sell in a year to cover its costs and earn a profit?
- How many employees should the company have working on each stage of the manufacturing process?
- How would purchasing automated equipment affect the costs of its guitars?

This chapter begins by describing the nature of managerial accounting and manufacturing operations. Basic cost terms and cost accounting systems are described for manufacturing operations. Using this as a basis, a job order cost accounting system for a manufacturing operation is described and illustrated. The chapter concludes by describing job order systems for service operations, just-in-time processing, and activity-based costing.

Sources: http://www.gibson.com/Gibson/History and www2.gibson.com

Managerial Accounting

Objective 1
Describe the nature of managerial accounting.

Managers make numerous decisions during the day-to-day operations of a business and in planning for the future. Managerial accounting provides much of the information used for these decisions. For example, managerial accounting provides useful information for addressing the following questions.

- What is the cost of manufacturing a product, and how can it be reduced?
- How many units of a product does the company have to sell to make a profit?
- What should be the selling price of a product?
- When two or more products use limited resources, how much of each product should be produced?
- Should the company purchase or lease an asset?
- Should the company discontinue an unprofitable segment?
- With limited investment monies, in which of several projects should the company invest for the long term?

Since **managerial accounting** focuses on preparing information that is useful for management, it is not constrained by rules such as generally accepted accounting principles. That is, managerial accounting information often reports information that is not recorded using generally accepted accounting principles. For example, managerial accountants might prepare reports that involve more subjective data such as the possibility of competitors' reactions to a company's new sales prices or marketing campaign. Also, managerial accounting is not constrained to reporting data in periodic intervals, but instead often prepares reports "as needed" by management.

Some of the ways financial and managerial accounting differ are summarized in Exhibit 1.

Exhibit 1 Financial and Managerial Accounting Differences

	Managerial Accounting	Financial Accounting
Type of information	Information that is useful to management for its decision making, which varies by type of decision and is not restricted by specific rules such as generally accepted accounting principles (GAAP).	Transactions and events recorded and reported using generally accepted accounting principles.
When reported	As needed by management for its decision making.	Required to be reported annually but may be reported monthly or quarterly.
Focus of report	Varies by type of decision and may be an employee, manufacturing unit or process, or product as well as the company as a whole or segments within the company.	Company as a whole or segments within the company.

The remainder of this text focuses on managerial accounting topics. For example, this chapter focuses on determining the cost of manufacturing a product. Such information would be used by management in setting prices and in determining the profitability of a product.

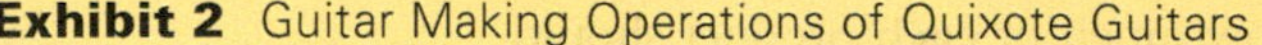

Objective 2
Describe and illustrate manufacturing operations, including different types and classifications of costs.

Manufacturing Operations and Costs

The operations of a business can be classified as service, merchandising, or manufacturing. The accounting for service and merchandising businesses has been described and illustrated in earlier chapters. For this reason, the remaining chapters of this text focus primarily on manufacturing businesses. However, most of the topics discussed also apply to service and merchandising businesses.

As a basis for illustration of manufacturing operations, a guitar manufacturer, Quixote Guitars, is used. Exhibit 2 is an overview of Quixote Guitar's manufacturing operations.

Exhibit 2 Guitar Making Operations of Quixote Guitars

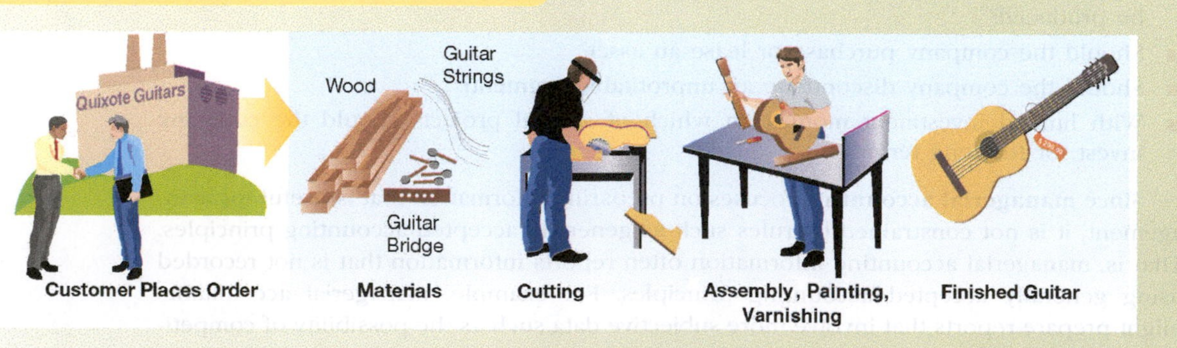

Gibson Guitars Connection
Gibson provides tours of its Memphis guitar factory located at 145 Lt. George W. Lee Avenue.

Quixote's guitar-making process begins when a customer places an order for a guitar. Once the order is accepted, the manufacturing process begins when the necessary materials are obtained. An employee then cuts the body and neck of the guitar out of raw lumber. Once the wood is cut, the body and neck of the guitar are assembled. When the assembly is complete, the guitar is painted and varnished.

A primary objective of managerial accounting is to accurately account for manufacturing costs. A **cost** is a payment of cash or the commitment to pay cash in the future for the purpose of generating revenues. For example, the cash (or credit) used to purchase equipment is the cost of the equipment. If equipment is purchased by exchanging assets other than cash, the current market value of the assets given up is the cost of the equipment purchased.

In managerial accounting, costs are classified according to the decision-making needs of management. For example, costs are often classified by their relationship to a segment of operations, called a **cost object**. A cost object may be a product, a sales territory, a department, or an activity, such as research and development.

The cost of a manufactured product includes the cost of materials used in making the product. In addition, the cost of a manufactured product includes the cost of converting the materials into a finished product. For example, Quixote Guitars uses employees and machines to convert wood (and other supplies) into finished guitars. Thus, the cost of a finished guitar (the cost object) includes the following:

1. Direct materials cost
2. Direct labor cost
3. Factory overhead cost

Direct Materials Cost

Manufactured products begin with raw materials that are converted into finished products. The cost of any material that is an integral part of the finished product is classified as a **direct materials cost**. For Quixote Guitars, direct materials cost includes the cost of the wood used in producing each guitar. Other examples of direct materials costs include the cost of electronic components for a television, silicon wafers for microcomputer chips, and tires for an automobile.

To be classified as a direct materials cost, the cost must be *both* of the following:

1. An integral part of the finished product
2. A significant portion of the total cost of the product

For Quixote Guitars, the cost of the guitar strings is not a direct materials cost. This is because the cost of guitar strings is an insignificant part of the total cost of each guitar. Instead, the cost of guitar strings is classified as a factory overhead cost, which is discussed later.

Materials costs such as the cost of the guitar strings are referred to as indirect materials costs. Another example of an indirect cost for Quixote Guitars is glue. Indirect materials costs are included in factory overhead.

Direct Labor Cost

Most manufacturing processes use employees to convert materials into finished products. The cost of employee wages that is an integral part of the finished product is classified as **direct labor cost**. For Quixote Guitars, direct labor cost includes the wages of the employees who cut each guitar out of raw lumber and assemble it. Other examples of direct labor costs include mechanics' wages for repairing an automobile, machine operators' wages for manufacturing tools, and assemblers' wages for assembling a laptop computer.

Like a direct materials cost, a direct labor cost must be *both* of the following:

1. An integral part of the finished product
2. A significant portion of the total cost of the product

For Quixote Guitars, the wages of the janitors who clean the factory are not a direct labor cost. This is because janitorial costs are not an integral part or a significant cost of each guitar. Instead, janitorial costs are classified as a factory overhead cost.

Labor costs such as janitorial costs are referred to as indirect labor costs. Another example of an indirect labor cost for Quixote Guitars is salaries of maintenance employees and plant supervisors. Indirect labor costs are included in factory overhead.

Factory Overhead Cost

Costs other than direct materials cost and direct labor cost that are incurred in the manufacturing process are combined and classified as **factory overhead cost**. Factory overhead is sometimes called *manufacturing overhead* or *factory burden.*

All factory overhead costs are indirect costs of the product. Some factory overhead costs include the following:

1. Heating and lighting the factory
2. Repairing and maintaining factory equipment
3. Property taxes on factory buildings and land
4. Insurance on factory buildings
5. Depreciation on factory plant and equipment

Factory overhead cost also includes materials and labor costs that do not enter directly into the finished product. Examples include the cost of oil used to lubricate machinery and the wages of janitorial and supervisory employees. Also, if the costs of direct materials or direct labor are not a significant portion of the total product cost, these costs may be classified as factory overhead costs.

For Quixote Guitars, the costs of guitar strings and janitorial wages are factory overhead costs. Additional factory overhead costs of making guitars are as follows:

1. Sandpaper
2. Buffing compound
3. Glue
4. Power (electricity) to run the machines
5. Depreciation of the machines and building
6. Salaries of production supervisors

Prime Costs and Conversion Costs

Direct materials, direct labor, and factory overhead costs may be grouped together for analysis and reporting. Two such common groupings are as follows:

1. **Prime costs**, which consist of direct materials and direct labor costs
2. **Conversion costs**, which consist of direct labor and factory overhead costs

Conversion costs are the costs of converting the materials into a finished product. Direct labor is both a prime cost and a conversion cost, as shown in Exhibit 3.

Exhibit 3 Prime Costs and Conversion Costs

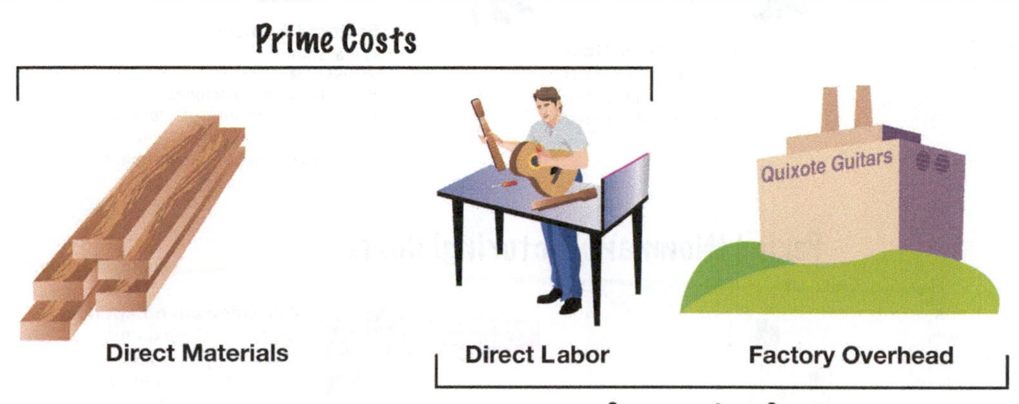

Product Costs and Period Costs

For financial reporting purposes, costs are classified as product costs or period costs.

1. **Product costs** consist of manufacturing costs: direct materials, direct labor, and factory overhead.
2. **Period costs** consist of selling and administrative expenses. *Selling expenses* are incurred in marketing the product and delivering the product to customers. *Administrative expenses* are incurred in managing the company and are not directly related to the manufacturing or selling functions.

Examples of product costs and period costs for Quixote Guitars are presented in Exhibit 4.

To facilitate control, selling and administrative expenses may be reported by level of responsibility. For example, selling expenses may be reported by products, salespersons, departments, divisions, or territories. Likewise, administrative expenses may be reported by areas such as human resources, computer services, legal, accounting, or finance.

Gibson Guitars Connection

In January 1986, guitar enthusiasts Henry Juszkiewicz and David Berryman purchased Gibson. Together they restored Gibson's reputation for innovation and quality. Under their leadership, Gibson began generating profits.

Exhibit 4 Examples of Product Costs and Period Costs—Quixote Guitars

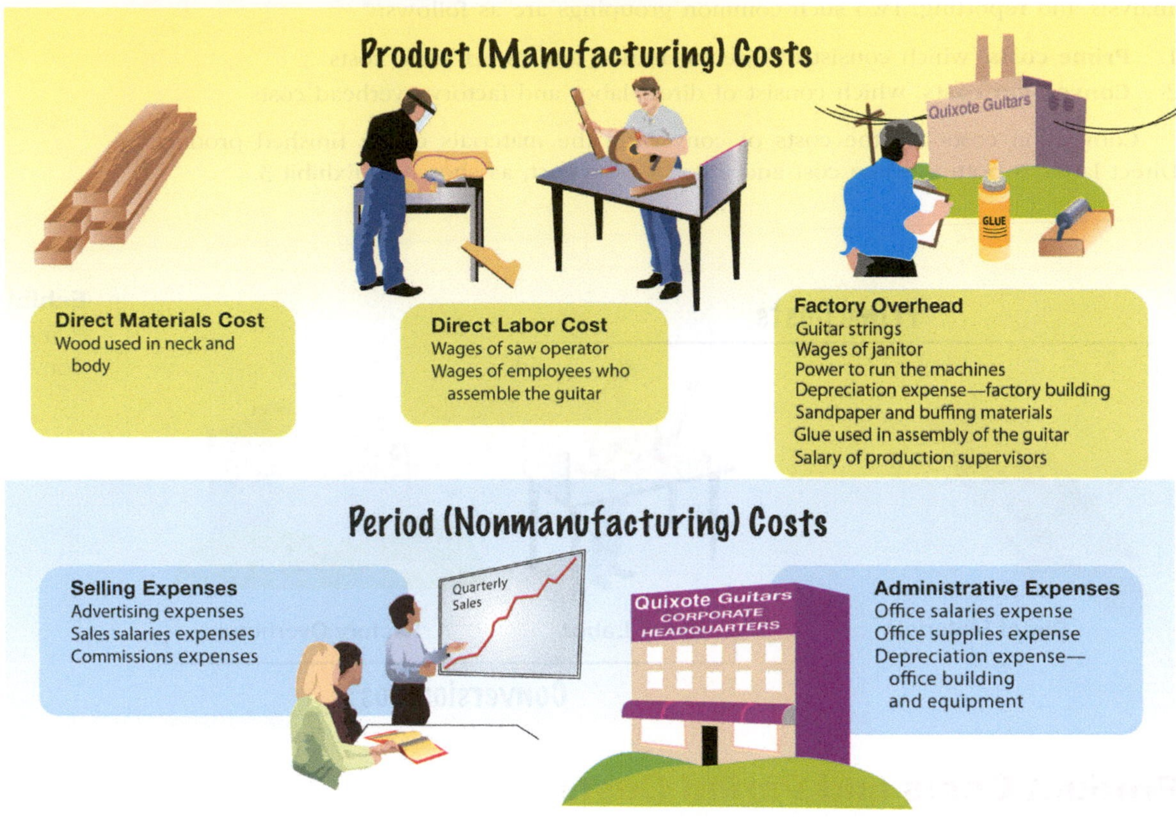

The impact on the financial statements of product and period costs is summarized in Exhibit 5. As product costs are incurred, they are recorded and reported on the balance sheet as *inventory*. When the inventory is sold, the cost of the manufactured product sold is reported as *cost of goods sold* on the income statement. Period costs are reported as *expenses* on the income statement in the period in which they are incurred and thus never appear on the balance sheet.

Exhibit 5 Product Costs, Period Costs, and the Financial Statements

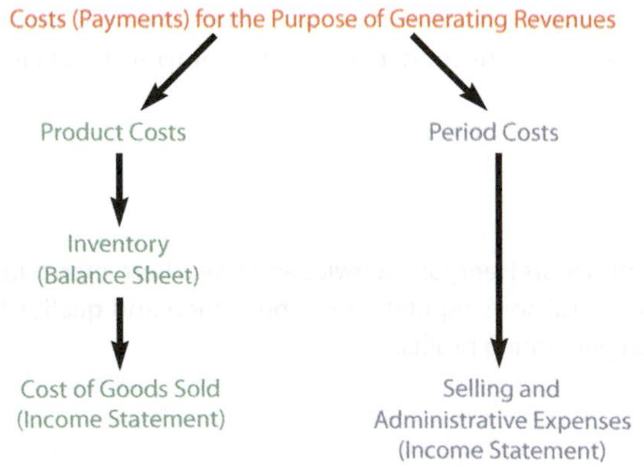

Cost Accounting Systems

Objective 3
Describe types of cost accounting systems.

Cost accounting systems measure, record, and report product costs. Managers use product costs for setting product prices, controlling operations, and developing financial statements.

The two main types of cost accounting systems for manufacturing operations are job order cost and process cost systems. Each system differs in how it accumulates and records manufacturing costs.

Job Cost Systems

A **job order cost system** provides product costs for each quantity of product that is manufactured. Each quantity of product that is manufactured is called a *job*. Job order cost systems are often used by companies that manufacture custom products for customers or batches of similar products. For example, an apparel manufacturer, such as **Levi Strauss & Co.**, or a guitar manufacturer, such as **Gibson Guitars**, would use a job order cost system.

Process Cost Systems

A **process cost system** provides product costs for each manufacturing department or process. Process cost systems are often used by companies that manufacture units of a product that are indistinguishable from each other and that are manufactured using a continuous production process. Examples would be oil refineries, paper producers, chemical processors, and food processors.

Job order and process cost systems are widely used. A company may use a job order cost system for some of its products and a process cost system for other products.

In this chapter, the job order cost system is illustrated. As a basis for illustration, Quixote Guitars, a manufacturer of guitars, is used. The process cost system is described and illustrated in Appendix B.

Job Order Cost Systems for Manufacturing Operations

Objective 5
Describe and illustrate a job order cost accounting system for manufacturing operations.

A job order cost system records and summarizes manufacturing costs by jobs. The flow of manufacturing costs in a job order system is illustrated in Exhibit 6.

Exhibit 6 Flow of Manufacturing Costs

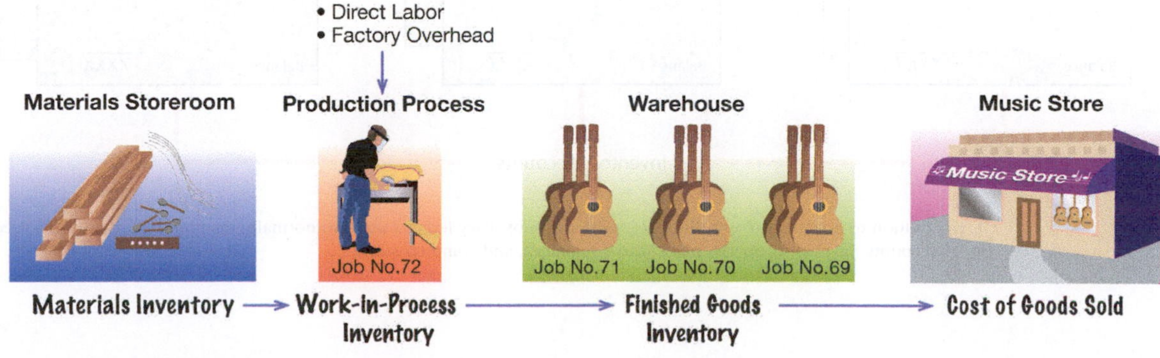

The **materials inventory**, sometimes called *raw materials inventory,* consists of the costs of the direct and indirect materials that have not yet entered the manufacturing process. For Quixote Guitars, the materials inventory would consist of wood, guitar strings, guitar bridges, and glue.

The **work-in-process inventory** consists of direct materials costs, direct labor costs, and factory overhead costs that have entered the manufacturing process but are associated with products that have not been completed. For example, although the materials for Job 72 have been added, it is still in the production process. Thus, Job 72 is in Work-in-Process Inventory as shown in Exhibit 6.

The **finished goods inventory** consists of completed jobs that have not been sold. Jobs 69, 70, and 71 have been completed and are included in Finished Goods Inventory as shown in Exhibit 6.

Upon sale, a manufacturer records the cost of the sale as *cost of goods sold.* An example is the guitars sold to the music store in Exhibit 6. The cost of goods sold for a manufacturer is comparable to the cost of merchandise sold for a merchandising business.

In a job order cost accounting system, perpetual inventory records are maintained for materials, work-in-process, and finished goods inventories. For example, materials inventory is supported by subsidiary inventory accounts that record the increase, decrease, and amount on hand for each type of material. These subsidiary materials accounts are kept in a ledger, called a **subsidiary ledger**. The sum of the subsidiary ledger accounts equals the balance of the materials account, called the **controlling account**.[1]

Gibson Guitars Connection

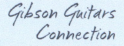

At any point in time, Gibson will have materials, work-in-process, and finished goods inventories.

The controlling accounts and subsidiary ledgers for materials, work-in-process, and finished goods inventories for Quixote Guitars are illustrated in Exhibit 7.

Exhibit 7 Inventory Ledger Accounts

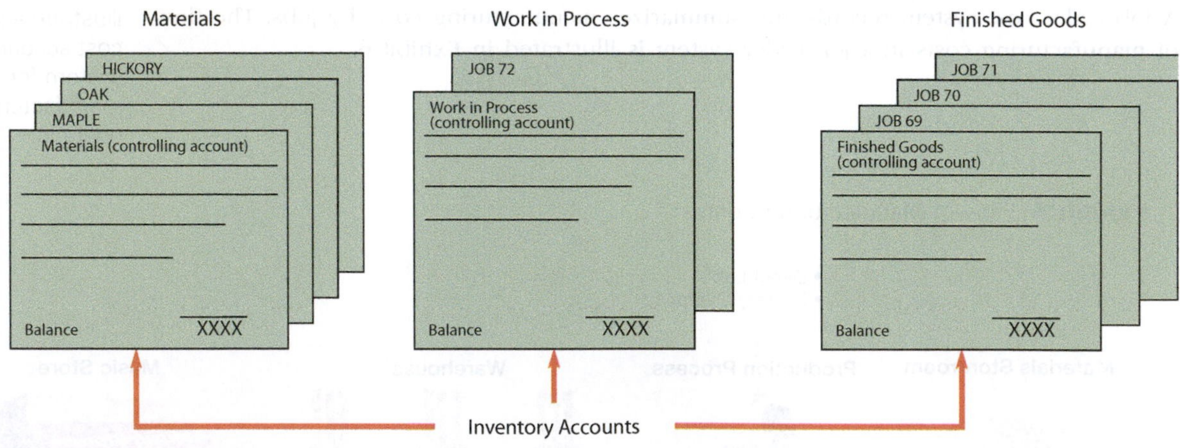

1. In addition to inventory, controlling accounts and subsidiary ledgers are also normally maintained for accounts receivable; accounts payable; property, plant, and equipment; and common stock.

Materials Cost

The materials account is a controlling account. A separate account for each type of material is maintained in a subsidiary **materials ledger**.

Exhibit 8 shows Quixote Guitars' materials subsidiary ledger account for maple. Increases and decreases to the account are as follows:

1. Increases are based on *receiving reports* such as Receiving Report No. 196 for $10,500, which is supported by the supplier's invoice.
2. Decreases are based on *materials requisitions* such as Requisition No. 672 for $2,000 for Job 71 and Requisition No. 704 for $11,000 for Job 72.

Exhibit 8
Materials Information and Cost Flows

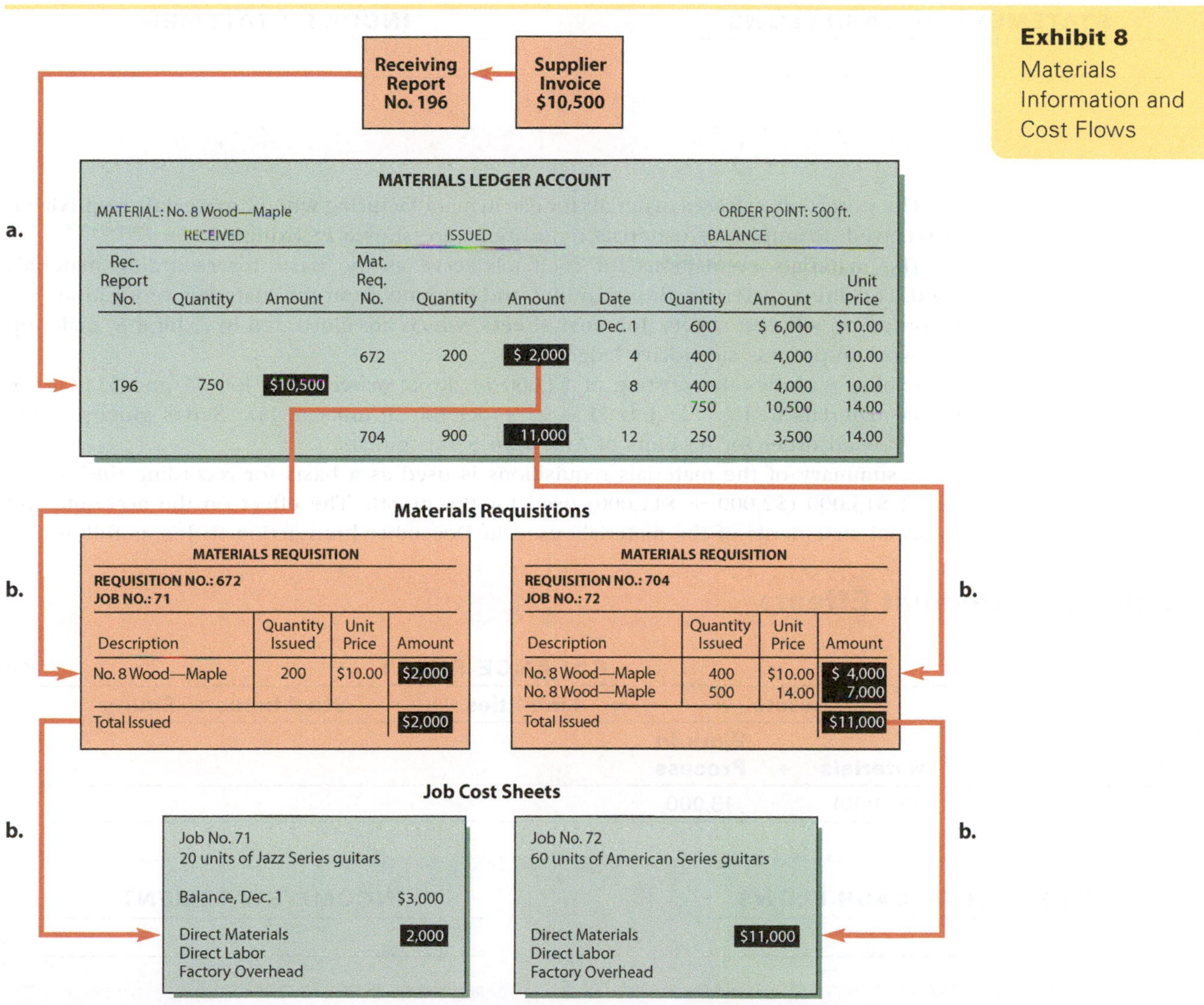

A **receiving report** is prepared when materials that have been ordered are received and inspected. The quantity received and the condition of the materials are entered on the receiving report. When the supplier's invoice is received, it is compared to the receiving report. If there are no discrepancies, the purchase is recorded.

The effect on the accounts and financial statements of recording the supplier invoice and Receiving Report No. 196 [transaction (a)] is as follows.

Gibson uses a variety of woods in making guitars, including cedar.

Gibson Guitars Connection

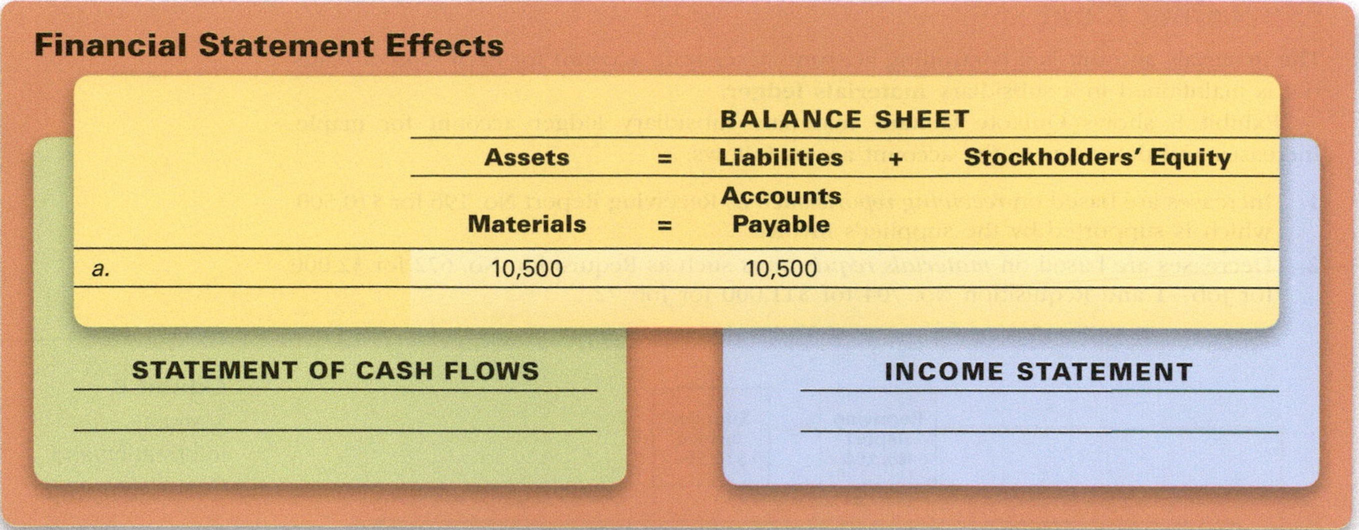

Financial Statement Effects
BALANCE SHEET
Assets = Liabilities + Stockholders' Equity
Materials = Accounts Payable
a. 10,500 10,500
STATEMENT OF CASH FLOWS
INCOME STATEMENT

The storeroom releases materials for use in manufacturing when a **materials requisition** is received. Examples of materials requisitions are shown in Exhibit 8.

The materials requisitions for each job serve as the basis for recording materials used. For direct materials, the quantities and amounts from the materials requisitions are recorded on job cost sheets. **Job cost sheets**, which are illustrated in Exhibit 8, make up the work-in-process subsidiary ledger.

Exhibit 8 shows the posting of $2,000 of direct materials to Job 71 and $11,000 of direct materials to Job 72.[2] Job 71 is an order for 20 units of Jazz Series guitars, while Job 72 is an order for 60 units of American Series guitars.

A summary of the materials requisitions is used as a basis for recording the materials of $13,000 ($2,000 + $11,000) used for the month. The effect on the accounts and financial statements of the materials used in December [transaction (b)] is as follows:

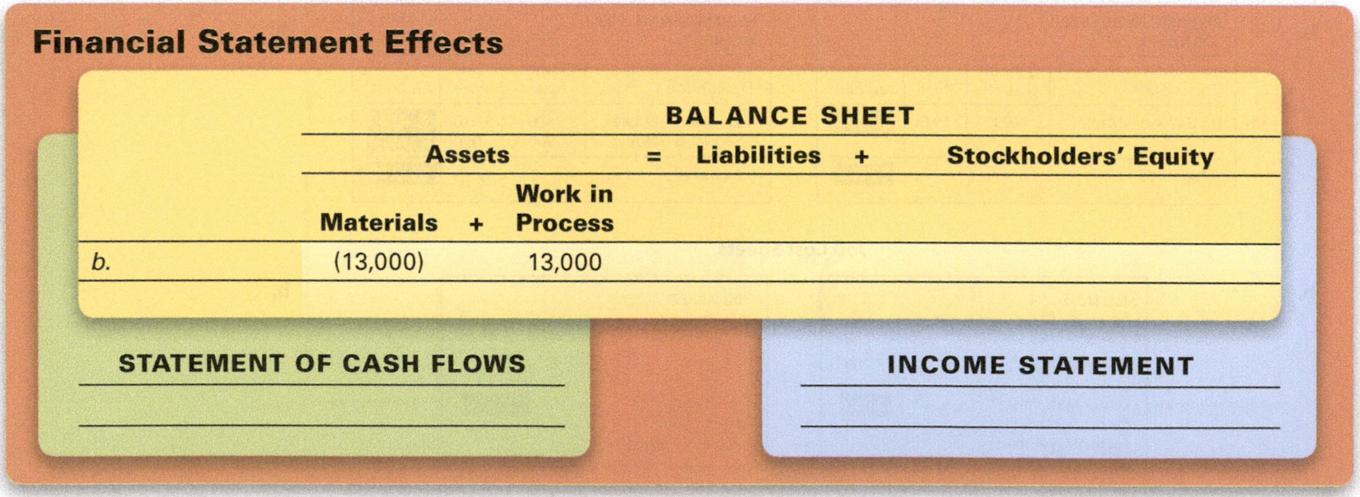

Financial Statement Effects
BALANCE SHEET
Assets = Liabilities + Stockholders' Equity
Materials + Work in Process
b. (13,000) 13,000
STATEMENT OF CASH FLOWS
INCOME STATEMENT

Many companies use computerized information processes to record the use of materials. In such cases, storeroom employees electronically record the release of materials, which automatically updates the materials ledger and job cost sheets.

Factory Labor Cost

When employees report for work, they may use *clock cards, in-and-out cards,* or *electronic badges* to clock in. When employees work on an individual job, they use **time tickets**. Exhibit 9 illustrates time tickets for Jobs 71 and 72.

2. To simplify, Exhibit 8 and this chapter use the first-in, first-out cost flow method.

Exhibit 9
Labor Information and Cost Flows

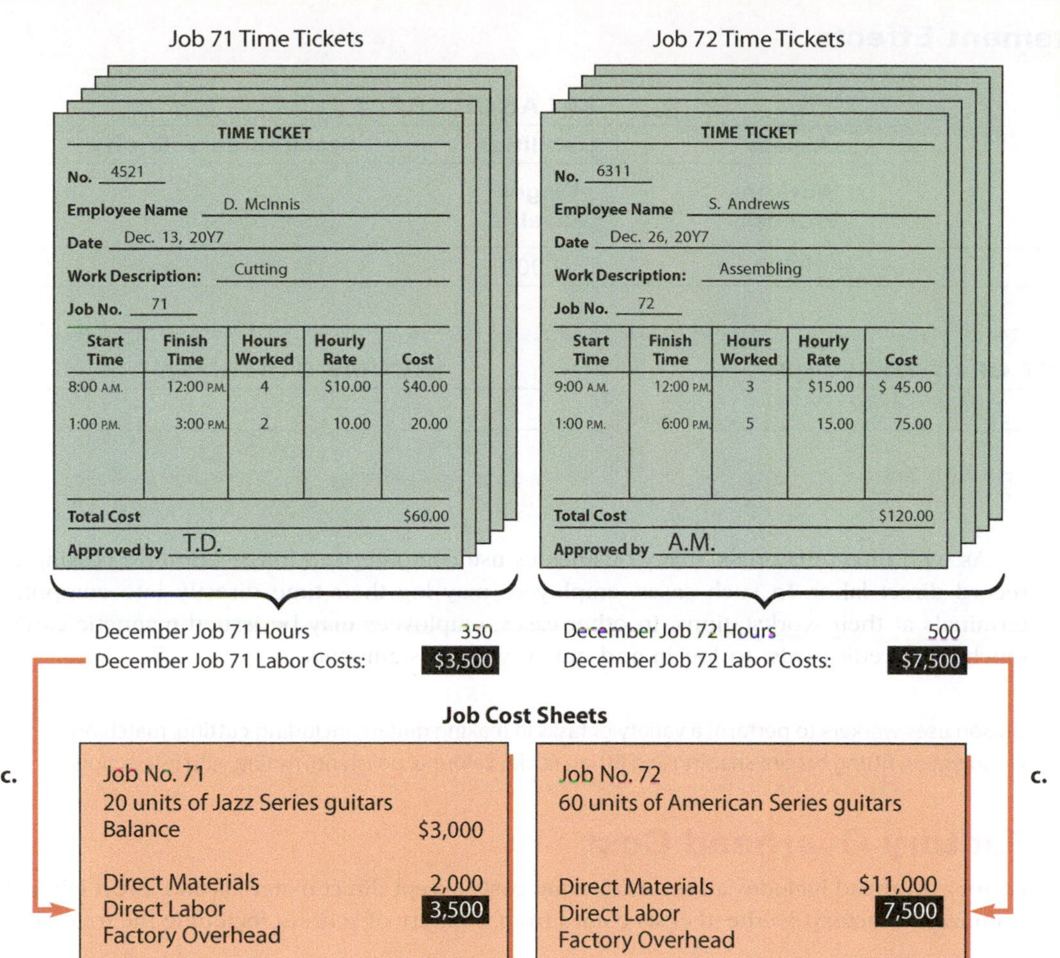

Exhibit 9 shows that on December 13, 20Y7, D. McInnis spent six hours working on Job 71 at an hourly rate of $10 for a cost of $60 (6 hrs. × $10). Exhibit 9 also indicates that a total of 350 hours was spent by employees on Job 71 during December for a total cost of $3,500. This total direct labor cost of $3,500 is recorded on the job cost sheet for Job 71, as shown in Exhibit 9.

Likewise, Exhibit 9 shows that on December 26, 20Y7, S. Andrews spent eight hours on Job 72 at an hourly rate of $15 for a cost of $120 (8 hrs. × $15). A total of 500 hours was spent by employees on Job 72 during December for a total cost of $7,500. This total direct labor cost of $7,500 is posted to the job cost sheet for Job 72, as shown in Exhibit 9.

A summary of the time tickets is used as the basis for recording direct labor of $11,000 ($3,500 + $7,500) for the month. The direct labor costs that flow into production increase Work in Process and Wages Payable. The effect on the accounts and financial statements of recording the direct labor for December [transaction (c)] is as shown at the top of the next page.

Integrity, Objectivity, and Ethics in Business

Phony Invoice Scams

A popular method for defrauding a company is to issue a phony invoice. The scam begins by initially contacting the target firm to discover details of key business contacts, business operations, and products. The swindler then uses this information to create a fictitious invoice. The invoice will include names, figures, and other details to give it the appearance of legitimacy. This type of scam can be avoided if invoices are matched with receiving documents prior to issuing a check.

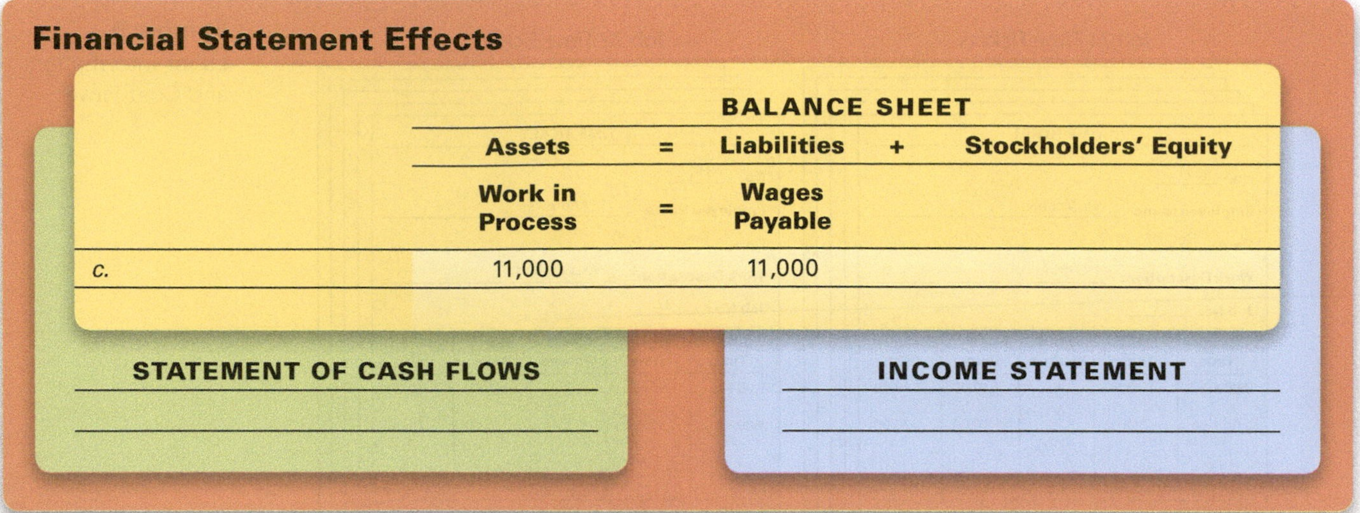

As with direct materials, many businesses use computerized information processing to record direct labor. In such cases, employees may log their time directly into computer terminals at their workstations. In other cases, employees may be issued magnetic cards, much like credit cards, to log in and out of work assignments.

Gibson Guitars Connection Gibson uses workers to perform a variety of tasks in making guitars, including cutting, matching wood grains, fitting braces, shaping and fitting necks, coloring, polishing, tuning, and inspecting.

Factory Overhead Cost

Factory overhead includes all manufacturing costs except direct materials and direct labor. A summary of factory overhead costs comes from a variety of sources including the following:

1. *Indirect materials* comes from a summary of materials requisitions.
2. *Indirect labor* comes from the salaries of production supervisors and the wages of other employees such as janitors.
3. *Factory power* comes from utility bills.
4. *Factory depreciation* comes from Accounting Department computations of depreciation.

To illustrate the recording of factory overhead, assume that Quixote Guitars incurred $4,600 of overhead in December, consisting of indirect materials of $500, factory depreciation of $1,200, indirect labor of $2,000, and factory utilities of $900. The effects on the accounts and financial statements of the December factory overhead of $4,600 [transaction (d)] are as shown at the top of the next page.

Gibson Guitars Connection Gibson incurs a variety of overhead costs in making guitars, including depreciation on buildings and equipment.

Integrity, Objectivity, and Ethics in Business

Ghost Employees

Companies must guard against the fraudulent creation and cashing of payroll checks. Numerous payroll frauds involve supervisors adding fictitious employees to or failing to remove departing employees from the payroll and then cashing the check. This type of fraud can be minimized by requiring proper authorization and approval of employee additions, removals, or changes in pay rates.

Financial Statement Effects

BALANCE SHEET

	Assets			=	Liabilities		+ Stockholders' Equity
	Materials +	Factory Overhead −	Accumulated Depreciation	=	Wages Payable +	Utilities Payable	
d.	(500)	4,600	(1,200)		2,000	900	

STATEMENT OF CASH FLOWS

INCOME STATEMENT

Allocating Factory Overhead Factory overhead is different from direct labor and direct materials in that it is *indirectly* related to the jobs. That is, factory overhead costs cannot be identified with or traced to specific jobs. For this reason, factory overhead costs are allocated to jobs. The process by which factory overhead or other costs are assigned to a cost object, such as a job, is called **cost allocation**.

The factory overhead costs are *allocated* to jobs using a common measure related to each job. This measure is called an **activity base**, *allocation base,* or *activity driver.* The activity base used to allocate overhead should reflect the consumption or use of factory overhead costs. For example, production supervisor salaries could be allocated on the basis of direct labor hours or direct labor cost of each job.

Predetermined Factory Overhead Rate Factory overhead costs are normally allocated or *applied* to jobs using a **predetermined factory overhead rate**. The predetermined factory overhead rate is computed as follows:

$$\text{Predetermined Factory Overhead Rate} = \frac{\text{Estimated Total Factory Overhead Costs}}{\text{Estimated Activity Base}}$$

To illustrate, assume that Quixote Guitars estimates total factory overhead cost of $50,000 for the year and an activity base of 10,000 direct labor hours. The predetermined factory overhead rate of $5 per direct labor hour is computed as follows:

$$\text{Predetermined Factory Overhead Rate} = \frac{\$50{,}000}{10{,}000 \text{ direct labor hours}} = \$5 \text{ per direct labor hour}$$

As shown above, the predetermined overhead rate is computed using *estimated* amounts at the beginning of the period. This is because managers need timely information on the product costs of each job. If a company waited until all overhead costs were known at the end of the period, the allocated factory overhead would be accurate, but not timely. Only through timely reporting can managers adjust manufacturing methods or product pricing.

Many companies use **activity-based costing** for accumulating and allocating factory overhead costs. This method uses a different overhead rate for each type of factory overhead activity, such as inspecting, moving, and machining. Activity-based costing is described and illustrated later in this chapter.

Applying Factory Overhead to Work in Process Quixote Guitars applies factory overhead using a rate of $5 per direct labor hour. The factory overhead applied to each job is recorded on the job cost sheets, as shown in Exhibit 10.

Exhibit 10 shows that 850 direct labor hours were used in Quixote Guitars' December operations. Based on the time tickets, 350 hours can be traced to Job 71, and 500 hours can be traced to Job 72.

Using a factory overhead rate of $5 per direct labor hour, $4,250 of factory overhead is applied as follows:

	Direct Labor Hours	Factory Overhead Rate	Factory Overhead Applied
Job 71	350	$5	$1,750 (350 hrs. × $5)
Job 72	500	5	2,500 (500 hrs. × $5)
Total	850		$4,250

As shown in Exhibit 10, the applied overhead is recorded on each job cost sheet. Factory overhead of $1,750 is recorded in Job Cost Sheet No. 71, which results in a total product cost on December 31, 20Y7, of $10,250. Factory overhead of $2,500 is recorded in Job Cost Sheet No. 72, which results in a total product cost on December 31, 20Y7, of $21,000.

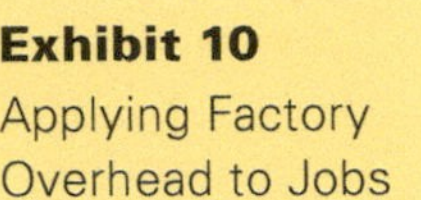

Exhibit 10 Applying Factory Overhead to Jobs

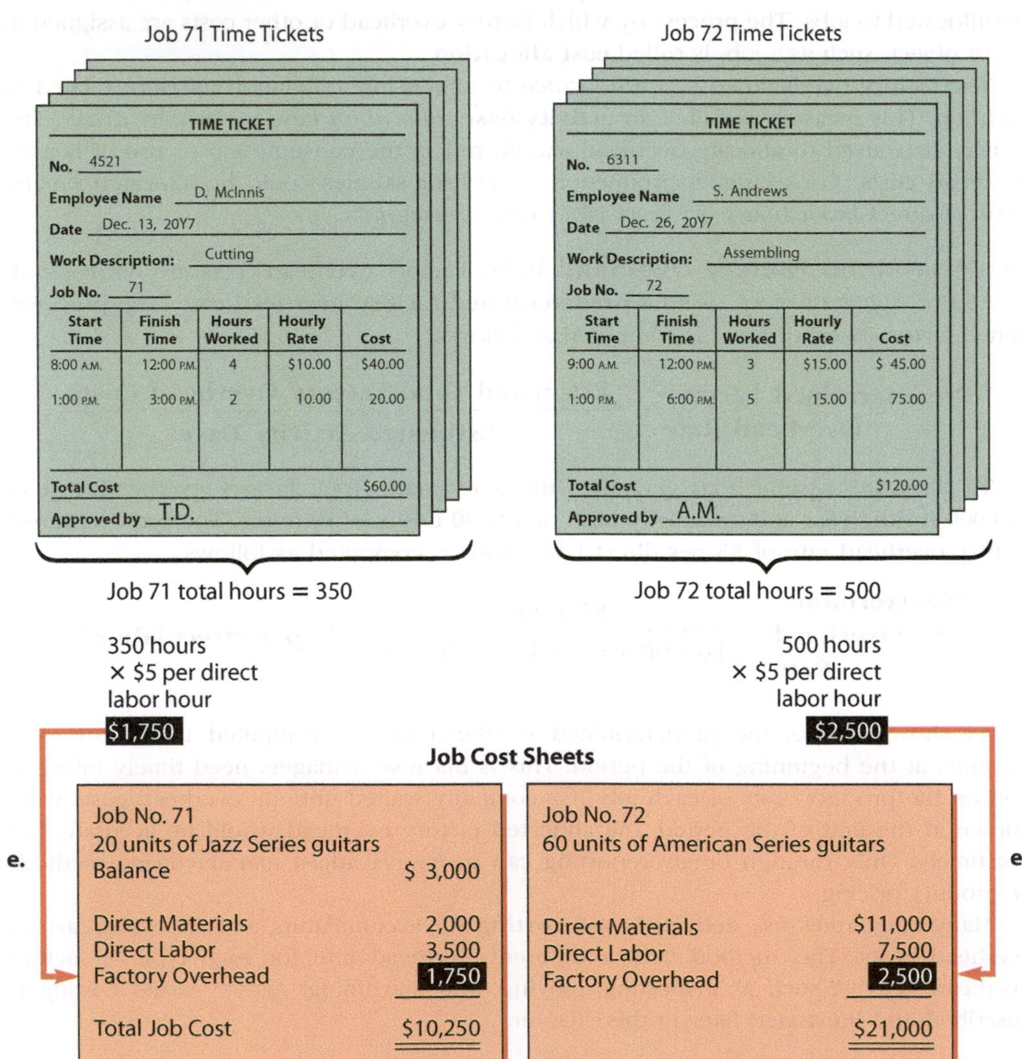

The factory overhead costs applied to production increase the work-in-process account and decrease the factory overhead account. The effect of applying the $4,250 ($1,750 + $2,500) of factory overhead to production [transaction (e)] on the accounts and financial statements for Quixote Guitars is shown below.

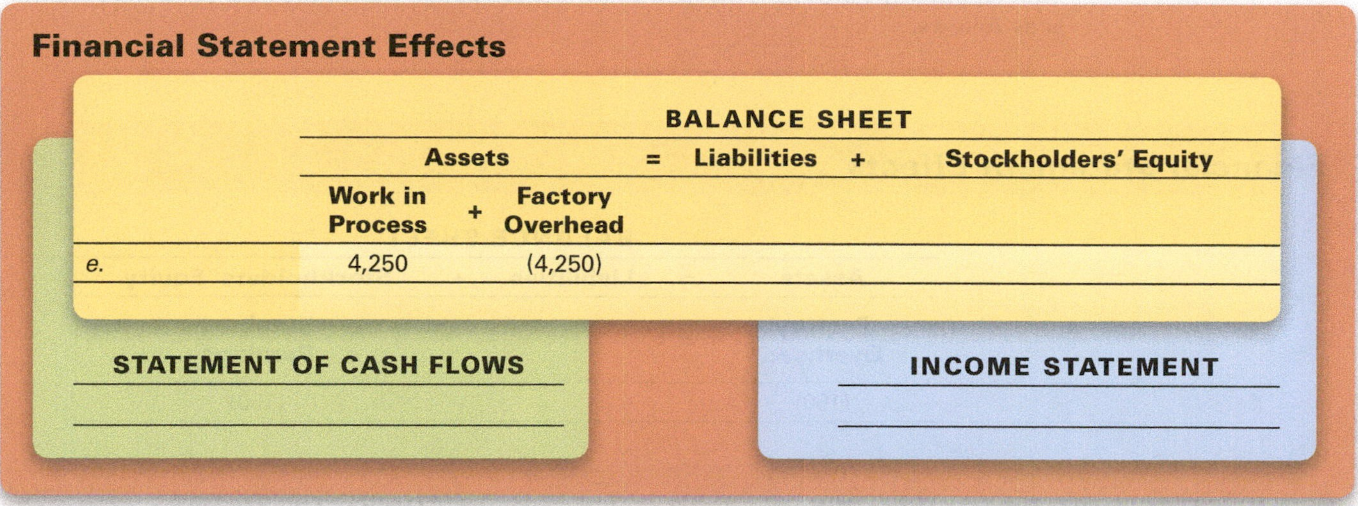

Financial Statement Effects

	BALANCE SHEET				
	Assets		= Liabilities	+	Stockholders' Equity
	Work in Process	+ Factory Overhead			
e.	4,250	(4,250)			

STATEMENT OF CASH FLOWS

INCOME STATEMENT

To summarize, the factory overhead account is:

1. Increased for the *actual overhead* costs incurred, as shown for transaction (d).
2. Decreased for the *applied overhead,* as shown for transaction (e).

The actual and applied overhead usually differ because the actual overhead costs are normally different from the estimated overhead costs. Depending on whether actual overhead is greater or less than applied overhead, the factory overhead account will either have a positive or negative ending balance as follows:

1. If the applied overhead is *less than* the actual overhead incurred, the factory overhead account will have a positive balance. This positive balance is called **underapplied factory overhead** or *underabsorbed factory overhead.*
2. If the applied overhead is *more than* the actual overhead incurred, the factory overhead account will have a negative balance. This negative balance is called **overapplied factory overhead** or *overabsorbed factory overhead.*

If the balance of factory overhead (either underapplied or overapplied) becomes large, the balance and related overhead rate should be investigated. For example, a large balance could be caused by changes in manufacturing methods. In this case, the factory overhead rate should be revised.

Disposal of Factory Overhead Balance During the year, the balance in the factory overhead account is carried forward and reported as a positive or negative amount on the monthly (interim) balance sheets. However, any balance in the factory overhead account should not be carried over to the next year. This is because any such balance applies only to operations of the current year.

If the estimates for computing the predetermined overhead rate are reasonably accurate, the ending balance of Factory Overhead should be relatively small. For this reason, the balance of Factory Overhead at the end of the year is disposed of by transferring it to the cost of goods sold account as follows:[3]

1. An ending positive balance (underapplied overhead) in the factory overhead account is disposed of by increasing Cost of Goods Sold and decreasing Factory Overhead.

3. An ending balance in the factory overhead account also may be allocated among the work-in-process, finished goods, and cost of goods sold accounts. This brings these accounts into agreement with the actual costs incurred. This approach is rarely used and is only required for large ending balances in the factory overhead account. For this reason, it will not be used in this text.

2. An ending negative balance (overapplied overhead) in the factory overhead account is disposed of by increasing Factory Overhead and decreasing Cost of Goods Sold.

To illustrate, the effect on the accounts and financial statements of eliminating an underapplied (positive) overhead balance of $150 at the end of the year [transaction (f)] is as follows.

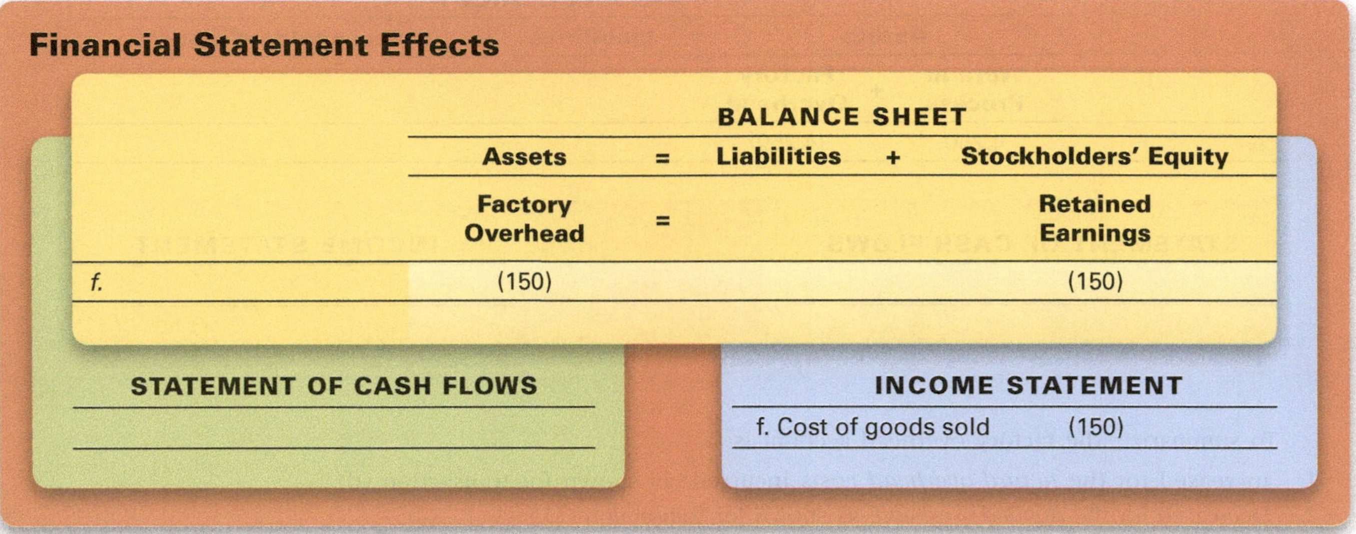

Financial Statement Effects

	BALANCE SHEET			
	Assets	=	Liabilities +	Stockholders' Equity
	Factory Overhead	=		Retained Earnings
f.	(150)			(150)

STATEMENT OF CASH FLOWS

INCOME STATEMENT	
f. Cost of goods sold	(150)

Work in Process

During the period, Work in Process is increased for the following:

1. Direct materials cost
2. Direct labor cost
3. Applied factory overhead cost

To illustrate, the balance of Work in Process for Quixote Guitars on December 1, 20Y7 (beginning balance), was $3,000. This balance relates to Job 71, which was the only job in process on this date. During December, Work in Process was increased for the following:

1. Direct materials cost of $13,000 [transaction (b)] based on materials requisitions.
2. Direct labor cost of $11,000 [transaction (c)] based on time tickets.
3. Applied factory overhead of $4,250 [transaction (e)] based on the predetermined overhead rate of $5 per direct labor hour.

The preceding increases in Work in Process are supported by the job cost sheets for Jobs 71 and 72, as shown in Exhibit 11.

During December, Job 71 was completed. Upon completion, the product costs (direct materials, direct labor, factory overhead) are totaled. This total is divided by the number of units produced to determine the cost per unit. Thus, the 20 Jazz Series guitars produced as Job 71 cost $512.50 ($10,250 ÷ 20) per guitar.

Exhibit 11 Job Cost Sheets and the Work-in-Process Controlling Account

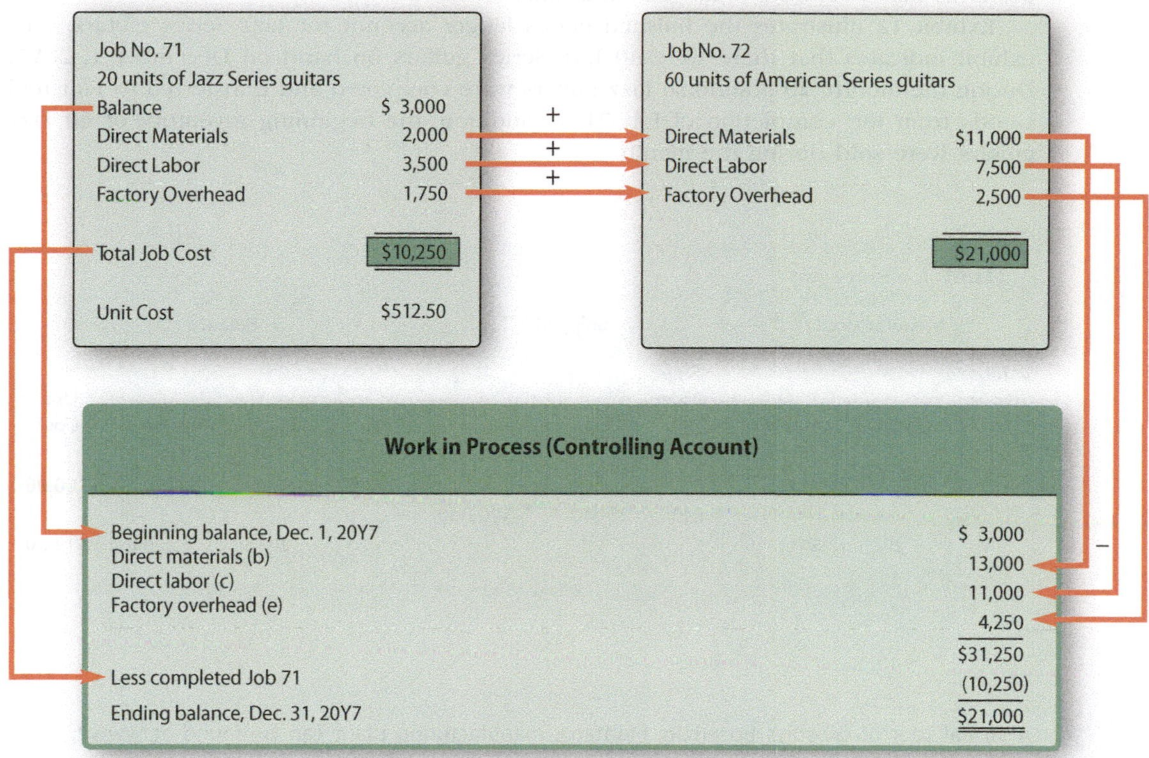

Job Cost Sheets
Job No. 71
20 units of Jazz Series guitars
Balance $ 3,000
Direct Materials 2,000
Direct Labor 3,500
Factory Overhead 1,750
Total Job Cost $10,250
Unit Cost $512.50
Job No. 72
60 units of American Series guitars
Direct Materials $11,000
Direct Labor 7,500
Factory Overhead 2,500
$21,000
Work in Process (Controlling Account)
Beginning balance, Dec. 1, 20Y7 $ 3,000
Direct materials (b) 13,000
Direct labor (c) 11,000
Factory overhead (e) 4,250
$31,250
Less completed Job 71 (10,250)
Ending balance, Dec. 31, 20Y7 $21,000

After completion, Job 71 is transferred from Work in Process to Finished Goods. For Job 71, this transfer of costs [transaction (g)] affects the accounts and financial statements as follows:

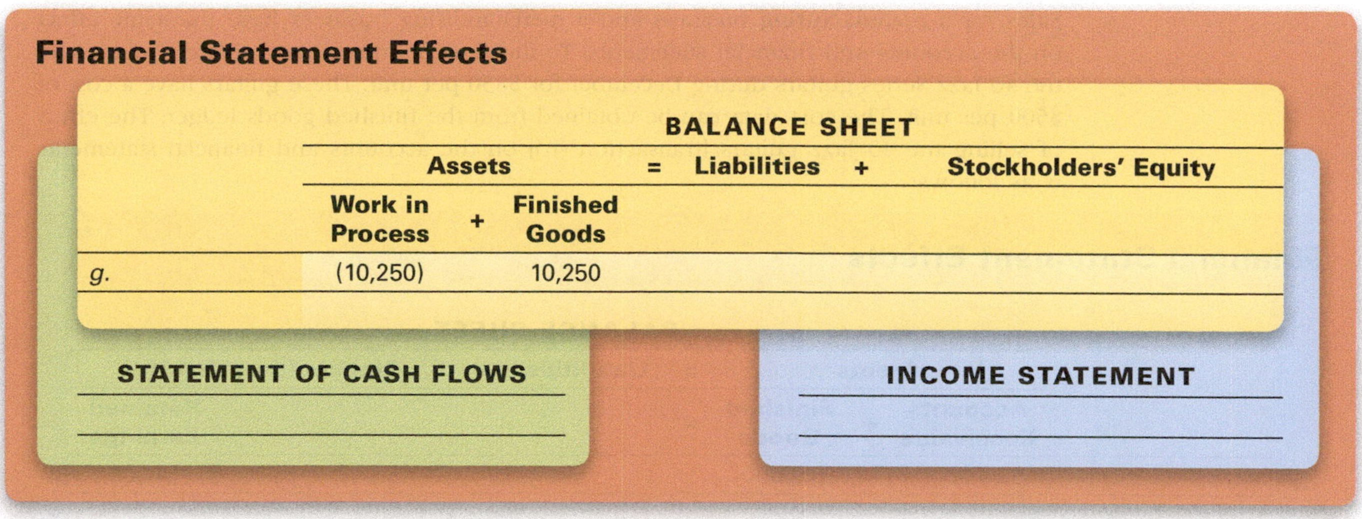

Job 72 was started in December but was not completed by December 31, 20Y7. Thus, Job 72 is still part of work in process on December 31, 20Y7. As shown in Exhibit 11, the balance of the job cost sheet for Job 72 ($21,000) is also the December 31, 20Y7, balance of Work in Process.

Finished Goods

The finished goods account is a controlling account for the subsidiary **finished goods ledger** or *stock ledger*. Each account in the finished goods ledger contains cost data for the units manufactured, units sold, and units on hand.

Exhibit 12 illustrates the finished goods ledger account for Jazz Series guitars. This exhibit indicates that there were 40 Jazz Series guitars on hand on December 1, 20Y7. During the month, 20 additional Jazz guitars were completed and transferred to Finished Goods from the completion of Job 71. In addition, the beginning inventory of 40 Jazz guitars were sold during the month.

Exhibit 12 Finished Goods Ledger Account

ITEM: *Jazz Series guitars*

Manufactured			Shipped			Balance			
Job Order No.	Quantity	Amount	Ship Order No.	Quantity	Amount	Date	Quantity	Amount	Unit Cost
						Dec. 1	40	$20,000	$500.00
			643	40	$20,000	9	—	—	—
71	20	$10,250				31	20	10,250	512.50

Gibson Guitars Connection

A virtual tour of Gibson's Bozeman, Montana, manufacturing plant can be found at www2.gibson.com. The Bozeman plant makes acoustic guitars similar to that illustrated in this chapter. Acoustic guitars do not require power or amps to produce music and are often used for folk and country music. Electric guitars are most often used for metal and rock music.

Sales and Cost of Goods Sold

Sales for a manufacturing business and a merchandising business have the same effect on the accounts and financial statements. To illustrate, assume that Quixote Guitars sold the 40 Jazz Series guitars during December for $850 per unit. These guitars have a cost of $500 per unit. The cost data can be obtained from the finished goods ledger. The effect of selling the 40 Jazz guitars [transaction (h)] on the accounts and financial statements is as follows:

Financial Statement Effects

BALANCE SHEET

	Assets			=	Liabilities	+	Stockholders' Equity
	Accounts Receivable	+	Finished Goods	=			Retained Earnings
h.	34,000		(20,000)				14,000

STATEMENT OF CASH FLOWS

INCOME STATEMENT

h. Sales	34,000
Cost of goods sold	(20,000)

Period Costs

Period costs are used in generating revenue during the current period but are not involved in the manufacturing process. Period costs are recorded as expenses of the current period as either selling or administrative expenses.

Selling expenses are incurred in marketing the product and delivering sold products to customers. Administrative expenses are incurred in managing the company but are not related to the manufacturing or selling functions. Exhibit 13 illustrates common selling and administrative expenses.

Exhibit 13 Examples of Period Costs

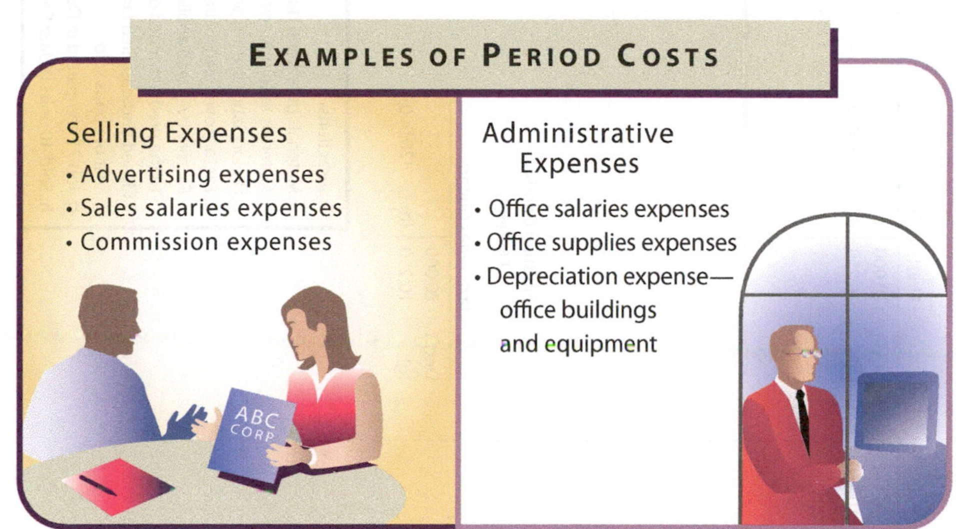

EXAMPLES OF PERIOD COSTS
Selling Expenses
• Advertising expenses
• Sales salaries expenses
• Commission expenses
ABC CORP
Administrative Expenses
• Office salaries expenses
• Office supplies expenses
• Depreciation expense—office buildings and equipment

During December, Quixote Guitars incurred sales salaries of $2,000 and office salaries of $1,500. The effect on the accounts and financial statements of recording the December salaries [transaction (i)] is as follows:

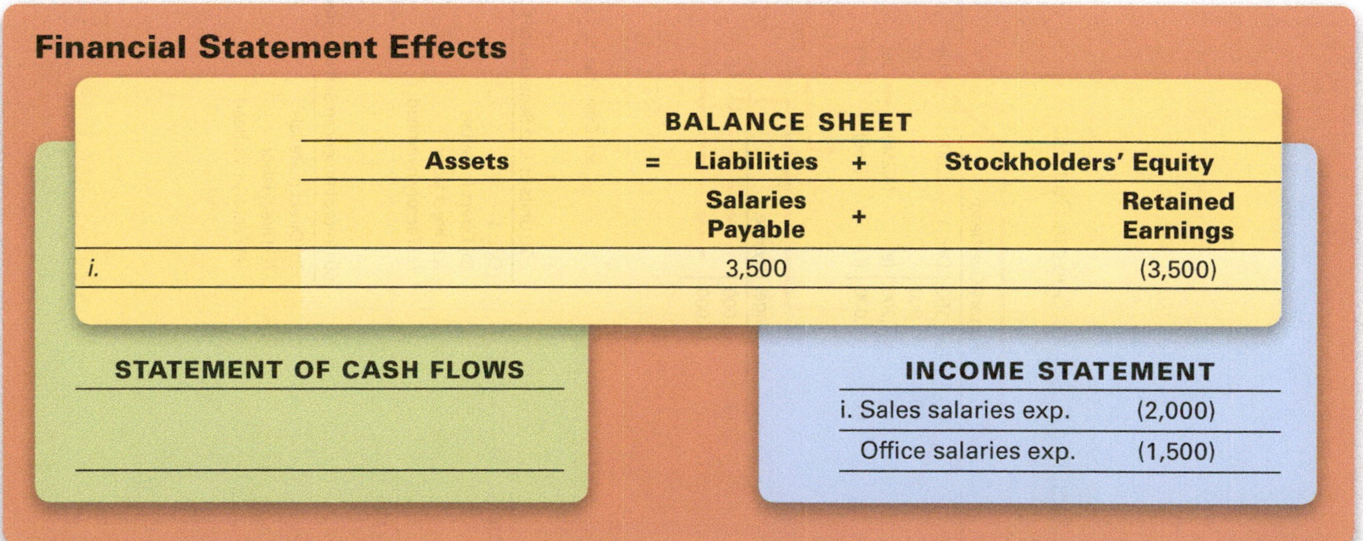

Financial Statement Effects

	BALANCE SHEET				
	Assets	=	Liabilities	+	Stockholders' Equity
			Salaries Payable	+	Retained Earnings
i.			3,500		(3,500)

STATEMENT OF CASH FLOWS

INCOME STATEMENT	
i. Sales salaries exp.	(2,000)
Office salaries exp.	(1,500)

Summary of Cost Flows for Quixote Guitars

Exhibit 14 shows the cost flows through the manufacturing accounts of Quixote Guitars for December. In Exhibit 14, increases are shown on the left side and decreases are shown on the right side of the accounts. In addition, summary details of the following subsidiary ledgers are shown:

1. *Materials Ledger*—the subsidiary ledger for Materials.
2. *Job Cost Sheets*—the subsidiary ledger for Work in Process.
3. *Finished Goods Ledger*—the subsidiary ledger for Finished Goods.

Exhibit 14 Flow of Manufacturing Costs for Quixote Guitars

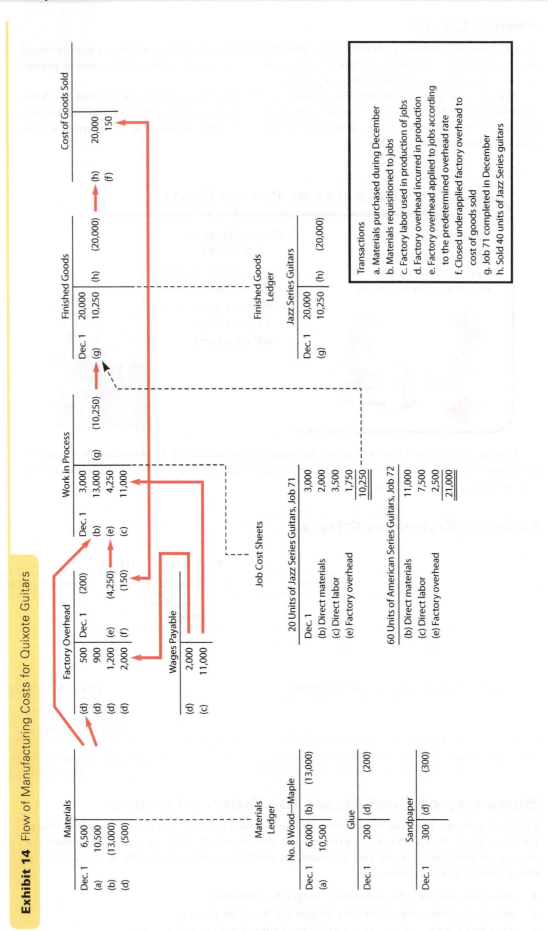

Materials

	Debit		Credit
Dec. 1	6,500		
(a)	10,500		
(b)	(13,000)		
(d)	(500)		

Factory Overhead

	Debit		Credit
(d)	500	Dec. 1	(200)
(d)	900		
(d)	1,200	(e)	(4,250)
(d)	2,000	(f)	(150)

Wages Payable

(d)	2,000
(c)	11,000

Work in Process

	Debit		Credit
Dec. 1	3,000		
(b)	13,000	(g)	(10,250)
(e)	4,250		
(c)	11,000		

Finished Goods

	Debit		Credit
Dec. 1	20,000		
(g)	10,250	(h)	(20,000)

Cost of Goods Sold

(h)	20,000
(f)	150

Materials Ledger

No. 8 Wood—Maple

	Debit		Credit
Dec. 1	6,000	(b)	(13,000)
(a)	10,500		

Glue

	Debit		Credit
Dec. 1	200	(d)	(200)

Sandpaper

	Debit		Credit
Dec. 1	300	(d)	(300)

Job Cost Sheets

20 Units of Jazz Series Guitars, Job 71

Dec. 1	3,000
(b) Direct materials	2,000
(c) Direct labor	3,500
(e) Factory overhead	1,750
	10,250

60 Units of American Series Guitars, Job 72

(b) Direct materials	11,000
(c) Direct labor	7,500
(e) Factory overhead	2,500
	21,000

Finished Goods Ledger

Jazz Series Guitars

	Debit		Credit
Dec. 1	20,000		
(g)	10,250	(h)	(20,000)

Transactions

a. Materials purchased during December
b. Materials requisitioned to jobs
c. Factory labor used in production of jobs
d. Factory overhead incurred in production
e. Factory overhead applied to jobs according to the predetermined overhead rate
f. Closed underapplied factory overhead to cost of goods sold
g. Job 71 completed in December
h. Sold 40 units of Jazz Series guitars

Entries in the accounts shown in Exhibit 14 are identified by letters. These letters refer to the entries described and illustrated in the chapter.

As shown in Exhibit 14, the balances of Materials, Work in Process, and Finished Goods are supported by their subsidiary ledgers. These balances are as follows:

Controlling Account	Balance and Total of Related Subsidiary Ledger
Materials	$ 3,500
Work in Process	21,000
Finished Goods	10,250

The income statement for Quixote Guitars is shown in Exhibit 15.

Exhibit 15 Income Statement of Quixote Guitars

Quixote Guitars Income Statement For the Month Ended December 31, 20Y7		
Sales		$ 34,000
Cost of goods sold		(20,150)
Gross profit		$ 13,850
Selling and administrative expenses:		
Sales salaries expense	$2,000	
Office salaries expense	1,500	
Total selling and administrative expenses		(3,500)
Operating income		$ 10,350

Job Order Cost Systems for Service Businesses

Objective 5

Describe a job order cost accounting system for service operations.

A job order cost accounting system may be used for a professional service business. For example, an advertising agency, an attorney, and a physician provide services to individual customers, clients, or patients. In such cases, the customer, client, or patient can be viewed as a job for which costs are accumulated and reported.

The primary product costs for a service business are direct labor and overhead costs. Any materials or supplies used in rendering services are normally insignificant. As a result, materials and supply costs are included as part of the overhead cost.

Like a manufacturing business, direct labor and overhead costs of rendering services to clients are accumulated in a work-in-process account. *Work in Process* is supported by a cost ledger with a job cost sheet for each client.

When a job is completed and the client is billed, the costs are transferred to a cost of services account. *Cost of Services* is similar to the cost of merchandise sold account for a merchandising business or the cost of goods sold account for a manufacturing business. A finished goods account and related finished goods ledger are not necessary. This is because the revenues for the services are recorded only after the services are provided.

The flow of costs through a service business using a job order cost accounting system is shown in Exhibit 16.

Exhibit 16 Flow of Costs Through a Service Business

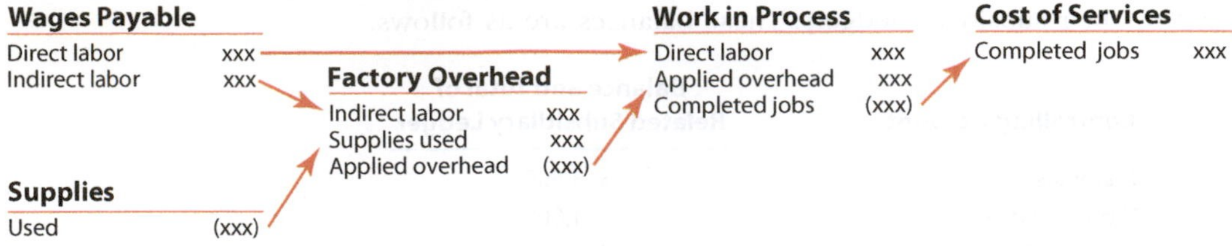

In practice, other considerations unique to service businesses may need to be considered. For example, a service business may bill clients on a weekly or monthly basis rather than when a job is completed. In such cases, a portion of the costs related to each billing is transferred from the work-in-process account to the cost of services account. A service business may also bill clients for services in advance, which would be accounted for as deferred revenue until the services are completed.

Objective 6
Describe just-in-time manufacturing processing.

Just-in-Time Processing

The objective of most manufacturers is to produce products with high quality, low cost, and instant availability. In attempting to achieve this objective, many manufacturers have implemented just-in-time processing. **Just-in-time (JIT) processing** is a management approach that focuses on reducing time and cost and eliminating poor quality. JIT processing achieves efficiencies and flexibility by reorganizing traditional production processes.

Traditional Production Process

A traditional manufacturing process for a furniture manufacturer is shown in Exhibit 17. The product (chair) moves through seven processes. In each process, workers are assigned a specific job, which is performed repeatedly as unfinished products are received from the preceding department. The product moves from process to process as each function or step is completed.

Exhibit 17 Traditional Production

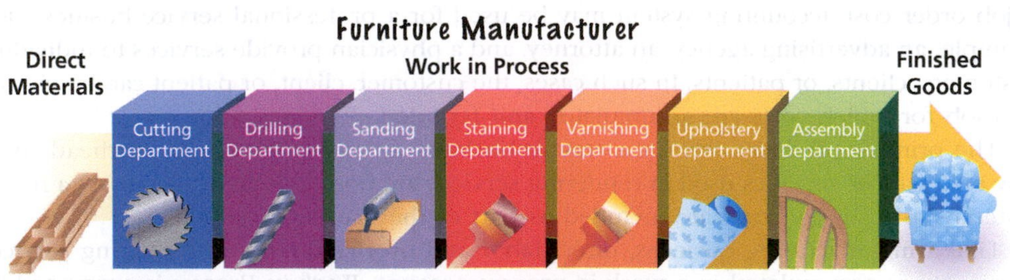

For the furniture maker in Exhibit 17, the product (chair) moves through the following seven steps:

1. In the Cutting Department, the wood is cut to design specifications.
2. In the Drilling Department, the wood is drilled to design specifications.
3. In the Sanding Department, the wood is sanded.
4. In the Staining Department, the wood is stained.
5. In the Varnishing Department, varnish and other protective coatings are applied.
6. In the Upholstery Department, fabric and other materials are added.
7. In the Assembly Department, the product (chair) is assembled.

In the traditional production process, supervisors enter materials into manufacturing so as to keep all the manufacturing departments (processes) operating. Some departments, however, may process materials more rapidly than others. In addition, if one department stops because of machine breakdowns, for example, the preceding departments usually continue production in order to avoid idle time. In such cases, a buildup of work-in-process inventories results in some departments.

Just-in-Time Production Process

In a just-in-time system, processing functions are combined into work centers, sometimes called **manufacturing cells**. For example, the seven departments illustrated in Exhibit 17 might be reorganized into the following three work centers:

1. Work Center 1 performs the cutting, drilling, and sanding functions.
2. Work Center 2 performs the staining and varnishing functions.
3. Work Center 3 performs the upholstery and assembly functions.

The preceding JIT manufacturing processing is illustrated in Exhibit 18.

Exhibit 18
Just-in-Time Processing

In traditional manufacturing, a worker typically performs only one function. However, in JIT manufacturing, work centers complete several functions. Thus, workers are often cross-trained to perform more than one function. Research has indicated that workers who perform several functions identify better with the end product. This creates pride in the product and improves quality and productivity.

The activities supporting the manufacturing process are called *service activities*. For example, repair and maintenance of manufacturing equipment are service activities. In a JIT manufacturing process, service activities may be assigned to individual work centers, rather than to centralized service departments. For example, each work center may be assigned responsibility for the repair and maintenance of its machinery and equipment. This creates an environment in which workers gain a better understanding of the production process and their machinery. In turn, workers tend to take better care of the machinery, which decreases repairs and maintenance costs, reduces machine downtime, and improves product quality.

In a JIT system, the product is often placed on a movable carrier that is centrally located in the work center. After the workers in a work center have completed their activities with the product, the entire carrier and any additional materials are moved just in time to satisfy the demand or need of the next work center. In this sense, the product is said to be "pulled through" production. Each work center is connected to other work centers through information contained on a **Kanban**, which is a Japanese term for cards.

In summary, the primary objective of JIT systems is to increase the efficiency of operations. This is achieved by eliminating waste and simplifying the production process. At the same time, JIT systems emphasize continually improving the manufacturing process and product quality.

Business Insight

Making Money in the Movie Business

Movie making is a high risk venture. The movie must be produced and marketed before the first dollar is received from the box office. If the movie is a hit, then all is well, but if the movie is a bomb, money will be lost. This is termed a "Blockbuster" business strategy and is common in businesses that have large up-front costs in the face of uncertain follow-up revenues, such as pharmaceuticals, video games, and publishing.

The profitability of a movie depends on its revenue and cost. A movie's cost is determined using job order costing; however, how costs are assigned to a movie is often complex and may be subject to disagreement. For example, in Hollywood's competitive environment, studios often negotiate payments to producers and actors based on a percentage of the film's gross revenues. This is termed "contingent compensation." As movies become hits, compensation costs increase in proportion to the movie's revenues, which eats into a hit's profitability.

iStockPhoto.com/mflippo

As the dollars involved get bigger, disagreements often develop between movie studios and actors or producers over the amount of contingent compensation. For example, the producer of the hit movie *Chicago* sued **Miramax Film Corp.** for failing to include foreign receipts and DVD sales in the revenue that was used to determine his payments. The controversial nature of contingent compensation is illustrated by the suit's claim that the accounting for contingent compensation led to confusing and meaningless results.

Integrity, Objectivity, and Ethics in Business

The Inventory Shift

Some managers take a shortcut to reducing inventory by shifting inventory to their suppliers. With this tactic, the hard work of improving processes is avoided. Enlightened managers realize that such tactics often have short-lived savings. Suppliers will eventually increase their prices to compensate for the additional inventory holding costs, thus resulting in no savings. Therefore, shifting a problem doesn't eliminate a problem.

Business Insight

P&G's "Pit Stops"

What do **Procter & Gamble (P&G)** and **Formula One** racing have in common? The answer begins with P&G's Packing Department, which is where detergents and other products are filled on a "pack line." Containers move down the pack line and are filled with products from a packing machine. When it was time to change from a 36-oz. to a 54-oz. Tide box, for example, the changeover involved stopping the line, adjusting guide rails, retrieving items from the tool room, placing items back in the tool room, changing and cleaning the pack heads, and performing routine maintenance. Changing the pack line could be a very difficult process and typically took up to several hours.

Management realized that it was important to reduce this time significantly in order to become more flexible and cost efficient in packing products. Where could they learn how to do setups faster? They turned to Formula One racing, reasoning that a pit stop was much like a setup. As a result, P&G videotaped actual Formula One pit stops. These videos were used to form the following principles for conducting a fast setup:

- Position the tools near their point of use on the line prior to stopping the line, to reduce time going back and forth to the tool room.
- Arrange the tools in the exact order of work, so that no time is wasted looking for a tool.
- Have each employee perform a very specific task during the setup.
- Design the workflow so that employees don't interfere with each other.
- Have each employee in position at the moment the line is stopped.
- Train each employee, and practice, practice, practice.
- Put a stop watch on the setup process.
- Plot improvements over time on a visible chart.

AP Images/PAUL SAKUMA

As a result of these changes, P&G was able to reduce pack-line setup time from several hours to 20 minutes. This allowed the company to reduce lead time and to improve the cost performance of the Packing Department.

Activity-Based Costing

Objective 7
Describe and illustrate activity-based costing.

In complex manufacturing systems, product costs can be distorted if inappropriate factory overhead rates are used. One way to avoid this distortion is by using the *activity-based costing (ABC) method*. This approach allocates factory overhead more accurately than does the single, plantwide overhead rate that was illustrated earlier in this chapter.

The activity-based costing method uses cost of activities to determine product costs. Under this method, factory overhead costs are initially accounted for in **activity cost pools**. These cost pools are related to a given activity, such as machine usage, inspections, moving, production setups, and engineering activities.

In order to simplify, a service business is used to illustrate the principles of activity-based costing. Like manufacturing businesses, service companies need to determine the cost of services in order to make pricing, promotional, and other decisions. Many service companies find that a single overhead rate can lead to service cost distortions. Thus, many service companies are now using activity-based costing for determining the cost of providing services to customers.

To illustrate, assume that Hopewell Hospital uses activity-based costing to allocate hospital overhead to patients. Hopewell Hospital applies activity-based costing by:

1. Identifying activity cost pools
2. Determining activity rates for each cost pool
3. Allocating overhead costs to patients based upon activity usage

Hopewell Hospital has identified the following activity cost pools:

1. Admission
2. Radiological testing
3. Operating room
4. Pathological testing
5. Dietary and laundry

Each activity cost pool has an estimated patient activity-base usage. Based on the budgeted costs for each activity and related estimated activity-base usage, the activity rates shown in Exhibit 19 were developed.

Exhibit 19 Activity-Based Costing Method—Hopewell Hospital

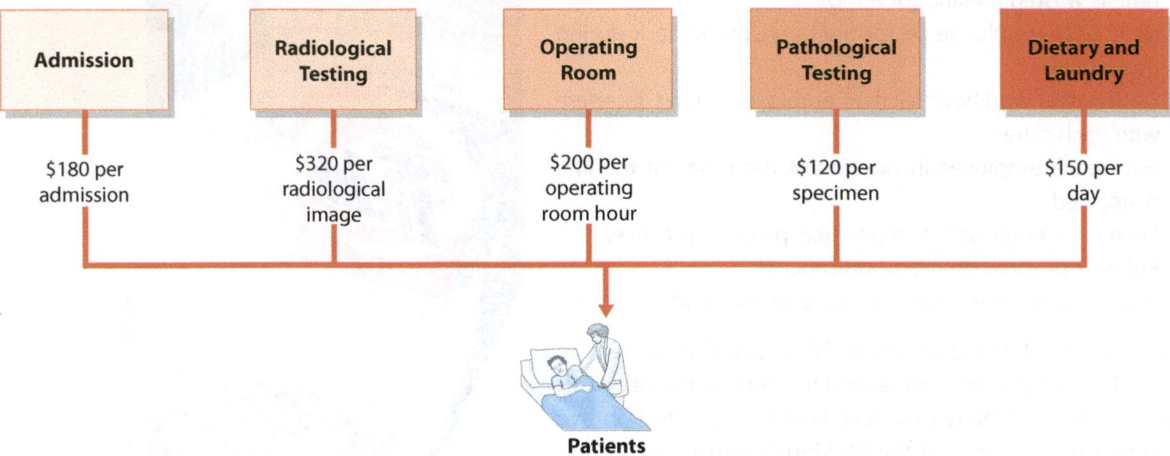

To illustrate, assume the following data for radiological testing:

Budgeted costs	$960,000
Total estimated activity-base usage	3,000 images

The activity rate of $320 per radiological image is computed as:

$$\textbf{Radiological Testing Activity Rate} = \frac{\textbf{Budgeted Activity Cost}}{\textbf{Activity-Base Usage}}$$

$$= \frac{\textbf{\$960,000}}{\textbf{3,000 images}} = \textbf{\$320 per image}$$

The activity rates for the other activities are determined in a similar manner. These activity rates along with the patient activity usage are used to allocate costs to patients as follows:

$$\textbf{Activity Cost Allocated to Patient} = \textbf{Patient Activity Usage} \times \textbf{Activity Rate}$$

To illustrate, assume that Mia Wilson was a patient of the hospital. The hospital overhead services (activities) performed for Mia Wilson are as follows.

	Patient (Mia Wilson) Activity Usage
Admission	1 admission
Radiological testing	2 images
Operating room	4 hours
Pathological testing	1 specimen
Dietary and laundry	7 days

Based on the preceding services (activities), the Hopewell Hospital overhead costs allocated to Mia Wilson total $2,790, as computed in Exhibit 20.

Exhibit 20 Overhead Allocation Using Activity-Based Costing

	A	B	C	D	E	F
1	Patient Name: Mia Wilson					
2		Activity-Base		Activity		Activity
3	Activity	Usage	×	Rate	=	Cost
4						
5	Admission	1 admission		$180 per admission		$ 180
6	Radiological testing	2 images		$320 per image		640
7	Operating room	4 hours		$200 per hour		800
8	Pathological testing	1 specimen		$120 per specimen		120
9	Dietary and laundry	7 days		$150 per day		1,050
10	Total					$2,790
11						

The patient activity costs can be combined with the direct costs, such as drugs and supplies. These costs and the related revenues can be reported for each patient in a patient (customer) profitability report. A partial patient profitability report for Hopewell Hospital is shown in Exhibit 21.

Exhibit 21 Patient Profitability Report

Hopewell Hospital
Patient (Customer) Profitability Report
For the Period Ending December 31, 20Y5

	Adcock, Kim	Birini, Brian	Conway, Don	Wilson, Mia
Revenues	$9,500	$21,400	$5,050	$3,300
Less patient costs:				
Drugs and supplies	$ 400	$ 1,000	$ 300	$ 200
Admission	180	180	180	180
Radiological testing	1,280	2,560	1,280	640
Operating room	2,400	6,400	1,600	800
Pathological testing	240	600	120	120
Dietary and laundry	4,200	14,700	1,050	1,050
Total patient costs	$8,700	$25,440	$4,530	$2,990
Operating income	$ 800	$ (4,040)	$ 520	$ 310

Exhibit 21 can be used by hospital administrators for decisions on pricing or services. For example, there was a large loss on services provided to Brian Birini. Investigation might reveal that some of the services provided to Birini were not reimbursed by insurance. As a result, Hopewell might lobby the insurance company to reimburse these services or request higher insurance reimbursement on other services.

Integrity, Objectivity, and Ethics in Business

University and Community Partnership—Learning Your ABC's

Students at Harvard's Kennedy School of Government joined with the city of Somerville, Massachusetts in building an activity-based cost system for the city. The students volunteered several hours a week in four-person teams, interviewing city officials within 18 departments. The students were able to determine activity costs, such as the cost of filling a pothole, processing a building permit, or responding to a four-alarm fire. Their study was used by the city in forming the city budget. As stated by some of the students participating in this project: "It makes sense to use the resources of the university for community building. . . . Real-world experience is a tremendous thing to have in your back pocket. We learned from the mayor and the fire chief, who are seasoned professionals in their own right."

Source: Kennedy School Bulletin, Spring 2005, "Easy as A-B-C: Students Take on the Somerville Budget Overhaul."

Business Insight

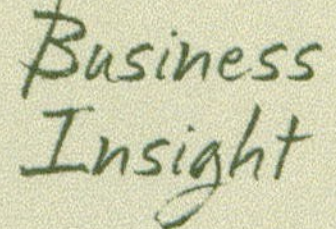

Finding the Right Niche

Businesses often attempt to divide a market into its unique characteristics, called market segmentation. Once a market segment is identified, product, price, promotion, and location strategies are tailored to fit that market. This is a better approach for many products and services than following a "one size fits all" strategy. Activity-based costing can be used to help tailor organizational efforts toward different segments. For example, **Fidelity Investments** uses activity-based costing to tailor its sales and marketing strategies to different wealth segments. Thus, a higher wealth segment could rely on personal sales activities, while less wealthy segments would rely on less costly sales activities, such as mass mail. The following table lists popular forms of segmentation and their common characteristics:

Form of Segmentation	Characteristics
Demographic	Age, education, gender, income, race
Geographic	Region, city, country
Psychographic	Lifestyle, values, attitudes
Benefit	Benefits provided
Volume	Light vs. heavy use

Examples for each of these forms of segmentation are as follows:

Demographic: **Fidelity Investments** markets growth to younger consumers while less aggressive investments are marketed to older consumers.

Geographic: **Chicago Cubs** markets its merchandise heavily in Chicago.

Psychographic: **The Body Shop** markets all-natural beauty products to consumers who value cosmetic products that have not been animal-tested.

Benefit: **Cold Stone Creamery** sells a premium ice cream product with customized toppings.

Volume: **Delta Air Lines** provides additional benefits, such as class upgrades, free air travel, and boarding priority, to its frequent fliers.

Metric-Based Analysis: Cost per Unit

Objective 8
Describe and illustrate the use of cost per unit for managerial decision making and performance analysis.

A job order cost accounting system accumulates and records product costs by jobs. The resulting total and unit product costs can be compared to similar jobs, compared over time, or compared to expected costs. In this way, a job order cost system can be used by managers for cost evaluation, decision making, and performance analysis.

To illustrate, Exhibit 22 shows the direct materials used for Jobs 54 and 63 for Quixote Guitars. The wood used in manufacturing the guitars is measured in board feet. Since Jobs 54 and 63 produced the same type and number of guitars, the direct materials cost per unit should be about the same. However, the materials cost per guitar for Job 54 is $100, while for Job 63 it is $125. Thus, the materials costs are more for Job 63.

Exhibit 22 Quixote Guitars Direct Materials Cost per Unit

Job 54
Item: 40 Jazz Series guitars

	Materials Quantity (board feet)	Materials Price	Materials Amount	Materials per Guitar
Direct materials:				
No. 8 Wood—Maple	400	$10.00	$4,000	$100

Job 63
Item: 40 Jazz Series guitars

	Materials Quantity (board feet)	Materials Price	Materials Amount	Materials per Guitar
Direct materials:				
No. 8 Wood—Maple	500	$10.00	$5,000	$125

The job cost sheets shown in Exhibit 22 can be analyzed for possible reasons for the increased materials cost for Job 63. Since the materials price did not change ($10 per board foot), the increased materials cost must be related to wood consumption.

Comparing wood consumed for Jobs 54 and 63 shows that 400 board feet were used in Job 54 to produce 40 guitars. In contrast, Job 63 used 500 board feet to produce the same number of guitars. Thus, an investigation should be undertaken to determine the cause of the extra 100 board feet used for Job 63.

Possible explanations could include the following:

1. A new employee, who was improperly trained, cut the wood for Job 63. As a result, excess waste and scrap was created.
2. The wood used for Job 63 was purchased from a new supplier. The wood was of poor quality, which created excessive waste and scrap.
3. The cutting tools needed repair and were improperly maintained. As a result, the wood was wrongly cut, which created excessive waste and scrap.
4. The instructions attached to the job were incorrect. The wood was cut according to the instructions. The incorrect instructions were discovered later in assembly. As a result, the wood had to be recut and the initial cuttings scrapped.

Based the results of the investigation, corrective actions should be taken to correct the underlying cause of the increased materials cost and improve performance.

Key Points

1. Describe the nature of managerial accounting.

Managerial accounting focuses on preparing information that is useful for management and is not constrained by rules such as generally accepted accounting principles (GAAP). The information reported varies the nature of the decision and when it is needed. The focus of the information may be for any item within the company such as an employee, product, or process.

2. Describe and illustrate manufacturing operations, including different types and classifications of costs.

In manufacturing operations, materials are converted into a finished product by using machinery and labor. A primary objective of managerial accounting is to accurately account for the costs of manufacturing products. The cost of materials that are an integral part of the manufactured product is direct materials cost. The cost of wages of employees who are involved in converting materials into the manufactured product is direct labor cost. Costs other than direct materials and direct labor costs are factory overhead costs, including indirect materials and labor. Direct materials, direct labor, and factory overhead costs are called product costs. Prime costs consist of direct materials and direct labor costs. Conversion costs consist of direct labor and factory overhead costs. Selling and administrative expenses are called period costs.

3. Describe types of cost accounting systems.

The two main types of cost accounting systems for manufacturing operations are job order cost and process cost systems. A job order cost system provides product costs for each quantity of product or job. A process cost system provides product costs for each manufacturing department or process.

4. Describe and illustrate a job order cost accounting system for manufacturing operations.

A job order cost system provides for a separate record of the cost of each particular quantity of product that passes through the factory. Direct materials, direct labor, and factory overhead costs are accumulated in a subsidiary cost ledger, in which each account is represented by a job cost sheet. Work in Process is the controlling account for the cost ledger. As a job is finished, its costs are transferred to the finished goods ledger, for which Finished Goods is the controlling account.

5. Describe the flow of costs for a service business that uses a job order cost accounting system.

A cost flow diagram for a service business using a job order cost accounting system is shown in Exhibit 16. For a service business, the cost of materials or supplies used is normally included as part of the overhead. The direct labor and overhead costs of rendering services are accumulated in a work-in-process account. When a job is completed and the client is billed, the costs are transferred to a cost of services account.

6. Describe just-in-time manufacturing processing.

The objective of JIT processing is to produce products with high quality, low cost, and instant availability. JIT processing combines traditional manufacturing functions into work centers where workers are cross-trained to complete several functions. Service activities such as repair and maintenance are also assigned to work centers. Finally, JIT processing emphasizes continuous improvement practices.

7. Describe and illustrate the use of activity-based costing.

In complex manufacturing systems, product costs can be distorted if a single factory overhead rate is used. One way to avoid this distortion is by using activity-based costing (ABC). Activity-based costing is illustrated in a service business setting by determining activity rates. The cost of each service offering is then determined by multiplying the activity rate by the amount of activity-base quantities consumed.

8. Describe and illustrate the use of cost per unit for managerial decision making and performance analysis.

A job order cost accounting system accumulates and records product costs by jobs. The resulting cost per unit can be compared to similar jobs, overtime, and to expected costs. In this way, cost per unit can be used for decision making and performance analysis.

Key Terms

Activity base (417)
Activity-based costing (417)
Activity cost pools (429)
Controlling account (412)
Conversion costs (409)
Cost (407)
Cost accounting system (411)
Cost allocation (417)
Cost object (407)
Direct labor cost (408)
Direct materials cost (407)
Factory overhead cost (408)
Finished goods inventory (412)
Finished goods ledger (422)
Job cost sheet (414)
Job order cost system (411)
Just-in-time (JIT) processing (426)
Kanban (427)
Managerial accounting (405)
Manufacturing cells (427)
Materials inventory (412)
Materials ledger (413)
Materials requisition (414)
Overapplied factory overhead (419)
Period costs (409)
Predetermined factory overhead rate (417)
Prime costs (409)
Process cost system (411)
Product costs (409)
Receiving report (413)
Subsidiary ledger (412)
Time tickets (414)
Underapplied factory overhead (419)
Work-in-process inventory (412)

Illustrative Problem

Derby Music Company specializes in producing and packaging compact discs (CDs) for the music recording industry. Derby uses a job order cost system. The following data summarize the operations related to production for March, the first month of operations:

a. Materials purchased on account, $15,500.

b. Materials requisitioned and labor used:

	Materials	Factory Labor
Job No. 100	$2,650	$1,770
Job No. 101	1,240	650
Job No. 102	980	420
Job No. 103	3,420	1,900
Job No. 104	1,000	500
Job No. 105	2,100	1,760
For general factory use	450	650

c. Factory overhead costs incurred on account, $2,700.

d. Depreciation of machinery, $1,750.

e. Factory overhead is applied at a rate of 70% of direct labor cost.

f. Jobs completed: Nos. 100, 101, 102, 104.

g. Jobs 100, 101, and 102 were shipped, and customers were billed for $8,100, $3,800, and $3,500, respectively.

Instructions

1. Prepare a schedule summarizing manufacturing costs by job during the month. Use the following form:

Job	Direct Materials	Direct Labor	Factory Overhead	Total

2. Prepare a schedule of jobs finished.
3. Prepare a schedule of jobs sold.
4. Prepare a schedule of completed jobs on hand at the end of the month.
5. Prepare a schedule of unfinished jobs at the end of the month.

Solution

1. Schedule of manufacturing costs incurred during month:

Job	Direct Materials	Direct Labor	Factory Overhead	Total
Job No. 100	$ 2,650	$1,770	$1,239	$ 5,659
Job No. 101	1,240	650	455	2,345
Job No. 102	980	420	294	1,694
Job No. 103	3,420	1,900	1,330	6,650
Job No. 104	1,000	500	350	1,850
Job No. 105	2,100	1,760	1,232	5,092
	$11,390	$7,000	$4,900	$23,290

2. Schedule of jobs finished:

Job	Direct Materials	Direct Labor	Factory Overhead	Total
Job No. 100	$2,650	$1,770	$1,239	$ 5,659
Job No. 101	1,240	650	455	2,345
Job No. 102	980	420	294	1,694
Job No. 104	1,000	500	350	1,850
				$11,548

3. Schedule of jobs sold:

Job No. 100	$5,659
Job No. 101	2,345
Job No. 102	1,694
	$9,698

4.

Schedule of Completed Jobs

Job No. 104:	
Direct materials	$1,000
Direct labor	500
Factory overhead	350
Balance of Finished Goods, March, 31	$1,850

5.

Schedule of Unfinished Jobs

Job	Direct Materials	Direct Labor	Factory Overhead	Total
Job No. 103	$3,420	$1,900	$1,330	$ 6,650
Job No. 105	2,100	1,760	1,232	5,092
Balance of Work in Process, March 31				$11,742

Self-Examination Questions

(Answers appear at the end of chapter)

1. Which of the following is *not* considered a cost of manufacturing a product?
   A. Direct materials cost
   B. Factory overhead cost
   C. Sales salaries
   D. Direct labor cost

2. Which of the following costs would be included as part of the factory overhead costs of a computer manufacturer?
   A. The cost of memory chips
   B. Depreciation of testing equipment
   C. Wages of computer assemblers
   D. The cost of disk drives

3. A company estimated $420,000 of factory overhead cost and 16,000 direct labor hours for the period. During the period, a job was completed with $4,500 of direct materials and $3,000 of direct labor. The direct labor rate was $15 per hour. What is the factory overhead applied to this job?
   A. $2,100
   B. $5,250
   C. $78,750
   D. $420,000

4. If the factory overhead account has a negative balance, factory overhead is said to be:
   A. Underapplied
   B. Overapplied
   C. Underabsorbed
   D. In error

5. When using job order costing for a professional service business, the primary product (service) costs are:
   A. Direct Materials and Overhead
   B. Direct Materials and Direct Labor
   C. Direct Materials, Direct Labor, and Overhead
   D. Direct Labor and Overhead

Class Discussion Questions

1. List three differences in how managerial accounting differs from financial accounting.

2. For a company that produces desktop computers, would memory chips be considered a direct or an indirect materials cost of each computer produced?

3. How is product cost information used by managers?

4. a. Name two principal types of cost accounting systems.
   b. Which system provides for a separate record of each particular quantity of product that passes through the factory?
   c. Which system accumulates the costs for each department or process within the factory?

5. What kind of firm would use a job order cost system?

6. How does the use of the materials requisition help control the issuance of materials from the storeroom?

7. a. Differentiate between the clock card and the time ticket.
   b. Why should the total time reported on an employee's time tickets for a payroll period be compared with the time reported on the employee's clock cards for the same period?

8. Describe the source of the data for increasing Work in Process for (a) direct materials, (b) direct labor, and (c) factory overhead.

9. Discuss how the predetermined factory overhead rate can be used in job order cost accounting to assist management in pricing jobs.

10. a. How is a predetermined factory overhead rate calculated?
    b. Name three common bases used in calculating the rate.

11. a. What is (1) overapplied factory overhead and (2) underapplied factory overhead?
    b. If the factory overhead account has a positive balance, was factory overhead underapplied or overapplied?

12. At the end of the fiscal year, there was a relatively minor balance in the factory overhead account. What procedure can be used for disposing of the balance in the account?
13. What is the difference between a product cost and a period cost?
14. Describe how a job order cost system can be used for professional service businesses.
15. a. What is the objective of just-in-time processing?
    b. How does just-in-time processing differ from traditional processing?
16. How can activity-based costing be used in service companies?

Exercises

Obj. 2

E10-1 Classifying costs as materials, labor, or factory overhead

Indicate whether each of the following costs of an airplane manufacturer would be classified as direct materials cost, direct labor cost, or factory overhead cost:

a. Aircraft engines
b. Controls for flight deck
c. Depreciation of equipment
d. Landing gear
e. Machine lubricants
f. Salary of plant superintendent
g. Tires
h. Wages of assembly line worker

Obj. 2

E10-2 Classifying costs as materials, labor, or factory overhead

Indicate whether the following costs of Colgate-Palmolive Company would be classified as direct materials cost, direct labor cost, or factory overhead cost:

a. Bottles in which mouthwashes are sold
b. Depreciation on production machinery
c. Depreciation on the soap plant
d. Maintenance supplies
e. Packaging department employees wages
f. Plant manager salary, toothpaste plant
g. Resins for soap and shampoo products
h. Salary of process engineers
i. Scents and fragrances
j. Wages of production line employees

Obj. 2

E10-3 Classifying costs as factory overhead

Which of the following items are properly classified as part of factory overhead for Caterpillar?

a. Amortization of patents on new assembly process
b. Consultant fees for a study of production line employee productivity
c. Depreciation on Peoria, Illinois, headquarters building
d. Factory supplies used in the Morganton, North Carolina, engine parts plant

e. Interest expense on debt
f. Plant manager's salary at Aurora, Illinois, manufacturing plant
g. Property taxes on the Danville, Kentucky, tractor tread plant
h. Sales incentive fees to dealers
i. Steel plate
j. Vice president of finance's salary

E10-4 Classifying costs as product or period costs

Obj. 2

For apparel manufacturer Ann Taylor, Inc., classify each of the following costs as either a product cost or a period cost:

a. Advertising expenses
b. Corporate controller's salary
c. Depreciation on office equipment
d. Depreciation on sewing machines
e. Fabric used during production
f. Factory janitorial supplies
g. Factory supervisors' salaries
h. Property taxes on factory building and equipment
i. Oil used to lubricate sewing machines
j. Repairs and maintenance costs for sewing machines
k. Research and development costs
l. Salaries of distribution center personnel
m. Salary of production quality control supervisor
n. Sales commissions
o. Utility costs for office building
p. Travel costs of salespersons
q. Wages of sewing machine operators

E10-5 Concepts and terminology

Obj. 2, 3

From the choices presented in the parentheses, choose the appropriate term for completing each of the following sentences:

a. Advertising expenses are usually viewed as (period, product) costs.
b. An example of factory overhead is (plant depreciation, sales office depreciation).
c. Direct materials costs and direct labor costs are called (prime, conversion) costs.
d. Implementing automatic factory robotics equipment normally (increases, decreases) the factory overhead component of product costs.
e. Materials that are an integral part of the manufactured product are classified as (direct materials, factory overhead).
f. An oil refinery would normally use a (job order, process) cost accounting system.
g. The balance sheet of a manufacturer would include an account for (cost of goods sold, work-in-process inventory).
h. The wages of an assembly worker are normally considered a (period, product) cost.

Obj. 4

E10-6 Transactions in a job order cost system

Five selected transactions for the current month are indicated by letters in the following accounts in a job order cost accounting system:

Cost of Goods Sold	Materials
(e) increase	(a) decrease

Factory Overhead	Wages Payable
(a) increase (b) increase (c) decrease	(b) increase

Finished Goods	Work in Process
(d) increase (e) decrease	(a) increase (b) increase (c) increase (d) decrease

Describe each of the five transactions.

Obj. 4
✔ c. $180,000

E10-7 Cost flow relationships

The following information is available for the first month of operations of Lane Inc., a manufacturer of art and craft items:

Sales	$750,000
Gross profit	240,000
Indirect labor	60,000
Indirect materials	30,000
Other factory overhead	10,000
Materials purchased	400,000
Total manufacturing costs for the period	600,000
Materials inventory, end of period	50,000

Using the above information, determine the following:

a. Cost of goods sold
b. Direct materials cost
c. Direct labor cost

Obj. 4

✔ b. $2,560

E10-8 Cost of materials issuances

An incomplete subsidiary ledger of wire cable for July is as follows:

RECEIVED			ISSUED			BALANCE			
Receiving Report Number	Quantity	Unit Price	Materials Requisition Number	Quantity	Amount	Date	Quantity	Amount	Unit Price
						July 1	250	$1,500	$6.00
309	400	$7.50				July 5			
			7401	480		July 10			
422	800	8.00				July 20			
			7639	650		July 26			

Note: The spreadsheet icon  indicates an Excel template is available on the student companion site.

a. Complete the materials issuances and balances for the wire cable subsidiary ledger. Assume a first-in, first-out cost flow.

b. Determine the balance of wire cable at the end of July.

c. Determine the total amount of materials transferred to Work in Process for July.

d. Explain how the materials ledger might be used as an aid in maintaining inventory quantities on hand.

E10-9 Recording issuing of materials

Obj. 4

Materials issued for the current month are as follows:

Requisition No.	Material	Job No.	Amount
945	Fiberglass	78	$112,850
946	Plastic	93	77,620
947	Glue	Indirect	3,330
948	Wood	99	28,550
949	Aluminium	108	49,100

a. Determine the amount of materials transferred to Work in Process and Factory Overhead for the current month.

b. Illustrate the effect on the accounts and financial statements of the materials transferred in (a).

E10-10 Amounts for materials

Obj. 4

✔ c. Fabric, $10,200

Big Timber Furniture Company manufactures furniture. Big Timber Furniture uses a job order cost system. Balances on June 1 from the materials ledger are as follows:

Fabric	$ 7,500
Polyester filling	18,000
Lumber	60,000
Glue	3,000

The materials purchased during June are summarized from the receiving reports as follows:

Fabric	$104,000
Polyester filling	200,000
Lumber	720,000
Glue	36,000

Materials were requisitioned to individual jobs as follows:

	Fabric	Polyester Filling	Lumber	Glue	Total
Job 304	$ 20,000	$ 52,300	$210,100		$ 282,400
Job 305	32,500	68,400	189,500		290,400
Job 306	48,800	78,400	313,200		440,400
Factory overhead—indirect materials				$37,700	37,700
Total	$101,300	$199,100	$712,800	$37,700	$1,050,900

The glue is not a significant cost, so it is treated as indirect materials (factory overhead).

a. Determine the total purchase of materials in June.

b. Determine the amounts of materials transferred to Work in Process and Factory Overhead during June.

c. Determine the June 30 balances that would be shown in the materials ledger accounts.

Obj. 4

E10-11 Recording factory labor costs

A summary of the time tickets for January is as follows:

Job No.	Amount	Job No.	Amount
3467	$ 2,500	3478	$ 9,030
3470	5,575	3480	10,100
3471	4,720	3497	6,625
Indirect labor	7,000	3501	1,800

a. Determine the amounts of factory labor costs transferred to Work in Process and Factory Overhead for January.

b. Illustrate the effect on the accounts and financial statements of the factory labor costs transferred in (a).

Obj. 4

E10-12 Recording factory labor costs

The weekly time tickets indicate the following distribution of labor hours for three direct labor employees:

	Hours			
	Job 560A	Job 560B	Job 560C	Process Improvement
Eva Leavitt	15	15	6	4
Micah Stone	10	15	13	2
Travis Hendrix	12	14	10	4

The direct labor rate earned by the three employees is as follows:

Leavitt	$31
Stone	28
Hendrix	20

The process improvement category includes training, quality improvement, housekeeping, and other indirect tasks.

a. Determine the amounts of factory labor costs transferred to Work in Process and Factory Overhead for the week.

b. Assume that Jobs 560A and 560B were completed but not sold during the week and that Job 560C remained incomplete at the end of the week. How would the direct labor costs for all three jobs be reflected on the financial statements at the end of the week?

Obj. 4

E10-13 Recording direct labor and factory overhead

Chamlee Industries Inc. manufactures recreational vehicles. Chamlee Industries uses a job order cost system. The time tickets from May jobs are summarized below.

Job 5-100	$6,400
Job 5-101	3,900
Job 5-102	4,800
Job 5-103	2,900
Factory supervision	1,750

Factory overhead is applied to jobs on the basis of a predetermined overhead rate of $30 per direct labor hour. The direct labor rate is $25 per hour.

a. Determine the total factory labor costs transferred to Work in Process and Factory Overhead for May.

b. Determine the amount of factory overhead applied to production for May.

c. Illustrate the effects of the factory overhead applied in (b) on the accounts and financial statements.

E10-14 Factory overhead rates and account balances

Obj. 4

✔ b. $9.50 per direct labor hour

Prostheses Industries operates two factories. The manufacturing operations of Factory 1 are machine intensive, while the manufacturing operations of Factory 2 are labor intensive. The company applies factory overhead to jobs on the basis of machine hours in Factory 1 and on the basis of direct labor hours in Factory 2. Estimated factory overhead costs, direct labor hours, and machine hours are as follows:

	Factory 1	Factory 2
Estimated factory overhead cost for fiscal year beginning August 1	$375,200	$2,660,000
Estimated direct labor hours for year		280,000
Estimated machine hours for year	22,400	
Actual factory overhead costs for August	$28,700	$230,000
Actual direct labor hours for August		24,000
Actual machine hours for August	1,800	

a. Determine the factory overhead rate for Factory 1.

b. Determine the factory overhead rate for Factory 2.

c. Determine the factory overhead applied to production in each factory for January.

d. Determine the balances of the factory accounts for each factory as of January 31, and indicate whether the amounts represent overapplied or underapplied factory overhead.

e. Explain why Factory 1 uses machine hours to allocate factory overhead while Factory 2 uses direct labor hours.

E10-15 Predetermined factory overhead rate

Obj. 4

Novus Engine Shop uses a job order cost system to determine the cost of performing engine repair work. Estimated costs and expenses for the coming period are as follows:

Engine parts	$1,257,500
Shop direct labor	550,000
Shop and repair equipment depreciation	91,000
Shop supervisor salaries	250,000
Shop property taxes	40,000
Shop supplies	15,000
Advertising expense	75,000
Administrative office salaries	175,000
Administrative office depreciation expense	12,500
Total costs and expenses	$2,466,000

The average shop direct labor rate is $25 per hour. Determine the predetermined shop overhead rate per direct labor hour.

Obj. 4

✔ a. $300 per hour

E10-16 Predetermined factory overhead rate

Mt Ellis Medical Center has a single operating room that is used by local physicians to perform surgical procedures. The cost of using the operating room is accumulated by each patient procedure and includes the direct materials costs (drugs and medical devices), physician surgical time, and operating room overhead. On March 1 of the current year, the annual operating room overhead is estimated to be:

Disposable supplies	$ 120,000
Depreciation expense	115,000
Utilities	90,000
Nurse salaries	675,000
Technician wages	260,000
Total operating room overhead	$1,260,000

The overhead costs will be assigned to procedures based on the number of surgical room hours. Mt Ellis Medical Center expects to use the operating room an average of 12 hours per day, seven days per week. In addition, the operating room will be shut down two weeks per year for general and maintenance repairs.

a. Determine the predetermined operating room overhead rate for the year.

b. Shirlee Greer had a 3.4-hour procedure on March 18. How much operating room overhead would be charged to her procedure, using the rate determined in part (a)?

c. During March, the operating room was used 330 hours. The actual overhead costs incurred for March were $101,750. Determine the overhead under- or overapplied for the period.

Obj. 4

✔ b. $85,000

E10-17 Recording jobs completed

The following account appears in the ledger after all postings have been completed except for the entries to transfer the costs of the jobs completed in October.

Work in Process	
Balance, October 1	$ 42,600
Direct materials	360,000
Direct labor	400,400
Factory overhead	107,000

Jobs finished during October are summarized as follows:

Job 1004	$180,000	Job 1037	$140,000
Job 1030	225,000	Job 1041	280,000

a. Determine the cost of jobs completed.

b. Determine the cost of the unfinished jobs at October 31.

Obj. 4

✔ d. $21,180

E10-18 Determining manufacturing costs

Wagner Printing Inc. began printing operations on July 1. Jobs 7-01 and 7-02 were completed during the month, and all costs applicable to them were recorded on the related cost sheets. Jobs 7-03 and 7-04 are still in process at the end of the month, and all applicable costs except factory overhead have been recorded on the related cost sheets. In addition to the materials and labor charged directly to the jobs, $2,000 of indirect materials and $1,650 of indirect labor were used during the month. The cost sheets, in summary form, for the four jobs during the month are as follows:

Job 7-01		Job 7-02	
Direct materials	4,000	Direct materials	5,000
Direct labor	3,600	Direct labor	4,800
Factory overhead	1,620	Factory overhead	2,160
Total	9,220	Total	11,960

Job 7-03		Job 7-04	
Direct materials	2,700	Direct materials	1,500
Direct labor	1,800	Direct labor	1,000
Factory overhead	?	Factory overhead	?

Determine each of the following for July:

a. Direct and indirect materials used.

b. Direct and indirect labor used.

c. Factory overhead applied (a single overhead rate is used based on direct labor cost).

d. Cost of completed Jobs 7-01 and 7-02.

e. Assume that in addition to indirect materials and indirect labor, factory overhead of $1,500 was incurred during July. Determine the overapplied or underapplied overhead for March.

E10-19 Financial statements of a manufacturing firm

Obj. 4

✔ a. Operating income, $155,500

The following events took place for Bridger Bikes Inc. during July 20Y6, the first month of operations, as a producer of road bikes:

- Purchased $340,000 of materials.
- Used $329,000 of direct materials in production.
- Incurred $160,000 of direct labor wages.
- Applied factory overhead at a rate of 80% of direct labor cost.
- Transferred $590,000 of work in process to finished goods.
- Sold goods with a cost of $550,000.
- Sold goods for $918,000.
- Incurred $132,500 of selling expenses.
- Incurred $80,000 of administrative expenses.

a. Prepare the July income statement for Bridger Bikes Inc. Assume that Bridger Bikes uses the perpetual inventory method.

b. Determine the inventory balances at the end of the first month of operations.

E10-20 Job order cost accounting entries for a service business

Obj. 5

✔ d. Cost of services completed, $1,377,000

Media Connect Inc. provides advertising services for clients across the nation. Media Connect is presently working on four projects, each for a different client. Media Connect accumulates costs for each account (client) on the basis of both direct costs and allocated indirect costs. The direct costs include the charged time of professional personnel and media purchases (air time and ad space). Overhead is allocated to each project as a percentage of media purchases. The predetermined overhead rate is 40% of media purchases. On April 1, the four advertising projects had the following accumulated costs:

	April 1 Balances
First Bank	$40,000
Reliable Airlines	18,000
Motel 26	33,000
Blue Mountain Beverages	27,000

During April, Media Connect incurred the following direct labor and media purchase costs related to preparing advertising for each of the four accounts:

	Direct Labor	Media Purchases
First Bank	$115,000	$ 480,000
Reliable Airlines	84,000	320,000
Motel 26	110,000	200,000
Blue Mountain Beverages	125,000	300,000

At the end of April, both the First Bank and Reliable Airlines campaigns were completed. The costs of completed campaigns are added to the cost of services account.

Determine each of the following for the month:

a. Direct labor costs.

b. Media purchases.

c. Overhead applied.

d. Cost of completed First Bank and Reliable Airlines campaigns.

Obj. 6

E10-21 Just-in-time principles

The chief executive officer (CEO) of Kankakee Industries has just returned from a management seminar describing the benefits of the just-in-time philosophy. The CEO issued the following statement after returning from the conference:

> ***This company will become a just-in-time manufacturing company. Presently, we have too much inventory. To become just-in-time, we need to eliminate the excess inventory. Therefore, I want all employees to begin reducing inventories until we are just-in-time. Thank you for your cooperation.***

How would you respond to the CEO's statement?

Obj. 6

E10-22 Just-in-time as a strategy

The American textile industry has moved much of its operations offshore in the pursuit of lower labor costs. Over the past 50 years, textile imports have risen from 2% of all textile production to over 70%. Offshore manufacturers make long runs of standard mass-market apparel items. These are then brought to the United States in container ships, requiring significant time between original order and delivery. As a result, retail customers must accurately forecast market demands for imported apparel items.

Assuming that you work for a U.S.-based textile company, how would you recommend responding to the low-cost imports?

Obj. 6

E10-23 Just-in-time principles

Jupiter Shirt Company manufactures various styles of men's casual wear. Shirts are cut and assembled by a workforce that is paid by piece rate. This means that workers are paid according to the amount of work completed during a period of time. To illustrate, if the piece rate is $0.18 per sleeve assembled, and the worker assembles 1,000 sleeves during the day, then the worker would be paid $180 (1,000 × $0.18) for the day's work.

The company is considering adopting a just-in-time manufacturing philosophy by organizing work cells around various types of products and employing pull manufacturing. However, no change is expected in the compensation policy. On this point, the manufacturing manager stated the following:

> ***Piecework compensation provides an incentive to work fast. Without it, the workers will just goof off and expect a full day's pay. We can't pay straight hourly wages—at least not in this industry.***

How would you respond to the manufacturing manager's comments?

E10-24 Activity-based costing for a hospital

Obj. 7

✔ a. Patient Franklin, $2,925

Deer Lodge Regional Hospital plans to use activity-based costing to assign hospital indirect costs to the care of patients. The hospital has identified the following activities and activity rates for the hospital indirect costs:

Activity	Activity Rate
Room and meals	$225 per day
Radiology	$300 per image
Pharmacy	$50 per physician order
Chemistry lab	$125 per test
Operating room	$3,000 per operating room hour

The records of two representative patients were analyzed, using the activity rates. The activity information associated with the two patients is as follows:

	Patient Franklin	Patient Kramer
Number of days	1 days	4 days
Number of images	2 images	5 images
Number of physician orders	1 orders	8 orders
Number of tests	2 tests	5 tests
Number of operating room hours	0.6 hour	2.8 hours

a. Determine the activity cost associated with each patient.

b. Why is the total activity cost different for the two patients?

E10-25 Activity-based costing in an insurance company

Obj. 7

✔ a. Auto, $1,440,500

Umbrella Insurance Company carries three major lines of insurance: auto, workers' compensation, and homeowners. The company has prepared the following report for 20Y2:

UMBRELLA INSURANCE COMPANY
Product Profitability Report
For the Year Ended December 31, 20Y2

	Auto	Workers' Compensation	Homeowners
Premium revenue	$ 7,200,000	$ 6,500,000	$ 9,200,000
Less estimated claims	(5,040,000)	(4,550,000)	(6,440,000)
Underwriting income	$ 2,160,000	$ 1,950,000	$ 2,760,000

Management is concerned that the administrative expenses may make some of the insurance lines unprofitable. However, the administrative expenses have not been allocated to the insurance lines. The controller has suggested that the administrative expenses could be assigned to the insurance lines using activity-based costing. The administrative expenses are comprised of five activities. The activities and their rates are as follows:

	Activity Rates
New policy processing	$160 per new policy
Cancellation processing	$240 per cancellation
Claim audits	$500 per claim audit
Claim disbursements processing	$120 per disbursement
Premium collection processing	$ 25 per premium collected

Activity-base usage data for each line of insurance were retrieved from the corporate records and are shown below.

	Auto	Workers' Comp.	Homeowners
Number of new policies	1,500	1,450	4,100
Number of canceled policies	350	250	2,000
Number of audited claims	320	100	700
Number of claim disbursements	400	180	750
Number of premiums collected	7,500	1,500	12,000

a. Complete the product profitability report through the administrative activities.

b. Determine the underwriting income as a percent of premium revenue.

c. Determine the operating income as a percent of premium revenue, rounded to one decimal place.

d. Interpret the report.

Problems

Obj. 2

P10-1 Classifying costs

The following is a list of costs that were incurred in the production and sale of all-terrain vehicles (ATVs).

a. Attorney fees for drafting a new lease for headquarters offices.

b. Cash paid to outside firm for janitorial services for factory.

c. Commissions paid to sales representatives, based on the number of ATVs sold.

d. Cost of advertising in a national magazine.

e. Cost of boxes used in packaging ATVs.

f. Electricity used to run the robotic machinery.

g. Engine oil used in engines prior to shipment.

h. Factory cafeteria cashier's wages.

i. Filter for spray gun used to paint the ATVs.

j. Gasoline engines used for ATVs.

k. Hourly wages of operators of robotic machinery used in production.

l. License fees for use of patent for transmission assembly, based on the number of ATVs produced.

m. Maintenance costs for new robotic factory equipment, based on hours of usage.

n. Paint used to coat the ATVs.

o. Payroll taxes on hourly assembly line employees.

p. Plastic for outside housing of ATVs.

q. Premiums on insurance policy for factory buildings.

r. Property taxes on the factory building and equipment.

s. Salary of factory supervisor.

t. Salary of quality control supervisor who inspects each ATV before it is shipped.

u. Salary of vice president of marketing.

v. Steering wheels for ATVs.

w. Straight-line depreciation on the robotic machinery used to manufacture the ATVs.

x. Steel used in producing the ATVs.

y. Telephone charges for company controller's office.

z. Tires for ATVs.

Instructions

Classify each cost as either a product cost or a period cost. Indicate whether each product cost is a direct materials cost, a direct labor cost, or a factory overhead cost. Indicate whether each period cost is a selling expense or an administrative expense. Use the following tabular headings for your answer, placing an "X" in the appropriate column.

	Product Costs			Period Costs	
Cost	Direct Materials Cost	Direct Labor Cost	Factory Overhead Cost	Selling Expense	Administrative Expense

P10-2 Schedules for unfinished jobs and completed jobs

Obj. 4

✔ 5. Work in Process, balance, $22,450

Waddell Equipment Company uses a job order cost system. The following data summarize the operations related to production for April 20Y4, the first month of operations:

a. Materials purchased on account, $36,000.

b. Materials requisitioned and factory labor used:

Job	Materials	Factory Labor
No. 401	$ 5,500	$6,650
No. 402	4,000	4,775
No. 403	2,400	1,875
No. 404	7,100	8,500
No. 405	3,200	4,000
No. 406	1,850	2,200
For general factory use	3,150	1,500

c. Factory overhead costs incurred on account, $6,000.

d. Depreciation of machinery and equipment, $1,550.

e. The factory overhead rate is $40 per machine hour. Machine hours used:

Job	Machine Hours
No. 401	38
No. 402	30
No. 403	18
No. 404	56
No. 405	24
No. 406	14
Total	180

f. Jobs completed: 401, 402, 403, and 405.

g. Jobs were shipped and customers were billed as follows: Job 401 $22,750, Job 402 $16,600, Job 403 $8,400.

Instructions

1. Prepare a schedule summarizing manufacturing costs by job for April. Use the following form:

Job	Direct Materials	Direct Labor	Factory Overhead	Total

2. Prepare a schedule of jobs finished in April.
3. Prepare a schedule of jobs sold in April. What account does this schedule support for the month of April?
4. Prepare a schedule of completed jobs on hand as of April 30, 20Y4. What account does this schedule support?
5. Prepare a schedule of unfinished jobs as of April 30, 20Y4. What account does this schedule support?
6. Determine the gross profit for April based upon the jobs sold. Ignore the difference between actual and applied factory overhead.

Obj. 4

P10-3 Job cost sheet

Hallmark Furniture Company refinishes and reupholsters furniture. Hallmark Furniture uses a job order cost system. When a prospective customer asks for a price quote on a job, the estimated cost data are inserted on an unnumbered job cost sheet. If the offer is accepted, a number is assigned to the job, and the costs incurred are recorded in the usual manner on the job cost sheet. After the job is completed, reasons for the variances between the estimated and actual costs are noted on the sheet. The data are then available to management in evaluating the efficiency of operations and in preparing quotes on future jobs.

On February 14, 20Y1, an estimate of $897.60 for reupholstering a chair and couch was given to Millard Schmidt. The estimate was based on the following data:

Estimated direct materials:	
12 meters at $9 per meter	$108.00
Estimated direct labor:	
32 hours at $16 per hour	512.00
Estimated factory overhead (25% of direct labor cost)	128.00
Total estimated costs	$748.00
Markup (20% of production costs)	149.60
Total estimate	$897.60

On February 17, the chair and couch were picked up from the residence of Millard Schmidt, 315 White Oak Drive, Columbus, Georgia, with a commitment to return them on March 15. The job was completed on March 9.

The related materials requisitions and time tickets are summarized as follows:

Materials Requisition No.	Description	Amount
122	9 meters at $9	$81
129	7 meters at $9	63

Time Ticket No.	Description	Amount
T344	20 hours at $14	$280
T348	18 hours at $14	252

Instructions

1. Prepare a job cost sheet showing the estimate given to the customer. Use the format shown on the next page.
2. Assign number 02-019 to the job, record the costs incurred, and complete the job cost sheet.

JOB COST SHEET

Customer	______	Date	______
Address	______	Date wanted	______
	______	Date completed	______
Item	______	Job No.	______

ESTIMATE

Direct Materials		Direct Labor		Summary	
	Amount		Amount		Amount
____meters at $____	____	____ hours at $____	____	Direct materials	____
____meters at $____	____	____ hours at $____	____	Direct labor	____
____meters at $____	____	____ hours at $____	____	Factory overhead	____
____meters at $____	____	____ hours at $____	____		
Total	____	Total	____	Total cost	____

ACTUAL

Direct Materials			Direct Labor			Summary	
Mat. Req. No.	Description	Amount	Time Tick. No.	Description	Amount	Item	Amount
____	____meters at $__	____	____	____hours at $__	____	Direct materials	____
____	____meters at $__	____	____	____hours at $__	____	Direct labor	____
____	____meters at $__	____	____	____hours at $__	____	Factory overhead	____
____	____meters at $__	____	____	____hours at $__	____		
Total		____	Total		____	Total cost	____

P10-4 Analyzing manufacturing cost accounts

Obj. 4

✔ 1. (G) $176,610

Summer Boards Company manufactures surf boards in a wide variety of sizes and styles. The following incomplete ledger accounts refer to transactions that are summarized for May:

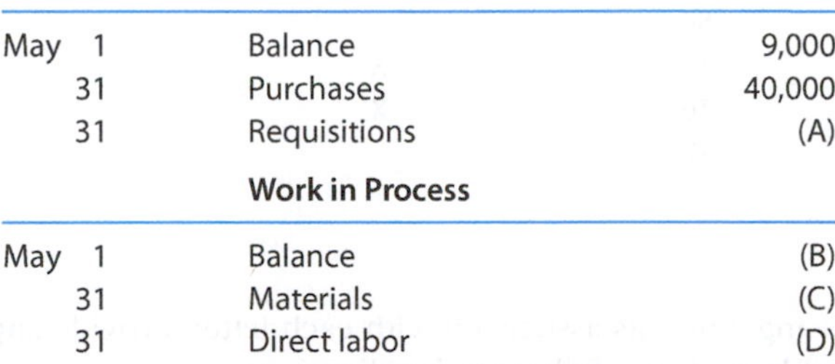

Materials

May	1	Balance	9,000
	31	Purchases	40,000
	31	Requisitions	(A)

Work in Process

May	1	Balance	(B)
	31	Materials	(C)
	31	Direct labor	(D)
	31	Factory overhead applied	(E)
	31	Completed jobs	(F)

Finished Goods

May 1	Balance	0
31	Completed jobs	(F)
31	Cost of goods sold	(G)

Wages Payable

May 31	Wages incurred	110,000

Factory Overhead

May 1	Balance	(3,000)
31	Indirect labor	(H)
31	Indirect materials	2,500
31	Other overhead	102,900
31	Factory overhead applied	(E)

In addition, the following information is available:

a. Materials and direct labor were applied to six jobs in May:

Job No.	Style	Quantity	Direct Materials	Direct Labor
No. 0521	SX	100	$ 5,000	$15,000
No. 0522	SJ	200	8,500	26,000
No. 0523	SK	100	3,500	8,000
No. 0524	T3	125	7,500	25,000
No. 0525	T6	90	5,600	17,500
No. 0526	SX	70	2,000	4,500
	Total	685	$32,100	$96,000

b. Factory overhead is applied to each job at a rate of 120% of direct labor cost.

c. The May 1 Work in Process balance consisted of two jobs, as follows:

Job No.	Style	Work in Process, May 1
Job 0521	SX	$1,500
Job 0522	SJ	4,000
Total		$5,500

d. Customer jobs completed and units sold in May were as follows:

Job No.	Style	Completed in May	Units Sold in May
No. 0521	SX	X	80
No. 0522	SJ	X	160
No. 0523	SK		0
No. 0524	T3	X	105
No. 0525	T6	X	75
No. 0526	SX		0

Instructions

1. Determine the missing amounts associated with each letter. Provide supporting calculations by completing a table with the following headings:

Job No.	Quantity	May 1 Work in Process	Direct Materials	Direct Labor	Factory Overhead	Total Cost	Unit Cost	Units Sold	Cost of Goods Sold

2. Determine the May 31 balances for each of the inventory accounts and factory overhead.

P10-5 Flow of costs and income statement

Obj. 4

✔ 1. Operating income, $184,500

R-Tunes Inc. is in the business of developing, promoting, and selling musical talent online and with compact discs (CDs). The company signed a new group, called *Cyclone Panic,* on January 1, 20Y8. For the first six months of 20Y8, the company spent $1,000,000 on a media campaign for *Cyclone Panic* and $175,000 in legal costs. The CD production began on April 1, 20Y8.

R-Tunes uses a job order cost system to accumulate costs associated with a CD title. The unit direct materials cost for the CD is:

Blank CD	$0.40
Case	0.25
Song lyric insert	0.18

The production process is straightforward. First, the blank CDs are brought to a production area where the digital soundtrack is copied onto the CD. The copying machine can copy 3,600 CDs per hour.

After the CDs are copied, they are brought to an assembly area where an employee packs the CD with a case and song lyric insert. The direct labor cost is $0.37 per CD.

The CDs are sold to record stores. Each record store is given promotional materials, such as posters and aisle displays. Promotional materials cost $30 per record store. In addition, shipping costs average $0.28 per CD.

Total completed production was 500,000 CDs during the year. Other information is as follows:

Number of customers (record stores)	50,000
Number of CDs sold	475,000
Wholesale price (to record store) per CD	$8

Factory overhead cost is applied to jobs at the rate of $1,800 per copy machine hour. There were an additional 18,000 copied CDs, packages, and inserts waiting to be assembled on December 31, 20Y8.

Instructions

1. Prepare an annual income statement for the *Cyclone Panic* CD, including supporting calculations, from the information above.
2. Determine the balances in the work-in-process and finished goods inventories for the *Cyclone Panic* CD on December 31, 20Y8.

Metric-Based Analysis

MBA 10-1 Unit cost analysis

The management of Colfax Manufacturing Inc. uses cost information from job sheets to assess its performance. Information on the total, product type, and quantity of items produced is as follows:

Date	Job No.	Quantity	Product	Amount
Jan. 13	1	180	Mercury	$ 4,500
Jan. 29	26	1,020	Venus	8,160
Feb. 3	38	1,330	Venus	13,300
Mar. 14	49	550	Mercury	12,100
Mar. 24	65	1,500	Pluto	6,000
May 11	74	1,750	Pluto	10,500
June 12	83	400	Mercury	7,200
Aug. 18	92	2,200	Pluto	19,800
Sept. 5	100	600	Venus	4,800
Nov. 14	109	725	Mercury	10,150
Dec. 15	116	2,000	Pluto	24,000

a. Develop a graph for *each* product (three graphs), with Job No. (in date order) on the horizontal axis and unit cost on the vertical axis. Use this information to determine Colfax Manufacturing's cost performance over time for the three products.

b. What additional information would you require to investigate Colfax Manufacturing's cost performance more precisely?

MBA 10-2 Unit cost analysis

Hathaway Trophies Inc. uses a job order cost system for determining the cost to manufacture award products (plaques and trophies). Among the company's products is an engraved plaque that is awarded to participants who complete an executive education program at a local university. The company sells the plaques to the university for $50 each.

Each plaque has a brass plate engraved with the name of the participant. Engraving requires approximately 30 minutes per name. Improperly engraved names must be redone. The plate is screwed to an oak backboard. This assembly takes approximately 6 minutes per unit. Improper assembly must be redone using a new oak backboard.

During the first half of the year, the university had two separate executive education classes. The job cost sheets for the two separate jobs indicated the following information:

Job 05-1	May 2		
	Cost per Unit	Units	Job Cost
Direct materials:			
Wood	$ 7.50/unit	75 units	$ 562.50
Brass	4.00/unit	75 units	300.00
Engraving labor	20.00/hr.	40 hrs.	800.00
Assembly labor	15.00/hr.	7.5 hrs.	112.50
Factory overhead	3.00/hr.	45 hrs.	135.00
Total			$1,910.00
Plaques shipped			÷ 75
Cost per plaque (rounded to nearest cent)			$ 25.47

Job 08-11	August 25		
	Cost per Unit	Units	Job Cost
Direct materials:			
Wood	$ 7.50/unit	85 units	$ 637.50
Brass	4.00/unit	85 units	340.00
Engraving labor	20.00/hr.	50 hrs.	1,000.00
Assembly labor	15.00/hr.	8 hrs.	120.00
Factory overhead	3.00/hr.	48 hrs.	144.00
Total			$2,241.50
Plaques shipped			÷ 80
Cost per plaque (rounded to nearest cent)			$ 28.02

a. Why did the cost per plaque increase from $25.47 to $28.02?

b. Based upon unit costs, what is an area of concern for Hathaway Trophies, Inc.?

MBA 10-3 Unit cost analysis

Using the data from P10-3, analyze and interpret the differences between the estimated and actual costs.

MBA 10-4 Unit cost analysis

The controller of the plant of Martz Industries prepared a graph of the unit costs from the job cost reports for Product M908t. The graph appeared as follows:

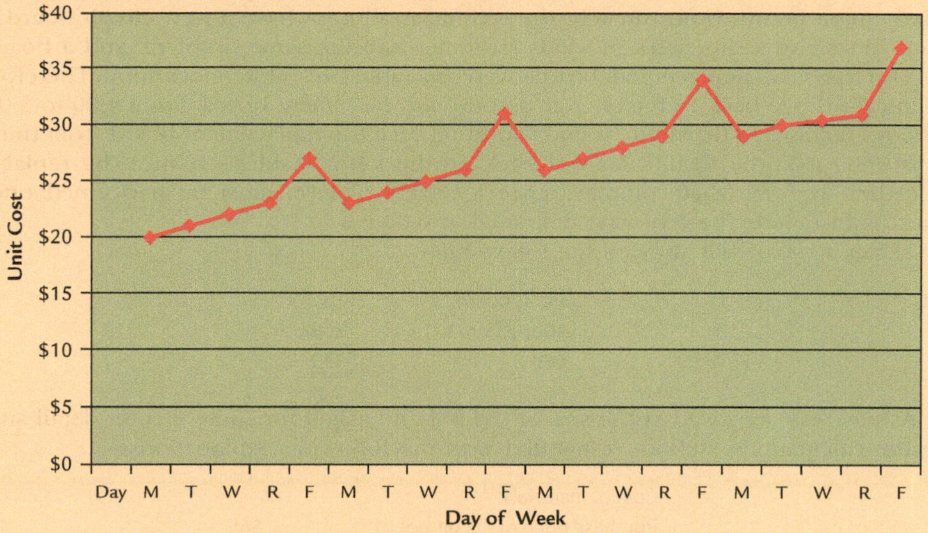

How would you interpret this information? What further information would you request?

Cases

Case 10-1 Ethics and professional conduct in business

Ebenezer Manufacturing Company allows employees to purchase, at cost, manufacturing materials, such as metal and lumber, for personal use. To purchase materials for personal use, an employee must complete a materials requisition form, which must then be approved by the employee's immediate supervisor. Beth Turner, an assistant cost accountant, charges the employee an amount based on Ebenezer's net purchase cost.

Beth Turner is in the process of replacing a deck on her home and has requisitioned lumber for personal use, which has been approved in accordance with company policy. In computing the cost of the lumber, Beth reviewed all the purchase invoices for the past year. She then used the lowest price to compute the amount due the company for the lumber.

Discuss whether Beth behaved in an ethical manner.

Case 10-2 Financial vs. managerial accounting

The following statement was made by the vice president of finance of Electro Inc.: "The managers of a company should use the same information as the shareholders of the firm. When managers use the same information in guiding their internal operations as shareholders use in evaluating their investments, the managers will be aligned with the stockholders' profit objectives."

Respond to the vice president's statement.

Case 10-3 Classifying costs

Reboot Inc. provides computer repair services for the community. Ashley DaCosta's computer was not working, and she called Reboot for a home repair visit. The Reboot Inc. technician arrived at 2:00 P.M. to begin work. By 4:00 P.M., the problem was diagnosed as a failed circuit board. Unfortunately, the technician did not have a new circuit board in the truck, since the technician's previous customer had the same problem, and a board was used on that visit. Replacement boards were available back at Reboot's shop. Therefore, the technician drove back to the shop to retrieve a replacement board. From 4:00 to 5:00 P.M., Reboot's technician drove the round trip to retrieve the replacement board from the shop.

At 5:00 P.M., the technician was back on the job at Ashley's home. The replacement procedure is somewhat complex, since a variety of tests must be performed once the board is installed. The job was completed at 6:00 P.M.

Ashley's repair bill showed the following:

Circuit board	$ 80
Labor charges	260
Total	$340

Ashley was surprised at the size of the bill and asked for some greater detail supporting the calculations. Reboot responded with the following explanations:

Cost of materials:	
Purchase price of circuit board	$65
Markup on purchase price to cover storage and handling	15
Total materials charge	$80

The labor charge per hour is detailed as follows:

2:00–3:00 P.M.	$ 65
3:00–4:00 P.M.	40
4:00–5:00 P.M.	95
5:00–6:00 P.M.	60
Total labor charge	$260

Further explanations in the differences in the hourly rates are as follows:

First hour:	
Base labor rate	$22
Fringe benefits	10
Overhead (other than storage and handling)	8
Total base labor rate	$40
Additional charge for first hour of any job to cover the cost of vehicle depreciation, fuel, and employee time in transit. A 30-minute transit time is assumed.	25
	$65
Second hour:	
Base labor rate	$40
Third hour:	
Base labor rate	$40
The trip back to the shop includes vehicle depreciation and fuel; therefore, a charge was added to the hourly rate to cover these costs. The round trip took an hour.	55
	$95
Fourth hour:	
Base labor rate	$40
Overtime premium for time worked in excess of an eight-hour day (starting at 5:00 P.M.) is equal to the base rate.	20
	$60

1. If you were in Ashley's position, how would you respond to the bill? Are there parts of the bill that appear incorrect to you? If so, what argument would you employ to convince Reboot that the bill is too high?
2. Use the headings below to construct a table. Fill in the table by first listing the costs identified in the activity in the left-hand column. For each cost, place a check mark in the appropriate column identifying the correct cost classification. Assume that each service call is a job.

Cost	Direct Materials	Direct Labor	Overhead

Case 10-4 Factory overhead rate

Fabricator Inc., a specialized equipment manufacturer, uses a job order cost system. The overhead is allocated to jobs on the basis of direct labor hours. The overhead rate is now $3,000 per direct labor hour. The design engineer thinks that this is illogical. The design engineer has stated the following:

> ***Our accounting system doesn't make any sense to me. It tells me that every labor hour carries an additional burden of $3,000. This means that while direct labor makes up only 5% of our total product cost, it drives all our costs. In addition, these rates give my design engineers incentives to "design out" direct labor by using machine technology. Yet, over the past years as we have had less and less direct labor, the overhead rate keeps going up and up. I won't be surprised if next year the rate is $4,000 per direct labor hour. I'm also concerned because small errors in our estimates of the direct labor content can have a large impact on our estimated costs. Just a 30-minute error in our estimate of assembly time is worth $1,500. Small mistakes in our direct labor time estimates really swing our bids around. I think this puts us at a disadvantage when we are going after business.***

1. What is the engineer's concern about the overhead rate going "up and up"?
2. What did the engineer mean about the large overhead rate being a disadvantage when placing bids and seeking new business?
3. What do you think is a possible solution?

Case 10-5 Classifying costs

GROUP PROJECT

With a group of students, visit a local copy and graphics shop or a take-out pizza restaurant. As you observe the operation, consider the costs associated with running the business. As a group, identify as many costs as you can and classify them according to the following table headings:

Cost	Direct Materials	Direct Labor	Overhead	Selling Expense

Case 10-6 Just-in-time principles

Warm Space Inc. manufactures electric space heaters. While the CEO, Gwen Willis, is visiting the production facility, the following conversation takes place with the plant manager, Tyra Chastain:

Gwen: As I walk around the facility, I can't help noticing all the materials inventories. What's going on?

Tyra: I have found our suppliers to be very unreliable in meeting their delivery commitments. Thus, I keep a lot of materials on hand so as to not risk running out and shutting down production.

Gwen: Not only do I see a lot of materials inventory, but there also seems to be a lot of finished goods inventory on hand. Why is this?

Tyra: As you know, I am evaluated on maintaining a low cost per unit. The one way that I am able to reduce my unit costs is by producing as many space heaters as possible. This allows me to spread my fixed costs over a larger base. When orders are down, the excess production builds up as inventory, as we are seeing now. But don't worry—I'm really keeping our unit costs down this way.

Gwen: I'm not so sure. It seems that this inventory must cost us something.

Tyra: Not really. I'll eventually use the materials, and we'll eventually sell the finished goods. By keeping the plant busy, I'm using our plant assets wisely. This is reflected in the low unit costs that I'm able to maintain.

If you were Gwen Willis, how would you respond to Tyra Chastain? What recommendations would you provide to Tyra Chastain?

Answers to Self-Examination Questions

1. **C** Sales salaries (answer C) is a selling expense and is not considered a cost of manufacturing a product. Direct materials cost (answer A), factory overhead cost (answer B), and direct labor cost (answer D) are costs of manufacturing a product.
2. **B** Depreciation of testing equipment (answer B) is included as part of the factory overhead costs of the computer manufacturer. The cost of memory chips (answer A) and the cost of disk drives (answer D) are both considered a part of direct materials cost. The wages of computer assemblers (answer C) are part of direct labor costs.
3. **B**

$$\text{Predetermined Factory Overhead Rate} = \frac{\text{Estimated Total Factory Overhead Costs}}{\text{Estimated Activity Base}}$$

$$\text{Predetermined Factory Overhead Rate} = \frac{\$420{,}000}{16{,}000 \text{ dlh}} = \$26.25$$

$$\text{Hours Applied to the Job} = \frac{\$3{,}000}{\$15 \text{ per hour}} = 200 \text{ hours}$$

Factory overhead applied to the job:

200 hours × \$26.25 = \$5,250

4. **B** If the amount of factory overhead applied during a particular period exceeds the actual overhead costs, the factory overhead account will have a negative balance and is said to be overapplied (answer B) or overabsorbed. If the amount applied is less than the actual costs, the account will have a positive balance and is said to be underapplied (answer A) or underabsorbed (answer C). Since an "estimated" predetermined overhead rate is used to apply overhead, a negative balance does not necessarily represent an error (answer D).
5. **D** When using job order costing for a professional service business, direct materials (answers A, B, and C) are normally insignificant. As a result, direct materials are normally included as part of overhead. Thus, the primary product costs are direct labor and overhead (answer D).

Chapter 11 Cost-Volume-Profit Analysis

What's Covered:

Topics: Cost-Volume-Profit Analysis

Cost Behavior
- Variable costs (Obj. 1)
- Fixed costs (Obj. 1)
- Mixed costs (Obj. 1)

Cost-Volume-Profit Relationships
- Contribution margin (Obj. 2)
- Contribution margin ratio (Obj. 2)
- Unit contribution margin (Obj. 2)

Cost-Volume-Profit Equations
- Break-even point (Obj. 3)
- Target profit (Obj. 3)

Cost-Volume-Profit Graphs
- Cost-volume-profit graph (Obj. 4)
- Profit-volume graph (Obj. 4)

Special Relationships
- Sales mix (Obj. 5)
- Operating leverage (Obj. 5)

Cost-Volume-Profit Assumptions
- Assumptions (Obj. 6)
- Sensitivity analysis (Obj. 6)

Metric-Based Analysis
- Margin of safety (Obj. 7)

Learning Objectives

Obj.1 Classify costs as variable costs, fixed costs, or mixed costs.

Obj.2 Compute the contribution margin, the contribution margin ratio, and the unit contribution margin.

Obj.3 Using cost-volume-profit equations, determine the break-even point and sales necessary to achieve a target profit.

Obj.4 Using cost-volume-profit and profit-volume graphs, determine the break-even point and sales necessary to achieve a target profit.

Obj.5 Apply cost-volume-profit relationships to more than one product and in computing operating leverage.

Obj.6 List the assumptions underlying cost-volume-profit analysis.

Obj.7 Describe and illustrate the use of the margin of safety for managerial decision making and performance analysis.

Chapter Metrics

The managerial decisionmaking and performance metric for this chapter is margin of safety.

Roberto Lusso/
Shutterstock.com

Ford Motor Company

Making a profit isn't easy for U.S. auto manufacturers like the **Ford Motor Company**. The cost of materials, labor, equipment, and advertising make it very expensive to produce cars and trucks.

How many cars does Ford need to produce and sell to break even? The answer depends on the relationship between Ford's sales revenue and costs. Some of Ford's costs, like direct labor and materials, will change in direct proportion to the number of vehicles that are built. Other costs, such as the costs of manufacturing equipment, are fixed and do not change with the number of vehicles that are produced. Ford will break even when it generates enough sales revenue to cover both its fixed and variable costs.

During the depths of the 2009 recession, Ford renegotiated labor contracts with their employees. These renegotiations reduced the direct labor cost incurred to build each car, which lowered the number of cars that the company needed to sell to break even by 45%.

As with Ford, understanding how costs behave, and the relationships between costs, profits, and volume, is important for all businesses. This chapter discusses commonly used methods for classifying costs according to how they change and techniques for determining how many units must be sold for a company to break even. Techniques that management can use to evaluate costs in order to make sound business decisions are also discussed.

Source: J. Booton, "Moody's Upgrades Ford's Credit Rating, Returns Blue Oval Trademark," Fox Business, May 22, 2012.

Objective 1
Classify costs as variable costs, fixed costs, or mixed costs.

Cost Behavior

Cost behavior is the manner in which a cost changes as a related activity changes. The behavior of costs is useful to managers for a variety of reasons. For example, knowing how costs behave allows managers to predict profits as sales and production volumes change. Knowing how costs behave is also useful for estimating costs, which affects a variety of decisions such as whether to replace a machine.

Understanding the behavior of a cost depends on:

1. Identifying the activities that cause the cost to change. These activities are called **activity bases** (or *activity drivers*).
2. Specifying the range of activity over which the changes in the cost are of interest. This range of activity is called the **relevant range**.

To illustrate, assume that a hospital is concerned about planning and controlling patient food costs. A good activity base is the number of patients who *stay* overnight in the hospital. The number of patients who are *treated* is not as good an activity base since some patients are outpatients and thus do not consume food. Once an activity base is identified, food costs can then be analyzed over the range of the number of patients who normally stay in the hospital (the relevant range).

Costs are normally classified as variable costs, fixed costs, or mixed costs.

Variable Costs

Variable costs are costs that vary in proportion to changes in the activity base. When the activity base is units produced, direct materials and direct labor costs are normally classified as variable costs.

Ford Motor Connection

The first vehicle built by Henry Ford in 1896 was a Quadricycle that consisted of four bicycle wheels powered by a four-horsepower engine. The first Ford Model A was sold by **Ford Motor Company** in 1903. In 1908, the Ford Model T was introduced, which sold 15 million units before its production was halted in 1927.

To illustrate, assume that Dynamic Sound Inc. produces stereo systems. The parts for the stereo systems are purchased from suppliers for $10 per unit and are assembled by Dynamic Sound Inc. For Model DS-300, the direct materials costs for the relevant range of 5,000 to 30,000 units of production are shown below.

Number of Units of Model DS-300 Produced	Direct Materials Cost per Unit	Total Direct Materials Cost
5,000 units	$10	$ 50,000
10,000	10	100,000
15,000	10	150,000
20,000	10	200,000
25,000	10	250,000
30,000	10	300,000

Variable costs have the following characteristics:

1. *Cost per unit* remains the same regardless of changes in the activity base. For Model DS-300, the cost per unit is $10.
2. *Total cost* changes in proportion to changes in the activity base. For Model DS-300, the direct materials cost for 10,000 units ($100,000) is twice the direct materials cost for 5,000 units ($50,000).

Exhibit 1 illustrates how the variable costs for direct materials for Model DS-300 behave in total and on a per-unit basis as production changes.

Exhibit 1 Variable Cost Graphs

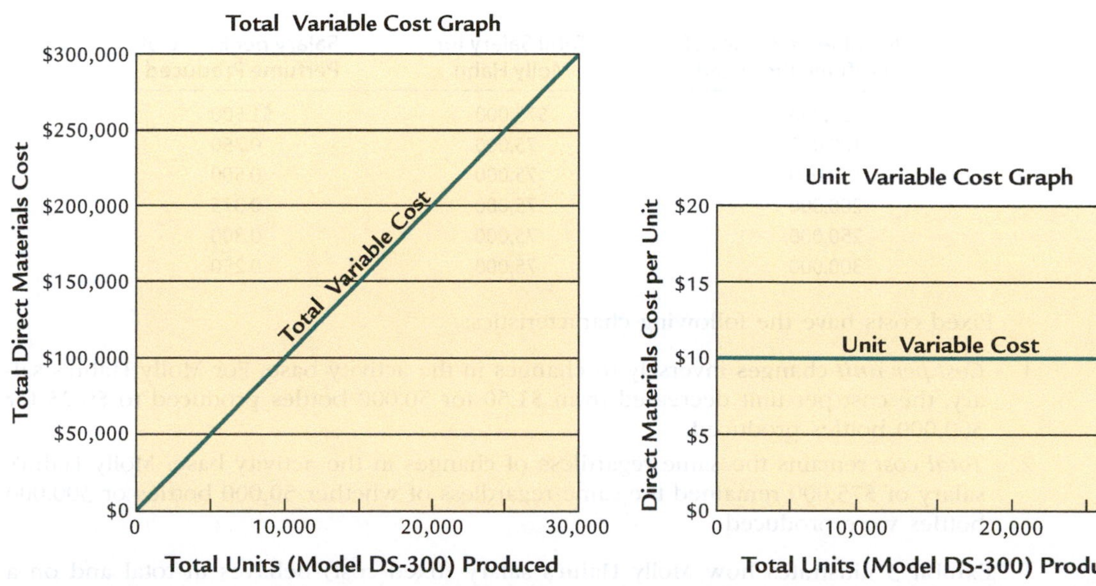

Changing emissions, fuel economy, and safety standards increase the variable cost of each vehicle manufactured by **Ford Motor Company**.

Ford Motor Connection

Some examples of variable costs and their related activity bases for various types of businesses are shown in Exhibit 2.

Exhibit 2
Variable Cost Examples

Type of Business	Cost	Activity Base
Passenger airline	Fuel	Number of miles flown
Manufacturing	Direct materials	Number of units produced
Hospital	Nurse wages	Number of patients
Hotel	Maid wages	Number of guests
Bank	Teller wages	Number of banking transactions

Fixed Costs

Fixed costs are costs that remain the same in total dollar amount as the activity base changes. When the activity base is units produced, many factory overhead costs such as straight-line depreciation are classified as fixed costs.

To illustrate, assume that Hahn Inc. manufactures, bottles, and distributes perfume. The production supervisor is Molly Hahn, who is paid a salary of $75,000 per year. For the relevant range of 50,000 to 300,000 bottles of perfume, the total fixed cost of $75,000 does not vary as production increases. However, the fixed cost per bottle decreases as the units produced increase because the fixed cost is spread over a larger number of bottles, as shown below.

Number of Bottles of Perfume Produced	Total Salary for Molly Hahn	Salary per Bottle of Perfume Produced
50,000 bottles	$75,000	$1.500
100,000	75,000	0.750
150,000	75,000	0.500
200,000	75,000	0.375
250,000	75,000	0.300
300,000	75,000	0.250

Fixed costs have the following characteristics:

1. *Cost per unit* changes inversely to changes in the activity base. For Molly Hahn's salary, the cost per unit decreased from $1.50 for 50,000 bottles produced to $0.25 for 300,000 bottles produced.
2. *Total cost* remains the same regardless of changes in the activity base. Molly Hahn's salary of $75,000 remained the same regardless of whether 50,000 bottles or 300,000 bottles were produced.

Exhibit 3 illustrates how Molly Hahn's salary (fixed cost) behaves in total and on a per-unit basis as production changes.

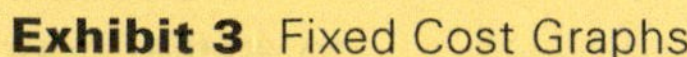

Exhibit 3 Fixed Cost Graphs

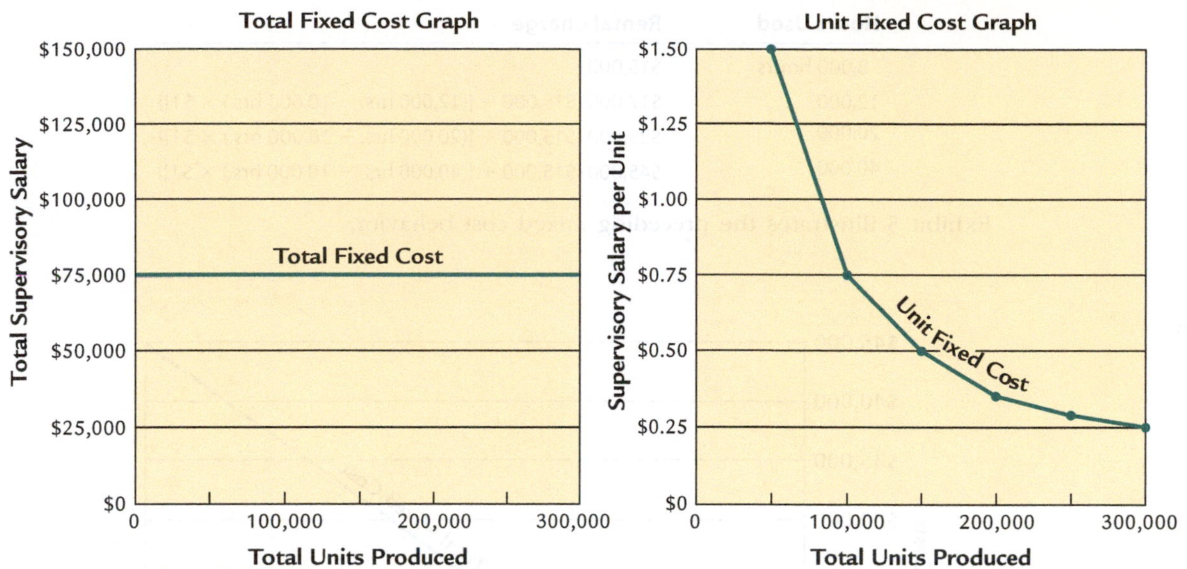

Some examples of fixed costs and their related activity bases for various types of businesses are shown in Exhibit 4.

Exhibit 4 Fixed Cost Examples

Type of Business	Fixed Cost	Activity Base
Passenger airline	Airplane (straight-line) depreciation	Number of miles flown
Manufacturing	Plant manager salary	Number of units produced
Hospital	Property insurance	Number of patients
Hotel	Property taxes	Number of guests
Bank	Branch manager salary	Number of customer accounts

A high proportion of **Ford Motor Company**'s costs are fixed in nature.

Ford Motor Connection

Mixed Costs

Mixed costs are costs that have characteristics of both a variable and a fixed cost. Mixed costs are sometimes called *semivariable* or *semifixed* costs.

To illustrate, assume that Simpson Inc. manufactures sails, using rented machinery. The rental charges are computed as follows:

Rental Charge = $15,000 per year + $1 times each machine hour over 10,000 hours

The rental charges for various hours used within the relevant range of 8,000 hours to 40,000 hours are as follows:

Hours Used	Rental Charge
8,000 hours	$15,000
12,000	$17,000 {$15,000 + [(12,000 hrs. − 10,000 hrs.) × $1]}
20,000	$25,000 {$15,000 + [(20,000 hrs. − 10,000 hrs.) × $1]}
40,000	$45,000 {$15,000 + [(40,000 hrs. − 10,000 hrs.) × $1]}

Exhibit 5 illustrates the preceding mixed cost behavior.

Exhibit 5
Mixed Cost

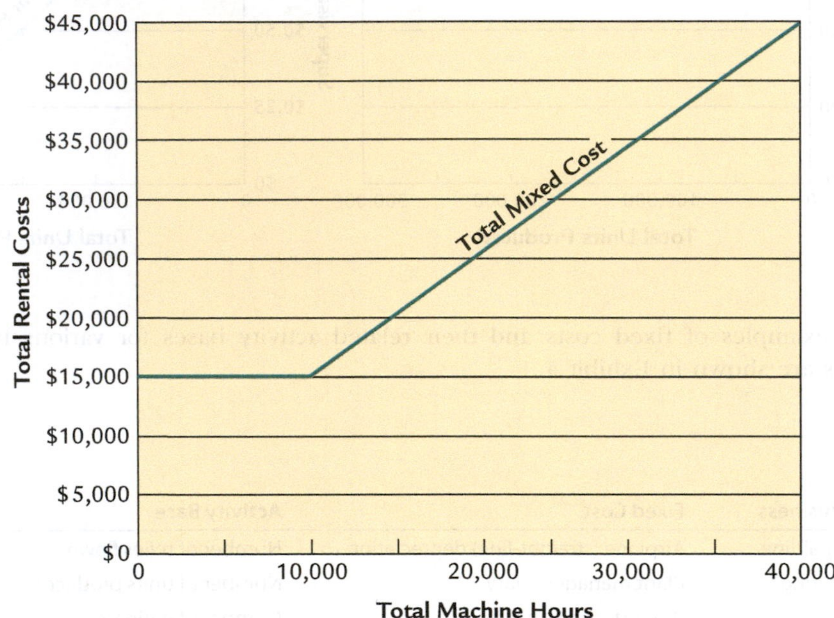

For purposes of analysis, mixed costs are usually separated into their fixed and variable components. The **high-low method** is a cost estimation method that may be used for this purpose.[1] The high-low method uses the highest and lowest activity levels and their related costs to estimate the variable cost per unit and the total fixed cost.

To illustrate, assume that the Equipment Maintenance Department of Elgen Inc. incurred the following costs during the past five months:

	Production	Total Cost
June	1,000 units	$45,550
July	1,500	52,000
August	2,100	61,500
September	1,800	57,500
October	750	41,250

The number of units produced is the activity base, and the relevant range is the units produced between June and October. For Elgen Inc., the difference between the

1. Other methods of estimating costs, such as the scattergraph method and the least squares method, are discussed in cost accounting textbooks.

units produced and total costs at the highest and lowest levels of production are as follows:

	Production	Total Cost
Highest level	2,100 units	\$ 61,500
Lowest level	(750)	(41,250)
Difference	1,350 units	\$ 20,250

The total fixed cost does not change with changes in production. Thus, the \$20,250 difference in the total cost is the change in the total variable cost. Dividing this difference of \$20,250 by the difference in production is an estimate of the variable cost per unit. For Elgen Inc., this estimate is \$15, as computed below.

$$\text{Variable Cost per Unit} = \frac{\text{Difference in Total Cost}}{\text{Difference in Production}}$$

$$= \frac{\$20{,}250}{1{,}350 \text{ units}} = \$15 \text{ per unit}$$

The fixed cost is estimated by subtracting the total variable costs from the total costs for the units produced as follows:

Fixed Cost = Total Cost − (Variable Cost per Unit × Units Produced)

The fixed cost is the same at the highest and the lowest levels of production as shown below for Elgen Inc.

Highest level (2,100 units):

Fixed Cost = Total Cost − (Variable Cost per Unit × Units Produced)
= \$61,500 − (\$15 × 2,100 units)
= \$61,500 − \$31,500
= \$30,000

Lowest level (750 units):

Fixed Cost = Total Cost − (Variable Cost per Unit × Units Produced)
= \$41,250 − (\$15 × 750 units)
= \$41,250 − \$11,250
= \$30,000

Using the variable cost per unit and the fixed cost, the total equipment maintenance cost for Elgen Inc. can be computed for various levels of production as follows:

Total Cost = (Variable Cost per Unit × Units Produced) + Fixed Costs
= (\$15 × Units Produced) + \$30,000

To illustrate, the estimated total cost of 2,000 units of production is \$60,000, as computed below.

Total Cost = (\$15 × Units Produced) + \$30,000
= (\$15 × 2,000 units) + \$30,000 = \$30,000 + \$30,000
= \$60,000

Summary of Cost Behavior Concepts

The cost behavior of variable costs and fixed costs is summarized in Exhibit 6.

Exhibit 6
Variable and Fixed Cost Summary

	Effect of Changing Activity Level	
Cost	**Total Amount**	**Per-Unit Amount**
Variable	Increases and decreases proportionately with activity level.	Remains the same regardless of activity level.
Fixed	Remains the same regardless of activity level.	Increases and decreases inversely with activity level.

Mixed costs contain a fixed cost component that is incurred even if nothing is produced. For analysis, the fixed and variable cost components of mixed costs are separated using the high-low method.

Exhibit 7 shows some examples of variable, fixed, and mixed costs for the activity base *units produced.*

Exhibit 7
Variable, Fixed, Mixed Cost Examples

Variable Cost	Fixed Cost	Mixed Cost
Direct materials	Straight-line depreciation	Quality Control Department wages
Direct labor	Property taxes	Purchasing Department wages
Electricity expense	Production supervisor salaries	Maintenance expenses
Supplies	Insurance expense	Warehouse expenses

One method of reporting variable and fixed costs is called **variable costing** or *direct costing.* Under variable costing, only the variable manufacturing costs (direct materials, direct labor, and variable factory overhead) are included in the product cost. The fixed factory overhead is treated as an expense of the period in which it is incurred. Variable costing is described and illustrated in advanced accounting courses.

Objective 2
Compute the contribution margin, the contribution margin ratio, and the unit contribution margin.

Cost-Volume-Profit Relationships

Cost-volume-profit analysis is the examination of the relationships among selling prices, sales and production volume, costs, expenses, and profits. Cost-volume-profit analysis is useful for managerial decision making. Some of the ways cost-volume-profit analysis may be used include:

1. Analyzing the effects of changes in selling prices on profits
2. Analyzing the effects of changes in costs on profits
3. Analyzing the effects of changes in volume on profits
4. Setting selling prices
5. Selecting the mix of products to sell
6. Choosing among marketing strategies

Contribution Margin

Contribution margin is especially useful because it provides insight into the profit potential of a company. **Contribution margin** is the excess of sales over variable costs, as shown below.

$$\textbf{Contribution Margin} = \textbf{Sales} - \textbf{Variable Costs}$$

To illustrate, assume the following data for Waddell Inc.:

Sales	50,000 units
Sales price per unit	$20 per unit
Variable cost per unit	$12 per unit
Fixed costs	$300,000

Exhibit 8 illustrates an income statement for Waddell Inc. prepared in a contribution margin format.

Exhibit 8
Contribution Margin Income Statement

Sales (50,000 units × $20)	$1,000,000
Variable costs (50,000 units × $12)	(600,000)
Contribution margin (50,000 units × $8)	$ 400,000
Fixed costs	(300,000)
Operating income	$ 100,000

Waddell's contribution margin of $400,000 is available to cover the fixed costs of $300,000. Once the fixed costs are covered, any additional contribution margin generated increases operating income.

Contribution Margin Ratio

The contribution margin can also be expressed as a percentage. The **contribution margin ratio**, sometimes called the *profit-volume ratio,* indicates the percentage of each sales dollar available to cover fixed costs and to provide operating income. The contribution margin ratio is computed as follows:

$$\textbf{Contribution Margin Ratio} = \frac{\textbf{Contribution Margin}}{\textbf{Sales}}$$

The contribution margin ratio is 40% for Waddell Inc., as computed below.

$$\textbf{Contribution Margin Ratio} = \frac{\$400{,}000}{\$1{,}000{,}000} = 40\%$$

The contribution margin ratio is most useful when the increase or decrease in sales volume is measured in sales *dollars.* In this case, the change in sales dollars multiplied by the contribution margin ratio equals the change in operating income, as shown below.

$$\textbf{Change in Operating Income} = \textbf{Change in Sales Dollars} \times \textbf{Contribution Margin Ratio}$$

To illustrate, if Waddell Inc. adds $80,000 in sales orders, its operating income will increase by $32,000, as computed below.

Change in Operating Income = $80,000 × 40% = $32,000

The preceding analysis is confirmed by the following contribution margin income statement of Waddell Inc.:

Sales (54,000 units × $20)	$1,080,000
Variable costs ($1,080,000 × 60%)	(648,000)
Contribution margin ($1,080,000 × 40%)	$ 432,000
Fixed costs	(300,000)
Operating income	$ 132,000

Operating income increased from $100,000 to $132,000 when sales increased from $1,000,000 to $1,080,000. Variable costs as a percentage of sales are equal to 100% minus the contribution margin ratio. Thus, in the above income statement, the variable costs are 60% (100% − 40%) of sales, or $648,000 ($1,080,000 × 60%). The total contribution margin, $432,000, can also be computed directly by multiplying the total sales by the contribution margin ratio ($1,080,000 × 40%).

In the preceding analysis, factors other than sales volume, such as variable cost per unit and sales price, are assumed to remain constant. If such factors change, their effect must also be considered.

The contribution margin ratio is also useful in developing business strategies. For example, assume that a company has a high contribution margin ratio and is producing below 100% of capacity. In this case, a large increase in operating income can be expected from an increase in sales volume. Therefore, the company might consider implementing a special sales campaign to increase sales. In contrast, a company with a small contribution margin ratio will probably want to give more attention to reducing costs before attempting to promote sales.

Unit Contribution Margin

The unit contribution margin is also useful for analyzing the profit potential of proposed decisions. The **unit contribution margin** is computed as follows:

Unit Contribution Margin = Sales Price per Unit − Variable Cost per Unit

To illustrate, if Waddell Inc.'s unit selling price is $20 and its variable cost per unit is $12, the unit contribution margin is $8 as shown below.

Unit Contribution Margin = $20 − $12 = $8

The unit contribution margin is most useful when the increase or decrease in sales volume is measured in sales *units* (quantities). In this case, the change in sales volume (units) multiplied by the unit contribution margin equals the change in operating income, as shown below.

Change in Operating Income = Change in Sales Units × Unit Contribution Margin

To illustrate, assume that Waddell Inc.'s sales could be increased by 15,000 units, from 50,000 units to 65,000 units. Waddell's operating income would increase by $120,000 (15,000 units × $8), as shown below.

Change in Operating Income = 15,000 units × $8 = $120,000

The preceding analysis is confirmed by the following contribution margin income statement of Waddell Inc., which shows that income increased to $220,000 when 65,000 units are sold.

Sales (65,000 units × $20)	$1,300,000
Variable costs (65,000 units × $12)	(780,000)
Contribution margin (65,000 units × $8)	$ 520,000
Fixed costs	(300,000)
Operating income	$ 220,000

The income statement in Exhibit 8 indicates income of $100,000 when 50,000 units are sold. Thus, selling an additional 15,000 units increases income by $120,000 ($220,000 − $100,000).

Unit contribution margin analysis provides useful information for managers. For example, in the preceding illustration, Waddell Inc. could spend up to $120,000 for special advertising or other product promotions to increase sales by 15,000 units. For example, if Waddell Inc. spent $90,000 to increase sales by 15,000, then income would increase by $30,000 ($120,000 − $90,000).

Cost-Volume-Profit Equations

Objective 3
Using cost-volume-profit equations, determine the break-even point and sales necessary to achieve a target profit.

The mathematical approach to cost-volume-profit analysis uses equations to determine the following:

- Sales necessary to break even
- Sales necessary to make a target or desired profit

Break-Even Point

The **break-even point** is the level of operations at which a company's revenues and expenses are equal as illustrated in Exhibit 9. At break-even, a company reports neither an income nor a loss from operations.

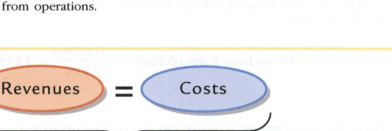

Exhibit 9
Break-Even Point

Revenues = Costs

Break-Even Point

The break-even point in *sales units* is computed as follows:

$$\textbf{Break-Even Sales (units)} = \frac{\textbf{Fixed Costs}}{\textbf{Unit Contribution Margin}}$$

To illustrate, assume the following data for Baker Corporation:

Unit selling price	$25
Unit variable cost	(15)
Unit contribution margin	$10
Fixed costs	$90,000

The break-even point is 9,000 units, as shown below.

$$\textbf{Break-Even Sales (units)} = \frac{\$90{,}000}{\$10} = 9{,}000 \text{ units}$$

The following income statement verifies the break-even point of 9,000 units:

Sales (9,000 units × \$25)	\$ 225,000
Variable costs (9,000 units × \$15)	(135,000)
Contribution margin	\$ 90,000
Fixed costs	(90,000)
Operating income	\$ 0

As shown in the preceding income statement, the break-even point is \$225,000 (9,000 units × \$25) of sales. The break-even point in *sales dollars* can be determined directly as follows:

$$\textbf{Break-Even Sales (dollars)} = \frac{\text{Fixed Costs}}{\text{Contribution Margin Ratio}}$$

The contribution margin ratio can be computed using the unit contribution margin and unit selling price as follows:

$$\textbf{Contribution Margin Ratio} = \frac{\text{Unit Contribution Margin}}{\text{Unit Selling Price}}$$

The contribution margin ratio for Baker Corporation is 40%, as follows:

$$\textbf{Contribution Margin Ratio} = \frac{\$10}{\$25} = 40\%$$

Thus, the break-even sales dollars for Baker Corporation of \$225,000 can be computed directly as follows:

$$\textbf{Break-Even Sales (dollars)} = \frac{\$90{,}000}{40\%} = \$225{,}000$$

Ford Motor Connection **Ford Motor Company** reported that its 2014 operations in the Middle East and Africa were at break-even.

The break-even point is affected by changes in the fixed costs, unit variable costs, and the unit selling price.

Effect of Changes in Fixed Costs Fixed costs do not change in total with changes in the level of activity. However, fixed costs may change because of other factors such as changes in property tax rates or factory supervisors' salaries. Changes in fixed costs affect the break-even point as follows:

- Increases in fixed costs increase the break-even point.
- Decreases in fixed costs decrease the break-even point.

The effect of changes in fixed costs on the break-even point is illustrated in Exhibit 10.

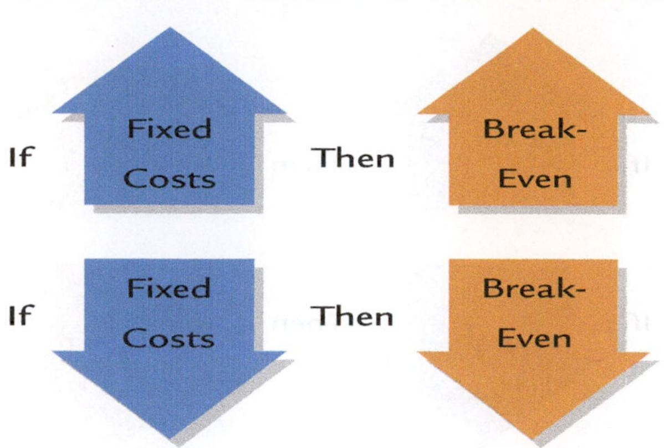

Exhibit 10
Effect of Changes in Fixed Costs on Break-Even Point

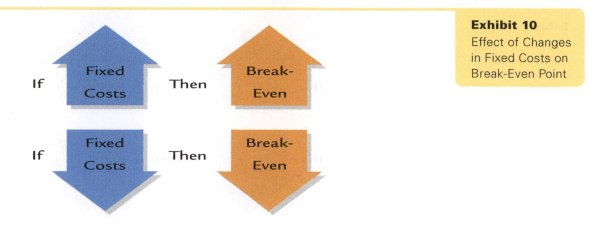

To illustrate, assume that Steiner Co. is evaluating a proposal to budget an additional $100,000 for advertising. The data for Steiner Co. are as follows:

	Current	Proposed
Unit selling price	$90	$90
Unit variable cost	(70)	(70)
Unit contribution margin	$20	$20
Fixed costs	$600,000	$700,000

Steiner Co.'s break-even point *before* the additional advertising expense of $100,000 is 30,000 units, as shown below.

$$\textbf{Break-Even Sales (units)} = \frac{\textbf{Fixed Costs}}{\textbf{Unit Contribution Margin}}$$

$$= \frac{\$600{,}000}{\$20} = \textbf{30,000 units}$$

Steiner Co.'s break-even point *after* the additional advertising expense of $100,000 is 35,000 units, as shown below.

$$\textbf{Break-Even Sales (units)} = \frac{\textbf{Fixed Costs}}{\textbf{Unit Contribution Margin}}$$

$$= \frac{\$700{,}000}{\$20} = \textbf{35,000 units}$$

As shown above, the $100,000 increase in advertising (fixed costs) requires an additional 5,000 units (35,000 − 30,000) of sales to break even.[2] In other words, an increase in sales of 5,000 units is required in order to generate an additional $100,000 of total contribution margin (5,000 units × $20) to cover the increased fixed costs.

Effect of Changes in Unit Variable Costs Unit variable costs do not change with changes in the level of activity. However, unit variable costs may be affected by other factors such as changes in the cost per unit of direct materials.

Changes in unit variable costs affect the break-even point as follows:

- Increases in unit variable costs increase the break-even point.
- Decreases in unit variable costs decrease the break-even point.

The effect of changes in variable costs on the break-even point is illustrated in Exhibit 11.

2. The increase of 5,000 units can also be computed by dividing the increase in fixed costs of $100,000 by the unit contribution margin, $20, as follows: 5,000 units = $100,000 ÷ $20.

Exhibit 11
Effect of Changes in Variable Costs on Break-Even Point

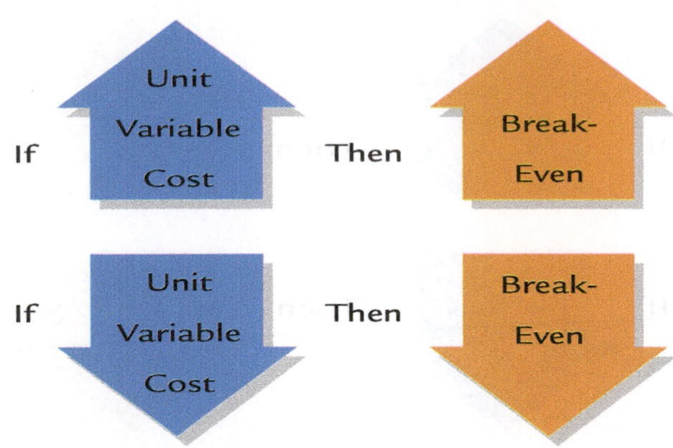

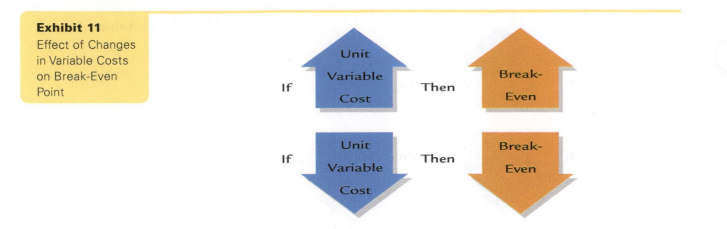

To illustrate, assume that Nagel Co. is evaluating a proposal to pay an additional 2% commission on sales to its salespeople as an incentive to increase sales. The data for Nagel Co. are as follows:

	Current	Proposed
Unit selling price	$ 250	$ 250
Unit variable cost	(145)	(150)
Unit contribution margin	$ 105	$ 100
Fixed costs	$840,000	$840,000

Nagel Co.'s break-even point *before* the additional 2% commission is 8,000 units, as shown below.

$$\textbf{Break-Even Sales (units)} = \frac{\textbf{Fixed Costs}}{\textbf{Unit Contribution Margin}}$$

$$= \frac{\$840{,}000}{\$105} = 8{,}000 \text{ units}$$

If the 2% sales commission proposal is adopted, unit variable costs will increase by $5 ($250 × 2%) from $145 to $150 per unit. This increase in unit variable costs will decrease the unit contribution margin from $105 to $100 ($250 − $150). Thus, Nagel Co.'s break-even point *after* the additional 2% commission is 8,400 units, as shown below.

$$\textbf{Break-Even Sales (units)} = \frac{\textbf{Fixed Costs}}{\textbf{Unit Contribution Margin}}$$

$$= \frac{\$840{,}000}{\$100} = 8{,}400 \text{ units}$$

As shown above, an additional 400 units of sales will be required in order to break even. This is because if 8,000 units are sold, the new unit contribution margin of $100 provides only $800,000 (8,000 units × $100) of contribution margin. Thus, $40,000 more contribution margin is necessary to cover the total fixed costs of $840,000. This additional $40,000 of contribution margin is provided by selling 400 more units (400 units × $100).

Effect of Changes in Unit Selling Price Changes in the unit selling price affect the unit contribution margin and thus the break-even point. Specifically, changes in the unit selling price affect the break-even point as follows:

- Increases in the unit selling price decrease the break-even point.
- Decreases in the unit selling price increase the break-even point.

The effect of changes in the selling price on the break-even point is shown in Exhibit 12.

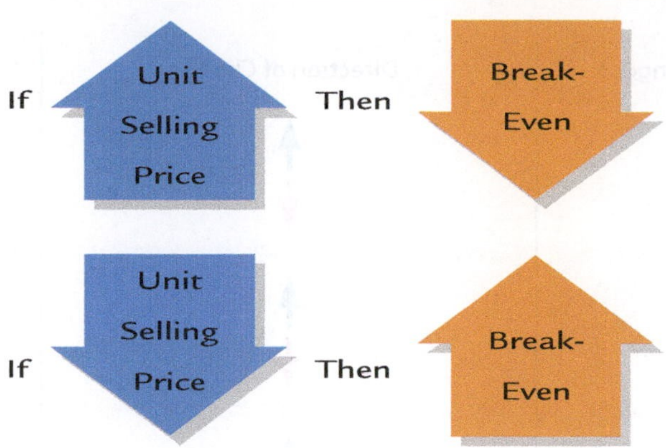

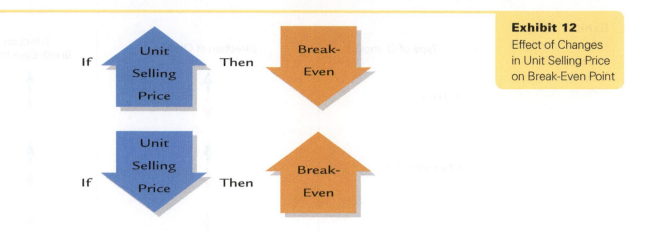

Exhibit 12 Effect of Changes in Unit Selling Price on Break-Even Point

To illustrate, assume that Fraser Co. is evaluating a proposal to increase the unit selling price of its product from $50 to $60. The data for Fraser Co. are as follows:

	Current	Proposed
Unit selling price	$ 50	$ 60
Unit variable cost	(30)	(30)
Unit contribution margin	$ 20	$ 30
Fixed costs	$600,000	$600,000

Fraser Co.'s break-even point *before* the price increase is 30,000 units, as shown below.

$$\textbf{Break-Even Sales (units)} = \frac{\textbf{Fixed Costs}}{\textbf{Unit Contribution Margin}}$$

$$= \frac{\$600{,}000}{\$20} = \textbf{30,000 units}$$

The increase of $10 per unit in the selling price increases the unit contribution margin by $10. Thus, Fraser Co.'s break-even point *after the* price increase is 20,000 units, as shown below.

$$\textbf{Break-Even Sales (units)} = \frac{\textbf{Fixed Costs}}{\textbf{Unit Contribution Margin}}$$

$$= \frac{\$600{,}000}{\$30} = \textbf{20,000 units}$$

As shown above, the price increase of $10 increased the unit contribution margin by $10, which decreased the break-even point by 10,000 units (30,000 units − 20,000 units).

Summary of Effects of Changes on Break-Even Point The break-even point changes in the same direction as changes in the variable cost per unit and fixed costs. In contrast, the break-even point changes in the opposite direction as changes in the unit selling price. These changes on the break-even point are summarized in Exhibit 13.

Exhibit 13
Effects of Changes in Selling Price, Fixed Costs, and Variable Costs on Break-Even Point

Type of Change	Direction of Change	Effect on Break-Even Point
Fixed cost	↑ ↓	↑ ↓
Unit variable cost	↑ ↓	↑ ↓
Unit selling price	↑ ↓	↓ ↑

Target Profit

At the break-even point, sales and costs are exactly equal. However, the goal of most companies is to make a profit.

By modifying the break-even equation, the sales required to earn a target or desired amount of profit may be computed. For this purpose, target profit is added to the break-even equation as shown below.

$$\textbf{Sales (units)} = \frac{\textbf{Fixed Costs + Target Proft}}{\textbf{Unit Contribution Margin}}$$

To illustrate, assume the following data for Waltham Co.:

Unit selling price	$75
Unit variable cost	(45)
Unit contribution margin	$30
Fixed costs	$200,000
Target profit	100,000

The sales necessary to earn the target profit of $100,000 would be 10,000 units, computed as follows:

$$\textbf{Sales (units)} = \frac{\$200{,}000 + \$100{,}000}{\$30} = \textbf{10,000 units}$$

The following income statement verifies this computation:

Sales (10,000 units × $75)	$ 750,000	
Variable costs (10,000 units × $45)	(450,000)	
Contribution margin (10,000 units × $30)	$ 300,000	
Fixed costs	(200,000)	
Operating income	$ 100,000	← Target profit

Breaking Even on Howard Stern

Satellite radio is one of the growing forms of entertainment. Customers are able to choose from a variety of types of music and talk radio and listen from just about anywhere in the country with limited commercials. The satellite radio market is dominated by **Sirius XM Radio Inc.** Prior to its merger with **XM Radio**, Sirius tripled its customer base by diversifying its product line and signing high-profile talk personalities. As part of this strategy, Sirius signed a five-year $500 million contract with radio "shock jock" Howard Stern. But how did Sirius determine that adding the self-proclaimed "King of All Media" to its play list was worth such a large amount of money? It used break-even analysis. Prior to signing with Sirius, 12 million listeners tuned in to Stern's show on **Infinity Broadcasting Corporation**. At the time the contract was signed, Sirius had about 600,000 subscribers. The company estimated that it would need 1 million of Stern's fans to subscribe to Sirius in order to break even on the $500 million fixed cost of the contract. Initial projections estimated that Stern's show would attract as many as 10 million listeners. It appears that the company's strategy worked as Sirius's subscriber base had grown to 20.2 million customers.

As shown in the preceding income statement, sales of $750,000 (10,000 units × $75) are necessary to earn the target profit of $100,000. The sales of $750,000 needed to earn the target profit of $100,000 can be computed directly using the contribution margin ratio, as shown below.

$$\textbf{Contribution Margin Ratio} = \frac{\textbf{Unit Contribution Margin}}{\textbf{Unit Selling Price}} = \frac{\$30}{\$75} = 40\%$$

$$\textbf{Sales (dollars)} = \frac{\textbf{Fixed Costs + Target Proft}}{\textbf{Contribution Margin Ratio}}$$

$$= \frac{\$200{,}000 + \$100{,}000}{40\%} = \frac{\$300{,}000}{40\%} = \$750{,}000$$

Integrity, Objectivity, and Ethics in Business

Orphan Drugs

Each year, pharmaceutical companies develop new drugs that cure a variety of physical conditions. In order to be profitable, drug companies must sell enough of a product to exceed break-even for a reasonable selling price. Break-even points, however, create a problem for drugs targeted at rare diseases, called "orphan drugs." These drugs are typically expensive to develop and have low sales volumes, making it impossible to achieve break-even. To ensure that orphan drugs are not overlooked, Congress passed the Orphan Drug Act, which provides incentives for pharmaceutical companies to develop drugs for rare diseases that might not generate enough sales to reach break-even. The program has been a great success. Since 1982, over 200 orphan drugs have come to market, including **Jacobus Pharmaceuticals Company, Inc.**'s drug for the treatment of tuberculosis and **Novartis AG**'s drug for the treatment of Paget's disease.

Objective 4
Using cost-volume-profit and a profit-volume graphs, determine the break-even point and sales necessary to achieve a target profit.

Cost-Volume-Profit Graphs

Cost-volume-profit analysis can be presented graphically as well as in equation form. Many managers prefer the graphic form because the operating profit or loss for different levels of sales can readily be seen.

Cost-Volume-Profit (Break-Even) Graph

A **cost-volume-profit graph**, sometimes called a *break-even graph*, graphically shows sales, costs, and the related profit or loss for various levels of units sold. It assists in understanding the relationship among sales, costs, and operating profit or loss.

To illustrate, the cost-volume-profit graph in Exhibit 14 is based on the following data:

Unit selling price	$ 50
Unit variable cost	(30)
Unit contribution margin	$ 20
Total fixed costs	$100,000

Exhibit 14
Cost-Volume-Profit Graph

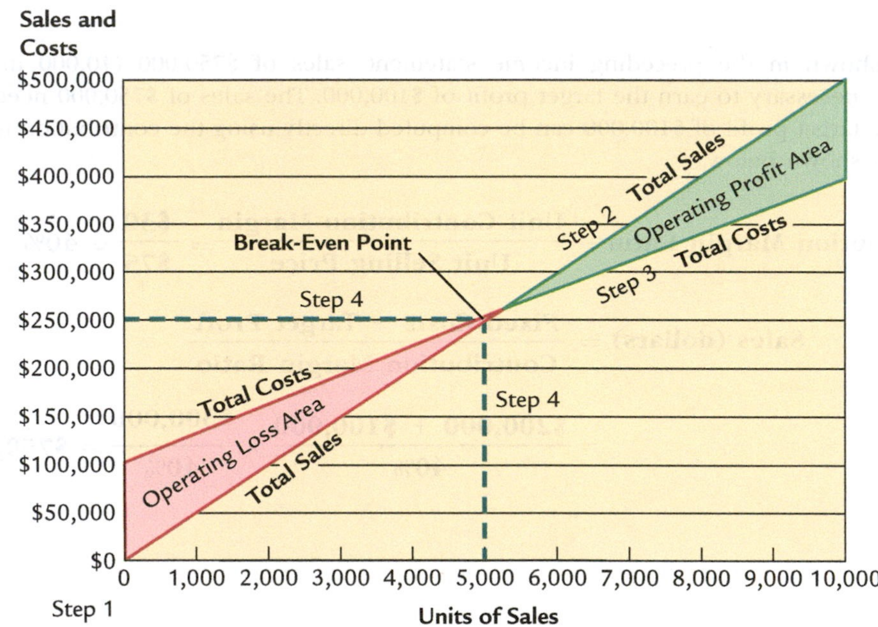

The cost-volume-profit graph in Exhibit 14 is constructed using the following steps:

Step 1. Volume in units of sales is indicated along the horizontal axis. The range of volume shown is the relevant range in which the company expects to operate. Dollar amounts of total sales and costs are indicated along the vertical axis.

Step 2. A sales line is plotted by beginning at zero on the left corner of the graph. A second point is determined by multiplying any units of sales on the horizontal axis by the unit sales price of $50. For example, for 10,000 units of sales, the total sales would be $500,000 (10,000 units × $50). The sales line is drawn upward to the right from zero through the $500,000 point.

Step 3. A cost line is plotted by beginning with total fixed costs, $100,000, on the vertical axis. A second point is determined by multiplying any units of sales on the horizontal axis by the unit variable costs and adding the fixed costs. For example, for 10,000 units of sales, the total estimated costs would be $400,000 [(10,000 units × $30) + $100,000]. The cost line is drawn upward to the right from $100,000 on the vertical axis through the $400,000 point.

Step 4. The break-even point is the intersection point of the total sales and total cost lines. A vertical dotted line drawn downward at the intersection point indicates the units of sales at the break-even point. A horizontal dotted line drawn to the left at the intersection point indicates the sales dollars and costs at the break-even point.

In Exhibit 14, the break-even point is $250,000 of sales, which represents sales of 5,000 units. Operating profits will be earned when sales levels are to the right of the break-even point *(operating profit area)*. Operating losses will be incurred when sales levels are to the left of the break-even point *(operating loss area)*.

Changes in the unit selling price, total fixed costs, and unit variable costs can be analyzed by using a cost-volume-profit graph Using the data in Exhibit 14 assume that a proposal to reduce fixed costs by $20,000 is to be evaluated. In this case, the total fixed costs would be $80,000 ($100,000 − $20,000).

As shown in Exhibit 15 the total cost line is redrawn, starting at the $80,000 point (total fixed costs) on the vertical axis. A second point is determined by multiplying any units of sales on the horizontal axis by the unit variable costs and adding the fixed costs. For example, for 10,000 units of sales, the total estimated costs would be $380,000 [(10,000 units × $30) + $80,000]. The cost line is drawn upward to the right from $80,000 on the vertical axis through the $380,000 point. The revised cost-volume-profit graph in Exhibit 15 indicates that the break-even point decreases to $200,000 and 4,000 units of sales.

Exhibit 15 Revised Cost-Volume-Profit Graph

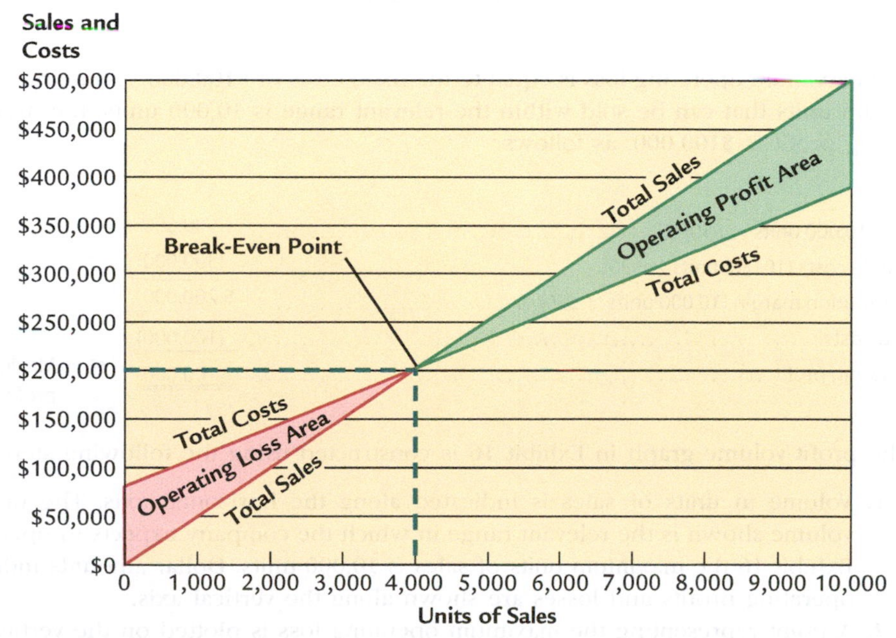

Profit-Volume Graph

Another graphic approach to cost-volume-profit analysis is the profit-volume graph. The **profit-volume graph** plots only the difference between total sales and total costs (or profits). In this way, the profit-volume graph allows managers to determine the operating profit (or loss) for various levels of units sold.

To illustrate, the profit-volume graph in Exhibit 16 is based on the same data as used in Exhibit 14. These data are as follows:

Unit selling price	$ 50
Unit variable cost	(30)
Unit contribution margin	$ 20
Total fixed costs	$100,000

Exhibit 16 Profit-Volume Graph

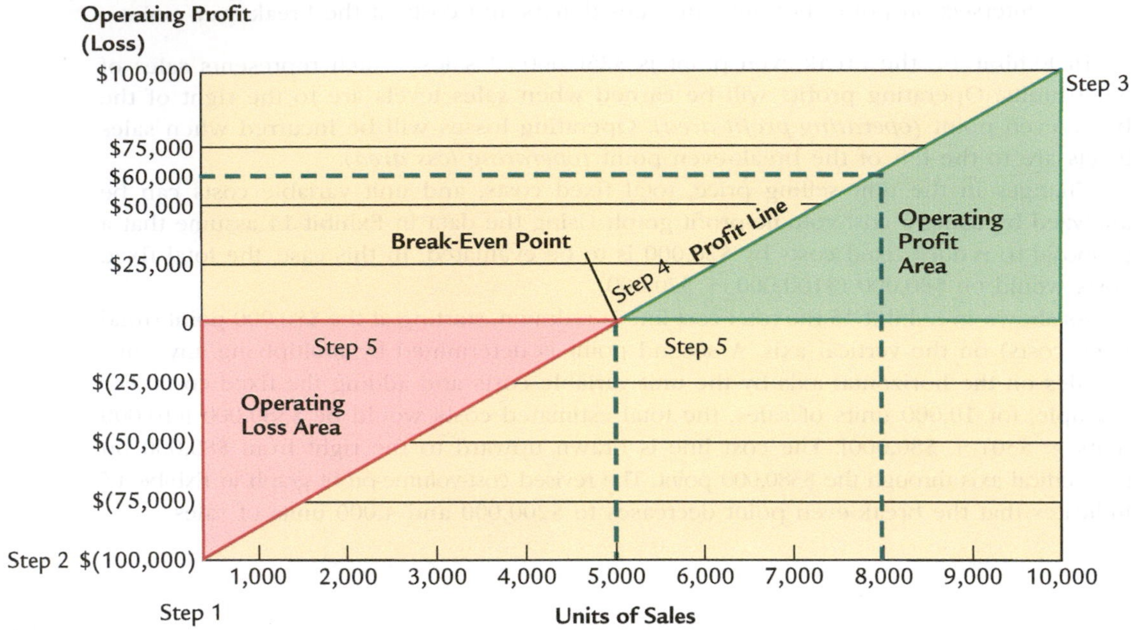

The maximum operating loss is equal to the fixed costs of $100,000. Assuming that the maximum units that can be sold within the relevant range is 10,000 units, the maximum operating profit is $100,000, as follows:

Sales (10,000 units × $50)	$ 500,000
Variable costs (10,000 units × $30)	(300,000)
Contribution margin (10,000 units × $20)	$ 200,000
Fixed costs	(100,000)
Operating profit	$ 100,000 ← Maximum profit

The profit-volume graph in Exhibit 16 is constructed using the following steps:

Step 1. Volume in units of sales is indicated along the horizontal axis. The range of volume shown is the relevant range in which the company expects to operate. In Exhibit 16 the maximum units of sales is 10,000 units. Dollar amounts indicating operating profits and losses are shown along the vertical axis.

Step 2. A point representing the maximum operating loss is plotted on the vertical axis at the left. This loss is equal to the total fixed costs at the zero level of sales. Thus, the maximum operating loss is equal to the fixed costs of $100,000.

Step 3. A point representing the maximum operating profit within the relevant range is plotted on the right. Assuming that the maximum unit sales within the relevant range is 10,000 units, the maximum operating profit is $100,000.

Step 4. A diagonal profit line is drawn connecting the maximum operating loss point with the maximum operating profit point.

Step 5. The profit line intersects the horizontal zero operating profit line at the break-even point in units of sales. The area indicating an operating profit is identified to the right of the intersection, and the area indicating an operating loss is identified to the left of the intersection.

In Exhibit 16, the break-even point is 5,000 units of sales, which is equal to total sales of $250,000 (5,000 units × $50). Operating profit will be earned when sales levels are to the right of the break-even point *(operating profit area)*. Operating losses will be incurred when sales levels are to the left of the break-even point *(operating loss area)*. For example, at sales of 8,000 units, an operating profit of $60,000 will be earned, as shown in Exhibit 16.

Changes in the unit selling price, total fixed costs, and unit variable costs on profit can be analyzed using a profit-volume graph. Using the data in Exhibit 16, assume the effect on profit of an increase of $20,000 in fixed costs is to be evaluated. In this case, the total fixed costs would be $120,000 ($100,000 + $20,000), and the maximum operating loss would also be $120,000. At the maximum sales of 10,000 units, the maximum operating profit would be $80,000, as follows.

Sales (10,000 units × $50)	$ 500,000
Variable costs (10,000 units × $30)	(300,000)
Contribution margin (10,000 units × $20)	$ 200,000
Fixed costs	(120,000)
Operating profit	$ 80,000 ← Revised maximum profit

A revised profit-volume graph is constructed by plotting the maximum operating loss and maximum operating profit points and drawing the revised profit line. The original and the revised profit-volume graphs are shown in Exhibit 17.

The revised profit-volume graph indicates that the break-even point is 6,000 units of sales. This is equal to total sales of $300,000 (6,000 units × $50). The operating loss area of the graph has increased, while the operating profit area has decreased.

PROFIT, LOSS, AND BREAK-EVEN IN MAJOR LEAGUE BASEBALL

Business Insight

Major League Baseball is a tough game and a tough business. Ticket prices, player salaries, stadium fees, and attendance converge to make it difficult for teams to make a profit, or at least break even. So, which major league baseball team was the most profitable in 2013? Well, it wasn't the World Champion Boston Red Sox. Nor was it the star-studded New York Yankees. Then, it had to be the recently turned around Los Angeles Angels, right? Not even close. It was actually the worst team in baseball—the Houston Astros.

Just how profitable were the Astros? They earned $99 million in 2013, which was more than the combined 2013 profits of the six most recent World Series champions. How could the team with the worst record in baseball since 2005 have one of the most profitable years in baseball history? By paying careful attention to costs and volume. Between 2011 and 2013, the Astros cut their player payroll from $56 million to less than $13 million. That's right, all of the players on the Houston Astros baseball team combined, made less in 2013 than Alex Rodriguez (New York Yankees), Cliff Lee (Philadelphia Phillies), Prince Fielder (Detroit Tigers), and Tim Lincecum (San Francisco Giants) made individually. While attendance at Astros games has dropped by around 20% since 2011, the cost reductions from reduced player salaries have far outpaced the drop in attendance, making the 2013 Astros the most profitable team in baseball history. While no one likes losing baseball games, the Houston Astros have shown that focusing on the relationship between cost and volume can yield a hefty profit, even when they aren't winning.

Source: D. Alexander, "2013 Houston Astros: Baseball's Worst Team is The Most Profitable in History," *Forbes*, August 26, 2013.

Exhibit 17
Original Profit-Volume Graph and Revised Profit-Volume Graph

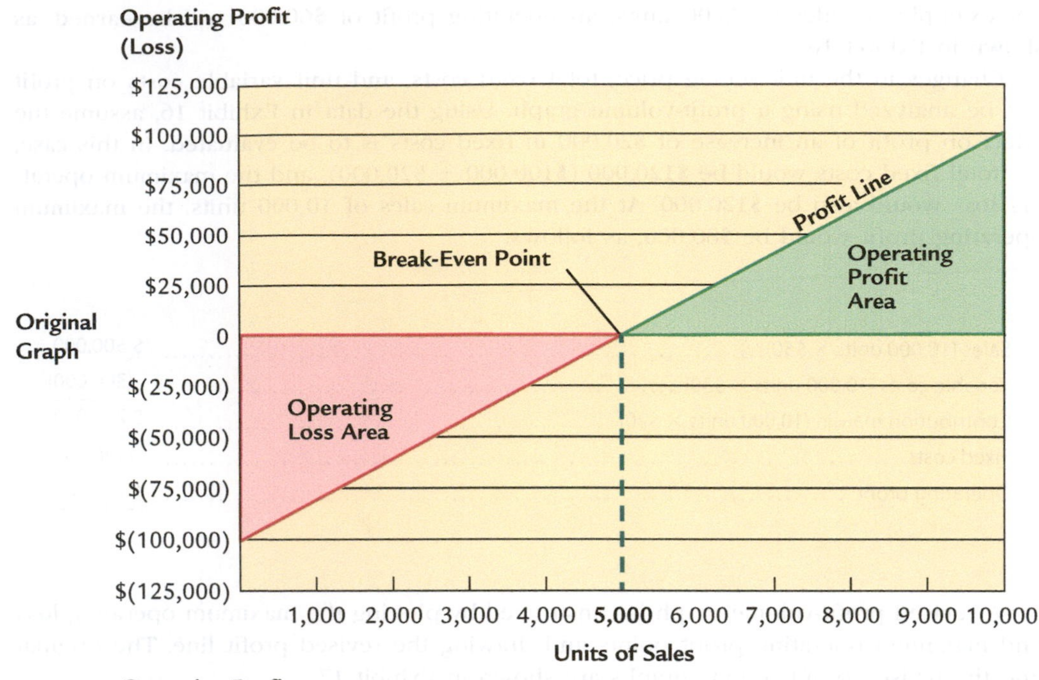

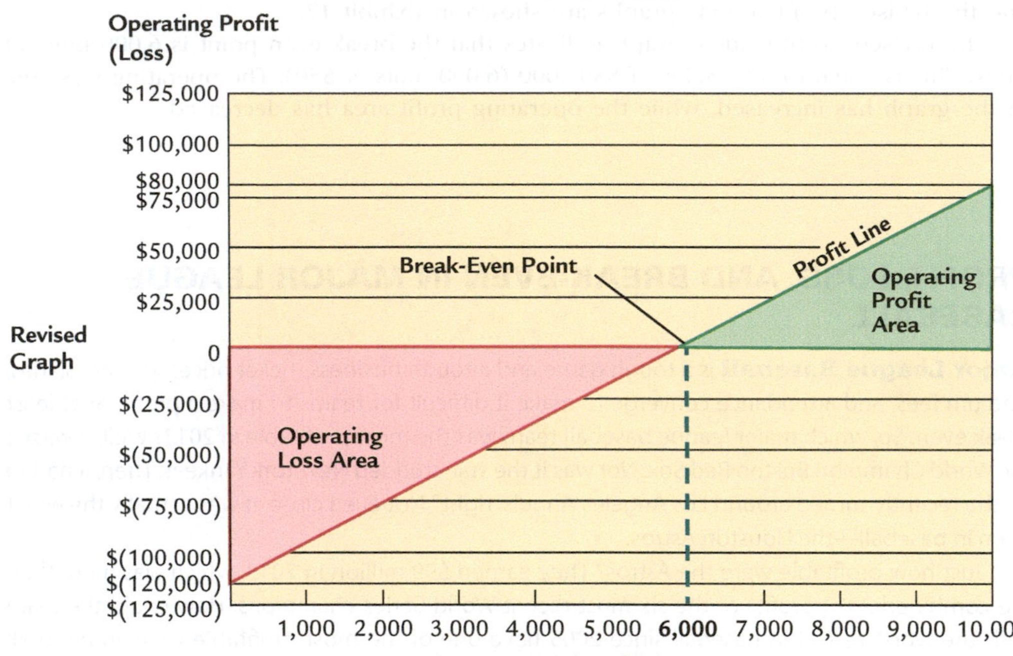

Objective 5
Apply cost-volume-profit relationships to more than one product and in computing operating leverage.

Special Relationships

Cost-volume-profit analysis can also be used when a company sells several products with different costs and prices. In addition, operating leverage is useful in analyzing cost-volume-profit relationships.

Sales Mix Considerations

Many companies sell more than one product at different selling prices. In addition, the products normally have different unit variable costs and thus different unit contribution margins. In such cases, cost-volume-profit analysis can still be performed by considering the sales mix. The **sales mix** is the relative distribution of sales among the products sold by a company.

To illustrate, assume that Burr Company sold Products A and B during the past year as follows:

	Product A	Product B
Unit selling price	$ 90	$140
Unit variable cost	(70)	(95)
Unit contribution margin	$ 20	$ 45
Units sold	8,000	2,000
Sales mix	80%	20%
Total fixed costs	$200,000	

The sales mix for Products A and B is expressed as a percentage of total units sold. For Burr Company, a total of 10,000 (8,000 + 2,000) units were sold during the year. Therefore, the sales mix is 80% (8,000 ÷ 10,000) for Product A and 20% for Product B (2,000 ÷ 10,000) as shown in Exhibit 18. The sales mix could also be expressed as the ratio 80:20.

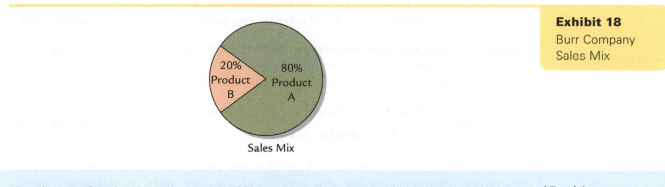

Exhibit 18
Burr Company Sales Mix

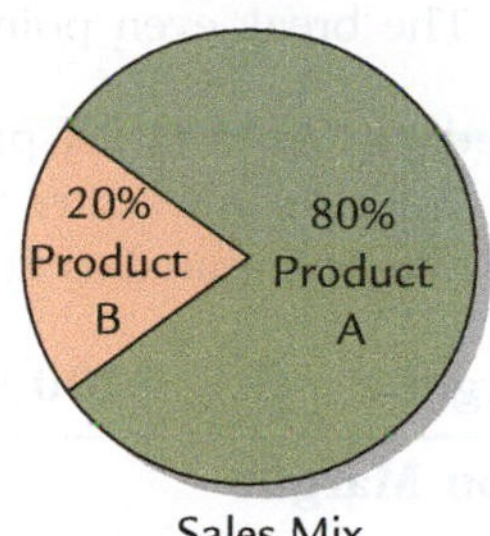

Sales Mix

The sales mix of Ford and Lincoln vehicles sold has a major impact on **Ford Motor Company**'s overall profitability.

Ford Motor Connection

Break-Even Analysis. For break-even analysis, it is useful to think of Products A and B as components of one overall enterprise product called E. The unit selling price of E equals the sum of the unit selling prices of each product multiplied by its sales mix percentage. Likewise, the unit variable cost and unit contribution margin of E equal the sum of the unit variable costs and unit contribution margins of each product multiplied by its sales mix percentage.

For Burr Company, the unit selling price, unit variable cost, and unit contribution margin for E are computed as follows:

Product E			Product A		Product B
Unit selling price of E	$100	=	($90 × 0.8)	+	($140 × 0.2)
Unit variable cost of E	(75)	=	($70 × 0.8)	+	($95 × 0.2)
Unit contribution margin of E	$ 25	=	($20 × 0.8)	+	($45 × 0.2)

The break-even point of 8,000 units of E can be determined in the normal manner as shown below.

$$\textbf{Break-Even Sales (units) for E} = \frac{\textbf{Fixed Costs}}{\textbf{Unit Contribution Margin}}$$

$$= \frac{\$200{,}000}{\$25} = 8{,}000 \text{ units}$$

Since the sales mix for Products A and B is 80% and 20% respectively, the break-even quantity of A is 6,400 units (8,000 units × 80%) and B is 1,600 units (8,000 units × 20%).

The preceding break-even analysis is verified by the following income statement:

	Product A	Product B	Total
Sales:			
6,400 units × $90	$ 576,000		$ 576,000
1,600 units × $140		$ 224,000	224,000
Total sales	$ 576,000	$ 224,000	$ 800,000
Variable costs:			
6,400 units × $70	$(448,000)		$ (448,000)
1,600 units × $95		$(152,000)	(152,000)
Total variable costs	$(448,000)	$(152,000)	$ (600,000)
Contribution margin	$ 128,000	$ 72,000	$ 200,000
Fixed costs			(200,000)
Operating income			$ 0 ← Break-even point

The effects of changes in the sales mix on the break-even point can be determined by assuming a different sales mix. The break-even point of E can then be recomputed.

Target Profit. The sales required to earn a target profit may also be computed for a sales mix of products. To illustrate, the sales necessary for Burr Company to earn a target profit of $50,000 would be 10,000 units, computed as follows:

$$\textbf{Sales (units)} = \frac{\textbf{Fixed Cots + Target Profit}}{\textbf{Unit Contribution Margin}} = \frac{\textbf{\$200,000 + \$50,000}}{\textbf{\$25}} = \textbf{10,000 units}$$

Since the sales mix for Products A and B is 80% and 20% respectively, the sales quantity of A is 8,000 units (10,000 units x 80%) and B is 2,000 units (10,000 units x 20%).

The preceding analysis is verified by the following income statement:

	Product A	Product B	Total
Sales:			
8,000 units × $90	$ 720,000		$ 720,000
2,000 units × $140		$ 280,000	280,000
Total sales	$ 720,000	$ 280,000	$ 1,000,000
Variable costs:			
8,000 units × $70	$(560,000)		$ (560,000)
2,000 units × $95		$(190,000)	(190,000)
Total variable costs	$(560,000)	$(190,000)	$ (750,000)
Contribution margin	$ 160,000	$ 90,000	$ 250,000
Fixed costs			(200,000)
Operating income			$ 50,000

Operating Leverage

The relationship of a company's contribution margin to operating income is measured by operating leverage. A company's **operating leverage** is computed as follows:

$$\textbf{Operating Leverage} = \frac{\textbf{Contribution Margin}}{\textbf{Operating Income}}$$

The difference between contribution margin and operating income is fixed costs. Thus, companies with high fixed costs will normally have a high operating leverage. Examples of such companies include airline and automotive companies. Low operating leverage is normal for companies that are labor intensive, such as professional service companies, which have low fixed costs.

To illustrate operating leverage, assume the following data for Lund Inc. and Yates Inc.:

	Lund Inc.	Yates Inc.
Sales	$ 400,000	$ 400,000
Variable costs	(300,000)	(300,000)
Contribution margin	$ 100,000	$ 100,000
Fixed costs	(80,000)	(50,000)
Operating income	$ 20,000	$ 50,000

As shown above, Lund Inc. and Yates Inc. have the same sales, the same variable costs, and the same contribution margin. However, Lund Inc. has larger fixed costs than Yates Inc. and thus a higher operating leverage. The operating leverage for each company is computed as follows:

$$\text{Operating Leverage for Lund Inc.} = \frac{\text{Contribution Margin}}{\text{Operating Income}} = \frac{\$100{,}000}{\$20{,}000} = 5$$

$$\text{Operating Leverage for Yates Inc.} = \frac{\text{Contribution Margin}}{\text{Operating Income}} = \frac{\$100{,}000}{\$50{,}000} = 2$$

Operating leverage can be used to measure the impact of changes in sales on operating income. Using operating leverage, the effect of changes in sales on operating income is computed as follows:

$$\text{Percent Change in Operating Income} = \text{Percent Change in Sales} \times \text{Operating Leverage}$$

To illustrate, assume that sales increased by 10%, or $40,000 ($400,000 × 10%), for Lund Inc. and Yates Inc. The percent increase in operating income for Lund Inc. and Yates Inc. is computed below.

$$\text{Percent Change in Operating Income for Lund Inc.} = 10\% \times 5 = 50\%$$

$$\text{Percent Change in Operating Income for Yates Inc.} = 10\% \times 2 = 20\%$$

As shown above, Lund Inc.'s operating income increases by 50%, while Yates Inc.'s operating income increases by only 20%. The validity of this analysis is shown in the following income statements for Lund Inc. and Yates Inc. based on the 10% increase in sales:

	Lund Inc.	Yates Inc.
Sales	$ 440,000	$440,000
Variable costs	(330,000)	(330,000)
Contribution margin	$ 110,000	$110,000
Fixed costs	(80,000)	(50,000)
Operating income	$ 30,000	$ 60,000

The preceding income statements indicate that Lund Inc.'s operating income increased from $20,000 to $30,000, a 50% increase ($10,000 ÷ $20,000). In contrast, Yates Inc.'s operating income increased from $50,000 to $60,000, a 20% increase ($10,000 ÷ $50,000).

Because even a small increase in sales will generate a large percentage increase in operating income, Lund Inc. might consider ways to increase sales. Such actions could include special advertising or sales promotions. In contrast, Yates Inc. might consider ways to increase operating leverage by reducing variable costs.

The impact of a change in sales on operating income for companies with high and low operating leverage can be summarized in Exhibit 19.

Exhibit 19 Effect of Operating Leverage on Operating Income

Operating Leverage	Percentage Impact on Operating Income from a Change in Sales
High	Large
Low	Small

Ford Motor Connection

Ford Motor Company has a high proportion of fixed costs with the result that small changes in units sold can significantly affect its overall profitability.

Objective 6
List the assumptions underlying cost-volume-profit analysis.

Cost-Volume-Profit Assumptions

The reliability of cost-volume-profit analysis depends upon several assumptions. These assumptions are as follows:

- Total sales and total costs can be represented by straight lines.
- Within the relevant range of operating activity, the efficiency of operations does not change.
- Costs can be divided into fixed and variable components.
- The sales mix is constant.
- There is no change in the inventory quantities during the period.

The preceding assumptions simplify cost-volume-profit analysis. Since these assumptions are often valid for the relevant range of operations, cost-volume-profit analysis is a useful management tool.[3]

In addition, managers can vary selling prices, costs, and volume and can observe the effects of each change on the break-even point and profit. Such analysis, often called *what if* or *sensitivity analysis,* is easy to perform using spreadsheet or other computerized programs.

[3] The impact of violating these assumptions is discussed in advanced accounting texts.

Objective 7
Describe and illustrate the use of the margin of safety for managerial decision making and performance analysis.

Metric-Based Analysis: Margin of Safety

The **margin of safety** indicates the possible decrease in sales that may occur before an operating loss results. Thus, if the margin of safety is low, even a small decline in sales revenue may result in an operating loss. The margin of safety may be expressed in the following ways:

1. Dollars of sales
2. Units of sales
3. Percent of current sales

To illustrate, assume the following data:

Sales	$250,000
Sales at the break-even point	200,000
Unit selling price	25

The margin of safety in dollars of sales, units of sales, and percent of current sales is computed as follows:

- **Margin of Safety in Dollars of Sales** = **Current Sales Dollars − Breakeven Sales Dollars**

  = $250,000 − $200,000 = $50,000

- **Margin of Safety in Units of Sales** = **Current Unit Sales − Breakeven Unit Sales**

  = ($250,000 ÷ $25) − ($200,000 ÷ $25)

  = 10,000 units − 8,000 units = 2,000 units

- **Margin of Safety in Percent of Current Sales** = $\frac{\textbf{Current Sales Dollars (or Units) − Breakeven Sales Dollars (or Units)}}{\textbf{Current Sales Dollars (or Units)}}$

$$= \frac{\$250{,}000 - \$200{,}000}{\$250{,}000} = \frac{\$50{,}000}{\$250{,}000} = 20\%$$

or

$$= \frac{10{,}000 \text{ units} - 8{,}000 \text{ units}}{10{,}000 \text{ units}} = \frac{2{,}000 \text{ units}}{10{,}000 \text{ units}} = 20\%$$

Therefore, the current sales may decline by $50,000, 2,000 units, or 20% before an operating loss occurs.

Key Points

1. Classify costs as variable costs, fixed costs, or mixed costs.

Cost behavior refers to the manner in which a cost changes as a related activity changes. Variable costs are costs that vary in total in proportion to changes in the level of activity. Fixed costs are costs that remain the same in total dollar amount as the level of activity changes. A mixed cost has attributes of both a variable and a fixed cost.

2. Compute the contribution margin, the contribution margin ratio, and the unit contribution margin.

The contribution margin concept is useful in business planning because it gives insight into the profit potential of a firm. The contribution margin is the excess of sales revenues over variable costs. Contribution margin can also be expressed as a percentage and is known as the contribution margin ratio.

$$\textbf{Contribution Margin Ratio} = \frac{\textbf{Sales} - \textbf{Variable Costs}}{\textbf{Sales}}$$

The unit contribution margin is the excess of the unit selling price over the unit variable cost.

3. Using cost-volume-profit equations, determine the break-even point and sales necessary to achieve a target profit.

The equation approach to cost-volume-profit analysis uses fixed costs and unit contribution margin to determine the break-even point. The equation approach can also be used to determine the sales necessary to achieve a target profit.

4. Using cost-volume-profit and profit-volume graphs, determine the break-even point and sales necessary to achieve a target profit.

A cost-volume-profit graph focuses on the relationships among costs, sales, and operating profit or loss. Preparing and using a cost-volume-profit graph to determine the break-even point and the volume necessary to achieve a target profit are illustrated in this chapter.

The profit-volume graph focuses on profits rather than on revenues and costs. Preparing and using a profit-volume graph to determine the break-even point and the volume necessary to achieve a target profit are illustrated in this chapter.

5. Apply cost-volume-profit relationships to more than one product and in computing operating leverage.

Computing the break-even point for a business selling two or more products is based on a specified sales mix. Given the sales mix, the break-even point can be computed, using the methods illustrated in this chapter.

Operating leverage is useful in measuring the impact of changes in sales on operating income without preparing formal income statements. It is computed by dividing contribution margin by operating income.

6. Describe and illustrate the use of the margin of safety for managerial decision making and performance analysis.

The margin of safety indicates the possible decrease in sales that may occur before an operating loss results. It may be expressed in dollars of sales, units of sales, or as a percent of current sales.

Key Terms

Activity base (460)
Break-even point (469)
Contribution margin (467)
Contribution margin ratio (467)
Cost behavior (460)
Cost-volume-profit analysis (466)
Cost-volume-profit graph (476)
Fixed costs (462)
High-low method (464)
Margin of safety (484)
Mixed costs (463)
Operating leverage (482)
Profit-volume graph (477)
Relevant range (460)
Sales mix (480)
Unit contribution margin (468)
Variable costing (466)
Variable costs (460)

Illustrative Problem

Jackson Inc. expects to maintain the same inventories at the end of the year as at the beginning of the year. The estimated fixed costs for the year are $288,000, and the estimated variable costs per unit are $14. It is expected that 60,000 units will be sold at a price of $20 per unit. Maximum sales within the relevant range are 70,000 units.

Instructions

1. What is (a) the contribution margin ratio and (b) the unit contribution margin?
2. Determine the break-even point in units.
3. Construct a cost-volume-profit graph indicating the break-even point.
4. Construct a profit-volume graph indicating the break-even point.

Solution

1\. a. Contribution Margin Ratio

$$= \frac{\text{Sales} - \text{Variable Costs}}{\text{Sales}}$$

$$= \frac{(60{,}000 \text{ units} \times \$20) - (60{,}000 \text{ units} \times \$14)}{(60{,}000 \text{ units} \times \$20)}$$

$$= \frac{\$1{,}200{,}000 - \$840{,}000}{\$1{,}200{,}000} = \frac{\$360{,}000}{\$1{,}200{,}000}$$

$$= 30\%$$

b. Unit Contribution Margin = Unit Selling Price − Unit Variable Costs
= \$20 − \$14 = \$6

2. $$\text{Break-Even Sales (units)} = \frac{\text{Fixed Costs}}{\text{Unit Contribution Margin}} = \frac{\$288{,}000}{\$6} = 48{,}000 \text{ units}$$

3.

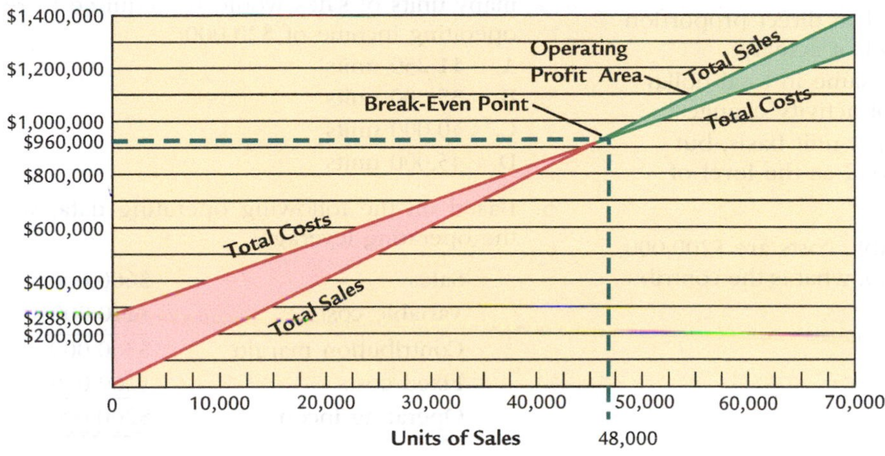

4.

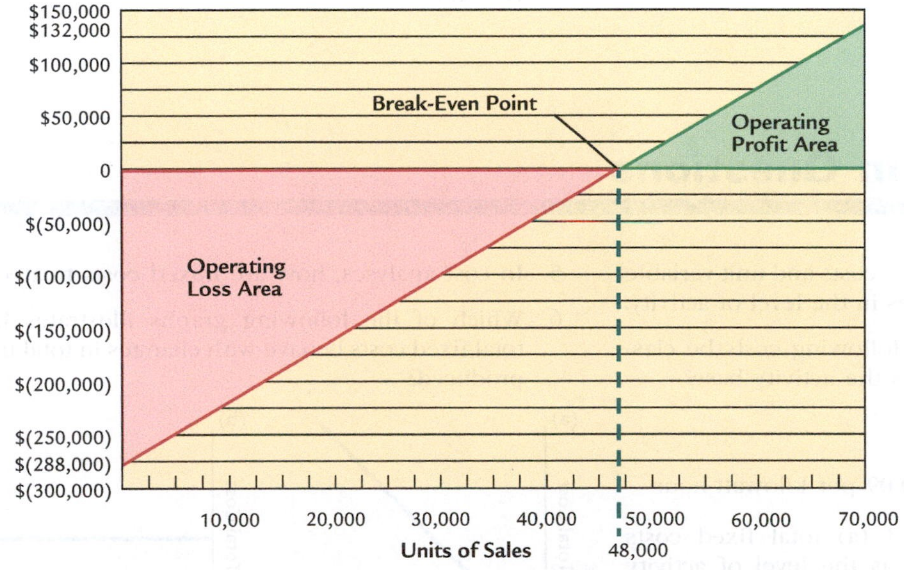

Self-Examination Questions

(Answers appear at the end of chapter)

1. Which of the following statements describes variable costs?
   A. Costs that vary on a per-unit basis as the level of activity changes
   B. Costs that vary in total in direct proportion to changes in the level of activity
   C. Costs that remain the same in total dollar amount as the level of activity changes
   D. Costs that vary on a per-unit basis, but remain the same in total as the level of activity changes

2. If sales are $500,000, variable costs are $200,000, and fixed costs are $240,000, what is the contribution margin ratio?
   A. 40%
   B. 48%
   C. 52%
   D. 60%

3. If the unit selling price is $16, the unit variable cost is $12, and fixed costs are $160,000, what are the break-even sales (units)?
   A. 5,714 units
   B. 10,000 units
   C. 13,333 units
   D. 40,000 units

4. Based on the data presented in Question 3, how many units of sales would be required to realize operating income of $20,000?
   A. 11,250 units
   B. 35,000 units
   C. 40,000 units
   D. 45,000 units

5. Based on the following operating data, what is the operating leverage?

Sales	$600,000
Variable costs	(240,000)
Contribution margin	$360,000
Fixed costs	(160,000)
Operating income	$200,000

   A. 0.8
   B. 1.2
   C. 1.8
   D. 4.0

Class Discussion Questions

1. Describe how total variable costs and unit variable costs behave with changes in the level of activity.
2. How would each of the following costs be classified if units produced is the activity base?
   a. Direct materials costs
   b. Direct labor costs
   c. Electricity costs of $0.09 per kilowatt-hour
3. Describe the behavior of (a) total fixed costs and (b) unit fixed costs as the level of activity increases.
4. How would each of the following costs be classified if units produced is the activity base?
   a. Salary of factory supervisor ($120,000 per year)
   b. Straight-line depreciation of plant and equipment
   c. Property rent of $11,500 per month on plant and equipment
5. In cost analyses, how are mixed costs treated?
6. Which of the following graphs illustrates how total fixed costs behave with changes in total units produced?

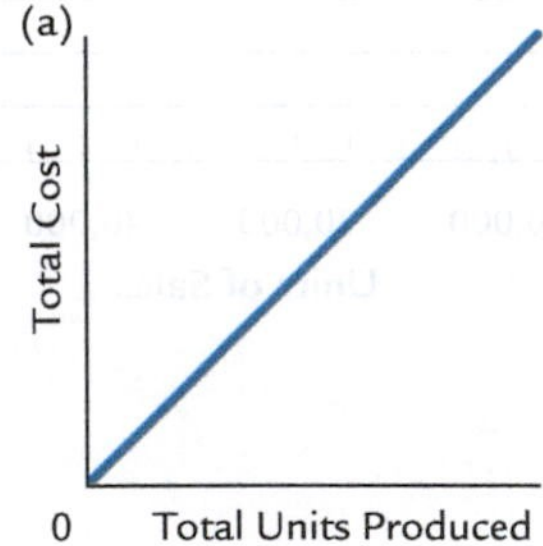

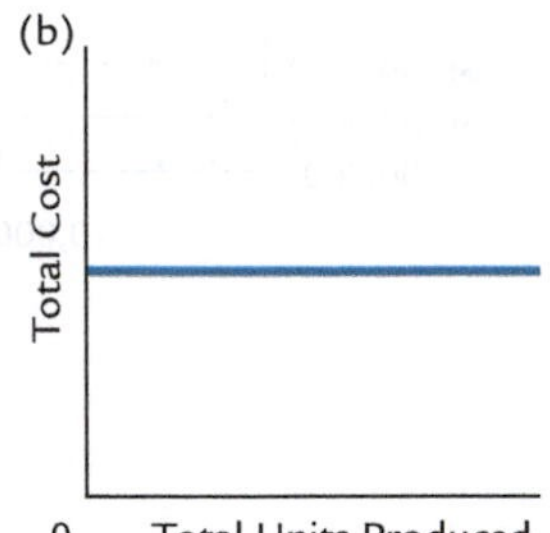

7. Which of the following graphs illustrates how unit variable costs behave with changes in total units produced?

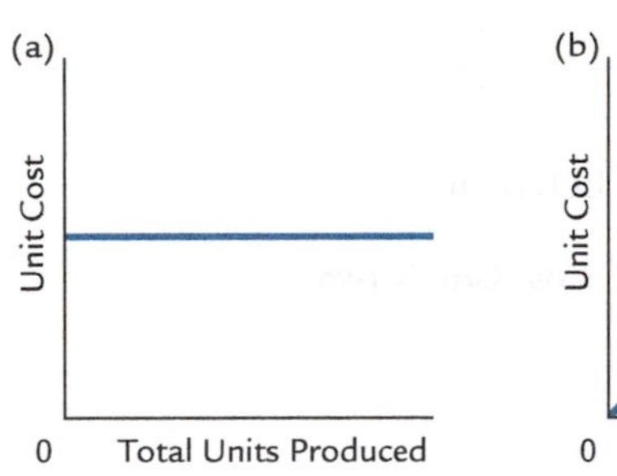

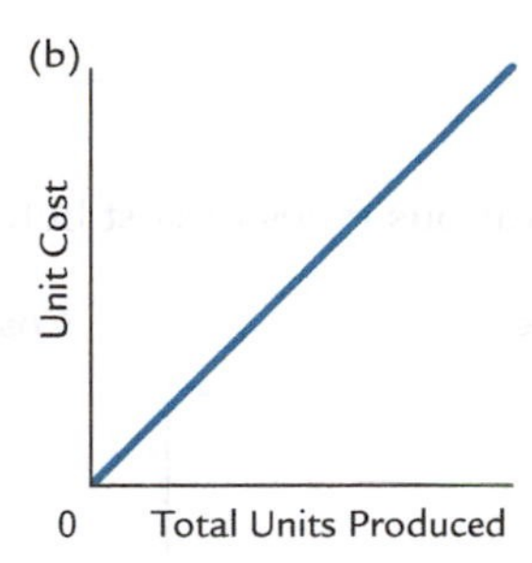

8. Which of the following graphs best illustrates fixed costs per unit as the activity base changes?

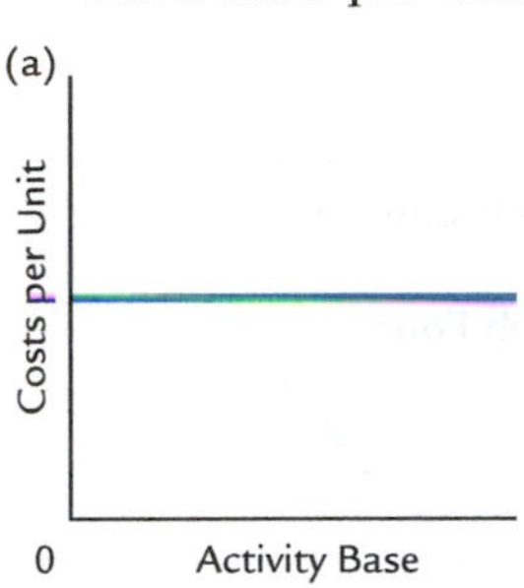

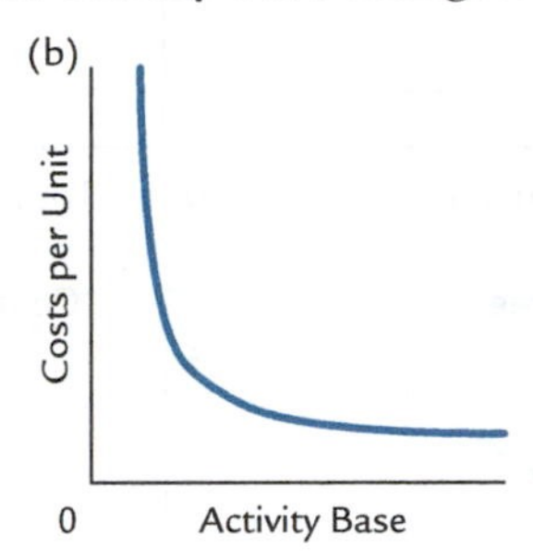

9. In applying the high-low method of cost estimation, how is the total fixed cost estimated?

10. If fixed costs increase, what would be the impact on the (a) contribution margin and (b) operating income?

11. An examination of the accounting records of Larredo Company disclosed a high contribution margin ratio and production at a level below maximum capacity. Based on this information, suggest a likely means of improving operating income.

12. If the unit cost of direct materials is decreased, what effect will this change have on the break-even point?

13. If insurance rates are increased, what effect will this change in fixed costs have on the break-even point?

14. Both Gouda Company and Cheddar Company had the same sales, total costs, and operating income for the current fiscal year; yet Gouda Company had a lower break-even point than Cheddar Company. Explain the reason for this difference in break-even points.

15. The reliability of cost-volume-profit (CVP) analysis depends on several key assumptions. What are those primary assumptions?

16. How does the sales mix affect the calculation of the break-even point?

17. What does operating leverage measure, and how is it computed?

Exercises

E11-1 Classify costs

Obj. 1

Following is a list of various costs incurred in producing and selling college textbooks. With respect to the production and sale of textbooks, classify each cost as either variable, fixed, or mixed.

1. Art commission of $36,000 paid for use of art on textbook cover.
2. Sales commissions paid sales representatives based upon number of textbooks sold.
3. Electricity costs, $0.04 per kilowatt-hour.
4. Hourly wages of operators of printing presses.
5. Janitorial costs, $5,000 per month.
6. Packaging for customized texts and texts shipped with software codes.
7. Paper used in printing the textbooks.
8. Property insurance premiums, $1,800 per month plus $0.05 for each dollar of property over $2,000,000
9. Property taxes, $615,000 per year on factory building and equipment.
10. Rent on warehouse, $12,800 per month plus $2.50 per square foot of storage used.
11. Royalty paid authors for each textbook sold.
12. Salary of plant manager.

13. Sales commission paid to Amazon.com of $100,000 plus $0.50 for each textbook sold online.
14. Straight-line depreciation on the production equipment.
15. Technology development costs of $1,200,000.

Obj. 1

E11-2 Identify cost graphs

The following cost graphs illustrate various types of cost behavior:

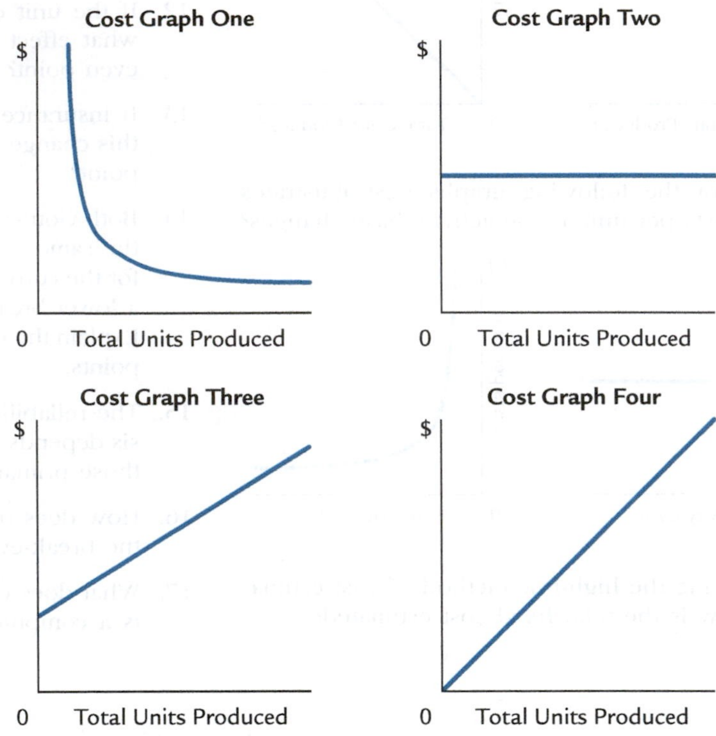

For each of the following costs, identify the cost graph that best illustrates its cost behavior as the number of units produced increases.

a. Direct material cost per unit.
b. Fees for using a patent of $500,000 plus $0.25 for each unit produced.
c. Salary of quality control supervisor.
d. Straight-line depreciation per unit on factory equipment.
e. Total direct materials cost.

Obj. 1

E11-3 Identify activity bases

For a major university, match each cost in the following table with the appropriate activity base. An activity base may only be used more than once.

Cost	Activity Base
1. Admissions mailing	a. Number of enrollment applications
2. Financial aid	b. Number of financial aid applications
3. Graduate teaching assistants	c. Number of student and faculty
4. Housing	d. Number of enrolled students and alumni
5. Identification cards	e. Number of students living on campus
6. Student records	f. Student credit hours

E11-4 Identify activity bases

Obj. 1

From the following list of activity bases for an automobile dealership, select the base that would be most appropriate for each of these costs: (1) preparation costs (cleaning, oil, and gasoline costs) for each car received, (2) salespersons' commission of 6% of the sales price for each car sold, and (3) administrative costs for ordering cars.

a. Dollar amount of cars on hand

b. Dollar amount of cars ordered

c. Dollar amount of cars received

d. Dollar amount of cars sold

e. Number of cars on hand

f. Number of cars ordered

g. Number of cars received

h. Number of cars sold

E11-5 Identify fixed and variable costs

Obj. 1

Intuit Inc. (INTU) develops and sells software products for the personal finance market, including popular titles such as Quicken® and TurboTax®. Classify each of the following costs and expenses for this company as either variable or fixed to the number of units produced and sold:

a. Advertising

b. CDs

c. Commissions for online sales personnel

d. Cost of registering each unit sold

e. Hourly wages of help desk employees

f. Packaging costs

g. Salaries of human resources personnel

h. Salaries of software developers

i. Salary of Chief Financial Officer

j. Shipping expenses

k. Straight-line depreciation on equipment

l. Writing of user's guides

E11-6 Relevant range and fixed and variable costs

Obj. 1

✔ a. $1.20

Third World Gamer Inc. manufactures components for computer games within a relevant range of 500,000 to 1,000,000 disks per year. Within this range, the following partially completed manufacturing cost schedule has been prepared:

Components produced	500,000	750,000	1,000,000
Total costs:			
Total variable costs	$ 600,000	(d)	(j)
Total fixed costs	600,000	(e)	(k)
Total costs	$1,200,000	(f)	(l)
Cost per unit:			
Variable cost per unit	(a)	(g)	(m)
Fixed cost per unit	(b)	(h)	(n)
Total cost per unit	(c)	(i)	(o)

Complete the cost schedule, identifying each cost by the appropriate letter (a) through (o).

Obj. 1

✔ a. 12.50 per unit

E11-7 High-low method

Liberty Inc. has decided to use the high-low method to estimate costs. The data for various levels of production are as follows:

Units Produced	Total Costs
100,000	$1,800,000
180,000	2,800,000
300,000	4,300,000

a. Determine the variable cost per unit and the fixed cost.

b. Based on part (a), estimate the total cost for 260,000 units of production.

Obj. 1

✔ Fixed cost, $3,600,000

E11-8 High-low method for service company

Miss River Railroad decided to use the high-low method and operating data from the past six months to estimate the fixed and variable components of transportation costs. The activity base used by Miss River Railroad is a measure of railroad operating activity, termed "gross-ton miles," which is the total number of tons multiplied by the miles moved.

	Transportation Costs	Gross-Ton Miles
January	$6,500,000	2,500,000
February	6,187,500	2,250,000
March	6,980,000	2,940,000
April	7,500,000	3,400,000
May	8,775,000	4,500,000
June	8,200,000	4,000,000

Determine the variable cost per gross-ton mile and the fixed costs.

Obj. 2

✔ a. 36%

E11-9 Contribution margin ratio

a. Matzinger Company budgets sales of $10,400,000, fixed costs of $1,100,000, and variable costs of $6,656,000. What is the contribution margin ratio for Matzinger Company?

b. If the contribution margin ratio for Raynor Company is 41%, sales are $6,200,000, and fixed costs are $1,350,000, what is the operating income?

Obj. 2

✔ b. 33.0%

E11-10 Contribution margin and contribution margin ratio

For a recent year, McDonald's (MCD) company-owned restaurants had the following sales and expenses (in millions):

Sales		$16,488
Food and packaging	$5,552	
Payroll	4,400	
Occupancy (rent, depreciation, etc.)	4,025	
General, selling, and admin. expenses	2,434	
Other expense	209	
Total expenses		(16,620)
Operating income (loss)		$ (132)

Assume that the variable costs consist of food and packaging, payroll, and 45% of the general, selling, and administrative expenses.

Note: The spreadsheet icon  indicates an Excel template is available on the student companion site at www.cengagebrain.com.

a. What is McDonald's contribution margin? Round to the nearest million.

b. What is McDonald's contribution margin ratio? Round to one decimal place.

c. How much would operating income increase if same-store sales increased by $500 million for the coming year, with no change in the contribution margin ratio or fixed costs?

d. What would have been the operating income or loss for the recent year if sales had been $500 million more?

e. To achieve break even for the recent year, by how much would sales need to increase?

E11-11 Break-even sales and sales to realize operating income

Obj. 3

✔ b. 118,000 units

For the current year ending December 31, McAdams Industries expects fixed costs of $1,860,000, a unit variable cost of $105, and a unit selling price of $125.

a. Compute the anticipated break-even sales (units).

b. Compute the sales (units) required to realize operating income of $500,000.

E11-12 Break-even sales

Obj. 3

✔ a. 94,147,059 barrels

Molson-Coors Brewing Company (TAP) reported the following operating information for a recent year (in millions):

Sales	$3,568
Cost of goods sold	(2,164)
Gross profit	$1,404
Marketing, general, and admin. expenses	(1,052)
Operating income	$ 352*

*Before special items

Assume that Molson-Coors sold 120 million barrels of beer during the year, variable costs were 70% of the cost of goods sold and 40% of marketing, general, and administrative expenses, and that the remaining costs are fixed. For the following year, assume that Molson-Coors expects pricing, variable costs per barrel, and fixed costs to remain constant, except that new distribution and general office facilities are expected to increase fixed costs by $100 million.

Rounding to the nearest cent:

a. Compute the break-even sales (barrels) for the current year.

b. Compute the anticipated break-even sales (barrels) for the following year.

E11-13 Break-even sales

Obj. 3

✔ a. 1,800 units

Currently, the unit selling price of a product is $1,350, the unit variable cost is $900, and the total fixed costs are $810,000. A proposal is being evaluated to increase the unit selling price to $1,400.

a. Compute the current break-even sales (units).

b. Compute the anticipated break-even sales (units), assuming that the unit selling price is increased and all costs remain constant.

Obj. 3

E11-14 Break-even analysis

The Garden Club of Palm Springs, California, collected recipes from members and published a cookbook entitled *Desert Dishes*. The book will sell for $40 per copy. The chairperson of the cookbook development committee estimated that the club needed to sell 8,000 books to break even on its $40,000 investment. What is the variable cost per unit assumed in the Garden Club's analysis?

Obj. 3

E11-15 Break-even analysis

Media outlets such as ESPN and Fox Sports often have Web sites that provide in-depth coverage of news and events. Portions of these Web sites are restricted to members who pay a monthly subscription to gain access to exclusive news and commentary. These Web sites typically offer a free trial period to introduce viewers to the Web site. Assume that during a recent fiscal year, ESPN.com spent $20,900,000 on a promotional campaign for its Web site, offering two free months of service for new subscribers. In addition, assume the following information:

Number of months an average new customer stays with the service (including the two free months)	18 months
Revenue per month per customer subscription	$9.95
Variable cost per month per customer subscription	$4.20

Determine the number of new customer accounts needed to break even on the cost of the promotional campaign. In forming your answer, (1) treat the cost of the promotional campaign as a fixed cost, and (2) treat the revenue less variable cost per account for the subscription period as the unit contribution margin.

Obj. 4
✔ b. $200,000

E11-16 Cost-volume-profit graph

For the coming year, Cabinet Inc. anticipates fixed costs of $60,000, a unit variable cost of $70, and a unit selling price of $100. The maximum sales within the relevant range are $500,000.

a. Construct a cost-volume-profit graph.
b. Estimate the break-even sales (dollars) by using the cost-volume-profit graph constructed in part (a).
c. What is the main advantage of presenting the cost-volume-profit analysis in graphic form rather than equation form?

Obj. 4
✔ b. $90,000

E11-17 Profit-volume graph

Using the data for Cabinet Inc. in Exercise 11-16, (a) determine the maximum possible operating loss, (b) compute the maximum possible operating income, (c) construct a profit-volume graph, and (d) estimate the break-even sales (units) by using the profit-volume graph constructed in part (c).

E11-18 Break-even graph

Obj. 4

Name the following graph, and identify the items represented by the letters (a) through (f).

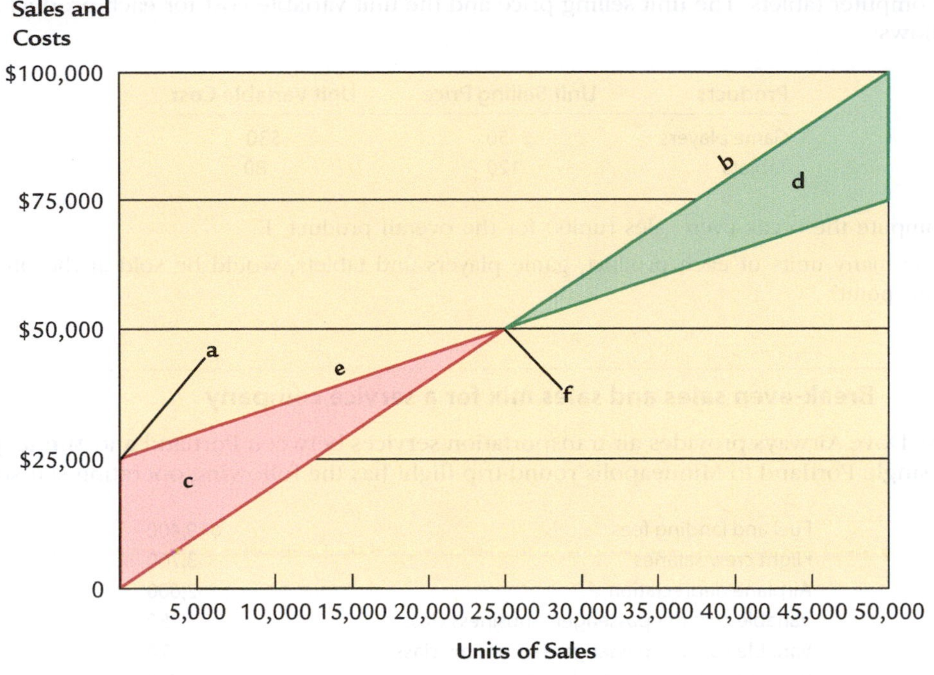

E11-19 Break-even graph

Obj. 4

Name the following graph and identify the items represented by the letters (a) through (f).

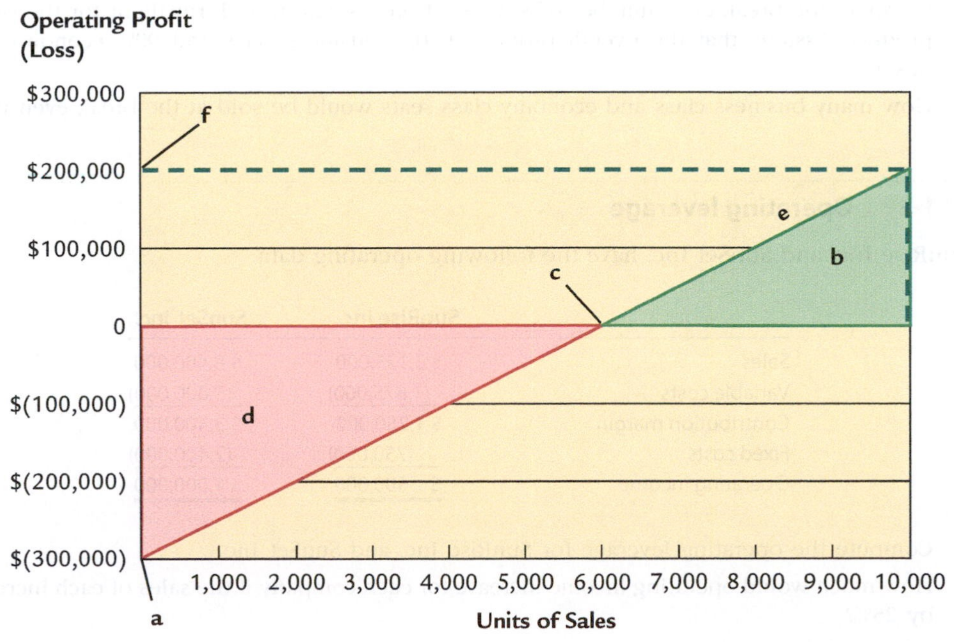

Obj. 5
✔ a. 36,000 units

E11-20 Sales mix and break-even sales

Northwest Technology Inc. manufactures and sells two products, digital game players and computer tablets. The fixed costs are $936,000, and the sales mix is 70% game players and 30% computer tablets. The unit selling price and the unit variable cost for each product are as follows:

Products	Unit Selling Price	Unit Variable Cost
Game players	$ 50	$30
Tablets	120	80

a. Compute the break-even sales (units) for the overall product, E.

b. How many units of each product, game players and tablets, would be sold at the break-even point?

Obj. 5
✔ a. 80 seats

E11-21 Break-even sales and sales mix for a service company

Yellow Dove Airways provides air transportation services between Portland and Minneapolis. A single Portland to Minneapolis round-trip flight has the following operating statistics:

Fuel and landing fees	$19,400
Flight crew salaries	3,760
Airplane depreciation	2,600
Variable cost per passenger—business class	50
Variable cost per passenger—economy class	20
Round-trip ticket price—business class	750
Round-trip ticket price—economy class	300

It is assumed that the fuel and landing fees, crew salaries, and airplane depreciation are fixed, regardless of the number of seats sold for the round-trip flight.

a. Compute the break-even number of seats sold on a single round-trip flight for the overall product. Assume that the overall product is 10% business class and 90% economy class tickets.

b. How many business class and economy class seats would be sold at the break-even point?

Obj. 5
✔ a. SunRise 2.5

E11-22 Operating leverage

SunRise Inc. and SunSet Inc. have the following operating data:

	SunRise Inc.	SunSet Inc.
Sales	$ 3,125,000	$ 8,400,000
Variable costs	(1,875,000)	(5,000,000)
Contribution margin	$ 1,250,000	$ 3,400,000
Fixed costs	(750,000)	(2,400,000)
Operating income	$ 500,000	$ 1,000,000

a. Compute the operating leverage for SunRise Inc. and SunSet Inc.

b. How much would operating income increase for each company if the sales of each increased by 25%?

c. Why is there a difference in the increase in operating income for the two companies? Explain.

Problems

P11-1 Classify costs

Obj. 1

Peak Apparel Co. manufactures a variety of clothing types for distribution to several major retail chains. The following costs are incurred in the production and sale of blue jeans:

a. Shipping boxes used to ship orders
b. Consulting fee of $200,000 paid to industry specialist for marketing advice
c. Straight-line depreciation on sewing machines
d. Salesperson's salary, $10,000 plus 2% of the total sales
e. Fabric
f. Dye
g. Thread
h. Salary of designers
i. Brass buttons
j. Legal fees paid to attorneys in defense of the company in a patent infringement suit, $50,000 plus $87 per hour
k. Insurance premiums on property, plant, and equipment, $70,000 per year plus $5 per $30,000 of insured value over $8,000,000
l. Rental costs of warehouse, $5,000 per month plus $4 per square foot of storage used
m. Supplies
n. Leather for patches identifying the brand on individual pieces of apparel
o. Rent on plant equipment, $50,000 per year
p. Salary of production vice president
q. Janitorial services, $2,200 per month
r. Wages of machine operators
s. Electricity costs of $0.10 per kilowatt-hour
t. Property taxes on property, plant, and equipment

Instructions

Classify the preceding costs as either fixed, variable, or mixed. Use the following tabular headings and place an "X" in the appropriate column. Identify each cost by letter in the cost column.

Cost	Fixed Cost	Variable Cost	Mixed Cost

P11-2 Break-even sales under present and proposed conditions

Obj. 2, 3
✔ 2. a. $96.60

Kearney Company, operating at full capacity, sold 400,000 units at a price of $246.60 per unit during 20Y5. Its income statement for 20Y5 is as follows:

Sales		$ 98,640,000
Cost of goods sold		(44,500,000)
Gross profit		$ 54,140,000
Expenses:		
Selling expenses	$8,000,000	
Administrative expenses	3,000,000	
Total expenses		(11,000,000)
Operating income		$ 43,140,000

The division of costs between fixed and variable is as follows:

	Fixed	Variable
Cost of goods sold	28%	72%
Selling expenses	25%	75%
Administrative expenses	80%	20%

Management is considering a plant expansion program that will permit an increase of $8,631,000 (35,000 units at $246.60) in yearly sales. The expansion will increase fixed costs by $3,600,000 but will not affect the relationship between sales and variable costs.

Instructions

1. Determine for 20Y5 the total fixed costs and the total variable costs.
2. Determine for 20Y5 (a) the unit variable cost and (b) the unit contribution margin.
3. Compute the break-even sales (units) for 20Y5.
4. Compute the break-even sales (units) under the proposed program.
5. Determine the amount of sales (units) that would be necessary under the proposed program to realize the $43,140,000 of operating income that was earned in 20Y5.
6. Determine the maximum operating income possible with the expanded plant.
7. If the proposal is accepted and sales remain at the 20Y5 level, what will be the operating income or loss for 20Y6?
8. Based on the data given, would you recommend accepting the proposal? Explain.

Obj. 3, 4

✔ 1. 6,000 units

P11-3 Break-even sales and cost-volume-profit graph

For the coming year, Bernardino Company anticipates a unit selling price of $85, a unit variable cost of $15, and fixed costs of $420,000.

Instructions

1. Compute the anticipated break-even sales (units).
2. Compute the sales (units) required to realize operating income of $70,000.
3. Construct a cost-volume-profit graph, assuming maximum sales of 10,000 units within the relevant range.
4. Determine the probable operating income (loss) if sales total 8,000 units.

Obj. 3, 4

✔ 1. 6,800 units

P11-4 Break-even sales and cost-volume-profit graph

Last year, Ridgecrest Inc. had sales of $3,200,000, based on a unit selling price of $400. The variable cost per unit was $240, and fixed costs were $1,088,000. The maximum sales within Ridgecrest Inc.'s relevant range are 10,000 units. Ridgecrest Inc. is considering a proposal to spend an additional $160,000 on billboard advertising during the current year in an attempt to increase sales and utilize unused capacity.

Instructions

1. Construct a cost-volume-profit graph indicating the break-even sales for last year. Verify your answer using the break-even equation.
2. Using the cost-volume-profit graph prepared in part (1), determine (a) the operating income for last year and (b) the maximum operating income that could have been realized during the year. Verify your answers arithmetically.
3. Construct a cost-volume-profit graph indicating the break-even sales for the current year, assuming that a noncancelable contract is signed for the additional billboard advertising. No changes are expected in the unit selling price or other costs. Verify your answer using the break-even equation.
4. Using the cost-volume-profit graph prepared in part (3), determine (a) the operating income if sales total 8,000 units and (b) the maximum operating income that could be realized during the year. Verify your answers arithmetically.

P11-5 Sales mix and break-even sales

Obj. 5

✔ 1. 7,500 units

Data related to the expected sales of kayaks and canoes for River Sports Inc. for the current year, which is typical of recent years, are as follows:

Products	Unit Selling Price	Unit Variable Cost	Sales Mix
Kayaks	$400	$240	80%
Canoes	800	480	20%

The estimated fixed costs for the current year are $1,440,000.

Instructions

1. Determine the estimated units of sales of the overall product necessary to reach the break-even point for the current year.
2. Based on the break-even sales (units) in part (1), determine the unit sales of kayaks and canoes for the current year.
3. Assume that the sales mix was 20% kayaks and 80% canoes. Determine the estimated units of sales of overall product necessary to reach the break-even point for the current year.
4. Based upon the break-even sales (units) in part (3), determine the unit sales of kayaks and canoes for the current year.
5. Why is the overall enterprise break-even point so different in (1) and (3)?

P11-6 Contribution margin, break-even sales, cost-volume-profit graph, and operating leverage

Obj. 2, 3, 4, 5

✔ 2. 40%

Organic Health Care Products Inc. expects to maintain the same inventories at the end of 20Y8 as at the beginning of the year. The total of all production costs for the year is therefore assumed to be equal to the cost of goods sold. With this in mind, the various department heads were asked to submit estimates of the costs for their departments during 20Y8. A summary report of these estimates is as follows:

	Estimated Fixed Cost	Estimated Variable Cost (per unit sold)
Production costs:		
Direct materials	—	$ 8.00
Direct labor	—	3.00
Factory overhead	$ 200,000	1.50
Selling expenses:		
Advertising	1,450,000	—
Sales salaries and commissions	93,000	1.85
Travel	340,000	—
Miscellaneous selling expense	2,000	0.10
Administrative expenses:		
Office and officers' salaries	300,000	—
Supplies	10,000	0.50
Miscellaneous administrative expense	5,000	0.05
Total	$2,400,000	$15.00

It is expected that 400,000 units will be sold at a price of $25 a unit. Maximum sales within the relevant range are 500,000 units.

Instructions

1. Prepare an estimated income statement for 20Y8.
2. What is the expected contribution margin ratio?
3. Determine the break-even sales in units.
4. Construct a cost-volume-profit graph indicating the break-even sales.
5. Determine the operating leverage.

Metric-Based Analysis

Obj. 3, 7
✔ a. (2) 25%

MBA 11-1 Margin of safety

a. If Go-Go Buggies Company, with a break-even point at $6,000,000 of sales, has actual sales of $8,000,000, what is the margin of safety expressed (1) in dollars and (2) as a percentage of sales?

b. If the margin of safety for Beartooth Company was 15%, fixed costs were $9,180,000, and variable costs were 60% of sales, what was the amount of actual sales (dollars)? (*Hint:* Determine the break-even in sales dollars first.)

Obj. 7

MBA 11-2 Break-even and margin of safety relationships

At a recent staff meeting, the management of Warp Time Technologies Inc. was considering discontinuing its Track Time line of electronic games. The chief financial analyst reported the following current monthly data for the Track Time:

Unit sales	1,250,000
Break-even units	1,300,000
Margin of safety in units	50,000

For what reason would you question the validity of these data?

Obj. 7

MBA 11-3 Margin of safety

Use the data from E11-12 and assume that break-even sales are $2,798 million.

Determine the following for Molson-Coors Brewing Company. Round to one decimal place.

1. Margin of safety expressed as dollar sales.
2. Margin of safety expressed as a percentage.

Obj. 5, 7

MBA 11-4 Sales mix and margin of safety

Use the data from E11-20, assume that 31,500 units of digital game players and 13,500 computer tablets were sold in the current year. Assuming no change in the sales mix, determine the following for Northwest Technology Inc. Round to one decimal place.

1. Margin of safety for game players expressed as (a) units sold, (b) sales dollars, and (c) a percentage.
2. Margin of safety for tablets expressed as (a) units sold, (b) sales dollars, and (c) a percentage.
3. Margin of safety for total sales expressed as (a) units sold, (b) sales dollars, and (c) a percentage.

Obj. 7

MBA 11-5 Margin of safety

Using the data from P11-2, determine the following for 20Y5.

1. Margin of safety for 20Y5.
2. Margin of safety under the proposed program assuming 20Y5 sales.

Obj. 7

MBA 11-6 Margin of safety

Using the data from P11-6, determine the following based upon the estimates for 20Y8:

1. Margin of safety for 20Y8 in units sold.
2. Margin of safety for 20Y8 in sales dollars.
3. Margin of safety for 20Y8 as a percentage of sales.

Cases

Case 11-1 Ethics and professional conduct in business

Phil Fritz is a financial consultant to Magna Properties Inc., a real estate syndicate. Magna Properties Inc. finances and develops commercial real estate (office buildings). The completed projects are then sold as limited partnership interests to individual investors. The syndicate makes a profit on the sale of these partnership interests. Phil provides financial information for the offering prospectus, which is a document that provides the financial and legal details of the limited partnership offerings. In one of the projects, the bank has financed the construction of a commercial office building at a rate of 7% for the first four years, after which time the rate jumps to 9% for the remaining 21 years of the mortgage. The interest costs are one of the major ongoing costs of a real estate project. Phil has reported prominently in the prospectus that the break-even occupancy for the first four years is 48%. This is the amount of office space that must be leased to cover the interest and general upkeep costs over the first four years. The 48% break-even is very low and thus communicates a low risk to potential investors. Phil uses the 48% break-even rate as a major marketing tool in selling the limited partnership interests. Buried in the fine print of the prospectus is additional information that would allow an astute investor to determine that the break-even occupancy will jump to 92% after the fourth year because of the contracted increase in the mortgage interest rate. Phil believes prospective investors are adequately informed as to the risk of the investment.

Comment on the ethical considerations of this situation.

Case 11-2 Break-even sales, contribution margin

"Every airline has what is called a break-even load factor. That is, the percentage of seats the airline . . . (flies) . . . that it must sell . . . to cover its costs. Since revenue and costs vary from one airline to another, so does the break-even factor. . . . Overall, the break-even load factor for the (airline) industry in recent years has been approximately 66 percent."

The airline industry is notorious for boom and bust cycles. Why is airline profitability very sensitive to these cycles? Do you think that during a down cycle the strategy to consolidate routes and raise ticket prices is reasonable? What would make this strategy succeed or fail? Why?

Source: http://www.avjobs.com/history/airline-economics.asp.

Case 11-3 Break-even analysis

Aquarius Games Inc. has finished a new video game, *Triathlon Challenge*. Management is now considering its marketing strategies. The following information is available:

Anticipated sales price per unit	$75
Variable cost per unit*	$45
Anticipated sales volume in units	800,000
Production costs	$9,000,000
Anticipated advertising costs	$15,000,000

*The video game, packaging, and copying costs.

Two managers, Haley Chipana and Dan Gillespie, had the following discussion of ways to increase the profitability of this new offering:

Haley: I think we need to think of some way to increase our profitability. Do you have any ideas?

Dan: Well, I think the best strategy would be to become aggressive on price.

Haley: How aggressive?

Dan: If we drop the price to $60 per unit and maintain our advertising budget at $15,000,000, I think we will generate sales of 2,000,000 units.

Haley: I think that's the wrong way to go. You're giving too much up on price. Instead, I think we need to follow an aggressive advertising strategy.

Dan: How aggressive?

Haley: If we increase our advertising to a total of $20,000,000, we should be able to increase sales volume to 1,200,000 units without any change in price.

Dan: I don't think that's reasonable. We'll never cover the increased advertising costs.

Which strategy is best: Do nothing? Follow the advice of Dan Gillespie? Or follow Haley Chipana's strategy?

Case 11-4 Variable costs and activity bases in decision making

The owner of Dawg Prints, a printing company, is planning direct labor needs for the upcoming year. The owner has provided you with the following information for next year's plans:

	One Color	Two Color	Three Color	Four Color	Total
Number of banners	198	250	352	400	1,200

Each color on the banner must be printed one at a time. Thus, for example, a four-color banner will need to be run through the printing operation four separate times. The total production volume last year was 600 banners, as shown below.

	One Color	Two Color	Three Color	Total
Number of banners	152	206	242	600

The four-color banner is a new product offering for the upcoming year. The owner believes that the expected 600-unit increase in volume from last year means that direct labor expenses should increase by 100% (600 ÷ 600). What do you think?

Case 11-5 Variable costs and activity bases in decision making

Sales volume has been dropping at Pinnacle Publishing Company. During this time, however, the Shipping Department manager has been under severe financial constraints. The manager knows that most of the Shipping Department's effort is related to pulling inventory from the warehouse for each order and performing the paperwork. The paperwork involves preparing shipping documents for each order. Thus, the pulling and paperwork effort associated with each sales order is essentially the same, regardless of the size of the order. The Shipping Department manager has discussed the financial situation with senior management. Senior management has responded by pointing out that sales volume has been dropping, so that the amount of work in the Shipping Department should be dropping. Thus, senior management told the Shipping Department manager that costs should be decreasing in the department.

The Shipping Department manager prepared the following information:

Month	Sales Volume	Number of Customer Orders	Sales Volume per Order
January	$500,000	1,400	250
February	460,000	1,440	230
March	440,000	1,460	220
April	400,000	1,500	200
May	380,000	1,570	190
June	370,000	1,650	185
July	360,000	1,700	180
August	350,000	1,750	175

Given this information, how would you respond to senior management?

Case 11-6 Break-even analysis

Break-even analysis is one of the most fundamental tools for managing any kind of business unit. Consider the management of your school. In a group, brainstorm some applications of break-even analysis at your school. Identify three areas where break-even analysis might be used. For each area, identify the revenues, variable costs, and fixed costs that would be used in the calculation.

Answers to Self-Examination Questions

1. **B** Variable costs vary in total in direct proportion to changes in the level of activity (answer B). Costs that vary on a per-unit basis as the level of activity changes (answer A) or remain constant in total dollar amount as the level of activity changes (answer C), or both (answer D), are fixed costs.

2. **D** The contribution margin ratio indicates the percentage of each sales dollar available to cover the fixed costs and provide operating income and is determined as follows:

$$\text{Contribution Margin Ratio} = \frac{\text{Sales} - \text{Variable Costs}}{\text{Sales}}$$

$$= \frac{\$500{,}000 - \$200{,}000}{\$500{,}000}$$

$$= 60\%$$

3. **D** The break-even sales of 40,000 units (answer D) is computed as follows:

$$\text{Break-Even Sales (units)} = \frac{\text{Fixed Costs}}{\text{Unit Contribution Margin}}$$

$$= \frac{\$160{,}000}{\$4}$$

$$= 40{,}000 \text{ units}$$

4. **D** Sales of 45,000 units are required to realize operating income of $20,000, computed as follows:

$$\text{Sales (units)} = \frac{\text{Fixed Costs} + \text{Target Profit}}{\text{Unit Contribution Margin}}$$

$$= \frac{\$160{,}000 + \$20{,}000}{\$4}$$

$$= 45{,}000 \text{ units}$$

5. **C** The operating leverage is 1.8, computed as follows:

$$\text{Operating Leverage} = \frac{\text{Contribution Margin}}{\text{Operating Income}}$$

$$= \frac{\$360{,}000}{\$200{,}000}$$

$$= 1.8$$

Chapter

12 Differential Analysis and Product Pricing

What's Covered:

Topics: Differential Analysis and Product Pricing

Nature of Differential Analysis
- Differential revenue (Obj. 1)
- Differential costs (Obj. 1)
- Differential income or loss (Obj. 1)

Applying Differential Analysis
- Lease or sell (Obj. 2)
- Discontinue segment or product (Obj. 2)
- Manufacture or purchase (Obj. 2)
- Replace fixed asset (Obj. 2)
- Process further or sell (Obj. 2)
- Sell at special price (Obj. 2)

Setting Product Prices
- Total cost concept (Obj. 3)
- Product cost concept (Obj. 3)
- Variable cost concept (Obj. 3)
- Target cost concept (Obj. 3)

Metric-Based Analysis
- Contribution margin per constrained resource (Obj. 4)

Learning Objectives

Obj. 1 Describe differential analysis for managerial decision making.

Obj. 2 Apply differential analysis for deciding whether to:
- Lease or sell
- Discontinue segment or product
- Manufacture or purchase
- Replace a fixed asset
- Process further or sell
- Sell at a special price

Obj. 3 Determine the selling price of a product, using the total cost, product cost, and variable cost concepts.

Obj. 4 Describe and illustrate the use of contribution margin per unit of production constraint for managerial decision making and performance analysis.

Chapter Metrics

The managerial decision-making and performance metric for this chapter is contribution margin per unit of constrained resource.

rvlsoft/Shutterstock.com

Facebook

Many of the decisions that you make depend on comparing the estimated costs of alternatives. The payoff from such comparisons is described in the following report from a University of Michigan study:

Richard Nisbett and two colleagues quizzed Michgan faculty members and university seniors on such questions as how often they walk out on a bad movie, refuse to finish a bad meal, start over on a weak term paper, or abandon a research project that no longer looks promising. They believe that people who cut their losses this way are following sound economic rules calculating the net benefits of alternative courses of action, writing off past costs that can't be recovered, and weighing the opportunity to use future time and effort more profitably elsewhere.

Among students, those who have learned to use cost-benefit analysis frequently are apt to have far better grades than their Scholastic Aptitude Test scores would have predicted. Again, the more economics courses the students have, the more likely they are to apply cost-benefit analysis outside the classroom.

Dr. Nisbett concedes that for many Americans, cost-benefit rules often appear to conflict with such traditional principles as "never give up" and "waste not, want not."

Managers must also evaluate the costs and benefits of alternative actions. **Facebook,** the largest social networking site in the world, was co-founded by Mark Zuckerberg in 2004. Since then, it has grown to more than 1 billion users and made Zuckerberg a multibillionaire.

Facebook has plans to grow to well over 1 billion users worldwide. Such growth involves decisions about where to expand. For example, expanding the site to new languages and countries involves software programming, marketing, and computer hardware costs. The benefits include adding new users to Facebook.

Analysis of the benefits and costs might lead Facebook to expand in some languages before others. For example, such an analysis might lead Facebook to expand in Swedish before it expands in Tok Pisin (the language of Papua New Guinea).

In this chapter, differential analysis, which reports the effects of decisions on total revenues and costs, is discussed. Practical approaches to setting product prices are also described and illustrated.

Source: Alan L. Otten, "Economic Persoective Produces Steady Yields," from People Patterns, *The Wall Street Journal*, March 31, 1992, p. B1.

Objective 1

Describe differential analysis for managerial decision making.

Nature of Differential Analysis

Managerial decision making involves choosing between alternative courses of action. Although the managerial decision-making process varies by the type of decision, it normally involves the steps shown in Exhibit 1.

The objective (Step 1) for most decisions is to maximize the company's profits. The alternative courses of action (Step 2) could include actions such as discontinuing an unprofitable segment, replacing equipment, or offering a product at a special price to an exporter. The relevant information (Step 3) varies by decision, but oftentimes includes estimates and data that are not available in the accounting records. Making decisions (Step 4) is the most important function of managers. Once the decision is made, the results of the decision (Step 5) should be reviewed, analyzed, and assessed in terms of the initial objective of the decision.

Accounting facilitates the preceding process by:

1. Gathering relevant information for managerial decisions
2. Reporting this information to management
3. Providing management feedback on the results of the decisions

For managerial decisions, estimated future revenues and costs are relevant.

Exhibit 1
Managerial Decision Making

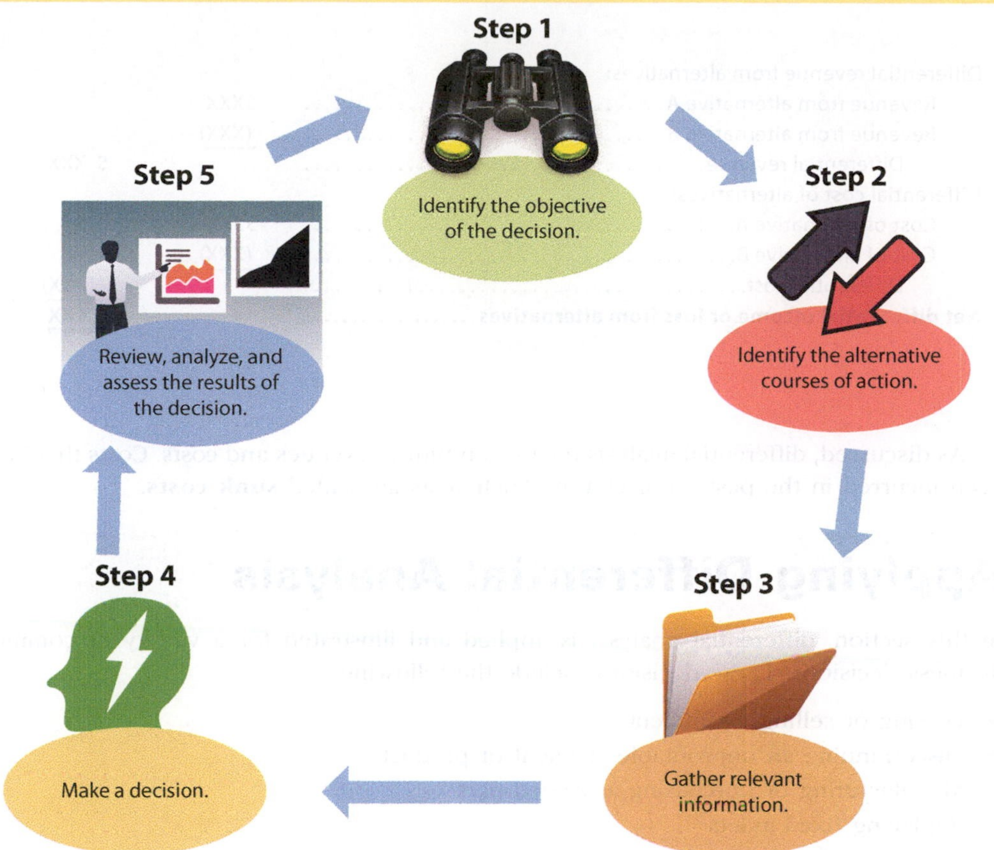
Step 1
Identify the objective of the decision.
Step 2
Identify the alternative courses of action.
Step 3
Gather relevant information.
Step 4
Make a decision.
Step 5
Review, analyze, and assess the results of the decision.

Differential revenue is the amount of increase or decrease in revenue that is expected from a course of action as compared to an alternative. To illustrate, assume that equipment can be used to manufacture digital clocks or calculators. The differential revenue from making and selling digital clocks is $25,000, determined as follows:

Product	Estimated Revenue
Digital clocks	$ 175,000
Calculators	(150,000)
Differential revenue	$ 25,000

Differential cost is the amount of increase or decrease in cost that is expected from a course of action as compared to an alternative. For example, if increasing advertising expenses from $100,000 to $150,000 is being considered, the differential cost is $50,000.

Differential income (or loss) is the difference between the differential revenue and the differential costs. Differential income indicates that a decision is expected to be profitable, while a differential loss indicates the opposite.

Facebook's purchase of WhatsApp in October 2014 was estimated to yield differential income.

Facebook Connection

Differential analysis, sometimes called *incremental analysis,* focuses on the effect of alternative courses of action on revenues and costs. An example of a reporting format for differential analysis is shown in Exhibit 2.

Exhibit 2
Differential Analysis—Report Format

Differential revenue from alternatives:		
Revenue from alternative A	$XXX	
Revenue from alternative B	(XXX)	
Differential revenue		$ XXX
Differential cost of alternatives:		
Cost of alternative A	$XXX	
Cost of alternative B	(XXX)	
Differential cost		(XXX)
Net differential income or loss from alternatives		**$ XXX**

As discussed, differential analysis focuses on future revenues and costs. Costs that have been incurred in the past are irrelevant. Such costs are called **sunk costs**.

Objective 2
Apply differential analysis for deciding whether to do the following:
Lease or sell
Discontinue segment or product
Manufacture or purchase
Replace a fixed asset
Process further or sell
Sell at a special price

Applying Differential Analysis

In this section, differential analysis is applied and illustrated for a variety of common business decisions. These decisions include the following:

- Leasing or selling equipment
- Discontinuing an unprofitable segment or product
- Manufacturing or purchasing a needed part
- Replacing fixed assets
- Processing further or selling a product
- Accepting additional business at a special price

Lease or Sell

Management may lease or sell a piece of equipment that is no longer needed. This may occur when a company changes its manufacturing process and can no longer use the equipment in the manufacturing process. In making a decision, differential analysis can be used.

To illustrate, assume that Karnes Company is considering leasing or disposing of the following equipment:

Cost of equipment	$ 200,000
Less accumulated depreciation	(120,000)
Book value	$ 80,000
Lease option:	
Total revenue for five-year lease	$ 160,000
Total estimated repair, insurance, and property tax expenses during life of lease	35,000
Residual value at end of fifth year of lease	0
Sell option:	
Sales price	$ 100,000
Commission on sales	6%

The differential analysis of whether to lease or sell the equipment is shown in Exhibit 3. Since the lease alternative generates a net differential income of $31,000, the equipment should be leased.

Exhibit 3 includes only the differential revenues and differential costs associated with the lease or sell decision. The $80,000 book value ($200,000 − $120,000) of the equipment is a *sunk* cost and is not considered in the differential analysis shown in Exhibit 3. In other words, the $80,000 does not affect the decision to lease or sell the equipment. This is illustrated in

Exhibit 3
Differential Analysis Report—Lease or Sell

Lease or Sell Equipment
Differential Analysis Report

Differential revenue from alternatives:		
Revenue from lease	$160,000	
Revenue from sale	(100,000)	
Differential revenue from lease		$ 60,000
Differential cost of alternatives:		
Repair, insurance, and property tax expenses from lease	$ 35,000	
Commission expense on sale ($100,000 × 6%)	(6,000)	
Differential cost of lease		(29,000)
Net differential income from the lease alternative		**$31,000**

Exhibit 4 using a more traditional analysis report that includes the book value of $80,000 in the lease and sell alternatives.

Exhibit 4
Traditional Analysis Report—Lease or Sell

Lease or Sell Equipment
Traditional Analysis Report

Lease alternative:			
Revenue from lease		$ 160,000	
Depreciation expense for remaining five years	$80,000		
Repair, insurance, and property tax expenses	35,000	(115,000)	
Net gain			$ 45,000
Sell alternative:			
Sales price		$ 100,000	
Book value of equipment	$80,000		
Commission expense	6,000	(86,000)	
Net gain			(14,000)
Net differential income from the lease alternative			**$31,000**

The differential analysis report in Exhibit 3 is preferable to the report shown in Exhibit 4. This is because Exhibit 3 simplifies the analysis by not including the $80,000 book value. In addition, Exhibit 3 avoids confusing the decision maker that the $80,000 is relevant for the decision. For these reasons, traditional analysis reports are not illustrated in the remainder of this chapter.

The following two factors were not considered in Exhibits 3 and 4:

1. Differential revenue from investing funds
2. Differential income tax

Differential revenue (interest) could arise from investing the cash created by the two alternatives. Differential income tax could arise from differences in the timing of the income from the two alternatives and differences in the amount that is taxed.

Discontinue a Segment or Product

A product, department, branch, territory, or other segment of a company may generate losses. As a result, the company may consider discontinuing (eliminating) the product or segment. In such cases, it may be incorrectly assumed that the company's income will increase by eliminating the segment.

Discontinuing the product or segment usually eliminates all of the segment's variable costs. Such costs include direct materials, direct labor, variable factory overhead, and sales commissions. However, fixed costs such as depreciation, insurance, and property taxes may not be eliminated. Thus, it is possible for company income to decrease rather than increase if the unprofitable segment is discontinued.

Facebook Connection

Facebook reports its financial results by geographic area (U.S. and rest of the world) but does not have separate business segments.

To illustrate, the income statement for Montana Wheat Cereal Co. is shown in Exhibit 5.

Exhibit 5
Condensed Income Statement

Montana Wheat Cereal Co.
Condensed Income Statement

	Corn Flakes	Toasted Oats	Bran Flakes	Total Company
Sales	$ 500,000	$ 400,000	$100,000	$1,000,000
Cost of goods sold:				
Variable costs	$(220,000)	$(200,000)	$ (60,000)	$ (480,000)
Fixed costs	(120,000)	(80,000)	(20,000)	(220,000)
Total cost of goods sold	$(340,000)	$(280,000)	$ (80,000)	$ (700,000)
Gross profit	$ 160,000	$ 120,000	$ 20,000	$ 300,000
Operating expenses:				
Variable expenses	$ (95,000)	$ (60,000)	$ (25,000)	$ (180,000)
Fixed expenses	(25,000)	(20,000)	(6,000)	(51,000)
Total operating expenses	$(120,000)	$ (80,000)	$ (31,000)	$ (231,000)
Operating income (loss)	$ 40,000	$ 40,000	$ (11,000)	$ 69,000

As shown in Exhibit 5, Bran Flakes incurred an operating loss of $11,000. Because Bran Flakes has incurred annual losses for several years, the company is considering discontinuing it.

If Bran Flakes is discontinued, what would be the total annual operating income of Montana Wheat Cereal? The first impression is that total annual operating income would be $80,000, as shown below.

	Corn Flakes	Toasted Oats	Total Company
Operating income	$40,000	$40,000	$80,000

However, assuming that discontinuing Bran Flakes has no effect on fixed costs and expenses, this will not be the case as shown in Exhibit 6.

Exhibit 6 Differential Analysis Report—Discontinue an Unprofitable Segment

Discontinue Brand Flakes Differential Analysis Report		
Differential revenue from annual sales of Bran Flakes:		
Revenue from sales		$100,000
Differential cost of annual sales of Bran Flakes:		
Variable cost of goods sold	$60,000	
Variable operating expenses	25,000	(85,000)
Annual differential income from sales of Bran Flakes		**$15,000**

Exhibit 6 indicates that Bran Flakes contributes $15,000 to company income. In other words, eliminating Bran Flakes will decrease company income from $69,000 to $54,000 as shown in Exhibit 7. Thus, Bran Flakes should not be discontinued.

Exhibit 7 Income Statement Without Bran Flakes

Montana Wheat Cereal Co.
Condensed Income Statement

	Corn Flakes	Toasted Oats	Total Company
Sales	$ 500,000	$ 400,000	$ 900,000
Cost of goods sold:			
Variable costs	$(220,000)	$(200,000)	$(420,000)
Fixed costs	(130,000)*	(90,000)*	(220,000)
Total cost of goods sold	$(350,000)	$(290,000)	$(640,000)
Gross profit	$ 150,000	$ 110,000	$ 260,000
Operating expenses:			
Variable expenses	$ (95,000)	$ (60,000)	$(155,000)
Fixed expenses	(28,000)*	(23,000)*	(51,000)
Total operating expenses	$(123,000)	$ (83,000)	$(206,000)
Operating income (loss)	**$ 27,000**	**$ 27,000**	**$ 54,000**

*Bran Flakes' fixed costs of $20,000 and $6,000 are allocated equally to Corn Flakes and Toasted Oats.

Exhibits 6 and 7 consider only the short-term (one-year) effects of discontinuing Bran Flakes. When discontinuing a segment, long-term effects should also be considered. For example, discontinuing Bran Flakes could decrease sales of other products. This might be the case if customers upset with the discontinuance of Bran Flakes quit buying other products from the company. Finally, employee morale and productivity might suffer if employees have to be laid off or relocated.

Make or Buy

Companies often manufacture products made up of components that are assembled into a final product. For example, an automobile manufacturer assembles tires, radios, motors, interior seats, transmissions, and other parts into a finished automobile. In such cases, the manufacturer must decide whether to make a part or purchase it from a supplier.

Differential analysis can be used to decide whether to make or buy a part. The analysis is similar whether management is considering making a part that is currently being purchased or purchasing a part that is currently being made.

Integrity, Objectivity, and Ethics in Business

Related-Party Deals

The make-or-buy decision can be complicated if the purchase (buy) is being made by a related party. A related party is one in which there is direct or indirect control of one party over another or the presence of a family member in a transaction. Such dependence or familiarity may interfere with the appropriateness of the business transaction. One investor has said, "Related parties are akin to steroids used by athletes. If you're an athlete and you can cut the mustard, you don't need steroids to make yourself stronger or faster. By the same token, if you're a good company, you don't need related parties or deals that don't make sense." While related-party transactions are legal, GAAP (*FASB Accounting Standards Codification*, Section 850, Related Party Disclosures) and the Sarbanes-Oxley Act require that they must be disclosed under the presumption that such transactions are less than arm's length.

Source: Herb Greenberg, "Poor Relations: The Problem with Related-Party Transactions," *Fortune Advisor* (February 5, 2001), p. 198.

or

To illustrate, assume that an automobile manufacturer has been purchasing instrument panels for $240 a unit. The factory is currently operating at 80% of capacity, and no major increase in production is expected in the near future. The cost per unit of manufacturing an instrument panel internally is estimated as follows:

Direct materials	$ 80
Direct labor	80
Variable factory overhead	52
Fixed factory overhead	68
Total cost per unit	$280

If the make price of $280 is simply compared with the buy price of $240, the decision is to buy the instrument panel. However, if unused capacity could be used in manufacturing the part, there would be no increase in the total fixed factory overhead costs. Thus, only the variable factory overhead costs would be incurred.

The differential report for this make-or-buy decision is shown in Exhibit 8.

Exhibit 8
Differential Analysis Report—Make or Buy

Make or Buy Instrument Panels Differential Analysis Report		
Purchase price of an instrument panel		$240
Differential cost to manufacture:		
Direct materials	$80	
Direct labor	80	
Variable factory overhead	52	(212)
Cost savings from manufacturing an instrument panel		**$ 28**

As shown in Exhibit 8, there is a cost savings from manufacturing the instrument panel of $28 per panel. However, other factors should also be considered. For example, production capacity used to make the instrument panel would not be available for other products. The decision may also affect the future business relationship with the instrument panel supplier. For example, if the supplier provides other parts, the company's decision to make instrument panels might jeopardize the timely delivery of other parts.

Replace Equipment

The usefulness of a fixed asset may decrease before it is worn out. For example, old equipment may no longer be as efficient as new equipment.

Differential analysis can be used for decisions to replace fixed assets such as equipment and machinery. The analysis normally focuses on the costs of continuing to use the old equipment versus replacing the equipment. The book value of the old equipment is a sunk cost and, thus, is irrelevant.

To illustrate, assume that a business is considering replacing the following machine:

Old Machine	
Book value	$100,000
Estimated annual variable manufacturing costs	225,000
Estimated selling price	25,000
Estimated remaining useful life	5 years
New Machine	
Cost of new machine	$250,000
Estimated annual variable manufacturing costs	150,000
Estimated residual value	0
Estimated useful life	5 years

The differential report for the decision to replace the old machine is shown in Exhibit 9.

Exhibit 9 Differential Analysis Report—Replace Machine

Replace Old Machine
Differential Analysis Report

Annual variable costs—present machine	$225,000	
Annual variable costs—new machine	(150,000)	
Annual differential decrease in cost	$ 75,000	
Number of years applicable	× 5	
Total differential decrease in cost	$375,000	
Proceeds from sale of present machine	25,000	$400,000
Cost of new machine		(250,000)
Net differential decrease in cost, five-year total		$150,000
Annual net differential decrease in cost—new machine ($150,000 ÷ 5 years)		**$ 30,000**

As shown in Exhibit 9, there is an annual decrease in cost of $30,000 ($150,000 ÷ 5 years) from replacing the old machine. Thus, the decision should be to purchase the new machine and sell the old machine.

Other factors are often important in equipment replacement decisions. For example, differences between the remaining useful life of the old equipment and the estimated

In a recent year, **Facebook** used cash to purchase $1,812 million of property and equipment.

Facebook Connection

life of the new equipment could exist. In addition, the new equipment might improve the overall quality of the product and, thus, increase sales.

The time value of money and other uses for the cash needed to purchase the new equipment could also affect the decision to replace equipment.[1] The revenue that is forgone from an alternative use of an asset, such as cash, is called an **opportunity cost**. Although the opportunity cost is not recorded in the accounting records, it is useful in analyzing alternative courses of action.

To illustrate, assume that in the preceding illustration the cash outlay of $250,000 for the new machine, less the $25,000 proceeds from the sale of the old machine, could be invested to yield a 15% return. Thus, the annual opportunity cost related to the purchase of the new machine is $33,750 (15% × $225,000). Since the opportunity cost of $33,750 exceeds the annual cost savings of $30,000, the old machine should not be replaced.

Process or Sell

During manufacturing, a product normally progresses through various stages or processes. In some cases, a product can be sold at an intermediate stage of production, or it can be processed further and then sold.

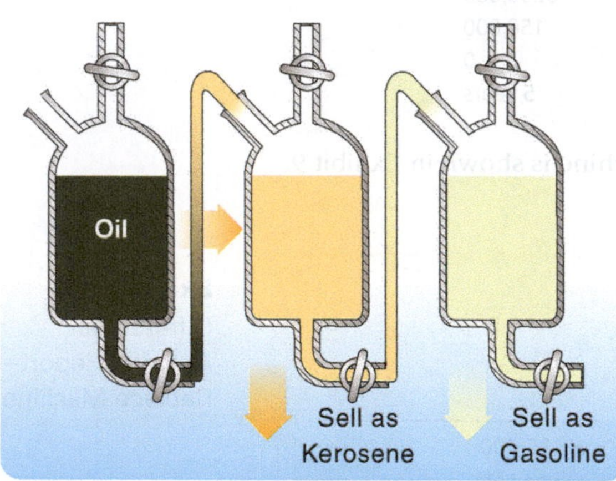

Differential analysis can be used to decide whether to sell a product at an intermediate stage or to process it further. In doing so, the differential revenues and costs from further processing are compared. The costs of producing the intermediate product do not change, regardless of whether the intermediate product is sold or processed further. These costs are sunk costs and are irrelevant to the decision.

To illustrate, assume that a business produces kerosene as follows:

Kerosene:	
Batch size	4,000 gallons
Cost of producing kerosene	$2,400 per batch
Selling price	$2.50 per gallon

The kerosene can be processed further to yield gasoline as follows:

Gasoline:		
Input batch size	4,000	gallons
Less evaporation (20%)	(800)	(4,000 × 20%)
Output batch size	3,200	gallons
Additional processing costs	$650	per batch
Selling price	$3.50	per gallon

The differential report for the decision to process the kerosene further is shown in Exhibit 10.

The initial cost of producing the kerosene of $2,400 is not considered in deciding whether to process kerosene further. This initial cost will be incurred, regardless of whether gasoline is produced and, thus, is a sunk cost.

1. The time value of money in purchasing equipment (capital assets) is discussed in Chapter 15.

Exhibit 10 Differential Analysis Report—Process or Sell

Process Kerosene Further
Differential Analysis Report

Differential revenue from further processing per batch:		
Revenue from sale of gasoline [(4,000 gallons − 800 gallons evaporation) × $3.50]	$11,200	
Revenue from sale of kerosene (4,000 gallons × $2.50)	(10,000)	
Differential revenue		$1,200
Differential cost per batch:		
Additional cost of producing gasoline		(650)
Differential income from further processing gasoline per batch		**$ 550**

As shown in Exhibit 10, there is additional income from further processing the kerosene into gasoline of $550 per batch. Therefore, the decision should be to process the kerosene further.

Facebook Connection

Facebook provides advertising and other services to its customers and does not manufacture a product.

Accept Business at a Special Price

A company may be offered the opportunity to sell its products at prices other than normal prices. For example, an exporter may offer to sell a company's products overseas at special discount prices.

Differential analysis can be used to decide whether to accept additional business at a special price. The differential revenue from accepting the additional business is compared to the differential costs of producing and delivering the product to the customer.

The differential costs of accepting additional business depend on whether the company is operating at full capacity.

1. If the company is *operating at full capacity*, any additional production increases fixed and variable manufacturing costs. Selling and administrative expenses may also increase because of the additional business.
2. If the company is *operating below full capacity*, any additional production does not increase fixed manufacturing costs. In this case, the differential costs of the additional production are the variable manufacturing costs. Selling and administrative expenses may also increase because of the additional business.

To illustrate, assume that Game Ball Inc. manufactures basketballs as follows:

Monthly productive capacity	12,500 basketballs
Current monthly sales	10,000 basketballs
Normal (domestic) selling price	$30.00 per basketball
Manufacturing costs:	
Variable costs	$12.50 per basketball
Fixed costs	7.50
Total	$20.00 per basketball

Game Ball Inc. has received an offer from an exporter for 5,000 basketballs at $18 each. Production can be spread over three months without interfering with normal production or incurring overtime costs. Pricing policies in the domestic market will not be affected.

Comparing the special offer sales price of $18 with the manufacturing cost of $20 per basketball indicates that the offer should be rejected. However, as shown in Exhibit 11, differential analysis indicates that the offer should be accepted.

Exhibit 11
Differential Analysis Report—Sell at Special Price

Sell Basketballs to Exporter
Differential Analysis Report

Differential revenue from accepting offer:	
Revenue from sale of 5,000 additional units at $18	$ 90,000
Differential cost of accepting offer:	
Variable costs of 5,000 additional units at $12.50	(62,500)
Differential income from accepting offer	**$27,500**

Proposals to sell products at special prices often require additional considerations. For example, special prices in one geographic area may result in price reductions in other areas with the result that total company sales decrease. Manufacturers must also conform to the Robinson-Patman Act, which prohibits price discrimination within the United States unless price differences can be justified by different costs.

Objective 3
Determine the selling price of a product, using the total cost, product cost, and variable cost concepts.

Setting Normal Product Selling Prices

The *normal* selling price is the target selling price to be achieved in the long term. The normal selling price must be set high enough to cover all costs and expenses (fixed and variable) and provide a reasonable profit. Otherwise, the business will not survive.

In contrast, in deciding whether to accept additional business at a special price, only differential costs are considered. Any price above the differential costs will increase profits in the short term. However, in the long term, products are sold at normal prices rather than special prices.

Managers can use one of two *market methods* to determine selling price:

- Demand-based concept
- Competition-based concept

The demand-based concept sets the price according to the demand for the product. If there is high demand for the product, then the price is set high. Likewise, if there is a low demand for the product, then the price is set low.

The competition-based concept sets the price according to the price offered by competitors. For example, if a competitor reduces the price, then management adjusts the price to meet the competition. The market-based pricing approaches are discussed in greater detail in marketing courses.

Facebook Connection

Facebook's prices are affected by its competitors, such as Google.

Managers can also use one of three cost-plus methods to determine the selling price:

- Total cost concept
- Product cost concept
- Variable cost concept

Cost-plus methods determine the normal selling price by estimating a cost amount per unit and adding a markup, as shown below.

Normal Selling Price = Cost Amount per Unit + Markup

The cost amount per unit depends on the cost concept used. Management determines the **markup** based on the desired profit for the product. The markup should be sufficient to earn the desired profit plus cover any costs and expenses that are not included in the cost amount.

Facebook Connection

Facebook generates advertising revenue based upon the number of clicks, impressions displayed, or the number of actions taken by people. It establishes prices for its customers for each of these options.

Total Cost Concept

Under the **total cost concept,** manufacturing cost plus the selling and administrative expenses are included in the total cost per unit. The markup per unit is then computed and added to total cost per unit to determine the normal selling price as shown in Exhibit 12.

Exhibit 12 Total Cost Concept of Pricing

TOTAL COST CONCEPT

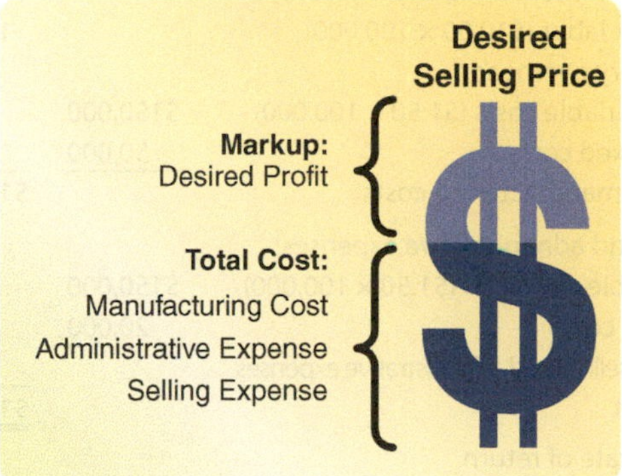

The total cost concept is applied using the following steps:

Step 1. Estimate the total manufacturing cost as follows:

Manufacturing costs:	
Direct materials	$XXX
Direct labor	XXX
Factory overhead	XXX
Total manufacturing cost	$XXX

Step 2. Estimate the total selling and administrative expenses.

Step 3. Estimate the total cost as follows:

Total manufacturing costs	$XXX
Selling and administrative expenses	XXX
Total cost	$XXX

Step 4. Divide the total cost by the number of units expected to be produced and sold to determine the total cost per unit, as follows:

$$\textbf{Total Cost per Unit} = \frac{\textbf{Total Cost}}{\textbf{Estimated Units Produced and Sold}}$$

Step 5. Compute the markup percentage as follows:

$$\textbf{Markup Percentage} = \frac{\textbf{Desired Profit}}{\textbf{Total Cost}}$$

The desired profit is normally computed based on a rate of return on assets as follows:

$$\textbf{Desired Profit} = \textbf{Desired Rate of Return} \times \textbf{Total Assets}$$

Step 6. Determine the markup per unit by multiplying the markup percentage times the total cost per unit as follows:

$$\textbf{Markup per Unit} = \textbf{Markup Percentage} \times \textbf{Total Cost per Unit}$$

Step 7. Determine the normal selling price by adding the markup per unit to the total cost per unit as follows:

Total cost per unit	$XXX
Markup per unit	XXX
Normal selling price per unit	$XXX

To illustrate, assume the following data for 100,000 digital projection clocks that Nebular Inc. expects to produce and sell during the current year:

Manufacturing costs:		
Direct materials ($3.00 × 100,000)		$ 300,000
Direct labor ($10.00 × 100,000)		1,000,000
Factory overhead:		
Variable costs ($1.50 × 100,000)	$150,000	
Fixed costs	50,000	200,000
Total manufacturing costs		$1,500,000
Selling and administrative expenses:		
Variable expenses ($1.50 × 100,000)	$150,000	
Fixed costs	20,000	
Total selling and administrative expenses		170,000
Total cost		$1,670,000
Desired rate of return		20%
Total assets		$ 800,000

Using the total cost concept, the normal selling price of $18.30 is determined as follows:

Step 1. Total manufacturing cost: $1,500,000

Step 2. Total selling and administrative expenses: $170,000

Step 3. Total cost: $1,670,000

Step 4. Total cost per unit: $16.70

$$\textbf{Total Cost per Unit} = \frac{\textbf{Total Cost}}{\textbf{Estimated Units Produced and Sold}}$$

$$= \frac{\textbf{\$1,670,000}}{\textbf{100,000 units}} = \textbf{\$16.70 per unit}$$

Step 5. Markup percentage: 9.6% (rounded)

$$\textbf{Desired Profit} = \textbf{Desired Rate of Return} \times \textbf{Total Assets}$$
$$= \textbf{20\%} \times \textbf{\$800,000} = \textbf{\$160,000}$$

$$\textbf{Markup Percentage} = \frac{\textbf{Desired Profit}}{\textbf{Total Cost}} = \frac{\textbf{\$160,000}}{\textbf{\$1,670,000}} = \textbf{9.6\% (rounded)}$$

Step 6. Markup per unit: $1.60

$$\textbf{Markup per Unit} = \textbf{Markup Percentage} \times \textbf{Total Cost per Unit}$$
$$= \textbf{9.6\%} \times \textbf{\$16.70} = \textbf{\$1.60 per unit}$$

Step 7. Normal selling price: $18.30

Total cost per unit	$16.70
Markup per unit	1.60
Normal selling price per unit	$18.30

The ability of the selling price of $18.30 to generate the desired profit of $160,000 is illustrated by the income statement shown as follows:

NEBULA INC.
Income Statement

Sales (100,000 units × $18.30)		$1,830,000
Expenses:		
Variable (100,000 units × $16.00)	$1,600,000	
Fixed ($50,000 + $20,000)	70,000	(1,670,000)
Operating income		$ 160,000

The total cost concept is often used by contractors who sell products to government agencies. This is because in many cases government contractors are required by law to be reimbursed for their products on a total-cost-plus-profit basis.

Product Cost Concept

Under the **product cost concept**, only the costs of manufacturing the product, termed the *product costs,* are included in the cost amount per unit to which the markup is added. Estimated selling expenses, administrative expenses, and desired profit are included in the markup. The markup per unit is then computed and added to the product cost per unit to determine the normal selling price as shown in Exhibit 13.

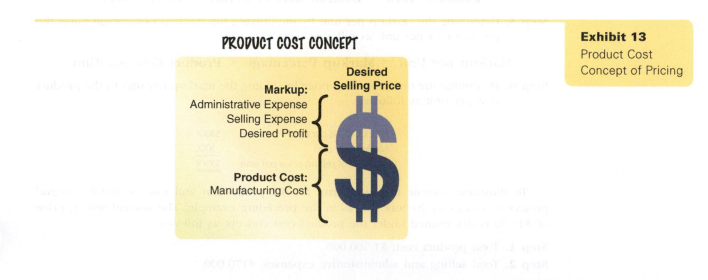

Exhibit 13
Product Cost Concept of Pricing

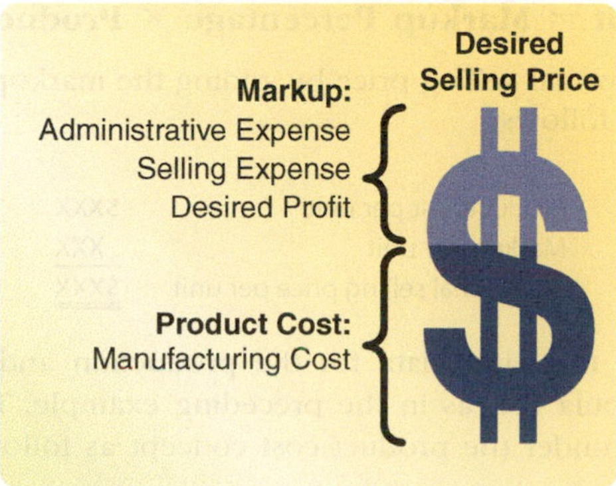

Integrity, Objectivity, and Ethics in Business

Price Fixing

Federal law prevents companies competing in similar markets from sharing cost and price information, or what is commonly termed "price fixing." For example, the Federal Trade Commission brought a suit against the major recording labels and music retailers for conspiring to set CD prices at a minimum level, or MAP (minimum advertised price). In settling the suit, the major labels ceased their MAP policies and provided $143 million in cash and CDs for consumers.

The product cost concept is applied using the following steps:

Step 1. Estimate the total product costs as follows:

Product costs:	
Direct materials	$XXX
Direct labor	XXX
Factory overhead	XXX
Total product cost	$XXX

Step 2. Estimate the total selling and administrative expenses.

Step 3. Divide the total product cost by the number of units expected to be produced and sold to determine the total product cost per unit, as shown below.

$$\textbf{Product Cost per Unit} = \frac{\textbf{Total Product Cost}}{\textbf{Estimated Units Produced and Sold}}$$

Step 4. Compute the markup percentage as follows:

$$\textbf{Markup Percentage} = \frac{\textbf{Desired Profit + Total Selling and Administrative Expenses}}{\textbf{Total Product Cost}}$$

The numerator of the markup percentage is the desired profit plus the total selling and administrative expenses. These expenses must be included in the markup percentage, since they are not included in the cost amount to which the markup is added.

As illustrated for the total cost concept, the desired profit is normally computed based on a rate of return on assets as follows:

$$\textbf{Desired Profit} = \textbf{Desired Rate of Return} \times \textbf{Total Assets}$$

Step 5. Determine the markup per unit by multiplying the markup percentage times the product cost per unit as follows:

$$\textbf{Markup per Unit} = \textbf{Markup Percentage} \times \textbf{Product Cost per Unit}$$

Step 6. Determine the normal selling price by adding the markup per unit to the product cost per unit as follows:

Product cost per unit	$XXX
Markup per unit	XXX
Normal selling price per unit	$XXX

To illustrate, assume the same data for the production and sale of 100,000 digital projection clocks by Nebula Inc. as in the preceding example. The normal selling price of $18.30 is determined under the product cost concept as follows:

Step 1. Total product cost: $1,500,000

Step 2. Total selling and administrative expenses: $170,000

Step 3. Total product cost per unit: $15.00

$$\textbf{Total Cost per Unit} = \frac{\textbf{Total Product Cost}}{\textbf{Estimated Units Produced and Sold}}$$

$$= \frac{\$1{,}500{,}000}{100{,}000 \text{ units}} = \$15.00 \text{ per unit}$$

Step 4. Markup percentage: 22%

$$\textbf{Desired Profit} = \textbf{Desired Rate of Return} \times \textbf{Total Assets}$$

$$= 20\% \times \$800{,}000 = \$160{,}000$$

$$\textbf{Markup Percentage} = \frac{\textbf{Desired Profit + Total Selling and Administrative Expenses}}{\textbf{Total Product Cost}}$$

$$= \frac{\$160{,}000 + \$170{,}000}{\$1{,}500{,}000} = \frac{\$330{,}000}{\$1{,}500{,}000} = 22\%$$

Step 5. Markup per unit: $3.30

$$\textbf{Markup per Unit} = \textbf{Markup Percentage} \times \textbf{Product Cost per Unit}$$

$$= 22\% \times \$15.00 = \$3.30 \text{ per unit}$$

Step 6. Normal selling price: $18.30

Total product cost per unit	$15.00
Markup per unit	3.30
Normal selling price per unit	$18.30

Variable Cost Concept

Under the **variable cost concept**, only variable costs are included in the cost amount per unit to which the markup is added. All variable manufacturing costs, as well as variable selling and administrative expenses, are included in the cost amount. Fixed manufacturing costs, fixed selling and administrative expenses, and desired profit are included in the markup. The markup per unit is then added to the variable cost per unit to determine the normal selling price as shown in Exhibit 14.

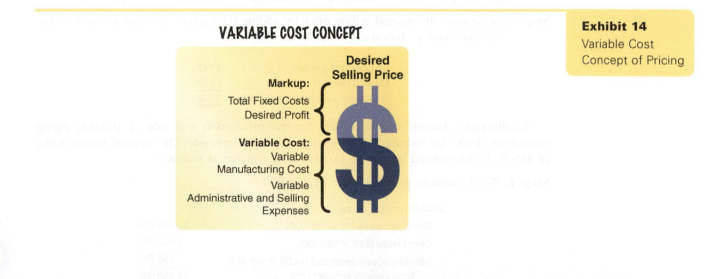

Exhibit 14
Variable Cost Concept of Pricing

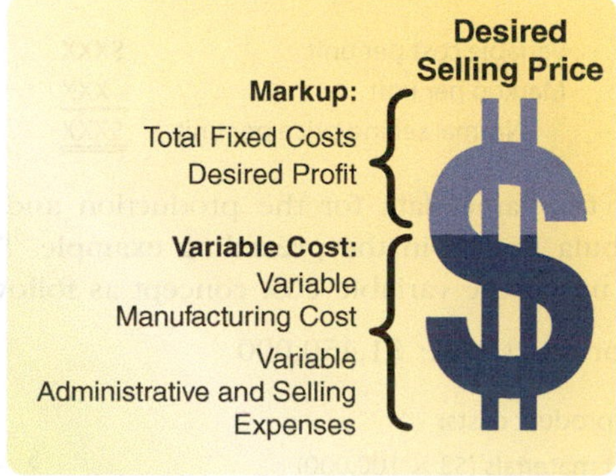

The variable cost concept is applied using the following steps:

Step 1. Estimate the total variable product cost as follows:

Variable product costs:	
Direct materials	$XXX
Direct labor	XXX
Variable factory overhead	XXX
Total variable product cost	$XXX

Step 2. Estimate the total variable selling and administrative expenses.

Step 3. Determine the total variable cost as follows:

Total variable product cost	$XXX
Total variable selling and administrative expenses	XXX
Total variable cost	$XXX

Step 4. Compute the variable cost per unit as follows:

$$\textbf{Variable Cost per Unit} = \frac{\textbf{Total Variable Cost}}{\textbf{Estimated Units Produced and Sold}}$$

Step 5. Compute the markup percentage as follows:

$$\textbf{Markup Percentage} = \frac{\textbf{Desired Profit + Total Fixed Costs and Expenses}}{\textbf{Total Variable Cost}}$$

The numerator of the markup percentage is the desired profit plus the total fixed costs (fixed factory overhead) and expenses (selling and administrative). These fixed costs and expenses must be included in the markup percentage, since they are not included in the cost amount to which the markup is added.

As illustrated for the total and product cost concepts, the desired profit is normally computed based on a rate of return on assets as follows:

$$\textbf{Desired Profit} = \textbf{Desired Rate of Return} \times \textbf{Total Assets}$$

Step 6. Determine the markup per unit by multiplying the markup percentage times the variable cost per unit as follows:

$$\textbf{Markup per Unit} = \textbf{Markup Percentage} \times \textbf{Variable Cost per Unit}$$

Step 7. Determine the normal selling price by adding the markup per unit to the variable cost per unit as follows:

Variable cost per unit	$XXX
Markup per unit	XXX
Normal selling price per unit	$XXX

To illustrate, assume the same data for the production and sale of 100,000 digital projection clocks by Nebula Inc. as in the preceding example. The normal selling price of $18.30 is determined under the variable cost concept as follows:

Step 1. Total variable product cost: $1,450,000

Variable product costs:	
Direct materials ($3 × 100,000)	$ 300,000
Direct labor ($10 × 100,000)	1,000,000
Variable factory overhead ($1.50 × 100,000)	150,000
Total variable product cost	$1,450,000

Step 2. Total variable selling and administrative expenses:
$150,000 ($1.50 × 100,000)

Step 3. Total variable cost: $1,600,000 ($1,450,000 + $150,000)

Step 4. Variable cost per unit: $16.00

$$\text{Variable Cost per Unit} = \frac{\text{Total Variable Cost}}{\text{Estimated Units Produced and Sold}}$$

$$= \frac{\$1{,}600{,}000}{100{,}000 \text{ units}} = \$16.00 \text{ per unit}$$

Step 5. Markup percentage: 14.4% (rounded)

$$\text{Desired Profit} = \text{Desired Rate of Return} \times \text{Total Assets}$$

$$= 20\% \times \$800{,}000 = \$160{,}000$$

$$\text{Markup Percentage} = \frac{\text{Desired Profit} + \text{Total Fixed Costs and Expenses}}{\text{Total Variable Cost}}$$

$$= \frac{\$160{,}000 + \$50{,}000 + \$20{,}000}{\$1{,}600{,}000} = \frac{\$230{,}000}{\$1{,}600{,}000}$$

$$= 14.4\% \text{ (rounded)}$$

Step 6. Markup per unit: $2.30

$$\text{Markup per Unit} = \text{Markup Percentage} \times \text{Variable Cost per Unit}$$

$$= 14.4\% \times \$16.00 = \$2.30 \text{ per unit}$$

Step 7. Normal selling price: $18.30

Total variable cost per unit	$16.00
Markup per unit	2.30
Normal selling price per unit	$18.30

Choosing a Cost-Plus Approach Cost Concept

All three cost-plus concepts produced the same selling price ($18.30) for Nebula Inc. The three cost-plus concepts are summarized in Exhibit 15.

Estimated, rather than actual, costs and expenses may be used with any of the three cost-plus concepts. Management should be careful, however, when using estimated or standard costs in applying the cost-plus approach. Specifically, estimates should be based on normal (attainable) operating levels and not theoretical (ideal) levels of performance. In product pricing, the use of estimates based on ideal or maximum-capacity operating levels could lead to setting product prices too low. In such cases, the costs of such factors as normal spoilage or normal periods of idle time might not be considered.

The decision-making needs of management are also an important factor in selecting a cost concept for product pricing. For example, managers who often make special pricing decisions are more likely to use the variable cost concept. In contrast, a government defense contractor would be more likely to use the total cost concept.

Exhibit 15 Cost-Plus Approach to Setting Normal Selling Prices

Normal Selling Price = Cost Amount per Unit + Markup

$$\text{Cost per Unit} = \frac{\text{Cost Amount}}{\text{Estimated Units Produced and Sold}}$$

Markup = Cost per Unit × Markup Percentage

Cost-Plus Concept	Cost	Markup Percentages
Total cost	Manufacturing (product) costs: Direct materials Direct labor Factory overhead Selling and administrative expenses	$\frac{\text{Desired Profit}}{\text{Total Cost}}$
Product cost	Manufacturing (product) costs: Direct materials Direct labor Factory overhead	$\frac{\text{Desired Profit} + \text{Total Selling and Administrative Expenses}}{\text{Total Product Cost}}$
Variable cost	Variable manufacturing (product) costs: Direct materials Direct labor Variable factory overhead Variable selling and administrative expenses	$\frac{\text{Desired Profit} + \text{Total Fixed Costs and Expenses}}{\text{Total Variable Cost}}$

Target Costing

Target costing is a method of setting prices that combines market-based pricing with a cost-reduction emphasis. Under target costing, a future selling price is anticipated, using the demand-based or the competition-based concepts. The target cost is then determined by subtracting a desired profit from the expected selling price, as shown below.

Target Cost = Expected Selling Price − Desired Profit

Target costing tries to reduce costs as shown in Exhibit 16. The bar at the left in Exhibit 16 shows the actual cost and profit that can be earned during the current period. The bar

Business Insight

Revenue Management

Did you know that is common to sit next to a person on a flight who paid much more for that seat than you did for yours (or vice versa)? While this may not seem fair, this practice is consistent with a type of differential analysis called revenue management. Revenue management strives to yield the maximum amount of profit from a perishable good. Examples of perishable goods in service include a seat on a flight, a hotel room for a given night, a ticket for a given event, or a cruise ship berth for a given voyage. The service is perishable because, once the date passes, the "product" expires.

Consider **Delta Air Lines**. Delta maximizes the profitability on a given flight by taking into account different customer behaviors and preferences. For example, a business person may pay a very high price for an airline ticket booked one day in advance to attend an emergency meeting. Next to her may be a college student on the same flight who booked two month's in advance at a very low price. The difference in behavior yields a different price. The airline sells early bookings at very favorable prices to fill out the flight. However, late emergency business bookings are priced high because the inventory of seats have diminished and, thus, have become valuable. However, if too many seats remain unoccupied very close to the flight time, the airline may release them at deep discounts to standby passengers to fill the flight. Thus, the flight is filled with different priced seats for different customers, all in attempt to fill the flight as profitably as possible.

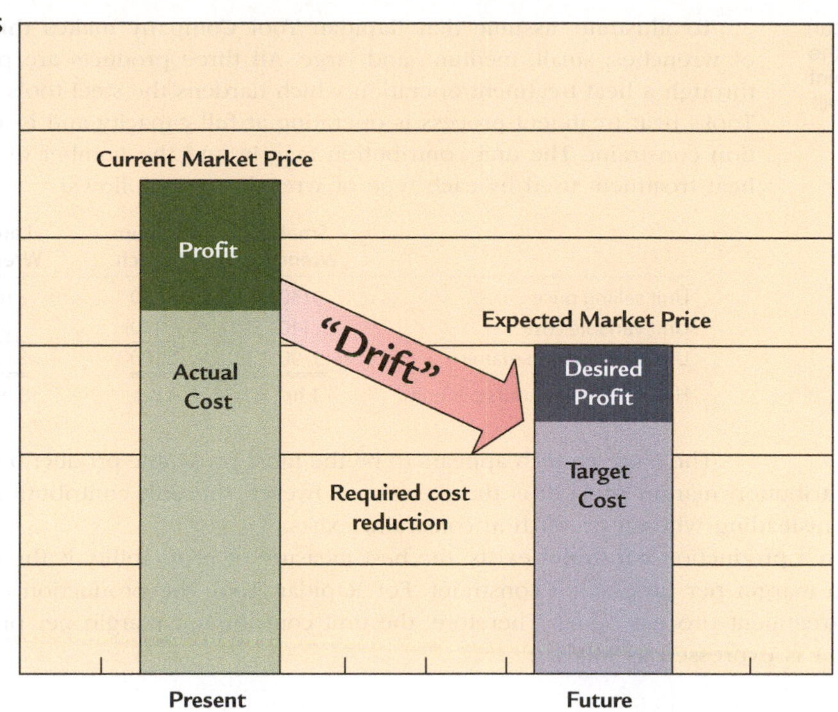

Exhibit 16 Target Cost Concept

at the right shows that the market price is expected to decline in the future. The target cost is estimated as the difference between the expected market price and the desired profit.

The target cost is normally less than the current cost. Thus, managers must try to reduce costs from the design and manufacture of the product.

The planned cost reduction is sometimes referred to as the cost "drift." Costs can be reduced in a variety of ways such as the following:

- Simplifying the design
- Reducing the cost of direct materials
- Reducing the direct labor costs
- Eliminating waste

Target costing is especially useful in highly competitive markets such as automobiles and the market for smartphones and computer tablets. Such markets require continual product cost reductions to remain competitive.

Metric-Based Analysis: Contribution Margin per Unit of Production Constraint

Objective 4
Describe and illustrate the use of contribution margin per unit of production constraint for managerial decision making and performance analysis.

A production **constraint (or bottleneck)** is a point in the manufacturing process where the demand for the company's products exceeds its ability to produce the products. The **theory of constraints (TOC)** is a manufacturing strategy that focuses on reducing the influence of constraints on production processes.

Production Constraints and Profits

When a company has a production constraint in its production process, it should attempt to maximize its profits, subject to the constraint. In doing so, the unit contribution margin of each product per production constraint is used.

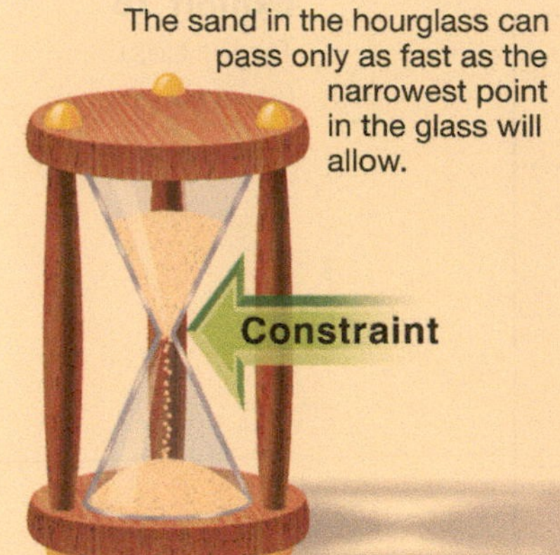

The sand in the hourglass can pass only as fast as the narrowest point in the glass will allow.

To illustrate, assume that Rapidan Tool Company makes three types of wrenches: small, medium, and large. All three products are processed through a heat treatment operation which hardens the steel tools. Rapidan Tool's heat treatment process is operating at full capacity and is a production constraint. The unit contribution margin and the number of hours of heat treatment used by each type of wrench are as follows:

	Small Wrench	Medium Wrench	Large Wrench
Unit selling price	$130	$140	$160
Unit variable cost	(40)	(40)	(40)
Unit contribution margin	$ 90	$100	$120
Heat treatment hours per unit	1 hr.	4 hrs.	8 hrs.

The large wrench appears to be the most profitable product because its unit contribution margin of $120 is the greatest. However, the unit contribution margin can be misleading when a production constraint exists.

When a production constraint exists, the best measure of profitability is the unit contribution margin per production constraint. For Rapidan Tool, the production constraint is heat treatment process hours. Therefore, the unit contribution margin per production constraint is expressed as follows:

$$\textbf{Unit Contribution Margin per Production Constraint Hour} = \frac{\textbf{Unit Contribution Margin}}{\textbf{Heat Treatment Hours per Unit}}$$

The unit contribution per heat treatment hour for each of the wrenches produced by Rapidan Tool is computed below.

Small Wrenches

$$\text{Unit Contribution Margin per Heat Treatment Hour} = \frac{\$90}{1 \text{ hr.}} = \$90 \text{ per hr.}$$

Medium Wrenches

$$\text{Unit Contribution Margin per Heat Treatment Hour} = \frac{\$100}{4 \text{ hrs.}} = \$25 \text{ per hr.}$$

Large Wrenches

$$\text{Unit Contribution Margin per Heat Treatment Hour} = \frac{\$120}{8 \text{ hrs.}} = \$15 \text{ per hr.}$$

The small wrench produces the highest unit contribution margin per heat treatment hour of $90 per hour. In contrast, the large wrench has the smallest unit contribution margin per heat treatment hour of $15 per hour. Thus, the small wrench is the most profitable product per heat treatment hour. In other words, the more heat treatment hours used for small wrench production, the higher the company's operating income will be.

Production Constraints and Pricing

When a company has a production constraint, the unit contribution margin per constraint is a measure of each product's profitability. This measure can be used to adjust product prices to reflect the product's use of the constraint.

To illustrate, the large wrench produced by Rapidan Tool Company uses eight heat treatment hours but produces a contribution margin per unit of only $120. As a result, the large wrench is the least profitable of the wrenches per constraint hour ($15 per hour).

Rapidan Tool Company can improve the profitability of producing large wrenches by any combination of the following:

1. Increasing the selling price of the large wrenches.
2. Decreasing the variable cost per unit of the large wrenches.
3. Decreasing the heat treatment hours required for the large wrenches.

Assume that the variable cost per unit and the heat treatment hours for the large wrench cannot be decreased. In this case, Rapidan Tool might be able to increase the selling price of the large wrenches.

The price of the large wrench that would make it as profitable as the small wrench is determined as follows:

$$\begin{array}{c}\textbf{Unit Contribution Margin}\\ \textbf{per Heat Treatment}\\ \textbf{Hour for Small Wrench}\end{array} = \frac{\begin{array}{c}\textbf{Revised Price of}\\ \textbf{Large Wrench}\end{array} - \begin{array}{c}\textbf{Unit Variable Cost}\\ \textbf{for Large Wrench}\end{array}}{\begin{array}{c}\textbf{Heat Treatment Hours per Unit}\\ \textbf{for Large Wrench}\end{array}}$$

$$\$90 = \frac{\text{Revised Price of Large Wrench} - \$40}{8}$$

$$\$720 = \text{Revised Price of Large Wrench} - \$40$$

$$\$760 = \text{Revised Price of Large Wrench}$$

If the large wrench's price is increased to \$760, it would provide the same unit contribution margin per heat treatment hour as the small wrench, as shown below.

$$\begin{array}{c}\textbf{Unit Contribution Margin}\\ \textbf{per Heat Treatment Hour}\end{array} = \frac{\textbf{Unit Contribution Margin}}{\textbf{Heat Treatment Hours per Unit}}$$

$$\$90 \text{ per hr.} = \frac{\$760 - \$40}{8 \text{ hrs.}}$$

At a price of \$760, Rapidan Tool Company would be indifferent between producing and selling the small wrench or the large wrench. This assumes that there is unlimited demand for the products. If the market were unwilling to purchase the large wrench at a price of \$760, then the company should produce and sell the small wrenches.

What Is a Product?

A product is often thought of in terms beyond just its physical attributes. For example, why a customer buys a product usually impacts how a business markets the product. Other considerations, such as warranty needs, servicing needs, and perceived quality, also affect business strategies.

Consider the four different types of products listed below. For these products, the frequency of purchase, the profit per unit, and the number of retailers differ. As a result, the sales and marketing approach for each product differs.

Product	Type of Product	Frequency of Purchase	Profit per Unit	Number of Retailers	Sales/Marketing Approach
Snickers®	Convenience	Often	Low	Many	Mass advertising
Sony® TV	Shopping	Occasional	Moderate	Many	Mass advertising; personal selling
Diamond ring	Specialty	Seldom	High	Few	Personal selling
Prearranged funeral	Unsought	Rare	High	Few	Aggressive selling

2. Assuming that the selling price of the large wrench cannot be increased, the same approach (equation) could be used to determine the decrease in variable cost per unit or decrease in bottleneck hours that is required to make the large wrench as profitable as the small wrench.

Key Points

1. Describe differential analysis for managerial decision making.

Differential analysis focuses on the effect of alternative courses of action on revenues and costs. Differential revenues, costs, and income are determined. Differential income indicates that a decision is expected to be profitable, and a differential loss indicates the opposite.

2. Prepare differential analysis reports for a variety of managerial decisions.

Differential analysis reports for leasing or selling, discontinuing a segment or product, making or buying, replacing equipment, processing or selling, and accepting business at a special price are illustrated in the text. Each analysis focuses on the differential revenues and/or costs of the alternative courses of action.

3. Determine the selling price of a product, using the total cost, product cost, and variable cost concepts.

The three cost concepts commonly used in applying the cost-plus approach to product pricing are summarized in Exhibit 14. The target costing method of product pricing combines market-based methods with a cost-reduction emphasis.

4. Describe and illustrate the use of contribution margin per unit per constrained resource for managerial decision making and performance analysis.

A production constraint (or bottleneck) is a point in the manufacturing process where the demand for the company's products exceeds its ability to produce the products. When a company has a production constraint, it should attempt to maximize its profits, subject to the constraint. In doing so, the unit contribution margin of each product per production constraint is used.

Key Terms

Constraint (or bottleneck) (525)
Differential analysis (507)
Differential cost (507)
Differential income (or loss) (507)
Differential revenue (507)
Markup (517)
Opportunity cost (514)
Product cost concept (519)
Sunk cost (508)
Target costing (524)
Theory of constraints (TOC) (525)
Total cost concept (517)
Variable cost concept (521)

Illustrative Problem

Hillard Company recently began production of a new product, SR10, which required an investment of $1,600,000 in assets. The costs of producing and selling 80,000 units of Product SR10 are estimated as follows:

Variable costs:	
Direct materials	$10.00 per unit
Direct labor	6.00
Factory overhead	4.00
Selling and administrative expenses	5.00
Total	$25.00 per unit
Fixed costs:	
Factory overhead	$800,000
Selling and administrative expenses	400,000

Hillard Company is currently considering how much should be charged for one unit of Product SR10. The president of Hillard Company has decided to use the cost-plus approach to product pricing and has indicated that Product SR10 must earn a 10% rate of return on invested assets.

Instructions

1. Determine the amount of desired profit from the production and sale of Product SR10.
2. Assuming that the total cost concept is used, determine (a) the cost amount per unit, (b) the markup percentage, and (c) the selling price of Product SR10.
3. Assuming that the product cost concept is used, determine (a) the cost amount per unit, (b) the markup percentage, and (c) the selling price of Product SR10.
4. Assuming that the variable cost concept is used, determine (a) the cost amount per unit, (b) the markup percentage, and (c) the selling price of Product SR10.
5. Assume that for the current year, the selling price of Product SR10 was $42 per unit. To date, 60,000 units have been produced and sold, and analysis of the domestic market indicates that 15,000 additional units are expected to be sold during the remainder of the year. Recently, Hillard Company received an offer from Ming Inc. for 4,000 units of Product SR10 at $28 each. Ming Inc. will market the units in China under its own brand name, and no additional selling and administrative expenses associated with the sale will be incurred by Hillard Company. The additional business is not expected to affect the domestic sales of Product SR10, and the additional units could be produced during the current year using existing capacity. (a) Prepare a differential analysis report of the proposed sale to Ming Inc. (b) Based on the differential analysis report in (a), should the proposal be accepted?

Solution

1. $160,000 ($1,600,000 × 10%)
2. a. Total costs:

Variable ($25 × 80,000 units)	$2,000,000
Fixed ($800,000 + $400,000)	1,200,000
Total	$3,200,000

Cost amount per unit: $3,200,000 ÷ 80,000 units = $40.00

b. $$\text{Markup Percentage} = \frac{\text{Desired Profit}}{\text{Total Costs}}$$

$$= \frac{\$160{,}000}{\$3{,}200{,}000} = 5\%$$

c.

Cost amount per unit	$40.00
Markup ($40 × 5%)	2.00
Selling price	$42.00

3. a. Total manufacturing costs:

Variable ($20 × 80,000 units)	$1,600,000
Fixed factory overhead	800,000
Total	$2,400,000

Cost amount per unit: $2,400,000 ÷ 80,000 units = $30.00

b. $$\text{Markup Percentage} = \frac{\text{Desired Profit} + \text{Total Selling and Administrative Expenses}}{\text{Total Manufacturing Costs}}$$

$$= \frac{\$160{,}000 + \$400{,}000 + (\$5 \times 80{,}000 \text{ units})}{\$2{,}400{,}000}$$

$$= \frac{\$160{,}000 + \$400{,}000 + \$400{,}000}{\$2{,}400{,}000}$$

$$= \frac{\$960{,}000}{\$2{,}400{,}000} = 40\%$$

c.

Cost amount per unit	$30.00
Markup ($30 × 40%)	12.00
Selling price	$42.00

4. a. Variable cost amount per unit: $25

   Total variable costs: $25 × 80,000 units = $2,000,000

   b. $$\text{Markup Percentage} = \frac{\text{Desired Profit} + \text{Total Fixed Costs}}{\text{Total Variable Costs}}$$

   $$= \frac{\$160{,}000 + \$800{,}000 + \$400{,}000}{\$2{,}000{,}000}$$

   $$= \frac{\$1{,}360{,}000}{\$2{,}000{,}000} = 68\%$$

   c.

Cost amount per unit	$25.00
Markup ($25 × 68%)	17.00
Selling price	$42.00

5. a. **Proposal to Sell to Ming Inc.**

Differential revenue from accepting offer:	
Revenue from sale of 4,000 additional units at $28	$112,000
Differential cost from accepting offer:	
Variable production costs of 4,000 additional units at $20	(80,000)
Differential income from accepting offer	$ 32,000

   b. The proposal should be accepted.

Self-Examination Questions

(Answers appear at the end of chapter)

1. Marlo Company is considering discontinuing a product. The costs of the product consist of $20,000 fixed costs and $15,000 variable costs. The variable operating expenses related to the product total $4,000. What is the differential cost?
   A. $19,000
   B. $15,000
   C. $35,000
   D. $39,000

2. Victor Company is considering disposing of equipment that was originally purchased for $200,000 and has $150,000 of accumulated depreciation to date. The same equipment would cost $310,000 to replace. What is the sunk cost?
   A. $50,000
   B. $150,000
   C. $200,000
   D. $310,000

3. Henry Company is considering spending $100,000 for a new grinding machine. This amount could be invested to yield a 12% return. What is the opportunity cost?
   A. $112,000
   B. $88,000
   C. $12,000
   D. $100,000

4. For which cost concept used in applying the cost-plus approach to product pricing are fixed manufacturing costs, fixed selling and administrative expenses, and desired profit allowed for in determining the markup?
   A. Total cost
   B. Product cost
   C. Variable cost
   D. Standard cost

5. Which of the following is a method of product pricing that combines market-based pricing with a cost-reduction emphasis?
   A. Product cost method
   B. Target cost method
   C. Total cost method
   D. Variable cost method

Class Discussion Questions

1. Explain the meaning of (a) differential revenue, (b) differential cost, and (c) differential income.
2. It was reported that Exabyte Corporation, a fast-growing Colorado marketer of computer devices has decided to purchase key components of its product from other suppliers. A former chief executive officer of Exabyte stated, "If we'd tried to build our own plants, we could never have grown that fast or maybe survived." The decision to purchase key product components is an example of what type of decision illustrated in this chapter?
3. A company could sell a building for $650,000 or lease it out for $5,000 per month. What would need to be considered in determining if the lease option would be preferred?
4. A chemical company has a commodity-grade and a premium-grade product. Why might the company elect to process the commodity-grade product further to the premium-grade product?
5. A company is offered incremental business at a special price that exceeds the variable cost. What other issues must the company consider in deciding whether to accept the business?
6. A company fabricates a component at a cost of $7.75. A supplier offers to supply the same component for $6.15. Under what circumstances is it reasonable to purchase from the supplier?
7. Many fast-food restaurant chains, such as McDonald's, occasionally discontinue restaurants in their system. What are some financial considerations in deciding to eliminate a store?
8. In the long run, the normal selling price must be set high enough to cover what factors?
9. Why might the use of ideal standards in applying the cost-plus approach to product pricing lead to setting product prices that are too low?
10. Although the cost-plus approach to product pricing may be used by management as a general guideline, what are some examples of other factors that managers should also consider in setting product prices?
11. How does the target cost concept differ from cost-plus approaches?
12. Under what circumstances is it appropriate to use the target cost concept?

Exercises

E12-1 Lease or sell decision

Obj. 1, 2

✔ **a. Differential revenue from lease, $70,000**

Orwell Industries is considering selling excess machinery with a book value of $300,000 (original cost of $950,000 less accumulated depreciation of $650,000) for $145,000 less a 5% brokerage commission. Alternatively, the machinery can be leased out for a total of $215,000 for five years, after which it is expected to have no residual value. During the period of the lease, Orwell Industries' costs of repairs, insurance, and property tax expenses are expected to be $80,000.

Note: The spreadsheet icon  indicates an Excel template is available on the student companion site.

a. Prepare a differential analysis report for the lease or sell decision.

b. On the basis of the data presented, would it be advisable to lease or sell the machinery? Explain.

Obj. 1, 2

✔ a. Total differential variable costs, $2,970,000

E12-2 Differential analysis report for a discontinued product

A condensed income statement by product line for Garcia Beverages Inc. indicated the following for Melon Cola for the past year:

Sales	$ 3,750,000
Cost of goods sold	(2,250,000)
Gross profit	$ 1,500,000
Operating expenses	(1,800,000)
Operating loss	$ (300,000)

It is estimated that 20% of the cost of goods sold represents fixed factory overhead costs and that 35% of the operating expenses are fixed. Since Melon Cola is only one of many products, the fixed costs will not be significantly affected if the product is discontinued.

a. Prepare a differential analysis report for the proposed discontinuance of Melon Cola.

b. Should Melon Cola be retained? Explain.

Obj. 1, 2

✔ a. Differential income: bowls, $738,600

E12-3 Differential analysis report for a discontinued product

The condensed product-line income statement for Dinner Ware Company is as follows:

DINNER WARE COMPANY
Product-Line Income Statement

	Bowls	Plates	Cups
Sales	$1,500,000	$ 2,350,000	$ 975,000
Cost of goods sold	(900,000)	(1,400,000)	(780,000)
Gross profit	$ 600,000	$ 950,000	$ 195,000
Selling and administrative expenses	(270,000)	(700,000)	(300,000)
Operating income (loss)	$ 330,000	$ 250,000	$(105,000)

Fixed costs are 40% of the cost of goods sold and 18% of the selling and administrative expenses. Dinner Ware assumes that fixed costs would not be significantly affected if the Cups line were discontinued.

a. Prepare a differential analysis report for all three products.

b. Should the Cups line be retained? Explain.

Obj. 1, 2

E12-4 Segment analysis

The Charles Schwab Corporation (SCHW) is one of the more innovative brokerage and financial service companies in the United States. The company provided information about its major business segments as follows (in millions) for a recent year.

	Investor (Retail) Services	Advisor Services
Revenues	$4,771	$1,609
Operating income before taxes	1,681	598
Depreciation and amortization	171	53

a. How do you believe Schwab defines the difference between the segments?

b. Provide a specific example of a variable and fixed cost in the "Investor (Retail) Services" segment.

c. Estimate the contribution margin for each segment.

d. If Schwab decided to sell its "advisory services" accounts to another company, estimate how much operating income would decline.

E12-5 Decision to discontinue a product

Obj. 1, 2

On the basis of the following data, the general manager of Sandals Industries Inc. decided to discontinue Children's Sandals because it reduced operating income by $65,000. What is the flaw in this decision?

SANDALS INDUSTRIES INC.
Product-Line Income Statement

	Children's Sandals	Women's Sandals	Men's Sandals	Total
Sales	$ 400,000	$1,200,000	$ 1,100,000	$ 2,700,000
Costs of goods sold:				
Variable costs	$(240,000)	$ (620,000)	$(580,000)	$(1,440,000)
Fixed costs	(100,000)	(300,000)	(300,000)	(700,000)
Total cost of goods sold	$(340,000)	$ (920,000)	$(880,000)	$(2,140,000)
Gross profit	$ 60,000	$ 280,000	$ 220,000	$ 560,000
Selling and administrative expenses:				
Variable selling and admin. expenses	$ (75,000)	$ (120,000)	$ (100,000)	$ (295,000)
Fixed selling and admin. expenses	(50,000)	(100,000)	(80,000)	(230,000)
Total selling and admin. expenses	$(125,000)	$ (220,000)	$ (180,000)	$ (525,000)
Operating income (loss)	$ (65,000)	$ 60,000	$ 40,000	$ 35,000

E12-6 Make-or-buy decision

Obj. 1, 2

✔ **a. Cost savings from making, $0.60 per case**

Watts Technologies Company has been purchasing carrying cases for its portable tablets at a delivered cost of $6.50 per unit. The company, which is currently operating below full capacity, charges factory overhead to production at the rate of 60% of direct labor cost. The fully absorbed unit costs to produce comparable carrying cases are expected to be as follows:

Direct materials	$ 2.00
Direct labor	3.25
Factory overhead (60% of direct labor)	1.95
Total cost per unit	$ 7.20

If Watts Technologies Company manufactures the carrying cases, fixed factory overhead costs will not increase and variable factory overhead costs associated with the cases are expected to be 20% of the direct labor costs.

a. Prepare a differential analysis report for the make-or-buy decision.

b. On the basis of the data presented, would it be advisable to make the carrying cases or to continue buying them? Explain.

E12-7 Make-or-buy decision

Obj. 1, 2

Wisconsin Arts of Milwaukee employs five people in its Publication Department. These people lay out pages for pamphlets, brochures, and other publications for the productions. The pages are delivered to an outside company for printing. The company is considering an outside publication service for the layout work. The outside service is quoting a price of $9.50 per layout page. The budget for the Publication Department is as follows:

Salaries	$185,000
Benefits	50,000
Supplies	30,000
Office expenses	25,000
Office depreciation	70,000
Computer depreciation	18,000
Total	$378,000

The department expects to lay out 30,000 pages. The computers used by the department have an estimated residual value of $6,500. The Publication Department office space would be used for future administrative needs if the department's function were purchased from the outside.

a. Prepare a differential analysis report for the make-or-buy decision, considering the differential revenues and costs.

b. On the basis of your analysis in part (a), should the page layout work be purchased from an outside company?

c. What additional considerations might factor into the decision making?

Obj. 1, 2

E12-8 Machine replacement decision

Creekside Products Inc. is considering replacing an old piece of machinery, which cost $315,000 and has $130,000 of accumulated depreciation to date, with a new machine that costs $275,000. The old machine could be sold for $140,000. The annual variable production costs associated with the old machine are estimated to be $30,000 for eight years. The annual variable production costs for the new machine are estimated to be $9,000 for eight years.

a. Determine the total and annualized differential income or loss anticipated from replacing the old machine.

b. What is the sunk cost in this situation?

Obj. 1, 2

✔ a. Annual differential decrease in costs and expenses, $23,000

E12-9 Differential analysis report for machine replacement

Lone Wolf Technologies Inc. assembles circuit boards by using a manually operated machine to insert electronic components. The original cost of the machine is $75,000, the accumulated depreciation is $30,000, its remaining useful life is eight years, and its residual value is zero. A proposal was made to replace the present manufacturing procedure with a fully automatic machine that will cost $160,000. The automatic machine has an estimated useful life of eight years and no significant residual value. For use in evaluating the proposal, the accountant accumulated the following annual data on current and proposed operations:

	Current Operations	Proposed Operations
Sales	$3,800,000	$3,800,000
Direct materials	$ 500,000	$ 500,000
Direct labor	150,000	50,000
Power and maintenance	10,000	60,000
Taxes, insurance, etc.	5,000	12,000
Selling and administrative expenses	200,000	200,000
Total expenses	$ 865,000	$ 822,000

a. Prepare a differential analysis report for the proposal to replace the machine. Include in the analysis both the net differential change in costs anticipated over the five years and the net annual differential change in costs anticipated.

b. Based only on the data presented, should the proposal be accepted?

c. What are some of the other factors that should be considered before a final decision is made?

E12-10 Sell or process further

Obj. 1, 2

✔ **a. Differential revenue, $95**

St. Paul Lumber Company incurs a cost of $280 per hundred board feet in processing certain "rough-cut" lumber, which it sells for $320 per hundred board feet. An alternative is to produce a "finished cut" at a total processing cost of $350 per hundred board feet, which can be sold for $415 per hundred board feet. What is the amount of (a) the differential revenue, (b) differential cost, and (c) differential income for processing rough-cut lumber into finished cut?

E12-11 Sell or process further

Obj. 1, 2

Bozeman Coffee Company produces Columbian coffee in batches of 10,000 pounds. The standard quantity of materials required in the process is 10,000 pounds, which cost $3.50 per pound. Columbian coffee can be sold without further processing for $8.00 per pound. Columbian coffee can also be processed further to yield Decaf Columbian, which can be sold for $9.50 per pound. The processing into Decaf Columbian requires additional processing costs of $7,500 per batch. The additional processing will also cause a 3% loss of product due to evaporation.

a. Prepare a differential analysis report for the decision to sell or process further.

b. Should Bozeman Coffee sell Columbian coffee or process further and sell Decaf Columbian?

c. Determine the price of Decaf Columbian that would cause neither an advantage nor a disadvantage for processing further and selling Decaf Columbian. Round to nearest cent.

E12-12 Decision on accepting additional business

Obj. 1, 2

✔ **a. Differential income, $625,000**

Madison Industries Inc. has an annual plant capacity of 800,000 units, and current production is 650,000 units. Monthly fixed costs are $1,200,000 and variable costs are $36 per unit. The present selling price is $50 per unit. The company received an offer from Story Mills Company for 125,000 units of the product at $41 each. Story Mills Company will market the units in a foreign country under its own brand name. The additional business is not expected to affect the domestic selling price or quantity of sales of Madison Industries Inc.

a. Prepare a differential analysis report for the proposed sale to Story Mills Company.

b. Briefly explain the reason why accepting this additional business will increase operating income.

c. What is the minimum price per unit that would produce a contribution margin?

E12-13 Accepting business at a special price

Obj. 1, 2

Palomar Battery Company expects to operate at 75% of full capacity during April. The total manufacturing costs for April for the production of 60,000 batteries are budgeted as follows:

Direct materials	$ 75,000
Direct labor	960,000
Variable factory overhead	111,000
Fixed factory overhead	288,000
Total manufacturing costs	$1,434,000

The company has an opportunity to submit a bid for 17,500 batteries to be delivered by April 30 to a government agency. If the contract is obtained, it is anticipated that the additional activity will not interfere with normal production during April or increase the selling or administrative expenses.

a. What is the April budgeted cost per battery for the production of 60,000 batteries?'

b. What is the unit cost below which Palomar Battery Company should not go in bidding on the government contract?

Obj. 1

✔ a. Total differential revenue, $800,000

E12-14 Decision on accepting additional business

Miramar Tire and Rubber Company has capacity to produce 250,000 tires. Miramar presently produces and sells 200,000 tires for the North American market at a price of $40 per tire. Miramar is evaluating a special order from a South American automobile company, Rio Motors. Rio Motors is offering to buy 40,000 tires for $20 per tire. Miramar's accounting system indicates that the total cost per tire is as follows:

Direct materials	$10.00
Direct labor	5.00
Factory overhead (45% variable)	4.00
Selling and administrative expenses (75% variable)	3.00
Total	$22.00

Miramar pays a sales commission equal to 4% of the selling price on North American orders, which is included in the variable portion of the selling and administrative expenses. However, this special order would not have a sales commission. If the order was accepted, the tires would be shipped overseas for an additional shipping cost of $1.50 per tire. In addition, Rio has made the order conditional on Miramar Tire and Rubber Company receiving a Brazilian safety certification. Rio estimates that this certification would cost Miramar Tire $20,000.

a. Prepare a differential analysis report for the proposed sale to Rio Motors.

b. What is the minimum price per unit that would be financially acceptable to Miramar?

Obj. 3

✔ d. Selling price, $262

E12-15 Total cost concept of product costing

Willis Products Inc. uses the total cost concept of applying the cost-plus approach to product pricing. The costs of producing and selling 200,000 units of medical tablets are as follows:

Variable costs per unit:		Fixed costs:	
Direct materials	$ 75	Factory overhead	$ 800,000
Direct labor	115	Selling and admin. exp.	1,200,000
Factory overhead	30		
Selling and admin. exp.	20		
Total	$240		

Willis Products desires a profit equal to a 20% rate of return on invested assets of $12,000,000.

a. Determine the amount of desired profit from the production and sale of 200,000 units.

b. Determine the total costs and the cost amount per unit for the production and sale of 200,000 units.

c. Determine the total cost markup percentage per unit.

d. Determine the selling price per unit.

E12-16 Product cost concept of product pricing

Obj. 3

✔ b. Markup percentage, 16.96%

Based on the data presented in Exercise 12-15, assume that Willis Products Inc. uses the product cost concept of applying the cost-plus approach to product pricing.

a. Determine the total manufacturing costs and the cost amount per unit for the production and sale of 200,000 units.

b. Determine the product cost markup percentage per unit. Round to two decimal place.

c. Determine the selling price per unit. Round to the nearest dollar.

E12-17 Variable cost concept of product pricing

Obj. 3

✔ b. Markup percentage, 9.17%

Based on the data presented in Exercise 12-15, assume that Willis Products Inc. uses the variable cost concept of applying the cost-plus approach to product pricing.

a. Determine the variable costs and the cost amount per unit for the production and sale of 200,000 units of medical tablets.

b. Determine the variable cost markup percentage per unit. Round to two decimal place.

c. Determine the selling price per unit. Round to the nearest dollar.

E12-18 Target costing

Obj. 3

Toyota Motor Corporation (TM) uses target costing. Assume that Toyota marketing personnel estimate that the competitive, average selling price for the Rav4 in the upcoming model year will need to be $25,000. Assume further that the Rav4's total unit cost for the upcoming model year is estimated to be $21,000 and that Toyota requires a 20% profit margin on selling price (which is equivalent to a 25% markup on total cost).

a. What price will Toyota establish for the Rav4 for the upcoming model year?

b. What impact will target costing have on Toyota, given the assumed information?

E12-19 Target costing

Obj. 3

✔ b. $14.40

Millennium Printers Inc. manufactures color laser printers. Model L-1819 presently sells for $200 and has a total product cost of $160, as follows:

Direct materials	$ 40
Direct labor	80
Factory overhead	40
Total	$160

It is estimated that the competitive selling price for color laser printers of this type will drop to $182 next year. Millennium Printers wants to establish a target cost to maintain its historical markup percentage on product cost. Engineers have provided the following cost reduction ideas:

1. Purchase a plastic printer cover with snap-on assembly. This will reduce the amount of direct labor by six minutes per unit.
2. Add an inspection step that will add nine minutes per unit of direct labor but reduce the materials cost by $7.25 per unit.
3. Decrease the cycle time of the injection molding machine from four minutes to three minutes per part. Thirty percent of the direct labor and 28% of the factory overhead is related to running injection molding machines.

The direct labor rate is $20 per hour.

a. Determine the target cost for Model L-1819 assuming that the historical markup on product cost is maintained.

b. Determine the required cost reduction.

c. Evaluate the three engineering improvements to determine if the required cost reduction (drift) can be achieved.

Problems

Obj. 1, 2

P12-1 Differential analysis report involving opportunity costs

Five Star is considering leasing a building and buying the necessary equipment to operate a public warehouse. Alternatively, the company could use the funds to invest in $900,000 of 4% U.S. Treasury bonds that mature in 15 years. The bonds could be purchased at face value. The following data have been assembled:

Cost of equipment	$900,000
Life of equipment	15 years
Estimated residual value of equipment	$100,000
Yearly costs to operate the warehouse, excluding depreciation of equipment	$175,000
Yearly expected revenues—years 1–7	$400,000
Yearly expected revenues—years 8–15	$250,000

Instructions

1. Prepare a differential analysis report of the proposed operation of the warehouse for the 15 years as compared with present conditions.
2. Based on the results disclosed by the differential analysis, should the proposal be accepted?
3. If the proposal is accepted, what is the total estimated operating income of the warehouse for the 15 years?

Obj. 1, 2

P12-2 Differential analysis report for machine replacement proposal

Catalina Tooling Company is considering replacing a machine that has been used in its factory for two years. Relevant data associated with the operations of the old machine and the new machine, neither of which has any estimated residual value, are as follows:

Old Machine	
Cost of machine, 10-year life	$75,000
Annual depreciation (straight-line)	7,500
Annual manufacturing costs, excluding depreciation	33,150
Annual nonmanufacturing operating expenses	10,000
Annual revenue	60,000
Current estimated selling price of the machine	24,000

New Machine	
Cost of machine, 8-year life	$90,000
Annual depreciation (straight-line)	11,250
Annual manufacturing costs, excluding depreciation	18,200
Annual nonmanufacturing operating expenses	10,000

Annual nonmanufacturing operating expenses and revenue are not expected to be affected by the purchase of the new machine.

Instructions

1. Prepare a differential analysis report comparing operations utilizing the new machine with operations using the old machine. The analysis should indicate the differential income that would result over the eight-year period if the new machine is acquired.
2. List other factors that should be considered before a final decision is reached.

P12-3 Differential analysis report for sales promotion proposal

Obj. 1, 2

✔ Differential income, cross-trainer shoe, $450,000

Rocket Shoe Company is planning a one-month campaign for August to promote sales of one of its two shoe products. A total of $500,000 has been budgeted for advertising, contests, redeemable coupons, and other promotional activities. The following data have been assembled for their possible usefulness in deciding which of the products to select for the campaign.

	Cross-Trainer Shoe	Running Shoe
Unit selling price	$ 90	$112
Unit production costs:		
Direct materials	$(24)	$ (30)
Direct labor	(10)	(8)
Variable factory overhead	(6)	(6)
Fixed factory overhead	(8)	(16)
Total unit production costs	$(48)	$ (60)
Unit variable selling expenses	(12)	(12)
Unit fixed selling expenses	(4)	(16)
Total unit costs	$(64)	$ (88)
Operating income per unit	$ 26	$ 24

No increase in facilities would be necessary to produce and sell the increased output. It is anticipated that 25,000 additional units of cross-trainer shoes or 18,000 additional units of running shoes could be sold without changing the unit selling price of either product.

Instructions

1. Prepare a differential analysis report presenting the additional revenue and additional costs anticipated from the promotion of cross-trainer shoes and running shoes.
2. The sales manager has tentatively decided to promote cross-trainer shoes, estimating that operating income will increase by $150,000 ($26 operating income per unit for 25,000 units, less promotion expenses of $500,000). The manager also believes that the selection of running shoes will decrease operating income by $68,000 ($24 operating income per unit for 18,000 units, less promotion expenses of $500,000). State briefly your reasons for supporting or opposing the tentative decision.

P12-4 Differential analysis report for further processing

Obj. 1, 2

✔ 1. Differential revenue, $70,400

The management of Dorsch Aluminum Co. is considering whether to process aluminum ingot further into rolled aluminum. Rolled aluminum can be sold for $4,100 per ton, and ingot can be sold without further processing for $2,400 per ton. Ingot is produced in batches of 80 tons by smelting 400 tons of bauxite, which costs $500 per ton. Rolled aluminum will require additional processing costs of $750 per ton of ingot, and 1.25 tons of ingot will produce 1 ton of rolled aluminum (due to trim losses).

Instructions

1. Prepare a report presenting a differential analysis associated with the further processing of aluminum ingot to produce rolled aluminum.
2. Briefly report your recommendations.

Obj. 1, 2, 3

✔ 2. b. Markup percentage, 16%

P12-5 Product pricing using the cost-plus approach concepts; differential analysis report for accepting additional business

Twilight Lumina Company recently began production of a new product, the halogen light, which required an investment of $1,200,000 in assets. The costs of producing and selling 20,000 halogen lights are estimated as follows:

Variable unit costs:		Fixed costs:	
Direct materials	$30	Factory overhead	$340,000
Direct labor	10	Selling and admin. exp.	160,000
Factory overhead	6		
Selling and admin. exp.	4		
Total	$50		

Twilight Lumina Company is currently considering establishing a selling price for the halogen light. The president of Twilight Lumina Company has decided to use the cost-plus approach to product pricing and has indicated that the halogen light must earn a 20% rate of return on invested assets.

Instructions

1. Determine the amount of desired profit from the production and sale of the halogen light.
2. Assuming that the total cost concept is used, determine (a) the cost amount per unit, (b) the markup percentage, and (c) the selling price of the halogen light.
3. Assuming that the product cost concept is used, determine (a) the cost amount per unit, (b) the markup percentage (round to the nearest two decimal places), and (c) the selling price of the halogen light (round to the nearest cent).
4. Assuming that the variable cost concept is used, determine (a) the cost amount per unit, (b) the markup percentage, and (c) the selling price of the halogen light.
5. Comment on any additional considerations that could influence establishing the selling price for the halogen light.
6. Assume that 15,000 units of the halogen light have been produced and sold during the current year. Analysis of the domestic market indicates that 2,000 additional units of the halogen light are expected to be sold during the remainder of the year at the normal product price determined under the total cost concept. Twilight Lumina Company received an offer from Contech Inc. for 3,000 units of the halogen light at $52 each. Contech Inc. will market the units in Southeast Asia under its own brand name, and no selling and administrative expenses associated with the sale will be incurred by Twilight Lumina Company. The additional business is not expected to affect the domestic sales of the halogen light, and the additional units could be produced using existing capacity.

   a. Prepare a differential analysis report of the proposed sale to Contech Inc.

   b. Based on the differential analysis report in part (a), should the proposal be accepted?

Metric-Based Analysis

MBA 12-1 Contribution margin per constraint

Obj. 4

Zion Metals Inc. has three grades of metal product, A1, B3, and E6. Financial data for the three grades are as follows:

	A1	B3	E6
Revenue	$ 400,000	$ 578,000	$ 300,000
Variable cost	$(250,000)	$(380,000)	$(270,000)
Fixed cost	(105,000)	(118,800)	(20,000)
Total cost	$(355,000)	$(498,800)	$(290,000)
Operating income	$ 45,000	$ 79,200	$ 10,000
Number of units	÷ 15,000	÷ 16,500	÷ 5,000
Operating income per unit	$ 3.00	$ 4.80	$ 2.00

Zion Metals' operations require all three grades to be melted in a furnace before being formed. The furnace runs 24 hours a day, 7 days a week, and is a production constraint. The furnace hours required per unit of each product are as follows:

A1:	8 hours
B3:	10 hours
E6:	6 hours

The Marketing Department is considering a new marketing and sales campaign. Which product should be emphasized in the marketing and sales campaign in order to maximize profitability?

MBA 12-2 Contribution margin per constraint

Obj. 4

Nygard Glass Company manufactures three types of safety plate glass: mirror, laminated, and regular. All three products have high demand. Thus, Nygard Glass is able to sell all the safety glass that it can make. The production process includes an autoclave operation, which is a pressurized heat treatment. The autoclave is a production constraint. Total fixed costs for the period are expected to be $90,000. In addition, the following information is available for the three products:

	Mirror	Laminated	Regular
Unit selling price	$90	$75	$60
Unit variable cost	(72)	(65)	(55)
Unit contribution margin	$18	$10	$ 5
Autoclave hours per unit	6	4	1
Total process hours per unit	20	15	8
Budgeted units of production	10,000	10,000	10,000

a. Determine the contribution margin by glass type and the total company operating income for the budgeted units of production.

b. Prepare an analysis showing which product is the most profitable per constraint hour.

Obj. 4

MBA 12-3 Contribution margin per constraint

Using the data and your answers from MBA 12-2, determine the following:

1. The selling price necessary for Mirror glass to be as profitable as Regular glass.
2. Assuming the selling price for Mirror glass cannot be changed, how much will the variable costs for Mirror glass need to be reduced so it is as profitable as Regular glass.
3. Assuming the selling price and variable costs for Mirror glass cannot be changed, how much will the furnace hours required for Mirror glass need to be reduced to make it as profitable as Regular glass.

Obj. 4

MBA 12-4 Contribution margin per constraint

Using the data and your answers from MBA 12-2, determine the following:

1. The selling price necessary for Laminated glass to be as profitable as Regular glass.
2. Assuming the selling price for Laminated glass cannot be changed, how much will the variable costs for Laminated glass need to be reduced so it is as profitable as Regular glass.
3. Assuming the selling price and variable costs for Laminated glass cannot be changed, how much will the furnace hours required for Laminated glass need to be reduced to make it as profitable as Regular glass.

Obj. 4

✔ 1. Ethylene contribution margin per unit, $100

MBA 12-5 Contributon margin per constraint

Chavez Chemical Company produces three products: ethylene, butane, and ester. Each of these products has high demand in the market, and Chavez Chemical is able to sell as much as it can produce of all three. The reaction operation is a bottleneck in the process and is running at 100% of capacity. Chavez Chemical wants to improve chemical operation profitability. The variable conversion cost is $20 per process hour. The fixed cost is $550,000. In addition, the cost analyst was able to determine the following information about the three products:

	Ethylene	Butane	Ester
Budgeted units produced	15,000	15,000	15,000
Total process hours per unit	6	6	4
Reactor hours per unit	1.0	0.8	0.5
Unit selling price	$400	$350	$250
Direct materials cost per unit	$180	$130	$90

The reaction operation is part of the total process for each of these three products. Thus, for example, 1.0 of the 6 hours required to process ethylene is associated with the reactor.

Instructions

1. Determine the unit contribution margin for each of the three products.
2. Provide an analysis to determine the relative product profitabilities, assuming that the reactor is a bottleneck.
3. Assume that management wishes to improve profitability by increasing prices on selected products. At what price would ethylene and butane need to be offered in order to produce the same relative profitability as ester?

Cases

Case 12-1 Product pricing

Bev Frazier is a cost accountant for Ocean Atlantic Apparel Inc. Jeff Rangel, vice president of marketing, has asked Bev to meet with representatives of Ocean Atlantic Apparel's major competitor to discuss product cost data. Jeff indicates that the sharing of these data will enable Ocean Atlantic to determine a fair and equitable price for its products.

Would it be ethical for Bev to attend the meeting and share the relevant cost data?

Case 12-2 Decision on accepting additional business

A manager of Coastal Sporting Goods Company is considering accepting an order from an overseas customer. This customer has requested an order for 50,000 dozen golf balls at a price of $12 per dozen. The variable cost to manufacture a dozen golf balls is $9 per dozen. The full cost is $14 per dozen. Coastal Sporting Goods has a normal selling price of $24 per dozen. Coastal's plant has just enough excess capacity on the second shift to make the overseas order.

What are some considerations in accepting or rejecting this order?

Case 12-3 Accept business at a special price

If you are not familiar with The Priceline Group Inc. (PCLN), go to its Web site. Assume that an individual "names a price" of $90 on Priceline.com for a room in Miami, Florida, on September 3. Assume that September 3 is a Saturday, with low expected room demand in Miami at a Marriott International, Inc. (MAR), hotel, so there is excess room capacity. The fully allocated cost per room per day is assumed from hotel records as follows:

Housekeeping labor cost*	$ 30
Hotel depreciation expense	50
Cost of room supplies (soap, paper, etc.)	2
Laundry labor and material cost*	6
Cost of desk staff	8
Utility cost (mostly air conditioning)	4
Total cost per room per day	$100

*Both housekeeping and laundry staff include many part-time workers, so that the workload is variable to demand.

Should Marriott accept the customer bid for a night in Miami on September 3 at a price of $90?

Case 12-4 Cost-plus and target costing concepts

The following conversation took place between Dean Lancaster, vice president of marketing, and Dina Conaway, controller of Redwood Computer Company:

Dean: I am really excited about our new computer coming out. I think it will be a real market success.

Dina: I'm really glad you think so. I know that our success will be determined by our price. If our price is too high, our competitors will be the ones with the market success.

Dean: Don't worry about it. We'll just mark our product cost up by 25% and it will all work out. I know we'll make money at those markups. By the way, what does the estimated product cost look like?

Dina: Well, there's the rub. The product cost looks as if it's going to come in at around $1,000. With a 25% markup, that will give us a selling price of $1,250.

Dean: I see your concern. That's a little high. Our research indicates that computer prices are dropping and that this type of computer should be selling for around $900 when we release it to the market.

Dina: I'm not sure what to do.

Dean: Let me see if I can help. How much of the $1,000 is fixed cost?

Dina: About $300.

Dean: There you go. The fixed cost is sunk. We don't need to consider it in our pricing decision. If we reduce the product cost by $300, the new price with a 25% markup would be right at $875. Boy, I was really worried for a minute there. I knew something wasn't right.

1. If you were Dina, how would you respond to Dean's solution to the pricing problem?
2. How might target costing be used to help solve this pricing dilemma?

Case 12-5 Pricing decisions and markup on variable costs

Many businesses are offering their products and services over the Internet. Two of these companies and their Internet addresses are listed below.

Company Name	Internet Address (URL)	Product
Delta Air Lines (DAL)	http://www.delta.com	Airline tickets
Amazon.com (AMZN)	http://www.amazon.com	Books

1. In groups of three, assign each person in your group to one of the Internet sites listed above. For each site, determine the following:
   a. A product (or service) description.
   b. A product price.
   c. A list of costs that are required to produce and sell the product selected in part (1) as listed in the annual report on SEC Form 10-K.
   d. Whether the costs identified in part (3) are fixed costs or variable costs.
2. Which of the products do you believe has the largest markup on variable cost?

Answers to Self-Examination Questions

1. **A** Differential cost is the amount of increase or decrease in cost that is expected from a particular course of action compared with an alternative. For Marlo Company, the differential cost is $19,000 (answer A). This is the total of the variable product costs ($15,000) and the variable operating expenses ($4,000), which would not be incurred if the product is discontinued.
2. **A** A sunk cost is not affected by later decisions. For Victor Company, the sunk cost is the $50,000 (answer A) book value of the equipment, which is equal to the original cost of $200,000 (answer C) less the accumulated depreciation of $150,000 (answer B).
3. **C** The amount of income that could have been earned from the best available alternative to a proposed use of cash is the opportunity cost. For Henry Company, the opportunity cost is 12% of $100,000, or $12,000 (answer C).

4. **C** Under the variable cost concept of product pricing (answer C), fixed manufacturing costs, fixed administrative and selling expenses, and desired profit are allowed for in determining the markup. Only desired profit is allowed for in the markup under the total cost concept (answer A). Under the product cost concept (answer B), total selling and administrative expenses and desired profit are allowed for in determining the markup. Standard cost (answer D) can be used under any of the cost-plus approaches to product pricing.

5. **B** The target cost method (answer B) combines market-based pricing with a cost-reduction emphasis. The product cost method (answer A) determines prices by adding a markup to a product cost amount that includes direct materials, direct labor, and factory overhead. The total cost method (answer C) determines prices by adding a markup to a total cost amount. The variable cost method (answer D) determines prices by adding a markup to a variable cost amount.

Chapter 13 Budgeting and Standard Costs

What's Covered:

Topics: Budgeting and Standard Costs

Nature of Budgeting
- Objectives (Obj. 1)
- Effects on human behavior (Obj. 1)
- Budgeting systems (Obj. 1)

Master Budget
- Sales budget (Obj. 2)
- Production budget (Obj. 2)
- Direct materials purchases budget (Obj. 2)
- Direct labor cost budget (Obj. 2)
- Factory overhead cost budget (Obj. 2)
- Cost of goods sold budget (Obj. 2)
- Selling and administrative expense budget (Obj. 2)
- Budgeted income statement (Obj. 2)
- Cash budget (Obj. 2)
- Capital expenditures budget (Obj. 2)
- Budgeted balance sheet (Obj. 2)

Standard Costs
- Setting standards (Obj. 3)
- Types of standards (Obj. 3)
- Performance reports (Obj. 4)
- Direct materials variances (Obj. 5)
- Direct labor variances (Obj. 5)

Metric-Based Analysis
- Process yield (Obj. 6)
- Utilization rate (Obj. 6)

Learning Objectives

Obj.1 Describe budgeting, its objectives, its impact on human behavior, and types of budget systems.

Obj.2 Describe and prepare a master budget for a manufacturing company.

Obj.3 Describe the types of standard costs and how they are established.

Obj.4 Describe and illustrate performance reporting for manufacturing operations.

Obj.5 Compute and interpret direct materials and direct labor variances.

Obj.6 Describe and illustrate process yield and utilization rate metrics.

Chapter Metrics

The managerial decision-making and performance metrics for this chapter are process yield and utilization rate.

Hendrick Motorsport

Daniel Huerlimann-BEELDE/Shutterstock.com

You may have financial goals for your life. To achieve these goals, it is necessary to plan for future expenses. For example, you may consider taking a part-time job to save money for school expenses for the coming school year. How much money would you need to earn and save in order to pay these expenses? One way to find an answer to this question would be to prepare a budget. A budget would show an estimate of your expenses associated with school, such as tuition, fees, and books. In addition, you would have expenses for day-to-day living, such as rent, food, and clothing. You might also have expenses for travel and entertainment. Once the school year begins, you can use the budget as a tool for guiding your spending priorities during the year.

The budget is used in businesses in much the same way it can be used in personal life. For example, **Hendrick Motorsport**, featuring drivers Dale Earnhardt, Jr., Jeff Gordon, and Jimmy Johnson, uses budget information to remain one of the most valuable racing teams in NASCAR. Hendrick uses budgets to keep revenues greater than expenses. For example, Hendrick plans revenues from car sponsorships and winnings. Primary and secondary sponsorships (car decals) can provide as much as 70% of the revenues for a typical race team. Costs include salaries, engines, tires, cars, travel, and research and development. In addition, star drivers, such as Dale Earnhardt, Jr., can earn as much as $28 million in salary, winnings, and endorsements. Overall, Hendrick is estimated to earn $179 million in revenues and $16.6 million in operating income from their four race teams. The budget provides the company with a "game plan" for the year. In this chapter, you will see how budgets can be used for financial planning and control.

Source: Kurt Badenhausen, "Hendrick Motorsports Tops list of Nascar's Most Valuable Teams," *Forbes*, March 13, 2013. Bob Pockrass, "NASCAR's Highest Paid drivers make their money from a variety of sources," *Sporting News*, December 4, 2012. Ed Hilton, "Under the Hood at Hendrick Motorsports", *Chicago Tribune*, July 13, 2007.

Nature and Objectives of Budgeting

Objective 1
Describe budgeting, its objectives, its impact on human behavior, and types of budget systems.

Budgets play an important role for organizations of all sizes and forms. For example, budgets are used in managing the operations of government agencies, churches, hospitals, and other nonprofit organizations. Individuals and families also use budgeting in managing their financial affairs. This chapter describes and illustrates budgeting for a manufacturing company.

Objectives of Budgeting

Budgeting involves (1) establishing specific goals, (2) executing plans to achieve the goals, and (3) periodically comparing actual results with the goals. In doing so, budgeting affects the following managerial functions:

1. Planning
2. Directing
3. Controlling

The relationships of these activities are illustrated in Exhibit 1.

Planning involves setting goals as a guide for making decisions. Budgeting supports the planning process by requiring all departments and other organizational units to establish their goals for the future. These goals help motivate employees. In addition, the budgeting process often identifies areas where operations can be improved or inefficiencies eliminated.

Directing involves decisions and actions to achieve budgeted goals. Budgeting aids in coordinating management's decisions and actions to achieve the company's budgeted goals. A budgetary unit of a company is called a **responsibility center**. Each responsibility center is led by a manager who has the authority and responsibility for achieving the center's budgeted goals.

Exhibit 1 Planning, Directing, and Controlling

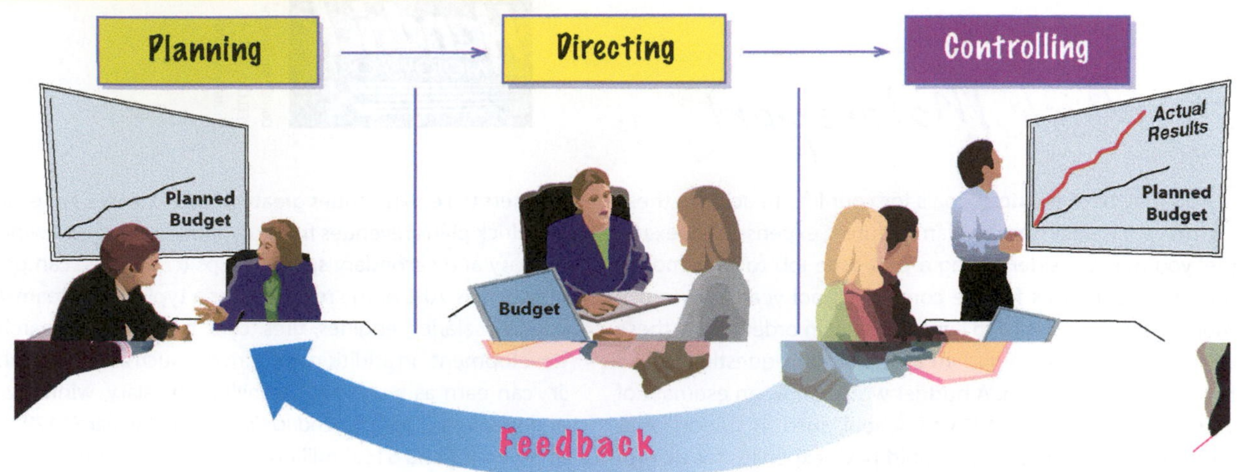

Controlling involves comparing actual performance against the budgeted goals. Such comparisons provide feedback to managers and employees about their performance. If necessary, responsibility centers can use such feedback to adjust their activities in the future.

Hendrick Motorsports Connection

Rick Hendrick started by selling used cars. At age 26, he invested all his assets in a struggling Chevrolet dealership becoming the youngest Chevrolet dearler in the United States. This dealership was the predecessor of the **Hendrick** Automotive Group.

Human Behavior and Budgeting

Human behavior problems can arise in the budgeting process in the following situations:

1. Budgeted goals are set too tight, which are very hard or impossible to achieve.
2. Budgeted goals are set too loose, which are very easy to achieve.
3. Budgeted goals conflict with the objectives of the company and employees.

These behavior problems are illustrated in Exhibit 2.

Exhibit 2 Human Behavior Problems in Budgeting

Setting Budget Goals Too Tightly Employees and managers may become discouraged if budgeted goals are set too high. That is, if budgeted goals are viewed as unrealistic or unachievable, the budget may have a negative effect on the ability of the company to achieve its goals.

Reasonable, attainable goals are more likely to motivate employees and managers. For this reason, it is important that employees and managers be involved in the budgeting process. Involving employees in the budgeting process provides employees with a sense of control and thus more of a commitment in meeting budgeted goals. Finally, involving employees and managers also encourages cooperation across departments and responsibility centers. Such cooperation increases awareness of each department's importance to the overall goals of the company.

Setting Budget Goals Too Loosely Although it is desirable to establish attainable goals, it is undesirable to plan lower goals than may be possible. Such budget "padding" is termed **budgetary slack**. Managers may plan slack in the budget in order to provide a "cushion" for unexpected events or improve the appearance of operations. Budgetary slack can be reduced by properly training employees and managers in the importance of realistic, attainable budgets.

Slack budgets may cause a "spend it or lose it" mentality. This often occurs at the end of the budget period when actual spending is less than the budget. Employees and managers may spend the remaining budget on unnecessary purchases in order to avoid having their budget reduced for the next period.

Setting Conflicting Budget Goals **Goal conflict** occurs when the employees' or managers' self-interest differs from the company's objectives or goals. Goal conflict may also occur among responsibility centers such as departments.

To illustrate, assume that the sales department manager is given an increased sales goal and as a result accepts customers who are poor credit risks. This, in turn, causes bad debt expense to increase and profitability to decline. Likewise, a manufacturing department manager may be told to reduce costs. As a result, the manufacturing department manager might use lower-cost direct materials, which are also of lower quality. As a result, customer complaints and returns might increase significantly, which would adversely affect the company's profitability.

Hendrick Motorsports Connection

Hendrick Motorsports sets high goals for its drivers. It holds a record of 11 NASCAR Sprint Cup Series Championships with 6 won by Jimmie Johnson, 4 won by Jeff Gordon, and 1 won by Terry Labonte.

Integrity, Objectivity, and Ethics in Business

Budget Games

The budgeting system is designed to plan and control a business. However, it is common for the budget to be "gamed" by its participants. For example, managers may pad their budgets with excess resources. In this way, the managers have additional resources for unexpected events during the period. If the budget is being used to establish the incentive plan, then sales managers have incentives to understate the sales potential of a territory in order to ensure hitting their quotas. Other times, managers engage in "land grabbing," which occurs when they overstate the sales potential of a territory in order to guarantee access to resources. If managers believe that unspent resources will not roll over to future periods, then they may be encouraged to "spend it or lose it," causing wasteful expenditures. These types of problems can be partially overcome by separating the budget into planning and incentive components. This is why many organizations have two budget processes, one for resource planning and another, more challenging budget, for motivating managers.

Budgeting Systems

Budgeting systems vary among companies and industries. For example, the budget system used by **Ford Motor Company** differs from that used by **Delta Air Lines**. However, the basic budgeting concepts discussed in this section apply to all types of businesses and organizations.

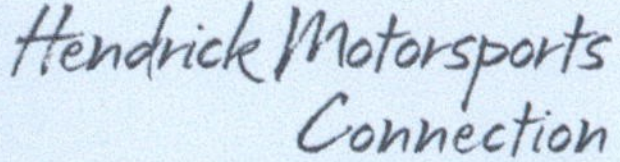

Rick Hendrick uses budgeting in **Hendrick Motorsports** as well as the Hendrick Automotive Group. The Hendrick Automotive Group is the largest privately held dealership group in the United States with 120 retail franchises.

The budgetary period for operating activities normally includes the fiscal year of a company. A year is short enough that future operations can be estimated fairly accurately, yet long enough that the future can be viewed in a broad context. However, for control purposes, annual budgets are usually subdivided into shorter time periods, such as quarters of the year, months, or weeks.

A variation of fiscal year budgeting, called **continuous budgeting**, maintains a 12-month projection into the future. The 12-month budget is continually revised by replacing the data for the month just ended with the budget data for the same month in the next year. A continuous budget is illustrated in Exhibit 3.

Exhibit 3 Continuous Budgeting

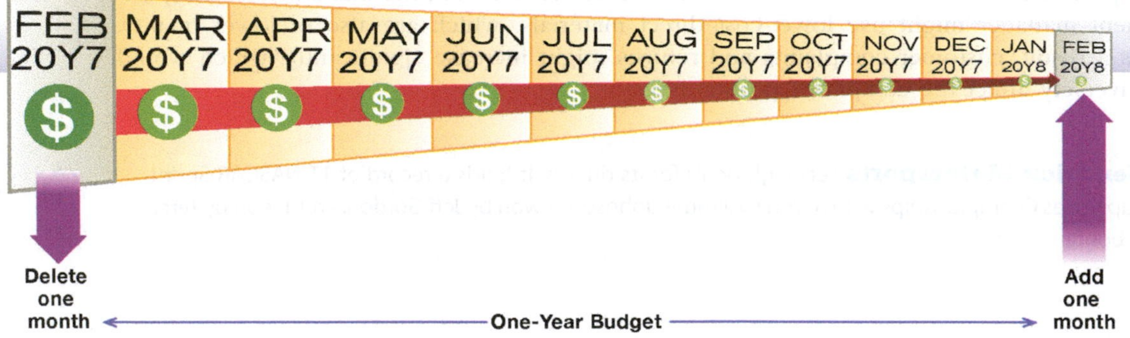

Developing an annual budget usually begins several months prior to the end of the current year. This responsibility is normally assigned to a budget committee. Such a committee often consists of the budget director, the controller, the treasurer, the production manager, and the sales manager. The budget process is monitored and summarized by the Accounting Department, which reports to the committee.

There are several methods of developing budget estimates. One method, termed **zero-based budgeting**, requires managers to estimate sales, production, and other operating data as though operations are being started for the first time. This approach has the benefit of taking a fresh view of operations each year. A more common approach is to start with last year's budget and revise it for actual results and expected changes for the coming year. Two major budgets using this approach are the static budget and the flexible budget.

Static Budget A **static budget** shows the expected results of a responsibility center for only one activity level. Once the budget has been determined, it is not changed, even if the activity changes. Static budgeting is used by many service companies and for some functions of manufacturing companies, such as purchasing, engineering, and accounting.

To illustrate, the static budget for the Assembly Department of Jewett Manufacturing Company is shown in Exhibit 4.

Exhibit 4
Static Budget

	A	B
1	Jewett Manufacturing Company	
2	Assembly Department Budget	
3	For the Year Ending July 31, 20Y7	
4	Direct labor	$40,000
5	Electric power	5,000
6	Supervisor salaries	15,000
7	Total department costs	$60,000
8		

A disadvantage of static budgets is that they do not adjust for changes in activity levels. For example, assume that the Assembly Department of Jewett Manufacturing spent $70,800 for the year ended July 31, 20Y7. Thus, the Assembly Department spent $10,800 ($70,800 − $60,000), or 18% ($10,800 ÷ $60,000) more than budgeted. Is this good news or bad news?

The first reaction is that this is bad news and the Assembly Department was inefficient in spending more than budgeted. However, assume that the Assembly Department's budget was based on plans to assemble 8,000 units during the year. If 10,000 units were actually assembled, the additional $10,800 spent in excess of budget might be good news. That is, the Assembly Department assembled 25% (2,000 units ÷ 8,000 units) more than planned for only 18% [$10,800 ÷ $60,000] more cost.

Flexible Budget Unlike static budgets, **flexible budgets** show the expected results of a responsibility center for several activity levels. A flexible budget is, in effect, a series of static budgets for different levels of activity.

To illustrate, a flexible budget for the Assembly Department of Jewett Manufacturing Company is shown in Exhibit 5.

Exhibit 5
Flexible Budget

	A	B	C	D
1	Jewett Manufacturing Company			
2	Assembly Department Budget			
3	For the Year Ending July 31, 20Y7			
4				
5	Units of production	8,000	9,000	10,000 ← Step 1
6	Variable cost:			
7	Direct labor ($5 per unit)	$40,000	$45,000	$50,000
8	Electric power ($0.50 per unit)	4,000	4,500	5,000
9	Total variable cost	$44,000	$49,500	$55,000
10	Fixed cost:			
11	Electric power	$ 1,000	$ 1,000	$ 1,000
12	Supervisor salaries	15,000	15,000	15,000
13	Total fixed cost	$16,000	$16,000	$16,000
14	Total department costs	$60,000	$65,500	$71,000

Step 2 (rows 6–12)

Step 3 (row 14)

A flexible budget is constructed as follows:

Step 1. Identify the relevant activity levels. The relevant levels of activity could be expressed in units, machine hours, direct labor hours, or some other activity base. In Exhibit 5, the levels of activity are 8,000, 9,000, and 10,000 units of production.

Step 2. Identify the fixed and variable cost components of the costs being budgeted. In Exhibit 5, the electric power cost is separated into its fixed cost ($1,000 per year) and variable cost ($0.50 per unit). The direct labor is a variable cost, and the supervisor salaries are fixed costs.

Step 3. Prepare the budget for each activity level by multiplying the variable cost per unit by the activity level and then adding the fixed cost.

With a flexible budget, actual costs can be compared to the budgeted costs for the actual activity level. To illustrate, assume that the Assembly Department spent $70,800 to produce 10,000 units. Exhibit 5 indicates that the Assembly Department was *under* budget by $200 ($71,000 − $70,800).

Under the static budget in Exhibit 4, the Assembly Department was $10,800 *over* budget. This comparison is illustrated in Exhibit 6.

Exhibit 6 Static and Flexible Budgets

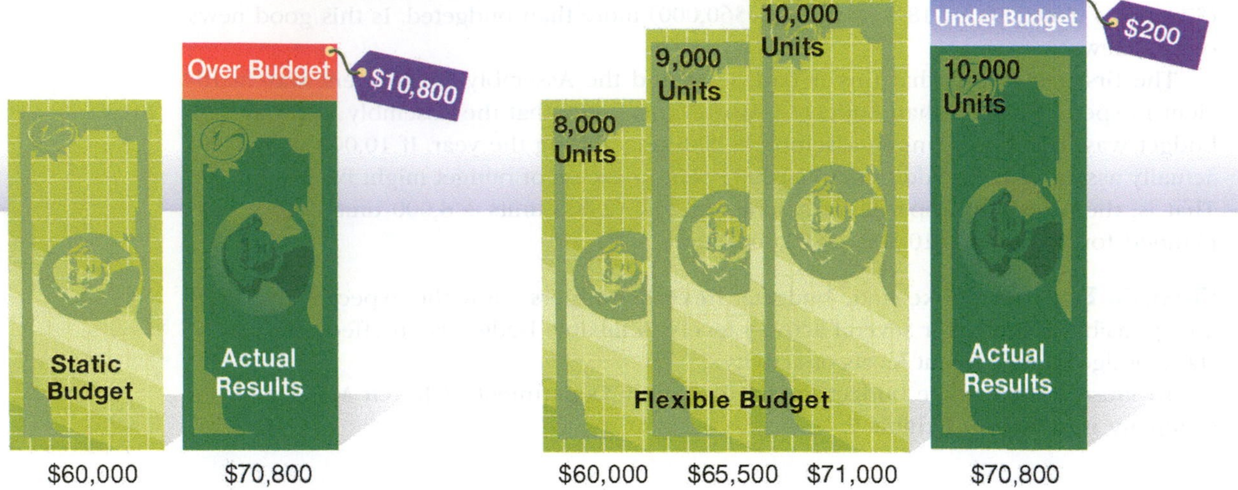

The flexible budget for the Assembly Department is much more accurate and useful than the static budget. This is because the flexible budget adjusts for changes in the level of activity.

Computerized Budgeting Systems

In developing budgets, companies use a variety of computerized approaches. Two of the most popular computerized approaches use:

1. Spreadsheet software such as **Microsoft** Excel
2. Integrated budget and planning (B&P) software systems

Integrated computerized budget and planning systems speed up and reduce the cost of preparing the budget. This is especially true when large quantities of data need to be processed.

B&P software systems are also useful in continuous budgeting. For example, the latest B&P systems use the Web to link thousands of employees together during the budget process. Employees can input budget data onto Web pages that are integrated and summarized throughout the company. In this way, a company can quickly and consistently integrate top-level strategies and goals with lower-level operational goals. These latest B&P software systems are moving companies closer to the real-time budget, wherein the budget is being "rolled" every day.[1]

Companies may also use computer simulation models to analyze the impact of various assumptions and operating alternatives on the budget. For example, the budget can be revised to show the impact of a proposed change in indirect labor wage rates. Likewise, the budgetary effect of a proposed product line can be determined.

1. Janet Kersnar, "Rolling Along," *CFO Europe*, September 14, 2004.

Build versus Harvest

NEIL FRASER/ALAMY STOCK PHOTO

Budgeting systems are not "one-size-fits-all" solutions but must adapt to the underlying business conditions. For example, a business can adopt either a build strategy or a harvest strategy. A *build* strategy is one where the business is designing, launching, and growing new products and markets. Build strategies often require short-term profit sacrifice in order to grow market share. **Apple Inc.**'s iPhone® is an example of a product managed under a build strategy. A *harvest* strategy is often employed for business units with mature products enjoying high market share in low-growth industries. **H.J. Heinz Company**'s Ketchup® and **P&G**'s *Ivory* soap are examples of such products. A build strategy often has greater uncertainty, unpredictability, and change than a harvest strategy. The difference between these strategies implies different budgeting approaches.

The build strategy should employ a budget approach that is flexible to the uncertainty of the business. Thus, budgets should adapt to changing conditions by allowing periodic revisions and flexible targets. The budget serves as a short-term planning tool to guide management in executing an uncertain and evolving product market strategy.

In a harvest strategy, the business is often much more stable and is managed to maximize profitability and cash flow. Because cost control is much more important in this strategy, the budget is used to restrict the actions of managers.

Master Budget

Objective 2
Describe and prepare a master budget for a manufacturing company.

The **master budget** is an integrated set of operating, investing, and financing budgets for a period of time. Most companies prepare the master budget on a yearly basis.

For a manufacturing company, the master budget consists of the following integrated budgets:

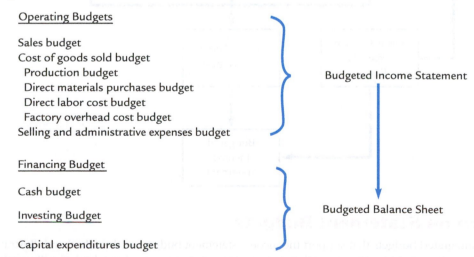

Operating Budgets

- Sales budget
- Cost of goods sold budget
  - Production budget
  - Direct materials purchases budget
  - Direct labor cost budget
  - Factory overhead cost budget
- Selling and administrative expenses budget

→ Budgeted Income Statement

Financing Budget

- Cash budget

Investing Budget

- Capital expenditures budget

→ Budgeted Balance Sheet

The master budget is an integrated set of budgets that tie together a company's operating, financing, and investing activities into an integrated plan for the coming year (period).

The master budget begins with preparing the operating budgets, which form the budgeted income statement. The income statement budgets are normally prepared in the following order beginning with the sales budget:

1. Sales budget
2. Production budget
3. Direct materials purchases budget
4. Direct labor cost budget
5. Factory overhead cost budget
6. Cost of goods sold budget
7. Selling and administrative expenses budget
8. Budgeted income statement

After the budgeted income statement is prepared, the budgeted balance sheet is prepared. Two major budgets comprising the budgeted balance sheet are the cash budget and the capital expenditures budget.

Exhibit 7 shows the relationships among the income statement budgets.

Exhibit 7
Income Statement Budgets

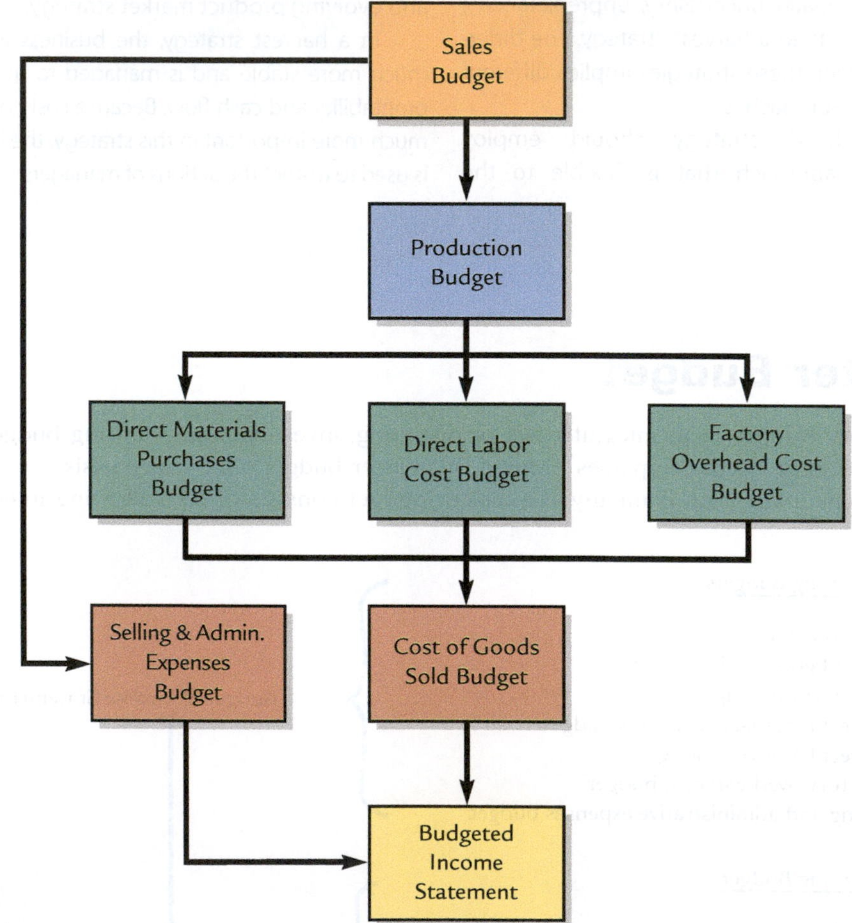

Income Statement Budgets

The integrated budgets that support the income statement budget are described and illustrated in this section. Cobbler Inc., a small manufacturing company, is used as a basis for illustration.

Sales Budget The **sales budget** begins by estimating the quantity of sales. As a starting point, the prior year's sales quantities are often used. These sales quantities are then revised for such factors as the following:

1. Backlog of unfilled sales orders from the prior period
2. Planned advertising and promotion
3. Productive capacity
4. Projected pricing changes
5. Findings of market research studies
6. Expected industry and general economic conditions

Once sales quantities are estimated, the expected sales revenue can be determined by multiplying the volume by the expected unit sales price.

To illustrate, Cobbler Inc. manufactures shoes and boots that are sold in two regions, the East and West Regions. Cobbler estimates the following sales quantities and prices for 20Y5:

	East Region	West Region	Unit Selling Price
Shoes	287,000	241,000	$12
Boots	156,400	123,600	25

Exhibit 8 illustrates the sales budget for Cobbler based on the preceding data.

Exhibit 8
Sales Budget

	A	B	C	D
1	Cobbler Inc.			
2	Sales Budget			
3	For the Year Ending December 31, 20Y5			
4		Unit Sales	Unit Selling	
5	Product and Region	Volume	Price	Total Sales
6	Shoes:			
7	East	287,000	$12.00	$ 3,444,000
8	West	241,000	12.00	2,892,000
9	Total	528,000		$ 6,336,000
10				
11	Boots:			
12	East	156,400	$25.00	$ 3,910,000
13	West	123,600	25.00	3,090,000
14	Total	280,000		$ 7,000,000
15				
16	Total revenue from sales			$13,336,000

In a recent year, **Hendrick** Automotive Group generated over $7 billion of revenue across 13 states.

Hendrick Motorsports Connection

Production Budget The production budget should be integrated with the sales budget to ensure that production and sales are kept in balance during the year. The **production budget** estimates the number of units to be manufactured to meet budgeted sales and desired inventory levels.

The budgeted units to be produced are determined as follows:

Expected units to be sold	XXX units
Plus desired units in ending inventory	XXX
Less estimated units in beginning inventory	(XXX)
Total units to be produced	XXX units

Cobbler Inc. expects the following inventories of shoes and boots:

	Estimated Inventory, January 1, 20Y5	Desired Inventory, December 31, 20Y5
Shoes	88,000	80,000
Boots	48,000	60,000

Exhibit 9 illustrates the production budget for Cobbler Inc.

Exhibit 9
Production Budget

	A	B	C
1	Cobbler Inc.		
2	Production Budget		
3	For the Year Ending December 31, 20Y5		
4		Units	
5		Shoes	Boots
6	Expected units to be sold (from Exhibit 8)	528,000	280,000
7	Plus desired ending inventory, December 31, 20Y5	80,000	60,000
8	Total	608,000	340,000
9	Less estimated beginning inventory, January 1, 20Y5	(88,000)	(48,000)
10	Total units to be produced	520,000	292,000

Direct Materials Purchases Budget The direct materials purchases budget should be integrated with the production budget to ensure that production is not interrupted during the year. The **direct materials purchases budget** estimates the quantities of direct materials to be purchased to support budgeted production and desired inventory levels.

The direct materials to be purchased are determined as follows:

Materials required for production	XXX
Plus desired ending materials inventory	XXX
Less estimated beginning materials inventory	(XXX)
Direct materials to be purchased	XXX

Cobbler Inc. uses leather and lining in producing shoes and boots. The quantity of direct materials expected to be used for each unit of product is as follows:

Shoes	Boots
Leather: 0.30 sq. yd. per unit	Leather: 1.25 sq. yds. per unit
Lining: 0.10 sq. yd. per unit	Lining: 0.50 sq. yd. per unit

Cobbler Inc. expects the following direct materials inventories of leather and lining:

	Estimated Direct Materials Inventory, January 1, 20Y5	Desired Direct Materials Inventory, December 31, 20Y5
Leather	18,000 sq. yds.	20,000 sq. yds.
Lining	15,000 sq. yds.	12,000 sq. yds.

The estimated price per square yard of leather and lining during 20Y5 is as follows:

	Price per Square Yard
Leather	$4.50
Lining	1.20

Exhibit 10 illustrates the direct materials purchases budget for Cobbler Inc.

Exhibit 10
Direct Materials Purchases Budget

	A	B	C	D	E
1		**Cobbler Inc.**			
2		**Direct Materials Purchases Budget**			
3		**For the Year Ending December 31, 20Y5**			
4			**Direct Materials**		
5			**Leather**	**Lining**	**Total**
6	Square yards required for production:				
7	Shoes (Note A)		156,000	52,000	
8	Boots (Note B)		365,000	146,000	
9	Plus desired inventory, December 31, 20Y5		20,000	12,000	
10	Total		541,000	210,000	
11	Less estimated inventory, January 1, 20Y5		(18,000)	(15,000)	
12	Total square yards to be purchased		523,000	195,000	
13	Unit price (per square yard)		× $4.50	× $1.20	
14	Total direct materials to be purchased		$2,353,500	$234,000	$2,587,500
15					
16	Note A:	Leather: 520,000 units × 0.30 sq. yd. per unit = 156,000 sq. yds.			
17		Lining: 520,000 units × 0.10 sq. yd. per unit = 52,000 sq. yds.			
18					
19	Note B:	Leather: 292,000 units × 1.25 sq. yds. per unit = 365,000 sq. yds.			
20		Lining: 292,000 units × 0.50 sq. yd. per unit = 146,000 sq. yds.			

The timing of the direct materials purchases should be coordinated between the Purchasing and Production departments so that production is not interrupted.

Hendrick Motorsports Connection

Hendrick Motorsports uses sheet metal in building its race cars. "Used" sections of sheet metal (from crashed cars) can be purchased from its online store.

Direct Labor Cost Budget The **direct labor cost budget** estimates the direct labor hours and related cost needed to support budgeted production.

Cobbler Inc. estimates that the following direct labor hours are needed to produce shoes and boots:

Shoes	Boots
Cutting Department: 0.10 hr. per unit	Cutting Department: 0.15 hr. per unit
Sewing Department: 0.25 hr. per unit	Sewing Department: 0.40 hr. per unit

The estimated direct labor hourly rates for the Cutting and Sewing departments during 20Y5 are as follows:

	Hourly Rate
Cutting Department	$12.00
Sewing Department	15.00

Exhibit 11 illustrates the direct labor cost budget for Cobbler Inc. For Cobbler Inc. to produce 520,000 shoes, 52,000 hours (520,000 units × 0.10 hr. per unit) of labor are required in the Cutting Department. Likewise, to produce 292,000 boots, 43,800 hours (292,000 units × 0.15 hour per unit) of labor are required in the Cutting Department. Thus, the estimated total direct labor cost for the Cutting Department is $1,149,600 [(52,000 hrs. + 43,800 hrs.) × $12.00 per hr.)]. In a similar manner, the direct labor hours and cost for the Sewing Department are determined.

Exhibit 11
Direct Labor Cost Budget

	A	B	C	D	E
1	Cobbler Inc.				
2	Direct Labor Cost Budget				
3	For the Year Ending December 31, 20Y5				
4			Cutting	Sewing	Total
5	Hours required for production:				
6	Shoes (Note A)		52,000	130,000	
7	Boots (Note B)		43,800	116,800	
8	Total		95,800	246,800	
9	Hourly rate		× $12.00	× $15.00	
10	Total direct labor cost		$1,149,600	$3,702,000	$4,851,600
11					
12	Note A:	Cutting Department: 520,000 units × 0.10 hr. per unit = 52,000 hrs.			
13		Sewing Department: 520,000 units × 0.25 hr. per unit = 130,000 hrs.			
14					
15	Note B:	Cutting Department: 292,000 units × 0.15 hr. per unit = 43,800 hrs.			
16		Sewing Department: 292,000 units × 0.40 hr. per unit = 116,800 hrs.			

The direct labor needs should be coordinated between the Production and Personnel departments so that there will be enough labor available for production.

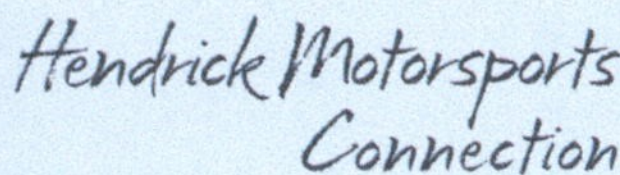

Hendrick Motorports offers an internship program for college students who want to experience and learn the operations of a NASCAR team.

Factory Overhead Cost Budget The **factory overhead cost budget** estimates the cost for each item of factory overhead needed to support budgeted production. Exhibit 12 illustrates the factory overhead cost budget for Cobbler Inc.

Exhibit 12
Factory Overhead Cost Budget

	A	B
1	Cobbler Inc.	
2	Factory Overhead Cost Budget	
3	For the Year Ending December 31, 20Y5	
4	Indirect factory wages	$ 732,800
5	Supervisor salaries	360,000
6	Power and light	306,000
7	Depreciation of plant and equipment	288,000
8	Indirect materials	182,800
9	Maintenance	140,280
10	Insurance and property taxes	79,200
11	Total factory overhead cost	$2,089,080

The factory overhead cost budget shown in Exhibit 12 may be supported by departmental schedules. Such schedules normally separate factory overhead costs into fixed and variable costs to better enable department managers to monitor and evaluate costs during the year.

The factory overhead cost budget should be integrated with the production budget to ensure that production is not interrupted during the year.

Cost of Goods Sold Budget The **cost of goods sold budget** is prepared by integrating the following budgets:

1. Direct materials purchases budget (Exhibit 10)
2. Direct labor cost budget (Exhibit 11)
3. Factory overhead cost budget (Exhibit 12)

In addition, the estimated and desired inventories for direct materials, work in process, and finished goods must be integrated into the cost of goods sold budget.

Cobbler Inc. expects the following direct materials, work in process, and finished goods inventories:

	Estimated Inventory, January 1, 20Y5		Desired Inventory, December 31, 20Y5	
Direct materials:				
Leather	$ 81,000	(18,000 sq. yds. × $4.50)	$ 90,000	(20,000 sq. yds. × $4.50)
Lining	18,000	(15,000 sq. yds. × $1.20)	14,400	(12,000 sq. yds. × $1.20)
Total direct materials	$ 99,000		$ 104,400	
Work in process:	$ 214,400		$ 220,000	
Finished goods:	$1,095,600		$1,565,000	

Exhibit 13 illustrates the cost of goods sold budget for Cobbler Inc. It indicates that total manufacturing costs of $9,522,780 are budgeted to be incurred in 20Y5. Of this total, $2,582,100 is budgeted for direct materials, $4,851,600 is budgeted for direct labor, and $2,089,080 is budgeted for factory overhead. After considering work in process inventories, the total budgeted cost of goods manufactured and transferred to finished goods during 20Y5 is $9,517,180. Based on expected sales, the budgeted cost of goods sold is $9,047,780.

Exhibit 13 Cost of Goods Sold Budget

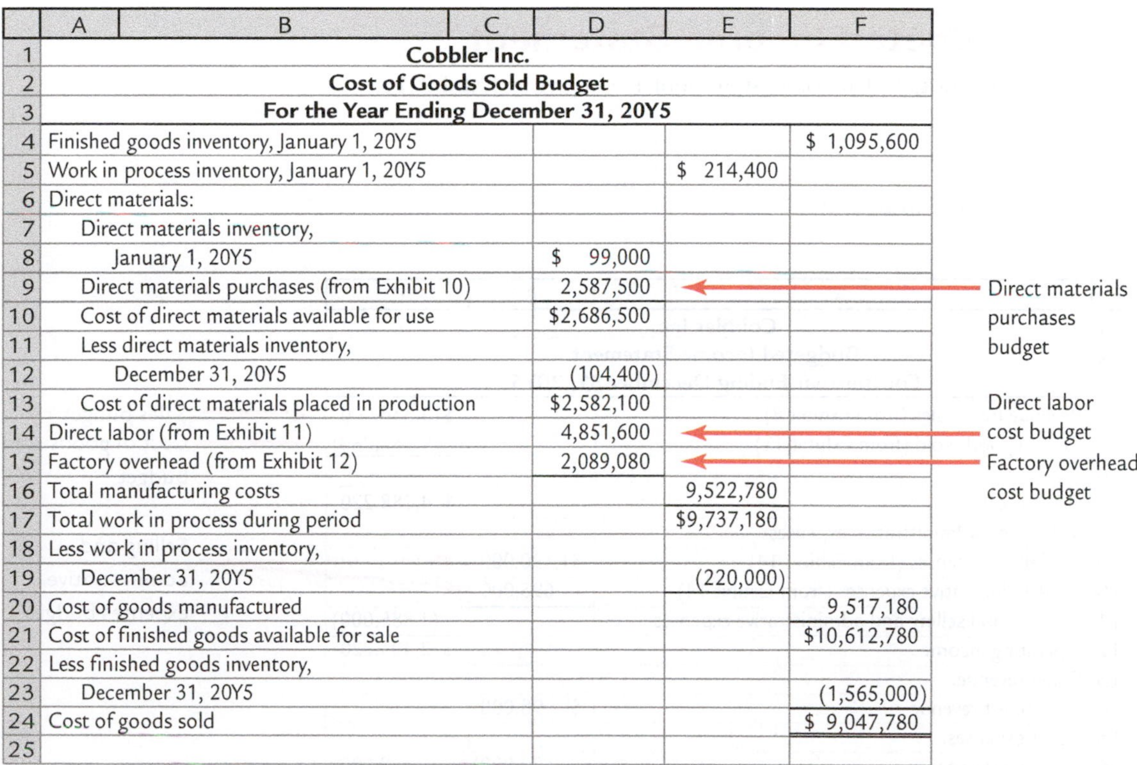

	A–C	D	E	F
1	**Cobbler Inc.**			
2	**Cost of Goods Sold Budget**			
3	**For the Year Ending December 31, 20Y5**			
4	Finished goods inventory, January 1, 20Y5			$ 1,095,600
5	Work in process inventory, January 1, 20Y5		$ 214,400	
6	Direct materials:			
7	Direct materials inventory,			
8	January 1, 20Y5	$ 99,000		
9	Direct materials purchases (from Exhibit 10)	2,587,500		
10	Cost of direct materials available for use	$2,686,500		
11	Less direct materials inventory,			
12	December 31, 20Y5	(104,400)		
13	Cost of direct materials placed in production	$2,582,100		
14	Direct labor (from Exhibit 11)	4,851,600		
15	Factory overhead (from Exhibit 12)	2,089,080		
16	Total manufacturing costs		9,522,780	
17	Total work in process during period		$9,737,180	
18	Less work in process inventory,			
19	December 31, 20Y5		(220,000)	
20	Cost of goods manufactured			9,517,180
21	Cost of finished goods available for sale			$10,612,780
22	Less finished goods inventory,			
23	December 31, 20Y5			(1,565,000)
24	Cost of goods sold			$ 9,047,780
25				

Selling and Administrative Expenses Budget The sales budget is often used as the starting point for the selling and administrative expenses budget. For example, a budgeted increase in sales may require more advertising expenses.

Exhibit 14 illustrates the selling and administrative expenses budget for Cobbler Inc. The selling and administrative expenses budget shown in Exhibit 14 is normally supported by departmental schedules. For example, an advertising expense schedule for the Marketing Department could include the advertising media to be used (newspaper, direct mail, television), quantities (column inches, number of pieces, minutes), the cost per unit, and related costs per unit.

Exhibit 14 Selling and Administrative Expenses Budget

	A	B	C
1	**Cobbler Inc.**		
2	**Selling and Administrative Expenses Budget**		
3	**For the Year Ending December 31, 20Y5**		
4	Selling expenses:		
5	Sales salaries expense	$715,000	
6	Advertising expense	360,000	
7	Travel expense	115,000	
8	Total selling expenses		$1,190,000
9	Administrative expenses:		
10	Officers' salaries expense	$360,000	
11	Office salaries expense	258,000	
12	Office rent expense	34,500	
13	Office supplies expense	17,500	
14	Miscellaneous administrative expenses	25,000	
15	Total administrative expenses		695,000
16	Total selling and administrative expenses		$1,885,000

Budgeted Income Statement

The budgeted income statement is shown in Exhibit 15.

Exhibit 15 Budgeted Income Statement

	A	B	C
1	**Cobbler Inc.**		
2	**Budgeted Income Statement**		
3	**For the Year Ending December 31, 20Y5**		
4	Revenue from sales (from Exhibit 8)		$13,336,000
5	Cost of goods sold (from Exhibit 13)		(9,047,780)
6			
7	Gross profit		$ 4,288,220
8	Selling and administrative expenses:		
9	Selling expenses (from Exhibit 14)	$1,190,000	
10	Administrative expenses (from Exhibit 14)	695,000	
11	Total selling and administrative expenses		(1,885,000)
12	Operating income		$ 2,403,220
13	Other revenue:		
14	Interest revenue	$ 98,000	
15	Other expenses:		
16	Interest expense	(90,000)	8,000
17	Income before income tax		$ 2,411,220
18	Income tax		(600,000)
19	Net income		$ 1,811,220
20			

Sales budget

Cost of goods sold budget

Selling and administrative expenses budget

The budgeted income statement is prepared by integrating the following budgets:

1. Sales budget (Exhibit 8)
2. Cost of goods sold budget (Exhibit 13)
3. Selling and administrative expenses budget (Exhibit 14)

In addition, estimates of other income, other expense, and income tax are also integrated into the budgeted income statement.

Exhibit 15 illustrates the budgeted income statement for Cobbler Inc. This budget summarizes the budgeted operating activities of the company. In doing so, the budgeted income statement allows management to assess the effects of estimated sales, costs, and expenses on profits for the year.

Balance Sheet Budgets

While the income statement budgets reflect the operating activities of the company, the balance sheet budgets reflect the financing and investing activities. In this section, the following balance sheet budgets are described and illustrated:

1. Cash budget (financing activity)
2. Capital expenditures budget (investing activity)

Cash Budget The **cash budget** estimates the expected receipts (inflows) and payments (outflows) of cash for a period of time. The cash budget is integrated with the various operating budgets. In addition, the capital expenditures budget, dividends, and equity or long-term debt financing plans of the company affect the cash budget.

To illustrate, a monthly cash budget for January, February, and March 20Y5 for Cobbler Inc. is prepared. The preparation of the cash budget begins by estimating cash receipts.

Estimated Cash Receipts The primary source of estimated cash receipts is from cash sales and collections on account. In addition, cash receipts may be obtained from plans to issue equity or debt financing as well as other sources such as interest revenue.

To estimate cash receipts from cash sales and collections on account, a *schedule of collections from sales* is prepared. To illustrate, the following data for Cobbler Inc. are used:

	January	February	March
Sales:			
Budgeted sales	$1,080,000	$1,240,000	$970,000
Percent of cash sales	10%	10%	10%
Accounts receivable, January 1, 20Y5	$ 370,000		
Receipts from sales on account:			
From prior month's sales on account	40%		
From current month's sales on account	60		
	100%		

Using the preceding data, the schedule of collections from sales is prepared, as shown in Exhibit 16. Cash sales are determined by multiplying the percent of cash sales by the monthly budgeted sales. The cash receipts from sales on account are determined by adding the cash received from the prior month's sales on account (40%) and the cash received from the current month's sales on account (60%). To simplify, it is assumed that all accounts receivable are collected.

Estimated Cash Payments Estimated cash payments must be budgeted for operating costs and expenses such as manufacturing costs, selling expenses, and administrative expenses. In addition, estimated cash payments may be planned for capital expenditures, dividends, interest payments, or long-term debt payments.

Exhibit 16
Schedule of Collections from Sales

	A	B	C	D	E
1		**Cobbler Inc.**			
2		**Schedule of Collections from Sales**			
3		**For the Three Months Ending March 31, 20Y5**			
4			**January**	**February**	**March**
5	Receipts from cash sales:				
6		Cash sales (10% × current month's sales—			
7		Note A)	$108,000	$ 124,000	$ 97,000
8					
9	Receipts from sales on account:				
10		Collections from prior month's sales (40% of			
11		previous month's credit sales—Note B)	$370,000	$ 388,800	$446,400
12		Collections from current month's sales (60%			
13		of current month's credit sales—Note C)	583,200	669,600	523,800
14	Total receipts from sales on account		$953,200	$1,058,400	$970,200
15					
16	Note A:	$108,000 = $1,080,000 × 10%			
17		$124,000 = $1,240,000 × 10%			
18		$ 97,000 = $ 970,000 × 10%			
19					
20	Note B:	$370,000, given as January 1, 20Y5, Accounts Receivable balance			
21		$388,800 = $1,080,000 × 90% × 40%			
22		$446,400 = $1,240,000 × 90% × 40%			
23					
24	Note C:	$583,200 = $1,080,000 × 90% × 60%			
25		$669,600 = $1,240,000 × 90% × 60%			
26		$523,800 = $ 970,000 × 90% × 60%			

To estimate cash payments for manufacturing costs, a *schedule of payments for manufacturing costs* is prepared. To illustrate, the following data for Cobbler Inc. are used:

	January	February	March
Manufacturing Costs:			
Budgeted manufacturing costs	$840,000	$780,000	$812,000
Depreciation on machines included in manufacturing costs	24,000	24,000	24,000
Accounts Payable:			
Accounts payable, January 1, 20Y5	$190,000		
Payments of manufacturing costs on account:			
From prior month's manufacturing costs	25%		
From current month's manufacturing costs	75		
	100%		

Using the preceding data, the schedule of payments for manufacturing costs is prepared, as shown in Exhibit 17. The cash payments are determined by adding the cash paid on costs incurred from the prior month (25%) to the cash paid on costs incurred in the current month (75%). The $24,000 of depreciation is excluded from all computations, since depreciation does not require a cash payment.

Completing the Cash Budget Assume the following additional data for Cobbler Inc.

Cash balance on January 1, 20Y5	$280,000
Quarterly taxes paid on March 31, 20Y5	150,000
Quarterly interest expense paid on January 10, 20Y5	22,500
Quarterly interest revenue received on March 21, 20Y5	24,500
Sewing equipment purchased in February 20Y5	274,000
Selling and administrative expenses (paid in month incurred):	

January	February	March
$160,000	$165,000	$145,000

Exhibit 17 Schedule of Payments for Manufacturing Costs

	A	B	C	D	E
1		**Cobbler Inc.**			
2		**Schedule of Payments for Manufacturing Costs**			
3		**For the Three Months Ending March 31, 20Y5**			
4			**January**	**February**	**March**
5	Payments of prior month's manufacturing costs				
6	{[25% × previous month's manufacturing costs				
7	(less depreciation)]—Note A}		$190,000	$204,000	$189,000
8	Payments of current month's manufacturing costs				
9	{[75% × current month's manufacturing costs				
10	(less depreciation)]—Note B}		612,000	567,000	591,000
11	Total payments		$802,000	$771,000	$780,000
12					
13	Note A:	$190,000, given as January 1, 20Y5, Accounts Payable balance			
14		$204,000 = ($840,000 − $24,000) × 25%			
15		$189,000 = ($780,000 − $24,000) × 25%			
16					
17	Note B:	$612,000 = ($840,000 − $24,000) × 75%			
18		$567,000 = ($780,000 − $24,000) × 75%			
19		$591,000 = ($812,000 − $24,000) × 75%			

Using the preceding data, the *cash budget* is prepared, as shown in Exhibit 18. Cobbler Inc. has estimated that a *minimum cash balance* of $340,000 is required at the end of each month to support its operations. This minimum cash balance is compared to the estimated ending cash balance for each month. In this way, any expected cash excess or deficiency is determined.

Exhibit 18 indicates that Cobbler expects a cash excess at the end of January of $16,700. This excess could be invested in temporary income-producing securities such as U.S. Treasury bills or notes. In contrast, the estimated cash deficiency at the end of February of $10,900 might require Cobbler Inc. to borrow cash from its bank.

Exhibit 18 Cash Budget

	A	B	C	D
1	**Cobbler Inc.**			
2	**Cash Budget**			
3	**For the Three Months Ending March 31, 20Y5**			
4		**January**	**February**	**March**
5	Estimated cash receipts from:			
6	Cash sales (from Exhibit 16)	$ 108,000	$ 124,000	$ 97,000
7	Collections of accounts receivable			
8	(from Exhibit 16)	953,200	1,058,400	970,200
9	Interest revenue			24,500
10	Total cash receipts	$1,061,200	$ 1,182,400	$ 1,091,700
11	Estimated cash payments for:			
12	Manufacturing costs (from Exhibit 17)	$ (802,000)	$ (771,000)	$ (780,000)
13	Selling and administrative expenses	(160,000)	(165,000)	(145,000)
14	Capital additions		(274,000)	
15	Interest expense	(22,500)		
16	Income taxes			(150,000)
17	Total cash payments	$ (984,500)	$(1,210,000)	$ (1,075,000)
18	Cash increase (decrease)	$ 76,700	$ (27,600)	$ 16,700
19	Cash balance at beginning of month	280,000	356,700	329,100
20	Cash balance at end of month	$ 356,700	$ 329,100	$ 345,800
21	Minimum cash balance	(340,000)	(340,000)	(340,000)
22	Excess (deficiency)	$ 16,700	$ (10,900)	$ 5,800

Schedule of collections from sales

Schedule of cash payments for manufacturing costs

Capital Expenditures Budget The **capital expenditures budget** summarizes plans for acquiring fixed assets. Such expenditures are necessary as machinery and other fixed assets wear out or become obsolete. In addition, purchasing additional fixed assets may be necessary to meet increasing demand for the company's product.

To illustrate, a five-year capital expenditures budget for Cobbler Inc. is shown in Exhibit 19.

Exhibit 19 Capital Expenditures Budget

	A	B	C	D	E	F
1	**Cobbler Inc.**					
2	**Capital Expenditures Budget**					
3	**For the Five Years Ending December 31, 20Y9**					
4	**Item**	**20Y5**	**20Y6**	**20Y7**	**20Y8**	**20Y9**
5	Machinery—Cutting Department	$400,000			$280,000	$360,000
6	Machinery—Sewing Department	274,000	$260,000	$560,000	200,000	
7	Office equipment		90,000			60,000
8	Total	$674,000	$350,000	$560,000	$480,000	$420,000

As shown in Exhibit 19, capital expenditures budgets are often prepared for five to ten years into the future. This is necessary since fixed assets often must be ordered years in advance. Likewise, it could take years to construct new buildings or other production facilities.

The capital expenditures budget should be integrated with the operating and financing budgets. For example, depreciation of new manufacturing equipment affects the factory overhead cost budget. The plans for financing the capital expenditures also affect the cash budget.

Budgeted Balance Sheet

The budgeted balance sheet is prepared based on the operating, financing, and investing budgets of the master budget. The budgeted balance sheet is dated as of the end of the budget period and is similar to a normal balance sheet except that estimated amounts are used. For this reason, a budgeted balance sheet for Cobbler Inc. is not illustrated.

Objective 3
Describe the types of standards and how they are established.

Standards

Standards are performance goals. Manufacturing companies normally use **standard cost** for each of the three following product costs:

1. Direct materials
2. Direct labor
3. Factory overhead

Accounting systems that use standards for product costs are called **standard cost systems**. Standard cost systems enable management to determine the following:

1. How much a product *should* cost (standard cost)
2. How much it does cost (actual cost)

When actual costs are compared with standard costs, the exceptions or cost variances are reported. This reporting by the *principle of exceptions* allows management to focus on correcting the cost variances.

Setting Standards

The standard-setting process normally requires the joint efforts of accountants, engineers, and other management personnel. The accountant converts the results of judgments and process studies into dollars and cents. Engineers with the aid of operation managers identify the materials, labor, and machine requirements needed to produce a product. For example, engineers estimate direct materials by studying the product specifications and estimating normal spoilage. Time and motion studies may be used to determine the direct labor required for each manufacturing operation. Engineering studies may also be used to determine standards for factory overhead, such as the amount of power needed to operate machinery.

Setting standards often begins with analyzing past operations. However, caution must be used when relying on past cost data. For example, inefficiencies may be contained within past costs. In addition, changes in technology, machinery, or production methods may make past costs irrelevant for future operations.

Types of Standards

Standards imply an acceptable level of production efficiency. One of the major objectives in setting standards is to motivate employees to achieve efficient operations.

Tight, unrealistic standards may have a negative impact on performance. This is because employees may become frustrated with an inability to meet the standards and may give up trying to do their best. Standards that can be achieved only under perfect operating conditions, such as no idle time, no machine breakdowns, and no materials spoilage, are called **ideal standards** or **theoretical standards**.

Standards that are too loose might not motivate employees to perform at their best. This is because the standard level of performance can be reached too easily. As a result, operating performance may be lower than what could be achieved.

Currently attainable standards, sometimes called *normal standards,* are standards that can be attained with reasonable effort. Such standards, which are used by most companies, allow for normal production difficulties and mistakes. For example, currently attainable standards allow for normal materials spoilage and machine breakdowns. When reasonable standards are used, employees focus more on cost and are more likely to put forth their best efforts.

An example from the game of golf illustrates the distinction between ideal and normal standards. In golf, "par" is an ideal standard for most players. Each player's USGA (United States Golf Association) handicap is the player's normal standard. The motivation of average players is to beat their handicaps because beating par is unrealistic for most players.

The difference between currently attainable and ideal standards is illustrated as follows.

Reviewing and Revising Standards

Standard costs should be periodically reviewed to ensure that they reflect current operating conditions. Standards should not be revised, however, just because they differ from actual costs. For example, the direct labor standard would not be revised just because employees are unable to meet properly set standards. On the other hand, standards should be revised when prices, product designs, labor rates, or manufacturing methods change.

Criticisms of Standard Costs

Some criticisms of using standard costs for performance evaluation include the following:

1. Standards limit operating improvements by discouraging improvement beyond the standard.
2. Standards are too difficult to maintain in a dynamic manufacturing environment, resulting in "stale standards."
3. Standards can cause employees to lose sight of the larger objectives of the organization by focusing only on efficiency improvement.
4. Standards can cause employees to unduly focus on their own operations to the possible harm of other operations that rely on them.

Regardless of these criticisms, standards are widely used. In addition, standard costs are only one part of the performance evaluation system used by most companies. As discussed in this chapter, other nonfinancial performance measures are often used to supplement standard costs, with the result that many of the preceding criticisms are overcome.

Hendrick Motorports must conform to NASCAR standards in building its race cars. For example, the rear deck fin of a car must be 3.5 inches tall and a minimum of 17 inches wide.

Integrity, Objectivity, and Ethics in Business

Company Reputation: The Best of the Best

Harris Interactive annually ranks American corporations in terms of reputation. The ranking is based on how respondents rate corporations on 20 attributes in six major areas. The six areas are emotional appeal, products and services, financial performance, workplace environment, social responsibility, and vision and leadership. What are the five highest ranked companies in its recent survey? The five highest (best) ranked companies were **Amazon, Apple, Alphabet (Google), USAA, and The Walt Disney Company.**

Source: Harris Interactive, February, 2016.

Objective 4

Describe and illustrate performance reporting for manufacturing operations.

Budgetary Performance Reporting

As discussed earlier in this chapter, the master budget assists a company in planning, directing, and controlling performance. The control function, or budgetary performance reporting, compares the actual performance against the budget.

To illustrate, Cowpoke Inc., a manufacturer of blue jeans, uses standard costs in its budgets. The standards for direct materials, direct labor, and factory overhead are separated into the following two components:

1. Standard price
2. Standard quantity

The standard cost per unit for direct materials, direct labor, and factory overhead is computed as follows:

Standard Cost per Unit = Standard Price × Standard Quantity

Cowpoke's standard costs per unit for its XL jeans are shown in Exhibit 20.

Exhibit 20
Standard Costs for XL Jeans

Manufacturing Costs	Standard Price	×	Standard Quantity per Pair	=	Standard Cost per Pair of XL Jeans
Direct materials	$5.00 per sq. yd.		1.5 sq. yds.		$ 7.50
Direct labor	$9.00 per hr.		0.80 hr. per pair		7.20
Factory overhead	$6.00 per hr.		0.80 hr. per pair		4.80
Total standard cost per pair					$19.50

As shown in Exhibit 20, the standard cost per pair of XL jeans is $19.50, which consists of $7.50 for direct materials, $7.20 for direct labor, and $4.80 for factory overhead.

The standard price and standard quantity are separated for each product cost. For example, Exhibit 20 indicates that for each pair of XL jeans, the standard price for direct materials is $5.00 per square yard and the standard quantity is 1.5 square yards. The standard price and quantity are separated because the department responsible for their control is normally different. For example, the direct materials price per square yard is controlled by the Purchasing Department, and the direct materials quantity per pair is controlled by the Production Department.

As illustrated earlier in this chapter, the master budget is prepared based on planned sales and production. The budgeted costs for materials purchases, direct labor, and factory overhead are determined by multiplying their standard costs per unit by the planned level of production. Budgeted (standard) costs are then compared to actual costs during the year for control purposes.

Budget Performance Report

The report that summarizes actual costs, standard costs, and the differences for the units produced is called a **budget performance report**. To illustrate, assume that Cowpoke Inc. produced the following pairs of jeans during June 20Y8:

XL jeans produced and sold	5,000 pairs
Actual costs incurred in June:	
Direct materials	$ 40,150
Direct labor	38,500
Factory overhead	22,400
Total costs incurred	$101,050

Exhibit 21 illustrates the budget performance report for June for Cowpoke Inc. The report summarizes the actual costs, standard costs, and the differences for each product cost. The differences between actual and standard costs are called **cost variances**. A **favorable cost variance** occurs when the actual cost is less than the standard cost. An **unfavorable cost variance** occurs when the actual cost exceeds the standard cost.

The budget performance report shown in Exhibit 21 is based on the actual units produced in June of 5,000 XL jeans. Even though 6,000 XL jeans might have been *planned* for production, the budget performance report is based on *actual* production.

Exhibit 21 Budget Performance Report

Cowpoke Inc.
Budget Performance Report
For the Month Ended June 30, 20Y8

Manufacturing Costs	Actual Costs	Standard Cost at Actual Volume (5,000 pairs of XL Jeans)*	Cost Variance—(Favorable) Unfavorable
Direct materials	$ 40,150	$37,500	$ 2,650
Direct labor	38,500	36,000	2,500
Factory overhead	22,400	24,000	(1,600)
Total manufacturing costs	$101,050	$97,500	$ 3,550

*5,000 pairs × $7.50 per pair = $37,500
5,000 pairs × $7.20 per pair = $36,000
5,000 pairs × $4.80 per pair = $24,000

Manufacturing Cost Variances

The **total manufacturing cost variance** is the difference between total standard costs and total actual cost for the units produced. As shown in Exhibit 21, the total manufacturing cost unfavorable variance and the variance for each product cost are as follows:

	Cost Variance (Favorable) Unfavorable
Direct materials	$ 2,650
Direct labor	2,500
Factory overhead	(1,600)
Total manufacturing variance	$ 3,550

For control purposes, each product cost variance is separated into two additional variances as shown in Exhibit 22. The total direct materials variance is separated into a

Exhibit 22 Manufacturing Cost Variances

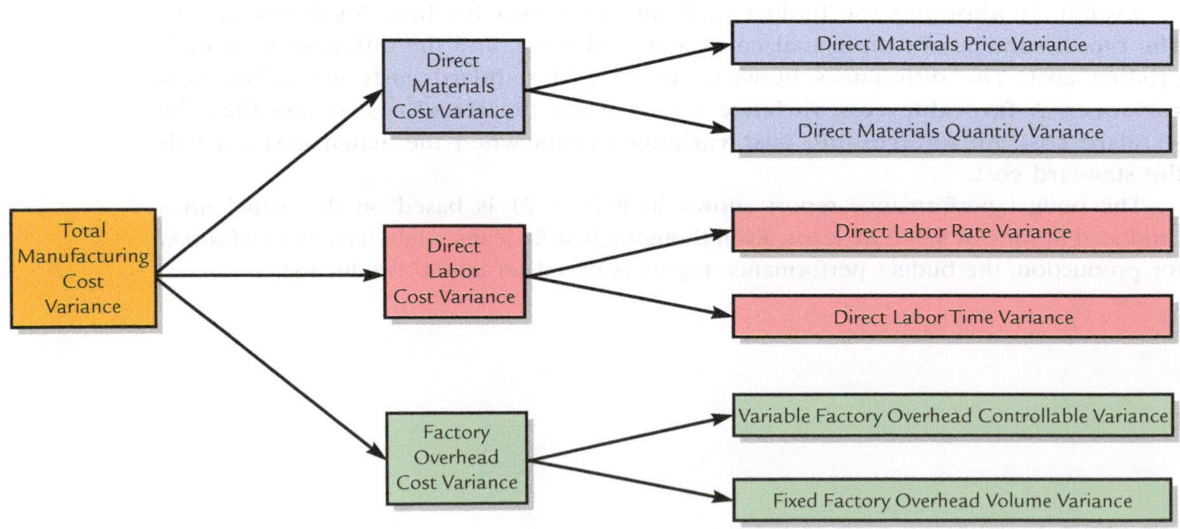

price and *quantity* variance. This is because standard and actual direct materials costs are computed as follows:

Cost		Price		Quantity
Actual Direct Materials Cost	=	Actual Price	×	Actual Quantity
(Standard Direct Materials Cost)	=	(Standard Price)	×	(Standard Quantity)
Direct Materials Cost Variance	=	Price Difference	×	Quantity Difference

Thus, the actual and standard direct materials costs may differ because of either a price difference (variance) or a quantity difference (variance).

Likewise, the total direct labor variance is separated into a *rate* and a *time* variance. This is because standard and actual direct labor costs are computed as follows:

Cost		Rate		Time
Actual Direct Labor Cost	=	Actual Rate	×	Actual Time
(Standard Direct Labor Cost)	=	(Standard Rate)	×	(Standard Time)
Direct Labor Cost Variance	=	Rate Difference	×	Time Difference

Therefore, the actual and standard direct labor costs may differ because of either a rate difference (variance) or a time difference (variance).

The total factory overhead variance is separated into a *controllable* and *volume* variance. Because factory overhead has fixed and variable cost elements, it is more complex to analyze than direct materials and direct labor, which are variable costs. The controllable variance is similar to a price or rate variance, and the volume variance is similar to the quantity or time variance.

In the next section, the price and quantity variances for direct materials and the rate and time variances for direct labor are described and illustrated. The controllable and volume variances for factory overhead are described and illustrated in the appendix to this chapter.

Direct Materials and Direct Labor Variances

Objective 5
Compute and interpret direct materials and direct labor variances.

As indicated in the prior section, the total direct materials and direct labor variances are separated into the following variances for analysis and control purposes:

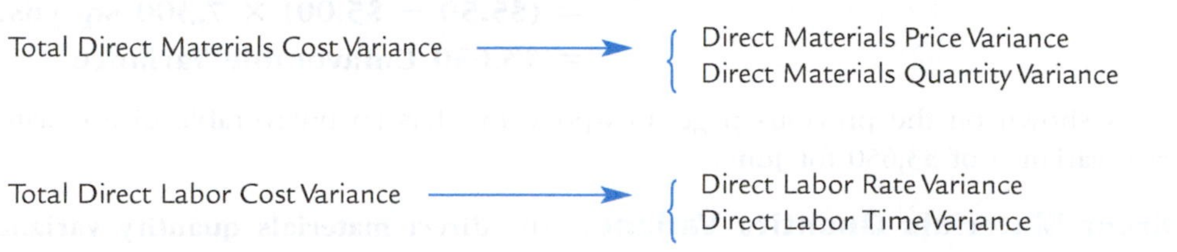

As a basis for illustration, the variances for Cowpoke Inc.'s June operations shown in Exhibit 21 are used.

Direct Materials Variances

During June, Cowpoke Inc. reported an unfavorable total direct materials cost variance of $2,650 for the production of 5,000 XL style jeans, as shown in Exhibit 21. This variance was based on the following actual and standard costs:

Actual costs	$40,150
Standard costs	(37,500)
Total direct materials cost variance	$ 2,650

The actual costs incurred of $40,150 consist of the following:

Actual Direct Materials Cost = Actual Price × Actual Quantity
= $5.50 per sq. yd. × 7,300 sq. yds.
= $40,150

The standard costs of $37,500 consist of the following:

Standard Direct Materials Cost = Standard Price × Standard Quantity
= $5.00 per sq. yd. × 7,500 sq. yds.
= $37,500

The standard price of $5.00 per square yard is taken from Exhibit 20. In addition, Exhibit 20 indicates that 1.5 square yards is the standard for producing one pair of XL jeans. Thus, 7,500 (5,000 × 1.5) square yards is the standard for producing 5,000 pairs of XL jeans.

Comparing the actual and standard cost computations shown above indicates that the total direct materials unfavorable cost variance of $2,650 is caused by the following:

1. A price per square yard of $0.50 ($5.50 − $5.00) more than standard
2. A quantity usage of 200 square yards (7,300 sq. yds. − 7,500 sq. yds.) less than standard

The impact of these differences from standard is reported and analyzed as a direct materials *price* variance and direct materials *quantity* variance.

Direct Materials Price Variance The **direct materials price variance** is computed as follows:

Direct Materials Price Variance = (Actual Price − Standard Price)
× Actual Quantity

If the actual price per unit exceeds the standard price per unit, the variance is unfavorable. This positive amount (unfavorable variance) can be thought of as increasing costs. If the actual price per unit is less than the standard price per unit, the variance is favorable. This negative amount (favorable variance) can be thought of as decreasing costs.

To illustrate, the direct materials price variance for Cowpoke Inc. is computed as follows:[2]

Direct Materials Price Variance = (Actual Price − Standard Price)
× Actual Quantity
= ($5.50 − $5.00) × 7,300 sq. yds.
= $3,650 Unfavorable Variance

As shown on the previous page, Cowpoke Inc. has an unfavorable direct materials price variance of $3,650 for June.

Direct Materials Quantity Variance The **direct materials quantity variance** is computed as follows:

Direct Materials Quantity Variance = (Actual Quantity − Standard Quantity)
× Standard Price

If the actual quantity for the units produced exceeds the standard quantity, the variance is unfavorable. This positive amount (unfavorable variance) can be thought of as increasing costs. If the actual quantity for the units produced is less than the standard quantity, the variance is favorable. This negative amount (favorable variance) can be thought of as decreasing costs.

2. To simplify, it is assumed that there is no change in the beginning and ending materials inventories. Thus, the amount of materials budgeted for production equals the amount purchased.

To illustrate, the direct materials quantity variance for Cowpoke Inc. is computed as follows:

Direct Materials Quantity Variance = (Actual Quantity − Standard Quantity) × Standard Price
= (7,300 sq. yds. − 7,500 sq. yds.) × $5.00
= $(1,000) Favorable Variance

As shown above, Cowpoke Inc. has a favorable direct materials quantity variance of $(1,000) for June.

Direct Materials Variance Relationships The relationship among the *total* direct materials cost variance, the direct materials *price* variance, and the direct materials *quantity* variance is shown in Exhibit 23.

Exhibit 23
Direct Materials Variance Relationships

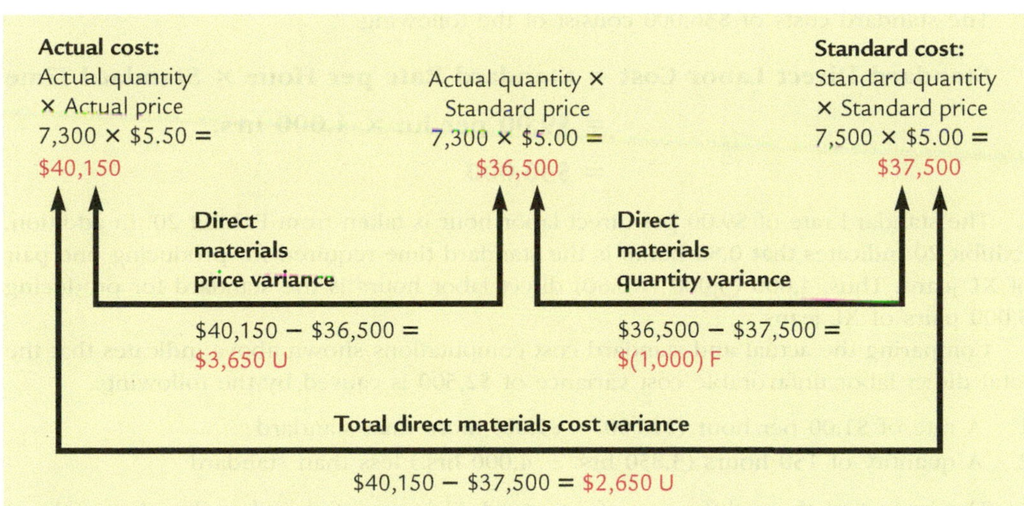

Reporting Direct Materials Variances The direct materials quantity variances should be reported to the manager responsible for the variance. For example, an unfavorable quantity variance might be caused by either of the following:

1. Equipment that has not been properly maintained
2. Low-quality (inferior) direct materials

In the first case, the operating department responsible for maintaining the equipment should be held responsible for the variance. In the second case, the Purchasing Department should be held responsible.

Not all variances are controllable. For example, an unfavorable materials price variance might be due to market-wide price increases. In this case, there is nothing the Purchasing Department might have done to avoid the unfavorable variance. On the other hand, if materials of the same quality could have been purchased from another supplier at the standard price, the variance was controllable.

Variances from NASCAR engine or equipment standards subjects race car teams to dollar fines and Championship point reductions.

Hendrick Motorsports Connection

Direct Labor Variances

During June, Cowpoke Inc. reported an unfavorable total direct labor cost variance of \$2,500 for the production of 5,000 XL style jeans, as shown in Exhibit 21. This variance was based on the following actual and standard costs:

Actual costs	\$38,500
Standard costs	36,000
Total direct labor cost variance	\$ 2,500

The actual costs incurred of \$38,500 consist of the following:

Actual Direct Labor Cost = Actual Rate per Hour × Actual Time
= \$10.00 per hr. × 3,850 hrs.
= \$38,500

The standard costs of \$36,000 consist of the following:

Standard Direct Labor Cost = Standard Rate per Hour × Standard Time
= \$9.00 per hr. × 4,000 hrs.
= \$36,000

The standard rate of \$9.00 per direct labor hour is taken from Exhibit 20. In addition, Exhibit 20 indicates that 0.80 hours is the standard time required for producing one pair of XL jeans. Thus, 4,000 (5,000 × 0.80) direct labor hours is the standard for producing 5,000 pairs of XL jeans.

Comparing the actual and standard cost computations shown above indicates that the total direct labor unfavorable cost variance of \$2,500 is caused by the following:

1. A rate of \$1.00 per hour (\$10.00 − \$9.00) more than standard
2. A quantity of 150 hours (3,850 hrs. − 4,000 hrs.) less than standard

The impact of these differences from standard is reported and analyzed as a direct labor *rate* variance and a direct labor *time* variance.

Direct Labor Rate Variance The **direct labor rate variance** is computed as follows:

Direct Labor Rate Variance = (Actual Rate per Hour − Standard Rate per Hour) × Actual Hours

If the actual rate per hour exeeds the standard rate per hour, the variance is unfavorable. This positive amount (unfavorable variance) can be thought of as increasing costs. If the actual rate per hour is less than the standard rate per hour, the variance is favorable. This negative amount (favorable variance) can be thought of as decreasing costs.

To illustrate, the direct labor rate variance for Cowpoke Inc. is computed as follows:

Direct Labor Rate Variance = (Actual Rate per Hour − Standard Rate per Hour) × Actual Hours
= (\$10.00 − \$9.00) × 3,850 hours
= \$3,850 Unfavorable Variance

As shown above, Cowpoke Inc. has an unfavorable direct labor rate variance of \$3,850 for June.

Direct Labor Time Variance The **direct labor time variance** is computed as follows:

$$\textbf{Direct Labor Time Variance} = (\textbf{Actual Direct Labor Hours} - \textbf{Standard Direct Labor Hours}) \times \textbf{Standard Rate per Hour}$$

If the actual direct labor hours for the units produced exceeds the standard direct labor hours, the variance is unfavorable. This positive amount (unfavorable variance) can be thought of as increasing costs. If the actual direct labor hours for the units produced is less than the standard direct labor hours, the variance is favorable. This negative amount (favorable variance) can be thought of as decreasing costs.

To illustrate, the direct labor time variance for Cowpoke Inc. is computed as follows:

$$\begin{aligned}\textbf{Direct Labor Time Variance} &= (\textbf{Actual Direct Labor Hours} - \textbf{Standard Direct Labor Hours}) \times \textbf{Standard Rate per Hour}\\ &= (\textbf{3,850 hours} - \textbf{4,000 direct labor hours}) \times \textbf{\$9.00}\\ &= \textbf{\$(1,350) Favorable Variance}\end{aligned}$$

As shown above, Cowpoke Inc. has a favorable direct labor time variance of $(1,350) for June.

Direct Labor Variance Relationships The relationship among the *total* direct labor cost variance, the direct labor *rate* variance, and the direct labor *time* variance is shown in Exhibit 24.

Exhibit 24 Direct Labor Variance Relationships

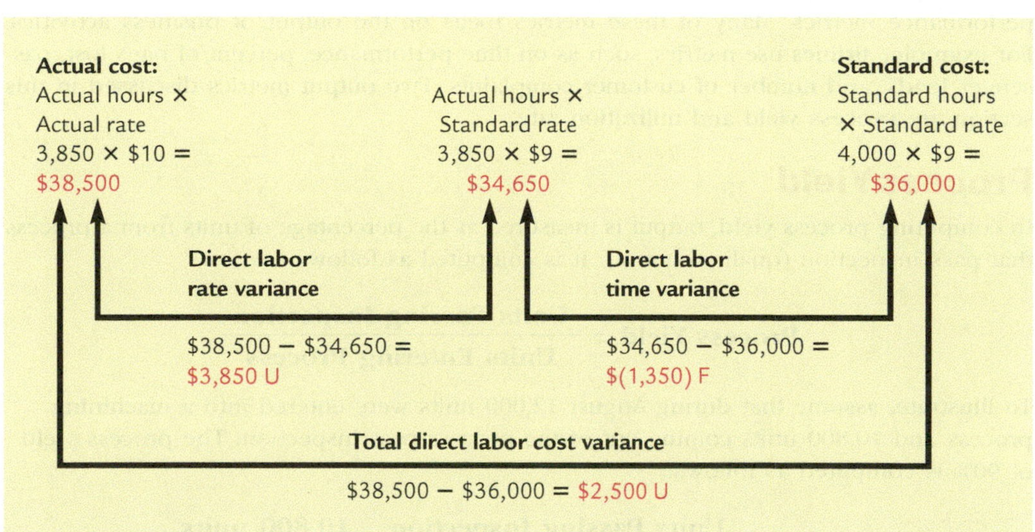

Reporting Direct Labor Variances Production supervisors are normally responsible for controlling direct labor cost. For example, an investigation could reveal the following causes for unfavorable rate and time variances:

1. An unfavorable rate variance may be caused by the improper scheduling and use of employees. In such cases, skilled, highly paid employees may be used in jobs that are normally performed by unskilled, lower-paid employees. In this case, the unfavorable rate variance should be reported to the managers who schedule work assignments.
2. An unfavorable time variance may be caused by a shortage of skilled employees. In such cases, there may be an abnormally high turnover rate among skilled employees. In this case, production supervisors with high turnover rates should be questioned as to why their employees are quitting.

Direct Labor Standards for Nonmanufacturing Activities Direct labor time standards can also be developed for use in administrative, selling, and service activities. This is most appropriate when the activity involves a repetitive task that produces a common output. In these cases, the use of standards is similar to that for a manufactured product.

To illustrate, standards could be developed for customer service personnel who process sales orders. A standard time for processing a sales order (the output) could be developed. The variance between the actual and the standard time could then be used to control sales order processing costs. Similar standards could be developed for computer help desk operators, nurses, and insurance application processors.

When labor-related activities are not repetitive, direct labor time standards are less commonly used. This often occurs when the time spent to perform the activity is not directly related to a unit of output. For example, the time spent by a senior executive or the work of a research and development scientist is not easily related to a measurable output. In these cases, the costs and expenses are normally controlled using static budgets.

Hendrick Motorsports Connection

NASCAR requires all drivers to attend a pre-race meeting. Failure of a driver to attend the meeting forces the driver to start at the rear of the field.

Metric-Based Analysis: Process Yield and Utilization Rate

Objective 6

Describe and illustrate the process yield and utilization rate metrics.

Most companies supplement budgets, standard costs, and variances with a variety of other performance metrics. Many of these metrics focus on the output of business activities. For example, airlines use metrics, such as on-time performance, percent of bags lost, passenger loads, and number of customer complaints. Two output metrics discussed in this section are process yield and utilization rate.

Process Yield

In computing process yield, output is measured as the percentage of units from a process that pass inspection (quality control). It is computed as follows:

$$\text{Process Yield} = \frac{\text{Units Passing Inspection}}{\text{Units Entering Process}}$$

To illustrate, assume that during August 12,000 units were entered into a machining process and 10,800 units coming out of the process pass inspection. The process yield of 90% is computed as follows:

$$\text{Process Yield} = \frac{\text{Units Passing Inspection}}{\text{Units Entering Process}} = \frac{10{,}800 \text{ units}}{12{,}000 \text{ units}} = 90\%$$

Process yield measures the efficiency of a process. In the preceding illustration, 10% of the units input into the machining process are either scrapped or reworked. A company's objective is to maximize process yield and reach a goal of zero defects.

In some processes, however, a yield of 100% is impossible because of the nature of the process. For example, processes that involve the heating of raw materials result in evaporation and process yields of less than 100 percent. In such cases, yield process goals are set with considering the uncontrollable losses caused by the process itself.

An overall process yield may be computed when several processes are required to manufacture a product. For example, assume that in the preceding illustration that the units pass from machining into painting and that the process yield for painting is 98%. The overall process yield of 88.2% is computed by multiplying the machining and painting process yields as follows:

$$\textbf{Overall Process Yield} = 90\% \times 98\% = 88.2\%$$

Utilization Rate

Instead of process yields, many service businesses use **utilization rates** for assessing performance and the efficient use of assets. For example, a hotel chain has a large investment in property and building. One measure of the efficiency of the use of a hotel's facilities is to compute a utilization rate. A normal utilization rate used for a hotel chain is an occupancy rate. Likewise, a normal utilization rate for an airline, which has a large investment in aircraft is the number of passengers occupying seats.

Utilization rates are normally computed as follows:

$$\text{Utilization Rate} = \frac{\text{Service Units Used}}{\text{Available Service Units}}$$

The computation must be adapted to each specific industry. For example, for a hotel chain, the utilization rate is referred to as an **occupancy rate**, which is computed as follows:

$$\text{Occupancy Rate} = \frac{\text{Rooms Occupied}}{\text{Available Room Nights}}$$

Available room nights is computed as the number of rooms times the number of nights during the period. For example, assuming that Slumber Motel has 80 rooms, the available room nights for June is 2,400 (80 rooms × 30 days). The rooms occupied is simply the number of rooms rented (occupied) during the period. Assume that during June 1,800 room nights were occupied by guests. The occupancy rate of 75% is computed as follows:

$$\text{Occupancy Rate} = \frac{\text{Room Nights Occupied}}{\text{Available Room Nights}} = \frac{1{,}800}{2{,}400} = 75\%$$

Service companies, like hotels and airlines, attempt to maximize their utilization rates and, thus, maximize the utilization of their investment in property, plant, and equipment.

Appendix

Factory Overhead Variances

Factory overhead costs are analyzed differently from direct labor and direct materials costs. This is because factory overhead costs have fixed and variable cost elements. For example, indirect materials and factory supplies normally behave as a variable cost as units produced changes. In contrast, straight-line plant depreciation on factory machinery is a fixed cost.

Factory overhead costs are budgeted and controlled by separating factory overhead into fixed and variable costs. Doing so allows the preparation of flexible budgets and analysis of factory overhead controllable and volume variances.

The Factory Overhead Flexible Budget

The preparation of a flexible budget was described and illustrated earlier in this chapter. Exhibit 25 illustrates a flexible factory overhead budget for Cowpoke Inc. for June 20Y8.

Exhibit 25
Factory Overhead Cost Budget Indicating Standard Factory Overhead Rate

	A	B	C	D	E
1	Cowpoke Inc.				
2	Factory Overhead Cost Budget				
3	For the Month Ending June 30, 20Y8				
4	Percent of normal capacity	80%	90%	100%	110%
5	Units produced	5,000	5,625	6,250	6,875
6	Direct labor hours (0.80 hr. per unit)	4,000	4,500	5,000	5,500
7	Budgeted factory overhead:				
8	Variable costs:				
9	Indirect factory wages	$ 8,000	$ 9,000	$10,000	$11,000
10	Power and light	4,000	4,500	5,000	5,500
11	Indirect materials	2,400	2,700	3,000	3,300
12	Total variable cost	$14,400	$16,200	$18,000	$19,800
13	Fixed costs:				
14	Supervisory salaries	$ 5,500	$ 5,500	$ 5,500	$ 5,500
15	Depreciation of plant				
16	and equipment	4,500	4,500	4,500	4,500
17	Insurance and property taxes	2,000	2,000	2,000	2,000
18	Total fixed cost	$12,000	$12,000	$12,000	$12,000
19	Total factory overhead cost	$26,400	$28,200	$30,000	$31,800
20					
21	Factory overhead rate per direct labor hour, $30,000 ÷ 5,000 hours = $6.00				
22					

Exhibit 25 indicates that the budgeted factory overhead rate for Cowpoke Inc. is $6.00, as computed as follows.

$$\textbf{Factory Overhead Rate} = \frac{\textbf{Budgeted Factory Overhead at Normal Capacity}}{\textbf{Normal Productive Capacity}}$$

$$= \frac{\$30{,}000}{5{,}000 \text{ direct labor hrs.}} = \$6.00 \text{ per direct labor hr.}$$

The normal productive capacity is expressed in terms of an activity base such as direct labor hours, direct labor cost, or machine hours. For Cowpoke Inc., 100% of normal capacity is 5,000 direct labor hours. The budgeted factory overhead cost at 100% of normal capacity is $30,000, which consists of variable overhead of $18,000 and fixed overhead of $12,000.

For analysis purposes, the budgeted factory overhead rate is subdivided into a variable factory overhead rate and a fixed factory overhead rate. For Cowpoke Inc., the variable overhead rate is $3.60 per direct labor hour, and the fixed overhead rate is $2.40 per direct labor hour, as computed as follows.

$$\textbf{Variable Factory Overhead} = \frac{\textbf{Budgeted Fixed Overhead at Normal Capacity}}{\textbf{Normal Productive Capacity}}$$

$$= \frac{\$18{,}000}{5{,}000 \text{ direct labor hrs.}} = \$3.60 \text{ per direct labor hr.}$$

$$\textbf{Fixed Factory Overhead Rate} = \frac{\textbf{Budgeted Variable Overhead at Normal Capacity}}{\textbf{Normal Productive Capacity}}$$

$$= \frac{\$12{,}000}{5{,}000 \text{ direct labor hrs.}} = \$2.40 \text{ per direct labor hr.}$$

To summarize, the budgeted factory overhead rates for Cowpoke Inc. are as follows:

Variable factory overhead rate	$3.60
Fixed factory overhead rate	2.40
Total factory overhead rate	$6.00

As mentioned earlier, factory overhead variances can be separated into a controllable variance and a volume variance as discussed in the next sections.

Variable Factory Overhead Controllable Variance

The variable factory overhead **controllable variance** is the difference between the actual variable overhead costs and the budgeted variable overhead for actual production. It is computed as follows:

$$\text{Variable Factory Overhead Controllable Variance} = \text{Actual Variable Factory Overhead} - \text{Budgeted Variable Factory Overhead}$$

If the actual variable overhead is less than the budgeted variable overhead, the variance is favorable. If the actual variable overhead exceeds the budgeted variable overhead, the variance is unfavorable.

The **budgeted variable factory overhead** is the standard variable overhead for the *actual* units produced. It is computed as follows:

$$\text{Budgeted Variable Factory Overhead} = \text{Standard Hours for Actual Units Produced} \times \text{Variable Factory Overhead Rate}$$

To illustrate, the budgeted variable overhead for Cowpoke Inc. for June is $14,400, computed as follows:

$$\text{Budgeted Variable Factory Overhead} = \text{Standard Hours for Actual Units Produced} \times \text{Variable Factory Overhead Rate}$$

$$= 4{,}000 \text{ direct labor hrs.} \times \$3.60$$

$$= \$14{,}400$$

The preceding computation is based on the fact that Cowpoke Inc. produced 5,000 XL jeans, which requires a standard of 4,000 (5,000 × 0.8 hr.) direct labor hours. The variable factory overhead rate of $3.60 was computed earlier. Thus, the budgeted variable factory overhead is $14,400 (4,000 direct labor hrs. × $3.60).

During June, assume that Cowpoke Inc. incurred the following actual factory overhead costs:

	Actual Costs in June
Variable factory overhead	$10,400
Fixed factory overhead	12,000
Total actual factory overhead	$22,400

Based on the actual variable factory overhead incurred in June, the variable factory overhead controllable variance is a $4,000 favorable variance, as computed as follows.

$$\text{Variable Factory Overhead Controllable Variance} = \text{Actual Variable Factory Overhead} - \text{Budgeted Variable Factory Overhead}$$

$$= \$10{,}400 - \$14{,}400$$

$$= \$(4{,}000) \text{ Favorable Variance}$$

The variable factory overhead controllable variance indicates the ability to keep the factory overhead costs within the budget limits. Since variable factory overhead costs are normally controllable at the department level, responsibility for controlling this variance usually rests with department supervisors.

Fixed Factory Overhead Volume Variance

Cowpoke Inc.'s budgeted factory overhead is based on a 100% normal capacity of 5,000 direct labor hours, as shown in Exhibit 25. This is the expected capacity that management believes will be used under normal business conditions. Exhibit 25 indicates that the 5,000 direct labor hours is less than the total available capacity of 110%, which is 5,500 direct labor hours.

The fixed factory overhead **volume variance** is the difference between the budgeted fixed overhead at 100% of normal capacity and the standard fixed overhead for the actual units produced. It is computed as follows:

$$\text{Fixed Factory Overhead Volume Variance} = \left(\text{Standard Hours for 100\% of Normal Capacity} - \text{Standard Hours for Actual Units Produced}\right) \times \text{Fixed Factory Overhead Rate}$$

The volume variance measures the use of fixed overhead resources (plant and equipment). The interpretation of an unfavorable and a favorable fixed factory overhead volume variance is as follows:

1. *Unfavorable* fixed factory overhead variance. The actual units produced is *less than* 100% of normal capacity; thus, the company used its fixed overhead resources (plant and equipment) less than would be expected under normal operating conditions.
2. *Favorable* fixed factory overhead variance. The actual units produced is *more than* 100% of normal capacity; thus, the company used its fixed overhead resources (plant and equipment) more than would be expected under normal operating conditions.

To illustrate, the volume variance for Cowpoke Inc. is a $2,400 unfavorable variance, as computed as follows.

$$\text{Fixed Factory Overhead Volume Variance} = \left(\text{Standard Hours for 100\% of Normal Capacity} - \text{Standard Hours for Actual Units Produced}\right) \times \text{Fixed Factory Overhead Rate}$$

$$= \left(\text{5,000 direct labor hrs.} - \text{4,000 direct labor hrs.}\right) \times \$2.40$$

$$= \$2{,}400 \text{ Unfavorable Variance}$$

Since Cowpoke Inc. produced 5,000 XL jeans during June, the standard for the actual units produced is 4,000 (5,000 × 0.80) direct labor hours. This is 1,000 hours less than the 5,000 standard hours of normal capacity. The fixed overhead rate of $2.40 was computed earlier. Thus, the unfavorable fixed factory overhead volume variance is $2,400 (1,000 direct labor hrs. × $2.40).

Exhibit 26 illustrates graphically the fixed factory overhead volume variance for Cowpoke Inc. The budgeted fixed overhead does not change and is $12,000 at all levels of production. At 100% of normal capacity (5,000 direct labor hours), the standard fixed overhead line intersects the budgeted fixed costs line. For production levels *more than* 100% of normal capacity (5,000 direct labor hours), the volume variance is *favorable*. For production levels *less than* 100% of normal capacity (5,000 direct labor hours), the volume variance is *unfavorable*.

Exhibit 26
Graph of Fixed Overhead Volume Variance

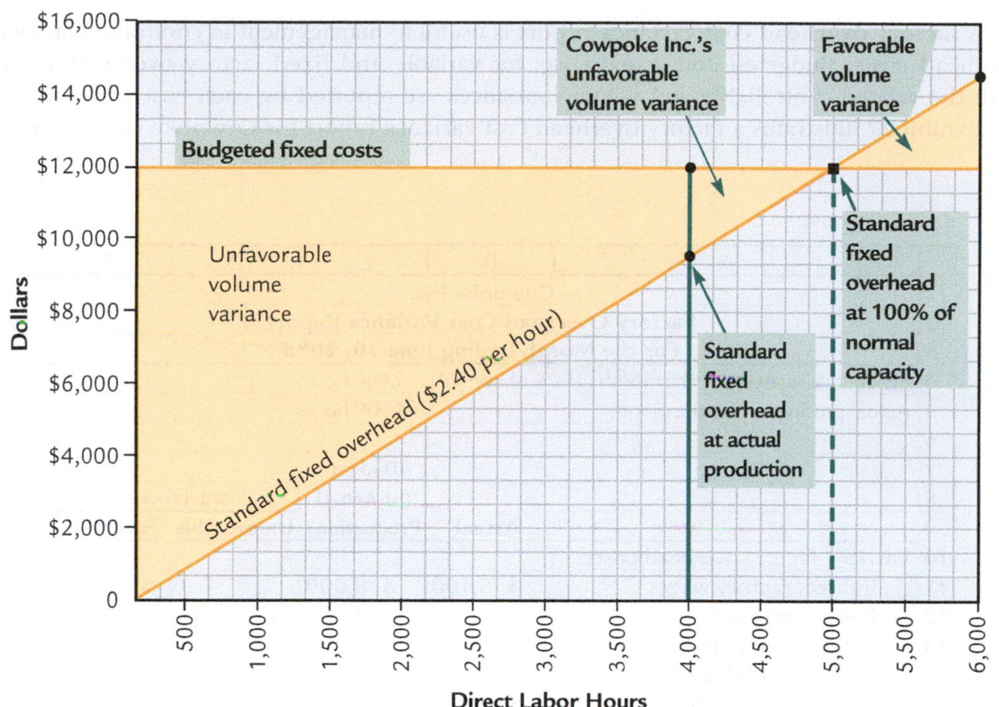

Exhibit 26 indicates that Cowpoke Inc.'s volume variance is unfavorable in June because the actual production is 4,000 direct labor hours, or 80% of normal volume. The unfavorable volume variance of $2,400 can be viewed as the cost of the unused capacity (1,000 direct labor hours).

An unfavorable volume variance may be due to factors such as the following:

1. Failure to maintain an even flow of work
2. Machine breakdowns
3. Work stoppages caused by lack of materials or skilled labor
4. Lack of enough sales orders to keep the factory operating at normal capacity

Management should determine the causes of the unfavorable variance and consider taking corrective action. For example, a volume variance caused by an uneven flow of work could be remedied by changing operating procedures. Lack of sales orders may be corrected through increased advertising.

Favorable volume variances may not always be desirable. For example, in an attempt to create a favorable volume variance, manufacturing managers might run the factory above the normal capacity. This is favorable when the additional production can be sold. However, if the additional production cannot be sold, it must be stored as inventory, which would incur storage costs. In this case, a favorable volume variance may actually reduce company profits.

Reporting Factory Overhead Variances

The total factory overhead cost variance can also be determined as the sum of the factory overhead controllable and volume variances, as follows for Cowpoke Inc.:

Variable factory overhead controllable variance	$(4,000)	Favorable Variance
Fixed factory overhead volume variance	2,400	Unfavorable Variance
Total factory overhead cost variance	($1,600)	Favorable Variance

A **factory overhead cost variance report** is useful to management in controlling factory overhead costs. Budgeted and actual costs for variable and fixed factory overhead along with the related controllable and volume variances are reported by each cost element.

Exhibit 27 illustrates a factory overhead cost variance report for Cowpoke Inc. for June.

Exhibit 27 Factory Overhead Cost Variance Report

	A	B	C	D	E
1	**Cowpoke Inc.**				
2	**Factory Overhead Cost Variance Report**				
3	**For the Month Ending June 30, 20Y8**				
4	Productive capacity for the month (100% of normal)		5,000 hours		
5	Actual production for the month		4,000 hours		
6					
7			**Budget**		
8			**(at Actual**	**Variances**	
9		**Actual**	**Production)**	**Unfavorable**	**Favorable**
10	Variable factory overhead costs:				
11	Indirect factory wages	$ 5,100	$ 8,000		$(2,900)
12	Power and light	4,200	4,000	$ 200	
13	Indirect materials	1,100	2,400		(1,300)
14	Total variable factory				
15	overhead cost	$10,400	$14,400		
16	Fixed factory overhead costs:				
17	Supervisory salaries	$ 5,500	$ 5,500		
18	Depreciation of plant and				
19	equipment	4,500	4,500		
20	Insurance and property taxes	2,000	2,000		
21	Total fixed factory				
22	overhead cost	$12,000	$12,000		
23	Total factory overhead cost	$22,400	$26,400		
24	Total controllable variances			$ 200	$(4,200)
25					
26					
27	Net controllable variance—favorable				$(4,000)
28	Volume variance—unfavorable:				
29	Capacity not used at the standard rate for fixed				
30	factory overhead—1,000 × $2.40				2,400
31	Total factory overhead cost variance—favorable				$(1,600)
32					

Factory Overhead Account

The total actual factory overhead for Cowpoke Inc. as shown in Exhibit 27 is $22,400. Thus, the total factory overhead cost variance for Cowpoke Inc. for June is a $1,600 favorable variance.

At the end of the period, the factory overhead account normally has a balance. A positive balance in Factory Overhead represents underapplied overhead. Underapplied overhead occurs when actual factory overhead costs exceed the applied factory overhead. A negative balance in Factory Overhead represents overapplied overhead. Overapplied overhead occurs when actual factory overhead costs are less than the applied factory overhead.

To illustrate, the applied factory overhead for Cowpoke Inc. for the 5,000 XL jeans produced in June is $24,000, as computed as follows.

$$\textbf{Applied Factory Overhead} = \textbf{Standard Hours for Actual Units Produced} \times \textbf{Total Factory Overhead Rate}$$

$$= \left(\textbf{5,000 jeans} \times \textbf{0.80 direct labor hr. per pair of jeans}\right) \times \textbf{\$6.00}$$

$$= \textbf{4,000 direct labor hrs.} \times \textbf{\$6.00} = \textbf{\$24,000}$$

The difference between the actual factory overhead and the applied factory overhead is the total factory overhead cost variance. Thus, underapplied and overapplied factory overhead account balances represent the following total factory overhead cost variances:

1. *Underapplied* Factory Overhead = *Unfavorable* Total Factory Overhead Cost Variance
2. *Overapplied* Factory Overhead = *Favorable* Total Factory Overhead Cost Variance

The factory overhead account for Cowpoke Inc. for the month ending June 30, 20Y8, is as follows:

Factory Overhead Account	
Actual factory overhead ($10,400 + $12,000)	$ 22,400
Less applied factory overhead (4,000 hours × 6.00 per hour)	(24,000)
Balance, overapplied factory overhead, June 30	$ (1,600)

The $1,600 overapplied factory overhead account balance shown above and the total factory cost variance shown in Exhibit 27 are the same.

The variable factory overhead controllable variance and the volume variance can be computed by comparing the factory overhead account with the budgeted total overhead for the actual level produced, as follows:

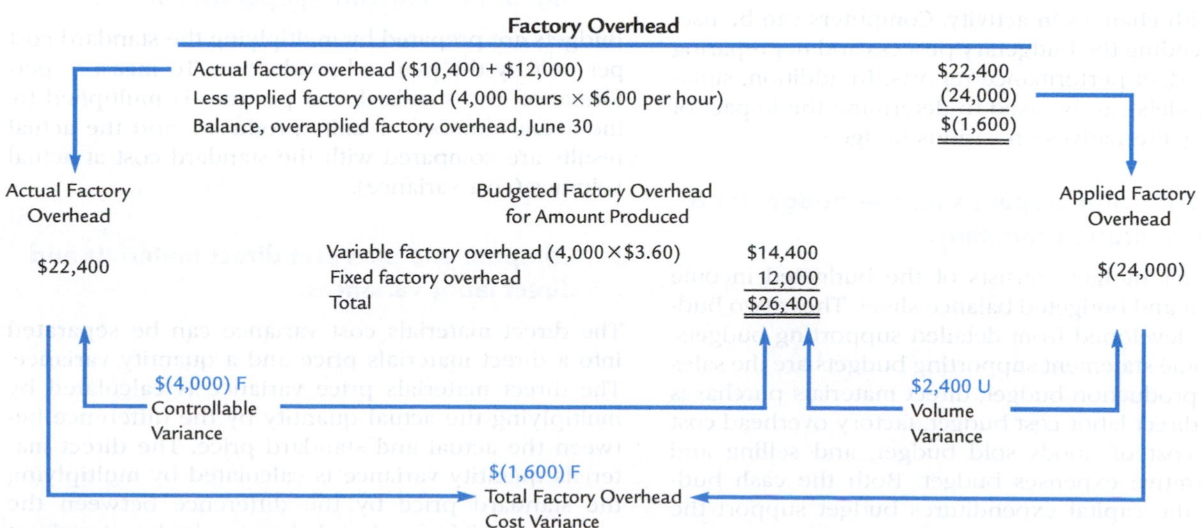

The controllable and volume variances are determined as follows:

1. The difference between the actual overhead incurred and the budgeted overhead is the *controllable* variance.
2. The difference between the applied overhead and the budgeted overhead is the *volume* variance.

If the actual factory overhead exceeds (is less than) the budgeted factory overhead, the controllable variance is unfavorable (favorable). In contrast, if the applied factory overhead is less than (exceeds) the budgeted factory overhead, the volume variance is unfavorable (favorable).

For many of the individual factory overhead costs, quantity and price variances can be computed similar to that for direct materials and direct labor. For example, the indirect factory labor cost variance may include both time and rate variances. Likewise, the indirect materials cost variance may include both a quantity variance and a price variance. Such variances are illustrated in advanced textbooks.

Key Points

1. Describe budgeting, its objectives, its impact on human behavior, and types of budget systems.

Budgeting involves (1) establishing specific goals, (2) executing plans to achieve the goals, and (3) periodically comparing actual results with these goals. In addition, budget goals should be established to avoid problems in human behavior. Thus, budgets should not be set too tightly, too loosely, or to cause goal conflict. Budgeting systems can use fiscal-year budgeting, continuous budgeting, or zero-based budgeting. Two major types of budgets are the static budget and the flexible budget. The static budget does not adjust with changes in activity while the flexible budget does adjust with changes in activity. Computers can be useful in speeding the budgetary process and in preparing timely budget performance reports. In addition, simulation models can be used to determine the impact of operating alternatives on various budgets.

2. Describe and prepare a master budget for a manufacturing company.

The master budget consists of the budgeted income statement and budgeted balance sheet. These two budgets are developed from detailed supporting budgets. The income statement supporting budgets are the sales budget, production budget, direct materials purchases budget, direct labor cost budget, factory overhead cost budget, cost of goods sold budget, and selling and administrative expenses budget. Both the cash budget and the capital expenditures budget support the budgeted balance sheet. The cash budget consists of budgeted cash receipts and budgeted cash payments. The capital expenditures budget is an important tool for planning expenditures for fixed assets.

3. Describe the types of standards and how they are established.

Standards represent performance benchmarks that can be compared to actual results in evaluating performance. Standards are developed, reviewed, and revised by accountants and engineers based on studies of operations. Standards are established so that they are neither too high nor too low but are attainable.

4. Describe and illustrate performance reporting for manufacturing operations.

Budgets are prepared by multiplying the standard cost per unit by the planned production. To measure performance, the standard cost per unit is multiplied by the actual number of units produced, and the actual results are compared with the standard cost at actual volumes (cost variance).

5. Compute and interpret direct materials and direct labor variances.

The direct materials cost variance can be separated into a direct materials price and a quantity variance. The direct materials price variance is calculated by multiplying the actual quantity by the difference between the actual and standard price. The direct materials quantity variance is calculated by multiplying the standard price by the difference between the actual materials used and the standard materials at actual volumes.

The direct labor cost variance can be separated into a direct labor rate and time variance. The direct labor rate variance is calculated by multiplying the actual hours worked by the difference between the actual labor rate and the standard labor rate. The direct labor time variance is calculated by multiplying the standard labor rate by the difference between the actual labor hours worked and the standard labor hours at actual volumes.

6. Describe and illustrate the process yield and utilization rate metrics.

Process yield is computed as units passing through a process divided by units entering the process. A utilization rate is computed as service units used divided by available service units. Process yields measure the efficiency of a process while utilization rates measure the efficiency of the use of property, plant, and equipment.

Key Terms

Budget (547)
Budget performance report (567)
Budgetary slack (549)
Budgeted variable factory overhead (577)
Capital expenditures budget (564)
Cash budget (561)
Continuous budgeting (550)
Controllable variance (577)
Cost of goods sold budget (558)
Cost variance (567)
Currently attainable standards (565)
Direct labor cost budget (557)
Direct labor rate variance (572)
Direct labor time variance (573)
Direct materials price variance (570)
Direct materials purchases budget (556)
Direct materials quantity variance (570)
Factory overhead cost budget (558)
Factory overhead cost variance report (580)
Favorable cost variance (567)
Flexible budget (551)
Goal conflict (549)
Ideal standards (565)
Master budget (553)
Occupancy rate (575)
Process yield (574)
Production budget (555)
Responsibility center (547)
Sales budget (554)
Standard cost (564)
Standard cost systems (564)
Standards (564)
Static budget (550)
Theoretical standards (565)
Total manufacturing cost variance (568)
Unfavorable cost variance (567)
Utilization rate (575)
Volume variance (578)
Zero-based budgeting (550)

Illustrative Problem

Mountain Art Inc. manufactures woven baskets for national distribution. The standard and actual costs for the manufacture of Folk Art style baskets were as follows:

	Standard Costs	Actual Costs
Direct materials	1,500 lbs. at $35	1,600 lbs. at $32
Direct labor	4,800 hrs. at $11	4,500 hrs. at $11.80
Factory overhead	Rates per labor hour, based on 100% of normal capacity of 5,500 labor hrs.:	
	Variable cost, $2.40	$12,300 variable cost
	Fixed cost, $3.50	$19,250 fixed cost

Instructions

1. Determine the quantity variance, price variance, and total direct materials cost variance for the Folk Art style baskets.
2. Determine the time variance, rate variance, and total direct labor cost variance for the Folk Art style baskets.

3. Appendix: Determine the controllable variance, volume variance, and total factory overhead cost variance for the Folk Art style baskets.

Solution

1. Direct Materials Cost Variance

Quantity variance:

Direct Materials Quantity Variance = (Actual Quantity − Standard Quantity) × Standard Price
= (1,600 lbs. − 1,500 lbs.) × \$35 per lb.
= \$3,500 Unfavorable Variance

Price variance:

Direct Materials Price Variance = (Actual Price − Standard Price) × Actual Quantity
= (\$32 per lb. − \$35 per lb.) × 1,600 lbs.
= \$(4,800) Favorable Variance

Total direct materials cost variance:

Direct Materials Cost Variance = Direct Materials Quantity Variance + Direct Materials Price Variance
= \$3,500 − \$4,800
= \$(1,300) Favorable Variance

2. Direct Labor Cost Variance

Time variance:

Direct Labor Time Variance = (Actual Direct Labor Hours − Standard Direct Labor Hours) × Standard Rate per Hour
= (4,500 hrs. − 4,800 hrs.) × \$11 per hour
= (\$3,300) Favorable Variance

Rate variance:

Direct Labor Rate Variance = (Actual Rate per Hour − Standard Rate per Hour) × Actual Hours
= (\$11.80 − \$11.00) × 4,500 hrs.
= \$3,600 Unfavorable Variance

Total direct labor cost variance:

Direct Labor Cost Variance = Direct Labor Time Variance + Direct Labor Rate Variance
= −\$3,300 + \$3,600
= \$300 Unfavorable Variance

3. Appendix **Factory Overhead Cost Variance**

Variable factory overhead controllable variance:

Variable Factory Overhead Controllable Variance = Actual Variable Factory Overhead − Budgeted Variable Factory Overhead
= \$12,300 − \$11,520*
= \$780 Unfavorable Variance

* 4,800 hrs. × \$2.40 per hour

Fixed factory overhead volume variance:

Fixed Factory Overhead Volume Variance = (Standard Hours for 100% of Normal Capacity − Standard Hours for Actual Units Produced) × Fixed Factory Overhead Rate
= (5,500 hrs. − 4,800 hrs.) × \$3.50 per hr.
= \$2,450 Unfavorable Variance

Total factory overhead cost variance:

Factory Overhead Cost Variance = Variable Factory Overhead Controllable Variance + Fixed Factory Overhead Volume Variance
= \$780 + \$2,450
= \$3,230 Unfavorable Variance

Self-Examination Questions

(Answers appear at the end of chapter)

1. Static budgets are often used:
   A. By production departments
   B. By administrative departments
   C. By responsibility centers
   D. For capital projects

2. The total estimated sales for the coming year is 250,000 units. The estimated inventory at the beginning of the year is 22,500 units, and the desired inventory at the end of the year is 30,000 units. The total production indicated in the production budget is:
   A. 242,500 units
   B. 257,500 units
   C. 280,000 units
   D. 302,500 units

3. Dixon Company expects $650,000 of credit sales in March and $800,000 of credit sales in April. Dixon historically collects 70% of its sales in the month of sale and 30% in the following month. How much cash does Dixon expect to collect in April?
   A. $800,000
   B. $560,000
   C. $755,000
   D. $1,015,000

4. The actual and standard direct materials costs for producing a specified quantity of product are as follows:

Actual:	51,000 pounds at $5.05	$257,550
Standard:	50,000 pounds at $5.00	$250,000

   The direct materials price variance is:
   A. $50 unfavorable
   B. $2,500 unfavorable
   C. $2,550 unfavorable
   D. $7,550 unfavorable

5. Bower Company produced 4,000 units of product. The direct labor standard quantity is 0.5 hours per unit. The standard labor rate is $12 per hour. Actual direct labor for the period was $22,000 (2,200 hours × $10 per hour). The direct labor time variance is:
   A. 200 hours unfavorable
   B. $2,000 unfavorable
   C. $4,000 favorable
   D. $2,400 unfavorable

Class Discussion Questions

1. What are the three major objectives of budgeting?
2. What is the manager's role in a responsibility center?
3. Briefly describe the type of human behavior problems that might arise if budget goals are set too tightly.
4. Give an example of budgetary slack.
5. What behavioral problems are associated with setting a budget too loosely?
6. What behavioral problems are associated with establishing conflicting goals within the budget?
7. When would a company use zero-based budgeting?
8. Under what circumstances would a static budget be appropriate?
9. How do computerized budgeting systems aid firms in the budgeting process?
10. What is the first step in preparing a master budget?
11. Why should the production requirements set forth in the production budget be carefully coordinated with the sales budget?
12. Why should the timing of direct materials purchases be closely coordinated with the production budget?
13. In preparing the budget for the cost of goods sold, what are the three budgets from which data on relevant estimates of quantities and costs are combined with data on estimated inventories?
14. a. Discuss the purpose of the cash budget.
    b. If the cash for the first quarter of the fiscal year indicates excess cash at the end of each of the first two months, how might the excess cash be used?
15. How does a schedule of collections from sales assist in preparing the cash budget?
16. Give an example of how the capital expenditures budget affects other operating budgets.

17. What are the basic objectives in the use of standard costs?
18. How can standards be used by management to help control costs?
19. What is meant by reporting by the "principle of exceptions," as the term is used in reference to cost control?
20. How often should standards be revised?
21. How are standards used in budgetary performance evaluation?
22. a. What are the two variances between the actual cost and the standard cost for direct materials?
    b. Discuss some possible causes of these variances.
23. The materials cost variance report for Nickols Inc. indicates a large favorable materials price variance and a significant unfavorable materials quantity variance. What might have caused these offsetting variances?
24. a. What are the two variances between the actual cost and the standard cost for direct labor?
    b. Who generally has control over the direct labor cost?
25. A new assistant controller recently said: "All the assembly workers in this plant are covered by union contracts, so there should be no labor variances." Was the controller's remark correct? Discuss.
26. Would the use of standards be appropriate in a nonmanufacturing setting, such as a fast-food restaurant?

Exercises

Obj. 1

✔ Total selling and administrative expenses at $600,000 sales, $327,000

E13-1 Flexible budget for selling and administrative expenses

Fuller Enterprises uses flexible budgets that are based on the following data:

Sales commissions	6% of sales
Advertising expense	20% of sales
Customer support expense	$2,000 plus 16% of sales
Office salaries expense	$30,000 per month
Miscellaneous administrative expense	$3,000 plus 5% of sales
Research and development expense	$10,000 per month

Prepare a flexible selling and administrative expenses budget for July for sales volumes of $600,000, $800,000, and $1,000,000. (Use Exhibit 5 as a model.)

Obj. 1

✔ b. Excess of actual over budget for March, $13,700

E13-2 Static budget vs. flexible budget

The production supervisor of the Machining Department for Lei Company agreed to the following monthly static budget for the upcoming year:

LEI COMPANY
Machining Department
Monthly Production Budget

Wages	$1,440,000
Utilities	92,000
Depreciation	32,500
Total	$1,564,500

Note: The spreadsheet icon indicates an Excel template is available on the student companion site.

The actual amount spent and the actual units produced in the first three months in the Machining Department were as follows:

	Amount Spent	Units Produced
January	$1,200,000	75,000
February	1,356,000	85,000
March	1,425,000	90,000

The Machining Department supervisor has been very pleased with this performance, since actual expenditures have been less than the monthly budget. However, the plant manager believes that the budget should not remain fixed for every month but should "flex" or adjust to the volume of work that is produced in the Machining Department. Additional budget information for the Machining Department is as follows:

Wages per hour	$18.00
Utility cost per direct labor hour	$1.15
Direct labor hours per unit	0.80 hrs.
Planned unit production	100,000 units

a. Prepare a flexible budget for the actual units produced for January, February, and March in the Machining Department. Assume depreciation is a fixed cost.

b. Compare the flexible budget with the actual expenditures for the first three months. What does this comparison suggest?

E13-3 Flexible budget for Fabrication Department

Obj. 1

✔ **Total department cost at 10,000 units, $315,000**

Steelcase Inc. is one of the largest manufacturers of office furniture in the United States. In Grand Rapids, Michigan, it produces filing cabinets in two departments: Fabrication and Assembly. Assume the following information for the Assembly Department:

Direct labor per filing cabinet	30 minutes
Supervisor salaries	$180,000 per month
Depreciation	$15,000 per month
Direct labor rate	$24 per hour

Prepare a flexible budget for 10,000, 25,000, and 40,000 filing cabinets for the month of August, similar to Exhibit 5, assuming that inventories are not significant.

E13-4 Sales and production budgets

Obj. 2

✔ **b. Model U500 total production, 305,000 units**

Ultimate Audio Company manufactures two models of speakers, U500 and S1000. Based on the following production and sales data for June, prepare (a) a sales budget and (b) a production budget.

	U500	S1000
Estimated inventory (units), June 1	25,000	10,000
Desired inventory (units), June 30	30,000	15,000
Expected sales volume (units):		
Northeast Region	140,000	100,000
Southwest Region	160,000	125,000
Unit sales price	$45	$80

Obj. 2

✔ Total professional fees earned, $38,100,000

E13-5 Professional fees earned budget

Day & Spieth, CPAs, offer three types of services to clients: auditing, tax, and small business accounting. Based on experience and projected growth, the following billable hours have been estimated for the year ending March 31, 20Y6:

	Billable Hours
Audit Department:	
Staff	50,000
Partners	10,000
Tax Department:	
Staff	75,000
Partners	16,000
Small Business Accounting Department:	
Staff	20,000
Partners	4,000

The average billing rate for staff is $180 per hour, and the average billing rate for partners is $400 per hour. Prepare a professional fees earned budget for Day & Spieth, CPAs, for the year ending March 31, 20Y6, using the following column headings and showing the estimated professional fees by type of service rendered:

Billable Hours	Hourly Rate	Total Revenue

Obj. 2

✔ Staff total labor cost, $5,220,000

E13-6 Professional labor cost budget

Based on the data in Exercise 13-5 and assuming that the average compensation per hour for staff is $36 and for partners is $300, prepare a professional labor cost budget for Day & Spieth, CPAs, for the year ending March 31, 20Y6. Use the following column headings:

Staff	Partners

Obj. 2

✔ Total cheese purchases, $19,884

E13-7 Direct materials purchases budget

Zippy's Frozen Pizza Inc. has determined from its production budget the following estimated production volumes for 12" and 16" frozen pizzas for September:

	Units	
	12" Pizza	16" Pizza
Budgeted production volume	9,000	15,000

There are three direct materials used in producing the two types of pizza. The quantities of direct materials expected to be used for each pizza are as follows:

	12" Pizza	16" Pizza
Direct materials:		
Dough	0.60 lb. per unit	1.00 lb. per unit
Tomato	0.30	0.45
Cheese	0.50	0.80

In addition, Zippy's has determined the following information about each material:

	Dough	Tomato	Cheese
Estimated inventory, September 1	500 lbs.	250 lbs.	480 lbs.
Desired inventory, September 30	600 lbs.	300 lbs.	550 lbs.
Price per pound	$0.75	$0.90	$1.20

Prepare September's direct materials purchases budget for Zippy's Frozen Pizza Inc.

E13-8 Direct materials purchases budget

Obj. 2

✔ Concentrate budgeted purchases, $630,000

Coca-Cola Enterprises is the largest bottler of Coca-Cola® in North America. The company purchases Coke® and Sprite® concentrate from The Coca-Cola Company, dilutes and mixes the concentrate with carbonated water, and then fills the blended beverage into cans or plastic two-liter bottles. Assume that the estimated production for Coke and Sprite two-liter bottles at the Dallas, Texas, bottling plant are as follows for the month of October:

Coke	1,500,000 two-liter bottles
Sprite	800,000 two-liter bottles

In addition, assume that the concentrate costs $75 per pound for Coke and Sprite. The concentrate is used at a rate of 0.20 pound per 100 liters of carbonated water in blending Coke and at a rate of 0.15 pound per 100 liters of carbonated water in blending Sprite. Assume that two-liter bottles cost $0.04 per bottle and carbonated water costs $0.03 per liter.

Prepare a direct materials purchases budget for October, assuming no changes between beginning and ending inventories for all three materials.

E13-9 Direct labor cost budget

Obj. 2

✔ Total direct labor cost, Assembly, $292,800

Donner Racket Company manufactures two types of tennis rackets, the Junior and Pro Striker models. The production budget for March for the two rackets is as follows:

	Junior	Pro Striker
Production budget	18,000 units	10,000 units

Both rackets are produced in two departments, Forming and Assembly. The direct labor hours required for each racket are estimated as follows:

	Forming Department	Assembly Department
Junior	0.20 hour per unit	0.60 hour per unit
Pro Striker	0.35 hour per unit	0.75 hour per unit

The direct labor rate for each department is as follows:

Forming Department	$21 per hour
Assembly Department	$16 per hour

Prepare the direct labor cost budget for March.

E13-10 Production and direct labor cost budgets

Obj. 2

✔ a. Total production of 501 Jeans, 240,000

Levi Strauss & Co. manufactures slacks and jeans under a variety of brand names, such as Dockers® and 501 Jeans®. Slacks and jeans are assembled by a variety of different sewing operations. Assume that the sales budget for Dockers and 501 Jeans shows estimated sales of 120,000 and 250,000 pairs, respectively, for May. The finished goods inventory is assumed as follows:

	Dockers	501 Jeans
May 1 estimated inventory	12,000	30,000
May 31 desired inventory	17,000	20,000

Assume the following direct labor data per 5 pairs of Dockers and 501 Jeans for four different sewing operations:

	Direct Labor per 5 Pairs	
	Dockers	**501 Jeans**
Inseam	15 minutes	10 minutes
Outerseam	18	15
Pockets	6	4
Zipper	3	2
Total	42 minutes	31 minutes

a. Prepare a production budget for February. Prepare the budget in two columns: Dockers and 501 Jeans.

b. Prepare the February direct labor cost budget for the four sewing operations, assuming a $15 wage per hour for the inseam and outerseam sewing operations and a $17 wage per hour for the pocket and zipper sewing operations. Prepare the direct labor cost budget in four columns: inseam, outerseam, pockets, and zipper.

Obj. 2

✔ Total variable factory overhead costs, $176,000

E13-11 Factory overhead cost budget

Nutty Candy Company budgeted the following costs for anticipated production for August:

Advertising expenses	$90,000	Production supervisor wages	$62,000
Manufacturing supplies	45,000	Production control wages	18,500
Power and light	28,000	Executive officer salaries	150,000
Sales commissions	115,000	Materials management wages	22,500
Factory insurance	8,000	Factory depreciation	16,000

Prepare a factory overhead cost budget, separating variable and fixed costs. Assume that factory insurance and depreciation are the only factory fixed costs.

Obj. 2

✔ Cost of goods sold, $491,900

E13-12 Cost of goods sold budget

The controller of Pueblo Ceramics Inc. wishes to prepare a cost of goods sold budget for April. The controller assembled the following information for constructing the cost of goods sold budget:

Direct materials:	**Enamel**	**Paint**	**Porcelain**	**Total**
Total direct materials purchases budgeted for April	$35,000	$6,000	$140,000	$181,000
Estimated inventory, April 1	3,000	750	9,250	13,000
Desired inventory, April 30	3,200	1,000	10,800	15,000

Direct labor cost:	**Kiln Department**	**Decorating Department**	**Total**
Total direct labor cost budgeted for April	$38,000	$162,000	$200,000

Budgeted factory overhead costs for April:	
Indirect factory wages	$ 71,500
Depreciation of plant and equipment	19,000
Power and light	12,300
Indirect materials	4,200
Total	$107,000

Work in process inventories:	
Estimated inventory, April 1	$ 11,400
Desired inventory, April 30	9,500

Finished goods inventories:	**Dish**	**Bowl**	**Figurine**	**Total**
Estimated inventory, April 1	$4,500	$3,000	$2,500	$10,000
Desired inventory, April 30	4,000	750	1,250	6,000

Use the preceding information to prepare a cost of goods sold budget for April.

E13-13 Schedule of cash collections of accounts receivable

Obj. 2

✔ Total cash collected in May, $720,000

Pet Stop Inc., a pet wholesale supplier, was organized on May 1. Projected sales for each of the first three months of operations are as follows:

May	$1,200,000
June	1,800,000
July	2,200,000

All sales are on account. Of sales on account, 60% are expected to be collected in the month of the sale, 30% in the first month following the sale, and the remainder in the second month following the sale.

Prepare a schedule indicating cash collections from sales for May, June, and July.

E13-14 Schedule of cash collections of accounts receivable

Obj. 2

✔ Total cash collected in January, $1,170,000

Innovative Office Inc. has "cash and carry" customers and credit customers. Innovative Office estimates that 30% of monthly sales are to cash customers, while the remaining sales are to credit customers. Of the credit customers, 75% pay their accounts in the month of sale, while the remaining 25% pay their accounts in the month following the month of sale. Projected sales for the first three months of 20Y4 are as follows:

January	$1,200,000
February	1,450,000
March	1,600,000

The Accounts Receivable balance on December 31, 20Y3, was $180,000.

Prepare a schedule of cash collections from sales for January, February, and March.

E13-15 Schedule of cash payments

Obj. 2

✔ Total cash payments in March, $77,000

Tadpole Learning Systems Inc. was organized on February 28. Projected selling and administrative expenses for each of the first three months of operations are as follows:

March	$120,000
April	140,000
May	160,000

Depreciation, insurance, and property taxes represent $10,000 of the estimated monthly expenses. The annual insurance premium was paid on February 28, and property taxes for the year will be paid in November. Seventy percent of the remainder of the expenses are expected to be paid in the month in which they are incurred, with the balance to be paid in the following month.

Prepare a schedule indicating cash payments for selling and administrative expenses for March, April, and May.

E13-16 Schedule of cash payments

Obj. 2

✔ Total cash payments in January, $52,500

Organic Physical Therapy Inc. is planning its cash payments for operations for the three months ending March 31. The Accrued Expenses Payable balance on January 1 is $12,000. The budgeted expenses for the next three months are as follows:

	January	February	March
Salaries	$40,000	$45,000	$60,000
Utilities	10,000	12,000	15,000
Other operating expenses	7,000	8,000	9,000
Total	$57,000	$65,000	$84,000

Other operating expenses include $2,000 of monthly depreciation expense and $1,000 of monthly insurance expense that was prepaid in the prior year. Of the remaining expenses, 75% are paid in the month in which they are incurred, with the remainder paid in the following month. The Accrued Expenses Payable balance on January 1 relates to the expenses incurred in December.

Prepare a schedule of cash payments for operations for January, February, and March.

Obj. 2

✔ Total capital expenditures in 20Y5, $5,000,000

E13-17 Capital expenditures budget

On August 1, 20Y4, the controller of Handy Dan Tools Inc. is planning capital expenditures for the years 20Y5–20Y8. The controller interviewed several Handy Dan executives to collect the necessary information for the capital expenditures budget. Excerpts of the interviews are as follows:

Director of Facilities: A construction contract was signed in May 20Y4 for the construction of a new factory building at a contract cost of $9,000,000. The construction is scheduled to begin in 20Y5 and completed in 20Y6.

Vice President of Manufacturing: Once the new factory building is finished, we plan to purchase $3.6 million in equipment in late 20Y6. I expect that an additional $500,000 will be needed early in the following year (20Y7) to test and install the equipment before we can begin production. If sales continue to grow, I expect we'll need to invest another half million in equipment in 20Y8.

Vice President of Marketing: We have really been growing lately. I wouldn't be surprised if we need to expand the size of our new factory building in 20Y8 by at least 25%. Fortunately, we expect inflation to have minimal impact on construction costs over the next four years. Additionally, I would expect the cost of the expansion to be proportional to the size of the expansion.

Director of Information Systems: We need to upgrade our information systems to wireless network technology. It doesn't make sense to do this until after the new factory building is completed and producing product. During 20Y7, once the factory is up and running, we should equip the whole facility with wireless technology. I think it would cost us $400,000 today to install the technology. However, prices have been dropping by 10% per year, so it should be less expensive at a later date.

President: I am excited about our long-term prospects. My only short-term concern is financing the $5,000,000 of construction costs on the portion of the new factory building scheduled to be completed in 20Y5.

Use the interview information above to prepare a capital expenditures budget for Handy Dan Tools Inc. for the years 20Y5–20Y8.

Obj. 4

E13-18 Standard product cost

Sorrento Furniture Company manufactures unfinished oak furniture. Sorrento uses a standard cost system. The direct labor, direct materials, and factory overhead standards for an unfinished dining room table are as follows:

Direct labor:	Standard rate	$21 per hr.
	Standard time per unit	2 hrs.
Direct materials (oak):	Standard price	$9.25 per bd. ft.
	Standard quantity	20 bd. ft.
Variable factory overhead:	Standard rate	$3.80 per direct labor hr.
Fixed factory overhead:	Standard rate	$4.25 per direct labor hr.

Determine the standard cost per dining room table.

E13-19 Budget performance report

Obj. 4

✔ **b. Direct labor cost variance, $475 U**

McAlisters Bottle Company manufactures plastic two-liter bottles for the beverage industry. The cost standards per 100 two-liter bottles are as follows:

Cost Category	Standard Cost per 100 Two-Liter Bottles
Direct labor	$2.75
Direct materials	1.20
Factory overhead	0.35
Total	$4.30

At the beginning of May, McAlisters Bottle's management planned to produce 800,000 bottles. The actual number of bottles produced for May was 750,000 bottles. The actual costs for May of the current year were as follows:

Cost Category	Actual Cost for the Month Ended May 31
Direct labor	$21,100
Direct materials	9,200
Factory overhead	2,700
Total	$33,000

a. Prepare the May manufacturing standard cost budget (direct labor, direct materials, and factory overhead) for McAlisters Bottle Company, assuming planned production.

b. Prepare a budget performance report for manufacturing costs, showing the total cost variances for direct materials, direct labor, and factory overhead for May.

c. Interpret the budget performance report.

E13-20 Direct materials variances

Obj. 5

✔ **a. Price variance, $12,000 U**

The following data relate to the direct materials cost for the production of 20,000 automobile tires:

Actual:	80,000 lbs. at $2.65	$212,000
Standard:	86,000 lbs. at $2.50	$215,000

a. Determine the price variance, quantity variance, and total direct materials cost variance.

b. To whom should the variances be reported for analysis and control?

E13-21 Standard direct materials cost per unit from variance data

Obj. 5

The following data relating to direct materials cost for August of the current year are taken from the records of Happy Tots Inc., a manufacturer of plastic toys:

Quantity of direct materials used	12,000 lbs.
Actual unit price of direct materials	$2.30 per lb.
Units of finished product manufactured	5,900 units
Standard direct materials per unit of finished product	2 lbs.
Direct materials quantity variance—unfavorable	$410
Direct materials price variance—unfavorable	$3,000

Determine the standard direct materials cost per unit of finished product, assuming that there was no work-in-process inventory at either the beginning or the end of the month.

Obj. 5

E13-22 Standard product cost, direct materials variance

H.J. Heinz Company uses standards to control its materials costs. Assume that a batch of ketchup (6,000 pounds) has the following standards:

	Standard Quantity	Standard Price
Whole tomatoes	7,500 lbs.	$0.40 per lb.
Vinegar	600 gal.	1.75 per gal.
Corn syrup	50 gal.	8.00 per gal.
Salt	500 lbs.	0.70 per lb.

The actual materials in a batch may vary from the standard due to tomato characteristics. Assume that the actual quantities of materials for batch H3001 were as follows:

7,850 lbs. of tomatoes
575 gal. of vinegar
63 gal. of corn syrup
480 lbs. of salt

a. Determine the standard unit materials cost per pound for a standard batch.

b. Determine the total direct materials quantity variance for batch H3001.

Obj. 5

✔ a. Rate variance, $(9,450) F

E13-23 Direct labor variances

The following data relate to direct labor costs for the production of smart tablets.

Actual:	6,300 hrs. at $23.00	$144,900
Standard:	6,000 hrs. at $24.50	$147,000

a. Determine the rate variance, time variance, and total direct labor cost variance.

b. Discuss what might have caused these variances.

Obj. 5

✔ Rate variance, $(550) F

E13-24 Direct labor variances

Death Valley Bicycle Company manufactures mountain bikes. The following data for October of the current year are available:

Quantity of direct labor used	1,100 hrs.
Actual rate for direct labor	$18.50 per hr.
Bicycles completed in October	350
Standard direct labor per bicycle	3 hrs.
Standard rate for direct labor	$19.00 per hr.
Planned bicycles for October	375

Determine the direct labor rate and time variances.

Obj. 5

✔ Direct materials quantity variance, $1,070 U

E13-25 Direct materials and direct labor variances

At the beginning of August, Havasu Printers Company budgeted 30,000 books to be printed in August at standard direct materials and direct labor costs as follows:

Direct materials	$15,000
Direct labor	72,000
Total	$87,000

The standard materials price is $0.40 per pound. The standard direct labor rate is $12 per hour. At the end of August, the actual direct materials and direct labor costs were as follows:

Actual direct materials	$13,320
Actual direct labor	60,000
Total	$73,320

There were no direct materials price or direct labor rate variances for August. In addition, assume no changes in the direct materials inventory balances in August. Havasu Printers Company actually produced 24,500 units during August.

Determine the direct materials quantity variance, the direct labor time variance, and the total variance.

E13-26 Direct labor standards for nonmanufacturing expenses

Obj. 5

✔ a. $1,512

Southwest Iowa Hospital began using standards to evaluate its Admissions Department. The standards were broken into two types of admissions as follows:

Type of Admission	Standard Time to Complete Admission Record
Unscheduled admission	30 min.
Scheduled admission	15 min.

The unscheduled admission took longer, since name, address, and insurance information needed to be determined at the time of admission. Information was collected on scheduled admissions prior to the admissions, which was less time consuming.

The Admissions Department employs two full-time people (36 hours per week, with no overtime) at $21 per hour. For the most recent week, the department handled 55 unscheduled and 210 scheduled admissions.

a. How much was actually spent on labor for the week?

b. What are the standard hours for the actual volume for the week?

c. Compute a time variance. How well did the department perform for the week?

E13-27 Factory overhead cost variances

✔ Volume variance, $36,000 U

app

The following data relate to factory overhead cost for the production of 8,000 computers:

Actual:	Variable factory overhead	$101,750
	Fixed factory overhead	180,000
Standard:	8,000 hrs. at $31	248,000

If productive capacity of 100% was 10,000 hours and the factory overhead cost budgeted at the level of 8,000 standard hours was $284,000, determine the variable factory overhead controllable variance, fixed factory overhead volume variance, and total factory overhead cost variance. The fixed factory overhead rate was $18 per hour.

E13-28 Factory overhead cost variances

✔ a. $(16,000) F

app

Osceola Textiles Corporation began May with a budget for 45,000 hours of production in the Weaving Department. The department has a full capacity of 60,000 hours under normal business conditions. The budgeted overhead at the planned volumes at the beginning of May was as follows:

Variable overhead	$ 990,000
Fixed overhead	300,000
Total	$1,290,000

The actual factory overhead was $1,428,000 for May. The actual fixed factory overhead was as budgeted. During May, the Weaving Department had standard hours at actual production volume of 52,000 hours.

a. Determine the variable factory overhead controllable variance.
b. Determine the fixed factory overhead volume variance.

app

E13-29 Factory overhead variance corrections

The data related to Danville Sporting Goods Company's factory overhead cost for the production of 40,000 units of product are as follows:

Actual:	Variable factory overhead	$269,000
	Fixed factory overhead	325,000
Standard:	105,000 hrs. at $9.00	945,000
	($5.75 for variable factory overhead)	

Productive capacity at 100% of normal was 100,000 hours, and the factory overhead cost budgeted at the level of 105,000 standard hours was $720,000. Based on these data, the chief cost accountant prepared the following variance analysis:

Variable factory overhead controllable variance:		
Actual variable factory overhead cost incurred	$600,000	
Budgeted variable factory overhead for 105,000 hours	(603,750)	
Variance—favorable		$(3,750)
Fixed factory overhead volume variance:		
Normal productive capacity at 100%	100,000 hrs.	
Standard for amount produced	105,000	
Productive capacity not used	5,000 hrs.	
Standard factory overhead rate	× $9.00	
Variance—unfavorable		45,000
Total factory overhead cost variance—unfavorable		$41,250

Identify the errors in the factory overhead cost variance analysis.

E13-30 Factory overhead cost variance report

✔ Net controllable variance, $1,710 U

app

Topeka Plastics Inc. prepared the following factory overhead cost budget for the Trim Department for July, during which it expected to use 25,000 hours for production:

Variable overhead cost:		
Indirect factory labor	$20,000	
Power and light	18,000	
Indirect materials	9,000	
Total variable cost		$ 47,000
Fixed overhead cost:		
Supervisory salaries	$50,000	
Depreciation of plant and equipment	33,100	
Insurance and property taxes	11,400	
Total fixed cost		94,500
Total factory overhead cost		$141,500

Topeka Plastics has 30,000 hours of monthly productive capacity available in the Trim Department under normal business conditions. During July, the Trim Department actually used 28,000 hours for production. The actual fixed costs were as budgeted. The actual variable overhead for July was as follows:

Actual variable factory overhead cost:	
Indirect factory labor	$23,250
Power and light	20,000
Indirect materials	11,100
Total variable cost	$54,350

Construct a factory overhead cost variance report for the Trim Department for July.

Problems

P13-1 Sales, production, direct materials purchases, and direct labor cost

Obj. 2

✔ 3. Total direct materials purchases, $3,894,830

The budget director of Royal British Furniture Company requests estimates of sales, production, and other operating data from the various administrative units every month. Selected information concerning sales and production for March is summarized as follows:

a. Estimated sales of William and Kate chairs for March by sales territory:

Eastern Domestic:	
William	7,500 units at $800 per unit
Kate	6,000 units at $650 per unit
Western Domestic:	
William	6,000 units at $700 per unit
Kate	5,000 units at $550 per unit
International:	
William	2,500 units at $600 per unit
Kate	1,000 units at $350 per unit

b. Estimated inventories at March 1:

Direct materials:		Finished products:	
Fabric	5,500 sq. yds.	William	1,500 units
Wood	13,700 lineal ft.	Kate	300 units
Filler	3,800 cu. ft.		
Springs	3,500 units		

c. Desired inventories at March 31:

Direct materials:		Finished products:	
Fabric	9,000 sq. yds.	William	2,000 units
Wood	20,000 lineal ft.	Kate	900 units
Filler	5,000 cu. ft.		
Springs	7,500 units		

d. Direct materials used in production:

In manufacture of William:

Fabric	4.0 sq. yds. per unit of product
Wood	16 lineal ft. per unit of product
Filler	3.8 cu. ft. per unit of product
Springs	14 units per unit of product

In manufacture of Kate:

Fabric	2.5 sq. yds. per unit of product
Wood	12 lineal ft. per unit of product
Filler	3.2 cu. ft. per unit of product
Springs	10 units per unit of product

e. Anticipated purchase price for direct materials:

Fabric	$9.00 per sq. yd.	Filler	$1.50 per cu. ft.
Wood	5.00 per lineal ft.	Springs	2.00 per unit

f. Direct labor requirements:

William:	
Framing Department	2.5 hrs. at $15 per hr.
Cutting Department	1.0 hr. at $12 per hr.
Upholstery Department	3.0 hrs. at $16 per hr.
Kate:	
Framing Department	1.5 hrs. at $15 per hr.
Cutting Department	0.5 hr. at $12 per hr.
Upholstery Department	2.0 hrs. at $16 per hr.

Instructions

1. Prepare a sales budget for March.
2. Prepare a production budget for March.
3. Prepare a direct materials purchases budget for March.
4. Prepare a direct labor cost budget for March.

Obj. 2

✔ 4. Total direct labor cost in Assembly Dept., $39,900

P13-2 Budgeted income statement and supporting budgets

The budget director of Jupiter Helmets Inc., with the assistance of the controller, treasurer, production manager, and sales manager, has gathered the following data for use in developing the budgeted income statement for May:

a. Estimated sales for May:

Bicycle helmet	7,500 units at $24 per unit
Motorcycle helmet	5,000 units at $175 per unit

b. Estimated inventories at May 1:

Direct materials:		Finished products:	
Plastic	1,480 lbs.	Bicycle helmet	200 units at $15 per unit
Foam lining	520 lbs.	Motorcycle helmet	100 units at $90 per unit

c. Desired inventories at May 31:

Direct materials:		Finished products:	
Plastic	2,000 lbs.	Bicycle helmet	400 units at $15 per unit
Foam lining	800 lbs.	Motorcycle helmet	300 units at $100 per unit

d. Direct materials used in production:

In manufacture of bicycle helmet:	
Plastic	0.90 lb. per unit of product
Foam lining	0.20 lb. per unit of product
In manufacture of motorcycle helmet:	
Plastic	3.50 lbs. per unit of product
Foam lining	1.40 lbs. per unit of product

e. Anticipated cost of purchases and beginning and ending inventory of direct materials:

Plastic	$4.40 per lb.
Foam lining	$0.90 per lb.

f. Direct labor requirements:

Bicycle helmet:	
Molding Department	0.30 hr. at $15 per hr.
Assembly Department	0.10 hr. at $14 per hr.
Motorcycle helmet:	
Molding Department	0.50 hr. at $15 per hr.
Assembly Department	0.40 hr. at $14 per hr.

g. Estimated factory overhead costs for May:

Indirect factory wages	$125,000	Power and light	$23,000
Depreciation of plant and equipment	45,000	Insurance and property tax	11,000

h. Estimated operating expenses for May:

Sales salaries expense	$175,000
Advertising expense	120,000
Office salaries expense	92,000
Depreciation expense—office equipment	6,000
Miscellaneous expense—selling	5,000
Utilities expense—administrative	3,000
Travel expense—selling	50,000
Office supplies expense	2,500
Miscellaneous administrative expense	1,500

i. Estimated other income and expense for May:

Interest revenue	$14,560
Interest expense	3,000

j. Estimated tax rate: 25%

Instructions

1. Prepare a sales budget for May.
2. Prepare a production budget for May.
3. Prepare a direct materials purchases budget for May.
4. Prepare a direct labor cost budget for May.
5. Prepare a factory overhead cost budget for May.
6. Prepare a cost of goods sold budget for May. Work in process at the beginning of May is estimated to be $4,200, and work in process at the end of May is desired to be $3,800.
7. Prepare a selling and administrative expenses budget for May.
8. Prepare a budgeted income statement for May.

P13-3 Cash budget

Obj. 2

✔ 1. March deficiency, $(26,000)

The controller of Shoe Mart Inc. asks you to prepare a monthly cash budget for the next three months. You are presented with the following budget information:

	January	February	March
Sales	$450,000	$550,000	$700,000
Manufacturing costs	260,000	330,000	420,000
Selling and administrative expenses	100,000	140,000	150,000
Capital expenditures	—	—	45,000

The company expects to sell about 20% of its merchandise for cash. Of sales on account, 75% are expected to be collected in full in the month following the sale and the remainder the following month. Depreciation, insurance, and property tax expense represent $40,000 of the estimated monthly manufacturing costs. The annual insurance premium is paid in June, and the annual property taxes are paid in October. Of the remainder of the manufacturing costs, 90% are expected to be paid in the month in which they are incurred and the balance in the following month. All sales and administrative expenses are paid in the month incurred.

Current assets as of January 1 include cash of $45,000, marketable securities of $65,000, and accounts receivable of $290,000 ($240,000 from December sales and $50,000 from November sales). Sales on account in November and December were $200,000 and $240,000, respectively. Current liabilities as of January 1 include a $50,000, 8%, 90-day note payable due March 20 and $18,000 of accounts payable incurred in December for manufacturing costs. All selling and administrative expenses are paid in cash in the period they are incurred. It is expected that $20,000 in dividends will be received in January. An estimated income tax payment of $15,000 will be made in February. Shoe Mart's regular quarterly dividend of $5,000 is expected to be declared in February and paid in March. Management desires to maintain a minimum cash balance of $35,000.

Instructions

1. Prepare a monthly cash budget and supporting schedules for January, February, and March.
2. On the basis of the cash budget prepared in part (1), what recommendation should be made to the controller?

Obj. 5

✔ c. Direct labor time variance, $(4,320) F

P13-4 Direct materials and direct labor variance analysis

Faucet Industries Inc. manufactures faucets in a small manufacturing facility. The faucets are made from zinc. Faucet Industries has 60 employees. Each employee presently provides 36 hours of labor per week. Information about a production week is as follows:

Standard wage per hr.	$18.00
Standard labor time per faucet	12 min.
Standard number of lbs. of zinc	0.80 lb.
Standard price per lb. of zinc	$1.25
Actual price per lb. of zinc	$1.40
Actual lbs. of zinc used during the week	10,200 lbs.
Number of faucets produced during the week	12,000
Actual wage per hr.	$18.75
Actual hrs. per week	2,160 hrs.

Instructions

Determine (a) the standard cost per unit for direct materials and direct labor; (b) the price variance, quantity variance, and total direct materials cost variance; and (c) the rate variance, time variance, and total direct labor cost variance.

Obj. 5

✔ a. Direct materials price variance, $(6,704) F

app

P13-5 Direct materials and direct labor, variance analysis; factory overhead cost variance analysis

Route 66 Tire Co. manufactures automobile tires. Standard costs and actual costs for direct materials, direct labor, and factory overhead incurred for the manufacture of 10,000 tires were as follows:

	Standard Costs	Actual Costs
Direct materials	85,000 lbs. at $6.25	83,800 lbs. at $6.17
Direct labor	4,000 hrs. at $20.80	4,450 hrs. at $21.00
Factory overhead	Rates per direct labor hr., based on 100% of normal capacity of 5,000 direct labor hrs.:	
	Variable cost, $2.90	$11,375 variable cost
	Fixed cost, $11.40	$57,000 fixed cost

Instructions

Determine (a) the price variance, quantity variance, and total direct materials cost variance; (b) the rate variance, time variance, and total direct labor cost variance; and (c) Appendix: variable factory overhead controllable variance, the fixed factory overhead volume variance, and total factory overhead cost variance.

P13-6 Standards for nonmanufacturing expenses

Obj. 5

✔ 2. $(144) F

The Radiology Department provides imaging services for Northeast Washington Medical Center. One important activity in the Radiology Department is transcribing digitally recorded analyses of images into a written report. The manager of the Radiology Department determined that the average transcriptionist could type 800 lines of a report in an hour. The plan for the first week in July called for 64,000 typed lines to be written. The Radiology Department has two transcriptionists. Each transcriptionist is hired from an employment firm that requires temporary employees to be hired for a minimum of a 40-hour week. Transcriptionists are paid $18.00 per hour. The manager offered a bonus if the department could type more than 70,000 lines for the week, without overtime. Due to high service demands, the transcriptionists typed more lines in the first week of July than planned. The actual amount of lines typed in the first week of July was 70,400 lines, without overtime. As a result, the bonus caused the average transcriptionist hourly rate to increase to $20.00 per hour during the first week in July.

Instructions

1. If the department typed 64,000 lines according to the original plan, what would have been the labor time variance?
2. What was the labor time variance as a result of typing 70,400 lines?
3. What was the labor rate variance as a result of the bonus?
4. The manager is trying to determine if a better decision would have been to hire a temporary transcriptionist to meet the higher typing demands in the first week of July, rather than paying out the bonus. If another employee was hired from the employment firm, what would have been the labor time variance in the first week?
5. Which decision is better, paying the bonus or hiring another transcriptionist?
6. Are there any performance-related issues that the labor time and rate variances fail to consider? Explain.

P13-7 Standard factory overhead variance report

✔ Controllable variance, $(390) F

app

Seabury, Inc., a manufacturer of disposable medical supplies, prepared the following factory overhead cost budget for the Assembly Department for October. The company expected to operate the department at 100% of normal capacity of 25,000 hours.

Variable costs:		
Indirect factory wages	$150,000	
Power and light	29,500	
Indirect materials	17,000	
Total variable cost		$196,500
Fixed costs:		
Supervisory salaries	$125,000	
Depreciation of plant and equipment	49,000	
Insurance and property taxes	29,750	
Total fixed cost		203,750
Total factory overhead cost		$400,250

During October, the department operated at 23,500 hours, and the factory overhead costs incurred were as follows: indirect factory wages, $140,500; power and light, $28,600; indirect materials, $15,220; supervisory salaries, $125,000; depreciation of plant and equipment, $49,000; and insurance and property taxes, $29,750.

Instructions

Prepare a factory overhead cost variance report for October. To be useful for cost control, the budgeted amounts should be based on 23,500 hours.

Metric-Based Analysis

Obj. 6

MBA 13-1 Process yield

Perez Inc. manufactures various types of furniture including couches, tables, and chairs. During April, wood for 1,000 tables entered into the cutting process where wood is cut to design specifications. After the cutting process, the tables entered into assembly, laminating/painting, and packaging processes. Quality control rejected the following tables from the cutting, assembly, laminating/painting, and packaging/shipping processes.

Manufacturing Process	Number of Tables Failing Inspection
Cutting	60
Assembly	15
Laminating/Painting	25
Packing/Shipping	5

1. Compute the process yield for cutting. Round to one decimal place.
2. Compute the process yield for assembly. Round to one decimal place.
3. Compute the process yield for laminating/painting. Round to one decimal place.
4. Compute the process yield for packing/shipping. Round to one decimal place.
5. Compute the overall process yield for April. Round to one decimal place.
6. Which processes require improvement?

Obj. 6

MBA 13-2 Process yield

Hendrick Motorsports sponsors cars and drivers in the National Association for Stock Car Auto Racing (NASCAR)'s Sprint Cup Series. Performance data for three recent years are as follows:

	Number of		
Year	Races	Wins	Top 10 Finishes
3	149	9	75
2	144	13	74
1	144	9	77

Performance data for Hendrick Motorsports' drivers are as follows:

	Number of		
Driver	Races	Wins	Top 10 Finishes
Jimmie Johnson	516	77	320
Terry Labonte	387	12	125
Dale Earnhardt, Jr.	295	9	130

1. Using the number of wins as a yield, determine the process yield for each of the three years. Round to one decimal place.
2. Using the number of "top ten finishes" as a yield, determine the process yield for each of the three years. Round to one decimal place.
3. Using the number of wins as a yield, determine the process yield for each driver. Round to one decimal place.
4. Using the number of "top ten finishes" as a yield, determine the process yield for each driver. Round to one decimal place.
5. Comment on the results from (1), (2), (3), and (4).

MBA 13-3 Utilization rate

Obj. 6

Hilton Worldwide Holdings Inc. (HLT) and Marriott International, Inc. (MAR) reported the following occupancy data for two recent years:

	Year 2	Year 1
Hilton	75.4%	74.6%
Marriott	73.7%	73.3%

1. Comment on Hilton's occupancy rate for Years 1 and 2.
2. Comment on Marriott's occupancy rate for Years 1 and 2.
3. Which company has the highest occupancy rate?
4. What other factors should be considered in comparing Hilton and Marriott?

MBA 13-4 Utilization rate

Obj. 6

Stop-N-Stay and Paradise Inn operate motels across the northwest. Operating data for each chain are as follows:

	Hotels	Rooms per Hotel	Total Rooms
Stop-N-Stay	50	180	9,000
Paradise Inn	60	175	10,500

For August, each chain reported the following:

	Room Nights Occupied	Average Daily Room Rate
Stop-N-Stay	239,940	$125
Paradise Inn	292,950	$ 95

1. Determine the occupancy rate for Stop-N-Stay for August.
2. Determine the occupancy rate for Paradise Inn for August.
3. Determine the total room revenue for each chain for August.
4. Compare and comment on the operating results for each chain.

MBA 13-5 Utilization rate

Obj. 6

The East Memorial Hospital measures occupancy using the number of patient beds used during a month. Patient data for the months of January, February, and March are as follow:

	January	February*	March
Admitted patients	24,500	23,000	25,200
Average nights per patient	2.0	1.8	2.2

*Assume February has 28 days.

East Memorial Hospital has 1,000 rooms, which includes 200 private rooms with one bed and 800 semi-private rooms with two beds.

1. Determine the number of patient beds used for each month.
2. Determine the available patient beds for each month.
3. Determine the occupancy (utilization) rate for each month. Round to one decimal place.
4. Comment on the occupancy (utilization) rates for January, February, and March.

Obj. 6

MBA 13-6 Utilization rate

Delta Air Lines (DAL) reported the following data (in millions) for three recent years.

	Year 3	Year 2	Year 1
Available seat miles	246,764	239,676	232,740
Passenger miles flown	209,625	202,925	194,974
Revenue	$34,782	$34,954	$32,942

Delta refers to its utilization rates as "passenger load factor."

1. Compute the passenger load factor (utilization rate) for each year.
2. Compute the passenger revenue per seat mile flown. Express in cents rounded to one decimal place.
3. Comment on (1) and (2).

Obj. 6

MBA 13-7 Utilization rate

Southwest Airlines Co. (LUV) reported the following data (in millions) for a recent year.

	Year 3	Year 2	Year 1
Available seat miles	140,501	131,004	130,344
Passenger miles flown	117,500	108,035	104,348
Revenue	$18,299	$17,658	$16,721

Southwest refers to its utilization rates as "passenger load factor."

1. Compute the passenger load factor (utilization rate) for each year.
2. Compute the passenger revenue per seat mile flown. Express in cents rounded to one decimal place.
3. Comment on (1) and (2).

Obj. 6

MBA 13-8 Utilization rate

Using the results of MBA 13-6 and MBA 13-7, compare the operating results of Delta Air Lines (DAL) and Southwest Airlines (LUV).

Cases

Case 13-1 Ethics and professional conduct in business

The director of marketing for Truss Industries Inc., Ellen Knutson, had the following discussion with the company controller, Bud Wyckoff, on February 26 of the current year:

Ellen: Bud, it looks like I'm going to spend much less than indicated on my February budget.

Bud: I'm glad to hear it.

Ellen: Well, I'm not so sure it's good news. I'm concerned that the president will see that I'm under budget and reduce my budget in the future. The only reason that I look good is that we've delayed an advertising campaign. Once the campaign hits in May, I'm sure my actual expenditures will go up. You see, we are also having our sales convention in May. Having the advertising campaign and the convention at the same time is going to kill my May numbers.

Bud: I don't think that's anything to worry about. We all expect some variation in actual spending month to month. What's really important is staying within the budgeted targets for the year. Does that look as if it's going to be a problem?

Ellen: I don't think so, but just the same, I'd like to be on the safe side.

Bud: What do you mean?

Ellen: Well, this is what I'd like to do. I want to pay the convention-related costs in advance this month. I'll pay the hotel for room and convention space and purchase the airline tickets in advance. In this way, I can charge all these expenditures to February's budget. This would cause my actual expenses to come close to budget for February. Moreover, when the big advertising campaign hits in May, I won't have to worry about expenditures for the convention on my May budget as well. The convention costs will already be paid. Thus, my May expenses should be pretty close to budget.

Bud: I can't tell you when to make your convention purchases, but I'm not too sure that it should be expensed on February's budget.

Ellen: What's the problem? It looks like "no harm, no foul" to me. I can't see that there's anything wrong with this—it's just smart management.

How should Bud Wyckoff respond to Ellen Knutson's request to expense the advanced payments for convention-related costs against February's budget?

Case 13-2 Evaluating budgeting systems

Children's Hospital of the King's Daughters Health System in Norfolk, Virginia, introduced a new budgeting method that allowed the hospital's annual plan to be updated for changes in actual operations. For example, if the budget was based on 1,000 patient-days (number of patients × number of days in the hospital) and the actual count rose to 1,200 patient-days, the variable costs of staffing, lab work, and medication costs could be adjusted to reflect this change. The budget manager stated, "I work with hospital directors to turn data into meaningful information and affect change before the month ends."

1. What budgeting methods are being used under the new approach?
2. Why are these methods superior to the former approaches?

Case 13-3 Service company static decision making

A bank manager of Oxford First Bank Inc. uses the managerial accounting system to track the costs of operating the various departments within the bank. The departments include Cash Management, Trust, Commercial Loans, Mortgage Loans, Operations, Credit Card, and Branch Services. The budget and actual results for the Operations Department are as follows:

Resources	Budget	Actual
Salaries	$300,000	$300,000
Benefits	40,000	40,000
Supplies	27,000	22,000
Travel	15,000	43,000
Training	13,000	15,000
Overtime	20,000	15,000
Total	$415,000	$435,000
Excess of actual over budget	$20,000	

1. What information is provided by the budget? Specifically, what questions can the bank manager ask of the Operations Department manager?
2. What information does the budget fail to provide? Specifically, could the budget information be presented differently to provide even more insight for the bank manager?

Case 13-4 Objectives of the master budget

Domino's Pizza LLC operates pizza delivery and carryout restaurants. The annual report describes its business as follows:

> *We offer a focused menu of high-quality, value priced pizza with three types of crust (Hand-Tossed, Thin Crust, and Deep Dish), along with buffalo wings, bread sticks, cheesy bread, CinnaStix®, and Coca Cola® products. Our hand-tossed pizza is made from fresh dough produced in our regional distribution centers. We prepare every pizza using real cheese, pizza sauce made from fresh tomatoes, and a choice of high-quality meat and vegetable toppings in generous portions. Our focused menu and use of premium ingredients enable us to consistently and efficiently produce the highest-quality pizza.*
>
> *Over the 41 years since our founding, we have developed a simple, cost-efficient model. We offer a limited menu, our stores are designed for delivery and carry-out, and we do not generally offer dine-in service. As a result, our stores require relatively small, lower-rent locations and limited capital expenditures.*

How would a master budget support planning, directing, and control for Domino's?

Case 13-5 Integrity and evaluating budgeting systems

The city of Rosebud has an annual budget cycle that begins on July 1 and ends on June 30. At the beginning of each budget year, an annual budget is established for each department. The annual budget is divided by 12 months to provide a constant monthly static budget. On June 30, all unspent budgeted monies for the budget year from the various city departments must be "returned" to the General Fund. Thus, if department heads fail to use their budget by year-end, they will lose it. A budget analyst prepared a chart of the difference between the monthly actual and budgeted amounts for the recent fiscal year. The chart was as follows:

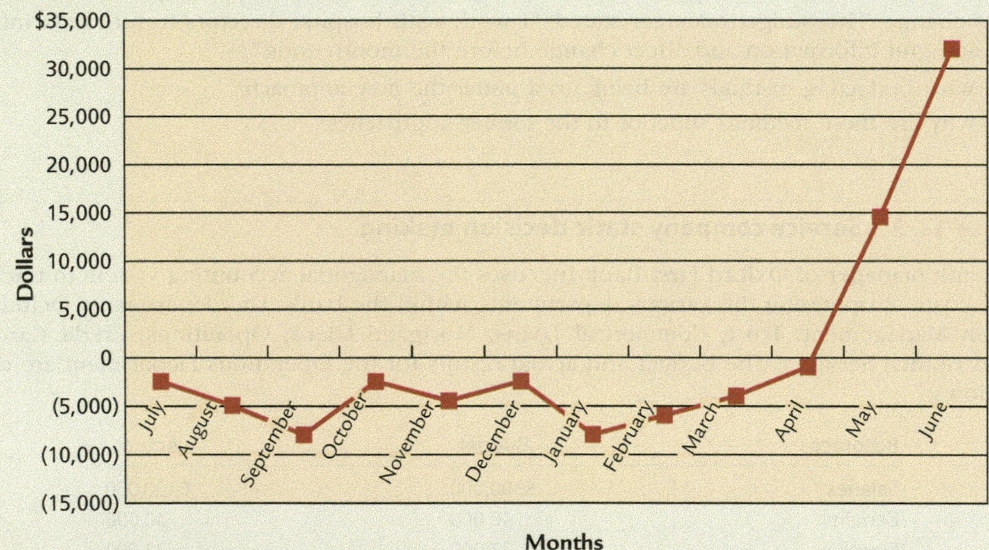

1. Interpret the chart.
2. Suggest an improvement in the budget system.

Case 13-6 Ethics and professional conduct in business using nonmanufacturing standards

Christy Eisenbeis is a cost analyst with Nations Insurance Company. Nations Insurance is applying standards to its claims payment operation. Claims payment is a repetitive operation that could be evaluated with standards. Christy used time and motion studies to identify an ideal standard of 24 claims processed per hour. The Claims Processing Department manager, Everett Boyle, has rejected this standard and has argued that the standard should be 18 claims processed per hour. Everett and Christy were unable to agree, so they decided to discuss this matter openly at a joint meeting with the vice president of operations, who would arbitrate a final decision. Prior to the meeting, Christy wrote the following memo to the VP.

To: *Megan Wilkins, Vice President of Operations*
From: *Christy Eisenbeis*
Re: *Standards in the Claims Processing Department*

As you know, Everett and I are scheduled to meet with you to discuss our disagreement with respect to the appropriate standards for the Claims Processing Department. I have conducted time and motion studies and have determined that the ideal standard is 24 claims processed per hour. Everett argues that 18 claims processed per hour would be more appropriate. I believe he is trying to "pad" the budget with some slack. I'm not sure what he is trying to get away with, but I believe a tight standard will drive efficiency up in his area. I hope you will agree when we meet with you next week.

Discuss the ethical and professional issues in this situation.

Case 13-7 Variance interpretation

Harmony Industries Inc. is a small manufacturer of electronic musical instruments. The plant manager received the following variable factory overhead report for the period:

	Actual	Budgeted Variable Factory Overhead at Actual Production	Controllable Variance
Indirect factory wages	$100,800	$ 72,000	$28,800 U
Power and light	38,000	40,000	(2,000) F
Supplies	21,000	18,000	3,000 U
Total	$159,800	$130,000	$29,800 U

Actual units produced: 15,000 (75% of practical capacity)

The plant manager is not pleased with the $29,800 unfavorable variable factory overhead controllable variance and has come to discuss the matter with the controller. The following discussion occurred:

Plant Manager: I just received this factory report for the latest month of operation. I'm not pleased with these figures. Before these numbers go to headquarters, you and I will need to reach an understanding.

Controller: Go ahead, what's the problem?

Plant Manager: What's the problem? Well, everything. Look at the variance. It's too large. If I understand the accounting approach being used here, you are assuming that my costs are variable to the units produced. Thus, as the production volume declines, so should these costs. Well, I don't believe that these costs are variable at all. I think they are fixed costs. As a result, when we operate below capacity, the costs really don't go down at all. I'm being penalized for costs I have no control over at all. I need this report to be redone to reflect this fact. If anything, the difference between actual and budget is essentially a volume variance. Listen, I know that you're a team player. You really need to reconsider your assumptions on this one.

If you were in the controller's position, how would you respond to the plant manager?

Answers to Self-Examination Questions

1. **B** Administrative departments (answer B), such as Purchasing or Human Resources, will often use static budgeting. Production departments (answer A) frequently use flexible budgets. Responsibility centers (answer C) can use either static or flexible budgeting. Capital expenditure budgets are used to plan capital projects (answer D).
2. **B** The total production indicated in the production budget is 257,500 units (answer B), which is computed as follows:

Sales	250,000	units
Plus desired ending inventory	30,000	units
Total	280,000	units
Less estimated beginning inventory	(22,500)	units
Total production	257,500	units

3. **C** Dixon expects to collect 70% of April sales ($560,000) plus 30% of the March sales ($195,000) in April, for a total of $755,000 (answer C). Answer A is 100% of April sales. Answer B is 70% of April sales. Answer D adds 70% of both March and April sales.
4. **C** The unfavorable direct materials price variance of $2,550 is determined as follows:

Actual price	$5.05 per pound
Standard price	(5.00)
Price variance—unfavorable	$0.05 per pound

Direct materials price variance: $2,550 = $0.05 × 51,000 actual pounds

5. **D** The unfavorable direct labor time variance of $2,400 is determined as follows:

Actual direct labor time	2,200 hours
Standard direct labor time	(2,000)
Direct labor time variance	200 hours

Direct labor time variance: Unfavorable
$2,400 = 200 × $12 standard rate

Chapter

14 Decentralized Operations

What's Covered:

Topics: Decentralized Operations

Operational Responsibility
- Centralized operations (Obj. 1)
- Decentralized operations (Obj. 1)
- Responsibility reporting (Obj. 1)

Cost Centers
- Nature (Obj. 2)
- Responsibility reporting (Obj. 2

Profit Centers
- Nature (Obj. 3)
- Service department allocations (Obj. 3)
- Responsibility reporting (Obj. 3)

Investment Centers
- Nature (Obj. 4)
- Return on investment (Obj. 4)
- Residual income (Obj. 4)

Transfer Pricing
- Market price approach (Obj. 5)
- Negotiated price approach (Obj. 5)
- Cost approach (Obj. 5)

Metric-Based Analysis
- Balanced scorecard (Obj. 6)

Learning Objectives

Obj.1 Describe types of operational responsibility.

Obj.2 Describe and illustrate responsibility reporting for a cost center.

Obj.3 Describe and illustrate responsibility reporting for a profit center.

Obj.4 Describe and illustrate responsibility reporting for an investment center.

Obj.5 Describe and illustrate transfer pricing for decentralized segments of a business.

Obj.6 Describe and illustrate balanced scorecard and related metrics.

Chapter Metrics

The managerial decision-making and performance metrics for this chapter are a balanced scorecard and related metrics.

Caterpillar

Have you ever wondered why large retail stores like Walmart, **Target, Cabela's**, and **Macy's** are divided into departments? Organizing into departments allows retailers to provide products and expertise in specialized areas while offering a wide range of products. Departments also allow companies to assign responsibility for financial performance. This information can be used to make product decisions, evaluate operations, and guide company strategy. Strong departmental performance might be attributable to a good department manager, and weak departmental performance may be the result of a product mix that has low customer appeal. By tracking departmental performance, companies can identify and reward excellent performance and take corrective action in departments that are performing poorly.

Like retailers, most businesses organize into operational units, such as divisions and departments. For example, **Caterpillar, Inc. (CAT)**, manufactures a variety of equipment and machinery and is organized into a number of different segments, including Construction Industries, Resource Industries, Energy and Transportation, and Financial Products. The Construction Industries segment manufactures construction equipment, such as tractors, dump trucks, and loaders. The Resource Industries segment makes equipment for the mining industry, such as off-highway and mining trucks. The Energy and Transportation segment manufactures equipment that is used to generate power, such as engines and turbines for power plants and railroads. The Financial Products segment provides financing for Caterpillar products to customers and dealers.

Managers at Caterpillar are responsible for running their business segment. Each segment is evaluated on segment profit. The company uses segment profit to determine how to allocate resources between business segments and to plan and control the company's operations. In this chapter, the role of accounting in assisting managers in planning and controlling organizational units, such as departments, divisions, and stores, is described and illustrated.

Objective 1
Describe types of operational responsibility.

Operational Responsibility

The Board of Directors and top management of a company assign responsibility for managing the day-to-day operations of the company. Operational responsibility can be assigned as follows:

- Centralized
- Decentralized

Centralized Operations

When operational responsibility is centralized all major planning and operating decisions are made by top management. For example, a one-person, owner-manager-operated company is centralized because all plans and decisions are made by one person. In a small owner-manager-operated business, centralization may be desirable. This is because the owner-manager's close supervision ensures the business will be operated in the way the owner-manager wishes.

Decentralized Operations

When operational responsibility is decentralized, managers of separate divisions or units are delegated the responsibility for managing their operations. For example, in a decentralized company, the division (unit) managers are responsible for planning and controlling the operations of their divisions. In such cases, the divisions are normally structured around products, customers, or regions.

The level of decentralization may vary from company to company and even within the same company. For example, in some companies, division managers have authority over all operations, including fixed asset purchases. In other companies, division managers only have authority over revenues and expenses.

Caterpillar uses a decentralized network of over a thousand dealers to sell its equipment.

Caterpillar Connection

Advantages of Decentralization. For large companies, it is difficult for top management to maintain the following:

- daily contact with all operations
- operating expertise in all product lines and services

In such cases, delegating authority to managers closest to the operations usually results in better decisions. For example, these managers can often anticipate and react more quickly to operating data than can top management. In addition, the time pressures on top managers prevent them from becoming experts in all areas of operations. In contrast, managers closest to the operations can focus on becoming "experts" in their area.

Decentralized operations also provide excellent training for managers. Delegating responsibility allows managers to develop managerial experience early in their careers. This helps a company retain managers, some of whom may be later promoted to top management positions.

Finally, managers of decentralized operations often work closely with customers. As a result, they tend to identify with customers and, thus, are often more creative in suggesting operating and product improvements. This helps create good customer relations.

Disadvantages of Decentralization. A primary disadvantage of decentralized operations is that decisions made by one manager may negatively affect the profits of the company. For example, managers of divisions whose products compete with one another might start a price war that decreases the profits of both divisions and, thus, the overall company.

Another disadvantage of decentralized operations is that assets and expenses may be duplicated across divisions. For example, each manager of a product line might have a separate sales force and office support staff.

The advantages and disadvantages of decentralization are summarized in Exhibit 1.

Exhibit 1 Advantages and Disadvantages of Decentralized Operations

Advantages of Decentralization

- Allows managers closest to the operations to make decisions
- Provides excellent training for managers
- Allows managers to become experts in their area of operation
- Helps retain managers
- Improves creativity and customer relations

Disadvantages of Decentralization

- Decisions made by managers may negatively affect the profits of the company
- Duplicates assets and expenses

Responsibility Accounting

In a decentralized business, accounting assists managers in evaluating and controlling their areas of responsibility, called *responsibility centers.* **Responsibility accounting** is the process of measuring and reporting operating data by responsibility center.

Three types of responsibility centers are:

1. Cost centers, which have responsibility over costs.
2. Profit centers, which have responsibility over revenues and costs.
3. Investment centers, which have responsibility over revenue, costs, and investment in assets.

Responsibility Accounting for Cost Centers

Objective 2

Describe and illustrate responsibility reporting for a cost center.

A **cost center** manager has responsibility for controlling costs. For example, the supervisor of the Power Department has responsibility for the costs of providing power. A cost center manager does not make decisions concerning sales or the amount of fixed assets invested in the center.

Cost centers may vary in size from a small department to an entire manufacturing plant. In addition, cost centers may exist within other cost centers. For example, an entire university or college could be viewed as a cost center, and each college and department within the university also could be a cost center, as shown in Exhibit 2.

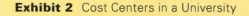

Exhibit 2 Cost Centers in a University

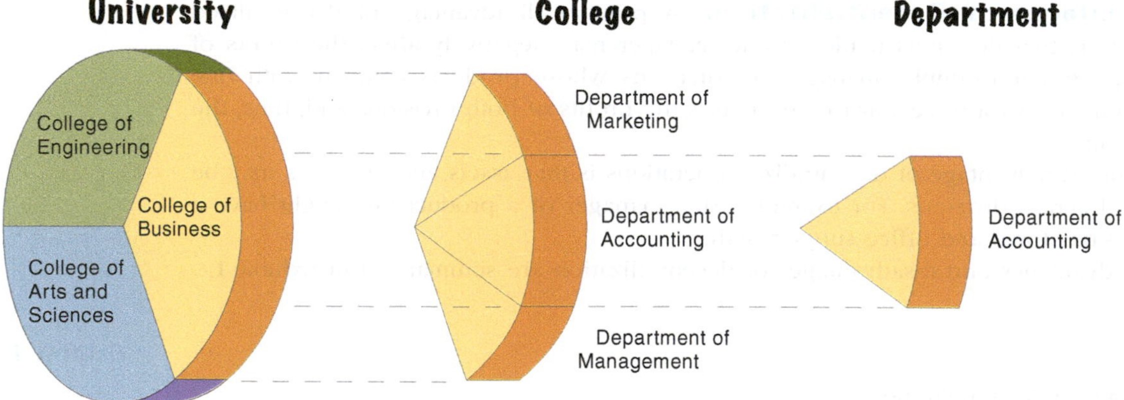

Responsibility accounting for cost centers focuses on controlling and reporting of costs. Budget performance reports that report budgeted and actual costs are normally prepared for each cost center.

Exhibit 3 illustrates budget performance reports for the following cost centers:

1. Vice President, Production
2. Manager, Plant A
3. Supervisor, Department 1—Plant A

Caterpillar Connection

Caterpillar's "Corporate Services" group performs support services to its operating segments and is organized as a cost center.

Exhibit 3 Responsibility Accounting Reports for Cost Centers

Budget Performance Report
Vice President, Production
For the Month Ended October 31, 20Y5

	Budget	Actual	Over Budget	(Under) Budget
Administration	$ 19,500	$ 19,700	$ 200	
Plant A	467,475	470,330	2,855	
Plant B	395,225	394,300		$(925)
	$882,200	$884,330	$3,055	$(925)

Budget Performance Report
Manager, Plant A
For the Month Ended October 31, 20Y5

	Budget	Actual	Over Budget	(Under) Budget
Administration	$ 17,500	$ 17,350		$(150)
Department 1	109,725	111,280	$1,555	
Department 2	190,500	192,600	2,100	
Department 3	149,750	149,100		(650)
	$467,475	$470,330	$3,655	$(800)

Budget Performance Report
Supervisor, Department 1—Plant A
For the Month Ended October 31, 20Y5

	Budget	Actual	Over Budget	(Under) Budget
Factory wages	$ 58,100	$ 58,000		$(100)
Materials	32,500	34,225	$1,725	
Supervisory salaries	6,400	6,400		
Power and light	5,750	5,690		(60)
Depreciation of plant and equipment	4,000	4,000		
Maintenance	2,000	1,990		(10)
Insurance and property taxes	975	975		
	$109,725	$111,280	$1,725	$(170)

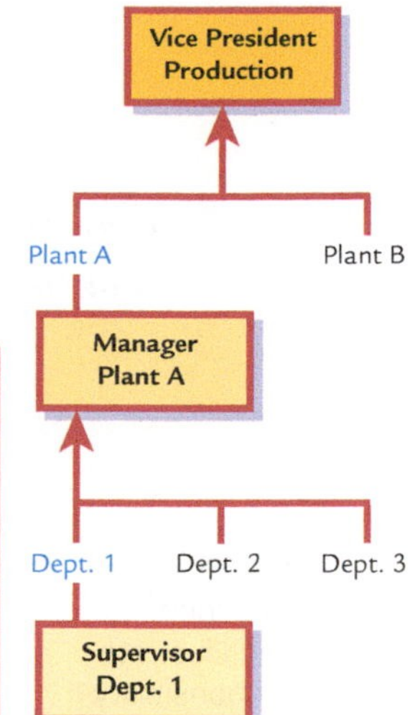

Exhibit 3 shows how cost centers are often linked together within a company. For example, the budget performance report for Department 1—Plant A supports the report for Plant A, which supports the report for the vice president of production.

The reports in Exhibit 3 show the budgeted costs and actual costs along with the differences. Each difference is classified as either *over* budget or *under* budget. Such reports allow cost center managers to focus on areas of significant differences.

For example, the supervisor for Department 1 of Plant A can focus on why the materials cost was over budget. The supervisor might discover that excess materials were scrapped. This could be due to such factors as machine malfunctions, improperly trained employees, or low quality materials.

As shown in Exhibit 3, responsibility accounting reports are usually more summarized for higher levels of management. For example, the budget performance report for the manager of Plant A shows only administration and departmental data. This report enables the plant manager to identify the departments responsible for major differences. Likewise, the report for the vice president of production summarizes the cost data for each plant.

Caterpillar Connection **Caterpillar**'s corporate headquarters are located in Peoria, Illinois.

Responsibility Accounting for Profit Centers

Objective 3
Describe and illustrate responsibility reporting for a profit center.

A **profit center** manager has the responsibility and authority for making decisions that affect revenues and costs and, thus, profits. Profit centers may be divisions, departments, or products. As a result, the manager of a profit center does not make decisions concerning the fixed assets invested in the center.

Responsibility accounting for profit centers focuses on reporting revenues, expenses, and operating income. Thus, responsibility accounting reports for profit centers take the form of income statements.

The profit center income statement should include only revenues and expenses that are controlled by the manager. **Controllable revenues** are revenues earned by the profit center. **Controllable expenses** are costs that can be influenced (controlled) by the decisions of profit center managers.

Service Department Charges

The controllable expenses of profit centers include *direct operating expenses* such as sales salaries and utility expenses. In addition, a profit center may incur expenses provided by internal centralized *service departments*. Examples of such service departments include the following:

1. Research and Development
2. Legal
3. Telecommunications
4. Information and Computer Systems
5. Facilities Management
6. Purchasing
7. Publications and Graphics
8. Payroll Accounting
9. Transportation
10. Personnel Administration

Caterpillar Connection **Caterpillar**'s research and development is conducted at its Technical Center in Mossville, Illinois.

Service department charges are *indirect* expenses to a profit center. They are similar to the expenses that would be incurred if the profit center purchased the services from outside the company. A profit center manager has control over service department expenses if the manager is free to choose how much service is used. In such cases, **service department charges** are allocated to profit centers based on the usage of the service by each profit center.

To illustrate, Tadpole Inc., a diversified entertainment company shown in Exhibit 4, is used. Tadpole Inc. has the following two operating divisions organized as profit centers:

1. Theme Park Division
2. Photography Division

Exhibit 4 Payroll Accounting Department Charges to Tadpole Inc.'s Theme Park and Photography Divisions

The revenues and direct operating expenses for Tadpole's two divisions are shown below. The operating expenses consist of direct expenses, such as the wages and salaries of a division's employees.

	Theme Park Division	Photography Division
Revenues	$6,000,000	$2,500,000
Operating expenses	2,495,000	405,000

Tadpole Inc.'s service departments and the expenses they incurred for the year ended December 31, 20Y7, are as follows:

Purchasing	$400,000
Payroll Accounting	255,000
Legal	250,000
Total	$905,000

An activity base for each service department is used to charge service department expenses to the Theme Park and Photography divisions. The activity base for each service department is a measure of the services performed. For Tadpole Inc., the service departments' activity bases are as follows:

Department	Activity Base
Purchasing	Number of purchase requisitions
Payroll Accounting	Number of payroll checks
Legal	Number of billed hours

The use of services by the Theme Park and Photography divisions is as follows:

	Service Usage		
Division	Purchasing	Payroll Accounting	Legal
Theme Park	25,000 purchase requisitions	12,000 payroll checks	100 billed hrs.
Photography	15,000	3,000	900
Total	40,000 purchase requisitions	15,000 payroll checks	1,000 billed hrs.

The rates at which services are charged to each division are called *service department charge rates*. These rates are computed as follows:

$$\textbf{Service Department Charge Rate} = \frac{\textbf{Service Department Expense}}{\textbf{Total Service Department Usage}}$$

Tadpole Inc.'s service department charge rates are computed as follows:

$$\textbf{Purchasing Charge Rate} = \frac{\$400{,}000}{40{,}000 \text{ purchase requisitions}} = \$10 \text{ per purchase requisition}$$

$$\textbf{Payroll Charge Rate} = \frac{\$255{,}000}{15{,}000 \text{ payroll checks}} = \$17 \text{ per payroll check}$$

$$\textbf{Legal Charge Rate} = \frac{\$250{,}000}{1{,}000 \text{ billed hrs.}} = \$250 \text{ per billed hr.}$$

The services used by each division are multiplied by the service department charge rates to determine the service charges for each division, as shown below.

$$\textbf{Service Department Charge} = \textbf{Service Usage} \times \textbf{Service Department Charge Rate}$$

Exhibit 5 illustrates the service department charges and related computations for Tadpole Inc.'s Theme Park and Photography divisions.

Exhibit 5 Service Department Charges to Tadpole Inc. Divisions

Tadpole Inc.
Service Department Charges to Tadpole Inc.'s Divisions
For the Year Ended December 31, 20Y7

Service Department	Theme Park Division	Photography Division
Purchasing (Note A)	$250,000	$150,000
Payroll Accounting (Note B)	204,000	51,000
Legal (Note C)	25,000	225,000
Total service department charges	$479,000	$426,000

Note A:
25,000 purchase requisitions × $10 per purchase requisition = $250,000
15,000 purchase requisitions × $10 per purchase requisition = $150,000

Note B:
12,000 payroll checks × $17 per payroll check = $204,000
3,000 payroll checks × $17 per payroll check = $51,000

Note C:
100 billed hours × $250 per billed hour = $25,000
900 billed hours × $250 per billed hour = $225,000

The differences in the service department charges between the two divisions can be explained by the nature of their operations and, thus, usage of services. For example, the Theme Park Division employs many part-time employees who are paid weekly. As a result, the Theme Park Division requires 12,000 payroll checks and incurs a $204,000 payroll service department charge (12,000 × $17). In contrast, the Photography Division has more permanent employees who are paid monthly. Thus, the Photography Division requires only 3,000 payroll checks and incurs a payroll service department charge of $51,000 (3,000 × $17).

Profit Center Reporting

The divisional income statements for Tadpole Inc. are shown in Exhibit 6. In evaluating the profit center manager, the operating income should be compared over time to a budget. However, it should not be compared across profit centers, since the profit centers are usually different in terms of size, products, and customers.

Exhibit 6 Divisional Income Statements—Tadpole Inc.

Tadpole Inc.
Divisional Income Statements
For the Year Ended December 31, 20Y7

	Theme Park Division	Photography Division
Revenues*	$6,000,000	$2,500,000
Operating expenses	(2,495,000)	(405,000)
Operating income before service department charges	$3,505,000	$2,095,000
Less service department charges:		
Purchasing	$ (250,000)	$ (150,000)
Payroll Accounting	(204,000)	(51,000)
Legal	(25,000)	(225,000)
Total service department charges	$ (479,000)	$ (426,000)
Operating income	$3,026,000	$1,669,000

*For a profit center that sells products, the income statement would report: Sales − cost of goods sold = gross profit. The operating expenses would be deducted from the gross profit to arrive at the operating income before service department charges.

Responsibility Accounting for Investment Centers

Objective 4
Describe and illustrate responsibility reporting for an investment center.

An **investment center** manager has the responsibility and the authority to make decisions that affect not only costs and revenues but also the assets invested in the center. Investment centers are often used in diversified companies organized by divisions. In such cases, the divisional manager has authority similar to that of a chief operating officer or president of a company.

Caterpillar has four Group Presidents who are responsible for the operations of each of its four segments: Construction, Resource, Power & Energy, and Financial Services. A fifth Group President is responsible for three smaller operating segments.

Caterpillar Connection

Since investment center managers have responsibility for revenues and expenses, *operating income* is part of investment center reporting. In addition, because the manager has responsibility for the assets invested in the center, the following two additional measures of performance are used:

1. Return on investment
2. Residual income

To illustrate, In-Touch Inc., a cellular phone company with three regional divisions, is used. Condensed divisional income statements for the Northern, Central, and Southern divisions of In-Touch are shown in Exhibit 7.

Using only operating income, the Central Division is the most profitable division. However, operating income does not reflect the amount of assets invested in each center. For example, the Central Division could have twice as many assets as the Northern Division. For this reason, performance measures that consider the amount of invested assets, such as the return on investment and residual income, are used.

Exhibit 7 Divisional Income Statements— In-Touch Inc.

In-Touch Inc.
Divisional Income Statements
For the Year Ended December 31, 20Y7

	Northern Division	Central Division	Southern Division
Revenues	$560,000	$672,000	$750,000
Operating expenses	(336,000)	(470,400)	(562,500)
Operating income before service department charges	$224,000	$201,600	$187,500
Service department charges	(154,000)	(117,600)	(112,500)
Operating income	$ 70,000	$ 84,000	$ 75,000

Return on Investment

Since investment center managers control the amount of assets invested in their centers, they should be evaluated based on the use of these assets. One measure that considers the amount of assets invested is the **return on investment (ROI)** or *return on assets*. It is computed as follows:

$$\textbf{Return on Investment (ROI)} = \frac{\textbf{Operating Income}}{\textbf{Invested Assets}}$$

The return on investment is useful because the three factors subject to control by divisional managers (revenues, expenses, and invested assets) are considered. The higher the rate of return on investment, the better the division is using its assets to generate income. In effect, the return on investment measures the income (return) on each dollar invested. As a result, the return on investment can be used as a common basis for comparing divisions with each other.

To illustrate, the invested assets of In-Touch's three divisions are as follows:

	Invested Assets
Northern Division	$350,000
Central Division	700,000
Southern Division	500,000

Using the operating income for each division shown in Exhibit 7, the return on investment for each division is computed below.

Northern Division:

$$\textbf{Return on Investment} = \frac{\textbf{Operating Income}}{\textbf{Invested Assets}} = \frac{\$70{,}000}{\$350{,}000} = 20\%$$

Central Division:

$$\textbf{Return on Investment} = \frac{\textbf{Operating Income}}{\textbf{Invested Assets}} = \frac{\$84{,}000}{\$700{,}000} = 12\%$$

Southern Division:

$$\textbf{Return on Investment} = \frac{\textbf{Operating Income}}{\textbf{Invested Assets}} = \frac{\$75{,}000}{\$500{,}000} = 15\%$$

Although the Central Division generated the largest operating income, its return on investment (12%) is the lowest. Thus, relative to the assets invested, the Central Division is the least profitable division. In comparison, the return on investment of the Northern Division is 20%, and the Southern Division is 15%.

Based upon recent financial statements, the return on investment for each of **Caterpillar**'s four segments was as follows:

Construction Industries	Resource Industries	Energy & Transportation	Financial Services
33.8%	5.2%	48.1%	2.7%

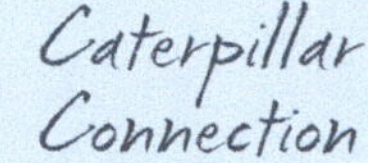

To analyze differences in the return on investment across divisions, the **DuPont formula** for the return on investment is often used.[1] The DuPont formula views the return on investment as the product of the following two factors:

1. **Profit margin**, which is the ratio of operating income to sales.
2. **Investment turnover**, which is the ratio of sales to invested assets.

Using the DuPont formula, the return on investment is expressed as follows:

$$\textbf{Return on Investment} = \textbf{Profit Margin} \times \textbf{Investment Turnover}$$

$$\textbf{Return on Investment} = \frac{\textbf{Operating Income}}{\textbf{Sales}} \times \frac{\textbf{Sales}}{\textbf{Invested Assets}}$$

The DuPont formula is useful in evaluating divisions. This is because the profit margin and the investment turnover reflect the following underlying operating relationships of each division:

1. Profit margin indicates *operating profitability* by computing the rate of profit earned on each sales dollar.
2. Investment turnover indicates *operating efficiency* by computing the number of sales dollars generated by each dollar of invested assets.

If a division's profit margin increases, and all other factors remain the same, the division's return on investment will increase. For example, a division might add more profitable products to its sales mix and thus increase its operating profit, profit margin, and return on investment.

1. The DuPont formula was created by a financial executive of **E. I. du Pont Nemours and Company** in 1919.

If a division's investment turnover increases, and all other factors remain the same, the division's return on investment will increase. For example, a division might attempt to increase sales through special sales promotions and thus increase operating efficiency, investment turnover, and return on investment.

The graphic in Exhibit 8 illustrates the relationship of the return on investment, the profit margin, and investment turnover. Specifically, more income can be earned (races won) by either increasing the investment turnover (installing a bigger engine), by increasing the profit margin (pressing the gas pedal), or both.

Exhibit 8 Profit Margin, Investment Turnover, and Return on Investment.

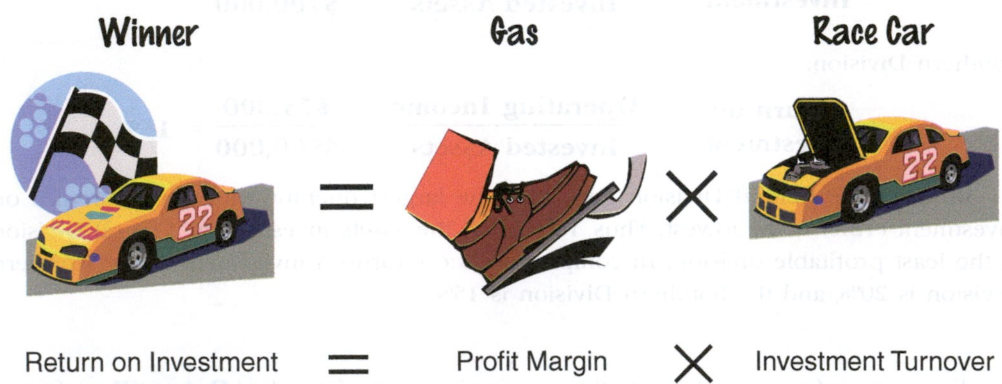

Return on Investment = Profit Margin × Investment Turnover

Using the DuPont formula yields the same return on investment for each of In-Touch's divisions, as shown below.

$$\textbf{Return on Investment} = \frac{\textbf{Operating Income}}{\textbf{Sales}} \times \frac{\textbf{Sales}}{\textbf{Invested Assets}}$$

Northern Division:

$$\textbf{Return on Investment} = \frac{\$70{,}000}{\$560{,}000} \times \frac{\$560{,}000}{\$350{,}000} = 12.5\% \times 1.6 = 20\%$$

Central Division:

$$\textbf{Return on Investment} = \frac{\$84{,}000}{\$672{,}000} \times \frac{\$672{,}000}{\$700{,}000} = 12.5\% \times 0.96 = 12\%$$

Southern Division:

$$\textbf{Return on Investment} = \frac{\$75{,}000}{\$750{,}000} \times \frac{\$750{,}000}{\$500{,}000} = 10\% \times 1.5 = 15\%$$

The Northern and Central divisions have the same profit margins of 12.5%. However, the Northern Division's investment turnover of 1.6 is larger than that of the Central Division's turnover of 0.96. By using its invested assets more efficiently, the Northern Division's return on investment of 20% is 8 percentage points higher than the Central Division's return on investment of 12%.

The Southern Division's profit margin of 10% and investment turnover of 1.5 are lower than those of the Northern Division. The product of these factors results in a return on investment of 15% for the Southern Division, compared to 20% for the Northern Division.

Even though the Southern Division's profit margin is lower than the Central Division's, its higher turnover of 1.5 results in a rate of return of 15%, which is greater than the Central Division's rate of return of 12%.

Caterpillar Connection

Based upon recent financial statements, the profit margin, investment turnover, and return on investment for each of **Caterpillar**'s four segments (rounded) was as follows:

	Construction Industries	Resource Industries	Energy & Transportation	Financial Services
Profit margin	11.3%	5.3%	16.9%	27.2%
Investment turnover	2.99	0.99	2.85	0.01
ROI	33.8%	5.2%	48.1%	2.7%

To increase the return on investment, the profit margin and investment turnover for a division may be analyzed. For example, assume that the Northern Division is in a highly competitive industry in which the profit margin cannot be easily increased. As a result, the division manager might focus on increasing the investment turnover.

To illustrate, assume that the revenues of the Northern Division could be increased by $56,000 through increasing operating expenses, such as advertising, to $385,000. The Northern Division's operating income will increase from $70,000 to $77,000, as shown below.

Revenues ($560,000 + $56,000)	$ 616,000
Operating expenses	(385,000)
Operating income before service department charges	$ 231,000
Service department charges	(154,000)
Operating income	$ 77,000

The return on investment for the Northern Division, using the DuPont formula, is recomputed as follows:

$$\textbf{Return on Investment} = \frac{\textbf{Operating Income}}{\textbf{Sales}} \times \frac{\textbf{Sales}}{\textbf{Invested Assets}}$$

$$\textbf{Return on Investment} = \frac{\$77{,}000}{\$616{,}000} \times \frac{\$616{,}000}{\$350{,}000} = 12.5\% \times 1.76 = 22\%$$

Although the Northern Division's profit margin remains the same (12.5%), the investment turnover has increased from 1.6 to 1.76, an increase of 10% (0.16 ÷ 1.6). The 10% increase in investment turnover increases the return on investment by 10% (from 20% to 22%).

The return on investment is also useful in deciding where to invest additional assets or expand operations. For example, In-Touch should give priority to expanding operations in the Northern Division because it earns the highest return on investment. In other words, an investment in the Northern Division will return 20 cents (20%) on each dollar invested. In contrast, investments in the Central and Southern divisions will earn only 12 cents and 15 cents, respectively, per dollar invested.

A disadvantage of the return on investment as a performance measure is that it may lead divisional managers to reject new investments that could be profitable for the company as a whole. To illustrate, assume the following returns for the Northern Division of In-Touch:

Current return on investment	20%
Minimum acceptable return on investment set by top management	10%
Expected return on investment for new project	14%

If the manager of the Northern Division invests in the new project, the Northern Division's overall return on investment will decrease from 20% due to averaging. Thus, the division manager might decide to reject the project, even though the new project's expected return of 14% exceeds In-Touch's minimum acceptable rate of return of 10%.

Residual Income

Residual income is useful in overcoming some of the disadvantages of the return on investment. **Residual income** is the excess of operating income over a minimum acceptable operating income, as follows:[2]

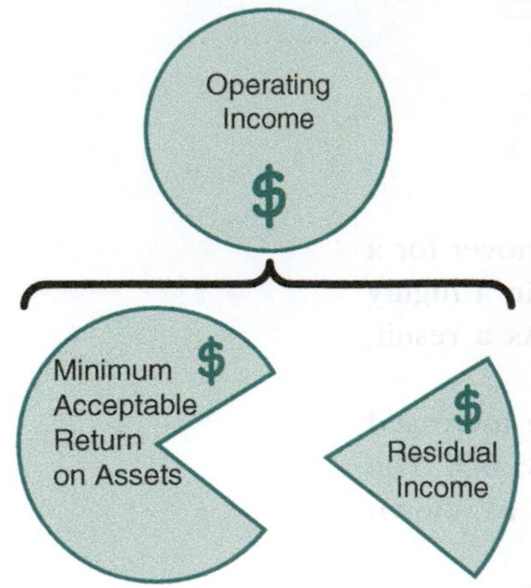

Operating income	$ XXX
Less minimum acceptable operating income as a percent of invested assets	(XXX)
Residual income	$ XXX

The minimum acceptable operating income is computed by multiplying the company minimum rate of return by the invested assets. The minimum rate is set by top management, based on such factors as the cost of financing.

To illustrate, assume that In-Touch Inc. has established 10% as the minimum acceptable return on divisional assets. The residual incomes for the three divisions are as follows:

	Northern Division	Central Division	Southern Division
Operating income	$ 70,000	$84,000	$ 75,000
Less minimum acceptable operating income as a percent of invested assets:			
$350,000 × 10%	(35,000)		
$700,000 × 10%		(70,000)	
$500,000 × 10%			(50,000)
Residual income	$ 35,000	$14,000	$ 25,000

The Northern Division has more residual income ($35,000) than the other divisions, even though it has the least amount of operating income ($70,000). This is because the invested assets are less for the Northern Division than for the other divisions.

The major advantage of residual income as a performance measure is that it considers both the minimum acceptable rate of return, invested assets, and the operating income for each division. In doing so, residual income encourages division managers to maximize operating income in excess of the minimum. This provides an incentive to accept any project that is expected to have a rate of return in excess of the minimum.

To illustrate, assume the following rates of return for the Northern Division of In-Touch:

Current return on investment	20%
Minimum acceptable return on investment, set by top management	10%
Expected return on investment for new project	14%

If the manager of the Northern Division is evaluated using only return on investment, the division manager might decide to reject the new project. This is because investing in the new project will decrease Northern's current rate of return of 20%. Thus, the manager might reject the new project, even though its expected rate of return of 14% exceeds In-Touch's minimum acceptable rate of return of 10%.

In contrast, if the manager of the Northern Division is evaluated using residual income, the new project would probably be accepted because it will increase the Northern Division's residual income. In this way, residual income supports both divisional and overall company objectives.

2. Another popular term for residual income is economic value added (EVA), which has been trademarked by the consulting firm **Stern Stewart & Co.**

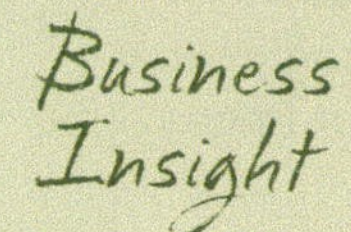

Return on Investment

The annual reports of public companies must provide segment disclosure information identifying revenues, operating income, and total assets. This information can be used to compute the return on investment for the segments of a company. For example, **The E.W. Scripps Company (SSP)**, a media company, operates three major segments:

Television: Includes 15 ABC, 5 NBC, 2 FOX, and 2 CBS affiliates that reach approximately 18% of U.S. television households.

Radio: Includes 34 radio stations (28 FM stations and 6 AM stations)

Digital: Includes digital operations of the television and radio segments such as the video news service and podcasts.

The DuPont formulas for these segments, as derived from a recent annual report, are as follows:

Segment	Profit Margin	×	Investment Turnover	=	Return on Investment
Television	22.9%		0.49		11.2%
Radio	21.8%		0.40		8.7%
Digital	(43.9)%		0.38		(16.7)%

The Scripps' television segment earns the highest return on investment of 11.2% compared to 8.7% for the radio and (16.7)% for the digital segments. The higher rate of return for the television segment is due to the higher profit margin and investment turnover. The investment turnovers for the radio and digital segments are comparable, but the digital segment has a negative profit margin of (43.9) percent. Management of Scripps should focus on improving the profit margin of the Digital segment.

Transfer Pricing

Objective 5

Describe and illustrate transfer pricing for decentralized segments of a business.

When divisions transfer products or render services to each other, a **transfer price** is used to charge for the products or services.[3] Since transfer prices will affect a division's financial performance, setting a transfer price is a sensitive matter for the managers of both the selling and buying divisions.

Caterpillar Connection

Inter-segment sales of **Caterpillar**'s Construction Industries, Resource Industries, and Engery & Transportation segments were $2.3 billion of Caterpillar's total sales of $47.5 billion.

Three common approaches to setting transfer prices are as follows:

1. Market price approach
2. Negotiated price approach
3. Cost approach

Transfer prices may be used for cost, profit, or investment centers. The objective of setting a transfer price is to motivate managers to behave in a manner that will increase the overall company income. As will be illustrated, however, transfer prices may be misused in such a way that overall company income suffers.

Transfer prices can be set as low as the variable cost per unit or as high as the market price. Often, transfer prices are negotiated at some point between variable cost per unit and market price. Exhibit 9 shows the possible range of transfer prices.

3. The discussion in this chapter highlights the essential concepts of transfer pricing. In-depth discussion of transfer pricing can be found in advanced texts.

Exhibit 9 Commonly Used Transfer Prices

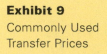

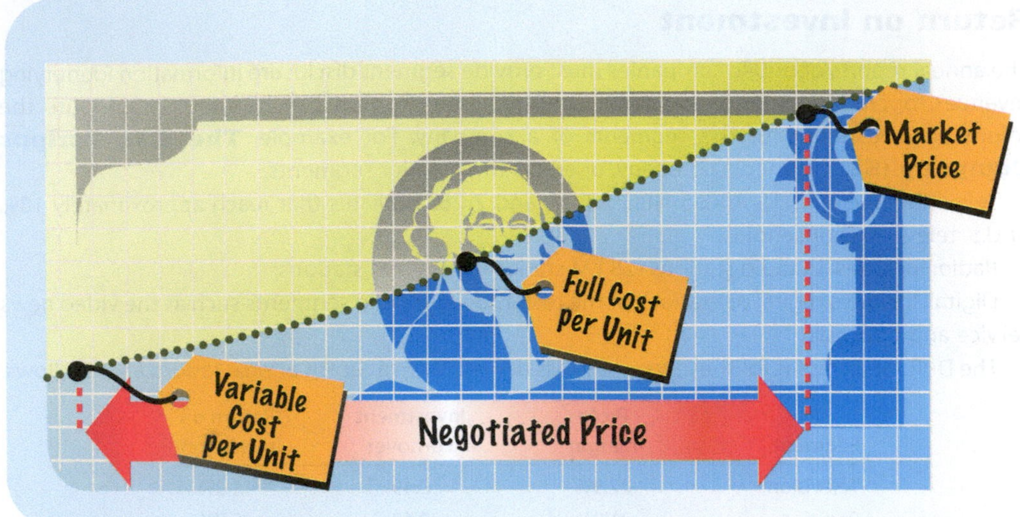

To illustrate, Wilson Company, a packaged snack food company with no service departments, is used. Wilson Company has two operating divisions (Eastern and Western) that are organized as investment centers. Condensed income statements for Wilson Company, assuming no transfers between divisions, are shown in Exhibit 10.

Exhibit 10 Income Statements—No Transfers Between Divisions

Wilson Company
Income Statements
For the Year Ended December 31, 20Y8

	Eastern Division	Western Division	Total Company
Sales:			
50,000 units × $20 per unit	$1,000,000		$1,000,000
20,000 units × $40 per unit		$ 800,000	800,000
			$1,800,000
Expenses:			
Variable:			
50,000 units × $10 per unit	$ (500,000)		$ (500,000)
20,000 units × $30* per unit		$(600,000)	(600,000)
Fixed	(300,000)	(100,000)	(400,000)
Total expenses	$ (800,000)	$(700,000)	$(1,500,000)
Operating income	$ 200,000	$ 100,000	$ 300,000

*$20 of the $30 per unit represents materials costs, and the remaining $10 per unit represents other variable conversion expenses incurred within the Western Division.

Market Price Approach

Using the **market price approach**, the transfer price is the price at which the product or service transferred could be sold to outside buyers. If an outside market exists for the product or service transferred, the current market price may be a proper transfer price.

Transfer Price = Market Price

To illustrate, assume that materials used by Wilson Company in producing snack food in the Western Division are currently purchased from an outside supplier at $20 per unit. The same materials are produced by the Eastern Division. The Eastern Division is operating at full capacity of 50,000 units and can sell all it produces to either the Western Division or to outside buyers.

A transfer price of $20 per unit (the market price) has no effect on the Eastern Division's income or total company income. The Eastern Division will earn revenues of $20 per unit on all its production and sales, regardless of who buys its product.

Likewise, the Western Division will pay $20 per unit for materials (the market price). Thus, the use of the market price as the transfer price has no effect on the Eastern Division's income or total company income.

In this situation, the use of the market price as the transfer price is proper. The condensed divisional income statements for Wilson Company would be the same as shown in Exhibit 10.

Negotiated Price Approach

If unused or excess capacity exists in the supplying division (the Eastern Division), and the transfer price is equal to the market price, total company profit may not be maximized. This is because the manager of the Western Division will be indifferent toward purchasing materials from the Eastern Division or from outside suppliers. That is, in both cases the Western Division manager pays $20 per unit (the market price). As a result, the Western Division may purchase the materials from outside suppliers.

If, however, the Western Division purchases the materials from the Eastern Division, the difference between the market price of $20 and the variable costs of the Eastern Division of $10 per unit (from Exhibit 10) can cover fixed costs and contribute to overall company profits. Thus, the Western Division manager should be encouraged to purchase the materials from the Eastern Division.

The **negotiated price approach** allows the managers to agree (negotiate) among themselves on a transfer price. The only constraint is that the transfer price be less than the market price but greater than the supplying division's variable costs per unit.

Variable Costs per Unit < Transfer Price < Market Price

To illustrate, assume that instead of a capacity of 50,000 units, the Eastern Division's capacity is 70,000 units. In addition, assume that the Eastern Division can continue to sell only 50,000 units to outside buyers.

A transfer price less than $20 would encourage the manager of the Western Division to purchase from the Eastern Division. This is because the Western Division is currently purchasing its materials from outside suppliers at a cost of $20 per unit. Thus, its materials cost would decrease, and its operating income would increase.

At the same time, a transfer price above the Eastern Division's variable costs per unit of $10 (from Exhibit 10) would encourage the manager of the Eastern Division to supply materials to the Western Division. In doing so, the Eastern Division's operating income would also increase.

Exhibit 11 illustrates the divisional and company income statements, assuming that the Eastern and Western division managers agree to a transfer price of $15.

Exhibit 11 Income Statements—Negotiated Transfer Price

Wilson Company
Income Statements
For the Year Ended December 31, 20Y8

	Eastern Division	Western Division	Total Company
Sales:			
50,000 units × $20 per unit	$1,000,000		$ 1,000,000
20,000 units × $15 per unit	300,000		300,000
20,000 units × $40 per unit		$ 800,000	800,000
Total sales	$ 1,300,000	$ 800,000	$ 2,100,000
Expenses:			
Variable:			
70,000 units × $10 per unit	$ (700,000)		$ (700,000)
20,000 units × $25* per unit		$(500,000)	(500,000)
Fixed	(300,000)	(100,000)	(400,000)
Total expenses	$(1,000,000)	$(600,000)	$(1,600,000)
Operating income	$ 300,000	$ 200,000	$ 500,000

*$10 of the $25 represents variable conversion expenses incurred solely within the Western Division, and $15 per unit represents the transfer price per unit from the Eastern Division.

The Eastern Division increases its sales by $300,000 (20,000 units × $15 per unit) to $1,300,000. As a result, the Eastern Division's operating income increases by $100,000 ($300,000 sales − $200,000 variable costs) to $300,000, as shown in Exhibit 11.

The increase of $100,000 in the Eastern Division's income can also be computed as follows:

$$\text{Increase in Eastern (Supplying) Division's Operating Income} = \left(\text{Transfer Price} - \text{Variable Cost per Unit}\right) \times \text{Units Transferred}$$

$$\text{Increase in Eastern (Supplying) Division's Operating Income} = (\$15 - \$10) \times 20{,}000 \text{ units} = \$100{,}000$$

The Western Division's materials cost decreases by $5 per unit ($20 − $15) for a total of $100,000 (20,000 units × $5 per unit). Thus, the Western Division's operating income increases by $100,000 to $200,000, as shown in Exhibit 11.

The increase of $100,000 in the Western Division's income can also be computed as follows:

$$\text{Increase in Western (Purchasing) Division's Operating Income} = (\text{Market Price} - \text{Transfer Price}) \times \text{Units Transferred}$$

$$\text{Increase in Western (Purchasing) Division's Operating Income} = (\$20 - \$15) \times 20{,}000 \text{ units} = \$100{,}000$$

Comparing Exhibits 10 and 11 shows that Wilson Company's operating income increased by $200,000, as shown below.

	Operating Income		
	No Units Transferred (Exhibit 10)	20,000 Units Transferred at $15 per Unit (Exhibit 11)	Increase (Decrease)
Eastern Division	$200,000	$300,000	$100,000
Western Division	100,000	200,000	100,000
Wilson Company	$300,000	$500,000	$200,000

In the preceding illustration, any negotiated transfer price between $10 and $20 is acceptable, as shown below.

$$\textbf{Variable Cost per Unit} < \textbf{Transfer Price} < \textbf{Market Price}$$

$$\$10 < \textbf{Transfer Price} < \$20$$

Any transfer price within this range will increase the overall operating income for Wilson Company by $200,000. However, the increases in the Eastern and Western divisions' operating income will vary depending on the transfer price.

To illustrate, a transfer price of $16 would increase the Eastern Division's operating income by $120,000, as shown below.

$$\text{Increase in Eastern (Supplying) Division's Operating Income} = \left(\text{Transfer Price} - \text{Variable Cost per Unit}\right) \times \text{Units Transferred}$$

$$\text{Increase in Eastern (Supplying) Division's Operating Income} = (\$16 - \$10) \times 20{,}000 \text{ units} = \$120{,}000$$

A transfer price of $16 would increase the Western Division's operating income by $80,000, as shown below.

$$\text{Increase in Western (Purchasing) Division's Operating Income} = (\text{Market Price} - \text{Transfer Price}) \times \text{Units Transferred}$$

$$\text{Increase in Western (Purchasing) Division's Operating Income} = (\$20 - \$16) \times 20{,}000 \text{ units} = \$80{,}000$$

With a transfer price of $16, Wilson Company's operating income still increases by $200,000, which consists of the Eastern Division's increase of $120,000 plus the Western Division's increase of $80,000.

As shown above, the negotiated price provides each division manager with an incentive to negotiate the transfer of materials. At the same time, the overall company's operating income will increase. However, the negotiated approach only applies when the supplying division has excess capacity and cannot sell all of its production to outside buyers at the market price.

Cost Price Approach

Under the **cost price approach**, cost is used to set transfer prices. A variety of costs may be used in this approach, including the following:

1. Total product cost per unit
2. Variable product per unit

If total product cost per unit is used, direct materials, direct labor, and factory overhead are included in the transfer price. If variable product cost per unit is used, the fixed factory overhead cost is excluded from the transfer price.

Actual costs or standard (budgeted) costs may be used in applying the cost price approach. If actual costs are used, inefficiencies of the producing (supplying) division are transferred to the purchasing division. Thus, there is little incentive for the producing (supplying) division to control costs. For this reason, most companies use standard costs in the cost price approach. In this way, differences between actual and standard costs remain with the producing (supplying) division for cost control purposes.

The cost price approach is most often used when the responsibility centers are organized as cost centers. When the responsibility centers are organized as profit or investment centers, the cost price approach is normally not used.

For example, using the cost price approach when the supplying division is organized as a profit center ignores the supplying division manager's responsibility for earning profits. In this case, using the cost price approach prevents the supplying division from reporting any profit (revenues – costs) on the units transferred. As a result, the division manager has little incentive to transfer units to another division, even though it may be in the best interests of the company.

Integrity, Objectivity, and Ethics in Business

Shifting Income Through Transfer Prices

Transfer prices allow companies to minimize taxes by shifting taxable income from countries with high tax rates to countries with low taxes. For example, **GlaxoSmithKline**, a British company and the second biggest drug maker in the world, had been in a dispute with the U.S. Internal Revenue Service (IRS) over international transfer prices. The company pays U.S. taxes on income from its U.S. Division and British taxes on income from the British Division. The IRS, however, claimed that the transfer prices on sales from the British Division to the U.S. Division were too high, which reduced profits and taxes in the U.S. Division. The company received a new tax bill from the IRS for almost $1.9 billion related to the transfer pricing issue, raising the total bill to almost $5 billion. The company agreed to settle this dispute with the IRS for $3.4 billion, one of the largest tax settlements in history.

Source: J. Whalen, "Glaxo Gets New IRS Bill Seeking Another $1.9 Billion in Back Tax," *The Wall Street Journal*, January 27, 2005.

Objective 6

Describe and illustrate a balanced scorecard and its related metrics.

Metric-Based Analysis: Balanced Scorecard

The **balanced scorecard**[4] is a set of multiple performance metrics for a company that include metrics in addition to traditional financial metrics. Balanced scorecards normally include performance metrics for the following four categories:

1. Learning and innovation
2. Internal processes
3. Customer service
4. Financial

4. The balanced scorecard was developed by R. S. Kaplan and D. P. Norton and explained in *The Balanced Scorecard: Translating Strategy into Action* (Cambridge: Harvard Business School Press, 1996).

Innovation and Learning

Innovation focuses on a company's research and development efforts in developing new products and improving current products. Examples of performance metrics for growth include the number of patents applied for during the year, the number of new products developed during a year, and the time it takes to bring new products to market.

In three recent years, **Caterpillar** spent 4.6%, 3.9%, and 3.7% of its sales on research and development.

Caterpillar Connection

Learning focuses on increasing the future value of the company by educating and training employees and managers. Examples of performance metrics for learning include the number of employee training sessions, the number of cross-trained employees, and employee turnover.

Internal Processes

Internal processes focus on improving the company's operations to eliminate waste and inefficiencies. Examples of performance metrics for internal processes include the time it takes to manufacture a product, the amount of scrap or waste, and the number of times a manufacturing process is shut down for repairs.

Caterpillar formed an Enterprise System Group to implement improvements in operational efficiency and reduce waste.

Caterpillar Connection

Customer Service

Customer service focuses on exceeding customer expectations. Examples of performance metrics for customer service include the number of customer complaints and the number of repeat customers. Customer surveys can also be used to gather measures of customer satisfaction with the company as compared to competitors.

Caterpillar is attempting to improve its order-to-delivery system to better reduce lead time and better align with customer requirements.

Caterpillar Connection

Financial

Financial focuses on traditional metrics of performance such as operating income, return on investment, and residual income. The assumption of the balanced scorecard is that traditional financial metrics are inadequate by themselves. Instead, financial metrics need to be supplemented and integrated with metrics from learning and innovation, internal processes, and customer service.

Some common performance metrics for each category of the balanced scorecard are shown in Exhibit 12.

Exhibit 12 Balanced Scorecard Performance Metrics

Innovation and Learning	Internal Process
• Number of new products • Number of new patents • Number of cross-trained employees • Number of training hours • Number of ethics violations • Employee turnover	• Wasted and scrap • Time to manufacture products • Number of defects • Number of rejected sales orders • Number of stockouts • Labor utilization
Customer Service	**Financial**
• Number of repeat customers • Customer brand recognition • Delivery time to customer • Customer satisfaction • Number of sales returns • Customer complaints	• Sales • Operating income • Return on investment • Profit margin and investment turnover • Residual income • Actual versus budgeted (standard) costs

Key Points

1. Describe types of operational responsibility.

A company may assign responsibility for its operations so they are centralized or decentralized. In centralized operations all major planning and control decisions are made by top management. When operational responsibility is decentralized, managers of separate divisions or units are delegated the responsibility for managing their operations. The advantages of decentralization include better decisions by the managers closest to the operations, more time for top management to focus on strategic planning, training for managers, improved ability to serve customers and respond to their needs, and improved manager morale. The disadvantages of decentralization include failure of the company to maximize profits because decisions made by one manager may affect other managers in such a way that the profitability of the entire company may suffer.

2. Describe and illustrate responsibility reporting for a cost center.

Since managers of cost centers have responsibility and authority to make decisions regarding costs, responsibility accounting for cost centers focuses on costs. The primary accounting tools for planning and controlling costs for a cost center are budgets and budget performance reports. An example of a budget performance report is shown in Exhibit 3.

3. Describe and illustrate responsibility reporting for a profit center.

In preparing a profitability report for a profit center, operating expenses are subtracted from revenues in order to determine the operating income before service department charges. Service department charges are then subtracted in order to determine the operating income of the profit center. An example of a divisional income statement is shown in Exhibit 6.

4. Describe and illustrate responsibility reporting for an investment center.

The return on investment for an investment center is the operating income divided by invested assets. The return on investment may also be computed as the product of (1) the profit margin and (2) the investment turnover. Residual income for an investment center is the excess of operating income over a minimum amount of desired operating income.

5. **Describe and illustrate transfer pricing for decentralized segments of a business.**

Under the market price approach, the transfer price is the price at which the product or service transferred could be sold to outside buyers. Market price should be used when the supplier division is able to sell to outsiders and is operating at capacity.

Under the negotiated price approach, the managers of decentralized units agree (negotiate) among themselves as to the transfer price. Negotiated prices should be used when the supplier division is operating below capacity.

Under the cost price approach, cost is used as the basis for setting transfer prices. A variety of cost concepts may be used, such as total product cost per unit or variable product cost per unit. In addition, actual costs or standard (budgeted) costs may be used. The cost price approach should be used for supplier divisions that are organized as cost centers.

6. **Describe and illustrate the balanced scorecard and related metrics.**

The balanced scorecard is a set of multiple performance metrics for a company related to the following four categories: learning and innovation, internal processes, customer service, and financial.

Key Terms

Balanced scorecard (628)
Controllable expenses (614)
Controllable revenues (614)
Cost center (612)
Cost price approach (628)
DuPont formula (619)
Investment center (617)
Investment turnover (619)
Market price approach (625)
Negotiated price approach (625)
Profit center (614)
Profit margin (619)
Return on investment (ROI) (618)
Residual income (622)
Responsibility accounting (612)
Service department charges (614)
Transfer price (623)

Illustrative Problem

Quinn Company has two divisions, Domestic and International. Invested assets and condensed income statement data for each division for the past year are as follows:

	Domestic Division	International Division
Revenues	$675,000	$480,000
Operating expenses	450,000	372,400
Service department charges	90,000	50,000
Invested assets	600,000	384,000

Instructions

1. Prepare condensed income statements for the past year for each division.
2. Using the DuPont formula, determine the profit margin, investment turnover, and return on investment for each division.
3. If management's minimum acceptable rate of return is 10%, determine the residual income for each division.

Solution

1.

QUINN COMPANY
Divisional Income Statements for the year just ended

	Domestic Division	International Division
Revenues	$675,000	$480,000
Operating expenses	(450,000)	(372,400)
Operating income before service department charges	$225,000	$107,600
Service department charges	(90,000)	(50,000)
Operating income	$135,000	$ 57,600

2. **Return on Investment (ROI) = Profit Margin × Investment Turnover**

$$\textbf{Return on Investment (ROI)} = \frac{\textbf{Operating Income}}{\textbf{Sales}} \times \frac{\textbf{Sales}}{\textbf{Invested Assets}}$$

$$\text{Domestic Division: ROI} = \frac{\$135{,}000}{\$675{,}000} \times \frac{\$675{,}000}{\$600{,}000}$$

$$\text{ROI} = 20\% \times 1.125$$

$$\text{ROI} = 22.5\%$$

$$\text{International Division: ROI} = \frac{\$57{,}600}{\$480{,}000} \times \frac{\$480{,}000}{\$384{,}000}$$

$$\text{ROI} = 12\% \times 1.25$$

$$\text{ROI} = 15\%$$

3. Domestic Division: $75,000 [$135,000 − (10% × $600,000)]
International Division: $19,200 [$57,600 − (10% × $384,000)]

Self-Examination Questions

(Answers appear at the end of chapter)

1. When the manager has the responsibility and authority to make decisions that affect costs and revenues but no responsibility for or authority over assets invested in the department, the department is called:
   A. A cost center
   B. A profit center
   C. An investment center
   D. A service department

2. The Accounts Payable Department has expenses of $600,000 and makes 150,000 payments to the various vendors who provide products and services to the divisions. Division A has operating income of $900,000 before service department charges and makes 60,000 payments to vendors. If the Accounts Payable Department is treated as a service department, what is Division A's operating income?
   A. $300,000
   B. $900,000
   C. $660,000
   D. $540,000

3. Division A of Kern Co. has sales of $350,000, cost of goods sold of $200,000, operating expenses of $30,000, and invested assets of $600,000. What is the return on investment for Division A?
   A. 20%
   B. 25%
   C. 33%
   D. 40%

4. Division L of Liddy Co. has a return on investment of 24% and an investment turnover of 1.6. What is the profit margin?
   A. 6%
   B. 15%
   C. 24%
   D. 38%

5. Which approach to transfer pricing uses the price at which the product or service transferred could be sold to outside buyers?
   A. Cost price approach
   B. Negotiated price approach
   C. Market price approach
   D. Standard cost approach

Class Discussion Questions

1. Differentiate between a cost center and a profit center.
2. Differentiate between a profit center and an investment center.
3. In what major respect would budget performance reports prepared for the use of plant managers of a manufacturing business with cost centers differ from those prepared for the use of the various department supervisors who report to the plant managers?
4. For what decisions is the manager of a cost center *not* responsible?
5. Weyerhaeuser developed a system that assigns service department expenses to user divisions on the basis of actual services consumed by the division. Here are a number of Weyerhaeuser's activities in its central Financial Services Department:
   - Payroll
   - Accounts payable
   - Accounts receivable
   - Database administration—report preparation

   For each activity, identify an activity base that could be used to charge user divisions for service.
6. What is the major shortcoming of using operating income as a performance measure for investment centers?
7. Why should the factors under the control of the investment center manager (revenues, expenses, and invested assets) be considered in computing the return on investment?
8. In a decentralized company in which the divisions are organized as investment centers, how could a division be considered the least profitable, even though it earned the largest amount of operating income?
9. How does using the return on investment facilitate comparability between divisions of decentralized companies?
10. The returns on investment for Shear Co.'s three divisions, North, South, and Midwest are 38%, 30%, and 22%, respectively. In expanding operations, which of Shear Co.'s divisions should be given priority? Explain.
11. What is the objective of transfer pricing?
12. When is the negotiated price approach preferred over the market price approach in setting transfer prices?
13. Why would standard cost be a more appropriate transfer cost between cost centers than actual cost?
14. When using the negotiated price approach to transfer pricing, within what range should the transfer price be established?

Exercises

E14-1 Budget performance reports for cost centers

Obj. 2

✔ a. (c) $22,950

Partially completed budget performance reports for Runquist Company, a manufacturer of air conditioners, are provided below.

RUNQUIST COMPANY
Budget Performance Report—Vice President, Production
For the Month Ended April 30

Plant	Budget	Actual	Over Budget	(Under) Budget
Daytona	$2,300,000	$2,287,900		$(12,100)
Little Rock	3,000,000	2,988,400		(11,600)
Oxford	(g)	(h)	(i)	
	$ (j)	$ (k)	$ (l)	$(23,700)

RUNQUIST COMPANY
Budget Peformance Report—Plant Manager, Oxford Plant
For the Month Ended April 30

Department	Budget	Actual	Over Budget	(Under) Budget
Condenser Assembly	$ (a)	$ (b)	$ (c)	
Electronic Assembly	700,000	703,200	3,200	
Final Assembly	525,000	516,600		$(8,400)
	$ (d)	$ (e)	$ (f)	$(8,400)

RUNQUIST COMPANY
Budget Performance Report—Supervisor, Condenser Assembly
For the Month Ended April 30

Department	Budget	Actual	Over Budget	(Under) Budget
Factory wages	$ 82,000	$ 95,500	$13,500	
Materials	120,000	115,300		$(4,700)
Power and light	45,000	49,950	4,950	
Maintenance	28,000	37,200	9,200	
	$275,000	$297,950	$27,650	$(4,700)

a. Complete the budget performance reports by determining the correct amounts for the lettered spaces.

b. Compose a memo to Jeff Kitchens, president of Meridian Company, explaining the performance of the Production Division for June.

Obj. 3

✔ Residential Division operating income, $125,000

E14-2 Divisional income statements

The following data were summarized from the accounting records for Vintage Construction Company for the year ended October 31, 20Y3.

Administrative expenses:		Sales:	
Commercial Division	$ 500,000	Commercial Division	$6,250,000
Residential Division	250,000	Residential Division	1,875,000
Cost of goods sold:		Service department charges:	
Commercial Division	$3,800,000	Commercial Division	$1,000,000
Residential Division	1,300,000	Residential Division	200,000

Prepare divisional income statements for Vintage Construction Company.

Obj. 3

E14-3 Service department charges and activity bases

For each of the following service departments, identify an activity base that could be used for charging the expense to the profit center.

a. Accounts Receivable
b. Central Purchasing
c. Duplication Services
d. Electronic Data Processing
e. Legal
f. Telecommunications

E14-4 Activity bases for service department charges

Obj. 3

For each of the following service departments, select the activity base listed that is most appropriate for charging service expenses to responsible units.

Service Department	Activity Base
a. Accounts Receivable	1. Number of computers
b. Central Purchasing	2. Number of conference attendees
c. Computer Support	3. Number of employees trained
d. Conferences	4. Number of payroll checks
e. Employee Travel	5. Number of purchase requisitions
f. Payroll Accounting	6. Number of sales invoices
g. Telecommunications	7. Number of telephone lines
h. Training	8. Number of travel claims

E14-5 Service department charges

Obj. 3

✔ b. Commercial payroll, $15,390

In divisional income statements prepared for Iguana Construction Company, the Payroll Department costs are charged back to user divisions on the basis of the number of payroll checks, and the Purchasing Department costs are charged back on the basis of the number of purchase requisitions. The Payroll Department had expenses of $42,750, and the Purchasing Department had expenses of $87,600 for the year. The following annual data for the Residential, Commercial, and Government Contract divisions were obtained from corporate records:

	Residential	Commercial	Government Contract
Sales	$9,400,000	$6,800,000	$2,400,000
Number of employees:			
Weekly payroll (52 weeks per year)	80	60	25
Monthly payroll	20	10	5
Number of purchase requisitions per year	12,400	8,900	2,700

a. Determine the total amount of payroll checks and purchase requisitions processed per year by each division.

b. Using the activity base information in (a), determine the annual amount of payroll and purchasing costs charged back to the Residential, Commercial, and Government Contract divisions from payroll and purchasing services.

c. Why does the Residential Division have a larger service department charge than the other two divisions?

E14-6 Service department charges and activity bases

Obj. 3

✔ b. Help desk, $14,580

Harris Corporation, a manufacturer of electronics and communications systems, uses a service department charge system to charge profit centers with Computing and Communications Services (CCS) service department costs. The following table identifies an abbreviated list of service categories and activity bases used by the CCS department. The table also includes some assumed cost and activity base quantity information for each service for February.

CCS Service Category	Activity Base	Assumed Cost	Assumed Activity Base Quantity
Help desk	Number of calls	$135,000	5,000
Network center	Number of devices monitored	363,000	7,500
Electronic mail	Number of user accounts	45,000	4,000
Local voice support	Number of phone extensions	39,000	3,000

One of the profit centers for Harris Corporation is the Electronics Systems sector. Assume the following information for the Electronics sector:

- The sector has 2,000 employees, of whom 60% are office employees.
- All the office employees have a phone, and all of them have a computer on the network.
- Ninety-five percent of the employees with a computer also have an e-mail account.
- The average number of help desk calls for February was 0.45 call per individual with a computer.
- There are 80 additional printers, servers, and peripherals on the network beyond the personal computers.

a. Determine the service charge rate for the four CCS service categories for February.

b. Determine the charges to the Electronics sector for the four CCS service categories for February.

Obj. 3

✔ Retail operating income, $4,624,000

E14-7 Divisional income statements with service department charges

Power Sports Company has two divisions, Wholesale and Retail, and two corporate service departments, Tech Support and Accounts Payable. The corporate expenses for the year ended December 31, 20Y7, are as follows:

Tech Support Department	$ 855,000
Accounts Payable Department	390,000
Other corporate administrative expenses	355,000
Total corporate expense	$1,600,000

The other corporate administrative expenses include officers' salaries and other expenses required by the corporation. The Tech Support Department charges the divisions for services rendered, based on the number of computers in the department, and the Accounts Payable Department charges divisions for services, based on the number of checks issued. The usage of service by the two divisions is as follows:

	Tech Support	Accounts Payable
Wholesale Division	250 computers	18,000 checks
Retail Division	500	12,000
Total	750 computers	30,000 checks

The service department charges of the Tech Support Department and the Accounts Payable Department are considered controllable by the divisions. Corporate administrative expenses are not considered controllable by the divisions. The revenues, cost of goods sold, and operating expenses for the two divisions are as follows:

	Wholesale	Retail
Revenues	$24,600,000	$13,750,000
Cost of goods sold	14,500,000	8,000,000
Operating expenses	1,500,000	400,000

Prepare the divisional income statements for the two divisions.

Note: The spreadsheet icon indicates an Excel template is available on the student companion site.

E14-8 Corrections to service department charges

Obj. 3

✔ b. Operating income, Cargo Division, $2,105,000

Panda Airlines Inc. has two divisions organized as profit centers, the Passenger Division and the Cargo Division. The following divisional income statements were prepared:

PANDA AIRLINES INC.
Divisional Income Statements
For the Year Ended April 30, 20Y9

	Passenger Division		Cargo Division	
Revenues		$7,500,000		$5,000,000
Operating expenses		(4,500,000)		(2,700,000)
Operating income before service department charges		$3,000,000		$2,300,000
Less service department charges:				
Training	$300,000		$200,000	
Flight scheduling	210,000		140,000	
Reservations	153,000	(663,000)	102,000	(442,000)
Operating income		$2,337,000		$1,858,000

The service department charge rate for the service department costs was based on revenues.

The following additional information is available:

	Passenger Division	Cargo Division	Total
Number of personnel trained	600	200	800
Number of flights	4,000	1,000	5,000
Number of reservations requested	750,000	0	750,000

a. Does the operating income for the two divisions accurately measure performance?

b. Using service charge rates for service department charges, correct the divisional income statements.

E14-9 Profit center responsibility reporting

Obj. 3

✔ Operating income, Action Sports Division, $2,823,000

On-Demand Sports Co. operates two divisions—the Action Sports Division and the Team Sports Division. The following income and expense accounts were provided as of November 30, 20Y1, the end of the current fiscal year, after all adjustments, including those for inventories, were recorded:

Sales—Action Sports (AS) Division	$18,500,000
Sales—Team Sports (TS) Division	30,600,000
Cost of Goods Sold—Action Sports (AS) Division	10,700,000
Cost of Goods Sold—Team Sports (TS) Division	19,200,000
Sales Expense—Action Sports (AS) Division	1,500,000
Sales Expense—Team Sports (TS) Division	2,100,000
Administrative Expense—Action Sports (AS) Division	1,250,000
Administrative Expense—Team Sports (TS) Division	1,450,000
Advertising Expense	3,000,000
Transportation Expense	654,900
Accounts Receivable Collection Expense	400,500
Warehouse Expense	800,000

The bases to be used in allocating expenses, together with other essential information, are as follows:

a. Advertising expense—incurred at headquarters, charged back to divisions on the basis of usage: Action Sports Division, $1,200,000; Team Sports Division, $1,800,000.

b. Transportation expense—charged back to divisions at a charge rate of $18.50 per bill of lading: Action Sports Division, 14,000 bills of lading; Team Sports Division, 21,400 bills of lading.

c. Accounts receivable collection expense—incurred at headquarters, charged back to divisions at a charge rate of $9.00 per invoice: Action Sports Division, 32,000 sales invoices; Team Sports Division, 12,500 sales invoices.

d. Warehouse expense—charged back to divisions on the basis of floor space used in storing division products: Action Sports Division, 120,000 square feet; Team Sports Division, 80,000 square feet.

Prepare divisional income statements with two column headings: Action Sports Division and Team Sports Division. Provide supporting schedules for determining service department charges.

Obj. 4

✔ a. Retail Division, 20%

E14-10 Return on investment

The operating income and the amount of invested assets in each division of Otte Industries are as follows:

	Operating Income	Invested Assets
Retail Division	$ 8,000,000	$40,000,000
Commercial Division	12,750,000	75,000,000
Internet Division	270,000	1,800,000

a. Compute the return on investment for each division.

b. Which division is the most profitable per dollar invested?

Obj. 4

✔ a. Commercial Division, $5,250,000

E14-11 Residual income

Based on the data in Exercise 14-10, assume that management has established a 10% minimum acceptable rate of return for invested assets.

a. Determine the residual income for each division.

b. Which division has the most residual income?

Obj. 4

✔ d. 1.50

E14-12 Determining missing items in return on investment computations

One item is omitted from each of the following computations of the return on investment:

Return on Investment	=	Profit Margin	×	Investment Turnover
12%	=	8%	×	(a)
(b)	=	16%	×	1.25
24%	=	(c)	×	1.20
15%	=	10%	×	(d)
(e)	=	10%	×	1.70

Determine the missing items, identifying each by the appropriate letter.

Obj. 4

✔ a. ROI, 19.2%

E14-13 Profit margin, investment turnover, and return on investment

The condensed income statement for the International Division of Valgenti Inc. is as follows (assuming no service department charges):

Sales	$24,000,000
Cost of goods sold	(14,100,000)
Gross profit	$ 9,900,000
Administrative expenses	(6,060,000)
Operating income	$ 3,840,000

The manager of the International Division is considering ways to increase the return on investment.

a. Using the DuPont formula for return on investment, determine the profit margin, investment turnover, and return on investment of the International Division, assuming that $20,000,000 of assets have been invested in the International Division.

b. If expenses could be reduced by $240,000 without decreasing sales, what would be the impact on the profit margin, investment turnover, and return on investment for the International Division?

E14-14 Return on investment

Obj. 4

✔ a. Parks and Resorts ROI, 11.8%

The Walt Disney Company has four major sectors, described as follows:

- **Media Networks:** The ABC television and radio network, Disney channel, ESPN, A&E, E!, and Disney.com.
- **Parks and Resorts:** Walt Disney World Resort, Disneyland, Disney Cruise Line, and other resort properties.
- **Studio Entertainment:** Walt Disney Pictures, Touchstone Pictures, Hollywood Pictures, Miramax Films, and Buena Vista Theatrical Productions.
- **Consumer Products:** Character merchandising, Disney stores, books, and magazines.

Disney recently reported sector operating income, revenue, and invested assets (in millions) as follows:

	Operating Income	Revenue	Invested Assets
Media Networks	$7,793	$23,264	$30,638
Parks and Resorts	3,031	16,162	25,510
Studio Entertainment	1,973	6,838	15,334
Consumer Products	1,752	5,027	7,591

a. Use the DuPont formula to determine the return on investment for the four Disney sectors. Round profit margin and return on investment to one decimal place and investment turnover to two decimal places.

b. How do the four sectors differ in their profit margin, investment turnover, and return on investment?

E14-15 Determining missing items in return on investment and residual income computations

Obj. 4

✔ c. $100,000

The following table presents various rates of return on investment and residual incomes:

Invested Assets	Operating Income	Return on Investment	Minimum Rate of Return	Minimum Acceptable Operating Income	Residual Income
$ 2,500,000	$ 400,000	(a)	12%	(b)	(c)
6,000,000	(d)	(e)	(f)	$600,000	$240,000
7,500,000	(g)	20%	(h)	900,000	(i)
14,000,000	2,380,000	(j)	13%	(k)	(l)

Determine the missing items, identifying each item by the appropriate letter.

Obj. 4

✔ a. (e) $9,000,000

E14-16 Determining missing items from computations

Data for the California, Midwest, Northwest, and Texas divisions of Firefly Industries are as follows:

	Sales	Operating Income	Invested Assets	Return on Investment	Profit Margin	Investment Turnover
California	$ 6,000,000	(a)	(b)	16%	20%	(c)
Midwest	(d)	$1,512,000	(e)	(f)	12%	1.4
Northwest	13,750,000	(g)	$11,000,000	17.5%	(h)	(i)
Texas	5,250,000	840,000	3,500,000	(j)	(k)	(l)

a. Determine the missing items, identifying each by the letters (a) through (l). Round profit margin to one decimal place and investment turnover to two decimal places.

b. Determine the residual income for each division, assuming that the minimum acceptable rate of return established by management is 10%.

c. Which division is the most profitable in terms of (1) return on investment and (2) residual income?

Obj. 5

✔ a. $750,000

E14-17 Transfer pricing

Wiring used by the Appliance Division of Kaufman Manufacturing is currently purchased from outside suppliers at a cost of $25 per unit. However, the same materials are available from the Electronic Division. The Electronic Division has unused capacity and can produce the materials needed by the Appliance Division at a variable cost of $20 per unit.

a. If a transfer price of $23 per unit is established and 150,000 units of materials are transferred, with no reduction in the Electronic Division's current sales, how much would Kaufman Manufacturing's total operating income increase?

b. How much would the Appliance Division's operating income increase?

c. How much would the Electronic Division's operating income increase?

Obj. 5

✔ b. $450,000

E14-18 Transfer pricing

Based on Kaufman Manufacturing's data in Exercise 14-17, assume that a transfer price of $22 has been established and that 150,000 units of materials are transferred, with no reduction in the Electronic Division's current sales.

a. How much would Kaufman Manufacturing's total operating income increase?

b. How much would the Appliance Division's operating income increase?

c. How much would the Electronic Division's operating income increase?

d. If the negotiated price approach is used, what would be the range of acceptable transfer prices and why?

Problems

Obj. 2

P14-1 Budget performance report for a cost center

Sneed Industries Company sells vehicle parts to manufacturers of heavy construction equipment. The Crane Division is organized as a cost center. The budget for the Crane Division for the month ended August 31, 20Y6, is as follows (in thousands):

Customer service salaries	$ 250,000
Insurance and property taxes	50,000
Distribution salaries	475,000
Marketing salaries	300,000
Engineer salaries	740,000
Warehouse wages	280,000
Equipment depreciation	155,000
Total	$2,250,000

During August, the costs incurred in the Crane Division were as follows:

Customer service salaries	$ 368,000
Insurance and property taxes	49,100
Distribution salaries	469,500
Marketing salaries	371,000
Engineer salaries	738,250
Warehouse wages	274,900
Equipment depreciation	155,000
Total	$2,425,750

Instructions

1. Prepare a budget performance report for the director of the Crane Division for the month of August.
2. For which costs might the director be expected to request supplemental reports?

P14-2 Profit center responsibility reporting

Obj. 3

✔ 1. Operating income, Air Division, $753,300

A-One Freight Inc. has three regional divisions organized as profit centers. The chief executive officer (CEO) evaluates divisional performance using operating income as a percent of revenues. The following quarterly income and expense accounts were provided from the trial balance as of December 31, 20Y3.

Revenues—Air Division	$5,000,000
Revenues—Rail Division	6,000,000
Revenues—Truck Division	9,000,000
Operating Expenses—Air Division	4,100,000
Operating Expenses—Rail Division	4,900,000
Operating Expenses—Truck Division	7,555,000
Corporate Expenses—Shareholder Relations	220,000
Corporate Expenses—Customer Support	990,000
Corporate Expenses—Legal	880,000
General Corporate Officers' Salaries	500,000

The company operates three service departments: Shareholder Relations, Customer Support, and Legal. The Shareholder Relations Department conducts a variety of services for shareholders of the company. The Customer Support Department is the company's point of contact for new service, complaints, and requests for repair. The department believes that the number of customer contacts is an activity base for this work. The Legal Department provides legal services for division management. The department believes that the number of hours billed is an activity base for this work. The following additional information has been gathered:

	Air	Rail	Truck
Number of customer contacts	1,500	4,500	16,000
Number of hours billed	900	2,400	6,700

Division management does not control activities related to the shareholder relations department and general corporate officers' salaries.

Instructions

1. Prepare quarterly income statements showing operating income for the three divisions. Use three column headings: Air, Rail, and Truck.
2. Identify the most successful division according to operating income as a percent of revenues. Round to one decimal place.
3. Provide a recommendation to the CEO for a better method for evaluating the performance of the divisions. In your recommendation, identify the major weakness of the present method.

Obj. 4

✔ 2. Breakfast Division, ROI, 10.8%

P14-3 Divisional income statements and return on investment analysis

High Country Foods Inc. is a diversified food products company with three operating divisions organized as investment centers. Condensed data taken from the records of the three divisions for the year ended June 30, 20Y7, are as follows:

	Breakfast Division	Bakery Division	Frozen Foods Division
Sales	$39,600,000	$18,500,000	$24,000,000
Cost of goods sold	32,500,000	13,500,000	14,400,000
Operating expenses	4,724,000	3,705,000	7,680,000
Invested assets	22,000,000	9,250,000	16,000,000

The management of High Country Foods Inc. is evaluating each division as a basis for planning a future expansion of operations.

Instructions

1. Prepare condensed divisional income statements for the three divisions, assuming that there were no service department charges.
2. Using the DuPont formula, compute the profit margin, investment turnover, and return on investment for each division.
3. If available funds permit the expansion of operations of only one division, which of the divisions would you recommend for expansion, based on parts (1) and (2)? Explain.

Obj. 4

✔ 1. ROI, 11.2%

P14-4 Effect of proposals on divisional performance

A condensed income statement for the Jet Ski Division of Amazing Rides Inc. for the year ended December 31, 20Y2, is as follows:

Sales	$12,000,000
Cost of goods sold	(7,200,000)
Gross profit	$ 4,800,000
Operating expenses	(3,120,000)
Operating income	$ 1,680,000
Invested assets	$15,000,000

Assume that the Jet Ski Division received no charges from service departments. The president of Amazing Rides has indicated that the division's rate of return on a $15,000,000 investment must be increased to at least 12% by the end of the next year if operations are to continue. The division manager is considering the following three proposals:

Proposal 1: Transfer equipment with a book value of $3,000,000 to other divisions at no gain or loss and lease similar equipment. The annual lease payments would exceed the amount of depreciation expense on the old equipment by $264,000. This increase in expense would be included as part of the cost of goods sold. Sales would remain unchanged.

Proposal 2: Purchase new and more efficient machining equipment and thereby reduce the cost of goods sold by $480,000. Sales would remain unchanged, and the old equipment, which has no remaining book value, would be scrapped at no gain or loss. The new equipment would increase invested assets by an additional $1,000,000 for the year.

Proposal 3: Reduce invested assets by discontinuing the tandem jet ski line. This action would eliminate sales of $2,280,000, cost of goods sold of $1,400,000, and operating expenses of $463,600. Assets of $4,200,000 would be transferred to other divisions at no gain or loss.

Instructions

1. Using the DuPont formula, determine the profit margin, investment turnover, and return on investment for the Jet Ski Division for the past year.
2. Prepare condensed estimated income statements and compute the invested assets for each proposal.

3. Using the DuPont formula, determine the profit margin, investment turnover, and return on investment for each proposal.
4. Which of the three proposals would meet the required 12% return on investment?
5. If the Jet Ski Division were in an industry where the profit margin could not be increased, how much would the investment turnover have to increase to meet the president's required 12% return on investment?

P14-5 Divisional performance analysis and evaluation

Obj. 4

✔ 2. Touring Bike Division ROI, 14.0%

The vice president of operations of Moab Bike Company is evaluating the performance of two divisions organized as investment centers. Invested assets and condensed income statement data for the past year ending October 31, 20Y9, for each division are as follows:

	Touring Bike Division	Trail Bike Division
Sales	$1,500,000	$5,400,000
Cost of goods sold	900,000	4,000,000
Operating expenses	495,000	968,000
Invested assets	750,000	3,600,000

Instructions

1. Prepare condensed divisional income statements for the year ended October 31, 20Y9, assuming that there were no service department charges.
2. Using the DuPont formula, determine the profit margin, investment turnover, and return on investment for each division.
3. If management desires a minimum acceptable rate of return of 10%, determine the residual income for each division.
4. Discuss the evaluation of the two divisions, using the performance measures determined in parts (1), (2), and (3).

P14-6 Transfer pricing

Obj. 5

✔ 3. Total operating income, $7,000,000

Birrell Scientific Inc. manufactures electronic products, with two operating divisions, GPS Systems and Communication Systems. Condensed divisional income statements, which involve no intracompany transfers and which include a breakdown of expenses into variable and fixed components, are as follows:

BIRRELL SCIENTIFIC INC.
Divisional Income Statements
For the Year Ended July 31, 20Y5

	GPS Systems Division	Communication Systems Division	Total
Sales:			
400,000 units @ $72 per unit	$ 28,800,000		$ 28,800,000
100,000 units @ $132 per unit		$ 13,200,000	13,200,000
	$ 28,800,000	$ 13,200,000	$ 42,000,000
Expenses:			
Variable:			
400,000 units @ $50 per unit	$(20,000,000)		$(20,000,000)
100,000 units @ $110* per unit		$(11,000,000)	(11,000,000)
Fixed	(5,000,000)	(1,000,000)	(6,000,000)
Total expenses	$(25,000,000)	$(12,000,000)	$(37,000,000)
Operating income	$ 3,800,000	$ 1,200,000	$ 5,000,000

*$70 of the $110 per unit represents materials costs, and the remaining $40 per unit represents other variable conversion expenses incurred within the Communication Systems Division.

The GPS Systems Division is presently producing 400,000 units out of a total capacity of 550,000 units. Materials used in producing the Communication Systems Division's product are currently purchased from outside suppliers at a price of $70 per unit. The GPS Systems Division is able to produce the materials used by the Communication Systems Division at a variable cost of $50 per unit. Except for the possible transfer of materials between divisions, no changes are expected in sales and expenses.

Instructions

1. Would the market price of $70 per unit be an appropriate transfer price for Birrell Scientific Inc.? Explain.
2. If the Communication Systems Division purchases 100,000 units from the GPS Systems Division, rather than externally, at a negotiated transfer price of $58 per unit, how much would the operating income of each division and the total company operating income increase?
3. Prepare condensed divisional income statements for Birrell Scientific Inc. based on the data in part (2).
4. If a transfer price of $64 per unit is negotiated, how much would the operating income of each division and the total company operating income increase?
5. a. What is the range of possible negotiated transfer prices that would be acceptable for Birrell Scientific Inc.?

   b. Assuming that the managers of the two divisions cannot agree on a transfer price, what price would you suggest as the transfer price?

Metric-Based Analysis

Obj. 6

MBA 14-1 Balanced scorecard

American Express Company (AXP) is a major financial services company, noted for its American Express card. Below are some of the performance measures used by the company in its balanced scorecard.

Average cardmember spending
Cards in force
Earnings growth
Hours of credit consultant training
Investment in information technology
Number of internet features
Number of merchant signings
Number of card choices
Number of new card launches
Return on equity
Revenue growth

For each measure, identify whether the measure best fits the innovation, customer, internal process, or financial dimension of the balanced scorecard.

Obj. 6

MBA 14-2 Balanced scorecard

Several years ago, United Parcel Service (UPS) believed that the Internet was going to change the parcel delivery market and would require UPS to become a more nimble and customer-focused organization. As a result, UPS replaced its old measurement system, which was 90% oriented toward financial performance, with a balanced scorecard. The scorecard emphasized four "point of arrival" measures, which were:

1. Customer satisfaction index—a measure of customer satisfaction.
2. Employee relations index—a measure of employee sentiment and morale.
3. Competitive position—delivery performance relative to competition.

4. Time in transit—the time from order entry to delivery.
   a. Why did UPS introduce a balanced scorecard and nonfinancial measures in its new performance measurement system?
   b. Why do you think UPS included a factor measuring employee sentiment?

MBA 14-3 Balanced scorecard **Obj. 6**

Delta Air Lines, Inc. (DAL) provides passenger services throughout the United States and the world. Fifteen Delta metrics and recent initiatives are as follows:

1. Using a mobile phone app that allows passengers to monitor their place in standby and first class upgrade lists
2. Improving the efficiency of aircraft maintenance
3. Increasing the number of check-in kiosks at major airports
4. Replacing less fuel-efficient aircraft with newer, more efficient aircraft
5. Reducing turnover of key employees
6. Reducing the number of cancelled flights
7. Investing in oil refinery that produces jet fuel
8. Offering cash incentive awards to employees
9. Awarding stock options to key employees that can be used over time
10. Increasing passenger revenue per available seat mile
11. Increasing the percentage of on-time arrivals
12. Reducing the number of passenger complaints
13. Reducing the number of lost passenger bags
14. Reducing the number of safety violations
15. Increasing the passenger load percentage

Assign each item to one of the four dimensions of the balanced scorecard:

1. learning and innovation
2. customer
3. internal process
4. financial

MBA 14-4 Balanced scorecard **Obj. 6**

Costco Wholesale Corporation (COST) operates membership warehouses throughout the United States and the world. Fifteen Costco metrics and recent initiatives are as follows:

1. Increasing same store sales
2. Improving safety procedures for warehouse prepared foods
3. Reducing the number of product returns
4. Researching consumer preferences
5. Increasing the number of warehouses with gas pumps
6. Offering training programs for all new employees
7. Offering awards for employees with more the five years of service
8. Improving Costco online consumer experience
9. Increasing gross profit percentage
10. Changing containers from square to round to increase the number of containers that can be shipped on a pallet
11. Developing a company-owned coffee roasting operation
12. Using floor-ready packaging from suppliers

13. Reducing warehouse energy usage for floor lighting
14. Increasing the use of automation to increase efficiencies
15. Increasing the average revenue per member

Assign each item to one of the four dimensions of the balanced scorecard:

1. learning and innovation
2. customer
3. internal process
4. financial

Obj. 6

MBA 14-5 Balanced scorecard

Divide responsibilities between two groups, with one group going to the home page of The Palladium Group at http://www.thepalladiumgroup.com, and the second group going to the home page of Stern Stewart & Co. at http://www.eva.com. The Palladium Group is a consulting firm that helped develop the balanced scorecard concept. Stern Stewart & Co. is a consulting firm that developed the concept of economic value added (EVA), another method of measuring corporate and divisional performance, similar to residual income.

After reading about the balanced scorecard at the palladiumgroup.com site, prepare a brief report describing the balanced scorecard and its claimed advantages. In the Stern group, use links in the home page of Stern Stewart & Co. to learn about EVA. After reading about EVA, prepare a brief report describing EVA and its claimed advantages. After preparing these reports, both groups should discuss their research and prepare a brief analysis comparing and contrasting these two approaches to corporate and divisional performance measurement.

Cases

Case 14-1 Ethics and professional conduct in business

Sisel Company has two divisions, the Optic Lens Division and the Camera Division. The Camera Division may purchase lenses from the Optic Lens Division or from outside suppliers. The Optic Lens Division sells products both internally and externally. The market price for lenses is $2,500 per carton (100). Newt Watt is the controller of the Camera Division, and Tani Trudeau is the controller of the Optic Lens Division. The following conversation took place between Newt and Tani:

Newt: I hear you are having problems selling lenses out of your division. Maybe I can help.

Tani: You've got that right. We're producing and selling at about 75% of our capacity to outsiders. Last year we were selling at capacity. Would it be possible for your division to pick up some of our excess capacity? After all, we are part of the same company.

Newt: What kind of price could you give me?

Tani: Well, you know as well as I that we are under strict profit responsibility in our divisions, so I would expect to get market price, $2,500 per carton (100).

Newt: I'm not so sure we can swing that. I was expecting a price break from a "sister" division.

Tani: Hey, I can only take this "sister" stuff so far. If I give you a price break, our profits will fall from last year's levels. I don't think I could explain that. I'm sorry, but I must remain firm—market price. After all, it's only fair—that's what you would have to pay from an external supplier.

Newt: Fair or not, I think we'll pass. Sorry we couldn't have helped.

Was Newt behaving ethically by trying to force the Optic Lens Division into a price break? Comment on Tani's reactions.

Case 14-2 Service department charges

The Customer Service Department of Bragg Inc. asked the Publications Department to prepare a brochure for its training program. The Publications Department delivered the brochures and charged the Customer Service Department a rate that was 15% higher than could be obtained from an outside printing company. The policy of the company required the Customer Service Department to use the internal publications group for brochures. The Publications Department claimed that it had a drop in demand for its services during the fiscal year, so it had to charge higher prices in order to recover its payroll and fixed costs.

Should the cost of the brochure be transferred to the Customer Service Department in order to hold the department head accountable for the cost of the brochure? What changes in policy would you recommend?

Case 14-3 Evaluating divisional performance

The three divisions of Dixie Foods are Cereal, Produce, and Snacks. The divisions are structured as investment centers. The following responsibility reports were prepared for the three divisions for the prior year:

	Cereal	Produce	Snacks
Revenues	$5,400,000	$16,000,000	$ 9,000,000
Operating expenses	(4,200,000)	(12,800,000)	(6,300,000)
Operating income before service department charges	$1,200,000	$ 3,200,000	$ 2,700,000
Service department charges:			
Promotion	$ (500,000)	$ (1,500,000)	$(1,200,000)
Legal	(268,000)	(740,000)	(420,000)
Total service department charges	$ (768,000)	$ (2,240,000)	$(1,620,000)
Operating income	$ 432,000	$ 960,000	$ 1,080,000
Invested assets	$4,500,000	$ 8,000,000	$ 5,000,000

1. Which division is making the best use of invested assets and thus should be given priority for future capital investments?
2. Assuming that the minimum acceptable rate of return on new projects is 10%, would all investments that produce a return in excess of 10% be accepted by the divisions?
3. Determine the overall return on investment for Dixie Foods. Round to one decimal place.
4. Can you identify opportunities for improving Dixie Foods' financial performance?

Case 14-4 Evaluating division performance over time

The Laser Division of FOX Technologies Inc. has been experiencing revenue and profit growth during the years 20Y6–20Y8. The divisional income statements are provided below.

FOX TECHNOLOGIES INC.
Divisional Income Statements, Laser Division
For the Years Ended December 31, 20Y6–20Y8

	20Y6	20Y7	20Y8
Sales	$3,000,000	$4,500,000	$7,000,000
Cost of goods sold	(1,800,000)	(2,625,000)	(3,800,000)
Gross profit	$1,200,000	$1,875,000	$3,200,000
Operating expenses	(300,000)	(300,000)	(400,000)
Operating income	$ 900,000	$1,575,000	$2,800,000

Assume that there are no charges from service departments. The vice president of the division, Stacy Harper, is proud of her division's performance over the last three years. The president of FOX Technologies Inc., Hal Nelson, is discussing the division's performance with Stacy, as follows:

Stacy: As you can see, we've had a successful three years in the Laser Division.

Hal: I'm not too sure.

Stacy: What do you mean? Look at our results. Our operating income has more than tripled, while our profit margins are improving.

Hal: I am looking at your results. However, your income statements fail to include one very important piece of information; namely, the invested assets. You have been investing a great deal of assets into the division. You had $2,000,000 in invested assets in 20Y6, $4,500,000 in 20Y7, and $10,000,000 in 20Y8.

Stacy: You are right. I've needed the assets in order to upgrade our technologies and expand our operations. The additional assets are one reason we have been able to grow and improve our profit margins. I don't see that this is a problem.

Hal: The problem is that we want to maintain a 30% rate of return on invested assets.

1. Determine the profit margins for the Laser Division for 20Y6–20Y8.
2. Compute the investment turnover for the Laser Division for 20Y6–20Y8.
3. Compute the return on investment for the Laser Division for 20Y6–20Y8.
4. Evaluate the division's performance over the 20Y6–20Y8 time period. Why was Hal concerned about the performance?

Case 14-5 Evaluating division performance

Modern Living Inc. is a privately held diversified company with five separate divisions organized as investment centers. A condensed income statement for the Patio Division for the past year, assuming no service department charges, is as follows:

MODERN LIVING INC.— PATIO DIVISION
Income Statement
For the Year Ended December 31, 20Y4

Sales	$ 18,000,000
Cost of goods sold	(13,000,000)
Gross profit	$ 5,000,000
Operating expenses	(1,400,000)
Operating income	$ 3,600,000
Invested assets	$ 15,000,000

The manager of the Patio Division was recently presented with the opportunity to add an outdoor fireplace product line, which would require invested assets of $4,500,000. A projected income statement for the new product line is as follows:

OUTDOOR FIREPLACE LINE
Projected Income Statement
For the Year Ended December 31, 20Y5

Sales	$ 4,050,000
Cost of goods sold	(2,340,000)
Gross profit	$ 1,710,000
Operating expenses	(900,000)
Operating income	$ 810,000

The Patio Division currently has $15,000,000 in invested assets, and Modern Living Inc.'s overall return on investment, including all divisions, is 14%. Each division manager is evaluated on the basis of divisional return on investment, and a bonus equal to $10,000 for each percentage point by which the division's return on investment exceeds the company average is awarded each year.

The president is concerned that the manager of the Patio Division rejected the addition of the new product line, when all estimates indicated that the product line would be profitable and would increase overall company income. You have been asked to analyze the possible reasons why the Patio Division manager rejected the new product line.

1. Determine the return on investment for the Patio Division for the past year.
2. Determine the Patio Division manager's bonus for the past year.
3. Determine the estimated return on investment for the new product line.
4. Determine the return for the Patio Division if the Outdoor Fireplace product line was added and the 20Y5 operating results were similar to those of 20Y4. Round to one decimal place.
5. Why might the manager of the Patio Division decide to reject the new product line?
6. Can you suggest an alternative performance measure for motivating division managers to accept new investment opportunities that would increase the overall company income and return on investment?

Answers to Self-Examination Questions

1. **B** The manager of a profit center (answer B) has responsibility for and authority over costs and revenues. If the manager has responsibility for only costs, the department is called a cost center (answer A). If the responsibility and authority extend to the investment in assets as well as costs and revenues, it is called an investment center (answer C). A service department (answer D) provides services to other departments. A service department could be a cost center, a profit center, or an investment center.

2. **C** \$600,000/150,000 = \$4 per payment. Division A anticipates 60,000 payments or \$240,000 (60,000 × \$4) in service department charges from the Accounts Payable Department. Operating income is thus \$900,000 − \$240,000, or \$660,000. Answer A assumes that all of the service department overhead is assigned to Division A, which would be incorrect, since Division A does not use all of the accounts payable service. Answer B incorrectly assumes that there are no service department charges from Accounts Payable. Answer D incorrectly determines the accounts payable transfer rate from Division A's operating income.

3. **A** The return on investment for Division A is 20% (answer A), computed as follows:

$$\text{Return on Investment (ROI)} = \frac{\text{Operating Income}}{\text{Invested Assets}}$$

$$= \frac{\$350{,}000 - \$200{,}000 - \$30{,}000}{\$600{,}000}$$

$$= 20\%$$

4. **B** The profit margin for Division L of Liddy Co. is 15% (answer B), computed as follows:

$$\text{Return on Investment (ROI)} = \text{Profit Margin} \times \text{Investment Turnover}$$

$$24\% = \text{Profit Margin} \times 1.6$$

$$15\% = \text{Profit Margin}$$

5. **C** The market price approach (answer C) to transfer pricing uses the price at which the product or service transferred could be sold to outside buyers. The cost price approach (answer A) uses cost as the basis for setting transfer prices. The negotiated price approach (answer B) allows managers of decentralized units to agree (negotiate) among themselves as to the proper transfer price. The standard cost approach (answer D) is a version of the cost price approach that uses standard costs in setting transfer prices.

Chapter

15 Capital Investment Analysis

What's Covered:

Topics: Capital Investment Analysis

Capital Investments
- Nature (Obj. 1)
- Importance (Obj. 1)

Non-Present Value Methods
- Average rate of return (Obj. 2)
- Cash payback (Obj. 2)

Present Value Methods
- Net present value method (Obj. 3)
- Internal rate of return method (Obj. 3)

Complications
- Income tax (Obj. 4)
- Unequal lives (Obj. 4)
- Lease versus purchase (Obj. 4)
- Uncertainty (Obj. 4)
- Changing prices (Obj. 4)
- Qualitative factors (Obj. 4)

Capital Rationing
- Competing proposals (Obj. 5)
- Decision process (Obj. 5)

Metric Analysis
- Financial leverage (Obj. 6)

Learning Objectives

Obj.1 Describe the nature and importance of capital investment analysis.

Obj.2 Evaluate capital investment proposals using the average rate of return and cash payback methods.

Obj.3 Evaluate capital investment proposals using the net present value and internal rate of return methods.

Obj.4 Describe factors that complicate capital investment analysis.

Obj.5 Describe and diagram the capital rationing process.

Obj.6 Describe and illustrate the impact of financial leverage (debt) on the return on stockholders' equity.

Chapter Metric

The managerial decision-making and performance metric for this chapter is financial leverage.

Vail Resorts, Inc.

Christian de Araujo/Shutterstock.com

Why are you paying tuition, studying this text, and spending time and money on a higher education? Most people believe the money and time spent now will return them more earnings in the future. That is, the cost of higher education is an investment in your future earning ability. How would you know if this investment is worth it?

One method would be for you to compare the cost of a higher education against the estimated increase in your future earning power. The bigger the difference between your expected future earnings and the cost of your education, the better the investment. A business also evaluates its investments in fixed assets by comparing the initial cost of the investment to its future earnings and cash flows.

For example, **Vail Resorts, Inc. (MTN)**, is one of the largest ski resort operators in the world. It is known for its Vail, Breckenridge, and Keystone ski resorts, among others. A ski resort requires significant investments in property and equipment. Thus, Vail routinely makes major investments in new or improved amenities, lodging, retail, lifts, snowmaking and grooming equipment, and technology infrastructure. These investments are evaluated by their ability to increase cash flows.

In this chapter, the methods used to make investment decisions, which may involve thousands, millions, or even billions of dollars, are described and illustrated. The similarities and differences among the most commonly used methods of evaluating investment proposals, as well as the benefits of each method, are emphasized. Factors that can complicate the analysis are also discussed.

Objective 1
Describe the nature and importance of capital investment analysis.

Nature of Capital Investment Analysis

Companies use capital investment analysis to evaluate long-term investments. **Capital investment analysis** (or *capital budgeting*) is the process by which management plans, evaluates, and controls investments in fixed assets. Capital investments use funds and affect operations for many years and must earn a reasonable rate of return. Thus, capital investment decisions are some of the most important decisions that management makes.

Capital investment evaluation methods can be grouped into the following categories:

Methods That Do Not Use Present Values

- Average rate of return method
- Cash payback method

Methods That Use Present Values

- Net present value method
- Internal rate of return method

The two methods that use present values consider the time value of money. The **time value of money concept** recognizes that an amount of cash invested today has the potential to earn income and increase in value over time.

Vail Inc. Connection **Vail Inc.** purchased the Park City Mountain Resort and ski area in Park City, Utah, for $182.5 million.

Use of Investment Analysis Methods

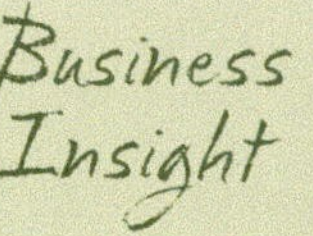

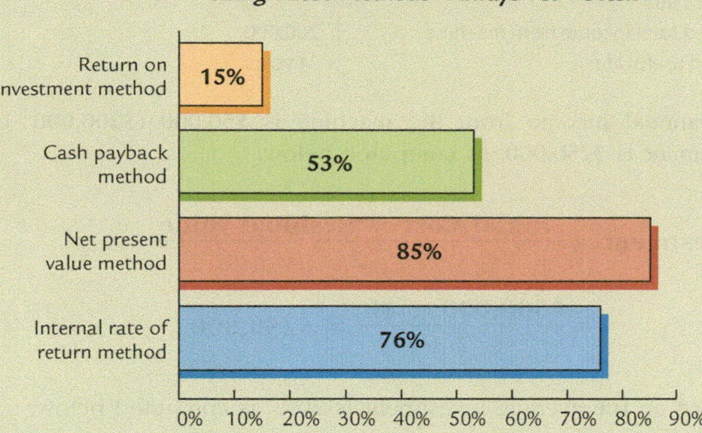

A survey of chief financial officers of large U.S. companies reported their use of the four investment methods as follows:

Source: Patricia A. Ryan and Glenn P. Ryan, "Capital Budgeting Practice of the Fortune 1000: How Have Things Changed?" *Journal of Business and Management* (Winter 2002).

Methods Not Using Present Values

Objective 2
Evaluate capital investment proposals using the average rate of return and cash payback methods.

The methods not using present values are often useful in evaluating capital investment proposals that have relatively short useful lives. In such cases, the timing of the cash flows (the time value of money) is less important.

Since the methods not using present values are easy to apply, they are often used to screen proposals. Minimum standards for accepting proposals are set, and proposals not meeting these standards are dropped. If a proposal meets the minimum standards, it may be subject to further analysis using the present value methods.

Average Rate of Return Method

The **average rate of return**, sometimes called the *accounting rate of return,* measures the average income as a percent of the average investment. The average rate of return is computed as follows:

$$\textbf{Average Rate of Return} = \frac{\textbf{Estimated Average Annual Income}}{\textbf{Average Investment}}$$

In the preceding equation, the numerator is the average of the annual income expected to be earned from the investment over its life after deducting depreciation. The denominator is the average investment (book value) over the life of the investment. Assuming straight-line depreciation, the average investment is computed as follows:

$$\textbf{Average Investment} = \frac{\textbf{Initial Cost} + \textbf{Residual Value}}{\textbf{2}}$$

To illustrate, assume that management is evaluating the purchase of a new machine as follows:

Cost of new machine	$500,000
Residual value	0
Estimated total income from machine	200,000
Expected useful life	4 years

The estimated average annual income from the machine is $50,000 ($200,000 ÷ 4 years). The average investment is $250,000, as computed below.

$$\text{Average Investment} = \frac{\text{Initial Cost} + \text{Residual Value}}{2}$$

$$= \frac{\$500{,}000 + \$0}{2} = \$250{,}000$$

The average rate of return on the average investment is 20%, as computed below.

$$\text{Average Rate of Return} = \frac{\text{Estimated Average Annual Income}}{\text{Average Investment}}$$

$$= \frac{\$50{,}000}{\$250{,}000} = 20\%$$

The average rate of return of 20% should be compared to the minimum rate of return required by management. If the average rate of return equals or exceeds the minimum rate, the machine should be purchased or considered for further analysis.

Capital investment proposals can be ranked by their rates of return. The higher the average rate of return, the more desirable the proposal. For example, assume that management is considering two capital investment proposals with the following average rates of return:

	Proposal A	Proposal B
Average rate of return	20%	25%

If only the average rate of return is considered, Proposal B, with a rate of return of 25%, is preferred over Proposal A.

The average rate of return has the following advantages:

- It is easy to compute.
- It includes the entire amount of income earned over the life of the proposal.
- It emphasizes accounting income, which is often used by investors and creditors in evaluating management performance.

The average rate of return has the following disadvantages:

- It does not directly consider the expected cash flows from the proposal.
- It does not directly consider the timing of the expected cash flows.

Vail Inc. Connection **Vail**'s overall rate of return on its investment in property, plant, and equipment is slightly more than 10 percent.

Cash Payback Method

A capital investment uses cash and must return cash in the future to be successful. The expected period of time between the date of an investment and the recovery in cash of the amount invested is the **cash payback period.**

When annual net cash inflows are equal, the cash payback period is computed as follows:

$$\textbf{Cash Payback Period} = \frac{\textbf{Initial Cost}}{\textbf{Annual Net Cash Inflow}}$$

To illustrate, assume that management is evaluating the purchase of the following new machine:

Cost of new machine	$200,000
Cash revenues from machine per year	50,000
Expenses of machine per year	30,000
Depreciation per year	20,000

To simplify, the revenues and expenses other than depreciation are assumed to be in cash. Hence, the net cash inflow per year from use of the machine is as follows:

Net cash inflow per year:		
Cash revenues from machine		$ 50,000
Less cash expenses of machine:		
Expenses of machine	$ 30,000	
Less depreciation	(20,000)	(10,000)
Net cash inflow per year		$ 40,000

The time required for the net cash flow to equal the cost of the new machine is the payback period. Thus, the estimated cash payback period for the investment is five years, as computed below.

$$\textbf{Cash Payback Period} = \frac{\textbf{Initial Cost}}{\textbf{Annual Net Cash Inflow}} = \frac{\textbf{\$200,000}}{\textbf{\$40,000}} = \textbf{5 years}$$

In the preceding illustration, the annual net cash inflows are equal ($40,000 per year). When the annual net cash inflows are not equal, the cash payback period is determined by adding the annual net cash inflows until the cumulative total equals the initial cost of the proposed investment.

To illustrate, assume that a proposed investment has an initial cost of $400,000. The annual and cumulative net cash inflows over the proposal's six-year life are as follows:

Year	Net Cash Flow	Cumulative Net Cash Flow
1	$ 60,000	$ 60,000
2	80,000	140,000
3	105,000	245,000
4	155,000	400,000
5	100,000	500,000
6	90,000	590,000

The cumulative net cash flow at the end of Year 4 equals the initial cost of the investment, $400,000. Thus, the payback period is four years, as shown in the following graph.

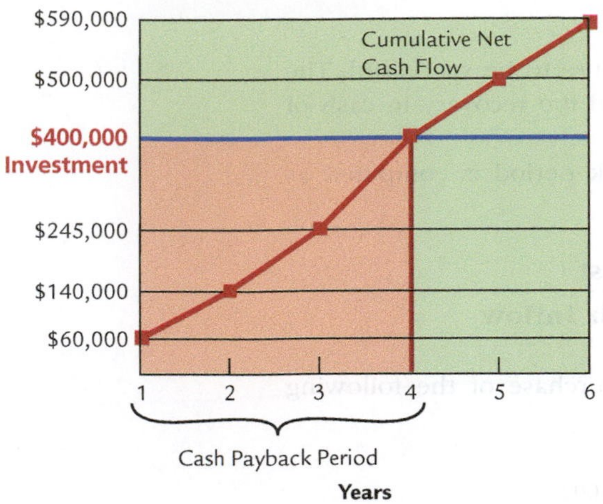

If the initial cost of the proposed investment had been $450,000, the cash payback period would occur during Year 5. Since $100,000 of net cash flow is expected during Year 5, the additional $50,000 to increase the cumulative total to $450,000 occurs halfway through the year ($50,000 ÷ $100,000). Thus, the cash payback period would be 4½ years.[1]

A short cash payback period is desirable. This is because the sooner cash is recovered, the sooner it can be reinvested in other projects. In addition, there is less chance of losses from changing economic conditions or other risks such as a decreasing customer demand when the payback period is short. A short cash payback period is also desirable for repaying debt used to purchase the investment.

The cash payback method has the following two advantages:

- It is simple to use and understand.
- It analyzes cash flows.

The cash payback method has the following two disadvantages:

- It ignores cash flows occurring after the payback period.
- It does not use present value concepts in valuing cash flows occurring in different periods.

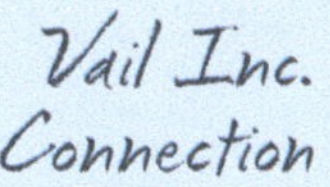

The ski operations are seasonal in nature and typically runs from mid-November to mid-April. To increase cash flows, **Vail Inc.** promotes non-ski activities in the summer months, including sightseeing, mountain biking, and zip tours.

Objective 3
Evaluate capital investment proposals using the net present value and internal rate of return methods.

Methods Using Present Values

An investment in fixed assets may be viewed as purchasing a series of net cash flows over a period of time. The timing of when the net cash flows will be received is important in determining the value of a proposed investment.

Present value methods use the amount and timing of the net cash flows in evaluating an investment. The two methods of evaluating capital investments using present values are as follows:

- Net present value method
- Internal rate of return method

Present Value Concepts

Both the net present value and the internal rate of return methods use the following **present value concepts**:

- Present value of an amount
- Present value of an annuity

Present Value of an Amount If you were given the choice, would you prefer to receive $1 now or $1 three years from now? You should prefer to receive $1 now, because you could invest the $1 and earn interest for three years. As a result, the amount you would have after three years would be greater than $1.

1. Unless otherwise stated, net cash inflows are received uniformly throughout the year.

To illustrate, assume that you have $1 to invest as follows:

Amount to be invested	$1
Period to be invested	3 years
Interest rate	12%

After one year, the $1 earns interest of $0.12 ($1 × 12%) and thus will grow to $1.12 ($1 × 1.12). In the second year, the $1.12 earns 12% interest of $0.134 ($1.12 × 12%) and thus will grow to $1.254 ($1.12 × 1.12) by the end of the second year. This process of interest earning interest is called *compounding*. By the end of the third year, your $1 investment will grow to $1.404 as shown in Exhibit 1.

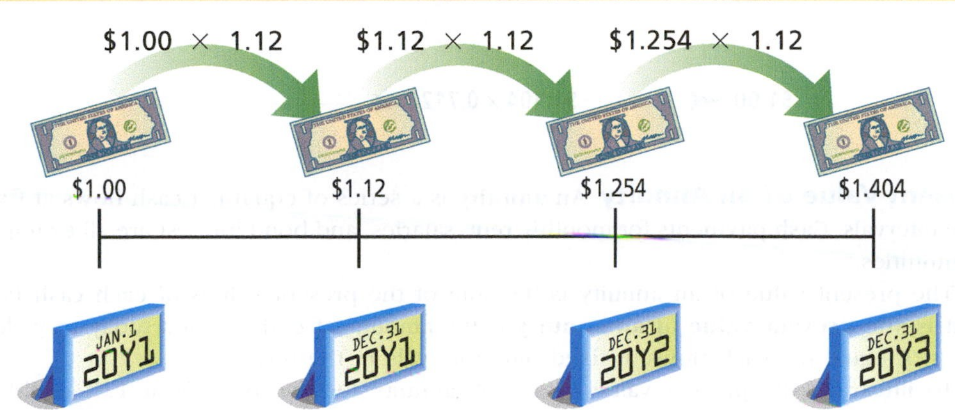

Exhibit 1 Compound Amount of $1 for Three Periods at 12%

On January 1, 20Y1, what is the present value of $1.404 to be received on December 31, 20Y3? This is a present value question. The answer can be determined with the aid of a present value of $1 table. For example, the partial table in Exhibit 2 indicates that the present value of $1 to be received in three years with earnings compounded at the rate of 12% a year is 0.712. Multiplying 0.712 by $1.404 yields $1 as follows:

Present Value		Amount to Be Received in 3 Years		Present Value of $1 to Be Received in 3 Years (from Exhibit 2)
$1	=	$1.404	×	0.712

Exhibit 2 Partial Present Value of $1 Table

Present Value of $1 at Compound Interest

Year	6%	10%	12%	15%	20%
1	0.943	0.909	0.893	0.870	0.833
2	0.890	0.826	0.797	0.756	0.694
3	0.840	0.751	0.712	0.658	0.579
4	0.792	0.683	0.636	0.572	0.482
5	0.747	0.621	0.567	0.497	0.402
6	0.705	0.564	0.507	0.432	0.335
7	0.665	0.513	0.452	0.376	0.279
8	0.627	0.467	0.404	0.327	0.233
9	0.592	0.424	0.361	0.284	0.194
10	0.558	0.386	0.322	0.247	0.162

In other words, the present value of $1.404 to be received in three years using a compound interest rate of 12% is $1, as shown in Exhibit 3.

Exhibit 3
Present Value of the Amount of $1.404 with Compound Interest of 12%

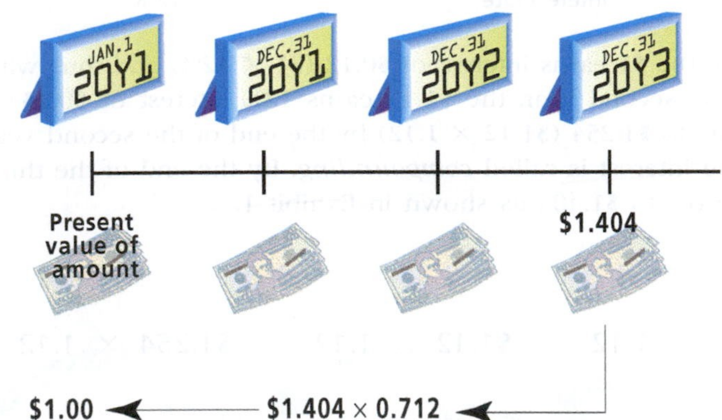

Present Value of an Annuity An **annuity** is a series of equal net cash flows at fixed time intervals. Cash payments for monthly rent, salaries, and bond interest are all examples of annuities.

The present value of an annuity is the sum of the present values of each cash flow. That is, the **present value of an annuity** is the amount of cash needed today to yield a series of equal net cash flows at fixed time intervals in the future.

To illustrate, the present value of a $100 annuity for five periods at 12% could be determined by using the present value factors in Exhibit 1. Each $100 net cash flow could be multiplied by the present value of $1 at a 12% factor for the appropriate period and summed to determine a present value of $360.50, as shown in Exhibit 4.

Exhibit 4
Present Value of $100 for Five Period with Compound Interest of 12%

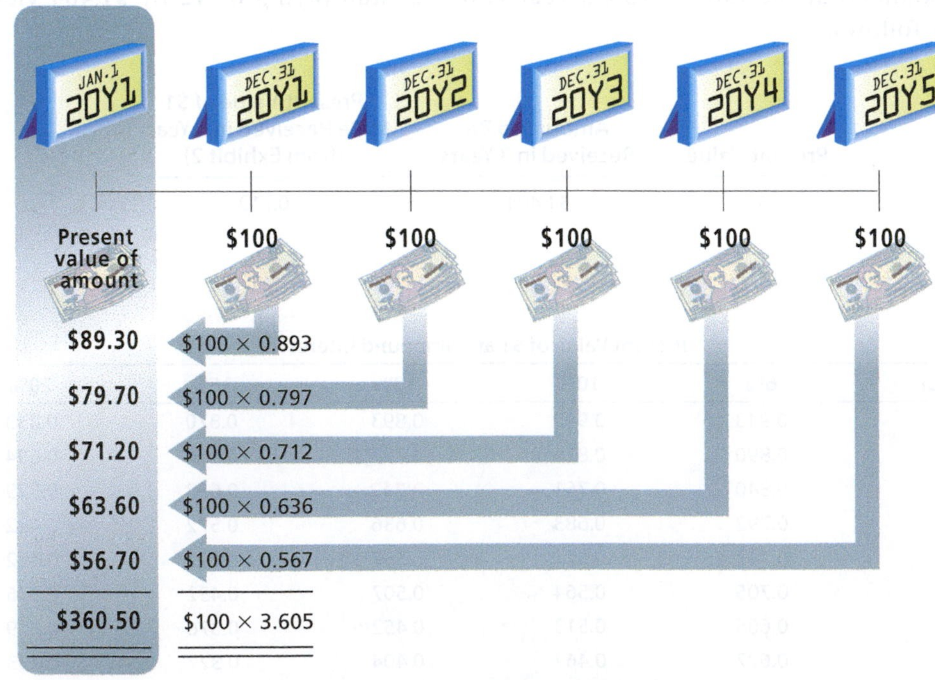

Using a present value of an annuity table is a simpler approach. Exhibit 5 is a partial table of present value of annuity factors.

Exhibit 5
Partial Present Value of an Annuity Table

Present Value of an Annuity of $1 at Compound Interest					
Year	6%	10%	12%	15%	20%
1	0.943	0.909	0.893	0.870	0.833
2	1.833	1.736	1.690	1.626	1.528
3	2.673	2.487	2.402	2.283	2.106
4	3.465	3.170	3.037	2.855	2.589
5	4.212	3.791	3.605	3.353	2.991
6	4.917	4.355	4.111	3.785	3.326
7	5.582	4.868	4.564	4.160	3.605
8	6.210	5.335	4.968	4.487	3.837
9	6.802	5.759	5.328	4.772	4.031
10	7.360	6.145	5.650	5.019	4.192

The present value factors in the table shown in Exhibit 5 are the sum of the present value of $1 factors in Exhibit 2 for the number of annuity periods. Thus, 3.605 in the annuity table (Exhibit 5) is the sum of the five present value of $1 factors at 12%, as shown below.

	Present Value of $1 (Exhibit 1)
Present value of $1 for 1 year @12%	0.893
Present value of $1 for 2 years @12%	0.797
Present value of $1 for 3 years @12%	0.712
Present value of $1 for 4 years @12%	0.636
Present value of $1 for 5 years @12%	0.567
Present value of an annuity of $1 for 5 years (from Exhibit 2)	3.605

Multiplying $100 by 3.605 yields the same amount ($360.50) as follows:

Present Value		Amount to Be Received Annually for 5 Years		Present Value of an Annuity of $1 to Be Received for 5 Years (Exhibit 2)
$360.50	=	$100	×	3.605

This amount ($360.50) is the same as what was determined in the preceding illustration by five successive multiplications.

Net Present Value Method The **net present value method** compares the amount to be invested with the present value of the net cash inflows. It is sometimes called the *discounted cash flow method.*

The interest rate (return) used in net present value analysis is the company's minimum desired rate of return. This rate, sometimes termed the *hurdle rate,* is based on such factors as the purpose of the investment and the cost of obtaining funds for the investment. If the present value of the cash inflows equals or exceeds the amount to be invested, the proposal is desirable.

To illustrate, assume the following data for a proposed investment in new equipment:

Cost of new equipment	$200,000
Expected useful life	5 years
Minimum desired rate of return	10%
Expected cash flows to be received each year:	
Year 1	$ 70,000
Year 2	60,000
Year 3	50,000
Year 4	40,000
Year 5	40,000
Total expected cash flows	$260,000

The present value of the net cash flow for each year is computed by multiplying the net cash flow for the year by the present value factor of $1 for that year as shown below.

Year	Present Value of $1 at 10%	Net Cash Flow	Present Value of Net Cash Flow
1	0.909	$ 70,000	$ 63,630
2	0.826	60,000	49,560
3	0.751	50,000	37,550
4	0.683	40,000	27,320
5	0.621	40,000	24,840
Total		$260,000	$202,900
Amount to be invested			(200,000)
Net present value			$ 2,900

The preceding computations are also graphically illustrated as shown in Exhibit 6.

Exhibit 6
Present Value of Cash Flows from New Equipment

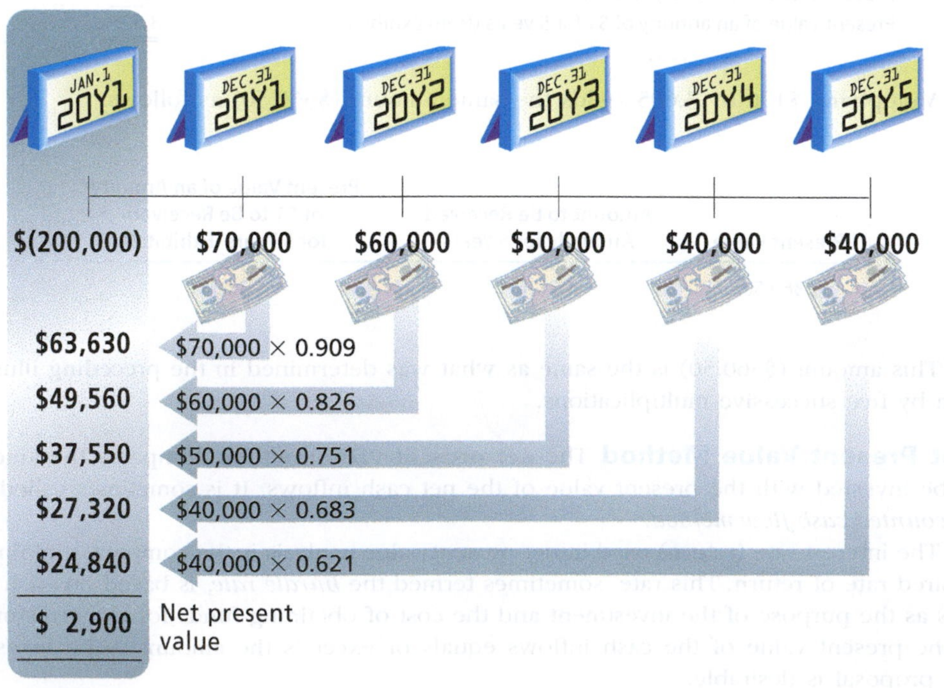

The net present value of $2,900 indicates that the purchase of the new equipment is expected to recover the investment and provide more than the minimum rate of return of 10%. Thus, the purchase of the new equipment is desirable.

The net present value method has the following advantages:

- It considers the cash flows of the investment.
- It considers the time value of money.
- It can rank projects with equal lives, using the present value index.

The net present value method has the following disadvantages:

- It has more complex computations than methods that don't use present value.
- It assumes the cash flows can be reinvested at the minimum desired rate of return, which may not be valid.

Vail Inc. uses present values in determining the value of assets and liabilities acquired in business acquisitions.

Net Present Value Index When capital investment funds are limited and the proposals involve different investments, a ranking of the proposals can be prepared by using a present value index. The **present value index** is computed as follows:

$$\text{Present Value Index} = \frac{\text{Total Present Value of Net Cash Flow}}{\text{Amount to Be Invested}}$$

The present value index for the investment in the preceding illustration is 1.0145, as computed below.

$$\text{Present Value Index} = \frac{\text{Total Present Value of Net Cash Flow}}{\text{Amount to Be Invested}}$$

$$\text{Present Value Index} = \frac{\$202{,}900}{\$200{,}000} = 1.0145$$

To illustrate, assume that a company is considering three proposals. The net present value and the present value index for each proposal are as follows:

	Proposal A	Proposal B	Proposal C
Total present value of net cash flow	$ 107,000	$ 86,400	$ 86,400
Amount to be invested	(100,000)	(80,000)	(90,000)
Net present value	$ 7,000	$ 6,400	$ (3,600)
Present value index:			
Proposal A ($107,000/$100,000)	1.07		
Proposal B ($86,400/$80,000)		1.08	
Proposal C ($86,400/$90,000)			0.96

A project will have a present value index greater than 1 when the net present value is positive. This is the case for Proposals A and B. When the net present value is negative, the present value index will be less than 1, as is the case for Proposal C.

Although Proposal A has the largest net present value, the present value indices indicate that it is not as desirable as Proposal B. That is, Proposal B returns $1.08 present value per dollar invested, whereas Proposal A returns only $1.07. Proposal B requires an investment of $80,000, compared to an investment of $100,000 for Proposal A. The possible use of the $20,000 difference between Proposals A and B investments should also be considered before making a final decision.

Internal Rate of Return Method The **internal rate of return (IRR) method** uses present value concepts to compute the rate of return from a capital investment proposal based on its expected net cash flows. This method, sometimes called the *time-adjusted rate of return method,* starts with the proposal's net cash flows and works backward to estimate the proposal's expected rate of return. To illustrate, assume that management is evaluating the following proposal to purchase new equipment:

Cost of new equipment	$33,530
Yearly expected cash flows to be received	10,000
Expected life	5 years
Minimum desired rate of return	12%

The present value of the net cash flows, using the present value of an annuity table in Exhibit 5, is $2,520, as shown in Exhibit 7.

Exhibit 7
Net Present Value Analysis at 12%

Annual net cash flow (at the end of each of five years)	$10,000
Present value of an annuity of $1 at 12% for five years (Exhibit 2)	× 3.605
Present value of annual net cash flows	$36,050
Less amount to be invested	(33,530)
Net present value	$ 2,520

In Exhibit 7, the $36,050 present value of the cash inflows, based on a 12% rate of return, is greater than the $33,530 to be invested. Thus, the internal rate of return must be greater than 12%. Through trial and error, the rate of return equating the $33,530 cost of the investment with the present value of the net cash flows can be determined to be 15%, as shown in Exhibit 8.

Exhibit 8
Present Value of an Annuity with an Internal Rate of Return of 15%

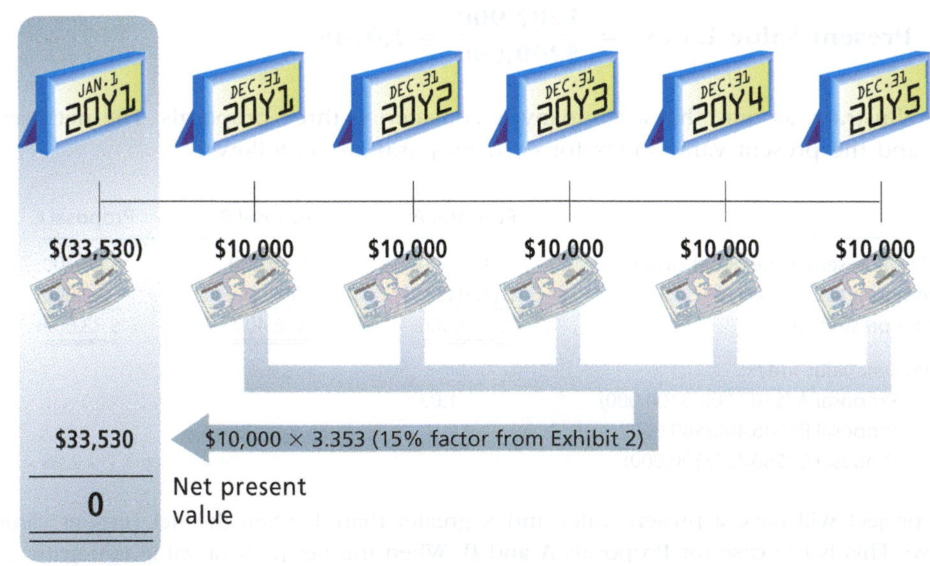

When equal annual net cash flows are expected from a proposal, as in the above example, the internal rate of return can be determined as follows:[2]

2. To simplify, equal annual net cash flows are assumed. If the net cash flows are not equal, spreadsheet software can be used to determine the rate of return.

Step 1. Determine a present value factor for an annuity of $1 as follows:

$$\textbf{Present Value Factor for an Annuity of \$1} = \frac{\textbf{Amount to Be Invested}}{\textbf{Equal Annual Net Cash Flows}}$$

Step 2. Locate the present value factor determined in Step 1 in the present value of an annuity of $1 table (Exhibit 2) as follows:

a. Locate the number of years of expected useful life of the investment in the Year column.

b. Proceed horizontally across the table until you find the present value factor computed in Step 1.

Step 3. Identify the internal rate of return by the heading of the column in which the present value factor in Step 2 is located.

To illustrate, assume that management is evaluating the following proposal to purchase new equipment:

Cost of new equipment	$97,360
Yearly expected cash flows to be received	20,000
Expected useful life	7 years

The present value factor for an annuity of $1 is 4.868, as shown below.

$$\textbf{Present Value Factor for an Annuity of \$1} = \frac{\textbf{Amount to Be Invested}}{\textbf{Equal Annual Net Cash Flows}}$$

$$\textbf{Present Value Factor for an Annuity \$1} = \frac{\textbf{\$97,360}}{\textbf{\$20,000}} = \textbf{4.868}$$

Using the following partial present value of an annuity of $1 table and a period of seven years, the factor 4.868 is related to 10% as shown in Exhibit 9. Thus, the internal rate of return for this proposal is 10%.

Exhibit 9
Determining Internal Rate of Return of 10%

Present Value of an Annuity of $1 at Compound Interest

	Year	6%		10% (Step 3)	12%
	1	0.943		0.909	0.893
	2	1.833		1.736	1.690
	3	2.673		2.487	2.402
	4	3.465		3.170	3.037
	5	4.212		3.791	3.605
	6	4.917	Step 2(b)	4.355	4.111
Step 2(a)	7	5.582	→	**4.868**	4.564
	8	6.210		5.335	4.968
	9	6.802		5.759	5.328
	10	7.360		6.145	5.650

Step 1: Determine present value factor for an annuity of $1 $= \frac{\$97,360}{\$20,000} = 4.868$

If the minimum acceptable rate of return is 10%, then the proposal is considered acceptable. Several proposals can be ranked by their internal rates of return. The proposal with the highest rate is the most desirable.

The internal rate of return method has the following advantages:

- It considers the cash flows of the investment.
- It considers the time value of money.
- It ranks proposals based upon the cash flows over their complete useful life, even if the project lives are not the same.

The internal rate of return method has the following disadvantages:

- It has complex computations, requiring a computer if the periodic cash flows are not equal.
- It assumes the cash received from a proposal can be reinvested at the internal rate of return, which may not be valid.

Factors That Complicate Capital Investment Analysis

Objective 4

Describe factors that complicate capital investment analysis.

Four widely used methods of evaluating capital investment proposals have been described and illustrated in this chapter. In practice, additional factors such as the following may impact capital investment decisions:

1. Income tax
2. Proposals with unequal lives
3. Leasing versus purchasing
4. Uncertainty
5. Changes in price levels
6. Qualitative factors

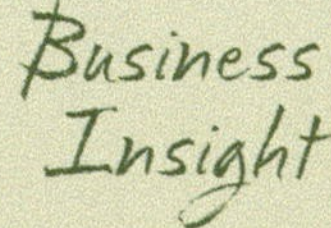

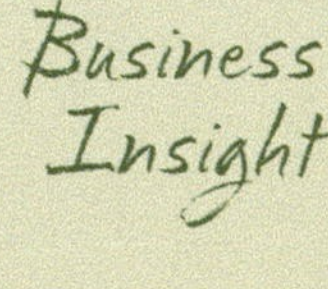

Panera Bread Store Rate of Return

RosalreneBetancourt 7/Alamy Stock Photo

Panera Bread owns, operates, and franchises bakery-cafes throughout the United States. An annual report to the Securities and Exchange Commission (SEC Form 10-K) disclosed the following information about an average company-owned store:

Operating profit	$ 302,000
Depreciation	98,000
Investment	1,000,000

Assume that the operating profit and depreciation will remain unchanged for the next 10 years. Assume operating profit plus depreciation approximates annual net cash flows, and that the investment's residual value will be zero. The average rate of return and internal rate of return can then be estimated. The average rate of return on a company-owned store is:

$$\frac{\$302{,}000}{\$1{,}000{,}000 \div 2} = 60.4\%$$

The internal rate of return is calculated by first determining the present value of an annuity of $1:

$$\text{Present value of an annuity of } \$1 = \frac{\$1{,}000{,}000}{\$302{,}000 + \$98{,}000} = 2.50$$

For a period of 10 years, this present value of an annuity of $1 implies an estimated internal rate of return of over 35%. Clearly, both the average rate of return and the internal rate of return methods indicate a highly successful business.

Income Tax

The impact of income taxes on capital investment decisions can be material. For example, in determining depreciation for federal income tax purposes, useful lives that are much shorter than the actual useful lives are often used. Also, depreciation for tax purposes often differs from depreciation for financial statement purposes. As a result, the timing of the cash flows for income taxes can have a significant impact on capital investment analysis.[3]

Unequal Proposal Lives

The prior capital investment illustrations assumed that the alternative proposals had the same useful lives. In practice, however, proposals often have different lives.

To illustrate, assume that a company is considering purchasing a new truck or a new computer network. The data for each proposal are shown below.

	Truck	Computer Network
Cost	$100,000	$100,000
Minimum desired rate of return	10%	10%
Expected useful life	8 years	5 years
Yearly expected cash flows to be received:		
Year 1	$ 30,000	$ 30,000
Year 2	30,000	30,000
Year 3	25,000	30,000
Year 4	20,000	30,000
Year 5	15,000	35,000
Year 6	15,000	0
Year 7	10,000	0
Year 8	10,000	0
Total	$155,000	$155,000

The expected cash flows and net present value for each proposal are shown in Exhibit 10. Because of the unequal useful lives, however, the net present values in Exhibit 10 are not comparable.

To make the proposals comparable, the useful lives are adjusted to end at the same time. In this illustration, this is done by assuming that the truck will be sold at the end of five years. The selling price (residual value) of the truck at the end of five years is estimated and included in the cash inflows. Both proposals will then cover five years; thus, the net present value analyses will be comparable.

To illustrate, assume that the truck's estimated selling price (residual value) at the end of Year 11 is $40,000. Exhibit 11 shows the truck's revised present value analysis assuming a five-year life.

As shown in Exhibit 5, the net present value for the truck exceeds the net present value for the computer network by $1,835 ($18,640 − $16,805). Thus, the truck is the more attractive of the two proposals.

Lease Versus Capital Investment

Leasing fixed assets is common in many industries. For example, hospitals often lease medical equipment. Some advantages of leasing a fixed asset include the following:

- The company has use of the fixed asset without spending large amounts of cash to purchase the asset.
- The company eliminates the risk of owning an obsolete asset.
- The company may deduct the annual lease payments for income tax purposes.

3. The impact of taxes on capital investment analysis is covered in advanced accounting textbooks.

Exhibit 10 Net Present Value Analysis—Unequal Lives of Proposals

	A	B	C	D
1			**Truck**	
2		**Present**	**Net**	**Present**
3		**Value of**	**Cash**	**Value of**
4	**Year**	**$1 at 10%**	**Flow**	**Net Cash Flow**
5	1	0.909	$ 30,000	$ 27,270
6	2	0.826	30,000	24,780
7	3	0.751	25,000	18,775
8	4	0.683	20,000	13,660
9	5	0.621	15,000	9,315
10	6	0.564	15,000	8,460
11	7	0.513	10,000	5,130
12	8	0.467	10,000	4,670
13	Total		$155,000	$112,060
14				
15	Amount to be invested			(100,000)
16	Net present value			$ 12,060
17				

	A	B	C	D
1			**Computer Network**	
2		**Present**	**Net**	**Present**
3		**Value of**	**Cash**	**Value of**
4	**Year**	**$1 at 10%**	**Flow**	**Net Cash Flow**
5	1	0.909	$ 30,000	$ 27,270
6	2	0.826	30,000	24,780
7	3	0.751	30,000	22,530
8	4	0.683	30,000	20,490
9	5	0.621	35,000	21,735
10	Total		$155,000	$116,805
11				
12	Amount to be invested			(100,000)
13	Net present value			$ 16,805
14				

Exhibit 11 Net Present Value Analysis—Equalized Lives of Proposals

	A	B	C	D
1			**Truck—Revised to 5-Year Life**	
2		**Present**	**Net**	**Present**
3		**Value of**	**Cash**	**Value of**
4	**Year**	**$1 at 10%**	**Flow**	**Net Cash Flow**
5	1	0.909	$ 30,000	$ 27,270
6	2	0.826	30,000	24,780
7	3	0.751	25,000	18,775
8	4	0.683	20,000	13,660
9	5	0.621	15,000	9,315
10	5 (Residual			
11	value)	0.621	40,000	24,840
12	Total		$160,000	$118,640
13				
14	Amount to be invested			(100,000)
15	Net present value			$ 18,640

Truck Net Present Value Greater than Computer Network Net Present Value by $1,835

A disadvantage of leasing a fixed asset is that it is normally more costly than purchasing the asset. This is because the lessor (owner of the asset) includes in the rental price not only the costs of owning the asset but also a profit.

The methods of evaluating capital investment proposals illustrated in this chapter also can be used to decide whether to lease or purchase a fixed asset.

Uncertainty

All capital investment analyses rely on factors that are uncertain. For example, estimates of revenues, expenses, and cash flows are uncertain. This is especially true for long-term capital investments. Errors in one or more of the estimates could lead to incorrect

decisions. Methods that consider the impact of uncertainty on capital investment analysis are discussed in advanced accounting and finance textbooks.

A variety of factors add uncertainty to **Vail**'s operations, including the effects of weather, gas and oil prices, economic conditions, and natural disasters, such as forest fires and earthquakes.

Vail Inc. Connection

Changes in Price Levels

Price levels normally change as the economy improves or deteriorates. General price levels often increase in a rapidly growing economy, which is called **inflation**. During such periods, the rate of return on an investment should exceed the rising price level. If this is not the case, the cash returned on the investment will be less than expected.

Some of **Vail**'s rental (lease) agreements include increases for inflation linked to the Consumer Price Index (CPI).

Vail Inc. Connection

Price levels may also change for foreign investments. This occurs as currency exchange rates change. **Currency exchange rates** are the rates at which currency in another country can be exchanged for U.S. dollars.

If the amount of local dollars that can be exchanged for one U.S. dollar increases, then the local currency is said to be weakening to the dollar. When a company has an investment in another country where the local currency is weakening, the return on the investment, as expressed in U.S. dollars, is adversely impacted. This is because the expected amount of local currency returned on the investment would purchase fewer U.S. dollars.

In a recent financial statement, **Vail** reported a negative foreign currency adjustment of $(132) million.

Vail Inc. Connection

Qualitative Considerations

Some benefits of capital investments are qualitative in nature and cannot be estimated in dollar terms. However, if a company does not consider qualitative considerations, an acceptable investment proposal could be rejected.

Some examples of qualitative considerations that may influence capital investment analysis include the impact of the investment proposal on the following:

- Product quality
- Manufacturing flexibility
- Employee morale
- Manufacturing productivity
- Market (strategic) opportunities

Qualitative factors may be as important as, if not more important than, quantitative factors.

Vail Inc. Connection The mission of **Vail** is to provide exceptional guest experiences at each of its resources.

Objective 5

Describe and diagram the capital rationing process.

Capital Rationing

Capital rationing is the process by which management allocates funds among competing capital investment proposals. In this process, management often uses a combination of the methods described in this chapter, as shown in Exhibit 12.

Exhibit 12 Capital Rationing Decision Process

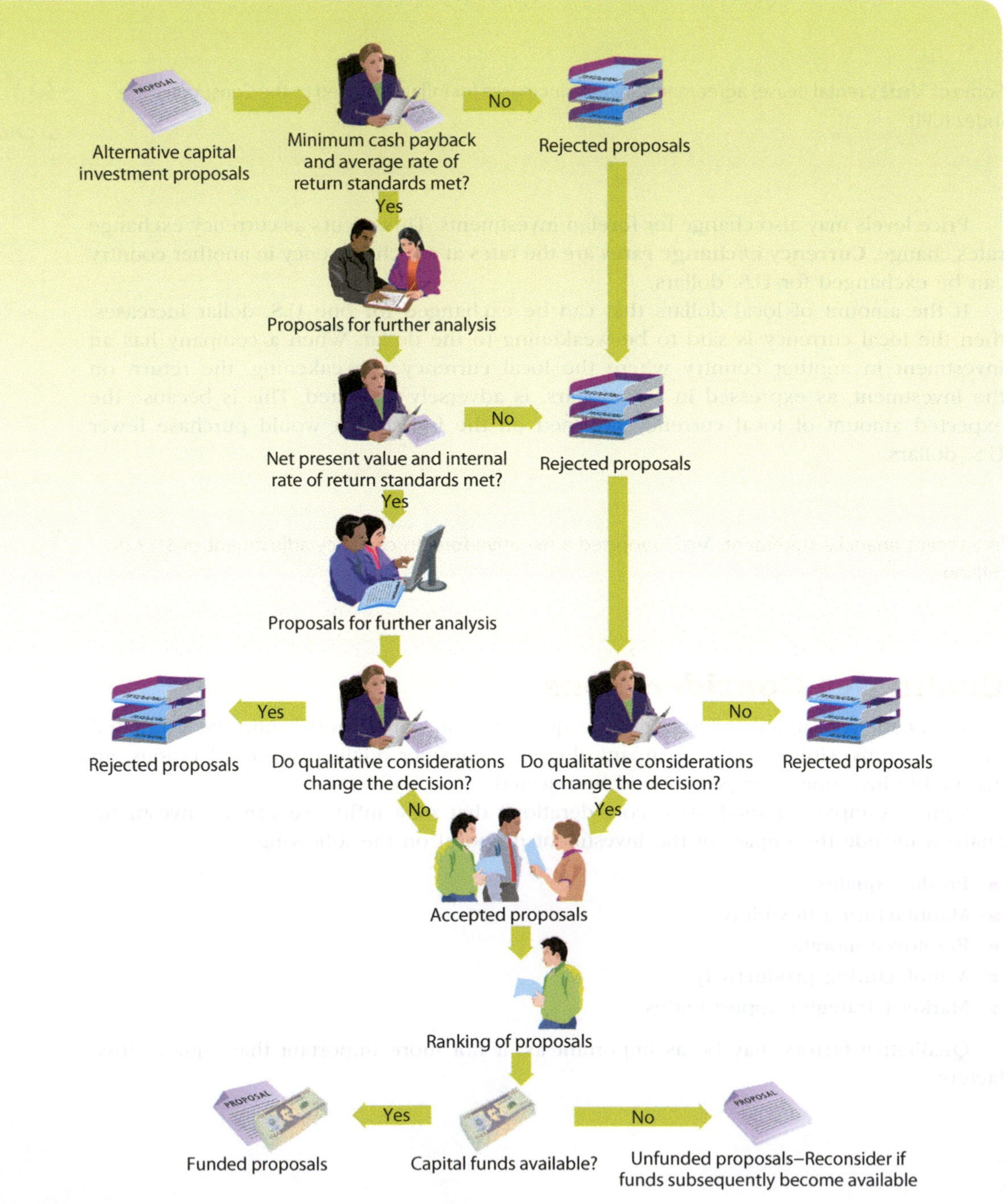

Integrity, Objectivity, and Ethics in Business

Assumption Fudging

The results of any capital budgeting analysis depend on many subjective estimates, such as the cash flows, discount rate, time period, and total investment amount. The results of the analysis should be used to either support or reject a project. Capital budgeting should not be used to justify an assumed net present value. That is, the analyst should not work backward, filling in assumed numbers that will produce the desired net present value. Such a reverse approach reduces the credibility of the entire process.

Exhibit 12 illustrates the capital rationing decision process. Alternative proposals are initially screened by establishing minimum standards using the cash payback and the average rate of return methods. The proposals that survive this screening are further analyzed using the net present value and internal rate of return methods.

Qualitative factors related to each proposal should also be considered throughout the capital rationing process. For example, new equipment might improve the quality of the product and thus increase consumer satisfaction and sales.

At the end of the capital rationing process, accepted proposals are ranked and compared with the funds available. Proposals that are selected for funding are included in the capital expenditures budget. Unfunded proposals may be reconsidered if funds later become available.

Metric-Based Analysis: Financial Leverage

Objective 6

Describe and illustrate the impact of financial leverage (debt) on the return on stockholders' equity.

The methods of capital investment analysis described and illustrated earlier in this chapter assumed that capital investments were purchased without using debt. In this section, the effects of using financial leverage (debt) to finance a company's operations are discussed. Specifically, the effects of financial leverage on a company's return on stockholders' equity are described and illustrated.

The **return on stockholders' equity** for a company is computed as follows:

$$\text{Return on Stockholders' Equity} = \frac{\text{Operating Income}}{\text{Average Stockholders' Equity}}$$

The return on stockholders' equity can also be expressed as the following:

$$\text{Return on Stockholders' Equity} = \frac{\text{Operating Income}}{\text{Sales}} \times \frac{\text{Sales}}{\text{Average Total Assets}} \times \frac{\text{Average Total Assets}}{\text{Average Stockholders' Equity}}$$

The preceding formula is an expansion of the DuPont formula for return on stockholders' equity discussed in Chapter 14. Specifically, operating income divided by sales is **profit margin**. Sales divided by average total assets is **asset turnover**. Average total assets divided by average stockholders' equity is **financial leverage**. Thus, the return on stockholders' equity can be expressed as follows:

$$\text{Return on Stockholders' Equity} = \text{Profit Margin} \times \text{Asset Turnover} \times \text{Financial Leverage}$$

To illustrate, for a recent year **Apple Inc. (AAPL)** reported the following data (in millions):

Sales	$233,715
Operating income	53,394
Average total assets	261,159
Average stockholders' equity	115,451

Apple earned a return on its total assets of 20.4% ($53,394 ÷ $261,159) and a return on stockholders' equity of 46.2% ($53,394 ÷ $115,451). The higher rate of return earned on stockholders' equity is due to Apple's use of financial leverage (debt). This will remain the case as long as Apple earns a higher rate of return on the use of its assets than the interest rate it is paying on its debt.

The effects of Apple's use of financial leverage can further be seen by using the expanded DuPont formula as follows:

	Profit Margin	×	Asset Turnover	×	Financial Leverage	=	Return on Stockholders' Equity
	22.8%		0.89		2.26		45.9%*
Computations:	$\frac{\$53,394}{\$233,715}$	×	$\frac{\$233,715}{\$261,159}$	×	$\frac{\$261,159}{\$115,451}$	=	46.2%*

*Differences due to rounding.

Apple has a profit margin of 22.8% but a relatively low asset turnover of 0.89. However, Apple's financial leverage of 2.26 results in a return on stockholders' equity of 45.9%. The use of financial leverage (debt) also increases financial risk of default, but Apple's strong operating results and financial position mitigates this increased risk.

Key Points

1. Describe the nature and importance of capital investment analysis.

Capital investment analysis is the process by which management plans, evaluates, and controls investments involving fixed assets. Capital investment analysis is important to a business because such investments affect profitability for a long period of time.

2. Evaluate capital investment proposals using the average rate of return and cash payback methods.

The average rate of return method measures the expected profitability of an investment in fixed assets. It is calculated using the following formula:

$$\text{Average Rate of Return} = \frac{\text{Estimated Average Annual Income}}{\text{Average Investment}}$$

The expected period of time that will pass between the date of an investment and the complete recovery in cash (or equivalent) of the amount invested is the cash payback period. Investment proposals with the shortest cash payback are considered the most desirable.

3. Evaluate capital investment proposals using the net present value and internal rate of return methods.

The net present value method uses present values to compute the net present value of the cash flows expected from a proposal. The net present values of the cash flows are then compared across proposals. The present value of a cash flow is computed by using a table of present values and multiplying it by the amount of the future cash flows, as shown in the text.

The internal rate of return method uses present values to compute the rate of return from the net cash flows expected from capital investment proposals. When equal annual net cash flows are expected from a proposal, the computations are simplified by using a table of the present value of an annuity, as shown in the text.

4. Describe factors that complicate capital investment analysis.

Factors that may complicate capital investment analysis include the impact of the federal income tax, unequal lives of alternative proposals, leasing, uncertainty, changes in price levels, and qualitative considerations. A brief description of the effect of each of these factors appears in the text.

5. Describe and diagram the capital rationing process.

Capital rationing refers to the process by which management allocates available investment funds among competing capital investment proposals. A diagram of the capital rationing process appears in Exhibit 12.

6. Describe and illustrate the impact of financial leverage on the return on stockholders' equity.

Financial leverage affects the return on stockholders' equity. Financial leverage can increase the return on stockholders' equity, but it can also increase the financial risk of being unable to pay periodic interest and the face value of the debt at its maturity.

Key Terms

Annuity (658)
Asset turnover (669)
Average rate of return (653)
Capital investment analysis (652)
Capital rationing (668)
Cash payback period (655)
Currency exchange rates (667)
Financial leverage (669)
Inflation (667)
Internal rate of return (IRR) method (662)
Net present value method (659)
Present value concepts (656)
Profit margin (669)
Present value index (661)
Present value of an annuity (658)
Return on stockholders' equity (669)
Time value of money concept (652)

Illustrative Problem

The capital investment committee of McEntyre Company is currently considering two projects. The estimated income from operations and net cash flows expected from each project are shown below.

	Project A		Project B	
Year	Income from Operations	Net Cash Flow	Income from Operations	Net Cash Flow
1	$ 6,000	$ 22,000	$13,000	$ 29,000
2	9,000	25,000	10,000	26,000
3	10,000	26,000	8,000	24,000
4	8,000	24,000	8,000	24,000
5	11,000	27,000	3,000	19,000
	$44,000	$124,000	$42,000	$122,000

Each project requires an investment of $80,000. Straight-line depreciation will be used, and no residual value is expected. The committee has selected a rate of 15% for purposes of the net present value analysis.

Instructions

1. Compute the following:
   a. The average rate of return for each project.
   b. The net present value for each project. Use the present value of $1 table appearing in this chapter.

2. Why is the net present value of Project B greater than Project A, even though its average rate of return is less?
3. Prepare a summary for the capital investment committee, advising it on the relative merits of the two projects.

Solution

1. a. Average rate of return for Project A:

$$\frac{\$44{,}000 \div 5}{(\$80{,}000 + \$0) \div 2} = 22\%$$

Average rate of return for Project B:

$$\frac{\$42{,}000 \div 5}{(\$80{,}000 + \$0) \div 2} = 21\%$$

b. Net present value analysis:

Year	Present Value of \$1 at 15%	Net Cash Flow Project A	Net Cash Flow Project B	Present Value of Net Cash Flow Project A	Present Value of Net Cash Flow Project B
1	0.870	\$ 22,000	\$ 29,000	\$19,140	\$25,230
2	0.756	25,000	26,000	18,900	19,656
3	0.658	26,000	24,000	17,108	15,792
4	0.572	24,000	24,000	13,728	13,728
5	0.497	27,000	19,000	13,419	9,443
Total		\$124,000	\$122,000	\$82,295	\$83,849
Amount to be invested				(80,000)	(80,000)
Net present value				\$ 2,295	\$ 3,849

2. Project B has a lower average rate of return than Project A because Project B's total income from operations for the five years is \$42,000, which is \$2,000 less than Project A's. Even so, the net present value of Project B is greater than that of Project A, because Project B has higher cash flows in the early years.
3. Both projects exceed the selected rate established for the net present value analysis. Project A has a higher average rate of return, but Project B offers a larger net present value. Thus, if only one of the two projects can be accepted, Project B would be the more attractive.

Self-Examination Questions

(Answers appear at the end of chapter)

1. Methods of evaluating capital investment proposals that ignore present value include:
   A. Average rate of return
   B. Cash payback
   C. Both A and B
   D. Neither A nor B
2. Management is considering a \$100,000 investment in a project with a five-year life and no residual value. If the total income from the project is expected to be \$60,000 and recognition is given to the effect of straight-line depreciation on the investment, the average rate of return is:
   A. 12%
   B. 24%
   C. 60%
   D. 75%

3. The expected period of time that will elapse between the date of a capital investment and the complete recovery of the amount of cash invested is called:
   A. The average rate of return period
   B. The cash payback period
   C. The net present value period
   D. The internal rate of return period

4. A project that will cost $120,000 is estimated to generate cash flows of $25,000 per year for eight years. What is the net present value of the project, assuming a 10% required rate of return? (Use the present value tables in this chapter.)
   A. $11,675
   B. $13,375
   C. $75,000
   D. $95,000

5. A project is estimated to generate cash flows of $40,000 per year for 10 years. The cost of the project is $226,000. What is the internal rate of return for this project?
   A. 8%
   B. 10%
   C. 12%
   D. 15%

Class Discussion Questions

1. What are the principal objections to the use of the average rate of return method in evaluating capital investment proposals?
2. Discuss the principal limitations of the cash payback method for evaluating capital investment proposals.
3. Why would the average rate of return differ from the internal rate of return on the same project?
4. What information does the cash payback period ignore that is included by the net present value method?
5. Your boss has suggested that a one-year payback period is the same as a 100% average rate of return. Do you agree?
6. Why would the cash payback method understate the value of a project with a large residual value?
7. Why might the use of the cash payback period for analyzing the financial performance of theatrical releases from a motion picture production studio be used over the net present value method?
8. A net present value analysis used to evaluate a proposed equipment acquisition indicated a $115,000 net present value. What is the meaning of the $115,000 as it relates to the desirability of the proposal?
9. Two projects have an identical net present value of $360,000. Are both projects equal in desirability?
10. What are the major disadvantages of the use of the net present value method of analyzing capital investment proposals?
11. What are the major disadvantages of the use of the internal rate of return method of analyzing capital investment proposals?
12. What provision of the Internal Revenue Code is especially important to consider in analyzing capital investment proposals?
13. What method can be used to place two capital investment proposals with unequal useful lives on a comparable basis?
14. What are the major advantages of leasing a fixed asset rather than purchasing it?
15. Give an example of a qualitative factor that should be considered in a capital investment analysis related to acquiring automated factory equipment.
16. Monsanto Company, a large chemical and fibers company, invested $37 million in state-of-the-art systems to improve process control, laboratory automation, and local area network (LAN) communications. The investment was not justified merely on cost savings but was also justified on the basis of qualitative considerations. Monsanto management viewed the investment as a critical element toward achieving its vision of the future. What qualitative and quantitative considerations do you believe Monsanto would have considered in its strategic evaluation of these investments?

Exercises

Obj. 2

✔ Testing equipment, 18%

E15-1 Average rate of return

The following data are accumulated by McDermott Motors Inc. evaluating two competing capital investment proposals:

	Testing Equipment	Diagnostic Software
Amount of investment	$300,000	$150,000
Useful life	8 years	5 years
Estimated residual value	$40,000	$5,000
Estimated total income over the useful life	$244,800	$85,250

Determine the expected average rate of return for each proposal.

Obj. 2

E15-2 Average rate of return—cost savings

Sager Industries is considering an investment in equipment that will replace direct labor. The equipment has a cost of $1,200,000 with a $300,000 residual value and a 10-year life. The equipment will replace three employees who has an average total wages of $180,000 per year. In addition, the equipment will have operating and energy costs of $7,500 per year.

Determine the average rate of return on the equipment, giving effect to straight-line depreciation on the investment.

Obj. 2

✔ Average annual income, $4,320,000

E15-3 Average rate of return—new product

Arrowhead Inc. is considering an investment in new equipment that will be used to manufacture a mobile communications product. The product is expected to generate additional annual sales of 24,000 units at $400 per unit. The equipment has a cost of $27,000,000, residual value of $1,800,000, and a 10-year life. The equipment only can be used to manufacture the product. The cost to manufacture the product is shown below.

Cost per unit:	
Direct labor	$ 40.00
Direct materials	60.00
Factory overhead (including depreciation)	120.00
Total cost per unit	$220.00

Determine the average rate of return on the equipment.

Obj. 2

✔ Year 1: $28,000

E15-4 Calculate cash flows

Daffodil Inc. is planning to invest in manufacturing equipment to make a new garden tool. The new garden tool is expected to generate additional annual sales of 120,000 units at $9 each. The new manufacturing equipment will cost $320,000, have a 10-year life, a residual value of $20,000, and will be depreciated using the straight-line method. Selling expenses related to the new product are expected to be 15% of sales revenue. The cost to manufacture the product includes the following on a per-unit basis:

Direct labor	$1.00
Direct materials	3.40
Fixed factory overhead—depreciation	0.25
Variable factory overhead	0.35
Total	$5.00

a. Determine the net cash flows for the first year of the project, Years 2–9, and for the last year of the project.

b. Assume that the operating cash flows occur evenly throughout the year and that the equipment is purchased on January 1, 20Y1. Determine when the cash payback will occur by year, month, and day.

E15-5 Cash payback period

Obj. 2

✔ Location 1: 4 years

Wyoming Woodworks is evaluating two capital investment proposals for a retail outlet store, each requiring an investment of $1,000,000 and each with a five-year life and expected total net cash flows of $1,250,000. Location 1 is expected to provide equal annual net cash flows of $250,000, and Location 2 is expected to have the following unequal annual net cash flows:

Year 1	$400,000
Year 2	375,000
Year 3	225,000
Year 4	175,000
Year 5	75,000

Determine the cash payback period for both location proposals.

E15-6 Cash payback method

Obj. 2

✔ a. Shampoo/ Conditioner: 5 years

Bliss Beauty Products is considering an investment in one of two new product lines. The investment required for either product line is $2,800,000. The net cash flows associated with each product are shown below.

Year	Shampoo/Conditioner	Body Wash
1	$ 700,000	$ 400,000
2	650,000	400,000
3	550,000	400,000
4	450,000	400,000
5	450,000	400,000
6	200,000	400,000
7	100,000	400,000
8	100,000	400,000
Total	$3,200,000	$3,200,000

a. Recommend a product offering to Bliss Beauty Products, based on the cash payback period for each product line.

b. Why is one product line preferred over the other, even though they both have the same total net cash flows?

c. Assume that instead of $550,000 of cash flows in Year 3 and $450,000 in Year 4, the Shampoo/Conditioner had cash flows of $600,000 in Year 3 and $550,000 in Year 4. What would be the cash payback period assuming that the cash flows occur uniformly throughout the year?

E15-7 Net present value method

Obj. 3

✔ a. NPV $12,545

The following data are accumulated by Wocester Hat Company in evaluating the purchase of $250,000 of equipment, having a four-year useful life with no residual value.

	Net Income (Loss)	Net Cash Flows
Year 1	$37,500	$100,000
Year 2	27,500	90,000
Year 3	12,500	75,000
Year 4	(2,500)	60,000

Note: The spreadsheet icon 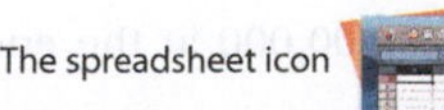 indicates an Excel template is available on the student companion site.

a. Assuming that the desired rate of return is 10%, determine the net present value for the proposal. Use the table of the present value of $1 appearing in Exhibit 2 of this chapter.

b. Would management be likely to look with favor on the proposal? Explain.

Obj. 3

✔ a. 20Y4, $36,000

E15-8 Net present value method

On Time Delivery Inc. is considering the purchase of an additional delivery truck for $85,000 on January 1, 20Y4. The truck is expected to have a five-year life with an expected residual value of $8,000 at the end of five years. The expected additional revenues from the added delivery capacity are anticipated to be $70,000 per year for each of the next five years. A driver will cost $25,000 in 20Y4, with an expected annual salary increase of $1,000 for each year thereafter. The operating costs for the truck is estimated to cost $9,000 per year.

a. Determine the expected annual net cash flows from the delivery truck investment for 20Y4–20Y8.

b. Calculate the net present value of the investment, assuming that the minimum desired rate of return is 12%. Use the present value of $1 table appearing in Exhibit 2 of this chapter.

c. Is the additional truck a good investment based on your analysis?

Obj. 3

✔ a. $13 million

E15-9 Net present value method—annuity

Model 99 Hotels is considering the construction of a new hotel for $80 million. The expected life of the hotel is 20 years with no residual value. The hotel is expected to earn revenues of $15 million per year. Total expenses, including straight-line depreciation, are expected to be $6 million per year. Model 99 management has set a minimum acceptable rate of return of 10%.

a. Determine the equal annual net cash flows from operating the hotel.

b. Calculate the net present value of the new hotel, using the present value factor of an annuity of $1 at 10% for 20 periods of 8.5136. Round to the nearest million dollars.

c. Does your analysis support construction of the new hotel?

Obj. 3

✔ a. $92,000

E15-10 Net present value method—annuity

Osborne Excavation Company is planning an investment of $315,000 for a bulldozer. The bulldozer is expected to operate for 1,850 hours per year for five years. Customers will be charged $140 per hour for bulldozer work. The bulldozer operator costs $37 per hour in wages and benefits. The bulldozer is expected to require annual maintenance costing $9,750. The bulldozer uses fuel that is expected to cost $48 per hour of bulldozer operation.

a. Determine the equal annual net cash flows from operating the bulldozer.

b. Determine the net present value of the investment, assuming that the desired rate of return is 10%. Use the table of present values of an annuity of $1 in the chapter. Round to the nearest dollar.

c. Should Osborne Excavation invest in the bulldozer, based on this analysis?

Obj. 3

✔ a. $288,800,000

E15-11 Net present value method

Carnival Corporation has recently placed into service some of the largest cruise ships in the world. One of these ships can hold up to 3,600 passengers and cost $750 million to build. Assume the following additional information:

- There will be 300 cruise days per year operated at a full capacity of 3,600 passengers.
- The variable expenses per passenger are estimated to be $90 per cruise day.
- The revenue per passenger is expected to be $450 per cruise day.
- The fixed expenses for running the ship, other than depreciation, are estimated to be $100,000,000 per year.
- The ship has a service life of 10 years, with a residual value of $120,000,000 at the end of 10 years.

a. Determine the annual net cash flows from operating the cruise ship.

b. Determine the net present value of this investment, assuming a 12% minimum rate of return. Use the present value tables provided in the chapter in determining your answer.

E15-12 Present value index

Obj. 3

✔ Billings Location: 0.98

Montana Grill has computed the net present value for capital expenditures for the Billings and Great Falls locations using the net present value method. Relevant data related to the computation are as follows:

	Billings	Great Falls
Total present value of net cash flow	$882,000	$1,050,000
Amount to be invested	900,000	750,000

a. Determine the present value index for each proposal. Round to two decimal places.

b. If Montana Grill can fund only one location, which location should be funded?

E15-13 Net present value method and present value index

Obj. 3

✔ b. Stitching Machine, 1.25

Ball Sports Inc. is considering an investment in one of two machines. The stitching machine will increase productivity from sewing 300 baseballs per hour to stitching 360 per hour. The contribution margin is $0.30 per baseball. Assume that any increased production of baseballs can be sold. The second machine applies a synthetic balata cover to golf balls. The golf ball machine will reduce labor cost. The labor cost saved is equivalent to $40 per hour. The stitching machine will cost $484,600, have an eight-year life, and will operate for 7,500 hours per year. The golf ball machine will cost $897,400, have an eight-year life, and will operate for 6,000 hours per year. Ball Sports Inc. seeks a minimum rate of return of 15% on its investments.

a. Determine the net present value for the two machines. Use the table of present values of an annuity of $1 in the chapter. Round to the nearest dollar.

b. Determine the present value index for the two machines. Round to two decimal places.

c. If Ball Sports Inc. has sufficient funds for only one of the machines and qualitative factors are equal between the two machines, in which machine should it invest?

E15-14 Average rate of return, cash payback period, net present value method

Obj. 2, 3

✔ b. 4 years

Southwest Transportation Inc. is considering a distribution facility at a cost of $10,000,000. The facility has an estimated life of 10 years and a $2,000,000 residual value. It is expected to provide yearly net cash flows of $2,500,000. The company's minimum desired rate of return for net present value analysis is 15%.

Compute the following:

a. The average rate of return, giving effect to straight-line depreciation on the investment. Round to one decimal place.

b. The cash payback period.

c. The net present value. Use the table of the present value of an annuity of $1 appearing in Exhibit 5.

E15-15 Payback period, net present value analysis, and qualitative considerations

Obj. 2, 3, 4

✔ a. 4.75 years

The plant manager of Jurassic Industries is considering the purchase of new automated assembly equipment. The new equipment will cost $2,375,000. The manager believes that the new investment will result in direct labor savings of $500,000 per year for 10 years.

a. What is the payback period on this project?

b. What is the net present value, assuming a 10% rate of return? Use the present value tables appearing in this chapter.

c. What else should the manager consider in the analysis?

Obj. 3

✔ a. 5.335

E15-16 Internal rate of return method

The internal rate of return method is used by Leach Construction Co. in analyzing a capital expenditure proposal that involves an investment of $400,125 and annual net cash flows of $75,000 for each of the eight years of its useful life.

a. Determine a present value factor for an annuity of $1 which can be used in determining the internal rate of return.

b. Using the factor determined in part (a) and the present value of an annuity of $1 table appearing Exhibit 5, determine the internal rate of return for the proposal.

Obj. 3

E15-17 Internal rate of return method

The Canyons Resort, a Utah ski resort, announced a $400 million expansion of lodging properties, lifts, and terrain. Assume that this investment is estimated to produce $79.7 million in equal annual cash flows for each of the first 10 years of the project life.

Determine the expected internal rate of return of this project for 10 years, using the present value of an annuity of $1 table found in Exhibit 5.

Obj. 3

✔ a. Delivery truck, 12%

E15-18 Internal rate of return method—two projects

Strahn Foods Inc. is considering two possible investments: a delivery truck or a bagging machine. The delivery truck would cost $65,970 and could be used to deliver an additional 90,000 bags of taquitos chips per year. Each bag of chips can be sold for a contribution margin of $0.35. The delivery truck operating expenses, excluding depreciation, are $0.55 per mile for 24,000 miles per year. The bagging machine would replace an old bagging machine, and its net investment cost would be $35,890. The new machine would require 2.5 fewer hours of direct labor per day. Direct labor is $20 per hour. There are 240 operating days in the year. Both the truck and the bagging machine are estimated to have five-year lives. The minimum rate of return is 14%. However, Strahn Foods has funds to invest in only one of the projects.

a. Compute the internal rate of return for each investment. Use the table of present values of an annuity of $1 in the chapter.

b. Provide a memo to management with a recommendation.

Obj. 3

✔ a. $(307,000)

E15-19 Net present value method and internal rate of return method

Wisconsin Healthcare Corp. is proposing to spend $3,810,000 on a project that has estimated net cash flows of $620,000 for each of the 10 years.

a. Compute the net present value, using a rate of return of 12%. Use the table of present values of an annuity of $1 in the chapter.

b. Based on the analysis prepared in part (a), is the rate of return (1) more than 12%, (2) 12%, or (3) less than 12%? Explain.

c. Determine the internal rate of return by computing a present value factor for an annuity of $1 and using the table of the present value of an annuity of $1 presented in the text.

Obj. 3

E15-20 Identify error in capital investment analysis calculations

Fireproofing Solutions Inc. is considering the purchase of automated machinery that is expected to have a useful life of eight years and no residual value. The average rate of return on the average investment has been computed to be 15%, and the cash payback period was computed to be 10 years.

Do you see any reason to question the validity of the data presented? Explain.

E15-21 Net present value—unequal lives

Obj. 3, 4

✔ Net present value, Office Building, $381,300

Healey Development Company has two competing projects: an office building and a condominium complex. Both projects have an initial investment of $2,000,000. The net cash flows estimated for the two projects are as follows:

	Net Cash Flow	
Year	Office Building	Condominium Complex
1	$950,000	$1,200,000
2	600,000	900,000
3	500,000	700,000
4	450,000	400,000
5	350,000	
6	350,000	
7	300,000	
8	300,000	

The estimated residual value of the office building at the end of Year 4 is $900,000.

Determine which project should be favored, comparing the net present values of the two projects and assuming a minimum rate of return of 15%. Use the table of present values in the chapter.

E15-22 Net present value—unequal lives

Obj. 3, 4

Buscho Industries is considering one of two investment options. Option 1 is a $45,000 investment in new blending equipment that is expected to produce equal annual cash flows of $18,000 for each of eight years. Option 2 is a $17,000 investment in a new computer system that is expected to produce equal annual cash flows (savings) of $10,000 for each of four years. The residual value of the blending equipment at the end of the fourth year is estimated to be $5,000. The computer system has no expected residual value at the end of the fourth year.

Assume there is sufficient capital to fund only one of the projects. Determine which project should be selected, comparing the (a) net present values and (b) present value indices of the two projects, assuming a minimum rate of return of 12%. Round the present value index to two decimal places. Use the present value tables in Exhibits 2 and 5.

Problems

P15-1 Average rate of return method, net present value method, and analysis

Obj. 2, 3

✔ 1. a. 16.5%

The capital investment committee of Overnight Express Inc. is considering two investment projects. The estimated income from operations and net cash flows from each investment are as follows:

	Distribution Center Expansion		Internet Tracking Technology	
Year	Income from Operations	Net Cash Flows	Income from Operations	Net Cash Flows
1	$ 66,000	$ 226,000	$200,000	$ 360,000
2	66,000	226,000	90,000	250,000
3	66,000	226,000	30,000	190,000
4	66,000	226,000	10,000	170,000
5	66,000	226,000	0	160,000
Total	$330,000	$1,130,000	$330,000	$1,130,000

Each project requires an investment of $800,000. Straight-line depreciation will be used, and no residual value is expected. The committee has selected a rate of 15% for purposes of the net present value analysis.

Instructions

1. Compute the following:
   a. The average rate of return for each investment.
   b. The net present value for each investment. Use the present value of $1 table appearing in this chapter.
2. Prepare a brief report for the capital investment committee, advising it on the relative merits of the two projects.

Obj. 2, 3

✔ 1. b. *European Hiking, $189,674*

P15-2 Cash payback period, net present value method, and analysis

McMorris Publications Inc. is considering two new magazine products. The estimated net cash flows from each product are as follows:

Year	*Canadian Cycling*	*European Hiking*
1	$220,000	$188,000
2	180,000	212,000
3	158,000	150,000
4	131,000	110,000
5	61,000	90,000
Total	$750,000	$750,000

Each product requires an investment of $400,000. A rate of 10% has been selected for the net present value analysis.

Instructions

1. Compute the following for each product:
   a. Cash payback period.
   b. The net present value. Use the present value of $1 table appearing in this chapter.
2. Prepare a brief report advising management on the relative merits of each of the two products.

Obj. 3

✔ 1. Product Line Expansion, net present value, $3,734,000

P15-3 Net present value method, present value index, and analysis

Donahue Industries Inc. wishes to evaluate three capital investment projects by using the net present value method. Relevant data related to the projects are summarized as follows:

	Product Line Expansion	Distribution Facilities	Computer Network
Amount to be invested	$4,000,000	$2,500,000	$500,000
Annual net cash flows:			
Year 1	4,200,000	1,000,000	600,000
Year 2	3,600,000	1,200,000	600,000
Year 3	3,000,000	1,300,000	550,000

Instructions

1. Assuming that the desired rate of return is 20%, prepare a net present value analysis for each project. Use the present value of $1 table appearing in this chapter.
2. Determine a present value index for each project. Round to two decimal places.
3. Which project offers the largest amount of present value per dollar of investment? Explain.

P15-4 Net present value method, internal rate of return method, and analysis

Obj. 3

✔ 1. a. Radio station, $176,400

The management of Heckel Communications Inc. is considering two capital investment projects. The estimated net cash flows from each project are as follows:

Year	Radio Station	TV Station
1	$560,000	$1,120,000
2	560,000	1,120,000
3	560,000	1,120,000
4	560,000	1,120,000

The radio station requires an investment of $1,598,800, while the TV station requires an investment of $3,401,440. No residual value is expected from either project.

Instructions

1. Compute the following for each project:
   a. The net present value. Use a rate of 10% and the present value of an annuity of $1 table appearing in this chapter.
   b. The present value index. Round to two decimal places.
2. Determine the internal rate of return for each project using the present value of an annuity of $1 table in Exhibit 5.
3. What advantage does the internal rate of return method have over the net present value method in comparing projects?

P15-5 Evaluate alternative capital investment decisions

Obj. 3, 4

✔ 1. Site B, $294,500

The investment committee of Iron Skillet Restaurants Inc. is evaluating two restaurant sites. The sites have different useful lives, but each requires an investment of $1,000,000. The estimated net cash flows from each site are as follows:

	Net Cash Flows	
Year	**Site A**	**Site B**
1	$400,000	$500,000
2	400,000	500,000
3	400,000	500,000
4	400,000	500,000
5	400,000	
6	400,000	

The committee has selected a rate of 20% for purposes of net present value analysis. It also estimates that the residual value at the end of each restaurant's useful life is $0, but at the end of the fourth year, Site A's residual value would be $300,000.

Instructions

1. For each site, compute the net present value. Use the present value of an annuity of $1 table appearing in this chapter. (Ignore the unequal lives of the projects.)
2. For each site, compute the net present value, assuming that Site A is adjusted to a four-year life for purposes of analysis. Use the present value of $1 table appearing in this chapter.
3. Prepare a report to the investment committee, providing your advice on the relative merits of the two sites.

Obj. 2, 3, 5

✔ 5. Proposal Tango, 1.28

P15-6 Capital rationing decision involving four proposals

Kopecky Industries Inc. is considering allocating a limited amount of capital investment funds among four proposals. The amount of proposed investment, estimated income from operations, and net cash flow for each proposal are as follows:

	Investment	Year	Income from Operations	Net Cash Flows
Proposal Sierra:	$850,000	1	$ 80,000	$ 250,000
		2	80,000	250,000
		3	80,000	250,000
		4	30,000	200,000
		5	(70,000)	100,000
			$200,000	$1,050,000
Proposal Tango:	$1,200,000	1	$320,000	$ 560,000
		2	320,000	540,000
		3	160,000	400,000
		4	60,000	300,000
		5	(40,000)	220,000
			$820,000	$2,020,000
Proposal Uniform:	$550,000	1	$ 90,000	$ 200,000
		2	90,000	200,000
		3	90,000	200,000
		4	90,000	200,000
		5	70,000	180,000
			$430,000	$ 980,000
Proposal Victor:	$380,000	1	$44,000	$ 120,000
		2	44,000	120,000
		3	44,000	120,000
		4	4,000	80,000
		5	4,000	80,000
			$140,000	$ 520,000

The company's capital rationing policy requires a maximum cash payback period of three years. In addition, a minimum average rate of return of 12% is required on all projects. If the preceding standards are met, the net present value method and present value indexes are used to rank the remaining proposals.

Instructions

1. Compute the cash payback period for each of the four proposals. Assume that net cash flows are uniform throughout the year.
2. Giving effect to straight-line depreciation on the investments and assuming no estimated residual value, compute the average rate of return for each of the four proposals. Round to one decimal place.
3. Using the following format, summarize the results of your computations in parts (1) and (2). By placing the calculated amounts in the first two columns on the left and by placing a check mark in the appropriate column to the right, indicate which proposals should be accepted for further analysis and which should be rejected.

Proposal	Cash Payback Period	Average Rate of Return	Accept for Further Analysis	Reject
Sierra				
Tango				
Uniform				
Victor				

4. For the proposals accepted for further analysis in part (3), compute the net present value. Use a rate of 12% and the present value of $1 table appearing in this chapter. Round to the nearest dollar.

5. Compute the present value index for each of the proposals in part (4). Round to two decimal places.
6. Rank the proposals from most attractive to least attractive, based on the present values of net cash flows computed in part (4).
7. Rank the proposals from most attractive to least attractive, based on the present value indexes computed in part (5).
8. Based on the analyses, comment on the relative attractiveness of the proposals ranked in parts (6) and (7).

Metric-Based Analysis

MBA 15-1 Financial leverage

Obj. 6

Microsoft Corporation (MSFT) reported the following data (in millions) for a recent year:

Sales	$ 93,580
Operating income	12,193
Average total assets	174,304
Average stockholders' equity	84,934

1. Compute the return on total assets. Round to one decimal place.
2. Compute the return on stockholders' equity. Round to one decimal place.
3. Compute the profit margin, asset turnover, and financial leverage metrics using the expanded DuPont formula. Round profit margin, asset turnover, and financial leverage to two decimal places. Round return on stockholders' equity to one decimal place.
4. Apple Inc. has a financial leverage metric of 2.26. Does Apple or Microsoft use more financial leverage in its operations?

MBA 15-2 Financial leverage

Obj. 6

Southwest Airlines Co. (LUV) reported the following data (in millions) for a recent year:

Sales	$ 19,820
Operating income	2,181
Average total assets	20,518
Average stockholders' equity	7,067

1. Compute the return on total assets. Round to one decimal place.
2. Compute the return on stockholders' equity. Round to one decimal place.
3. Compute the profit margin, asset turnover, and financial leverage metrics using the expanded DuPont formula. Round profit margin, asset turnover, and financial leverage to two decimal places. Round return on stockholders' equity to one decimal place.

MBA 15-3 Financial leverage

Obj. 6

Delta Air Lines, Inc. (DAL) reported the following data (in millions) for a recent year:

Sales	$40,704
Operating income	4,526
Average total assets	53,570
Average stockholders' equity	9,832

1. Compute the return on total assets. Round to one decimal place.
2. Compute the return on stockholders' equity. Round to one decimal place.
3. Compute the profit margin, asset turnover, and financial leverage metrics using the expanded DuPont formula. Round profit margin, asset turnover, and financial leverage to two decimal places. Round return on stockholders' equity to one decimal place.

Obj. 6

MBA 15-4 Financial leverage

Using the answers to MBA 15-2 and MBA 15-3, compare and comment on the operations for **Southwest Airlines (LUV)** and **Delta Air Lines (DAL).**

Obj. 6

MBA 15-5 Financial leverage

Costco Wholesale Corporation (COST) and **Wal-Mart Stores Inc. (WMT)** reported the following data (in millions) for a recent year:

	Costco	Wal-Mart
Sales	$116,199	$482,130
Operating income	2,377	15,080
Average total assets	33,232	201,536
Average stockholders' equity	11,460	80,970

1. Compute the return on total assets. Round to one decimal place.
2. Compute the return on stockholders' equity. Round to one decimal place.
3. Compute the profit margin, asset turnover, and financial leverage metrics. Round profit margin, asset turnover, and financial leverage to two decimal places. Round return on stockholders' equity to one decimal place.
4. Comment on the results of 1, 2, and 3.

Cases

Case 15-1 Ethics and professional conduct in business

Erin Haywood was recently hired as a cost analyst by Wind River Medical Supplies Inc. One of Erin's first assignments was to perform a net present value analysis for a new warehouse. Erin performed the analysis and calculated a present value index of 0.8. The plant manager, Zuhair Barbat, is very intent on purchasing the warehouse because he believes that more storage space is needed. Zuhair asks Erin into his office and the following conversation takes place:

Zuhair: Erin, you're new here, aren't you?

Erin: Yes, sir.

Zuhair: Well, Erin, let me tell you something. I'm not at all pleased with the capital investment analysis that you performed on this new warehouse. I need that warehouse for my production. If I don't get it, where am I going to place our output?

Erin: Hopefully with the customer, sir.

Zuhair: Now don't get smart with me.

Erin: No, really, I was being serious. My analysis does not support constructing a new warehouse. The numbers don't lie; the warehouse does not meet our investment return targets. In fact, it seems to me that purchasing a warehouse does not add much value to the business. We need to be producing product to satisfy customer orders, not to fill a warehouse.

Zubair: Listen, you need to understand something. The headquarters people will not allow me to build the warehouse if the numbers don't add up. You know as well as I that many assumptions go into your net present value analysis. Why don't you relax some of your assumptions so that the financial savings will offset the cost?

Erin: I'm willing to discuss my assumptions with you. Maybe I overlooked something.

Zubair: Good. Here's what I want you to do. I see in your analysis that you don't project greater sales as a result of the warehouse. It seems to me, if we can store more goods, then we will have more to sell. Thus, logically, a larger warehouse translates into more sales. If you incorporate this into your analysis, I think you'll see that the numbers will work out. Why don't you work it through and come back with a new analysis? I'm really counting on you on this one. Let's get off to a good start together and see if we can get this project accepted.

What is your advice to Erin?

Case 15-2 Personal investment analysis

A Masters of Accountancy degree at Jalapeno University would cost $15,000 for an additional fifth year of education beyond the bachelor's degree. Assume that all tuition is paid at the beginning of the year. A student considering this investment must evaluate the present value of cash flows from possessing a graduate degree versus holding only the undergraduate degree. Assume that the average student with an undergraduate degree is expected to earn an annual salary of $50,000 per year (assumed to be paid at the end of the year) for 10 years. Assume that the average student with a graduate Masters of Accountancy degree is expected to earn an annual salary of $65,000 per year (assumed to be paid at the end of the year) for nine years after graduation. Assume a minimum rate of return of 10%.

1. Determine the net present value of cash flows from an undergraduate degree. Use the present value tables provided in this chapter. Round to nearest dollar.
2. Determine the net present value of cash flows from a Masters of Accountancy degree, assuming no salary is earned during the graduate year of schooling. Round to nearest dollar.
3. What is the net advantage or disadvantage of pursuing a graduate degree under these assumptions?

Case 15-3 Changing prices

World Electronics Inc. invested $16,000,000 to build a plant in a foreign country. The labor and materials used in production are purchased locally. The plant expansion was estimated to produce an internal rate of return of 20% in U.S. dollar terms. Due to a currency crisis, the currency exchange rate between the local currency and the U.S. dollar doubled from two local units per U.S. dollar to four local units per U.S. dollar.

1. Assume that the plant produced and sold product in the local economy. Explain what impact this change in the currency exchange rate would have on the project's internal rate of return.
2. Assume that the plant produced product in the local economy but exported the product back to the United States for sale. Explain what impact the change in the currency exchange rate would have on the project's internal rate of return under this assumption.

Case 15-4 Qualitative issues in investment analysis

The following are some selected quotes from senior executives:

CEO, Worthington Industries (a high technology steel company): "We try to find the best technology, stay ahead of the competition, and serve the customer. . . . We'll make any investment

that will pay back quickly . . . but if it is something that we really see as a must down the road, payback is not going to be that important."

Chairman of Amgen Inc. (a biotech company): "You cannot really run the numbers, do net present value calculations, because the uncertainties are really gigantic. . . . You decide on a project you want to run, and then you run the numbers [as a reality check on your assumptions]. Success in a business like this is much more dependent on tracking rather than on predicting, much more dependent on seeing results over time, tracking and adjusting and readjusting, much more dynamic, much more flexible."

Chief Financial Officer of Merck & Co., Inc. (a pharmaceutical company): ". . . at the individual product level—the development of a successful new product requires on the order of $230 million in R&D, spread over more than a decade—discounted cash flow style analysis does not become a factor until development is near the point of manufacturing scale-up effort. Prior to that point, given the uncertainties associated with new product development, it would be lunacy in our business to decide that we know exactly what's going to happen to a product once it gets out."

Explain the role of capital investment analysis for these companies.

Case 15-5 Net present value method

Metro-Goldwyn-Mayer Studios Inc. (MGM) is a major producer and distributor of theatrical and television filmed entertainment. Regarding theatrical films, MGM states, "Our feature films are exploited through a series of sequential domestic and international distribution channels, typically beginning with theatrical exhibition. Thereafter, feature films are first made available for home video generally six months after theatrical release; for pay television, one year after theatrical release; and for syndication, approximately three to five years after theatrical release."

Assume that MGM produces a film during early 20Y5 at a cost of $200 million, and releases it halfway through the year. During the last half of 20Y5, the film earns revenues of $240 million at the box office. The film requires $80 million of advertising during the release. One year later, by the end of 20Y6, the film is expected to earn MGM net cash flows from home video sales of $50 million. By the end of 20Y7, the film is expected to earn MGM $25 million from pay TV; and by the end of 20Y8, the film is expected to earn $10 million from syndication.

1. Determine the net present value of the film as of the beginning of 20Y5 if the desired rate of return is 20%. To simplify present value calculations, assume all annual net cash flows occur at the end of each year. Use the table of the present value of $1 appearing in Exhibit 2 of this chapter. Round to the nearest whole million dollars.
2. Under the assumptions provided here, is the film expected to be financially successful?

Case 15-6 Capital investment analysis

In one group, find a local business, such as a copy shop, that charges for printing, faxing, copying, and scanning documents. In the other group, determine the price of a mid-range printer/copier/scanner/fax machine. Combine this information from the two groups and perform a capital budgeting analysis. Assume that one student will use the machine for 1,000 documents per semester for the next three years. Also assume that the minimum rate of return is 10%. In performing your analysis, use the present value factor for 5% compounded for six semiannual periods of 5.08.

Does your analysis support the student purchasing the printer/copier/scanner/fax machine?

Answers to Self-Examination Questions

1. **C** Methods of evaluating capital investment proposals that ignore the time value of money are categorized as methods that ignore present value. This category includes the average rate of return method (answer A) and the cash payback method (answer B).

2. **B** The average rate of return is 24% (answer B), determined by dividing the expected average annual earnings by the average investment, as follows:

$$\frac{\$60{,}000 \div 5}{(\$100{,}000 + \$0) \div 2} = 24\%$$

3. **B** Of the four methods of analyzing proposals for capital investments, the cash payback period (answer B) refers to the expected period of time required to recover the amount of cash to be invested. The average rate of return (answer A) is a measure of the anticipated profitability of a proposal. The net present value method (answer C) reduces the expected future net cash flows originating from a proposal to their present values. The internal rate of return method (answer D) uses present value concepts to compute the rate of return from the net cash flows expected from the investment.

4. **B** The net present value is determined as follows:

Present value of $25,000 for 8 years at 10% ($25,000 × 5.335)	$133,375
Less: Project cost	120,000
Net present value	$ 13,375

5. **C** The internal rate of return for this project is determined by solving for the present value of an annuity factor that when multiplied by $40,000 will equal $226,000. By division, the factor is:

$$\frac{\$226{,}000}{\$40{,}000} = 5.65$$

In Exhibit 5, scan along the n = 10 years row until finding the 5.65 factor. The column for this factor is 12%.

Appendix A

Double-Entry Accounting Systems

Throughout this text, transactions are recorded and summarized by using the accounting equation and the integrated financial statement framework. Transactions were recorded as pluses or minuses for each item affected by a transaction. At the same time, the effects of the transaction on the financial statements were shown. The equality of the accounting equation aided in preventing and detecting errors. That is, total assets must always equal total liabilities plus stockholders' equity.

Double-entry accounting also uses the accounting equation. However, double-entry accounting uses debit and credit rules as an additional control on the accuracy of recording transactions. This appendix describes and illustrates the basic elements of double-entry accounting.

In a double-entry accounting system, transactions are recorded in accounts. An **account**, in its simplest form, has three parts:

1. A title, which identifies the accounting equation element recorded in the account
2. A space for recording increases in the amount of the element
3. A space for recording decreases in the amount of the element

The account form presented below is called a **T account** because it resembles the letter T. The left side of the account is called the debit side, and the right side is called the credit side.[1]

Title	
Left side *debit*	Right side *credit*

Amounts entered on the left side of an account, regardless of the account title, are called debits to the account. When debits are entered in an account, the account is said to be *debited*. Amounts entered on the right side of an account are called credits, and the account is said to be *credited*. Debits and credits are sometimes abbreviated as *Dr.* and *Cr.*

To illustrate, a T account for Cash is shown below.

Cash

Debit side of account	(a)	25,000	(b)	20,000	Credit side of account
	(d)	7,500	(e)	3,650	
			(f)	950	
			(h)	2,000	
	Balance	5,900			

Balance of account → 5,900

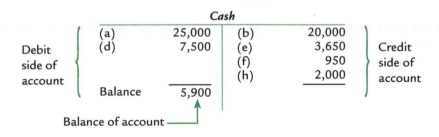

Recording transactions in accounts using double-entry accounting follows certain rules. For example, increases in assets are recorded on the debit (left) side of the account. Likewise, decreases in assets are recorded on the credit (right) side of the account. With an asset account, the excess of debits over its credits is the balance of the account.

To illustrate, the preceding cash account is used. The receipt of cash (increase in Cash) of $25,000 in transaction (a) is entered on the debit (left) side of the cash account. A reference notation (letter or date of the transaction) is also entered into the account. The reference notation provides a means of backtracking to the underlying transaction data, should any questions arise.

1. The terms *debit* and *credit* are derived from the Latin *debere* and *credere*.

The payment of cash (decrease in Cash) of $20,000 in transaction (b) is entered on the credit (right) side of the account. The balance of the cash account of $5,900 is the excess of debits over credits, as shown below:

Debits ($25,000 + $7,500)	$ 32,500
Less credits ($20,000 + $3,650 + $950 + $2,000)	(26,600)
Balance of Cash	$ 5,900

The balance of the cash account is inserted in the Debit column. In this way, the balance is identified as a debit balance.

Rules of Debit and Credit

A standard method of recording debits and credits in accounts is essential to ensure that businesses record transactions in a similar manner. The rules of debit and credit are shown in Exhibit 1.

Exhibit 1 Rules of Debit and Credit; Normal Balances of Accounts

ASSETS		=	LIABILITIES		+	STOCKHOLDERS' EQUITY			
Asset Accounts			Liability Accounts			Common Stock		+ Retained Earnings	
Debit for increases (+)	Credit for decreases (−)		Debit for decreases (−)	Credit for increases (+)		Debit for decreases (−)	Credit for increases (+)	Debit for decreases (−)	Credit for increases (+)
Balance				Balance			Balance		Balance

Income Statement Accounts

− Dividends		+ Revenue Accounts		− Expense Accounts	
Debit for increases (+)	Credit for decreases (−)	Debit for decreases (−)	Credit for increases (+)	Debit for increases (+)	Credit for decreases (−)
Balance			Balance	Balance	

The side of the account for recording increases and the normal balance is shown in dark blue shading.

Exhibit 1 illustrates the following characteristics of the rules of debit and credit:

1. The normal balance of an account is the side of the account used to record increases. Thus, the normal balance of an asset account is a debit balance; the normal balance of a liability account is a credit balance. This characteristic is often useful in detecting errors in the recording process. That is, when an account normally having a debit balance actually has a credit balance, or vice versa, an error has occurred or an unusual situation exists.
2. Asset accounts (on the left side of the accounting equation) are increased by debits and have a normal debit balance. The only exception is that some asset accounts, called *contra asset accounts,* are increased by credits and have normal credit balances. As the words *contra asset* imply, these accounts offset the normal debit balances of asset accounts. For example, accumulated depreciation, an offset to plant assets, is increased by credits and has a normal credit balance. Thus, accumulated depreciation is a contra asset account.
3. Liability and stockholders' equity accounts (on the right side of the accounting equation) are increased by credits and have normal credit balances.
4. Dividend accounts appear on the right side of the accounting equation and decrease stockholders' equity (retained earnings). Thus, dividends accounts are increased by debits and have a normal debit balance. In this sense, the dividends accounts can be thought of as a type of contra account to retained earnings.

5. Revenue accounts appear on the right side of the accounting equation and increase stockholders' equity (retained earnings). Thus, revenue accounts are increased by credits and have normal credit balances.
6. Expense accounts appear on the right side of the accounting equation and decrease stockholders' equity (retained earnings). Thus, expense accounts are increased by debits and have a normal debit balance. Expense accounts can be thought of as a type of contra account. In this case, expense accounts can be thought of as contra accounts to revenues.

The rules of debit and credit require that for each transaction, the total debits equal the total credits. That is, each transaction must be recorded so the total debits for the transaction equal the total credits.

To illustrate, assume a company pays cash of $500 for supplies. The asset account Supplies is debited (increased) by $500 and Cash is credited (decreased) by $500. Likewise, if the company provides services and receives $2,000 from customers, Cash is debited (increased) and Fees Earned is credited (increased) by $2,000. This equality of debits and credits for each transaction provides a control over the recording of transactions.

To summarize, under double-entry accounting each transaction is recorded using the rules shown in Exhibit 1. In doing so, the total debits equal the total credits for each transaction.

The Journal

Under double-entry accounting, each transaction is initially entered in chronological order in a record called a **journal**. In this way, the journal documents the history of the company. The process of recording transactions in the journal is called **journalizing**. The specific transaction record entered in the journal is called a **journal entry**.

In practice, companies use a variety of formats for recording journal entries. A small company may use one all-purpose journal, sometimes called a **general journal**. Alternatively, another company may use **special journals** for recording different types of transactions. To simplify, a basic two-column general journal is used in this appendix.

Illustration of Double-Entry Accounting

Assume that on November 1, 20Y7, Lee Dunbar organizes a corporation that will be known as Web Solutions. The first phase of Lee's business plan is to operate Web Solutions as a service business providing assistance to individuals and small businesses by developing Web pages and configuring and installing application software. Lee expects this initial phase of the business to last one to two years. During this period, Web Solutions will gather information on the software and hardware needs of customers. During the second phase of the business plan, Web Solutions will expand into an Internet-based retailer of software and hardware to individuals and small business markets.

To start the business, Lee deposits $25,000 in a bank account in the name of Web Solutions in return for shares of stock in the corporation. This first transaction increases Cash and Common Stock by $25,000. This transaction is recorded in the journal using the following three steps:

Step 1. The date of the transaction is entered in the Date column.
Step 2. The title of the account to be debited is recorded at the left-hand margin under the Description column, and the amount to be debited is entered in the Debit column.
Step 3. The title of the account to be credited is listed below and to the right of the debited account title, and the amount to be credited is entered in the Credit column.

Using the preceding steps, the transaction is recorded in the journal as follows:

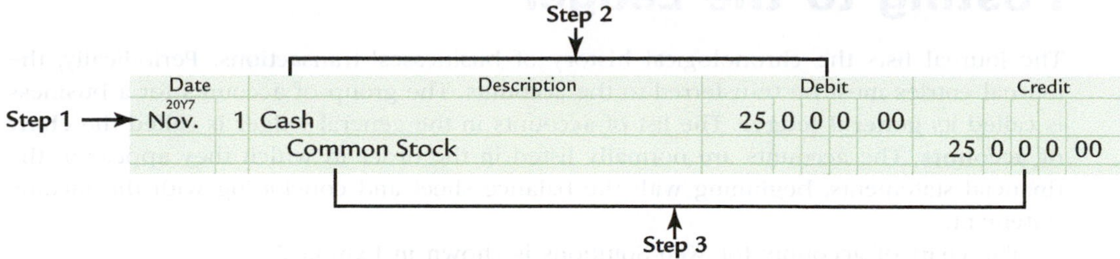

The increase in the asset is debited to the cash account. The increase in stockholders' equity (capital stock) is credited to the capital stock account. As other assets are acquired, the increases are also recorded as debits to asset accounts. Likewise, other increases in stockholders' equity will be recorded as credits to stockholders' equity accounts.

Web Solutions entered into the following additional transactions during the remainder of November:

Nov. 5 Purchased land for $20,000, paying cash. The land is located in a new business park with convenient access to transportation facilities. Web Solutions plans to rent office space and equipment during the first phase of its business plan. During the second phase, the company plans to build an office and a warehouse on the land.

10 Purchased supplies on account for $1,350.

18 Received $7,500 for services provided to customers for cash.

30 Paid expenses as follows: wages, $2,125; rent, $800; utilities, $450; and miscellaneous, $275.

30 Paid creditors on account, $950.

30 Paid stockholder (Lee Dunbar) dividends of $2,000.

The journal entries to record these transactions follow.

Date		Description	Debit	Credit
Nov.	5	Land	20 0 0 0 00	
		Cash		20 0 0 0 00
	10	Supplies	1 3 5 0 00	
		Accounts Payable		1 3 5 0 00
	18	Cash	7 5 0 0 00	
		Fees Earned		7 5 0 0 00
	30	Wages Expense	2 1 2 5 00	
		Rent Expense	8 0 0 00	
		Utilities Expense	4 5 0 00	
		Miscellaneous Expense	2 7 5 00	
		Cash		3 6 5 0 00
	30	Accounts Payable	9 5 0 00	
		Cash		9 5 0 00
	30	Dividends	2 0 0 0 00	
		Cash		2 0 0 0 00

Posting to the Ledger

The journal lists the chronological history of businesses' transactions. Periodically, the journal entries must be transferred to the accounts. The group of accounts for a business is called its **general ledger**. The list of accounts in the general ledger is called the **chart of accounts**. The accounts are normally listed in the order in which they appear in the financial statements, beginning with the balance sheet and concluding with the income statement.

The chart of accounts for Web Solutions is shown in Exhibit 2.

Exhibit 2
Chart of Accounts for Web Solutions

Balance Sheet Accounts	**Income Statement Accounts**
Assets	**Revenue**
Cash	Fees Earned
Accounts Receivable	Rent Revenue
Supplies	**Expenses**
Prepaid Insurance	Wages Expense
Office Equipment	Rent Expense
Accumulated Depreciation	Depreciation Expense
Land	Utilities Expense
Liabilities	Supplies Expense
Accounts Payable	Insurance Expense
Wages Payable	Miscellaneous Expense
Unearned Rent	
Stockholders' Equity	
Common Stock	
Retained Earnings	
Dividends	

The process of transferring the journal entry debits and credits to the accounts in the ledger is called **posting**. To illustrate the posting process, Web Solutions' November 1 transaction, along with its posting to the cash and common stock accounts, is shown in Exhibit 3.

Exhibit 3
Posting a Journal Entry

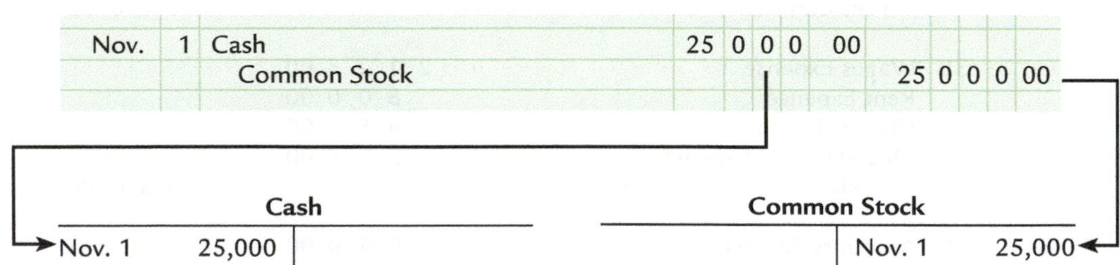

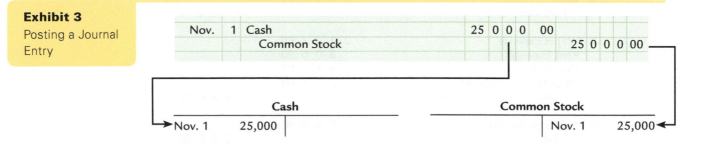

The debits and credits for each journal entry are posted to the accounts in the order in which they occur in the journal. In posting to the accounts, the date is entered followed by the amount of the entry. After the journal entries have been posted, the ledger becomes a chronological history of transactions by account. The posting of Web Solutions' remaining journal entries is shown in Exhibit 7 on page 696.

Trial Balance and Financial Statements

Errors may occur in posting debits and credits from the journal to the ledger. One way to detect such errors is by preparing a **trial balance**. Double-entry accounting requires that debits must always equal credits. The trial balance verifies this equality. The four steps in preparing a trial balance are as follows:

Step 1. List the name of the company, the title of the trial balance, and the date the trial balance is prepared.
Step 2. List the accounts from the ledger and enter their debit or credit balance in the Debit or Credit column of the trial balance.
Step 3. Total the Debit and Credit columns of the trial balance.
Step 4. Verify that the total of the Debit column equals the total of the Credit column.

The trial balance for Web Solutions as of December 31, 20Y7, is shown in Exhibit 4. The account balances in Exhibit 4 are taken from the November 30 balances, which are shown in a darker green screen in the ledger shown in Exhibit 7.

The trial balance does not provide complete proof of the accuracy of the ledger. It indicates only that the debits and the credits are equal. However, this proof is still of value as errors often affect the equality of debits and credits.

If the two totals of a trial balance are not equal, an error has occurred. In such a case, the error must be located and corrected before financial statements are prepared. This ability to detect errors in recording when the trial balance totals are not equal is a primary control feature of the double-entry accounting system.

The trial balance can be used as the source of data for preparing financial statements. The financial statements prepared in a double-entry accounting system are similar to those described and illustrated in the text. For this reason, the financial statements are not illustrated in this appendix.

Exhibit 4 Trial Balance

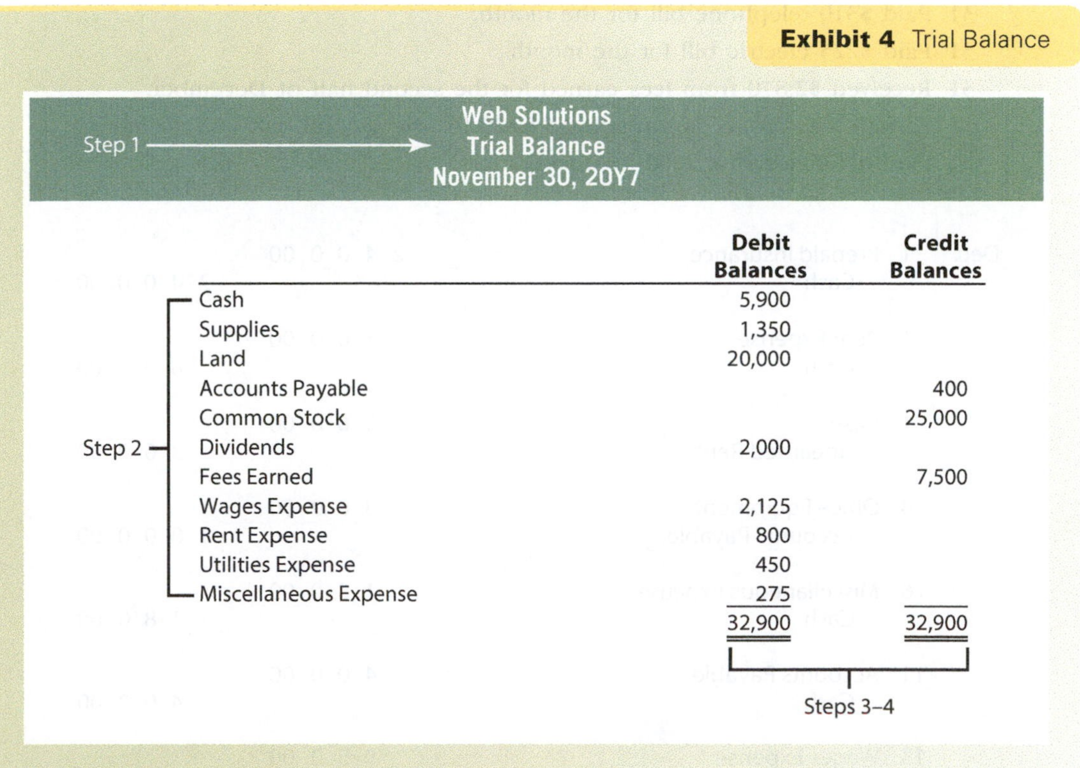

Step 1 → Web Solutions
Trial Balance
November 30, 20Y7

Step 2	Account	Debit Balances	Credit Balances
	Cash	5,900	
	Supplies	1,350	
	Land	20,000	
	Accounts Payable		400
	Common Stock		25,000
	Dividends	2,000	
	Fees Earned		7,500
	Wages Expense	2,125	
	Rent Expense	800	
	Utilities Expense	450	
	Miscellaneous Expense	275	
		32,900	32,900

Steps 3–4

Review of Double-Entry Accounting

As a review of the double-entry accounting financial reporting system, Web Solutions' transactions for December are used. The journal entries for the following December transactions are shown in Exhibit 5.

Dec. 1 Paid a premium of $2,400 for a comprehensive insurance policy covering liability, theft, and fire. The policy covers a two-year period.

1 Paid rent for December, $800. The company from which Web Solutions is renting its store space now requires the payment of rent on the first day of each month rather than at the end of the month.

1 Received an offer from a local retailer to rent the land purchased on November 5. The retailer plans to use the land as a parking lot for its employees and customers. Web Solutions agreed to rent the land to the retailer for three months with the rent payable in advance. Web Solutions received $360 for three months' rent beginning December 1.

4 Purchased office equipment on account from Executive Supply Co. for $1,800.

6 Paid $180 for a newspaper advertisement.

11 Paid creditors $400.

13 Paid a receptionist and a part-time assistant $950 for two weeks' wages.

16 Received $3,100 from fees earned for the first half of December.

16 Earned fees on account totaling $1,750 for the first half of December.

20 Paid $1,800 to Executive Supply Co. on the debt owed from the December 4 transaction.

21 Received $650 from customers in payment of their accounts.

23 Purchased $1,450 of supplies by paying $550 cash and charging the remainder on account.

27 Paid the receptionist and the part-time assistant $1,200 for two weeks' wages.

31 Paid $310 telephone bill for the month.

31 Paid $225 electric bill for the month.

31 Received $2,870 from fees earned for the second half of December.

31 Earned fees on account totaling $1,120 for the second half of December.

31 Paid dividends of $2,000 to stockholders.

Exhibit 5
Journal Entries: December Transactions for Web Solutions

Dec.	1	Prepaid Insurance	2,400.00	
		Cash		2,400.00
	1	Rent Expense	800.00	
		Cash		800.00
	1	Cash	360.00	
		Unearned Rent		360.00
	4	Office Equipment	1,800.00	
		Accounts Payable		1,800.00
	6	Miscellaneous Expense	180.00	
		Cash		180.00
	11	Accounts Payable	400.00	
		Cash		400.00
	13	Wages Expense	950.00	
		Cash		950.00

Exhibit 5
Continued

			Debit	Credit
Dec.	16	Cash	3,100.00	
		Fees Earned		3,100.00
	16	Accounts Receivable	1,750.00	
		Fees Earned		1,750.00
	20	Accounts Payable	1,800.00	
		Cash		1,800.00
	21	Cash	650.00	
		Accounts Receivable		650.00
	23	Supplies	1,450.00	
		Cash		550.00
		Accounts Payable		900.00
	27	Wages Expense	1,200.00	
		Cash		1,200.00
	31	Utilities Expense	310.00	
		Cash		310.00
	31	Utilities Expense	225.00	
		Cash		225.00
	31	Cash	2,870.00	
		Fees Earned		2,870.00
	31	Accounts Receivable	1,120.00	
		Fees Earned		1,120.00
	31	Dividends	2,000.00	
		Cash		2,000.00

The posting of the journal entries to the ledger accounts is shown in Exhibit 6.

Exhibit 6
Ledger for Web Solutions

Cash

Debit		Credit	
Nov. 1	25,000	Nov. 5	20,000
18	7,500	30	3,650
		30	950
		30	2,000
	32,500		26,600
Nov. 30 Bal.	5,900	Dec. 1	2,400
Dec. 1	360	1	800
16	3,100	6	180
21	650	11	400
31	2,870	13	950
		20	1,800
		23	550
		27	1,200
		31	310
		31	225
		31	2,000
	12,880		10,815
Dec. 31 Bal.	2,065		

Accounts Receivable

Debit		Credit	
Dec. 16	1,750	Dec. 21	650
31	1,120		
Dec. 31 Bal.	2,220		

Supplies

Debit		Credit	
Nov. 10	1,350		
Dec. 23	1,450		
Dec. 31 Bal.	2,800		

Prepaid Insurance

Debit		Credit	
Dec. 1	2,400		

Office Equipment

Debit		Credit	
Dec. 4	1,800		

Land

Debit		Credit	
Nov. 5	20,000		

Accounts Payable

Debit		Credit	
Nov. 30	950	Nov. 10	1,350
		Nov. 30 Bal.	400
Dec. 11	400	Dec. 4	1,800
20	1,800	23	900
	2,200		3,100
		Dec. 31 Bal.	900

Exhibit 6 Continued

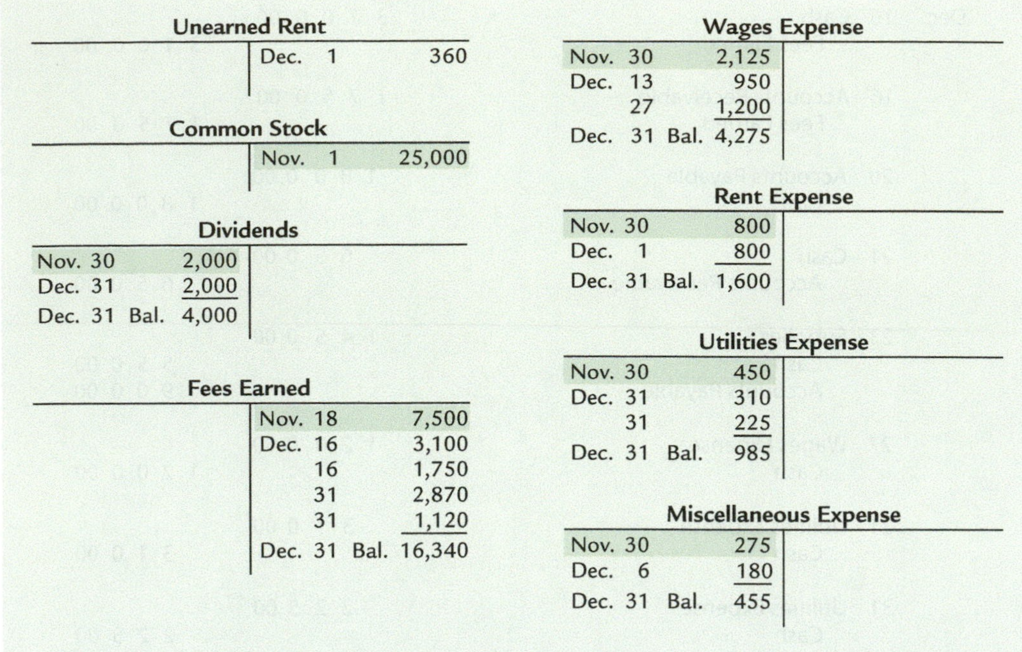

The trial balance shown in Exhibit 7 indicates that after posting December transactions to the general ledger, the total of the debit balances of accounts equals the total of the credit balances.

Exhibit 7 Trial Balance for Web Solutions

Web Solutions
Trial Balance
December 31, 20Y7

	Debit Balances	Credit Balances
Cash	2,065	
Accounts Receivable	2,220	
Supplies	2,800	
Prepaid Insurance	2,400	
Office Equipment	1,800	
Land	20,000	
Accounts Payable		900
Unearned Rent		360
Common Stock		25,000
Dividends	4,000	
Fees Earned		16,340
Wages Expense	4,275	
Rent Expense	1,600	
Utilities Expense	985	
Miscellaneous Expense	455	
	42,600	42,600

Exercises

E-1 Rules of debit and credit

The following table summarizes the rules of debit and credit. For each of the items (a) through (l), indicate whether the proper answer is a debit or a credit.

	Increase	Decrease	Normal Balance
Balance sheet accounts:			
Asset	Debit	(a)	(b)
Liability	Credit	(c)	(d)
Stockholders' equity:			
Common stock	(e)	Debit	(f)
Retained earnings	(g)	Debit	Credit
Dividends	Debit	(h)	Debit
Income statement accounts:			
Revenue	(i)	(j)	(k)
Expense	(l)	Credit	Debit

E-2 Identifying transactions

Wild River Tours Co. is a travel agency. The nine transactions recorded by Wild River Tours during May 20Y5, its first month of operations, are indicated in the following T accounts:

Cash

Debit		Credit	
(1)	25,000	(2)	1,750
(7)	10,000	(3)	3,600
		(4)	2,700
		(6)	7,500
		(9)	2,500

Equipment

Debit		Credit	
(3)	18,000		

Dividends

Debit		Credit	
(9)	2,500		

Accounts Receivable

Debit		Credit	
(5)	13,500	(7)	10,000

Accounts Payable

Debit		Credit	
(6)	7,500	(3)	14,400

Service Revenue

Debit		Credit	
		(5)	13,500

Supplies

Debit		Credit	
(2)	1,750	(8)	1,050

Common Stock

Debit		Credit	
		(1)	25,000

Operating Expenses

Debit		Credit	
(4)	2,700		
(8)	1,050		

Indicate the following for each debit and each credit: (a) whether an asset, liability, capital stock, dividend, revenue, or expense account was affected and (b) whether the account was increased (+) or decreased (−). Present your answers in the following form, with transaction (1) given as an example:

	Account Debited		Account Credited	
Transaction	Type	Effect	Type	Effect
(1)	asset	+	capital stock	+

E-3 Journal entries

Based upon the T accounts in Exercise 2, prepare the nine journal entries from which the postings were made.

E-4 Trial balance

Based upon the data presented in Exercise 2, prepare a trial balance, listing the accounts in their proper order.

✔ Total Debit column: $45,400

E-5 Normal entries for accounts

During the month, Demko Labs Co. has a substantial number of transactions affecting each of the following accounts. State for each account whether it is likely to have (a) debit entries only, (b) credit entries only, or (c) both debit and credit entries.

1. Accounts Payable
2. Accounts Receivable
3. Cash
4. Fees Earned
5. Insurance Expense
6. Dividends
7. Supplies Expense

E-6 Normal balances of accounts

Identify each of the following accounts of Shredder Services Co. as an asset, liability, stockholders' equity, revenue, or expense, and state in each case whether the normal balance is a debit or a credit.

a. Accounts Payable
b. Accounts Receivable
c. Common Stock
d. Cash
e. Dividends
f. Fees Earned
g. Office Equipment
h. Rent Expense
i. Supplies
j. Wages Expense

E-7 Cash account balance

During the month, Shogun Co. received $515,000 in cash and paid out $331,000 in cash.

a. Do the data indicate that Shogun Co. had net income of $184,000 during the month? Explain.
b. If the balance of the cash account is $222,350 at the end of the month, what was the cash balance at the beginning of the month?

✔ c. $283,600

E-8 Account balances

a. During October, $100,000 was paid to creditors on account, and purchases on account were $115,150. Assuming the October 31 balance of Accounts Payable was $39,000, determine the account balance on October 1.
b. On May 1, the accounts receivable account balance was $36,200. During May, $315,000 was collected from customers on account. Assuming the May 31 balance was $41,600, determine the fees billed to customers on account during May.
c. On June 1, the cash account balance was $20,000. During June, cash receipts totaled $279,100 and the June 30 balance was $15,500. Determine the cash payments made during June.

E-9 Transactions

Off-Peak Co. has the following accounts in its ledger: Cash, Accounts Receivable, Supplies, Office Equipment, Accounts Payable, Common Stock, Retained Earnings, Dividends, Fees Earned, Rent Expense, Advertising Expense, Utilities Expense, and Miscellaneous Expense.

Journalize the following selected transactions for July 20Y9 in a two-column journal.

July 1 Paid rent for the month, $4,500.
2 Paid advertising expense, $1,800.

Note: The spreadsheet icon indicates an Excel template is available on the student companion site at www.cengagebrain.com.

July 5 Paid cash for supplies, $900.
6 Purchased office equipment on account, $12,300.
10 Received cash from customers on account, $4,100.
15 Paid creditor on account, $1,200.
27 Paid cash for repairs to office equipment, $500.
30 Paid telephone bill for the month, $180.
31 Fees earned and billed to customers for the month, $26,800.
31 Paid electricity bill for the month, $315.
31 Paid dividends, $2,000.

E-10 Journalizing and posting

On November 2, 20Y3, Fibrosis Co. purchased $1,800 of supplies on account.

a. Journalize the November 2, 20Y3, transaction.

b. Prepare a T account for Supplies. Enter a debit balance of $1,050 as of November 1, 20Y3.

c. Prepare a T account for Accounts Payable. Enter a credit balance of $15,600 as of November 1, 20Y3.

d. Post the November 2, 20Y3, transaction to the accounts and determine November 30 balances.

E-11 Transactions and T accounts

The following selected transactions were completed during January of the current year:

1. Billed customers for fees earned, $41,730.
2. Purchased supplies on account, $1,800.
3. Received cash from customers on account, $39,150.
4. Paid creditors on account, $1,100.

a. Journalize the above transactions in a two-column journal, using the appropriate number to identify the transactions.

b. Post the entries prepared in (a) to the following T accounts: Cash, Supplies, Accounts Receivable, Accounts Payable, and Fees Earned. To the left of each amount posted in the accounts, place the appropriate number to identify the transactions.

E-12 Trial balance

✔ Total of Credit column: $700,000

The accounts in the ledger of Cupid Co. as of December 31, 20Y7, are listed in alphabetical order as follows. All accounts have normal balances. The balance of the cash account has been intentionally omitted.

Accounts Payable	$ 28,000	Notes Payable	$ 60,000
Accounts Receivable	59,900	Prepaid Insurance	4,500
Common Stock	50,000	Rent Expense	90,000
Cash	?	Retained Earnings	83,500
Dividends	30,000	Supplies	3,150
Fees Earned	465,000	Supplies Expense	11,850
Insurance Expense	9,000	Unearned Rent	13,500
Land	127,500	Utilities Expense	62,250
Miscellaneous Expense	13,350	Wages Expense	262,500

Prepare a trial balance, listing the accounts in their proper order and inserting the missing figure for cash.

Problems

P-1 Journal entries and trial balance

✔ 3. Total of credit column: $32,650

On March 1, 20Y1, Larry Kinyon established Valley Realty, which completed the following transactions during the month:

a. Larry Kinyon transferred cash from a personal bank account to an account to be used for the business in exchange for common stock, $20,000.
b. Purchased supplies on account, $1,000.
c. Earned sales commissions, receiving cash, $12,250.
d. Paid rent on office and equipment for the month, $3,800.
e. Paid creditor on account, $600.
f. Paid dividends, $3,000.
g. Paid automobile expenses (including rental charge) for month, $1,500, and miscellaneous expenses, $400.
h. Paid office salaries, $3,100.
i. Determined that the cost of supplies used was $725.

Instructions

1. Journalize entries for transactions (a) through (i), using the following account titles: Cash, Supplies, Accounts Payable, Common Stock, Dividends, Sales Commissions, Rent Expense, Office Salaries Expense, Automobile Expense, Supplies Expense, and Miscellaneous Expense.
2. Prepare T accounts, using the account titles in part (1). Post the journal entries to these accounts, placing the appropriate letter to the left of each amount to identify the transaction. Determine the account balances, after all posting is complete. Accounts containing only a single entry do not need a balance.
3. Prepare a trial balance as of March 31, 20Y1.

P-2 Journal entries and trial balance

✔ 4. Total of Debit column: $573,350

Apple Realty acts as an agent in buying, selling, renting, and managing real estate. The trial balance on October 31, 20Y4, is shown below.

APPLE REALTY
Trial Balance
October 31, 20Y4

	Debit Balances	Credit Balances
Cash	33,920	
Accounts Receivable	69,800	
Prepaid Insurance	7,200	
Office Supplies	1,600	
Land	—	
Accounts Payable		9,920
Unearned Rent		—
Notes Payable		—
Common Stock		10,000
Retained Earnings		53,080
Dividends	25,600	
Fees Earned		352,000
Salary and Commission Expense	224,000	
Rent Expense	28,000	
Advertising Expense	22,880	
Automobile Expense	10,240	
Miscellaneous Expense	1,760	
	425,000	425,000

The following business transactions were completed by Apple Realty during November 20Y4:

Nov. 1 Purchased office supplies on account, $2,100.

2 Paid rent on office for month, $4,000.

3 Received cash from clients on account, $44,600.

5 Paid annual insurance premiums, $5,700.

9 Returned a portion of the office supplies purchased on November 1, receiving full credit for their cost, $400.

17 Paid advertising expense, $5,500.

23 Paid creditors on account, $4,950.

29 Paid miscellaneous expenses, $500.

30 Paid automobile expense (including rental charges for an automobile), $1,500.

30 Discovered an error in computing a commission; received cash from the salesperson for the overpayment, $1,000.

30 Paid salaries and commissions for the month, $27,800.

30 Recorded revenue earned and billed to clients during the month, $83,000.

30 Purchased land for a future building site for $75,000, paying $10,000 in cash and giving a note payable for the remainder.

30 Paid dividends, $5,000.

30 Rented land purchased on November 30 to a local university for use as a parking lot for athletic events; received advance payment of $3,600.

Instructions

1. Record the November 1, 20Y4, balance of each account in the appropriate balance column of a T account, and write Balance to identify the opening amounts.
2. Journalize the transactions for November in a two-column journal.
3. Post the journal entries to the T accounts, placing the date to the left of each amount to identify the transaction. Determine the balances for all accounts with more than one posting.
4. Prepare a trial balance of the ledger as of November 30, 20Y4.

Appendix B

Process Cost Systems

A **process manufacturer** produces products that are indistinguishable from each other, using a continuous production process. For example, an oil refinery processes crude oil through a series of steps to produce a barrel of gasoline. One barrel of gasoline, the product, cannot be distinguished from another barrel. Other examples of process manufacturers include paper producers, chemical processors, aluminum smelters, and food processors.

The cost accounting system used by process manufacturers is called the **process cost system**. A process cost system records product costs for each manufacturing department or process.

In contrast, a job order manufacturer produces custom products for customers or small batches of similar products. For example, a custom printer produces wedding invitations, graduation announcements, or other special print items that are tailored to the specifications of each customer. Each item manufactured is unique to itself. Other examples of job order manufacturers include furniture manufacturers, shipbuilders, and home builders.

As described and illustrated in Chapter 10, the cost accounting system used by job order manufacturers is called the *job order cost system.* A job order cost system records product costs for each job using job cost sheets.

Some examples of process and job order manufacturers are shown below:

Process Manufacturers		Job Order Manufacturers	
Company	Product	Company	Product
Pepsi	soft drinks	**Walt Disney**	movies
Alcoa	aluminum	**Nike, Inc.**	athletic shoes
Intel	computer chips	**Tiger Woods Design**	golf courses
Apple	iPhone	**Heritage Log Homes**	log homes
Hershey Foods	chocolate bars	**DDB Advertising Agency**	advertising

Comparing Job Order and Process Cost Systems

Process and job order cost systems are similar in the following five ways:

1. Records and summarizes product costs
2. Classifies product costs as direct materials, direct labor, and factory overhead
3. Allocates factory overhead costs to products
4. Uses a perpetual inventory system for materials, work in process, and finished goods
5. Provides useful product cost information for decision making

Process and job costing systems are different in several ways. As a basis for illustrating these differences, the cost systems for La Scoop and Quixote Guitars are used.

Exhibit 1 illustrates the process cost system for La Scoop, an ice cream manufacturer. As a basis for comparison, Exhibit 1 also illustrates the job order cost system for Quixote Guitars, a custom guitar manufacturer. Quixote Guitars was described and illustrated in Chapter 10.

Exhibit 1 Process Cost and Job Order Cost Systems

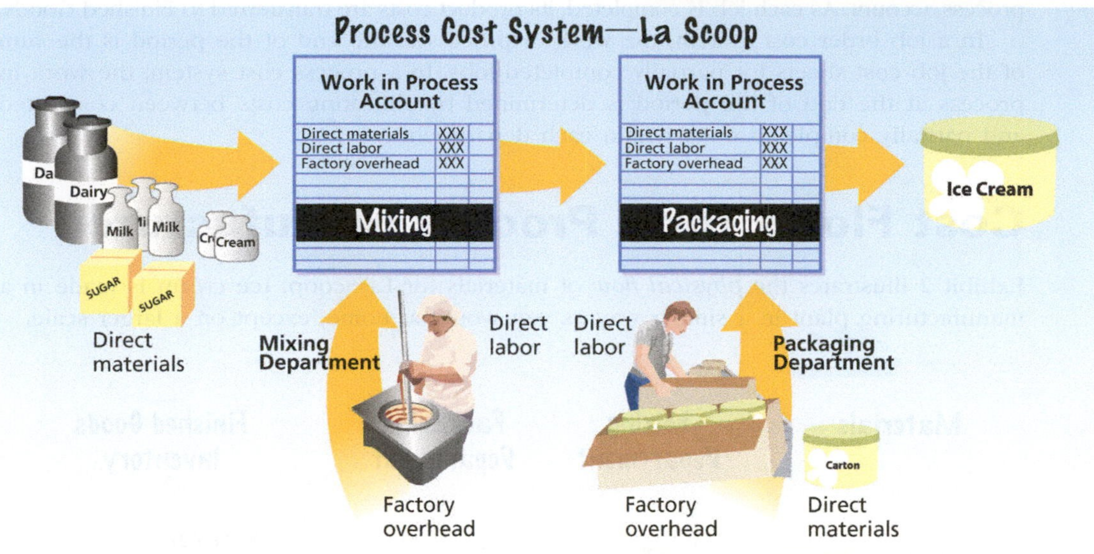

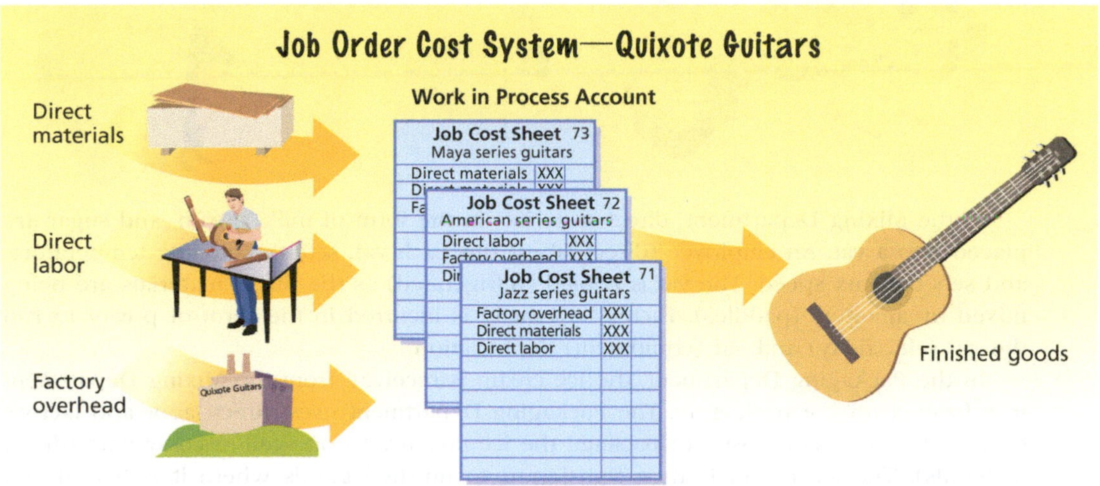

Exhibit 1 indicates that La Scoop manufactures ice cream using two departments:

1. Mixing Department mixes the ingredients using large vats.
2. Packaging Department puts the ice cream into cartons for shipping to customers.

Since each gallon of ice cream is similar, product costs are recorded in each department's work-in-process account. As shown in Exhibit 1, La Scoop accumulates (records) the cost of making ice cream in *work-in-process accounts* for the Mixing and Packaging departments. The product costs of making a gallon of ice cream include the following:

1. *Direct materials cost,* which includes milk, cream, sugar, and packing cartons. All materials costs are added at the beginning of the process for both the Mixing Department and the Packaging Department.
2. *Direct labor cost,* which is incurred by employees in each department who run the equipment and load and unload product.
3. *Factory overhead costs,* which include the utility costs (power) and depreciation on the equipment.

When the Mixing Department completes the mixing process, its product costs are transferred to the Packaging Department. When the Packaging Department completes its process, the product costs are transferred to Finished Goods. In this way, the cost of the product (a gallon of ice cream) accumulates across the entire production process.

In contrast, Exhibit 1 shows that Quixote Guitars accumulates (records) product costs by jobs using a job cost sheet for each type of guitar. Thus, Quixote Guitars uses just one work-in-process account. As each job is completed, its product costs are transferred to Finished Goods.

In a job order cost system, the work in process at the end of the period is the sum of the job cost sheets for partially completed jobs. In a process cost system, the work in process at the end of the period is determined by allocating costs between completed and partially completed units within each department.

Cost Flows for a Process Manufacturer

Exhibit 2 illustrates the *physical flow* of materials for La Scoop. Ice cream is made in a manufacturing plant in a similar way as you would at home, except on a larger scale.

Exhibit 2 Physical Flows for a Process Manufacturer

In the Mixing Department, direct materials in the form of milk, cream, and sugar are placed into a vat. An employee (direct labor) fills each vat, sets the cooling temperature, and sets the mix speed. The vat is cooled (refrigerated) as the direct materials are being mixed by agitators (paddles). Factory overhead is incurred in the form of power to run the vat (electricity) and vat (equipment) depreciation.

In the Packaging Department, the ice cream is received from the Mixing Department in a form ready for packaging. The Packaging Department uses direct labor and factory overhead (conversion costs) to package the ice cream into one-gallon containers (direct materials). The ice cream is then transferred to finished goods where it is frozen and stored in refrigerators prior to shipment to customers (stores).

The *cost flows* in a process cost accounting system are similar to the *physical flow* of materials described above. The cost flows for La Scoop are illustrated in Exhibit 3.

Exhibit 3 Cost Flows for a Process Manufacturer—La Scoop

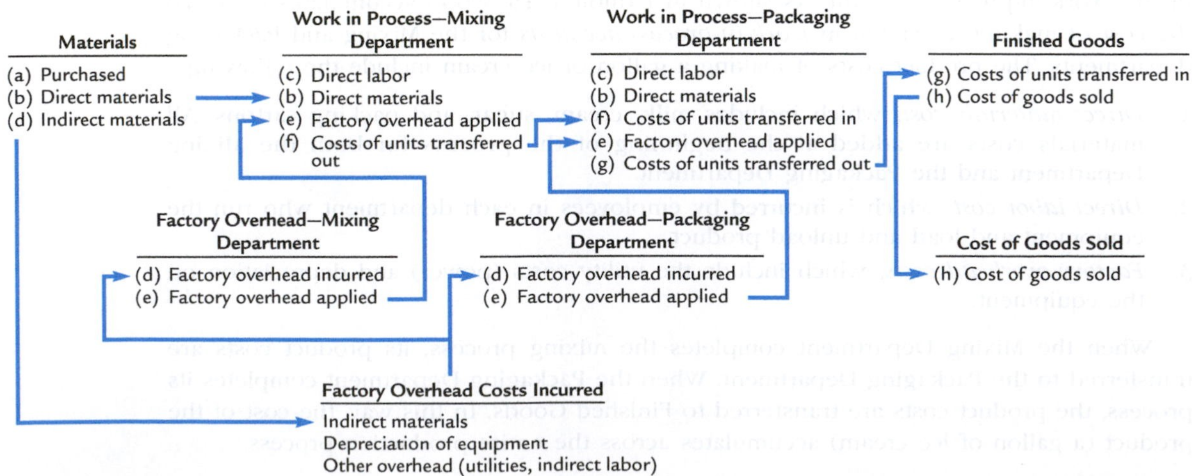

Transactions (a) through (h) in Exhibit 3 are described and explained below:

a. The cost of materials purchased is recorded in the materials account.
b. The cost of direct materials used by the Mixing and Packaging departments is recorded in the work-in-process accounts for each department.
c. The cost of direct labor used by the Mixing and Packaging departments is recorded in work-in-process accounts for each department.
d. The cost of factory overhead incurred for indirect materials and other factory overhead, such as depreciation, is recorded in the factory overhead accounts for each department.
e. The factory overhead incurred in the Mixing and Packaging departments is applied to the work-in-process accounts for each department.
f. The cost of units completed in the Mixing Department is transferred to the Packaging Department.
g. The cost of units completed in the Packaging Department is transferred to Finished Goods.
h. The cost of units sold is transferred to Cost of Goods Sold.

As shown in Exhibit 3, the Mixing and Packaging departments have separate factory overhead accounts. The factory overhead costs incurred for indirect materials, depreciation, and other overhead are recorded as an increase to each department's factory overhead account. The overhead is applied to work in process by increasing each department's work-in-process account and decreasing the department's factory overhead account.

Exhibit 3 illustrates how the Mixing and Packaging departments have separate work-in-process accounts. Each work-in-process account is increased for the direct materials, direct labor, and applied factory overhead. In addition, the work-in-process account for the Packaging Department is increased for the cost of the units transferred in from the Mixing Department. Each work-in-process account is decreased for the cost of the units transferred to the next department.

Exhibit 3 also shows that the finished goods account is increased for the cost of the units transferred from the Packaging Department. The finished goods account is decreased for the cost of the units sold, which is recorded as an increase to the cost of goods sold account.

Weighted Average Cost Method

A cost flow assumption must be used as product costs flow through manufacturing processes. In this appendix, the weighted average cost flow method is illustrated for Granny's Ice Cream Company.[1]

Determining Costs Using the Weighted Average Cost Method

Granny's operations are similar to those of La Scoop. Like La Scoop, Granny's mixes direct materials (milk, cream, sugar) in refrigerated vessels and has two manufacturing departments, Mixing and Packaging. All direct materials are entered at the beginning of the process for both Mixing and Packaging Departments.

The manufacturing data for the Mixing Department for July are as follows:

Work-in-process inventory, July 1, 5,000 gallons (70% completed)		$ 6,200
Direct materials cost incurred in July, 60,000 gallons	$66,000	
Direct labor cost incurred in July	10,500	
Factory overhead applied in July	6,405	82,905
Total production costs to account for		$89,105
Cost of goods transferred to Packaging in July (includes units in process on July 1), 62,000 gallons	?	
Cost of work-in-process inventory, July 31, 3,000 gallons, 25% completed as to conversion costs	?	

1. The first-in, first-out and last-in, first-out cost flow assumptions are described and illustrated in advanced cost accounting textbooks and courses.

Using the weighted average cost (WAC) method, the objective is to allocate the total costs of production of $89,105 to the following:

1. The 62,000 gallons completed and transferred to the Packaging Department
2. The 3,000 gallons in the July 31 (ending) work-in-process inventory

The preceding costs show two question marks. These amounts are determined by preparing a cost of production report using the following four steps:

Step 1. Determine the units to be assigned costs
Step 2. Compute equivalent units of production
Step 3. Determine the cost per equivalent unit
Step 4. Allocate costs to transferred out and partially completed units

Under the WAC method, all production costs (materials and conversion costs) are combined for determining equivalent units and cost per equivalent unit.

Step 1: Determine the Units to Be Assigned Costs

The first step is to determine the units to be assigned costs. A unit can be any measure of completed production, such as tons, gallons, pounds, barrels, or cases. For Granny's, a unit is a gallon of ice cream.

Granny's Mixing Department had 65,000 gallons of direct materials to account for during July, as shown here:

Total gallons to account for:	
Work in process, July	5,000 gallons
Received from materials storeroom	60,000
Total units to account for by the Packaging Department	65,000 gallons

There are two groups of units to be assigned costs for the period:

Group 1	Units completed and transferred out
Group 2	Units in the July 31 (ending) work-in-process inventory

During July, the Mixing Department completed and transferred 62,000 gallons to the Packaging Department. Of the 60,000 gallons started in July, 57,000 (60,000 − 3,000) gallons were completed and transferred to the Packaging Department. Thus, the ending work-in-process inventory consists of 3,000 gallons.

The total units (gallons) to be assigned costs for Granny's can be summarized as follows:

Group 1	Units transferred out to the Packaging Department in July	62,000 gallons
Group 2	Work-in-process inventory, July 31	3,000
	Total gallons to be assigned costs	65,000 gallons

The total units (gallons) to be assigned costs (65,000 gallons) equal the total units to account for (65,000 gallons).

Step 2: Compute Equivalent Units of Production

Granny's has 3,000 gallons of units in the work-in-process inventory for the Mixing Department on July 31. Since these units are 25% complete, the number of equivalent units in process in the Mixing Department on July 31 is 750 gallons (3,000 gallons × 25%).

Since the units transferred to the Packaging Department have been completed, the units (62,000 gallons) transferred out are the same as the equivalent units transferred.

The total equivalent units of production for the Mixing Department are determined by adding the equivalent units in the ending work-in-process inventory to the units transferred and completed during the period as shown below:

Equivalent units completed and transferred to the Packaging Department during July	62,000 gallons
Equivalent units in ending work in process, July 31	750
Total equivalent units	62,750 gallons

Step 3: Determine the Cost per Equivalent Unit

Materials and conversion costs are combined under the WAC method. The cost per equivalent unit is determined by dividing the total production costs by the total equivalent units of production as follows:

$$\textbf{Cost per Equivalent Unit} = \frac{\textbf{Total Production Costs}}{\textbf{Total Equivalent Units}}$$

$$\textbf{Cost per Equivalent Unit} = \frac{\textbf{Total Production Costs}}{\textbf{Total Equivalent Units}} = \frac{\textbf{\$89,105}}{\textbf{62,750 gallons}} = \textbf{\$1.42}$$

The cost per equivalent unit shown above is used in Step 4 to allocate the production costs to the completed and partially completed units.

Step 4: Allocate Costs to Transferred Out and Partially Completed Units

The cost of transferred out and partially completed units is determined by multiplying the cost per equivalent unit times the equivalent units of production. For the Mixing Department, these costs are determined as follows:

Group 1	Transferred out to the Packaging Department (62,000 gallons × $1.42)	$88,040
Group 2	Work-in-process inventory, July 31 (750 equivalent units × $1.42)	1,065
	Total production costs assigned	$89,105

The Cost of Production Report

The July cost of production report for Granny's Mixing Department is shown in Exhibit 4. This cost of production report summarizes the following:

1. The units for which the department is accountable and the disposition of those units
2. The production costs incurred by the department and the allocation of those costs between completed and partially completed units

Cost Flows for a Process Cost System

Exhibit 5 shows the flow of costs for each transaction. The highlighted amounts in Exhibit 5 were determined from assigning the costs charged to production in the Mixing Department. These amounts were computed and are shown at the bottom of the cost of production report for the department in Exhibit 4. Likewise, the amount transferred out of the Packaging Department to Finished Goods also would have been determined from a cost of production report for the Packaging Department.

Exhibit 4 Cost of Production Report for Granny's Mixing Department— Weighted Average Cost

	A	B	C
1	**Granny's Ice Cream Company**		
2	**Cost of Production Report—Mixing Department**		
3	**For the Month Ended July 31**		
4	**UNITS**	Step 1	Step 2
5		Units	Equivalent Units
6			of Production
7	Units to account for during production:		
8	Work-in-process inventory, July 1	5,000	
9	Received from materials storeroom	60,000	
10	Total units accounted for by the Mixing Department	65,000	
11			
12	Units to be assigned costs:		
13	Transferred to Packaging Department in July	62,000	62,000
14	Inventory in process, July 31 (25% completed)	3,000	750
15	Total units to be assigned costs	65,000	62,750
16			
17	**COSTS**		
18			
19	Cost per equivalent unit:		
20	Total production costs for July in Mixing Department		$89,105
21	Total equivalent units (from Step 2 above)		÷62,750
22	Cost per equivalent unit		$ 1.42
23			
24	Costs assigned to production:		
25	Inventory in process, July 1		$ 6,200
26	Direct materials, direct labor, and factory overhead incurred in July		82,905
27	Total costs accounted for by the Mixing Department		$89,105
28			
29			
30	Costs allocated to completed and partially completed units:		
31	Transferred to Packaging Department in July (62,000 gallons × $1.42)		$88,040
32	Inventory in process, July 31 (750 equivalent units × $1.42)		1,065
33	Total costs assigned by the Mixing Department		$89,105
34			

Step 3 (rows 19–27)
Step 4 (rows 30–33)

Exhibit 5 Granny's Cost Flows

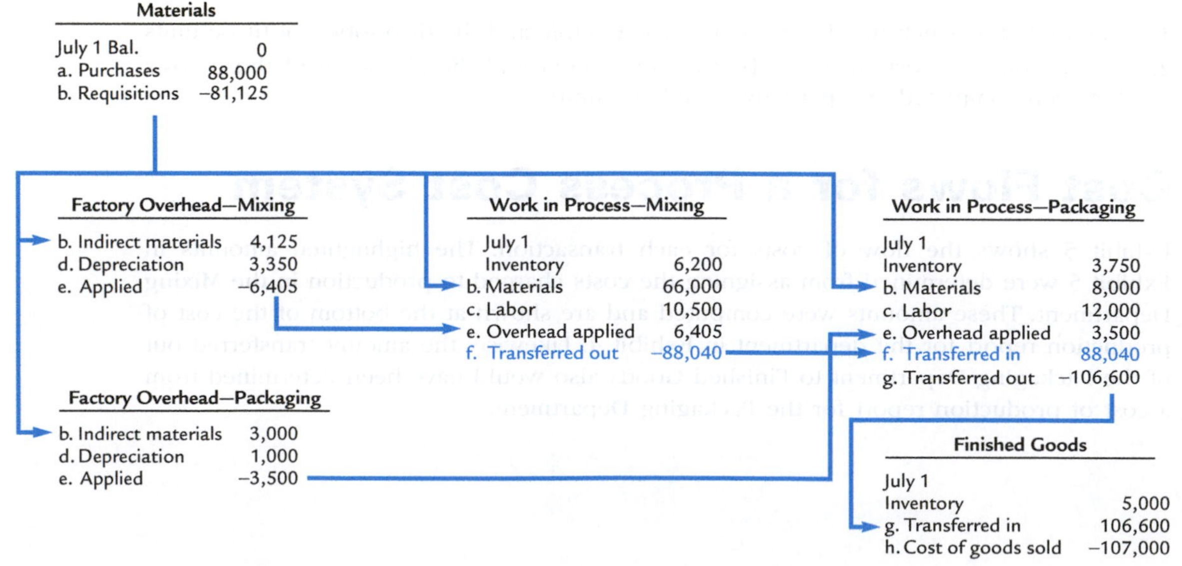

Using the Cost of Production Report for Decision Making

The cost of production report is often used by managers for decisions involving the control and improvement of operations. To illustrate, cost of production reports for Soda Butte Beverage Company are used. Finally, the computation and use of yield is discussed.

Soda Butte Beverage Company

A cost of production report may be prepared in greater detail than shown in Exhibit 4. This greater detail can help managers isolate problems and identify opportunities for improvement.

To illustrate, the Blending Department of Soda Butte Beverage Company prepared cost of production reports for April and May. To simplify, assume that the Blending Department had no beginning or ending work-in-process inventory in either month. In other words, all units started were completed in each month. The cost of production reports for April and May in the Blending Department are as follows:

	A	B	C
1	**Cost of Production Reports**		
2	**Soda Butte Beverage Company—Blending Department**		
3	**For the Months Ended April 30 and May 31**		
4		**April**	**May**
5	Direct materials	$ 20,000	$ 40,600
6	Direct labor	15,000	29,400
7	Energy	8,000	20,000
8	Repairs	4,000	8,000
9	Tank cleaning	3,000	8,000
10	Total	$ 50,000	$106,000
11	Units completed	÷100,000	÷200,000
12	Cost per unit	$ 0.50	$ 0.53
13			

The May results indicate that total unit costs have increased from $0.50 to $0.53, or 6% from April. To determine the possible causes for this increase, the cost of production report is restated in per-unit terms by dividing the costs by the number of units completed, as shown below:

	A	B	C	D
1	**Blending Department**			
2	**Per-Unit Expense Comparisons**			
3		**April**	**May**	**% Change**
4	Direct materials	$0.200	$0.203	1.50%
5	Direct labor	0.150	0.147	−2.00%
6	Energy	0.080	0.100	25.00%
7	Repairs	0.040	0.040	0.00%
8	Tank cleaning	0.030	0.040	33.33%
9	Total	$0.500	$0.530	6.00%
10				

Per-unit costs for energy (25% change) and tank cleaning (33.33% change) have increased significantly in May. These increases should be further investigated. For example, the increase in energy may be due to the machines losing fuel efficiency. This could lead management to repair the machines. The tank cleaning costs could be investigated in a similar fashion.

Exercises

E-1 Entries for materials cost flows in a process cost system

The Hershey Foods Company manufactures chocolate confectionery products. The three largest raw materials are cocoa beans, sugar, and dehydrated milk. These raw materials first go into the Blending Department. The blended product is sent to the Molding Department, where the bars of candy are formed. The candy is sent to the Packing Department, where the bars are wrapped and boxed. The boxed candy is sent to the distribution center, where it is sold to food brokers and retailers.

Show the accounts increased and decreased for each of the following four business events:

a. Materials used by the Blending Department

b. Transfer of blended product to the Molding Department

c. Transfer of chocolate to the Packing Department

d Transfer of boxed chocolate to the distribution center

e. Sale of boxed chocolate

E-2 Flowchart of accounts related to service and processing departments

Alcoa Inc. is the world's largest producer of aluminum products. One product that Alcoa manufactures is aluminum sheet products for the aerospace industry. The entire output of the Smelting Department is transferred to the Rolling Department. Part of the fully processed goods from the Rolling Department are sold as rolled sheet, and the remainder of the goods are transferred to the Converting Department for further processing into sheared sheet.

Prepare a chart of the flow of costs from the processing department accounts into the finished goods accounts and then into the cost of goods sold account. The relevant accounts are as follows:

Cost of Goods Sold
Materials
Factory Overhead—Smelting Department
Factory Overhead—Rolling Department
Factory Overhead—Converting Department
Finished Goods—Rolled Sheet
Finished Goods—Sheared Sheet
Work in Process—Smelting Department
Work in Process—Rolling Department
Work in Process—Converting Department

E-3 Equivalent units of production

✔ a. 28,400

The Converting Department of Girders Company uses the weighted average cost (WAC) method and had 3,500 units in work in process that were 60% complete at the beginning of the period. During the period, 24,900 units were started and 25,200 units were completed and transferred to the Packing Department. There were 3,200 units in process that were 30% complete at the end of the period.

a. Determine the number of units to be accounted for and to be assigned costs for the period.

b. Determine the number of equivalent units of production for the period.

Note: The spreadsheet icon indicates an Excel template is available on the student companion site at www.cengagebrain.com.

E-4 Equivalent units of production

✔ a. 94,000 units to be accounted for

Units of production data for the two departments of Alaska Cable and Wire Company for May of the current fiscal year are as follows:

	Drawing Department	Winding Department
Work in process, May 1	3,000 units, 50% completed	2,000 units, 30% completed
Units started during May	91,000 units	90,000 units
Completed and transferred to next processing department during May	90,000 units	89,200 units
Work in process, May 31	4,000 units, 55% completed	2,800 units, 25% completed

Each department uses the weighted average cost (WAC) method.

a. Determine the number of units to be accounted for and to be assigned costs and the equivalent units of production for the Drawing Department.

b. Determine the number of units to be accounted for and to be assigned costs and the equivalent units of production for the Winding Department.

E-5 Equivalent units of production

✔ a. 21,500

The following information concerns production in the Finishing Department for July. The Finishing Department uses the weighted average cost (WAC) method.

ACCOUNT Work in Process—Finishing Department

Date		Item	
July	1	Bal., 20,000 units, 40% completed	24,600
	31	Direct materials, 144,000 units started	345,000
	31	Direct labor	163,200
	31	Factory overhead	86,700
	31	Goods transferred, 142,500 units	−578,550
	31	Bal., ? units, 60% completed	40,950

a. Determine the number of units in work-in-process inventory at the end of the month.

b. Determine the number of units to be accounted for and to be assigned costs and the equivalent units of production for July.

E-6 Equivalent units of production and related costs

✔ b. 84,600 units

The charges to Work in Process—Baking Department for a period, as well as information concerning production are as follows. The Baking Department uses the weighted average cost (WAC) method, and all direct materials are placed in process during production.

Work in Process—Baking Department

Bal., 10,000 units, 70% completed	12,280
Direct materials, 82,300 units started	161,000
Direct labor	91,800
Factory overhead	81,780
To Finished Goods, 81,300 units	?
Bal., 11,000 units, 30% completed	?

Determine the following:

a. The number of units to be accounted for and to be assigned costs

b. The number of equivalent units of production

(Continued)

c. The cost per equivalent unit
d. The cost of the units transferred to Finished Goods
e. The cost of units in the ending Work in Process

E-7 Cost per equivalent unit

✔ a. $11.50

The following information concerns production in the Forging Department for April. The Forging Department uses the weighted average cost (WAC) method.

ACCOUNT Work in Process—Forging Department

Date		Item	
Apr.	1	Bal., 2,000 units, 40% completed	9,120
	30	Direct materials, 46,200 units started	324,800
	30	Direct labor	137,045
	30	Factory overhead	75,400
	30	Goods transferred, 45,900 units	?
	30	Bal., 2,300 units, 70% completed	?

Determine the following:

a. The cost per equivalent unit
b. The cost of the units transferred to Finished Goods
c. The cost of units in the ending Work in Process

E-8 Cost of production report

✔ Cost per equivalent unit, $6.20

The increases to Work in Process—Roasting Department for Colonel Dirks Coffee Company for August, as well as information concerning production, are as follows:

Work in process, August 1, 2,000 pounds, 40% completed	$ 8,130
Coffee beans added during August, 93,000 pounds	391,420
Conversion costs during August	187,900
Work in process, August 31, 1,250 pounds, 80% completed	?
Goods finished during August, 93,750 pounds	?

Prepare a cost of production report using the weighted average cost (WAC) method.

E-9 Cost of production report

✔ Cost per equivalent unit, $12.00

Prepare a cost of production report for the Cutting Department of Oriental Carpet Company for May. Use the weighted average cost (WAC) method with the following data:

Work in process, May 1, 8,000 units, 75% completed		$ 75,000
Materials added during May from Weaving Department, 105,000 units	$807,750	
Direct labor for May	275,200	
Factory overhead for May	100,850	1,183,800
Total production costs to account for		$1,258,800
Goods finished during May (includes goods in process, May 1), 104,000 units		?
Work in process, May 31, 9,000 units, 10% completed		?

E-10 Decision making

Ganges Bottling Company bottles popular beverages in the Bottling Department. The beverages are produced by blending concentrate with water and sugar. The concentrate is purchased from a concentrate producer. The concentrate producer sets higher prices for the more popular concentrate flavors. Below is a simplified Bottling Department cost of production report separating the costs of bottling the four flavors.

	A	B	C	D	E
1		**Grape**	**Cola**	**Orange**	**Root Beer**
2	Concentrate	$ 6,650	$135,000	$ 99,000	$ 3,600
3	Water	2,100	36,000	27,000	1,200
4	Sugar	3,500	60,000	45,000	2,000
5	Bottles	7,700	132,000	99,000	4,400
6	Flavor changeover	3,500	6,000	4,500	5,000
7	Conversion cost	2,625	24,000	18,000	1,500
8	Total cost transferred to Finished Goods	$26,075	$393,000	$292,500	$17,700
9	Number of cases	3,500	60,000	45,000	2,000
10					

Beginning and ending work-in-process inventories are negligible, so they are omitted from the cost of production report. The flavor changeover cost represents the cost of cleaning the bottling machines between production runs of different flavors.

Prepare a memo to the production manager analyzing this comparative cost information. In your memo, provide recommendations for further action, along with supporting schedules showing the total cost per case and the cost per case by cost element.

E-11 Decision making

Lasting Memories Inc. produces photographic paper for printing digital images. One of the processes for this operation is a coating (solvent spreading) operation, where chemicals are coated onto paper stock. There has been some concern about the cost performance of this operation. As a result, you have begun an investigation. You first discover that all materials and conversion prices have been stable for the last six months. Thus, increases in prices for inputs are not an explanation for increasing costs. However, you have discovered three possible problems from some of the operating personnel whose quotes follow:

Operator 1: "I've been keeping an eye on my operating room instruments. I feel as though our energy consumption is becoming less efficient."

Operator 2: "Every time the coating machine goes down, we produce waste on shutdown and subsequent startup. It seems like during the last half year we have had more unscheduled machine shutdowns than in the past. Thus, I feel as though our yields must be dropping."

Operator 3: "My sense is that our coating costs are going up. It seems to me like we are spreading a thicker coating than we should. Perhaps the coating machine needs to be recalibrated."

The Coating Department had no beginning or ending inventories for any month during the study period. The following data from the cost of production report are made available:

	A	B	C	D	E	F	G
1		**April**	**May**	**June**	**July**	**August**	**September**
2	Paper stock	$72,960	$69,120	$76,800	$69,120	$65,280	$61,440
3	Coating	$16,416	$17,280	$21,120	$21,600	$21,216	$23,040
4	Conversion cost (incl. energy)	$36,480	$34,560	$38,400	$34,560	$32,640	$30,720
5	Pounds input to the process	95,000	90,000	100,000	90,000	85,000	80,000
6	Pounds transferred out	91,200	86,400	96,000	86,400	81,600	76,800
7							

a. Prepare a table showing the paper cost per output pound, coating cost per output pound, conversion cost per output pound, and yield for each month.

b. Interpret your table results.

Problems

P1 Equivalent units and related costs; cost of production report: weighted average cost method

✔ Transferred to Packaging Dept., $67,050

Joshua Flour Company manufactures flour by a series of three processes, beginning in the Milling Department. From the Milling Department, the materials pass through the Sifting and Packaging departments, emerging as packaged refined flour.

The balance in the account Work in Process—Sifting Department was as follows on March 1:

Work in Process—Sifting Department (3,200 units, 75% completed)	$3,500

The following costs were charged to Work in Process—Sifting Department during March:

Direct materials transferred from Milling Department: 14,500 units	$51,400
Direct labor	13,325
Factory overhead	5,125

During March, 14,900 units of flour were completed. The balance of Work in Process—Sifting Department on March 31 was 2,800 units, 50% completed.

Instructions

Prepare a cost of production report for the Sifting Department for March, using the weighted average cost (WAC) method.

P2 Cost of production report: Weighted average cost method

✔ Cost per equivalent unit, $5.00

Sergeant Wilkes Coffee Company roasts and packs coffee beans. The process begins in the Roasting Department. From the Roasting Department, the coffee beans are transferred to the Packaging Department.

On October 1, the balance of the account Work in Process—Roasting Department was as follows:

Work in Process—Roasting Department (7,500 units, 80% completed)	$27,600

The account Work in Process—Roasting Department was increased during October by the following costs:

Direct materials (64,500 units)	$135,600
Direct labor	118,900
Factory overhead	67,900

During October, 64,000 units were completed and transferred to the Packaging Department. As of October 31, there were 8,000 units, 75% complete in the Roasting Department.

Instructions

Prepare a cost of production report for the Roasting Department for October, using the weighted average cost method.

Glossary

A

Accelerated depreciation method A depreciation method that provides for a higher depreciation amount in the first year of the asset's use, followed by a gradually declining amount of depreciation.

Account A record in which increases and decreases in a financial statement element are recorded.

Accounting An information system that provides reports to stakeholders about the economic activities and condition of a business.

Accounting cycle The process that begins with analzing transactions and ends with preparing the financial statements.

Accounting equation Assets = Liabilities + Stockholders' Equity

Accounting period concept An accounting concept in which accounting data are recorded and summarized in a period process.

Accounts payable Liabilities for amounts incurred from purchases of products or services in the normal operations of a business.

Accounts receivable Receivables created by selling merchandise or services on credit.

Accounts receivable turnover The relationship between net sales and accounts receivable computed by dividing the net sales by the average net accounts receivable; measures how frequently during the year the accounts receivable are being converted to cash.

Accrual basis of accounting A system of accounting in which revenue is recorded as it is earned and expenses are recorded and matched against the revenue they generate.

Accruals Recognition of revenue when earned or expenses when incurred regardless of when cash is received or disbursed.

Accrued assets Revenues that have been earned at the end of an accounting period but have not been recorded in the accounts; sometimes called *accrued revenues*.

Accrued expenses Expenses that have been incurred at the end of an accounting period but have not been recorded in the accounts; sometimes called *accrued liabilities*.

Accrued liabilities Expenses that have been incurred at the end of an accounting period but have not been recorded in the accounts; sometimes called *accrued expenses*.

Accrued revenues Revenues that have been earned at the end of an accounting period but have not been recorded in the accounts; sometimes called *accrued assets*.

Accumulated depreciation An offsetting or contra asset account used to record depreciation on a fixed asset.

Activity base A measure of activity that is related to changes in cost and is used in the denominator in calculating the predetermined factory overhead rate to assign factory overhead costs to cost objects; also called an *allocation base* or *activity driver*.

Activity-based costing (ABC) An accounting framework based on determining the cost of activities and allocating these costs to products using activity rates.

Activity cost pools Cost accumulations that are associated with a given activity, such as machine usage, inspections, moving, and production setups.

Adequate disclosure concept An accounting concept that requires financial statements to include all relevant data a reader needs to understand the financial condition and performance of a business.

Adjustment process A process required by the accrual basis of accounting in which the accounts are updated prior to preparing financial statements.

Administrative expenses Expenses incurred in the administration or general operations of the business; costs not directly related to selling, such as officer salaries.

Aging the receivables The process of analyzing the accounts receivable and classifying them according to various age groupings, with the due date being the base point for determining age.

Allowance for doubtful accounts The contra asset account for accounts receivable.

Allowance method The method of accounting for uncollectible accounts that provides an expense for uncollectible receivables in advance of their write-off.

Amortization The periodic transfer of the cost of an intangible asset to expense.

Annuity A series of equal cash flows at fixed intervals.

Assets The resources owned by a business.

Asset turnover A profitability metric used to assess how efficiently a company is using its operating assets to generate sales, computed as sales divided by average long-term operating assets.

Average rate of return A method of evaluating capital investment proposals that focuses on the expected profitability of the investment.

B

Bad debt expense The operating expense incurred because of the failure to collect receivables.

Balanced scorecard A performance evaluation approach that incorporates multiple performance dimensions by combining financial and nonfinancial measures.

Balance sheet A list of the assets, liabilities, and owner's equity as of a specific date, usually at the close of the last day of a month or a year.

Bank reconciliation The analysis that details the items responsible for the difference between the cash balance reported in the bank statement and the cash balance in the ledger.

Bank statement A summary of all transactions mailed to the depositor by the bank each month.

Bond A form of interest-bearing note requiring periodic interest payments with the face amount due at the maturity date.

Bond indenture The contract between a corporation issuing bonds and the bondholders.

Bonds payable A type of long-term debt financing with a face amount that is in the future with interest that is normally paid semiannually.

Book value The cost of a fixed asset minus accumulated depreciation on the asset.

Book value of a fixed asset The value of an asset as indicated by the company's records of historical cost less accumulated depreciation.

Break-even point The level of business operations at which revenues and expired costs are equal.

Budget An accounting device used to plan and control resources of operational departments and divisions.

Budgetary slack Excess resources set within a budget to provide for uncertain events.

Budgeted variable factory overhead The standard variable overhead for the actual units produced.

Budget performance report A report comparing actual results with budget figures.

Business An organization in which basic resources (inputs), such as materials and labor, are assembled and processed to provide goods and services (outputs) to customers.

Business entity concept An accounting concept that limits the economic data in the accounting system of a specific business or entity to data related directly to the activities of that business or entity.

Business stakeholder A person or entity that has an interest in the economic performance of a business.

C

Capital expenditures The costs of acquiring fixed assets, adding a component, or replacing a component of a fixed asset.

Capital expenditures budget The budget summarizing future plans for acquiring plant facilities and equipment.

Capital investment analysis The process by which management plans, evaluates, and controls long-term capital investments involving fixed assets.

Capital rationing The process by which management allocates available investment funds among competing capital investment proposals.

Cash Coins, currency (paper money), checks, money orders, and money on deposit available for unrestricted withdrawal from banks and other financial institutions.

Cash basis of accounting A system of accounting in which only transactions involving increases or decreases of the entity's cash are recorded.

Cash budget A budget of estimated cash receipts and payments.

Cash dividend A cash distribution of earnings by a corporation to its shareholders.

Cash equivalents Highly liquid investments that are usually reported with cash on the balance sheet.

Cash payback period The expected period of time that will elapse between the date of a capital expenditure and the complete recovery in cash (or equivalent) of the amount invested.

Cash short and over The account used to record the difference between the amount of cash in a cash register and the amount of cash that should be on hand according to the records.

Chief financial officer The head of the accounting department in a company; also called the *comptroller*.

Classified balance sheet A balance sheet prepared with various sections, subsections, and captions that aid in its interpretation and analysis.

Common-sized balance sheet A balance sheet where each amount is expressed as a percent of total assets or total liabilities plus stockholders' equity.

Common-sized financial statements Financial statements that express each amount as a percent of a base amount.

Common-sized income statement An income statement where each amount is expressed as a percent of sales.

Common-sized statement A financial statement in which all items are expressed only in relative terms.

Common stock The basic type of stock issued to stockholders of a corporation when a corporation has issued only one class of stock.

Compensating balance A requirement by some banks that depositors maintain minimum cash balances in their bank accounts.

Component analysis A method of analysis that computes metrics for liquidity, solvency, and profitability for components of financial statements.

Comptroller The head of the accounting department in a company; also called the *chief financial officer*.

Constraint (or bottleneck) A point in the manufacturing process where the demand for the company's products exceeds its ability to produce the products.

Contingent liabilities Potential liabilities if certain events occur in the future.

Continuous budgeting A method of budgeting that provides for maintaining a 12-month projection into the future.

Contract rate The periodic interest to be paid on the bonds that is identified in the bond indenture; expressed as a percentage of the face amount of the bond.

Contribution margin Sales less variable cost of goods sold and variable selling and administrative expenses.

Contribution margin ratio The percentage of each sales dollar that is available to cover the fixed costs and provide income from operations.

Controllable expenses Costs that can be influenced by the decisions of a manager of a cost, profit, or investment center.

Controllable revenues Revenues that can be influenced by the decisions of a manager of a profit or investment center.

Controllable variance The difference between the actual amount of variable factory overhead cost incurred and the amount of variable factory overhead budgeted for the standard product.

Controlling account The account in the general ledger that summarizes the balances of the accounts in the subsidiary ledger.

Conversion costs The combination of direct labor and factory overhead costs.

Copyright An exclusive right to publish and sell a literary, artistic, or musical composition.

Corporation A business organized under state or federal statutes as a separate legal entity.

Cost A payment of cash (or a commitment to pay cash in the future) for the purpose of generating revenues.

Cost accounting system A system used to accumulate manufacturing costs for decision-making and financial reporting purposes.

Cost allocation The process of assigning indirect costs to a cost object, such as a job.

Cost behavior The manner in which a cost changes in relation to its activity base (driver).

Cost center A decentralized unit in which the department or division manager has responsibility for the control of costs incurred and the authority to make decisions that affect these costs.

Cost concept An accounting concept that determines the amount initially entered into the accounting records for purchases.

Cost object A product, a sales territory, a department, or an activity by which costs are classified and assigned.

Cost of goods sold budget A budget of the estimated direct materials, direct labor, and factory overhead consumed by sold products.

Cost of goods sold The cost of products sold; also may be referred to as *cost of merchandise sold* or *cost of sales*.

Cost of merchandise sold The cost of products sold; also may be referred to as *cost of sales* or *cost of goods sold*.

Cost of sales The cost of products sold; also may be referred to as *cost of merchandise sold* or *cost of goods sold*.

Cost price approach An approach to transfer pricing that uses cost as the basis for setting the transfer price.

Cost variance The difference between the actual cost and the standard cost at actual volumes.

Cost-volume-profit analysis The systematic examination of the relationships among costs, expenses, sales, and operating profit or loss.

Cost-volume-profit graph A chart that graphically shows the sales, costs, and related profit or loss for various levels of units sold; also called a *break-even graph*.

Creditors The businesses or people to whom debt is owed.

Credit memorandum A form used by a seller to inform the buyer of the amount the seller proposes to decrease the account receivable due from the buyer.

Credit period The amount of time the buyer is allowed in which to pay the seller.

Credit terms Terms for payment on account by the buyer to the seller.

Currency exchange rates The rates at which currency in another country can be exchanged for U.S. dollars.

Current assets Cash and other assets that are expected to be converted to cash or sold or used up through the normal operations of the business within 1 year or less.

Current liabilities Liabilities that will be due within a short time (usually 1 year or less) and that are to be paid out of current assets.

Currently attainable standards Standards that represent levels of operation that can be attained with reasonable effort.

Current position analysis Analysis of a company's ability to pay its current liabilities.

Current ratio A financial ratio that is computed by dividing current assets by current liabilities.

Customer Refunds Payable A liability recording the amount of refunds and allowances expected to be granted in the future, which is estimated at the end of the period as part of the adjusting process.

D

Days' sales in inventory An estimate of the average number of days it takes to sell inventory, determined by dividing the average inventory by the average daily cost of goods sold.

Days' sales in receivables An estimate of the average number of days it takes to collect accounts receivable, determined by dividing the average accounts receivable by the average daily sales.

Debit memorandum A form used by a buyer to inform the seller of the amount the buyer proposes to decrease the account payable due the seller.

Debt ratio A solvency metric that indicates the percent of a company's assets financed by debt, computed as total liabilities divided by total assets.

Deferrals Delayed recordings of expenses or revenues.

Deferred expenses Items that are initially recorded as assets but are expected to become expenses over time or through the normal operations of the business; sometimes called *prepaid expenses*.

Deferred revenues Items that are initially recorded as liabilities but are expected to become revenues over time or through the normal operations of the business; sometimes called *unearned revenues*.

Depletion expense The portion of the cost of a natural resource that has been harvested or mined.

Depreciable cost The amount of an asset's cost that is allocated over its useful life as depreciation expense; calculated as initial cost less residual value.

Depreciation The systematic periodic transfer of the cost of a fixed asset to an expense account during its expected useful life.

Differential analysis The area of accounting concerned with the effect of alternative courses of action on revenues and costs.

Differential cost The amount of increase or decrease in cost expected from a particular course of action compared with an alternative.

Differential income (or loss) The difference between differential revenue and differential cost.

Differential revenue The amount of increase or decrease in revenue expected from a particular course of action as compared with an alternative.

Direct labor cost Wages of factory workers who are directly involved in converting materials into a finished product.

Direct labor cost budget A budget that estimates the direct labor hours and related costs needed to support budgeted production.

Direct labor rate variance The cost associated with the difference between the standard rate and the actual rate paid for direct labor used in producing a commodity.

Direct labor time variance The cost associated with the difference between the standard hours and the actual hours of direct labor spent producing a commodity.

Direct materials cost The cost of materials that are an integral part of the finished product.

Direct materials price variance The difference between the actual price and standard price times the actual quantity.

Direct materials purchases budget A budget that uses the production budget as a starting point.

Direct materials quantity variance The cost associated with the difference between the standard quantity and the actual quantity of direct materials used in producing a commodity.

Direct write-off method The method of accounting for uncollectible accounts that recognizes the expense only when accounts are judged to be worthless.

Discount on bonds payable The excess of the face amount of bonds over their issue price.

Dividends per share Measures the extent to which earnings are being distributed to common shareholders.

Dividend yield A ratio, computed by dividing the annual dividends paid per share of common stock by the market price per share at a specific date, which indicates the rate of return to stockholders in terms of cash dividend distributions.

Dividends Distributions of the earnings of a corporation to its stockholders.

Double-declining balance method A method of depreciation that provides periodic depreciation expense based on the declining book value of a fixed asset over its estimated life.

DuPont formula An expanded expression of return on investment determined by multiplying the profit margin by the investment turnover.

E

Earnings per share (EPS) A measure of profitability computed by dividing net income, reduced by preferred dividends, by the number of shares outstanding.

Earnings per share (EPS) on common stock Net income per share of common stock outstanding during a period.

Electronic funds transfer (EFT) A system in which computers rather than paper (money, checks, etc.) are used to effect cash transactions.

Elements of internal control The control environment, risk assessment, control activities, information and communication, and monitoring.

Employee fraud The intentional act of deceiving an employer for personal gain.

Estimated Returns Inventory An asset representing inventory expected to be returned in the future, which is estimated at the end of the period as part of the adjusting process.

Expected useful life An estimate of the duration that an asset will be in service or provide benefit to the company.

Expenses Costs used to earn (generate) revenues.

Expense recognition principle An accounting principle that states that the expenses incurred in generating revenue should be reported in the same period as the related revenue; by matching revenues and expenses, net income or loss for the period can properly be determined and reported.

F

Factory overhead cost All of the costs of operating the factory except for direct materials and direct labor.

Factory overhead cost budget A budget that estimates the cost for each item of factory overhead needed to support budgeted production.

Factory overhead cost variance report Reports budgeted and actual costs for variable and fixed factory overhead for each cost element along with the related controllable and volume variances.

Factory overhead cost variance report Reports budgeted and actual costs for variable and fixed factory overhead for each cost element along with the related controllable and volume variances.

Favorable cost variance Actual cost is less than standard cost.

Fees earned Revenues received from providing services.

Financial Accounting Standards Board (FASB) The authoritative body that has the primary responsibility for developing accounting principles.

Financial accounting system A system that includes (1) a set of rules for determining what, when, and the amount that should be recorded for an economic event; (2) a framework for facilitating preparing financial statements; and (3) one or more controls to determine whether errors could have occurred in the recording process.

Financial accounting The area of accounting that focuses on recording transactions and events so that general-purpose financial statements can be prepared.

Financial leverage The use of debt to finance a company's operations so as to enhance the earnings of stockholders.

Financial statements Financial reports that summarize the effects of events on a business.

Financing activities Business activities that involve obtaining funds to begin and operate a business.

Finished goods inventory The cost of finished products on hand that have not been sold.

Finished goods ledger The subsidiary ledger that contains the individual accounts for each kind of commodity or product produced.

First-in, first-out (FIFO) inventory cost flow method A method of inventory costing based on the assumption that the costs of merchandise sold should be charged against revenue in the order in which the costs were incurred.

Fixed assets Long-lived or relatively permanent tangible assets that are used in the normal business operations; sometimes called *plant assets*.

Flexible budget A budget that adjusts for varying rates of activity.

Fixed Costs Costs that tend to remain the same in amount, regardless of variations in the level of activity.

FOB (free on board) destination Freight terms in which the seller pays the transportation costs from the shipping point to the final destination.

FOB (free on board) shipping point Freight terms in which the buyer pays the transportation costs from the shipping point to the final destination.

Free cash flow A liquidity metric that represents the cash available after maintaining and expanding current operating capacity; computed as operating cash flows less investing cash flows.

Freight The cost of transportation when shipping or receiving goods.

Fringe benefits Benefits provided to employees in addition to wages and salaries.

G

General expenses Expenses incurred in the administration or general operations of the business; sometimes called administrative expenses.

General-purpose financial statements Basic financial statements, such as the balance sheet and income statement, which are made available to a wide range of potential users so that the company's financial condition and performance may be assessed.

Generally accepted accounting principles (GAAP) Rules for the way financial statements should be prepared.

Global analysis A method of analysis that computes changes in amounts, percentages of amounts, and percentage changes in amounts for each financial statement.

Goal conflict Situation when individual self-interest differs from business objectives.

Going concern concept An accounting concept that assumes that a company will continue in business indefinitely.

Goodwill An intangible asset of a business that is created from favorable factors such as location, product quality, reputation, and managerial skill, as verified from a merger transaction.

Gross pay The total earnings of an employee for a payroll period.

Gross profit Sales minus the cost of merchandise sold.

Gross profit percent Gross profit divided by net sales.

H

High-low method A technique that uses the highest and lowest total cost as a basis for estimating the variable cost per unit and the fixed cost component of a mixed cost.

Horizontal analysis Financial analysis that compares an item in a current statement with the same item in prior statements.

I

Ideal standards Standards that can be achieved only under perfect operating conditions, such as no idle time, no machine breakdowns, and no materials spoilage; also called *theoretical standards*.

Income from operations The excess of gross profit over total operating expenses; sometimes called *operating income*.

Income statement A summary of the revenue and expenses for a specific period of time, such as a month or a year.

Indirect method A method of preparing the statement of cash flows that reconciles net income with net cash flows from operating activities.

Inflation A period when prices in general are rising and the purchasing power of money is declining.

Initial cost of a fixed asset The purchase price of a fixed asset plus all the costs incurred to obtain and ready it for use.

Insolvent The state of a company when it cannot pay its liabilities as they become due or if its total liabilities exceed its total assets.

Intangible assets Long-lived assets that are useful in the operations of a business, are not held for sale, and are without physical qualities.

Interest payable A liability to pay interest on a due date.

Internal control The policies and procedures used to safeguard assets, ensure accurate business information, and ensure compliance with laws and regulations.

Internal rate of return (IRR) method A method of analyzing proposed capital investments that focuses on using present value concepts to compute the rate of return from the net cash flows expected from the investment.

International Accounting Standards Board (IASB) An authoritative body that establishes accounting principles and practices for companies in many countries outside of the United States.

Inventory Merchandise on hand (not sold) at the end of an accounting period.

Inventory shortage The amount by which the merchandise for sale, as indicated by the balance of the merchandise inventory account, is larger than the total amount of merchandise counted during the physical inventory; sometimes called *inventory shrinkage*.

Inventory shrinkage The amount by which the merchandise for sale, as indicated by the balance of the merchandise inventory account, is larger than the total amount of merchandise counted during the physical inventory; sometimes called *inventory shortage*.

Inventory turnover The relationship between the volume of goods sold and inventory, computed by dividing the cost of goods sold by the average inventory.

Investing activities Business activities that involve obtaining the necessary resources to start and operate the business.

Investment center A decentralized unit in which the manager has the responsibility and authority to make decisions that affect not only costs and revenues but also the fixed assets available to the center.

Investment turnover A component of the rate of return on investment computed as the ratio of sales to invested assets.

Invoice The bill that the seller sends to the buyer.

J

Job cost sheet An account in the work-in-process subsidiary ledger in which the costs charged to a particular job order are recorded.

Job order cost system A type of cost accounting system that provides for a separate record of the cost of each particular quantity of product that passes through the factory.

Just-in-time (JIT) processing A business philosophy that focuses on eliminating time, cost, and poor quality within manufacturing processes.

K

Kanban A Japanese term for cards; the cards used to signal the need to move materials within a just-in-time (JIT) manufacturing system.

L

Last-in, first-out (LIFO) inventory cost flow method A method of inventory costing based on the assumption that the most recent merchandise inventory costs should be charged against revenue.

Lease A contract for the use of an asset for a period of time.

Liabilities The rights of creditors that represent a legal obligation to repay an amount borrowed according to terms of the borrowing agreement.

LIFO conformity rule A financial reporting rule requiring a firm that elects to use LIFO inventory valuation for tax purposes to also use LIFO for external financial reporting.

LIFO reserve A required disclosure for LIFO firms, showing the difference between inventory valued under FIFO and inventory valued under LIFO.

Limited liability company (LLC) A form of corporation that combines attributes of a partnership and a corporation.

Liquidity Refers to the ability to convert an asset to cash.

Long-term liabilities Liabilities due beyond one year or liabilities that will be paid out of noncurrent assets.

Low-cost strategy A strategy where a company designs and produces products or services at a lower cost than its competitors.

Lower-of-cost-or-market (LCM) method A method of valuing inventory that reports the inventory at the lower of its cost or current market (net realizable) value.

M

Management's Discussion and Analysis (MD&A) An annual report disclosure that provides management's analysis of the results of operations and financial condition.

Managerial accounting The branch of accounting that aids management in making financing, investing, and operating decisions for the company.

Manufacturing business A type of business that changes basic inputs into products that are sold to customers.

Manufacturing cells Work centers in a just-in-time (JIT) manufacturing system.

Margin of safety The difference between current sales revenue and the sales at the break-even point.

Market price approach An approach to transfer pricing that uses the price at which the product or service transferred could be sold to outside buyers as the transfer price.

Market rate of interest The effective rate of interest at the time the bonds were issued.

Markup An amount that is added to a "cost" amount to determine product price.

Markup percent The amount expressed as a percentage that is added to the cost of a product to determine its selling price.

Master budget The comprehensive budget plan linking the individual budgets related to sales, cost of goods sold, operating expenses, capital expenditures, and cash.

Matching concept An accounting concept that requires expenses of a period to be matched with the revenue generated during that period.

Materials inventory The cost of materials that have not yet entered into the manufacturing process.

Materials ledger The subsidiary ledger containing the individual accounts for each type of material.

Materials requisition The form or electronic transmission used by a manufacturing department to authorize the issuance of materials from the storeroom.

Maturity value The amount that is due at the maturity or due date of a note.

Merchandising business A type of business that purchases finished products from other businesses to sell to its customers.

Metric A quantitative measure.

Metric-based analysis The use of metrics to assess a business's financial condition, performance, and decisions.

Mixed costs Costs with both variable and fixed characteristics.

Monthly cash burn The net cash outflow used for expenses, also called *monthly cash expenses*.

Monthly cash expenses Computed for companies with negative cash flows from operations as net cash flows from operations divided by 12.

Multiple-step income statement A form of income statement that contains several sections, subsections, and subtotals.

N

Negotiated price approach An approach to transfer pricing that allows managers of decentralized units to agree (negotiate) among themselves as to the transfer price.

Net assets A company's stockholders' equity, computed as total assets less total liabilities.

Net income The excess of revenues over expenses.

Net Income – Accrual Basis A profitability metric determined as the excess of revenues over expenses in an accounting system in which revenue is recorded as it is earned and expenses are recorded and matched against the revenue they generate.

Net loss The excess of expenses over revenues.

Net pay Gross pay less payroll deductions; the amount the employer is obligated to pay the employee.

Net present value method A method of analyzing proposed capital investments that focuses on the present value of the cash flows expected from the investments.

Net realizable value of accounts receivable The amount of receivables that is expected to be collected or realized after deducting an allowance for doubtful accounts (bad debts).

Net realizable value of inventory The value of inventory determined by its estimated selling price less the direct costs of disposal, such as special advertising or sales commissions.

Note payable A type of short- or long- term financing that requires payment of the amount borrowed plus interest.

Notes receivable Written claims against debtors who promise to pay the amount of the note plus interest at an agreed upon rate.

O

Objectivity concept An accounting concept that requires accounting records and data reported in financial statements be based on objective evidence.

Occupancy rate An output metric for assessing the performance and the efficient use of assets for the hotel industry, computed as rooms occupied by the available room nights; also known as the *utilization rate*.

Operating activities Business activities that involve using the business's resources to implement its business strategy.

Operating cycle The business process of spending cash to acquire assets used to generate revenue, earning revenues, and receiving cash from customers.

Operating income The excess of gross profit over total operating expenses; also called *income from operations*.

Operating leverage A measure of the relative mix of a business's variable costs and fixed costs, computed as contribution margin divided by income from operations.

Opportunity cost The amount of income forgone from an alternative to a proposed use of cash or its equivalent.

Other expense Expenses that cannot be traced directly to operations.

Other revenue Revenue from sources other than the primary operating activities of a business.

Outstanding stock The stock in the hands of stockholders.

Overapplied factory overhead The amount of factory overhead applied in excess of the actual factory overhead costs incurred for production during a period.

Owner's equity The financial rights of the owner.

P

Par The monetary amount printed on a stock certificate.

Partnership A business owned by two or more individuals.

Patents Exclusive rights to produce and sell goods with one or more unique features.

Payroll The total amount paid to employees for a certain period.

Period costs Those costs that are used up in generating revenue during the current period and that are not involved in the manufacturing process.

Periodic inventory system The inventory method in which the inventory records do not show the amount available for sale or sold during the period.

Perpetual inventory system The inventory system in which each purchase and sale of merchandise is recorded in an inventory account.

Petty cash fund A special-purpose cash fund to pay relatively small amounts.

Physical inventory A physical count and listing of goods on hand used to determine the balance of the inventory account at the end of an accounting period.

Predetermined factory overhead rate The rate used to apply factory overhead costs to the goods manufactured. The rate is determined from budgeted overhead cost and estimated activity usage data at the beginning of the fiscal period.

Preferred stock A class of stock with preferential rights over common stock.

Premium on bonds payable The excess of the issue price of bonds over their face amount.

Premium on stock The excess of the issue price of a stock over its par value.

Premium-price strategy A strategy where a company tries to design and produce products or services that serve unique market needs, allowing it to charge premium prices.

Prepaid expenses Assets resulting from the prepayment of future expenses such as insurance or rent that are expected to become expenses over time or through the normal operations of the business; often called *deferred expenses*.

Present value concept Cash today is not the equivalent of the same amount of money to be received in the future.

Present value index An index computed by dividing the total present value of the next cash flow to be received from a proposed capital investment by the amount to be invested.

Present value of an annuity The sum of the present values of a series of equal cash flows to be received at fixed intervals.

Price-earnings (P/E) ratio A financial metric that indicates the market's assessment of the future earnings potential of a company; computed as the market price per share of common stock divided by the earnings per share of common stock; also called the *earnings multiple*.

Prime costs The combination of direct materials and direct labor costs.

Process cost system A type of cost accounting system in which costs are accumulated by department or process within a factory.

Process yield An output metric that indicates the efficiency of a process, computed as units passing inspection divided by units entering the process.

Product cost concept A concept used in applying the cost-plus approach to product pricing in which only the costs of manufacturing the product, termed the *product costs*, are included in the cost amount to which the markup is added.

Product costs The three components of manufacturing costs: direct materials, direct labor, and factory overhead costs.

Production budget A budget of estimated unit production.

Profit The excess of the amounts received from customers for goods or services and the amounts paid for the inputs used to provide the goods or services.

Profit center A decentralized unit in which the manager has the responsibility and the authority to make decisions that affect both costs and revenues (and thus profits).

Profit margin The ratio of operating income to sales.

Profit-volume graph A chart that graphically shows only the difference between total sales and total costs (or profits) and allows managers to determine the operating profit (or loss) for various levels of units sold.

Proprietorship A business owned by one individual.

Purchases discounts Discounts taken by the buyer for early payment of an invoice.

Purchases returns and allowances From the buyer's perspective, returned merchandise or an adjustment for defective merchandise.

Pull manufacturing A just-in-time method wherein customer orders trigger the release of finished goods, which triggers production, which triggers release of materials from suppliers.

Q

Quick assets Cash and other current assets that can be quickly converted to cash, such as marketable securities and receivables.

Quick ratio A financial ratio that measures the ability to pay current liabilities with quick assets (cash, marketable securities, accounts receivable).

R

Rate of return on investment (ROI) A measure of managerial efficiency in the use of investments in assets computed as income from operations divided by invested assets.

Ratio of cash to monthly cash expenses A ratio that is useful in assessing how a company with negative cash flows from operations can continue to operate. Computed as cash and cash equivalents divided by monthly cash expenses.

Ratio of fixed assets to long-term liabilities A leverage ratio that measures the margin of safety of long-term creditors, calculated as the net fixed assets divided by the long-term liabilities.

Ratio of liabilities to stockholders' equity A comprehensive leverage ratio that measures the relationship of the claims of creditors to stockholders' equity.

Receivables All money claims against other entities, including people, business firms, and other organizations.

Receiving report The form or electronic transmission used by the receiving personnel to indicate that materials have been received and inspected.

Relevant range The range of activity over which changes in cost are of interest to management.

Residual income The excess of divisional income from operations over a "minimum" acceptable income from operations.

Residual value The estimated value of a fixed asset at the end of its useful life.

Responsibility accounting The process of measuring and reporting operating data by areas of responsibility.

Responsibility center A budgetary unit within a company for which a manager is assigned responsibility over costs, revenues, or assets.

Retained earnings Net income retained in a corporation.

Return on assets A profitability metric often used to compare a company's performance over time and with competitors, computed by dividing net income by average total assets.

Return on common stockholders' equity A profitability metric that indicates the rate of profits earned on the amount invested by the common stockholders; computed by dividing net income less preferred dividends by average common stockholders' equity.

Return on sales A profitability metric computed by dividing net income by total sales.

Return on stockholders' equity A profitability metric that indicates the rate of profits earned on the amount invested by stockholders; computed by dividing net income by average total stockholders' equity.

Return on investment (ROI) A measure of managerial efficiency in the use of investments in assets, computed as operating income divided by invested assets.

Return on total assets A profitability metric that indicates the rate of profits earned on total assets without considering how the assets are financed; computed as the sum of net income plus interest expense divided by average total assets.

Revenue The increase in assets from selling products or services to customers.

Revenue expenditures Costs that benefit only the current period or costs incurred for normal maintenance and repairs of fixed assets.

Revenue recognition principle An accounting principle that states that revenues should be recorded at the time a product is sold or a service is rendered.

S

Sales Revenues received from selling products; the total amount charged to customers for merchandise sold, including cash sales and sales on account.

Sales budget A budget that indicates for each product (1) the quantity of estimated sales, and (2) the expected unit selling price.

Sales discounts From the seller's perspective, discounts that a seller can offer the buyer for early payment.

Sales mix The relative distribution of sales among the various products available for sale.

Sarbanes-Oxley Act An act passed by Congress in 2002 designed to reduce the likelihood and mitigate the impact of financial fraud so as to restore public confidence and trust in the financial statements of companies.

Securities and Exchange Commission (SEC) An agency of the U.S. government that has authority over the accounting and financial disclosures for corporations whose stock is traded and sold to the public.

Selling expenses Costs directly related to the selling of a product or service such as sales salaries and advertising expenses.

Service business A type of business that provides services rather than products to customers.

Service department charges The costs of services provided by an internal service department and transferred to a responsibility center.

Single-step income statement A form of income statement that deducts the total of all expenses in one step from the total of all revenues.

Solvency The ability of a company to pay its debts as they become due over the long term.

Special-purpose funds Cash funds designated for special needs, such as payroll or travel expenses.

Specific identification inventory cost flow method An inventory cost flow method where the cost of each inventory unit is separately identified.

Standard cost A detailed estimate of what a product should cost.

Standard cost systems Accounting systems that use standards for each manufacturing cost entering into the finished product.

Standards Performance goals.

Stated value A value, similar to par value, approved by the board of directors of a corporation for no-par stock.

Statement of cash flows A financial statement that provides a summary of the cash receipts and cash payments and reports the change in financial condition due to the change in cash during a specific period of time.

Statement of financial condition Reports the financial condition as of a point in time; often referred to as the *balance sheet*.

Statement of stockholders' equity A financial statement that reports the change in financial condition due to the changes in stockholders' equity items for a specific period of time.

Static budget A budget that does not adjust to changes in activity levels.

Stock dividend A distribution of shares of stock to stockholders.

Stock split The reduction in the par or stated value of common stock and issuance of a proportionate number of additional shares.

Stockholders Investors who purchase stock in a corporation.

Stockholders' equity The stockholders' rights to the assets of a business.

Straight-line method A method of depreciation that provides for equal periodic depreciation expense over the estimated life of a fixed asset.

Subsidiary ledger A ledger containing individual accounts with a common characteristic.

Sunk cost A cost that is not affected by subsequent decisions.

T

Tangible assets Assets such as machinery, buildings, computers, office furnishings, trucks, and automobiles that have physical characteristics.

Target costing A concept used to design and manufacture a product at a cost that will deliver a target profit for a given market-determined price.

Theoretical standards Standards that can be achieved only under perfect operating conditions, such as no idle time, no machine breakdowns, and no materials spoilage; also called *ideal standards*.

Theory of constraints (TOC) A manufacturing strategy that attempts to remove the influence of bottlenecks (constraints) on a process.

Times interest earned A solvency metric that determines the degree of risk that interest payments will not be made if earnings decrease, computed as income before interest and taxes divided by interest expense; also known as the *fixed charge coverage ratio*.

Time tickets The form on which the amount of time spent by each employee and the labor costs incurred for each individual job, or for factory overhead, are recorded.

Time value of money concept The concept that an amount of money invested today will earn interest.

Total cost concept A concept used in applying the cost-plus approach to product pricing in which all the costs of manufacturing the product plus the selling and administrative expenses are included in the cost amount to which the markup is added.

Total manufacturing cost variance The difference between the total actual cost and the total standard cost for the units produced.

Trademark A name, term, or symbol used to identify a business and its products.

Transaction An economic event that under generally accepted accounting principles (GAAP), affects an element of the accounting equation and must be recorded.

Transfer price The price charged one decentralized unit by another for the goods or services provided.

Treasury stock Stock that a corporation has once issued and then reacquired.

U

Underapplied factory overhead The actual factory overhead costs incurred in excess of the amount of factory overhead applied for production during a period.

Unearned revenues Items that are initially recorded as liabilities but are expected to become revenues over time or through the normal operations of the business.

Unfavorable cost variance Actual cost exceeds standard cost.

Unit contribution margin The dollars available from each unit of sales to cover fixed costs and provide income from operations.

Unit of measure concept An accounting concept requiring that all economic data be recorded in dollars.

Utilization rate An output metric for assessing the performance and the efficient use of assets, computed as service units used divided by available service units.

V

Variable cost concept Often referred to as *variable costing*, a method of reporting variable and fixed costs that includes only the variable manufacturing costs in the cost of the product.

Variable costing A method of reporting variable and fixed costs that includes only the variable manufacturing costs in the cost of the product.

Variable costs Costs that vary in total dollar amount as the level of activity changes.

Vertical analysis An analysis that compares each item in a current statement with a total amount within the same statement.

Volume variance The difference between the budgeted fixed overhead at 100% of normal capacity and the standard fixed overhead for the actual units produced.

Voucher Any document that serves as proof of authority to pay cash.

Voucher system A set of procedures for authorizing and recording liabilities and cash payments.

W

Weighted average cost inventory cost flow method A method of inventory costing that is based upon the assumption that costs should be charged against revenue by using the weighted average unit cost of the items sold.

Working capital The excess of the current assets of a business over its current liabilities.

Work-in-process (WIP) inventory The direct materials costs, the direct labor costs, and the factory overhead costs that have entered into the manufacturing process but are associated with products that have not been finished.

Z

Zero-based budgeting A concept of budgeting that requires all levels of management to start from zero and estimate budget data as if there had been no previous activities in their units.

Subject Index

D

E

J

K

L

M

Company Index